P9-AGG-315

ENCYCLOPEDIA OF WORLD BIOGRAPHY

3

ENCYCLOPEDIA OF WORLD BIOGRAPHY

SECOND EDITION

Brice
Ch'i Pai-Shih 3

GALE

DETROIT • NEW YORK • TORONTO • LONDON

Editorial Staff: Luann Brennan, Frank V. Castronova, Laura S. Hightower, Karen E. Lemerand, Stacy A. McConnell, Jennifer Mossman, Maria L. Munoz, Katherine H. Nemeh, Terrie M. Rooney, Geri Speace

Permissions Manager: Susan M. Tosky
Permissions Specialist: Maria L. Franklin
Permissions Associate: Michele M. Lonoconus
Image Cataloger: Mary K. Grimes

Production Director: Mary Beth Trimper
Production Manager: Evi Seoud
Production Associate: Shanna Heilveil
Product Design Manager: Cynthia Baldwin
Senior Art Director: Mary Claire Krzewinski

Research Manager: Victoria B. Cariappa
Research Specialists: Michele P. LaMeau, Andrew Guy Malonis, Barbara McNeil, Gary J. Oudersluys
Research Associates: Julia C. Daniel, Tamara C. Nott, Norma Sawaya, Cheryl L. Warnock
Research Assistant: Talitha A. Jean

Graphic Services Supervisor: Barbara Yarrow
Image Database Supervisor: Randy Bassett
Imaging Specialist: Mike Lugosz

Manager of Data Entry Services: Eleanor M. Allison
Data Entry Coordinator: Kenneth D. Benson

Manager of Technology Support Services: Theresa A. Rocklin
Programmers/Analysts: Mira Bossowska, Jeffrey Muhr, Christopher Ward

Gale Research
835 Penobscot Bldg.
Detroit, MI 48226-4094

ISBN 0-7876-2221-4 (Set)
ISBN 0-7876-2543-4 (Volume 3)

Library of Congress Cataloging-in-Publication data is available.

Printed in the United States of America
10 9 8 7 6 5 4 3 2 1

ENCYCLOPEDIA OF WORLD BIOGRAPHY

3

B

Fanny Brice

Fanny Brice (1891-1951) was a vaudeville, Broadway, film, and radio singer and comedienne.

Fanny Brice was born on October 29, 1891, on New York's Lower East Side. She was the daughter of Charles Borach, a saloonkeeper, and Rose Stern, a real estate agent. As a child she sang and danced in her father's saloon, and at the age of 13, after winning an amateur contest, she sang and played piano in a movie theater. Brice's acute sense of humor made its way into her act early on. She began to work parody into her songs and toured in burlesque. In 1910 she was asked by Max Spiegel to be in *The College Girls* at a major New York theater and also to do a benefit he was producing. Since this was an important job for her she asked Irving Berlin to write her some songs, one of which—"Sadie Salome, Go Home"—became a Brice trademark. The song told the story of a Jewish dancer who shocked her family by going on the stage. It required a Jewish accent for its comic effect. The audiences loved this character, and from then on Brice's most successful characters would be drawn from her own Jewish background.

Aside from discovering her forte, Brice was rewarded for this performance with a job on Broadway in Florenz Ziegfeld's *Follies* of 1910. This was the beginning of an association between the famous impresario and the talented comedienne that would last for 14 years. In 1911 she left New York and toured the vaudeville circuit, during which time she created two more characters which became her hallmarks: the "vamp" and the pretentious "dancer."

Following the tour she appeared as the major attraction at two important theaters: the Victoria in Times Square and the Victoria Palace in London. She also played a Yiddish soubrette, a part specifically written for her, in Shubert's *The Whirl of Society,* which also starred Al Jolson. She played the same part in another Shubert hit, *Honeymoon Express,* and she played the female lead in Jerome Kern's *Nobody Home.*

In 1916 Brice returned to the *Ziegfeld Follies* with her popular skit "The Blushing Bride." She remained with Ziegfeld until 1924, in all appearing in seven editions of the *Follies* and four revues.

Brice was considered to be one of the greatest comediennes on Broadway. Although she was an attractive, graceful woman offstage, she elicited the audience's sympathy and laughter by bringing out the imperfections of her characters. She could be ugly, lack grace, and be mischievous—all for a laugh. She could bring out pathos and at the same time mock sentimentality. In her vaudeville number "You Made Me Love You" the first half was a heart rending song, followed by Brice laughing at her own sentiment by kicking her heels, winking her eyes, swinging on the curtain, and then lifting her skirt to show off her knock knees Not only did she make fun of herself but she parodied standard theatrical styles and actors of the period, such as the Barrymores. Brice also appeared several times with W. C. Fields in a popular family sketch.

In 1921 Brice introduced "My Man" to American audiences. She stood on an empty stage against a lamppost and sang the painful song about a woman whose total devotion to her "man" had brought nothing but unhappiness. Perhaps the pathos she brought to that character was from her personal experience—her husband, Nickie Arnstein, had just been jailed for embezzlement and she had to stand by

him. This was one of her few totally straight performances, and it is one for which she will be remembered.

In 1924 Brice, displeased with the material Ziegfeld was giving her, returned to vaudeville for a time. She played the lead role in the film "My Man" and then appeared in Billy Rose's (her third husband) *Sweet and Low* (1930) in which she introduced "Babykins," a three year old in a high chair. This character was the starting point for another Brice trademark, "Baby Snooks."

In the Shubert's 1936 *Follies* she did a spoof of "My Man" in which she said that she had been singing about "that bum" for more than 15 years. This satire on the sentiment in the song was much more her style than the straight emotionality of the earlier delivery. In the same show she did a parody of Shirley Temple in an act with Bob Hope in which she played a child star who couldn't remember her lines.

Due to ill health Brice left Broadway for Los Angeles, where she made a few film appearance, including MGM's *Ziegfeld Follies* (1946) (she was the only Ziegfeld star who appeared in this film). She also immortalized "Baby Snooks" during her ten year radio series.

Despite her work in film Brice was a daughter of the stage. She knew exactly how to reach an audience and she gave her whole self with no reserves. During each performance she would get bigger and bigger until she seemed to envelop the audience with her whole being.

In 1938 *Rose of Washington Square,* a film suggesting the life of Brice, was made and Brice sued the producer. Yet it was through another film and Broadway show, *Funny Girl,* in which Brice was played by Barbra Streisand, that Brice's unique contributions to the theater became known to later generations. A fantasized version of her life focussing on her Ziegfeld days and her marriage to Nickie Arnstein, the play brings back to life her favorite characters and songs. Through this play her life has become inextricably linked with that of her characters, Sadie and "Second Hand Rose"—the poor but spunky Jewish city girls.

Aside from her theater career, Brice was a dress designer, painter, and interior decorator. She had two children, William and Frances. She died May 19, 1951, of cerebral hemorrhage, at the age of 59.

Further Reading

A concise biography and analysis of Fanny Brice's work is included in *The Great Clowns of Broadway* (1984) by Stanley Green. Reviews, an interview, and a short biography can be found in *Famous Actors and Actresses on the American Stage,* Vol. 1 (1975) by William C. Young. Daniel Blum's *Great Stars of the American Stage* (1952) includes a short biography and photographs. For background information on the *Ziegfeld Follies* and Brice's role in their creation, see Randolph Carter's *The World of Flo Ziegfeld* (1974).

Additional Sources

Goldman, Herbert G., *Fanny Brice: the original funny girl,* New York: Oxford University Press, 1992.

Grossman, Barbara Wallace, *Funny woman: the life and times of Fanny Brice,* Bloomington: Indiana University Press, 1991. □

James Bridger

American trapper, fur trader, and wilderness guide, James Bridger (1804-1881), was one of the most famous frontiersmen. He is credited with discovering the Great Salt Lake, Utah.

James Bridger was born on March 17, 1804, at Richmond, Va. In 1812 the family moved west to Missouri, where all but Jim soon died. At 13 he became a blacksmith's apprentice and apparently learned how to handle machinery, horses, and guns. In March 1822 Bridger started his frontier life by joining the party of trappers being organized at St. Louis by William H. Ashley. That year the men traveled up the Missouri to trap along its tributaries in the Rocky Mountains.

For the next 20 years Bridger and other mountain men roamed throughout the western third of the United States. While trapping in late 1824, Bridger reached the Great Salt Lake, which he thought was part of the Pacific Ocean. Historians are unsure if Bridger was alone when he found the lake but credit him with first reporting it.

During his years in the West, Bridger trapped for several leading fur companies and in 1830 became one of five partners in the Rocky Mountain Fur Company. By the early 1840s, however, he realized that the supply of furs was nearly exhausted, and with Louis Vasquez he established Ft. Bridger. Built on the Green River in south-western Wyoming, this post became a major way station on the Oregon and California trails, a military fort, and a Pony Express station. In 1853 the Mormons drove Bridger and his partner away and confiscated their property because they purportedly had provided guns and anti-Mormon information to the Native Americans.

Bridger's career as a guide spanned from 1849 to 1868. During this time he led Capt. Howard Stansbury to Utah, Col. Albert S. Johnston during the so-called Mormon War, and Capt. William Raynolds to the Yellowstone. In 1861 he led Capt. E.L. Berthoud and his survey party west from Denver through the mountains to Salt Lake City, and for the next several years he guided army units sent west to guard overland mail. Between 1865 and 1868 he guided several expeditions and survey parties over the Bozeman, or Powder River, Trail. In 1868 he retired to his farm in Missouri, where he died on July 17, 1881.

During his years on the frontier Bridger had been married three times to Native American women. In 1835 he married the daughter of a Flathead chief. When she died, he acquired a Ute wife, and after her death he wed the daughter of a Shoshone chief. Described as tall and muscular by his contemporaries, Bridger was considered shrewd, honest, and brave. His life exemplifies the achievements of a leading frontiersman of the mid-19th century.

Further Reading

The best study of Bridger's career is J. Cecil Alter, *James Bridger, Trapper, Frontiersman, Scout, and Guide* (1925; rev. ed. 1962). This includes a thorough discussion of his actions and an evaluation of the many folktales surrounding his life. An earlier account is Grenville M. Dodge, *Biographical Sketch of James Bridger* (1905), supposedly based on stories Bridger told to the author. Dale L. Morgan, *Jedediah Smith and the Opening of the West* (1953), examines many of the same people and events from a different perspective and provides additional insight into Bridger's life and contributions. □

Harry A.R. Bridges

The American labor leader Harry A.R. Bridges (1901-1990) became one of the best known radical trade unionists during the 1930s and was thereafter a subject of political controversy. He devoted most of his life and career to the cause of maritime industry workers on the Pacific Coast.

For more than 40 years (1934 to 1979) Harry Bridges earned a reputation as one of the most radical, astute, and successful leaders in the American labor movement. He first came to national attention during the combined waterfront and general strikes which paralyzed San Francisco in 1934. Bridges emerged from this labor conflict as the dominant leader and spokesperson for Pacific Coast waterfront workers. Then, and for many years afterward, his enemies accused him of serving Communist purposes and the federal government several times tried unsuccessfully to deport Bridges. Bridges built his union, the International Longshoremen and Warehousemen's Union (ILWU), into one of the most militant and successful in the nation. Before he retired from active union service in 1979, Bridges also won plaudits from employers for his role as a labor statesman, which meant accepting technological innovations and less total employment on the waterfront in return for union and job security.

Harry Bridges was born in Melbourne, Australia, on July 28, 1901, the oldest of six children in a solidly middle-class family. His father, Alfred Earnest, was a successful suburban realtor, and his mother, Julia Dorgan, was a devout Catholic. Harry received a firm Catholic upbringing, serving four years as an altar boy and attending parochial schools from one of which he earned a secondary diploma in 1917. After leaving school he tried his hand at clerking but was bored by white-collar work.

The sea, however, enthralled Bridges. In late 1917, he found employment as a merchant seaman and remained at sea for the next five years. As a sailor Bridges saw the world, experienced exploitation, became friendly with his more radical workmates, and, for a time, even joined the Industrial Workers of the World (IWW), a left-wing, syndicalist American labor organization. When one of his ships made port in the United States in 1920, Bridges decided to be-

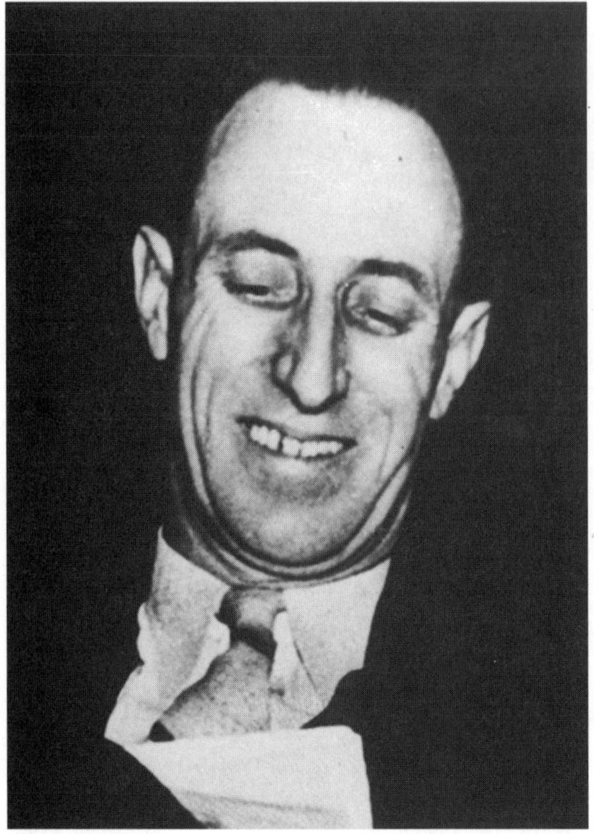

come an immigrant. He even took out his first papers as part of the process of establishing U.S. citizenship. But Bridges' carelessness in meeting the statutory timetable for filing final citizenship papers (as well as his alleged links to communism) became the basis for the government's later attempts to deport him.

Having settled in the United States, Bridges left the sea in 1922 and took up work as a longshoreman in San Francisco. He labored for more than ten years in one of the nation's most exploitative job markets and in a city whose waterfront employers had established a closed-shop company union. During that decade (1922 to 1933) Bridges lived in relative obscurity as an ordinary longshoreman, marrying for the first time in 1923 (he was to be divorced twice and married a third time) and leading a conventional working-class life.

President Franklin D. Roosevelt's New Deal changed all that. The labor upheaval of the 1930s lifted Bridges from obscurity to prominence. When discontent erupted among West Coast waterfront workers in 1933 and 1934, Bridges seized the moment and became a militant union agitator. In 1934 when labor conflict spread up and down the Pacific Coast and culminated in the San Francisco general strike, Bridges acted as the waterfront strikers' most effective leader. He led his followers to a great victory in 1934. The longshoremen in San Francisco won not only union recognition but also a union hiring hall to replace the traditional shape-up in which workers obtained jobs in a demeaning and discriminatory manner.

Building on this success, Bridges next tried to unite all the maritime workers of the Pacific Coast in the Maritime Federation of the Pacific (1935). His plans for waterfront labor solidarity were disrupted by the outbreak of a union civil war between the American Federation of Labor (AFL) and the Congress of Industrial Organizations (CIO). Bridges chose the CIO side, took his union members out of the International Longshoremen's Association (ILA)-AFL, and reorganized them as the ILWU. John L. Lewis, president of the CIO, appointed Bridges to the new union federation's executive board and also as regional director for the entire Pacific Coast. By 1939 Bridges had won a deserved reputation as one of the CIO's new labor men of power.

He had also won many more enemies. Employers found the ILWU to be an especially militant and demanding negotiating partner. Foes in the AFL, among public officials, and even within the CIO used Bridges' links to communism to undercut his influence as a labor leader. Secretary of Labor Frances Perkins tried to deport him in 1939. Through votes and investigations, Congress sought to accomplish the same goal. Not until 1953 when the Supreme Court ruled in Bridges' favor did the government cease its deportation efforts. The charges against Bridges were dropped, and the Supreme Court said, "Seldom, if ever, in the history of this nation has there been such a concentrated and relentless crusade to deport an individual because he dared to exercise the freedom that belongs to him as a human being, and is guaranteed to him under the Consistution." While different branches of the federal government hounded Bridges, Lewis, in 1939, limited Bridges' sphere as a CIO leader to the state of California.

Despite his enemies inside and outside the CIO, Bridges led his union from victory to victory. The labor shortages associated with World War II, the Korean War, and the war in Vietnam, combined with the strategic importance of Pacific Coast ports in the shipping of war-related goods, provided the ILWU with enormous bargaining power which Bridges used to the fullest. He used the power his union amassed on the West Coast as a base from which to organize waterfront and plantation workers in Hawaii. The ILWU brought stable mass unionism to the islands for the first time in their history and thus transformed Hawaii's economic and political balance of power.

Bridges meantime initiated a long strike among Pacific Coast waterfront workers in 1948 that would win them the best labor contract such workers had ever had. But that was to be the last strike Bridges led as a militant labor leader. Shortly after that success for the ILWU, the CIO in 1949-1950 expelled Bridges' union as one of eleven charged with being under communist control and serving the interests of the Soviet Union. By 1960, however, Bridges won a new reputation for himself as a labor statesman. In that year he negotiated a contract with the Pacific Maritime Association which eliminated many union work rules, accepted labor-saving machinery, and tolerated a reduced labor force in return for either guaranteed jobs or annual earnings for more senior union members. A decade later, in 1971-1972, Bridges led his last long strike of 135 days, but it aimed mostly to ratify and strengthen the agreement of 1960, rather than to dilute it. Bridges had made his peace with employers and relished his role as a labor statesman.

In 1968, Bridges was appointed to a city Charter Commission, and then in 1970 he was appointed to the San Francisco Port Commission. In 1977 he retired as ILWU president. During his last eight years as a union leader, Bridges had left far behind the radicalism and controversy that marked his earlier career. But both Bridges and his union remained distinctive. In an era of highly-paid union officials, many of whom lived ostentatious private lives, Bridges remained as abstemious as ever, living frugally on an atypically modest union salary; he had earned only 27,000 dollars a year. In an age of more conservative trade unionism, the ILWU still behaved as a union with a social conscience, promoting racial solidarity, opposing the war in Vietnam, and supporting disarmament and world peace. The ILWU built by Bridges was a legacy in which any trade unionist could take pride, but he always downplayed his role. In 1985 he said, "I just got the credit . . . I just happened to be around at the right time." Bridges died on March 30, 1990, in San Francisco.

Further Reading

The standard biography is Charles P. Larrowe, *Harry Bridges, The Rise and Fall of Radical Labor in the United States* (1972). The same author's *Shape-Up and Hiring Hall* (1955) is the best scholarly treatment of labor on the West Coast waterfront. Irving Bernstein, *Turbulent Years: A History of the American Worker, 1933-1941* (1969) includes a fine brief sketch of Bridges. Gary M. Fink, editor, *Biographical Dictionary of American Labor Leaders* (1984) provides essential facts. □

Percy Williams Bridgman

The American experimental physicist Percy Williams Bridgman (1882-1961) was a pioneer in investigating the effects of enormous pressures on the behavior of matter—solid, liquid, and gas.

Percy Bridgman was born in Cambridge, Mass., on April 21, 1882, the son of Raymond Landon and Mary Ann Maria Williams Bridgman. At high school in Newton, Mass., he was led into the field of science by the influence of one of his teachers.

Bridgman received his doctorate from Harvard University in 1908 and remained there as a research fellow in physics. He married Olive Ware in 1912, with whom he had a daughter and a son. By 1919 he rose to a full professorship, and 7 years later the university appointed him Hollis professor of mathematics and natural philosophy.

In 1946 Bridgman received the Nobel Prize in physics. He was a fellow of the American Academy of Arts and Sciences and at one time served as president of the American Physical Society. He continued to work at Harvard several years after his official retirement, until he died on Aug. 20, 1961.

Bridgman's major work dealt with the building of apparatus for the investigation of the effects of high pressures, apparatus that would not burst under pressures never reached before. Quite by accident he discovered that a packed plug automatically became tighter as more pressure was applied. This proved a key to his further experimentation. Using the steel alloy Carboloy and new methods of construction and immersing the vessel itself in a fluid maintained at a pressure of approximately 450,000 pounds per square inch (psi), which Bridgman later increased to more than 1,500,000 psi, he reached, inside the vessel, 6,000,000 psi by 1950. To measure such hitherto unattainable pressures, Bridgman invented new measuring methods.

The most striking effect of these enormous pressures was the change in the melting point of many substances. Bridgman also found different crystalline forms of matter which are stable under very high pressure but unstable under low pressure. Ordinary ice, for example, becomes unstable at pressures above about 29,000 psi and is replaced by stable forms. One of these forms is stable under a pressure of 290,000 psi at a temperature as high as 180°F. This "hot ice" is more dense than ordinary ice and sinks completely in water.

In 1955 the General Electric Company announced the production of synthetic diamonds, which their scientists, working on methods and information derived from Bridgman's work, had produced from ordinary carbon subjected to extremely high pressures and temperatures.

Further Reading

Reflections of a Physicist (1950; 2d ed. 1955) is a collection of Bridgman's nontechnical writings on science. A detailed biography of Bridgman is in National Academy of Sciences, *Biographical Memoirs,* vol. 41 (1970). Niels H. de V. Heathcote, *Nobel Prize Winners in Physics: 1901-1950* (1954), contains a chapter on Bridgman. He is included in Royal Society, *Biographical Memoirs of Fellows of the Royal Society,* vol. 8 (1962), and in National Academy of Sciences, *Biographical Memoirs,* vol. 12 (1970).

Additional Sources

Walter, Maila L., *Science and cultural crisis: an intellectual biography of Percy Williams Bridgman (1882-1961),* Stanford, Calif.: Stanford University Press, 1990. ☐

John Bright

The English politician John Bright (1811-1889) was one of the leading figures in 19th-century British radicalism. An outstanding orator, he was the most prominent British supporter of the North during the American Civil War.

Born at Rochdale, Lancashire, on Nov. 16, 1811, John Bright was strongly influenced first by the Quaker religion of his family and second by the industrial environment in which he was brought up. His father was a textile manufacturer, and he himself went into the business when he was 16 years old. He revealed a growing interest in the politics of reform throughout the early 1830s, but it required an exceptional sense of commitment to break away from Quaker quietism into platform agitations.

The turning point of Bright's life was his meeting with the reformer Richard Cobden and his involvement in the Anti-Corn Law League, founded in 1839. He was returned to Parliament in 1843, and although his share in the affairs of the League was far smaller than that of Cobden, with whom his name was later bracketed both by contemporaries and historians, his share in following up the work of the league after the repeal of the Corn Laws in 1846 was greater. He pressed not only for further measures of free trade but for further extension of the franchise. He was also bitterly critical of aristocratic influences in British political life and of active British foreign policies which cost money and lives.

Although Bright's political career was lengthy, it was also fitful and interrupted. He was unpopular with most sections of political opinion for his opposition to the Crimean War, and in 1857, for local as well as national reasons, he lost his parliamentary seat at Manchester, the symbolic center of free trade. Instead, he secured a seat at Birmingham, which he represented until his death. Between 1858 and 1867 he was at the head of a reform agitation which he did much to inspire and to guide. He extended his appeal from religious dissenters to workingmen and in the course of devoted campaigns won disciples and made enemies. There was no subtlety in his approach, but he appealed with supreme confidence to underlying moral principles.

More interested in political activism than in administration, Bright nonetheless served under Gladstone as president of the Board of Trade (1868-1870) and in a later government as chancellor of the duchy of Lancaster (1880-1882). He admired Gladstone and contributed to the mobilization of working-class support for Gladstone in the industrial districts. Yet he resigned in 1882, when Gladstone intervened in Egypt, and opposed him in 1886 in the crucial debates on Irish home rule.

During the last phases of his career Bright was dogged by illness, and an element of conservatism, which had never been entirely missing from his temperament, came to the forefront. Animosity toward him disappeared in his last years, when he had the reputation of a patriarch. Yet he was a lonely man after the death of his second wife in 1878—his first had died in 1841 after less than 2 years of marriage—and he was out of touch with new forces in national politics. He died on March 27, 1889, and was buried simply in the Friends' Meeting House in Rochdale.

Further Reading

Bright's speeches, which must be carefully studied to understand the kind of appeal he made, were edited by James E. Thorold Rogers in 1879, his letters by H. J. Leech in 1885, and his diaries by R. A. J. Walling in 1930. The standard biography of Bright is George Macaulay Trevelyan, *The Life of John Bright*

(1913), but it is circumscribed and dated in its approach and needs to be supplemented by Herman Ausubel, *John Bright, Victorian Reformer* (1966), and Donald Read, *Cobden and Bright: A Victorian Political Partnership* (1967). The most penetrating account of Bright's political milieu and claim to leadership is given in J. Vincent, *The Formation of the Liberal Party, 1857-1868* (1966). See also the essay on Bright in Asa Briggs, *Victorian People: Some Reassessments of People, Institutions, Ideas and Events, 1851-1867* (1954; rev. ed. 1970).

Additional Sources

Joyce, Patrick, *Democratic subjects: the self and the social in nineteenth-century England,* Cambridge; New York: Cambridge University Press, 1994.

Robbins, Keith, *John Bright,* London; Boston: Routledge & K. Paul, 1979.

Trevelyan, George Macaulay, *The life of John Bright,* London: Routledge/Thoemmes Press; Tokyo: Kinokuniya Co., 1993. □

Richard Bright

The English physician Richard Bright (1789-1858) discovered the relationship of fluid retention and the appearance of albumin in the urine to kidney disease.

On Sept. 28, 1789, Richard Bright was born in Bristol, the third son of a wealthy merchant and banker. Richard Bright was educated at Exeter, matriculated in Edinburgh University in 1808, and began his medical studies there the following year. In 1810 he joined George Mackenzie on a trip to Iceland and contributed a chapter on botany and zoology to Mackenzie's *Travels in Iceland* (1811). Two years of training in clinical medicine at Guy's Hospital in London followed, and then he returned to Edinburgh, where he received his medical degree in 1813.

Bright studied in Berlin and in Vienna and first became known for his travelog, *Travels from Vienna* (1818), which contained his own illustrations. In 1816 he became a licentiate of the Royal College of Physicians and assistant physician at the London Fever Hospital. Four years later he was appointed assistant physician at Guy's Hospital and opened a private practice at the same time. He advanced to full physician by 1824 and became physician extraordinary to Queen Victoria in 1837.

As a student at Guy's Hospital, one of the world's foremost medical schools, Bright was exposed to the best teaching available. He was impressed with the importance of careful descriptions of disease. His instructors also emphasized the need for correlating clinical observations with gross pathological changes of specific organs after death. A reaction to the theoretical systems which had flourished in the previous century, this approach provided the first sound basis for diagnosis and a modern concept of disease; it contributed little to treatment.

In the first volume of *Reports of Medical Cases* (1827) Bright related dropsy with albuminuria with changes in the kidney and differentiated it from excess accumulation of fluid in cases with heart or liver disease. Although others had demonstrated earlier the presence of albumin in the urine of some patients with dropsy, Bright was the first to relate its presence to kidney pathology. What he described was chronic nephritis, later known as Bright's disease. A collaborative study of 100 cases in 1842, for which two wards and a laboratory were specially set aside, confirmed his thesis. The second volume of *Reports* (1831) dealt with diseases of the nervous system. Bright also published on other diseases, such as acute yellow atrophy of the liver.

Well liked as a teacher and much sought after as a consultant, Bright devoted most of his later years to private practice. At the time of his death from heart disease on Dec. 16, 1858, he had a worldwide reputation as a teacher of pathological anatomy and medicine, an author, and a physician.

Further Reading

William Hale-White, *Great Doctors of the Nineteenth Century* (1935), has a detailed account of Bright's life and work. Essays on Bright are in Samuel Wilks and G.T. Bettany, *A Biographical History of Guy's Hospital* (1892), and in R.T. Williamson, *English Physicians of the Past* (1923). A contemporary appreciation of Bright is in Thomas Joseph Pettigrew, *Medical Portrait Gallery* (4 vols., 1838-1840).

Additional Sources

Berry, Diana, *Richard Bright 1789-1858: physician in an age of revolution and reform,* London: Royal Society of Medicine Services, 1992.

Bright, Pamela, *Dr. Richard Bright, (1789-1858),* London: Bodley Head, 1983. □

Edgar Sheffield Brightman

A leading exponent of American Personalism, Edgar Sheffield Brightman (1884-1953) was an eminent philosopher of religion. His provocative idea of a God limited in power was a unique effort to solve the problem of suffering and evil.

Born in a Methodist parsonage in Holbrook, Massachusetts, on September 20, 1884, Edgar Sheffield Brightman showed an early interest in the scholarly life. He studied Greek in after-school hours when in high school in Whitman, Massachusetts, and began writing articles on stamp collecting when he was 16. By the time he was 18, he had had 46 such articles published. Before he entered Brown University in 1902, he worked for a year in a grocery store earning $3 a week. After receiving his bachelor's degree in 1906, he stayed on at Brown as an assistant in philosophy and Greek and completed his M.A. in philosophy in 1908.

Later that year he began studying for the ministry at Boston University and there came under the influence of Borden P. Bowne (1847-1910), the founder of the philosophy of Personalism. He was awarded a fellowship in 1910 and went to Germany to study with Adolf Harnack in Berlin and Wilhelm Herrman in Marburg. In 1912 he began teaching at Nebraska Wesleyan and, despite arduous responsibilities, completed his doctoral degree. He married Charlotte Hülsen, a young woman he had met in Germany, and one son was born to the couple just a year before the young bride died of cancer.

In 1915 he took a position at Wesleyan University in Connecticut and was so successful that he was made a full professor after only two years. Here he wrote his first book, *The Sources of the Hexateuch* (1918), a study of the documents of the early books of the Old Testament, a hypothesis which challenged the traditional view that Moses was their sole author. He promptly learned what it meant to be criticized by conservative fundamentalists. His second marriage, to Irma B. Fall, took place during this period, and two more children were born, Miriam and Robert.

In 1919 he was called to Boston University, where he taught until his death on February 25, 1953. He was named Borden Parker Bowne Professor of Philosophy in 1925 and also served as chairman of the board of the graduate school for 18 years. Some 80 students received their doctorates under him. His most famous student was Nobel Prize winner Martin Luther King, Jr., who later wrote how much he owed to the personalistic philosophy of Brightman and Bowne.

As a teacher Brightman was close to the ideal. Rigorous planning enabled him to do an amazing amount of scholarly work and yet give personal attention to his many students. Some attended weekly prayer meetings in his office. His religious outlook was one of thoughtful, committed reverence, and while he learned much from religions other than his own, especially Hinduism, he remained an active churchman and had widespread influence on clergymen and church leaders. He spoke of God as "Christlike" and believed that: "To have faith in God is to have faith in the eternal power of truth, of love, and of persuasion as more potent than selfishness, trickery, and competition. A world in which men believe in God is totally different from a world of atheists." He was an opponent of literalism in religion and of irrationalism in theology. His liberalism extended into social and political thought. He knew what it meant to be black-listed by super patriots who could not understand why he opposed war and certain injustices in capitalism.

In demand as a lecturer, Brightman was an active participant and officer in professional associations, serving a term as president of the American Philosophical Association in 1936. He was an early champion of Latin American thought in the northern hemisphere and supported scholars who had to flee Europe or were oppressed by totalitarian regimes in South America. He wrote 16 books and over 100 scholarly articles. His challenging essay on Bertrand Russell's atheistic views earned high praise from Russell himself. His best known book was *A Philosophy of Religion* (1940), which went through 17 printings. His *Introduction to Philosophy* (1925, revised twice, and translated into Chinese, Spanish, and Portuguese) has been used as a college text for over 50 years. He died before he could complete his major systematic work, *Person and Reality,* but former students brought it to fruition in 1958.

His treatise on ethics, *Moral Laws* (1933), was a strikingly original effort to show how broad ethical principles such as the Law of Altruism and the Law of the Best Possible can be formulated. The best short statement of his philosophy may be found in *Nature and Values* (1945). Here he contrasted idealistic Personalism with scientific Naturalism. A selection of his writings was scheduled to appear in 1986, co-edited by the author of this biography.

His approach in philosophy was broadly empirical and his standard of truth was coherence—"inclusive systematic consistency." This truth criterion led him away from abstract theories of the self or soul as a substance to the view that the self is simply consciousness as it knows itself to be,—"the shining present." All knowing is a result of inference from immediate awareness. Practical certainty takes the place of logical necessity. Brightman's idealistic roots went back to Plato and included the thought of Leibniz, Berkeley, Kant, Hegel, and Bowne. His social thought may be characterized as "communitarian Personalism." "Persons are the only profits," he once wrote.

One of the clearest theistic thinkers of the century, Brightman's empirical approach to God by-passed traditional barren arguments and led to his conclusion that God was not an eternal absolute above the temporal process but an immanent spirit present in the world working out his purposes. He wondered why a God who is all-powerful and totally good did not put a stop to the pain, suffering, and deformities of his creatures. Traditional theism sees things like natural catastrophes and severe birth defects as willed by God and as somehow serving an unknown goal.

Brightman, who knew suffering first-hand and was aware of the slow, wasteful process of evolution, could not attribute evils to a good God. He offered the unique proposal that God, though perfect in goodness and wisdom, was not infinite in power. The horrors of our world are not intended by him, but occur because there are certain brutish facts that are "given" in his nature. God creatively works with them but cannot suddenly decree that heavy objects will not fall or hurricanes will cease to blow. With this idea of God, religious people can have trust in a divine companion whose power is sufficient to guide the universe towards "inexhaustible perfectibility" and whose will is ever directed to his children's good.

Further Reading

Edgar Sheffield Brightman is listed in *The Encyclopedia of Philosophy*, Vol. 1. In addition to his key books, many of which are in public libraries and most in university libraries, there are two essays of interest: Andrew Reck, "The Philosophy of Edgar Sheffield Brightman," in *Recent American Philosophy* (1962) and Daniel Callahan's "Human Experience and God: Brightman's Personalistic Theism," in Michael Novack (editor) *American Philosophy and the Future* (1968). Martin Luther King, Jr. speaks of his debt to Brightman in his *Stride Toward Freedom* (1958). □

Albert Brisbane

The American social theorist Albert Brisbane (1809-1890) was the leading advocate of the kind of socialism known in the United States as Fourierism.

Albert Brisbane was born on Aug. 22, 1809, in Batavia, N.Y. His father was an influential landowner and his mother a talented and cultivated woman. At the age of 18, already concerned with the progress of man and society, he decided to pursue his studies with the great social thinkers in Europe and left for Paris.

In France, Brisbane studied under such distinguished philosophers as Victor Cousin and François Guizot but could not seem to find what he sought. He moved to Berlin, took instruction from G. W. F. Hegel, the grandest theorist of all, and enjoyed the city's progressive intellectual circles. Still unsatisfied, he traveled through eastern Europe and the Turkish Empire.

On returning to Paris, Brisbane's interest in ending human degradation was greatly intensified. He read a treatise by Charles Fourier and wrote that after finishing it he "commenced pacing the floor in a tumult of emotion . . . carried away into a world of new conceptions." He then studied under Fourier himself for 2 years. In 1834 Brisbane returned to the United States as a disciple of the French socialists.

What had excited Brisbane were Fourier's ideas about the organization of labor. Brisbane simplified the theories, avoided the bizarre aspects, and emphasized the practical, seizing on the idea of "attractive industry." In an ideal society, types of work would be assigned according to individuals' interests instead of by the cruel accidents of the marketplace and class structure. All work would be respected and paid for according to its usefulness, with the most disagreeable being the most highly paid. The reward for labor would be the gratification an individual found in doing it rather than in differences of prestige. This could be brought about only in new associations of men and women, called phalanxes.

In 1839 Brisbane began lecturing. His *Social Destiny of Man* (1840) and *Association* (1843) explained Fourier's new system of labor. Horace Greeley, an immediate and influential convert, helped Brisbane establish a newspaper, the *Future,* and when it failed gave him a column in his own *New York Tribune* that gained a national audience for Fourierism.

The 1840s were filled with rampant enthusiasm for utopian communities. Quickly, over 40 ventures calling themselves phalanxes were launched. Other communities, like George Ripley's Brook Farm, were converted to Fourierism. Brisbane, however, took no responsibility for them, for they met none of the requirements of careful preparation and financing. Most failed swiftly, and enthusiam for the ideas disappeared.

Though Brisbane could say truthfully that there had been no real trial of Fourierism, the times had moved on. He retired from his propagandizing; only in 1876, in a *General Introduction to Social Sciences,* did he try again to explain Fourierism to Americans.

Brisbane was married twice and had three children. He died on May 1, 1890, in Richmond, Va.

Further Reading

Brisbane's own *Albert Brisbane* (1893) is an autobiography to which a character study by his second wife, Redelia, has been added. For background on American socialism see chapters in Morris Hillquit, *History of Socialism in the United States* (1903; 5th rev. ed. 1910; repr. 1965), and Alice Felt Tyler, *Freedom's Ferment: Phases of American Social History from the Colonial Period to the Outbreak of the Civil War* (1944). A wide-ranging set of essays and an extensive bibliography is in Donald Drew Egbert and Stow Persons, eds., *Socialism and American Life* (2 vols., 1952). □

Benjamin Helm Bristow

Benjamin Helm Bristow (1832-1896) was an American lawyer, Kentucky unionist, and Federal official. As U.S. attorney in Kentucky, he fought the Ku Klux

Klan, and as U.S. secretary of the Treasury, he crushed the Whiskey Ring.

On June 20, 1832, Benjamin H. Bristow was born in Elkton, Ky. His choice of career and politics was influenced by his father, a lawyer and Whig unionist who served in the U.S. Congress. Bristow graduated from Jefferson College in Pennsylvania in 1851, read law in his father's office, and was admitted to the bar in 1853. When Kentucky was torn apart by the outbreak of the Civil War, Bristow raised a regiment for the Union—the 25th Kentucky Infantry—and became its lieutenant colonel. He was wounded at Shiloh but returned to service as lieutenant colonel and then colonel of the 8th Kentucky Cavalry.

The need for Union men in the Kentucky Legislature brought him election to that body in 1863, where he urged emancipation of slaves and ratification of the 13th Amendment. In 1865 he moved to Louisville, where he was appointed assistant U.S. attorney and promoted to U.S. attorney for the Kentucky district. In this post he was confronted by clashes between former secessionists and unionists, racial conflict, and the growing power of the Ku Klux Klan. With the courage and determination that marked his career, he moved against the Klan and against corruption in the Internal Revenue Service. He secured 29 convictions for violations of the Civil Rights Act of 1866, including one capital sentence for murder—putting a crimp in the Klan's style.

After President Ulysses S. Grant appointed Bristow U.S. solicitor general in 1870, he argued several important constitutional cases before the Supreme Court. He resigned in 1872. After a brief tenure as counsel of the Texas and Pacific Railroad, he was again called to Washington as secretary of the Treasury on June 1, 1874. The Treasury Department was riddled with corruption, and he began a housecleaning that made him the talk of Washington and nearly earned him a presidential nomination. His greatest achievement was the dissolution of the Whiskey Ring, an intricate network of collusion and bribery between Federal revenue officers and distillers by which the government was cheated of millions of dollars in taxes. By means of ingenious detective work using secret codes, Bristow's agents infiltrated the ring and obtained voluminous evidence of fraud. In May 1875 distilleries in St. Louis, Chicago, and Milwaukee were seized and their owners arrested. The government indicted 176 men, convicted 110, and collected more than $3,000,000 in back taxes.

Because Bristow's activities endangered members of Grant's inner circle, these men forced his resignation in June 1876. Meanwhile Bristow had emerged as the 1876 presidential candidate of Reform Republicans, but he fell short of the nomination. In 1878 he formed a distinguished law firm in New York. Bristow was elected the second president of the American Bar Association a year later. He died suddenly of appendicitis at his home in New York on June 22, 1896.

Further Reading

A full-length biography of Bristow is Ross A. Webb, *Benjamin Helm Bristow: Border State Politician* (1969). An excellent account of his activities in wartime and postwar Kentucky is in E. Merton Coulter, *The Civil War and Readjustment in Kentucky* (1926). Two large histories of the Grant administration discuss Bristow's prosecution of the Whiskey Ring: William B. Hesseltine, *Ulysses S. Grant: Politician* (1935), and Allan Nevins, *Hamilton Fish: The Inner History of the Grant Administration* (1936). ☐

Benjamin Britten

The English composer, pianist, and conductor Benjamin Britten (1913-1976) revitalized English opera after 1945.

Born in Lowestoft, Suffolk, Benjamin Britten had a normal preparatory school education, at the same time studying with some of the best musicians in England. At the age of 16 he entered the Royal College of Music on a scholarship. By then he had already composed a large quantity of music, and before long he was represented in print with the publication of the *Sinfonietta* for chamber orchestra, written when he was 19.

Prior to World War II Britten furnished music for a number of plays and documentary films. He also continued with other composing, the most prominent item being the *Variations on a Theme by Frank Bridge* (1937), his first major success. He lived in the United States from 1939 to 1942. Despite the turmoil of war, the period from 1939 to 1945 was a highly creative one for him, climaxed by the production of his opera *Peter Grimes* (1945). A year later Britten helped to form the English Opera Company, devoted to the production of chamber opera and in 1948 he founded the summer festival at Aldeburgh, where he made his home. He performed frequently in public as pianist and conductor.

Britten's performance skills were impressive, but even more so were the amount and variety of music he composed. Early in his career he wrote a moderate amount of solo and ensemble music for instruments, among which is *The Young Person's Guide to the Orchestra* (1946), comprising variations and fugue on a theme by Henry Purcell, and later he composed several big works for the cello. Quite in the British tradition, though, music employing voices far outweighs the purely instrumental in his output. He wrote over 100 songs, mainly organized in the form of song cycles or solo cantatas, which he called "canticles," and he made arrangements of several volumes of folk songs. Representative examples are the excellent *Serenade* for tenor, horn, and strings (1943); Canticle No. 3, *Still Falls the Rain* (1954); and *The Poet's Echo* (1967), six songs to poems of Aleksandr Pushkin. Complementing the solo pieces for voice are numerous large works involving chorus, such as A *Ceremony of Carols* (1942), the *Spring Symphony* (1949), the *Cantata Academica* (1960), and especially the *War Requiem* (1962), which are among his best and most popular compositions.

But it is his operas that carried Britten's name farthest. Beginning rather poorly with *Paul Bunyan* (1941), he made a spectacular turnabout with *Peter Grimes*. Following these operas came two chamber operas, *The Rape of Lucretia* (1946) and *Albert Herring* (1947); a new version of *The Beggar's Opera* (1948); *Let's Make an Opera* (1949), a work for children; *Billy Budd* (1951); Gloriana (1953), written for the coronation of Queen Elizabeth II; *The Turn of the Screw* (1954); *A Midsummer Night's Dream* (1960); and three dramatized parables for church performance. While by no means uniformly successful, they represent the most sustained and influential attempt by an Englishman to create an English repertory since the time of Purcell.

With so much music to his credit, Britten must certainly be counted among the most fluent of modern composers. He is also one of the least problematical. Leaving polemics and innovation to others, he settled for a conservative tonal idiom that offers few surprises in vocabulary, textures, or formal organization. His roots are strongly in the English past, centering on Purcell and earlier composers of the Elizabethan and Tudor periods. From Purcell, Britten said he learned how to set English words to music. From this source he also may have derived his attachment to vocal music, including opera, as well as his preference for baroque forms, such as the suite and the theme and variations. Britten's strengths are his masterful handling of choral sonorities, alone or in conjunction with instruments, his imaginative treatment of the word-music relationship, his sharp sense for the immediate theatrical effect, and his unusual interest and skill in writing music for children.

Britten's example stimulated English composition, particularly in the operatic field, as it had not been stirred for ages. The United States recognized his contributions to music when, in 1963, he was the first winner of the $30,000 Robert O. Anderson Award in the Humanities.

In addition to being remembered for his compositions, Britten also gained fame as an accompanist and as a conductor. In 1976 he was declared a life peer (the granting of a non-hereditary title of nobility in Great Britain). He died later that year.

Further Reading

The most recent study of Britten is Mervyn Cooke *Britten and the Far East,* Boydell & Brewer, 1997. Other recent sources are Peter J. Hodgson *Benjamin Britten: A Guide to Research,* Garland Publishing, Inc., 1996; and Peter Evans *The Music of Benjamin Britten,* Oxford University Press, 1996. Hans Keller and Donald Mitchell, eds., *Benjamin Britten: A Commentary on His Works from a Group of Specialists* (1952), is somewhat lavish in its praise but otherwise gives illuminating remarks on Britten's first 40 years. A good general treatment of his works is Patricia Howard, *The Operas of Benjamin Britten: An Introduction* (1969). There is a chapter on Britten in Joseph Machlis, *Introduction to Contemporary Music* (1961). Eric Salzman, *Twentieth Century Music: An Introduction* (1967), provides a good general survey of Britten's period. R. Murray Schafer, *British Composers in Interview* (1963), is a revealing exposition of the tastes and ideas of Britten and his contemporaries. □

Charlie Dunbar Broad

The English philosopher Charlie Dunbar Broad (1887-1971) published in all the major fields of philosophy but is known chiefly for his work in epistemology and the philosophy of science.

On December 30, 1887, C.D. Broad was born at Harlesden in Middlesex, now a suburb of London. He was the only child of middle-class parents and was brought up in comfortable circumstances in a household that included several adult relatives. His early education was at Dulwich College. There he was encouraged to concentrate on scientific subjects and mathematics. He earned a science scholarship to Cambridge University in 1906.

His work in science at Trinity College, Cambridge, was distinguished, but Broad felt that he would never be outstanding as a scientist. Partly owing to the powerful influence of a roster of eminent philosophers at Trinity, a group which included J. M. E. McTaggart, W. E. Johnson, G. E. Moore, and Bertrand Russell, Broad shifted his studies to philosophy. Here too he took first-class honors. In 1911 he won a Trinity fellowship for his dissertation, later published as *Perception, Physics and Reality.* There followed a decade of teaching in Scotland. During World War I, Broad worked as a consultant to the Ministry of Munitions, exempting him from military service in a war he did not support.

In 1920 he was elected to the chair of philosophy at Bristol University, and 3 years later he was invited back to Cambridge to succeed McTaggart as lecturer. There, having decided that marriage was not for him, he settled into rooms once occupied by Isaac Newton and into a fixed, routine life. Lecturing and writing were his chief concerns, and he avoided the famous weekly meetings of the Moral Science Club, which were dominated by the more articulate Ludwig Wittgenstein and Moore. In 1933 he was elected Knightbridge professor of moral philosophy at Cambridge.

Broad's lecture notes formed the basis of his numerous books, of which *Scientific Thought* (1923) and *Mind and Its Place in Nature* (1925) are perhaps the most important. His philosophical work is always competent and well informed if not highly original, and it is expressed in language of admirable lucidity and style. In addition to the usual academic subjects, Broad long pursued an interest in psychical research and urged other philosophers to do the same.

After his retirement from teaching in 1953, Broad lectured for a year in the United States. He then returned to Cambridge to live "an exceptionally sheltered life." There he died on March 11, 1971.

Further Reading

Paul A. Schilpp, ed., *The Philosophy of C. D. Broad* (1959), includes a lengthy autobiographical essay in which Broad gives a very candid and rather unflattering appraisal of his own character and accomplishments. The same volume includes a number of critical, but more appreciative, essays by contemporaries, together with detailed replies by Broad. It also features a complete bibliography through 1959. Also worth consulting is the critical study of Broad's theory of perception, Martin Lean, *Sense Perception and Matter: A Critical Analysis of C. D. Broad's Theory of Perception* (1953). □

Sir Isaac Brock

The British general Sir Isaac Brock (1769-1812) captured Detroit and became known as the "hero of Upper Canada" during the War of 1812 against the United States.

Isaac Brock, born on Oct. 6, 1769, at St. Peter Port on the island of Guernsey, entered the army as an ensign in 1785. Rising by purchase according to the custom of the time, he became a lieutenant colonel in 1797, commanded his regiment in the North Holland expedition in 1799, and later fought in the naval battle of Copenhagen. Sent to Canada with his regiment in 1802, he was promoted to colonel in 1805 and commanded the garrison at Quebec until 1810. He then was placed in charge of all British troops in Upper Canada and was promoted to major general in 1811; after October of that year he was also in charge of the civil government.

Brock brought to his job military skill, magnetic personal character, and expert knowledge of the land and people. Many of the Canadian settlers were former Americans, and one of Brock's problems was keeping the loyalty of the volunteer militia. The local tribes posed another problem. Brock had to influence them against raiding the American frontier, at the same time keeping them loyal to Britain. As for the regular army, Brock wrote that although his own regiment had been in Canada for 10 years, "drinking rum without bounds, it is still respectable, and apparently ardent for an opportunity to acquire distinction."

When the United States declared war on Great Britain in 1812, Brock organized the defense of Upper Canada. He called a special session of the legislature at York (present Toronto), and although it refused to suspend habeas corpus, it did vote supplies. After an American invasion was repelled by the newly formed militia, Brock launched a counterattack. Commanding an army of 1,330 men, including 600 natives led by Chief Tecumseh, Brock sailed down Lake Erie to Detroit, where Gen. William Hull had an American army of 2,500 men. Although Brock was outmanned, he did not hold his ground or retreat but in a daring move advanced on Ft. Detroit, and Hull surrendered without firing a shot. For this achievement Brock was acclaimed the "hero of Upper Canada" and named a knight commander of the Order of the Bath.

From Detroit, Brock hurried to the Niagara frontier to repel another American invasion of Canada, but on Oct. 13, 1812, he was killed at the battle of Queenston Heights. As he fell, his last words were, "Never mind me—push on the York Volunteers." The war continued for over 2 more years, but Upper Canada was saved for Britain because of Brock's victories at Detroit and Queenston Heights.

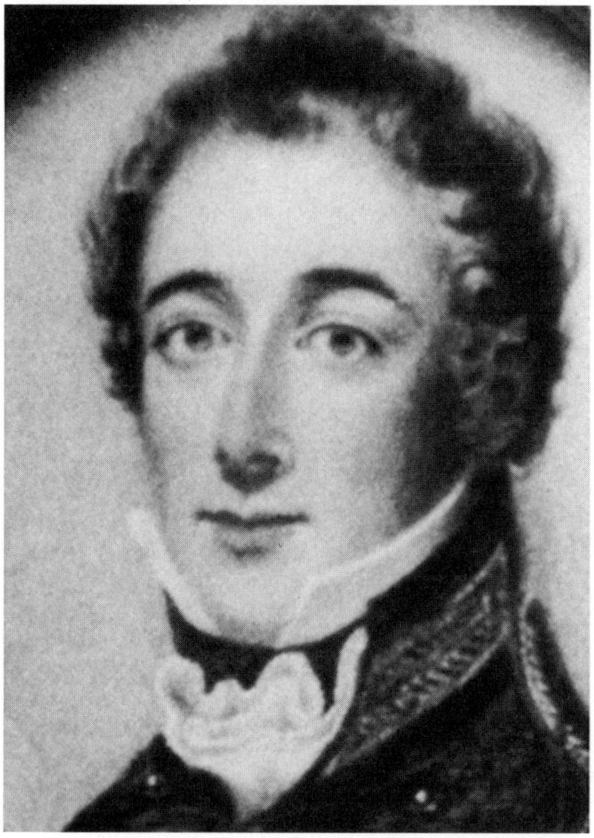

In 1824, on the twelfth anniversary of his death, his remains were placed beneath a monument at Queenston Heights erected by the provincial legislature. In 1840 a fanatic blew up the monument, but in 1841 a new and more stately monument was erected, a tall shaft supporting a statue of Brock.

Further Reading

A biography of Brock is D. J. Goodspeed, *The Good Soldier: The Story of Isaac Brock* (1964). The best account of Brock's role in the War of 1812 is Morris Zaslow, ed., *The Defended Border: Upper Canada and the War of 1812* (1964).

Additional Sources

Richardson, John, *Major Richardson's Major-General Sir Isaac Brock and the 41st regiment,* Burke Falls Ont.: Old Rectory Press, 1976. □

Joseph Brodsky

Nobel Prize winner and fifth U.S. poet laureate, Russian-born Joseph Brodsky (born Iosif Alexandrovich Brodsky; 1940-1996) was imprisoned for his poetry in the former Soviet Union but was greatly honored in the West.

Joseph (Iosif Alexandrovich) Brodsky was born on May 24, 1940, in Leningrad (now St. Petersburg), where he attended school until about 1956. His father was an officer in the old Soviet Navy. The family fell into poverty when the government stripped the older Brodsky, a Jew, of his rank.

When he left school, Joseph began an intensive program of self education, reading widely and studying English and Polish. He worked in photography and as an aid to a coroner and a geologist. He translated into Russian the work of John Donne, the 17th-century English poet, and Czeslaw Milosz, a modern Polish poet. He also wrote his own poetry, which impressed Anna Akhmatova, one of the country's leading literary figures.

His powerful, highly individualistic writing troubled the Communist political and literary establishments, and he was arrested in 1964 for being a "vagrant" and "parasite" devoted to translating and writing poetry instead of to useful work. "It looked like what I've seen of a Nuremberg trial," Brodsky reported years later of his hearing, "in terms of the number of police in the room. It was absolutely studded with police and state security people." The court sentenced him to five years on a prison farm.

One member of the Leningrad Writers' Union, Frieda Vigdorova, dissenting from her colleagues and the court, outraged by the trial and sentence, made available to the outside world her stenographic record of the event. Brodsky's poems and translations were also circulated out-

side the boundaries of what was then the Soviet Union. The resulting protest against his incarceration by leading writers inside and outside the country forced his release after a year and a half. In 1972 the authorities suggested he emigrate to Israel.

After stopping in Vienna, he went on to the United States, where he took up a series of academic posts at the University of Michigan, Columbia University, and Mount Holyoke College. He became an American citizen in 1977. The Soviet Government did not allow him to visit his parents before they died.

Yale University awarded him a Doctor of Letters degree in 1978. In 1979 Italy bestowed him the Mondello Prize. He was named a MacArthur fellow in 1981. The National Book Critics Circle first nominated him for a poetry prize in 1980 for his book *A Part of Speech,* and then awarded him its prize for nonfiction prose in 1984 for a selection of his essays, *Less Than One.* In 1987 he received both a Guggenheim fellowship and the Nobel Prize for Literature. The Library of Congress appointed him poet laureate in 1991.

A London Times Literary Supplement review of his poetry emphasized its "religious, intimate, depressed, sometimes confused, sometimes martyr-conscious, sometimes elitist" nature. Olga Carlisle, in her book *Poets on Street Corners* (1968), wrote, "Not long ago while in Moscow I heard Brodsky's voice on tape, reading his 'The Great Elegy for John Donne.' The voice was extremely youthful and frenzied with anguish. The poet was reciting the elegy's detailed catalogue of household objects in a breathless, rhetorical manner, in the tradition of the poets of the Revolutionary generation. . . . There was a touch of Surrealism to this work—a new, Soviet kind of Surrealism—in the intrusion of everyday detail into the poem."

Stephen Spender, the prominent English poet and critic, writing in the *New Statesman and Nation,* characterized Brodsky's poetry as having "the air of being ground out between his teeth." He went on: "[Brodsky] deals in unpleasing, hostile truths and is a realist of the least comforting and comfortable kind. Everything nice that you would like him to think, he does not think. But he is utterly truthful, deeply religious, fearless and pure. Loving, as well as hating."

In an extended interview with David Montenegro, published in full in *Partisan Review* in 1987, Brodsky reveals his easy grasp of classical and colloquial English as well as his rich understanding of the technical nature of poetry both in its roots and its delicate complexity. Following are excerpts of questions and answers.

(Montenegro) What problems and pleasures do you find in writing prose that you don't find in writing poetry? (Brodsky) In prose you have a more leisurely pace, but in principle prose is simply spilling some beans, which poetry sort of contains in a tight pod. . . . In prose there is nothing that prevents you from going sideways, from digressing.

(Montenegro) What new problems does the modern poet face . . . ? (Brodsky) To think that you can say something qualitatively new after people like Tsvetaeva, Akhmatova, Auden, Pasternak, Mandelstam, Frost, Eliot, and others after Eliot—and let's not leave out Thomas Hardy—reveals either a very enterprising fellow or a very ignorant one. And I would bill myself as the latter.

(Montenegro) What is the power of language through poetry? (Brodsky) I think if we have a notion of Rome and of the human sensibility of the time it's based on—Horace, for instance, the way he sees the world, or Ovid or Propertius. And we don't have any other record, frankly. . . . I don't really know what the function of poetry is. It's simply the way, so to speak, the light or dark refracts for you. That is, you open the mouth. You open the mouth to scream, you open the mouth to pray, you open the mouth to talk. Or you open the mouth to confess.

(Montenegro) Some poets now don't use rhyme and meter, they say, because they feel such form is no longer relevant. . . . (Brodsky) They're entitled to their views, but I think it's pure garbage. Art basically is an operation within a certain contract, and you have to abide by all the clauses of the contract. . . . Meter and rhyme are basically mnemonic devices.

(Montenegro) Do you feel your work's been well translated into English? (Brodsky) Sometimes it has; sometimes it hasn't. On the whole, I think I have less to complain about than any of my fellow Russians, dead or alive, or poets in other languages. My luck, my fortune, is that I've been able to sort of watch over the translations. And at times I would do them myself.

(Montenegro) You knew Auden and Akhmatova, and they seem to have been very important to you. Could you say something about . . . how they struck you or how they affected you? (Brodsky) I can tell you how. They turned out to be people whom I found that I could love. Or, that is, if I have a capacity for loving, those two allowed me to exercise it, presumably to the fullest. . . . Auden, in my mind, in my heart, occupies far greater room than anything or anybody else on the earth. As simple as that. Dead or alive or whatever. . . . Both of them I think gave me, whatever was given me, almost the cue or the key for the voice, for the tonality, for the posture toward reality.

In his Nobel acceptance speech, published in *Poets & Writers,* Brodsky made the following comments on the relation between poetry and politics: "Language and, presumably, literature are things that are more ancient and inevitable, more durable than any form of social organization. The revulsion, irony, or indifference often expressed by literature toward the state is essentially the reaction of the permanent—better yet, the infinite, against the temporary, against the infinite. . . . Every new esthetic experience . . . can in itself turn out to be, if not a guarantee, then a form of defense, against enslavement." He declared that the power of literature helps us "understand Dostoyevsky's remark that beauty will save the world, or Matthew Arnold's belief that we shall be saved by poetry."

Brodsky was a master in creating tension between seemingly arbitrarily summoned images and tight subtle rhyming. A good example appears in the last stanza of his poem "Porta San Pancrazio," which appeared in the *New Yorker* of March 14, 1994. (The poem, which he wrote in Russian, was translated by himself.)

> Life without us is, darling, thinkable. It exists as
> honeybees, horsemen, bars, habitues, columns,
> vistas and clouds over this battlefield whose
> every standing statue triumphs, with its physique,
> over a chance to touch you.

"The Jewish Cemetery," translated by the prominent American poet W. S. Merwin, appears in Olga Carlisle's book *Poets on Street Corners.* It expresses succinctly his ethnic roots and transcendent humanity.

> The Jewish Cemetery near Leningrad
> a lame fence of rotten planks
> and lying behind it side by side
> lawyers, businessmen, musicians,
> revolutionaries.
> They sang for themselves,
> got rich for themselves,
> died for others.
> But always paid their taxes first;
> heeded the constabulary,
> and in this inescapably material world
> studied the Talmud,
> remained idealists.
> Maybe they saw something more,
> maybe they believed blindly.
> In any case they taught their children
> tolerance. But
> obstinacy. They
> sowed no wheat.
> Never sowed wheat,
> simply lay down in the earth
> like grain
> and fell asleep forever.
> Earth was heaped over them,
> candles were lit for them,
> and on their day of the dead raw voices of
> famished
> old men, the cold at their throats,
> shrieked at them, "Eternal peace!"
> Which they have found
> in the disintegration of matter,
> remembering nothing
> forgetting nothing
> behind the lame fence of rotten planks
> four kilometers past the streetcar terminal.

Joseph Brodsky succumbed to a sudden heart attack on January 28, 1996. In a unique memorial service Brodsky was eulogized exclusively in his own words, in the words of other poets, and with music. Brodsky's essays on Robert Frost were published in *Homage to Frost,* after his death.

Further Reading

Brodsky's work and comment on it have been published throughout the world. His books in English include *Elegy to John Donne and Other Poems* (1967; selected, introduced, and translated by Nicholas Bethell); *Selected Poems* (1973; translated by George L. Kline); and *Verses on the Winter Campaign 1980* (1981; translated by Alan Meyers). His Nobel acceptance speech appeared in *Poets & writers* for March/April 1988. The *Partisan Review* interview is reprinted in Montenegro's book *Points of Departure: International Writers on Writing and Politics* (1991). Carlisle's *Poets on Street Corners: Portraits of Fifteen Russian Poets* (1968) has a short summary of Brodsky's career and the texts of several of his poems in Russian with the English translation on facing pages. See also Jacob Weisberg, "Rhymed Ambition" in *The Washington Post Magazine* (January 19, 1992).

Additional Sources

Brodsky, Joseph; Heaney, Seamus; Walcott, Derek, *Homage to Frost,* Farrar, Straus, and Giroux, 1996.

Knight-Ridder/Tribune News Service, March 12, 1996; October 16, 1996. □

Louis Victor Pierre Raymond de Broglie

The French theoretical physicist Louis Victor Pierre Raymond de Broglie (1892-1987) was awarded the Nobel Prize in Physics for his discovery of the wave nature of electrons. He was the founder of wave mechanics.

Louis de Broglie the son of Victor, 5th Duc de Broglie, was born at Dieppe on August 15, 1892. After early education in Paris he entered the Sorbonne, where, as he intended to become a civil servant, he read history and graduated in that subject in 1910. He then studied the physical sciences at the Sorbonne and graduated in them in 1913. In the army during World War I he was active in wireless telegraphy. After the war he did research on theoretical physics at the Sorbonne, and in 1924 he was awarded his doctorate in science with a thesis on the quantum theory which already contained the basis of all his future work.

Origin of De Broglie's Theories

The discovery just before 1900 of the electron, x-rays, and the photoelectric effect had led to doubts regarding the accuracy of the hitherto accepted wave theory of light. Then Max Planck enunciated his quantum theory, according to which radiant energy is always absorbed in finite quantities, or quanta. In 1905 Albert Einstein postulated that light must consist of wave packets, or minute corpuscles in rapid motion, later called photons. By 1911 Lord Rutherford had explained his concept of the atom, and in 1913 Niels Bohr incorporated Planck's ideas into the Rutherford atom. The concept of the Bohr atom led at first to important results, but by about 1920 its usefulness in explaining experimental observations was rapidly declining.

De Broglie's Early Work

At the start of his researches in the early 1920s, De Broglie realized that neither the quantum theory of light nor the corpuscular theory of electrons appeared to be satisfactory. From his theoretical researches he suspected that an electron could not be regarded merely as a corpuscle, but that a wave must be associated with it. He then considered the possibility that in the case of matter, as well as light and radiation generally, it must be assumed that corpuscles are associated with waves.

De Broglie then assumed that any particle of matter, such as an electron, has "matter waves" associated with it. The velocities of propagation of these waves associated with any one particle differ slightly from each other. As a result, these waves combine at regular intervals along the direction of propagation to form a wave crest. This wave crest therefore also travels along the line of propagation, and its velocity (the "group velocity") is quite different from the velocities of the individual waves that combine to form it. The distance between two successive crests of the De Broglie matter wave is known as the De Broglie wavelength (λ).

The nature of the new matter wave postulated by De Broglie was not generally understood. But his hypothesis was not simply an imaginative attempt to envisage a vague possibility, because his theory was backed up by an elaborate mathematical analysis. The wavelength determines the character of the wave, and the moving particle is characterized by its momentum, that is, its mass multiplied by its velocity (*mv*). He was able to deduce a very important equation for the wavelength of the De Broglie wave associated with a particle having a known momentum.

De Broglie's first two papers were published in 1922. The beginning of his theory of wave mechanics, marked by the introduction of his conception of phase waves, was made public by him in September 1923, and within a few months he published three more papers extending his views. His theoretical work was further coordinated and amplified in his doctoral thesis, published in 1924. The thesis attracted the attention of Einstein, who publicly expressed his high regard for this work. As a result, De Broglie's theory received much attention from theoretical physicists. But, as far as was then realized, there was no experimental confirmation of the theory.

Experimental Confirmation

From his theoretical work De Broglie predicted the interference phenomena that would result when a stream of electrons was directed against a solid screen having apertures approximating in size to the matter waves of the electrons. No one had then deliberately attempted such an experiment, as the technical difficulties were too great. But in 1925 Clinton J. Davisson and L. H. Germer had an accident while bombarding a sheet of nickel with electrons. To restore the nickel they heated it; they then found that it had become crystalline and that, relative to the electrons, it behaved as a diffraction grating. Their new results proved that an electron behaves not only as a particle of matter but also as a wave. The calculations made from these experimental results agreed perfectly with those obtained by using De Broglie's formula. These experimental results were not confirmed until 1927, but after that year experimental evidence favoring De Broglie's views greatly increased. This experimental confirmation was vital to the survival of his theoretical work.

De Broglie's Development of Wave Mechanics

Up to this time the De Broglie wave could be determined only in the immediate vicinity of the trajectory. De Broglie now investigated the mechanics of a swarm of particles and was thus able to define the characteristics of the matter waves in space. He was also able to predict accurately the splitting of a beam of electrons in a magnetic field and to explain this phenomenon without reference to any hypothetical electron spin.

In 1927 De Broglie put forward his "theory of the double solution" of the linear equations of wave mechanics, from which he deduced the law that a particle moves in its wave in such a manner that its internal vibration is constantly in phase with the wave that carries it. He soon modified this to his "pilot-wave theory." As a result of criticisms, he temporarily abandoned these theories. But in 1954 he developed his original theory, which now envisaged the particle as constantly jumping from one trajectory to another.

Later Life

From 1924 De Broglie taught theoretical physics in the University of Paris and from 1932 he occupied the chair in that subject for 30 years. He was awarded the Nobel Prize for Physics in 1929. In 1933 he was elected to the Académie des Sciences, and in 1942 he became its Permanent Secretary. In 1944 he was elected to the Académie Française. He was elected a Foreign Member of the Royal Society of London in 1953 and was a member of many other foreign academies, including the National Academy of Sciences of the United States and the American Academy of Arts and Sciences. He received honorary degrees from six universities.

A far-seeing man, De Broglie saw by the middle of World War II that stronger links between industry and science were becoming necessary. In an effort to forge those links, and also to give the theoretical science a practical application, he established a center for applied mechanics at the Henri Poincare Institute, where research into optics, cybernetics, and atomic energy were carried out. His efforts to bring industry and science closer together were highly appreciated by the French government, which rewarded him a post as counselor to the French High Commission of Atomic Energy in 1945.

Among De Broglie's works for theoretical physicists are *Recherches sur la théorie des quanta* (1924), *Nonlinear Wave Mechanics* (1960), *The Current Interpretation of Wave Mechanics* (1964), and *La Thermodynamique de la particule isolée* (1964). Less difficult works are *Ondes et mouvements* (1926), *Matter and Light: The New Physics* (1939), and *New Perspectives in Physics* (1962).

In 1960 de Broglie succeeded his brother Maurice as the 7th Duc. He died in 1987.

Further Reading

For a short biography of De Broglie see *Nobel Lectures, Physics, 1922-1941* (1965), which also contains his Nobel Lecture of 1929. For a discussion of his work see N. H. deV. Heathcote, *Nobel Prize Winners: Physics, 1901-1950* (1953); and A. d'Abro, *The Rise of the New Physics,* vol. 2 (1939). □

Charlotte Brontë

The English novelist Charlotte Brontë (1816-1855) portrayed the struggle of the individual to maintain his integrity with a dramatic intensity entirely new to English fiction.

Charlotte Brontë was born in Thornton in the West Riding of Yorkshire on April 21, 1816, the daughter of an Anglican minister. Except for a brief unhappy spell at a charity school, later portrayed in the grim and gloomy Lowood of the opening chapters of *Jane Eyre,* most of her early education was guided at home by her father.

After the early death of her mother, followed by that of the two older sisters, Brontë lived in relative isolation with her father, aunt, sisters Anne and Emily, and brother Branwell. The children created fantasy worlds whose doings they recorded in miniature script on tiny sheets of paper. Anne and Emily devised the essentially realistic kingdom of Gondal, while she and Branwell created the realm of Angria, which was dominated by the Duke of Zamorna. Zamorna's lawless passions and amorous conquests make up the greater part of her contributions. Created in the image of Byronic satanism, he was proud, disillusioned, and masterful. He ruled by strength of will and feeling and easily conquered women, who recognized the evil in him but were drawn into helpless subjection by their own passion.

This dreamworld of unrestricted titanic emotions possessed Brontë with a terrible intensity, and the conflict between it and the realities of her life caused her great suffering. Thus, although her life was outwardly placid, she had inner experience of the struggles of will with circumstance and of desire with conscience that are the subject of her novels. Her conscience was an exceptionally powerful monitor. During a year at a school in Brussels (1843/1844) she seems to have fallen in love with the married headmaster but never fully acknowledged the fact to herself.

Brontë's first novel was *The Professor,* based upon her Brussels experience. It was not published during her lifetime, but encouraged by the friendly criticism of one publisher she published *Jane Eyre* in 1847. It became the literary success of the year. Hiding at first behind the pseudonym Currer Bell, she was brought to reveal herself by the embar-

rassment caused by inaccurate speculation about her true identity. Of all Brontë's novels, *Jane Eyre* most clearly shows the traces of her earlier Angrian fantasies in the masterful Rochester with his mysterious ways and lurid past. But the governess, Jane, who loves him, does not surrender helplessly; instead she struggles to maintain her integrity between the opposing demands of passion and inhumanly ascetic religion.

Within 8 months during 1848/1849, Brontë's remaining two sisters and brother died. Despite her grief she managed to finish a new novel, *Shirley* (1849). Set in her native Yorkshire during the Luddite industrial riots of 1812, it uses social issues as a ground for a psychological study in which the bold and active heroine is contrasted with a friend who typifies a conventionally passive and emotional female. In her last completed novel, *Villette* (1853), Brontë again turned to the Brussels affair, treating it now more directly and with greater art. But in this bleak book the clear-sighted balance the heroine achieves after living through extremes of cold detachment and emotion is not rewarded by a rich fulfillment.

Despite her literary success Brontë continued to live a retired life at home in Yorkshire. She married a former curate of her father in 1854, but died within a year on March 31, 1855.

Further Reading

Still standard is Elizabeth Gaskell, *The Life of Charlotte Brontë* (2 vols., 1857). Winifred Gérin, *Charlotte Brontë* (1967), is reliable and more complete. Robert B. Martin, *The Accents of Persuasion: Charlotte Brontë's Novels* (1966), is the only book-length critical study. □

Emily Brontë

The English novelist Emily Brontë (1818-1848) wrote only one novel, "Wuthering Heights." A unique achievement in its time, this work dramatizes a vision of life controlled by elemental forces which transcend conventional categories of good and evil.

Emily Brontë was born in Thornton on Aug. 20, 1818, the daughter of an Anglican minister. She grew up in Haworth in the bleak West Riding of Yorkshire. Except for an unhappy year at a charity school (described by her sister Charlotte as the Lowood Institution in *Jane Eyre*), her education was directed at home by her father, who let his children read freely and treated them as intellectual equals. The early death of their mother and two older sisters drove the remaining children into an intense and private intimacy.

Living in an isolated village, separated socially and intellectually from the local people, the Brontë sisters (Charlotte, Emily, and Anne) and their brother Branwell gave themselves wholly to fantasy worlds, which they chronicled in poems and tales and in "magazines" written in miniature script on tiny pieces of paper. As the children matured, their personalities diverged. She and Anne created the realm of Gondal. Located somewhere in the north, it was, like the West Riding, a land of wild moors. Unlike Charlotte and Branwell's emotional dreamworld Angria, Gondal's psychological and moral laws reflected those of the real world. But this did not mean that she found it any easier than her sister to submit herself to the confined life of a governess or schoolmistress to which she seemed inevitably bound. When at the age of 17 she attempted formal schooling for the second time, she broke down after 3 months, and a position as a teacher the following year proved equally insupportable despite a sincere struggle. In 1842 she accompanied Charlotte to Brussels for a year at school. During this time she impressed the master as having the finer, more powerful mind of the two.

The isolation of Haworth meant for Brontë not frustration as for her sister, but the freedom of the open moors. Here she experienced the world in terms of elemental forces outside of conventional categories of good and evil. Her vision was essentially mystical, rooted in the experience of a supernatural power, which she expressed in poems such as "To Imagination," "The Prisoner," "The Visionary," "The Old Stoic," and "No Coward Soul."

Brontë's first publication consisted of poems contributed under the pseudonym Ellis Bell to a volume of verses (1846) in which she collaborated with Anne and Charlotte. These remained unnoticed, and *Wuthering Heights* (1847) was unfavorably received. Set in the moors, it is the story of the effect of a foundling named Heathcliff on two neigh-

boring families. Loving and hating with elemental intensity, he impinges on the conventions of civilization with demonic power.

Brontë died of consumption on Dec. 19, 1848. Refusing all medical attention, she struggled to perform her household tasks until the end.

Further Reading

Elizabeth Gaskell, *The Life of Charlotte Brontë* (2 vols., 1857), is a basic source. Charles W. Simpson, *Emily Brontë* (1929), is reliable and incorporates subsequently revealed material. See also Muriel Spark and Derek Stanford, *Emily Brontë: Her Life and Work* (1953). □

Bronzino

The Italian painter Bronzino (1503-1572) was one of the leaders of the second generation of Florentine mannerists. He is noted chiefly for his stylized portraits, cold in color but impeccable in realism of detail.

Born at Monticelli near Florence on Nov. 17, 1503, Angelo di Cosimo, called Bronzino was trained principally under Raffaellino del Garbo and Pontormo. According to Giorgio Vasari, Bronzino's portrait appears in Pontormo's *Joseph in Egypt* (ca. 1515). In his earliest works, often produced in collaboration with Pontormo, Bronzino's style reconciles influences from his two masters. Intellectual dependence on the late-15th-century style of Raffaellino prevented Bronzino from fully understanding the visionary imagination of Pontormo, and Bronzino's fresco *St. Benedict* (ca. 1526-1530) in the Badia, Florence, with its hard modeling, classicizing types, and objectivity of form and detail shows the beginnings of his lifelong academicism.

After the siege of Florence in 1530 Bronzino fled to Urbino, but he was soon recalled to collaborate again with Pontormo on the frescoes for several Medici villas. Bronzino's contributions to the ceremonial decorations for the triumphal entry of Eleanor of Toledo into Florence in 1539 resulted in his appointment that year as official court painter to the grand duchy of Tuscany. The autocratic, sophisticated atmosphere of Cosimo I's court, precisely reflected in Bronzino's formal and frigid portraits of the 1540s, was already hinted at in the detached impersonality of the still-Pontormesque *Ugolino Martelli* (ca. 1535-1538). In *Eleanor of Toledo and Her Son* (ca. 1545) the emotionless, carved faces are set off against a brittle, cold display of color and brilliantly observed realistic detail. Such portraits, and works like the *Allegory with Venus, Cupid, Folly, and Time* (ca. 1546), disturbing in its ice-cold, fragile sensuality, had a farflung impact in courtly circles throughout Europe.

Although his study of Michelangelo's Florentine works was evident in Bronzino's works of the 1530s when he was forming his court style, later on Bronzino developed comparatively little within the general tendencies of painting under the repressive conditions of the Counter Reformation, even remaining apparently unaffected by such revolutionary works as Michelangelo's *Last Judgment.* The academic, as opposed to imaginative, qualities of Bronzino's style, clearly dominant in the confused compositions and overdesigned figures of such late narrative works as the fresco *Martyrdom of St. Lawrence* (1565-1569) in S. Lorenzo, Florence, brought him into sympathetic contact with such Florentine academic mannerists as Vasari and Francesco Salviati, who were, like Bronzino, prominent members of the Florentine Academy. Bronzino died in Florence on Nov. 23, 1572.

Further Reading

The standard monograph on Bronzino is in Italian. In English see Arthur McComb, *Agnolo Bronzino: His Life and Works* (1928). Useful background material is in Giuliano Briganti, *Italian Mannerism* (trans. 1962).

Additional Sources

McCorquodale, Charles, *Bronzino,* New York: Harper & Row, 1981. □

Peter Brook

Peter Brook (born 1925) was a world renowned theater director, staging innovative productions of the works of famous playwrights.

Peter Brook was born in London in 1925, the son of immigrant scientists from Russia. A precocious child with a distaste for formal education but a love of learning, Brook performed his own four-hour version of Shakespeare's *Hamlet* at the age of seven. After spending two years in Switzerland recovering from a glandular infection, Brook became one of the youngest undergraduates at Oxford University. At the same time he wrote scripts for television commercials and introduced to London audiences his first professional stage production, Marlowe's *Dr. Faustus.*

Brook, called the "golden boy," did his first production at Stratford Theatre, one of the world's most prestigious stages, at the young age of 21. It was Shakespeare's *Loves Labours Lost.* He spent the next several years staging acclaimed productions of plays. He worked at the Covent Garden directing opera, as well as designing the sets and costumes for his productions. Always seeking innovations and styles which would make his productions speak to modern audiences, he ended this experience with opera by calling it "deadly theater." He directed plays with prominent actors, including Laurence Olivier in *Titus Andronicus* and Paul Schofield in *King Lear.* (Brook also directed the film version of this production.) In 1961 Peter Brook directed one of his seven films, the chilling Peter Shaffer adaptation of *Lord of the Flies.*

Despite his successes and the fact that he was named as one of the directors of the famous Royal Shakespeare Company in 1962, Brook continued to seek out alternative ways to create vibrant, meaningful theater. This search led him to direct a season of experimental theater with the Royal Shakespeare Company in which he was free from the commercial constraints of box office concerns. The season was called "Theatre of Cruelty," a name taken from the works of Antonin Artaud, one of this century's most influential theater men. Brook's desire was to turn away from stars and to create an ensemble of actors who improvised during a long rehearsal period in a search of the meaning of "holy theater."

Out of this search would come the director's finest work. In 1964 Brook directed Genet's *The Screens* and Peter Weiss' *Marat Sade,* for which he received seven major awards and introduced Glenda Jackson to the theater. Influenced by Bertolt Brecht and Artaud, *Marat Sade* shocked the audience with its insane asylum environment. In 1966 he developed *US,* a play about the Vietnam experience and the horrors of war. The production reflected a collective statement by all of the artists involved and was certainly a departure from traditional theater. Jerzy Grotowski, one of the most important theater directors of this century and a man who profoundly influenced Brook, came to work with the company during this production. Brook also did an adaptation of Seneca's *Oedipus* by Ted Hughes, a renowned English poet who continued to collaborate with the director for many years. The culmination of this phase of Brook's work was his production of *A Midsummer Night's Dream* (1970). Using trapezes, juggling, and circus effects, Brook and his actors created a sense of magic, joy, and celebration in this interpretation of Shakespeare's play. It was a masterpiece of the theater.

After this highly successful production, Brook went to Paris and founded the International Center of Theatre Research. He wanted to find a new form of theater that could speak to people worldwide—theater which was truly universal. He also wanted to work in an environment of unlimited rehearsal time in order to allow for a deep search-of-self for all involved. The first production that came out of this third phase was *Orghast* (1971), which employed a new language based on sound developed by Ted Hughes. This production, performed at the ruins of Persepolis in Persia, used actors from many different cultures. Brook sought a communication that transcends language, to find the common experience of all of us. In 1972 and 1973 his group traveled across the Sahara and elsewhere in Africa with the *Conference of the Birds* project, performing in each village and learning their ancient rituals.

In the 1980s and 1990s, Brook saw a variety of his productions staged, both in Europe and America. He directed *The Cherry Orchard,* first in Paris in 1981, then later in New York in 1988. Other works during this time included *Tchin, Tchin* (1984), *Qui Est La* (1996), and *The Director Who . . .* (1996).

Qui Est La was staged in Paris and was a reinterpretation of *Hamlet.* Typically for Brook, his choices were anything but traditional. At one point in the play, a character delivered a speech in Japanese, which led James Fenton to observe in *The New York Review of Books* (1996), "You are going to have to rely on your memory now, and on your imagination, as much as on what you see and hear." The play was not a complete *Hamlet,* as many might have hoped, but rather a combination of Shakespeare and Brook's dialogue about theater. Of the production, Fenton further observed, "What is tantalizing - frustrating even - is to see suggested a whole production of *Hamlet.* . . . only to have it whisked away again as we return to the dialogue about theater."

Brook never relied on traditional approaches in his direction. Although his next work, *The Man Who . . .* (1996), met better critical acclaim than *Qui Est La,* it too relied heavily on theory. Brook's objective with the play, as with many of his other works, was to transcend what separates all people, whether culturally or intellectually, and find a common language within the context of the play. In *The Man Who . . . ,* he painted portraits of insanity, taken from the case studies of Oliver Sacks, a psychiatrist whose work formed the basis for the opera *The Man Who Mistook His Wife for a Hat,* as well as the film *Awakenings* (1991). In the play's program notes Brook wrote, "For a long while, within our theater work, I have been searching for a common ground that could involve the spectator directly. . . . whatever the social and national barriers, we all have a brain and we think we know it." His experiment met much critical success when performed at the Brooklyn Academy of Music in spring of 1996, though some reviewers didn't find the work entirely gratifying. In *The New Republic*

Robert Brustein wrote, "[Brook] . . . persists in seeking One Worldism through theater experiments . . . The problem is that, whatever Brook's prodigious theatrical gifts, playwrighting is not among them. The piece grows tedious because it displays no dramatic progress."

This type of work was highly experimental in the world of theater and was not accepted by all. Undeterred by opinion, Brook proceeded into exploration of this little known area of the theater. He believed that traditional theater had lost its meaning, and his journey was to learn about his own barriers and his own deceptions and to face them. Essentially a theater scientist with an intellectual approach to theater, he wanted to discover the soul. Brook had the courage to be an innovator in the world of the theater.

Brook wrote an important book, *The Empty Space* (1968), and was the director of over 60 productions, including an acclaimed production of Bizet's opera *Carmen.*

Further Reading

In 1988 Brook published his autobiography, *The Shifting Point. Peter Brook, A Biography* (1971) by J.C. Trewin is a thorough examination of Brook's work, and *A Midsummer Night's Dream. Directors' Theatre* (1968) by Judith Cook includes a short biography of the director. In 1996 several biographies were published, including *Peter Brook: Directors in Perspective,* edited by Albert Hunt and Geoffrey Reeves, as well as *Into Brook's Rehearsal - And Beyond - An Actor Adrift,* by Yoshi Oida with Lorna Marshall. The following books are examinations of individual productions or projects: *Peter Brook's production of William Shakespeare's* A Midsummer Night's Dream (1974) by Glen Loney; *The Making of* A Midsummer Night's Dream (1982) by David Selbourne; Orghast *at Persepolis* (1973) by Anthony Smith; *US: The Book of the Royal Shakespeare Production* (1968) by Peter Brook; and *Conference of the Birds: the Story of Peter Brook in Africa* (1977) by John Herlpern. For insight into Brook's theories see his book *The Empty Space* (1968). □

Sir James Brooke

Sir James Brooke (1803-1868) was a British empire builder and the first "white ruler" of Sarawak, Borneo. Founder of a dynasty, Brooke ruled with integrity, justice, and a sympathetic understanding of the indigenous population.

James Brooke was born on April 29, 1803, in Benares, India, son of Thomas Brooke, a judge of the High Court of India. At 15 James was sent to England for his schooling, and in 1819 he joined the armed forces of the East India Company. He was seriously wounded in the First Burmese War of 1824 and returned to England to recuperate. Upon his return to India in 1829, he resigned from the East India Company, and en route home again to England he visited China and Malaya.

Greatly impressed with the Malay Archipelago, Brooke invested in a yacht, the *Royalist,* and a trained crew, and in 1839 he arrived in northern Borneo to carry out scientific research and exploration. In Sarawak he met Pangeran an Muda Hashim, to whom he gave assistance in crushing a rebellion, thereby winning the allegiance of the Malays and Dayaks. In 1841 Muda Hashim offered Brooke the governorship of Sarawak in return for his help.

Raja Brooke was highly successful in suppressing the widespread piracy of the region. Malay nobles in Brunei, unhappy over Brooke's measures against piracy, arranged for the murder of Muda Hashim and his followers. Brooke, with assistance from a unit of Britain's China squadron, took over Brunei and restored its sultan to the throne. In return the sultan ceded complete sovereignty of Sarawak to Brooke, who in 1846 presented the island of Labuan to the British government.

Piracy, mainly by Sea Dayaks, continued to be a major problem, and in 1849, at the request of the sultan of Brunei, Brooke and his Malays raided the Sea Dayak area but did not gain a decisive victory. Shortly afterward, several vessels of the China squadron succeeded in stamping out piracy.

Early in his rule Brooke was concerned with the status of his dominion. The Chinese uprising, and the later Malay rebellion, made him aware of the need for foreign protection, and after the British government refused to provide a protective relationship, he toyed with the idea of turning Sarawak over to the Dutch. His heir designate and nephew, Capt. James Brooke (who had changed his name from Charles Johnson), was completely against any cession. Sir James continued his efforts to obtain England's recognition

but without success. In 1863 he retired to England, where he died after a stroke on June 11, 1868.

It is generally conceded that Brooke was a poor administrator and incompetent at finances, but his understanding of the Malays, Dayaks, and other people of Sarawak was profound, and his improvement of their status was undeniable.

Further Reading

A biography of Brooke is Emily Hahn, *James Brooke of Sarawak* (1953). He is treated in some detail in Robert Payne, *The White Rajahs of Sarawak* (1960), and Steve Runciman, *The White Rajahs: A History of Sarawak from 1841 to 1946* (1960).

Additional Sources

Ingleson, John, *Expanding the empire: James Brooke and the Sarawak lobby, 1839-1868,* Nedlands, W.A.: Centre for South and Southeast Asian Studies, University of Western Australia, 1979.

St. John, Spenser, Sir, *The life of Sir James Brooke: rajah of Sarawak: from his personal papers and correspondence,* Kuala Lumpur; New York: Oxford University Press, 1994.

Tarling, Nicholas, *The burthen, the risk, and the glory: a biography of Sir James Brooke,* Kuala Lumpur; New York: Oxford University Press, 1982. □

Rupert Brooke

The English poet Rupert Brooke (1887-1915) was the poet-patriot hero of World War I. He is the most famous representative of Georgian poetry, a short-lived literary movement of the early 20th century.

Rupert Brooke was born on Aug. 3, 1887, at Rugby, where his father was a master at the school. At Cambridge University, Rupert achieved distinction as a scholar. Remarkably handsome and a superb athlete, he had a romantic disposition, evident in his undergraduate poetry, which ranged from the exuberantly amorous to the fashionably cynical. Like other youthful poets of this period, he vowed a rebellion against Victorianism. Mistrustful of Victorian sentimentalism and the devotion to beauty of the fin de siècle, the new poets dedicated themselves to achieve "realism" or "truth to life." The intent of this rebellion was to produce vigorous and simple poetry which shunned affectedly literary phrasing and relied on a diction appropriate to the incidents of life which it portrayed.

This "realism" in Brooke's first volume, *Poems* (1911), was to excite some opposition from critics who found it too "coarse," but otherwise it received little attention. Brooke and his friend and mentor Edward Marsh conceived the idea of an anthology of the works of contemporary new poets in order to develop a new audience for poetry. Walter de la Mare, John Masefield, D. H. Lawrence, and others contributed poems, and the resulting volume, *Georgian Poetry,* appeared at the end of 1912. The volume was instantly and continuously successful, and Georgian poetry became a recognized movement, with Brooke as its dominant figure.

But before the second volume of *Georgian Poetry* was published in 1915, Brooke had died. Disenchanted, after some years of travel, with "a world grown old and cold and weary," he had, like many of his young and idealistic contemporaries, responded to the declaration of war in 1914 with enthusiastic idealism. While not on active service, Brooke died of blood poisoning at Skyros in the Aegean Sea on April 23, 1915. His death in the midst of popular success as a poet and within a year of the publication of his war sonnet "The Soldier" excited a deep response not only from contemporary poets, who published moving tributes, but also from politicians and from the general public.

Despite the banner of poetic revolution under which it was published, Brooke's verse is seen in retrospect to consist only in the simple, direct expression of sentiments traditional to the young romantic of English poetry, or sometimes, as in "The Great Lover," merely in the rhetorical exaggeration of the commonplace. Like most of the poems in *Georgian Poetry,* his work is often meditative, imbued with a love of the English countryside, spiced by an easy sense of disillusionment at the transience of deeply cherished earthly experiences, and moved by an expressed desire for order and certainty and peace in a world seemingly less ordered than the playing fields and gardens and villages of Brooke's childhood.

Further Reading

Brooke inspired many biographical, personal, and critical tributes from his friends and contemporaries. The most distinguished work is Edward Marsh, *Rupert Brooke: A Memoir* (1918). Norman Douglas offers some interesting comments on Brooke in *Looking Back: An Autobiographical Excursion* (1933). Henry James's introduction to Brooke's *Letters from America* (1916) indicates the esteem in which contemporary men of letters held Brooke. An early study of Brooke is Walter de la Mare, *Rupert Brooke and the Intellectual Imagination: A Lecture* (1919). A more recent book is Christopher Hassall, *Rupert Brooke: A Biography* (1964). The most scholarly study of Brooke in relation to his literary milieu is in Robert H. Ross, *The Georgian Revolt: 1910-1922* (1965). Geoffrey Keynes compiled *A Bibliography of Rupert Brooke* (1954).

Additional Sources

Brooke, Rupert, *Letters from America,* New York: Beaufort Books, 1988.

Brooke, Rupert, *Rupert Brooke in Canada,* Toronto: PMA Books, 1978.

Clark, Keith., *The muse colony: Rupert Brooke, Edward Thomas, Robert Frost, and friends: Dymock, 1914,* Bristol England: Redcliffe, 1992.

Delany, Paul, *The Neo-pagans: Rupert Brooke and the ordeal of youth,* New York: Free Press, 1987.

Laskowski, William E., *Rupert Brooke,* New York: Twayne; Toronto: Maxwell Macmillan Canada; New York: Maxwell Macmillan International, 1994.

Lehmann, John, *Rupert Brooke: his life and his legend,* London: Weidenfeld & Nicolson, 1980.

Lehmann, John, *The strange destiny of Rupert Brooke,* New York: Holt, Rinehart, and Winston, 1980.

Pearsall, Robert Brainard, *Rupert Brooke; the man and poe,* Amsterdam, Rodopi, 1974. □

Anita Brookner

Anita Brookner (born 1928), a British art historian specializing in 18th-and 19th-century painting, was the first woman to hold the rank of Slade Professor at Cambridge University (1967-68). Brookner is also a successful author, publishing several scholarly works, as well as seventeen novels. Her novel, *Hotel du Lac* (1984) won the Booker Prize, England's highest award for fiction.

Anita Brookner was born on July 16, 1928, in London, England. Her mother was a former professional singer and her father was a Polish emigré businessman. Brookner once admitted that her family's Jewish roots often made her feel like an outsider in her native land, that she could not be English no matter how she tried. "I have never learned the custom of the country. We were aliens . . . tribal. I doubt that you ever get away from the people before you."

After earning her B.A. from King's College, University of London, and her Ph.D. in art history at the Courtauld Institute of Art in London, Brookner went on to develop a successful career as lecturer and teacher of eighteenth and nineteenth century French art and culture. She was an instructor at the University of Reading (1959-64), Lecturer in Art History at Courtauld, and the first woman to achieve the prestigious title of Slade Professor at Cambridge University (1967-68).

Brookner wrote several scholarly books including *Watteau* (1968), *The Genius of the Future: Studies in French Art Criticism* (1971), *Greuze: The Rise and Fall of an Eighteenth Century Phenomenon* (1972), and *Jacques-Louis David* (1980). Although Brookner's works were generally well-received by academia, not all scholars agreed on the academic merits of her research. Dr. Graham Smith, retired professor and vice-principal of Wulfrun College (Wolverhampton, England), wrote the following for Wulfrun's *American Studies Resource Guide* (1996). "Some very poor history in this [*Jacques-Louis David*] but it's an accessible biography and if treated with caution does have some useful material on the Revolution's pageant master. Take no notice of anything she says on the Revolution as a whole."

A general malaise of spirit coupled with the boredom of a summer vacation prompted Brookner to write her first novel, *A Start in Life* (1981). During an interview for *The Paris Review* (Fall, 1987), Shusha Guppy quoted Brookner as saying, "My life seemed to be drifting in predictable channels and I wanted to know how I deserved such a fate. I thought if I could write about it I would be able to impose some structure on my experience."

Throughout her books, several parallels clearly exist between Brookner and her protagonists, who are almost always highly intellectual, emotionally reserved women alienated from the mainstream of life. Brookner herself made the comment, "If my novels contain a certain amount of grief, it is to do with my not being what I would wish to be . . . more popular . . . socially more graceful . . . . " This struggle to find a balance between inner acceptance and social acceptance is reflected in the strongly female themes that dominate Brookner's novels.

Brookner's second novel, *The Debut* (1981), received praise for perceptive character development and the clever intermingling of narrative and literary background. The protagonist, Ruth Weiss, a specialist in French literature, struggles to break free from the moral obligations that restrict her life. Weiss, hoping to emulate Balzac's female protagonist, Eugenie Grandet, goes to Paris to study. But Weiss' dream of being rescued by a hero fails. Weiss resigns herself to fate and returns to London to care for her querulous, aging parents.

Kitty Maule, protagonist in *Providence* (1984), is another intelligent woman disillusioned by the discrepancies between literature and reality. When Maule's affair with a colleague fails to earn his love, her yearnings for love and social acceptance into the British social milieu which he represents remain unfulfilled.

In *Hotel du Lac* (1984) Brookner uses melancholy wit, sharp observations, and ironically misdirected passions to relate another quiet victory of a lonely woman over emotional predators. The novel won England's prestigious Booker Prize, the highest honor bestowed on books of fiction.

The main character of *Hotel du Lac* is middle-aged Edith Hope, best-selling author of romance novels. She is an industrious woman with literary sensibilities, trapped in doomed romantic yearnings. Single and financially independent, Hope leads a wellordered life that includes a socially desirable but boring fiance, whom she mocks; monthly trysts with her married love; and regular lunches with her best friend. Hope's deliberate avoidance of her own wedding transgresses the firm but unwritten conventions of her society. She becomes a social and emotional outcast, exiled to the secluded Hotel du Lac.

Hope views the other women residing at the hotel as social misfits. When the only male guest at the hotel, Mr. Neville, accuses Hope of living a wretched life because she is single, her sense of self-worth is further diminished. She is tempted by the thought that if she accepts a marriage of convenience with Neville she will regain her position in society.

Although Hope rejects his proposal, Neville's philosophy towards life causes Hope to reevaluate her own understanding of femininity, sex, and motherhood. By the end of the novel, Hope has come to a new acceptance of what she wants from life and returns to London and her married lover.

In *Family and Friends* (1985), the focus is not on a solitary woman but on a large Jewish-European family. Brookner explores the familial bonds of dependence that create a network of enduring and complex emotional relationships. Her prose style is tightly controlled and intelligent.

A Misalliance (1986) returns to familiar Brookner territory, the world of a professionally acclaimed woman who views herself as a failure. In Brookner's earlier novels, literature provided the novel's witty counterpoint. In *A Misalliance* Brookner calls upon her own world of art history to enrich the narrative.

Other Brookner novels include *Look At Me* (1983), *A Friend From England* (1987), *Latecomers* (1988), *Lewis Percy* (1989), *Brief Lives* (1990), *A Closed Eye* (1991), *Fraud* (1992), *Dolly* (1993), *A Family Romance* (1994), *A Private View* (1994), and *Incidents in the Rue Laugier* (1996).

Brookner's observant stories about British society have been compared to the works of Henry James and Jane Austen, while the wry isolation and secretive passions of her heroines are reminiscent of stories written by the Emily and Charlotte Brontë.

Further Reading

Reviews by Adam Mans-Jones (January 31, 1985), D.J. Enright (December 5, 1985), and Rosemary Dinnage (June 1, 1989) in *New York Review of Books* provide detailed critiques of several Brookner's novels. John Updike reviews of *Latecomers* in *The New Yorker* (May 1, 1989). Interviews with Brookner have appeared in *Publishers Weekly* (September 6, 1985), *Saturday Review* ("Self-Reflecting," May/June 1985), and *The Paris Review* (Fall, 1987). □

Gwendolyn Brooks

Gwendolyn Brooks (born 1917) was the first African American to receive a Pulitzer Prize for Poetry and is best known for her intense poetic portraits of urban African Americans.

Gwendolyn Brooks was born on June 7, 1917, in Topeka, Kansas. The eldest child of Keziah (Wims) Brooks, a schoolteacher, and David Anderson Brooks, a janitor who, because he lacked the funds to finish school, did not achieve his dream of becoming a doctor. Brooks grew up in Chicago and, according to George Kent, was "spurned by members of her own race because she lacked social or athletic abilities, a light skin, and good grade hair." She was deeply hurt by this rejection and took solace in her writing. She became known to her family and friends as "the female Paul Lawrence Dunbar" and received compliments on her poems and encouragement from James Weldon Johnson and Langston Hughes, prominent writers with whom she initiated correspondence and whose readings she attended in Chicago. By the age of sixteen, she had compiled a substantial portfolio, consisting of over 75 poems.

Early Career

After graduating from Wilson Junior College in 1936, she worked briefly at "The Mecca," a Chicago tenement building. She participated in poetry readings and workshops at Chicago's South Side Community Art Center, producing verse that would appear in her first published volume, *A Street in Bronzeville* in 1945.

In 1939 she married Henry L. Blakeley, and together they would raise two children: Henry, Jr., and Nora. When she married she became a housewife and mother. But instead of directing her creative energy entirely to domestic chores, Brooks wrote poetry when the children were asleep or later while they were in school. In this way she wrote several collections of poetry, which constitutes her early work: *A Street in Bronzeville, Annie Allen* (1949), *The Bean Eaters* (1960), and *Selected Poems* (1962). During this time she also wrote a novel, *Maud Martha* (1953).

The work of this period is characterized by her portraits of urban African American people involved in their day-to-day activities and by her technical form, lofty diction, and intricate word play. Critics have frequently labeled her early work as intellectual, sophisticated, and academic. Although these poems sing out against social and sexual oppression, they are frequently complex and, therefore, in need of close textual reading to uncover their protest and Brooks' own social commentary. In many of these works she criticized the color prejudice which African American people inflict on one another by calling attention to their tendency to prefer light-skinned African American people. In *Annie Allen* and *Maud Martha* she examined the conventional gender roles of mother and father, husband and wife, and found that they frequently stifle creativity out of those who try to

live up to artificial ideals. But this social criticism tends to be pushed back into the complicated language.

In recognition of these works, in 1950, Brooks was awarded a Pulitzer Prize for Poetry, and became the first African American to be granted this honor.

New Tone

In 1967, Brooks' work achieved a new tone and vision. She simplified her technique so that her themes, rather than her techniques, stood in the forefront. This change can be traced to her growing political conscienceness, previously hinted at in *Selected Poems,* after witnessing the combative spirit of several young African American authors at the Second Black Writers' Conference held at Fisk University that year. These works include: *In the Mecca* (1968), *Riot* (1969), *Aloneness* (1971), *Family Pictures* (1971), the autobiographical *Report from Part One* (1972), *The Tiger Who Wore White Gloves: Or, What You Are You Are* (1974), *Beckonings* (1975), and *Primer for Blacks* (1980). These works are much more direct, and they are designed to sting the mind into a higher level of racial awareness. Foregoing the traditional poetic forms, she favored free verse and increased the use of her vernacular to make her works more accessible to African Americans and not just academic audiences and poetry magazines.

During the 1970s, Brooks taught poetry at numerous institutions for higher learning, including Northeastern Illinois State College (now Northeastern Illinois University), University of Wisconsin at Madison, and the City College of the City University of New York. She continued to write, and while her concern for the African American nationalist movement and racial solidarity continued to dominate her verse in the early-1970s, the energy and optimism of *Riot* and *Family Pictures* were replaced in the late-1970s with an impression of disenchantment resulting from the divisiveness of the civil rights and "Black Power" movements. This mood was reflected in *Beckonings* (1975) and *To Disembark* (1980), where she urged African Americans to break free from the repression of white American society and advocated violence and anarchy as acceptable means.

Later, Brooks spent her time encouraging others to write by sponsoring writers' workshops in Chicago and poetry contests at correctional facilities. In 1985, she was named as the consultant in poetry for the Library of Congress. In short, she has taken poetry to her people, continuing to test its relevance by reading her poetry and lecturing in taverns, barrooms, lounges, and other public places as well as in academic circles.

In later years Brooks continued to write, with *Children Coming Home* (1992) and *Blacks* (1992). In 1990 Brooks' works were ensured a home when Chicago State University established the Gwendolyn Brooks Center on its campus. She continued to inspire others to write, focusing on young children by speaking and giving poetry readings at schools around the country.

In 1997, on the occasion of her 80th birthday, she was honored with tributes from Chicago to Washington D.C. Although she was honored by many, perhaps the best description of Brooks' life and career came from her publisher, Haki Madhubuti, when he said, "She is undoubtedly one of the top 100 writers in the world. She has been a chronicler of black life, specifically black life on the South Side of Chicago. She has become almost a legend in her own time."

Honors

In addition to her Pulitzer Prize, Brooks has been awarded an American Academy of Arts and Letters Award (1946), a Guggenheim Fellowship (1946 and 1947), a *Poetry* magazine award (1949), a Friend of Literature Award (1963), a Black Academy of Arts and Letters Award (1971), a Shelley Memorial Award (1976), an *Essence* Award (1988), a Frost Medal from the Poetry Society of America (1989), a Lifetime Achievement Award from the National Endowment for the Arts (1989), a Jefferson Award from the National Endowment for the Humanities (1994), as well as some 49 honorary degrees from universities and colleges, including Columbia College in 1964, Lake Forest College in 1965, and Brown University in 1974. Moreover, she was named poet laureate of Illinois in 1969 and was inducted into the National Women's Hall of Fame in 1988. In 1985 she reached the pinnacle of her career when she became the poetry consultant at the Library of Congress, the second African American and the first African American woman to hold that position.

Further Reading

The best source of biographical information is Brooks' own autobiography, *Report from Part One* (1972). Critical information on Brooks includes Don L. Lee "The Achievement of Gwendolyn Brooks," in *Black Scholar* (Summer, 1972); Gloria T. Hill "A Note on the Poetic Technique of Gwendolyn Brooks," in *College Languages Association Journal* (December, 1975); Suzanne Juhasz "A Sweet Inspiration . . . of My People: The Poetry of Gwendolyn Brooks and Nikki Giovanni," in *Naked and Fiery Forms* (1976); Hortense J. Spillers "Gwendolyn the Terrible: Propositions on Eleven Poems," in *Shakespeare's Sisters* (1979); George E. Kent "Aesthetic Values in the Poetry of Gwendolyn Brooks," in *Black American Literature and Humanism,* edited by R. Baxter Miller (1981); Mari Evans "Gwendolyn Brooks," in *Black Women Writers, 1950-1980* (1983); and Claudia Tate "Gwendolyn Brooks," in *Black Women Writers at Work* (1983).

Further biographical information on Brooks can found in Shirley Henderson "Our Miss Brooks on Eve of Her 80th Birthday, Poet Offers Some Answers," in the June 6, 1997 issue of the *Chicago Tribune* and in Heather Lalley "Paying Tribute to Illinois' Poet Laureate as Brooks Turns 80, City Finds Words to Describe Her Power to Inspire," in the June 5, 1997 issue of the *Chicago Tribune*. Her life and works are also the subject of George E. Kent *A Life of Gwendolyn Brooks* (1990). □

Phillips Brooks

American Protestantism's most respected figure in the last half of the 19th century, Phillips Brooks (1835-1893) derived his stature from his personal qualities rather than from his position as scholar, saint, or ecclesiastical statesman.

Phillips Brooks was born on Dec. 13, 1835, in Boston, the second of six sons of a family of affluence, respectability, piety, and learning. After graduation from Harvard and a brief, wretched teaching experience, he prepared himself for the Episcopal ministry at the Alexander, Va., seminary. Ordained a deacon in 1859, he served with growing distinction in two churches in Philadelphia, a city he loved. In 1869 he was called to Boston's Church of the Holy Trinity.

Brooks quickly became Boston's first citizen, knowing the sheer adulation of the worshipers who regularly packed Trinity to hear his compelling sermons and to view his serene yet radiant presence. His fame spread. In the entire annals of the Episcopal Church the power of his preaching is unmatched. Invitation after invitation to preach came his way, as did honorary degrees from the nation's leading universities and England's Oxford. Greatly admired abroad (he was an inveterate world traveler), he was the first American to preach in the Royal Chapel at Windsor. In 1891 he was elected bishop of Massachusetts, the culmination of a life of nobility. His unexpected death in 1893 caused Lord Bryce to observe that not since Lincoln's assassination had America so widely mourned the loss of a leader.

Brooks's mind was poetic rather than analytical. It is revealing that his pen produced the carol "O Little Town of Bethlehem" rather than enduring theological works. Although learned, Brooks was not an academician. He neither anguished over the shattering new findings of science and scholarship nor argued the case for Christianity philosophically. Rather, luminously and passionately, he presented to his people the full and joyous life open to all who accepted Christ as the revelation of what God is and man may be.

Brooks was not a narrow sectarian, however. One of his great services to the Protestant Episcopal Church was in moderating High Church tendencies and also in helping to prevent a change of name to "The American Church."

Standing an imposing six feet four inches and weighing 300 pounds, quite without effort on his own part Brooks commanded respect. He was also loved, for his manner was sunny and nonchalant, never pompous. Brooks never married, a decision he regretted in his last years; despite a legion of friends, he remained lonly without a wife or children.

Born to social and economic security and preaching primarily to "proper Bostonians," Brooks had little to say about the problems challenging post-Civil War America. He probably had little comprehension of the exploitation, bitterness, and injustice at work in urban, industrial America. He was not a reactionary, but his conception of reform was of the most limited, patrician variety. Indeed in the year of his death, a year of desperate economic depression, both the manner of the man and the message of his preaching already seemed outmoded.

Further Reading

The most illuminating of Brooks's own writings is *Lectures on Preaching, Delivered before the Divinity School of Yale College* (1877). Alexander V. G. Allen, *Life and Letters of Phillips Brooks* (2 vols., 1900), is massive, splendidly written, and totally admiring. Two briefer but equally uncritical biographies are William Lawrence, *Phillips Brooks: A Study* (1903), and Raymond W. Albright, *Focus on Infinity* (1961). Albright's *A History of the Protestant Episcopal Church* (1964) is the standard study of that denomination. □

Joyce Brothers

The psychologist Joyce Brothers (born 1927) pioneered the trend to phone-in questions for professional psychological advice. Her rise to prominence in "pop-psych" in electronic media followed her unusual success on a television quiz show in the mid-1950s.

Joyce Brothers, popular psychologist of a radio, television, and reading audience since 1958, was born about 1927, one of two daughters to Morris K. and Estelle (Rapoport) Bauer. Both her lawyer parents taught their children the importance of academic excellence and the work ethic.

As a bright child, Brothers displayed many of the qualities that would help establish her professional career. She was an honors student in high school, received a B.S. degree with honors in psychology from Cornell University (1947), and obtained her M.A. degree from Columbia University in 1949. She then married a medical student, Milton Brothers, and continued her research and teaching. In 1953 she earned her Ph.D. from Columbia, having completed her dissertation on the topic of anxiety avoidance and escape behavior.

After their daughter was born, Brothers gave up her teaching posts at Columbia and Hunter College (New York City) because she believed it vital in the early development of children to have one parent at home. (In 1974 she said that a father could be that parent, but generally the mother got that responsibility.)

Without her teaching salary the family was soon in financial straits because her husband's resident's income was minimal. To supplement their funds Joyce determined to try for an appearance on the television quiz show *The $64,000 Question* (1955). By laboriously memorizing 20 volumes of a boxing encyclopedia, Joyce Brothers became the only woman and the second person ever to win the top prize. She later remarked that she had good motivation "because we were hungry."

When the *$64,000 CHALLENGE,* which pitted experts in certain fields with the contestant, replaced *The $64,000 Question,* Brothers' boxing knowledge dismayed the seven ex-boxer experts. She answered each question correctly and brought her total earnings to $134,000, making her one of the biggest winners in the history of television quiz shows.

In spite of accusations of quiz show corruption and subsequent investigations which exposed the fact that some

contestants were given answers prior to the shows, Brothers emerged unscathed in the quiz-fix scandal. She later revealed that the producers had planned to "knock me out" with impossible questions, but she had memorized her subject so thoroughly that she could provide all the right answers.

Her fame in the quiz shows led to her public psychologist career. In 1956 Brothers cohosted *Sports Showcase ,* in which she interviewed prominent sports figures and discussed sports events. Her charm, dignity, and intelligence led to several appearances on television "talk shows."

By 1958 NBC offered her a trial on local afternoon programs in which she advised on the topics of love, marriage, sex, and child-rearing. When she proved an instant success, the same format was telecast nationally. Soon Brothers had several late-night shows (under various titles and formats) which included topics which had been tabooed earlier, such as menopause, frigidity, impotence, and sexual satisfaction. Much of her success was attributed to her sympathetic manner and her ability to discuss issues in laymen's terms rather than professional jargon. Brothers also gave personal advice on a number of phone-in radio programs. Some were taped, while others were "live," which sometimes provided on-the-air drama.

To her colleagues who criticized her for giving advice without knowing her callers well enough, Brothers responded that she did not attempt to treat mental illness, nor did she practice therapy on the air, and that when needed she advised callers to seek professional help. Her supporters also suggested that her public performance approximated group therapy with its many advantages.

Brothers also wrote a syndicated newspaper column for 350 daily newspapers, authored magazine articles, and advised several manufacturers on women's needs. She authored several books, including *Ten Days To A Successful Memory* (1964), *How To Get Whatever You Want Out of Life, What Every Woman Should Know About Men,* and *What Every Woman Ought to Know About Love and Marriage* (1985).

In the 1970s Brothers spoke against sexist bias, citing the need to change textbooks because children quickly pick up sexist attitudes from them. She noted that non-sexist cultures tend to be less war-like because the man does not have to prove that he is big and strong and needs to protect the weaker woman. She called for children to learn that it is fine to be either male or female, thereby developing more positive attitudes about themselves.

Without tremendous organizational ability, Brothers could scarcely have managed her many and varied professional activities. Without her keen interest in learning new things (she taught herself plumbing in college and could do her own electrical wiring), her multi-faceted life would have been less stimulating and her impact on American society less significant. Since she pioneered the psychological phone-in show in the 1960s, the idea proliferated to the extent that by 1985 there was an Association of Media Psychologists to monitor for abuses.

In the 1990s Brothers authored several books, including *Positive Plus: The Practical Plan for Liking Yourself Better* (1995), and *Widowed* (1992). She wrote the latter after losing her husband in 1990, and it is a guide to dealing with grief for women who have lost their spouses. The movie rights to the story were optioned by ABC -TV, and a television movie is scheduled. Brothers also appeared in Garry Marshall's 1996 film, Dear God.

Brothers' books have been translated into 26 different languages, and she was a regular columnist for *Good Housekeeping* magazine. In her columns, she addressed family-oriented topics such time together and the secret to a successful marriage. In her June 1994 *Good Housekeeping* article she said, "We are beginning to realize that real solutions to many of the nation's difficult problems may in fact be found in the home." Brothers also regularly wrote on other topical issues such as obsession and the elements of a healthy patient-doctor relationship. Throughout her career, Brothers guest-lectured at colleges and universities.

Further Reading

Biographical information on Joyce Brothers is limited primarily to interviews given in periodicals, her comments in electronic media, and newspaper accounts of her press conferences. A brief section entitled "The Joyce Brothers Story" in her book *Ten Days To A Successful Memory* (1964) gives insights into that period of her life when she became a successful quiz-show contestant. Additional materials may be gleaned from *Authors In The News,* Vol. 1 (1976); *Coronet* (November 1968), *New York Times* (January 5, 1971), *Newsday* (June 22, 1970), and *Good Housekeeping* (December 1980). A Web site with biographical information can be accessed at www.clark.net/pub/speakers/on-line/spkr1069.html. □

Harry Samuel Broudy

American philosopher and educator Harry Samuel Broudy (born 1905) received world-wide recognition for his philosophical theories about education, education in a democracy, the aesthetics of education as a dimension of learning, and the presuppositions of competency-based and performance-based teacher education.

Harry Samuel Broudy (born on July 27, 1905) emigrated with his parents, Michael and Mollie (nee Wyzanski) Broudy, from Filipowa, Poland to the United States in 1912 and took up residence in Milford, Massachusetts. After his high school graduation, Broudy chose to enroll at Massachusetts Institute of Technology (MIT), rather than follow his father's wishes and enter into rabbinical studies.

Broudy soon discovered that his real interests lay with literature, philosophy, and psychology, not with chemical engineering. He left MIT and earned his B.A. from Boston University in 1929; he was valedictorian for his graduating class. Broudy worked as a reporter for the *Milford Daily News* after his graduation. In 1932, he enrolled at Harvard University where he studied under the well-known philosophers William E. Hocking, C.I. Lewis, and Alfred North Whitehead. Broudy earned his M.A. from Harvard in 1933 and his Ph.D. in 1936.

It was the height of the Great Depression when Broudy graduated. Unable to find a position as a college instructor, he went to work as a supervisor at the Massachusetts Department of Education. In 1937, Broudy secured a faculty position at Massachusetts State College at North Adams where he taught psychology and philosophy. He transferred to Framingham State Teachers College in 1949 and remained there until 1957. Broudy married Dorothy L. Hogarth in 1947 and they had one child, a son named Richard.

It was during his years at Framingham State Teachers College that Broudy wrote *Psychology for General Education* (with E.L. Freel, 1956). He also served as president in both the Philosophy of Education Society (1953) and the Association for Realistic Philosophy (1955).

Broudy's philosophical views were based on a tradition of classical realism. He viewed philosophy as a classical discipline concerned with truth, goodness, and beauty. But he was also influenced by the modern philosophies, especially existentialism and instrumentalism. In his popular textbook, *Building a Philosophy of Education* (1954, 1961), Broudy put forth two major ideas central to his philosophical outlook; first, truth is independent of the individual knower, and second, there are universal structures to be found in humanity's struggle for education and the good life.

In 1957, Broudy was appointed professor of Philosophy of Education at the University of Illinois where he gained a reputation as one of America's leading educational philosophers. One issue which he frequently addressed was a concern for education in a democracy. (*Democracy and Excellence in American Secondary Education* with B.O. Smith and J.R. Burnette, 1964, and *Truth and Credibility: The Citizen's Dilemma,* 1981.) He believed that for a democracy to flourish, all citizens must have general knowledge (education) and moral commitment.

Broudy also studied the issues centered around society's demands on schools. (*The Real World of the Public Schools,* 1972, and *The Uses of Schooling,* 1988.) He saw education as the common link that united a diverse society and he urged the society to renew its commitment to the schools.

In his classic study *Enlightened Cherishing: An Essay in Aesthetic Education* (1972), Broudy sought to establish the relationship between the aesthetic dimension of learning and education. Broudy strongly believed that imagery held a central role in a child's ability to develop concepts, values, and language skills. In *The Role of Imagery in Learning* (1987) and *The Role of Art in General Education* (video, 1988) Broudy stressed the role of images in everyday experiences, particularly in the development of the educated mind.

Although he recognized the importance of John Dewey's philosophy of "warranted assertion as an outcome of reflective thought," Broudy believed in "warranted commitment," a rational process in which individuals decide upon principles and ideals to which they can then make a moral committment.

Broudy further believed that warranted commitment could best be achieved through a common formal study of the arts and sciences. According to this philosophy, schools could best withstand societal demands by remaining focused on the experiences and enduring aspects of human nature found in the arts and sciences. Broudy's philosophy was that of the classical realist; let the demands of external reality support individual rationality and social well-being.

A prolific author, Broudy was a major contributor to several collaborative works including *Exemplars of Teaching Method* with J.R. Palmer (1965); *Philosophy of Education: An Organization of Topics and Selected Sources* with M.J. Parsons, I.A. Snook, and R.D. Szoke (1967); and *Philosophy of Educational Research* with Robert Ennis and L.I. Krimerman (1973).

Broudy was also editor of the acclaimed educational journal *Educational Forum* (1964-72) and was a regular contributor to yearbooks for the National Society for the Study of Education.

Broudy's work brought him widespread recognition, including honorary doctorate degrees from Oakland University (1969), Eastern Kentucky State University (1979), and Massachusetts State College at North Adams (1981). He was distinguished visiting professor at Memorial University of Newfoundland (1974) and at California State University (1978). He filled several distinguished lectureships including the Bode Lecture (1960), the Kappa Delta Phi Lecture (1972), the Damon Lecture (1976), the De Garmo Lecture (1979), and the John Dewey Lecture (1983). He was a fellow at the Center for Advanced Study in the Behavioral Sciences (1967-1968), and he received a grant from the Spencer Foundation in 1983.

Broudy officially retired from University of Illinois in 1974, but remained active as professor *emeritus* in the College of Education. He wrote, lectured, and participated in other educational projects until the early 1990s when Alzheimer's disease forced him into full retirement.

Further Reading

Harry Samuel Broudy is listed in the *Biographical Dictionary of American Educators* (1978), the *Dictionary of American Scholars* (1982), *Leaders in Education* (1974), and *Who's Who in America* (1988-1989). A more detailed accounting of his philosophical beliefs is found in his autobiographical statement, "Unfinishable Business," in *Mid-Twentieth Century American Philosophy,* edited by P.A. Bertocci (1974). A brief biographical review of Broudy's theory of aesthetic education is Ronald H. Silverman's "Harry S. Broudy: Super Advocate for the Arts," *School Arts* (March 1979). □

Adriaen Brouwer

The Flemish painter Adriaen Brouwer (c. 1605-1638) exerted an immense influence on his contemporaries. His success as a painter of genre subjects ensured the popularity of scenes of peasant life in Dutch and Flemish painting of the 17th century.

Adriaen Brouwer was born at Oudenaarde in the southern Netherlands. There is no reliable account of his training as an artist. He lived in Holland, working in Haarlem and Amsterdam, from about 1625 until 1631. In Haarlem he undoubtedly knew and was influenced by Frans Hals. An early painting, typical of Brouwer's Dutch period, is the *Pancake Man,* which, with its lumpish, misshapen peasant types and strong local colors, recalls the 16th-century Flemish master Pieter Bruegel the Elder.

In 1631 Brouwer was in Antwerp, where he was listed as a master in the Guild of St. Luke (the painters' guild) and where he remained until his death, at only 32 years of age, in 1638. During these few years the artist produced some masterpieces. In works such as the *Peasants Playing Cards* the sharp local colors of the early period have been replaced by an all-embracing tonality and a more painterly handling, probably derived from Hals; and the observation of human foibles and passions has likewise become more acute and sympathetic. Despite their sometimes coarse subject matter, Brouwer's figure paintings are remarkable for their sensitive color and refinement of execution. Not to be overlooked among the works of the last Antwerp years are his landscape paintings, which have a surprising freshness and poetic quality.

The records plainly show that Brouwer was a man of unconventional behavior: he undoubtedly led a rather bohemian existence and was frequently in debt. Nevertheless, it should be emphasized that the traditional picture of the artist as a dissolute and irresponsible buffoon is largely an invention of early biographers, who seem to have believed that Brouwer's manner of life resembled that of the uncouth boors in some of his tavern scenes.

Both Peter Paul Rubens and Rembrandt paid Brouwer the compliment of acquiring paintings by his hand for their own collections. Brouwer's principal followers in the rendering of peasant subjects were the Dutch painter Adriaen van Ostade and the Flemish painter David Teniers the Younger.

Further Reading

The best books on Brouwer are by Dutch and German scholars. An early attempt to define the artist's output is C. Hofstede de Groot, *Catalogue Raisonné of the Works of the Most Eminent Dutch Painters,* vol. 3 (trans. 1911). The fundamental study, still not supplanted, is Wilhelm von Bode's monograph in German, *Adriaen Brouwer, sein Leben und seine Werke* (1924), which contains all the documents relating to the artist's life; Bode regarded Brouwer as "the most gifted Netherlandish master of the 17th century after Rembrandt and Rubens," and this assessment of the painter and his work has not been seriously modified by subsequent scholarly investigation. Gerard Knuttel, *Adriaen Brouwer, the Master and His Work* (trans. 1962), is a well-illustrated monograph which seeks to present a new critical evaluation of the painter and his artistic development. □

Earl Russell Browder

Earl Russell Browder (1891-1973) was the head of the Communist party of the United States during its most influential and prosperous period, 1930-1945. He was the best-known native-born Communist in American history.

Earl Browder was born on May 20, 1891, in Wichita, Kansas, one of 10 children. His father was a teacher in the local schools who had also been a Methodist minister and farmer and whose political convictions were avidly Populist. Browder's formal education ended with the third grade when, because of his father's poor health, he went to work to help support the family. At the age of 15 Browder followed his father into the Socialist party, but within a few years he moved on to the still more radical Syndicalist League of North America, led by William Z. Foster. After working briefly on a Syndicalist magazine, he took a correspondence course in law and became manager of a cooperative store in Olathe, Kansas.

Browder resisted conscription in World War I, like many other political radicals, and as a result he spent 16 months in state and federal prisons. Soon after he left prison, he joined the newly organized Communist party, which was forced to operate clandestinely because of steady government harassment during the "Red Scare" of the immediate postwar years. He also went to work as an editor for Foster's Trade Union Educational League (TUEL) in New York City. In 1921 Browder and Foster represented the TUEL at the Communist-inspired International of Labor Unions in Moscow. Two years later, after the underground Communist party merged with the legal Workers party to form what eventually became the Communist party of the United States, Browder became a top aide to Foster in his efforts to gain the leadership of the new organization.

In 1926 Browder returned to Moscow for another trade union conference and from there journeyed to China as part of an international Communist delegation. In China he edited an underground newspaper for a Communist propaganda agency called the Pan-Pacific Trade Union Secretariat, until shortly before the stock market crash in the fall of 1929. Returning to the United States, Browder helped Foster become general secretary of the party. When poor health soon forced Foster to assume the less strenuous post of party chairman, as Foster's protégé (and perhaps at the behest of the Stalin regime) Browder easily succeeded to the party leadership.

The mild-mannered Browder seemed an unlikely revolutionary. Yet during the 15 years of his leadership, the Communist party gained many new members and consider-

able respectability, especially within the American intellectual community. Browder managed to ride out several sudden and spectacular changes in the official Communist line that emanated from Moscow. From violent denunciation of the New Deal as the precursor of fascist dictatorship, the party moved in the "Popular Front" period (1935-1939) to temporary cooperation with non-Communist leftists and the New Deal; then in the 20 months following the Nazi-Soviet pact of August 1939, to insistence on strict American neutrality toward the European war; and finally, after Germany invaded the Soviet Union, to wholehearted support for the Roosevelt administration and the American war effort. In 1942 Roosevelt commuted a four-year Federal prison sentence Browder had received two years earlier for falsifying his passport. On the eve of the 1944 presidential campaign, Browder announced that the Communist party, to demonstrate its patriotism and to solidify bipartisan backing for Roosevelt, had been transformed into the Communist Political Association.

At the close of the war the party's membership, boosted by the wartime American-Soviet alliance and the party's apparent patriotic fervor, stood at an all-time peak of more than 75,000. But in the spring of 1945, with the war almost over, the party officially shifted once again, from cooperation with liberal capitalism to militant opposition to both the capitalist system and to the further expansion of United States power in the world. But Browder, an enthusiastic advocate of postwar cooperation with the established order, could not survive this latest shift in Moscow's thinking. That July a special convention of the Communist Political Association repudiated "Browderism," dissolved the association, reestablished the Communist party of the United States, and denied Browder a place on the party's national committee. Early in 1946 the party officially expelled him.

After 1946 Browder, no longer even a rank-and-file Communist party member, continued to live in Yonkers, N.Y., earning a living mainly from writing and occasional editing jobs. His wife, the former Raissa Irene Berkman, whom he had married in Moscow during the 1920s, died in 1955. The Browders had three sons, none of whom followed a political career. The Federal government permitted Browder to live in peace after 1959, when it dropped an indictment returned against him 7 years earlier on the grounds that he had lied on his wife's citizenship application about her membership in the Communist party. Browder died on June 27, 1973, at the home of his son William, in Princeton, New Jersey.

Further Reading

There is no adequate biography of Browder. For information on his career—and on the history of the American Communist party, from which his career is inseparable—see Irving Howe and Lewis Coser, *The American Communist Party: A Critical History, 1919-1957* (1957); Theodore Draper, *The Roots of American Communism* (1957) and *American Communism and Soviet Russia, the Formative Period* (1960); and David A. Shannon, *The Decline of American Communism* (1959). ☐

Alexander Brown

The merchant and banker Alexander Brown (1764-1834) became one of America's first millionaires. He was a leading promoter of the city of Baltimore.

Alexander Brown was born and raised in Ireland, where he established himself as a linen merchant in Belfast. In 1800 he, his wife, and his sons emigrated to Baltimore, Md. He brought with him not only his stock of goods, but, evidently, a considerable amount of capital and advantageous connections with family members in business in England.

Brown's mercantile interests developed rapidly. One source reports that he obtained a monopoly of the linen trade in the Baltimore area. From an importer of foreign goods, Alexander Brown and Sons became an exporter of cotton and tobacco, a major shipper commanding a fleet of sailing vessels, and a commission brokerage and banking establishment with agents in all the major Southern ports.

Continuous growth was achieved despite the hazards of business in a developing country, the danger to shipping during the War of 1812, and economic panics, like that of 1819. Native caution, substantial capital, and a policy of strategic expansion seem to account for Brown's spectacular success. In 1810 he established a Liverpool branch of the business under his eldest son, William (later Sir William Brown). The English office, through which American remittances, credit instruments, and securities flowed, enabled the firm to take a large role in international trade and finance. In 1818 a Philadelphia office was opened by another son, John, and in 1825 a New York branch under still another son, James. Both of these firms were to continue in operation for more than a century under the name of Brown Brothers and Company.

In addition to his private banking concerns, Alexander Brown was a leading advocate of the Second Bank of the United States. He himself owned a large block of its stock, and he sold more to other buyers. Brown led the fight against the Bank's first officers, who were speculating in its stock, and helped to gain the appointment of more reliable businessmen to its board. He was a director of the Mechanics Bank of Baltimore and of the Baltimore branch of the Bank of the United States.

Brown and his son George were among the principal architects and persistent supporters of the Baltimore and Ohio Railroad, the first significant railroad line in America. It had been undertaken to maintain Baltimore's competitive advantage in an era when New York City had acquired the Erie Canal, and Philadelphia the Susquehanna Canal, to link them with markets in the West. By the mid-1820s the Browns were clearly Baltimore's most prominent capitalists.

From his first years in the city, Alexander Brown had also taken an active role in civic life. In 1804 he had helped organize a municipal waterworks; in 1825 he was one of the incorporators of the Maryland Institute of Art. In 1834, the year of his death, his credit helped save Baltimore's Bank of Maryland.

Brown was one of America's very few millionaires in the antebellum period, leaving a personal fortune estimated at more than $2 million. After his death the mercantile aspects of his business were gradually diminished, and the companies he had founded became exclusively banking concerns.

Further Reading

Most of the sources for Brown's life are privately printed company histories, such as Frank R. Kent, *The Story of Alexander Brown and Sons* (1925). Bray Hammond, *Banks and Politics in America: From the Revolution to the Civil War* (1957), is recommended for general historical background. See also John Crosby Brown, *A Hundred Years of Merchant Banking* (1909). □

Benjamin Gratz Brown

The American politician Benjamin Gratz Brown (1826-1885) served Missouri as senator and governor and gained national prominence in 1872 as the vice-presidential nominee on the Liberal Republican ticket.

On May 28, 1826, B. Gratz Brown was born in Frankfort, Ky. He studied at Transylvania College and the Yale Law School, from which he graduated in 1847, and then settled in St. Louis, Mo., becoming a partner in a law firm. He quickly became involved in Missouri politics as a supporter of Thomas Hart Benton and spokesman for the Benton wing of the divided state Democratic party. Brown served in the Missouri Legislature (1852-1858) and furthered his political career as editor of the *Missouri Democrat* (1854-1859).

After the election of 1856 Brown's opposition to the expansion of slavery into American territories and to sectionalism, nullification, and secessionism led him to break with the proslavery Democrats and become one of the founders of the Missouri Republican party.

During the Civil War, Brown became a leading Radical Republican and served in the U.S. Senate (1863-1866). Influenced by John C. Frémont, whose drastic antislavery measures he approved, and seeking the support of antislavery German-Americans in St. Louis, Brown advocated a vigorous prosecution of the war and the passage of stringent wartime measures. He opposed Lincoln's moderation and objected to the Emancipation Proclamation because it did not free slaves in Missouri and other loyal border states. In 1864 Brown supported an abortive movement to replace Lincoln with Frémont as the Republican nominee for president. Later he opposed President Andrew Johnson's moderate plan of reconstruction and supported the Radical-sponsored Civil Rights Bill and Freedmen's Bureau Bill.

In 1864, however, Brown began his movement away from the Radical Republicans and in 1866 urged leniency toward former rebels and Confederate sympathizers. After his retirement from the Senate, he helped organize the Liberal Republican party in Missouri in association with Carl Schurz. In 1870 Brown was elected Liberal Republican governor of Missouri. His attempts to attract Democrats into the Liberal Republican party caused a split with Schurz.

In 1872 Brown was instrumental in expanding Liberal Republicanism into a national party, although Schurz quickly assumed leadership. At the Liberal Republican convention Brown threw his support for a presidential candidate to Horace Greeley, securing the vice-presidential nomination for himself. The Liberal Republicans acquired Democratic support but were badly beaten by the regular Republicans. Shortly afterward Brown retired from politics and devoted himself to business and law. By 1874 he had rejoined the Democratic party.

Brown's career reflected the turbulence and political chaos of the years from 1848 to 1877. While many of his political shifts were based on expediency and reflected the transient passions of the times, his commitment to nationalism and his advocacy of liberal reforms provided a measure of consistency beneath his political wandering.

Further Reading

The only full biography of Brown is Norma L. Peterson, *Freedom and Franchise: The Political Career of B. Gratz Brown* (1965), which is excellent not only in tracing Brown's tortuous career but also in relating Brown to the history of the period. This work can be supplemented by Thomas S. Barclay, *The Liberal Republican Movement in Missouri, 1865-1871* (1926), and John V. Mering, *The Whig Party in Missouri* (1967). □

Charles Brockden Brown

The American novelist and magazine editor Charles Brockden Brown (1771-1810) was a predecessor of Edgar Allan Poe in horror fiction and a critic of contemporary literature.

Charles Brockden Brown was born in Philadelphia, Pa., on Jan. 17, 1771, the fifth son of Elijah and Elizabeth Armitt Brown, wealthy and liberal Quakers. Charles attended the Friends' Latin School, began the study of law, but soon gave evidence of the traits of melancholy, an interest in morbid psychology, and a commitment to literature that governed all of his short life.

With the brilliant and gifted Dr. Elihu Hubbard Smith, the dramatist William Dunlap, and others, Brown formed literary and scientific clubs in Philadelphia and New York to discuss current ideas and issues. This intellectual sociability, however, provided only interludes between long periods of introspective retreat when he read widely and wrote with almost fanatic intensity.

Brown was deeply affected by the yellow fever epidemics which broke out in both cities during this time and took the life of Dr. Smith in 1798. Mainly because of his parents' objection to marriage "out of meeting," he remained a bachelor until 1804, when he married the Presbyterian Elizabeth Linn.

After the experimental novel *Alcuin* (1798), in which he expressed William Godwin's ideas on social justice and woman's rights, he undertook to Americanize the then popular Gothic novel of horrors. He gave it a local setting in the towns and untamed countryside he knew so well and added to its horrors from his knowledge of the pseudosciences and morbid psychology of his day. His was a complex personality, and his intense concern for moral issues was reflected in swift-moving plots; he produced in rapid succession *Wieland* (1798), *Arthur Merwyn* (1798-1799), *Ormond* (1799), and *Edgar Huntly* (1799).

Spontaneous combustion, sleepwalking, ventriloquism, compulsive behavior, and other scientific interests of the time often provided rational explanations for the seemingly occult mysteries that held suspense at a high level throughout the complex and often unresolved plots of these novels. Brown's skills, however, in dealing with extremes of character, swift-moving action, and a shifting narrative point of view gave them reader interest far beyond any other writing of the day.

Although recognized in his own time as a promising novelist, Brown was soon forced by illness and lack of financial success to turn to the editing of journals, in which his literary nationalism was tempered by his sound esthetic judgment of the work of others. His last years were devoted to the more commonplace novels *Clara Howard* and *Jane Talbot* (both 1804) and to effective tracts on current national problems.

Living at a time when a professional literary life was impractical because of the disorganized state of American intellectual society, Brown used his powerful, though imperfect, gifts to open many of the avenues which later writers like Poe, Nathaniel Hawthorne, and Herman Melville followed to achieve their masterworks.

Further Reading

The best general biography of Brown is Harry R. Warfel, *Charles Brockden Brown: American Gothic Novelist* (1949). Donald A. Ringe, *Charles Brockden Brown* (1966), provides a critical analysis of his major works, in biographical form.

Additional Sources

Warfel, Harry Redcay, *Charles Brockden Brown, American Gothic novelist,* New York, Octagon Books, 1974.

Allen, Paul, *The life of Charles Brockden Brown,* Delmar, N.Y.: Scholars' Facsimiles & Reprints, 1975.

Watts, Steven, *The romance of real life: Charles Brockden Brown and the origins of American culture,* Baltimore: Johns Hopkins University Press, 1994. □

Charlotte Eugenia Hawkins Brown

The African American educator and humanitarian Charlotte Eugenia Hawkins Brown (born Lottie Hawkins; 1882-1961) founded the Palmer Memorial Institute in North Carolina as a preparatory school for African Americans in the early 1900s and served as its president for over half a century.

The rural community of Sedalia, North Carolina, is the site of a memorial to Dr. Charlotte Hawkins Brown, African American educator-humanitarian. Sedalia is 90 miles from Henderson, where Brown was born in 1882. The granddaughter of slaves, Lottie moved to Cambridge, Massachusetts, during her childhood. There she attended the Alston Grammar School, Cambridge English High School, and Salem State Normal School. She changed her name to Charlotte Eugenia in 1900 and acquired the name Brown through her brief marriage to Edward S. Brown whom she met at Cambridge.

Also in 1900, Brown met Alice Freeman Palmer, then president of Wellesley College, who became her friend and mentor. Toward the end of her first year at Salem, in 1901, Brown was introduced to a representative of the American Missionary Association, a philanthropic organization which operated schools for African Americans in the South. The AMA representative offered her a job as teacher of its school in Sedalia, Guilford County, North Carolina. Even as a teenager, Brown was a visionary. Troubled by the lack of educational opportunities for Blacks in the southern region, she accepted the AMA's offer and returned to her native state in 1901 to teach African American children.

The school was housed in Bethany Congregational Church, but closed only one term after Brown's arrival. Many Sedalia residents wanted the school to continue and appealed to Brown to stay as its principal. She accepted their offer and vowed to justify their faith in her capability. To maintain Palmer's growth and contribute to its further development, Brown continually engaged in fund-raising efforts which were directed primarily toward northern supporters. Her appeals were undergirded with singing and persuasive speeches, and she touched the hearts of people who were responsive to an opportunity to provide an educational facility for southern African Americans.

The renamed Palmer Memorial Institute gained national recognition as a preparatory school for African Americans. In the beginning the school's curriculum emphasized manual training and industrial education for rural living. Later the curriculum was changed to emphasize cultural education. As Palmer and its dynamic founder-president became nationally known, Brown's circle of associates expanded to include Mary McLeod Bethune, Nannie Burroughs, Eleanor Roosevelt, W.E.B. DuBois, and Booker T. Washington.

In 1911 Palmer Memorial Institute was fully accepted by the Southern Association of Colleges and Secondary Schools at a time when few schools for southern African Americans had achieved such recognition. Over one thousand students graduated from Palmer during the presidency of Brown. Each student had been the beneficiary of counsel by a proud and able educator-humanitarian whose career was characterized by a determination to make them "educationally efficient, religiously sincere and culturally secure." After more than half a century as the school's director, she resigned in 1952.

A recipient of honorary doctorates from several colleges, including Wilberforce, Howard, and Lincoln, Brown became the first African American woman to be elected (1928) to the 20th Century Club of Boston, organized to honor leaders in education, art, science, and religion. Brown died in 1961. Palmer Memorial Institute was closed ten years later.

Further Reading

Published biographical information on Charlotte Hawkins Brown is sketchy and extremely limited in number. Alva Stewart's article on "The Charlotte Hawkins Brown Memorial Historic Site—Remembering the History of Black Education," *Wilson Library Bulletin* (October 1989); Constance Marteena's *The Lengthening Shadow of a Woman* (1977); *The Negro Almanac—A Reference on the African American,* Fifth Edition (1989); and the *Encyclopedia of Black America* (1981) are the best sources available at this time. Additional unpublished information is available through the Department of Cultural Resources, Historic Sites Section, Raleigh, North Carolina. □

George Brown

George Brown (1818-1880) was a Canadian politician and newspaper editor who stood for the principle of majority rule, favored expansion into the West, and gave powerful support to the movement for the federation of British North America.

George Brown was born in Alloa near Edinburgh, Scotland, on Nov. 20, 1818. Educated in Edinburgh, he emigrated to the United States with his father at the age of 20 and settled in New York. There the Browns began a newspaper, the *British Chronicle.* Not finding life in New York to their liking, they moved in 1843 to Toronto, Canada, where they established a Presbyterian newspaper, the *Banner.*

A year later the younger Brown founded the *Globe,* a political journal designed to appeal to the residents of Toronto and the Protestant rural area in the western part of the province. In this newspaper Brown began to expound the views that made him a power in politics: dissatisfaction with the system of equal representation in the legislature for the French-and English-speaking parts of the province and the favoring of its replacement by "representation by population" ("rep. by pop."), which would ensure an English-speaking majority. He also thundered against the dominant influence which he felt was exercised by French-Canadians in the Conservative ministries of John Macdonald, and he criticized the power of the Roman Catholic Church in political affairs.

In Canada West, Brown was particularly concerned about the attempt to establish separate Roman Catholic schools with state support. Brown also urged the annexation of the Hudson's Bay Company territories to Canada, regarding them as a new agricultural frontier for the province and hoping to see Toronto outbid Montreal to become the commercial center for the West. His attitudes coincided with those of the Reform, or "Grit," party in Canada West, and Brown slipped naturally into a position of leadership in the party. The *Globe* took over other Reform papers and soon became the official organ of the movement. It eventually became a daily, very widely read throughout Canada West. No editor or newspaper has since possessed the influence in central Canada which was wielded by Brown and the *Globe.*

Brown entered politics in 1851, being elected as a Reform candidate for the county of Kent, Canada West. In the legislature he soon made his mark as a critic and formidable debater, but his views about French-speaking Canadians made for an uneasy relationship with the reformers of Canada East, the Rouges. In 1858 there was a short-lived attempt to construct a Reform ministry headed by Brown and A.-A. Dorion, but the new administration could not win the confidence of the House. The next year Brown and the Reform party adopted the goal of a federal union for the two Canadas, leaving each part free to manage its local affairs.

In June 1864 the increasing political difficulties and frustrations of the early 1860s finally led to the creation of a coalition ministry to carry forward the plan of the union of all the British North American colonies. Brown's adherence was critical to the purpose of the new government, and there was much satisfaction when he swallowed his personal dislike of the Conservative leader, Macdonald, and joined the coalition. Throughout 1865 Brown worked for the cause of federation, resigning from the ministry at the end of the year, when he found he could no longer work with Macdonald and his Conservative colleagues. The break did not interrupt Brown's powerful support, on the platform and through the pages of the *Globe,* for the realization of a federal union in British America.

The first election after the formation of the Dominion of Canada, in July 1867, saw the Conservatives under Macdonald installed as the national government. Brown was defeated in this election, although he continued to play an active role in Ontario provincial politics. In 1873, with the accession to power of the Reformers, or Liberals as they were now beginning to be called, Brown was named to the Senate of Canada. Although relatively inactive in the upper house, he exerted a strong influence over the new Liberal prime minister, Alexander Mackenzie, who had been his protégé. In 1874 Brown was sent to Washington to negotiate a new reciprocity treaty with the United States, but the agreement was turned down by the U.S. Senate.

Brown's last years saw him much involved in the management of his newspaper, now a large enterprise. His life ended tragically when he was shot and fatally wounded by a disgruntled employee whom he had recently discharged. Brown died on May 9, 1880.

Further Reading

The official biography of Brown, published shortly after his death, is Alexander Mackenzie, *The Life and Speeches of Hon. George Brown* (1882). The modern biography is J. M. S. Careless, *Brown of the Globe* (2 vols., 1959-1963). Brown is discussed by a fellow journalist, Sir J. S. Willison, in *Reminiscences, Political and Personal* (1919). A good background study of the period is Edgar Wardwell McInnis, *Canada: A Political and Social History* (1947; rev. ed. 1959). □

Helen Gurley Brown

American author and editor Helen Gurley Brown (born 1922) first achieved fame for her book *Sex and the Single Girl,* an immediate best-seller. After Gurley Brown became editor of the faltering *Cosmopolitan,* she transformed it into a sexy, upbeat top-selling magazine for young women in over 27 different countries.

Helen Gurley Brown was born in Green Forest, Arkansas, on February 18, 1922, and lived in Little Rock, Arkansas until her father, Ira M. Gurley, a schoolteacher, was killed in an elevator accident. Gurley Brown's mother, Cleo (nee Sisco), was left to raise their two daughters. (Helen's sister was partially paralyzed from polio.) "I never liked the looks of the life that was programmed for me—ordinary, hillbilly, and poor," Gurley Brown wrote later, "and I repudiated it from the time I was seven years old." She attended Texas State College for Women (1939-1941), Woodbury College (1942) and received her LL.D from Woodbury University in 1987.

Gurley Brown's first job was with radio station KHJ where she answered fan mail for six dollars per week. From 1942-1945 she worked as an executive secretary at Music Corp. of America, a Beverly Hills talent agency. Once, while reminiscing about her early career days, Gurley Brown recalled how secretaries were required to use the back stairs because the ornate lobby staircase was only for clients and/or male executives.

A major career move for Gurley Brown occurred in 1948 when she became the first woman to hold a copywriter position at Foote, Cone & Belding, a Los Angeles advertising agency. Her ability to produce bright, arresting prose won her two Francis Holmes Advertising Copywriters awards during her tenure at the firm (1948-1958).

She worked for Kenyon & Eckhardt, a Hollywood advertising agency as an account executive and copywriter from 1958-1962.

In 1959, at the age of 37, Helen Gurley married David Brown, then vice president for production at 20th Century Fox. (In later years Brown co-produced *Jaws, Cocoon,* and *The Sting.*) The couple had no children. Gurley Brown once remarked that one secret of their marital success was that her husband never interrupted her on Saturdays and Sundays when she was working upstairs in her office.

Gurley Brown's first book, *Sex and the Single Girl* (1962) revolutionized single women's attitudes towards their own lifestyle. The book became a national best-seller. At a time when *Reader's Digest* and *The Ladies Home Journal* still insisted that a "nice" girl had only two choices, "she can marry him or she can say no," Gurley Brown openly proclaimed that sex was an important part of a single woman's lifestyle. According to Gurley Brown, "The single girl is the new glamour girl." For emphasis, Gurley Brown recounted her own story, the saga of a self-proclaimed "mouseburger," who through persistence, patience, and planning, advanced in her chosen field and then married the man of her dreams.

In 1965, Gurley Brown was hired as editor-in-chief of Hearst Corp.'s faltering general interest magazine *Cosmopolitan* . She revised the magazine's cover image, creating a devil-may-care, sexy *Cosmo* girl. "A million times a year I defend my covers," Gurley Brown admitted. "I like skin, I like pretty. I don't want to photograph the girl next door." The new *Cosmopolitan* often provoked controversy, especially when it published a nude male centerfold of actor Burt Reynolds in 1972.

Relentlessly upbeat, the magazine, like its editor, was filled with advice on how to move ahead in a career, meet men, lose weight, and be an imaginative sexual partner.

There was no time for the negative. "I wasn't allowed to write critical reviews," movie critic Liz Smith confessed.

By 1990, *Cosmopolitan* had grown from a circulation of 800,000 in the United States to over 2.5 million. Hearst Corp. claimed that with its 27 international editions *Cosmopolitan* was now one of the most widely read women's magazines in the world and had become the sixth best-selling newsstand magazine in any category.

In the 20 years between publication of *Sex and the Single Girl* and *Having It All* (1982), Gurley Brown's advice changed little. She still refused to print four letter words but graphically described techniques for oral stimulation. "I am still preoccupied with sex," she confessed. "If you want to enchant a man and eventually marry him, you are good to him, easy with him, adorable to be around."

During a *Fortune* magazine interview in Oct. of 1996, Gurley Brown shared several of her rules for being a good executive. "These are my rules, written with some incredulity about being one [an executive] and with probably not enough modesty," she stated. Her guidelines included saying something complimentary before criticizing, saying "no" to time wasters, doing what you dread first, and working harder than anybody else.

In addition to her Francis Holmes Achievement awards (1956-59), Gurley Brown received several awards for journalism, including a Distinguished Achievement Award from the University of Southern California in 1971, an award for editorial leadership from the American Newspaper Woman's Club of Washington, D.C., in 1972, and the Distinguished Achievement Award in Journalism from Stanford University in 1977. In 1985 she received the New York Women in Communications matrix award. She has been dedicated as a "living landmark" by the New York Landmarks Conservancy and the Helen Gurley Brown Research professorship was established in her name at Northwestern University's Medill School of Journalism in 1986. She was inducted into the Publisher's Hall of Fame in 1988.

In January, 1996, Bonnie Fuller, founding editor of Hearst Corp.'s magazine *Marie Claire,* was named Gurley Brown's successor and new editor-in-chief of *Cosmopolitan.* "She [Fuller] thoroughly understands the *Cosmo* girl, and her success . . . certainly prepared her to succeed to the editorship of *Cosmopolitan,*" said Gurley Brown. Fuller served an eighteen-month internship under Gurley Brown while Gurley Brown continued as editor-in-chief of *Cosmopolitan's* international publishing program.

Further Reading

The best glimpse of Helen Gurley Brown is provided through her own books. In addition to *Sex and the Single Girl* (1962), Gurley Brown authored *Sex and the Office* (1965), *Outrageous Opinions* (1967), *Helen Gurley Brown's Single Girl's Cookbook* (1969), *Sex and the New Single Girl* (1970), *Cosmopolitan's Love Book, A Guide to Ecstasy in Bed* (1978), and *Having It All* (1982). See also "What the Women's Movement Means to Me" in *Ms.* (July 1985). ☐

James Brown

"Godfather of Soul" James Brown (born 1933) is also known as "the hardest-working man in show business."

In the book about his life, *Living in America,* James Brown told the author, "I never try to express what I actually did," regarding his influence on the American soul scene. "I wouldn't try to do that, 'cause definition's such a funny thing. What's put together to make my music—it's something which has real power. It can stir people up and involve 'em. But it's just something I came to hear."

The music that James Brown heard in his head—and conveyed to his extraordinary musicians with an odd combination of near-telepathic signals and vicious browbeating—changed the face of soul. By stripping away much of the pop focus that had clouded pure rhythm and blues, Brown found a rhythmic core that was at once primally sexual and powerfully spiritual. Shouting like a preacher over bad-to-the-bone grooves and wicked horn lines, he unleashed a string of hits through the 1960s and early 1970s; he was also a formative influence on such rock and soul superstars as Parliament-Funkadelic leader George Clinton, Rolling Stones frontman Mick Jagger, Prince, and Michael Jackson, among countless others.

By the late 1970s, however, Brown's career was waning, and he was plagued by demands for back taxes, a nagging drug problem, and a combative relationship with his third wife. In 1988 he went to prison after leading police on a high-speed chase. And even as the advent of hip-hop has made him perhaps the most sampled artist in the genre, he has had frequent scrapes with the law since his release in 1991. Even so, his legacy—as bandleader, singer, dancer, and pop music visionary—is assured.

Brown was born in the South—sources vary, but generally have him hailing from Georgia or South Carolina—and grew up in Augusta, Georgia, struggling to survive. At the age of four, he was sent to live with his aunt, who oversaw a brothel. Under such circumstances, he grew up fast; by his teens he drifted into crime. In the words of Timothy White, who profiled the singer in his book *Rock Stars,* "Brown became a shoeshine boy. Then a pool-hall attendant. Then a thief." At 16 he went to jail for multiple car thefts. Though initially sentenced to 8-16 years of hard labor, he got out in under four for good behavior. After unsuccessful forays into boxing and baseball, he formed a gospel group called the Swanees with his prison pal Johnny Terry.

The Swanees shifted toward the popular mid-1950s doo-wop style and away from gospel, changing their name to the Famous Flames. Brown sang lead and played drums; their song "Please, Please, Please"—a wrenchingly passionate number in which Brown wailed the titular word over and over—was released as a single in 1956 and became a million-seller. By 1960 the group had become the James Brown Revue and was generating proto-funk dance hits like "(Do the) Mashed Potato." Deemed the "King of

Soul" at the Apollo Theater, New York's black music mecca, Brown proceeded over the ensuing years to burn up the charts with singles like "Papa's Got a Brand New Bag," "I Got You (I Feel Good)," "It's a Man's Man's Man's World," "Cold Sweat," "Funky Drummer," and many others. In the meantime, he signed with the Mercury subsidiary Smash Records and released a string of mostly instrumental albums, on which he often played organ.

Brown's declamatory style mixed a handful of seminal influences, but his intensity and repertoire of punctuating vocal sounds—groans, grunts, wails, and screams—came right out of the southern church. His exhortations to sax player Maceo Parker to "blow your horn," and trademark cries of "Good God!" and "Take it to the bridge!" became among the most recognizable catchphrases in popular music. The fire of his delivery was fanned by his amazingly agile dancing, without which Michael Jackson's fancy footwork is unimaginable. And his band—though its personnel shifted constantly—maintained a reputation as one of the tightest in the business. Starting and stopping on a dime, laying down merciless grooves, it followed Brown's lead as he worked crowds the world over into a fine froth. "It was like being in the army," William "Bootsy" Collins—who served as Brown's bassist during the late 1960s—told *Musician,* adding that the soul legend "was just a perfectionist at what he was doing." Brown adopted a series of extravagant titles over the years, but during this period he was known primarily as "The Hardest-Working Man in Show Business."

At the same time, Brown's harshness as a leader meant that bandmembers were constantly facing fines for lateness, flubbed notes, missed cues, violating his strict dress code, or even for talking back to him. His musicians also complained of overwork and insufficient pay, and some alleged that Brown took credit for ideas they had developed. The singer-bandleader's temper is legendary; as trombonist Fred Wesley told *Living in America* author Cynthia Rose, "James was bossy and paranoid. I didn't see why someone of his stature would be so defensive. I couldn't understand the way he treated his band, why he was so evil."

Charles Shaar Murray ventured in his book *Crosstown Traffic* that "playing with James Brown was a great way to learn the business and to participate in the greatest rhythm machine of the sixties. It was a very poor way to get rich, to get famous, or to try out one's own ideas." Even so, the group—which included, at various times, funk wizards like Maceo Parker, guitarist Jimmy Nolen, and drummer Clyde Stubblefield—reached unprecedented heights of inspiration under Brown. "He has no real musical skills," Wesley remarked to Rose, "yet he could hold his own onstage with any jazz virtuoso—because of his guts."

The increasingly militant stance of many black activists in the late 1960s led Brown—by now among an elite group of influential African Americans—to flirt with the "Black Power" movement. Even so, the singer generally counseled nonviolence and won a commendation from President Lyndon B. Johnson when a broadcast of his words helped head off a race riot. He was also saluted by Vice-President Hubert Humphrey for his pro-education song "Don't Be a Dropout." Brown's music did begin to incorporate more overtly political messages, many of which reiterated his belief that black people needed to take control of their economic destinies. He was a walking example of this principle, having gained control of his master tapes by the mid-1960s.

The year 1970 saw the release of Brown's powerful single "(Get Up, I Feel Like Being a) Sex Machine," a relentless funk groove featuring several hot young players, notably Bootsy Collins and his brother Phelps, aka "Catfish." Brown soon signed with Polydor Records and took on the moniker the "Godfather of Soul," after the highly successful mafia movie *The Godfather.* Further refining his hard funk sound, he released hits like "Get on the Good Foot," "Talking Loud and Saying Nothing," and "Soul Power." With the 1970s box-office success of black action films—known within the industry as "blaxploitation" pictures—Brown began writing movie soundtracks, scoring such features as Slaughter's Big Rip-Off and Black Caesar.

James Brown may have been one of the biggest pop stars in the world—the marquees labeled him "Minister of New New Super Heavy Funk"—but he was not immune to trouble. In 1975 the Internal Revenue Service claimed that he owed $4.5 million in taxes from 1969-70, and many of his other investments collapsed. His band quit after a punishing tour of Africa, and most tragically, his son Teddy died in an automobile accident. Brown's wife later left him, taking their two daughters.

By the late 1970s, the advent of disco music created career problems for the Godfather of Soul. Though he dubbed himself "The Original Disco Man (a.k.a. The Sex Machine)," he saw fewer and fewer of his singles charting significantly. Things improved slightly after he appeared as a preacher in the smash 1980 comedy film *The Blues Brothers,* and he demonstrated his importance to the burgeoning hip-hop form with *Unity (The Third Coming),* his 1983 EP with rapper Afrika Bambaataa. But Brown's big comeback of the 1980s came with the release of "Living in America," the theme from the film *Rocky IV,* which he performed at the request of star Sylvester Stallone. The single was his first million-selling hit in 13 years. As a result, Brown inked a new deal with CBS Records; in 1986 he was inducted into the Rock 'n' Roll Hall of Fame. "Living in America" earned him a Grammy Award for best R&B performance by a male artist.

Through it all, Brown had been struggling with substance abuse, despite his participation in the President's Council against Drugs. His and his third wife Adrienne's use of the drug known as PCP or "angel dust" led to frequent encounters with the law; in May of 1988 he faced charges of assault, weapons and drug possession, and resisting arrest. In December he was arrested again after leading police on a two-state car chase and was sentenced to six years in State Park Correctional Facility in Columbia, South Carolina. His confinement became a political issue for his fans, and Brown was ultimately released in early 1991. "We've got lots of plans," the soul legend declared to *Rolling Stone,* adding that the experience "has opened James Brown's eyes about things he has to do." He later announced plans to tape a cable special with pop-rap sensation M.C. Hammer.

That same year saw the release of Star Time, a four-CD boxed set that meticulously collected Brown's finest moments; much of which had never been released on compact disc before. The project's release date was set to coincide with the 35th anniversary of "Please, Please, Please." Brown, meanwhile, set to work on a new album, *Universal James,* which included production by British soul star Jazzie B. "It'll be the biggest album I ever had," he declared to *Spin,* though this was not to be the case. The 1990s did, however, reveal just how influential James Brown's work had been in rap and hip-hop circles: hundreds of his records were sampled for beats, horn stabs, and screams; the group Public Enemy, which had taken its name from one of his singles, often elaborated on the political themes he had raised.

Meanwhile—thanks in part to his participation in *The Blues Brothers* and the use of his music in feature films like *Good Morning, Vietnam*—Brown emerged as a "classic" mainstream artist. Indeed, *Time* magazine listed 32 appearances of "I Got You (I Feel Good)" in films, movie trailers, and television commercials, and this list was probably not exhaustive. In 1993 the people of Steamboat Springs, Colorado, christened the James Brown Soul Center of the Universe Bridge. The following year a street running alongside New York's Apollo Theater was temporarily named James Brown Blvd., and he performed at Radio City Music Hall; superstar actress Sharon Stone sang "Happy Birthday" to him on the occasion of his 61st. "I'm wherever God wants me to be and wherever the people need for me to be," he told the *New York Times.*

Unfortunately, his troubles were not at an end. In December of 1994, he was charged with misdemeanor domestic violence after yet another conflagration with Adrienne. And on October 31, 1995, Brown was once again arrested for spousal abuse. He later blamed the incident on his wife's addiction to drugs, stating in a press release, "She'll do anything to get them." Just over two months later, Adrienne died at the age of 47 after undergoing cosmetic surgery.

Brown's penchant for survival and the shining legacy of his work managed to overshadow such ugly incidents. "No one in the world makes me want to dance like James Brown," wrote producer and record executive Jerry Wexler—one of the architects of modern soul—in his book *Rhythm and the Blues* . "I came from nothing and I made something out of myself," Brown commented in a *New York Times* interview. "I dance and I sing and I make it happen. I've made people feel better. I want people to be happy." The Godfather of Soul released a new live album in 1995.

In 1997 Brown appeared in *When We Were Kings,* a documentary also starring Muhammad Ali and George Foreman. The film by Leon Gast is about Ali and Foreman's 1974 fight in Zaire (now Congo).

Further Reading

Brown, James, *The Godfather of Soul,* 1990.

Murray, Charles Shaar, *Crosstown Traffic: Jimi Hendrix and the Rock 'n' Roll Revolution,* St. Martin's, 1989.

Rees, Dafydd, and Luke Crampton, *Rock Movers & Shakers,* ABC/CLIO, 1991.

Rose, Cynthia, Living in America: *The Soul Saga of James Brown, Serpent's Tail,* 1990.

Wexler, Jerry, *Rhythm and the Blues,* Knopf, 1993.

White, Timothy, *Rock Stars,* Stewart, Tabori & Chang, 1984.

Augusta Chronicle (Augusta, GA), April 30, 1995.

Entertainment Weekly, December 23, 1994.

Los Angeles Times, September 10, 1994; December 10, 1994.

Musician, November 1994, .

New York Times, April 13, 1994.

Oakland Press (Oakland County, MI), November 4, 1995; January 7, 1996.

Rolling Stone, April 18, 1991.

Spin, December 1992; December 1993.

Starwave, "http://web.3starwave.com/starbios/jamesbrown/b.html," July 18, 1997.

Time, April 25, 1994; May 16, 1994.

Additional information for this profile was taken from Scotti Bros. Records publicity materials, 1995. □

John Brown

John Brown (1800-1859) has been revered for generations as a martyr to the American antislavery cause. His attack on Harpers Ferry, Va., just before the Civil War freed no slaves and resulted in his own trial and death.

John Brown was born at Torrington, Conn., on May 4, 1800, to Owen Brown, a tanner, and Ruth Mills Brown, whose family had a history of mental instability. He spent his childhood there and on the family farm at Hudson, Ohio. A devoutly religious youth, Brown studied briefly for the ministry but quit to learn the tanner's trade. He married Dianthe Lusk in 1820, who bore him 7 children (two mentally deficient) before her death in 1832; a year later he married Mary Ann Day, who bore 13 children in the next 21 years. Of Brown's 20 children, 12 survived.

He said later that he had realized the sin of slavery, "the sum of all villainies," at 12, and that seeing an African American boy mistreated had "led him to declare, or *swear:* eternal war with slavery." He also developed a great interest in military history, especially in the guerrilla warfare of the Napoleonic Wars and in the Haitian slave rebellion. According to family testimony, he finally concluded that slavery could be destroyed only by atonement in blood, deciding in 1839 that the South, "Africa itself," should be invaded and the slaves freed at gunpoint. If he actually made such a plan, he kept it to himself for another decade, meanwhile trying and failing at a number of business ventures, always in debt. He moved his family 10 times until in 1849 he settled on a farm at North Elba, N.Y., that was part of a project financed by philanthropist Gerrit Smith for the training of free African Americans.

Kansas Controversy

After the Kansas-Nebraska Act of 1854 the territory hung in the balance between slave- and free-state status while pro- and antislavery settlers contested for control. Five of Brown's sons went to Kansas, joined the free-staters, and appealed to their father for help. Brown traveled through the East, speaking on the Kansas question and gathering money for arms, for "without the shedding of blood," he said, there could be "no remission of sin" in Kansas. In September he went to Kansas, settling near Osawatomie. "I am here," he said grimly, "to promote the killing of slavery." In spring of 1856 he led a retaliatory raid on a proslavery settlement at Pottawatomie, killing five men in cold blood. John Junior spent 3 months in jail as an accomplice, but Brown himself escaped. The Pottawatomie affair made him nationally known, and while some antislavery sympathizers disowned him, to others he seemed a hero.

First Raid: Osawatomie

Brown spent the summer of 1856 collecting money for Kansas in New England, where prominent public figures, some not wholly aware of the details of his Kansas activities, were impressed by his dedication to the abolitionist cause. The Massachusetts Kansas Committee, whose directors included such civic leaders as Theodore Parker, Samuel Gridley Howe, and Thomas W. Higginson, helped him to gather recruits, guns, and money. In August he led a skirmish at Osawatomie in which his son Frederick was killed. "I will die fighting for this cause," Brown wrote. "There will be no peace in this land until slavery is done for."

He went East in early 1857 with plans for a Southern invasion apparently in hand, ordered a thousand 6-foot pikes from a Connecticut firm, and in late summer gathered a band of recruits at Tabor, Iowa, for training. He held frequent conferences with Eastern abolitionists and in early 1858 sent John Junior to survey the country around Harpers Ferry, Va., the site of a Federal arsenal. In April he held a curious 10-day meeting of sympathizers in Chatham, Ontario, Canada, during which he explained his plan to invade the South, arm the slaves, and set up a free state under a new constitution; the meeting adopted his plan and then voted him commander in chief. He returned to Kansas under the name of Shubel Morgan to lead a raid into Missouri, killing one man and taking some slaves back to Canada.

Brown was now considered a criminal in the eyes of Missouri and the U.S. government, and both offered rewards for his capture; still he was hailed in parts of the North as a liberator, and donations poured in. In early 1859 he again toured the East to raise money, and in July he rented a farm 5 miles north of Harpers Ferry, where he recruited 21 men (16 white and 5 black) for final training. He intended to seize the arsenal, distribute arms to the slaves he thought would rally to him, and set up a free state for african Americans within the South. Though Harpers Ferry was an isolated mountain town, with few slaves in the vicinity, the irrationality of his plan seemed to occur to no one.

Raid on Harpers Ferry

On the night of Oct. 16, 1859, Brown set out for Harpers Ferry with 18 men and a wagonload of supplies, leaving 3 men behind to guard the farm. After cutting the telegraph wires, Brown's party slipped into the town and easily captured the armory watchmen. Inexplicably, Brown allowed the midnight train to go through; the conductor telegraphed an alarm the next morning. Shooting broke out early on the 17th between Brown's men and local residents, while militia soon arrived from Charles Town. By nightfall Brown's band lay trapped in the armory enginehouse, all but 5 wounded, Brown's sons Oliver and Watson fatally. That night Col. Robert E. Lee and Lt. J. E. B. Stuart, commanding 90 marines, arrived from Washington. The next morning the marines stormed the enginehouse, bayoneting 2 men and slashing Brown severely with sabers. Of Brown's original party 10 died and 7 were captured; on the other side the toll was a marine and 4 civilians, one of them, ironically, a free African American killed by mistake.

Brown was jailed at Charles Town and tried a week later, lying wounded on a stretcher, in a fair trial which some, however, felt to be unduly hasty. He put up no defense. "I believe that to have interfered as I have done," he said, "in behalf of His despised poor, I did no wrong, but right. . . . I am ready for my fate." The jury indicted him on three counts—treason against Virginia, conspiracy with african Americans, and first-degree murder. The court imposed the death sentence on November 2, to be executed a month later.

Beginning of a Legend

News of Brown's deed—"so surprising, so mixed, so confounding," Bronson Alcott called it—shocked the nation. Was he martyr or murderer? Many praised him (Ralph Waldo Emerson called him "that new saint who will make the gallows like a cross"), and many condemned him. Seventeen of Brown's acquaintances sent affidavits to Governor Wise of Virginia raising, on good evidence, the issue of Brown's sanity, but Wise did not act on them. Brown was hanged at Charles Town on Dec. 2, 1859, with four of his men, after handing a prophetic note to his jailer on his way to the gallows: "I John Brown am now quite certain that the crimes of *this guilty land: will* never be purged *away;* but with Blood." Mass meetings of mourning were held throughout the North, and church bells tolled at the hour of his execution. He was buried at North Elba, N.Y., and the cause of abolition had its martyr. When a penny ballad about him, set to the music of an old revival hymn and named "John Brown's Body," appeared on the streets of Boston in early 1861, he was already a legend.

Further Reading

The best book on Brown, well written and soundly researched, is Joseph C. Furnas, *The Road to Harper's Ferry* (1959). James C. Malin, *John Brown and the Legend of Fifty-Six* (1942), is a study of the Kansas years. David Karsner, *John Brown: Terrible Saint* (1934), and Oswald Garrison Villard, *John Brown* (1943), are good biographies. Allan Keller, *Thunder at Harper's Ferry* (1958), is an hour-by-hour account of the raid. One of the Massachusetts Kansas Committee leaders, Franklin B. Sanborn, published *The Life and Letters of John Brown* (1885; 4th ed. 1910), which is still interesting reading. ☐

Joseph Emerson Brown

Georgia governor and U.S. senator Joseph Emerson Brown (1821-1894) is chiefly remembered for his political representation of the common man and his obstructionist attitude toward the policies of Confederate president Jefferson Davis.

Joseph E. Brown was born in Pickens District, S.C., on April 15, 1821, but his family soon moved to the mountains of northern Georgia. At the age of 19 Brown attended school in Anderson District, S.C. He returned to Canton, Ga., where he directed the local academy and read law. In 1845, after admission to the Georgia bar, he left to attend Yale Law School. He graduated in 1846, settled in Canton, and began practicing law.

In 1849 Brown was elected to the state senate, where he demonstrated a capacity for work and innate political skill. In 1855 he became judge of the Blue Ridge circuit. A Democrat, Brown was elected governor in 1857, 1859, 1861, and 1863—a record never equaled before in the history of Georgia.

Brown protected the interests of the average Georgian and sought measures to extend benefits to the plain people. He opposed legislation especially favorable to the banks of the state, advocated the establishment of free schools and endowment of the state university, reformed the administration of the state-owned Western and Atlantic Railroad, and improved the militia system.

Though Brown consistently maintained proslavery and secessionist attitudes, he was in constant conflict with the Confederate government: he was nearly fanatical in adhering to the doctrine of state sovereignty, while the exigencies of the Civil War forced President Davis to promote centralization of government. Brown opposed Davis's acceptance of state troops without the governor's permission and the appointment of officers to command Georgia troops. He disputed both the wisdom and constitutionality of the conscription law and at times obstructed its application; he protested against seizure of property without compensation; and he opposed the suspension of the writ of habeas corpus.

At the end of the war in 1865, Brown was imprisoned briefly and then resigned the governorship. During Reconstruction he advised compliance with the congressional plan, an attitude which subjected him to widespread denunciation. He even joined the Republican party. In 1868 he was named chief justice of the state supreme court but 2 years later resigned to become president of the Western and Atlantic Company. By 1872 Brown had rejoined the Democratic party. He was elected U.S. senator in 1880 and twice reelected, serving until 1891. Brown died on Nov. 30, 1894.

Further Reading

The best full-length work on Brown is Louise Biles Hill, *Joseph E. Brown and the Confederacy* (1939). This is a well-documented study of Brown's career as Georgia's wartime gover-

nor and his significance in the failure of the Confederacy. Elizabeth Studley Nathans, *Losing the Peace* (1969), contains useful information on Brown's railroad interests and on his activities as a Republican. Brown is a prominent figure in E. Merton Coulter, *Georgia: A Short History* (1947; rev. ed. 1960).

Additional Sources

Parks, Joseph Howard, *Joseph E. Brown of Georgia,* Baton Rouge: Louisiana State University Press, 1977. □

Moses Brown

Moses Brown (1738-1836) was an American manufacturer and merchant. Quaker discipline tempered the career of this successful New England businessman.

Moses Brown was born into a family of merchants of Providence, R.I. He began his business education as apprentice to his uncle, Obadiah Brown. The elder Brown's interests included not only the West Indies trade but also insurance, moneylending, and the manufacture of spermaceti candles—diversification typical of the era of merchant capitalism. On the death of his uncle in 1762, Moses joined his three older brothers in the firm of Nicholas Brown and Company. To candlemaking and the shipping trade they added an ironworks. By the 1770s the Browns were one of the great mercantile families of New England.

After the death of his first wife in 1773, Brown withdrew from his business commitments and remained inactive until the end of the decade. He became a Quaker, a faith shared by his second and third wives, Mary Olney and Phoebe Lockwood. During this period he took part in the antislavery movement in Rhode Island. He freed his own slaves, aided other slaves to escape, and helped freedmen of Arican descent maintain themselves.

Then Brown became an early sponsor of textile manufacturing. In 1789 he formed a company with his son-in-law, William Almy, to manufacture cotton cloth. His interest in this phase of manufacturing led him to invite Samuel Slater, who had worked at the famed Arkwright Mills in England, to re-create their advanced cloth-producing machinery in Rhode Island. When completed, this was the first water-powered cotton mill in America, and the success of the Almy, Brown and Slater Firm was ensured. Brown helped found the Providence Bank in 1791, then once more withdrew from business management.

Brown's deliberate withdrawals from the business world indicated his anxiety to achieve religious peace by escaping worldly preoccupations. He never achieved quietism, however; instead, his religious impulse was channeled into programs aimed at improving the physical and moral health of his fellows. He had sponsored an unsuccessful effort to found a public school in Providence in the

1760s, and in 1770 he had helped bring Rhode Island College, now Brown University, to Providence. Although to some degree he shared the Quaker suspicion that higher education weakened the fundamentals of piety, he worked for decades to found a Friends' school. In 1819 the New England Yearly Meeting Boarding School became a reality, and in 1904 it was renamed the Moses Brown School.

Brown's interest in business enterprises was conditioned by a concern as statesmanlike as it was business-like. He was actively involved in distributing relief to the poor. He was conscious of the impact of any interruption of commerce, and he hoped that textile manufactures would provide a source of continuous employment for the poor. He urged tariffs, bounties, and child labor in a report prepared for Alexander Hamilton when the secretary of the Treasury was drafting his famous position paper on the state of American manufactures.

Further Reading

The most comprehensive biography of Brown is Mack Thompson, *Moses Brown: Reluctant Reformer* (1962). James B. Hedges, *The Browns of Providence Plantations* (2 vols., 1952-1968), provides an exciting and detailed history of the business ventures of the Brown brothers. Robert M. Hazelton, *Let Freedom Ring!* (1957), discusses Brown as a Quaker. □

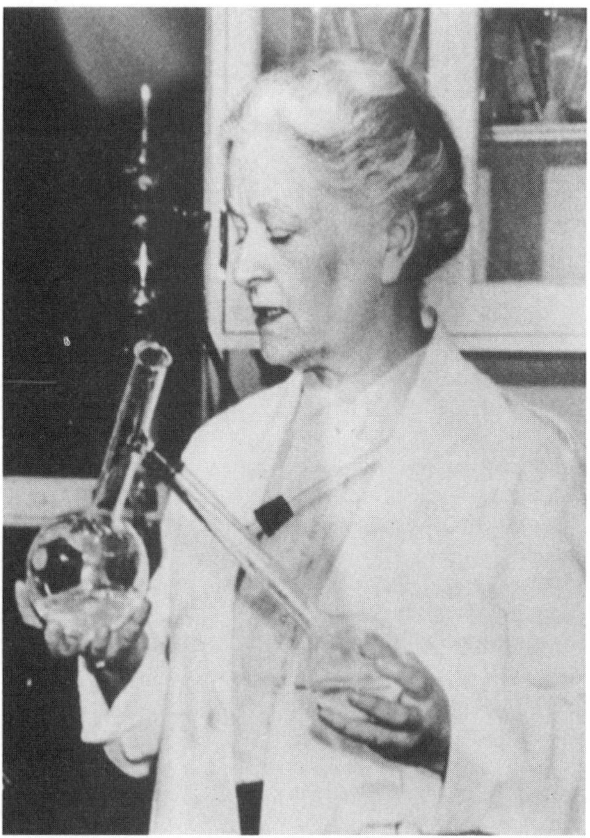

Rachel Fuller Brown

With Elizabeth Lee Hazen, Brown (1898-1980) developed the first effective antibiotic against fungal disease in humans—the most important biomedical breakthrough since the discovery of penicillin two decades earlier.

Rachel Fuller Brown, with her associate Elizabeth Hazen, developed the first effective antibiotic against fungal disease in humans—the most important biomedical breakthrough since the discovery of penicillin two decades earlier. The antibiotic, called nystatin, has cured sufferers of life-threatening fungal infections, vaginal yeast infections, and athlete's foot. Nystatin earned more than $13 million in royalties during Brown's lifetime, which she and Hazen dedicated to scientific research.

Brown was born in Springfield, Massachusetts, on November 23, 1898, to Annie Fuller and George Hamilton Brown. Her father, a real estate and insurance agent, moved the family to Webster Groves, Missouri, where she attended grammar school. In 1912, her father left the family. Brown and her younger brother returned to Springfield with their mother, who worked to support them. When Brown graduated from high school, a wealthy friend of the family financed her attendance at Mount Holyoke College in Massachusetts.

At Mount Holyoke, Brown was initially a history major, but she discovered chemistry when fulfilling a science requirement. She decided to double-major in history and chemistry, earning her A.B. degree in 1920. She subsequently went to the University of Chicago to complete her M.A. in organic chemistry. For three years, she taught chemistry and physics at the Francis Shimer School near Chicago. With her savings, she returned to the University to complete her Ph.D. in organic chemistry, with a minor in bacteriology. She submitted her thesis in 1926, but there was a delay in arranging her oral examinations. As her funds ran low, Brown took a job as an assistant chemist at the Division of Laboratories and Research of the New York State Department of Health in Albany, New York. Seven years later, when she returned to Chicago for a scientific meeting, Brown arranged to take her oral examinations and was awarded her Ph.D.

Brown's early work at the Department of Health focused on identifying the types of bacteria that caused pneumonia, and in this capacity she helped to develop a pneumonia vaccine still in use today. In 1948, she embarked on the project with Hazen, a leading authority on fungus, that would bring them their greatest acclaim: the discovery of an antibiotic to fight fungal infections. Penicillin had been discovered in 1928, and in the ensuing years antibiotics were increasingly used to fight bacterial illnesses. One side effect, however, was the rapid growth of fungus that could lead to sore mouths or upset stomachs. Other fungal diseases without cures included infections attacking the central nervous system, athlete's foot, and ringworm. Microorganisms called actinomycetes that lived in soil were known to produce antibiotics. Although some killed fungus, they also proved fatal to test mice. Hazen ultimately narrowed the search down to a microorganism taken from soil near a barn on a friend's dairy farm in Virginia, later named streptomyces norsei. Brown's chemical analyses revealed that the microorganism produced two antifungal substances, one of which proved too toxic with test animals to pursue for human medical use. The other, however, seemed to have promise; it wasn't toxic to test animals and attacked both a fungus that invaded the lungs and central nervous system and candidiasis, an infection of the mouth, lungs, and vagina.

Brown purified this second antibiotic into small white crystals, and in 1950 Brown and Hazen announced at a meeting of the National Academy of Sciences that they had found a new antifungal agent. They patented it through the nonprofit Research Corporation, naming it "nystatin" in honor of the New York State Division of Laboratories and Research. The license for the patent was issued to E. R. Squibb and Sons, which developed a safe and effective method of mass production. The product—called Mycostatin—became available in tablet form in 1954 to patients suffering from candidiasis. Nystatin has also proved valuable in agricultural and livestock applications, and has even been used to restore valuable works of art.

In 1951, the Department of Health laboratories promoted Brown to associate biochemist. Brown and Hazen, in continuing their research, discovered two additional antibiotics, phalamycin and capacidin. Brown and Hazen were awarded the 1955 Squibb Award in Chemotherapy. Brown won the Distinguished Service Award of the New York State Department of Health when she retired in 1968, and the Rhoda Benham Award of the Medical Mycological Society of the Americas in 1972. In 1975, Brown and Hazen became the first women to receive the Chemical Pioneer Award from the American Institute of Chemists. In a statement publised in the *Chemist* the month of her death, Brown hoped for a future of "equal opportunities and accomplishments for all scientists regardless of sex."

On retirement, Brown maintained an active community life, and became the first female vestry member of her Episcopalian church. By her death on January 14, 1980, she had paid back the wealthy woman who had made it possible for her to attend college. Using the royalties from nystatin, more importantly, she helped designate new funds for scientific research and scholarships.

Further Reading

Baldwin, Richard S., *The Fungus Fighters: Two Women Scientists and Their Discovery,* Cornell University Press, 1981.

Vare, Ethlie Ann and Greg Ptacek, *Mothers of Invention,* Morrow, 1988, pp. 124–126.

Yost, Edna, *Women of Modern Science,* Greenwood, 1959, pp. 64–79.

New York Times, June 29, 1957, p. 22–26; January 16, 1980, p. D19. □

Ronald H. Brown

After a very successful tenure as Chairman of the Democratic National Committee, Ronald Brown (1941-1996) was appointed Commerce Secretary by President Bill Clinton. His reign as Secretary was cut short when his plane crashed during a mission to Bosnia-Herzegovina, killing all on board.

Ron Brown made history in 1989 when he became the first African American chosen to lead a major U.S. political party. From 1989 through 1992, Brown served as the highly visible deputy chairman of the Democratic National Committee (DNC). Prior to that, he was Jesse Jackson's manager at the 1988 Democratic National Convention. But Brown's liberal roots go even deeper: he was earlier the National Urban League's chief Washington lobbyist, the deputy campaign manager for U.S. Senator Edward (Ted) Kennedy's 1980 presidential bid, and a chief counsel for the Senate Committee on the Judiciary. Brown's confirmation in 1993 as President Bill Clinton's secretary of commerce, however, focused the nation's attention on him even further.

As a boy growing up in the Theresa Hotel in Harlem managed by his father—boxer Joe Louis and actor Paul Robeson were guests there—Ronald Harmon Brown learned early to straddle two worlds. The Theresa, near the famed Apollo Theater, was an oasis for the black entertainment and professional classes of the day. Brown, whose parents were graduates of Howard University, was bused to exclusive preparatory schools and attended the virtually all-white Middlebury College in Vermont. Because of such a background, Brown, unlike many black political leaders of his generation, had for the most part no involvement in the civil rights movement of the 1960s. While Jesse Jackson led 278 students arrested at sit-ins over civil rights at all-black North Carolina A and T State University, Brown was fulfilling ROTC responsibilities at his private rural college.

One instance of activism came far from the beaten paths of Southern civil rights battlefields but would characterize his later skill at nonconfrontational negotiations. The only black student in his freshman class at Middlebury, Brown was rushed by white classmates from the Sigma Phi Epsilon fraternity, the campus "jock house." But the national organization objected because of an exclusionary clause that barred blacks. As the debate dragged on, reported *Time* magazine, "Brown let it be known that he was unwilling to finesse the issue by accepting house privileges without full membership." Finally, fraternity members rallied to his side, provoking their expulsion by the national chapter leaders. Middlebury then barred all exclusionary charters from campus. Brown became a trustee at the mostly white school.

After college Brown served as the only black officer at his U.S. Army post in West Germany. Back home, he earned a law degree, worked as an inner-city social worker, and then joined the National Urban League—considered the most moderate of civil rights groups—as its Washington lobbyist. Later, he became the first African American attorney at the high-powered Washington law firm of Patton, Boggs and Blow.

Political Savvy Paid Off

Brown's election as head of the Democratic party came despite his carrying all the wrong credentials as far as many party regulars were concerned: he had served as Jesse Jackson's campaign manager in the 1988 bid for the party's presidential nomination. Brown's ties to the aggressive and somewhat controversial Jackson made some observers feel he was too volatile for the job, but his role as peacemaker between the Jackson and Michael Dukakis camps during the 1988 Democratic Convention helped cement his reputation as a suave negotiator. Jackson, who knew his '88 bid for the Democratic nomination was out of gas, at least wanted respect from Dukakis.

Such respect, however, was hard to elicit from the Dukakis camp, since it seemed to have the nomination—if not that 1988 general election against the Republicans—all wrapped up. Divisiveness within the party could have been a disaster for the Democrats, with even worse repercussions than Dukakis's eventual defeat against George Bush. But Brown helped to avoid an irreparable split in the party along color lines. "He is not bragging when he says that his conciliation efforts 'played a part in turning a potential disaster into a love-in,'" wrote David Broder in the *Washington Post.* And Donna Brazile, a Democratic activist aligned with Michael Dukakis in the 1988 election campaign, told the *Atlanta Journal and Constitution,* "If Ron was a pop singer, he would have crossover appeal."

Brown was the consummate Washington insider who learned how to work the levers of power by being a team player. Before becoming party chairman, he served on the DNC's Executive Committee as deputy chairman and chief counsel for the party and worked for Ted Kennedy and other Democrats in Congress. "His political formation is within national political processes and not within ethnic political processes," Harvard professor Martin Kilson told the *Washington Post.* "Brown is the new black transethnic politician." Soon after his election to the DNC in 1989, Brown made a vow to the committee, stating, as reprinted in the *Washington Post,* "I promise you, my chairmanship will not be about race, it will be about the races we win."

Brown's political savvy was evident in his engineering of his own election as party chairman. He began the campaign as just one of five candidates for the post, but he deployed his lobbying skills early. One call Brown made looking for support went to his former boss, Senator Kennedy, chair of the crucial Labor Committee. Soon after the call, the AFL-CIO endorsed Brown. The *New York Times* wrote, "Mr. Brown's election, the product of a meticulously organized campaign, gave him such an overwhelming advantage that his four competitors dropped out of the contest weeks before the voting."

However, Brown faced scrutiny for trying to be too many different things to too many people. "If you asked people in the Fifties and Sixties what it was to be a Democrat, they could easily tell you," Brown told *Gentleman's Quarterly.* "Somehow in recent years, it has become harder and harder. If we continue to let our opponents . . . define us . . . there's no way we're going to win elections." But some critics feel that Brown's own self-analysis betrays just that weakness. When the magazine asked him to define his own beliefs, Brown replied, "Let's see, what did we come up with? I'm a mainstream progressive Democrat . . . meaning I embrace the traditional values of the Democratic party, but I'm progressive."

Chairman of Democratic National Committee

The role of Democratic National Committee chairman became increasingly important during the dozen years between 1980 and 1992 when Democrats were out of the White House. As party chairman, Brown was successful in raising funds against the odds and helping to elect approved candidates. The 1989 off-year elections were, in Brown's own words, "a slam dunk," according to the *New York Times.* Democrats registered two firsts: a black governor in Virginia and a black mayor in New York City. Just as significantly, the Democrats picked up four congressional seats in special elections, including winning former Vice-President Dan Quayle's seat in heavily Republican Indiana. Brown remarked to the *New York Times,* "What the party does over here and over there should be strategically connected. The voter registration, the redistricting, the state party building and the campaigns—everything should be connected to winning elections." That the party, and Brown, succeeded in that to a good degree is made even more impressive given President Bush's sky-high approval ratings during that period.

Still, potentially thorny racial questions—exactly the kind that could alienate jumpy white Southern Democrats—always threatened to grab headlines. There too, though, Brown found a way to defuse the many pressures facing him. In the Chicago mayoral election of 1989, for instance, Brown dodged a tricky, racially-charged issue—whether to support white Democratic nominee Richard Daley, son of the late mayor, over black alderman Tim Evans, a Jackson ally running as an independent. He vowed to toe the party line and back the Democratic nominee, Daley.

But there was nowhere to escape to, no corner of America in which Brown could hide, when the political theater expanded from local elections to the presidential campaign of 1992. After the Persian Gulf War with Iraq, President Bush was enjoying high favorability ratings with the American electorate, and it appeared the Democratic party would again face an uphill battle to wrest White House control from the Republicans. Initially, because of Bush's popularity, Brown had difficulty raising money for the Democratic National Committee. Another problem was that, in the eyes of some Jewish contributors, Brown had not sufficiently distanced himself from Jesse Jackson, whose anti-Semitic remarks several years earlier were still a festering sore spot in Jewish/African American relations.

Worked for Democratic Unity

But Brown's greatest challenge, in terms of attracting dollars and, ultimately, the votes of Americans, was to remold the image of the party, shedding the "tax and spend" label that the Republicans had successfully applied to democratic candidates in the past. "We need to define ourselves as a party," Brown was quoted as telling *Black Enterprise.* "When you allow your adversaries to define you, you can be assured that the definition is going to be a very unpleasant one and that you find yourself on the defensive trying to dig yourself out of a hole. We can't let that happen again."

The answer, as many political observers had long known, lay in the middle. Brown understood that for the party to reclaim the so-called Reagan Democrats, it would need a candidate with fiscally conservative economic policies that would not adversely affect the struggling middle class. While he could not keep liberals such as Iowa senator Tom Harkin out of the primaries, Brown did muzzle the potential candidacy of Jesse Jackson, who, Brown feared, would unwittingly tarnish the new, moderate image that the party desperately needed.

Brown's plan was to minimize any acrimony among the primary candidates, hoping to focus their disparate voices on the need to unseat the Republican president. Bush, meanwhile, had suffered a precipitous fall in popularity, as his success in the Persian Gulf was overshadowed by a lingering recession in the United States. At a time when the citizenry had grown tired of politics as usual and were calling on the U.S. president to focus on domestic affairs, the Democratic party became the agent of "change."

In addition to nudging the party toward the center of the political spectrum, Brown's plan was to throw the party's support behind its candidate early in the political season. Indeed, one primary candidate, former California governor Jerry Brown, accused the party chairman of coddling to then-Arkansas governor Bill Clinton, who was emerging as the leading democratic figure, in spite of several personal and professional scandals in the Clinton camp that might have led to yet another Democratic loss in the general elections.

At the Democratic National Convention in July of 1992, Clinton won the nomination despite the various controversies surrounding him, and Brown, having calmed many of the voices of dissent, earned widespread praise for a smooth democratic crowning whose central messages were unity and enthusiasm for the party candidate. "Ron sensed what he had to do right from the start," former DNC chairman Kirk was quoted as saying in the *New York Times.* "He knew the party had to show it could govern itself before it could hope to govern the country." Brown's public trumpeting about a redefined Democratic party, and his behind-the-scenes maneuvering to generate support for Clinton, were seen as key to the first democratic presidential victory since 1976.

Named Secretary of Commerce

Brown's departure from the DNC was as controversial as his election as its chairman. In what some skeptics viewed as a political payback and an effort to create a racially diverse cabinet, Clinton nominated Brown as secretary of commerce. Immediately, Brown's past experience as a lobbyist took on the weight of a political liability. As secretary, he would make administrative and policy decisions that might affect his former clients, to whom, it was feared, he would feel some sort of allegiance. Moreover, several political commentators found it ironic that Clinton, who had campaigned against the status quo and the government-insider lobbyist crowd, had nominated Brown, the Washington power broker who played the political game with expert finesse. Illustrative of the ethical questions raised by Brown's nomination was a celebration in his honor that several of the largest American and Japanese corporations had planned. These companies, whose financial interests are impacted by decisions of the commerce secretary, were to have donated $10,000 each for the gala, which was abruptly canceled by Brown after Clinton expressed disapproval. Despite these setbacks, Brown was confirmed by the U.S. Senate in 1993 as the nation's first African American secretary of commerce. He pledged to make the department more responsive to the country's needs and concentrate on the promotion of American business interests both at home and in the international arena.

Brown's tenure as commerce secretary was a troubled one, however, as he was the target of numerous allegations that he acted improperly in his business dealings prior to his cabinet appointment. These allegations included charges that he failed to disclose his investment in a low-income apartment complex and that he did not report a $400,000 payment from a former business partner. By May of 1995, Brown was being investigated by the Justice Department, the Federal Deposit Insurance Corporation, and Congressional Republicans.

Brown's policy at the commerce department was one which emphasized trade over nuclear proliferation and human rights. His backslapping friendly manner resulted in American businessmen signing memoranda for new projects worth $4 billion in India on a January 1995 visit and over $6 billion in China during a September 1994 visit. On the China trip, Brown had 24 American CEOs accompany him to insure that the potential for some dealmaking would exist. He also led delegations bringing CEOs to South Africa, Northern Ireland, and Gaza. As a result of this policy Brown managed to acquire more foreign business for the United States than had any of his predecessors.

It was on a similar trip to Croatia, hoping to rebuild the war-torn region's infrastructure and economy, that Ron Brown died. Thirty-three people, including the secretary, business executives, and commerce staffers, were killed when their plane went down in the midst of a storm between Kalamota, near Dubrovnik, and the Cilipi airport on April 3, 1996. There were no survivors. As quoted in *USA Today,* President Clinton called Brown "one of the best advisers and ablest people I ever knew."

Further Reading

Atlanta Journal and Constitution, January 7, 1989; February 12, 1989; May 22, 1989.
Black Enterprise, March 1992, p. 48.
Boston Globe Magazine, October 22, 1989.
Business Week February 13, 1989, p. 54; June 18, 1990, p. 30; January 11, 1993, p. 31; September 12, 1994, p. 54.
The Economist January 21, 1995, p. 37.
Gentleman's Quarterly, July 1989.
Nation, February 20, 1989.
Newsweek, February 6, 1989, p. 20.
New York Times, February 11, 1989; March 28, 1992, p. A9; July 20, 1992, p. A11; January 14, 1993, p. A1.
New York Times Magazine, December 12, 1989.
Oakland Press (Oakland County, MI), December 13, 1992, p. A12.
Time, January 30, 1989, p. 56.
USA Today, April 4, 1996, pp. 1A, 2A, 13A.
Wall Street Journal, January 8, 1993, p. A14.
Washington Post, February 5, 1989; February 11, 1989. □

Tina Brown

Jumping onto journalism's fast track in 1974, British-born Tina Brown (Christina Hambly Brown, born 1953) transformed the English magazine *Tatler,* then the U.S. magazines *Vanity Fair* and the *New Yorker,* using controversial topics and challenging images. Her editorial rabbit punches knocked all three magazines into top-seller realm by boosting circulation, ad revenues, and reader interest.

Assuming the post of editor-in-chief of *Vanity Fair* magazine in 1984, Tina Brown, formerly with Britain's *Tatler,* delighted both skeptics and devotees. *Vanity Fair,* an art and literary magazine popular before World War II, had been reintroduced in 1983 by publisher S.I. Newhouse, Jr., but suffered from weak editorial focus and limp enthusiasm among media critics. As editor, Brown employed a saucy cleverness to both tighten that focus and rouse apathetic critics.

Born in Maidenhead, England, on November 21, 1953, Christina Hambly Brown and her brother, Christopher, were raised by George Hambly Brown and Bettina (Kohr) Brown in Little Marlow, Buckinghamshire. Her film-producer father and her mother (once a press agent for Sir Laurence Olivier) gave Tina not only a loving, comfortable, upper-middle-class home, but the inevitable excitement deriving from close association with the film community. Brown later enjoyed the full range of experience provided by a boarding school education. Attractive, articulate, and intelligent, she was also a known cut-up and quite mischievous on occasion.

While yet in college, Brown won the 1973 drama award given by the (London) *Sunday Times* for her play *Under the Bamboo Tree.* In 1974 she graduated from St. Anne's, Oxford, and soon thereafter landed various assignments with the *Times, Punch,* the *Sunday Telegraph,* and the *New Statesman* on numerous topics focusing on the United States. Brown's sharp, witty prose garnered her the Young Journalist of the Year Award given in 1978 by *Punch,* where she was for several years a columnist. In 1978 Brown became the housemate of *Times* editor Harold Evans, whom she subsequently married on August 20, 1981. They had two children, a son born in 1986 and a daughter born in 1990.

In 1979 Brown took the reins of the *Tatler,* a venerable British publication founded in 1709. Her choice as editor was a gamble on the part of Gary Bogard, the moribund magazine's new owner. Interjecting new life into *Tatler* was a challenge to which Brown was more than equal; as she noted at the time, one of her goals was to achieve "irreverence" in treating certain topics, including the British monarchy, formerly sacred among readers. That this was just the approach needed to expand *Tatler's* readership was only a hunch, but one that paid off handsomely.

Brown's adroit blend of elegant sass, tongue-in-cheek primness, and cutting-edge intelligence saw *Tatler* quadruple its circulation in four years. More important, it ensured the magazine's appeal. Millionaire publisher S.I. Newhouse, Jr., decided to buy the wildly successful *Tatler* in 1982. The following year Brown left as editor, but returned to Newhouse several months later as an editorial adviser to the faltering *Vanity Fair* .

Asked to enhance the flavor of a magazine others had failed to make palatable, Brown served forth a publication that not only bespoke good taste, but whetted the reader's appetite for more. As a result, in January 1984 Brown was named *Vanity Fair's* editor-in-chief, replacing Leo Lerman. It took over a year for her influence to take effect, but money eventually poured in from advertisers and subscribers alike. In 1986 the magazine was cited as "hottest" by the trade journal *Adweek;* in 1988 Brown was named Editor of the Year by *Advertising Age.*

Thanks to Brown, *Vanity Fair* threw off its stodgy image by covering, courting, and occasionally excoriating celebrities, in much the same way that *Tatler* had done earlier. Some decisions, such as the 1991 cover choice of nude and pregnant actress Demi Moore, were predictably controversial. But it was Brown's use of the unexpected and the titillating that boosted *Vanity Fair*'s readership to one million, reversed drooping ad sales, and promoted Brown to virtual celebrity stardom.

Precisely because of their profitability, her strategies were destined to leave *Vanity Fair;* another Newhouse publication, *The New Yorker,* was ailing and needed assistance. Despite the editorial expertise of Robert Gottlieb, whom S.I. Newhouse had put in charge in 1987, *The New Yorker* was in trouble. To salvage a $147 million investment, Newhouse switched editors again. In an outrageous gamble, in July 1992 he announced Gottlieb's resignation and named Tina Brown as *The New Yorker* editor. He later shifted Graydon Carter (founder of *Spy,* another Newhouse publication) into place as head of *Vanity Fair.*

These announcements scandalized and angered *The New Yorker* faithful. Although Brown won admiration for reviving flagging sales of once-healthy magazines, few believed she had the skills to succeed as *The New Yorker* editor, and many felt her previous triumphs were due to lack of discrimination among *Tatler* and *Vanity Fair* readers.

The transition from *Vanity Fair* to *The New Yorker* was not an easy one for Brown, which was evident in her emotional good-bye to *Vanity Fair* staff. Also, some said she worried about being unwelcome at *The New Yorker.* Commenting with scrupulous care about editorial changes, Brown used such terms as "irreverent" and "more timely" to signal her intentions. She denied, though, any desire to promulgate a wholesale transformation of what remained (despite the previously unheard-of use of color on editorial pages) America's most exalted, highly respected literary magazine.

The New Yorker continues to draw attention, mainly due to Brown's pannache for drawing it. In 1995 Brown shocked the writing world by inviting Roseanne, the controversial television star, to contribute to the issue on American women.

Further Reading

Various articles and interviews detail Tina Brown's meteoric rise as magazine editor *par excellence.* These articles can be found in *The American Spectator* (December 1992); *Newsweek* (October 26 and July 13, 1992; September 18, 1995); *TIME* (July 13, 1992); *New York* (July 20, 1992); and *Newsweek* (May 1, 1989). □

William Wells Brown

Born a slave, William Wells Brown (1815-1884) escaped to freedom and became the first African American to publish a novel or a play. He was also an abolitionist and an internationally acclaimed lecturer.

William Wells Brown was born in Lexington, Ky. His mother was a slave and, according to tradition, the daughter of Daniel Boone, the frontiersman. His father was the owner of the plantation on which William was born. While still a boy William was hired out to the captain of a St. Louis steamboat in the booming Mississippi River trade. After a year he was put to work in the printing office of Elijah P. Lovejoy, a well-known abolitionist.

While working again on a steamboat, Brown escaped, and by 1834 he had made his way to freedom in Canada. He became a steward aboard a ship plying the Great Lakes. In the course of his travels he was befriended by a Quaker, and he named himself after his benefactor. Brown taught himself to read and write. He also became an important link in the Underground Railroad, helping slaves escape to freedom, sometimes concealing them aboard his ship until they could be put ashore in a friendly port. In 1834 he had married a free African American woman, and they had two daughters.

In 1843 Brown was invited to lecture for the Anti-Slavery Society and soon gained renown as a public speaker. The American Peace Society chose him as their representative to the Peace Congress in Paris in 1849. The American Anti-Slavery Society provided him with letters of commendation introducing him to many distinguished Europeans, and he was soon well known in intellectual circles in Europe. Among his friends were the English statesman Richard Cobden and the French novelist Victor Hugo. Brown remained in Europe for several years. He found time to study medicine and was active in the temperance, woman's-suffrage, and prison reform movements.

Brown's first work, *The Narrative of William W. Brown, a Fugitive Slave* (1842), was a recollection of his life. He published a collection of his poems, *The Anti-Slavery Harp,* in 1843. His *Three Years in Europe* and his first novel, *Clotelle, or the President's Daughter,* a melodramatic commentary on interracial love, were published in London in 1853. The following year he produced *Sketches of Places and People Abroad,* in which he offered impressions of Cobden, Alexis de Tocqueville, Hugo, and other European notables of the day. His play, *The Escape, or a Leap for Freedom,* was published in 1858.

Other works by Brown include *The Black Man: His Antecedents, His Genius and His Achievements,* written in support of emancipation (1863); *The Negro in the American Rebellion* (1866); *The Rising Sun* (1874); and *My Southern*

Home (1884). He was a contributor to Frederick Douglass's paper, the *Liberator,* and to the *National Anti-Slavery Standard* and the *London Daily News.* Brown died on Nov. 6, 1884, at his home in Chelsea, Mass.

Further Reading

Many of Brown's works have been reprinted. J. Noel Heermance, *William Wells Brown and Clotelle: A Portrait of the Artist in the First Negro Novel* (1969), reprints the 1864 version of *Clotelle,* together with a discussion of its literary, biographical, and antislavery background. A good study is William E. Farrison, *William Wells Brown, Author and Reformer* (1969), although it fails to mention much of the criticism of Brown's works. Probably the best source on Brown is William J. Simmons, *Men of Mark: Eminent, Progressive and Rising* (1887; repr. 1968). See also Harry A. Ploski and Roscoe C. Brown, Jr., eds., *The Negro Almanac* (1967).

Additional Sources

Brown, William Wells, *From fugitive slave to free man: the autobiographies of William Wells Brown,* New York: Mentor Books, 1993.

Brown, William Wells, *The travels of William Wells Brown, including The narrative of William Wells Brown, a fugitive slave, and The American fugitive in Europe, sketches of places and people abroad,* New York: M. Weiner Pub., 1991.

Two biographies by African-American women, New York: Oxford University Press, 1991.

Whelchel, L. H. (Love Henry), *My chains fell off: William Wells Brown, fugitive abolitionist,* Lanham, MD: University Press of America, 1985. □

Sir Thomas Browne

The works of the English author Sir Thomas Browne (1605-1682) are in large part inquiries into religion, morality, science, and human error. A doctor and scholar, he is chiefly famed for *Religio medici,* which is marked by his masterly prose style.

Thomas Browne was born in Cheapside, London, on Oct. 19, 1605. He was the son of a mercer of genteel Cheshire ancestry who died 8 years later, leaving "a plentifull Fortune." After earning a master's degree at Oxford in 1629, Browne studied medicine in Montpellier, Padua, and Leiden, where he received a degree in medicine in 1633. About 1635, while a young doctor in Yorkshire, he composed *Religio medici* (A Doctor's Religion) "as a personal exercise." In 1637 he settled in Norwich and gained esteem as a doctor who kept abreast of current revolutionary developments in medicine, such as William Harvey's discovery of blood circulation. In 1641 Browne married Dorothy Mileham, who bore him 12 children in 18 years, though he had professed in the *Religio* that he "could be content" if men procreated "like trees without conjunction."

Although Norwich was a Parliamentary stronghold, Browne remained a staunch royalist throughout the Puritan Revolution (1642-1660). His *Religio,* published without his permission in 1642 but in an authorized edition the next year, contrasts with the doctrinaire religious rigidity of his contemporaries. He writes as a humane Anglican, convinced of his own faith, enraptured by the wonders of theology, but open-minded and aware of the limitations of human reason and the folly of pious prejudices. In an age of intolerance he respected every man's right to decide on his own beliefs: "I could never divide myself from any man upon the difference of an opinion."

The *Religio* is a deliberately digressive, eclectic, charmingly erudite testimonial of Browne's experiences in religion and thought. He explores such topics as the relations of reason and faith, nature as God's art, musical harmonies, witchcraft, and man as inhabiting the "divided and distinguished worlds" of soul and spirit, reason and sense. The treatise is a revelation of self, reminiscent of Montaigne, but it is written from the perspective of eternity and couched in richly cadenced, imaginative, ornate, and flexible prose.

Pseudodoxia epidemica, or Vulgar Errors (1646) now seems more quaint than scientific, but it was practical in an age bound by traditional fallacies. Its purpose was to induce inquiries into popular delusions; for example, Browne denies that elephants lack knees, that crystal is hard ice, and that rubbing with garlic inhibits a magnet's power to attract.

In 1658 Browne published *Hydriotaphia, or Urn Burial* and its companion, *The Garden of Cyrus.* The first reflects on ancient burial customs, life's mystery, and the futility of pagan piety. The second discovers quincunxes (patterns of

fives) throughout nature and man's works and thus probes into the mysteriously intricate unity of things.

After the Restoration, Browne was elected a fellow of the Royal Society of Physicians, and in 1671 Charles II knighted him. Browne died on his birthday in 1682. His *Letter to a Friend* and *Christian Morals* found posthumous publication. Since then his works have been persistently reprinted, and he has won ever-increasing respect as a man of virtuous life dedicated to the progress of medicine and scientific experimentation and to appreciation of the mysteries of God, man, and nature. Above all, he is esteemed for a style rich in tone, exquisite in prose poetry, and superbly flexible in rhetoric.

Further Reading

Sir Geoffrey Keynes, ed., *The Works of Sir Thomas Browne* (6 vols., 1928-1931; new ed., 4 vols., entitled *Works,* 1964), is the standard collection and includes Browne's fascinating letters and miscellaneous writings as well as the major works. A wide selection is conveniently available in *The Prose of Sir Thomas Browne,* edited by Norman Endicott (1968). Jeremiah S. Finch, *Sir Thomas Browne: A Doctor's Life of Science and Faith* (1950), is an interesting, well-informed survey. Readers who find Browne's style and erudition baffling may turn for guidance to Joan Bennett, *Sir Thomas Browne: A Man of Achievement in Literature* (1962). Of the numerous scholarly treatments, among the most recent is Leonard Nathanson, *The Strategy of Truth: A Study of Sir Thomas Browne* (1967). For general background and further bibliography Douglas Bush, *English Literature in the Earlier 17th Century, 1600-1660* (1945; 2d ed. 1962), is useful. □

Carol M. Browner

When President-elect Bill Clinton named Carol Browner (born 1955) as his choice to head up the Environmental Protection Agency (EPA), environmentalists were pleased. Members of the business community, on the other hand, were somewhat skeptical because they feared increased regulations.

It is no secret that the EPA and the business community have been long-standing adversaries. During her confirmation hearings, however, Browner promised the business community that the regulatory climate would not be hostile toward them. Her experience in Florida had proven that the regulatory burdens on business could be eased without compromising the environment. Browner has been credited by both environmentalists as well as the Florida business community for being fair, knowledgeable, intelligent, and balanced in her approach to the environment and economics.

During her tenure as secretary of the Florida Department of Environmental Regulations, Browner drew both criticism and accolades from environmentalists, agriculturalists, and the business community. Browner's role as a strong negotiator and as an environmental visionary won her much respect in two specific cases in which she was involved while she served as Florida's secretary of Environmental Regulations. Browner was the chief negotiator for the state of Florida in a suit filed by the Federal Government to restore the Everglades by purifying and restoring the natural water flow to Everglades National Park. This was considered the largest ecological restoration effort ever undertaken in the United States and was projected to cost the state of Florida, the federal government, and sugar cane farmers about $1 billion. While the outcome pleased environmentalists, it infuriated the sugar farmers who would bear the burden of much of the cost. Andy Rackley, vice-president and general manager of the Florida Sugar Cane League, said of Browner in a *New York Times* article, "Having been on the opposite side of the table from her on the Everglades issue, I can tell you she is a formidable opponent."

Disney Does Wetlands

Browner is also credited with negotiating a successful landmark agreement with the Walt Disney Company that allowed them to develop 400 acres of wetlands on their property in Disney World in exchange for their investment of $40 million to purchase and protect more than 8500 acres of wetlands in central Florida. "[Browner] is a tremendous environmental leader," said Todd W. Mansfield, senior vice-president of Walt Disney Development Company. "She had a vision of protecting an entire ecosystem. She is a very, very long-term thinker." Browner's approach not only responded to the needs of the business community for ongoing development but insured and protected the balance

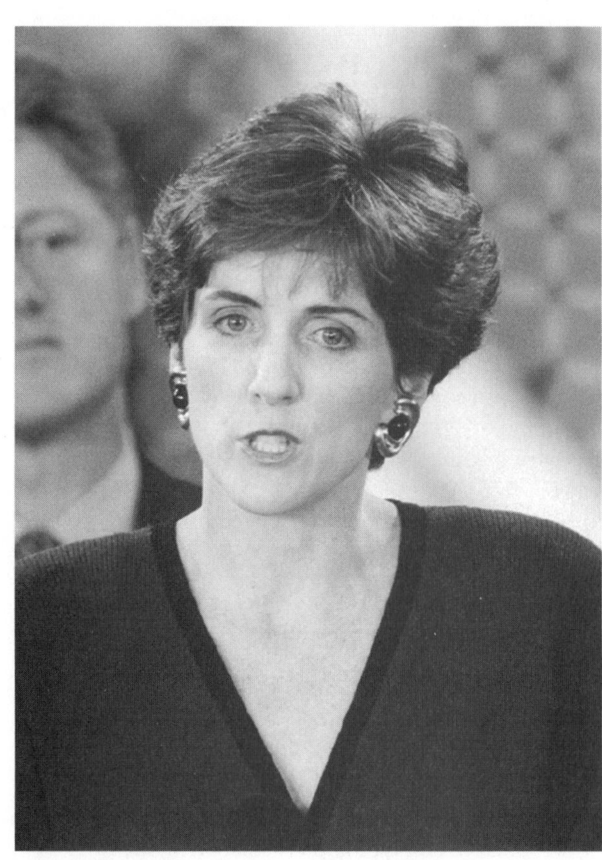

of an ecological system—the wetlands—that would provide a refuge for wildlife spanning thousands of acres in central Florida for decades to come.

Browner is the oldest of three daughters born to Michael Browner and Isabella Harty-Hugues, both academicians whose respect for education undoubtedly had a strong influence on their three daughters. The Browners limited their daughters' television viewing time and encouraged them, instead, to read and pursue their interests.

Browner was born and raised in Florida and her love of the state's natural beauty certainly played into her strong environmentalist attitudes. Growing up in the 1950s and '60s, Browner spent many hours hiking around the Everglades searching out the many species that inhabited the area. It is even said that she once missed school so that she could stay home and finish a watercolor painting of a rare water fowl that landed in a pond near her home.

Browner received both her undergraduate degree in English and her law degree from the University of Florida in Gainesville. Her sister, Michelle, the middle Browner daughter, is a biochemist at the University of California at San Francisco. The third and youngest of the Browner sisters, Stephanie, is completing her doctoral studies at the University of Indiana in American literature. Carol Browner's family feels that her position with the EPA not only allows her to continue to marvel at the natural world she loves but to have a profound and lasting impact on its future.

Focus on Prevention

Browner is being called one of a new breed of environmentalists because she believes that there can and should be a balance between environmental protection and economic development. She feels that the EPA, in the past, has not brought issues to conclusion quickly enough for businesses to act upon them. "I've found business leaders don't oppose strong environmental programs," said Browner during her confirmation hearings, as stated in the *New York Times*. "What drives them crazy is a lack of certainty." She vowed that the current administration will not hold up federal regulations considered anti-business as the previous administration had done. Her goal is to make the regulatory process more business-friendly. Browner's focus is on preventing pollution rather than on cleanup. Instead of an authoritarian and repressive regulatory environment, Browner looks for economic incentives in pollution prevention. She also works toward greater coordination with the other regulatory agencies within the federal government—energy, interior, transportation, agriculture—to develop a more unified environmental position. Browner also encourages giving individual states the freedom to develop their own environmental protection plans while keeping them under the auspices of the EPA. Browner made her point as stated by Max Gates in *Automotive News* when she said, "No one can tell me that Hawaii and Maine should have the same rules in all cases."

Browner had a formidable task facing her as the new EPA chief, but she also had the support of the Clinton administration. During the presidential campaign, Clinton, along with vice-presidential candidate Al Gore—a noted environmentalist and author of best seller *Earth in the Balance*—promised to make the environment a priority during their administration.

Browner introduced the Common Sense Initiative in 1994. The initiative updates the old method of regulating the environment—dealing with air, water, and land pollution separately—to an industry-by industry approach. Browner, President Clinton, and Vice President Gore announced a package of 25 reforms to streamline environmental regulation in March 1995.

An issue of paramount importance waiting for Browner when she stepped into her new position as EPA chief was that of toxic-waste disposal. Unlike the previous administrations' stances that incineration was the best way to handle the disposal of toxic waste, the new administration announced an 18-month moratorium on the licensing of new incinerators in order to give itself time to study the overall impact of incinerators on the environment. Further, this time enabled the EPA to tighten regulations on 171 unlicensed boilers and industrial furnaces that dispose of nearly five million tons of hazardous waste each year. Browner expanded the Toxic Release Inventory, which ensures the public's awareness of toxic emissions. She also issued the Chemical Manufacturing Rule, which aims to cut smog-producing chemicals by 1 million tons per year.

As Florida's secretary of Environmental Regulations, Browner had a solid foundation from which to approach her new post as chief of the Environmental Protection Agency. While in Florida, Browner managed the country's third-largest state environmental agency with a budget of $650 million and a staff of 1,500 employees. She is credited with revitalizing the department's demoralized workforce and making the agency one of the most active in the state. To date, Browner is the youngest administrator ever to serve with the EPA and only the second woman to hold the top post. As head of the Environmental Protection Agency, Browner oversees 17,000 individuals and is responsible for a budget of $7 billion. It has been said that she listens well, is a strong negotiator, and will compromise when necessary. Similar qualities have been attributed to her boss, Bill Clinton. And like President Clinton, she has opponents and critics on all sides.

Browner is a very organized individual both in her professional career and in her personal life, but she also has a lighter side to her personality, according to her father Michael Browner—a side that the public may never see. He laughingly recalls a time when he and other members of the family were invited to a party at Carol's new house shortly after she and Michael Podhorzer were married. Upon their arrival, and much to their surprise, they were all handed paint brushes. They painted all day and all night according to Mr. Browner.

Carol Browner bikes, skis, and jogs. The jogging is done mostly on a treadmill now because Browner usually arrives home after dark. The family is very active. Five days after her son Zachary was born, the family, including baby, went cross-country skiing. Browner says it was just a short trip and she doesn't want people to get the idea that she's superhuman, but she loves spending time with her family. Family is important to Browner and her husband Michael. Spending time with them continues to be a priority with Browner, even though it requires careful planning, since her position as EPA chief exacts more of her time and energy.

Browner is also very proud of the fact that she and husband Podhorzer, whom she met while both were working for the nonprofit advocacy Citizen Action group and whom she married in 1987, have never employed a housekeeper or a nanny for Zachary. They both share housekeeping chores and they both take equal responsibility for their child. Browner does not want to be branded as "eco-obsessed," but she admits she would consider the availability of curb-side recycling when purchasing a home. She also tries to buy in bulk to lessen packaging waste. Browner believes small things would make a big difference if everyone did them. She also feels that it is crucial to teach our young people how to be good stewards of the land, air and water. When she and Zachary walk to the store she lets him know that it is to save energy. When she gardens, she teaches her young son how to grow things and to respect the environment. When asked by a reporter for *USA Weekend Magazine* what his mom did for a living, Zachary simply said, "she saves things." What Browner wants for her son is not so different from what most parents want for their children. "I want my son to be able to grow up and enjoy the natural wonders of the United States in the same way that I have," stated Browner in the *New York Times.* With everything going on around her, Browner has not lost her idealism. She still wants to leave the world a better place for all of our children.

Further Reading

Amicus Journal, spring 1993.

Automotive News, December 14, 1992; February 22, 1993.

Chemical & Engineering News, December 21, 1992; March 1, 1993; May 24, 1993.

Congressional Quarterly Weekly Report, January 16, 1993.

Economist, January 9, 1993.

Fortune, March 22, 1993.

Good Housekeeping, March 1993.

Insight, February 8, 1993.

National Journal, February 13, 1993.

National Parks, March 1993.

Nation's Business, June 1993.

Nation's Cities Weekly, January 18, 1993.

New York Times, December 12, 1992; December 17, 1992; February 2, 1993; February 7, 1993; February 8, 1993; February 9, 1993; February 12, 1993; May 22, 1993.

Science, March 12, 1993.

Time, December 21, 1992; February 15, 1993.

USA Weekend, May 21-23, 1993.

Wall Street Journal, December 11, 1992; January 8, 1993; January 25, 1993; February 8, 1993; February 10, 1993; March 23, 1993; April 5, 1993. □

Elizabeth Barrett Browning

The works of the English poet Elizabeth Barrett Browning (1806-1861) enjoyed great popularity during her lifetime. Her most enduring poetry has proved to be *Sonnets from the Portuguese.*

Elizabeth Barrett was born on March 6, 1806, near Durham. She was the eldest of the 12 children of Edward Moulton Barrett, a possessive and autocratic man loved by his children even though he rigidly controlled their lives. Though she never received any formal education, Elizabeth was a precocious reader, and she began writing poetry at an early age. In 1819 her father had printed 50 copies of her epic "The Battle of Marathon," which she later referred to as "Pope's *Homer* done over again, or rather undone." In 1826 she published anonymously *An Essay on Mind, with Other Poems,* an attempt, as she later noted, to survey history, science, metaphysics, and poetry from classical Greece to the Victorian day in 88 pages.

Elizabeth's youthful happiness was not to last. In 1821 she began to suffer from a nervous disorder which was to cause headaches, weakness, and fainting spells for the rest of her life. Barrett continued her poetic career in 1833 with the anonymous publication of *Prometheus Bound: Translated from the Greek of Aeschylus, and Miscellaneous Poems.* Two years later, the Barretts moved to London and in 1838 settled permanently at 50 Wimpole Street. In the same year Elizabeth published her first book under her own name, *The Seraphim and Other Poems.* Though these poems are often filled with heavy-handed pathos and moralizing, the critics hailed her as a new poet of "extraordinary ability."

In 1838 Barrett became seriously ill. Two years later her favorite brother, Edward, drowned, and this shock seriously aggravated her poor health. For the next 5 years she remained in her room and saw no one except her family and a few close friends. In 1844, however, the publication of *Poems* secured her fame. Such poems as "The Dead Pan" and "Lady Geraldine's Courtship" seem strident and sentimental to modern readers, but they were very popular with Victorian readers and won high praise from critics in England and the United States.

But the most significant result of *Poems* was the beginning of Barrett's relationship with the poet Robert Browning. Attracted by her praise of his poetry, Browning wrote to her on Jan. 10, 1845, and thus began England's most famous literary love affair. Barrett's illness had led her to feel "completely dead to hope of any kind." Her progress out of this despair to hope and finally joy can be traced in her letters to Browning and in her *Sonnets from the Portuguese,* written during their courtship and expressing her love for him. Because Elizabeth's father had forbidden any of his children to marry, the couple were secretly married on Sept. 12, 1846. In anger and frustration, Mr. Barrett refused ever to see his daughter again.

The Brownings journeyed south through France to Italy. Casa Guidi in Florence was their home for the rest of Mrs. Browning's life. There her health was so improved that on March 9, 1849, she gave birth to a son, Robert Wiedeman Barrett Browning. In 1850 Browning issued a revised edition of *Poems* containing the *Sonnets from the Portuguese,* which her husband had urged her to publish. Modern readers usually find these sonnets her best work. But Victorian readers much preferred her *Aurora Leigh,* a long poem in blank verse published in 1856.

The major interest of Browning's later years was the Italian struggle for unity and independence. Both *Casa Guidi Windows* (1851) and *Poems before Congress* (1860) attempted to win sympathy for the Italian cause. On June 29, 1861, she died quietly in her husband's arms, with a "smile on her face."

Further Reading

The best biography of Mrs. Browning is Gardner B. Taplin, *The Life of Elizabeth Barrett Browning* (1957). Also useful is Dorothy Hewlett, *Elizabeth Barrett Browning: A Life* (1952). A detailed and moving account of the courtship of the Brownings can be obtained from *The Letters of Robert Browning and Elizabeth Barrett, 1845-1846,* first edited by their son (2 vols., 1899) and recently re-edited by Elvan Kintner (2 vols., 1969). More of Browning's extensive correspondence is collected in Sir Frederick G. Kenyon's edition of *The Letters of Elizabeth Barrett Browning* (2 vols., 1897). □

Robert Browning

The English poet Robert Browning (1812-1889) is best known for his dramatic monologues. By vividly portraying a central character against a social background, these poems probe complex human motives in a variety of historical periods.

Robert Browning was born on May 7, 1812, in Camberwell, London. His father, a senior clerk in the Bank of England, provided a comfortable living for his family and passed on a love of art and literature to Robert. His mother, an excellent amateur pianist, gave him a love of music, while her strong and simple piety provided him with an enduring conviction of the existence of God. In 1828 Browning entered the University of London, but he dropped out after half a year. The Brownings were a small, close-knit family and Robert apparently preferred to remain at home, reading in his father's library of over 7,000 volumes.

Early Poems and Plays

Browning began to write verses at the age of 6. His first published work was *Pauline: A Fragment of a Confession,* issued anonymously in 1833. The hero of the poem is a young poet, obviously Browning himself, who bares his soul to a patient heroine. When John Stuart Mill commented that the anonymous author seemed "possessed with a more intense and morbid self-consciousness than I ever knew in any sane human being," Browning resolved never again to reveal his thoughts directly to his readers. Henceforth, he would "only make men and women speak."

This major step in Browning's poetic development was evident in his next long poem, *Paracelsus* (1835), whose hero was a Renaissance alchemist. Though Browning later called the poem "a failure," it received favorable reviews and brought about important friendships with the authors William Wordsworth and Thomas Carlyle and with the actor William C. Macready. Encouraged by these friendships, Browning began to emerge in the London social scene. Mrs. Bridell-Fox, another friend of Browning's, described him at this time as "slim and dark, and very handsome . . . just a trifle of a dandy, addicted to lemon-coloured kid gloves." He seemed to her "determined to conquer fame and to achieve success."

Encouraged by Macready, Browning turned to writing drama. But his first play, *Strafford* (1837), closed after only five performances. During the next 10 years he wrote six other plays, none of which were successfully produced. All of Browning's plays are marred by overemphasis of character analysis and lack of dramatic action.

In 1838 Browning traveled to northern Italy to acquire firsthand knowledge of its setting and atmosphere for his next long poem. But the publication of *Sordello* in 1840 was a disaster which dealt Browning's growing reputation a severe blow. Critics unanimously declared the poem totally obscure and unreadable, and modern readers still find it difficult.

Development of the Dramatic Monologue

After the disappointing reception of *Strafford* and *Sordello,* Browning turned to the dramatic monologue. He experimented with and perfected this form in the long poem *Pippa Passes* (1841) and two collections of shorter poems, *Dramatic Lyrics* (1842) and *Dramatic Romances and Lyrics* (1845).

Usually written in blank verse, the dramatic monologue is the speech of a single character in a moment of some dramatic significance. In the course of his monologue, the speaker reveals what this situation is, as well as the setting of the situation and to whom he is speaking. Of greatest interest, however, is what he reveals about his own motives and personality. Often the speaker, while trying to justify himself to his listeners, actually reveals the faults or even depravity of his character to the reader. Such poems as "My Last Duchess," "Soliloquy of the Spanish Cloister," and "The Bishop Orders His Tomb," in which this ironic revelation is fully developed, give the reader the pleasure of discovering more about the speaker than he perceives about himself.

Marriage to Elizabeth Barrett

After reading Elizabeth Barrett's flattering reference to him in her *Poems,* Browning wrote to her in January 1845. At that time, Barrett was an invalid confined to her room by a nervous disorder. But the two became frequent correspondents, and on May 20, 1845, Browning made his first personal visit. With his constant urging, she gained steadily in strength, hope, and will until she agreed to a secret marriage on Sept. 12, 1846. Such secrecy was necessary because Barrett's father had forbidden all of his children "the iniquity of love affairs."

Shortly after their marriage, the Brownings left London for Italy, and they made Casa Guidi in Florence their home from 1847 until 1861. It was there that their son, Robert Wiedeman Barrett Browning, was born on March 9, 1849.

Mature Poetry

In 1855 Browning published *Men and Women,* a collection of 51 poems. Though the volume contained many of the dramatic monologues that are best known and loved by modern readers, it was not popular with Browning's contemporaries. But it did receive several favorable critical reviews and made Browning the idol of Dante Gabriel Rossetti and the Pre-Raphaelite Brotherhood.

After gradually declining in health for several years, Elizabeth Browning died on June 29, 1861. Browning found that he could no longer remain in Florence because of the memories it evoked. He resolved to "go to England, and live and work and write." In 1864 he published *Dramatis Personae* . Though some of the dramatic monologues in the collection are complex and difficult or overlong, this was the first of Browning's works to be popular with the general reading public. His popularity increased with the publication of *The Ring and the Book* in 1868-1869. This long poem is based on a murder and subsequent trial in Rome in 1698. In a Florentine bookstall Browning had found an "old Yellow Book" that contained records of these events. The poem is composed of 12 dramatic monologues, in which the major characters give their interpretations of the crime. The accounts contradict each other, but eventually the truth emerges from behind the tangled web of deceit and self-justification.

The Ring and the Book was enthusiastically received by the public, and Browning became a prominent figure in London society. He was a frequent guest at dinners, concerts, and receptions. In the next 10 years Browning wrote with great energy, publishing a volume almost every year. But none of these works match the quality of *Men and Women,* and they are little read today.

Though in the early stages of his career Browning's poetic reputation was far less than that of his wife, by 1870 he had achieved equal status with Tennyson, the poet laureate. The energy and roughness of Browning's poetry, however, contrast sharply with the melancholy and polish of Tennyson's. Today, through his influence on Ezra Pound and T. S. Eliot, Browning seems the most modern and enduring of all the mid-Victorian poets.

Browning died at his son's home in Venice on Dec. 12, 1889. In the "Epilogue" to his last collection of lyrics Browning described himself as "One who never turned his back but marched breast forward,/ Never doubted clouds would break." He was buried in Westminster Abbey.

Further Reading

The standard biography of Browning is W. Hall Griffin and Harry C. Minchin, *The Life of Robert Browning* (1910; 3d rev. ed. 1938). Mrs. Sutherland Orr, *Life and Letters of Robert Browning* (1891; revised by Frederic G. Kenyon, 1908), contains important additional information. An interesting modern psychological study is Betty B. Miller, *Robert Browning: A Portrait* (1952). William DeVane, *A Browning Handbook* (1935; 2d ed. 1955), is a useful source of information about Browning's poetry. Three of the best critical studies of his work are Roma A. King, *The Bow and the Lyre: The Art of Robert Browning* (1957); Robert W. Langbaum, *The Poetry of Experience: The Dramatic Monologue in Modern Literary Tradition* (1957); and Park Honan, *Browning's Characters: A Study in Poetic Techniques* (1961). Recommended for general historical background are George M. Trevelyan, *British History in the Nineteenth Century and After, 1782-1919* (1922; new ed. 1962); G. M. Young, *Victorian England: Portrait of an Age* (1936; 2d ed. 1953); and David Thomson, *England in the Nineteenth Century, 1815-1914* (1950).

Additional Sources

Maynard, John, *Browning's youth,* Cambridge, Mass.: Harvard University Press, 1977.

Thomas, Donald Serrell, *Robert Browning, a life within life,* New York: Viking Press, 1983, 1982.

Mason, Cyrus, *The poet Robert Browning and his kinsfolk,* Waco, Tex.: Baylor University Press, Markham Press Fund, 1983.

Irvine, William, *The book, the ring, & the poet; a biography of Robert Browni,* New York, McGraw-Hill 1974.

Ryals, Clyde de L., *The life of Robert Browning: a critical biography,* Oxford, UK; Cambridge, Mass.: Blackwell, 1993. □

William Gannaway Brownlow

The American preacher William Gannaway Brownlow (1805-1877) became the voice of strongly pro-Union East Tennessee before and during the Civil War through his speeches, writings, and newspapers. He was known as "the fighting parson."

William G. Brownlow was born on Aug. 29, 1805, in Wythe County, Va., and grew up in East Tennessee. After a brief period of schooling he became a Methodist circuit rider in 1826 and developed into an aggressive and controversial writer and speaker. In 1838 he added politics to his activities by purchasing a newspaper, the *Tennessee Whig,* which became an enthusiastic supporter of the Whig party under his guidance. Brownlow's newspaper used even more ridicule, cartoons, and abuse to attack opponents than was customary and gained a reputation that went far beyond East Tennessee. Extracts were reprinted in leading Whig newspapers all over the country. Brownlow also wrote pamphlets and books dealing with religious and political controversies.

When the Civil War began, most people in East Tennessee wanted to remain in the Union, even though the majority of Tennesseans had voted to join the Confederacy. Brownlow fearlessly printed their pro-Union views. He continued to publish in defiance of the state and Confederate governments until October 1861, when his press was confiscated and he was sent through the battle lines to the North. He returned to Knoxville with the Union Army in 1863 and resumed publication of his newspaper.

In 1865 he was elected governor of the newly restored state of Tennessee and was reelected in 1867. His two administrations were turbulent because of the problems of reconstructing a war-devastated state, the terrorist activities of the Ku Klux Klan, and his own forceful and controversial character. Before the war he had supported slavery, but during the war he embraced emancipation, and as governor he supported legislation to enfranchise African Americans. In 1869 Brownlow became a member of the U.S. Senate, but owing to failing health he took little part in the disputes of the times.

Upon his return to Tennessee he acquired half interest in another newspaper, and although by now an invalid, he continued active in its management until his death on April 29, 1877.

Further Reading

The only book-length biography, E. Merton Coulter, *William G. Brownlow: Fighting Parson of the Southern Highlands* (1937), is critical of Brownlow and the Reconstruction period. Oliver P. Temple, *Notable Men of Tennessee, from 1833 to 1875: Their Times and Their Contemporaries* (1912), contains a sympathetic biography. Temple was a contemporary of Brownlow, and his account is based on personal recollections.

Additional Sources

Humphrey, Steve, *"That d——d Brownlow": being a saucy and malicious description of William Gannaway Brownlow . . . ,* Boone, N.C.: Appalachian Consortium Press, 1978. □

Susan Brownmiller

A career feminist whose work spans the distance from political activism to historical research and novel writing, Susan Brownmiller (born 1935) is most recognized for raising public awareness of violent crimes against women and children.

Brownmiller was born in Brooklyn on February 15, 1935. She returned to New York City twenty years later, after graduating from Cornell University. She worked for four years as an actress before beginning her journalistic career as assistant to the managing editor of *Coronet.* During the 1960s she worked as a freelance writer with feminist leanings, and also in various capacities for *Newsweek, Village Voice,* NBC, and ABC. Especially relevant to the themes of her later writing, in 1968 Brownmiller cofounded the New York Radical Feminists among whose political stunts was a sit-in at the offices of *Ladies Home Journal.* Her first book, *Shirley Chisholm* (1970), a biography of the first African-American Congresswoman, was expanded from a cover story for *The New York Times Magazine* into a book aimed at adolescent audiences. During her work for a 1971 "Speak-Out," Brownmiller so radically revised her own opinions on rape that she began drafting the book which would eventually become *Against Our Will.* Her next book, *Femininity* (1984), was written against the "fear of not being feminine," a fear she feels has been historically imposed upon women. She was inspired to write her first novel, *Waverly Place* (1989), while covering the trial of Joel Steinman for *Ms.* magazine. As she told *Publisher's Weekly* in an interview, "I wrote the novel in a white heat because I was possessed. I had never given myself permission to invent before. It was very liberating." Her most recent work, *Seeing Vietnam: Encounters of the Road and Heart* (1994), also was born from a reporting assignment, this time for *Travel and Leisure.*

Against Our Will is perhaps most remarkable for its absolute lack of precedent, for as of 1975 such a comprehensive study of rape's genealogy had yet to be written. Indeed, the book created a clamor against this vast silence. Dredging up facts from the Trojan War to the Vietnam War, Brownmiller uncovered rape as a traditional military strategy. Pouring over centuries of legal history, she described rape as an openly or quietly advocated privilege of husbands over wives, fathers over daughters. The book is broadly and meticulously researched, presenting facts that are indispensable to fields of psychoanalysis, sociology, criminology, and law. Its rhetoric does not shy from its controversial claim that rape "is nothing more or less than a conscious process of intimidation by which *all men* keep *all women* in a state of fear." Behind her commitment to expose rape as a pervasive quality within all cultures stands Brownmiller's interest in empowering an immense society historically paralyzed and atomized by fear. Her third book, *Femininity,* also addresses the societal confinement of women, but the subject matter is considerably more subtle. Femininity, Brownmiller writes, "in essence, is a romantic sentiment, a nostalgic tradition of imposed limitations." According to this book, these limitations have taken the forms of clothing, games, manners, and popular metaphors for the "feminine" body, all of which debilitate women in their efforts to succeed.

Following the calm reception of *Shirley Chisholm,* which *Booklist* reviewed as a "chatty, narrative account," came the critical torrent surrounding *Against Our Will.* Although some reviews praised its "informed" and "compelling" "vision," as does Mary Ellen Gates for *The New York Times Book Review,* many more have left Brownmiller's work with more mixed responses. Amanda Heller of *The Atlantic Monthly* declared it to be "intelligent" and "ambitious" but in places given to "a kind of feminist pornography that overwhelms the book's more thoughtful passages." Diane Johnson, writing for *The New York Review of Books,* looked more seriously at the risk of these latter passages, suggesting Brownmiller's rhetoric effectively divides her audience between discouraged women and alienated men. Coming from a radically different perspective, M. J. Sobran, writing for *National Review,* rejected Brownmiller's very premises: "What she is engaged in, really, is not scholarship but henpecking—that conscious process of intimidation by which all women keep all men in terror."

The critical reception of *Femininity* was likewise divided. Anne Collins believed it to be "neither self-deprecating enough to be funny nor winsome enough to evoke rueful empathy." Laura Shapiro agreed, stating, "Brownmiller skips along with a great armful of cliches and truisms and scatters them like rose petals until they're all gone." In stark contrast to such comments, Elizabeth Wheeler announced "Brownmiller has written an important book." Carol Gilligan agreed, writing, "The critical questions are of perspective, power, and judgment."

Further Reading

Against Our Will: Men, Women, and Rape, Brownmiller, Susan, Simon & Schuster, 1975.

Waverly Place, Brownmiller, Susan, Grove, 1989.

Commentary, February, 1976.

Commonweal, December 5, 1975.

Detroit News, February 1, 1984.

Nation, November 29, 1975.

National Review, March 5, 1976. □

Orestes Augustus Brownson

Orestes Augustus Brownson (1803-1876) was an American clergyman, transcendentalist, and social activist. He passed through the whole range of American religion, from nebulous Unitarianism to firmly disciplined Catholicism.

Orestes A. Brownson was born in Stockbridge, Vt., on Sept. 16, 1803, to Sylvester Augustus and Relief Metcalf Brownson. He was entrusted to the care of neighbors after his father died and his mother could not support him. Brownson grew up on a small farm, educated only by his own reading; farm work toughened him and self-education trained his mind. From the start, his bent was toward the church. In 1822 he became a Presbyterian, but he was uncomfortable with the Presbyterian doctrines of election and reprobation. Universalism, on the other hand, preached that all men could be saved and that over the universe presided a loving rather than a just God. In 1826 he became a Universalist minister.

The following year Brownson married Sally Healy and embarked on a restless pastorate. He preached in Vermont, New Hampshire, and upstate New York, seeking not only the ideal pulpit but the ideal theology. In 1829 he became the editor of a church paper, the *Gospel Advocate.* But he gradually developed doubts about Universalism too, questioning Christ's divinity, the Bible's authenticity, and the idea of eternal life. The one denomination more open than Universalism was Unitarianism, so from 1832 he served as a Unitarian minister. In 1836 he shook off this last affiliation and formed his own congregation in Boston.

Significantly, the new congregation was made up of poor people. Brownson had shown increasing interest in social action, particularly in bettering the condition of New England's urban poor. Before forming his Boston church, he had been a socialist and had helped set up the Workingmen's party. Now he found that he could make his best contribution not through political activity but through the church. He expressed his ideas in *New Views of Christianity, Society and the Church* (1836).

Brownson founded the *Boston Quarterly Review* in 1838. It outraged many New England conservatives by attacking inherited wealth, harsh criminal codes, and organized religion and espousing the cause of the poor and the Democratic party. In 1842 he merged his magazine with the *Democratic Review;* the merger proved unsuccessful, and 2 years later he reestablished his own journal as *Brownson's Quarterly Review.*

Meanwhile, though he remained an individualist, he found friends and allies among members of the transcendentalist movement. Their rather vague philosophy had little appeal for him, but he admired their unconventional stance and joined in their occasional efforts at social reform. Among his friends were Ralph Waldo Emerson, Henry Thoreau, George Ripley, and William Ellery Channing. Brownson sent his son Orestes to the transcendentalist commune Brook Farm.

In 1844 Brownson's supporters experienced a shock. The man they had systematically identified with individualism and dissent suddenly joined the Roman Catholic Church. He embraced his new denomination with more ardor than he had shown for any other, becoming that classic figure, the convert with more zeal than any cradle Catholic. The steps in his conversion are described in *The Convert; or Leaves from My Experience* (1857).

Brownson's conversion dealt a blow to the *Review,* which lost many Protestant and agnostic readers but failed to add many Catholic ones. It endured as an essentially Catholic journal until January 1865, and he revived it again in 1872 for 3 years.

Brownson was extraordinarily active throughout his life. His pen was seldom still. He contributed to other magazines besides his own and published several books. In old age, still driven by abundant energy, Brownson moved from place to place restlessly, as in his early days. He died in Detroit on April 17, 1876.

Further Reading

The Works of Orestes A. Brownson (20 vols., 1882-1907) was edited by Brownson's son, Henry F. Brownson, who also wrote *Orestes A. Brownson's Life* (3 vols., 1898-1900). Two good biographies of Brownson exist: Arthur M. Schlesinger, Jr., *Orestes A. Brownson: A Pilgrim's Progress* (1939), traces Brownson's life especially as it related to his religious and social ideas; Theodore Maynard, *Orestes Brownson: Yankee, Radical, Catholic* (1943), written by a Catholic, emphasizes the years after Brownson's conversion. See also Lawrence Roemer, *Brownson on Democracy and the Trend toward Socialism* (1953).

Additional Sources

Ryan, Thomas R. (Thomas Richard), *Orestes A. Brownson: a definitive biography,* Huntington, Ind.: Our Sunday Visitor, 1976.

McDonnell, James M. (James Michael), *Orestes A. Brownson and nineteenth-century Catholic education,* New York: Garland, 1988. □

John Seiler Brubacher

A major figure in the field of history and philosophy of education in the 20th century, John Seiler Brubacher (1898-1988) helped shaped the direction of the field through his teaching and writing. His books were used to prepare many teachers, school administrators, and professors across the United States.

John Seiler Brubacher was born on October 18, 1898, in Easthampton, Massachusetts, the only child of Abram Royer and Rosa (Haas) Brubacher. A descendant of Pennsylvania Mennonites, Brubacher grew up in New York where his father served as a public school administrator and as president of New York State Teachers College at Albany. His mother was a former music teacher. Thus, Brubacher was reared by parents who strongly supported his academic endeavors.

Brubacher went to the public schools of New York in the various places of his father's work. He attended public high school in Schenectady, but when the family moved to Albany, he completed his secondary education at the private Albany Boys Academy. From there he entered Yale, where he received the B.A. degree with Phi Beta Kappa rank in 1920. After completing the J.D. degree at Harvard Law School in 1923, he served a brief stint with a law firm, but after deciding that education was his true interest, he entered Teachers College, Columbia University, completing the M.A. degree in 1924. In August he married Winifred Wemple, a Schenectady classmate, and began his teaching career at Dartmouth College. In 1925 he returned to Teachers College for the Ph.D., and after studying under such leading figures as John Dewey and I. L. Kandel he completed his studies in 1927. In 1928 he joined the faculty at Yale and over the ensuing years became a nationally prominent professor and author in the field of history and philosophy of education.

Of all his publications, perhaps the two most important were *Modern Philosophies of Education* (1939, 1950, 1962, 1969) and *A History of the Problems of Education* (1947, 1966). In each he took a rather novel approach. For example, the standard approach to writing philosophy of education textbooks was to organize them by a school of thought such as idealism, realism, or pragmatism according to its implications for education. The result, Brubacher argued, was that students learned more about academic philosophy than the philosophical problems of education; instead, education should be the primary focus, and philosophy—studied with scholarly rigor—should be used to shed light on the problems of education. He never completely abandoned reference to schools of thought, however, for he felt that those traditions reflected educational ideologies that were woven into the culture.

Brubacher's influence became such that he was elected president of the Philosophy of Education Society from 1942 to 1946, and he was selected to chair the committees for two important yearbooks of the National Society for the Study of Education: *Philosophies of Education* (1942) and *Modern Philosophies and Education* (1955). In addition to these works, he also edited *Eclectic Philosophy of Education* (1951, 1962) and produced numerous articles and scholarly papers. Brubacher's popular textbook, *Modern Philosophies of Education,* went through four editions, but by the time of the fourth edition in 1969 views such as his were receiving mounting criticism, primarily from Anglo-American analytic philosophers. They agreed that the old "schools" approach was inadequate; however, they argued that analytic philosophy had so revolutionized the field that the major task now was to clarify educational terms and statements through language analysis. Brubacher recognized that clarification was a very important function of philosophy of education, but he would not concede that analytic philosophy was truly revolutionary or that the need to examine ideological considerations had lost its usefulness.

In teaching the history of education, Brubacher found the traditional chronological approach too restrictive. Educators needed chronology, but they also needed to know the history of specific topics, such as the historical development of curriculum or the evolution of an institutional form. To meet this need, he wrote *A History of the Problems of Education,* which has been called one of the few genuinely novel approaches because it breaks that history into some 19 topical areas, including educational aims, the politics of education, elementary and secondary education, and public and private education, to name a few.

After Yale president A. Whitney Griswold dismantled the education department in a preemptory fashion, Brubacher resigned in 1958 and took a position at the University of Michigan's Center for the Study of Higher Education. Even before leaving Yale, he and Willis Rudy had completed *Higher Education in Transition: An American History, 1636-1956* (1958). Now, addressing the lack of an adequate contemporary philosophy of higher education, Brubacher wrote *Bases for Policy in Higher Education* in 1965 and *On the Philosophy of Higher Education* in 1977 (revised 1982). This new interest connected with his legal background and led to *The Courts and Higher Education* (1971) and the two-volume *The Law and Higher Education: A Casebook* (1971).

Brubacher retired from the University of Michigan in 1969, and subsequently moved to Bridgeport, Connecticut. Some time after the death of his first wife, Winifred, he married Dorothy Kohler in 1972. He died on March 8, 1988. His many honors included the Reuben Post Halleck professorship at Yale in 1947; two terms as visiting professor at the American University in Beirut, Lebanon, in 1951-1952 and 1956-1957; a Fulbright fellowship at the University of Kyushu, Japan, in 1957; a series of lectures at the invitation of Brazil's National Research Institute in both Sao Paulo and Rio de Janeiro in 1959; and the distinguished service award from the John Dewey Society in 1973. During his years as a professor at Yale and at Michigan he taught hundreds of students, many of whom became important leaders in education, and his many books and articles influenced countless others.

Further Reading

John Seiler Brubacher is listed in *Leaders in Education,* 5th edition (1974) and in the *Biographical Dictionary of American Educators* (1978). The best and most extensive treatments, however, may be found in Brubacher's autobiographical statement, "John S. Brubacher: An Autobiography," and Maxine Greene's "John S. Brubacher: A Biographical Essay," both found in *Leaders in Education,* Seventieth Yearbook of the Society for the Study of Education, Part II (1971). □

Dave Brubeck

Dave Brubeck (born 1920), who is considered the most widely acclaimed jazz musician of his time period, has been described as everything from mystical to methodical.

According to Robert Rice of the *New Yorker,* the combo led by jazz pianist Dave Brubeck during the 1950s and 1960s was "the world's best-paid, most widely travelled, most highly publicized, and most popular small group." While Brubeck can be considered the world's most widely acclaimed musician of his period, he is also quite possibly its most criticized, having been described as everything from mystical to methodical. Stanley H. White wrote in *Jazz Journal* in 1958 that Brubeck's "ability to improvise fluently on almost any given theme, and his ability to swing with both drive and imagination make him a jazz musician of singular merit"; two years later Joe Goldberg declared in *Jazz Review* "that jazz is not [Brubeck's] natural form of expression, but he is determined to play jazz, as if a man who knew five hundred words of French were to attempt a novel in that language."

Perhaps Rice's statement on the importance of Brubeck's music, that "it is impossible to make a comment—pro, con, or merely factual—that would not be disputed by a majority of the people who habitually play, listen to, or write about jazz," sums up the critical commentary that surrounds Brubeck's body of work. What can be asserted is that Brubeck, beyond the praise and fault-finding, beyond even the unexamined end result of his music, has always been an intelligent musician thoughtful of the process, an artist constantly seeking a new and justifiable means of creative expression.

"Perhaps the most significant contribution made by the Brubeck Quartet has been the integration of jazz and classical elements," Al Zeiger noted in *Metronome.* But Brubeck's precarious marriage of these two divergent styles has frequently offended stylists and aficionados of the pure jazz form. "He cannot always maintain the balance between jazz and classical music without forsaking an element vital to either one form," White appraised in *Jazz Journal.* More often than not, Brubeck's improvisations slip from jazz into classical colors, bringing up "a little canon a la Bach or some dissonant counterpoint a la Bartok or even a thrashing crisis a la Beethoven," a reporter for *Time* pointed out.

Brubeck's tendency toward peppering his jazz speech with classical tones is rooted in his childhood. His mother, a classically trained piano teacher, was a believer in prenatal influence. "She practiced all through her pregnancies," Brubeck related, according to Len Lyons in *The Great Jazz Pianists: Speaking of Their Lives and Music.* "When we were born, we were all put near the piano to listen to her practicing. I heard Chopin, Liszt, Mozart, and Bach from infancy." While his brothers took to classical training, Brubeck rebelled against his mother's teachings, preferring instead to make up his own songs. "There can be little doubt that his original interest in jazz arose as a protest against the idea of playing notes that were written on paper instead of the notes that were in his head," Rice wrote in the *New Yorker.* It is noteworthy that Brubeck did not learn to read music until later in life. Because of his acute musical ear, he was able to fool his mother by reproducing any piece after listening to it once or twice.

Despite Brubeck's early protestations, classical music informed his subsequent musical approach. He attested to this in an article he wrote for *Down Beat* at the beginning of his career: "Because the jazz musician creates music, interprets music as he hears it, it is natural that his improvised compositions should reflect every kind of music to which he has been exposed." Further exposure to the classical realm came through studies with the French composer Darius Milhaud.

After graduating with a degree in music and serving in the U.S. Army during World War II, Brubeck studied composition under Milhaud at Mills College for three years. From this classical instructor, Brubeck learned one important point about composing, as he explained to Michael Bourne in *Down Beat:* "One lesson was never give up jazz. And he told me I would be a composer on my own terms. . . . He said, 'If you don't reflect your own country and use the jazz idiom, you'll never be a part of this culture.' And, of course, Copland used it, Bernstein used it. Most of the important American composers have used jazz." But it seems that jazz was just a tool used to build his compositions, for in addition, Brubeck learned from Milhaud the usage of modern European polytonal harmonies on which he was to base his style.

After his apprenticeship under Milhaud, Brubeck sought a group sound for his compositions in 1949, first with an octet, then pared down to a trio. He also helped form Fantasy Records, the label on which he first recorded. But his definition of jazz—"an improvised musical expression based on European harmony and African rhythms," as he described it in *Down Beat* —was not fulfilled until Brubeck added alto saxophonist Paul Desmond to the group in 1951. "Desmond's yearning lyricism proved the perfect foil for Brubeck's percussive approach," Amy Duncan pointed out in the *Christian Science Monitor.* Another indication of Brubeck's keen judgement was his decision at the time to forego the night club circuit in favor of college campuses. The 1954 recording of one such tour, *Jazz Goes to College,* was the quartet's breakthrough, selling over a million copies and earning Brubeck the cover of *Time*'s November 8, 1954, issue.

In *Time*'s accompanying profile Brubeck was described as "a wigging cat with a far-out wail" who produces "some of the strangest and loveliest music ever played since jazz was born." His music and approach, which the article proclaimed heralded a new jazz age, "is neither chaotic nor abandoned. It evokes neither swinging hips nor hip flasks. It goes to the head and the heart more than to the feet."

But accompanying the rising acclaim was also rising derision. The debate over the purpose and sound of jazz divided the critical camps. *Metronome*'s Zeiger lauded Brubeck's technique: "his texture has a refinement and lightness to it which, at times, is characteristic of the grace and elegance of Mozart"; but *Jazz Journal*'s White stressed that "the unavoidable lack of beat, the absence of the jazz spirit—these indispensable jazz attributes—bring defeat to an otherwise highly intelligent and musicianly artist." Dave Gelly, writing in his book *The Giants of Jazz,* summed up the reasons for critical disapproval: "Brubeck's studious manner, his copious references to Milhaud and Hindemith in press interviews, his little lectures at concerts on how very complicated and demanding the next number was going to be, his quotations from Bach, the galloping pomposity of his piano solos." The public, however, continued its almost unanimous approval of the quartet. "The fact that it is admired by the public may explain the fact that it is scorned by many of the adepts," Rice assessed in the *New Yorker.* "'Popular' is an extreme [negative] in certain jazz circles."

With the substitution of Joe Morello on drums and Eugene Wright on bass in the late 1950s, Brubeck formed the classic Dave Brubeck Quartet, which performed unchanged for almost ten years. Len Lyons and Don Perlo, in their book *Jazz Portraits: The Lives and Music of the Jazz Masters,* described the basic elements of the quartet's music: "Fuguelike interplay among the instruments; clear (sometimes simplistic) thematic statements; excursions into polytonality; and a tight group sound." This definitive Dave Brubeck Quartet sound also bore the mark of irregular time signatures. Brubeck's belief that "new and complex rhythm patterns, more akin to the African parents, is the natural direction for jazz to develop," as he wrote in *Down Beat,* was fully realized on his famous 1959 recording, *Time Out,* which featured the hits "Take Five" (in 5/4 meter) and "Blue Rondo a la Turk" (in 9/8 meter). "Take Five" was so well received that it even made the popular music charts, unheard of for an instrumental jazz recording. *Time Out* went on to become the first instrumental jazz album certified gold.

The quartet continued to record and tour successfully until 1967, when Brubeck decided to disband the group to fully concentrate on composing sacred music and jazz-influenced symphonic works. Among his compositions is the cantata *Truth Is Fallen,* commissioned in 1971 and dedicated "to the slain students of Kent State University and Jackson State, and all other innocent victims caught in the cross fire between repression and rebellion," Leonard Feather noted in his book *The Pleasures of Jazz.*

But Brubeck couldn't stay away from the quartet format and the improvisational element of jazz. "Jazz stands for freedom," he told Duncan of the *Christian Science Monitor.* "It's supposed to be the voice of freedom: Get out there and improvise, and take chances." Since the early 1970s, Brubeck has recorded and toured with his quartet composed of various musicians, including a combination of his sons, and labeled Two Generations of Brubeck. Although not quite the force he was in the 1950s and 1960s, Brubeck continued to produce vital music, as *Stereo Review*'s Chris Albertson attested to in a review of Brubeck's 1986 offering, *Reflections,* stating that "the album only partly reflects the past: the present is also strongly represented, and the blend is good. . . . There was always a lyrical side to Brubeck, and that—as several selections here demonstrate—is an aspect of his music that time has enhanced."

For over four decades Dave Brubeck has created music, both written and unwritten. He led one of the most successful quartets in the history of jazz without pandering to either popular or critical dictates, remaining "a paragon of obstinacy, and [playing], stolidly or not, as he pleases," Rice observed in the *New Yorker.* He has persisted in seeking a voice for his creations with an informed intellectual purpose. "Far from being a born jazz man, Brubeck is a creative artist, an artist who uses jazz as his means of self-impression and as a source of unbounded inspiration," wrote *Jazz Journal'* s White, adding that "the fundamental reason for Brubeck's failure to convince the jazz masses is simply that he attempted to bring something new into jazz."

Further Reading

Feather, Leonard, *The Pleasures of Jazz,* Horizon, 1976.
Gelly, Dave, *The Giants of Jazz,* Schirmer Books, 1986.
Lyons, Len, *The Great Jazz Pianists: Speaking of Their Lives and Music,* Morrow, 1983.
Lyons, Len and Don Perlo, *Jazz Portraits: The Lives and Music of the Jazz Masters,* Morrow, 1989.
Christian Science Monitor, January 18, 1989; August 17, 1989.
Down Beat, January 27, 1950; February 10, 1950; February 6, 1957; October, 1982; March, 1991.
Jazz Journal, February 1958.
Jazz Journal International, December 1988.
Jazz Review, February 1960.
Metronome, August 1955.
New Yorker, June 3, 1961.
New York Times, July 1, 1990.
Stereo Review, February 1980; November 1986.
Time, November 8, 1954. □

1st Viscount Bruce of Melbourne

Stanley Melbourne Bruce, 1st Viscount Bruce of Melbourne (1883-1967), was an Australian statesman, diplomat, and international administrator. He believed in close ties with the British Empire without diminishing Australia's self-government.

Stanley Bruce was born in Melbourne on April 15, 1883, the son of a successful merchant. He was educated in Melbourne and Trinity Hall, Cambridge, where he graduated in law, and from 1906 practiced in London at Middle Temple. Bruce enlisted in 1914 and served in a British regiment; he was twice wounded before his discharge in 1917.

Returning to Melbourne to direct the family business, Bruce was elected as a Nationalist party candidate to the House of Representatives in 1918. He was on a private visit to Europe when asked to represent Australia at the League of Nations Assembly meeting in 1921. On his return to Australia he became treasurer under Premier William Morris Hughes.

Leader of the Government

After the general election of 1922 Bruce was chosen as Nationalist party leader, and in 1923 he became prime minister in a Nationalist-Country coalition of generally conservative complexion. Bruce called for economies in all phases of economic life and particularly for cost reduction, which he believed could be achieved through wage restraint.

By inclination and experience Bruce favored an "empire" approach dedicated to rebuilding Britain's diminished strength through "all pulling together" in the imperial cause. As part of an attack on economic problems at home and abroad, he promoted immigration from Britain to Australia, with emphasis on rural settlement. State governments were encouraged to maximize their role in such plans, but the Development and Migration Act of 1926 was an ambitious federal attempt to initiate resource surveys, promote investment, and coordinate labor requirements.

Lasting achievements of Bruce's government were the establishment of a national scientific research body and the federal-states compact of 1928, under which a loan council was set up with powers to regulate the borrowings of all government agencies. Administration of the government-owned Commonwealth Bank was revamped by placing the bank under an eight-man board drawn almost wholly from the private sector. To advise on fiscal policy, an independent tariff board was created, while grower-dominated boards were established to regulate the marketing of various agricultural products.

Returned in 1928 with a narrow majority, Bruce's administration faced a deteriorating economic situation. Commodity prices had fallen overseas, the country had to meet heavy overseas interest payments with shrunken export earnings, and unemployment was widespread. In 1929 there were numerous strikes and a serious lockout in the coal industry. Bruce intensified pressures on labor by strengthening coercive laws and demanding fines on striking unions.

There was sharp political disagreement concerning the proper role of federal and state authorities in handling labor disputes, and Bruce took the unprecedented step of proposing that the federal government virtually withdraw from industrial arbitration. Deserted by some of his shocked followers in September 1929, Bruce called a special election in which his administration was soundly defeated; he lost his own seat in the debacle.

International Statesman

Bruce was reelected in 1931 but remained in Parliament only a year before returning to London, where he represented Australia at the World Monetary and Economic Conference of 1933. Later that year he became Australian high commissioner, a post he retained until 1945.

From 1942 to 1945 Bruce was the representative of the Australian government in the United Kingdom War Cabinet and the Pacific War Council in London. Under instructions from the government of John Curtin he accented Australia's claims to full prior consultation on matters affecting basic strategy on the conduct of the war, and he pressed the case for a buildup of Allied forces in Australia as the major base for launching a counteroffensive against Japan.

In 1947 Bruce was made 1st Viscount Bruce of Melbourne—the second Australian raised to the peerage. Lord Bruce was chairman of the World Food Council of the Food and Agriculture Organization from 1947 to 1951, and in 1952 he became the first chancellor of the Australian National University, retaining that office until 1961. He died in London on Aug. 25, 1967.

Further Reading

A full biography, written by a newspaperman who knew Bruce throughout his public life, is Cecil Edwards, *Bruce of Melbourne: Man of Two Worlds* (1965). The legislative record is contained in A. N. Smith, *Thirty Years: The Commonwealth of Australia, 1901-31* (1933). Political aspects are explored in Louise Overacker, *The Australian Party System* (1952), and Dagmar Carboch, *The Fall of the Bruce-Page Government* (1958).

The views of Bruce's coalition partner are given in U. R. Ellis, *A History of the Australian Country Party* (1963), and Earle Page, *Truant Surgeon: The Inside Story of Forty Years of Australian Political Life* (1963). Wider references are in J. G. Latham, *Australia and the British Commonwealth* (1929). Background material is in Brian Fitzpatrick, *The British Empire in Australia: An Economic History, 1834-1939* (1941). The effect of the 1924 banking legislation is given in L. F. Giblin, *The Growth of a Central Bank: The Development of the Commonwealth Bank of Australia, 1924-45* (1951).

Additional Sources

Stirling, Alfred Thorpe, *Lord Bruce, the London years,* Melbourne: Hawthorn Press, 1974. □

Blanche Kelso Bruce

Blanche Kelso Bruce (1841-1898), African American political leader in Mississippi, was the first member of his race to serve a full term in the U.S. Senate.

On March 1, 1841, Blanche Kelso Bruce was born a slave near Farmville, Prince Edward County, Va. His master had him educated, and before the Civil War he went to Missouri, where he organized the first school for African Americans in the state. In 1868, after 2 years at Oberlin College, he moved to Floreyville, Bolivar County, Miss., where he became a planter in the rich Mississippi Delta and acquired considerable property.

Soon after his arrival, Military Governor Adelbert Ames appointed him conductor of elections for a nearby county, and in 1870 he became sergeant at arms in the state senate. Bruce was highly regarded in Bolivar County, where he served as assessor, sheriff, county school superintendent, and member of the Board of Levee Commissioners. He was also tax collector, with prominent Republicans and Democrats posting the bond required for the position. When Ku Klux Klan-inspired violence began to rise, he was able to use his influence to prevent race riots in his home county. As a leader of the Republican party in Mississippi, he was elected in 1874 to the U.S. Senate.

Bruce was a handsome man with erect bearing and polished manners, and he and his wife were active in Washington society. In the Senate he served on important committees, spoke on behalf of the Native Americans and Chinese, advocated improvements on the Mississippi River, and worked to obtain pensions for African American Union Army veterans. He tried to prevent the removal of Federal troops from Mississippi, where their presence acted as a deterrent to terrorism. After the Democrats took over control of the state through intimidation and violence at the polls in 1875, he was instrumental in providing for an investigation of the election.

At the end of his 6-year term in the Senate he was appointed register of the Treasury by President James A. Garfield and later served as recorder of deeds for the District of Columbia during the Harrison administration. Bruce continued to be a leader of the Republican party in Mississippi in the 1880s, often speaking from the same platform with white political friends and opponents, and he was a trustee of Howard University. President McKinley appointed him register of the Treasury again in 1895. He died in Washington, D.C., on March 17, 1898.

Further Reading

A sketch of Bruce's life is in Benjamin G. Brawley, *Negro Builders and Heroes* (1937). More detailed information on his career is in Vernon Lane Wharton, *The Negro in Mississippi: 1865-1890* (1947). See also Philip Sterling and Rayford Logan, *Four Took Freedom: The Lives of Harriet Tubman, Frederick Douglass, Robert Smalls, and Blanche K. Bruce* (1967), and Wil-

liam J. Simmons, *Men of Mark: Eminent, Progressive and Rising* (1887; repr. 1968). □

David Bruce

The Australian parasitologist David Bruce (1855-1931) discovered the causes of Malta, or undulant, fever and of sleeping sickness.

David Bruce was born on May 29, 1855, in Melbourne, Australia. His family went to Scotland when David was 5. He attended the medical school at Edinburgh University. In 1883 he married Mary Elizabeth Steele, who assisted him in his work throughout his life. Shortly thereafter Bruce was commissioned in the Royal Medical Service and was posted to Malta in 1884. There he studied a serious, often fatal disease, known as Malta or Mediterranean fever, which was prevalent among civilians and military personnel.

Malta fever is characterized by a continuous long-lasting fever which rises and falls irregularly, and which has been known in the Mediterranean region since the time of Hippocrates, who accurately described it. Within two years of his arrival in Malta, Bruce found a bacterium in the spleen of a number of fatal human cases of the disease. He named the organism *Micrococcus melitensis* because of its small size. He also found that human beings became infected from goats' milk and cheese and that abortions were common in diseased goats as well as in pregnant women who contracted the fever. This and later work led eventually to the eradication of the disease.

In 1894 Bruce went to Zululand, South Africa, where he studied nagana, a common disease of domestic animals. By 1895 he discovered trypanosomes, minute wormlike protozoans, living in the blood of sick cattle, and he showed that this parasite was transmitted by the bite of the tsetse fly. He had actually found a mixture of three species, which are now identified as *Trypanosoma brucei* (named after him), *T. congolense,* and *T. vivax*. Bruce's work was with animals at that time, and he was not directly concerned with human disease; but in 1890 trypanosomes were found in human blood and in 1901 were named *T. gambiense.*

A mysterious lethargy that had long been known in regions of tropical Africa first began to attract considerable attention when slaves exported to the West Indies often developed this disease. In Uganda alone in 1900, about two-thirds of the population died from it; they called it sleeping sickness. In 1902 the Royal Society sent a Sleeping Sickness Commission to Uganda, and one of its members, Aldo Castellani, reported finding trypanosomes in the cerebrospinal fluid of a patient. The following year a second commission was dispatched, with Bruce at its head. Following Castellani's lead and aided by his experience with nagana, Bruce proved that trypanosomes, transmitted by the tsetse fly, were the cause of sleeping sickness. Bruce was engaged in sleeping sickness investigations until 1911, when he was posted to the Royal Army Medical College, where during World War I he directed research on louse-carried trench fever and tetanus. He retired in 1919; he died on Nov. 20, 1931, in London.

Further Reading

There is no book-length biography of Bruce. Frederick Eberson, *Man against Microbes: The Story of Preventive Medicine* (1963), gives an account of Bruce's work in combating trypanosomiasis. Paul de Kruif's popular *Men against Death* (1932) offers an interesting account of Bruce's role in the scientific battle against Malta fever. □

James Bruce

The Scottish explorer James Bruce (1730-1794) introduced Ethiopia to the Western world and confirmed the source of the Blue Nile. He was the first modern explorer of tropical Africa.

James Bruce was born on Dec. 14, 1730, near Larbert in Stirlingshire. His father, the laird of Kinnaird House and a descendant of the prominent Bruce family, sent young James to school in England partly because his mother was dead and partly to keep him away from Jacobite influences.

In 1747 Bruce enrolled at the University of Edinburgh to study law, but after graduating he decided not to practice.

In 1754 he married Adriana Allan, who died of consumption a year later.

Bruce visited Andalusia in 1757, where he became interested in the history of Moorish Spain and of the Arabs who had created it, and then toured northern Europe. On his father's death the following year, Bruce became the laird of Kinnaird. In 1760 the pit coal on his land was used by the inventor John Roebuck for a new steelmaking process. Although Bruce, a large, florid, quarrelsome man, argued incessantly with Roebuck, his immediate financial gain was considerable and, with Bruce's tastes for adventure and travel, liberating.

Bruce obtained the post of consul general in Algiers in 1762, but he took nearly a year to reach the city. He traveled through France and Italy, investigating and sketching Roman ruins and writing essays on classical civilization. As consul general in Algiers to 1765, the ever-querulous Bruce succeeded primarily in alienating both the local rulers and his British associates. However, he acquired a knowledge of Arabic, skill as a horseman, and experience in Oriental society. In 1765 he made two journeys among the Berber peoples of the interior and then traveled through North Africa, the Aegean, and the Levant.

From 1768 to 1772 Bruce was engaged in the adventures on which his fame depends. Traveling first up the Nile in 1769 and then along the Red Sea, he finally reached Massawa, the main port of what became the Eritrean province of Ethiopia. He spent the major portion of his Ethiopian period in and around Gondar, the imperial capital. This epoch coincided with political upheavals in the empire and the rise of provincial warlords, the chronicle of which is narrated at some length in Bruce's five-volume *Travels to Discover the Source of the Nile* (1790). He also discussed Ethiopia's history, monuments, art, geography, and natural history.

Bruce gathered detailed and still significant orally derived accounts of the Ethiopian past and made observations on the state of the nation in the late 18th century. During the course of his stay in Ethiopia he also observed the flow of the Blue Nile from its source in Lake Tana. On his way home in 1772 he spent some months in the Funj kingdom of Sennar (now the Sudan), for which his published writings again constitute a valuable record.

Bruce returned to Britain in 1774 and was elected a fellow of the Royal Society. His arrogance and temperament made him difficult to bear and his tales hard to credit. He retired to Kinnaird, in 1776 married Mary Dundas, who died in 1785, and only then began to write the account of his Ethiopian saga. Bruce was working on second edition when, on April 27, 1794, he fell down a flight of steps and died without regaining consciousness.

Further Reading

The most substantial account of Bruce and his work is still the second edition of the original *Travels to Discover the Source of the Nile,* which was prepared and supplemented by Alexander Murray (8 vols., 1805); an abridged version, edited by Charles F. Beckingham (1964), contains an excellent introduction. The only modern, though racy, biography of Bruce is James Macarthur Reid, *Traveller Extraordinary: The Life of James Bruce of Kinnaird* (1968). □

Joseph Anton Bruckner

The Austrian composer Joseph Anton Bruckner (1824-1896) is best known for his nine monumental symphonies and his religious compositions.

Anton Bruckner was born on Sept. 4, 1824, at Ansfelden in Upper Austria. He was the first of 11 children of the village schoolmaster. At an early age Anton had his first music lessons from his father and began to help him with his teaching duties. When he was 11, he began to study with his cousin, and his earliest compositions date from this time. Two years later, at the death of his father, Anton was transferred to the monastery of St. Florian, where he remained as a chorister until 1840. St. Florian was always to be a spiritual refuge for him; at his own request, he was buried under the great organ there.

After preparatory courses at Linz, Bruckner was certified as an assistant teacher for elementary schools. He taught in a small village near Steyr, where he continued his organ studies. In 1845 he became a teacher and assistant organist at St. Florian and was finally appointed first organist in 1855. During the years at St. Florian, Bruckner composed many liturgical works. Typical of the larger-scale compositions are the *Requiem* (1849) and the *Missa solemnis* (1854), both first performed at St. Florian.

In 1856 Bruckner became principal organist at Linz Cathedral. He studied with the Viennese theorist and organist Simon Sechter, traveling to Vienna every year for 6 weeks of concentrated study. During his 5 years of strict contrapuntal studies, he did not compose. Bruckner completed his course with Sechter in 1861 and began to study orchestration and form with the conductor Otto Kitzler. Through him, Bruckner came to know Wagner's music. Stimulated by this new experience, he began to write instrumental works: an overture, two unnumbered symphonies, and a string quartet.

Bruckner's first mature work was the Mass in D Minor (1864); it was followed by the Mass in E Minor and the First Symphony (1866). Partly because of overwork, the composer suffered a severe nervous breakdown in 1867. A sojourn at Bad Kreuzen brought him relief, and grateful for his recovery, he began his third, and last, great Mass, in F Minor, which he completed the following year.

Bruckner became professor of thorough bass, counterpoint, and organ at the Vienna Conservatory in 1868, a position he retained till 1891. He held other important posts in Vienna: organist of the Imperial Court Chapel (1868-1892) and lecturer in harmony and counterpoint at the University of Vienna (1875-1894). He also found time to write his huge symphonies, which are pervaded by a deep religious feeling. At first, they were not successful. His partisanship of Wagner brought him the enmity of Eduard Hanslick and other influential critics in Vienna, who preferred the music of Brahms. However, Bruckner's work gradually won recognition, especially outside Austria.

Bruckner's last eight symphonies were composed in Vienna beginning in 1871. He frequently revised his work; for example, there are three versions of the Second, Third, and Eighth Symphonies and four of the Fourth (*Romantic*) Symphony. Since other revisions were also made, with or without his authorization, by his disciples, it has been extremely hard to establish the accurate text of his symphonies. The International Bruckner Society has published critical editions.

Bruckner's health failed during his last years. In 1895 the emperor Franz Josef offered him free quarters in the Belvedere Palace. There, after a morning spent working on the Ninth Symphony (the finale is incomplete), Bruckner died on Oct. 11, 1896.

Further Reading

Two enthusiastic and sentimental biographies of Bruckner are Gabriel Engel, *The Life of Anton Bruckner* (1931), and Werner Wolff, *Anton Bruckner: Rustic Genius* (1942). Hans F. Redlich, *Bruckner and Mahler* (1955), is a well-balanced presentation of the two composers. Erwin Doernberg, *The Life and Symphonies of Anton Bruckner* (1960), is more opinionated. Robert Simpson, *The Essence of Bruckner* (1968), gives impressionistic analyses of the nine symphonies. Dika Newlin, *Bruckner, Mahler, Schoenberg* (1947), presents Bruckner in his cultural environment and includes analyses of his major works. □

Pieter Bruegel the Elder

Pieter Bruegel the Elder (c. 1525-1569) was a Netherlandish painter and designer for engravings. His works provide a profound and elemental insight into man and his relationship to the world of nature.

Pieter Bruegel lived at a time when northern art was strongly influenced by Italian mannerism, but despite the requisite journey to Italy for purposes of study, he was astonishingly independent of the dominant artistic interests of his day. Instead, he deliberately revived the late Gothic style of Hieronymus Bosch as the point of departure for his own highly complex and original art.

Our major source of information concerning Bruegel is the Dutch biographer Karel van Mander, who wrote in 1604. This near-contemporary of the painter claims that Bruegel was born in a town of the same name near Breda on the modern Dutch-Belgian border. Most recent authorities, however, follow the Italian writer Guicciardini in designating the painter's birthplace as Breda itself.

From the fact that Bruegel entered the Antwerp painters' guild in 1551, we may infer that he was born between 1525 and 1530. His master, according to Van Mander, was the Antwerp painter Pieter Coecke van Aelst, whose daughter Bruegel married in 1563. Between 1552 and 1553 Bruegel went to Italy, probably by way of France. He visited Rome, where he met the miniaturist Giulio Clovio, whose will of 1578 lists three paintings by Bruegel. These works, which apparently were landscapes, have not survived.

About 1555 Bruegel returned to Antwerp by way of the Alps, which resulted in a number of exquisite drawings of mountain landscapes. These sketches, which form the basis for many of his later paintings, are not records of actual places but "composites" made in order to investigate the organic life of forms in nature.

Early Antwerp Style

In 1556 Bruegel entered the house of the Antwerp publisher Hieronymus Cock as a designer for engravings. His pen drawing of that year entitled *Big Fish Eat Little Fish* was published in 1557 as an engraving by Cock, who substituted Bosch's name for Bruegel's in order to exploit the fashion for Bosch's works then current at Antwerp. The series *Seven Deadly Sins,* engraved in 1558, however, carries the artist's own signature, a sign of Bruegel's increasing importance. In these works Bruegel, unlike any of his Antwerp contemporaries, achieved a truly creative synthesis of Bosch's demonic symbolism with his own personal vision of human folly and depravity. Despite efforts to dismiss these engravings as "fascinating drolleries," there is evidence to suggest that Bruegel was attempting to substitute a new and more relevant eschatology for Bosch's traditional view of the Christian cosmos.

In Bruegel's earliest signed and dated painting, the *Combat of Carnival and Lent* (1559), the influence of Bosch is still strongly felt. The high-horizoned landscape, the decorative surface patterning, and many of the iconographic details derive from the earlier Dutch master. There is, however, a new sensitivity to color, particularly in the use of bright, primary hues, and a rhythmic organization of forms that is uniquely Bruegel's. This painting, the *Netherlandish Proverbs* (1559), and the highly involved *Children's Games* (1560) form the body of the early "encyclopedic" works which, despite their superficial gaiety, have been shown to be allegories of a foolish and sinful world.

Also related in conception to the encyclopedic paintings are Bruegel's two most phantasmagoric works: the *Dulle Griet* and the *Triumph of Death* (both probably executed in 1562). The *Dulle Griet* is still related to Bosch stylistically, but unlike the works of that painter it is not intended so much as a moral sermon against the depravity of the world as a recognition of the existence of evil in it. This capacity to see evil as inseparable from the human condition carries over into the *Triumph of Death,* which has also been interpreted as a reference to the outbreak at that time of religious persecutions in the Netherlands.

The last of Bruegel's great "figurative anthologies" is the *Tower of Babel* (1563). Intended to symbolize the futility of human ambition and perhaps more specifically to criticize the spirit of commercialism then reigning in Antwerp, the panel also contains a new panoramic vista of a vast world. Only distantly related to Bosch's cosmic landscapes, this new world view was to inform most of the artist's subsequent works.

Mature Style

Whatever his reasons for leaving Antwerp, Bruegel took up residence in Brussels in 1563, where he was to remain until his death in 1569. His reputation as one of the greatest of all Netherlandish painters is mainly founded upon the works of this brief but highly productive period.

The *Road to Calvary* (1564) inaugurates this phase, in which man is increasingly subordinated to the rhythms and patterns of nature. A lower horizon and a new feeling for atmospheric perspective are important stylistic features of this panel, which is one of the few surviving religious works in Bruegel's oeuvre.

In 1565 Bruegel was commissioned to execute a series of pictures of the months for Niclaes Jonghelinck of Antwerp. Based upon the medieval idea of the labors of the seasons as seen, for example, in cathedral sculpture or the illuminations of late Gothic books of hours, Bruegel's series represents a magnificient culmination of this tradition. Of the original group, five paintings have survived. De Tolnay (1935) has very plausibly suggested that each panel portrayed the activities of 2 months, so that only the painting for April and May is lost.

In these beautifully conceived and executed panels Bruegel has achieved a moment of resolution of the previously existing duality between man and nature. The central theme of the cycle is that man, if he follows the order of nature, can avoid the folly for which he is otherwise destined. The role of mankind is portrayed by peasants—anonymous symbols of humanity—who live and work close to the soil in a state of beneficent unity with nature.

The months of December and January are represented by the *Hunters in the Snow.* A work of great compositional unity, it demonstrates that the activities of men, in order to be good, must conform to the seasonal patterns of nature.

The *Dark Day* and the *Hay Harvest* depict the labors of February-March and June-July respectively. In both panels broad panoramic landscapes dominate visually as well as in terms of content the affairs of men, which once again accord with the will of nature.

The months of August and September are portrayed by the golden-hued *Wheat Harvest,* one of the most lyrical panels in the series. Here Bruegel achieves a greater degree of spatial and figural integration than in the previous paintings, as well as heightened atmospheric effects.

The most brilliant panel in the series is the *Return of the Herd,* which represents October and November. A magnificent composition, organized along a sequence of intersecting diagonal movements, this painting evokes with unparalleled actuality the scope and grandeur of the natural world.

Through the striking beauty and originality of these seasonal pictures Bruegel enunciated a new coherency in man's relationship to the natural scheme. Casting off the established order and hierarchy of the medieval and Renaissance cosmologies, he substituted a view of a dynamically evolving world that is fundamentally modern in its conception.

Van Mander thought Bruegel's *Massacre of the Innocents* (ca. 1566) was a criticism of the mounting atrocities of the Spanish Inquisition in the Netherlands. In view of the artist's deliberate use of the setting of a contemporary Flemish village to stage the events, this view has gained acceptance from most recent authorities. Similar in conception, though differing in spirit, is the *Numbering at Bethlehem* (1566). In this instance, however, Bruegel contemporizes the religious events in order to investigate the varieties of rural life in a winter setting. Here again the religious theme is at best a pretext for Bruegel's basically secular art.

Late Style

The *Peasant Dance* (ca. 1566-1567) represents a new and important direction that Bruegel was to develop in the last years of his career. In this work the painter changed to a "large-figure" style in which highly animated peasants are organized to convey the rhythms and patterns of the dance. Also, by reducing forms to their elemental essences Bruegel achieved a clarity of design and coloration that has seldom been rivaled in Western painting.

At about the same time Bruegel completed one of his most famous and beloved works, the *Peasant Wedding Feast.* Conceived in a spirit of sympathy and affection for country folk, this panel reveals the artist's delightfully droll sense of humor as well as his genius in making universal even the most trivial events.

One of Bruegel's most bizarre works is the *Land of Cockaigne* (1567). The composition is made up principally of three recumbent figures—a knight, a peasant, and a burgher—whose forms radiate outward from the center of the picture and are intended to produce a sensation of nausea and dislocation in the spectator. In this connection, it has also been observed that the sophisticated device of tilting the ground plane and all the other elements of the design is one aspect of mannerist influence on Bruegel's art.

The *Parable of the Blind* illustrates the verse from Matthew (14:14): "If the blind lead the blind, both shall fall into the ditch." In this great work the descending diagonal formed by the figures of the blind men is enlivened and activated by the use of color, strong hues for the foreground and cooler tones toward the rear. Another development of this period is a heightened sense of atmosphere, the landscape being one of the most vaporous in Bruegel's oeuvre.

This highly sensitive landscape style carries over into what is probably the painter's last work, the *Magpie on the Gallows,* a panel which, according to Van Mander, Bruegel willed to his wife. The seeming accord between the peasant and his natural environment, one of the main tenets of Bruegel's art, is oddly vitiated by the presence of a gallows at the center of the composition. Brooding over a group of dancing peasants, it forms a striking contrast to the beauties of the setting and serves as a grim reminder of the basic human condition. Whatever interpretation is placed on this panel, Bruegel's painting summarizes all that had gone before and stands at the threshold of the modern era. In its timeless validity, Bruegel's art finds no rival before Rembrandt.

The master may have represented himself in a drawing (ca. 1567) entitled *The Artist and the Connoisseur,* which portrays two half-length figures: a cynical and embittered painter at work and an oafish, uncritical onlooker. The former, probably a self-portrait, makes no effort to disguise his contempt for the latter, whose conspicuous moneybag reveals his philistine nature.

Bruegel's Influence

Bruegel's legacy was most directly transmitted through his two painter sons: Pieter the Younger (1564-1638) and Jan (1568-1625). Well into the 17th century, however, almost all Flemish painters, including Peter Paul Rubens, were indebted to Bruegel's vision of the landscape.

Further Reading

The most authoritative book in English on Bruegel is Fritz Grossmann, *Bruegel: The Paintings* (1955). It contains an exhaustive account of the artist's life and works as well as a thoughtful interpretation of the meaning of the paintings. A brilliant, though controversial, essay on Bruegel's art and its relation to the thought of the period is in Charles de Tolnay, *The Drawings of Pieter Bruegel, the Elder, with a Critical Catalogue* (1935; trans. 1952). For information on the engraved works see H. Arthur Klein, ed., *Graphic Works of Pieter Bruegel the Elder* (1963). Useful general surveys are Robert L. Delevoy, *Bruegel: Historical and Critical Study* (1954; trans. 1959), and the excellent essay in Charles D. Cuttler, *Northern Painting: From Pucelle to Bruegel* (1968). □

Étienne Brûlé

Étienne Brûlé (ca. 1592-1633) was a French explorer in North America. He was the first European to voyage through the Great Lakes and the Susquehanna Valley.

Etienne Brûlé was born reputedly at Champigny-sur-Marne. When, in 1608, Samuel de Champlain went to the New World and founded a trading post at Quebec, Brûlé was probably a member of that expedition. In 1610 Brûlé voyaged west with a band of Algonquians to learn their language, a vital necessity in the fur trade. Where Brûlé traveled is not known, but when he returned to Quebec the following year, Champlain was well pleased with Brûlé's knowledge of the Indian country and the Algonquin language. Shortly afterward Brûlé returned to the west; and when Champlain, in 1615, assisted the Hurons in a campaign against the Onondagas near presentday Syracuse, N.Y., Brûlé volunteered to accompany a Huron delegation across the enemy's country to enlist the aid of the Susquehannas. The reinforcements the delegation brought arrived too late, for Champlain and the Hurons had been defeated and forced to retreat.

Brûlé spent the following year or more with the Susquehanna tribe and apparently traveled down the river bearing their name to Chesapeake Bay, the first European to traverse that part of present-day Pennsylvania. According to the account of his journey that Brûlé later gave Champlain, on the way back he was captured by the Senecas, tortured, and subsequently released and sent to Quebec to assist in concluding a peace treaty and establishing trade relations between the Iroquois and the French. In 1621 or 1622 Brûlé returned to the west and appears to have voyaged to Lake Superior. There is some evidence to indicate that he went as far as the site of present-day Duluth.

By this time Brûlé appears to have been more attuned to the permissive Indian way of life than to that of the more puritanical French. The missionaries complained that he was leading a scandalous life and making their efforts to impose Christian morals and religious beliefs on the Native Americans more difficult. In 1629 Brûlé threw in his lot with the English trader Sir David Kirke, who forced Champlain to surrender Quebec. In 1632 Canada was returned to France, but Brûlé was not brought to account. He had returned to the west, where in 1633 he was killed by the Hurons under obscure circumstances.

Brûlé left no record of his travels, and his activities can be gleaned only from passing references in the accounts of others. He spent most of his active life with Native Americans and was assimilated by them. According to the account of the missionary Gabriel Sagard, Brûlé was eaten by his Huron murderers; if indeed this is true, then no one could have been more completely assimilated than he was.

Further Reading

The most reliable account of Brûlé is Consul Willshire Butterfield, *History of Brûlé's Discoveries and Explorations, 1610-1626* (1898). J. H. Cranston, *Étienne Brûlé Immortal Scoundrel* (1949), is romanticized. Brûlé figures in John Bartlet Brebner, *The Explorers of North America, 1492-1806* (1933), and in Morris Bishop, *Champlain: The Life of Fortitude* (1948).

Additional Sources

Burbey, Louis H., *Michigan's pioneer of pioneers: the dramatic, tragic destiny of Étienne Brûlé,* Royal Oak, Mich.: L.H. Burbey, 1987. □

Gro Harlem Brundtland

Norwegian political leader Gro Harlem Brundtland (born 1939) was the first Scandinavian woman to serve as a prime minister (1981; 1986-1989; 1990-1997). Brundtland also paved the way for women in the United Nations when she was asked by UN Secretary General Javier Perez de Cuellar to establish and chair the World Commission for Environment and Development in 1983.

Norwegian prime minister Gro Harlem Brundtland, born in Oslo in 1939, was both the first woman and the youngest person ever to hold Norway's highest ranking political office. Her father, Gudmund Harlem, Norway's Minister of Social Affairs (1955-61) and Minister of Defense (1961-63, 63-65) was a strong influence on her early political development and as a young adult Brundtland was actively involved in the Labour party's student movement.

Brundtland earned her medical degree from the University of Oslo in 1963 and earned a Master of Public Health degree from Harvard University in 1965. Returning to Norway after graduation, she first served as a medical officer at the Norwegian Directorate of Health (1966-68) and then became assistant medical director to Oslo's Board of Health (1968-74).

In 1974, Brundtland was "discovered" by Prime Minister Trygve Brattelishe and appointed Minister of the Environment, a position she held until her resignation in 1979. She served as deputy leader of Labour's parliamentary group from 1975-81 and was elected to the Storting (Norway's Parliament) for the city of Oslo in 1977. While in the Storting, Bruntland headed two important standing committees, finance and foreign affairs. (She was leader of the Committee on Foreign and Constitutional Affairs for the years 1980-81, 1981-86, and 1989-90.)

In February of 1981 the acting Labour prime minister retired. Urged on by Labour party members, Bruntland claimed the prime minister's seat. Two months later she also took control of the party chairmanship. However, Brundtland's first term as prime minister was short-lived.

The Labour party lost the October 1981 elections to a Conservative coalition which named Kåre Willoch to the post of prime minister.

In May 1986, Brundtland was reelected as Labour party prime minister. This time she remained in office until 1989 when the Conservative party again defeated the Labour government.

With the collapse of the Conservative party's administration in 1990, Brundtland became prime minister for the third time. This time she was forced to build a coalition with minor parties to hold a majority in the 165-seat National Assembly. Bruntland's fourth term as Norway's prime minister, begun in 1993, drew to a close in October, 1996, when she submitted her resignation. She stepped down from office on 25 October 1997.

As a leader of the Norwegian Labour Party, Brundtland became the single most influential politician in Norway during the 1980s and early 1990s. Her extraordinary career can be explained in terms of both her own political and personal beliefs as well as the political times in which she lived. In contrast to the typical working-class style of the Labour movement, Brundtland was a young, professional, female candidate. She was the most likely candidate at a time when the Labour party felt an urgent need to modernize its image.

Bruntland's sound analytical skills, good humor, and charm earned her a reputation as someone able to deal with difficult conflicts. Brundtland would thoroughly study the background of all contenders, as well as their positions on an issue. She would carefully avoid any commitment on an issue until the conflicting sides reached a joint resolution. As a final step, she would quickly implement any resolutions reached by the opposing sides.

Brundtland's approach to conflict resolution was a major factor in resolution of the "Rocket Crisis," the debate led by the European Socialist party following the North Atlantic Treaty Organization's decision on missile deployment in Europe (1981). She also played an instrumental role in resolving the devastating disagreement among Norwegian Socialists on the European Community question. Both issues threatened to split the Labour party and would almost certainly have done so without "the Gro grip," the nickname given to describe Bruntland's approach to conflict resolution.

In 1983, United Nations Secretary General Javier Perez de Cuellar asked Bruntland to establish and chair the World Commission on Environment and Development. Bruntland approached the task of hammering out compromises on international environmental issues in the same way she handled other conflicts. The Commission's 1987 report, *Our Common Future,* identified the future of global ecology as sustainable growth through environment protection *and* economic growth.

By 1990, Bruntland was well-known internationally because of her participation in the Independent Commission on Disarmament and Security (the Palme Commission), her vice-presidency of Socialist International, and her role in the first UN Conference on Environment and Development held in Rio de Janeiro (1992). Bruntland, often referred to in media releases as "mother earth," wrote several articles on political, environmental, and developmental issues.

Brundtland has received several international awards, including the Third World Prize (1988), the Indira Gandhi Prize (1988), the Onassis Foundation's Delphi Prize (1992), and the Charlemagne Prize (1994). She is married to Arne Olav Brundtland, a research director at the Oslo Institute of Foreign Studies, and has four children.

Further Reading

For additional information on Brundtland see *Ms.* (January 1988) and *Time* (September 23, 1989). Also see the World Commission on Ecology and Development report *Our Common Future,* Oxford University Press (1987). For a general background survey of Scandinavian politics, strategies, and social developments see *Daedalus* (Summer 1988). □

Isambard Kingdom Brunel

Isambard Kingdom Brunel (1806-1859) was a leading English civil engineer in the railway age with an original and unprejudiced approach to problems in railway and marine engineering.

Isambard Kingdom Brunel was born on April 9, 1806, near Portsmouth, the only son of Marc Isambard Brunel, known for his machine for making ships' blocks and as the engineer of the Thames Tunnel. After attending the Collège Henri Quatre in Paris, Brunel served a short apprenticeship under the Paris instrument maker Louis Breguet. Brunel returned to London in 1822 and entered his father's office in 1823, where he received practical training by assisting with the Thames Tunnel until 1828.

Brunel's first important commission was the 630-foot-span Clifton suspension bridge near Bristol (1831). Unfinished in his lifetime, it was completed in 1864 as his memorial. He also built the Hungerford (London) suspension bridge (1841-1845); its wrought-iron chains were used to complete the bridge at Clifton.

Railway Engineer

In 1833 Brunel was appointed engineer for the Great Western Railway and began surveys for a line between Bristol and London. Construction of the line (1835-1841) included the famous flat-arch bridge over the Thames at Maidenhead and the 3,200-yard Box Tunnel outside Bath (through which the sun is said to shine on Brunel's birthday). With the aim of smooth, high-speed running and locomotive-fuel economy for the line, he introduced the 7-foot gage, which, while technically sound, was commercial folly. However, it was not entirely superseded by the British standard 4-foot 8 1/2-inch gage until 1892. He also designed railroad terminals and a series of bridges, culminating in the Royal Albert Bridge near Plymouth (1853-1859),

which combines a tubular arch with suspension chains in the two main spans.

Designer of Steamships

In 1835 Brunel suggested, half in jest, a transatlantic steamship service. The idea found support, and the outcome was the *Great Western,* a timber-built paddle steamer of 2,300 tons' displacement. In April 1838 it steamed from Bristol to New York in 15 days and then maintained a regular service. His *Great Britain* (1839-1845) was a 3,600-ton iron-hulled, screw-driven steamship. Brunel's last great ship was the *Great Eastern* (1854-1859), for which he was the sole architect. Displacing 32,000 tons, the largest ship afloat, it was intended to make the round trip to Australia without recoaling. The *Great Eastern* had a double hull, and with engines to drive both paddles and screw, it had outstanding maneuverability. That its cost was excessive, its completion delayed, and the launch difficult was largely due to the machinations of the building contractor. Brunel never saw the trials, for he suffered a stroke and died on Sept. 15, 1859, in London. A liability to its owners, the ship showed twice the calculated fuel consumption. The *Great Eastern* was sold and eventually used to lay the first Atlantic telegraph cable (1865-1866).

Further Reading

Of three worthwhile biographical studies, the latest, L. T. C. Rolt, *Isambard Kingdom Brunel: A Biography* (1959), is the most carefully written. The others are by Brunel's son, Isambard Brunel, *The Life of Isambard Kingdom Brunel: Civil Engineer* (1870), and by his granddaughter, Celia Brunel Noble, *The Brunels, Father and Son* (1938). An account of the building of the *Great Eastern* is James Dugan, *The Great Iron Ship* (1954).

Additional Sources

Pudney, John, *Brunel and his world,* London, Thames and Hudson 1974.

Jenkins, David, *Isambard Kingdom Brunel, engineer extraordinary,* Hove: Priory Press, 1977.

Vaughan, Adrian, *Isambard Kingdom Brunel, engineering knight-errant,* London: J. Murray, 1993.

The Works of Isambard Kingdom Brunel: an engineering appreciation, Cambridge Eng.; New York: Cambridge University Press, 1980, 1976. □

Filippo Brunelleschi

Filippo Brunelleschi (1377-1446) was an Italian architect, goldsmith, and sculptor. The first Renaissance architect, he also formulated the principles of linear perspective which governed pictorial depiction of space until the late 19th century.

In Florence during the second and third decades of the 15th century, the visual arts were transformed into the Renaissance style. The concept of the Renaissance, whose aim was the re-creation of ancient classical culture, occasioned in painting and sculpture a revival of naturalism based primarily on antique statuary and in architecture a revival of classical forms and ornament. All the arts revealed an increased concern for the delineation and unification of space, which the development of linear perspective satisfied. Three Florentine artists—the architect Filippo Brunelleschi the sculptor Donatello, and the painter Masaccio—were the leaders in this new movement and soon made Florence the artistic capital of Europe.

Brunelleschi was born in Florence, the son of an eminent notary. Filippo entered the silk guild as a goldsmith in 1398. The following year he was employed by a goldsmith in Pistoia, where he made several silver figures for the altar of St. James in the Cathedral. Brunelleschi entered the competition of 1401 for a new set of portals for the Baptistery in Florence; his trial piece, the *Sacrifice of Isaac,* compared very favorably with that of Lorenzo Ghiberti, who was awarded the commission. Brunelleschi's relief is derived stylistically from the work of his predecessor Andrea Pisano, but it already reveals an interest in classical antiquity, as the servant in the relief was inspired by the Hellenistic statue *Spinario* , or "thorn-puller." In 1404 Brunelleschi was admitted as master to the goldsmiths' guild in Florence, and later that year he was consulted regarding a buttress of the Cathedral.

Method of Constructing Linear Perspective

During the next decade the details of Brunelleschi's life are very vague. He undoubtedly made several trips to Rome to survey its ancient monuments. A wooden crucifix in S. Maria Novella, Florence, perhaps from this period, is sometimes attributed to him. In 1415 he repaired the Ponte a Mare in Pisa, and 2 years later he and other masters presented opinions on the design and construction of the great dome projected for the Gothic Cathedral of Florence. It was perhaps at this time that Brunelleschi devised the method of constructing linear perspective, which he illustrated in two perspective panels (now lost): one depicted the Florentine Baptistery as viewed from the Cathedral portal, and the other illustrated the Palazzo Vecchio.

Early Architecture

Beginning in 1418 Brunelleschi concentrated on architecture. In two small domed chapels in S. Jacopo Soprarno and S. Felicità (now destroyed or altered), Florence, he experimented with domical construction. That same year he began the church of S. Lorenzo (1418-ca. 1470), commencing with the Old Sacristy (1418-1428), a cubical chapel with an umbrella dome. The church is a Latin-cross basilica with three arcaded aisles, side chapels, and a dome over the crossing. All the ornamentation is classical, with Corinthian columns, pilasters, and classical moldings of a soft blue-gray stone (*pietra serena*) against light stucco walls. The loggia of the Ospedale degli Innocenti (designed 1419, constructed 1421-1451), Florence, usually considered the first Renaissance building, is a graceful arcade with Composite columns and windows with triangular pediments regularly spaced above each of the arches. It may have been at this time that Brunelleschi worked on the Palazzo di Parte Guelfa, Florence; he designed giant pilasters at each end of the exterior (altered in completion).

In 1420 Brunelleschi began to erect the great dome of the Florentine Cathedral in collaboration with Ghiberti, who eventually withdrew from the project. The dome has a skeleton of eight large stone ribs closed by two shells, of which the lower portions are of stone and the upper parts of brick laid in a herringbone design probably derived from ancient Roman construction. In its rib construction and pointed arch form, the dome still belongs within the Gothic tradition. With the closing of the oculus in 1436, Brunelleschi designed the lantern (completed in 1467). Meanwhile he was consulted on projects elsewhere; he was in Pisa during 1426 to work on the Citadel and in Volterra in 1427 to advise on the dome of the Baptistery.

The Pazzi Chapel (1429-1467), in the medieval cloister of Santa Croce, Florence, has a charming porch with six Corinthian columns supporting an entablature broken in the center by a semicircular arch, reflecting the dome behind it. The upper part of the facade is incomplete. The interior is rectangular with a large umbrella dome at the center covered by a conical roof with a lantern. As in all his architecture, Brunelleschi used the darker *pietra serena* for the classical details. The glazed terra-cotta reliefs of the four Evangelists in the pendentives of the dome were designed by Brunelleschi; the remaining decoration was by Luca della Robbia. In 1432 Brunelleschi went to Mantua and Ferrara on unknown commissions, and in 1433 he was again in Rome to study the antiquities.

Later Architecture

During the Renaissance the ideal church plan was centralized as a circle or Greek cross with four equal arms. On his return to Florence in 1434 Brunelleschi began a central-plan church, S. Maria degli Angeli, which was never completed. It would have been the first central plan of the Renaissance. Octagonal on the interior with eight chapels, it was 16-sided on the exterior; a domical vault was probably intended to cover the center. In 1435 Brunelleschi was again in Pisa working on the bastion of the Porta al Parlascio.

In 1436 Brunelleschi designed another basilican church in Florence, Santo Spirito (constructed 1444-1482), which shows a much greater concern for a unified composition than S. Lorenzo does. The arcaded side aisles are continued around the transept arms and choir and were intended to go across the interior of the facade (never executed), which gives a very unified and centralized impression around the crossing dome. The shallow chapels are curvilinear in plan and were to be so expressed on the exterior, but after Brunelleschi's death a straight external wall masked the chapels. The interior is carefully organized in simple proportional relationships which result in a very harmonious space that is the ideal of Renaissance architecture. In 1440 Brunelleschi returned to Pisa for further work on the Citadel. On April 15, 1446, he died at Florence and received the unusual honor of being buried in the Cathedral.

Style and Influence

Brunelleschi was particularly adept in solving engineering problems, as the construction of the Cathedral dome reveals. His architectural style is of a very refined classicism and was inspired as much by the Tuscan Romanesque or proto-Renaissance style of the 12th century as by ancient Roman architecture. He used the Corinthian order, the most decorative of the classical orders, almost exclusively, and he made sure that all the decorative elements of his architecture were cut in a very crisp style.

Because of Brunelleschi's innovation of linear perspective and his adaptation of the classical style to architecture, he is one of the major figures of the early Renaissance period. His architecture remained influential in Florence through the 16th century.

Further Reading

The only monograph on Brunelleschi in English is Leader Scott, *Filippo di Ser Brunellesco* (1901); although out of date, it is still informative. More recent scholarly studies are in Italian: Piero Sanpaolesi, *Brunelleschi* (1962), and Eugenio Luporini, *Brunelleschi* (1964). Antonio Manetti's 15th-century biography of Brunelleschi was published in English, with an introduction by Howard Saalman, *The Life of Brunelleschi* (1969). See also Frank D. Prager and Gustina Scaglia, *Brunelleschi: Studies of His Technology and Inventions* (1970). General works which include references to Brunelleschi are Wallace K. Ferguson, *The Renaissance in Historical Thought: Five Centuries of Interpretation* (1948); Rudolf Wittkower, *Architectural Principles in the Age of Humanism* (1949; 3d rev. ed.

1962); and Peter Murray, *The Architecture of the Italian Renaissance* (1963).

Additional Sources

Battisti, Eugenio, *Filippo Brunelleschi: the complete works,* New York: Rizzoli, 1981.

Brunelleschi, Filippo, *Brunelleschi: the complete works,* London: Thames and Hudson, 1981. □

Jerome Seymour Bruner

An American psychologist, Jerome Seymour Bruner (born 1915) made outstanding contributions to the study of perception, cognition, and education. He taught in universities in both the United States and England and was the author of many articles and books in the field of psychology and education.

Jerome Seymour Bruner was born on October 1, 1915, to Polish immigrant parents, Herman and Rose (Gluckmann) Bruner. He was born blind and did not achieve sight until after two cataract operations while he was still an infant. He attended public schools, graduating from high school in 1933, and entered Duke University where he majored in psychology, earning the AB degree in 1937. Bruner then pursued graduate study at Harvard University, receiving the MA in 1939 and the Ph.D. in 1941. During World War II, he served under General Eisenhower in the Psychological Warfare Division of Supreme Headquarters Allied Expeditionary Force Europe. After the war he joined the faculty at Harvard University in 1945.

When Bruner entered the field of psychology, it was roughly divided between the study of perception and the analysis of learning. The first was mentalistic and subjective, while the second was behavioristic and objective. At Harvard the psychology department was dominated by behaviorists who followed a research program called psychophysics, the view that psychology is the study of the senses and how they react to the world of physical energies or stimuli. Bruner revolted against behaviorism and psychophysics and, together with Leo Postman, set out on a series of experiments that would result in the "New Look," a new theory of perception. The New Look held that perception is not something that occurs immediately, as had been assumed in older theories. Rather, perception is a form of information processing that involves interpretation and selection. It was a view that psychology must concern itself with how people view and interpret the world, as well as how they respond to stimuli.

Bruner's interest moved from perception to cognition— how people think. This new direction was stimulated by Bruner's discussions in the early 1950s with Robert Oppenheimer, the nuclear physicist, around whether the idea in the scientist's mind determined the natural phenomenon being observed. A major publication to come out of this period was *A Study of Thinking* (1956), written with Jacqueline Goodnow and George Austin. It explored how people think about and group things into classes and categories. Bruner found that the choice to group things almost invariably involves notions of procedures and criteria for grouping. It may also involve focusing on a single indicator as a "home base" and grouping things according to the presence of that indicator. Furthermore, people will group things according to their own attention and memory capacity; they will choose positive over negative information; and they will seek repeated confirmation of hypotheses when it is often not needed. *A Study of Thinking* has been called one of the initiators of the cognitive sciences.

Center for Cognitive Studies

Soon Bruner began collaborating with George Miller on how people develop conceptual models and how they code information about those models. In 1960 the two opened the Center for Cognitive Studies at Harvard. Both shared a conviction that psychology should be concerned with the cognitive processes—the distinct human forms of gaining, storing, and working over knowledge. Bruner was drawn toward new developments in philosophy and anthropology: linguistic philosophy for insight into human language capacities and how thoughts are organized into logical syntax and cultural anthropology for insight into how thinking is culturally conditioned. To the center came some of the leading figures in psychology, philosophy, anthropology, and related disciplines who made contributions to the study of cognitive processes. In retrospect, Bruner said of those years that what he and his colleagues most sought was to show "a higher order principle" that human thought included language capacities and cultural conditions and not only a mere response to a stimulus.

In spite of his many contributions to academic psychology, Bruner is perhaps best known for his work in education, most of which he undertook during his years with the Center for Cognitive Studies. He held the position that the human species had taken charge of its own evolution by technologically shaping the environment. The passing on of this technology and cultural heritage involved the very survival of the species. Hence, education was of supreme importance. As Bruner admitted, he was not fully appreciative of this importance until he was drawn into the educational debate gripping the United States following the launching of Sputnik, the first satellite, in 1957 by the former Soviet Union.

In 1959 Bruner was asked to head a National Academy of Sciences curriculum reform group that met at Woods Hole on Cape Cod. Some 34 prominent scientists, scholars, and educators met to hammer out the outlines of a new science curriculum for America's schools. Although numerous work area reports were issued, to Bruner fell the task of writing a chairman's report. The end result was *The Process of Education,* which became an immediate best-seller and was eventually translated into 19 languages. Bruner centered on three major considerations: a concept of mind as method applied to tasks—e.g., one does not think *about* physics, one thinks physics, the influence of Jean Piaget, particularly that the child's understanding of any idea will be contingent upon the level of intellectual operations he has achieved, and the notion of the structure of knowledge—the important thing to learn is how an idea or discipline is put together. Perhaps the element that is most remembered is Bruner's statement that "any subject can be taught effectively in some intellectually honest form to any child at any stage of development."

A Controversial Curriculum

Bruner's educational work led to an appointment on the Education Panel of the President's Science Advisory Committee. He also worked on a new social studies curriculum for Educational Services, Incorporated. Called "Man: A Course of Study," the controversial, federally funded project drew the ire of various conservative and rightwing pressure groups because it did not push values and traditions they felt were important. The controversy led some school districts to drop the program, and federal funds were withdrawn from any additional development. The program was continued in some American school districts, and it was also adopted by many schools in Britain and Australia.

In 1972 the Center for Cognitive Studies was closed, and Bruner moved to England upon being appointed Watts Professor of Psychology and Fellow of Wolfson College at Oxford University. His research now came to focus on cognitive development in early infancy. In 1980 he returned to the United States and for a short time served again at Harvard until, in 1981, he was appointed to the position of the George Herbert Mead professorship at the New School for Social Research in New York and director of the New York Institute for the Humanities.

Bruner never tried, in his own words, to construct "a 'grand' or overarching system of thought." His main interest was on "psychology of the mind," particularly perception and cognition, as well as education, during a long and productive career.

Later Works and Publications

Bruner published a series of lectures in 1990, *Acts of Meaning,* wherein he refutes the "digital processing" approach to studies of the human mind. He reemphasizes the fundamental cultural and environmental aspects to human cognitive response. In 1986 he had put his own professional slant on varied topics such as literature and anthropology in his book *Actual Minds, Possible Worlds.* During that same year he participated in a symposium at Yale University on the implications of affirmative action within the context of the university. Bruner also contributed to an educational videocassette, *Baby Talk* (1986), which provides excellent insight to the processes by which children acquire language skills.

Further Reading

The single best source on Bruner's life is his autobiography, *In Search of Mind* (1983). A good, concise overview of his work up to 1972 may be found by Jeremy Anglin in the introduction to *Beyond the Information Given* (1973). This volume is a collection of some of Bruner's more important essays, edited and arranged by Anglin. For a collection of essays on some of Bruner's speculative thought, see *On Knowing: Essays for the Left Hand* (Expanded Edition, 1979). For additional reading on Bruner's educational ideas, see *The Relevance of Education* (1971).

Additional Sources

Bruner, Jerome, *Actual Minds, Possible Worlds,* Harvard University Press, 1986.

Bruner, Jerome, *Acts of Meaning,* Harvard University Press, 1990.

America, March 9, 1991.

Library Journal, March 15, 1987; October 15, 1990. □

Alois Brunner

Nazi German officer Alois Brunner (born 1912) helped engineer the Nazi destruction of European Jews, sending over 125,000 people to death camps.

SS (Schutzstaffel) Captain Alois Brunner served Adolf Eichmann in organizing the Nazi destruction of European Jews. Eichmann called Brunner "one of my best men." Born in Rohrbrunn, Austria, on April 8, 1912, Brunner joined the Nazi Party at age 19 and the SS at 26 (1938). He worked with Eichmann in the Central Office for Jewish Emigration in Vienna, which forced Jews to emigrate. Then, in October 1939, Brunner organized the first transports to Poland, a pilot project for mass deportation of Jews to ghettoes and death camps in the East. As director of the Vienna Central Office for Jewish Emigration (1940-1942), Brunner deported people that might have received exemptions, such as invalids and orphans. Brunner's personal torture of Jews exceeded the needs of Nazi policy. He knew the fate of those he deported, for he visited the ghettoes and camps. The combination of tactics Brunner used in Vienna—efficiency, deception, and terror—was noted by higher authorities and activated elsewhere.

Brunner proved his worth to Eichmann, who posted him next to Salonica, Greece, the center of Sephardic Jewish culture in Europe. Salonica Jews, whose ancestors fled the Inquisition, had retained the language and some of the customs of 15th century Spain. Brunner forced Salonica's Jews into a ghetto, while he settled into a mansion with luxury gardens outside and torture chambers below. Witnesses have called Brunner the "most ferocious" of all the torturers. He packed 2,000 Jewish prisoners into each transport of sealed boxcars, which after ten days arrived at the gas chambers of Auschwitz. In six weeks Brunner destroyed a community that had persisted for five centuries.

In his next assignment as deportation expert in France (June 1943-August 1944), Brunner took over the transit camp of Drancy, northeast of Paris. He ruled by torture, reprisal, and deception (for example, encouraging prisoners to take personal belongings on transports to a so-called labor colony in Poland). Before Brunner's arrival, only Jews born outside France were deported. But Brunner began sending French Jews to death camps as well. He specifically

marked Jewish children as targets, calling them "future terrorists," raiding children's centers, deporting hundreds of unaccompanied infants. Of the 23,500 people Brunner deported from France, only 1,645 survived.

As Germany faced defeat in the West in August 1944, Brunner left France for Slovakia (part of Czechoslovakia). Here he instituted a brutal camp regime and continued to deport Jews until the German retreat before the Russian attack.

Brunner was imprisoned by the Allies, but, using a false name, he got released. After working in Germany, he escaped in 1954 to Damascus, Syria, where he lived for over 40 years under Syrian protection. Beginning in the 1960s, monitors of Nazi activities asserted Brunner's presence in Damascus (under the name Georg Fischer) and his services to the Syrian secret service. In a 1985 interview Brunner showed no remorse for his wartime activities.

Warrants for Brunner's arrest and requests to Syria for his extradition were on the books in Germany, Austria, and elsewhere for many years. In 1954 France sentenced him to death in absentia, and in 1984 West Germany renewed a request for Brunner's extradition. Syrian authorities gave no sign of willingness to comply with such requests. Shortly after the in absentia verdict Brunner had four fingers blown from his left hand and was left partially blind when he opened a powerful mail bomb postmarked from Vienna. Armed government guards were outside his third floor apartment for many years. He was reported to carry cyanide with him at all times to be ingested in the event of his capture.

Brunner's mastery of deportation prevented resistance from his victims and showed his superiors how far the "Final Solution" could go. By a conservative estimate, Brunner deported 47,000 from Austria, 44,000 from Greece, 23,500 from France, and 14,000 from Slovakia. Very few of Brunner's victims survived.

Further Reading

Little has been written about Alois Brunner, and sources often confuse him with a Nazi named Anton Brunner. Information can be found in Raul Hilberg, *The Destruction of the European Jews* (1961, 1985). Documents which mention Brunner are reproduced and translated in *The Holocaust: Selected Documents,* edited by John Mendelsohn (1982), Vol. 8; *Trial of the Major War Criminals* (Nuremberg, 1946-1951), Vol. 4; and *Nazi Conspiracy and Aggression* (1946-1948), Vol. 8. A brief account of Brunner in Syria appeared in *Newsweek* (November 11, 1985). For more details, see Mary Felstiner, "Alois Brunner: 'Eichmann's Best Tool,'" *Simon Wiesenthal Center Annual* (1986).

Additional Sources

Reader's Digest June 1990.

U.S. News & World Report, November 25, 1991.

Josephs, Jeremy, *Swastika Over Paris,* Arcade Publishing Incorporated (1989). □

Emil Brunner

Emil Brunner (1889-1966), Swiss Reformed theologian, was a principal contributor to what came to be known popularly (though inaccurately) as "neo-orthodoxy," which was in opposition to late 19th and early 20th century "liberal" Protestant theology.

Emil Brunner was born at Winterthur, near Zurich, Switzerland, on December 23, 1889. After completing his early education at the *Gymnasium* in Zurich in 1908, he pursued advanced studies at the Universities of Zurich and Berlin, receiving the Doctor of Theology degree from the former institution in 1913. His formal education included a year of post-doctoral studies at Union Theological Seminary in New York in 1919-1920. In later years he was to receive honorary degrees from a number of the most prestigious centers of learning on the continent of Europe, in Great Britain, and in the United States.

From 1916 to 1924 Brunner was pastor of a small congregation in the mountain village of Obstalden in the Canton of Glarus in Switzerland. From 1945 to 1955 he occupied the Chair of Systematic and Practical Theology at the University of Zurich.

In the early 1920s Brunner became loosely associated with a small group of theologians who like himself had become disillusioned by the reigning "liberal" religious thought in which they had been trained. The group (which included Karl Barth, Eduard Thurneysen, Georg Merz, and Rudolf Bultmann) was to initiate a revolution in Protestant theology. Awakened to the inadequacies of liberalism by the catastrophe of World War I and appalled in particular by the pervasive notion of human "progress," these men (in the spirit of the Reformation of the 16th century) set about the task of regrounding faith firmly and solely in the self revelation of God in Christ. The movement begun by these men is variously alluded to as "the theology of crisis," "dialectical theology," "neo-orthodoxy," "neo-Protestantism," "Barthian Theology," or any one of several other designations. It was publicized through a new journal of religion entitled *Zwischen den Zeiten* ("Between the Times") which the group had established for that purpose.

Some of these men turned their attention to problems of New Testament hermeneutics (interpretaton of the Bible) or to a reinterpretation of culture and civilization. Brunner and Barth, however, each working independently, began intensive life-long labors in the area of systematic theology.

In Christian theology Brunner was unquestionably one of the two or three most eminent system builders of the 20th century. His method was to publish a preparatory volume on each of the cardinal doctrines of the faith and then to distill the whole in a comprehensive system of dogmatics. The titles of his books, and numerous phrases in them, became favorite modes of expression of key ideas for a whole generation of professionals in theology. Always the exponent of a living faith, he was sensitive to the great issues of that faith as demonstrated in distinguished performance at the writing desk, in the classroom and pulpit, on the lecture platform, and at conference tables around the world.

He was a theologians' theologian, yet he was a simple believer and churchman who spoke meaningfully to the generality of men. He professed to regard himself as first a preacher of the gospel and only then as also a theologian. He was critically sensitive, moreover, to the actual contest within which theology must take place. He wrote and spoke consciously, therefore, to 20th century man, believing that no artificial barriers should hinder the faith of those who belong by destiny to this particular stage of history. Holding that the gospel has its own inherent "offence," he was unwilling that any extraneous material should unnecessarily scandalize modern thinking men.

Apart from the Reformed tradition in which he was nurtured, three contemporary movements helped to mold his thought. The first was the religious socialist movement, which in its Swiss form had a firm Christological grounding. A second was the Oxford Group Movement, which for a time seemed to offer insights for the renewal of the church. And a third was the "I-Thou philosophy" of Soren Kierkegaard, Ferdinand Ebner, and Martin Buber, which helped Brunner toward a new understanding of truth.

From 1930 until the end of his life he was at the forefront of the ecumenical movement. From 1953 to 1955 he labored in the establishment of the International Christian University in Japan, thus crowning a career-long concern for missionary service.

Brunner was married and had four sons. He died, following a lengthy illness, on April 6, 1966.

Among his writings were: *The Mediator; The Divine Imperative; Our Faith; Man in Revolt; Truth as Encounter; Revelation and Reason: The Christian Doctrine of Creation and Redemption; The Christian Doctrine of the Church, Faith, and the Consummation; The Misunderstanding of the Church;* and *Eternal Hope.*

Further Reading

There is no extended biography of Emil Brunner in print. He left two autobiographical sketches: See "a Spiritual Autobiography" in the *Japan Christian Quarterly* (July 1955) and "Intellectual Autobiography" in Charles W. Kegley, editor, *The Theology of Emil Brunner.* Limited biographical data are available in a number of books and journal articles which are devoted primarily to his thought. See Dale Moody, "An Introduction to Emil Brunner," in *The Review and Expositor* (July 1947); J. R. Nelson, "Emil Brunner: Teacher Unsurpassed," in *Theology Today* (January 1963); and "Emil Brunner—The Final Encounter," in *The Christian Century* (April 20, 1966). See also Paul K. Jewett, *Emil Brunner: An Introduction to the Man and His Thought* (1961) and J. Edward Humphrey, *Emil Brunner* (1976). □

Giordano Bruno

The Italian philosopher and poet Giordano Bruno (1548-1600) attempted to deal with the implications of the Copernican universe. Although he made no scientific discoveries, his ideas had much influence on later scientists and philosophers.

Giordano Bruno was born at Nola in southern Italy. His baptismal name was Filippo, but he took the name Giordano when he entered a Dominican monastery in Naples in 1565. During his stay in different monastic houses in southern Italy, he acquired a vast knowledge of philosophy, theology, and science. Because he developed unorthodox views on some Catholic teachings, Bruno was suspected of heresy and finally fled the monastic life in 1576. This experience reveals much about Bruno's personality. His love for knowledge and hatred of ignorance led him to become a rebel, unwilling to accept traditional authority. The price he paid for this independence was persecution and condemnation in many countries.

After making his way through northern Italy, Bruno sought refuge at Geneva in 1579. His criticism of a Genevan professor, however, forced his withdrawal from that city. The next 2 years were spent in Toulouse, where he was granted a master's degree and lectured on Aristotle. In 1581-1582 he stayed in Paris and published his first significant set of writings, in which he explained a new method for memory training and commented on the logical system of Raymond Lully.

In 1583 Bruno traveled to England, where he lived for 2 years. While there, he became friendly with some prominent Englishmen, publicly praised Queen Elizabeth I, and held a disputation at Oxford on the Copernican and

Aristotelian conceptions of the universe. Most important, he published some of his best works in England during 1584-1585, namely, *La Cena de le Ceneri* (*The Ash Wednesday Supper*); *De l'infinito universo et mondi* (*On the Infinite Universe and Worlds*); and *De la causa, principio et uno* (*Concerning the Cause, Principle, and One*). In these works Bruno attempted to come to grips with the meaning of the new conception of the universe that Copernicus had developed. Bruno conceived of the universe as infinite, composed of a plurality of worlds. For him the universe has a unity that signifies a prevailing order-individual things are not isolated but are animated by a common life and a common cause. This cause is immanent, not transcendent, and the soul which gives life to the whole is God. It is God who "is not above, and not outside, but within and through, all things." It is not surprising that later examiners of Bruno's system described it as pantheistic. Bruno also published an Italian dialogue, *De gli eroici furori* (1585; *The Heroic Furies*), in which he presents the Renaissance conception of Platonic love.

Returning to France in 1585, Bruno was forced to leave that country in 1586 because of his attacks on Aristotelian philosophy. He then went to Germany, where he achieved some acclaim as a result of his lectures at the University of Wittenberg and published some works centered primarily on logic. After further travels he settled briefly in Frankfurt am Main, where he wrote a series of poems in Latin. In the three most important ones (all 1591), *De minimo* (*On the Minimum*), *De monade* (*On the Monad*), and *De immenso* (*On the Immense*), he examined what is infinitely small and infinitely great in the universe.

In 1592 Bruno went to Venice on the invitation of a Venetian nobleman who later betrayed him to the Catholic Inquisition. Bruno was arrested and imprisoned in Rome, where after a lengthy confinement and a trial for heresy he was burned at the stake on Feb. 17, 1600.

Further Reading

There is an extensive literature on Bruno in many languages. The best English biography is Dorothea Waley Singer, *Giordano Bruno: His Life and Thought* (1950). This work also includes a translation of Bruno's important work *On the Infinite Universe and Worlds* . Older biographies are J. Lewis McIntyre, *Giordano Bruno* (1903), and William Boulting, *Giordano Bruno: His Life, Thought, and Martyrdom* (1916). The former is divided into two sections, one on his life, the other on his philosophy. Among the specialized works on Bruno are Sidney Greenberg, *The Infinite in Giordano Bruno, with a Translation of His Dialogue: Concerning the Cause, Principle, and One* (1950); Irving Louis Horowitz, *The Renaissance Philosophy of Giordano Bruno* (1952); John Nelson, *Renaissance Theory of Love: The Context of Giordano Bruno's Eroici furori* (1958); and Frances A. Yates, *Giordano Bruno and the Hermetic Tradition* (1964).

Additional Sources

Yates, Frances Amelia, *Lull & Bruno,* London; Boston: Routledge & K. Paul, 1982.

Bossy, John, *Giordano Bruno and the embassy affair,* New Haven: Yale University Press, 1991. □

John Gerard Bruton

Prime Minister of Ireland John Bruton (born 1947), who served in parliament since 1969, has earned a reputation as a no-nonsense, forthright leader. One of Bruton's goals is to establish peace between the Irish Republican Army (IRA) and its opposition, mainly Britain and Southern Ireland.

The 1990s has seen much change in Ireland—from a cultural and economic upturn to the overtures of peace, after nearly three decades of turmoil. Into this wellspring of hope came Ireland's newly elected prime minister, John Bruton.

A Fresh Perspective

Bruton has served in the Irish parliament since 1969. With his election to the highest governing office in the land (there is a president of Ireland, but that position serves primarily as head of state), Bruton, head of the Fine Gael party, served notice of a fresh perspective. For one thing, Bruton is no "media-driven politician," as one associate was quoted as saying in a *National Review* article by Conor Cruise O'Brien. Indeed, added O'Brien, "the Irish media don't like him and have consistently underestimated him."

Conor points to Bruton's sometimes brusque manner in delivering policy, especially noticeable on television, which thrives on more upbeat personalities. But to those who run the parliament, Bruton represents "a person whose word is his bond."

The Bruton government, O'Brien went on to say, "has a lot going for it." High on the prime minister's agenda is the prospect of establishing and maintaining peaceful relations between the Irish Republican Army (IRA) and its opposition—mainly, Britian and Southern Ireland. In a 1995 St. Patrick's Day speech, U.S. President Bill Clinton himself praised Bruton "for his tireless efforts for peace and for continuing the work of his predecessor [former Prime Minister Albert Reynolds] in completing the Joint Framework Document for Northern Ireland" along with British Prime Minister John Major. Bruton, for his part, thanked Clinton for instilling in the IRA "the sense of confidence in itself and a glimpse of the political dividend that was there for them by pursuing a peaceful rather than a violent path."

Tried to Maintain a Delicate Balance

But tragic bombings in the metropolitan London area in the Spring of 1996 underscored the fragile nature of cease-fire efforts promoted by Bruton and by Gerry Adams, head of the IRA's political party, Sinn Fein. After one of the bombings, Bruton delivered a parliamentary speech denouncing the radical actions, but added that his government's door was open to Sinn Fein. In stating this, Bruton demonstrated that his approach was complementary to United States policy on Irish politics. (President Clinton's granting of a visa to Gerry Adams in 1995 is considered an important step in promoting peace.)

A former Deputy Leader of the Fine Gael party, Bruton, trained in law, served on numerous parliamentary committees, chiefly on topics of finance, industry and agriculture. A graduate of the University College, Dublin, Bruton married Finola Gill in 1981; the couple have four children.

Further Reading

National Review, January 23, 1995, p. 22.

U.S. Department of State Dispatch, March 27, 1995, p. 234. □

Dennis Brutus

The South African poet in exile Dennis Brutus (born 1924) is known both as a creative artist and as a political activist opposed to apartheid.

Dennis Brutus was born in Salisbury, Southern Rhodesia, of South African parents. Educated at Fort Hare College and the University of the Witwatersrand, he taught for 14 years in South Africa and participated in many anti-apartheid campaigns, particularly those concerned with sports. The South African government eventually banned him from attending political and social meetings and made it illegal for any of his writings to be published in South Africa.

In 1963 he was arrested for attending a sports meeting. When released on bail, he fled to Swaziland and from there tried to make his way to Germany to meet with the world Olympic executive committee, but the Portuguese secret police at the Mozambique border handed him back to the South African security police. Realizing that no one would know of his capture, he made a desperate attempt to escape, only to be shot in the back on a Johannesburg street. On recovery he was sentenced to 18 months hard labor on Robben Island.

When he finished his term in prison, Brutus was permitted to leave South Africa with his wife and children on an "exit permit," a document which made it illegal for him to return. He lived in London from 1966 to 1970, where he worked as a teacher and a journalist. In 1970 he took a position as a visiting professor of English at the University of Denver for a year, after which he moved to Northwestern University in Evanston, Illinois. He was a professor of English at Northwestern from 1971 to 1985, then took a position at the University of Pittsburgh in 1986. In 1983 Brutus was granted political asylum in the United States. During the 1970s and 1980s he remained active in a number of anti-apartheid organizations, particularly SANROC (South African Non-Racial Olympic Committee), which led the movement to have South Africa excluded from the Olympic Games because of its discriminatory sports policies. He was also on the staff of the International Defense and Aid Fund. Brutus was as famous for his political activities as he was for his poetry.

There were five distinct phases in his development as a poet, each marked by formal and thematic shifts which tended not only to reflect his changing preoccupations and professional concerns, but also to document profound transformations in his conception of the nature and function of poetry. Each new phase grew out of a personal experience which made him question his previous attitudes toward verbal art and seek a more satisfying outlet for his energies of articulation.

His first book of poems, *Sirens, Knuckles, Boots* (1963), contained a variety of lyric forms invested with many of the standard poetic conventions. This was highbrow poetry—tight, mannered, formal, and sometimes formidably difficult. Schooled in classic English verse, Brutus attempted to compose multi-leveled lyrics that would challenge the mind, poems sufficiently subtle and intricate to interest any well-educated lover of poetry. He frequently sought to achieve an ambiguous idiom that allowed him to make a political and an erotic statement in the same breath. It was during this early phase in his career that he wrote nearly all of his most complex verse.

While he was in prison Brutus decided to stop writing this kind of poetry. The five months he spent in solitary confinement caused him to reexamine his verse and his attitudes toward creative self-expression, and he resolved thereafter to write simple, unornamented poetry that ordinary people could comprehend immediately. His *Letters to Martha and Other Poems from a South African Prison* (1968) contains brief, laconic statements deriving from his experiences as a prisoner. The diction is deliberately conversational and devoid of poetic devices. Instead of seeking to express two or three thoughts simultaneously, Brutus was striving to say only one thing at a time and to say it directly.

After he left South Africa and began his life in exile, Brutus' poetry changed again. This time a change appeared as a balance between the complexity of his early verse and the simplicity of his prison poems. While traveling the world as an anti-apartheid crusader, he wrote many nostalgic, plaintive lyrics recalling the beauties and terrors of his native land. This homesick verse, collected in *Poems from Algiers* (1970), *Thoughts Abroad* (1970), and *A Simple Lust* (1973), was more richly textured than what he had written in prison, yet he continued to aim for lucidity rather than symbolic nuances.

In the summer of 1973 Brutus visited the People's Republic of China to attend a sports meeting. Impressed by the extreme economy of Chinese verse, he began experimenting with epigrammatic poetic forms resembling Japanese *haiku* and Chinese *chueh chu,* in which very little is said and much suggested. The results were brought together in a pamphlet called *China Poems* (1975).

Brutus's later collections, *Strains* (1975), *Stubborn Hope* (1978), and *Salutes and Censures* (1980), contained poems written over a span of years and thus in a variety of poetic idioms. But in his later verse he appeared once again to be moving toward a balanced position, this time between the extreme density of his complex early verse and the extraordinary economy of his nearly wordless Chinese experiments. However, despite these remarkable changes in poetic posture, Brutus's political stance never altered. He devoted his life and his art to opposing apartheid in South Africa.

Until the dissolution of the apartheid system in 1993, Brutus' work was systematically banned in South Africa. He did manage to publish his collection, *Thought Abroad* under the pseudonym John Bruin for a short while. Until the government learned Brutus was the author, the poems were actually studied in South African universities. The banning of Brutus' work was so thorough, literary critic Colin Gardner observed in *Research in African Literatures,* "it seems likely that many well-read South Africans, even some of those with a distinct interest in South African poetry, are wholly or largely unacquainted with his writing."

In the late 1980s, Brutus published *Airs and Tributes* (1989). The end of apartheid brought a surge in creativity for South African writers, and in 1993 Brutus visited his native country for the first time since 1966.

Further Reading

No books have yet been written on Dennis Brutus, but he is discussed in most books dealing with African poetry or with South African literature. Informed critical commentary can be found in Ken Goodwin, *Understanding African Poetry* (1982); Ursula A. Barnett, *A Vision of Order: A Study of Black South African Literature in English* (1983); and Jacques Alvarez-Pereyre, *The Poetry of Commitment in South Africa* (1984). □

Marcus Junius Brutus

Marcus Junius Brutus (ca. 85-42 B.C.) was a Roman statesman and one of the conspirators who assassinated Julius Caesar. Brutus's contemporaries admired him for his political integrity and intellectual and literary attainments.

The father of Brutus took part in the unsuccessful attempt of M. Aemilius Lepidus to overthrow the government of L. Cornelius Sulla and was killed by Pompey in 78 B.C. Brutus's mother, Servilia, was the niece of the reformer M. Livius Drusus and half sister of M. Porcius Cato the Younger. She became notorious as the mistress of Julius Caesar. After the death of his father, Brutus was adopted by his uncle and took the name Quintus Caepio Brutus. But Cato exercised the dominant influence over him in his youth. Under Cato's direction Brutus began his philosophical studies in Rome and continued them in Athens.

Brutus may have been the Q. Caepio who had been engaged to Julia, daughter of Julius Caesar, until Caesar broke the engagement a few days before the marriage in 59 B.C. in order to give her to Pompey. That same year the informer P. Vettius named Brutus as a member of a plot to murder Pompey. But Vettius's story lacked credibility and was ridiculed in the Senate. In 58 Brutus accompanied Cato to Cyprus, where he earned the confidence of prominent Cypriots. On his return to Rome he abused that confidence by lending money to the Cypriot Senate at the extortionate rate of 48 percent and by using force to exact its payment. Elected quaestor for 53 B.C., Brutus refused to join Caesar's staff in Gaul but went to Cilicia with his father-in-law, Appius Claudius Pulcher.

In Rome after 52 Brutus joined in attacks on Pompey, but as the civil war approached, he chose the senatorial side, accepting appointment as legate to P. Sestius in Cilicia in 49. Cato persuaded Brutus to bury his differences with Pompey and fight with him in Greece.

After the Battle of Pharsalus Brutus requested and readily received pardon from Caesar. He later met Caesar at Tarsus in Cilicia and accompanied him on his triumphal campaign in Asia. Back in Rome Caesar continued to show Brutus favor, appointing him governor of Cisalpine Gaul in 46 and choosing him over Cassius for the important post of city praetor for 44.

The Conspiracy

Brutus's reasons for joining the conspiracy against Caesar were complex: the persuasiveness of its chief organizer, Cassius; the martyrdom of Cato, whose daughter Brutus had married in 45 B.C.; consciousness of his descent from L. Junius Brutus, who slew the last king of Rome; and Stoic dogma, which declared the murder of a tyrant not only just but obligatory. At the time no one accused him of acting out of personal antagonism. It was Brutus's personality and idealism which gave the conspiracy its force and direction, and Brutus insisted that action be taken against Caesar

alone. The death of the dictator, he naively believed, would automatically restore liberty and the republic.

After the death of Caesar the conspirators soon found themselves outmaneuvered by Antony. Although the Senate voted them amnesty on March 17, 44, and Brutus was allowed to address the people, he and Cassius left Rome in April in the face of mounting hostility. Eventually Brutus was assigned the province of Cyprus, and Cassius, Cyrene. At the end of August both men went to the East.

Building a Base of Power

Establishing himself at Athens, Brutus conscripted troops, requisitioned money on its way to Rome from Asia, seized arms, accepted illegally the governorship of Macedonia, took over the province of Illyricum, and defeated Antony's brother Gaius, sent out to check him. In February 43 the Senate recognized Brutus's position in Macedonia, Illyricum, and Greece. After the defeat of Antony at Mutina the Senate voted Brutus and Cassius command over the entire East.

But fortune soon changed for the worse. When Octavian seized the consulship in August 43, one of his first acts was to revoke the amnesty given to the assassins of Caesar. When Antony, Octavian, and Lepidus formed the Second Triumvirate to avenge Caesar, Brutus left Greece to join forces with Cassius in Asia and prepare for war. From Asia the two men returned to Europe and met the forces of Antony and Octavian at Philippi in October 42. In the first engagement Brutus overran the camp of Octavian, but

Cassius in a fit of despair after being defeated by Antony committed suicide. Brutus rallied his legions, but he too was defeated in a second battle and took his own life.

Brutus's Philosophy and Character

Brutus was eclectic in his philosophical beliefs, following the teachings of the Academy and the Stoics. He wrote treatises on virtue, on duties, and on patience which were much admired. He was also a powerful orator and pamphleteer. He composed partisan tracts against Pompey and in praise of Cato and Appius Claudius. In the 50s Cicero and Q. Hortensius, the leading orators of the day, cultivated Brutus. Cicero thought so highly of his talents and learning that he dedicated two treatises on oratory, the *Brutus* and *Orator,* to him. There survives a small part of the extensive correspondence between Brutus and Cicero, dating from the period after the death of Caesar.

Shakespeare's portrayal of Brutus as the "noblest Roman of them all" is highly idealized. Steadfast and determined in large matters, he was petty and cruel in small. For all his admiration of Brutus, Cicero found him obstinate, aloof, and arrogant. The narrow moral and patriotic idealism in which he cloaked the murder of Caesar ensured the futility of the deed. Brutus, in fact, acted in defense of his own class and a system which was already dying. He was the last of the republicans, and when he fell, the republic fell with him.

Further Reading

The chief ancient sources for Brutus are Cicero, Plutarch, and Appian. Max Radin, *Marcus Brutus* (1939), is a popular biography marred by occasional factual errors. S. A. Cook, F. E. Adcock, and M. P. Charlesworth, eds., *Cambridge Ancient History,* vol. 10 (1934), gives a balanced and penetrating assessment of Brutus as a politician and statesman. For a less charitable view see Sir Ronald Syme, *The Roman Revolution* (1939), which stresses Brutus's personal and political motives in murdering Caesar.

Additional Sources

Clarke, M. L. (Martin Lowther), *The noblest Roman: Marcus Brutus and his reputation,* Ithaca, N.Y.: Cornell University Press, 1981. □

William Jennings Bryan

The American lawyer, editor, and politician William Jennings Bryan (1860-1925) was the Democratic party's presidential nominee three times and became secretary of state. Called the "Great Commoner," Bryan advocated an agrarian democracy.

For 30 years William Jennings Bryan was active in American politics, emerging first as a spokesman for those who felt disregarded or slighted by the urban, industrial forces revolutionizing the United States in the period after the Civil War. Giving voice to their values and protests, Bryan advocated measures which he believed would give the people more direct control of the government and would allow the common man more economic advantages. Seeking simple solutions to complex social and economic problems, Bryan talked in pietistic terms: the controversy over coinage was viewed as a struggle between good and evil, not merely between men of conflicting points of view.

Although the increasing industrialization and urbanization of American society and greater United States participation in world affairs made Bryan an anachronism and finally thrust him aside, his attacks helped to focus public attention on serious problems and indirectly led to measures of correction and reform in the early 20th century.

Bryan was born in Salem, Ill. In his middle-class family, great emphasis was placed on religion and morality, not only in one's personal life but in politics and in the conduct of national affairs. After graduating from Illinois College in 1881 and studying for 2 years at Union College of Law in Chicago, he opened a law office in Jacksonville. Shortly afterward he married Mary Baird.

Early Career

In 1887 Bryan moved to Lincoln, Nebr., practicing law and simultaneously turning toward politics. He won a seat in Congress in 1890 and was reelected in 1892. As a congressman, he was a foe of high tariffs and an exponent of free coinage of silver, both popular positions with Nebraska voters.

In the 1880s and 1890s debtors, farmers, and silver mine owners urged the expansion of the amount of money in circulation in the United States, arguing that more money in circulation would mean better times and that when money was scarce the wealthy benefited at the expense of the less well-to-do. Exponents of silver coinage argued that the Federal government should buy large quantities of silver, issue currency based on silver, and put 16 times as much silver in a silver dollar as the amount of gold in a gold dollar. The movement had a magnetic appeal for those suffering from the agricultural depression of the 1880s and 1890s. Bryan took its rallying cries—"free silver" and "16 to 1"—as his own. A dynamic and dedicated speaker, he toured the country speaking on silver, as well as urging its merits in the *Omaha World Herald.* Defeated for the Senate in 1894, he had become editor of the paper. Known for his oratory rather than his brilliance or shrewdness, Bryan captured the imagination of small-town and rural people who were bewildered by the changes occurring around them, devastated by the depression of 1893, and angry with President Grover Cleveland's policies toward Coxey's Army and the Homestead strike.

Presidential Candidate and Political Leader

The silver forces, centered chiefly in western and southern states, had virtual control of the Democratic convention of 1896 before it opened in Chicago. Bryan's dramatic "Cross of Gold" speech helped him secure the presidential nomination, and he prosecuted the campaign against former Ohio governor William McKinley with unprecedented vigor. When the Populist party also nominated Bryan, the conservative "Gold Democrats" were alarmed and seceded from their traditional party and nominated another candidate. The campaign was extremely heated. To Bryan the "money men of the East" were agents of evil; to Republicans and conservative Democrats, Bryan was equally abhorrent. Bryan was the first presidential candidate to travel extensively and to use the railroads to take his case to the people.

Bryan lost the election but remained the Democratic party leader and immediately began campaigning for 1900. His activities were varied, designed to keep him before the public eye: he wrote magazine articles, made extensive speaking tours on the Chautauqua circuit, and, with his wife, compiled an account of the 1896 campaign called *The First Battle.*

When the Spanish-American War began, Bryan enlisted and served briefly, raising a regiment in Nebraska. The paramount issue arising from the war (which the United States won quickly) was whether the country should annex any of the overseas territories Spain had been forced to relinquish—whether the nation should embark on a policy of imperialism, as had most of the other major nations of the world. Bryan, a dedicated anti-imperialist, felt certain that by referendum the people would repudiate any administration that declared for annexation. But he argued for approving the Treaty of Paris ending the war, by which the Spanish would cede Puerto Rico and the Philippines to the United States, saying that the United States should first secure the freedom of the Philippines from Spain and then award them independence when the international situation was more favorable.

Bryan coupled anti-imperialism with free silver as the major issues of the 1900 campaign, in which he again opposed President McKinley and was again defeated. The gradual disappearance of hard times had lessened the appeal of free silver, and the American people were too pleased with the outcome of the Spanish-American War to support anti-imperialism.

Bryan launched a weekly newspaper, the *Commoner,* in 1901 and kept himself before the public, although many Democratic party leaders considered him a failure as a candidate. Bypassed in 1904 by the Democratic party, Bryan supported the presidential candidacy of conservative Judge Alton B. Parker. Parker and the conservatives did so poorly in the election that Bryan was able to secure the 1908 nomination for himself. Another defeat, this time at the hands of William Howard Taft, ensued, but Bryan remained active in the Democratic party. In 1912 he helped to secure the nomination of Woodrow Wilson for the presidency, and Wilson named the Great Commoner secretary of state in 1913.

Bryan's durability as a political leader stemmed from a number of sources: his control of a party faction, his appeal to the common man and his personification of traditional American values, his identification with a large number of reform issues, his constant and unremitting labor, and the paucity of successful Democratic leaders. In particular, his capacity for pointing out areas of reform turned the public's attention toward problems of trusts and monopolies, paving the way for corrective legislation. Many of the reforms he suggested were carried out, several by President Theodore Roosevelt. Federal income tax, popular election of senators, woman's suffrage, stricter railroad regulation, initiative and referendum provisions, and publicity of campaign contributions were all reforms for which Bryan had worked.

Secretary of State

Bryan helped to obtain passage of domestic legislation, most notably the Federal Reserve Act. He strove to master foreign policy, bringing more energy and dedication than insight. He had no experience in foreign policy and had been chosen secretary of state because that was the most important position in the Cabinet. For Latin America he advocated a policy of protection of American business interests, suggesting that more financial intervention by the U.S. government might prevent European influence. He was particularly interested in negotiating arbitration treaties with some 30 countries, for he believed that such treaties would prevent war. He advocated a policy of neutrality in World War I, hoping that the United States might play the role of arbitrator between the opposing sides. Wilson, however, did not follow his advice; in protest over the tone of the President's second note about the sinking of the *Lusitania,* Bryan resigned in June 1915.

Last Decade

Bryan remained active in politics and also promoted Florida real estate, wrote copiously, and lectured on prohibition. The old-fashioned Protestantism that had made him a hero to many people became more prominent in his thinking even as it became less prevalent in American society; he spoke out for the fundamentalists, even to the point of refusing to condemn the Ku Klux Klan because of their Christian guise. Shortly after he was howled down at the 1924 Democratic convention, he appeared for the prosecution in the Scopes trial in Tennessee, opposing the teaching of theories of evolution in public schools. The naiveté and narrowness of his thinking emerged clearly in this trial, which was Bryan's last appearance in public before his death in 1925.

Further Reading

Books about Bryan, like books by him, are abundant. The most detailed biography is Paolo E. Coletta, *William Jennings Bryan: Political Evangelist, 1860-1908* (1964). Louis W. Koenig, *Bryan: A Political Biography of William Jennings Bryan* (1971), is a useful study. Paul W. Glad, *The Trumpet Soundeth: William Jennings Bryan and His Democracy, 1896-1912* (1960), treats the rural context from which Bryan emerged. Glad's *McKinley, Bryan and the People* (1964) focuses on the election. The last years of Bryan's life are handled skillfully by Lawrence W. Levine, *Defender of the Faith: William Jennings Bryan; The Last Decade, 1915-1925* (1965). By far the best brief treatment of Bryan is Richard Hofstadter, "The Democrat as Revivalist," in Paul W. Glad, ed., *William Jennings Bryan: A Profile* (1968). □

Paul Bryant

At the time of his retirement in 1982, Paul "Bear" Bryant (1919-1983), legendary coach of the University of Alabama's "Crimson Tide" football team, then had the best record of any coach in college football history: 323 wins, 85 losses, and 17 ties. Sixty-five of his former college players were in professional football, and 44 more were head coaches of college or professional teams.

The future coach was born Paul William Bryant on September 11, 1919, in a rural area of Arkansas known as Moro Bottom, the 11th of 12 children of William Monroe and Ida Bryant. He received the nickname "Bear" after wrestling a muzzled bear at a carnival. After the death of his father, the family moved to nearby Fordyce, Arkansas. In high school there Bryant participated in football, basketball, baseball, and track. He played on the 1930 Arkansas state high school football champion team as an offensive end and defensive tackle. He was scouted and recruited by the University of Alabama.

From 1932 to 1936 he attended Alabama and played on the football team. During the 1933-1934 season he was the starting offensive end. In 1935 he played on the Alabama team that defeated Stanford University in the Rose Bowl. After graduation in 1936 he stayed at Alabama as an assistant football coach. In 1940 he left to accept a similar position at Vanderbilt University. World War II interrupted his football career and he enlisted in the U.S. Navy, achieving the rank of lieutenant commander. After the war he accepted the head football coaching position at the University of Maryland. He stayed at Maryland one year, leaving to become the head football coach at the University of Kentucky. In his years at Kentucky he compiled a record of 60 wins, 23 losses, and 5 ties. In 1950 Kentucky won the Southeast Conference title by defeating Oklahoma University. During his tenure there Kentucky went to the Great Lakes, Orange, Sugar, and Cotton bowls.

He left Kentucky in 1954 to accept the head coaching position at Texas A&M University. There he had his only losing season. After four years, however, his record stood at 25 wins, 14 losses, and 2 ties. In 1954 his team won the Southwest Conference title. Texas A&M won the conference title again in 1956, but was barred from participating in the Cotton Bowl because of recruiting violations. In 1957 the Aggies lost to Tennessee in the Gator Bowl, but Bryant had coached his first Heisman Trophy winner, John David Crow.

Bryant returned to Alabama as head football coach in 1958. In his first year back at Alabama went 5-4-1. In his second year they went to the Liberty Bowl, the first of 24 consecutive trips to bowl games. He became known as a tough disciplinarian who demanded the best from his players. He had them live together in a special dormitory, and

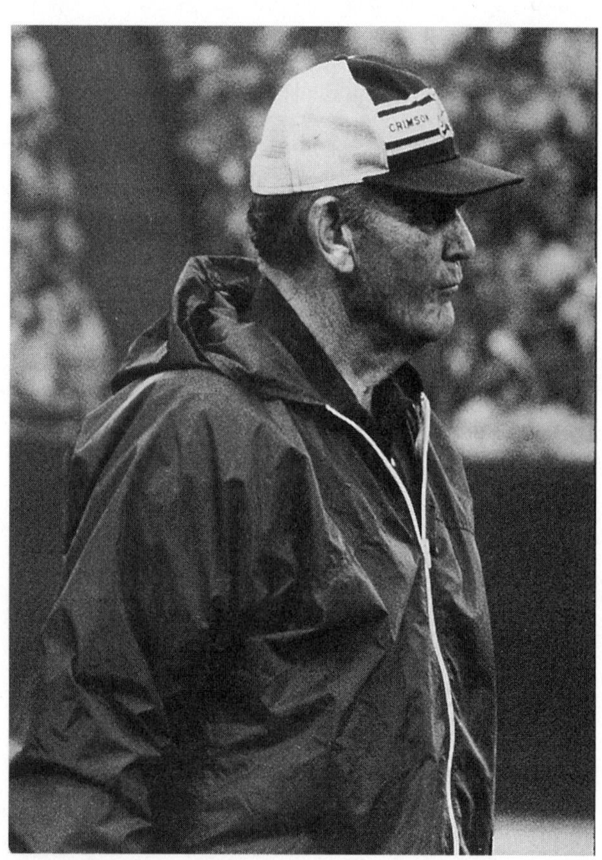

they all ate together. This toughness, however, was bolstered by integrity and fairness. He expected nothing from his players that he was not willing to give of himself. And his approach to the game paid off. Alabama football teams won six national championships and 13 Southeastern Conference titles. This remarkable accomplishment brought national attention to Alabama, and Bryant, wearing his trademark houndstooth hat, became a familiar figure on the sidelines during televised games.

In 1962 the *Saturday Evening Post* published an article that accused Bryant of coaching in a manner that encouraged unsportsmanlike conduct. The article was apparently prompted by an incident that had occurred during the game between Alabama and Georgia Tech played on November 18, 1961. A Tech player going downfield to cover a punt was blocked out of bounds by an Alabama player who used what is called a forearm shiver. The blow to the face broke the Tech player's jaw. As a result, the friendship between Bryant and Tech's coach Bobby Dodd was ruined. Georgia Tech dropped Alabama from its schedule and later left the Southeastern Conference. Bryant filed suit against the magazine.

The *Post* then published another article accusing Bryant and coach Wallie Butts of the University of Georgia's football team of rigging a game, a game that Alabama had won 35-0. Bryant again filed suit against the *Post.* One of the best known public figures in Alabama, Bryant went on statewide television to proclaim his innocence. Bryant's lawyers protested to the *Post* and asked that the charges be withdrawn. The *Post,* however, stood by the story, and Bryant filed his third lawsuit against the magazine.

Wallie Butts had filed suit against the *Post* as well, and his suit went to trial first. Bryant appeared to testify in support of Butts. He displayed the same style on the witness stand as he did on the football field sidelines. Confident and dignified, he still could not suppress his rage at the charges, and appeared near tears at times during his testimony. The jury ruled in favor of Coach Butts and awarded general as well as punitive damages. Bryant's suits never made it to the courtroom. Curtis Publishing, publisher of the *Post,* published a retraction and awarded a cash settlement.

Bryant was named Southeastern Conference (SEC) "Coach of the Year" eight times. In 1968 sportswriters voted him all-time SEC coach. Bryant, however, believed that a head coach was only as good as his assistants. On December 15, 1982, Bryant retired as head coach position and became athletic director at Alabama. He was succeeded by Ray Perkins, a former coach of the New York Giants of the National Football League. Less than two months later, on January 26, 1983, Bryant died of a heart attack. In 1986 he was elected to the College Football Hall of Fame, in his first year of eligibility. The Bear Bryant Award is given each year to the top college football coach.

Further Reading

Bear, Bryant's autobiography, was published in 1974. It is a remarkably modest story of his life, in which he gives all of the credit for his success to his mother. *The Legend of "Bear" Bryant* (1987) by Mickey Herskowitz is an emotional tribute to Bryant by one of his greatest admirers. Another good book, this one about the entire Alabama program, is *The Crimson Tide: A Story of Alabama Football* (1973) by Clyde Balton.

Additional Sources

Bryant, Paul W, *Bear; the hard life and good times of Alabama's Coach Bryant,* Boston, Little, Brown 1975.

Bynum, Mike, *Bryant, the man, the myth,* Atlanta, Ga.: Cross Roads Books, 1979.

Bynum, Mike, *We believe—Bear Bryant's boys talk,* College Station, Tex.: We Believe Trust Fund at the Bank of A&M, 1980.

Ford, Tommy, *Bama under Bear: Alabama's family Tides,* Huntsville, Ala.: Strode Publishers, 1983.

Reed, Delbert, *Paul "Bear" Bryant, what made him a winner: analyses, comments, and memories by those who knew him best,* Northport, Ala.: Vision Press, 1995. □

William Cullen Bryant

The American poet and newspaper editor William Cullen Bryant (1794-1878) helped introduce European romanticism into American poetry. As an editor, he championed liberal causes. He was one of the most influential and popular figures of mid-19th-century America.

William Cullen Bryant was born on Nov. 3, 1794, in Cummington, Mass. His well-established New England family was staunchly Federalist in politics and Calvinist in religion. Encouraged to write poetry by his father, a physician of wide learning, the boy reflected in his earliest poems his family's political and religious attitudes. Bryant's Federalist satire on Thomas Jefferson, *The Embargo, or Sketches of the Times* (1808), by a "Youth of Thirteen" was published through his father's influence. In later years the liberal, democratic, Unitarian Bryant understandably wished to forget this youthful indiscretion, and he did not reprint it in any of his collections.

"Thanatopsis" and Other Poems

Bryant entered Williams College in 1810 and left after a year. In 1811 he wrote the first draft of his best-known poem, "Thanatopsis" (literally, view of death), reflecting the influence of English "graveyard" poets such as Thomas Gray.

Perhaps the most remarkable feature of "Thanotopsis" is its anti-Christian, stoical view of death. There is no heaven or hell beyond the grave; death ends life, and that is all: "Thine individual being, shalt thou go/ To mix forever with the elements,/ To be a brother to the insensible rock/ And to the sluggish clod. . . . " Published in 1817, the poem was a marked success; it was reprinted in 1821 in the final, revised version familiar today.

A few years later Bryant modified his attitude to death in "To a Waterfowl," in which a "Power" (God) is omnipresent and beneficent. The later English poet Matthew

Arnold considered this to be the finest short poem in the English language. As the 1876 poem "The Flood of Years" makes clear, Bryant held this view of death to the end of his life.

Shortly after Bryant wrote the first draft of "Thanotopsis," he came under the influence of the romantic British poets William Wordsworth and Samuel Taylor Coleridge. In the opening lines of "Inscription for the Entrance to a Wood," Bryant conveyed a love of nature that he retained throughout his career: "Thou wilt find nothing here [in nature]/ Of all that pained thee in the haunts of men,/ And made thee loathe thy life." However, like Wordsworth and other romantics, Bryant saw the world of nature less as an escape from the evils of life in the city than as a positive, vital force in itself. He explored this idea in other poems of this period, such as "The Yellow Violet," "I Cannot Forget with What Fervid Devotion," "Green River," and "A Winter Piece," and later in "A Forest Hymn," "The Death of Flowers," and "The Prairies."

Following his year at Williams College, Bryant read for the law and in 1815 was admitted to the Massachusetts bar. From 1816 to 1825 he practiced law in Great Barrington, Mass. He also kept up his literary activities, writing poetry and essays. In 1821 he published his first volume, *Poems,* and read his Phi Beta Kappa poem "The Ages" at Harvard. That same year he married Frances Fairchild, his "Fairest of the Rural Maids."

In 1826 Bryant became assistant editor of the liberal *New York Evening Post* and in 1829 editor in chief. He served in this capacity for 50 years.

Poetic Theories

Bryant formulated his poetic theories in a series of four lectures on poetry, which he delivered in 1826 before the New York Athenaeum Society (they were published in 1884). He stressed, "The most beautiful poetry is that which takes the strongest hold of the feelings. . . . Important, therefore, as may be the office of the imagination [and of understanding, as well] in poetry, the great spring of poetry is emotion." (He expressed a similar view in the 1864 poem "The Poet.") Models from the past which the poet chooses to follow should be used only as guides to his own originality. While acknowledging that America's historical and cultural past was not as rich for the creation of poetry as England's, Bryant nevertheless felt that when America did produce a great poet he would draw on the best the young country had to offer.

The Editor

As an editor espousing liberal causes, Bryant had considerable impact on the life of New York and of the nation. Typical of his editorials was "The Right of Workmen to Strike" (1836), in which he upheld the workers' right to collective bargaining and ridiculed the prosecution of labor unions: "Can any thing be imagined more abhorrent to every sentiment of generosity or justice, than the law which arms the rich with the legal right to fix . . . the wages of the poor? If this is not *slavery,* we have forgotten its definition."

Similarly, Bryant was firmly committed to many other liberal causes of the day, including the antislavery movement, the "free-soil" concept, and free trade among nations. He also helped in the formation of the new Republican party in 1855.

Bryant published nine volumes of poetry from 1832 on. He also translated the *Iliad* (1870) and the *Odyssey* (1871-1872). He died in New York City on June 12, 1878.

Though Bryant was not a great poet, his poems were much admired in his own time, and a number of them are eminently readable today. As the guiding force of the *Evening Post,* he left his mark not only on the city his liberal paper served but on the nation as well.

Further Reading

Parke Godwin, Bryant's son-in-law, edited the standard editions of both *The Poetical Works of William Cullen Bryant* (2 vols., 1883) and Bryant's *Prose Writings* (2 vols., 1884). The best one-volume edition of the poems is Henry C. Sturges and Richard Henry Stoddard, eds., *The Poetical Works of William Cullen Bryant* (1903). The standard biography of Bryant is Parke Godwin, *A Biography of William Cullen Bryant, with Extracts from His Private Correspondence* (2 vols., 1883). A more balanced assessment is Harry H. Peckham, *Gotham Yankee: A Biography of William Cullen Bryant* (1950). Tremaine McDowell edited and wrote an excellent introduction to *William Cullen Bryant: Representative Selections* (1935). Allan Nevins, *The Evening Post: A Century of Journalism* (1922), discusses Bryant as an editor. Recommended for general background are Roy Harvey Pearce, *The Continuity of American Poetry* (1961), and Hyatt H. Waggoner, *American Poets, from the Puritans to the Present* (1968). □

James Bryce

The British historian, jurist, and statesman James Bryce, Viscount Bryce (1838-1922), is best known for "The American Commonwealth," a significant study of United States political institutions. He also fostered a revival of interest in Roman law.

James Bryce was born on May 10, 1838, in Belfast, Ireland, the son of a Scottish schoolmaster. In 1846 the family moved to Glasgow, Scotland, where James attended secondary school and studied at the university. In 1857 he entered Trinity College, Oxford, where he had a brilliant scholastic career. In 1862 he was elected a fellow of Oriel College, Oxford, and was the first fellow who did not take the Anglican oaths.

Bryce's *The Holy Roman Empire* (1864) established his reputation as a legal historian. After practicing law in London for several years, he returned to Oxford in 1870 as regius professor of civil law, a post he held until 1893. His lectures at Oxford (published in 1901 as *Studies in History and Jurisprudence*) led to a revival in the study of Roman law.

An avid traveler, Bryce made the first of many trips to the United States in 1870. His interest in the life of the Armenians, which was acquired during a climbing holiday in 1876, led him to write *Transcaucasia and Ararat* (1877). A close friend and adviser of William Gladstone, Bryce entered the House of Commons in 1880 and from 1885 to 1907 sat as a Liberal member. During this period he completed his most important work, *The American Commonwealth* (1888). In this classic study, Bryce's legal training, historical knowledge, and firsthand experience of American life contribute to his cogent and influential analysis of the governmental process in the United States.

After serving as undersecretary for foreign affairs in 1886 and again in 1892, Bryce served as president of the Board of Trade and chairman of the Royal Commission on Secondary Education in 1894-1895. His visit to South Africa in 1895 led him to protest the handling of negotiations with the Boer republics, and his *Impressions of South Africa* (1897) influenced the Liberal position on the Boer War.

After serving as chief secretary for Ireland (1905-1906), Bryce was the British ambassador to the United States (1907-1913). During his ambassadorship he dealt with many United States-Canadian problems. He was elevated to the peerage on his return to England in 1913. During the remaining 9 years of his life, Bryce served on the International Court at The Hague, supported the establishment of the League of Nations, and published *Modern Democracy* (1921). He died on Jan. 22, 1922.

Further Reading

The best book on Bryce is H. A. L. Fisher, *James Bryce* (2 vols., 1927). It emphasizes Bryce's connections with the United States but also discusses his parliamentary career, writings, and influence on legal studies. See also Edmund S. Ions's study, *James Bryce and American Democracy, 1870-1922* (1968).

Additional Sources

Bernard, Burton C., *James Bryce and St. Louis: a bibliographic introduction to the writings of James Bryce, May 10, 1988*, Granite City, Ill.: B.C. Bernard, 1988.

Bernard, Burton C., *The James Bryce Collection at Washington University, St. Louis, October 22, 1988,* Granite City, Ill.: B.C. Bernard, c1988. □

Zbigniew Brzezinski

Zbigniew Brzezinski (born 1928) was assistant to the president of the United States for national security affairs during the Carter administration (1977-1980). Later he was associated with the Center for Strategic and International Studies in Washington D.C. He authored several books through which he expounded his philosophies as well as his political beliefs and ideals.

Zbigniew Brzezinski was born in Warsaw, Poland, on March 28, 1928. After obtaining his B.A. and M.A. degrees from McGill University in Montreal, Canada, he came to the United States in 1953. He was awarded the Ph.D. at Harvard the same year and remained there, first as a research fellow at the Russian Research Center and then as assistant professor of government, until 1960. He became a naturalized American citizen in 1958.

In 1960 Brzezinski moved to Columbia where he continued his rapid climb up the academic ladder. He was promoted to full professor in 1962 and directed the Research Institute in Communist Affairs (later the Research Institute on International Change) from 1962 to 1977. From 1966 to 1968 he had gained valuable experience as a member of the Department of State's Policy Planning Council during the Lyndon B. Johnson administration. Identified as a Democrat and a rival of Henry Kissinger, Brzezinski saw little action during Richard Nixon's presidency. In 1973 he became director of the Trilateral Commission and had the foresight to recruit a young and generally unknown governor of Georgia, Jimmy Carter. For Brzezinski, the early contact with Carter brought handsome rewards.

Carter declared his candidacy for president in 1974, and Brzezinski quickly approached him with an offer of advice. Of the potential candidates, Henry Jackson of Washington had views on foreign policy that appealed to Brzezinski more than those of Carter, but Jackson did not look like a winner. To most other Democratic presidential aspirants, Brzezinski's reputation as a "hard-liner" was un-

acceptable. By 1975 Brzezinski emerged as Carter's principal adviser on foreign policy issues.

National Security Adviser

Brzezinski was openly eager to be appointed assistant to the president for national security affairs and delighted when President-elect Carter offered him the position in December 1976. He had not wanted to be secretary of state, confident that he would be more effective in the White House, at the president's side. From the outset he was uneasy about the president's idealism and the absence of other appointees likely to give Carter the "realistic and hard-nosed" advice needed in world affairs.

Carter had campaigned against the Ford administration's "Lone Ranger" diplomacy, the unchecked activities of Henry Kissinger. He intended to have a more balanced organization reporting to the president, who would decide policy questions. A triumvirate composed of the secretary of state, the secretary of defense, and the national security adviser, such as had existed in the Kennedy years, seemed ideal. Cyrus Vance, Harold Brown, and Brzezinski would do the job.

Brzezinski agreed with Carter's ideas on organizational structure, but never doubted that his presence in the White House and his daily briefing of the president gave him the upper hand. He moved quickly to assert himself, and neither Vance nor Brown was equal to the challenge. What balance existed—and it was considerable—was provided, as it had to be, by Carter.

Brzezinski's differences with Vance were often substantive as well, especially on policy toward what was then the Soviet Union. Although Vance had few illusions about the Soviet leadership, he believed that improvement of Soviet-American relations was both necessary and possible. Further arms limitation agreements and cooperation in crisis areas such as the Middle East were essential to avoid nuclear war. He was not willing to jeopardize progress toward a sounder Soviet-American detente by disregarding Soviet interests in the Middle East or fears of Chinese-American rapprochement. Brzezinski shared Vance's conception of the Soviet Union and the United States as permanent competitors, but perceived little hope for significant improvement in the relationship. The United States had to be firm, seek every advantage it could garner at Soviet expense, and play on Soviet fears by "playing the China card." Although Carter initially leaned toward Vance's view, by the end of 1978 Brzezinski appeared to have prevailed. The handling of the decision to normalize relations with China marked the ascendency of Brzezinski and the increasing alienation of the secretary of state from the policies of the administration.

Another arena in which Brzezinski succeeded in establishing his primacy was in the public presentation of Carter administration policy. Initially, all concerned had agreed that other than the president, the secretary of state would be the sole spokesman on foreign policy. Brzezinski quickly concluded, however, that Vance was not adequate to the task and took it upon himself. The result, given the policy differences that emerged between Vance and Brzezinski, was increased public confusion about America's course and a decline in confidence in the president's ability to keep his team running in tandem.

Hostage Crisis in Iran

Although disagreement over the handling of the hostage crisis in Iran finally drove Vance from the administration, Brzezinski had been unhappy with the original course Vance had plotted and Carter had approved during the last days of the Shah's rule. Brzezinski was a sincere advocate of a foreign policy that stressed concern for human rights, but when he perceived a need to choose between enhancing human rights or projecting American power, power came first. As the Shah's regime disintegrated in late 1978, Brzezinski wanted the United States to urge the Shah to act aggressively, to use force against his opponents, to carry out a military coup. Carter refused, sharing the distaste within the administration, generally for the repressive means the Shah had already undertaken. After the Shah's abdication, the return of Khomeini, and the seizure of the American hostages, a desperate president accepted a rescue plan that Brzezinski supported and Vance opposed. Vance resigned. The plan failed.

Brzezinski saw Iran as Carter's "only" fatal error. Probably more than any other single issue, the prolongation of the hostage crisis cost Carter the election of 1980 (to Ronald Reagan) and resulted in Brzezinski's return to private life in 1981. Of the accomplishments of the Carter administration, Brzezinski was proudest of its success in the Middle East (the

Camp David accords), the normalization of relations with the People's Republic of China, the Panama Canal treaties, SALT II, the commitment to majority rule in Africa, the identification of American policy with the human rights issue, and the plan to strengthen the military and strategic position of the United States by building the MX missile.

Adviser, Author, and Observer

Brzezinski remained a prominent personage during the Reagan administration. During this time he conceived and advocated a form of detente which he called "Mutual Strategic Security." This proposal involved both space-based Strategically Deployed Interballistic missiles (SDI) and ground-based systems to be maintained by the United States. The United States, in turn, would limit its nuclear arsenal to a level well below "first-strike" capability. His conservative politics were notoriously in sync with right-wing Republican views, with regard to virtually every aspect of foreign affairs. His highly academic approach to foreign policy led some to see him as immature and insecure. In his various writings he occasionally criticized other politicians for petty idiosyncrasies.

After leaving government service, Brzezinski, still a young man, wrote a memoir, joined the Center for Strategic and International Studies at Georgetown University, served as a consultant to Dean, Witter, Reynolds, Inc., and waited for another opportunity to exercise power.

Brzezinski was widely interviewed in 1989 with respect to the Solidarity movement which arose in Poland, as well as the imminent dissolution of the Soviet Union. He expressed guarded optimism for the success of the Solidarity movement in his native Poland, and he avowed emphatic support for the demise of Communism. He further advocated some degree of laissez-faire policy by the United States in dealing with Eastern Europe at such a fragile moment in history. He published his thoughts on these matters in a book, *The Grand Failure: The Birth and Death of Communism in the Twentieth Century.* Brzezinski then took a peek into the 21st century, based on a retrospective of the past 100 years, in his provocative publication, *Out of Control: Global Turmoil on the Eve of the Twenty-first Century.*

Throughout his career Brzezinski has utilized his aggressive perseverance to foster his policies, keeping him in the forefront as a respected political advisor and critic. He has established himself as a deep thinker, as well as a philosopher through his many writings. His published opinions range from cold war politics to human rights to genetic engineering. His ideas are at once pessimistic and moralistic, especially with respect to the culture of the United States. In a 1993 interview he stated that the "self-indulgent, hedonistic, consumption-oriented society cannot project a moral imperative onto the world . . . Our moral consciousness has been corrupted by . . . the equal indifference we assign to all values as if they were competing products on the supermarket shelf."

Further Reading

The most useful source of biographical material is his memoir, *Power and Principle: Memoirs of the National Security Adviser, 1977-1981* (1983). See also Cyrus Vance, *Hard Choices: Critical Years in America's Foreign Policy* (1983) and Jimmy Carter, *Keeping Faith-Memoirs of a President* (1982).

Additional Sources

Washington Monthly, October 1987.
Maclean's, August 18, 1989.
People Weekly, November 27, 1989.
Time, December 18, 1989.
New Perspectives Quarterly, Summer 1993.
USA Today Magazine, November 1993.
Insight on the News, August 21, 1995.
The Economist, March 11, 1989; March 12, 1994.
Brzezinski, Zbigniew, *The Grand Failure: The Birth and Death of Communism in the Twentieth Century,* Scribner, 1989.
Brzezinski, Zbigniew, *Out of Control: Global Turmoil on the Eve of the Twenty-first Century,* Scribner, 1993. □

Martin Buber

The Jewish theologian and philosopher Martin Buber (1878-1965) was one of the most creative and influential religious thinkers of the 20th century. His book "I and Thou" has had a wide impact on people of all faiths.

The life and thought of Martin Buber are intimately related to the problems and the fate of modern Judaism. He experienced as a young man the spiritual estrangement and confusion which have often been the lot of modern Jews; as a Jewish scholar and teacher in Germany during the 1930s, the increasingly ruthless suppression of Jews by the Nazis; and as a Zionist, the building of the nation of Israel during and after World War II. Yet precisely in and through his reverent exploration of the Jewish tradition and his concrete identification with his people's destiny, Buber was a truly universal man whose life and insights belong to everyone.

Martin Buber was born on Feb. 8, 1878, in Vienna. When he was 3 his parents were divorced, and he was raised by his paternal grandparents in what is now Lvov in the Ukraine. The natural piety and learning of both his grandparents were an important influence on Buber, although he gave up Jewish religious practices shortly after he celebrated his bar mitzvah (at age 13).

From 1896 to 1904 Buber studied philosophy, religion, and art history at the universities of Vienna, Berlin, Leipzig, and Zurich, receiving a doctorate from Vienna in 1904. His dissertation was on mysticism, which attracted him both intellectually and personally. He was also influenced by existentialism through the writings of Kierkegaard, Nietzsche, and Dostoevsky.

Although religiously estranged from Judaism, Buber as a student became a member of the Zionist movement, which sought a center and sanctuary for the world's Jews in the ancient Palestinian homeland. In 1901 Buber edited the

Zionist journal *Die Welt,* but he soon found himself out of sympathy with the purely political program of the majority, aligning himself instead with a smaller group who believed that Zionism must be built upon a Jewish cultural and spiritual renaissance. He retired from active participation for a number of years but returned to the movement in 1916 by founding and editing the very influential journal *Der Jude.*

Relevance of Hasidism

Buber's explorations into Hasidism, the result of his resolve to become better acquainted with the Jewish tradition, led him into the spiritual dimension of Judaism and thereby into his mature philosophy. The Hasidic movement (*hasid* means pious) revitalized eastern European Jewry in the 18th century, although by Buber's time it had become isolated and fossilzed. Original Hasidism was a deeply joyous, world-affirming mysticism which sought God in a "hallowing of the everyday" and in human community. Buber believed this to be the essence of Judaism and of religion itself. Buber believed that the peculiar genius of Hasidic piety was the encounter with the divine in the midst of everyday life with its neighbor-to-neighbor responsibilities and joys. This insight, reinforced by existentialism's intense focus on concrete human life and ethical decision, provided the basis for Buber's "philosophy of dialogue," in which the presence of the divine Thou is encountered within, and for the sake of, the concrete relationships "between man and man."

Buber became an eminent authority on Hasidism, preserving its treasures by translating its literature and interpreting its spiritual genius to the contemporary Western world. Among his translations of Hasidic classics and studies of Hasidism are *For the Sake of Heaven* (1945), *Hasidism* (1948), *Tales of the Hasidim: The Early Masters* (1947) and *The Later Masters* (1948), *The Way of Man according to the Teachings of Hasidism* (1950), *The Legend of the Baal-Shem* (1955), and *Hasidism and Modern Man* (1958).

"I and Thou"

Buber contributed importantly to 20th-century philosophy by offering a creative alternative to the impasse between science-dominated philosophies which reduce human reality to mechanistic terms and idealistic philosophies which abstract the human spirit from its embeddedness in the world and human community. In *I and Thou* (1922) he analyzes man's two types of relationship to reality, I-It and I-Thou. In the I-It relation, I deal with the world and other persons functionally, manipulatively, as "things" to be investigated and used. This is an inescapable and necessary relation to reality which is not evil in itself but becomes evil insofar as it constantly tends to dominate and shut out another, more profound relation, the I-Thou. In the I-Thou relation, I encounter the world, other persons, and God as Thou in interpersonal dialogue which opens up the true depths of reality and summons to ethical responsibility in the midst of life. Among Buber's philosophical writings, besides *I and Thou,* mention should be made of *Between Man and Man* (1947) and *Eclipse of God* (1952).

Career as a Teacher

In 1923 Buber became the first appointee to the chair of Jewish religious thought at the University of Frankfurt, where he taught for 10 years. During this period he collaborated with his friend, the distinguished Jewish thinker Franz Rosenzweig, on a new translation of the Hebrew Bible into German which was acclaimed a masterpiece. Buber's deep involvement with the biblical literature led to profound studies in biblical interpretation, such as *Moses* (1946) and *The Prophetic Faith* (1949).

In 1933 Buber was made director of the Central Office for Jewish Adult Education in Germany, carrying out a "spiritual war against Nazism" until forced to leave in 1938. He went to Palestine to become professor of social philosophy at the Hebrew University, where he taught until his retirement in 1951. Buber worked tirelessly until the end of his life for the new nation of Israel and was widely respected for his integrity and moral passion. Ranging over a wide variety of modern issues, such as education and politics, Buber's writings focus especially on the state of Israel, as in *Israel and the World* (1948). Buber also dialogued sensitively with Christians and deeply admired Jesus. His book *Two Types of Faith* (1951) compares Judaism and Christianity. Honored by people all over the world, he died on June 13, 1965.

Further Reading

Full-length studies of Buber's life and thought in English include Maurice S. Friedman, *Martin Buber: The Life of Dialogue* (1955); Malcolm L. Diamond, *Martin Buber: Jewish Existen-*

tialist (1960); Maurice Friedman and Paul Arthur Schilpp, eds., *The Philosophy of Martin Buber* (1967); Ronald G. Smith, *Martin Buber* (1967); and Lowell D. Streiker, *The Promise of Buber: Desultory Philippics and Irenic Affirmations* (1969). Aubrey Hodes, *Martin Buber: An Intimate Portrait* (1971), is a personal study by a close friend.

Additional Sources

Friedman, Maurice S., *Encounter on the narrow ridge: a life of Martin Buber,* New York: Paragon House, 1991.

Friedman, Maurice S., *Martin Buber's life and work,* Detroit: Wayne State University Press, 1988.

Friedman, Maurice S., *Martin Buber's life and work: the early years, 1878-1923,* New York: Dutton, 1981.

Friedman, Maurice S., *Martin Buber's life and work: the later years, 1945-1965,* New York: Dutton, 1983.

Friedman, Maurice S., *Martin Buber's life and work: the middle years, 1923-1945,* New York: Dutton, 1983.

The other Martin Buber: recollections of his contemporaries, Athens, Ohio: Ohio University Press, 1988. □

James Buchanan

James Buchanan (1791-1868) was the fifteenth president of the United States. His administration was dominated by fighting between pro-and antislavery forces. In 1860, at the close of his term in office, South Carolina became the first state to secede from the Union.

James Buchanan was born on April 23, 1791, on a farm in Lancaster, Pa., the son of a Scotch-Irish immigrant. After graduating from Dickinson College in 1809, Buchanan became a lawyer. As a Federalist, he was elected to the Pennsylvania Assembly in 1814 and to the U.S. House of Representatives in 1820. He was an early supporter of Andrew Jackson's presidential aspirations and became a leading member of the new Democratic party in Pennsylvania. Buchanan was elected to the U.S. Senate in 1834, serving there until 1845. As a senator, he supported Southern demands that all abolitionist petitions to the Senate be immediately tabled without consideration.

Presidential Contender

At the 1844 Democratic convention, Buchanan was one of the leading contenders for the presidential nomination but lost out to James K. Polk. When Polk won the presidency and formed his Cabinet, Buchanan was named secretary of state. In this position he played a key role in Polk's expansionist policies. He successfully negotiated a treaty with England over the Oregon Territory, thus avoiding a possible war. At the beginning of the administration, he often acted as a moderating influence on the President, but later Buchanan became a leading imperialist. He urged rejection of the Treaty of Guadalupe Hidalgo (1848) in favor of annexation of large areas of Mexico. He also tried to secure the purchase of Cuba from Spain for $120 million.

At the 1848 and 1852 Democratic conventions, Buchanan was a leading contender for the presidential nomination but was again passed over. In 1853, he was appointed ambassador to England by President Franklin Pierce. While on this mission, in order to win Southern support for his nomination in 1856 he helped draft the Ostend Manifesto, which called for United States acquisition of Cuba, by force of arms if necessary. Returning to the United States in 1856, he received the Democratic nomination for president, and won the election.

A Crisis President

Buchanan sought to restore unity within his party and within the country by appointing Democrats from all geographical sections to the Cabinet. He was doomed to failure. A week after he was inaugurated, the Supreme Court handed down the Dred Scott decision, which upheld the Southern position that Congress had no right to legislate on the question of slavery in the territories. The decision alienated a great many Northerners.

Another stumbling block of Buchanan's administration was the constitution submitted by the territory of Kansas to Congress. A proslavery convention had drawn up the Lecompton Constitution. Governor Robert Walker warned that unless the whole document was submitted for a vote, Congress would reject it. In defiance of the threat, only one section of the constitution was submitted. Buchanan put great pressure on Congress to accept it and to admit Kansas as a state but ran into opposition from Stephen A. Douglas, his party's most powerful senator. Douglas argued that the document was fraudulent and violated the provisions of the Kansas-Nebraska Act, which had provided for popular sovereignty. This dispute split the Northern and Southern wings of the Democratic party.

Buchanan's handling of the Kansas problem was complicated by several other difficulties. Shortly after he had taken office, the country went into a depression. Adhering to a strict states'-rights doctrine, Buchanan cut the budget and urged stricter regulation of banks but refused to commit the Federal government to relief measures. He also had difficulty with the Mormons, who had settled in the Utah Territory. As a consequence of Brigham Young's refusal to accept a governor appointed in Washington, the President sent 2,500 troops to bring Utah under Federal control. After the Mormons fled Salt Lake City and threatened a scorched-earth policy, Buchanan reached a compromise with Young that granted the Mormons a high degree of autonomy.

The administration also failed to achieve its diplomatic goals, which were to repudiate the Clayton-Bulwer Treaty and to establish American control over Central American and Cuba. In his last year and a half of the presidency, Buchanan faced a hostile Republican majority in Congress and had no hopes of securing ratification of a treaty on either subject, even had one been negotiated.

By the time of the Democratic convention in April 1860, the administration had been completely repudiated. The Democratic party broke into two factions—the North supporting Douglas for president and the South supporting Vice President John C. Breckinridge of Kentucky.

When Lincoln won in November 1860, Buchanan faced his final crisis—the secession of South Carolina. Unable to secure support in Congress and unable to overcome his own scruples against the use of force to restore the Union, Buchanan found his administration paralyzed. This paralysis was compounded by Lincoln's refusal to agree to any policy before actually becoming president. Buchanan did support efforts to conciliate the two sides, especially the Crittenden Compromise and the Peace Conference called by Virginia in 1861, but when these failed, so did the Union. Many Northerners blamed him for the dissolution of the Union and the ensuing Civil War. Thus, as the new president took office, Buchanan left Washington, a bitter and tired old man. He returned to Lancaster, where he died on June 1, 1868, at the age of 77.

Further Reading

The best biography of Buchanan is Philip Shriver Klein, *President James Buchanan* (1962), a well-researched work sympathetic to the subject. For the problems of the Buchanan administration see Allan Nevins, *The Emergence of Lincoln* (2 vols., 1950). For a summation of Buchanan's work as secretary of state see the chapter on Buchanan by St. George L. Sioussat in Samuel Flagg Bemis, ed., *The American Secretaries of State and Their Diplomacy,* vol. 5 (1928). □

Patrick Joseph Buchanan

Commentator, journalist, and presidential candidate Patrick Joseph Buchanan (born 1938) represented the hard-line conservative wing of the Republican Party.

Patrick Buchanan was born in Washington, D.C., on November 2, 1938. His father, William Baldwin Buchanan, was a partner in a Washington, D.C., accounting firm. His mother, Catherine Elizabeth (Crum) Buchanan, was a nurse, an active mother, and a homemaker.

Buchanan traced his father's family as coming from Scotland and Ireland and settling in the southern region of America in the late 1700s. He related how some of his ancestors fought for the Confederacy, while another family branch lived in the North. His mother's side of the family were of German immigrant heritage and had settled in the Midwest.

Buchanan grew up in an energetic household. He was the third of nine children. He had six brothers and two sisters. He learned his combatative personality from his father. The elder Buchanan encouraged good manners, debates, sibling rivalries, and fisticuffs.

As did all his siblings, he attended a local Catholic elementary school. He went on to Jesuit-run Gonzaga High

School, following in the steps of his father and brothers. Deciding to stay in Washington and to continue at a Catholic school, he enrolled in Georgetown University in 1956 on a scholarship. While there, Buchanan majored in English, lived at home, and had an active social life. He joined intramural boxing and tore the cartilage in his knee during a fight. The damage was later to keep him out of military service.

In his senior year he received a traffic violation. Believing that his ticket was wrongfully given, he verbally and physically assaulted the police. He was arrested, fined, and had a minor police record. The incident had a marked effect on his life. The university suspended him for a year. During that period he learned accounting and took a serious look at his future. He decided on a career in journalism and returned to complete his undergraduate education with a more mature attitude. He graduated with a Bachelor of Arts degree, with honors, in 1961.

Buchanan entered the journalism school at Columbia University with a fellowship. He enjoyed writing, but disliked studying the technical side of newspaper publishing. He earned his Master of Science degree in 1962.

The future media personality began his career as a reporter with the *St. Louis Globe-Democrat.* He quickly became an editorial writer for this conservative Midwest newspaper. He was appointed the paper's assistant editorial editor in 1964. Thinking it would be years before he could become an editor, and wanting some challenges in his life, he thought about a new career direction.

In 1966 he arranged a meeting with Richard Nixon, whom he impressed with his conservative outlook and aggressive political style. Nixon hired him as an assistant. At that time the former vice-president (1953-1961) was a partner in a New York City law firm, was involved in Republican Party activities, and was anticipating a run for the 1968 presidential nomination. Buchanan assisted Nixon on his speeches, newspaper articles, study tours, and campaign.

Following Nixon's 1968 election, Buchanan joined the new presidential administration as a special assistant. He wrote speeches for Nixon and for Vice President Spiro Agnew. He helped plan strategies for the 1972 reelection campaign. During this time he met Shelly Ann Scarney, who was a receptionist at the White House. They married in 1971.

In 1973 Buchanan was appointed a special consultant to President Nixon. He devoted his attention to the Watergate crisis, which revolved around political sabotage in the 1972 presidential campaign. He testified before the Senate Watergate Committee later that year. Although he was not accused of any wrongdoing by the committee members, Buchanan denied suggesting or using any illegal or unethical tactics.

After Nixon's resignation from office in August 1974, Buchanan stayed on for several months as an adviser to President Gerald Ford. Buchanan then left the White House and became a syndicated columnist and lecturer. He later worked as a radio and television commentator on political and social issues. With his style and viewpoints, he became nationally known as a spokesman for a right-wing conservative philosophy.

He returned to the White House in 1985 as director of communications at the start of President Ronald Reagan's second term. His sister, Angela Marie Buchanan-Jackson, had served as treasurer of the United States in Reagan's first term. Buchanan took a major loss of income in his switch back to public service. He stayed only two years, then went back to broadcasting, writing, and lecturing.

In 1992 Buchanan declared his candidacy for the Republican Party presidential nomination. His campaign against President George Bush, who sought reelection, was designed to position himself as an "outsider" and to promote a strong conservative program. He ran with an "American First" theme, arguing that the country should limit its obligations abroad in the post-Cold War decade.

Buchanan attracted attention from a public facing an economic recession, lay-offs of workers, depressed real estate values, increased taxes, and general frustration with government. He spoke against abortion on demand, homosexual rights, women in combat, pornography, racial quotas, free trade, and an activist U.S. Supreme Court. He spoke for aid to religious schools, prayer in public schools, and curbs on illegal immigrants. Buchanan called his political beliefs "street corner" conservatism, which he learned at the dinner table, soaked up in parochial schools, and picked up on the street corners of his youth.

In the early 1992 New Hampshire primary he won 37 percent of the votes. That was his highest percentage of support. The figure dropped in each succeeding primary. In some primaries where Republican voters could vote uncommitted, "uncommitted" finished ahead of Buchanan. He found it difficult to maintain a campaign organization and to raise funds, but he pressed on through the spring and summer.

Buchanan vied for the White House a second time in 1995, basing his campaign on conservatism. However, he lost once again. Buchanan also founded and directs The American Cause, an educational foundation that emphasizes his political beliefs.

Further Reading

Buchanan has written a lively autobiography, *Right from the Beginning* (1988), which describes the life and times of growing up in Washington, D.C., and attending Catholic schools in the mid-to-late 20th century. His conservative call to arms is colorfully written in his book *Conservative Votes, Liberal Victories: Why the Right Has Failed* (1975). The 1992 election campaign can be reviewed in the 1992 *Congressional Quarterly* weekly reports. Many facts about Buchanan can be obtained from his Web site entitled "The Buchanan Brigade" available at http://www.buchanan.org. □

Pearl Sydenstricker Buck

Pearl Sydenstricker Buck (1892-1973), an American Nobel Prize-winning novelist, dedicated her books

and her personal activities to the improvement of relations between Americans and Asians.

Pearl Sydenstricker was born in Hillsboro, West Virginia, on June 26, 1892. Her parents were Presbyterian missionaries, on furlough at the time of her birth from their activities in Chinkiang, China, although they soon returned there. During the anti-foreign Boxer Rebellion of 1900, the family was forced to flee to Shanghai where, from 1907 to 1909, Buck attended boarding school. She moved to the United States the following year to enter Randolph-Macon Woman's College in Virginia. After receiving a bachelor's degree in 1914, she took a teaching assistantship at the college but almost immediately returned to Chinkiang to care for her ailing mother.

In 1917 she married John Lossing Buck, an American agricultural specialist, with whom she settled in northern China. From 1921 until 1934 they lived chiefly in Nanking, where her husband taught agricultural theory. Buck occasionally taught English literature at several universities in the city, although most of her time was spent caring for her mentally disabled daughter and her infirm parents. In 1925 Buck returned to the United States to pursue graduate studies at Cornell University, where she received a master's degree in English in 1926. Back in Nanking the following year, she barely escaped a revolutionary army attack on the city. Meanwhile, because of her family's financial difficulties, she resolved to begin writing.

Novels Reflect Love of China

Buck's first novel, *East Wind: West Wind* (1930), a study of the conflict between the old China and the new, was followed by *The Good Earth* (1931), a profoundly affecting novel of Chinese peasant life, which won her a Pulitzer Prize. In 1933 Buck received a second master's degree, this time from Yale University, and in 1934 she took up permanent residence in the United States. In 1935 she divorced John Buck and married Richard J. Walsh, her publisher. Her extensive literary output—*Sons* (1932), *The First Wife and Other Stories* (1933), *The Mother* (1934), *A House Divided* (1935), and biographies of her father and mother, *The Exile* (1936) and *Fighting Angel* (1936) respectively—culminated in a 1938 Nobel Prize for literature, the first ever awarded to a woman.

Humanitarian Efforts Occupy Later Life

In the next three decades, while continuing to write prolifically, Buck worked to promote racial tolerance and ease the plight of disadvantaged Asians, particularly children. In 1941 she founded the East and West Association to promote greater understanding among the world's peoples, and in 1949 she established Welcome House, an adoption agency for Asian-American children. She always had a special interest in children, and among her many books for them are *The Water-Buffalo Children* (1943), *The Man Who Changed China: The Story of Sun Yat Sen* (1953), *The Beech Tree* (1955), *Christmas Miniature* (1957), and *The Christmas Ghost* (1960). A steadfast supporter of multiracial families, in 1964 she organized the Pearl S. Buck Foundation, which supports Asian-American children and their mothers living abroad.

Although Buck's literary career embraced a variety of genres, almost all of her stories are set in China: the extremely popular novel *Dragon Seed,* its less popular sequel, *The Promise* (1943), and a raft of later novels, including *Peony* (1948), *Letter from Peking* (1957), and *The New Year* (1968). Among her other works, the highly acclaimed *The Living Reed* (1963) details the history of a Korean family during the late 19th and early 20th century. In the late 1940s Buck also authored a trilogy under the pseudonym John Sedges. The novels were later published as *American Triptych* (1958).

Lauded for Generous Spirit

Buck's play *A Desert Incident* was produced in New York City in 1959. Her ability as an essayist is exemplified by *American Argument* (with Eslanda Goode Robeson, 1949) and *Friend to Friend* (1958), "a candid exchange" with Philippine president Carlos P. Rómulo. Buck died of lung cancer in 1973, with more than one hundred written works to her credit. But even more significant, perhaps, were the over three hundred awards she received for her humanitarian efforts on behalf of improved race relations worldwide.

Further Reading

There has been very little critical attention given to Mrs. Buck's work. Her autobiography is *My Several Worlds* (1954). The best biographical sources are Cornelia Spencer, *The Exile's Daughter: A Biography of Pearl S. Buck* (1944), Paul A. Doyle, *Pearl S. Buck* (1965), and Nora Stirling, *Pearl Buck: A Woman in Conflict* (1983). □

1st Duke of Buckingham

The English courtier and military leader George Villiers, 1st Duke of Buckingham (1592-1628), greatly influenced kings James I and Charles I. His power was such that he virtually controlled the British government from 1618 to 1628.

George Villiers was born in 1592, the son of Sir George Villiers of Brooksby, Leicestershire. After the death of his father when the boy was 13, his mother had him learn the essential arts of the courtier—fencing and dancing-and sent him to France. Villiers returned to London in 1614, was introduced to King James I, and became cupbearer, a low member of the royal household. His rise to importance at court he owed to his good looks and bright personality and to the King's powerful, and probably homosexual, attraction to him.

In a short time Villiers became the dominant influence on the King. He gained the titles of Viscount Villiers and Baron Waddon in 1616 and Earl of Buckingham in 1617. In 1618 he was made Marquess of Buckingham and 5 years later Duke. His chief office during this period was lord high admiral, but his influence ranged over a wide area of foreign and domestic policy. His vast pride prevented him from sharing authority with wiser and more experienced officials. He possessed no capacity for self-criticism and sought to turn each new fiasco aright with another equally ill-conceived scheme.

Buckingham's rise to power coincided with James's decision to seek an alliance with Spain through the marriage of Prince Charles to the Spanish Infanta. In this way James hoped to obtain Spanish support for his Protestant son-in-law, Frederick, the Elector Palatine, against the Catholic Holy Roman Emperor. Buckingham vacillated between advocating direct military aid to Frederick and supporting the Spanish alliance. In 1623 he accompanied the prince to Madrid. But when the Spaniards insisted that Prince Charles convert to Catholicism and that James repeal the English anti-Catholic laws, the marriage negotiations ended. After returning to England, Buckingham and Charles steered the aged king toward a pro-French alliance and active military campaigns against the German Catholics and the Spaniards.

The Parliament of 1624 saw Buckingham at the height of his popularity, as the nation favored the new foreign policy. He took advantage of his power to procure the condemnation of Middlesex, the lord treasurer, the most able of the King's advisers, of whom Buckingham was jealous. James sought vainly to save his valued treasurer, finally exclaiming to Buckingham: "By God, Steenie, you are a fool and will shortly repent this folly and will find that in this fit of popularity you are making a rod with which you will be scourged yourself."

Buckingham soon squandered his popularity. His military campaigns were poorly financed and precipitous. He was unable to obtain parliamentary subsidies for them because he insisted on personal control over all details. A Continental campaign led by Lord Mansfeld was stranded in 1625; a naval attack on Cadiz accomplished nothing and returned in 1626. Sir John Eliot, formerly one of Buckingham's chief supporters in the Commons, turned against the duke after the Cadiz fiasco. Eliot's demands for a complete accounting by Buckingham in the Parliament of 1626 led to an attempt to impeach the duke, but Charles, now king, protected his favorite by dissolving Parliament.

During 1626 and 1627 the Crown took high-handed measures to obtain funds without calling Parliament, and the proceeds were wasted by Buckingham in an expedition to aid French Protestants on the Isle of Rhé. In the wake of this new disaster, in 1628 Parliament drafted a Petition of Right, by which it hoped to place some restraints on monarchical power. To avoid another attack on his favorite, Charles assented. The Commons voted substantial subsidies for the King, and once again Buckingham planned to sail for France. While at Plymouth preparing for embarkation, on Nov. 27, 1628, Buckingham was stabbed to death by a sailor, John Felton, one of the survivors of the Cadiz campaign.

Further Reading

Buckingham has been the subject of many biographies. Among the better portraits are M. A. Gibbs, *Buckingham* (1935); Charles Richard Cammell, *The Great Duke of Buckingham* (1939); and Philippe Erlanger, *George Villiers, Duke of Buckingham* (1951; trans. 1953). Nowhere does Buckingham come to life more than in David Harris Willson, *James VI and I* (1956). For a competent and lucid account of Buckingham's influence during the early years of Charles I's reign see G. M. Trevelyan, *England under the Stuarts* (1904; 21st ed. 1961).

Additional Sources

Lockyer, Roger, *Buckingham, the life and political career of George Villiers, first Duke of Buckingham, 1592-1628,* London; New York: Longman, 1981. □

2d Duke of Buckingham

The English statesman George Villiers, 2d Duke of Buckingham (1628-1687), was influential in Restoration England. An advocate of religious toleration, he was also known as a rake and as the author of lewd poetry and prose.

Elder son of the Duke of Buckingham, Charles I's most powerful subject, George Villiers was born on Jan. 30, 1628. In November his father was assassinated by a Puritan fanatic, and George, his brother Francis, and his sisters became wards of the King. Educated with the royal princes, Buckingham and his brother then attended Trinity College, Cambridge, and George received a master of arts degree in 1642. With the outbreak of civil war in the same year, George (age 15) and Francis (13) left their studies to fight for their guardian. Their youthful valor resulted in the sequestration of their estates by Parliament.

By summer 1643 anxious relatives had prevailed upon the boys to abandon the fighting and to complete their educations abroad. For the next 4 years they came under the influence of the dissolute Ferdinand II, Grand Duke of Tuscany, and George began his long career of debauchery. On his way back to England, Buckingham renewed his friendship with Prince Charles in Paris.

Support of Charles II

Upon the conclusion of the civil war in 1646, Buckingham's lands were restored to him. During the renewed hostilities of 1648, his brother was killed in battle. Buckingham fled to Holland, and his estates were again seized by Parliament. After the execution of Charles I, the young Prince Charles became a king in exile. Charles II gave what recompense he could to his friend and follower—Buckingham was made a knight of the Garter in 1649 and became a member of the Privy Council the next year. He soon proved to have a great deal of influence over the King.

The combination of Buckingham's influence, insolence, and outspokenness alienated many in Charles's entourage. Among those who were less than enchanted with the young duke was Edward Hyde, Earl of Clarendon, the King's chief adviser. Over the older man's objections Buckingham convinced the King to ally himself with the Scottish Presbyterians and, accompanying Charles to Scotland, helped to keep him firm in his alliance.

Charles's projected invasion of England had no chance of success. Buckingham was with the King at the battle of Worcester in 1651 and, with some difficulty, managed to escape overseas, as he had done 3 years earlier. By 1657 Buckingham had tired of his life in Holland and returned to England. Convincing Oliver Cromwell that he was harmless, Buckingham sought to win back his property by wooing and marrying the heiress of the man who held most of his lands—Lord Fairfax, late general of the parliamentary forces. To everyone's surprise the duke's scheme succeeded, and Mary Fairfax broke off an engagement to marry Buckingham.

Cromwell's suspicions of the duke's intentions were soon aroused, and Buckingham was subjected first to house arrest and, then, having broken his oath not to escape, to close imprisonment in the Tower, where he remained until Cromwell's death in 1659. He then joined his father-in-law and Gen. George Monck in the task of suppressing the more radical Puritan forces and clearing the way for Charles's restoration to the throne in 1660.

For the next decade the duke was at the height of his power. He was in favor with Charles, his lands were restored, and he entered government service as lord lieutenant in Yorkshire. Buckingham wanted more than the trappings of favor, however. He sought to exercise power in the state but was, at first, blocked in his attempts by Clarendon. He then devoted much of his energy to bringing about Clarendon's ruin. By 1667 an unsuccessful war against the Dutch, a rising tide of discontent at home, and the unceasing attacks of Buckingham had brought Clarendon's government down and had sent the old statesman into what proved permanent exile. Seemingly, at least, Buckingham was now supreme.

At this time, however, Charles began to direct his own policy; surrounded by five chief ministers (Clifford, Arlington, Buckingham, Ashley, Lauderdale—whose initials spelled Cabal), the King confided fully in none and made use of them all.

Buckingham favored an alliance with France; in this his wishes accorded with those of his sovereign. Buckingham, however, sought only a political and military treaty, while Charles had his Catholic members of the Cabal negotiate a secret agreement with Louis XIV in which he promised to return England to the Catholic faith. Buckingham, unaware of Charles's real intentions, was given the task of overseeing the signing of the public treaty, which ostensibly marked the end of negotiations between the English and the French.

When Buckingham learned of the existence of the secret treaty in 1673, he sought to have Arlington impeached but was himself subjected to scathing attacks in the Commons (where it was thought that he was the papist) and in the Lords (where the vagaries of his private life were under attack). But the resultant confusion served his purpose—the Cabal was destroyed, and England was no longer the ally of France.

During the period of Buckingham's greatest authority his public career had been made more difficult by his private life. His feuds with literate such as John Dryden had led him to compose the brilliant, slashing satire *The Rehearsal*. His changing relationships with the King's several mistresses intruded onto the public scene as well. It was, however, his long-standing affair with the Countess of Shrewsbury that formed the basis for the attack in the Lords in the 1670s. Buckingham had killed his mistress's husband in a duel, had then moved her into his own home, and had sired a son by her. When the infant died, the parents, with incredible effrontery, had the child buried in Westminster Abbey. Buckingham was forced to abjure his mistress and apologize to the Lords for his behavior.

Later Career

Buckingham now retired for a time to private life and contented himself with spending one of the largest fortunes in England. But he soon became active in the Country party (the opposition party to Charles II), which had been founded by Lord Shaftesbury (formerly Lord Ashley, a member of the Cabal). Buckingham's support of religious toleration appears to have been one of his few constant beliefs; he had supported the King's Declarations of Indulgence in the past and now opposed Parliament's narrow religious beliefs.

In 1677 his opposition to the government led Buckingham to be imprisoned in the Tower for a short time. Upon his release he was restored to Charles's personal favor but was not reconciled to the government. Indeed his hostility to Charles's chief minister, Lord Danby, led him to solicit funds from Louis XIV to bring about Danby's downfall. It also led him to join with Shaftesbury in promoting the monstrous accusations of Titus Oates—the "Popish Plot." Quite cynically Buckingham used Oates's preposterous accusations to destroy Danby's government.

But as Shaftesbury's schemes grew wilder and as the idea of excluding James from the succession grew, Buckingham tended to withdraw from active participation in events. He played no role in the events of Shaftesbury's last Parliament but defended the earl when the latter was arrested by Charles's order. This defense was his last public role, for in 1682, his health ruined by his vices, he retired finally into private life. His own words provide his best epitaph: "Fortune filled him too full, and he run over."

Further Reading

The most readable biography of Buckingham is Hester W. Chapman, *Great Villiers: A Study of George Villiers, Second Duke of Buckingham, 1628-1687* (1949). Other biographies include Robert P. Tristram Coffin, *The Dukes of Buckingham: Playboys of the Stuart World* (1931), and John Harold Wilson, *A Rake and His Times: George Villiers, 2nd Duke of Buckingham* (1954). Valuable insights into his life can be found in the works of his contemporaries, such as Pepys, Chesterfield, Clarendon, Rochester, and Burnet.

Additional Sources

National Trust (Great Britain), *Cliveden, Buckinghamshire*, London: The Trust, 1978.

O'Neill, John H., *George Villiers, Second Duke of Buckingham*, Boston: Twayne Publishers, 1984. □

Henry Thomas Buckle

The English historian Henry Thomas Buckle (1821-1862) was a major figure in the positivist movement in historical scholarship. He applied the methods of natural science to history in an effort to discover scientific laws governing the historical process.

Henry Thomas Buckle was born in Lee, Kent, on Nov. 24, 1821. Owing to his delicate health, he did not attend school but educated himself through extensive reading and traveling. Before the age of 20 he had become one of the foremost chess players in England. After his father's death in 1840, he traveled on the Continent, and during this period he resolved to turn his energies to the preparation of a great historical work. He first decided to write a history of the Middle Ages, but by 1851 he had expanded his original plan and had begun work on a history of civilization. He published the first volume of the *History of Civilization in England* in 1857 and the second volume in 1861.

Buckle felt that there was a need to demonstrate that historical development occurs in accordance with universal laws, and perhaps more than any other historian of the 19th century he popularized the belief that scientific laws of history could be formulated. Thus the aim of his work was to discover by inductive inquiry the causal uniformities governing society and its development. Buckle's historiographical method was influenced by John Stuart Mill's empiricism and by Auguste Comte's belief that society should be studied through the application of scientific procedures.

In his *History of Civilization in England* Buckle argued that in order to develop a scientific study of history, it is necessary to take into account not only how man modified the natural world but also how the natural world modified man. In particular, he believed that physical factors (climate and food, among others) are the most important force in determining how a civilization will develop. Thus for Buckle the differences among the world's civilizations are due in large part to the unique physical circumstances in which each culture evolved. He held that the high level to which European civilization had developed was due to a combination of environmental factors that had encouraged full use of man's intellectual capabilities. The key to human progress was, therefore, the development of knowledge.

Buckle's work enjoyed an immediate success, but his failure to assimilate Charles Darwin's and Herbert Spencer's evolutionary theories resulted in a rapid decline in his fame.

While traveling in the Middle East in 1862, he contracted a fever and died in Damascus.

Further Reading

The best book on Buckle is Giles St. Aubyn, *A Victorian Eminence: The Life and Works of Henry Thomas Buckle* (1958), an account of his life and thought against the background of Victorian England. An older but reliable work is Alfred Henry Huth, *The Life and Writings of Henry Thomas Buckle* (1880). □

William F. Buckley Jr.

Author, editor, and political activist, William F. Buckley, Jr. (born 1925) helped to create the modern conservative political movement. His journal, *National Review,* prepared the way for the presidential terms of Ronald Reagan and George Bush.

William F. Buckley, Jr., was born in New York City on November 24, 1925. His father made a fortune in the oil fields of Mexico and gave his ten children personal tutors and exclusive Roman Catholic private schools for their educations. Buckley spent his early years in England and France and inherited his father's self-confidence and strong convictions. As a child of six, for instance, he wrote the king of England demanding that Great Britain pay its World War I debts to the United States.

Buckley served in the U.S. Army from 1944 to 1946, then entered Yale University and graduated with honors in 1950. In 1951 he examined his university education in his first book, *God and Man at Yale.* The 25-year-old Buckley wrote that he entered Yale with a firm belief in Christianity, limited government, and the free enterprise system. But he found Yale's teachers, courses, and textbooks showed little sympathy for Christianity and private property. Instead, they favored secular values and advocated centralized government planning. Buckley urged his fellow Yale alumni to elect university trustees who would reform the university and fire atheist and socialist faculty. Academic freedom, Buckley argued, was a superstition that denied the university's right to promote ideas and values essential to a good education.

Buckley's criticism of higher education was followed by an equally controversial defense of Wisconsin Senator Joseph McCarthy. In *McCarthy and his Enemies* (1954) co-authors Buckley and L. Brent Bozell argued that the senator deserved credit for alerting Americans to the danger of Communist subversion. This achievement, they reasoned, overshadowed McCarthy's rough tactics and excesses.

In 1955 Buckley established the biweekly journal *National Review* to promote conservative ideas and influence national affairs. Conservatives such as Buckley believed American politics was still dominated by liberal New Deal Democrats and by Republicans such as President Dwight Eisenhower who continued their policies. *National Review* published sharp polemical articles and reflective essays challenging conventional political ideas and proposing conservative alternatives.

As editor, the youthful Buckley brought together older established writers from three schools of thought. Libertarian writers such as Max Eastman and free market economists such as Milton Friedman favored individual freedom over social equality and opposed government regulation of the economy. Traditionalist scholars such as Russell Kirk valued religion and classical education and lamented the results of secular thinking and technical education. Anti-communist writers such as Whittaker Chambers urged Americans to guard against the power of the Soviet Union and the ideas of Karl Marx. *National Review* provided a forum for these conservative thinkers and created a popular audience for their ideas.

While *National Review* concentrated its attacks on liberalism, the journal also helped to define modern conservatism by rejecting anti-semitism, the individualist philosophy of the writer Ayn Rand, and the conspiracy theories of the right-wing John Birch Society and its founder, Robert Welch.

In the 1960s conservatism changed from a set of political ideas to an organized political movement. While continuing to edit *National Review,* Buckley turned to political activism. In 1960 he helped found a national student activist group, Young Americans for Freedom (YAF). YAF members were prominent in opposing the 1960s student protest movement against the Vietnam War. In 1961 Buckley and several others formed the New York Conservative Party to challenge the state's liberal Republican governor, Nelson Rockefeller. And in 1965 Buckley was the Conservative Party's candidate for mayor of New York City.

Although he received only 13.4 percent of the vote, Buckley's campaign for mayor undermined the influence of liberal ideas on New York politics. With sharp arguments and a keen wit, Buckley questioned the role of government in solving urban problems. His published an account of the campaign, *The Unmaking of a Mayor* (1966), ridiculed New York City's divided politics of race, religion, and ethnicity and offered innovative approaches to the problems of poverty and welfare dependency.

Buckley's many writings reflected his active engagement with the world of social and political events. He confessed that he had little interest in personal introspection. And he did not write a major study of conservative political philosophy, preferring to focus his debater's skills on current affairs.

In national politics Buckley promoted the presidential candidacies of Barry Goldwater, Richard Nixon, and Ronald Reagan. In 1971, however, he suspended his support of Nixon over the president's domestic policy of wage and price controls and his foreign policy of detente with the Soviet Union and China. He also attacked President Gerald Ford for failing to meet with the Russian dissident writer Alexander Solzhenitsyn. And he angered many fellow conservatives by supporting the Carter administration's Panama Canal treaties. Buckley's controversial reactions to public events were aired on his weekly television interview program *Firing Line,* in his syndicated newspaper columns, *National Review* articles, and in the several volumes collecting his journalistic writings which appeared every few years starting in 1963. His political stances often surprised those who believed they could predict his political outlook. For instance, in 1996 he asserted in *National Review,* along with six other writers, that drugs should be legalized because of the United States' losing battle in the drug war. Buckley also published *Cruising Speed* (1971) and *Overdrive* (1983), amusing event-filled diaries of single weeks in his busy life.

Buckley later moved in new directions. He showed no interest in holding political office even though his friend Ronald Reagan was elected president in 1980. Beginning in the mid-1970s, Buckley began writing a series of bestselling spy novels. Their central character is a dashing CIA agent named Blackford Oakes who uncovers Communist treachery during the Cold War years of the early 1960s. Oakes is a man of intellect and wit determined to resist the leftward movement of modern politics. He is not unlike his creator; Buckley has even stated that the first novel in the series, *Saving the Queen* (1976), is based largely on Buckley's own experiences within the Central Intelligence Agency during his service with their Mexican division from 1951 to 1952. Later novels in the Blackford Oakes series focus on famous Cold War incidents such as the construction of the Berlin Wall and the Cuban Missile Crisis. In these novels, which include *Stained Glass, Who's On First, High Jinx,* and *Mongoose, R.I.P.,* Buckley creates fictional scenarios against these historical backdrops. He dares to let his imagination roam, contemplating different political choices on the part of real-life world leaders such as John F. Kennedy. In *The New York Times* Anatole Broyard wrote, "He says, What if-' and then proposes something that is as attractive as it is preposterous, something so nearly commonsensical that it throws the entire Western world into pandemonium."

Buckley also wrote books about one of his most beloved pastimes, sailing. He published *Airborne: A Sentimental Journey* (1976), *Atlantic High: A Celebration* (1982), and *Racing through Paradise: A Pacific Passage* (1987). These books transcended political barriers, appealing to anyone who shared Buckley's love of yachting.

Buckley was honored with a variety of awards, including an Emmy in 1969 from the National Academy of Television Arts and Sciences for *Firing Line,* Man of the Decade Award in 1970 from the Young Americans for Freedom, and the American Book Award in 1980 for *Stained Glass.* He also received numerous honorary degrees from institutions such as Syracuse University, Notre Dame, and New York Law School.

Further Reading

Buckley's many books and, perhaps more importantly, his many contributions to *National Review* are the best introduction to his life and thought. George Nash's *The Conservative Intellectual Movement in America since 1945* (1976) is a comprehensive summary of conservative ideas and activities before the Reagan presidency. Other good sources are John Jurdis' biography, *William F. Buckley, Jr.: Patron Saint of the Conservatives* (1988) and *The Buckleys: A Family Examined* (1973) by Charles Markmann. □

The Buddha

The Buddha (ca. 560-480 B.C.) was an Indian philosopher, religious teacher, and the historical founder of Buddhism. He is regarded variously as a human spiritual teacher or an omniscient, active deity.

India during the 6th century B.C. was a land of religious and political turmoil. The Northwest was dominated by the Indo-Aryan invaders who had entered India in the 2d millennium, bringing their own religious and social institutions, which were dominated by a great sacrificial cult and hereditary priestly elite, the Brahmins. Their cultural influence was wide-spread even in areas to the east beyond their political authority. But their claims to religious and social superiority were often regarded as pretentious and superficial by the older, indigenous aristocracy.

It was an era of great brutality which undermined traditional religious moorings and, for men of deeper religious sensibilities, called into question the value of all worldly activities and the meaning of life itself. In these circumstances emerged many new religious teachers and schools—all searching for deeper insights into the meaning of existence, the nature of man, and programs of spiritual reconstruction. It was in this environment that young Prince Gautama matured and grew to manhood.

The Buddha ("enlightened one") was born Siddhartha Gautama in northern India near the town of Kapilavastu. His father was ruler of an indigenous Indian tribe, the Shakyas—hence one of the Buddha's traditional epithets, Shakyamuni, or "sage of the Shakyas"—and he was expected to follow in the tradition of a worldly raja.

The traditions relate that his father was disturbed by Gautama's excessive—seemingly morbid—preoccupation with the great spiritual enigmas of life: the problems of suffering, death, and the inequities of human existence. The King tried in vain to insulate him from these harsh realities and built a special palace for him surrounded with distracting luxuries. Gautama married and had a son. But his preoccupation with the great religious questions could not be suppressed, and at the age of 29 he made a decisive move. He formally renounced his worldly commitments, left his family and clan, and embarked on a search for the answers to the massive spiritual questions which perplexed him.

Spiritual Struggles and Enlightenment

Gautama was just one of many wandering ascetics, philosophers, and teachers in India during this period who were searching for religious truth. For many of these teachers the basic religious problem was defined by the theory of transmigration, which, in its most general form, asserts that

the human soul (*atman*) is entrapped in the phenomenal world by an endless cycle of rebirths (*samsara*). After death the soul is reborn in a new physical form depending on the ethical quality of deeds (*karma*) in the preceding life. The ultimate religious goal is to obtain complete salvation or "release" (*moksha*) from bondage to this phenomenal process. For this purpose the spiritual adept practices the yoga—a system of inward, ascetic discipline over body, mind, and motivations designed to cleanse and finally eliminate the debilitating sources of *karma* and transmigration. This basic teaching was presupposed as the dominant religious problem, though there were sharp disagreements over which teacher had most accurately analyzed the situation and evolved the most efficacious yoga.

The traditions relate that for 7 years Gautama experimented with many different teachings, including extreme bodily self-mortification, but found none of them adequate. He set them all aside; and at last in a single night of intensive meditation he achieved a radical breakthrough, an absolutely clear perception of the real spiritual enigmas of life and the unique religious means for dealing with them. This realization culminated in a transcendental mystical experience—his own enlightenment (*bodhi*) —which simultaneously confirmed the integrity of his insight and unqualified spiritual salvation. At this point he became the Buddha.

The Buddha's Teaching

There is an interesting legend which reveals some of the problems inherent in formulating the Buddha's teaching. It is told that at the moment of his enlightenment he was entitled to its immediate rewards—complete salvation and spiritual release from the bonds of existence. This would have meant that the doctrine would never have been made known to other men. And there was the additional problem that the inner spiritual meaning of the teaching and its ultimate mystical consequences could not be adequately communicated in any case, except paradoxically through silence. But after debating these issues, the Buddha decided to preach the doctrine anyway, out of his love and compassion for all men. This legend presents a psychological and historical truth: the formal exposition of the teaching is just the top of the iceberg. Understanding the mystical essence of the teaching and putting it into practice varies greatly, depending on the capacity of its hearers, their needs, and their historical and cultural situation. In a sense, the subsequent history of Buddhism, in all of its immensely varied forms, is proof of this fact.

The earliest tradition represents the Buddha as teaching a yoga which was exoteric—open to all men—and, at least on the surface, simple and eminently practical. It was called the Middle Path, a qualitative mean between the extremes of physical self-indulgence and self-mortification. The teaching is specifically embodied in the Four Noble Truths. The first of these truths lies in the recognition that all existence is fundamentally sorrow and pain (*duhkha*), bound to birth, old age, death, and rebirth and (collectively, *samsara*) and marked by impermanence (*anitya*) without lasting essence (*anatman*). The second truth asserts that this condition is caused by ignorance (*avidya*) of the nature of reality, especially of the Buddha's teachings, and by sensual craving (*trishna*) for worldly existence. This craving in turn is the prime element which at death binds together the heterogeneous components of the individual human being, including the soul itself, and ties it once again inexorably to the causal sequence of phenomenal composition and rebirth. The third truth promises that the elimination of these pernicious factors will finally break the chain of causation and bring about final salvation, *Nirvana* (the "blowing out"), release from the transmigrational process and achievement of a state of mystical transcendence beyond expression. The fourth truth shows that to gain this end, the appropriate yoga is the Eightfold Path, a combination of moral and mental self-discipline which will root out the conceptual and libidinal perversions of the mind that are inimical to salvation.

Despite its apparent simplicity the yoga is described as very demanding, "subtle and hard to understand," since it is only through arduous practice that real insight, the inner meaning of the truths, self-transformation, and final enlightenment can be attained. Consequenlty, in this form of the teaching there is a premium placed on total commitment expressed in the person of the celibate monk who has withdrawn from the world for full-time pursuit of the spiritual goal. A perfected monk is an *arahat,* or "noble one," who has given his whole life to the yoga.

It is important to realize that the teaching is basically optimistic. It places the broken and disrupted forms of the phenomenal world in perspective and teaches that every human being—irrespective of his social position or past life—can through his own exertions obtain therapeutic control of himself, of his preconceptions and passions, and of his destiny. The ethical principles gravitate around concepts of compassion (*karuna*), love (*maitri*), and noninjury (*ahimsa*) to living creatures, and they stress the obligation to promote friendship and concord. They are basically universal standards of behavior with obvious constructive consequences for stabilization of interpersonal relationships and social order.

Mission and Monastic Order

The traditions relate that the Buddha first preached his doctrine (*Dharma*) in Benares, India's great holy city on the Ganges. He began his missionary work soon after with a handful of disciples, offering the teaching to all who would hear and understand. The life and discipline of this little band were at first centered on the spiritual authority of the Buddha himself. But as the number of converts and monastic centers grew, the loosely structured community (*Sangha*) began to take on more formal characteristics. It seems probable that by the time of the Buddha's death, at the age of 80, a number of basic institutional patterns had been set. These included a disciplinary code, later expanded into the full monastic rule (*Vinaya*), and a collection of the Buddha's sayings and discourses (*Sutra*). The major ceremonies included the bimonthly *uposatha,* a confessional assembly of the monks in each monastery to recite the monastic rules.

Despite this appearance of routine orthodoxy, the early *Sangha* was not a centralized church under a bureaucratic hierarchy. In one of his last sermons the Buddha is depicted as rejecting all forms of magisterial authority or patriarchal succession: "Be lamps unto yourselves, O monks." The main purpose of the monastic rule was to guard the independence of each monk in his own spiritual quest. All fully ordained monks had an equal vote on matters affecting the welfare of the community. When internal disagreements could not be resolved, the dissenters simply left and formed a new community. Monks guilty of infractions against the monastic code were expected to confess and discipline themselves. No form of coercion could legitimately be invoked.

Nevertheless, the institutional problems must have been burdensome. The Buddha is occasionally represented as perplexed and disgusted by the contentious and often selfish behavior of the monks. On at least one occasion he took time to wash and care for a sick monk who had been callously neglected by his fellows; and his own cousin, Devadatta, is reputed to have started a schismatic movement to replace him as head of the order. He was equally irritated by abstruse philosophical speculation about topics not specifically relevant to the practice of the yoga, and he likened this kind of distraction to a man, struck by a poisoned arrow, speculating at length about its point of origin and ballistic curve before trying to pull it out.

In keeping with the principle of personal conversion women were admitted to the order; within the monastic community all barriers of caste, race, sex, and previous background were swept under the impact of the universal thrust of the teaching.

The Laity

Although the ascetic ideal and rigors of the yoga tended to limit monastic membership to those who were fulltime practitioners, the power of the Buddha's personality attracted many lay followers—the "householders." The tradition relates that the Buddha said only that it was harder for the laity to attain *Nirvana;* but the bulk of lay piety gravitated toward a merit-making ethic which could at least guarantee a better rebirth.

The Buddhist ethic was significantly oriented to the economic and political needs of urban mercantile and artisan groups. At the outset, lay devotees promised to adhere to the five precepts: no killing, stealing, lying, adultery, or consumption of alcoholic beverages. In a sermon attributed to the Buddha he advises a well-to-do young layman to pursue ethical self-discipline for the sake of "well-being in this world and the next," especially the elimination of economically wasteful vices such as sloth, self-indulgence, and sensuality. The Buddha is also represented as preaching openly against hereditary caste distinctions, which he regarded as social conventions based originally on occupational differences. "A Brahmin is not such by his deeds, an Outcaste is such by his deeds." And, typically, he reserved the words "Aryan" and "true Brahmin" for members of the monastic community.

Buddha's political teachings are basically contractual and were probably drawn from the oligarchical patrimonialism of his own clan. The king has the obligation to care for his people and, especially, to set high moral standards. A man who fails in this is not worthy to rule. No cult of divine kingship is proposed. In the traditions the Buddha is represented as consulting frequently with the monarchs of the great states and petty kingdoms, teaching his doctrine and seeking to ameliorate the conditions of endemic warfare.

Later Developments

One of the most ancient forms of the teaching is in the texts of the Theravada Buddhists, now dominant in Ceylon and the Southeast Asian mainland. But Theravada is the only living remnant of a number of ancient Indian schools. There were schismatic movements both during and after the Buddha's life. One of these gave birth to the forerunners of another great and very different tradition, the Mahayana ("great vehicle"). This tradition stretches from India through China to Japan and appears in an immense variety of schools ranging from abstruse philosophies to popular theism and magic. Though its exponents have often stigmatized the Theravada school as Hinayana ("small vehicle"), it has produced a massively diverse body of literature which defies uniform characterization.

Mahayana is itself closely related to another tradition—the Tantrayana ("esoteric vehicle"), which found one of its central locations in Tibet. Consequently the historical reality of the Buddha's teaching has been vastly complicated and often obscured over the past 2500 years.

Though there were always signs of tension and disagreements over the appropriate interpretation of the Buddha's teaching, it was not until a century after his death that a major schism developed, based on longstanding points of contention, basic elements of which are most prominently developed in Mahayana doctrine. Although Mahayana literature emerged later, beginning in the 1st century B.C., it claims to present the true and restored teaching of the Buddha.

The first point is directed against the conservative ideal of the monk, the *arahat,* who attains enlightenment only after long and solitary practice of the yoga. For the Mahayana teachers this ideal is a self-centered perversion of the spirit of the Buddha's teaching, especially his outgoing love for all men, and instead these teachers developed the notion of the Bodhisattva ("being of enlightement"). This concept originally denoted previous incarnations of the historical Buddha. In Mahayana it signifies one who is essentially worthy of *Nirvana* but, like the Buddha himself, gives up this right in order to teach and assist all sentient creatures with compassion and love. All men, including the laity, are held capable of this great role. Typically, one of the great Mahayana texts speaks of a precocious layman—Vimalakirti—who achieves spiritual perfection far in excess of that of the monks while living a normal householder's life.

The second and related point concerns the concept of *Nirvana.* In his wisdom (*prajha*) the Bodhisattva knows that *Nirvana* cannot be conceived of as a simple goal or reward for spiritual striving in the fashion of the *arahat.* This misconception subtly reinforces the craving (*trishna*) for personal satisfaction and therefore is the antithesis of salvation. *Nirvana* is beyond all spatiotemporal polarities. It is "void" (*shunya*), and its realization is inseparable from the compassionate wisdom which is the distinctive mark of the Bodhisattva.

The third point concerns the status of the Buddha himself. In the Hinayana (Theravada) tradition, he is the human founder of the historical teaching, but in Mahayana he is an omniscient, omnipresent, loving deity. These theistic developments had their roots in lay worship practices which emerged very early in the tradition—perhaps even in the Buddha's own lifetime—as his personal spiritual power promoted the notion that he was a reincarnation of an eternal sacred reality. The bulk of popular Mahayana throughout Asia became centered on the theistic cult. Believers worshiped many transcendent Buddhas and Bodhisattvas who had the power to answer prayers of petition and to magically transfer merit for the welfare of the pious. The new mythologies even included a heavenly paradise—a "Pure Land"—available to the faithful through the active grace of the savior Amitabha (endless light) Buddha.

While certain features of these theistic developments are present in the early Indian traditions, altogether they represent later changes and accretions which seem remote from the earliest teaching. But in another sense they are not untrue to the spirit of the whole. The Buddha is represented, even in the earliest traditions, as tolerant of the necessity of adjusting the teaching to the capacities and background of his adherents. His "skill in means" (*upayakaushalya*) refers to the technique of doctrinal and institutional adjustment out of compassion for diverse human needs and limitations. And this principle was an important factor in facilitating the missionary diffusion of Buddhism throughout Asia.

Buddha's Modern Significance

The immense diversity of Buddhist faith and practice is perhaps its most striking feature. In Tibet the political system was until recently a theocracy, ruled by spiritual leaders, the Dalai and Panchen Lamas who were regarded as supreme Bodhisattvas, worldly incarnations of the Buddha; and Tibetan Tantrism is a rich synthesis of Buddhist and primitive indigenous teachings.

In China and Japan, Zen Buddhism represents a special adaptation of the meditational yoga strongly influenced by Chinese values and regarded as uniquely efficacious by its adherents. In Ceylon and the Indochinese mainland, orthodox Theravada has served as an effective state religion while often richly infused with primitive animism and magic.

In looking for a single point of unity in this extraordinarily complex matrix, it is to be found only in the paradigmatic grandeur of the Buddha himself, who persists in all the traditions as a model of spiritual perfection and transcendent saving power.

Further Reading

Edward J. Thomas, *The Life of Buddha as Legend and History* (1927; 3d ed. 1952), is a scholarly study of the Buddha and of

Buddhist thought. A biography based on an evaluation of the ancient texts, which includes a social analysis of the Buddha's times, is Alfred Foucher, *The Life of the Buddha: According to the Ancient Texts and Monuments of India* (abr. trans. 1963). Two scholarly studies of Buddhist thought are Sukumar Dutt, *Early Buddhist Monachism: 600 B.C.-100 B.C.* (1924), and Edward J. Thomas, *The History of Buddhist Thought* (1933; 2d ed. 1951). See also Beatrice Lane Suzuki, *Mahayana Buddhism* (1938; 2d ed. 1948); Edward Conze, *Buddhism: Its Essence and Development* (1951); and Edward Conze, ed., *Buddhist Texts through the Ages* (1954). □

Buddhadāsa Bhikkhu

Buddhadāsa Bhikkhu (1906-1993), the founder of Wat Suan Mokkhabalārama, outside of Chaiya, Surat Thani Province, southern Thailand, established himself as the most creative and controversial interpreter of Theravāda Buddhism in the modern period.

Born on May 21, 1906, as Nguam Phanich, Buddhadāsa Bhikkhu completed his lower secondary education in Chaiya and went to work at age 15 in his family's business after his father's untimely death. Ordained a Buddhist monk in 1927 at Wat Ubon, he rapidly gained a reputation for his intellectual prowess, interest in meditation, and ability as a preacher. Taking the name Buddhadāsa, Servant of the Buddha, he furthered his studies in Bangkok at Wat Pathum Khongkha, where he distinguished himself in Pāli and Buddhist studies. Returning to Chaiya to lead a more contemplative life, he settled down at a deserted monastery (Thai: *wat;* Pali: *vasa*) outside of town. After ten years, as farmers gradually took over the land around the temple, Buddhadāsa established his meditation and study center in a 150 acre plot of virgin jungle about five kilometers outside of town.

The new center of Suan Mokkhabalārama, or Suan Mokh as it was more generally known, combined aspects of early Buddhist monastic life with modern methods of propagating the Dhamma (the Buddha's teachings). The 50 to 60 monks residing at Suan Mokh at any given time lived in simple wooden structures with few of the amenities characteristic of monks who lived in large urban monasteries. While they observed the traditional precepts of the monastic life, most monks at Suan Mokh spent more time in meditation and study than the typical Thai monk. Moreover, many engaged in appropriate forms of manual labor such as casting bas-reliefs copied from such ancient Indian Buddhist sites as Sañchi and Barhut. These were then shipped to monasteries around the country.

While the setting of Suan Mokh and the life style of the monks residing there seemed close to the ideal associated with the Buddha and his disciples, other structures were quite modern. For example, there was a "Spiritual Theater" equipped to teach the Dhamma with modern audiovisual equipment. The walls were covered with mural paintings not only from the Theravāda Buddhist tradition of Thailand, but also from the Zen Buddhism of China and Japan and from other religious traditions including Christianity. The paintings taught the basic Buddhist precepts, in particular the importance of non-attachment, an attitude which frees one from egoistic preoccupations and the greed and hatred stemming from them.

Buddhadāsa's teachings from the 1950s on were collected and published in nearly 50 substantial volumes. They include his written work, as well as numerous talks and lectures which were recorded and transcribed. The oral nature of Buddhadāsa's thoughts tends to give the material an informal and contextual cast. Very little has been translated into English or other foreign languages, which accounts for the fact that he was not as well known as Buddhist interpreters who write in English. Part of Buddhadāsa's unique genius, however, stemmed from the fact that, with the exception of a pilgrimage to Buddhist sites in India, he lived exclusively in Thailand. He read widely, particularly in the Zen Buddhist tradition which he admired, and had rather extensive contacts with Americans and Europeans, several of whom were monks in residence at Suan Mokh. Many of the Thai monks associated with Suan Mokh were, furthermore, well educated, helping to make Buddhadāsa's monastery an outstanding place for Buddhist practice and study.

Buddhadāsa was controversial for several reasons. In the first place he was quite critical of conventional Thai Buddhism, which he saw as dominated by a desire to use religion for one's own personal, worldly benefit. In the Thai Buddhist context this is called "making merit" (Thai: *tham puñña*). Buddhadāsa found the preoccupation with the externals of religious rituals and ceremonials with the intent of bettering one's self in the world to be a kind of materialism rather than true religious practice. Buddhadāsa was equally critical of a kind of mindless philosophizing which has no transformative effect on one's attitudes and actions. Specifically, he thought that the memorization of endless categories of Abhidhamma philosophy was not only useless, but led one away from genuine religious practice and understanding.

However, Buddhadāsa was more than a critic of Thai Buddhism. His system of thought represented one of the most comprehensive interpretations of Theravāda Buddhism of the modern period, or, as some admirers claimed, ever since Buddhagosha standardized Theravāda doctrine in the 5th century A.D. It was an influence comparable to St.Thomas Aquinas in Roman Catholicism. The originality of his thought stemmed from a profound understanding of such seminal Buddhist concepts as interdependent co-arising (*paticca samuppāda*), impermanence (*aniccā*), not-self (*anattā*), and, of course, Nirvāna. His thought was characterized by the use of language in a way which provoked deep insight into these ideas. For example, he made the ordinary Thai term for "nature" (*dhamma-jāti*) into a means of understanding the difficult but fundamental concept of Theravāda Buddhism, interdependent co-arising (*paticca samuppāda*).

While Buddhadāsa should be seen as a reinterpreter of his own Theravāda tradition, he also studied and was influenced by other religions. At the deepest level, Buddhadāsa saw all religions standing for something quite similar. For example, he argued that terms like God, Tao, and Dharma all point to the same underlying truth which transcends all the ordinary distinctions on which conventional language is built. Hence, the religious journey or path should be toward an understanding of things the way they really are, a universal state of being in which we are able to realize our essential oneness with human beings of all kinds and persuasions as well as with the universe. This is a kind of religious socialism in which our own personal well-being is realized in terms of the good of the whole. It is an ideal, to be sure, but one which Buddhadāsa hoped would inspire people to work for the peace and harmony of the entire human community.

Buddhadāsa Bhikkhu suffered from heart attacks and strokes as he grew older, but his ardent desire to teach helped to keep him alive. He finally succumbed to a stroke just before his birthday celebration in 1993. Shortly before he died, he enhanced the Suan Mokkh center by establishing the International Dhamma Hermitage to foster principles of Buddhism among visitors to Thailand. The Hermitage provides instructional curricula for foreign students and meeting facilities for religious leaders from all nations. A final project which he conceived, and which was undertaken by his followers after his death, was the establishment of the small Dawn Kiam monastery (Suan Atammayatārāmā). Dawn Kiam is a missionary training facility for monks from other lands.

Further Reading

Unfortunately, at the present time only a small portion of the extensive writings by Buddhadāsa have been translated from Thai into English. The most extensive collection has been translated under the title *Toward the Truth,* translated and edited by Donald K. Swearer (1971). Some of his shorter essays have been translated and published in English in Thailand but are not generally available in the West—e.g., *Christianity and Buddhism,* translated by B. Siamwala and Hajji Prayoon Vadanyakul (Bangkok, 1967). A major portion of Buddhadāsa's lectures on Christianity and Buddhism has been reprinted as a chapter in Donald K. Swearer, *Dialogue. The Key to Understanding Other Religions* (1980). Buddhadāsa has figured into some scholarly work on Theravāda Buddhism—e.g., Donald K. Swearer, "Bhikkhu Buddhadāsa on Ethics and Society," in *Journal of Religious Ethics* (July 1, 1979)—and has been the subject of several doctoral dissertations in German, French, and English—e.g., Patarporn Sirikanchana, *The Concept of Dhamma in the Writings of Vajirañāna and Buddhadāsa* (1985). □

Guillaume Budé

The French Renaissance humanist Guillaume Budé (1467-1540) is best known for his influence on the revival of Greek studies in France through his scholarly works and success in persuading the King to establish the Collège de France.

Guillaume Budé was born in Paris on Jan. 26, 1467. His university education at Orléans and Paris centered on the study of law and the "liberal studies," especially Greek. He was basically a lawyer turned humanist. His interest in the classics was demonstrated by his translation of three of Plutarch's treatises into Latin (1502-1505). Budé's abilities brought him to the attention of King Louis XII, who sent him to Rome as his ambassador at the coronation of Pope Julius II in 1502. After this mission Budé became secretary to the King, a position he held until 1515.

During this period Budé produced two works that displayed his superb scholarly abilities and his interest in law and classical antiquity. His work on Roman law, *Annotationes in XXIV Pandectarum libros* (1508; *Notes on Twenty-four books of the Pandects*), was a milestone in the Renaissance humanist attack on medieval jurisprudence. Budé's aim was to eliminate corruptions and misreadings from the medieval versions of Roman law. His second work of this period was *De asse et partibus* (1515; *On the As and Its Parts*), a treatise on ancient coins and measures, in which he attempted to determine their exact values in antiquity and their modern equivalents. This work required an exhausting and critical examination of the ancient authors, and it earned Budé the reputation of being among the foremost scholars of his day.

In 1515 Budé was again sent to Rome, this time on a diplomatic mission to Pope Leo X. Under the new king, Francis I, Budé was eventually made master of the royal library. In this position he urged the King to establish a college for the study of Greek, Latin, and Hebrew. Since

Francis I did not immediately respond, Budé gave supplementary encouragement in additional literary works. In the preface to his *Commentarii linguae Graecae* (1529; *Commentaries on the Greek Language*), which he intended as a Greek lexicon, he criticized Francis publicly for not beginning the endeavor. The King finally responded in 1530 by establishing the Collège Royal, later known as the Collège de France. The foundation of this institution was an important step in the revival of classical studies in France.

Budé's position as royal librarian also enabled him to establish the royal library at Fontainebleau, which, when later moved to Paris, became the Bibliothèque Nationale. His later years were clouded with the unfounded accusation that he was inclined to Calvinism. He died in Paris on Aug. 22, 1540.

Further Reading

The standard works on Budé are in French. For his role in French humanistic education see William H. Woodward, *Studies in Education during the Age of the Renaissance, 1400-1600* (1906; repr. 1966). For background material Paul O. Kristeller, *Renaissance Thought: The Classic, Scholastic, and Humanistic Strains* (1955; rev. ed. 1961), is recommended.

Additional Sources

McNeil, David O., *Guillaume Budé and humanism in the reign of Francis I,* Genéve: Droz, 1975. □

Frederick Buechner

The American novelist Frederick Buechner (born 1926) was also a Presbyterian minister and theologian whose novels and essays after his conversion explored the grace and healing which "now and then" surprisingly and even comically penetrate the everyday darkness of human estrangement.

Carl Frederick Buechner was born on July 11, 1926, in New York City, the older of two sons of Carl Frederick and Katherine Kuhn Buechner. Although both of Buechner's parents' families were wealthly and connected with the upper-class, his immediate family was never more than modestly well situated. His father, a Princeton graduate and minor executive who moved from job to job and place to place on the East Coast during the Depression years, committed suicide by carbon monoxide poisoning when Buechner was ten. The event had a lasting impact on Frederick, who with his brother James saw the body on the driveway as their mother and grandmother tried frantically to revive their father. Relationships between parents and children are important in all of Buechner's novels, and the father-son relationship of which he was early deprived dominates several of them.

Buechner graduated from Lawrenceville School in New Jersey in 1943 and entered Princeton the same year. He interrupted his studies to serve with the U.S. Army from 1944 to 1946, returning to Princeton in 1946 and completing the A.B. degree in 1948. Buechner taught English at Lawrenceville School from 1948 to 1953, during which time he also wrote his first two novels: *A Long Day's Dying* (1950), begun while he was still at Princeton; and *The Seasons' Difference* (1952). Most of the small groups of main characters in his first novels occupy a typically modern-affluent spiritual and moral vacuum, deeply isolated from one another beneath their genteel pleasantries and polite deceptions.

Upon its publication *A Long Day's Dying* was both a critical and a popular success. Some literary critics of the 1950s included Buechner among the most promising of the new generation of American writers, sometimes extravagantly comparing him to Henry James, Marcel Proust, and Elizabeth Bowen and pairing him with Truman Capote among his contemporaries.

After his initial success Buechner lived in New York City from 1953 to 1955, trying for awhile unsuccessfully to work as a full-time writer. Having had an almost completely secular upbringing, Buechner had long experienced a kind of spiritual emptiness and restlessness. While living in New York he started attending regularly the Madison Avenue Presbyterian Church, whose pastor was the celebrated preacher George Buttrick. During one of Buttrick's sermons Buechner had a conversion experience. The following week he talked with Buttrick about attending seminary and entered Union Theological Seminary in New York in the fall of 1954. Among his distinguished teachers, he was particu-

larly influenced by Paul Tillich, Reinhold Niebuhr, and James Muilenberg.

Buechner decided to take the 1955-1956 academic year off to work on another novel. During that period his *New Yorker* short story "The Tiger" won the O. Henry Prize (1955), and he courted and married Judith Friedrike Merck. Buechner returned to Union Seminary and graduated in 1958. His third novel, *The Return of Ansel Gibbs,* a story about a former statesman called out of retirement to be nominated for a Cabinet post, appeared in 1958 and received the Rosenthal award that year. In *Ansel Gibbs* and succeeding novels, Buechner's intense preoccupation in his earlier fiction with the hidden and labyrinthine complexities, the coincidences, and the might-have-beens of human behavior and relationships became increasingly enlarged and embraced within a wondering and finally comic vision of the elusive strangeness of both the self and the world.

Ordained to the ministry of the United Presbyterian Church in the United States, Buechner was invited to develop a department of religion at Phillips Exeter Academy. He chaired the department from 1959 to 1960 and served as school minister and teacher of religion from 1960 to 1967. The Buechners' three daughters—Katherine, Dinah, and Sharman—were all born during the Exeter years.

In 1965 Buechner's fourth novel, *The Final Beast,* appeared. It is about a young minister and widower in a small New England town and the woman the local newspaper editor tries to link together with him in a scandal. During this period Buechner also published his first theological work, a collection of school sermons entitled *The Magnificent Defeat* (1966).

After 1967 Buechner and his family lived in rural Vermont, and he devoted himself entirely to writing. In 1969 he published a second book of sermons, *The Hungering Dark.* That same year he was the William Belden Noble Lecturer at Harvard. His lectures were published in 1970 as *The Alphabet of Grace,* a kind of theological autobiography which examined a day in his life. All of Buechner's theological works are short, highly literary productions in most of which he draws explicit links with fiction writing generally and his own fiction in particular. He also published his fifth novel, *The Entrance to Porlock* in 1970, a retelling of *The Wizard of Oz.* The other Oz books played a large role in forming Buechner's early imagination. For example, his father, his uncle, and his grandfather set out for the same place but on very different personal quests during Buechner's childhood.

In 1971 Buechner published *Lion Country,* the first of what was to become a tetralogy of novels whose main character is a remarkable Southern evangelist named Leo Bebb. *Lion Country* was nominated for the National Book Award, and the succeeding novels in the tetralogy followed rapidly: *Open Heart* (1972), *Love Feast* (1974), and *Treasure Hunt* (1977). It is in the Bebb novels that Buechner comes the closest to a fully balanced artistic portrayal of that inseparable mix of the ridiculous and the sublime, the absurd and the gracious, the accidental and the providential, which he sees as the human condition in the light of Christianity. In an interview in *The Christian Century,* he said that with the Bebb series he was able to find his true voice, "And the other great loosening up of my life, besides writing in my own voice, was to allow myself to be funny. That was for other times, not for literary work. But with the Bebb books, I had such tremendous fun. I still remember the pure joy of writing those books."

During the 1970s and 1980s Buechner continued to write theological books. *Wishful Thinking: A Theological ABC* and *The Faces of Jesus,* a book of pictures with text by Buechner, both appeared in 1974. In 1977 he was the Lyman Beecher Lecturer at Yale, and his lectures were published the same year as *Telling the Truth: The Gospel as Tragedy, Comedy, and Fairy Tale.* In 1979 Buechner published *Peculiar Treasures: A Biblical Who's Who,* with illustrations by his daughter Katherine. *Godric,* a historical novel about the 11th century English hermit-saint who may have been England's first lyric poet, appeared in 1980. In 1982 Buechner published the first volume of an autobiography, *The Sacred Journey;* the second volume, *Now and Then,* followed in 1983. Later, he continued his autobiographical work with *Telling Secrets* (1991) and *The Longing For Home* (1996). Each of these books delved into aspects of Buechner's life in an honest way. *The Sacred Journey* dealt with his relationship with his father, who committed suicide. Writing in *The Christian Century,* Buechner commented on the book, "Much of the insight of the book came out of therapy, and as I told some of these things I was moved to the very foundation of my being." Similarly, he wrote about his mother after her death, in *Telling Secrets.* Of his autobiographical forays, Buechner said, "My work became spiritual autobiography because that was the only part of my life I was interested in talking about. I also had a sense of my life as a plot, not just incident following incident, as in a newspaper. It was trying to take me somewhere."

Other works during the 1980s and 1990s consisted of several novels, including *Brendan* (1987), *Wizard's Tide* (1990), and *The Son of Laughter* (1996). The latter met with mixed reviews, some feeling that his retelling of the Biblical story of Jacob was a bit thin. On the whole, however, Buechner's fiction was lauded by critics. In *America,* Alan Davis wrote that *Wizard's Tide,* " . . . is not merely inspirational, which suggests an unacceptable sentimentality, but is part of a dialogue with the mythic unknown that fiction at its best always pursues."

Buechner's mature religious vision was characterized by what has been called the "higher naivete" because his lifelong love of fantasy was allowed free play in his fiction and his artist's sense of reality revealed in the narrative and metaphorical character of the biblical literature. Theologically, his writings after his conversion came more and more to sound the theme that beneath the dark and ambivalent appearances, human life and the cosmos are actors in a divine comedy; that at the heart of reality is a wild, ineffable joy, that faith in its self-transcendence is very close to humor, and our fumbling efforts at living lives of faith are repeatedly startled by the comic incongruities of the "crazy, holy grace" which against all expectation wells up to sustain, challenge, and renew human life.

Further Reading

The most complete biographical information about Frederick Buechner is to be found in his four volumes of autobiography, *The Sacred Journey* (1982), *Now and Then* (1983), *Telling Secrets* (1991), and *The Longing For Home.* The only published book-length study of Buechner's writings is Marie-Helene Davies, *Laughter in a Genevan Gown: The Works of Frederick Buechner 1970-1980* (1983). A brief introduction to Buechner's life and writings is James Woelfel, "Frederick Buechner: The Novelist as Theologian," in *Theology Today* (1983). An excellent interview with Buechner can be found in *The Christian Century,* October 14, 1992. □

Jesse Buel

The American agriculturalist and journalist Jesse Buel (1778-1839) pioneered in the effort to make farming more scientific and more productive. The new agricultural methods he developed were disseminated to other farmers through his journal.

Jesse Buel was born on Jan. 4, 1778, in Coventry, Conn., the youngest of the 14 children of farming parents. When Jesse was 12 years old, the family moved to Rutland, Vt., where he was apprenticed to a printer 2 years later. He worked as a journeyman printer on newspapers in New York City and upstate New York, and in 1797 he began publishing his own newspapers.

Buel's newspaper career lasted until 1821; he published papers in Lansingburgh, Troy, Poughkeepsie, Kingston, and Albany. During his residence in Albany he was the printer for the state. By the age of 43 Buel had acquired a reputation as an editor and built up a sizable fortune in personal property and real estate. He then turned to the work which constituted his major achievement: the improvement of agriculture.

Like Thomas Jefferson, Buel believed that the nation's well-being ultimately depended upon agriculture, which he called "the great wheel which moves all the machinery of society." He also felt that American farming was wasteful, too often merely exhausting the soil of successive farms, much in the manner of the southern cotton planters' ruthless exploitation of successive fertile areas. To improve American agriculture, Buel created an experimental farm on an 85-acre tract just west of Albany. He utilized scientific farming methods, including deep plowing, drainage, the use of manure and the plowingunder of green crops for fertilizers, and crop rotation. The farm became extremely productive and soon gained fame as the "Albany Nursery."

Once Buel had demonstrated the validity of his farming methods, he set out to disseminate the principles of the new husbandry. He became secretary of the state board of agriculture, campaigned for the creation of a state agricultural school, and was instrumental in the founding of the state Agricultural Society in 1832, becoming its first recording secretary. In 1834 Buel began publishing the *Cultivator,* which soon became the most popular farm journal in the United States. In 1839 he published the *Farmer's Companion,* a book which embodied the results of his work on farming and went through 11 editions.

Buel served in the New York Assembly in the 1820s and ran unsuccessfully as a Whig for the governorship of the state. He used his political career, like his publishing talents, in the service of improved agriculture.

Further Reading

The best source on the life and thought of Buel is Harry J. Carman, ed., *Jesse Buel, Agricultural Reformer* (1947), which contains selections from his voluminous writings. William Edward Ogilvie includes a biographical sketch in *Pioneer Agricultural Journalists* (1927). See also Percy Wells Bidwell and John I. Falconer, *History of Agriculture in the Northern United States, 1620-1860* (1925). □

Buffalo Bill

The controversial, half-fictitious career of William Frederick Buffalo Bill' Cody (1846-1917), American scout and publicist, helped create the prototype "Wild West" hero.

William Cody, born in Scott County, Iowa, and raised on a farm, served briefly in the Civil War. Hunting buffalo for construction crews of the Kansas Pacific Railroad, he was dubbed "Buffalo Bill" because of his proficiency. He also served as civilian scout for U.S. generals Sheridan and Carr. Though he went east to begin a stage career in 1873, he returned west in 1876 to avenge Gen. Custer's defeat. Claiming to have killed Chief Tall Bull, he later brought the Wild West indoors and toured widely with his Wild West Show. Clever publicists, like Ned Buntline, Prentiss Ingraham, and John Burke, billed him as "Prince of the Plains" and made him the hero of countless stories and novels.

Often in trouble and always in debt, Buffalo Bill toured Europe to recoup his fortunes. He became the darling of Queen Victoria's Jubilee in England and went on to France, Spain, and Italy, spreading the legend of the American West, depicting the wild yet romantic life which Europeans liked to think of as uniquely American, and paving the way for the 20th-century cowboy movie. The name Buffalo Bill was magic; in Victorian days he personified the American dream.

But triumph turned to ashes. Tired of sham hero worship, Buffalo Bill drank heavily and involved himself in many foolish liaisons. Women doted on him, but his wife wanted a divorce. Sick children sought his touch, but his only son died in his arms. Manipulated by shrewd men, he had to perform his Wild West act daily to avoid bankruptcy. Finally, disillusioned, he petitioned the Federal government for the $10 monthly Congressional Medal-holders' dole. All his dreams had become nightmares.

In 1910 Sam Goldberg released a slide series showing Buffalo Bill in action, and Harry Powers made the first moving picture of the Wild West Show, "300 thrills in 300 reels." But Bill himself was not able to utilize the new mass-media opportunities. Instead, the old man watched William S. Hart, Harry Carey, and Tom Mix fill the heroic void. When he died he was buried in Cody, Wyo.; since citizens of Denver plotted to steal the body, tons of concrete were poured over it. Thus the man whose life revolved in frantic motion had found his resting place.

Buffalo Bill epitomized a whole phase of the American western movement and the final winning of the Great West. His reputation had been contrived and half-fictitious, but to his own code and image he remained faithful.

Further Reading

The best contemporary accounts of Buffalo Bill are Henry L. Williams, "*Buffalo Bill*" (1887), and Helen Cody Wetmore, *Last of the Great Scouts* (1899). The only thorough and scholarly biography is Richard J. Walsh, *The Making of Buffalo Bill: A Study in Heroics* (1928). Dan Muller, *My Life with Buffalo Bill* (1948), is a convincing apologia, while James Monaghan, *The Great Rascal* (1952), concentrates on the feet of clay. For the Cody literature see Albert Johannsen, *The House of Beadle and Adams and Its Dime and Nickel Novels: The Story of a Vanished Literature* (1950). □

Warren Buffett

Warren Buffett (born 1930) is America's most brilliant investor, compiling a year-after-year record of phenomenal returns for the shareholders of his holding company, Berkshire Hathaway, Inc.

For example, if someone had given him $10,000 to invest in 1956 he or she would be worth over $60 million by 1994. Buffett is one of the richest men in America, and he is a success story in the classic mold. As of 1995 Buffett, with a personal fortune of some $12 billion in Berkshire stock, was the second-wealthiest individual in America, right after his friend, Microsoft chairman Bill Gates.

Throughout it all Buffett has retained a seeming simplicity that goes along with his down-home, Midwestern roots. His associates, however, say his hayseed manner disguises a brilliant sophisticate. He shuns New York and Los Angeles, preferring to run his far-flung empire from modest offices in Omaha, Nebraska. The periodic insights into his success that he dispenses are usually witty and simple. However, each time Buffett—known in the financial world as the "Oracle of Omaha"—speaks, just about everyone, from the most accomplished professional prognosticator to the stock-playing hobbyist, pays attention.

Born in 1930 in Omaha, Nebraska, Buffett always "wanted to be very, very rich," as a *Time* article put it. The boy received an early, close-up look at the stock market: his father Howard was a broker, and young Warren, just nine years old, often visited the shop and charted stock performances. He chalked in stock prices on the big blackboard at his father's office, and at age 13 ran paper routes and published his own horse-racing tip sheet.

In 1942 Buffett's father was elected to the U.S. House of Representatives and the family moved to Fredricksburg, Virginia. Young Warren Buffett expanded his business interests by placing pinball machines in Washington, D.C. barbershops. At age 16, a prodigy in statistics and mathematics, he enrolled at the University of Pennsylvania. He stayed two years, moved to the University of Nebraska to finish up his degree, and emerged from college at age 20 with $9,800 in cash from his childhood businesses. Harvard Business School rejected him, but Columbia University's Graduate School of Business accepted his application.

Finds Niche

Columbia was a key turning point in Buffett's life, for it was there that he met Benjamin Graham, co-author with David Dodd of the landmark textbook *Security Analysis*. "I don't want to sound like a religious fanatic or anything, but it really did get me," Buffett was quoted as saying in the *New York Times Magazine* about Graham's writings.

Graham's philosophy has permeated most of Buffett's decision in the 40-plus years since they first met. Essentially,

Graham's theory, called value investing, urges stock pickers to buy shares that are much cheaper than a company's net worth would indicate. That is, look for stocks that sell below their "intrinsic value," a measurement Graham calculated by subtracting a company's liabilities from its assets. Eventually, Graham theorized, the stock market will catch on to the true value of a company and its share price will rise; by that time, a savvy investor following Graham's principles already will be locked into the stock at a low price. It's a simple enough theory, but one that requires much research into companies to determine their net worth, their "book value," and other factors. It is research for which Buffett is eminently suited.

After graduate school, at his father's brokerage firm, Buffett would often travel to Lincoln, Nebraska and pore through company reports. As he told *Forbes* magazine, "I read from page to page. I didn't read brokers' reports or anything. I just looked at raw data. And I would get all excited about these things." Today, he conducts his business the same way. Buffett does not have a stock ticker in his office, nor a computer or calculator. According to numerous published reports, he spends about five to six hours each day reading annual reports and trade publications. *Fortune* magazine reported that in Omaha, Buffett "does what he pleases, leading an unhurried, unhassled, largely unscheduled life. . . . He spends hours at a stretch in his office, reading, talking on the phone, and, in the December to March period, agonizing over his annual report, whose fame is one of the profound satisfactions in his life."

Buffett left Omaha and joined Graham's investment firm on Wall Street in 1954. There he was able to view his mentor's work first-hand. Over the next two years, Buffett got married, fathered two children, and made $140,000 by the time he was 25. Graham shut down his investment firm in 1956 and Buffett gladly left New York. When he returned to Omaha family members asked him for advice, so Buffett set up an investment partnership. As he told the *New York Times Magazine,* he said to his investors, "I'll run it like I run my own money, and I'll take part of the losses and part of the profits. And I won't tell you what I'm doing."

While he might have kept investors in the dark about his methods, Buffet's bottom-line returns were crystal clear: over the next 13 years Buffett Partnership Ltd. generated a 29.5 percent compounded annual return. He raised $105,000 from investors to start the partnership, and when he closed it 13 years later, the partnership was worth $105 million, and Buffett worth $25 million.

One of the investments along the way was Berkshire Hathaway, a textile manufacturer in Massachusetts. Buffett would create his multibillion-dollar empire around that business, although the textile company itself remains—in Buffett's opinion—one of the biggest investment mistakes he made. Sure, Berkshire Hathaway's stock price was cheap, satisfying a requirement of the Graham strategy. But the textile industry as a whole, and the company itself, was weak. In one of his much-anticipated annual reports, quoted in *Fortune* magazine, Buffett summed up part of his philosophy in the wake of that mistaken textile purchase: "It's far better to buy a wonderful company at a fair price than a fair company at a wonderful price." (He would shut down the textile mill in the mid-1980s.)

Buffett ended the lucrative partnership in 1969. As the *New York Times Magazine* reported, "The partnership's capital had grown so large that small investments were no longer reasonable, and he could find no big investments to his liking. In addition, the market was too speculative for his taste." He then focused on Berkshire Hathaway, buying up companies under its umbrella, investing "where and when he pleased," according to the *Times*.

Buffett's holdings, and his strategies, from the late 1960s on are clear. He first bought a series of insurance companies, which are considered excellent sources of cash. (People regularly pay insurance premiums; insurance companies usually pay claims on those insurance policies—if they have to pay them at all—years down the line. Therefore, there is usually a great amount of cash on hand for the company owners.) Buffett used that cash to buy a series of businesses, which have remained at the core of his investments.

His so-called "Sainted Seven Plus One" are sizeable, profitable companies that, according to the *Wall Street Journal,* "provide a steady stream of profits and capital to fund the investments that bring him renown." Among the eight core businesses are: the *Buffalo News,* World Books, Kirby vacuum cleaners, Fechheimer Brothers uniform company, and See's Candies. According to *Money* magazine, those businesses alone generated $173 million in cash in 1990, and the *New York Times* estimated in 1991 that their combined worth was approximately $1.6 billion. The cash generated by the eight companies is, in turn, invested in other corporations, which comprise the other core chunk of Berkshire Hathaway's holdings.

All of the companies in which Buffett invested are businesses he understands, underlining one of Buffett's main rules: "Stick to what you know." *Forbes* once quoted him as explaining why he had not invested in the immensely profitable computer company, Microsoft: "Bill Gates is a good friend, and I think he may be the smartest guy I ever met. But I don't know what those little things do."

Instead Buffett bought into what the *New York Times Magazine* called his "permanent holdings": The *Washington Post,* Geico (an insurance company), Capital Cities/ABC, and Coca Cola. He bought $45 million of Geico stock, which by 1989, according to the *New York Times,* was worth $1.4 billion. His $10.6 million investment in the *Washington Post* group of publications ballooned to an investment worth $486 million 16 years later. When he purchased seven percent of Coca Cola for $1 billion in 1988, some said he had bought too high, too late. But Buffett predicted Coke's expansion into foreign markets and thought the company could grow. It did, more than doubling his investment.

Investments in the big, brand-name companies is an example of how Buffett's buying strategy has evolved from the teachings of his mentor, Graham. Buffett became interested in what he called "franchise" businesses, or companies that are well-managed, with an established product line, and which are not subject to low-cost competition. His strategy changed because the market changed. The companies that Graham liked—companies trading far below their actual value—are rarer.

White Knight

Also in the 1980s, Buffett engaged in a series of transactions that are available only to someone with enormous wealth. He stepped in as a so-called "white knight" to help companies fend off hostile takeovers by other corporations. Buffett's strategy works like this: a company, such as Gillette, faces a takeover and needs an infusion of cash. Buffett invests in the company's "preferred stock." According to the *Wall Street Journal,* the preferred stock options are "not available to other investors. Typically [Buffett] gets preferred stock bearing a healthy dividend—assuring a modest return no matter what happens—and the ability to convert to common stock if the company's fortunes rise." In the case of Gillette, Buffett invested $600 million in 1989, and in converting the stock two years later, received 11 percent of the company, which was worth, at the time, $1.05 billion.

In 1991 Buffett stepped in as interim chairman of Solomon Brothers brokerage firm after that it was accused of making false bids at Treasury auctions. Buffett, who had invested $700 million of Berkshire Hathaway cash in Solomon Brothers, was its largest shareholder. He is credited with streamlining the company and, over his six-month tenure as interim chairman, helping to rebuild its reputation after the scandal.

But the shareholders are not complaining. Berkshire Hathaway stock was trading for $12 a share in 1965. As of December, 1994, a single share of the investment company was the most expensive traded on the New York Stock Exchange: it cost $19,900 a share. Buffett owns over 40 percent of Berkshire Hathaway, which accounts for his $8.3 billion net worth. (Incidentally, Buffett does his own taxes.) And in August 1995, Buffett brokered a spectacular deal when his Berkshire Hathaway arranged the $19 billion purchase of Cap Cities/ABC by the Walt Disney Company. While the brokerage already had a $345 million in investments, this one merger raised the value to $2.3 billion.

Those not fortunate enough to own Berkshire Hathaway often mimic Buffett's buys. *Fortune* reported that when the general public learns Buffett has bought a particular stock, the public also buys the stock, running up the price. That led the magazine to quip: "Now there are two ways to make a killing in the stock market. The first, goes the old saw, is to shoot your broker. The second, it seems, is to shadow Warren Buffett."

The strategy doesn't always work, as a 1995 *Money* article warned. "Awe-inspiring though Buffett's record is, he's had a few clunkers. The $322 million investment he made last spring in Salomon common stock is down roughly 26%, and an albeit tiny (for him) $38.7 million stake in [an aircraft leasing company] has plummeted 68% since 1990." Prior to that, Buffett had bought Disney low and sold it later for a small profit; but that company rose spectacularly after Buffett's sale. He bought a $358-million chunk of USAir only to see the investment sour. (He was later quoted in *Fortune* as telling a group of business students at Columbia, "Don't invest in airlines.") In his 1989 annual report, quoted in *Fortune,* Buffett candidly wrote, "It's no sin to miss a great opportunity outside one's area of competence. But I have passed on a couple of really big purchases that were served up to me on a platter and that I was fully capable of understanding. For Berkshire's shareholders, myself included, the cost of this thumb-sucking has been huge."

Aside from his business acumen and opinions, many people are interested in Buffett himself, asking: What's a billionaire like? He does not give frequent interviews, preferring to let his corporate report speak for him. He lives in the same Omaha home he bought in 1958 for $31,500. He lives in that home with his girlfriend and former housekeeper, Astrid Menks, 17 years his junior. His wife of 40-plus years lives in California and is friends with his girlfriend. (Mrs. Buffett is the second largest shareholder of Berkshire Hathaway and is slated to take over the company after Buffett's death.)

One of his few extravagances is his corporate jet, and playing bridge by computer with friends from around the country. According to the *Wall Street Journal,* he wears rumpled suits, although very expensive Italian ones, and drinks about five cherry Cokes a day. He says he is an agnostic. As Roger Lowenstein related in his unauthorized biography *Buffett: The Making of an American Capitalist,* the investor once promised his young daughter a $10,000 check if he didn't lose a certain number of pounds by a certain date. He lost the weight, and kept the cash.

"He is a standard bearer for long-term investing, the perfect antidote to the get-rich-quick schemers of *Wall Street,*" the *Wall Street Journal* said of Buffett. *Forbes* opined that "He has not the psychological need for the constant wheeling and dealing, buying and selling that afflicts so many successful business and financial people." His philosophy—as well as his enormous wealth—allows him to be pickier and choosier. As he stated in his 1989 annual report, "We do not wish to join with managers who lack admirable qualities, no matter how attractive the prospects of their business. We've never succeeded in making a good deal with a bad person."

Which leads to the obvious question he is often asked: How do you succeed in the stock market? Throughout the years Buffett has offered bits of advice, such as: 1) If you buy into a great business, stick with it no matter how high the stock price goes; 2) avoid staggering debt; 3) think long term and don't hop in and out of the market; 4) in a bidding war between companies, buy stock in the side you think will lose; 5) easy does it (meaning, avoid businesses with big problems), and 6) concentrate on a small number of stocks.

Buffett has already made preparations for his money when he dies. He intends to set up a philanthropic foundation which, given the 23 percent annual rate of return he has averaged throughout his career, could generate a multibillion-dollar legacy to put the Ford and Rockefeller foundations to shame. He wants the fund's trustees to focus on halting population growth and nuclear proliferation. His three children will not make out that well; Buffett has said he plans to leave them "only" about $5 million apiece. He was quoted in *Esquire* as saying, "I think kids should have enough money to be able to do what they want to do, to learn what they want to do, but not enough money to do nothing."

Further Reading

Lowenstein, Roger, *Buffett: The Making of an American Capitalist* (unauthorized biography), Random House, 1995.

Business Week, May 10, 1993, p. 30; July 18, 1994, p. 46.

Economist, May 23, 1992, p. 86.

Esquire, October 1988, p. 103.

Forbes, March 19, 1990, p. 92; October 18, 1993, p. 40, p. 112.

Fortune, April 11, 1988, p. 26; April 9, 1990, p. 95; January 11, 1993, p. 101; November 29, 1993, p. 10; April 18, 1994, p. 14; July 25, 1994, p. 17.

Money, November 1990, p. 72; August 1991, p. 70; April 1995, p. 106.

New York Times, March 26, 1992, p. D1.

New York Times Magazine, April 1, 1990, part 2, p. 16.

Time, August 21, 1995.

U.S. News & World Report, June 20, 1994, p. 58.

Wall Street Journal, November 8, 1991, p. A1. □

Comte de Buffon

The French naturalist Georges Louis Leclerc, Comte de Buffon (1707-1788), wrote the major general work on natural history of the 18th century and made the Royal Garden in Paris a center for scientific research.

On Sept. 7, 1707, Georges Louis Leclerc was born in Montbard, the son of a magistrate in the local sovereign court of justice (*parlement*). While information regarding Buffon's early career is scant, it is probable that he graduated from the Jesuit college in Dijon and later received a diploma from the Faculty of Law located in Dijon. He was preparing for his father's calling, a career in the law being the expected activity of one of Buffon's particular noble background; but the law never interested him.

Intellectual Apprenticeship

Buffon's first work in the sciences gave little indication of the future naturalist. Evidently having early set as his goal a career in mathematics, he made a close study of various problems in mechanics and paid particular attention to Isaac Newton's new system of the world. Newtonian physics and cosmology were at this time finally displacing the Cartesian system as the focus of French interest in the physical sciences.

During the late 1730s and 1740s Buffon performed notable experiments on the strength of wood and on other aspects of the preparation of forest products. These studies were related to the exploitation of his lands. He read reports to the Academy of Sciences in Paris on various scientific matters and also an occasional mathematical note. It was

soon clear, however, that Buffon was not destined to become a mathematician; his talents lay elsewhere. He entered the Academy of Sciences, the center of Parisian scientific activity, in 1733. In 1739 he was appointed director of the Royal Garden (Jardin du Roi; later the Jardin des Plantes). During the years of Buffon's command the Royal Garden stood supreme in France in the study of botany, zoology, chemistry, and mineralogy.

Buffon married Marie Françoise de Saint-Belin Malain in 1752. They had one son, who conducted himself and his financial affairs in such a scandalous manner that he was executed in 1794. With him the direct succession of the family ends.

"Natural History"

The principal product of Buffon's scientific and literary labors was a work of vast magnitude (44 volumes) and exceptional influence. The first volumes of the *Histoire naturelle, générale et particulière* appeared in 1749; the set was completed posthumously in 1804. Not being a field naturalist or a skilled anatomist, Buffon sought an interpretation of nature and clearly felt that, for this purpose, exhaustive enumeration of animal characteristics was of secondary importance. The great value of the *Natural History* resides in the anatomical descriptions contributed not by Buffon but by his assistants, above all, the classical studies of mammalian anatomy presented by Louis Daubenton.

Catalog of Nature

Buffon distinguished civil history from natural history. "Natural history," he then announced, "is the source of the other physical sciences and mother of all the arts." This was a call to catalog nature, but a catalog singularly unlike, in form and intention, the compendiums traditionally cast by botanists and zoologists, for Buffon was genuinely uninterested in problems of plant and animal classification. It is customary to contrast the *Natural History* with the publications of the Swedish botanist Carl Linnaeus. Linnaeus sought above all a practicable manner of distributing the bewildering diversity of plants and animals into classificatory units (genera, species) which were sharply defined and comprehensible to all.

Linnaeus's *System of Nature* (1735 and later editions) was thus a remarkable elaboration on traditional practice in natural history. Buffon, however, would have none of this kind of classification. He was impressed by the individuality of nature's productions and even more struck by the fecundity of the productive process itself. He evinced no desire in, and saw no possibility of, forcing nature and its product—the varying host of animals spread over the earth's surface—into the rigid classificatory categories of conventional natural history. In truth, he adopted a general pattern of classification (Mammals, Birds, Reptiles), but that pattern was wholly conventional.

Organic Molecule and Evolution

"Epochs of Nature" (1779) most fully expounds Buffon's cosmological schema and best reveals his speculative genius. Thousands of years ago, Buffon claimed, a passing comet sheared great masses from a molten sun. These masses scattered in space, congealed, and became planets (including the earth) revolving about the sun. At a later date life appeared on earth. The production of life required one of Buffon's most disputed explanatory concepts—organic molecules, minute centers of attractive force and heat which constituted indestructible building blocks for all living organisms. He claimed that the molecules were marshaled to form the various kinds of plants and animals by a totally obscure agent, the internal mold (*moule intérièure*), and that there was a determinate number of such molds, each related to an individual or species.

Many efforts have been made to represent Buffon as an evolutionist. The complementary ideas of organic molecule and formative molds do not serve this purpose. More germane is Buffon's notorious conception of the *dégénération* of animals. The principal instance of degeneration was the purported smaller stature and weaker constitution of American animals compared with those of the Old World. He claimed the transforming agents to be climate, nurture, and domestication. But his evidence was, at best, questionable, and the proffered agencies of change no less uncertain. While degeneration was thus a limited idea, it had the great merit of turning attention to the possibility of such changes and, even more so, to the interest and importance of the geographical distribution of animals.

All of these questions impinged upon religious matters. While Buffon evidently satisfied all the outward forms of

Christian practice, he almost certainly was a deist in the 1730s and may very well have become an atheist in his later years. He recognized that the wonderful intricacies of nature's productions, especially plants and animals, and the astonishing fertility of natural processes could not be used as evidence of God's existence or of His providential concern and powers. By the 1780s Buffon regarded events in nature as the mere result of blind chance and believed that "nature" itself was no more than an assemblage of regular but probably inscrutable laws. Their delimitation remained the naturalist's foremost task.

Further Reading

There is no biography of Buffon in English. His life and work are recounted in detail in Donald Culross Peattie, *Green Laurels: The Lives and Achievements of the Great Naturalists* (1936), and Alexander B. Adams, *Eternal Quest: The Story of the Great Naturalists* (1969). A useful study of Buffon's scientific views and their context is J. S. Wilkie's "Buffon, Lamarck and Darwin" in P. R. Bell, ed., *Darwin's Biological Work* (1959). In French an excellent selection of Buffon's writings and an exhaustive bibliographical guide, including English editions, to all aspects of Buffon's work are in J. Piveteau, *Oeuvres philosophiques* (1954).

Additional Sources

From natural history to the history of nature: readings from Buffon and his critics, Notre Dame: University of Notre Dame Press, 1981. □

Thomas Robert Bugeaud de la Piconnerie

Thomas Robert Bugeaud de la Piconnerie, Duke of Isly (1784-1849), was a French national hero as a result of his role in conquering Algeria.

Thomas Bugeaud was born in Limoges on Oct. 15, 1784, into a family of country squires who were later ruined by the Revolution of 1789. Growing up in rural France, he guarded his rustic manners and attachment to the land throughout his life. His education was cursory and prevented him from entering a military academy.

Bugeaud's army career nevertheless began in 1804, and he quickly rose in the ranks during Napoleon's Imperial wars. He participated in the difficult Spanish campaigns, in which he encountered widespread guerrilla warfare and became the foremost expert in counterinsurgency techniques on the European continent. Later he applied these lessons against Abd el-Kadir.

In 1831 Bugeaud was named marshal of the French army and also became the deputy from Dordogne. In 1834 he harshly repressed popular uprisings in Paris.

Although initially hostile to the conquest of Algeria, Bugeaud went there in 1836 and defeated Abd el-Kadir, the leader of Algerian resistance. This first African campaign was a military success, but by the Treaty of Tafna (1837), Bugeaud handed his adversary the sovereignty over the major portion of Algeria. Despite a scandal which erupted over secret financial clauses of this treaty, Bugeaud was named governor general of Algeria in 1840. Aided by his powerful Parisian friends, especially L. A. Thiers, Bugeaud established a veritable proconsulate over Algeria.

Militarily, Bugeaud imposed his conceptions of offensive warfare on the army. He trimmed heavy artillery from his contingents, adding to the mobility of his columns, and introduced the practice of burning the crops and the villages of all Algerians suspected of aiding Abd el-Kadir. Chased from his capital, Tagdempt, Abd el-Kadir took refuge in Morocco. His presence there provoked a war with France. Bugeaud defeated the Moroccan troops at the battle of Isly in 1844—a turning point in modern Moroccan history—after which he acquired the title Duke of Isly.

During the respite which Bugeaud gained when the defeated Moroccans evicted Abd el-Kadir and declared him an outlaw, the marshal repressed with ferocity a new insurrection in Algeria led by Bou Maza. Abd el-Kadir, profiting from this diversion, reappeared in western Algeria, only to be defeated for a last time in 1847. That same year Bugeaud, on his own authority, led a military campaign into the Kabylie mountains south of Algiers. Disillusioned at being reprimanded by the French government for this independent action, he demanded to be replaced.

During the Revolution of 1848 Bugeaud received from King Louis Philippe the command of the Parisian troops, but Bugeaud's presence did not stop the monarchy from falling. He died of cholera on June 18, 1849.

Further Reading

There is no book-length biography of Bugeaud in English, although there are several in French. Background studies that discuss Bugeaud include John P. T. Bury, *France, 1814-1940* (1949; 4th ed. 1969), and John Plamenatz, *The Revolutionary Movement in France, 1815-71* (1952).

Additional Sources

Sullivan, Antony Thrall, *Thomas-Robert Bugeaud, France and Algeria, 1784-1849: politics, power, and the good society,* Hamden, Conn.: Archon Books, 1983. □

Muhammad ibn Ismail al-Bukhari

Muhammad ibn Ismail al-Bukhari (810-870) was a Moslem traditionist. He was the compiler of the "Sahih," one of the six canonical collections of traditions (hadiths) in Sunnite Islam that report the sayings and actions of the prophet Mohammed.

Al-Bukhari was born at Bukhara into a family of Persian origin. At the age of 10 he began to memorize traditions. His prodigious memory became evident early for he is reported to have corrected his teachers and the traditions written down by his companions. At 16 he made the pilgrimage to Mecca and then stayed there and in Medina in order to hear the famous scholars of tradition. During the following 16 years he visited the centers of learning in Egypt, Palestine, Syria, Iraq, and Persia, collecting as well as transmitting traditions.

Al-Bukhari claimed to have received traditions from over 1,000 traditionists, and his fame as a scholar grew rapidly. In Nishapur he attracted larger crowds than the leading scholar of tradition, who out of jealousy accused al-Bukhari of heresy. He had to leave and returned to Bukhara, where he completed his famous *Sahih.* Students came from all parts of the Moslem world to hear him. When the governor of the city asked al-Bukhari to give him and his children private lessons, al-Bukhari refused. The governor encouraged other scholars to charge al-Bukhari with heresy and expelled him from the city. Al-Bukhari left for Khartank, near Samarkand, where he lived until his death on Aug. 1, 870.

The "Sahih"

The title of al-Bukhari's collection of traditions, *Sahih,* means "sound," and it refers to his precept of including only traditions which he considered as being of certain authenticity according to his own rigid criteria. These criteria were mainly concerned with the reliability of the transmitters mentioned in the chain of transmission of the traditions leading back to the original relator and with the formal perfection of this chain. Al-Bukhari is reported to have chosen his "sound" traditions from among some 600,000. His collection contains 7,397 traditions with complete chains of transmission, of which 4,635 are repetitions. The great mass of the traditions relate sayings or actions of the prophet Mohammed, though a few relate statements of his Companions.

The work is divided into 97 books subdivided into 3,450 chapters, in which the traditions are arranged according to subject matter. The greater part deals with the ritual and legal matters of Islamic law, though some sections deal with questions of theology, Koran exegesis, and the life of Mohammed. Since many traditions were relevant to more than one subject, they were repeated in other chapters.

Al-Bukhari has sometimes been criticized for stretching the meaning of traditions for his purpose. A few chapters contain titles without traditions, indicating that he did not find any well-authenticated ones relevant to the subject. The titles show al-Bukhari to be independent in his doctrine of any of the Sunnite schools of the law. His work became authoritative for the traditions it contained, not for the views expressed by the author, and it is generally accepted by Sunnite Moslems as the most authoritative book after the Koran.

Further Reading

A complete translation of al-Bukhari's *Sahih* is available in French. There is an annotated English translation of a few sections by Muhammad Asad, *Sahih al-Bukhari* (1938). General works include A. Guillaume, *The Traditions of Islam: An Introduction to the Study of the Hadith Literature* (1924); U. Wayriffe, *Arabica and Islamica* (1936; rev. ed. 1940); and H. A. R. Gibb, *Mohammedanism: An Historical Survey* (1949; 2d ed. 1953). □

Nikolai Ivanovich Bukharin

The Soviet politician and writer Nikolai Ivanovich Bukharin (1858-1938) was a leading theorist of the Communist movement during the Revolutionary period in Russia and throughout the 1920s.

Nikolai Bukharin was born in Moscow, the son of a schoolteacher. As a university student, he became interested in the anticzarist political movement. In 1906 he joined the Leninist faction of the Russian Social Democratic Workers' party, then known as the Bolsheviks. He worked for the party as a successful propagandist and organizer. In 1911 he emigrated to Germany and remained abroad, either in Europe or the United States, until the Revolution began in 1917. At this time he began to establish himself as a major theorist, writing *Political Economy of the Leisure Class* (1912-1913) and *World Economy and Imperialism* (1915). Gradually, a split emerged between the position taken by Lenin and that of Bukharin with respect to the conditions under which revolution would succeed in Russia. Bukharin and others, who came to be known as the Left Bolsheviks, took the view that the coming socialist revolution could be successful only in a European-wide context, with the emergence of a socialist United States of Europe.

In 1917 Bukharin returned to Russia, but in 1918 his left-wing attitudes caused him to part company temporarily with Lenin. In the face of Lenin's proposal to end World War I for Russia by a separate peace with Germany, Bukharin, Trotsky, Dzerzhinsky, and others argued strongly for changing the world war into a European revolutionary war. But by the time of the Tenth Party Congress (1921), Bukharin's views had begun to undergo extensive change. He supported Lenin's proposal to consolidate the victories of the party inside Russia by means of the New Economic Policy. During this period and the remainder of the 1920s, Bukharin held numerous high party and government posts, including the editorships of *Pravda* (1918-1929), the journal *Bolshevik* (1924-1929), and the *Great Soviet Encyclopedia.* In addition, he was chairman of the Communist International (Comintern, 1919-1929) and a member of the Political Bureau (executive committee) of the party's Central Committee. At the same time he continued his work in Marxist-Leninist political theory, publishing his *Theory of Historical Materialism* (1921).

After the death of Lenin in 1924, a struggle for power ensued, and the ideological positions as well as the political

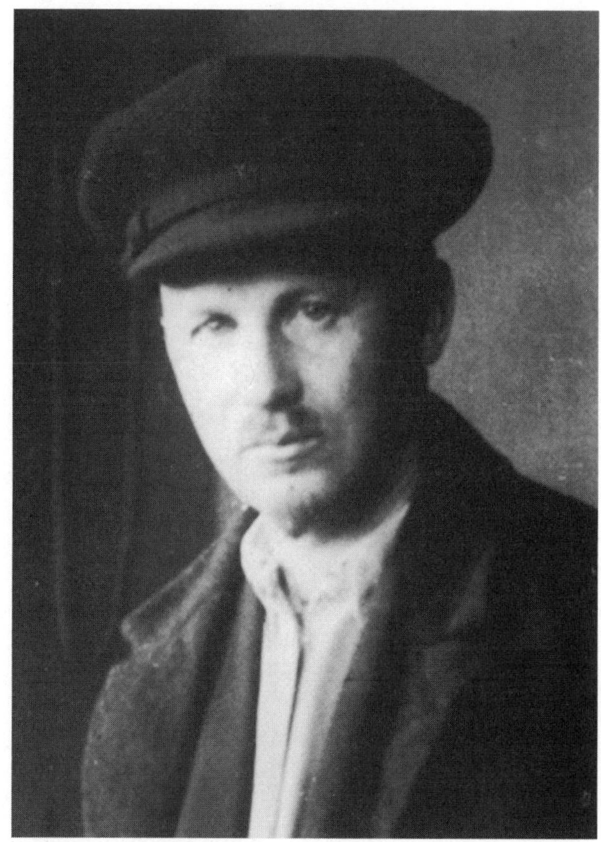

self-interests of Bukharin and Stalin dictated their cooperation in the defeat of Trotsky, Zinoviev, and Kamenev. Ultimately, however, Bukharin himself fell victim to Stalin's tactics when he was condemned as a leader of the so-called Right Deviation (1928-1929). As a result, Bukharin was removed from his high positions by mid-1929, though he continued to be a potential threat to Stalin. By 1934 Bukharin had regained a measure of his former power. His position continued to be precarious, however, and he was finally arrested during the Great Purge in 1937. Brought to trial with 20 others, he was accused of plotting the overthrow of the state. Bukharin was condemned to death and was executed in March 1938.

Further Reading

There is no definitive study of Bukharin in English. The definitive bibliography of Bukharin's published works is in German. In English see Sidney Heitman, *Nikolai I. Bukharin: A Bibliography* (1969). A short synopsis of Bukharin's philosophical viewpoint is in S. V. Utechin, *Russian Political Thought: A Concise History* (1964). Background reading includes Leonard Schapiro, *The Origin of the Communist Autocracy: Political Opposition in the Soviet State; First Phase, 1917-1922* (1955), and Robert V. Daniels, *The Conscience of the Revolution* (1960). An extensive discussion, together with stenographic reports, of Bukharin's trial for treason is in Robert C. Tucker and Stephen F. Cohen, eds., *The Great Purge Trial* (1965); see also George Katkov, *Trial of Bukharin* (1969).

Additional Sources

Bukharin in retrospect, Armonk, N.Y.: M.E. Sharpe, 1994.

Coates, Ken, *The case of Nikolai Bukharin,* Nottingham: Spokesman Books, 1978.

Cohen, Stephen F., *Bukharin and the Bolshevik Revolution: a political biography, 1888-19,* New York, Vintage Books 1975, 1973.

Gluckstein, Donny, *The tragedy of Bukharin,* London; Boulder, Co.: Pluto Press, 1993.

Larina, Anna, *This I cannot forget: the memoirs of Nikolai Bukharin's widow,* New York: W.W. Norton & Co., 1993.

Medvedev, Roy Aleksandrovich, *Nikolai Bukharin: the last years,* New York: Norton, 1980. □

Charles Bukowski

A prolific and seminal figure in underground literature, Charles Bukowski (1920-1994) is best known for poetry and fiction in which he caustically indicts bourgeois society while celebrating the desperate lives of alcoholics, prostitutes, decadent writers, and other disreputable characters in and around Los Angeles.

Born in 1920 in Andernach, Germany, Bukowski emigrated to Los Angeles in 1922 with his father, an American soldier, and his German mother. As an adolescent he was distanced from his peers by a disfiguring case of acne and he resisted the attempts of his abusive and uncompromising father to instill in him the American ideals of hard work and patriotism. Following high school, Bukowski attended Los Angeles City College from 1939 to 1941 but left without obtaining a degree. He began writing hundreds of unsuccessful short stories while drifting from city to city in a succession of low-paying jobs—including work as a mailman, post office clerk, Red Cross orderly, and laborer in a slaughterhouse and a dog biscuit factory. Although he published his first short story, "Aftermath of a Lengthy Rejection Slip," in a 1944 issue of *Story* magazine at the age of twenty-four, Bukowski virtually stopped writing for a decade, choosing instead to live as an alcoholic on skid row. After being hospitalized with a bleeding ulcer in 1955, Bukowski began writing poetry and resolved to drink less heavily. During this period he discovered the literature of Upton Sinclair, Sinclair Lewis, and especially Ernest Hemingway, which offered him an alternative to alcoholism and aided in the development of his own concise, realistic prose style.

Bukowski published his first collection of poetry, *Flower, Fist, and Bestial Wail,* in 1960. He quickly produced a series of poetry chapbooks, including *Longshot Poems for Broke Players* and *Run with the Hunted,* featuring surreal verse that expresses sentimentality for the West's Romantic past as well as disgust for the vacuousness of modern culture. While these poems garnered him a small but loyal following over the next decade, Bukowski's work in the short story genre first gained him a wide readership and established his literary reputation. Beginning in 1967, when the antiwar and counterculture movements flourished

in the United States, Bukowski began contributing a weekly column, "Notes of a Dirty Old Man," to the Los Angeles alternative newspaper *Open City,* and later, to the Los Angeles *Free Press.* Combining journalism, fiction, and philosophy in a rambling, disjointed style, these pieces established his philosophy and defiant, anarchic persona. Perceiving American culture as hypocritical, Bukowski censured American films and television as escapist wish-fulfillment, morality as organized hypocrisy, patriotism as conformism, and academic writers, scholars, and intellectuals as self-righteous charlatans who attack American society while reaping its benefits.

Bukowski began his career writing poetry critical of American bourgeois institutions while disclaiming the title of writer: "To say I'm a poet puts me in the company of versifiers, neontasters, fools, clods, and skoundrels [sic] masquerading as wise men." In *Longshot Poems for Broke Players,* Bukowski introduces his characteristic outsider protagonist: the unstudied, self-exiled poet who provokes public enmity through his apparent rudeness to writers and other socialites, and maintains his freedom and uniqueness as a writer by rejecting the public literary world. In "Letter from the North," for example, the narrator responds to a despondent writer's request for sympathy with the question: "write you? about what my friend? / I'm only interested in poetry." In ensuing collections such as *It Catches My Heart in Its Hands* and *Crucifix in a Deathhand,* Bukowski's narrator retains his hostility to the outer world while revealing a paradoxical inner gentleness. In "Fuzz," the unsteady protagonist unexpectedly empathizes with a group of children who are taunting him: "when I go into the liquor store / they whirl around outside / like bees / shut out from their nest. / I buy a fifth of cheap / whiskey / and / 3 / candy bars." Much of Bukowski's subsequent poetry, collected in such volumes as *Poems Written before Jumping out of an 8-story Window, The Days Run Away Like Wild Horses over the Hills,* and *Fire Station,* deals in concrete, realistic terms with acts of rape, sodomy, deceit, and violence, particularly focusing on sexual relationships characterized by physical and emotional abuse in which women seek to enslave men through marriage and men attempt to avoid such enslavement through the equally imprisoning pursuit of wealth and material pleasures.

Many of the events described in Bukowski's poetry recur in the autobiographical short stories and novels he began writing in the 1970s. While his earlier stories, many of which were published in men's pornographic magazines, generally employ stock formulas, Bukowski's later fiction, published in *Erections, Ejaculations, Exhibitions, and General Tales of Ordinary Madness* and *South of No North: Stories of the Buried Life,* is more sophisticated, philosophical, and pointedly critical of American society. Many of these stories focus on sexual relationships that feminist and other critics have faulted as misogynistic. Other critics, however, believe these works expose the short-sightedness, pettiness, and spiritual bankruptcy of a dysfunctional society.

During the 1970s Bukowski began writing semiautobiographical novels featuring the first-person narrator Henry ("Hank") Chinaski, a hard-boiled, alcoholic survivor who trades a mediocre, normal life for a position that allows for unromanticized self-awareness in the socially unrestricted environment of the ghetto. Bukowski's first novel, *Post Office,* contrasts the mindlessness and monotony of Chinaski's work life as an employee of the United States Post Office with the varying degradation and vitality of his unconventional personal life. *Factotum* chronicles Chinaski's experiences as a young man before the events related in *Post Office,* while *Ham on Rye* recounts his adolescent years and conflicts with his tyrannical father. *Women* details Chinaski's sexual exploits after the events chronicled in *Post Office* and his eventual desire for a monogamous relationship. Chinaski is also a central character in Bukowski's novel *Barfly,* which he adapted into a screenplay for the film directed by Barbet Schroeder and starring Mickey Rourke and Faye Dunaway. Bukowski's encounters with California's film industry are also detailed in *Hollywood,* another novel featuring Chinaski. Bukowski died of leukemia in Los Angeles in 1994

Further Reading

Contemporary Literary Criticism, Gale, Volume 2, 1974, Volume 5, 1976, Volume 9, 1978, Volume 41, 1987.

Contemporary Novelists, 4th edition, edited by D. L. Kirkpatrick, St. James Press, 1986.

Dictionary of Literary Biography, Volume 5: *American Poets since World War II,* Gale, 1980.

A Bibliography of Charles Bukowski, Dorbin, Sanford, Black Sparrow Press, 1969.

Charles Bukowski: A Critical and Bibliographical Study, Fox, Hugh, Abyss Publications, 1969.

Bukowski: Friendship, Fame, and Bestial Myth, Sherman, Jory, Blue Horse Press, 1982.

A Charles Bukowski Checklist, Weinberg, Jeffrey, editor, Water Row Press, 1987. □

Momir Bulatovic

Momir Bulatovic (born 1956) became president of Montenegro in 1990 in the first democratic multiparty elections held there. Heading a left-wing Democratic party of Socialists, he won again in the elections of 1992 as part of the newly organized Federal Republic of Yugoslavia.

Momir Bulatovic was born on September 26, 1956, in Belgrade, capital city of Yugoslavia. His family belonged to the Vasojevici clan from Montenegro, a small mountainous region in southern Yugoslavia. Although similar to Serbs with whom they share the same language and religion under the auspices of the Serbian Orthodox Church, many people of Montenegro are proud of their rich history and consider themselves as Montenegrins rather than Serbs.

The childhood of Momir Bulatovic did not substantially differ from that of the majority of the youngsters who grew up during the 1960s and early 1970s, the most prosperous period in Yugoslav history. After finishing compulsory primary and secondary school, Bulatovic was accepted at the "Veljko Vlahovic" University in Podgorica (former Titograd) where he began his studies in economics in 1975. Diligent and methodical, he graduated as the best student in his generation in 1980. After the completion of his undergraduate studies he became a lecturer of political economy in the school of economics at the same university. As a lecturer he worked under the supervision and mentorship of professor Bosko Gluscevic, a prominent Yugoslav economist with strong political connections. In 1987 Momir successfully defended his Masters thesis, titled "The Role of Rent in the Economy of Montenegro." He published several articles and three books. In 1991 he published a political essay titled "Less than a Game—More than a Life."

Despite the fact that he was active in the Socialist Youth Organization during the 1980s and quite certainly connected to some political circles, the real political career of Bulatovic began in January 1989. After the death of Josip Broz Tito in 1980, Yugoslavia fell into a deep economic and political crisis. The constitutional crisis in Yugoslavia fully opened in 1988 with Serbia's attempt to reinstate its authority over the autonomous provinces of Kosovo and Vojvodina. The opposition from Croatia and Slovenia precluded any political solution within the existing framework of a crumbling federation. The inability of the ruling bureaucracy to cope with the problem fueled public outrage, which became especially dramatic in Serbia and Montenegro.

On January 10, 1989, more than 120,000 people rallied in Titograd and demanded the immediate resignation of the ruling Communist elite—an event without a precedent in Yugoslav history. Bulatovic and a group of young people, many of whom occupied less visible positions within the League of Communists (official name for the Communist party) seized the moment and came into power in Montenegro. Although there are several interpretations of these events, some question the authenticity of the popular discontent and imply that the whole affair was staged by Serbia's president, Slobodan Milosevic. Bulatovic and his group proved to be more capable, realistic, and progressive than their predecessors.

Soon after Bulatovic became president of the League of Communists of Montenegro, broad and sweeping reforms were introduced. He emphasized the necessity of movement toward a market economy and Western-style democracy. Under his leadership the old League of Communists of Montenegro was reorganized and changed into the Democratic party of Socialists. In the first democratic multiparty elections, held in 1990, his party won an absolute majority of seats in the Montenegrin Parliament, and Bulatovic became president of Montenegro.

Following the collapse of the old defunct Yugoslav federation that came after the unilateral secessions of four republics (Slovenia, Croatia, Bosnia and Herzegovina, and Macedonia) and the violent civil war that followed, Serbia and Montenegro formed a new federation under the name Federal Republic of Yugoslavia on April 27, 1992. In the early elections in December 1992 Bulatovic won a decisive victory over Branko Kostic, who ran as a candidate of the ultranationalist Radical party and remained the president of Montenegro. Bulatovic's Democratic party of Socialists again gained an absolute majority of seats in the Montenegrin Parliament.

Bulatovic was perceived as a moderate left-wing politician by many Montenegrins. He and his party faced many challenges, especially after the imposition of the crippling sanctions against the Federal Republic of Yugoslavia in 1992. Bulatovic succeeded in confronting and defeating the open calls for secession from Yugoslavia that came from the Liberal party, as well as the demands for the inclusion of Montenegro in a Serbian state, which mainly originated from the ultra right-wing Radical party. In an effort to normalize the unstable relationship between Yugoslavia and Albania, he visited Tirana in 1993 and met with the Albanian president, Sali Berisa. In his commitment to keep a united Yugoslavia, he was nonetheless persistent in his refusal to compromise the special interests of Montenegrins.

Bulatovic's reputation in the United States was seriously prejudiced by his strict censorship policies and by his dubious support of free elections. He frequently came under fire by his own people, as well as the press, for actions in these areas.

Although often overlooked by the Western media, Bulatovic took an active role in the negotiations about ending the civil war in Bosnia and Herzegovina. He was a member of the Yugoslav delegation to the peace negotiations in Dayton, Ohio during the final eventful weeks of

1995 when a fragile accord was reached. Bulatovic then spoke out repeatedly against Bosnian Serb leader Radovan Karadzic who persisted in violating the Dayton accord.

Bulatovic was often described as an honest and modest person. Momo, as friends simply called him, liked to emphasize that despite the nationalistic frenzy in the Balkan states, Montenegro "remains the state of all its citizens regardless of their respective nationality and political affiliation." Many people still remember his open letter to Slovenian president Milan Kucan in which he questioned the ethics of the policy of violent secessions. Married and the father of two children, he lived in Podgorica.

Further Reading

Daily Digest of the Open Media Research Institute, January 23, 1995; October 9, 1995; December 20, 1995; January 2, 1996; June 27, 1996; July 1, 1996; July 29, 1996; August 23, 1996; September 16, 1996; October 21, 1996; November 19, 1996; December 13, 1996; December 18, 1996; February 27, 1997; March 13, 1997; March 26, 1997.

Pursuing Balkan Peace, July 2, 1996; September 3, 1996; October 22, 1996. □

Charles Bulfinch

Possibly the best known of all American "colonial" architects, Charles Bulfinch (1763-1844) approached design as an 18th-century amateur gentleman of taste rather than as a 19th-century professional architect.

Charles Bulfinch was born into a well-connected and well-to-do Boston family; his father was a physician and a graduate of Harvard College and Edinburg University. Bulfinch took a degree at Harvard in 1781; then, as soon as political conditions permitted, he took the 18th-century gentleman's grand tour of Europe (1785-1787). On his return, according to his autobiography, he "passed a season of leisure, pursuing no business but giving gratuitous advice in architecture, and looking forward to an establishment in life."

In 1788 he married Hannah Apthorp and designed his first building, the Hollis Street Church in Boston. The following year he provided plans for churches in Taunton and Pittsfield and executed a Revolutionary memorial in Boston, a Roman Doric column of stucco-covered brick, 60 feet high, capped with an eagle doubling as a weather vane (it was destroyed when Beacon Hill was cut away in 1811). In 1792 he designed the statehouse in Hartford, Conn. (still extant though changed in function), and several houses for friends.

All these works were in the fashionable rococo version of the 18th-century classical style popularized in Britain by Robert Adam from the 1760s on, which Bulfinch had seen during his travels in England—heavier and more provincial than the originals, but for that very reason all the more acceptable. They were so well received that Bulfinch was encouraged to erect, on speculation, a 16-house block of uniform proportion, scale, and composition in the manner made famous and fashionable by New Town in Edinburgh, Scotland. Eventually this project, named Tontine Crescent and begun in 1793, was an enormous success, and it set a pattern for similar blocks which give the Beacon Hill area of Boston its distinctive character. But Bulfinch was caught in the brief depression following Jay's Treaty in November 1794 and could not raise enough money to finish it immediately; he went bankrupt in January 1796.

The experience had practical results, which Bulfinch records in his autobiography: "My inexperience and that of my agents in conducting business of this nature . . . led me to surrender all my property . . . and I found myself reduced to my personal exertions for support. . . . " He became dependent on architectural fees for his living. Fortunately, his reputation was unaffected; his friends rallied round, and he soon had plenty of commissions.

Bulfinch had submitted a plan for the proposed new Massachusetts statehouse in 1787, and in 1795 Governor Samuel Adams authorized construction to proceed under Bulfinch's supervision; the building was completed 3 years later. For Boston he also designed an almshouse (1799), churches (Holy Cross, 1803; New North, 1804; Federal Street, 1809; New South, 1814), markets (Faneuil Hall, 1805; Boylston, 1809), five bank buildings (1800-1815), a prison (Charlestown, 1803-1805), a courthouse (1810), a hospital (1818-1820), and residences (the three for Harrison Gray Otis, built in 1796, 1801, and 1805, are still standing).

Recognized as a "genius" who had made fashionable Boston over into his own stylistic image, he received commissions from all over the region and inspired followers and imitators, notably Samuel McIntire and Asher Benjamin.

In 1817 Bulfinch was appointed architect of the Capitol in Washington, D.C.. In all his previous work there had been no fundamental change in his style of architecture, and he remained essentially what he had always been, the gentleman amateur designing in a tasteful variant of the classical mode. That is how he approached the U.S. Capitol. But there, on the national scene, he was forced to meet a new concept of architecture, and it frustrated him. On first studying the drawings of Benjamin Henry Latrobe, one of the original designers, he wrote: "My courage almost failed me . . . the design is in the boldest stile." As he completed the center section of the Capitol, the design was much more traditional than Latrobe and William Thornton, the other original designer, had envisaged. In particular, Bulfinch was criticized for making the dome higher than they had planned. Yet it was his changes that made the design all the more acceptable generally. As far as the contemporary public was concerned, Bulfinch was the "designer of the Capitol" and, though little is left of his work because of later alterations, he still enjoys that reputation.

During the 1820s Bulfinch executed several more important commissions: a Unitarian church in Washington (1822), a prison in Alexandria, Va. (1826), and a capitol for the new state of Maine, at Augusta (1829, remodeled 1911). He effectively retired about 1829 and died in Boston in 1844.

Further Reading

Two early biographies on which most writings about Bulfinch have been based are Ellen S. Bulfinch, ed., *Life and Letters of Charles Bulfinch* (1896), and Charles A. Place, *Charles Bulfinch, Architect and Citizen* (1925). Bulfinch's work on the Capitol is described by Talbot F. Hamlin in *Greek Revival Architecture* (1944) and *Benjamin Henry Latrobe* (1955). For a general presentation of Bulfinch's place in the evolution of American architecture see Alan Gowans, *Images of American Living* (1964). □

Mikhail Afanasievich Bulgakov

The Soviet novelist and playwright Mikhail Afanasievich Bulgakov (1891-1940) was a satirist with an outstanding talent for depicting the grotesque, the comic, and the fantastic.

Mikhail Bulgakov was born on May 2, 1891, in Kiev of a middle-class intellectual family. He graduated in medicine from the University of Kiev but soon abandoned his medical career for journalism. His first literary efforts were short stories, such as "The Fatal Eggs" and "Devilry," in which the real world is mixed with science fantasy for the purpose of social and moral satire.

The realistic novel *The White Guard* (1924) was Bulgakov's first major triumph and is notable as one of the few works published in the Soviet Union which sympathetically portray the supporters of the White cause during the civil war. This outstanding novel was never reprinted in Russia, but Bulgakov's dramatic adaptation of it, *The Days of the Turbins* (1926), became a fixture on the Soviet stage. From 1926 until his death Bulgakov was closely associated with the Moscow Art Theater, for which he wrote over 30 plays, only 8 of which were performed in his lifetime.

During the 1930s Bulgakov's partiality for satire and his independence as a writer kept him under a political cloud. At one time the pressure on him became so great that he asked Stalin for permission to leave the Soviet Union permanently, but Stalin refused. He also suffered from poor health and became blind the year before his death in 1940.

It was not until the 1960s that Bulgakov was fully rehabilitated by the Soviet authorities. At that time the manuscripts of numerous stories and plays and of three novels were discovered and published; these works established him as one of the finest 20th-century Russian writers. The first of the novels to appear was *Black Snow* (written in the late 1930s), a satire on the Soviet theatrical world. The second, *The Heart of a Dog* (written in 1925), is a science fantasy in which human organs are transplanted into a dog, giving it the most disgusting qualities of mankind.

The third novel, *The Master and Margarita,* was written in his last years and is Bulgakov's greatest work. It is a complex, grotesque, and fantastic satire, combining a unique interpretation of the story of Jesus with descriptions of the literary and theatrical circles of Moscow and with weird adventures caused by the mischief of the devil. The novel has many symbolic elements, which can be interpreted in a great variety of ways. A number of Bulgakov's manuscripts remain unpublished.

Further Reading

There is no full-length study of Bulgakov in English. Most of the English-language editions of his works, however, contain valuable introductory material. Shorter treatments of Bulgakov are in Gleb Struve, *Soviet Russian Literature, 1917-50* (1951); Marc Lvovich Slonim, *Modern Russian Literature from Chekhov to the Present* (1953); Viacheslav Zavalishin, *Early Soviet Writers* (1958); and Edward J. Brown, *Russian Literature since the Revolution* (1969).

Additional Sources

My life with Mikhail Bulgakov, Ann Arbor: Ardis, 1983.

Milne, Lesley, *Mikhail Bulgakov: a critical biography,* Cambridge England; New York: Cambridge University Press, 1990.

A pictorial biography of Mikhail Bulgakov, Ann Arbor, MI: Ardis, 1984. □

Nikolai Bulganin

Nikolai Bulganin (1885-1975) was chairman of the Soviet Council of Ministers from 1955 until 1958 and for a brief period of time he was one of the world's most prominent political figures.

Nikolai Aleksandrovich Bulganin was born June 11, 1885, in Gorky, formerly called Nizhni Novgorod, a trade and industrial center on the Volga river. His father worked as an accountant, but little has been revealed about Bulganin's youth, perhaps because he came from a fairly well-to-do family and was given an excellent private school education. In 1917, the midst of the revolution, he joined the Bolshevik (Communist) Party. For several months he worked as a party organizer in the region's textile factories, and in early 1918, when civil war broke out, he joined other young Communist enthusiasts in the newly formed Cheka, forerunner of the secret police.

As a Chekist in Gorky, Turkestan, and Moscow, Nikolai Aleksandrovich became closely associated with a number of future party leaders, including Lazar Kaganovich, Viacheslav Molotov, Georgy Malenkov, Nikolai Ezhov, and Anastas Mikoian. These relationships undoubtedly helped further his career, but so did his own intelligence and administrative competence. In 1922 Bulganin became a member of the important National Economic Council charged with planning and directing the Soviet economy. He was soon given other important posts, including control in 1927 over the Soviet Union's "General Electric," the Moscow electrical components factory "Electrozavod." Here Bulganin distinguished himself during Stalin's industrialization drive, gaining national attention by completing his assigned Five Year Plan in less than three years.

Survives Stalin's Purges

Bulganin's success as a practical administrator and his personal friendships led in 1931 to his becoming chairman of the Moscow city soviet, the capital's mayor. Here he again worked closely with Lazar Kaganovich, at the time secretary of the all-important Moscow party committee. In 1934, the year Kaganovich was followed in the Moscow party apparatus by Nikita Sergeevich Khrushchev, Bulganin was elected a candidate member of the Central Committee.

Shortly thereafter, as Bulganin and Khrushchev plunged energetically into the task of Moscow's rapid growth (including the construction of the city's famous subway system), Stalin's massive purges began; and in 1936 Bulganin's old colleague Ezhov became head of the dreaded police. Patronage was not always protection in these years, but in Bulganin's case it clearly helped consolidate his position as a bright young Stalinist at a time when "Old Bolsheviks" were arrested and killed by the tens of thousands. Advancement came rapidly. In July 1937, at the height of the purges, he became premier of the Russian republic, the largest and most important of the country's 16 constituent units. One year later he was appointed deputy premier of the U.S.S.R. and simultaneously head of the State Bank.

With the German invasion in 1941 Bulganin's experience and ability led to his assuming a number of important posts, first as the principal party administrator for the Western front, and later, in 1944, as a member of the all-important State Defense Committee. Immediately after the war, while such other prominent figures as Marshal Zhukov were being removed from positions of power, Bulganin was appointed first deputy minister of defense and himself became a marshal. In 1949 he was promoted to vice-premier of the U.S.S.R., a position he held when Stalin died in 1953.

Teams Up with Khrushchev

Bulganin apparently played a key role in the weeks following Stalin's death in helping Khrushchev become first secretary, using his influence in the military to assure the removal and execution of their mutual rival Lavrenti Beria, Ezhov's successor. As vice-premier, Bulganin was also able to stand somewhat on the sidelines as Khrushchev jockeyed for power with another old friend, Malenkov; and in February 1955 Bulganin himself replaced Malenkov as Soviet premier. Given now to welltailored clothes (in marked contrast to Khrushchev) and able to handle himself with ease on the Western embassy cocktail circuit, Bulganin soon became widely known in the west as a man of quick wit and intelligence. Late in 1955 he also became, with Khrushchev, the Soviet Union's leading exponent of peaceful coexistence and better relations with the West.

Bulganin and Khrushchev "teamed up" in these months to make a number of trips to Western Europe and Asia, including visits to Burma, India, Yugoslavia, England, and Finland. In July 1955 he led the Soviet delegation to the four power conference in Geneva, where he met Eisenhower and toasted the end of war. As head of state, Bulganin also assumed a principal role in the Soviet Union's major peace offensive throughout 1956 and 1957, corresponding frequently with Eisenhower and in one celebrated letter on the eve of the 1956 elections urging an end to nuclear tests. Westerners generally perceived Bulganin as a man of reason and worldly sophistication, although Poles, Hungarians, and his own countrymen also knew his tough-mindedness and understood first-hand his willingness to clamp down Stalinist fashion when he thought such measures were required.

Choosing the Wrong Side

June 1957 proved an important turning point in Bulganin's career. Khrushchev's de-stalinization campaign and his effort to stimulate rapid industrial growth by introducing a number of rapid-fire domestic reforms led to the formation of a solid opposition bloc in the Politburo, the Communist Party's leading council. The opposition was led by Kaganovich, Molotov, and Malenkov and soon secured a majority of seven to four in favor of Khrushchev's ouster. Bulganin apparently felt bound to side with the majority, although he remained supportive of Khrushchev's policies. In any event, the decision to replace Khrushchev was made in his office.

Khrushchev, however, refused to accept the Politburo's decision. According to reports (perhaps leaked self-servingly by Khrushchev himself), it was Bulganin who insisted that a seven to four vote left Khrushchev no choice, drawing the famous retort that "politics is not arithmetic." When Khrushchev boldly assembled the Central Committee and assured his power, Bulganin's days were numbered. In March 1958 he was ousted as premier (a position now assumed by Khrushchev himself) and demoted to head the State Bank. Despite abject public and private apologies for his "incorrect" behavior, further humiliation followed quickly. In August 1958 he was transferred to a minor economic post at Stavropol in the northern Caucasus, where his authority was limited and he was constantly exposed to ridicule. His subsequent plea in February 1960 to be allowed to retire was granted, perhaps as a favor by his former friend Khrushchev. In increasingly ill health, he lived the rest of his years as a pensioner in a small dacha outside Moscow, only once, in 1964, appearing again at an official party gathering.

Although Bulganin held a number of important party positions and received every major award and honor, the *Great Soviet Encyclopedia* allots him less than half the space devoted to S. N. Bulgakov, a "bourgeois" philosopher who disagreed sharply with Lenin and became a leading anti-communist writer, and only two lines more than Andrei Boulainvilliers, an obscure 18th century French historian. At one time tens of millions of Soviet schoolchildren saw Bulganin's picture every day of their young lives. Millions more of their elders paid close attention to his speeches. And during the American election campaign of 1956, Bulganin's correspondence with President Eisenhower was front page news in every major American newspaper. Nevertheless, when he died on February 24, 1975, there was not even a formal obituary in the Soviet newspapers *Pravda* or *Izvestiia.*

Further Reading

Nikolai Aleksandrovich Bulganin has no Western biographer. Material relating to his rise to power can be found in a number of general texts, including Leonard Schapiro, *History of the Communist Party of the Soviet Union* (1960); Carl A. Linden, *Khrushchev and the Soviet Leadership, 1957-1964* (1966); Edward Crankshaw, *Khrushchev: A Career* (1966); and Wolfgang Leonard, *The Kremlin Since Stalin* (1962). An interesting analysis of the 1957 crisis appears in Roger Pethybridge, *A Key to Soviet Politics: The Crisis of the "Anti-Party" Group* (London, 1962). See also the collection of essays edited by Stephen Cohen, Alexander Rabinowitch, and Robaert Sharlet, *The Soviet Union Since Stalin* (1980), especially Roy Medvedev's "The Stalin Question." The best source for Bulganin's many public speeches during his years as premier is the *Current Digest of the Soviet Press,* issued weekly since 1949, with quarterly and cumulative indices. □

Rudolf Karl Bultmann

The German theologian Rudolf Karl Bultmann (1884-1976) altered the direction of biblical studies by his work in the interpretation of the New Testament.

Rudolf Bultmann was born August 20, 1884, in Wiefelstede, the eldest son of an Evangelical Lutheran pastor. He attended the humanistic gymnasium in Oldenburg and in 1903 began to study theology at Tübingen. In the manner of German university students, he spent several semesters at Berlin and later at Marburg and thus studied with most of the leading German scholars of biblical and dogmatic theology. His degree was awarded in 1910, and after submitting a qualifying essay two years later, he was admitted at Marburg as a lecturer on the New Testament. After brief lectureships at Breslau and Giessen, he returned to Marburg in 1921 as a full professor. He retained this position until his retirement in 1951.

Bultmann applied to his exegesis of Scripture certain key ideas borrowed from the "existential analysis" of the philosopher Martin Heidegger. Heidegger attempted to discover the fundamental concepts which must be used in any understanding of human existence. Thus, for example, his treatment of "authentic" existence was adopted by Bultmann to illuminate the biblical conception of the life of faith. Bultmann also used Heidegger's treatment of alienation and anxiety to clarify the biblical notions of sin and guilt, and the philosopher's emphasis of human mortality influenced Bultmann's ideas of dying to the world and to oneself.

Another important aspect of Bultmann's biblical interpretation was his effort to separate the essential gospel message from the 1st-century world view. This "demythologizing" did not mean the elimination of the miracle stories or the account of demonic powers. Rather, it meant their reinterpretation "existentially" in terms of man's understanding of his own situation and its fundamental possibilities. To Bultmann the story of the Resurrection is not an account of the reanimation of a corpse; instead, it expresses the possibility of man's entrance into a new dimension of existence, free from guilt and anxiety and open to all people in love. Less plausibly, Bultmann argued that Paul began this process of demythologizing by giving an existential interpretation to the Gnostic mythology of demons. The most complete statement of Bultmann's biblical exegesis is found in his *Theology of the New Testament* (trans. 1951).

In his later writings Bultmann continued with his form-critical analysis of New Testament sources. *The History of the Synoptic Tradition* (1968) was an influential examination of the compositions of the Gospels of Matthew, Mark, and Luke. *The Gospel of John: A Commentary* (1971) was considered a significant new interpretation of the difficult fourth Gospel. One of Bultmann's last works, *Jesus and the Word* (1975), was an investigation of the teachings of Jesus that provides readers a glimpse of the theologian's theory of history, as well as Biblical interpretation.

During the Nazi regime Bultmann was one of the most outspoken members of the "Confessing Church," which refused to follow the "German Christian" clergy in supporting Hitler's non-Aryan exclusion policies. Throughout his career Bultmann continued to preach as well as teach. Bultmann married and became the father of three daughters. He died on July 30, 1976, in Marburg, (then West) Germany.

Further Reading

The literature on Bultmann's work has grown enormously since the end of World War II. Charles Kegley, ed., *The Theology of Rudolf Bultmann* (1966), contains a brief autobiographical sketch by Bultmann, important essays of interpretation, and criticism of his major ideas, together with Bultmann's replies. It also contains an exhaustive bibliography of his works to 1965. André Malet, *The Thought of Rudolf Bultmann* (trans. 1971), is comprehensive and very readable. More recent studies include Gareth Jones, *Bultmann: Towards a Critical Theology* (1991) and Schubert M. Ogden, *Christ Without Myth: A Study Based on the Theology of Rudolf Bultmann* (1991). □

Philippe Jean Bunau-Varilla

Philippe Jean Bunau-Varilla (1859-1940) was a French engineer and soldier. He influenced the United States decision to build a waterway through Panama and encouraged Panama's successful revolution against Colombia.

Philippe Bunau-Varilla, born in Paris on July 26, 1859, graduated from the École Polytechnique in 1880 and 3 years later left the École des Ponts et Chaussées. After serving a year as an engineer in the French department of public works, he went to Panama to head one of the three divisions of Ferdinand de Lesseps' Panama Canal Company. By the age of 26, Bunau-Varilla had temporarily assumed general management of the company.

When, amid charges of fraud, Lesseps' company went bankrupt in 1888, Bunau-Varilla, working to revitalize French interest, zealously defended the canal idea. He also, unsuccessfully, attempted to gain Russian support. Meanwhile there developed in France the New Panama Company, in which Bunau-Varilla purchased stock. Eventually abandoning hopes of finishing the canal, the new company tried to sell it to the United States. The American government was initially unresponsive, but through determined efforts first of Nelson W. Cromwell, the company's New York lawyer, and later of Bunau-Varilla, the United States eventually selected the Panamanian route.

In various trips to the United States, Bunau-Varilla met prominent people, lectured, and published a booklet entitled *Panama or Nicaragua*. To illustrate his charge that volcanoes would threaten the Nicaraguan route, he purchased Nicaraguan postage stamps picturing Momotombo belching ashes and smoke and distributed them to every U.S. Senator. Influenced by such efforts, the U.S. Congress in 1902 passed the Spooner Act, which provided for canal construction in Panama if reasonable arrangements could

be made with Colombia, of which Panama was a part at that time.

When the treaty with Colombia failed ratification in that country's Senate, Bunau-Varilla supported a Panamanian revolution. In New York he plotted with a representative of the revolutionary junta and provided a proclamation of independence, draft of a constitution, plan of military operations, flag, and promise of money. The United States quickly recognized the independent Panama and received its first minister, Philippe Bunau-Varilla, who negotiated the Hay-Bunau-Varilla Treaty (1903), giving the United States the right to build a canal in Panama.

An officer in the French army during World War I, Bunau-Varilla lost a leg at Verdun. In his later years he continued his interest in the Panama Canal and advocated changing it from a lock to a sea-level waterway. He died in Paris on May 18, 1940.

Further Reading

Bunau-Varilla's *Panama: The Creation, Destruction, and Resurrection* (trans. 1914) and *From Panama to Verdun: My Fight for France* (trans. 1940) reveal a man of strong opinions, ardently anti-German, confident of his beliefs, and certain of his enemies. Background studies on the Panama Canal that discuss Bunau-Varilla are Dwight Carroll Miner, *The Fight for the Panama Route* (1940), and Gerstle Mack, *The Land Divided* (1944).

Additional Sources

Anguizola, G. A., *Philippe Bunau-Varilla, the man behind the Panama Canal,* Chicago: Nelson-Hall, 1980. □

Ralph Johnson Bunche

Ralph Johnson Bunche (1904-1971) was the highest American official in the United Nations. For his conduct of negotiations leading to an armistice in the First Arab-Israeli War, he received the Nobel Peace Prize in 1950, the first African American to do so.

A barber's son, Ralph Bunche was born in Detroit, Mich., on Aug. 7, 1904. His parents died when he was 13, and his maternal grandmother took Ralph and his young sister to live in Los Angeles. While going to school Ralph helped support the family by working as a janitor, carpet-layer, and seaman. His grandmother's indomitable will and her wisdom had a lasting influence on him.

Bunche attended the University of California at Los Angeles on scholarships and graduated in 1927. He earned a master's degree at Harvard University in 1928 and a doctorate in government and international relations at Harvard in 1934. His doctoral dissertation won the Tappan Prize as the best one in the social sciences that year. Later he did advanced work in anthropology at Northwestern University, the London School of Economics, and the University of Cape Town.

From 1928 to 1942 Bunche was a member (and chairman from 1937) of the department of political science at Howard University. He married Ruth Harris, one of his students, in 1930; the couple had three children. In 1950 he was appointed to the faculty of Harvard University, but after two successive leaves of absence he resigned in 1952 without having taught there.

An expert on colonialism, Bunche worked during World War II in the Office of Strategic Services as an analyst of African and Far Eastern affairs, moving in 1944 to the State Department, where he became head of the Division of Dependent Area Affairs. At Dumbarton Oaks in 1944, San Francisco in 1945, and London in 1946, he was active as an authority on trusteeship in the planning and establishment of the United Nations (UN). In 1947, at the invitation of Secretary General Trygve Lie, Bunche joined the UN Secretariat as director of the Trusteeship Division.

Lie and his successors, Dag Hammarskjöld and U Thant, gave special troubleshooting assignments to Bunche. In 1947 he was a member of the UN Special Committee on Palestine that recommended partition of the country into Jewish and Arab states. Arab refusal to accept the UN plan resulted in the First Arab-Israeli War. When the UN's chief mediator in that conflict, Count Folke Bernadotte, was assassinated in 1948, Bunche took his place. From January to June 1949 he presided over the difficult negotiations be-

tween Arab and Israeli delegations on the island of Rhodes that led eventually to an armistice. Both sides praised his achievement, and in 1950 he was awarded the Nobel Peace Prize for his work.

In 1955 Bunche was named undersecretary without portfolio in the UN Secretariat and in 1957 undersecretary for special political affairs (in 1969 this title was changed to undersecretary general). He directed UN peace-keeping operations in the Suez area (1956), in the Congo (1960), and on the island of Cyprus (1964) and was also responsible for the UN's program in the peaceful uses of atomic energy. He became U Thant's most influential political adviser. In June 1971, fatally ill, Bunche retired from his post. He died in New York City on December 9.

The grandson of a slave, Bunche bore with great reserve the indignities of racial prejudice that he experienced. His lifelong concern about race relations was the source of his early desire to be a teacher and his later specialization in colonial problems. In 1936 he was codirector of the Institute of Race Relations at Swarthmore College. From 1938 to 1940, as a staff member of the Carnegie Corporation of New York, he served as chief aide to Swedish sociologist Gunnar Myrdal in his investigation of the race problem in the United States that led to Myrdal's influential book *An American Dilemma*. Bunche wrote or supervised 13 of the 81 volumes of manuscripts and memoranda submitted to Myrdal for the book. For 22 years Bunche was a member of the board of directors of the National Association for the Advancement of Colored People. In 1965 he participated in marches in Selma and Montgomery, Ala., led by Martin Luther King, Jr., to protest racial discrimination.

Bunche received many honorary degrees and awards, and President John F. Kennedy presented him with the Medal of Freedom in 1963. Bunche was president of the American Political Science Association and a member of the Harvard University board of overseers.

Further Reading

Bunche wrote *A World View of Race* (1936; repr. 1968). Howard P. Linton compiled *Ralph Johnson Bunche: Writings by and about Him from 1928 to 1966* (1967). A biography is J. Alvin Kugelmass, *Ralph J. Bunche: Fighter for Peace* (1962). There is a short biography of him in Wilhelmina S. Robinson, *Historical Negro Biographies* (1968). For examinations of the UN Secretariat and the UN's peace-keeping efforts see Sydney D. Bailey, *The Secretariat of the United Nations* (1962; rev. ed. 1964), and James M. Boyd, *United Nations Peace-keeping Operations: A Military and Political Appraisal* (1971). □

McGeorge Bundy

McGeorge Bundy (1919-1996) served as national security adviser to both President John F. Kennedy and President Lyndon B. Johnson. He later was president of the Ford Foundation and was instrumental in expanding its programs to emphasize equal opportunity in the United States. When he died at the age of 77, he was serving as a scholar in residence at the Carnegie Corporation.

McGeorge Bundy was born in Boston, Massachusetts, on March 30, 1919. His father was a close associate of Henry L. Stimson, who served Herbert Hoover as secretary of state and Franklin D. Roosevelt as secretary of war. Bundy graduated first in his class at Yale in 1940 and became a junior fellow at Harvard in 1941. He served in the U.S. Army during World War II as an aide to Admiral Alan Kirk. In that capacity he assisted with the planning for the invasions of Sicily and France.

After he left the armed forces in 1946 Bundy had the opportunity of working with Stimson on the latter's autobiography, *On Active Service* (1948). He then worked briefly in Washington on implementation of the Marshall Plan before joining Thomas E. Dewey's presidential campaign as a consultant on foreign policy issues. Any doubt that he was a rising star of the foreign policy establishment was dispelled by his appointment as a political analyst for the Council on Foreign Relations in late 1948.

Bundy stayed with the Council for less than a year and then accepted an appointment to teach foreign policy at Harvard. There, despite the absence of the usual graduate degrees or scholarly publications, he rose rapidly, becoming a full professor within five years. Even before that, at the age of 34, he was appointed dean of the faculty of arts and

sciences. Popular with students and faculty, Bundy had an extraordinary academic career.

Although he considered himself a Republican and campaigned for Dwight Eisenhower in 1952 and 1956, Bundy rejected Richard M. Nixon in favor of John F. Kennedy in 1960. In 1961 Kennedy appointed him special assistant to the president for national security, a post he held until his resignation five years later.

Bundy assembled a brilliant staff and, with Secretary of State Dean Rusk and Secretary of Defense Robert McNamara, he shared responsibility for advising the president on foreign policy. Unlike his successors Henry Kissinger and Zbigniew Brzezinski, Bundy engaged in no ostentatious struggle for power with the secretary of state. He deferred publicly to the courtly Rusk, content with the knowledge that he was closer to the president, had superior access to him, and controlled much of what the president heard or saw. More than anyone else, Bundy controlled the process by which decisions were made. Anyone unaware and/or unappreciative of his *modus operandi* was unworthy of his concern. He was confident that those who mattered—establishment figures such as Dean Acheson, Robert Lovett, and John McCloy and great journalists like Walter Lippmann and James Reston—all recognized the advantages of mind and position he held.

In temperament Bundy was closer to Kennedy than Rusk. Rusk perceived some of the world's problems as intractable. They had antedated his appointment and would doubtless persist long after he was gone. He did not believe that there was an American action that would soothe Indian and Pakistani, Arab and Israel relations. Some problems were best left unaddressed. Bundy, like Kennedy, had little patience for Rusk's approach. They were men of action, always ready to take the necessary risks, confident that as long as they were leading, the United States could fashion the world as it chose. And they did not hesitate to use American power. Kennedy liked action and quick decisions. Bundy's staff was more likely to provide both than was the Department of State.

After Kennedy's death, Bundy stayed on to serve Lyndon Johnson. He played a central role in the decision to escalate the war in Vietnam, joining McNamara in urging the president to approve the bombing of North Vietnam opposed by Rusk. Bundy was also instrumental in the decision to send American troops into the Dominican Republic in 1965.

Although Bundy and Johnson worked well together initially, by 1966 the relationship had deteriorated. Johnson was more comfortable with Rusk, also from the South, than with the upper-class Eastern intellectuals Bundy seemed to personify. Bundy found Johnson's style of leadership disorderly and irritating. He was offended by Texas hyperbole and the concomitant loss of credibility so essential to maintain public support of policy. When offered the presidency of the Ford Foundation in 1966, Bundy was less eager to stay in Washington than he had been in the days of the Kennedy administration and found Johnson less determined to keep him there than Kennedy had been. Bundy accepted the Ford Foundation offer in February 1966.

The Ford Foundation had long played an important role in international development and education. During Bundy's presidency the foundation continued those activities, but it also added major new programs to fight racism at home. The struggle for equal opportunity became its highest domestic concern.

Bundy retired from the presidency of the Ford Foundation in 1979 and joined the Department of History at New York University. Throughout those years, both at Ford and at NYU, he retained his interest in foreign policy and his prestige in the foreign policy community. He was one of the "wise men" who advised Johnson to end the war in Vietnam in 1968. In the 1980s he joined forces with McNamara and George Kennan in an effort to alert Americans to the growing danger of nuclear war and to the need to end the arms race. They failed to persuade President Ronald Reagan.

Bundy later became a scholar in residence at the Carnegie Corporation. While he was there he was deeply concerned with issues of science and survival in the age of nuclear technology. He espoused the importance of proper understanding and implementation of nuclear technology on the part of the President of the United States, and he bemoaned the apparent lack of direction in this regard at the highest echelons of government. He was listed as a contributor to Brown University's *Journal of World Affairs* in 1995. He died of a heart attack in 1996. Journalist Walter Isaacson said that Bundy "came to personify the hubris of an intellectual elite that marched America with a cool and confident brilliance into the quagmire of Vietnam."

Further Reading

Among the most useful books touching on Bundy's role are David Halberstam, *The Best and the Brightest* (1972) and Arthur Schlesinger, Jr., *A Thousand Days* (1965). See also Warren I. Cohen, *Dean Rusk,* Vol. 19 in Samuel F. Bemis and Robert H. Ferrell, editors, *The American Secretaries of State and Their Diplomacy* (1980) and Lyndon B. Johnson, *The Vantage Point* (1971).

Additional Sources

Bundy, McGeorge, *Reducing Nuclear Danger: The Road Away from the Brink,* Council on Foreign Relations Press, 1993.

Newsweek, September 30, 1996.

The Scientist, June 24, 1996.

Time Magazine, September 30, 1996. □

Ivan Alekseevich Bunin

Ivan Alekseevich Bunin (1870-1953) was the first Russian to receive the Nobel Prize in literature, in 1933. Although a noted poet, he is perhaps best known for the delicate "brocaded" prose of his short stories and his novels on Russian rural life and bourgeois stupidity.

Ivan Bunin was born on his impoverished but proud family's estate near Voronezh in Oryol Province on Oct. 10/22, 1870. He grew up with a love for family traditions and a high regard for the works of Aleksandr Pushkin. In 1881 he entered the gymnasium (secondary school) in Elets but withdrew after 3 years and was tutored by his older brother. In 1889, however, family poverty forced Bunin to go to work. He held various technical and clerical jobs on provincial newspapers.

In 1891 Bunin published *Poems,* a volume that celebrated the natural world and was classical in style. Other collections of poetry followed—*In the Open Air* (1898) and *Falling Leaves* (1901), which won the Academy of Sciences' Pushkin Prize in 1903. At the same time Bunin wrote stories and sketches about Russian rural life, among the most notable of which are "Tank," "At the World's End," and "News from Home." During the 1890s he was becoming a well-known figure in literary circles. The year 1891 marked the beginning of his friendship with Anton Chekhov. And in 1899 Bunin met Maxim Gorky, who introduced him to the Znaniye group, a circle of young liberal writers.

With the opening years of the 20th century, Bunin began to concentrate on prose forms. "Antonov Apples" (1900), "The Pines" (1901), and "The Black Earth" (1904) are among his finest stories. They are marked by love for the land as well as by social awareness. In his novels *The Village* (1910) and *Sukhodol* (1911), Bunin contrasts man's aspirations with the dismal record of failure seen in human history. These works display Bunin's use of striking metaphors and penetrating understatement. Bunin's prose style has been widely admired for its delicacy, subtlety, clarity, and strong musical quality.

Bunin's work was both popular and critically respected, and in 1909 the Academy of Sciences elected him to honorary membership. He traveled widely, and from 1907 to 1911 he published a series of sketches on the Mediterranean and the Near East. At the same time, his energetic talent explored urban themes (the satirical "A Good Life," told entirely in Elets dialect), presented psychological portraits of fierce intensity ("The Dreams of Chang," 1916), and exposed the internal contradictions of bourgeois civilization ("The Gentleman from San Francisco," 1916). His translations of *The Song of Hiawatha,* Lord Byron's plays, and other works were extremely successful.

Bunin opposed the Russian Revolution, and in 1920 he emigrated to France, where he lived until his death. Bunin's early themes often reappear in the works he wrote in exile-especially his use of autobiographical material in fiction (*Arseniyev's Life,* 1930) and his strong interest in death and idealistic passion ("Mitya's Love," 1925). During this period he also wrote books on Leo Tolstoy and Anton Chekhov. In his *Memories and Portraits* (1950) he attacked Soviet cultural debasement. Bunin died in Paris, on Nov. 8, 1953.

Further Reading

Bunin's *Memories and Portraits* was translated by Vera Traill and Robin Chancellor (1951), and most of his stories and short novels have also been translated. There is no book in English on Bunin; he is, however, discussed in Renato Poggioli, *The Poets of Russia, 1890-1930* (1960). For background material see Ernest J. Simmons, *An Outline of Modern Russian Literature, 1880-1940* (1944), and Helen Muchnic, *An Introduction to Russian Literature* (1947; rev. ed. 1963). □

Robert Wilhelm Bunsen

The German chemist and physicist Robert Wilhelm Bunsen (1811-1899) was one of the great experimental chemists and a pioneer of chemical spectroscopy.

Robert Bunsen was born on March 31, 1811, in the university town of Göttingen. His father was professor of linguistics and librarian at the university. Bunsen completed his advanced education at Göttingen, developing an extensive mastery of mathematics, physics, chemistry, and mineralogy. In later years, when his fame as an experimentalist was worldwide, Bunsen stated that "a chemist who is not a physicist is nothing."

With his strong practical bent and interest in the expanding industrial revolution, Bunsen studied blast furnace operations, the working of steam engines, and the physiochemical processes of the famed porcelain works at Sèvres. In later years his scientific discoveries contributed to the increased efficiency of some of these basic industries.

Bunsen established his reputation through his work in inorganic chemistry and his classical set of experiments in organic chemistry which involved the properties of the cacodyl series of compounds. These organic arsenic bodies were highly dangerous, and his work with them nearly cost Bunsen his life. A useful by-product of this research was his discovery of the antidote for arsenic poisoning.

In 1852 Bunsen succeeded Leopold Gmelin in Heidelberg. There he established his Institute of Chemistry, which soon attracted the most brilliant students from all over the world, including Edward Frankland, the developer of the theory of chemical valency, and Victor Meyer, the pioneer in the chemistry of benzene compounds.

A master craftsman, Bunsen developed many of the instruments for analytical chemistry, including the burner which bears his name but which had been used first in a primitive form by Michael Faraday. The ice calorimeter and many devices for gas analysis were the product of Bunsen's personal skill.

Bunsen contributed to the foundations of photochemistry in collaboration with H. E. Roscoe, determining the effect of light on the combining reactions of hydrogen and chlorine. This led Bunsen to the first effort to estimate the radiant energy of the sun.

The most fruitful collaboration of Bunsen was his work with Gustav Kirchhoff, the German physicist. By combining the Bunsen burner with the optical system pioneered by Joseph von Fraunhofer, the two scientists developed the science and art of spectroscopy. Since each chemical element rendered radiant by the heat source emitted a characteristic pattern of lines (spectrum), there had been developed the supreme instrument of chemical analysis. Bunsen and Kirchhoff soon discovered two hitherto-unknown elements, cesium and rubidium.

Further Reading

A good account of Bunsen appears in volume 4 of J. R. Partington, *A History of Chemistry* (1964). Eduard Farber, ed., *Great Chemists* (1961), contains a short biographical sketch. Henry M. Leicester and Herbert S. Klickstein, *A Source Book in Chemistry, 1400-1900* (1952), includes a description of Bunsen's work. □

Gordon Bunshaft

The American architect Gordon Bunshaft (1909-1990) as chief designer for Skidmore, Owings & Merrill in New York designed major buildings from skyscrapers to museums. Bunshaft shared the esteemed Pritzker Architecture Prize with fellow architect Oscar Niemeyer in 1988.

The son of Russian Jewish immigrants, Gordon Bunshaft was born May 9, 1909, and raised in Buffalo, New York. He was determined to become an architect from childhood and eventually earned a B.Arch. (1933) and M.Arch. (1935) from the Massachusetts Institute of Technology (MIT). This education was followed by a study tour of Europe on a Rotch Traveling Fellowship (1935-1937). In 1937, after working briefly for the architect Edward Durell Stone and the industrial designer Raymond Loewy, Bunshaft entered the New York City office of Louis Skidmore. Skidmore had formed an architectural firm with Nathaniel Owings in 1936, which John O. Merrill joined in 1939 to form Skidmore, Owings & Merrill (SOM). Other than serving in the U.S. Army Corps of Engineers between 1942 and 1946, Bunshaft remained with SOM until his retirement in 1979. By the late 1940s he was a partner and chief designer in the New York office.

As a member of the large architectural firm of SOM, Bunshaft's designs benefited from SOM's extensive staff of experts in all areas of the art and business of architecture. Because of SOM's emphasis on teamwork, and the fact that his name was not a part of the firm's name, Bunshaft was perhaps not as well known as many of the other major architects of the post-1945 period. Nonetheless, several of his designs have become landmarks in the history of architecture. He preferred to express his ideas primarily through building, rather than writing or speaking.

Bunshaft's most significant early design was Lever House (1951-1952) on Park Avenue in New York. Breaking from the ziggurat-like masses of the previous generation of New York skyscrapers, Bunshaft's tower was a seemingly weightless glass box. Bunshaft juxtaposed a low, horizontal block, raised on pilotis (stilt-like supports), with a slablike,

vertical tower, which covered only 25 percent of the site. The pilotis, roof garden on the lower block, and dramatic sculptural quality of these pristine geometric forms were reminiscent of the architecture of Le Corbusier, whom Bunshaft had met in Paris during World War II. However, the use of large areas of glass, metal frames, and a meticulous concern for precise details were closer to another master of modern architecture, Ludwig Mies van der Rohe, whose masterpiece—the Seagram Building—would rise across the intersection from Lever House later in the 1950s. In its emphasis of volume over mass, regularity over symmetry, and the elimination of ornament, Lever House was one of the central links in transforming the radical International Style of the 1920s and 1930s into the dominant architectural expression for American corporations during the 1950s and 1960s. For the soap company of Lever Brothers, this perpetually shining tower of blue/green glass with stainless steel frames seemed an appropriate symbol for the cleaning properties of their products.

The era of the "glass box" skyscraper, which Lever House helped to foster, was often criticized for its redundancy and lack of originality. However, in the hands of Bunshaft this minimal approach to skyscraper design often became a high art form, such as his simple and elegant composition for the Pepsi-Cola Company (1958-1959) in New York. In the design for the Chase Manhattan Bank and Plaza (1957-1961) in New York, Bunshaft showed finesse in housing diverse functions within the clarity and order of a single rectangular block of steel and glass rising up 60 stories. On the much smaller scale of a branch bank for the Manufacturers Hanover Trust Company (1953-1954), New York, Bunshaft reversed traditional notions of a bank's appearance by enclosing it with glass curtain walls. Rather than stressing impregnable solidity, this bank suggested accessibility to the public, and security was provided for the vault by having it on view for all to see, behind plate glass at the sidewalk level.

Along with defining the architectural character of corporate America in cities, Bunshaft built several significant designs for corporate headquarters in suburban and rural areas. Rather than rising vertically, these modern buildings spread out horizontally across arcadian settings in a palace-like manner, such as the two examples in Bloomfield, Connecticut: the Connecticut General Life Insurance Company Headquarters (1954-1957) and the Emhard Manufacturing Company Administration and Research Building (1963).

Bunshaft was an avid collector of modern art and often worked with artists to bring sculptures into a correspondence with buildings. An excellent example of such a collaboration was the placement of Isamu Noguchi's red *Cube* on one of its corners in front of SOM's somberly rational Marine Midland Bank (1967) in New York.

Bunshaft's interest in sculpture was further suggested in the monumental character of many of his designs for institutions. The exhibition hall for his Beinecke Rare Book and Manuscript Library (1960-1963) at Yale University, New Haven, Connecticut, was a large, elevated block whose one and one-fourth inch thick, translucent marble walls (held in place by granite encased Vierendeel steel trusses) allowed a mysteriously soft light to penetrate the majestically scaled room within. Bunshaft further explored the bold and dramatic use of singular monumental forms in his formalist temple, with Egyptian-like sloping walls, for the Lyndon Baines Johnson Library (1968-1971) at the University of Texas, Austin, and the cylindrical, bunker-like Hirshhorn Museum (1974) in Washington, D.C.

Before his retirement in 1979, Bunshaft helped other SOM partners design the Haj Terminal at King Abdul Aziz International Airport (1975-1982) in Jeddah, Saudi Arabia.The most striking feature of this design was an extensive open area covered by conical fiberglass tents supported by cables from steel pylons to provide temporary shelter for Moslem pilgrims. Bunshaft also designed for Jeddah a National Commercial Bank in 1977. In response to the strong desert heat and sunshine, this skyscraper, triangular in plan, turned inward to large courts, which were expressed on the exterior with monumental openings, a creative reinterpretation of the skyscraper for a foreign climate.

Along with Bunshaft's activities as an architect, he was a visiting critic at MIT, Harvard, and Yale, a member of the President's Commission on the Fine Arts, a trustee of the Museum of Modern Art, and a trustee of Carnegie-Mellon University. He also received numerous awards, including the 1984 Gold Medal of the American Academy and Institute of Arts and Letters. In 1988 he and fellow architect Oscar Niemeyer of Brazil shared the highly prestigious Pritzker Architecture Prize. Bunshaft died in the summer of 1990 at the age of 81.

Further Reading

The best single source on Bunshaft is David Jacobs, "The Establishment's Architect-Plus," *New York Times Magazine* (July 23, 1972). His buildings are illustrated and discussed in Henry Russell Hitchcock (introduction to) and Ernst Danz (author), *Architecture of Skidmore, Owings & Merrill, 1950-1962* (1962); Christopher Woodward, *Skidmore, Owings & Merrill* (1970); Arthur Drexler (introduction to) and Axel Menges (commentaries by), in *Architecture of Skidmore, Owings & Merrill, 1963-1973* (1974); and Albert Bush-Brown, *Skidmore, Owings & Merrill: Architecture and Urbanism, 1973-1983* (1983). Two books with limited but interesting discussions of Bunshaft are Cranston Jones, *Architecture Today and Tomorrow* (1961) and Nathaniel Alexander Owings, *The Spaces In Between: An Architect's Journey* (1973). Also see *Time,* May 30, 1988; August 20, 1990. □

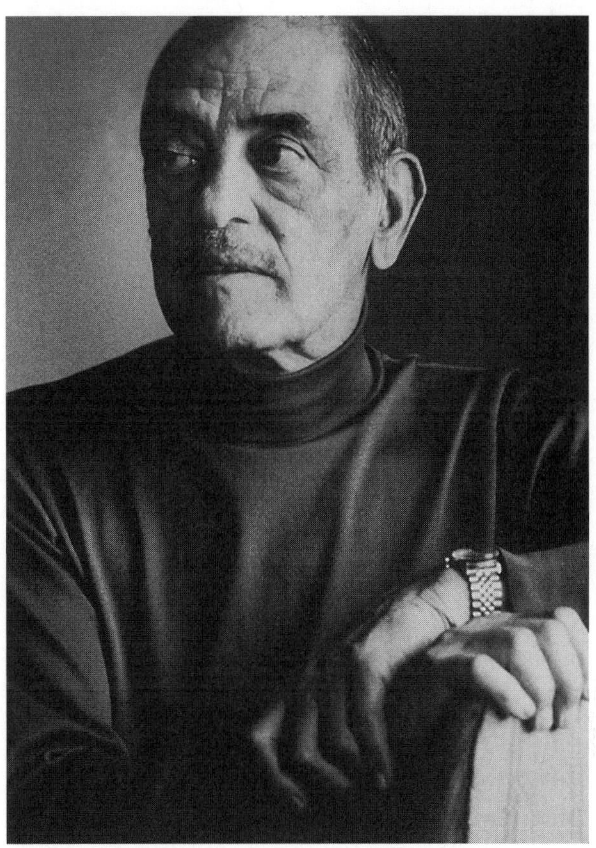

Luis Buñuel

The films of the Spanish director Luis Buñuel (1900-1983) emphasize the hypocrisy of conventional morality.

Luis Buñuel was born in Calanda, the first of seven children in a prosperous, landowning family. After being educated by the Jesuits in Saragossa, he studied philosophy and literature at the University of Madrid.

In 1925 Buñuel traveled to Paris, where he came under the influence of the surrealist André Breton and the film director Jean Epstein. In 1928 he returned to Spain to collaborate with Salvador Dali on *Un Chien Andalou* (1928) and *L'âge d'or* (1929), two innovative surrealist films. The following year Buñuel journeyed to Hollywood. He completed only two short films during the next 10 years: *Land without Bread* (1932), a realistic study of Spanish provincial poverty, and *Madrid 36 to Spain in Arms,* a documentary supporting the Loyalist struggle against Franco.

During the early 1940s Buñuel supervised the production of anti-Nazi propaganda films, and in 1946 he wrote the screenplay for *The Beast with Five Fingers.* He then undertook a series of films set in Mexico. The initial efforts were poorly executed commercial pieces, but *Los olvidados* (1950), a mordant portrayal of an urchin gang brutalized beyond hope of recovery, was perhaps the first cinematic expression of Buñuel's emotional and intellectual vision.

In 1952 Buñuel directed in English *The Adventures of Robinson Crusoe,* an imaginative translation of the Defoe classic. The same year *El* appeared; like several subsequent Buñuel works, this film is a bitter attack on Catholic Spain's sexual mores. After a succession of inconsequential efforts, he produced his first cinematic masterpiece, *Nazarin* (1958), a lyrically moving, atheistic parable on the impossibility of a modern Christ.

In 1961 Buñuel returned to Spain to produce his most celebrated work, *Viridiana.* This film contains a detailed foray into the sexual deviations, physical cruelty, and religious psychoses fostered by Spain's repressive and decadent climate. Returning to Mexico, he filmed *The Exterminating Angel* (1962), a claustrophobic study of the human condition, flawed by occasional philosophical obfuscation and banal use of surrealist elements.

In 1965 Buñuel directed one of his poorest efforts, *The Diary of a Chambermaid,* and one of his best, *Simon of the Desert.* The latter is a trenchant analysis of the psychology of sainthood, containing a superb blending of ironic satire with sincere religious feeling. In 1967 he filmed the flawed *Belle de jour,* a dream fantasy with metaphysical-sexual content. Three years later *The Milky Way* presented with freshness and charm Buñuel's quintessential statement on the flesh-spirit duality.

Buñuel rang up the curtain on the new decade with *Tristana* (1970), a film about an unconventional relationship which featured two of his favorite players, Fernando Rey and Catherine Deneuve. It was nominated for an Oscar as Best Foreign Language Film, an honor by which the iconoclastic director declined to be flattered. "Nothing would disgust me more, morally, than receiving an Oscar," he declared. He did win an Academy statuette for his next film, *The Discreet Charm of the Bourgeoisie* (1972), a charming satire about a dinner party that is ranked among his master works. His follow-up, *The Phantom of Liberty* (1974) was less well-received, but his final film, *That Obscure Object of Desire* (1977), a raucous erotic comedy, is one of his most accessible works.

In January 1983, Buñuel received the *Grand Cross of Isabel,* Spain's highest civilian honor, for his contributions to cinema and for his steadfast opposition to Spanish Fascism. By that time he had lived abroad for almost 40 years, an exile from his homeland. He died on July 29, 1983, shortly before the publication of his autobiography, *My Last Sigh.*

Further Reading

Raymond Durgnat, *Luis Buñuel* (1968), is an admiring study of the director's film career. Varying shades of critical opinion can be found in John Russell Taylor, *Cinema Eye, Cinema Ear: Some Key Film-makers of the Sixties* (1964); Stanley Kauffmann, *A World of Film: Criticism and Comment* (1966); Pauline Kael, *Kiss Kiss Bang Bang* (1968); and Dwight Macdonald, *Dwight Macdonald on Movies* (1969). Buñuel's autobiography *My Last Sigh* (1983) was published posthumously. Peter William Evans, *The Films of Luis Buñuel: Subjectivity and Desire* (1995) offers an extended analysis of Buñuel's films in the context of contemporary debates in film studies. □

John Bunyan

The English author and Baptist preacher John Bunyan (1628-1688) wrote "The Pilgrim's Progress" and some 60 other pious works. The sincere evangelical urgency of his religious thought and the vivid clarity of his prose have won wide admiration.

John Bunyan, born in Elstow near Bedford, was baptized on Nov. 30, 1628. His father, the brazier-tinker "Thomas Bonnion," derived from an old Bedfordshire family which had declined in fortune and status. Bunyan had a rudimentary education and at an early age became a tinker. From 1644 to 1647 he served with the parliamentary army during the Puritan Revolution, but he saw little or no fighting.

Religious Development

About 1649 Bunyan married a pious Anglican who introduced him to Arthur Dent's *The Plain Man's Pathway to Heaven.* Under their combined influence Bunyan became an attentive churchgoer and delighted in Anglican ceremonial and bell ringing. But he soon recognized that he was desperately bound by sin and that only Christ could provide redemption. He turned for guidance to John Gifford; once a roistering Cavalier, Gifford had been rescued from debauchery by the Gospel and was pastor of the Congregational Church in Bedford. "Mr. Gifford's doctrine," wrote Bunyan, "was much for my stability." Like Joan of Arc and St. Theresa, Bunyan heard voices, and like William Blake, he had visions. He saw Jesus looking "through the tiles on the roof" and felt Satan pluck his clothes to stop him from praying.

Bunyan was no fornicator, drunkard, or thief; but so urgent was his religion, so passionate his nature, that any sin, however small, was an enormous burden. With Gifford's guidance he made a spiritual pilgrimage and in 1653 was baptized in the Ouse River. Two years later, induced by his Baptist coreligionists, he started "the mighty work of preaching the Gospel." Soon his pen became as active as his tongue, and in 1658-1659 he published *Sighs from Hell* and other tracts.

Triumph in Adversity

The restoration of monarchy and Anglicanism in 1660 meant that Bunyan could no longer preach freely as he had under the Puritan Commonwealth. In January 1661 he was jailed for "pertinaciously abstaining" from Anglican services and for holding "unlawful meetings." Because he was unwilling to promise silence, his 3-month sentence stretched to 12 years with a few respites. After his wife's death he had remarried, and he worked while in prison to support his second wife and children. He also preached to his fellow sufferers and wrote a variety of religious works, including *Grace Abounding* published in 1666—one of the world's most poignant spiritual autobiographies. During this period he also wrote most of Part I of *The Pilgrim's Progress,* but he hesitated to release it because of its fictional structure.

After the Declaration of Indulgence (1672), Bunyan was freed and licensed as a preacher. He built a Nonconformist congregation of 3,000 or 4,000 souls in Bedfordshire; he ministered assiduously to his flock and helped to found about 30 other congregations. But in 1673 the edict of toleration was repealed. When Bunyan was imprisoned for about 6 months in 1675, he again worked on his masterpiece, and Part I of *The Pilgrim's Progress* was published in

1678. It won immediate popularity, and before Bunyan's death there were 13 editions, with some additions. Since then it has been continuously in print and has been translated into well over a hundred languages.

Bunyan's own experience and the language of the Bible were the sources of *The Pilgrim's Progress.* Unlike *Grace Abounding,* this work reveals his spiritual development through allegory. The countryside through which the hero, Christian, progresses is a blend of the English countryside, the world of the Bible, and the land of dreams. Despite his assertion that "manner and matter too was all my own," Bunyan owed a good deal to oral tradition and wide reading—folk tales, books of emblems and characters, sermons, homilies in dialogue form, and traditional allegories.

Bunyan's last decade was fertile. Like *The Pilgrim's Progress, The Life and Death of Mr. Badman* (1680) made a significant advance toward the English novel. *The Holy War* (1682) is a dramatic, allegorical account of siege warfare against the town of Mansoul. Although, like all his works, it is based on Calvinist theology, Bunyan should not be considered a rigid determinist but should be viewed as a Christian humanist who assigned personal responsibility to his characters. Part II of *The Pilgrim's Progress* (1684) emphasizes human relationships and the sanctification of the world, especially through marriage and family life. Bunyan produced 14 more books before he died at the age of 60 on Aug. 31, 1688. He was buried in Bunhill Fields, where he lies near other great Nonconformists—William Blake, George Fox, and Daniel Defoe.

Despite the Protestant evangelical cast of his mind, Bunyan transcended Puritanism and remains relevant in an age of ecumenism. Nor was he a pessimistic prophet: if his Pilgrim knew the Hill of Difficulty and the Slough of Despair, he also enjoyed the Delectable Mountains and reached the Celestial City.

Further Reading

Because there is no complete modern edition of Bunyan's works, students rely on *The Works of John Bunyan,* edited by George Offor (1853-1855). Roger Sharrock's edition of *The Pilgrim's Progress* (1960) is textually definitive. James F. Forrest's admirable edition of *The Holy War* (1968) emphasizes Bunyan's modern relevance. There are several excellent biographies of Bunyan. The fullest treatment is John Brown, *John Bunyan: His Life, Times, and Work* (1885; rev. ed. by Frank Mott Harrison, 1928). Roger Sharrock, *John Bunyan* (1954), is a brilliant brief survey. Henri Antoine Talon, *John Bunyan: The Man and His Work* (1948; trans. 1951), is a scholarly interpretation. Bunyan's personality is emphasized in George Bagshawe H. Harrison, *John Bunyan* (1928). Robert Hay Coats, *John Bunyan* (1927), is a popularized account. William York Tindall, *John Bunyan* (1934), places Bunyan in the tradition of "mechanick" preachers. Richard L. Greaves, *John Bunyan* (1969), focuses on Bunyan's theology. Bunyan's place in the history of fiction is explored in Dorothy Van Ghent, *The English Novel: Form and Function* (1953). There is a brief appreciation of Bunyan's style in George Bernard Shaw, *Dramatic Opinions and Essays* (1906).

Additional Sources

Arnott, Anne, *Valiant for truth: the story of John Bunyan,* Grand Rapids, Mich.: W.B. Eerdmans Pub. Co., 1986, 1985.

Bunyan, John, *The trial of John Bunyan & the persecution of the Puritans: selections from the writings of John Bunyan and Agnes Beaumont,* London: Folio Society, 1978.

Griffith, Gwilym Oswald, *John Bunyan,* Folcroft, Pa.: Folcroft Library Editions, 1979.

Harding, Richard Winboult, *John Bunyan, his life and times,* Philadelphia: R. West, 1978.

Venables, Edmund, *Life of John Bunyan,* Folcroft, Pa.: Folcroft Library Editions, 1977.

Williams, Charles, *A bi-centenary memorial of John Bunyan, who died A. D. 1688,* Philadelphia: R. West, 1978. □

Luther Burbank

The American plant breeder Luther Burbank (1849-1926) originated many varieties of garden plants, grains, and fruits. He was popularly known as a "wizard" because of the stream of new and improved forms that came from his experimental farm.

In Luther Burbank's youth, botany was beginning to shed its taxonomic preoccupation and the interest of scientists was shifting to questions related to the theory of evolution—variation, species formation, modes of reproduction, and environmental effects. To a long-standing American interest in importation of foreign plant varieties was added an interest in the experimental production of improved forms. Agricultural experimental stations began to dot the country during the 1890s. Although Burbank was not a scientist and was essentially uninterested in scientific questions, he nevertheless drew his inspiration from this new scientific work, and his own success served to intensify public interest in such investigations.

Burbank was born on March 7, 1849, in Lancaster, Mass., the son of a farmer and maker of brick and pottery. He attended the district school until he was 15 and then spent four winters at the Lancaster Academy. Most of his scientific education, however, was obtained from reading at the public library in Lancaster. According to his own account, his reading of Charles Darwin's *Variation of Animals and Plants under Domestication* in 1868 proved the turning point in his career, causing him to take the production of new species and varieties of plants as his life's work.

Beginning the Work

In 1870, 2 years after the death of his father, Burbank used his inheritance to help purchase a tract of 17 acres near the small town of Lunenburg, where he took up the business of market gardening. Here he produced his first "creation," the Burbank potato, and began the work that was to make him famous.

Despite his success as a market gardener, in 1875 Burbank decided to sell his land and move to California, where his three older brothers had already moved. He set-

tled in Santa Rosa, where he would carry on his work for the next 50 years. Later he added a small amount of acreage adjoining a nearby town.

Following the Empirical Method

Although Burbank had read the scientific literature, he never operated as a scientist and apparently never thought of himself as one. His methods were empirical; he imported plants from foreign countries, made crosses of every conceivable kind—often for no apparent reason except, as he said, to get "perturbation" in the plants so as to get as wide and as large a variation as possible—and grew hundreds of thousands of plants under differing environmental conditions. He kept records only for his own use; once a project was completed and a new plant on the market, the records were generally destroyed. An effort made by the Carnegie Institution of Washington to collate the scientific data that came out of Burbank's experiments collapsed after a few years.

Although Burbank's methods were empirical, he did develop a store of knowledge that proved invaluable. This special knowledge (as emphasized by two scholars who studied the scientific aspects of his work) concerned correlations. Thus a minute, almost undetectable, variation in a young leaf, for example, may imply (or correlate with) a sweeter or plumper fruit, or a larger and more perfect flower. In his years of experimentation, Burbank gained an unrivaled mastery of such correlations, which, combined with his unusually keen sensory abilities, largely accounted for his success.

Originating New Forms

Burbank's creative work ranged over a long list of plants, but his strongest interests were in plums, berries, and lilies. He originated more than 40 new varieties of plums and prunes, mostly from multiple crossings in which Japanese plums played a prominent part. His work with berries, extending over 35 years, resulted in the introduction of at least 10 new varieties, mostly obtained through hybridizations of dewberries, blackberries, and raspberries. His years of experimentation with lilies resulted in a brilliant array of new forms, many of which became the most popular varieties in American gardens.

Best known among Burbank's flowers are the Shasta daisy, the blue Shirley poppy and the Fire poppy, and the fragrant calla. His wide range of techniques is illustrated by these. The Shasta daisy, a favorite of Burbank, was the result of a multiple crossing between a European and an American species of field daisy and then between these hybrids and a Japanese variety. The Shirley poppy was obtained by long selection from a crimson European poppy. The Fire poppy was a hybrid from a butter-colored species and a pure-white species that had a dull red in its ancestry. The fragrant calla, which has a perfume resembling that of the violet, was discovered by accident in a flat of Little Gem calla seedlings. His new fruits, besides the many plums and prunes, included varieties of apples, peaches, quinces, and nectarines. One of his less profitable creations, the result of an effort to excite "perturbations," was a cross between the peach and the almond. At one time or another, he worked with virtually all the common garden vegetables. One of his most unusual experiments resulted in the production of a series of spineless cacti useful for feeding cattle in arid regions.

Applying Principles to Humans

Burbank's work with plants convinced him that the key to good breeding was selection and environment, and he, like so many others of his time, tried to apply his concepts to human society. The product of his thinking on this subject was first published in 1907 as *The Training of the Human Plant.* Yet despite his vast experience in plant breeding, this book revealed his firm belief in the then-discredited theory of the inheritance of acquired characteristics; accordingly, unlike most eugenists of the period, he stressed education and the provision of a good environment generally as the best way to remake human society.

Burbank was an honorary member of leading scientific societies all over the world. He was a fellow of the American Association for the Advancement of Science and of the Royal Horticultural Society. In 1905 he was awarded an honorary doctor of science degree by Tufts College. He died on April 11, 1926.

Further Reading

Luther Burbank: His Methods and Discoveries and Their Practical Application, edited by John Witson (12 vols., 1914-1915), was written under Burbank's direction. For an intimate account by Burbank's sister, Emma Burbank Beeson, see *The Early Life and Letters of Luther Burbank* (1927), which had been published in 1926 as *The Harvest of the Years.* Biographical material is also in Henry Smith Williams, *Luther Burbank: His Life and Work* (1915). For a favorable assessment of Burbank's scientific work see David Starr Jordan and Vernon L. Kellogg, *The Scientific Aspects of Luther Burbank's Work* (1909).

Additional Sources

Dreyer, Peter, *A gardener touched with genius: the life of Luther Burbank,* New York: Coward, McCann & Geoghegan, 1975, Santa Rosa, Calif.: L. Burbank Home & Gardens, 1993. □

Charles Burchfield

The American painter Charles Burchfield (1893-1967) was an expressionist nature painter, although many of his fine early works are of city or small-town subjects.

Charles Burchfield was born on April 9, 1893, in Ashtabula Harbor, OH. He grew up in the nearby town of Salem, where the family had moved after the father's death. There, on the edge of a small midwestern industrial town, Burchfield discovered nature. He walked continually in the woods and marshes around the town. He had begun drawing and painting before he entered the first grade.

Burchfield graduated from high school with a scholarship award of $120 and in a year had earned enough money to enter the Cleveland School of Art (now the Cleveland Institute of Art). He studied there for four years, supporting himself by working during vacations. His chief discovery there was Asian art, particularly the work of Hiroshige and Hokusai. When he graduated from Cleveland, the school awarded him a scholarship to the National Academy of Design in New York City. He arrived for the fall term of 1916. His trepidation about New York and the academy proved justified, and he went back to Salem at the end of November.

Back home, he continued to paint on weekends and during lunch hours. He married, moved to Buffalo, NY, to work as a wallpaper designer, and persisted as a part-time painter until 1929. He raised five children in the Buffalo suburb of Gardenville and continued living there long after he had achieved national recognition. He painted evocative pictures of small-town houses. *Six O'Clock,* for example, conveys a feeling of an imprisoned place remarkably like that evoked in Sherwood Anderson's stories. Burchfield also painted many straight-on industrial subjects with great feeling for their monumental strength.

Because he limited himself to scenes around his home during the 1930s, he was welcomed into the American Scene, or Regionalist, movement, though he firmly rejected any such identification. His best work, in watercolor, is distinguished by a strong sense of the life-force hidden behind the appearances of nature, pulsing in the atmosphere, often forming a nimbus of colored light around trees, flowers, bushes, and water.

Long overlooked because he placed himself outside the art establishment of his time, Burchfield lived to see his reputation solidified by a comprehensive exhibition at the Whitney Museum of American Art in 1956. The ensuing national tour helped put an end to the financial worries that had plagued him for much of his life.

Late in his life, Burchfield created a series of dynamic free-form watercolors, again using nature as his subject matter. Working almost entirely from memory because heart trouble limited his movements, Burchfield found a new freedom and spontaneity in these later paintings. The art historian Matthew Baigell called them "some of the finest celebrations of landscape moods ever done by an American artist." As his health continued to deteriorate, Burchfield grew increasingly contemplative, often wondering at the nature of the afterlife. In 1967, while having lunch with his wife in a Buffalo restaurant, Burchfield suffered a fatal heart attack. He was 73 years old.

A small-town resident all his life, Burchfield reminded one interviewer of a backwater businessman, another of a family doctor. Essentially, Burchfield was always the boy alone in the woods, sensing the presence of cosmic forces within the forms of nature. He usually painted outdoors, face-to- face with the nature he loved. Burchfield more than any other American artist created his art out of a nature studied, loved, observed, and finally, revealed. Too often dismissed as a regionalist, Burchfield was in fact a cartographer of the human spirit. In 1997, the Columbus Museum of Art mounted a large and comprehensive exhibition of his work. The national tour that followed was designed to return Burchfield to his rightful place among the front ranks of twentieth-century American painters.

Further Reading

The basic work on Burchfield is John I. H. Baur, *Charles Burchfield* (1956), written following a major exhibition at the Whitney Museum of American Art; it is greatly enriched by Burchfield's private journal and by his conversations with the author. Burchfield is treated sympathetically in E. P. Richardson, *Painting in America: The Story of 450 Years* (1956), and in Alexander Eliot, *Three Hundred Years of American Painting* (1957). Baur's later book is *The Inlander: Life and Work of Charles Burchfield, 1893-1967* (1982). Nannette V. Maclejunes and Michael D. Hall, *The Paintings of Charles Burchfield: North by Midwest* (1997) is an interdisciplinary study of Burchfield's oeuvre written to accompany a traveling exhibition organized by the Columbus Museum of Art. □

Jacob Christoph Burckhardt

The Swiss historian Jacob Christoph Burckhardt (1818-1897) was a philosophical historian whose books dealt with cultural and artistic history and whose lectures examined the forces that had shaped European history.

Through the use of eyewitness accounts, diplomatic documents, and the contents of government archives, the teachers and contemporaries of Jacob Christoph Burckhardt sought to reconstruct political events "as they had really happened." Burckhardt, however, viewed history as the record of the achievement of the human spirit. Politics was only part of that record. The highest expression of any age was to be found in its poetry, art, literature, and philosophy. The historian's task was to seek the spirit these works expressed, so the reader might be "not smarter for the next time but wiser forever."

Burckhardt was born in Basel on May 25, 1818. His father, a pastor at the Basel Minster, was elected administrative head of the Reformed Church in the canton in 1838. The year before, Jacob had begun theological studies at the University of Basel. Within 18 months, however, he lost his orthodox religious beliefs and turned from theology to history. He studied in Berlin for 4 years, attending the lectures of Johann Droysen, August Boeckh, and Franz Kugler, and Leopold von Ranke's seminar. Burckhardt formed close friendships with a group of poets and students of revolutionary liberal political views.

In 1843 Burckhardt returned to Basel, where he took a post as political correspondent with the conservative *Basler Zeitung,* and lectured at the university on art history. He immersed himself in the political crisis then shaking Switzerland, a crisis brought on by the return of the Jesuits to the Catholic canton of Lucerne. Then in 1846, disgusted by what he had seen, he left for Italy. His political views had turned to cultural and aristocratic conservatism. During the next 12 years he taught and wrote in Berlin, Basel, and Zurich, with lengthy trips to Italy in 1847, 1848, and again in 1853 to prepare the *Cicerone.*

"The Age of Constantine" and "Cicerone"

During the winter of 1847-1848 Burckhardt planned a series of cultural histories, beginning with the age of Pericles and ending with the age of Raphael. The first to appear was *The Age of Constantine the Great* (1852). The structure of this work was one that Burckhardt would use again in his later cultural histories and analyze in detail in his *Reflections on World History:* the "three great powers"—state, religion, and culture—and the ways in which they determine each other. The book is thus concerned as much with art and literature as with politics and religion.

Burckhardt's *Cicerone* (1854) was "a guide for the enjoyment of art in Italy." In form a traveler's guidebook, it was in reality a history of Italian art. In it Burckhardt first tried to solve the problem of systematic art history, tried, as he later put it, to get away from "the mess of art history as the history of artists," to go beyond biography to the analysis of historical and geographical styles.

"The Civilization of the Renaissance"

While still a student in Berlin, Burckhardt had come to the conclusion that the French Revolution had "pulled the historical ground from under the feet" of all European peoples. Just as in art the styles of every age now coexisted, "one beside the other," with no single tradition dominating, so with the state "the nineteenth century began with a clean slate." The individual now had free choice in politics, and nothing to fall back on but his own "inner truth." The application of this insight to the culture of Renaissance Italy resulted in Burckhardt's masterpiece, *The Civilization of the Renaissance in Italy* (1860).

In this work Burckhardt proposed that the conflict between popes and emperors had deprived 13th-century Italy of legitimate political rule, had left it with that "clean slate" he saw in his own times. This climate allowed political units to appear "whose existence was founded simply on their power to maintain it." But it also freed the individual of all traditional constraints, whether political, religious, or social. Expressed through artistic and literary forms revived from antiquity, this freed and self-conscious individualism, this "genius of the Italian people . . . achieved the conquest of the western world." In the Italian Renaissance, Burckhardt saw the major characteristics of the modern world, its evil as well as its good.

Later Years

Burckhardt explained his thesis in his lectures of 1868-1869, "On the Study of History," in the course of a wide-ranging analysis of the "three powers" at the heart of his historical vision. Culture, in contrast to the constants, state and religion, "is the sum of those spiritual developments that appear spontaneously." Its form and its vehicle—

language—are the product of societies and epochs, but its source is always the individual. To study culture is thus to study the individual giving expression to his place and his age as well as himself.

After publishing his notes on Italian architecture in 1867, Burckhardt prepared nothing more for the press but devoted himself until his retirement in 1893 to lecturing at the university. His series of cultural histories was never completed, but his lectures covered the entire sweep of European history from the ancient Greeks to the European crisis of 1870. In an age of ever-narrower nationalisms, Burckhardt reached back to the universal humanism of Goethe.

After 1870 Burckhardt became increasingly pessimistic about the future of European culture. Though he hoped for another Renaissance, he feared the arrival of the "fearful simplifiers," the demogogues who would lead the "masses" to tyranny and destroy the European culture he loved. "The world is moving toward the alternative of complete democracy or absolute, ruthless despotism," he wrote to a friend in 1882. The day would come when "the military state will turn industrialist." He withdrew to two sparsely furnished rooms above a bakery shop and devoted himself to his work on Italian art, which he never completed. He died on Aug. 8, 1897.

Further Reading

The definitive biography of Burckhardt is in German. In English, analyses of Burckhardt's work on the Renaissance are presented in Wallace K. Ferguson, *The Renaissance in Historical Thought: Five Centuries of Interpretation* (1948), and Karl J. Weintraub, *Visons of Culture* (1966). George P. Gooch, *History and Historians in the Nineteenth Century* (1913; 3d ed. 1935; with new preface, 1959), analyzes Burckhardt's life and work. Hans Kohn, *The Mind of Germany: The Education of a Nation* (1960), and H. Hearder, *Europe in the Nineteenth Century, 1830-1880* (1966), are recommended for general historical background. □

Johann Ludwig Burckhardt

Johann Ludwig Burckhardt (1784–1817) was a Swiss-born, British-sponsored explorer of the Near East and Africa who anticipated the great explorers of the 19th century.

Johann Ludwig Burckhardt was born in Lausanne and grew up in his ancestral city, Basel. After study at the universities of Leipzig and Göttingen, he went to England in 1806. A letter from the anthropologist Johann Friedrich Blumenbach introduced him to Sir Joseph Banks, the moving spirit in the Association for Promoting the Discovery of the Interior Parts of Africa.

Failing to find other employment, Burckhardt offered his services to the "African Association" for an attempt to penetrate the Moslem-dominated central and western Sudan, and he was accepted. To prepare himself, Burckhardt went to Cambridge, where he studied Arabic, attended lectures on science and medicine, and adopted Arabian costume.

Burckhardt left England for Aleppo, Syria, in 1809. At a safe distance from the intended scene of his endeavors, he perfected himself in Arabic and in Moslem customs. As a test of his disguise, he made three journeys, traveling as the poorest of Arabs, sleeping on the ground, and eating with the camel drivers.

His apprenticeship completed, Burckhardt journeyed to Cairo, became the first modern European to visit Petra, and wrote an account of his journeys for the association. As no westbound caravan was available at Cairo, Burckhardt followed the Nile southward, hoping to reach Dongola. After he had traveled over a thousand miles by donkey, insurrectionaries blocked him less than a hundred miles from his goal.

Burckhardt then returned to Isna and decided to follow the caravan route over the Nubian Desert and cross the Red Sea. He crossed from Suakin to Jidda and explored the northeast coast of the Red Sea. His report on the Hejaz and the holy cities of Islam was the fullest and most accurate then available in Europe.

In 1815 Burckhardt returned to Cairo, suffering from the dysentery which had cut short his Arabian explorations. Burckhardt wrote up his later journals, continued to collect manuscripts and antiquities, and, to escape the plague, made a 2-month journey to the Sinai Peninsula, where he took notes on manuscripts at the Mount Sinai monastery. He also traced the Gulf of Aqaba.

In late 1817 Burckhardt's illness recurred. He died at Cairo on October 15 as he was preparing to join a caravan for Timbuktu. "Sheikh Ibrahim," as the Moslems knew him, was buried with Islamic rites.

Further Reading

There is no full-length biography of Burckhardt. Robin Hallett, *The Penetration of Africa . . . to 1830* (1965), contains a chapter on Burckhardt, furnishes an excellent introduction to African exploration, and has an extensive bibliography. □

Warren E. Burger

As Chief Justice of the U.S. Supreme Court (1969-1986), Warren E. Burger (born 1907) was tough on criminal defendants and generally negative toward civil rights and civil liberties claims, but did much to improve the administration of justice.

During the 1968 presidential campaign, Richard Nixon told a public worried about the rising crime rate that the Supreme Court was "seriously hamstringing the peace forces in our society and strengthening the criminal forces." He promised, if elected, to ensure that the Court would no longer hamper law enforcement. The victorious Nixon's first step toward that goal was appointing Warren E. Burger to succeed Earl Warren as chief justice. Liberals worried that Burger would soon sweep away the many legal reforms initiated during the Warren era, but their fears proved unfounded. Although more conservative than his predecessor, he led no counterrevolution, but rather made his mark as an administrative reformer.

Indeed the contrast between the Burger and Warren courts was less striking than that between the humble origins of the new chief and the background of the typical appointee. Most members of the Court have come from prominent or well-to-do families and have attended prestigious colleges and law schools. Burger, though, was the son of a railroad cargo inspector and travelling salesman. He was born on September 17, 1907, in St. Paul, Minnesota, and grew up in modest circumstances. By age nine he was delivering newspapers to help his family financially. When Burger graduated from high school, where he was student council president and engaged in a wide range of extracurricular activities, Princeton offered him a partial scholarship. Because of his family's limited resources, he had to decline it. Burger took extension courses at the University of Minnesota for two years and then enrolled in a night law school. Combining study with work as a life insurance salesman, he earned his LL.B. *magna cum laude* from St. Paul College of Law in 1931.

After admission to the bar, Burger joined the St. Paul law firm of Boyesen, Otis & Faricy. In 1935 he became a partner in the successor firm of Faricy, Burger, Moore & Costello, with which he remained affiliated until 1953. In addition to handling a variety of civil and criminal cases, he taught contract law at his alma mater for a dozen years.

Political Career

Burger was active in Republican politics. He helped to organize the Minnesota Young Republicans in 1934 and played an important role in Harold Stassen's successful 1938 campaign for governor. Rejected for World War II military service because of a spinal injury, he served from 1942 to 1947 on his state's Emergency War Labor Board. At both the 1948 and 1952 Republican National Conventions, Burger acted as floor manager for Stassen's presidential campaign. At a crucial moment during the 1952 gathering he threw his support to Gen. Dwight Eisenhower, helping Ike to win the nomination on the first ballot.

After the election President Eisenhower made him head of the Justice Department's Civil Division. Assistant Attorney General Burger supervised a staff of about 180 lawyers who handled all civil cases except antitrust and land litigation. When Solicitor General Simon E. Sobeloff refused to defend the dismissal of Yale professor John Peters from a part-time position with the Public Health Service as a security risk, Burger volunteered to argue the case before the Supreme Court. He lost and, by involving himself in the matter, aroused the ire of liberals.

Law and Order Judge

Nevertheless, in 1955 Eisenhower named him to the U.S. Court of Appeals for the District of Columbia. While on that prestigious bench, Burger demonstrated a capacity for legal scholarship, writing several law review articles and lecturing on a variety of topics ranging from the insanity defense to judicial administration. His opinions in criminal procedure cases attracted more attention. They were consistently pro-prosecution. He urged that confessions be admitted into evidence even when the police who obtained them had violated legal rules requiring the prompt arraignment of suspects and that physical evidence not be excluded because it had been obtained through forcible entry. Pragmatic rather than legalistic, Judge Burger sought to ensure that the judiciary would not interfere with law enforcement.

He was just what Nixon wanted in a chief justice. Ironically, in Burger's most famous criminal case the loser was the president. In *United States* v. *Nixon* (1974) Burger ordered his patron to turn over to Watergate special prosecutor Leon Jaworski tape recordings, one of which contained unequivocal evidence that Nixon had committed the crime of obstruction of justice. This ruling led directly to the president's resignation.

In more routine criminal cases, Burger was everything Nixon had hoped for. He spent his first years on the Court dissenting as holdovers from the Warren era continued to expand the rights of defendants. When other Nixon appointees joined him on the bench, Burger launched a successful counterattack, which lasted from 1971 until 1976. It resulted in decisions partially undercutting Warren Court precedents, such as *Harris* v. *New York* (1971), in which he announced that a statement obtained without giving the warnings required by *Miranda* v. *Arizona* (1966) could be used to impeach a defendant's testimony. About 1977 the Burger Court's hostility toward the work of its predecessor seemed to subside, but the chief justice frequently dissented when it rendered decisions favorable to defendants. He also continued to criticize the "exclusionary rule," which made illegally obtained evidence inadmissible. Prodded by Burger, the Court returned to the attack in 1981. During the years that followed, it handed down decisions which, among other things, created significant exceptions to both the exclusionary rule and the requirement that police give suspects *Miranda* warnings before interrogating them.

During the same period, Burger also helped give new life to the death penalty, which for several years after the Court re-legalized it in 1976 had existed more in theory than in practice. With the chief justice lashing out at lawyers who resorted to endless legal maneuvering to keep their clients alive, the Supreme Court rejected almost all appeals in such cases. Executions began to occur again with relative frequency.

Civil Rights and Liberties

Besides being a law and order hard-liner, Burger also proved to be a conservative authoritarian. He believed "the community" (which he tended to equate with those having a bare majority in the legislature) had a right to impose its values on nonconforming individuals. Consequently, he was far less sympathetic toward civil liberties claims than Earl Warren had been.

That held for those claims based on the First Amendment's establishment of religion clause. In *Lemon* v. *Kurtzman* (1971) Burger announced a test for determining whether state attempts to subsidize parochial education violated that constitutional prohibition. This generated a collage of inconsistent decisions, striking down some and upholding others. The results of *March* v. *Chambers* (1983) and *Lynch* v. *Donnelly* (1984) were clearer but even more difficult to reconcile with the language of the establishment clause. In those cases Burger upheld respectively Nebraska's practice of opening legislative sessions with a prayer delivered by a state-paid Protestant chaplain and Pawtucket, Rhode Island's right to display a nativity scene in front of its city hall.

He was also, despite a background of service in Minnesota with groups seeking to improve race relations, an inconsistent supporter of claims based on the equal protection clause of the Fourteenth Amendment. Use of that provision against gender-based discrimination began with the Burger Court, and it was the chief justice who wrote the seminal opinion in *Reed* v. *Reed* (1971). On the other hand, he refused to support Justice William Brennan's effort to have the Court adopt for sex cases the same stringent constitutional test already employed in racial ones, and he accepted as valid policies which penalized pregnancy.

Also indicative of Burger's lack of sympathy for civil rights and civil liberties was his support of procedural innovations making it more difficult to litigate such claims in federal court. The Burger Court's decisions on such technical issues as standing, justicability, abstention, and the requirements for bringing class action suits all tended toward closing the courthouse door. In addition, the Court lengthened the list of officials immune from suits for damages for violating citizens' constitutional rights and expanded the "good faith" defense available to those who can still be sued.

Reformer or Counterrevolutionary?

Yet, despite being less receptive to civil rights and civil liberties claims, the Burger Court was not as different from the Warren Court as casual observers supposed. It was, for example, equally "activist." That is, it proved equally willing to substitute its own value judgments for those of popularly elected lawmakers. In *Roe* v. *Wade* (1973), for example, the Burger Court on tenuous constitutional grounds invalidated the states' abortion laws and spelled out precisely how they might regulate abortion in the future.

Furthermore, although often critical of its predecessor's work, the Burger Court did not undo it. Not a single one of the Warren Court's landmark decisions was reversed. Neither segregation, nor malapportioned legislatures, nor prayer in public schools became constitutional again. Even in the area of criminal procedure, the Burger Court limited the effect of, rather than overturned, Warren Court precedents.

Ironically, after 17 years on the Court the "conservative" chief justice had better credentials as a reformer than as a counterrevolutionary. Early in his tenure he launched a crusade to reshape and improve the administration of justice, which had broken down under the burden of a vastly expanded volume of litigation. At his urging many courts began to employ professional administrators, and an institute was set up to train them. Burger got continuing education for judges whose numbers had increased substantially, and his attacks on the competency of trial lawyers inspired innovations in the training of litigators. He also improved the coordination between federal and state courts serving the same geographic areas. In 1986 Warren Burger resigned as chief justice to spend full time as head of the U.S. Constitution Bicentennial Commission.

Further Reading

Although the literature on the Burger Court is extensive, that on Warren Burger himself is not. Andrew Norman, "Warren E. Burger," in *The Burger Court 1969-1978,* ed. Leon Friedman (1978) is a disappointing article which does no more than analyze Burger's work on the Supreme Court. Although poorly focused, Dennis E. Everette's "Overcoming Occupational Heredity on the Supreme Court," *American Bar Association Journal* (January 1980), is a spirited defense of Burger's humble origins. Charles M. Lamb analyzes his work on the court of appeals in "The Making of a Chief Justice: Warren Burger on Criminal Procedure, 1956-1969," *Cornell Law Review* (June 1975). Robert Douglas Chesler, "Imagery of Community, Ideology of Authority: The Moral Reasoning of Chief Justice Burger," *Harvard Civil Rights/Civil Liberties Law Review* (Summer 1983) is helpful in understanding Burger's negative attitude toward civil rights and civil liberties claims. Edward A. Tamm and Paul C. Reardon, "Warren E. Burger and the Administration of Justice," *Brigham Young University*

Law Review (1981), is a good survey of Burger's efforts to promote judicial efficiency.

The book which provides the most insights into the inner workings of the Burger Court and the sometimes highhanded conduct of its chief justice is Bob Woodward and Scott Armstrong, *The Brethren* (1979), written by two investigative journalists. For scholarly evaluations of the Burger Court's decisions and direction, see Richard Y. Funston, *Constitutional Counterrevolution? The Warren Court and the Burger Court: Judicial Policy Making in Modern America* (1977); Vincent Blasi, editor, *The Burger Court: The Counter-Revolution That Wasn't* (1983); and Alpheus Thomas Mason, "Whence and Whither the Burger Court? Judicial Self Restraint: A Beguiling Myth," *Review of Politics* (January 1979). *The Nation* devoted its entire September 29, 1984, issue to an assessment of the Burger Court's first 15 years. The articles it contained examine numerous facets of the Court's work and are easy for readers with little legal background to understand. □

Anthony Burgess

Anthony Burgess (1917-1993) was one of the most prolific literary figures of the 20th century, producing a large number of novels, plays, biographies, screenplays, criticism, and articles.

John Anthony Burgess Wilson was born on February 25, 1917, in Manchester, England. As a child he demonstrated talent as a writer, artist, and musician. He studied the violin and taught himself piano as well as musical notation. Though he regarded himself as a "failed composer," his efforts were not altogether unsuccessful. He created classical pieces and scores for television, film, and theater. His third symphony was performed in Iowa City in 1975. In his lifetime, Burgess composed choral works, concertos, and even operas. Writing was initially a "hobby," then, after he recognized his gift and found it remunerative, a "full time job."

The experiences of Burgess' first 32 years provided inspiration for his novels. He was raised in an Irish Catholic family and attended Bishop Bilsborrow School and Xaverian College. Ironically, he lost his faith at Xaverian but considered himself "a lapsed Catholic," never completely free of his background. In 1940, after graduating from Manchester University with a degree in literature, he entered the Army Educational Corps. From 1943 to 1946 he was a training college lecturer in speech and drama on Gibraltar. Afterwards he held a variety of teaching positions including member of the Central Advisory Council for Adult Education in the Armed Forces, Birmingham, 1946-1948, teacher of phonetics, drama, and literature for the Ministry of Education, Preston, Lancashire, 1948-1950, and teacher of literature, phonetics, Spanish, and music, Banbury Grammar School, Oxfordshire, 1950-1954.

In 1954 he joined the Colonial Service as a lecturer in English in Malaya. In 1957 he became an educational officer and English language specialist in Borneo. It was as an observer of these politically and socially complex cultures that Burgess began his writing career. His first published novels, *Time for a Tiger* (1956), *Enemy in the Blanket* (1958), and *Beds in the East* (1959) are set in Malaya. *Devil of a State* (1961) is set in Borneo. He took the name Anthony Burgess because he thought his superiors would disapprove of his writing fiction.

In 1959 Burgess was ill and returned to England. He was told he probably had a brain tumor and would survive only a year. Luckily, this was a misdiagnosis. But the prospect of death prompted him to turn full-time to writing, and during this "terminal year" he completed *The Doctor Is Sick, Inside Mr. Enderby, The Wanting Seed* and *One Hand Clapping*. Later, Burgess stated in *The Economist* that his objective during that year had been to provide an inheritance for his wife by writing ten novels. But, he said, "I couldn't do it. I did produce five and a half though . . . And some of them are still around. But it was too much. I don't think anybody should do quite as much as that." The five novels that Burgess completed during his "terminal year" proved a fitting overview of themes he would return to frequently throughout his career. Once recovered from his misdiagnosed illness, Burgess continued writing novels. Among the most acclaimed were three that followed F.X. Enderby, a poet misplaced in society who was introduced in 1963's *Inside Mr. Enderby*. Those three books were *Enderby Outside* (1968), *The Clockwork Testament, or Enderby's End* (1974), and *Enderby's Dark Lady* (1984). When Enderby died in *The Clockwork Testament, or Enderby's*

End, readers were so dismayed that the author "resurrected" him in *Enderby's Dark Lady.*

Other of Burgess' well-regarded works include *Nothing Like the Sun* (1964), a story about William Shakespeare, and *Napoleon Symphony* (1974), a fictional biography of Napoleon structured to follow the form of Beethoven's *Eroica.* Burgess' most famous, though not his favorite, novel was *A Clockwork Orange* (1962), which was made into a movie. Its violent anti-hero, Alex, is subdued when he undergoes behavior modification treatment administered by the state. The novel haunted Burgess throughout his life because his publisher, W.W. Norton, dropped a final chapter in which Alex remained reformed. Instead, the book was published with Alex returning to a life of crime, and when Stanley Kubrick made the film version of the novel in 1971, he adhered to the publisher's ending. Burgess said in *The Economist* that he felt, " . . . when the film was made the theological element almost completely disappeared." The film was so violent that it was permanently banned in Britain.

Burgess also published other books during this time, including *The Novel Now* (1967), *Shakespeare* (1970), and two studies of James Joyce: *ReJoyce* (1965) and *Joysprick* (1973).

Burgess married twice. In 1968 his first wife died of pscerosis of the liver as a result of severe alcoholism, and he married Liliana Macelli, a linguist. Discontent with life in England, and particularly with excessive taxation, they moved with their son to Malta and then lived in Italy and Monaco. Burgess visited the United States and taught at the University of North Carolina, Princeton, and City College, New York.

Burgess was acutely sensitive to evil in modern life. He called himself a "Manichee," a believer in the duality, the inter-connection of good and evil, of reality. Typically, his protagonists represent relatively decent people caught in the conflicts and absurdities of their environments. They confront chaos, as in the Malayan trilogy, espionage, as in *Tremor of Intent* (1966), and authoritarian institutions, as in *The Wanting Seed, A Clockwork Orange,* and *Honey for the Bears* (1963). Burgess distrusted government. The socialized state which "cures" Alex destroys his free will. Other novels, such as the Enderby books, *The Right to an Answer* (1960), *One Hand Clapping* (1961), and *Beard's Roman Women* (1976)—about Hollywood—satirized materialism, corruption, and vacuousness in contemporary culture.

People, too, are seen as evil. One of Burgess' interests was the conflict between Pelagias, who believed man is ultimately perfectible, and Augustine, who believed man is irredeemably sinful. In novels such as *Earthly Powers* (1980), Augustine generally prevails. There are characters, however, who learn and grow and artistic ones who create order from chaos and suggest hope.

Burgess' comic style softened his pessimism. Characters lurch from outlandish adventure to adventure. Farcical figures, surreal coincidences, and inventive allusions to history and fiction supplement his novels. Language—puns, poetic images, distorted syntax—distance one from the gloom. *Nothing Like the Sun* was written in Elizabethan style. For *A Clockwork Orange* Burgess invented a dialect. Some books are considered more intellectually than emotionally stimulating, rendering illustrations of theses and complicated reading puzzles. Consequently, Burgess' vitality and originality were widely admired.

Burgess published two volumes of memoirs, *Little Wilson and Big God* (1987) and *You've Had Your Time* (1990). While both volumes were generally well-received by critics, some complained that they spent too much time on abstract thought, and not enough on the author's life. In his review of *You've Had Your Time,* William F. Buckley, Jr. remarked in *The New York Times Book Review,* " . . . is there a human narrative under this truckload of cultural petit point? Not a whole lot, to tell the truth, but some."

Although Burgess did not begin writing until age 32, publishing his first novel at 39, he became one of the busiest authors of his time. In addition to over 25 novels, he produced biographies, plays, screenplays, criticism, and articles. His translation of *Cyrano de Bergerac* had a successful run at the Guthrie Theatre, Minneapolis, in 1971 and on Broadway in 1984. For television he wrote *Jesus of Nazareth,* based on his novel *Man of Nazareth* (1979), and *AD.* Even in 1993, when he was suffering from a long illness, Burgess published two works: *Dead Man in Deptford* and *A Mouthful of Air: Languages, Languages—Especially English.* He was also a regular contributor to periodicals, such as *Atlantic Monthly* and *The New York Times Book Review.* Burgess died on November 25, 1993 after a long battle with cancer.

Further Reading

Geoffrey Aggeler, *Anthony Burgess: The Artist as Novelist* (1979) and Samuel Coale, *Anthony Burgess* (1981) contain biographies and criticism. Coale included a bibliography. His selected checklist of Anthony Burgess criticism also appeared in *Modern Fiction Studies* (Autumn 1981). Burgess' autobiography, *This Man and His Music* (1982), examined music in his life and writing. Richard Mathews, *The Clockwork Universe of Anthony Burgess* (1978) and Robert Morris, *The Consolations of Ambiguity* (1971) discussed themes in the novels. □

John Burgoyne

British general and statesman John Burgoyne (1723-1792) is mainly remembered for his disastrous campaign in the American Revolution, which ended in his surrender to the American forces in 1777.

The son of a British army captain, John Burgoyne received his education at Westminster and then went into the military. While still an impecunious junior officer, he eloped with the daughter of Lord Derby. After a brief period of ill will, there emerged a firm friendship between Burgoyne and his influential, noble father-in-law. During Derby's hostility, however, Burgoyne had been so poor that he had sold his commission, fled from his creditors to France, and there studied French literature and Continental military practices. After their reconciliation, Derby's influence enabled Burgoyne to return to military life.

In the Seven Years War (1756-1763), Burgoyne promoted the raising of light cavalry similar to some Continental forces. He drafted elaborate instructions advising his officers to deal with their men as "thinking beings." After action in France, he acquired favorable notice for his leadership of the Anglo-Portuguese forces in 1762. He was then promoted to a regular colonelcy—a mark as much of Derby's power as of Burgoyne's ability.

Burgoyne was long active in politics. He held a seat in the House of Commons from 1761 until his death. Although he occasionally joined the opposition, he generally enjoyed royal favor until 1777. In Commons he spoke frequently and showed considerable interest in the troubles of the East India Company. He received profitable military appointments. While differing on some issues with Lord North, he supported a repressive American policy.

After brief service in America, Burgoyne—visiting home—drew up plans for invading New York from Canada. In March 1777 he was named commander of an invasion force that was about half as strong as he had desired. There was little or no coordination of the efforts to be made between this army and the troops under Sir Henry Clinton and William Howe. Nonetheless, Burgoyne with great confidence—expressed in bombastic fashion—started his campaign with the capture of Ft. Ticonderoga in early July. He soon encountered unexpectedly heavy American resistance. Yet he persisted in moving his troops in a rather leisurely fashion, rather than marching rapidly toward Albany. Inadequate strength, overconfidence, general bumbling, the appearance of large numbers of Americans—all contributed to disaster for the British. Burgoyne belatedly realized that he was surrounded and outnumbered, unable either to advance or retreat. He surrendered at Saratoga on Oct. 17, 1777.

Burgoyne's defeat was followed by his apostasy from Lord North's ministry. Greeted with criticism at home, he replied by blaming others. He lost favor at court and went so far as to resign from military offices which had netted him £3,500 a year. Finding new friends among the supporters of Charles James Fox, he became a kind of opposition martyr, and his fate rose or fell along with the fortunes of Fox. He gained some position in 1782 but remained on the fringes of real power. Though a frequent speaker on military matters in Parliament, he made little impact on political life of the 1780s.

Instead, Burgoyne turned increasingly to literary and social pursuits. He mingled with theater friends and took as his mistress a popular singer. A series of stage successes culminated in *The Heiress,* a popular triumph after its first performance in 1786. More successful as an author than he had been as a soldier, Burgoyne died in London on June 4, 1792.

Further Reading

The standard, older biography of Burgoyne is E. B. de Fonblanque, *Political and Military Episodes Derived from the Life and Correspondence of John Burgoyne* (1876). A less substantial biography is Francis J. Hudleston, *Gentleman Johnny Burgoyne* (1927). Howard H. Peckham, *The War for Independence: A Military History* (1958), provides a general military perspective.

Additional Sources

Glover, Michael, *General Burgoyne in Canada and America: scapegoat for a system,* London: Gordon & Cremonesi; New York: distributed by Atheneum Publishers, 1976.

Hargrove, Richard J., *General John Burgoyne,* Newark: University of Delaware Press, 1983.

Howson, Gerald, *Burgoyne of Saratoga: a biography,* New York: Times Books, 1979.

Lunt, James D., *John Burgoyne of Saratoga,* London: Macdonald and Jane's, 1976.

Mintz, Max M., *The generals of Saratoga: John Burgoyne & Horatio Gates,* New Haven: Yale University Press, 1990.

Paine, Lauran, *Gentleman Johnny: the life of General John Burgoyne,* London: Hale, 1973. □

Edmund Burke

The British statesman Edmund Burke (1729-1797) was a noted political theorist and philosophical writer. He was born in Ireland, spent most of his active life in English politics, and died the political oracle of conservative Europe.

Edmund Burke's view of society was hierarchical and authoritarian, yet one of his noblest characteristics was his repeated defense of those who were too weak to defend themselves. Outstanding in 18th-century British politics for intellect, oratory, and drive, he lacked the ability either to lead or to conciliate men and never exerted an influence commensurate with his capabilities. His career as a practical politician was a failure; his political theories found favor only with posterity.

Burke was born on Jan. 12, 1729, in Dublin of middleclass parents. His mother suffered from what Burke called "a cruel nervous disorder," and his relations with his authoritarian father, a Dublin attorney, were unhappy. After attending Trinity College, Dublin, Burke in 1750 crossed to England to study law at the Middle Temple. But he unconsciously resisted his father's plans for him and made little progress in the law. Indecision marked his life at this time: he described himself as "a runaway son" and his "manner of life" as "chequered with various designs." In 1755 he considered applying for a post in the Colonies but dropped the idea when his father objected.

In 1756 Burke published two philosophical treatises, *A Vindication of Natural Society* and *A Philosophical Enquiry into the Origin of Our Ideas of the Sublime and Beautiful.* In the *Vindication* Burke exposed the futility of demanding a reason for moral and social institutions and, with the foresight which was one of the most remarkable of his gifts, distinguished the coming attack of rationalistic criticism on the established order. The *Enquiry,* which he had begun when only 19, was considered by Samuel Johnson to be "an example of true criticism." These works were followed in 1757 by *An Account of the European Settlement in America,* to which Burke, although he denied authorship, clearly contributed a great deal. The early sheets of *The Abridgement of the History of England* were also printed in 1757, although the book itself was not published until after Burke's death. These works introduced Burke's name into London literary circles and seemed to open up a reputable career.

Family unity, which he had never known as a boy, became an article of Burke's adult philosophy. In 1757 he married the daughter of his physician and settled into family life with his father-in-law, his brother Richard, and his so-called cousin William. With them he found a domestic harmony he had never known in his father's home.

Early Political Career

Financial security, however, was elusive, and Burke was forced to take a minor secretarial post in the government establishment in Ireland. But contact with the depressed and persecuted Irish Catholics unsettled him, and early in 1765 he resigned his position. Necessity now led Burke into politics. In July 1765, when the Whig administration of Lord Rockingham was being formed, he was recommended to Rockingham, who took him on as his private secretary. In December, Burke entered Parliament as member for the Buckinghamshire constituency of Wendover.

Burke's subsequent political career was bound inextricably to the fortunes of the Rockingham group. Emotional and hysterical by nature, without a profession or a secure income, he found stability and independence through his attachment to the Whig aristocrats. When Rockingham lost the premiership in 1766, Burke, though offered employment under the new administration, followed him into opposition. "I believe in any body of men in England I should have been in the minority," he later said. "I have always been in the minority." Certainly the dominant characteristic of his political career was an overwhelming impulse to argue and oppose; to that was added enormous persistence, courage, concentration, and energy. Endowed with many of the qualities of leadership, he lacked the sensitivity to gauge and respect the feelings and opinions of others. Hence his political life was a series of negative crusades—against the American war, Warren Hastings, and the French Revolution—and his reputation as a statesman rests on his wisdom in opposition, not on his achievements in office.

Burke's theory of government was essentially conservative. He profoundly distrusted the people and believed in the divine right of the aristocracy to govern. "All direction of public humour and opinion must originate in a few," he wrote in 1775. "God and nature never meant [the people] to think or act without guidance or direction." Yet all Burke's writings, despite their rather narrow propaganda purpose, include valuable generalizations on human conduct.

Views on America and Ireland

Burke found difficulty in applying his political philosophy to practical issues. He was one of the first to realize the implications of Britain's problems with colonial America. He saw the British Empire as a family, with the parent exercising a benevolent authority over the children. Perhaps influenced by his own upbringing, he believed the British government to have been harsh and tyrannical when it should have been lenient. "When any community is subordinately connected with another," he wrote, "the great danger of the connexion is the extreme pride and self-complacency of the superior."

In 1774 Burke argued against retaining the tea duty on the Colonies in his celebrated *Speech on American Taxation,* and twice in 1775 he proposed conciliation with the Colonies. His conception of the British Empire as an "aggregate of many states under one common head" came as near as was possible in the 18th century to reconciling British authority with colonial autonomy. Yet at the same time he repeatedly declared his belief in the legislative supremacy of the British Parliament. Thus the American war split Burke in two. He could face neither American independence nor the prospect of a British victory. "I do not know," he wrote in August 1776, "how to wish success to those whose victory is to separate us from a large and noble part of our empire. Still less do I wish success to injustice, oppression, and absurdity . . . No good can come of any event in this war to any virtuous interest."

In Ireland, Burke's sympathies were with the persecuted Roman Catholics, who were "reduced to beasts of burden" and asked only for that elementary justice all subjects had a right to expect from their government. He preferred their cause to that of the Protestant Anglo-Irish, who were striving to throw off the authority of the British Parliament. With Irish nationalism and its constitutional grievances he had little sympathy. "I am sure the people ought to eat whether they have septennial Parliaments or not," he wrote in 1766. As on the American problem, Burke always counseled moderation in Ireland. "I believe," he said only 2 months before his death, "there are very few cases which will justify a revolt against the established government of a country, let its constitution be what it will."

Hastings Incident

On the formation of the short-lived Rockingham ministry in March 1782, Burke was appointed paymaster general. But now, when he seemed on the threshold of political achievement, everything seemed to go wrong for Burke. In particular, his conduct at this time showed signs of mental disturbance, a tendency aggravated by the death of Rockingham in July 1782. James Boswell told Samuel Johnson in 1783 that Burke had been represented as "actually mad"; to which Johnson replied, "If a man will appear extravagant as he does, and cry, can he wonder that he is represented as mad?" A series of intemperate speeches in the Commons branded Burke as politically unreliable, an impression confirmed by his conduct in the impeachment of Warren Hastings, the governor general of Bengal, in 1790.

Ever since Rockingham had taken office, the punishment of those accused of corruption in India had been uppermost in Burke's mind. His strong aggressive instincts, sharpened by public and private disappointments, needed an enemy against which they could concentrate. Always inclined to favor the unfortunate, he became convinced that Hastings was the principal source of misrule in India and that one striking example of retribution would deter other potential offenders. In Burke's disordered mind, Hastings appeared as a monster of iniquity; he listened uncritically to any complaint against him; and the vehemence with which he prosecuted the impeachment indicates the depth of his emotions. His violent language and intemperate charges alienated independent men and convinced his own party that he was a political liability.

Last Years

Disappointment and nostalgia colored Burke's later years. He was the first to appreciate the significance of the French Revolution and to apply it to English conditions. In February 1790 he warned the Commons: "In France a cruel, blind, and ferocious democracy had carried all before them; their conduct, marked with the most savage and unfeeling barbarity, had manifested no other system than a determination to destroy all order, subvert all arrangement, and reduce every rank and description of men to one common level."

Burke had England and his own disappointments in mind when he published *Reflections on the Revolution in France and on the Proceedings of Certain Societies in London* in 1790. "You seem in everything to have strayed out of the high road of nature," he wrote. "The property of France does not govern it"; and in the *Letters on a Regicide Peace* (1796) he defined Jacobinism as "the revolt of the enterprising talents of a country against its property." If England, following the French example, was not to be governed by property, what would become of Burke's most cherished principles? In part the *Reflections* is also Burke's apologia for his devotion to Rockingham. For Rockingham's cause Burke had sacrificed his material interests through 16 long years of profitless opposition, and when his party at last came to power he failed to obtain any lasting advantage for himself or his family. In the famous passage on Marie Antoinette in the *Reflections,* Burke, lamenting the passing of the "age of chivalry," perhaps unconsciously described his own relations with the Whig aristocrats: "Never, never more, shall we behold that generous loyalty to rank and sex, that proud submission, that dignified obedience, that subordination of the heart, which kept alive, even in servitude itself, the spirit of an exalted freedom."

For the last 5 years of his life Burke occupied a unique position. "He is," remarked a contemporary, "a sort of power in Europe, though totally without any of those means . . . which give or maintain power in other men." He corresponded with Louis XVIII and the French royalists and counseled Stanislaus of Poland to pursue a liberal policy. The Irish Catholics regarded him as their champion. As each succeeding act of revolution became more bloody, his foresight was praised more widely. He urged the necessity of war with France, and the declaration of hostilities further increased his prestige. On the last day of his life he spoke of his hatred for the revolutionary spirit in France and of his belief that the war was for the good of humanity. He died on

July 9, 1797, and in accordance with his wishes was buried in the parish church of Beaconsfield in Buckinghamshire.

Further Reading

There are many editions of Burke's writings. *The Correspondence of Edmund Burke,* edited by Thomas W. Copeland and others (8 vols., 1958-1969), is the definitive edition of Burke's letters. Of the smaller collections, *Speeches and Letters on American Affairs,* with an introduction by Peter McKevitt (1961), is of particular interest. *A Philosophical Enquiry into the Origin of Our Ideas of the Sublime and Beautiful,* edited by J. T. Boulton (1958), and *Reflections on the Revolution in France,* edited by William B. Todd (1965), are definitive editions of two major works. See also Walter J. Bate, ed., *Selected Works* (1960).

Thomas *E. Utley, Edmund Burke* (1957), is the most useful modern biography. Studies of Burke's political philosophy include Charles W. Parkin, *The Moral Basis of Burke's Political Thought: An Essay* (1956); Francis P. Canavan, *The Political Reason of Edmund Burke* (1960); Peter J. Stanlis, ed., *The Relevance of Edmund Burke* (1964) and his own *Edmund Burke and the Natural Law* (1958); Gerald W. Chapman, *Edmund Burke: The Practical Imagination* (1967); and Burleigh T. Wilkins, *The Problem of Burke's Political Philosophy* (1967). Of the many works setting Burke in the context of the 18th century, the most useful are Carl B. Cone, *Burke and the Nature of Politics* (2 vols., 1957-1964); Alfred Cobban, *Edmund Burke and the Revolt against the 18th Century* (2d ed. 1960); and R. R. Fennessy, *Burke, Paine and the Rights of Man* (1963).

Additional Sources

Ayling, Stanley Edward, *Edmund Burke: his life and opinions,* New York: St. Martin's Press, 1988.

Kirk, Russell, *Edmund Burke: a genius reconsidered,* Peru, Ill.: Sherwood Sugden, 1988.

Kramnick, Isaac, comp., *Edmund Burke,* Englewood Cliffs, N.J.: Prentice-Hall, 1974.

Macpherson, C. B. (Crawford Brough), *Burke,* Oxford; New York: Oxford University Press, 1980.

Miller, Alice P., *Edmund Burke: a biography,* New York: Allwyn Press, 1976.

Miller, Alice P., *Edmund Burke and his world,* Old Greenwich, Conn.: Devin-Adair Co., 1979.

Morley, John, *Edmund Burke,* Belfast: Athol Books, 1993. □

Kenneth Burke

Kenneth Burke (1897-1993) was a literary theorist and critic whose work was influential in several fields of knowledge where symbols are a central focus of study.

Kenneth Duva Burke was born in Pittsburgh, Pennsylvania, on May 5, 1897. Burke dropped out of college twice, first from Ohio State and then from Columbia, preferring to study on his own. He wanted to write rather than follow the path toward a college professorship. He became part of the literary culture of Greenwich Village, supported by a small allowance from his father. In 1919 Burke married Lillian Batterham, with whom he had three daughters. In 1933 he divorced Lillian and married her sister, Elizabeth, with whom he had two sons.

Burke participated fully in the literary and academic culture of the 1920s. Thereafter, although he was influenced by both Marx and Freud and held several academic positions, he never allowed himself the ease of dogmatism or the security of a permanent academic appointment. His many books are an unusual combination of powerful and original theory marked throughout by paradox, erudition, and a comic spirit.

Burke's early interest in poetry, music, and literature soon turned theoretical, and he began to explore the ways in which poetry and criticism could explain human relations in general. In a series of major works Burke began to explore literature not only as a potential social influence and reflection of social attitudes, but as a model of the structure of human action. Human action, said Burke, is essentially symbolic action, shaped and motivated as if it were drama. Hence, he used the term dramatism to describe a way of studying human motivation. The key to dramatism is that human action is free and purposeful, as opposed to motion, which is simply the physical movement of objects. Humans act, said Burke, and objects move. The structure of human action is dramatic, based on interaction of the five sources of motive that Burke identified in *A Grammar of Motives* (1945) as the pentad: act, agent, agency, purpose, scene (what was done, who did it, by what means, to what end, and where and when?).

In *A Rhetoric of Motives* (1950), Burke wrote that rhetoric, or persuasion, is central to any study of the human condition, defining rhetoric as "the use of language as a symbolic means of inducing cooperation in beings that by nature respond to symbols." The key to Burke's concept of rhetoric is *identification,* a recognition of common interests or common "substance," with other humans and is based on the ever-present opposite of identification, division. Rhetoric preserves or alters social order by influencing the way people perceive their symbolic relations. Although rhetoric is historically rooted in language, Burke extended its operation to any human activity in which meaning could be found, and that means all human action. "Wherever there is persuasion, there is rhetoric. And wherever there is 'meaning,' there is 'persuasion.'"

Because all human action is meaningful and therefore persuasive, both for its author and its audience, Burke thought of all symbolic behavior as strategic action that is directed at defining situations and attitudes for ourselves and others. But Burke noted that though rhetoric is inherently aimed at inducing cooperation by healing division, it can also lead to the futile and coercive attempt to create perfect unity.

In *The Rhetoric of Religion* (1961), Burke turned his attention to what he called *logology,* his term for the general study of language and symbols. In this and other works, Burke showed that humans organize their perceptions, their languages, their societies, and their religions on the basis of hierarchies, as in the religious ascent from earthly to eternal life. Burke claimed that a major human invention is the negative, which is what makes symbolic meaning and consequent human society possible, because all notions that something *is* depend on the implicit claim that it *is not* something else. The human desire for order and perfection leads to cycles of guilt-victimage-purification-redemption, such as that embodied in the Christian religion and re-enacted, said Burke, throughout our history and daily experience. A life's work led Burke to his definition of man, set forth in *Language as Symbolic Action* (1966). He claimed, "Man is/the symbol-using (symbol making, symbol-misusing) animal/inventor of the negative (or moralized by the negative)/separated from his natural condition by instruments of his own making/goaded by the spirit of hierarchy (or moved by the sense of order)/and rotten with perfection."

Burke's work was distinguished by its application of elements from both anthropology and psychoanalysis. Many hailed his use of these sciences, but others felt he neglected to fully apply their methodologies, instead, opting for a sort of smorgasbord approach, in which he took only the aspects that he wanted. In *Psychoanalysis & American Literary Criticism,* Louis Fraiberg describes Burke's approach. Fraiberg contends, "Psychoanalysis cannot exist without words, but this does not mean that words are the only things in it that matter. Burke has been guilty of taking the part for the whole, and this has thrown his entire critical view out of focus." While Burke had some detractors, he also had the support of notable literary figures such as W.H. Auden and John Crowe Ransom.

Burke received many awards in his lifetime, including the Creative Arts Award from Brandeis University in 1967, the National Endowment for the Arts award in 1968, the National Council on the Arts award in 1969, the gold medal from the National Institute of Arts and Letters in 1975, and the National Medal for Literature in 1981. He also received the Elmer Holmes Bobst Award in 1984. Burke received fellowships from numerous organizations, such as the Princeton Institute for Advanced Study (1949), Stanford University (1957), and the Rockefeller Foundation (1966). He died of heart failure on November 19, 1993, in Andover, New Jersey.

Further Reading

Burke's works may be dipped into at almost any point, depending on the reader's interest. Burke's major works were *Counter-Statement* (1931); *Towards a Better Life* (1932); *Permanence and Change: An Anatomy of Purpose* (1935); *Attitudes Toward History* (1937); *Philosophy of Literary Form: Studies in Symbolic Action* (1941); *A Grammar of Motives* (1945); *A Rhetoric of Motives* (1950); *The Rhetoric of Religion: Studies in Logology* (1961); *Language as Symbolic Action* (1966); *Collected Poems, 1915-1967* (1968); and *The Complete White Oxen: Collected Short Fiction* (1924, 1968). Some of Burke's later works include, *Dramatism and Development* (1972) and *On Symbols and Society* (1989). He contributed to regularly to a variety of publications, such as *Dial, Poetry, Kenyon Review, New Republic,* and *Critical Inquiry.*

There are a number of books about Burke or heavily influenced by Burke. A good introduction is William H. Rueckert, *Kenneth Burke and the Drama of Human Relations* (2nd edition, 1982). On Burke as a rhetorical theorist, a good introduction and excellent bibliography are provided in Sonja K. Foss, Karen A. Foss, and Robert Trapp, *Contemporary Perspectives on Rhetoric* (1985). For Burke's influence on rhetorical criticism, see also Martin J. Medhurst and Thomas W. Benson, *Rhetorical Dimensions in Media: A Critical Casebook* (1984). For Burke's place in literary and social theory, see also Hugh D. Duncan, *Communication and Social Order* (1962); Stanley Edgar Hyman, *The Armed Vision: A Study in the Methods of Modern Literary Criticism* (1947); and Hayden White and Margaret Brose (editors), *Representing Kenneth Burke* (1982). Other biographical sources are *Contemporary Authors* (1994) Volume 143, Robert Heath's *Realism and Relativism: A Perspective on Kenneth Burke* (1986), and Greig Henderson's *Kenneth Burke: Literature and Language as Symbolic Action* (1989). □

Robert O'Hara Burke

Robert O'Hara Burke (1820-1861) was a British policeman and explorer who led the first expedition to cross the Australian continent.

Robert O'Hara Burke was born in County Galway, Ireland, the son of a British army officer. After attending Woolwich Military Academy, Burke served in an Austrian cavalry regiment until 1848, when he joined the mounted Irish constabulary. Migrating to Australia in

1853, he became a police inspector in the Victorian goldfields. After the outbreak of the Crimean War, he returned to Europe, hoping to distinguish himself as a soldier. Disappointed, he returned to Victoria in 1858 as superintendent of police at Castlemaine.

The South Australian government offered a prize in 1859 to the first explorer to cross the continent. John McDouall Stuart reached Mount Attack in 1860 before returning to Adelaide. Spurred by intercolonial rivalry, the rich colony of Victoria financed its own scientific expedition, and the flamboyant Burke, who wanted desperately to improve his fortunes, was chosen to lead it despite his inexperience.

Equipped with camels, horses, and supplies for 2 years, 15 men left Melbourne on Aug. 20, 1860. The party reached Menindee along the Darling River in October without mishap. Burke, with seven men, then pushed rapidly ahead to Cooper's Creek, 400 miles north. The remainder of the expedition, conveying heavy stores, made such slow progress that the impetuous Burke decided to make a dash for the coast with three companions. Because of exceptional rains they encountered no water shortage and in February 1861 sighted the Gulf of Carpentaria beyond impenetrable mangrove swamps. Marching 12 hours a day, the party covered the return journey of 1500 miles in 4 months. One man, Gray, died.

The rest regained Cooper's Creek April 21, 1861, only hours after the depot party had headed south. Instead of pursuing them, Burke mistakenly decided to head for a police station 150 miles away at Mount Hopeless. Exhausted, Burke and Wills died in Cooper's Creek. King, the only survivor, lived with aborigines until rescued in September.

This most costly expedition in Australian history accomplished little. Burke allowed no time for scientific work and kept no journal, but fortunately William John Wills kept a record. Four relief expeditions contributed considerably more knowledge about the north-central zone, particularly about its grazing potential, and in 1862 Stuart pioneered the principal all-weather route to the Indian Ocean. Nevertheless the tragedy of Burke and Wills became an Australian legend.

Further Reading

An interesting contemporary apologia for Burke with extensive excerpts from Wills's diary and the Royal Commission of 1861-1862 is Andrew Jackson, *Robert O'Hara Burke and the Australian Exploring Expedition of 1860* (1862). Alan Moorehead's attractively written *Cooper's Creek* (1963) is a well-balanced popular account. Ernest Favenc, *The History of Australian Exploration from 1788 to 1888* (1967), is a general study well worth consulting. Ian Mudie in *The Heroic Journey of John McDouall Stuart* (1968) discusses Burke. See also Charles George Douglas Roberts, *Discoveries and Explorations in the Century* (1903).

Additional Sources

Colwell, Max, *The journey of Burke and Wills,* Brookvale, NSW, Australia: Child & Associates, 1987, 1971. □

Selma Burke

An African American sculptor, Selma Burke (1900–1995) created the relief sculpture rendering of Franklin Delano Roosevelt which appears on the dime.

Selma Burke is an artist whose career has spanned more than sixty years. She was born in Mooresville, North Carolina, in 1900, and received her training as a sculptor at Columbia University in New York. She also studied with Maillol in Paris and in Vienna with Povoley. World War II interrupted her work in Europe and she returned to the United States to continue her artistic and humanitarian pursuits. She is best known for her relief sculpture rendering of Franklin Delano Roosevelt that was minted on the American dime.

Founder of the Selma Burke Art Center in Pittsburgh, Pennsylvania, she has taught many and supported numerous artists from the period of the Depression through the present day.

The Pearl S. Buck Foundation Woman's Award was given to her in 1987 for her professional distinction and devotion to family and humanity. Notable works include *Falling Angel; Peace;* and *Jim.*

Burke died of cancer August 29, 1995 in New Hope, Pennsylvania.

Further Reading

New York Times, September 2, 1995.
Washington Post, September 1, 1995. □

Anson Burlingame

American diplomat Anson Burlingame (1820-1870) served as U.S. minister to China and later as a Chinese envoy to the United States.

Anson Burlingame was born on Nov. 14, 1820, in New Berlin, N.Y., a descendant of Roger Burlingame, who had emigrated from England in 1654 and helped settle Providence, R.I. Anson's father, a farmer and Methodist lay preacher, moved his family westward in 1823 to Seneca Country, Ohio, to Detroit in 1833, and in 1835 to a farm at Branch, Mich.

Educated in common schools and at the Detroit branch of the newly formed University of Michigan, Burlingame graduated from Harvard Law School in 1846. He began to practice law in Boston with the son of the governor of Massachusetts. A gifted and popular public speaker, he soon became active in politics. In 1848 he toured Massachusetts on behalf of the third-party Free Soil ticket, Martin Van Buren and Charles Francis Adams. He was elected to the state senate in 1852 and to the state constitutional convention in 1853. He joined the American party when it was formed in 1854, and he won election to Congress in 1854, 1856, and 1858 but lost the election of 1860. In Congress, Burlingame actively supported the antislavery cause and in 1856 helped form the Republican party on Free Soil principles. At the end of his congressional term in March 1861, President Lincoln appointed him minister to Austria. Owing to Burlingame's unacceptability to the Austrian government because of his speeches favoring independence for Hungary and Sardinia, Lincoln changed his assignment, naming him minister to China.

China had only recently granted foreigners the right to reside and trade within its borders, and the mercantile community was anxious to extend its influence. Burlingame, despite his lack of experience, quickly assumed leadership of the diplomatic corps in Peking. He successfully furthered a policy of cooperating with the European powers in defending the weak imperial government of China against the overbearing demands of the foreign merchants. For example, he helped thwart foreigners' efforts to establish in the treaty ports governments that were wholly independent of the imperial government. He tried to settle disputes by diplomacy instead of force, and his policies were "based upon justness and freed from prejudice of race." Throughout, his goal was the modernization of China.

Burlingame had long urged China to send diplomatic representatives to the Western powers, and when he resigned as minister in November 1867, the imperial govern-

ment named him and two Chinese colleagues to head an official delegation to visit the United States and the European capitals. In the United States the result was the Burlingame Treaty of 1868, which restated the principles of the 1858 treaty and pledged an American policy of respect for the territorial integrity of China. One article of the treaty provided for reciprocal immigration and was designed to promote the importation of Chinese laborers to work on the transcontinental railroad. Unfortunately, anti-Chinese agitation in America resulted in congressional restriction of Chinese immigration and strained Sino-American relations.

Burlingame continued his mission in London, where he secured a declaration that China was "entitled to count upon the forbearance of foreign nations." He was less successful in the other European capitals. He caught pneumonia while in St. Petersburg and died there on Feb. 23, 1870.

Further Reading

There is no full-length biography of Burlingame. The standard account of his mission to the Western powers for China is Frederick Wells Williams, *Anson Burlingame and the First Chinese Mission to Foreign Powers* (1912). There is also material on Burlingame in John W. Foster, *American Diplomacy in the Orient* (1903); Tyler Dennett, *Americans in Eastern Asia* (1922); and Foster Rhea Dulles, *China and America: The Story of Their Relations since 1784* (1946). □

Sir Edward Coley Burne-Jones

The English painter and designer Sir Edward Coley Burne-Jones (1833-1898) inherited some of the tradition and preoccupations of the Pre-Raphaelite painters. He was a designer for the firm of Morris & Co.

Edward Burne-Jones was born on Aug. 28, 1833, and was originally destined for the Church. With that intention he went to Oxford University in 1852, where he met William Morris, who became his lifelong colleague. When Burne-Jones met Dante Gabriel Rossetti in 1855, Rossetti persuaded him to leave Oxford and become a painter. The following year Burne-Jones became Rossetti's pupil.

Burne-Jones and Morris collaborated in 1857 on Rossetti's mural paintings in the Oxford Union. The earliest works of Burne-Jones, such as the watercolor *Clerk Sanders* (1861), closely resemble Rossetti's in style and technique but only distantly echo the teacher's vivid, mystical expressiveness: Rossetti's passion gives way to a delicate, meditative nostalgia.

Visits to Italy in 1859 and 1862 resulted in a noticeable change in Burne-Jones's style, under the influence of such Renaissance painters as Andrea Mantegna, Sandro Botticelli, and Michelangelo. A stylistically uneasy amalgam of these influences with his pale variant of Rossetti's imaginative intensity can be seen in the *Perseus* series (begun 1875) and later in the well-known *King Cophetua and the Beggar Maid* (1884), which in subject matter conform to the romanticizing view of the past that Burne-Jones inherited from the Pre-Raphaelites.

Burne-Jones was a founder-partner of Morris & Co., established in April 1861 to produce individually designed, handmade objects; this was the origin of the Arts and Crafts movement. Burne-Jones's first designs for Morris had been for stained glass used in the decoration of Morris's own house in 1857; later he made innumerable designs, especially for stained glass, tapestry, and book illustration, for Morris's firm. In 1862 Burne-Jones was at his best, producing designs of fresh simplicity, but after about 1870, under increasing Renaissance influence, the rich primary colors of medieval glass gave way to anemic, stylized figures in pallid colors. Burne-Jones lacked Rossetti's rich imaginative power, and his art sank into the calm sentimentality of estheticism and marked the final demise of the Pre-Raphaelite movement. Burne-Jones well deserved W. G. Gilbert's characterization as that "Greenery-yallery, Grosvenor Gallery, Foot-in-the-grave young man."

Burne-Jones was instrumental in founding the Grosvenor Gallery in 1877 to provide an exhibition forum for young, unacademic painters. The Royal Academy elected Burne-Jones a member in 1885, but he resigned in 1893. In 1894 he was created baronet, and he died on June 17, 1898.

Further Reading

There is no recent monograph on Burne-Jones. The basic biographical work is by his wife, Georgiana Burne-Jones, *Memorials of Edward Burne-Jones* (1904; new ed. 1906). His work is sketchily discussed in early monographs, including Malcolm Bell, *Sir Edward Burne-Jones* (1901). Robin Ironside, *Pre-Raphaelite Painters* (1948), and John D. Hunt, *The Pre-Raphaelite Imagination, 1848 to 1900* (1969), include useful sections on Burne-Jones. His work in connection with Morris & Co. is discussed by Paul Thompson in *The Work of William Morris* (1967).

Additional Sources

Fitzgerald, Penelope, *Edward Burne-Jones: a biography,* London: Joseph, 1975.

Harrison, Martin, *Burne-Jones/material,* London: Barrie and Jenkins, 1979. □

Sir Frank Macfarlane Burnet

The Australian virologist and physician Sir Frank Macfarlane Burnet (1899-1985) made important contributions to virology, immunology, and human biology.

On Sept. 3, 1899, F. Macfarlane Burnet was born in the country town of Traralgon. He was a naturalist at heart, wandering in the bush to study animals, birds, and insects. After graduating as a doctor of medicine from Melbourne University in 1922, he studied staphylococcal infections at the Walter and Eliza Hall Institute of Medical Research, Melbourne. He worked at the institute for 41 years, becoming director in 1942.

In 1930 Burnet discovered the existence of multiple strains of the poliomyelitis virus, essential knowledge for the production of vaccine. While visiting Sir Henry Dale in London in 1931, he observed the discovery of the influenza virus and mastered the developing-chick-embryo technique for virus culture. Returning to Australia in 1932, Burnet and his colleagues were the first to make influenza virus vaccine by the egg technique. In 1936 they discovered that Q fever, an infection in slaughter house workers, which had a worldwide distribution in humans, cattle, and sheep, was caused by a rickettsial organism. They also discovered, in 1952, the virus that causes the brain disease Murray Valley encephalitis, finding that it was carried by migrating birds from New Guinea and transmitted by mosquitoes to man.

Burnet possessed an insatiable desire to explore the unknown. He often thought of the inadequately explored field of immunology and theorized that at birth a person learned to tolerate his or her own tissues ("self") and to reject foreign tissues ("not-self"). A failure by a person to tolerate his or her own tissues might be produced by a freak mutation in the antibody-producing system, and a person would then attack his or her own organs to produce autoimmune disease. To prove these beliefs, in 1957 Burnet turned his researches to immunology with immediate success. His findings stimulated worldwide research in autoimmune disease. In 1960 he received the Nobel Prize for work on immunological tolerance.

In 1964 Burnet retired to write and lecture. From 1965 to 1969 he served as the president of the Australian Academy of Science. In 1969 he was made knight commander of the British Empire. That same year, he was named an Honorary Fellow of the Royal College of Surgeons. He was made a Knight of the Order of Australia in 1978. Burnet's published works during this period included the books *Immunology, Aging, and Cancer* (1976) and *Endurance of Life* (1978). His own productive life came to an end on August 31, 1985, when he died of cancer in Melbourne.

On his seventieth birthday Burnet's disciples proclaimed him a charming colleague and a great scientist who had made a major contribution to the good of humankind. On that day Burnet concluded, "The real objective today is to use the ability of men and women . . . to devise ways by which patterns of behavior, laid down in a million years, can be modified—tricked and twisted if necessary—to allow tolerable human existence in a crowded world."

Further Reading

Burnet's life and work are delightfully described in his *Changing Patterns: An Atypical Autobiography* (1968); his studies in immunology are treated in his *Self and Not-Self: Cellular Immunology* (1969). Sarah R. Riedman and Elton T. Gustafson, *Portraits of Nobel Laureates in Medicine and Physiology* (1963), includes a discussion of Burnet. A short biography and his Nobel lecture is in the Nobel Foundation,

Physiology or Medicine: Nobel Lectures, Including Presentation Speeches and Laureates' Biographies (3 vols., 1964-1967). Burnet's obituary appeared in *The Lancet* on 14 September 1985. A more recent biography is Frank Fenner, *Sir Macfarlane Burnet, Scientist and Thinker* (1987). □

Gilbert Burnet

The British prelate Gilbert Burnet (1643-1715) was a noted historian and a political and spiritual adviser to the British monarchs William and Mary.

Gilbert Burnet was born in Edinburgh, where his father was an advocate. He was educated by his father until the age of 10; he then entered the University of Aberdeen. By 14 Burnet had mastered Latin, Greek, and Aristotelian philosophy and had received a master's degree. He then studied civil law, but at his father's behest he turned to theology. By 18 Burnet had mastered the subject and was offered a church living. He declined it, however, on the grounds that he was too young for the pastoral calling.

In 1663 Burnet visited England, where he met the leading intellectual figures at Oxford and in London. He traveled to Europe in 1664, where his bent toward toleration was strengthened in Holland and his hatred of tyranny confirmed in France. In 1665 he accepted a church living in Scotland, and in 1669 he became a professor of divinity at the University of Glasgow. His patron was Lord Lauderdale, Charles II's chief adviser on Scottish affairs. By 1672, however, Burnet came to oppose Lauderdale's ruthless policy of government and turned to the Duke of Hamilton as his patron.

To avoid Lauderdale's wrath, Burnet settled in London. His testimony was crucial in the impeachment of Lauderdale by the House of Commons in 1674. During this period Burnet began his *History of the Reformation in England,* and the first volume was published during the uproar over the Popish Plot. He defended many of the victims of the plot, however, and did not favor the exclusion of Charles II's Catholic brother James from the succession. He had long been acquainted with James, who treated him well, even though Burnet repeatedly tried to persuade him to renounce Catholicism. Burnet's solution for the exclusion crisis was that James should keep the crown but that the Protestant William of Orange should exercise power as protector. When exclusion was defeated, Burnet fell out of favor. In 1683 he was forbidden to preach, and he left England for France.

By 1687 Burnet had moved to Utrecht and become a political adviser to William of Orange and religious guide to William's wife, Mary. In 1688 he accompanied William on his invasion of England; upon the entry into London he preached on the text, "It is the Lord's doing and it is marvelous in our eyes." After the accession of William and Mary in 1689, Burnet was made bishop of Salisbury. His episcopate was marked by his strong spirit of tolerance and by vigorous efforts to improve the clergy in the diocese.

Burnet influenced William's successor, Anne, to augment the income of poor Anglican clergymen; the fund became known as "Queen Anne's Bounty." Otherwise Burnet's tolerance was not congenial to Anne, and he devoted his last years to his diocese and the completion of *History of His Own Times,* the record of an intelligent, tolerant, and moderate man in an age of passionate religious and political antagonisms.

Further Reading

The best biography of Burnet is still his *History of His Own Times* (many editions). See also T. E. S. Clarke, *A Life of Gilbert Burnet* (1907). Background studies which discuss Burnet include Geoffrey S. Holmes and W. A. Speck, eds., *The Divided Society: Parties and Politics in England, 1694-1716* (1967), and Geoffrey S. Holmes, ed., *Britain after the Glorious Revolution, 1689-1714* (1969). □

Fanny Burney

The English novelist and diarist Fanny Burney (1752-1840) was one of the most popular novelists of the late 18th century. She was also an important chronicler of English manners, morals, and society.

Fanny Burney, originally named Frances, was the daughter of Dr. Charles Burney, the distinguished historian of music. She captured London's literary society with the publication of *Evelina, or the History of a Young Lady's Entrance into the World,* the best of her four extant novels. Although she had begun to compose *Evelina* as early as 1767, she did not publish it until 1778, and then only anonymously. The heroine's search for a father and a husband exposes both the vanity and affectation of life among the upper class and the vulgarity and lack of feeling which she associates with low life. An effective novel told in letters, it displays Burney's wit, knowledge of English society, technical versatility, sentiment, interest in contemporary theater, and gift for depicting character.

Evelina won Burney admission to the salons of the great and famous, many of whom she described vividly in her diaries and journals. From 1787 to 1791 she served as second keeper of the robes to Queen Charlotte. In 1793 she married Gen. d'Arblay, a French refugee, with whom she lived in France from 1802 to 1812.

Her priceless record of life in the late 18th and early 19th centuries is preserved in what she called an "immense Mass of Manuscripts," consisting of diaries, journals, notebooks, and a voluminous correspondence begun in her fifteenth year.

Before publishing her second novel, *Cecilia,* in 1782, Burney had written and abandoned a comedy entitled *The Witlings.* While the immensely popular *Cecilia* again shows Burney's mastery of plot, it is both less comic and more sentimental than *Evelina.* Melodramatic scenes, revealing the influence of the contemporary stage, frame Cecilia Beverley's efforts to marry young Delvile.

Camilla (1796) and *The Wanderer* (1814) lack narrative interest and are perhaps better considered courtesy books than novels. *Camilla* teaches the lessons of propriety, prudence, and fortitude to a young girl; *The Wanderer* depicts the difficulties faced by a penniless and unprotected spinster trying to earn her living in England.

In 1832 Fanny Burney published three volumes of the *Memoirs of Dr. Burney,* a project begun in 1814. Seven volumes of *The Diary and Letters of Madame d'Arblay,* published between 1842 and 1846, and two volumes of *The Early Diary of Francis Burney,* not published until 1907, reveal her pert and astute observations about fashionable life in Georgian England.

Further Reading

The authoritative biographical study of Fanny Burney is Joyce Hemlow, *The History of Fanny Burney* (1958). Her major works are discussed in J. M. S. Tompkins, *The Popular Novel in England, 1770-1800* (1932); Lionel Stevenson, *The English Novel: A Panorama* (1960); and Ronald Paulson, *Satire and the Novel in Eighteenth Century England* (1967). Recommended for general background reading are J. H. Plumb, *England in the Eighteenth Century* (1951); A. R. Humphreys, *The Augustan World: Life and Letters in Eighteenth Century England* (1954); and Ian P. Watt, *The Rise of the Novel* (1957). □

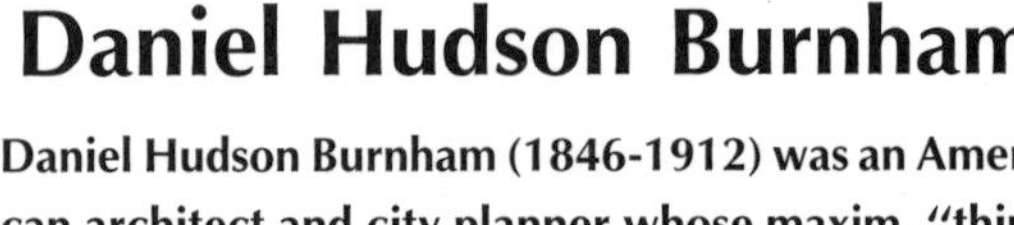

Daniel Hudson Burnham

Daniel Hudson Burnham (1846-1912) was an American architect and city planner whose maxim, "think big," dominated his successful career. The firm of Burnham & Root was important in developing the skyscraper.

Daniel H. Burnham was born in Henderson, N.Y. In 1868 he worked for the architect William Le Baron Jenney in Chicago and then for Carter, Drake & Wight, where he met John Welborn Root. In 1873 the firm of Burnham & Root was established, and Burnham's career until 1891, the year of Root's death, was inseparable from that of his talented, innovative partner.

The firm, which employed as many as 60 draftsmen, moved into the just-completed Montauk Block (1882-1883) in Chicago, which they had designed. Although load-bearing masonry walls were outdated by 1889, Burnham & Root designed the 16-story Monadnock Building in Chicago (completed in 1891) of brick construction. The walls enclosed a portal-braced iron frame consisting of girders riveted to the columns for wind bracing and structural stability; this was the first example of portal bracing. Burnham & Root's further development of this structural innovation was the completely steel structure of the Rand McNally Building (1889-1890) in Chicago. Their four-story Reliance

Building (1890; increased to 13 stories in 1895), also in Chicago, with terracotta facing material, gave expression to the steel-and-glass skyscrapers of the 1890s.

Burnham and Root were to have been the coordinators of the World's Columbian Exposition to be held in 1893 in Chicago, but on the day of the first planning conference Root contracted pneumonia, and died. Charles Follen McKim of the noted architectural firm of McKim, Mead & White filled the void left by Root and influenced Burnham in his "think big" attitude. Numerous architectural firms from Chicago, New York, Boston, and Kansas City designed specific buildings, and Frederick Law Olmsted was the landscape architect. The classical style provided the unifying element in the architecture of the exposition.

In 1891 Burnham established the firm of D. H. Burnham, which was replaced in 1896 by D. H. Burnham & Co. In 1894 he became president of the American Institute of Architects.

After the Chicago exposition of 1893 Burnham devoted his efforts to the "City Beautiful" movement of civic planning. "Make no little plans," he said, "for they have no magic to stir men's blood ... Make big plans, aim high. . . . " His city planning aimed at creating beauty in a geometry of streets, with large parks and recreational areas and boulevards leading from a civic center to other nodal points of the city. In 1903 Burnham replanned Manila in the Philippines in this manner, ridding the city of its chaos and yet retaining its picturesque image. Baguio, 160 miles away, was planned as a summer retreat in the hills, with a dominant geometry adapted to the contours. Three days before the great earthquake of April 15, 1906, Burnham submitted his plan for San Francisco. Never implemented, it attempted to circumnavigate the hills and tie the whole street pattern together by an outer ring road. Chicago was replanned, and Burnham's ideas for a coordinated system of surface and subsurface freight distribution, linked to the waterfront activities, were partially realized. Washington, D.C., was "beatified" and railroads were removed from the Mall; Burnham built Union Station there.

Burnham's firm designed over 100 major projects: civic centers, office blocks, department stores, libraries, and numerous stations for the Penn Central Railroad. The station in Pittsburgh has been described as "Burnham baroque," and one critic sees the beginnings of Art Nouveau in its flowing lines.

Further Reading

One biography of Burnham is Charles Moore, *Daniel H. Burnham, Architect, Planner of Cities* (2 vols., 1921). Structural innovations by Burnham and Root are discussed in Carl W. Condit's publications, including *American Building Art: The Nineteenth Century* (1960) and *The Chicago School of Architecture* (1964).

Additional Sources

Hines, Thomas S., *Burnham of Chicago, architect and planner,* New York: Oxford University Press, 1974. □

Forbes Burnham

Forbes Burnham (1923-1985) led the coalition government which won independence for British Guiana in 1966 and was Guyana's first prime minister. He established himself as president of Guyana in 1970.

Linden Forbes Sampson Burnham was born at Kitty in then British Guiana on February 20, 1923. His father, James Ethelbert Burnham, was the local elementary school headmaster. His mother was Rachel Abigail (Sampson) Burnham. Burnham attended the local elementary school in Kitty, then went on to Queen's College in Georgetown where he excelled both academically and in debating. He won a British Guiana scholarship which permitted him to attend the University of London in 1942. Awarded a Bachelor of Arts degree in 1944, Burnham proceeded to study law, completing all the requirements brilliantly. He was called to the bar in 1948. Always a politically active student, Burnham served as president of the West Indian Students Union of London University for the academic year, 1947-1948. He was a delegate to the meeting of the International Union of Students in Paris in 1947 and in Prague in 1948.

Burnham returned to his native land in 1949 with a reputation as a gifted speaker with a passion for politics and as a moderate socialist. He immediately became active in local politics and remained until his death Guyana's most active and influential politician. He was co-founder, along with Cheddi Jagan, Jainarine Singh, J. B. Latchmansingh, Martin Carter, and Sydney King (later Eusi Kwayana), of the People's Progressive Party, which won a resounding victory in the first elections held in Guiana under universal adult suffrage in 1953. By then Burnham was chairman of the party, an elected member of the Georgetown city council, and the unofficial leader of the urban section of the party.

In a country where the racial divisions between Guyanese of African and East Indian descent tended to coincide with the geographical divisions of urban-coastal (Georgetown) and rural-interior, respectively, Burnham's political base gave him great strength within the party. Indeed this emerged early when, at the age of 30, he challenged Jagan for the position of leader of the House of Representatives. Burnham eventually accepted the position of minister of education, but after only a few months the British government suspended the constitution and imposed an interim government until 1957.

In 1955 Burnham and others defected from the People's Progressive Party, but their wing, though strong, lost to the Jagan faction in the new elections of 1957. That year Burnham, a sitting member of Parliament, founded the People's National Congress, designed to be a multi-racial moderately socialist party to the right of Cheddi Jagan. Meanwhile, Burnham's political star began to rise. He was elected mayor of Georgetown in 1959 and again in 1964 and served as president of the Guyana Bar Association in 1959. Moreover, he was the leader of the opposition from 1957 to 1964 and president of the Guyana Labor Union.

Burnham's party won the general elections of 1964 on a modified system of proportional representation. Instead of the usual winner-take-all of the conventional "Westminster Model" election, each party was given a number of seats in Parliament in direct relationship to their proportion of the popular vote. With the 12 percent won by the United Party, Burnham was able to form a coalition government. This government led Guyana into independence in 1966, and Forbes Burnham became the first prime minister.

The coalition did not last long, and after 1967 Burnham manipulated the electoral system to maintain his party in power. The main instrument was an overseas voting system based on registration lists of nationals. In the 1968 elections the People's National Congress gained 93.7 percent of the total of 36,745 foreign votes, allowing it to claim an absolute majority of 55.8 percent of the ballots and to dispense with the coalition. However, research done by the reliable Opinion Research Center of London could verify only 15 percent of the entries on the overseas registration lists.

Buoyed by the result of the 1968 general elections, Burnham established the Co-Operative Republic of Guyana in 1970 with himself as president. He still maintained his Commonwealth contacts, but Guyanese politics in the 1970s and early 1980s was the will of a singular individual. Indeed, in 1973 Burnham announced that his party had won two-thirds of the votes in the general election and with its corresponding proportion of the unicameral legislature had the requisite legal means to alter the constitution. To further reinforce his position, Burnham engineered a referendum in 1978 which made referenda unnecessary to amend the constitution once the proposed amendment got a two-third vote in the National Assembly. A new constitution made Burnham executive president with a wide range of powers to dissolve Parliament, to veto legislation, and to appoint or dismiss the prime minister, any minister of the cabinet, the vice-president, the leader of the opposition, and/or any member of the bureaucracy.

As Burnham consolidated his political power and created a new variant of ethnic politics in Guyana, the national economy went from bad to worse. Although Guyana is potentially rich, possessing extensive fertile coastal lands and a vast interior with deposits of gold, emeralds, bauxite, lumber, and other natural resources, the country had been bankrupt for nearly a decade. The massive schemes of nationalization of industry in the 1970s increased neither employment nor production nor income for the state. Opponents of the government—which by 1980 had virtually become synonymous with Burnham—were crudely beaten by thugs, hounded out of the country, or, as in the case of Walter Rodney, the leader of the Working People's Alliance, boldly assassinated.

Despite a confused rhetoric suggesting Marxist orientation and amicable relationships with the Soviet Union, China, Cuba, and the government of Maurice Bishop in Grenada, Burnham succeeded in retaining open, if exasperating, relations with the United States, the British Commonwealth, and the Caribbean community. Foreign support of the Burnham regime merely facilitated the consolidation of power by the People's National Congress and further demoralized the opposition.

President Burnham succumbed to heart failure while undergoing a throat operation on August 6, 1985. His successor was Prime Minister Ptolemy Reid.

Further Reading

Burnham is listed in the *International Who's Who* and *Personalities Caribbean, 1982-1983.* His political opinion-cum-autobiography is *A Destiny to Mould* (1970). Critical accounts of his policies and his government may be found in Clive Thomas, *Plantations, peasants, and state: a study of the mode of sugar production in Guyana* (1984); and J. E. Greene, *Race vs. Politics in Guyana—Racial Cleavages and Political Mobilization in the 1968 General Election* (1974). □

Anthony Burns

Anthony Burns (1834-1862) was a fugitive African American slave whose recapture in Boston forced his return to slavery, thus angering many Northerners and increasing the moral force of the abolitionists.

Anthony Burns was born in Stafford Country, Va., on May 31, 1834. By the age of 6 he had learned the alphabet from neighboring white children and could read. After a youthful conversion, he became a Baptist slave preacher. While working in Richmond, he escaped from his owner, C. T. Suttle, by stowing away on a ship. Arriving in Boston in March 1854, Burns found friendship and employment among the free blacks.

Suttle learned the whereabouts of Burns through an intercepted letter and determined to recover his slave, valued at $1,000. Armed with a court order, Suttle had Burns arrested in May 1854 under the Fugitive Slave Act of 1850, which required only "positive identification" before a Federal commissioner to award custody of an African American to an "owner"; there was no jury trial or possibility of appeal.

On the night preceding the formal hearing before the commissioner, an abolitionist meeting was held. Theodore Parker and Wendell Phillips urged that Burns be freed, by force if necessary. Thomas Wentworth Higginson led a group of blacks and whites in a badly timed charge on the jail. Although one guard was killed, Burns was not freed. On the next day Richard Henry Dana, Burn's counsel, argued brilliantly for his client but failed to prevent the slave's return to Virginia. Mass hostility regarding the decision forced the governor to use militia, marines, and regular army troops when Burns was marched across Boston to a waiting ship. To prevent a repetition of similar cases, several Northern states enacted "personal liberty laws" designed to block the capture and return of fugitive slaves.

After 5 months in a Richmond prison, Burns was sold to a speculator who made a handsome profit by reselling the slave to a group of Bostonians who, in turn, freed him in March 1855. He returned to a hero's welcome in Boston, where he assisted C. E. Stevens in compiling *Anthony Burns: A History* (1856).

Late in 1855, with the aid of antislavery people, Burns entered the preparatory department of Oberlin College in Ohio. After a year there he attended Fairmont Theological Seminary in Cincinnati for a year's study and returned again to Oberlin. During 1858-1859 he reportedly served as pastor of an African American congregation in Indianapolis, Ind. He returned to Oberlin once more, remaining there until June 1862. During his holidays, in addition to preaching, Burns traveled on the abolitionist circuit, speaking against the evils of slavery and selling copies of his book. In the spring of 1862 he went to St. Catharines, Ontario, to become pastor of a congregation of freedmen. He died there on July 27, 1862, after a short illness.

Further Reading

In addition to the biography by Charles Emery Stevens, *Anthony Burns: A History* (1856), the trial of Burns is described in an anonymous pamphlet, *The Boston Slave Riot, and Trial of Anthony Burns* (1854). More recent accounts appear in the biographies of the prominent Bostonians who participated: Oscar Sherwin, *Prophet of Liberty: The Life and Times of Wendell Phillips* (1958); Samuel Shapiro, *Richard Henry Dana, Jr., 1815-1882* (1961); John L. Thomas, *The Liberator, William Lloyd Garrison* (1963); and Tilden G. Edelstein, *Strange Enthusiasm: A Life of Thomas Wentworth Higginson* (1968). □

Arthur Burns

Having occupied important positions in every Republican administration from the end of World War II to the mid-1980s, Arthur Burns (1904-1987) was one of the most influential economic statesmen of his times.

Born in Stanislau, Austria, Arthur Burns soon immigrated with his Austro-Hungarian Jewish parents to New Jersey. He grew up in Bayonne, where he showed particular promise in debate and languages. He attended Columbia University on a scholarship, and while a student worked as a painter, sailor, writer, and clerk. Occasionally, he published articles in *New York Herald Tribune.*

Burns studied under Wesley Clair Mitchell, one of the nation's leading economists who pioneered in the development of statistics. Mitchell had organized the National Bureau of Economic Research at Columbia and, after receiving his Ph.D. in economics, Burns joined him there. His first important publication, *Production Trends in the United States Since 1870,* was released by the National Bureau in 1934 and established him as a coming scholar in that field.

During the 1930s economic debate in America centered on the concepts of John Maynard Keynes, who held that a vigorous governmental role was needed to direct the economy. Because the United States then was mired in a deep depression, this meant large-scale government spending programs such as those sponsored by President Franklin D. Roosevelt's New Deal. While accepting some of Keynes' ideas, Burns believed the American Keynesians were far too simplistic in their approaches. Along with Mitchell, he believed economic action must be preceded by careful gatherings of facts and not based upon some abstract idea. Each industry has its own cycle, he wrote, and when several head downward at the same time, we will have a recession or depression. What is needed then is some intervention, but on a highly selective basis.

By the late 1940s, by which time he had succeeded Mitchell as director of research at the National Bureau of Economic Research, Burns had come to believe that the maintenance of employment was a prime goal of government, but that inflation was another serious problem which had to be addressed. This would be accomplished by "leaning" against the economy whenever one or the other threatened. Gentle stimulative pressures would be applied when recession threatened, and restrictive ones when inflation seemed about to rise or accelerate. This placed Burns squarely in the camp of moderate Republicans who then were supporting General Dwight D. Eisenhower for the presidency.

When Eisenhower became president in 1953 he selected Burns to head the Council of Economic Advisors. A recession developed later that year, and Eisenhower was willing to embark upon a major recovery program. Burns urged him to hold back. The economic indicators seemed to point to a milder correction than most other economists expected. He proved correct. Without major intervention the economy turned upward in 1954, leading Eisenhower to remark, "Arthur, you'd have made a fine chief of staff during the war."

Burns resigned from the administration after the 1956 election and returned to the National Bureau of Economic Research and Columbia. He advised Eisenhower from there and later took on temporary assignments from his successors, John F. Kennedy and Lyndon B. Johnson. In addition, he kept in close contact with Richard Nixon, formerly Eisenhower's vice president and then a New York attorney.

When Nixon won the 1968 election he asked Burns to return to Washington as counselor to the president, a position which would carry cabinet rank and give him wide responsibilities in domestic affairs. At the time the nation was in the midst of a crisis of confidence due to anti-Vietnam War sentiment, high inflation, and the largest budget deficit of the post-World War II period. Burns recommended a slowdown in the growth of the money supply through Federal Reserve Board policies and cutbacks in spending, which he hoped would dampen the inflation rate without causing a recession. Nixon accepted the broad outlines of the program, and at first it seemed to be working. Then the Federal Reserve tightened up sharply on the money supply, causing interest rates to rise and leading to an economic downturn while inflation was still deemed a problem. Thus was born "stagflation," a problem which would haunt the nation throughout the 1970s and cause economists to rethink many of their earlier ideas.

With the coming of stagflation Burns' position in the Nixon White House declined, and his views started to change. Now he supported wage and price "guidelines" as a means of controlling inflation and seemed to inch away from his earlier stance.

In late 1969 President Nixon named Burns to become chairman of the Federal Reserve, where he would be able to act independently. Burns expanded the currency supply, which gave the economy a boost. When the Penn Central Railroad collapsed in 1970, Burns proclaimed that the Federal Reserve would provide sufficient funds to prevent a panic, and his calm behavior in this crisis not only enhanced his reputation but made him one of the most powerful men in the country insofar as economic matters were concerned. Burns continued to support wage and price guidelines and was credited with having helped prompt President Nixon to impose them in 1971. That same year he expanded the money supply considerably, so that by Election Day 1972 the economy was growing while prices were being contained, making the economy appear quite healthy and helping Nixon win a second term. Burns was accused of having used the Federal Reserve for political purposes, which he vehemently denied.

Burns served as chairman of the Federal Reserve until the conclusion of his term in 1978, at which time he was not reappointed by Democratic President Jimmy Carter. This caused the dollar to plummet and shook the new administration. Burns left government to take a post at the American Enterprise Institute and also lectured and wrote, becoming an elder statesman of moderate economics. During that time he published *Reflections of an Economic Policy Maker* (1978).

In 1981 President Ronald Reagan named Burns ambassador to the Federal Republic of Germany. He took the post during a time of strong anti-American sentiment in Europe, because of U.S. deployment of cruise and Pershing missiles. Reagan proved wise in his decision to appoint Burns, who was well-respected throughout Europe for his past performance in economic matters. He was able to quell European concerns, arriving at an agreement with the West German foreign minister that significantly eased tensions within NATO. Burns served as Ambassador to Germany for four years, then returned to the American Economic Institute to pursue writing and teaching.

Arthur Burns died in Baltimore, Maryland on June 26, 1987, leaving a tremendous legacy. Not only did his economic policies dramatically influence the American and world economies, he also inspired people, such as his famous pupil, Milton Friedman. He was clearly an approachable man, being described by one reporter as "a small-town druggist circa 1910."

Further Reading

There is no biography of Arthur Burns. A discussion and analysis of his life and ideas may be found in Robert Sobel, *The Worldly Economists* (1980); William Breit and Roger Ransom, *The Academic Scribblers* (1971); Edward Flash, Jr., *Economic Advice and Presidential Leadership* (1965); and Herbert Stein, *The Fiscal Revolution in America* (1969). For his work during the Eisenhower administration see Sherman Adams, *Firsthand Report: The Story of the Eisenhower Administration* (1961), while William Safire, *Before the Fall* contains material on his work during the Nixon administration. Among the more accessible works by Burns himself is *Reflections on an Economic Policy Maker* (1978), which is a collection of his papers and speeches through the years. Also see Wyatt C. Wells, *Economist in an Uncertain World: Arthur F. Burns and the Federal Reserve, 1970–78*, Columbia University Press, 1994. □

George Burns

Comedian and actor George Burns (1896–1996) is a show business legend. When he died at the age of 100 in 1996, he had spent 90 years as a comic entertainer, making numerous television and film appearances and earning an enduring popularity with his obligatory-cigar-in-hand comedy routines.

In his ninety years in show business, George Burns had time for three careers. His first two decades were spent as a small-time vaudeville performer. Later, as part of a comedy duo with his wife, Gracie Allen, he achieved wide popularity on the stage, radio, television, and in films. Finally, after Allen's death, Burns performed as a stand-up comedian and comic actor, winning an Academy Award at the age of 80.

George Burns was born Nathan Birnbaum on January 20, 1896, the ninth of twelve children of an Orthodox Jewish family. The Birnbaums, recent immigrants from Eastern Europe, lived on New York City's impoverished lower East Side. His father was a cantor (a painfully out-of-tune one, according to Burns's account), who worked as a last-minute substitute at various New York synagogues.

After his father's death, Burns began a career in show business at the age of seven. To help support the family, he formed the Pee Wee quartet, a group of child performers who sang and told jokes on street corners. He and his brothers also helped out by stealing coal from a nearby coal yard—earning the nickname the Burns Brothers. He would later settle on this as a stage name, changing his first name to George after an idolized older brother.

Burns's early performing years were spent doing whatever he could to earn money. In 1916, under the name Willy Delight, he performed as a trick roller-skater on the Keith Vaudeville Circuit. Later, as Pedro Lopez, he taught ballroom dancing. Over the years, he tried several other names—Billy Pierce, Captain Betts, Jed Jackson, Jimmy Malone, Buddy Lanks—appearing in a wide range of vaudeville acts with many different partners. "When I first started in vaudeville I was strictly small-time," he reminisced in his book, *How to Live to be 100—or More.* "I'd be

lying if I said I was the worst act in the world; I wasn't that good."

Formed Partnership with Gracie Allen

By 1923, he was appearing at the Union Theatre as George Burns, comedian, when he met his future partner, Gracie Allen. Allen, ten years younger than Burns, came from a San Francisco show business family, and had also been performing since she was a child. However, by the early 1920s, she had given up her fledgling career in entertainment to train as a stenographer. Allen was accompanying a friend on a backstage visit at the theater when she was introduced to Burns. In tune with her scatterbrained image, she confused him with someone else, and called him by the wrong name for several days.

Burns and Allen made their performing debut in 1924. In his previous act, Burns was both the writer and the comedian, while his partner played the straight man. Burns initially stuck to this format in his act with Allen, but quickly learned that she was the funny one. "Even her straight lines got laughs," Burns was quoted as saying in *The Guardian.* "She had a very funny delivery . . . . they laughed at her straight lines and didn't laugh at my jokes."

Soon Burns and Allen developed the act that would make them famous: he played the bemused, cigar-smoking boyfriend and comic foil to her dizzy, muddled girlfriend. In a distracted, little-girl voice, Allen told rambling stories about her family, while Burns asked questions. "I just asked Gracie a question, and she kept talking for the next 37 years," he later recalled (quoted in *The Daily Telegraph*).

After performing together in vaudeville for three years, Burns and Allen were married in Cleveland on January 7, 1926. Theirs was a famously happy marriage. "I'm the brains and Gracie is everything else, especially to me," Burns once said (quoted in *The Daily Mail*). Later, they adopted two children, Sandra Jean and Ronald John.

Around the time of their marriage they were signed to a six-year contract with Keith theaters, which took them on tours of the United States and Europe. In 1930 Burns and Allen joined Eddie Cantor, George Jessel, and others in a headline bill marking the end of vaudeville at the Palace Theatre in New York. After this appearance, as well as appearances on the Rudy Vallee and Guy Lombardo shows, CBS signed the team for their own radio program.

Launched Successful Radio Show

The George Burns and Gracie Allen Show debuted on February 15, 1932. The team became famous for one exchange that ended that show, and every show. After a program filled with one non sequitur after another, Burns would say, long sufferingly, "Say goodnight, Gracie" and Allen would respond brightly, "Goodnight, Gracie."

During nineteen years in radio, Burns and Allen attracted an audience estimated at more than 45 million listeners. In 1940 their salary was reported to be $9,000 a week. Always modest about his role in the series, Burns claimed that Allen was solely responsible for their enduring success. "With Gracie, I had the easiest job of any straight man in history," he said (quoted in *The Guardian*). "I only had to know two lines—'How's your brother?' and 'Your brother did *what?*'"

Meanwhile, in 1931 they signed a contract with Paramount Studios to star in short films and, when not making pictures, to play on the stage of the Publix theaters. Their first full-length movie was *The Big Broadcast of 1932.* In addition to many short films, the team made an average of two films a year for Paramount. Their last film for Paramount was *Honolulu* (1939), which starred Eleanor Powell and Robert Young.

To attract attention for their radio show, Burns masterminded several publicity stunts. In 1933, Allen appeared on radio shows throughout the country, searching for her imaginary lost brother. The joke was so convincing that her real brother, an accountant in San Francisco, had to go into hiding until public interest in him had waned. During the 1940 election, Allen declared herself a nominee for the "Surprise Party," and campaigned on various radio shows, even holding a three-day convention in Omaha. She received several thousand write-in votes.

In October 1950, *The Burns and Allen Show* made the transition to television. The program used the same format as the successful radio program. The following exchange was typical of their humor: "Did the maid ever drop you on your head when you were a baby?" "Don't be silly, George. We couldn't afford a maid. My mother had to do it" (quoted in *The Independent*).

Began to Perform as Solo Act

In 1958, angina forced Allen to retire—an event that merited the cover of *Life* magazine. At the time, *The George Burns and Gracie Allen Show* was then television's longest-running sitcom. Burns continued to perform in *The George Burns Show,* but the series only lasted one season. "The show had everything it needed to be successful, except Gracie," Burns recalled (quoted in *The Independent*).

Six years later, Allen died of cancer at the age of 59. Burns was devastated, and made almost daily visits to her grave. "The good things for me started with Gracie and for the next 38 years they only got better," he was quoted as saying in *The Guardian.* "But everything has a price. It still doesn't seem right that she went so young, and that I've been given so many years to spend without her."

After Allen's death, Burns devoted his time to McCadden, his television production company, which made such popular programs as *The People's Choice* (1955-58) and *Mr. Ed* (1961-66). Burns also appeared as a guest in various television specials throughout the sixties. However, his attempts to develop a new double act failed; he was unacceptable to the public with new partners like Carol Channing or Connie Stevens.

Won Academy Award at Age 80

It was not until 1975 that Burns was given the opportunity to re-launch his performing career. After the death of Jack Benny, a contemporary and close friend from the vaudeville days, Burns took Benny's role opposite Walter

Matthau in Neil Simon's film, *The Sunshine Boys.* The role of the ancient straight man, coming out of retirement for one last get-together with his shambling former partner, could not have been more perfect for Burns. At age 80, he won an Academy Award for best supporting actor—the oldest person to do so. "My last film was in 1939," he said at the time (quoted in *The Daily Telegraph*). "My agent didn't want me to suffer from over-exposure."

He followed his success with *Oh God!,* in which he played the deity wearing baggy pants, sneakers, and a golf cap. Two sequels followed, *Oh God! II* (1980) and *Oh God! You Devil* (1984), as well as several other comedies. None of these films was very successful, but Burns was undisturbed. "I just like to be working," he was quoted as saying in *The Daily Telegraph.*

Throughout the 1980s, Burns appeared often on television, hosting *100 Years of America's Popular Music* (1981), *George Burns and Other Sex Symbols* (1982) and *George Burns Celebrates 80 Years in Show Business* (1983). By this time, his comic material, mostly one-liners, centered almost exclusively on his age and longevity.

Burns also published various books, including *Dr. Burns' Prescription for Happiness* (1985) and a tribute to his wife, *Gracie, A Love Story* (1988), in which he revealed that Allen was actually his second wife. During his vaudeville days, Burns had formed a dancing act with Hannah Siegel, whom he had rechristened Hermosa Jose, after his favorite cigar. When their act was booked for a 26-week tour, her parents refused to let her travel the country with Burns unless he married her. The marriage lasted as long as the tour, and then was dissolved.

Although Burns never remarried, during his 80s and 90s he developed an enthusiasm for taking out young women—which became another endless source for comic material. At 97, Burns was still writing, making stage appearances, and numbering Sharon Stone among his escorts.

Burns had planned shows to celebrate his 100th birthday at the London Palladium for January 20, 1996. However, after a bad fall in 1994, his health declined, and the performances were canceled. A few days before his 100th birthday, he was suffering from the flu, and was unable to attend a party in his honor. Burns died at his home in Los Angeles on March 9, 1996.

Further Reading

Daily Mail, March 11, 1996, p. 23.
The Daily Telegraph, March 11, 1996, p. 23.
The Guardian, March 11, 1996, p. 12.
The Independent, March 11, 1996, p. 16.
The Times (London), March 11, 1996. □

Robert Burns

The work of the Scottish poet Robert Burns (1759-1796) is characterized by realism, intense feeling, and metrical virtuosity. His best work is in Scots, the vernacular of southern Scotland, and he is one of the greatest authors in that language of the last 4 centuries.

Robert Burns was born in Alloway, Ayrshire, on Jan. 25, 1759, in the cottage of hard-working farmer parents. He grew up in the general atmosphere of dour Scottish Calvinism, but his father's moderate religious views helped instill in Burns a spirit of tolerance and of rebellion against the grimmer doctrines of Calvinism. Although Burns's formal schooling was skimpy, he read avidly and for a time had a good tutor in John Murdoch, who gave him a thorough grounding in the 18th-century genteel tradition of English literature.

The family worked hard on their Ayrshire farm, and the arduousness of his labor in adolescence was to have a crippling effect in the long run on Robert's health. And troubles with landlords and their agents were helping to foster in him the egalitarianism and rebelliousness against privilege which became prominent themes in his poetry. In 1784 his father died in bankruptcy, and the family then moved a few miles away to Mossgiel. Here and in nearby Mauchline the gregarious and attractive Burns embarked on his notorious career as womanizer, which extended to about 1790. (By the end of his short life he was to have fathered fourteen children, nine of them out of wedlock, by six different mothers.)

Achievement and Sudden Fame

At Mossgiel, Burns's poetic powers developed spectacularly, and in 1786 he published *Poems, Chiefly in the Scottish Dialect* at nearby Kilmarnock. At this time Burns was 27, and he had written some of the most effective and biting satires in the language. Among them were "Holy Willie's Prayer" (a dramatic monologue which exposes the hypocrisy of a Calvinist pharisee) and "The Holy Fair" (a cynically humorous description of the Scottish equivalent of a religious camp meeting). Other important poems which appeared in his first volume were "Address to the Unco Guid" (a moving appeal to the rigidly upright to show tolerance for the fallen); "The Jolly Beggars" (a dramatic poem celebrating ragged havenots and ending with one of the most exhilarating paeans to anarchism in any language); the masterful "Address to the Deil" (that is, to the Devil); "The Cotter's Saturday Night" (an idealization of rural Scottish virtues); the sentimental but moving "Auld Farmer's Salutation to His Mare"; and the poignant "To a Mouse" (a poem that treats the human condition through presenting a field mouse unearthed by the plow). These and other typical poems by Burns are almost unparalleled in their combination of direct colloquialism and profundity of feeling or shrewd satirical characterization. Not for centuries had such fine poetry been written in the Scots tongue, poetry of feeling that exhibited great metrical virtuosity.

But 1786 was also a year of great distress for Burns. His liaison with Jean Armour, a Mauchline girl, had resulted in the birth of twins, and the two unwed parents were exposed to public penance. In addition, Burns was in love with Mary Campbell, the "Highland Mary" of his lyric, but she died in 1786, apparently in giving birth to his child. He contemplated emigrating to Jamaica, but he abandoned the plan and spent the winter in Edinburgh, where he was lionized. Early in 1787 a new edition of his poems was published which made him famous not only throughout Scotland but also in England and internationally. After a summer and fall spent in touring Scotland (the only real traveling he ever did), and incidentally in a renewal of his affair with Jean, Burns spent a second winter in Edinburgh. The limelight had begun to dim, but the sojourn was highlighted by the tragicomic love episode with Mrs. M'Lehose, the "Clarinda" of the "Sylvander-Clarinda" letters. This episode ended in March 1788 with Burns's decision to return to Mauchline and marry Jean, who had borne him a second set of twins.

Later Years and His Songs

After his marriage Burns turned his efforts to supporting his family. In 1788 he leased a farm at Ellisland, 45 miles from Mauchline. After frustrating delays in house building and an equally frustrating few years trying to wring an income from reluctant farmland, he moved with Jean and the children to Dumfries. In 1789 he had begun duties as a tax inspector, a profession in which he continued until his death.

At Ellisland, Burns had little leisure, but it was there that he wrote his masterpiece of comic humor "Tam o'Shanter," his one outstanding piece of narrative verse. He also wrote numerous songs (some of them original lyrics for old tunes, some refurbishings of old lyrics) for *The Scots Musical Museum,* an anthology of Scottish songs with which he had been associated since 1787. From 1792 until his death he also collaborated on a similar work, *A Select Collection of Original Scottish Airs.* Most of Burns's poetic effort in the Ellisland and Dumfries periods was in this area of song writing and song editing (he had written songs earlier but had usually not published them), and his achievement was spectacular. Among the lyrics, early and late, that he composed or reworked are "Mary Morison," "Highland Mary," "Duncan Gray," "Green Grow the Rashes, O," "Auld Lang Syne," "John Anderson, My Jo," "Scots Wha Hae Wi' Wallace Bled," "A Man's a Man for A' That," "A Red, Red Rose," and "Ye Banks and Braes o' Bonie Doon." These are true song lyrics; that is, they are not poems meant to be set to music but rather are poems written to melodies that define the rhythm.

Burns's years in Dumfries were years of hard work and hardship but not (as posthumous legend soon began to insist) of ostracism and moral decline. He was respected by his fellow townsmen and his colleagues. His health, always precarious, began to fail, and he died of heart disease on July 21, 1796. As if in witness to his vitality, his wife gave birth to their last child on the day of the funeral.

Further Reading

Two dependable biographies of Burns are Hans Hecht, *Robert Burns: The Man and His Work* (1919; trans. 1936; 2d ed. 1950); and Franklyn Bliss Snyder, *The Life of Robert Burns* (1932). Catherine Carswell, *The Life of Robert Burns* (1931; 2d ed. 1951), lacks documentation but is sensitive and interesting. Good critical studies include David Daiches, *Robert Burns* (1950; rev. ed. 1967), and Thomas Crawford, *Burns: A Study of the Poems and Songs* (1960). On the songs see James C. Dick, ed., *The Songs of Robert Burns* (1903; rev. ed. 1962). For Burns's place in Scots literature see Kurt Wittig, *The Scottish Tradition in Literature* (1958), as well as Daiches's book. □

Aaron Burr

American lawyer and politician Aaron Burr (1756-1836) was vice president under Thomas Jefferson. After his term of office he conspired to invade Spanish territory in the Southwest and to separate certain western areas from the United States.

Aaron Burr was born in Newark, N.J., on Feb. 6, 1756, the grandson of the Calvinist theologian Johathan Edwards, and the son of a Presbyterian minister. The family soon moved to Princeton, where the Reverend Burr became president of the College of New Jersey (later Princeton University). Burr was soon orphaned.

From an early age Burr prepared for an education at the College of New Jersey. Denied admission at the age of age 11, the precocious youth was accepted as a sophomore 2 years later. An eager and industrious student, he graduated with distinction in 3 years. He studied theology for a while but found himself disenchanted with the religious controversies generated by the Great Awakening. He turned instead to the study of law and for a period worked under the famous jurist Tapping Reeve.

Officer in the Revolution

Attracted by the drama and opportunity of the Revolutionary War, Burr secured a letter of recommendation from John Hancock, the president of the Continental Congress, and appeared before Gen. Washington to request a commission in the Continental Army. Washington refused, thus opening the first in a series of conflicts between the two men. Burr, however, persisted. He joined the Army and behaved commendably in the illfated expedition against Quebec. In the spring of 1776 he secured appointment, with the rank of major, to Washington's official household in New York. Mutual distrust quickly deepened between the two men, partly because of Burr's disenchantment with the tedium of administrative duties and partly because of the glaring contrast between his own spontaneous behavior and Washington's stiff and humorless manner.

Again through the intercession of Hancock, Burr transferred to the staff of Gen. Israel Putnam. For the next several years he served effectively in a variety of posts, developing a reputation both for vigilance and the effective disciplining of his troops.

In March 1779, his health impaired by exhaustion and exposure, Burr resigned his commission. By 1780, however, he was ready to launch a heavy program of legal study. Burr was licensed as an attorney in January 1782 and 2 months later was admitted to the bar.

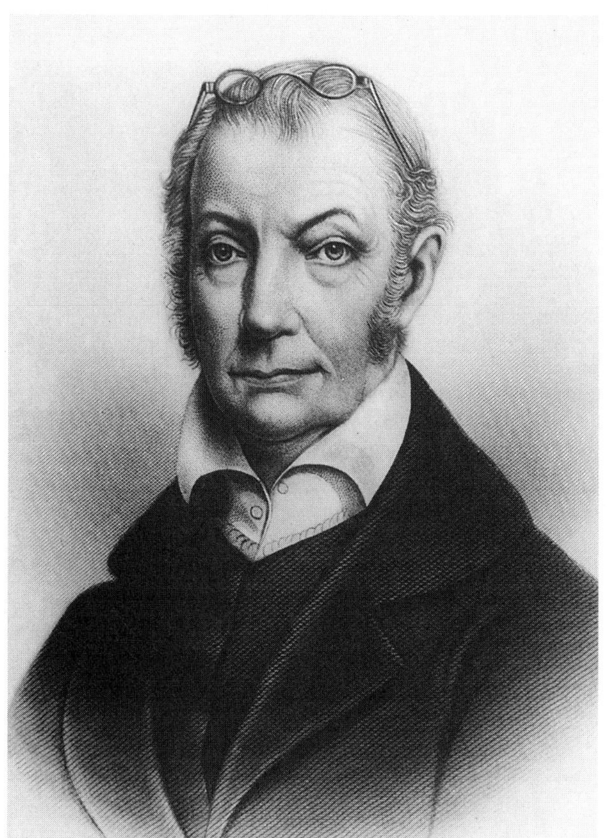

At least equal to Burr's pursuit of fame and fortune was his passion for women. Throughout his long life he carried on numerous affairs. Though he was only 5 feet 6 inches tall, his erect military bearing and graceful manner, his sparkling conversation and elegant appearance made him very attractive to women. In July 1777 he began regular visits to Mrs. Theodosia Prevost, 10 years his senior and wife of a British officer frequently away on duty. In July 1781 she was widowed; 9 months later she and Burr were married. The marriage lasted until her death in 1794, though Burr carried on a number of amours during the interval. In 1783 a daughter, Theodosia, was born, with whom Burr developed a deep and affectionate relationship. Indeed, much of Burr's life came to revolve around his ambitions and concerns for her.

Lawyer in New York

After establishing a successful legal practice in the booming town of Albany, Burr moved in 1783 to New York City. For 6 years he stuck to his practice, generating a substantial reputation and income. He never compiled a large fortune, however, for his generosity and his own lifestyle drained his money away.

Local and National Politics

Gradually during the 1790s Burr worked his way into New York politics. Nominally a member of the emerging Jeffersonian opposition, he took care not to break completely with the Federalists. The results of this were twofold. By carefully balancing group against group, he could present himself as a nonsectarian, coalition candidate. On the other hand, this generated suspicions among both Jeffersonians and Federalists about his "unsettled" political loyalties. In 1791 Burr won election to the U.S. Senate, defeating Philip Schuyler, Alexander Hamilton's father-in-law. Burr and Hamilton had been for some time political and professional antagonists; this election elicited Hamilton's unrelenting hatred. In the Senate, Burr occupied a somewhat ambiguous position, opposing Hamilton's financial program and the Jay Treaty, yet not becoming a full Jeffersonian partisan.

Burr failed to drum up support for the vice presidency in 1796 and also lost his seat in the Senate. From 1797 to 1799 he served in the New York Legislature but was defeated for reelection when he came under fire for promoting legislation to aid a land company and banking corporation in which he had financial interests.

Vice Presidency

Burr's opportunity to fashion a national political career came with the presidential election of 1800. With the support of the Tammany organization (which he never formally joined), he organized New York City and enabled Jefferson to carry the state's crucial electoral votes. Meanwhile Burr had secured a pledge from the Jeffersonians in Congress to support him equally with Jefferson in the election as a way of ensuring that neither of the Federalist candidates would have a chance. (In 1800 presidential electors simply cast two ballots, making no distinction between presidential and vice-presidential preferences.) The result was a tie. Jefferson and Burr each received 73 votes, and the election shifted to the House of Representatives. For 35 ballots neither man received a majority, while rumors circulated that Burr was scheming for Federalist support. A number of Federalists did state their strong preference for him, but Hamilton argued just as strongly that Jefferson was a more honorable man. Finally several Federalists withheld their votes and permitted Jefferson's election, thus ending a major constitutional crisis.

Burr was now vice president, but his political career was near its end. His relations with Jefferson's supporters were further strained during his 4 years in office. In 1804 Burr was passed over by the Jeffersonian congressional caucus and was not renominated for vice president.

Hamilton-Burr Duel

In July 1804 the famous duel with Hamilton took place. Burr had tried to avoid it, but it was forced upon him by Hamilton's mounting public attacks. As word of Hamilton's death spread, the public outcry forced Burr to flee for his safety. His political base, both within New York and in the Jeffersonian party, was now completely gone. To fulfill his obligation as vice president, Burr returned to Washington to preside over the impeachment proceedings against Justice Samuel Chase, a task he carried out with justice and impartiality. The day after the trial was over, Burr left the Senate chamber for the last time.

Burr's Conspiracy

For at least a year prior to this, Burr had been making plans to recoup in the West some of the power denied him in the East. The precise motive behind his western adventures has never been clarified. There seems to have been two options: to gather a force to invade Spanish–held territory across the Mississippi out of which an independent republic was to be fashioned, or to separate certain southwestern territories (east of the Mississippi) from the United States and incorporate them with the Spanish lands to form an independent nation. Burr's primary goal seems to have been the Spanish venture, though he was clearly interested in including New Orleans and territory along the Mississippi. If his proposals to England to aid in dismembering the Union had met with support, Burr might well have placed separation at the center of his planning. Whatever the case, his western adventure had the gravest implications for the young republic.

Burr's involved intrigue took form in 1804-1805, when he divulged his plans to various persons, among them Gen. James Wilkinson, commander of American forces in the West, and Anthony Merry, British minister to the United States, whom Burr asked for half a million dollars and the promise of aid from the British fleet. After a scouting trip down the Ohio and Mississippi rivers, Burr returned east and made further attempts to organize support. Failing to secure funds from England, he turned to various private sources.

When Jefferson's purchase of Spanish Florida ended the prospect of the Spanish-American border war that Burr had hoped to use as the occasion for his own invasion of Spanish territory, he decided to launch his enterprise. In August 1806 he started west into the Ohio Valley to rally men and supplies. Increasingly alarmed by rumors of Burr's operations, President Jefferson sent warnings to western officials to keep Burr under careful surveillance. Receiving a communication from Wilkinson (who had now turned against Burr), the President issued a proclamation describing the intended expedition and warning American citizens not to participate. At the beginning of 1807, unaware of Wilkinson's betrayal, Burr started down the Ohio with about 100 men. Within a few weeks the whole thing was over. Behind Burr, units of the Ohio militia organized for pursuit, and ahead of him Wilkinson was frantically arranging New Orleans's defense while preparing a force to intercept Burr. Learning of Wilkinson's opposition, Burr fled toward Mobile, Ala., leaving his force to be placed under detention. Burr was arrested a few miles from Spanish Florida and returned east for trial.

On Trial

Charged with the high misdemeanor of launching a military expedition against Spanish territory and the treasonous act of attempting to separate areas from the United States, Burr stood trial before Chief Justice John Marshall in the U.S. Circuit Court at Richmond, Va. The outcome hung upon Marshall's instructions to the jury concerning the technicalities of American treason law. Burr was acquitted on the treason charge, and the misdemeanor indictment was eventually canceled. The acquittal was extremely unpopular; Marshall was burned in effigy as a result.

Burr's Decline

Although Burr was legally free, his political career was finished. For the next 4 years he wandered through Europe, vainly trying to find support for plans to revolutionize Mexico, free the Spanish colonies, and instigate war between England and the United States. Finally, in 1812, he returned to America, broken in health and financially destitute. After some discreet inquiries, he decided it was safe to return to New York. There he set about the task of reestablishing his legal practice. He was moderately successful, but his final years were not easy. In December 1812 his cherished daughter, Theodosia, was lost at sea. As the years passed, his fortunes again declined. By 1830 he had come to depend heavily upon contributions from a few friends for his survival. In 1833, at the age of 77, Burr married a wealthy widow 20 years his junior who quickly divorced him when it became apparent he would run through her fortune. Over the next several years a series of strokes left him paralyzed and utterly dependent for his care upon a cousin. Burr died on Staten Island, N.Y., on Sept. 14, 1836.

Further Reading

The best modern biography of Burr is Herbert S. Parmet and Marie B. Hecht, *Aaron Burr: Portrait of an Ambitious Man* (1967). The most detailed biographical study, however, is still James Parton, *The Life and Times of Aaron Burr* (1858; repr. 1967). Other biographies of Burr include Samuel H. Wandell and Meade Minnigerode, *Aaron Burr* (2 vols., 1925); Walter Flavius McCaleb, *The Aaron Burr Conspiracy* (1936); and Nathan Schachner, *Aaron Burr* (1937). For the fullest treatment of Burr's western adventures see Thomas P. Abernethy, *The Burr Conspiracy* (1954). Bradley Chapin explains many of the technicalities surrounding the famous trial of Aaron Burr in *The American Law of Treason* (1964).

Additional Sources

Lomask, Milton, *Aaron Burr,* New York: Farrar, Straus & Giroux, 1979-c1982.

Keunstler, Laurence S, *The unpredictable Mr. Aaron Burr,* New York: Vantage Press, 1974.

Chidsey, Donald Barr, *The great conspiracy; Aaron Burr and his strange doings in the West,* New York: Crown Publishers, 1967. □

Alberto Burri

The Italian painter Alberto Burri (1915-1995) worked in the collage tradition of Schwitters and the Dadaists. His art is characterized by a love for textural effects and by evocative images of war and industrial waste.

Alberto Burri was born in Città di Castello. He studied medicine and served as a surgeon in World War II. Captured by the Allies, he began painting in 1944 in a Texas prisoner-of-war camp. There he developed his surgeon's skill into artistic creation. He sewed together scraps of burlap, metal, and wood to create metaphors for torn and bleeding flesh.

When Burri returned to Rome in 1945, he gave up medicine. His early paintings, with their images of gashes, wounds, and torn and putrefying flesh, recall his wartime impressions. He ripped his materials, burned them, and then deftly stitched them together, working both as a soldier, mutilating, and as a surgeon, lovingly healing. He often discretely spattered the composition with red paint, black oil, or small touches of yellow or white.

Burri's work recalls in form cubist collages, Kurt Schwitters's *Merzbild,* and surrealist fantasy constructions. Burri's collages, however, lack Schwitters's nihilism and anger and become poetic metaphors for suffering. Burri resurrected the wastes and excretions of technology, war, and time, and with a sure sense for texture and composition he evolved a work both sensual and brutal.

In the late 1950s Burri enriched the early textile, wood, paint, and plaster collages with metal scraps. In these "ferris" (from the Italian word for iron, *ferro*) he subjected the metal to the same mutilations, burnings, and healings to which he had subjected the previous materials. He combined the corroded and oxidized metal with ashes, burlap, wood, and paint. The works thus blend natural colors and textures with burned, oxidized, welded, and painted surfaces.

The ferris were perhaps less organic, less directly evocative of injured flesh and increasingly a comment on industrial, technological ravages and wastes. The beauty of the early works was replaced by an inorganic presence, the carnal by the technological: a commentary on modern industrialization.

The ferris of the late 1950s gave way in late 1963 to the "plastiche." Here Burri stretched transparent plastic sheets over the canvas, then perforated, shriveled, and charred them.The plastic, with its evocations of the supermarket, of packaging, of life in the technological society, was subjected to the same mutilation, the characteristic slashing, charring, and healing, to create shriveled, scarlike edges and gaping craters revealing the painted canvas beneath, punctuated by reflections from the translucent surfaces. Burri experimented with wood in the same manner. The 1970s marked a stylistic shift as Burri began painting large, brightly-colored abstracts on monumental sheets of particle board.

Burri scrupulously avoided the spotlight, rarely granting interviews and dividing his time between homes in Città di Castello and Los Angeles. In 1981, he settled in Beaulieu, France, near Nice, and shuttled between there and Italy. In the late 1980s and 1990s, Burri chose Cellotex, a compound derived from the scission of cellulose, as his preferred medium. In a series of black on black abstracts, he employed the Cellotex to support pigment to create subtle variations in the tone and texture of the paint. Showing the influence of trompe l'oeil, the geometric shapes thus created morph into stylized letters that form an anagram of the series' title.

Burri lived to enjoy his reputation as one of the preeminent figures of post-war Italian art. He was the subject of a major retrospective in Milan in 1985, and his work was displayed at the 1988 Venice Biennale, the survey of twentieth-century Italian art mounted in London in 1989, and as part of an overview of post-war Italian art organized in 1994 by New York's Guggenheim Museum. In his last years, he suffered from emphysema. He died of respiratory failure at Pasteur Hospital in Nice on February 13, 1995.

The essence of Burri's work is a sensitivity to texture and a compassion for the wastes of civilization. He subjected these wastes to further humiliations before he healed them, but out of the whole there emerges a poetic, esthetic metaphor for suffering, and the compositions themselves become evocative objects of compassion.

Further Reading

James Johnson Sweeney, *Burri* (1955), in Italian, has many good color reproductions, though the text is inadequate. Cesare Brandi, *Burri* (trans. 1963), includes color reproductions, text, and a short biographical note. Burri receives brief mention in William C. Seitz, *The Art of Assemblage* (1961). *Alberto Burri: Prints 1959-1977* (1977) is a worthwhile retrospective. A more recent study of the artist is G. Butterfield, *Alberto Burri* (1982). A comprehensive English/Italian edition of his works from Art Books is *Alberto Burri* (1997). His obituary ran in the *New York Times* on 16 February 1995. □

Elihu Burritt

The American advocate of world peace Elihu Burritt (1810-1879), called the "Learned Blacksmith," conceived measures that helped internationalize the 19th-century pacifist movement.

Elihu Burritt was born in New Britain, Conn., on Dec. 8, 1810. Though he possessed a good mind, he was forced by his father's death to leave school and apprentice himself to a blacksmith when he was 15 years old. He began so intensive a program of self-education, especially in languages, that his health suffered.

Following some business experiences, Burritt settled in Worcester, Mass., as a blacksmith and there began a serious study of European and Oriental languages. He gained command of numerous tongues, including Hebrew, Chaldaic, and Syriac. Word of the abilities of the Learned Blacksmith reached the Massachusetts governor, himself a scholar, who referred to Burritt as exemplifying democratic values. Burritt, a shy and earnest young man, was offered a chance to study at Harvard but refused on the grounds that his place was with the common people.

He developed into a successor of William Ladd, who saw peace as necessarily a world movement. In 1844 Burritt began one of a number of publications in behalf of peace, the *Christian Citizen*. The Oregon crisis between the United States and Great Britain inspired him to publish *Advocate of Peace and Universal Brotherhood* and to exchange "Friendly Addresses" with English pacifists. Invited by them to visit England in 1847, he there organized the League of Universal Brotherhood. His innovations as a propagandist, as expressed in *Sparks from the Anvil* (1847), aimed at influencing a broad public opinion. In the Oregon crisis, and also in 1852, when war was threatened between Great Britain and France, Burritt made personal visits and inspired civilian correspondence to encourage peace sentiment on both sides. He also sponsored "Olive Branch" advertisement in European newspapers which were widely reprinted.

His next approach to the peace crusade entailed organizing conferences of eloquent and distinguished individuals from various nations. The Friends of Peace met in 1848 in Brussels. Successive congresses in Frankfurt, London, Manchester, and Edinburgh were widely approved and created a tradition of conferences and adjudications.

Burritt returned to the United States to publicize his campaign for penny postage, intended to aid amicable correspondence. His plans lost momentum because of the outbreak of the Crimean War in 1854 and the impending Civil War at home. In his *Citizen of the World,* Burritt

advocated an end to slavery through peaceful purchase of slaves by the government. The Compensated Emancipation Convention, held in Cleveland, Ohio, in August 1856, drew such notables as Gerrit Smith and Mark Hopkins but failed to affect events.

Disheartened, Burritt turned to farming in New Britain. His publications increasingly summarized his experience, as in *Thoughts of Things at Home and Abroad* (1854), and he now turned his efforts toward reaching influential statesman and leaders of society, rather than the common man. In 1863 he made lengthy tours in Great Britain and memorialized these in publications such as *A Walk from John O'Groats to Land's End* (1864). In 1865-1870 he served as U.S. consular agent for Birmingham, England. Burritt returned home to New Britain in 1870. He continued to farm, teach, and write until his death on March 6, 1879.

Further Reading

Merle E. Curti, *The American Peace Crusade, 1815-1860* (1929), and his edited selections from Burritt's letters and journals, *The Learned Blacksmith* (1937), are the leading modern works on Burritt. See also Charles Northend, ed., *Elihu Burritt: A Memorial Volume* (1880). □

John Burroughs

The American naturalist and essayist John Burroughs (1837-1921) wrote prolifically of his experiences in

nature and was one of America's most honored writers at the beginning of the 20th century.

The seventh of 10 children of Chauncy and Amy Kelly Burroughs, John Burroughs was born on the family dairy farm in the Catskill Mountains near Roxbury, N.Y., on April 3, 1837. He left school at 17 to become a teacher, and he alternated periods of teaching with brief studies at such institutions as Cooperstown Seminary, where he developed enthusiasm for the work of William Wordsworth and Ralph Waldo Emerson. At 20, he married Ursula North, but 2 years passed before his teaching yielded enough money for the couple to set up housekeeping. He was only 23 when James Russell Lowell accepted his essay "Expression" for the *Atlantic Monthly.* The essay sounded so much like Emerson's work that Lowell at first suspected it had been plagiarized.

In 1863 Burroughs gave up teaching to become a clerk in the Currency Bureau of the Treasury Department in Washington. There the young man of 26 met Walt Whitman, who was 18 years his senior. Of their friendship Burroughs wrote: "I owe more to him than to any other man in the world. He brooded me; he gave me things to think of; he taught me generosity, breadth, and an all-embracing charity." *Notes on Walt Whitman as Poet and Person* (1867), Burroughs's first book, was written in part by Whitman himself. In his Washington years Burroughs gave himself up to an avid study of birds. His second book, *Wake-Robin* (1871), a collection of essays on birds, was given its title by Whitman. In 1871 the Treasury Department sent him to England, and he later recorded his impressions of that country in *Winter Sunshine* (1875). By the time the book appeared, Burroughs had left Washington and government service for a home he had built at West Park on the Hudson. There he began fruit farming; he also began keeping the journal in which much of his finest prose was written. His son, Julian, was born in 1878; his wife died in 1917. Few other events disturbed the even pace of his domestic life on the farm, which was his laboratory, his inspiration, and the principal subject of the nature essays which made him famous.

Locusts and Wild Honey (1879) was the first book to reflect the more scientific and less poetic approach that Burroughs took toward nature in his mature work. In 1903 he traveled to Yellowstone Park with President Theodore Roosevelt, who had allied himself with the writer in a campaign for scientifically accurate observation in writing on nature. *Camping and Tramping with Roosevelt* (1907) recorded the trip. Attracted both to the poetic response to nature, which Emerson represented for him, and to its opposite, the scientific, which he admired in the writings of the English biologist T. H. Huxley, Burroughs found a reconciliation of the two in the work of French philosopher Henri Bergson. Bergson's influence is evident in such books as *Under the Apple-Trees* (1916) and *The Summit of the Years* (1917).

For the last 20 years of his life Burroughs was one of America's most popular and most revered authors. He grew ill while wintering in California in 1921, and he died on March 29 aboard the train on which he was returning to his home.

Further Reading

After Burroughs's death, Clara Barrus published *The Life and Letters of John Burroughs* (2 vols., 1925) and *Whitman and Burroughs, Comrades* (1931). She also wrote *John Burroughs: Boy and Man* (1920) and edited *The Heart of Burroughs' Journals* (1928). See also Clifton Johnson, *John Burroughs Talks: His Reminiscences and Comments* (1922), and Elizabeth B. Kelley, *John Burroughs, Naturalist* (1959). The best study of Burroughs's writings is in Norman Foerster, *Nature in American Literature* (1923).

Additional Sources

Renehan, Edward, *John Burroughs: an American naturalist,* Post Mills, Vt.: Chelsea Green Pub. Co., 1992.

Kelley, Elizabeth Burroughs, *John Burroughs' Slabsides,* West Park, N.Y.: Riverby Books, 1987.

Kelley, Elizabeth Burroughs, *John Burroughs: naturalist: the story of his work and family,* West Park, N.Y.: Riverby Books, 1986, 1959.

Kanze, Edward, *The world of John Burroughs,* New York: H.N. Abrams, 1993.

Burroughs, John, *The birds of John Burroughs: a great naturalist's meditations and essays on bird watching,* Woodstock, N.Y.: Overlook Press, 1988. ☐

William S. Burroughs

An innovative and controversial author of experimental fiction, William S. Burroughs (1914–1997) is best known for *Naked Lunch* (1959), a bizarre account of his fourteen-year drug addiction and a surrealistic indictment of middle-class American mores.

William S. Burroughs is the grandson of the industrialist who modernized the adding machine and the son of a woman who claimed descent from Civil War General Robert E. Lee. In 1936, he received his bachelor's degree in English from Harvard University. In 1944, after abortive attempts at, among other things, graduate study in anthropology, medical school in Vienna, Austria, and military service, he met Allen Ginsberg and Jack Kerouac and began using morphine. The meeting of these three writers is generally regarded as the beginning of the Beat movement; the writers who later became part of this group produced works that attacked moral and artistic conventions. The escalation of Burroughs's drug addiction, his unsuccessful search for cures, and his travels to Mexico to elude legal authorities are recounted in his first novel, *Junkie: The Confessions of an Unredeemed Drug Addict* (1953; republished as *Junky*). Written in the confessional style of pulp magazines under the pseudonym William Lee, the novel received little critical notice. In 1957, Burroughs traveled to London to undergo a controversial drug treatment known as apomorphine. Following two relapses, he was successfully cured of his addiction.

Ostensibly the story of junkie William Lee, *Naked Lunch* features no consistent narrative or point of view. The novel has been variously interpreted as a condemnation of the addict's lifestyle, as an allegory satirizing the repressiveness of American society, and as an experiment in literary form, exemplified by its attacks upon language as a narrow, symbolic tool of normative control. Consisting of elements from diverse genres, including the detective novel and science fiction, *Naked Lunch* depicts a blackly humorous, sinister world dominated by addiction, madness, grotesque physical metamorphoses, sadomasochistic homosexuality, and cartoon-like characters, including Dr. Benway, who utilizes weird surgical and chemical alterations to cure his patients. Escape from the imprisoning concepts of time and space are dominant themes in this work and in Burroughs's later fiction, reflecting the addict's absolute need for drugs and his dependency on what Burroughs termed "junk time." Burroughs explained the book's title as "the frozen moment when everyone sees what is on the end of every fork."

Naked Lunch represents a selection from the wealth of material Burroughs had been writing for many years. The remaining work makes up the bulk of his immediately subsequent novels, *The Soft Machine* (1961), *The Ticket That Exploded* (1962), and *Nova Express* (1964). During the process of writing these works, Burroughs, influenced by artist Brion Gysin, developed his "cut-up" and "fold-in" techniques, experiments similar in effect to collage painting. Collecting manuscript pages of his narrative episodes, or "routines," in random order, Burroughs folds some pages vertically, juxtaposing these with other passages to form new pages. This material, sometimes drawn from the works of other authors, is edited and rearranged to evoke new associations and break with traditional narrative patterns. In the surrealistic, quasi-science fiction sequels to *Naked Lunch,* Burroughs likens addiction to the infestation of a malignant alien virus, which preys upon the deep-seated fears of human beings and threatens to destroy the earth through parasitic possession of its inhabitants. The title of *The Soft Machine,* a novel emphasizing sexuality and drugs as a means of normative control throughout history, indicates the innate biological device which allows the virus entry into the human body. Mind control through word and image is the subject of *The Ticket That Exploded.* In this novel and in *Nova Express,* Burroughs suggests a number of remedies to the viral infestation. Although he expresses a cautious optimism, the crisis remains unresolved, and humanity's fate is uncertain at the saga's end.

In 1970, Burroughs announced his intention to write a second " mythology for the space age." Although his recent novels have generally received less acclaim than *Naked Lunch* and its sequels, critics have discerned a remarkably straightforward approach to these works, which rely less on cut-up strategies and horrific elements and more on complex, interrelated plots and positive solutions to escaping societal constraints. As Jennie Skerl noted: "In Burroughs's recent fiction, pleasure and freedom through fantasy balance the experience of repression, bondage, and death that the earlier works had emphasized." The universe of *The Wild Boys: A Book of the Dead* (1971) is similar to that of Burroughs's earlier books but is epic in proportion, encompassing galactic history and the whole of humanity in its scope. Time and space travel figure prominently in *Cities of the Red Night: A Boys' Book* (1981), in which detective Clem Snide traces the source of the alien virus to an ancient dystopian society. *The Place of Dead Roads* (1984) transfers the conflict to near-future South America, where descendants of the wild boys ally themselves with Venusian rebels in an escalating battle for galactic liberation.

Burroughs's novel *Queer* (1985) was written at the same time as *Junkie* and is considered its companion piece. According to Burroughs, the book was "motivated and formulated" by the accidental death of his wife in Mexico in 1951, for which Burroughs was held accountable. The novel centers once again on William Lee, chronicling a month of withdrawal in South America and his bitter, unrealized pursuit of a young American male expatriate. Harry Marten stated that the book functions as "neither a love story nor a tale of seduction but a revelation of rituals of communication which substitute for contact in a hostile or indifferent environment."

Burroughs is also well known for his nonfiction works. *The Yage Letters* (1963) contains his mid-1950s correspondence with Allen Ginsberg concerning his pursuit in Colombia of the legendary hallucinogen *yage*. Further correspondence is collected in *Letters to Allen Ginsberg, 1953-1957* (1982). During the mid-1960s, Burroughs became an outspoken proponent of the apomorphine treatment, claiming that its illegal status in the United States was the result of a conspiracy between the Food and Drug Administration, police, and legal authorities. His arguments are presented in *Health Bulletin, APO 33: A Report on the Synthesis of the Apomorphine Formula* (1965) and *APO 33, a Metabolic Regulator* (1966). Burroughs's observations on literary, political, and esoteric topics appear in a collaborative venture with Daniel Odier, *Entretiens avec William Burroughs* (1969; revised and translated as *The Job: Interviews with William Burroughs*), and in his collection *The Adding Machine: Collected Essays* (1985). *The Third Mind* (1979), written in collaboration with Brion Gysin, is a theoretical manifesto of their early "cut-up" experiments. Burroughs has also written a screenplay, *The Last Words of Dutch Schultz* (1970).

Burroughs's controversial novels have provoked extreme critical reactions, ranging from claims of genius to allegations that he is little more than a pornographer. While his work can be offensive, it has elicited much serious criticism, and Burroughs is regarded by many scholars as an innovative, even visionary writer. Critics credit Burroughs's hallucinatory prose and antiestablishment views with inspiring the Beat movement and such counterculture groups as hippies and punks. Among other accomplishments, Burroughs has, perhaps more effectively than any other author, rendered the nightmarish, paranoid mindset of the drug addict. Harry Marten observed that Burroughs "has been mixing the satirist's impulse toward invective with the cartoonist's relish for exaggerated gesture, the collage artist's penchant for radical juxtapositions with the slam-bang pace of the carnival barker. In the process, he has mapped a grotesque modern landscape of disintegration whose violence and vulgarity is laced with manic humor."

The former heroin addict lived in the quiet town of Lawrence, Kansas with several cats and a collection of guns until his death from a heart attack on August 2, 1997. Although his business affairs were handled by his staff at the high tech William Burroughs Communications, the writer himself still used a typewriter. One of his more recent publications, *The Letters of William S. Burroughs: 1945-1959* was used both as a journal and a sketchbook for his early work.

Further Reading

Bartlett, Lee, editor, *The Beats: Essays in Criticism,* McFarland, 1981.

Bowles, Paul, *Without Stopping,* Putnam, 1972.

Bryant, Jerry H., *The Open Decision: The Contemporary American Novel and Its Intellectual Background,* Free Press, 1970.

Burgess, Anthony, *The Novel Now: A Guide to Contemporary Fiction,* Norton, 1967.

Burroughs, William, Jr., *Kentucky Ham,* Dutton, 1973.

Burroughs, William S., *Junky,* Penguin, 1977.

Burroughs, William S., *Cities of the Red Night,* Holt, 1981. □

Richard Burton

Richard Burton (1925-1984) was known for his outstanding abilities as a Shakespearean actor, his commanding presence on Broadway, and his compelling screen portrayals. He was almost as famous for his romance with actress Elizabeth Taylor, to whom he was twice married.

Richard Burton was born on November 10, 1925, in the Welsh coal-mining town of Pontrhydfen. One of 13 children in the family of Thomas and Edith Jenkins, he was born Richard Jenkins. As a child, he was permitted a "normal" life, which included swimming and rugby. His father, a coal miner, wanted one of his sons to "live in sunshine," so he was sent to school rather than to the mines. He changed his last name upon becoming a professional actor to honor Philip Burton, his high school drama coach and mentor, who became his guardian. The young man spoke no English until the age of ten. His mentor taught him to speak English without a Welsh accent, to read the classics, and to hold a knife and fork.

Burton entered Exeter College, Oxford, on scholarship and, after one year, joined the Royal Air Force in 1944. Training as a navigator in Canada, he was discharged in 1947, after which he accepted a $30 weekly salary with a London theater company. In May 1949 Burton played at London's Globe Theatre in *The Lady's Not For Burning.* On February 5, 1949, he married actress Sybil Williams, and

the couple subsequently had two daughters, Kate and Jessica.

Burton went to New York City in November 1950 to play in the Broadway production of *The Lady's Not For Burning.* He then went to Hollywood in 1952 and starred in *My Cousin Rachel* opposite Olivia de Havilland. For this film he received an Oscar nomination.

Between 1950 and 1960 Burton appeared in many stage productions, playing most of the great Shakespearean roles. In 1960 Burton's role of King Arthur in *Camelot,* then on Broadway, landed him a Twentieth Century Fox contract to play opposite Elizabeth Taylor in *Cleopatra.*

After divorcing his wife in April 1963, Richard Burton married Taylor on March 15, 1964. She had divorced actor Eddie Fisher, and so great was the scandal surrounding the Burton-Taylor romance that the U.S. State Department was requested to revoke Burton's visa on grounds that he was "detrimental to the morals of the youth of our nation."

Liz and Dick, as they were known, lived on a grand scale. He bought her jewels, including the 69-carat Cartier diamond. They bought a yacht for $500,000. On a more conventional note, they adopted a daughter, Maria.

Partly because Burton was a tempestuous alcoholic, he and Taylor divorced in 1974. So great was the pull between them, however, that on October 10, 1975, they remarried. Burton once said of Taylor, "Our love is so furious we burn each other out." As if to prove the point, the couple once more divorced, in July 1976. Burton then married former model Suzy Hunt.

Burton and Taylor appeared in almost a dozen films between 1962 and 1972. She won several Oscars. He never received any although he was nominated seven times, most notably for his role in *Who's Afraid of Virginia Woolf?* in 1966.

Troubled by a drinking problem that he kept under control for brief periods of time, Burton also suffered acute spinal pain. In 1980 he underwent neck surgery to alleviate the discomfort. In 1983 he and Taylor appeared together on Broadway in Noel Coward's *Private Lives.* Burton, divorced from Hunt, was married by then to Sally Hay.

On August 5, 1984, Richard Burton died suddenly of a cerebral hemorrhage in Geneva, Switzerland.

Further Reading

Several biographies about Richard Burton have appeared. They include *Richard Burton: A Biography* (1971) by John Cottrell, and *Richard Burton* (1981) by Paul Ferris. There is also a substantial amount of information about Burton's life in Kitty Kelley's *Elizabeth Taylor, The Last Star* (1981) and in David Lester's *Richard and Elizabeth* (1977). A later, gossipy biography was Hollis Alpert's *Burton* (1986). □

Sir Richard Francis Burton

Sir Richard Francis Burton (1821-1890), English explorer, scholar, poet, translator, and diplomat, explored in Africa and Asia and studied Oriental literature and American religions.

Richard Burton was born on March 19, 1821, in the west of England into the family of a ne'er-do-well gentleman soldier and a putative descendant of an illegitimate son of Louis XIV. Soon the family moved to Tours, France, where Burton received a classical education. As a boy, he exhibited courage, derring-do, and a wavering self-control. When he was 10, Burton's family returned briefly to England. He went to school in Richmond, his days punctuated by fighting and wild escapades. Back in France and then in Italy, where Burton spent his adolescent years, his wildness was more characteristic than learning.

Burton attended Trinity College, Oxford, from 1840 to 1842, when he was dismissed for disobedience. Entering the Indian army, he spent the next 7 years studying 11 languages (passing examinations in most and publishing original grammars in 2), practicing his gifts for disguise, learning geodesy, and gathering the material for a book on Goa, two books on Sindh, a discourse on falconry, and a book on bayonet exercise which was ultimately adopted as a British army manual.

In 1852, having begun the courtship of Isabel Arundell which was to result in marriage in 1861, Burton concocted a scheme (he was then on sick leave from the Indian army) to learn the secrets of Mecca and Medina, the jealously guarded shrines of Islam. In April 1853 a bearded Burton stained himself with henna, called himself an Afghani doc-

tor, and for many months sustained the disguise despite varied opportunities of detection. The result of this spectacular exploit was a readable and learned book of travel, *Personal Narrative of a Pilgrimage to Mecca and El Medina* (1855).

Explorations in Africa

The Arabian adventure whetted Burton's ambitions as an explorer. He turned his attention to the Horn of Africa and, in company with John Speke and others, Burton began an exploration of Somalia and eastern Ethiopia that, for him, culminated in a dangerous foray to the "forbidden" Moslem city-state of Harar, which he was the first white man to visit. Afterward, near Berbera, Burton and Speke had to flee the country after an attack by Somali which left them both wounded. The published account of this African escapade was contained in *First Footsteps in East Africa; or An Exploration of Harar* (1856).

After participating in the Crimean War, Burton persuaded the Royal Geographical Society in 1855 to appoint him leader of an expedition to ascertain the limits of the "Sea of Ujiji," which had been outlined by missionaries in East Africa, and to "determine the exportable produce of the interior and the enthnography of its tribes." He was urged to seek the source of the Nile and the location of the mountains of the Moon. First Burton visited Kilwa, Mombasa, and the Usambara mountains; these minor exploits formed the basis of *Zanzibar: City, Island, and Coast* (2 vols., 1872).

Then, in 1857, from Bagamoyo on the Indian Ocean, Burton, Speke, and African guides and porters followed the traditional route to Tabora, where they arrived 10 months later. Burton had begun to suffer intermittent bouts of fever, but he proceeded westward to the trading town of Ujiji, where, early in 1858, he became the first European in modern times to view Lake Tanganyika; what Burton saw was but one of the three components, Lakes Victoria and Nyasa being the others, of the Sea of Ujiji. This was the conclusion of Burton's greatest African performance, appropriately expressed in the lavishly written, intellectually expansive pages of *The Lake Regions of Central Africa* (2 vols., 1860). There are copious notes on the peoples with whom Burton had become acquainted, on the Arab and Indian traders of the interior, on the topography of what was to become Tanganyika, on its flora and fauna, and on a vast miscellany which Burton—a true encyclopedist—had recorded.

After returning to Britain and publishing his book, Burton, by way of diversion, crossed North America, particularly focusing upon the Church of Jesus Christ of the Latter Day Saints (Mormons); *The City of the Saints and Across the Rocky Mountains to California* (1861) is jammed with random but important information.

Consular Career and West African Explorations

Burton married Isabel in 1861 and, presumably because of his new responsibilities, decided to take a position in the British consular service. He wanted to go to Damascus but, instead, was offered the comparatively lowly post of consul to the Bights of Benin and Biafra, with a base on Fernando Po. This was known as the Foreign Office grave, but Burton used it to visit Abeokuta, the Egba Yoruba capital in western Nigeria; to climb Mt. Cameroons; to venture up the Gabon River in search of gorillas and to learn about a native people called the Pahouin or Fang; to explore the estuary of the Congo River; and to visit the Portuguese colony of Angola.

In 1864 he paid an official call upon Gelele, King of the Fon of Dahomey. The slave trade still flourished there, and the Foreign Office was determined to negotiate its conclusion. Burton, unhappily, failed to persuade the Fon to cease participating in the trade, but he did acquire a typically full and valuable knowledge of the kingdom, its religion, its culture, and even its Amazons. The published record of these West African years includes a two-volume account of Nigeria and the Cameroons (1863), reminiscences of his wanderings throughout the region (1863), *A Mission to Gelele, King of Dahome* (2 vols., 1864), and a book on Gabon and the Congo (2 vols., 1876).

Burton spent the rest of his life far from Africa. He was a consul in Brazil, in Damascus, and finally in Trieste. And he wrote, translated, or edited 35 more books, not least of which were his famous translations *The Book of the Thousand Nights and a Night* (10 vols., 1885-1888) and *The Kama Sutra* (1883). He died in Trieste on Oct. 20, 1890.

Further Reading

The standard modern biographies of Burton are Byron Farwell, *Burton* (1963), and Fawn H. Brodie, *The Devil Drives* (1967). Among the older biographies, Georgiana M. Stisted, *The True Life of Capt. Sir Richard F. Burton* (1896), is valuable. The standard bibliography is Norman M. Penzer, *An Annotated Bibliography of Sir Richard Francis Burton* (1923). Sir Reginald Coupland, *The Exploitation of East Africa, 1856-1890: The Slave Trade and the Scramble* (1939; 2d ed. 1968), includes material on Burton.

Additional Sources

Rice, Edward, *Captain Sir Richard Francis Burton: the secret agent who made the pilgrimage to Mecca, discovered the Kama Sutra, and brought the Arabian nights to the West,* New York, NY: HarperPerennial, 1991.

McLynn, F. J., *Burton: snow upon the desert,* London: John Murray, 1990.

Hastings, Michael, *Sir Richard Burton: a biography,* London: Hodder and Stoughton, 1978.

Farwell, Byron, *Burton: a biography of Sir Richard Francis Burton,* Middlesex, England; New York, N.Y., U.S.A.: Viking, 1988, 1963.

Dearden, Seton, *Burton of Arabia: the life story of Sir Richard Francis Burton,* Norwood, Pa.: Norwood Editions, 1978, c1937.

Burton, Isabel, Lady, *The life of Captain Sir Richard F. Burton,* Boston: Longwood Press, 1977.

Brodie, Fawn McKay, *The Devil drives: a life of Sir Richard Burton,* New York: Norton, 1984. □

Robert Burton

The English scholar and clergyman Robert Burton (1577-1640) wrote "The Anatomy of Melancholy," an analysis of the symptoms, causes, and cures of the melancholic temperament.

Robert Burton was born at Lindley, Leicestershire, on Feb. 8, 1577. He entered Brasenose College, Oxford, in 1593 but transferred to Christ Church. In 1599 he was elected a fellow at Christ Church, where he remained until his death on Jan. 25, 1640. He received three degrees: bachelor of arts, master of arts, and finally bachelor of divinity in 1611. He presumably did some tutoring at Christ Church, and from 1626 he acted as its librarian. He served as vicar of St. Thomas's Church in suburban Oxford (1616-1640) and conducted some services there. He was a bright conversationalist, took delight in nature, and enjoyed visits to relatives and friends.

Burton's Latin comedy *Philosophaster* (written in 1605 and later revised) was performed successfully at Christ Church in 1618. But he devoted most of his life to composing and augmenting his major opus, *The Anatomy of Melancholy.* This work was first published in 1621, and later editions (1624, 1628, 1632, 1638, and 1651) incorporated Burton's revisions. Its modern relevance would be obvious if it were retitled "An Analysis of the Blues" or "The Psychology and Cure of Depression."

In the *Anatomy* Burton uses the device of a fictitious author, Democritus Junior. The utopia, which he includes in the introductory section and which is the first example of this genre to be written by an English author, shows acute awareness of economic abuses and practical remedies. He advocates a planned, capitalistic society which makes maximum use of resources of men and materials, and he cogently analyzes England's faults, treating them as a sort of national melancholia.

Burton then presents an exhaustive medical analysis of the disease of melancholy based on the old theory that a healthy body contains a proper balance of four "humors," or fluids: phlegm, blood, choler, and black bile. Imbalance makes a man phlegmatic, sanguine, choleric, or, if the excess is black bile, melancholy. The melancholy man could be introspective like Hamlet, or mildly eccentric and able to enjoy a good cry like Jacques in Shakespeare's *As You Like It,* or healthily contemplative like Milton's Il Penseroso.

Next, larding his text with quotations from "authorities," Burton explores the cures of melancholy. Underlying his jaunty erudition is common sense: be moderate in diet; enjoy sex reasonably and morally; get plenty of fresh air and exercise; keep the bowels moving; and avoid strain and worry or learn how to cope with them. The final section deals with the melancholy evoked by love, jealousy, and religion.

Burton's usual style is diffuse and amiable, but he is also capable of magnificent, carefully structured baroque prose—for example, the section "Man's Excellency." His

style and persona owe a debt to Montaigne, his satire to Erasmus. His contents include a variety of prose genres, the equivalents of essays, character sketches, sermons, and treatises.

Burton's range is encyclopedic, including the new and the old science, medical lore of previous ages, geography, philosophy, and current literature. John Milton echoed him; Laurence Sterne pillaged his erudition; the *Anatomy* got Samuel Johnson "out of bed two hours earlier"; Lord Byron found it the easiest means of acquiring "a reputation of being well read"; Charles Lamb loved the "fantastic, great old man"; John Keats based "Lamia" on one of Burton's passages; and Sir William Osler praised the "golden compilation" as the greatest medical treatise written by a layman.

The *Anatomy* is a tome to be browsed in for delight or to be mined for 17th-century views on almost any subject, from witchcraft and attitudes toward women to theories on laughter and concepts of imagination and fancy. It is both a key to the early Stuart period and, because of its underlying common sense and humanity, a book for all times.

Further Reading

The three-volume edition of Burton's *The Anatomy of Melancholy,* edited by Holbrook Jackson (1932), retains Burton's quotations in Latin and inserts English translations of them. A well-chosen volume of selections from this work is Lawrence Babb, ed., *The Anatomy of Melancholy* (1965). Babb's *Sanity in Bedlam: A Study of Robert Burton's Anatomy of Melancholy* (1959) is an excellent introduction to the scholarship on Burton's work. Bergen Evans, *The Psychiatry of Robert Burton* (1944), dispels the old notion that the Anatomy is quaint erudition and finds Burton a sound psychologist and relevant today. William R. Mueller, *The Anatomy of Robert Burton's England* (1952), is useful on style and social ideas. □

George Bush

A successful businessman, George Bush (born 1924) emerged as a national political leader during the 1970s. After holding several important foreign policy and administrative assignments in Republican politics, he served two terms as vice president (1980, 1984) under Ronald Reagan. In 1988, he was elected the 41st president of the United States.

George Herbert Walker Bush was born on June 12, 1924, in Milton, Massachusetts. His father, Prescott Bush, was a managing partner in the Wall Street investment firm of Brown Brothers, Harriman and also served as U.S. senator from Connecticut from 1952 to 1962. His mother, Dorothy Walker Bush, was the daughter of another prominent Wall Street investment banker, George Herbert Walker (George Bush's namesake), and the founder of the Walker Cup for international golfing competition. George Bush grew up in the affluent New York City suburb of Greenwich, Connecticut, vacationing in the summers in Kennebunkport, Maine, where he later maintained a home.

Bush attended the Greenwich Country Day School and Phillips Academy, exclusive private schools, where he excelled both in the classroom and on the athletic field. After graduating from Phillips in 1942, he enrolled in the U.S. Navy Reserve and was commissioned a navy flight pilot in 1943, serving in the Pacific for the duration of World War II. Secretly engaged to Barbara Pierce, Bush married this daughter of the publisher of *Redbook* and *McCall's* in Rye, New York, on January 6, 1945. The Bushes became the parents of six children (one of whom died of leukemia when three years old).

Following severance from the navy, Bush enrolled at Yale University in September 1945. An ambitious, highly competitive student, he earned a B.A. in economics within three years. Although a married military veteran, Bush was nonetheless active in campus social and athletic activities (playing three years of varsity baseball and captaining the team). Following graduation in 1948, Bush became an oilfield supply salesman for Dresser Industries in Odessa, Texas. Rising quickly in an industry then in the midst of a postwar boom, in 1953 Bush started his own oil and gas drilling firm. After merging with another firm in 1955, Bush eventually (in September 1958) moved the corporate headquarters to Houston, Texas.

In addition to having become a millionaire in his own right, Bush was also active in local Republican politics and served as Houston County party chairman. In 1964 he took a leave of absence from his firm, Zapata Petroleum, to challenge incumbent Democratic Senator Ralph Yarborough. Bush campaigned as a Goldwater Republican,

opposing civil rights legislation, calling for U.S. withdrawal from the United Nations should the Peoples Republic of China be admitted, and demanding a cutback in foreign aid spending. The strategy of Goldwater Republicans had been to promote a conservative realignment, specifically leading to Republican congressional victories in the South and Southwest. This strategy failed, and Bush also lost decisively in what was a nationwide Democratic landslide.

Bush did not withdraw from politics, however, and in 1966 he won election to the House of Representatives from a Houston suburban district. A two-term congressman, serving from 1966 through 1970, Bush compiled a conservative voting record (earning a 77 percent approval rating from the conservative Americans for Constitutional Action), specifically championing "right to work" anti-labor union legislation and a "freedom of choice" alternative to school desegregation. In an exception to an otherwise conservative record, in 1968, despite opposition from his constituents, Bush voted for the open housing bill recommended by President Lyndon Johnson.

A loyal adherent of the Nixon administration during 1969 and 1970, Bush supported the president's major legislative initiatives, including the family assistance plan. In 1970 he again sought election to the Senate, campaigning as an outspoken Nixon supporter on a "law and order" theme. His election chances, however, were submarined when the more moderate Lloyd Bentsen defeated Yarborough in the Democratic primary. Although Bush's electoral support had increased since 1966 (from 43 to 47 percent), he was once again defeated.

As a reward for his loyalty, in February 1971 President Nixon appointed Bush U.S. ambassador to the United Nations. Given the nominee's lack of foreign policy experience, this appointment was initially viewed as a political favor. Bush, however, proved to be an able and popular diplomat, particularly in his handling of the difficult, if ultimately unsuccessful, task of ensuring the continued seating of the Taiwan delegation when the United Nations in a dramatic reversal voted to seat the Peoples Republic of China.

In December 1972 Bush resigned his United Nations appointment to accept, again at Nixon's request, the post of chairman of the Republican National Committee. This largely administrative appointment proved to be a demanding assignment when the Senate, in the spring of 1973, initiated a highly publicized investigation into the so-called Watergate Affair and then, in the winter/spring of 1973, when the House debated whether to impeach President Nixon. Throughout this period Bush publicly championed the president, affirming Nixon's innocence and questioning the motives of the president's detractors. As the scandal unfolded, Bush sought to minimize its adverse consequences for the political fortunes of the Republican party. Following Nixon's forced resignation in August 1974 his successor, Gerald Ford, appointed Bush in September 1974 to head the U.S. liaison office in Peking, China.

Serving until December 1975, Bush proved again to be a popular and accessible "ambassador" (formal diplomatic relations with the People's Republic had not at this time been established). He left this post to accept appointment in January 1976 as director of the Central Intelligence Agency. Bush served as a caretaker director, acting to restore morale within the agency and to deflect public and congressional criticisms of the agency's past role and authority. Resigning as CIA director in January 1977 following the election of Democratic presidential candidate Jimmy Carter, Bush returned to Houston to accept the chairmanship of the First National Bank of Houston.

Bush was an unannounced candidate for the Republican presidential nomination of 1980 starting in 1977. He sought to exploit the contacts he had made as Republican National Committee chairman and as a businessman in Texas with family and corporate interests in the East as well as his record of public service. Travelling to all 50 states and establishing his own fund-raising organization, the Fund for Limited Government, Bush formally announced his candidacy in May 1979. Modeling his campaign after Jimmy Carter's successful strategy of 1975-1976 of building a well-organized grass roots organization in the early primary/caucus states of Iowa and New Hampshire, Bush quickly emerged as the principal opponent of former governor of California Ronald Reagan, the Republican frontrunner.

While as conservative as Reagan in his economic and foreign policy views, Bush nonetheless successfully projected the image of a moderate candidate. He lacked substantive programmatic differences from Reagan except for his support for the Equal Rights Amendment, his qualified stand on abortion, and his questioning of Reagan's proposed intention to increase defense spending sharply while reducing taxes and balancing the budget. His failure to find a major issue and his lackluster campaign style eventually forestalled his candidacy. Although recognizing that he did not have the needed delegate votes, Bush did not drop out of the race before the Republican National Convention. In a surprise decision, made on the eve of the balloting, Reagan announced his selection of Bush as his vice presidential running mate.

Becoming vice president with Reagan's decisive victory over incumbent Democratic President Jimmy Carter in 1980, Bush proved to be a loyal, hard working supporter of the president. Careful to demonstrate his loyalty and to accept the largely ceremonial public responsibilities of the vice presidency, Bush provided quiet counsel to the president and thereby gained his respect. Renominated in 1984, Bush retained the vice presidency with the resultant Reagan landslide. Bush's record of demonstrated loyalty and competence, and the series of important administrative offices he had held since 1971, nonetheless had not created for him a broad-based nationwide constituency. As such, he was not assured the Republican presidential nomination in 1988. Despite his nationwide campaign for the Republican presidential nomination in 1980, Bush remained an untested vote getter, his only electoral victory coming as a candidate from a safe Republican congressional district. Bush's other governmental positions were all attained through appointment. His career was thus marked by the ability to handle difficult administrative assignments, and yet a seeming failure to demonstrate the promise of leadership with the voters.

In 1988, Bush defeated Massachusetts governor Michael Dukakis to become the 41st president of the United States. With this victory, many felt he had overcome his weak image and allegations that he had known more than he admitted about the Iran-Contra (arms-for-hostages trade with Iran) scandal. As chief executive he was widely viewed as a foreign policy president. He was in office when the Communist governments of the Soviet Union and eastern Europe fell. The Persian Gulf War of 1990 also boosted Bush's popularity to a point where many thought he would be unbeatable in the next election.

However, Bush also had his share of problems. Many historians believe that Bush ran a negative campaign in 1988 which affected his ability to govern the country. Congress refused to confirm his nomination of former Texas senator John Tower for secretary of defense. He inherited problems with the Department of Housing and Urban Development (HUD). Other critics said he lacked vision and leadership. He also had a relatively inexperienced vice president in former Indiana Senator Dan Quayle. In 1992, in the midst of a recession, he lost his re-election bid in a three-way race to Democrat Bill Clinton.

In retirement, Bush kept a relatively low profile, preferring to travel and spend time with his grandchildren. He did make the news when, in March 1997, at the age of 72, he became (many believe) the first American President to jump out of an airplane. He also received a honorary doctorate from Hofstra University in April 1997.

Bush the politician will always be remembered. On November 30, 1994, the ground breaking ceremony for the George Bush Presidential Library and Museum was held. This facility was constructed on the campus of Texas A & M University, in College Station, Texas, and opened in November 1997. It is the tenth presidential library administered by National Archives and documents Bush's long public career, from ambassador to world leader. Located within the complex will be The Bush School of Government & Public Service, which will provide graduate education to those who wish to lead and manage organizations serving the public interest.

Further Reading

Having been married for over 50 years, Barbara Bush's *Barbara Bush: A Memoir* (1994) will provide insight to the "real" George Bush. Michael Duffy's *Marching in Place: The Status Quo Presidency of George Bush* (1992) will also offer an interesting perspective. George Bush has also been profiled on the television show *A&E Biography.* Information on The George Bush Presidential Library and Museum can be accessed through the World Wide Web at http://www.csdl.tamu.edu/bushlib/ (July 29, 1997). Readers also might profitably consult Eleanora Schoenebaum (editor), *Political Profiles: The Nixon/Ford Years,* Vol. 5 (1979); Roy Reed, "George Bush on the Move," *New York Times Magazine* (February 10, 1980); and Elizabeth Drew, "A Reporter at Large: Bush 1980," *The New Yorker* (March 3, 1980); *New York Times* (March 26, 1997 and April 20, 1997). □

Vannevar Bush

Vannevar Bush (1890-1974) was a leader of American science and engineering during and after World War II. He was instrumental in the development of the atomic bomb and the analogue computer, as well as an administrator of government scientific activities.

By any standard, Vannevar Bush was one of the movers of the 20th century. A prominent engineer, he rose through the ranks to become the first vice president and dean of engineering at the Massachusetts Institute of Technology (MIT). In 1939 he moved to Washington, D.C. to assume the presidency of the Carnegie Institution, one of the country's most prestigious and important private foundations and sources of support for scientific research. Within a year, however, the gathering clouds of war turned his energies in other directions. With the advantage of location in Washington and drawing on acquaintanceships with the leaders of American science and engineering, Bush moved quickly into the lead mobilizing the scientific community for war.

The roots of this man who became the czar of wartime science reach deeply into the soil of New England. Bush was the descendant of a long line of sea captains who made their home in Provincetown and he always kept something of the salty independence of the sea about him. He returned frequently to Cape Cod throughout his life, and often found himself drawing upon images of the sea in talking of his work in engineering. His father had left Provincetown in the 1870s, probably to escape religious tensions and a declining economy, and taken up residence in the suburbs of Boston in the small community of Everett to be near the new Universalist Tufts College. There he studied for his degree in divinity and over the next decades became one of the area's well known and well loved pastors. And there Vannevar was born to Richard Perry and Emma Linwood Bush March 11, 1890, one of three children.

For over two decades Bush was associated with two of the country's best engineering schools. One was MIT; the earlier and, in some ways, the more formative was Tufts. While small, this Universalist school had nevertheless towards the end of the century encouraged the development of a strong and innovative engineering program under the guidance of Gardner Anthony, a master of drawing and mechanical design. Here Bush developed a lifelong romance with invention which eventually culminated in a series of pioneering analogue computers during the 1920s and 1930s. Here also he acquired that graphic mathematical approach to things which became a characteristic of his work in engineering. Not least, the profoundly ethical context in which the profession of engineering gestated at Tufts combined with the pastoral commitments of his father to shape Bush's deep belief that engineering could, in fact, be a ministry devoted to social welfare and public good. Bush

graduated from Tufts in 1913 with both bachelor's and master's degrees.

Between 1913 and 1919 he worked at General Electric, taught mathematics to the women at Tufts, worked as an electrical inspector in the New York Navy Yard, earned his doctorate in electrical engineering at MIT in one year in 1916, and returned again to Tufts as a young assistant professor. Here he taught for part of his time and consulted for the rest with a small company devoted to the development of radio equipment. From these modest beginnings came the Raytheon Corporation, one of New England's largest companies and a mainstay of its defense industry. Bush was one of the company's founders in the early 1920s and maintained his connections until World War II.

In 1919, just as the academic market for engineering was turning bullish after World War I, Bush joined the faculty of MIT. Starting as an associate professor of electric power transmission, he rose rapidly through the department, bypassing the chairmanship to become in 1932 MIT's first vice president and dean of engineering under the new president, Karl Compton. During these years Bush became involved in many of the issues percolating through the country's community of engineers. They ranged over the curricula and conceptual development of electrical engineering, the relationship of the engineer and the government, the characteristics of professionalism, and the large role of the engineer in American society. In his early years at the institute, Bush cooperated with the department's dynamic chairman, Dugald Jackson, in modernizing the curriculum; assumed direction of graduate training; and coordinated the research activities of the department. By the middle 1930s, as Compton's righthand man, Bush had become not only a major figure at MIT but a respected spokesman within the country's technical community.

His inventive activity during these years revolved around the notion of mechanical analysis and the development of machine methods for the solution of mathematical problems in engineering. Between 1927 and 1943 Bush developed a series of electromechanical analogue computers which greatly facilitated the solution of complex mathematical problems. In 1936 the Rockefeller Foundation awarded a major grant to MIT which resulted in the famous Rockefeller differential analyzer of World War II. The analyzer was quickly superseded by faster digital computers, but in its time it was a significant achievement and clearly revealed the possibilities for machine computation not only in engineering but in more basic fields of science. Moreover, it embodied in a concrete way the culture of engineering in which Bush had come of age.

During the war Bush headed the vital National Defense Research Committee and its successor, the Office of Scientific Research and Development. From these organizations and the laboratories they oversaw came radar, the proximity fuse, penicillin, and, of course, the atomic bomb. Such accomplishments brought fame to Bush and enormous public respect to the country's scientists. They also provided Bush great influence in the public debates and legislative battles which followed the war and which eventually gave birth to the Atomic Energy Commission in 1947 and the National Science Foundation in 1950.

In the calmer times after the war, Bush returned to his responsibilities at the Carnegie Institution. When he retired in 1955 he went home to Cambridge. He took up duties as a member of the boards of directors of Merck and Company, AT&T, the Metals and Controls Corporation, and the MIT Corporation, becoming honorary chairman of the last in 1959. He died in 1974.

After his career took its pronounced public turn with the events of World War II, Bush became a prolific and popular author of books dealing with the nature of science and the problems of science and public policy in the period of the Cold War. *Science—The Endless Frontier* (1945), a report written for President F. D. Roosevelt dealing with the organization of postwar science, quickly became an influential bestseller, as did his 1949 book, *Modern Arms and Free Men: A Discussion of the Role of Science in Preserving Democracy.*

In many ways, Bush is the outstanding example of the expert whose role at the hub of an increasingly complex society captured the imagination of American society in the early part of the 20th century. These were years in which the figure of the engineer became not only a necessary fact of life but a value-laden symbol which presaged the contributions of science and technology to human progress. If the consequences of this turning to science and engineering, especially in the light of the nuclear predicaments which followed the war, have proved ambiguous blessings, Bush himself never lost faith. The pioneering spirit helped us conquer plains and forest, Bush wrote at the end of his life in his autobiographical *Pieces of the Action.* Given the chance, it would do so again.

Further Reading

The best account of Bush's life, which contains as well an extensive bibliography of his writings, is Jerome Wiesner's short biography in volume 50 of the National Academy of Science's *Biographical Memoirs.* More anecdotal material can be found in Bush's own collection of autobiographical reminiscences, *Pieces of the Action* (1970), as well as in *My Several Lives* (1970), the autobiography of James Conant, his closest wartime collaborator. Bush's importance as a wartime administrator, as well as his general significance in the history of modern American science, have been treated in Daniel Kevles' interpretative survey, *The Physicists—The Development of a Scientific Community.* □

Horace Bushnell

The Congregational clergyman Horace Bushnell (1802-1876) was the pivotal American theologian who freed mainstream Protestant theology from its Puritan scholasticism and established the basis for religious liberalism.

Horace Bushnell was born April 14, 1802, at Bantam, Conn. He graduated from Yale College in 1827. For a time he taught school and served as an editor, but in 1829 he returned to Yale to study law. A spiritual revival in 1831 led him to transfer to the Divinity School, from which he graduated in 1833. He studied under Nathaniel W. Taylor, leader of the "New Haven theology" in vogue then, but he was unimpressed by the dry theological scholasticism. In 1833 Bushnell was ordained as pastor of North Church, Hartford, Conn., where he remained for 26 years until poor health forced him to retire.

It was as a theologian rather than as a pastor that Bushnell was most significant. Primarily, he provided the intellectual method and content to break the dogmatic system-building approach of Puritan theology. His first major work, *Christian Nurture* (1847, rev. 1861), refuted the prevalent focus on the necessity of conversion by arguing that a child of believing parents should grow up so that he never knows he is anything but a Christian. A profound mystical experience during 1848 led him to overlook the hostility his views had aroused.

In *God in Christ* (1848) Bushnell included a preliminary discourse on language which is the crucial explanation of his basic method. Maintaining that language consists of symbols agreed on by social groups, he insisted that the historical context of words is crucial for understanding and that changing situations require new definitions. Conservative clergymen immediately saw the threat this posed to their use of traditional doctrine, and charges of heresy were prepared. Only the withdrawal of Bushnell's congregation from the local consociation in 1852 enabled him to avoid trial.

Bushnell's *Nature and the Supernatural* (1858) was so sweeping in scope that it contained all creation in one divine system, which laid the basis of the Kingdom of God emphasis of liberalism. In *The Vicarious Sacrifice* (1866) and *Forgiveness and Law* (1874) he stressed the moral theory of the atonement, which liberalism embraced. At his death on Feb. 17, 1876, his views were still considered heretical by most contemporaries, but within a few decades his works became regarded as the basic literature for Christ-centered liberalism. Though later liberals altered his ideas, he may rightly be called the father of the liberal movement, which has been so important in Protestant theology in the past century.

Further Reading

Bushnell's life and theology have recently attracted renewed attention. Barbara M. Cross, *Horace Bushnell: Minister to a Changing America* (1958), provides a biographical reinterpretation. H. Shelton Smith, ed., *Horace Bushnell: Twelve Selections* (1965), contains selections from Bushnell's writings; introductory materials and bibliography make this work an important contribution. Sydney Ahlstrom's essay on Bushnell in Dean G. Peerman and Martin E. Marty, eds., *A Handbook of Christian Theologians* (1965), gives a brief but accurate appraisal.

Additional Sources

Barnes, Howard A., *Horace Bushnell and the virtuous republic,* Philadelphia: American Theological Library Association; Metuchen, N.J.: Scarecrow Press, 1991.

Edwards, Robert Lansing, *Of singular genius, of singular grace: a biography of Horace Bushnell,* Cleveland, Ohio: Pilgrim Press, 1992.

Haddorff, David W. (David Wayne), *Dependence and freedom: the moral thought of Horace Bushnell,* Lanham, Md.: University Press of America, 1994. □

Kofi Abrefa Busia

Kofi Abrefa Busia (1914-1978) was a Ghanaian political leader and sociologist. A scholar by inclination and temperament, he symbolized the dilemma of the intellectual in politics—the man of thought forced by events to become the man of action.

Kofi Busia was born a member of the royal house of Wenchi, a subgroup of the Ashanti, Ghana's largest tribe. Educated at church missions and at Mfantsipim School, he became a teacher at Achimoto, Ghana's leading secondary school. After three years he attained his goal of a scholarship to Oxford, where he went in 1939. His subsequent career alternated between, and sometimes combined, scholarship, government, and politics.

In 1941 Busia returned to the Gold Coast to begin research on the Ashanti political system. In 1942 he became one of the two first African administrative officers in the colonial service. Finding the experience frustrating, he returned to Oxford, where he received a doctorate. Afterward he undertook for the colonial government a social survey of the towns of Sekondi-Takoradi. This was followed by an appointment at the University College in 1949, where in 1954 he became the first African professor.

Political Career

Busia became concerned when the nationalism of Ghana's strong man, Prime Minister Kwame Nkrumah, became increasingly radical. In 1951 Busia had stood for Parliament in his home district of Wenchi in the Gold Coast's first real elections and had been defeated. Yet the chiefs still had powers. Those in Ashanti could choose six additional members of the Legislative Council, of whom Busia became one. In 1952, when the opposition attempted to regroup, it elected Busia as leader, less by choice than by elimination, and for his eminence as a scholar.

The opposition had little effect, until there arose in Ashanti a violent "National Liberation Movement" determined to rid the country of Nkrumah at any cost. Its emergence forced the holding of a new election in 1956. Busia was the movement's unlikely leader, unable to restrain or control it. This was the first real threat to Nkrumah, but his party still emerged victorious, as well as vengeful.

Ghana's independence in 1957 brought Nkrumah new power, which he used systematically to decimate the opposition. Busia regrouped the opposition into a united party and tried to develop a constructive program, but their tactics played into Nkrumah's hands. Their inability to sense the mood of the country, which at its base was still in support of Nkrumah, made of them an unconstructive opposition and of Busia a voiceless leader. By late 1958 Nkrumah was prepared to detain their leading members, and by the next year he had passed a law unseating any Council member absent for more than 20 sessions. The law was aimed directly at Busia, whose scholarly commitments took him all over the world. Threatened by immediate detention, Busia left Ghana, in circumstances that have never been explained, but probably on the advice of Krobo Edusei, a fellow Ashanti in Nkrumah's government.

Years of Exile

The next seven years were spent in exile, with Leiden and then St. Antony's College, Oxford, as Busia's academic base. If Busia had been an unlikely opposition leader in Ghana, he was even more so in exile. But he was now too committed to the struggle against Nkrumah to settle easily into the scholarly life, although he published one book, *The Challenge of Africa,* and some articles during these years. The steadily increasing number of other exiles failed to rally around Busia, least of all Komla Gbedemah, Nkrumah's principal lieutenant turned exile. Nor did Western governments, before 1964, give Busia any tangible support or even encouragement. His testimony to the U.S. Congress against American aid to Ghana caused some resentment. Except perhaps in French circles, it was felt everywhere that if Nkrumah were overthrown it would not be by forces that Busia could hope to command. What was underestimated was the extent to which a revulsion had spread in Ghana against everything Nkrumah symbolized, which would rebound to Busia's benefit.

Return to Triumph

Several months after the soldiers and policemen had overthrown Nkrumah in February 1966, Busia returned to Ghana after careful negotiations with the ruling National Liberation Council (NLC). Politics were banned, and the NLC was at best divided as to how much room for maneuver Busia should be given. Its most powerful member in any event favored Komla Gbedemah, who was no doubt a more skillful politician. Busia was made chairman of a new council on higher education after he was passed over for the vice chancellorship of the University of Ghana. Tactically, Gbedemah always outmaneuvered Busia and his party was better organized, but he was tainted by his association with Nkrumah. Busia, on the other hand, was an Ashanti, and the Ashanti wanted power after so many years. Thus, with their bloc vote, Busia won the premiership in a landslide victory at the end of August 1969.

Once in office, Busia wielded strong executive powers. He instituted a stringent austerity program. The chief question that was posed by the election and Busia's years in power was whether this once reluctant politician was sufficiently in control of his own party, increasingly dominated by little-known but strong-willed younger men, and whether he was sufficiently farsighted to lead Ghana out of its economic troubles and its tribal and political bitterness. Although his commitment to a parliamentary system was nowhere in question, he authorized some actions and tolerated others that gave rise to the old doubts and some new ones as well. The defeated opposition was further enfeebled by the successful barring of Gbedemah even from membership in the new Assembly, a seat he had overwhelmingly won in his district.

Widespread discontent led to a second military coup on January 13, 1972. The presidency was abolished and the National Assembly dissolved under the regime of Lieutenant Colonel Ignatius Kutu Acheampong. Busia, who was in London receiving medical treatment at the time of the coup, was forced into exile for a second time. By the late 1970s, Ghana's economy had slid into chaos, and corruption was rife. The Supreme Military Council, which assumed power in 1975, ousted Colonel Ignatius Kutu Acheampong in 1978.

Busia spent his final years as a lecturer in sociology at Oxford University. Busia's scholarly contribution proved valuable, not only intrinsically, but also for what it has done for the African seeking his identity after centuries of colonial rule. Of the colonial period, Busia wrote that "physical enslavement is tragic enough; but the mental and spiritual bondage that makes people despise their own culture is much worse, for it makes them lose self-respect and, with it, faith in themselves." Part of the intellectual liberation in Africa has come through the systematic analysis of African institutions by Africans; Busia's major study, *The Position of the Chief in the Modern Political System of the Ashanti* (1951), was a ground breaker in this regard. Moreover, Busia personalized the commitment to freedom of the African intellectual, and his writings on the relevance of democratic institutions to modern Africa found a wide audience. He died in London on August 28, 1978.

Further Reading

Busia's doctoral dissertation, *The Position of the Chief in the Modern Political System of the Ashanti: A Study of the Influence of Contemporary Social Changes on Ashanti Political Institutions* (1951), remains both his most important scholarly contribution and a standard work. Busia's *The Challenge of Africa* (1962), written in exile, is a short testimonial to the importance of, and difficulty in, implementing democratic traditions. For an understanding of Busia's political career up to his exile, Dennis Austin, *Politics in Ghana, 1946-1960* (1964), is the definitive work. An account of Busia's term as prime minister is contained in Youry Petchenkine, *Ghana: In Search of Stability, 1957-1992* (1992). Busia's collected speeches have been compiled by M.K. Akyeampong, *Ghana's Struggle for Democracy and Freedom: 1957-1969* (1970-79). □

Ferruccio Benvenuto Busoni

The Italian musician Ferruccio Benvenuto Busoni (1866-1924) was one of the most distinguished and versatile musicians of his time, active as a pianist, conductor, teacher, and composer. His speculations about future developments of music were prophetic.

Ferruccio Busoni, "Italian by birth and instinct, German by education and choice," was born in Empoli, near Florence, where his father was a professional clarinetist and his Italian-German mother was a pianist who gave Ferruccio his first lessons. He was a prodigy, and his childhood was similar to Mozart's in that Busoni composed and went on concert tours throughout Austria and Italy, playing his own compositions for both violin and piano. Although he was largely self-taught, he became one of the greatest pianists of his day and spent many years concertizing.

Busoni was professor of piano at the Helsinki Conservatory in 1889, then in Moscow, and in Boston at the New England Conservatory. He lived in Berlin from 1894 to 1913, when he was appointed director of the Liceo Musicale, a conservatory in Bologna, Italy. This post lasted only a year because Busoni was unhappy when he was unable to change the ultraconservative policies there. He spent the war years in Switzerland, returning to Berlin in 1920 to become professor of composition at the Academy of Arts, a position he held until his death in 1924.

Busoni's contemporaries thought of him primarily as a pianist. Because he lived before the era of effective recording, there is little actual evidence of the quality of his playing. From all accounts he had a prodigious technique and a big, "orchestral" style of playing. He specialized in large works and had no interest in the smaller salon pieces. He was an intellectual pianist and not a charmer. Through-

out his life he taught piano. Among his best-known students was Egon Petri, who in turn was the teacher of many prominent pianists of the next generation.

Busoni thought of himself more as a composer than a pianist, but his compositions never became popular. Among the most important are a huge, five-movement Piano Concerto (the last movement with male chorus), the *Indian Fantasy* for piano and orchestra, based on Native American melodies, and a *Fantasia contrappuntistica* for piano solo. He also wrote several operas; the unfinished last one, *Dr. Faustus,* is occasionally performed.

In his last years Busoni was an influential composition teacher who espoused neoclassic ideals counter to the expressionism that dominated German music of the time. He was always an original thinker. In *The New Esthetic of Music* (1907; trans. 1911) he urged the expansion of musical resources and the use of microtones such as third and sixth tones as well as synthetic scales. Such ideas were much ahead of their time, and in the 1960s, when many composers explored such resources, interest in Busoni revived.

Edgard Varèse, one of the pioneers of electronic music, knew Busoni in Berlin in 1907. In 1966 he wrote that his reading of Busoni's book was a "milestone in my musical development, and when I came upon 'Music is born free; and to win freedom is its destiny,' it was like hearing the echo of my thought."

Further Reading

One study of Busoni in English, Edward J. Dent, *Ferruccio Busoni* (1933), is very good. The chapter on Busoni in David Ewen, *The World of Twentieth-Century Music* (1968), deals mainly with the composer's piano music. Joseph Machlis, *Introduction to Contemporary Music* (1961), contains a chapter discussing Busoni's classical orientation.

Additional Sources

Dent, Edward Joseph, *Ferruccio Busoni, a biography,* London: Eulenburg Books, 1974.

Sablich, Sergio, *Busoni,* Torino: EDT/musica, 1982.

Stuckenschmidt, Hans Heinz, *Ferruccio Busoni; chronicle of a European,* New York, St. Martin's Press 1972, 1970. □

Sylvano Bussotti

Sylvano Bussotti (born 1931), an Italian avant-garde composer, was one of the most audacious of the experimental composers of his generation. His ability to discover new sounds in conventional instruments was unsurpassed.

Sylvano Bussotti was born in Florence and received his early education there. Between 1941 and 1948 he studied at the Florence Conservatory, and in 1957 he became a student of Max Deutsch, a disciple of Arnold Schoenberg, in Paris. At the same time Bussotti studied painting and became acquainted with the principles of abstract expressionism and the concepts of aleatory (or "chance") music championed by John Cage and others.

In abstract expressionist painting a great deal was left to chance. The painter worked without a preconceived plan or drawing and sometimes dripped or slashed paint on his canvas. In the corresponding movement in music, composers believed that the traditional composer-performer relationship, in which the composer "controls" performance through the exactitude of his notation, should be changed. Instead, they held that the composer should establish only certain general situations and then allow the performer great liberty in fulfilling them.

As a result, traditional notation had to be abandoned because it was too precise. Probably because of his training as a painter, Bussotti was very ingenious in devising new notation. His scores often have no staffs, clefs, notes, or anything resembling conventional music. Instead, there are doodles, blots, or intricate line drawings. In his *Five Pieces for David Tudor* (1959) the score looks like Rorschach inkblots; the performer is asked to approximate the shapes in sound. Naturally, no two performances, even by the same pianist, will ever be the same. In these pieces Bussotti extends normal piano technique in requiring that the fingernails be rattled against the keys and that the strings be plucked, hit by table-tennis balls, and rubbed.

In *Frammento* (1959), for soprano and piano, the singer intones a wide variety of fragmentary texts in several different languages while the piano punctuates with highly percussive sounds. At times, the singer sings directly onto the piano strings so as to make them vibrate sympathetically.

Bussotti, like other avant-garde composers of his generation, was interested in multimedia theatrical performances. His "opera" *Passion, according to Sade* was presented in Sweden in 1968. Without a plot and without characterization in the usual sense, it is in the tradition of the theater of the absurd. Another piece, written in the same year, is called *Instrumental Theater*. When the curtain opens, a piano, a harp, an electric organ, and a harpsichord are seen, along with a clothes rack on which there are numerous costumes. The performers change costumes from time to time, while projections are shown on the back wall of the stage, and tapes of distorted words and music are played. Here, too, every performance is different. Success depends on the ability of the performers to improvise and on the empathy of the audience.

Passion, according to Sade piqued Bussotti's interest in theater, which came increasingly to occupy his imagination in the 1970s. Turning his back on the radical experimentation that had marked his work in the 1960s, Bussotti began to incorporate more theatrical and operatic elements into his work. His *Rara Requiem* (1970) marked the beginning of this stylistic shift, which culminated in 1972 with *Lorenzaccio*, a virtuoso blending of dramatic genres most plainly influenced by 19th century grand opera. The work incorporates elements of ballet, film, spoken passages, and off–stage events into a seamless unity of which music is only one part. Eschewing experimentation for the craftsman's devices of the traditional theater, Bussotti manages to use all of the artistic tools at his disposal. As much a departure as it is, however, the composition's theme of memory and its quotation of the entirety of *Rara Requiem* as its fourth and fifth acts hearken back to earlier Bussotti works.

Bussotti continued to work with the techniques and eclectic mixing of styles perfected in *Lorenzaccio* for the remainder of the decade. He also found time for a wide range of academic and administrative commitments. In 1972 he traveled to Berlin on an award from the Deitscher Akademischer Austauschdienst. From 1971 to 1974 he was a professor of history of music drama at the L'Aquila Academy of Fine Arts and in 1974 held an open course in music analysis at the Milan Conservatory. In 1975, Bussotti was named artistic director of the Teatro La Fenice in Venice. Throughout this period he worked as director and designer on numerous stage works by himself and other composers. His major works during this period include the ballet, *Bergkristall* (1974), and the opera, *Nottetempo* (1976).

More recently, Bussotti has kept up his breakneck pace and astonishing command of genres. *Il catalogo è questo* is a cycle of symphonic movements for orchestra which the composer began working on the late 1970s. A series of operas centered around the character of Racine's Phèdre commenced with *Le Racine* (1980). *Fedra* (1988) transformed and expanded upon this piece, while *L'inspirazione* (1988) explores the theme of artistic creation, as its elderly protagonist oversees the production of a new opera in the year 2031.

Further Reading

Paul Henry Lang and Nathan Broder, eds., *Contemporary Music in Europe: A Comprehensive Survey* (1965), includes a short discussion on Bussotti and his work. An excellent background study is Joseph Machlis, *Introduction to Contemporary Music* (1961). A more recent work is A. Lucioli's *Sylvano Bussotti* (1988). A valuable essay on Bussotti's work, "'Auf der Suche nach der verloren Oper' Mozart's Musiktheater und sein Winfluss auf Luciano Berio und Sylvano Bussotti" appears in S. Mauser, *Mozart in der Musik des 20. Jahrhunderts: Formen asthetischer und kompositionstechnischer Rezeption* (1996) □

William Alexander Bustamante

William Alexander Bustamante (1884-1977) was a Jamaican labor leader who became Jamaica's first chief minister under limited self-government and the first prime minister after independence in 1962.

William Alexander Bustamante, perhaps Jamaica's most flamboyant and charismatic politician, was born William Alexander Clarke on February 24, 1884. His father, Robert Constantine Clarke, a member of the declining white plantocracy, was the overseer of a small, mixed-crop plantation called Blenheim, in the parish of Hanover on the then-isolated northwestern coast of the island. By virtue of the second marriage of Elsie Hunter, his paternal grandmother, to Alexander Shearer, he became distantly related to both Norman Washington Manley and Michael Manley, as well as to Hugh Shearer—all of whom were to be chief ministers or prime ministers of Jamaica. His mother, Mary Wilson, descended from the sturdy, independent Black peasantry of rural Hanover.

Bustamante is the surname which he formally adopted in September 1944, although he had been using that name regularly since the 1920s. Bustamante's own apochryphal explanation of the name is that it derives from the Spanish mariner who adopted him at the age of five, taking him to Spain where he was sent to school and where he saw active military service. However, Bustamante did not leave Jamaica until 1905, when he was 21 years old—and he left as part of the early Jamaican migration to Cuba, where employment opportunities were expanding in the sugar industry.

Of Bustamante's early life little is known. He attended elementary school in rural Hanover, once even in his mother's native village of Dalmally. Those few who recall his youth remember him as a fine horseman, who even as a teenager owned his personal horse and raced regularly with his numerous male cousins and others. He was restless, extremely extroverted and gregarious. Although intelligent, he had little formal education beyond the elementary level in Jamaica and resisted the apprenticeship which would

have led him to succeed his father as an overseer of the Jamaican landed interests.

Between 1905 and 1934 Bustamante lived outside of Jamaica, returning to his homeland for only brief visits. Most of this time was spent in Cuba, where he eventually gained employment in the security police of Presidents Alfredo Zayas and Gerardo Machado in the 1920s. Earlier he had spent nearly ten years in Panama (probably between 1908 and 1919) working as a traffic inspector. There he met Mildred Edith Blanck, the widow of an English consulting engineer, whom he married in the Kingston Parish Church on December 12, 1910, while on one of his short visits to the island.

The Jamaica to which Bustamante returned in 1934 was a cauldron of social and economic discontent. The decline of the old colonial system, hastened by the enormous difficulties which Great Britain had encountered during World War I and during the Great Depression, had saddled Jamaica with a type of politics and a bureaucracy which could not respond to the many problems which the island encountered. Wages and working conditions had declined steadily, and the government had consistently refused to provide relief. Workers were being organized and militantly politicized not only by the race and color conscious supporters of Marcus Garvey but also by the articulate socialist-oriented committees of Norman Manley, Frank Hill, Ken Hill, Arthur Henry, Richard Hart, Allan Coombs, Wills O. Isaacs, and Noel Nethersole. To this situation Bustamante brought great charisma, an attractive, empathetic eloquence spiced with rapier-like humor, carnival-like flair, boundless enthusiasm, energy, and an unflagging support for the working classes and the underprivileged. Along with his famous half-cousin Norman Washington Manley he became the dominant political figure in Jamaica until his retirement in the late 1960s.

After his return to Jamaica, Bustamante established himself as a money-lender in modest offices on Duke Street, then the desired cachet for all business addresses in Kingston. He installed Gladys Longbridge as his private secretary, and she was to accompany him for the rest of his life as confidante, assistant, companion, and, finally, after September 6, 1962, his second wife. Bustamante described himself as a dietician and businessman with North American experience, but while he might have returned with some wealth to the island, his formal training and experience were mostly his own fantastic fabrication.

Spokesman for Labor

He began his political involvement by writing long, almost daily letters to the press, especially the venerable *Daily Gleaner,* the island's leading newspaper—then more than a century in continuous publication—and its smaller rival, *The Jamaica Standard.* He wrote on many subjects, but most had to do with the conditions of the lower orders of the working classes and the political ineptness of the local administrators. Gradually he became involved in the protest marches and other demonstrations of the urban masses. He was interned briefly for this activity. The widespread labor disturbances of the years 1937 and 1938 provided the opportunity to establish himself as the foremost labor leader in the island. He combined the oratory of Marcus Garvey with the modified messianic spirit of the former millenialists Alexander Bedward and Solomon Hewitt, but he made the new movement his own instrument.

On January 23, 1939, he registered the Bustamante Industrial Trade Union over the opposition of the governor and others who declared that a union should not possess the name of an individual. Within four years the union represented more than 80 percent of all organized workers in Jamaica, mainly among the rural agricultural workers. The constitution of the union made Bustamante president for life, with unrestricted control of its finances.

Between September 8, 1939, and February 8, 1942, Bustamante was imprisoned by the governor of Jamaica, Sir Arthur Richards, under wartime emergency powers for incitement to riot for addressing a group of longshoremen on the Kingston waterfront. The internment made a political martyr of Bustamante and enhanced the position of his union among the masses. During Bustamante's internment Norman Manley and his followers rebuilt and expanded the organization of the Bustamante Industrial Trade Union. The eventual release of Bustamante from prison derived from the unceasing efforts of Manley, who had earlier founded the People's National Party as the political instrument for forging a new nationalism in Jamaica. And indeed, it was through the efforts of the People's National Party, modeled after the British Labor Party, that Jamaica gained a new political status in 1944 with universal adult suffrage and an elected legislature with limited self-government.

Working for an Independent Jamaica

Immediately after his release Bustamante broke with Manley, reorganized the union, and formally launched the Jamaica Labor Party on July 1943 to rival the People's National Party and the Jamaica Democratic Party in the first general elections held in December 1944. The Jamaica Labor Party won 23 of the 32 seats in the House of Representatives, with 41 percent of the votes, and Bustamante became Jamaica's first chief minister.

Along with being head of the government, Bustamante served as mayor of Kingston and Saint Andrew Corporation in 1947. His Jamaica Labor Party won re-election in the national elections of 1949 with a reduced parliamentary representation. More significantly, the party gained less popular votes than the opposition People's National Party. Although Bustamante lost the general elections of 1955 and 1959, he remained leader of the opposition in the Jamaican Parliament until 1962. His was a prominent voice and effective presence in the political life of the country. He established the vital link between the trade union base and the political party and made this combination the most effective instrument of political operation in Jamaica.

Bustamante virtually single-handedly destroyed the West Indian Federation, established in 1958 to unify and order the political evolution of the English West Indian territories. His decision not to participate in the federation and to orchestrate the Jamaican opposition to it in a 1961 referendum led to the demise of the federation in 1962, the year in which Bustamante's party, riding the crest of its successful campaign to withdraw Jamaica from the federation, won the general elections once more and made Bustamante the prime minister of independent Jamaica.

In 1967 he retired from politics, having reduced his participation during the previous three years because of failing health. The following year the Jamaican Parliament honored him by declaring him a national hero. He died on August 6, 1977, at the age of 93 and was buried in the shrine for prime ministers of Jamaica in the national park in Kingston.

Further Reading

An excellent balanced account is *Alexander Bustamante and Modern Jamaica* by George Eaton (1975). Unflattering synoptic portraits can be found in Paul Blanshard, *Democracy and Empire in the Caribbean* (1977) and *Personal and Controversial: An Autobiography* (1973). Norman Manley's portrait is more insightful in *The New Jamaica: Selected Speeches and Writings, 1938-1968,* edited with notes and introduction by Rex Nettleford (1971).

Additional Sources

Hamilton, B. L. St. John, *Bustamante: anthology of a hero,* Kingston, Jamaica: Produced for B. St. J. Hamilton by Publication & Productions, 1978.

Hill, Frank, *Bustamante and his letters,* Kingston, Jamaica: Kingston Publishers, 1976.

Ranston, Jackie, *From we were boys: the story of the magnificent cousins, the Rt. Excellent Sir William Alexander Bustamante and the Rt. Excellent Norman Washington Manley,* Kingston, Jamaica: Bustamante Institute of Public & International Affairs, 1989. □

3d Earl of Bute

The British statesman John Stuart, 3d Earl of Bute (1713-1792), served as prime minister under George III, over whom he exercised an unpopular influence.

John Stuart was born in Edinburgh of aristocratic Scottish parents. His father died when John was 10, and the boy was raised in England under the guardianship of two maternal uncles. In 1737, when he was 24, Bute was elected to the English Parliament as one of the Scottish peers nominated by Lord Islay. Two years later he entered the opposition, thereby severing his connection with his patron and losing his seat at the next election in 1741. He remained excluded from Parliament for the next 20 years.

For 5 years after this setback, Bute lived in retirement on the island of Bute. Though better educated than most English aristocrats—an unsympathetic contemporary described him as having "a great deal of superficial knowledge . . . upon matters of natural philosophy, mines, fossils, a smattering of mechanics, a little metaphysics, and a very false taste in everything"—he was much worse off financially. His Scottish estates were poor, and his immediate financial prospects had not been improved by his marriage to the daughter of Edward Wortley Montagu, a notorious miser. In 1736 she had eloped with Bute. Hence Bute failed to get anything from his father-in-law except advice to continue to live economically in Scotland.

In 1746 Bute decided to return to London. There, despite his poverty, he appeared often in aristocratic society, where he attracted attention by his great physical beauty. The most important outcome of this was an introduction to the Prince of Wales, later George III, who quickly became utterly dependent upon him. After the prince succeeded to the throne in October 1760, his dependence on Bute continued. But although Bute's views completely dominated the King's conduct, he did not become prime minister until May 1762. Then he quickly found the strain of office too great. In April 1763, despite the King's entreaties, Bute resigned. His hysterical excuses of ill health and distaste for politics have no substance; he committed political suicide because he was on the verge of a nervous breakdown.

For another 3 years Bute retained the confidence of George III, and his influence over the King continued to be a major source of political friction and popular grievance. He was constantly lampooned and caricatured and could not appear in public without risk of injury. Repeatedly the King undertook to end Bute's irresponsible meddling, but not until 1766 did he finally sacrifice the relationship in the interests of governmental stability. Subsequently Bute played little part in active politics, and in 1780 he retired from Parliament to spend the last years of his life in the study

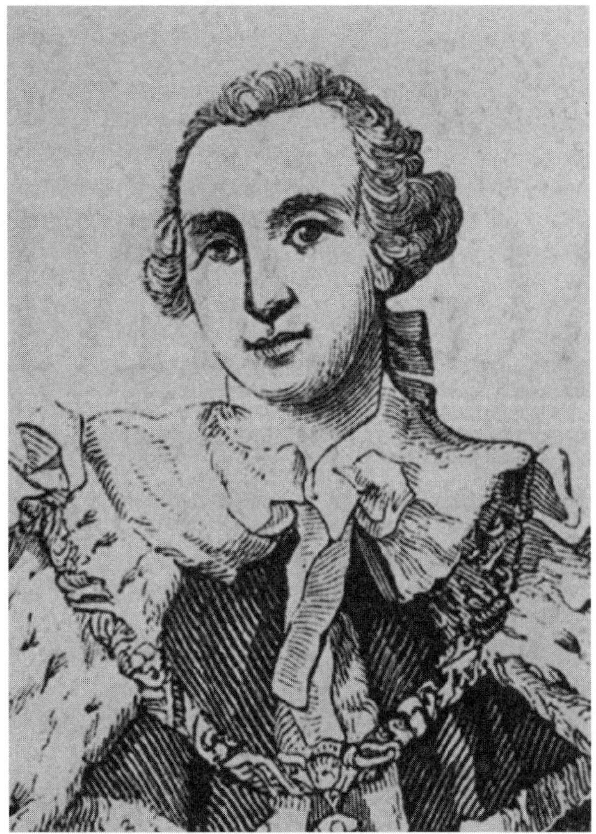

of literature and science. He died on March 10, 1792, and was buried on the island of Bute.

Further Reading

There is no modern biography of Bute. A useful study is James A. Lovat-Fraser, *John Stuart, Earl of Bute* (1912). Fascinating insights into his relationship with George III are provided in Romney Sedgwick, ed., *Letters from George III to Lord Bute, 1756-1766* (1939). For background material see Sir Lewis B. Namier, *England in the Age of the American Revolution* (1930; 2d ed. 1962), and Richard Pares, *King George III and the Politicians* (1953).

Additional Sources

Lord Bute: essays in re-interpretation, Leicester: Leicester University Press, 1988. □

Mangosuthu Gatsha Buthelezi

Dr. Mangosuthu Gatsha Buthelezi (born 1928), played a leading role in South Africa's political history. Founder of the Inkatha Freedom Party (IFP) and heir to the Chieftainship of the Buzelezi tribe, Buthelezi was elected Chief Executive Officer of the KwaZulu Territory in 1970, Chief Executive Councillor of the KwaZulu Legistative Assembly in 1972, and Chief Minister of KwaZulu in 1976. He is also Chancellor of the University of Zululand and was appointed Minister of Home Affairs (1994) in Nelson Mandela's coalition government.

Mangosuthu Gatsha Buthelezi, great-grandson of King Dinizulu and direct descendent of warrior-king Shaka, was born August 27, 1928, at Mahlabatini, near the traditional Zulu capital of Ulundi. (Dinizulu was banished and died in exile after the 1906 Zulu rebellion against British rule.) As heir to the Chieftainship of the Buzelezi tribe, Buthelezi's ancestry is as important to his current political standing as are his own political skills. He married to Irene Mzila, a nurse from Johannesburg, and has three sons and four daughters.

In 1948, Buthelezi enrolled at Fort Hare University and majored in History and Bantu Administration. While at the University Buthelezi joined the predominantly Xhosa African National Congress (ANC) Youth League and participated in anti-discrimination protests. After leaving the University Buthelezi took a position with the Department of Native Affairs.

Apartheid became firmly established in South Africa during the 1950s and racial segration was strictly enforced. Then in the 1960s the government declared that native Africans would be franchised in one of ten homelands corresponding to their ethnic affiliation. Buthelezi strongly

opposed the government's homeland plan. He contended, as did other critics, that the economic bases of the homelands were inadequate and that the homeland plan was simply another way of enforcing apartheid.

Approximately six million Zulu (1/4 of the country's native population) were declared citizens of KwaZulu, now known as KwaZulu-Natal. In 1970, Dr. Buthelezi was elected Chief Executive Officer of the newly established KwaZulu Territorial Authority. He became Chief Executive Councillor of the KwaZulu Legistative Assembly in 1972, and Chief Minister of KwaZulu, which he continues to hold, in 1976.

Buthelezi was in an ambiguous political position. Although he was a strong critic of apartheid, and thus the government, he also was a government-approved homeland leader, a role that many saw as an integral part of apartheid. Buthelezi found himself at odds with the government-banned ANC, of which he had once been a member. In 1975 Buthelezi revived Inkatha we Sizwe, a cultural organization originally founded in the 1920s, and transformed Inkatha, as it was commonly known, into the Inkatha Freedom Party (IFP). By continuing to identify itself as a cultural organization rather than a political organization the IFP avoided being banned by the government. Membership in the IFP was almost entirely Zulu.

Political differences as well as tribal differences made the IFP and the ANC bitter rivals. During the years 1987-91, as the two groups competed for control over the KwaZulu-Natal province, there were more than 18,000 deaths.

The ANC was unbanned after leader Nelson Mandela was released from prison in February, 1990. Many of the ANC's previous socialist economic policies and strictures against freedom of speech and freedom of religion were revised. However, the ANC also gained control of the media; anyone not belonging to the ANC was "retrenched." Bloodshed continued as clandestine support for the IFP came from security police and military intelligence and the ANC continued deadly raids on IFP supporters.

In information provided by several witness affadavits, it was shown that in 1993 the IFP, which was controlled by Buthelezi, used taxpayer money to train and arm an 8,000 member paramilitary force. The KwaZulu Police (KZP) commissioner, Roy During, was ordered to merge trainees into the KZP as special constables. The merger effectively bypassed government restrictions forbidding territories from establishing their own armies. Then, just days before the April 1994 election, the IFP joined the elections and withdrew the paramilitary from the police force. (The KZP itself was later disbanded.)

Although IFP legislator Senator Philip Powell claimed that the special force was meant to increase the KZP's ability to handle any large-scale civil unrest due to the election, testimony in 1996 by Col. Eugene de Kock at his mitigation hearing suggests that the underlying purpose of the paramilitary organization was to provide a readily-mobilized warrior network that would prevent KwaZulu-Natal from being absorbed into an ANC-ruled South Africa.

The first democratic, multi-racial election was held in South Africa in April, 1994. The ANC won the majority and Mandela was elected President of South Africa. As required by the Interim Constitution, Mandela formed a coalition government, the Government of National Unity (GNU). The coalition included the ANC, the IFP, and the National Party (NP). Buthelezi was appointed Minister of Home Affairs.

Documents submitted during the 1996 trial of NP's Defence Minister Gen. Magnus Malan confirmed Buthelezi's knowledge of the IFP's plans to establish a paramilitary force. However, documents showing the paramilitary's operations for October 1986 through February 1988 disappeared. Malan was acquitted and no legal action was taken against Buthelezi.

In a move designed to position the IFP for a 1999 electoral victory, Buthelezi nominated moderate Ben Ngubane as KwaZulu-Natal's premier. Ngubane, who is viewed as a skilled negotiator well-versed in the IFP's constitutional demands, was described by Betheluzi as "his right hand man." In late 1996 at an IFP youth rally, Buthelezi reminded participants of his earlier warning - that with the destruction of apartheid, the real struggle for economic empowerment of black South Africans would begin.

Violence in the KwaZulu-Natal province had been diminishing for months as IFP Premier Ngubane and ANC provincial leader Jacob Zume met in secret to discuss a peace pact. According to IFP parliamentarian Powell, a way to provide amnesty for people involved on both sides of the violence was a key element of the talks. ANC leaders were unwilling to discuss the peace talks. In mid-1997, Buthelezi appeared to endorse a possible merger of the IFP with the ANC and other nationalist movements. He was quoted as saying in the *Sunday Times,* that "Unity [between the rival nationalist movements in KwaZulu-Natal] would be an ideal thing. I do not see why it should not happen."

In addition to being leader of the IFP, Dr. Buthelezi currently holds the position of Minister of Home Affairs in Mandela's coalition government (GNU), and is Chief Minister of KwaZulu-Natal. He is Chancellor of the University of Zululand and has served on the standing committee of the Zululand Anglican Diocese, of the council of St. Peter's Seminary, of the council of the Inanda Seminary, and of the KwaZulu Conservation Trust. Buthelezi has received several awards and honorary doctorate degrees including Knight Commander of the Star of Africa for outstanding leadership (1975), Honorary doctorate of law, University of Zululand (1976), and the George Meaney Human Rights Award from the United States American Federation of Labor & Congress of Industrial Organizations (AFL/CIO) (1983).

Further Reading

Biographies of Buthelezi are generally polemical. Ben Temkin, *Gatsha Buthelezi, Zulu Statesman* (1976) is laudatory. Gerhard Mare and Georgina Hamilton, *An Appetite for Power: Buthelezi's Inkatha and South Africa* (Johannesburg: 1987) is critical. Michael Massing, "The Chief," *New York Review of Books* (February 12, 1987), is sober and critical. Jeff Guy, *The Destruction of the Zulu Kingdom* (London: 1979), presents an important aspect of Zulu history, as does J. D. Omer-Cooper, *The Zulu Aftermath* (1969). □

John Butler

John Butler (1728-1796), British Indian agent and loyalist leader during the American Revolution, was famous for his military exploits along the New York and Pennsylvania frontiers.

Born in Connecticut, the son of Capt. Walter Butler and Deborah Butler, John moved with his family to the Mohawk Valley of New York in 1742. As a captain in the British military, he served in the French and Indian War (1754-1763) in engagements at Crown Point, Ticonderoga, and Ft. Frontenac. He became a trusted representative of Sir William Johnson, at first commanding Native American auxiliaries and later conducting Indian affairs.

With the coming of the American Revolution, Butler fled with his son and other loyalists (American colonials who felt allegiance to the English crown rather than the urge for independence of the Colonies) to Canada. He continued to take an active role in Indian affairs and in military activities along the frontier of New York. He participated in St. Leger's fruitless British expedition of 1777. Then he began the recruitment of a band of refugee loyalists, called Butler's Rangers. As a major, he commanded these and other loyalists and their Native American allies in an invasion of Pennsylvania's Wyoming Valley in the spring of 1778. His march culminated in an encounter with American colonial troops near Forty Fort, with the subsequent surrender of that post on July 4, 1778. The slaughter of some of the captives (the Wyoming Valley "massacre") has been the occasion of later, highly colored criticism of Butler. Actually, he seems to have tried, with some success, to limit the scope of the atrocities. In the following year Butler's Rangers and the Native American allies were defeated at Newton during the only pitched battle of the American general John Sullivan on his expedition into Iroquois country. In 1780 Butler reached his highest rank, that of lieutenant colonel. His military career was an exceptional one for a loyalist leader: he and his fellow exiles, his son and Sir John Johnson, were successful in raising, commanding, and making real use for the British of the loyalists who had fled from the rebel forces among the Americans. The Revolutionaries responded with the Act of Attainder in 1779 and by confiscating all Butler's property in New York. His wife and younger children were held temporarily as hostages but were eventually exchanged for other prisoners. Butler's eldest son also participated in loyalist military activities until he was killed in action in 1781.

After the war the British rewarded Butler's services with a pension and a grant of land near Niagara. Butler was prominent in the development of a Tory settlement there and served as Indian commissioner. Variously described as sturdy or fat, he lived the remainder of his years in exile, respected by the British and by other refugees for his loyalty and detested by his former fellow colonists in the United States. He died in 1796.

Further Reading

The best account of the activities of John and Walter Butler is Howard Swiggett, *War out of Niagara: Walter Butler and the Tory Rangers* (1933). □

Joseph Butler

The English philosopher and theologian Joseph Butler (1692-1752) developed a moral philosophy based on human nature and a natural theology that emphasized the validity of Christian beliefs.

Joseph Butler was born on May 18, 1692, at Wantage, Berkshire, to Presbyterian parents. His father, wishing his son to be a minister, sent him to a Dissenting academy, which was first located at Gloucester and then at Tewkesbury. While at this academy Butler's keen aptitude for theological speculation became evident. In his correspondence with Samuel Clarke he indicated two flaws in the reasoning of Clarke's recently published *a priori* demonstrations concerning the proof of the divine omnipresence and of the unity of the "necessarily existent being." Also while at the academy, for reasons not fully known, young Butler left the Presbyterian communion and joined the Church of England. After securing his father's reluctant consent, in 1714 he entered Oriel College, Oxford; after taking his degree, he was ordained a priest in 1718.

During his lifetime Butler served the Anglican Church in a number of different offices. He was preacher at Rolls Chapel, rector of Haughton and Stanhope, clerk of the closet to Queen Caroline, bishop of Bristol, dean of St. Paul's Cathedral, clerk of the closet to King George II, and, for the last 2 years of his life, bishop of Durham. He died in Bath on June 16, 1752, and was buried in Bristol Cathedral.

Philosophical Thought

A systematic statement of Butler's moral philosophy is found in his "Three Sermons on Human Nature" in *Fifteen Sermons* and in Dissertation II ("Of the Nature of Virtue") in *The Analogy*. Butler, believing that revelation and nature are complementary, argues in Aristotelian fashion from the nature of man to conclusions on how man should live to be in accord with that nature. By nature men have both self-regarding and benevolent affections. The intrinsic character of the self-regarding affection is not incompatible with a benevolent attitude. In fact, more often than is commonly supposed, these affections reinforce each other.

But the affections are only one facet of human nature; far more important is the capacity to judge the affections and the behavior issuing from them. This superior faculty is conscience or reflection. As Butler himself indicates, his view of conscience is drawn from Arrian's *Discourses of Epictetus*. Conscience, Butler insists, keeps man from being the captive of his passions, approves or condemns his actions, and constitutes man as a morally self-legislating being.

The Analogy offers the clearest statement of Butler's natural theology. This work was apparently intended to convince deists, who acknowledged God's existence, that their beliefs could reasonably lead them to Christianity. It shows the importance of the Christian revelation and the reasonableness of belief in immortality.

Further Reading

G. W. Kitchin, *Seven Sages of Durham* (1911), includes a biographical sketch of Butler. The following works consider particular aspects of Butler's thinking: Ernest Campbell Mossner, *Bishop Butler and the Age of Reason: A Study in the History of Thought* (1936); Austin Duncan-Jones, *Butler's Moral Philosophy* (1952); and P. Allan Carlsson, *Butler's Ethics* (1964).

Additional Sources

Penelhum, Terence, *Butler,* London; Boston: Routledge & Kegan Paul, 1985. □

Nicholas Murray Butler

The American educator Nicholas Murray Butler (1862-1947) was president of Columbia University during its period of greatest expansion, in which it acquired an international reputation as a center of research and scholarship.

Nicholas Murray Butler was born in Elizabeth, N.J., on April 2, 1862, the son of a manufacturer. He graduated from Columbia College, New York City, in 1882 and earned his doctorate there in 1884. After a year's study in Berlin and Paris he returned to Columbia to become an assistant in philosophy. His interest in the education of teachers led him to help organize, and to head from 1886 to 1891, the institution which later became Teachers College of Columbia University. In 1890 he was promoted to professor of philosophy and also became dean of the newly created faculty of philosophy, a position he held until his elevation to the acting presidency in 1901.

In 1902 Butler became permanent president and remained in office until his retirement in 1945. The transformation of Columbia into a modern university had already begun under his predecessors, but under Butler's leadership the school experienced a tremendous increase in endowment, buildings, size of student body, and number and quality of faculty. An indefatigable speechmaker, clubman, and fund raiser, Butler strove to expand and deepen the material and intellectual resources of his institution, building it into an international leader in advanced study and research.

An active worker for the Republican party for most of his life, Butler attended national conventions from 1880 on, frequently as a voting delegate. He was chosen as candidate for vice president of the United States in 1912, when the vice president died in office. In the 1920 Republican convention he was nominated by the New York delegation as a candidate for the presidency and received 69 1/2 votes. Although a firm proponent of liquor regulation, he opposed prohibition and fought the 18th Amendment to the Constitution. Many presidents sought his advice on matters of public policy.

Butler became interested in the international peace movement well before World War I, becoming chairman of the American branch of Conciliation Internationale in 1907. He strongly supported the League of Nations. From 1925 to 1945 he headed the Carnegie Endowment for International Peace. He won a Nobel Peace Prize in 1931, which he shared with Jane Addams. Butler died in New York City on Dec. 7, 1947.

Further Reading

Butler's life is best studied in his autobiography, *Across the Busy Years: Recollections and Reflections* (2 vols., 1939-1940). Richard Whittemore, *Nicholas Murray Butler and Public Education* (1970), is a useful study. Butler's career is also recounted in Horace Coon, *Columbia: Colossus on the Hudson* (1947). A guide to his written work was compiled by Milton Halsey Thomas, *Bibliography of Nicholas Murray Butler, 1872-1932* (1934). His work at Columbia is recorded in Edward C. Elliot, ed., *The Rise of a University,* vol. 2: *The University in Action* (1937), which is composed of excerpts from Butler's annual reports as president of Columbia, topically arranged.

Additional Sources

Marrin, Albert, *Nicholas Murray Butler,* Boston: Twayne Publishers, 1976. □

Octavia E. Butler

Octavia Butler (born 1947) is best known as the author of the Patternist series of science fiction novels in which she explores topics traditionally given only cursory treatment in the genre, including sexual identity and racial conflict. Butler's heroines are black women who are both mentally and physically powerful .

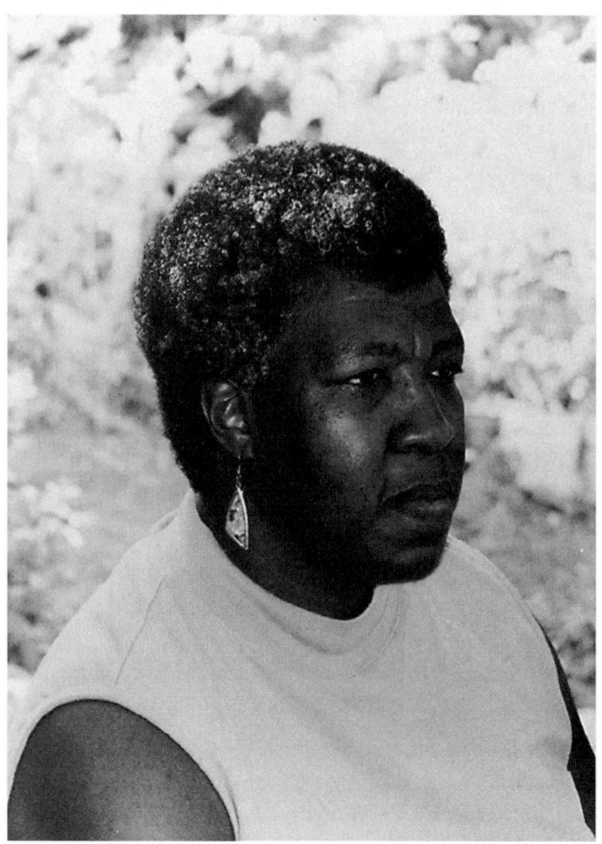

Butler grew up in a racially mixed neighborhood in Pasadena, California. Her father died while she was very young, and her mother worked as a maid to support the two of them. Butler has written memoirs of her mother's sacrifices: buying her a typewriter of her own when she was ten years old, and to paying a large fee to an unscrupulous agent so Butler's stories could be read. Butler entered student contests as a teenager, and after attending workshops like the Writers Guild of America, West "open door" program during the late 1960s and the Clarion Science Fiction Writer's Workshop in 1970, Butler sold her first science fiction stories.This early training brought her into contact with a range of well-known science fiction writers, including Joanna Russ and Harlan Ellison, who became Butler's mentor.

Four of Butler's six novels revolve around the Patternists, a group of mentally superior beings who are telepathically connected to one another. These beings are the descendants of Doro, a four thousand-year-old Nubian male who has selectively bred with humans throughout time with the intention of establishing a race of superhumans. He prolongs his life by killing others, including his family members, and inhabiting their bodies. The origin of the Patternists is outlined in *Wild Seed,* which begins in seventeenth-century Africa and spans more than two centuries. The Novel recounts Doro's uneasy alliance with Anyanwu, an earth-mother figure whose extraordinary powers he covets. Their relationship progresses from power struggles and tests of will to mutual need and dependency. Doro's tyranny ends when one of his children, the heroine of *Mind of My Mind,* destroys him and united the Patternists with care and compassion. *Patternmaster* and *Survivor* are also part of the Patternist series. The first book set in the future, concerns two brothers vying for their dying father's legacy. However, the pivotal character in the novel is Amber, one of Butler's most heroic women, whose unconventional relationship with one of her brothers is often interpreted in feminist contexts. In *Survivor,* set on an alien planet, Butler examines human attitudes toward racial and ethnic differences and their effects on two alien creatures. Alanna, the human protagonist, triumphs over racial prejudice and enslavement by teaching her alien captors tolerance and respect for individuality. *Kindred* departs from the Patternist series yet shares its focus on male/female relationships and racial matters. The protagonist, Dana, is a contemporary writer who is telepathically transported to a pre-Civil War plantation. She is a victim both of the slave-owning ancestor who summons her when he is in danger and of the slave-holding age in which she is trapped for increasing periods. *Clay's Ark* (1984) reflects Butler's interest in the psychological traits of men and women in a story of a space virus that threatens the earth's population with disease and genetic mutation. In an interview, Butler commented on how Ronald Reagan's vision of a winnable nuclear war encouraged her to write more dystopic material. This shift in focus is most evident in *Parable of the Sower* (1994), a novel which depicts a religious sea-change, set against the backdrop of a strife-ridden inner city in 2025.

Critics have often applauded Butler's lack of sentimentality, and have responded favorably on her direct treatment of subjects not previously addressed in science fiction, such as sexuality, male/female relationships, racial inequity, and contemporary politics. Frances Smith Foster has commented: "Octavia Butler is not just another woman science fiction writer. Her major characters are black women, and through her characters and through the structure of her imagined social order, Butler consciously explores the impact of race and sex upon future society."

Further Reading

Contemporary Literary Criticism, Volume 38, Gale, 1986.

Dictionary of Literary Biography, Volume 33: *Afro-American Fiction Writers After 1955,* Gale, 1984.

Analog: Science Fiction/Science Fact, January 5, 1981; November, 1984; December 15, 1987; December, 1988.

Black American Literature Forum, summer, 1984.

Black Scholar, March/April, 1986.

Equal Opportunity Forum Magazine, Number 8, 1980.

Essence, April, 1979; May, 1989, pp. 74, 79, 132, 134.
Extrapolation, spring, 1982.
Fantasy Review, July, 1984.
Janus, winter, 1978-79.
Los Angeles Times, January 30, 1981.
Magazine of Fantasy and Science Fiction, February, 1980; August, 1984.
Ms., March, 1986; June, 1987.
Salaga, 1981.
Science Fiction Review, May, 1984.
Thrust: Science Fiction in Review, summer, 1979.
Washington Post Book World, September 28, 1980; June 28, 1987; July 31, 1988; June 25, 1989. □

Samuel Butler

The English novelist and essayist Samuel Butler (1835-1902) was a critic of established religious, social, and scientific ideas.

Samuel Butler was born on Dec. 4, 1835, in Langar, near Bingham, Nottinghamshire, the son of the local vicar. In a time of common paternal absolutism, his childhood seems to have been bleak and graceless. After taking a degree at Cambridge, he came into open conflict with his father over the question of his future profession, and at last he emigrated to New Zealand to become a sheep farmer. But though free of his father, he was not free of revolt, and the spirit of resentful rebelliousness marked much of his later life. In New Zealand he read Charles Darwin's *Origin of Species* and wrote a series of newspaper articles setting forth Darwin's ideas and ingeniously applying the evolutionary hypothesis to machines. Having made a modest fortune, he returned to England in 1864.

Erewhon (1872), Butler's first book, is a mixture of satire, utopian theories, and serious speculation masked as whimsy. Set in the frame of a trip to an unknown land (Erewhon is an anagram of "no-where"), it has no real plot but is rather a description and discussion of the customs and institutions of Erewhon. In this land moral failings are treated as mental illness and cured by a "straightener," but physical illness and misfortune are considered crimes and severely punished. Children sign certificates absolving their parents of responsibility for their birth, and education is carried on in the College of Unreason.

Butler's reflections on orthodox religion, begun in New Zealand, issued in *The Fair Haven* (1873), an ironic attempt to reconcile the New Testament with rationalistic criticism. In *Life and Habit* he returned to the question of evolution. In *Evolution Old and New* (1879), *Unconscious Memory* (1880), and *Luck, or Cunning?* (1887), he developed his ideas with an increasingly self-righteous resentment of what he conceived to be the Darwinians' deliberate concealment of the truth. Butler hoped to be able to restore will, intelligence, and design to a universe apparently made meaningless by the blind process of natural selection.

The novel *The Way of All Flesh,* Butler's most famous work, was written between 1872 and 1885. It is the supposed biography of Ernest Pontifex, narrated by an older friend with an unrelenting candor deliberately affronting conventional pieties. The account of a grimly repressive childhood is based on Butler's own youth. As a young man, Ernest swings from naive religious zeal to despairing disillusionment, is imprisoned for propositioning an innocent girl, and upon his release makes a disastrous marriage. Finally free, he turns to a career as writer and intellectual gadfly, exposing the evils and hypocrisies of the established institutions and values that had twisted his own life.

Erewhon Revisited (1901) returns to the problem of religion and examines the relationship between rational truth and religious faith.

Further Reading

The primary biographical source is Henry Festing Jones, *Samuel Butler: A Memoir* (2 vols., 1919). A shorter, more critical biography is Clara G. Stillman, *Samuel Butler: A Mid-Victorian Modern* (1932). Two good studies of Butler's ideas are P. N. Furbank, *Samuel Butler* (1948), and Basil Willey, *Darwin and Butler: Two Versions of Evolution* (1960).

Additional Sources

Butler, Samuel, *Butleriana,* Folcroft, Pa.: Folcroft Library Editions, 1976.
Jones, Henry Festing, *Samuel Butler: a sketch,* Norwood, Pa.: Norwood Editions, 1977.
Raby, Peter, *Samuel Butler: a biography,* Iowa City: University of Iowa Press, 1991. □

Samuel Butler

The English poet Samuel Butler (ca. 1613-1680) is best known as the author of "Hudibras," a long comic poem that satirizes the Puritans.

The exact date of Samuel Butler's birth is unknown. He was baptized Feb. 14, 1613, in Strensham, Worcestershire. The son of a yeoman farmer, he attended the King's School in Worcester. Shortly after leaving school, about 1628, he entered the service of Elizabeth, Countess of Kent, at her home at Wrest, Bedfordshire. At Wrest he enjoyed the use of the countess's magnificent library and met some of the most learned men of his time.

During the period of the Commonwealth, Butler served as clerk to a number of country magistrates, several of whom were dedicated Puritans. While in the households of these men, he seems to have suppressed his own religious and political convictions and to have busied himself with the writing of *Hudibras.* It seems probable that Butler modeled his character of the ridiculous Sir Hudibras on the characters of at least two of his Puritan employers.

It was not until after the death of Cromwell that Butler published his first essay, *Mola asinaria* (1659), pleading for the restoration of the Stuarts. In 1662 Butler began publishing *Hudibras* in installments. The first part, written in rhyming octosyllabic couplets, appeared late in 1662, the second in 1663, and the third in 1677. It was an immediate success, particularly with the King and his court. Many of the surviving copies of the first edition are inscribed as gifts of Charles II to members of the court, and the number of pirated versions and spurious sequels of the poem testify to its popularity with the general public.

Although *Hudibras* brought Butler fame, he seems to have lived in relative obscurity after 1663. Little is known of his character and occupation during the years in which he produced the bulk of his writings. Of moderate height and strong build, he is said to have been "a good fellow" possessing "severe and sound judgment." Records show that he was employed as secretary to secretary to George Villiers, 2d Duke of Buckingham, for some time in the early 1670s. It is believed that he remained in London after 1677, occupying a room in Rose Alley, Covent Garden. He died Sept. 25, 1680.

Butler's contemporaries seem to have held Charles II responsible for the poverty in which the poet spent his last years. But in 1677 Charles granted Butler an annual pension of £100. He was buried at the expense of William Longueville, who later collected his unpublished manuscripts. These were kept intact by Longueville's heirs and published in 1759. The volumes contained much occasional poetry, a satire on the Royal Society entitled "The Elephant on the Moon," and a series of prose character sketches.

Further Reading

The most interesting discussion of Butler and his work is by John Wilders in his edition of *Hudibras* (1967). An earlier biographical account is Jan Veldkamp, *Samuel Butler: The Author of Hudibras* (1923). Critical discussions of *Hudibras* and its place in English literary tradition include Edward Ames Richards, *Hudibras in the Burlesque Tradition* (1937), and Ian Jack, *Augustan Satire: Intention and Idiom in English Poetry, 1660-1750* (1952).

Additional Sources

Veldkamp, Jan, *Samuel Butler, the author of Hudibras,* Norwood, Pa.: Norwood Editions, 1978. □

John Butterfield

The American financier, politician, and businessman John Butterfield (1801-1869) is best known for his energetic role in developing American transportation and communication facilities. He organized the American Express Company.

John Butterfield was born on Nov. 18, 1801, to an obscure family which had settled in New York in the early 17th century. Irregular attendance during winters at primitive public schools provided him with a limited formal education. While still a boy he found employment as a stage driver. Later he became a small proprietor and eventually the organizer of the first great transcontinental stage line, the Overland Mail, in 1857. He was also involved at various times and in various places with packet boats, plank roads, Great Lakes steamers, telegraph lines, street railways, transportation facilities across the Isthmus of Panama, banking, and railroads.

Butterfield's involvement in stage driving led directly to his participation in the express business. He was among the first to see the commercial possibilities in the multiple services rendered by the express companies, ranging from delivery of diversified freight to collection of accounts. He also came to the industry when it was on the eve of great growth, as both the national economy and the areas serviced by Butterfield's enterprises were expanding rapidly. His initial venture in the express business was Butterfield, Wasson and Company, which merged with several other firms in 1850 to become the American Express Company. It quickly became the largest business of its kind in the United States.

In 1857 Butterfield and the American Express Company were awarded a $600,000 annual contract by the Federal government to establish and operate the first transcontinental stage line, the Overland Mail. Its establishment was lauded, although the route was criticized on the grounds that it deviated from the most direct route between St. Louis and San Francisco, and covered a distance of 2,800 miles en route to the Pacific (via El Paso, Yuma, and Los Angeles). Within a year hundreds of men and thousands of

head of stock were procured, scores of way stations built, and rolling equipment secured. Butterfield supervised the operation, and soon service on a semiweekly basis began, with mail coaches departing on Sept. 15, 1858, from San Francisco and St. Louis. Regular service continued—in spite of the long distances and occasional attacks by Indians—until the outbreak of the Civil War forced the closing of the line in 1861 to avoid interference by Confederate forces.

Butterfield was also involved in a number of railroad developments, telegraph facilities, and banks. A lifelong Democrat, he was interested in the city of Utica, N.Y., where he built an elaborate home and commercial buildings, and also a business. He was elected mayor in 1865.

Butterfield combined great energy and minute attention to details with keen insight into the significance of impending change in the fields of communication and transportation. The result was spectacular success in enterprises which varied from plank roads to telegraph lines and touched widely scattered points in an area bounded by the Isthmus of Panama, the Great Lakes, and the Atlantic and the Pacific oceans. His wife, Malinde Harriet Baker Butterfield, whom he married in 1822, bore nine children, including Daniel Butterfield, who became a distinguished Union general in the Civil War.

Upon his death on Nov. 14, 1869, Butterfield was hailed for his contributions to the general growth and development of New York State.

Further Reading

There is no biography of Butterfield. Considerable information on him can be found in a biography of his son: Julia Lorrillard Butterfield, ed., *A Biographical Memorial of General Daniel Butterfield* (1904). See also LeRoy Hafen, *The Overland Mail, 1849-1869* (1926); Edward Hungerford, *Wells Fargo: Advancing the American Frontier* (1949); and Noel M. Loomis, *Wells Fargo* (1968). □

Dietrich Buxtehude

The organ works and sacred vocal compositions of the Danish composer Dietrich Buxtehude (1637-1707) are the culmination of the North German school of composition in the 17th century.

Dietrich Buxtehude was born in either Holstein or Sweden (both were Danish territories at the time), the son of an organist. The family was of German extraction, and branches were located in various parts of Scandinavia, which had close cultural ties with Germany at the time. Buxtehude thus was exposed to the forms and styles typical of North German music.

Little is known of Buxtehude's early life, but he apparently received musical instruction from his father. He accepted positions as organist in 1657 at Helsingborg and in 1660 at Helsingör. On April 11, 1668, he succeeded the illustrious Franz Tunder to the prestigious post of organist at St. Mary's Church in Lübeck (marrying Tunder's daughter as one of the terms of succession) and remained in this post for the rest of his career.

Buxtehude was a truly inventive and imaginative composer in an era often marked by solid, workmanlike technique devoid of any profound inspiration. His extant works represent but a small portion of his production, and many of them exist only in secondary sources. Dating his work is close to impossible on any but stylistic grounds, and his flamboyant imagination led to a wide variety of stylistic treatment. Italian and South German music was known in his area, broadening the stock upon which he drew. With the growing emphasis of the time on individuality, he turned his back on authoritarian formulas and allowed his fiery imagination free rein.

Recent scholarship has shown that Buxtehude's sacred vocal works are, historically, his most important contribution, rather than the organ works as was previously thought. Few are liturgical. Most fall under the heading of cantata, if by this term one understands the earlier form as practiced by Tunder rather than the later genre represented by most of Johann Sebastian Bach's cantatas.

In 1673 Buxtehude established the famous *Abendmusiken,* or evening musicals, in St. Mary's; they took place from 4 to 5 P.M. on the five Sundays before Christmas. These performances included organ music as well as sacred works of a dramatic-allegorical nature for chorus, soloists, and orchestra; the bulk of the latter has disappeared.

Most of Buxtehude's 124 extant cantatas were probably written between 1676 and 1687. The solo portions exhibit operatic styles ranging from recitative to arias. There are also songlike pieces on lyric texts. Especially notable among the choral sections are the closing portions with closely imitative introductions, followed by fugal Alleluia or Amen sections. Throughout there is the strongest possible expression of the text content, achieved through the free exercise of musical fantasy. Buxtehude also wrote works based on melodies and texts of chorales (the traditional hymnody of Lutheranism), in some of which the melody is varied in each movement.

This wealth of expression made a profound impression on the young Johann Sebastian Bach, who in 1705 journeyed 200 miles on foot to hear Buxtehude's music and remained for 4 months. Thereafter Bach seems to have been determined to employ this expressive potential in church works.

Equally impressive for Bach must have been Buxtehude's organ music. Certainly the older composer comes closer than anyone else to Bach in the composition of the small-scale, subjective-interpretive chorale prelude (a free organ composition based on the melody of a Lutheran chorale, originally used to introduce congregational singing). This was a more southerly form. Buxtehude brought to its most advanced state the North German chorale fantasia, in which the chorale melody is so freely treated in a series of rhapsodic sections as to nearly disappear. For the most part his toccatas are in the then standard form, consisting of a sequence of diverse sections, including free fantasy, virtuoso pedal solos, and at least two fugues. Here, especially, his penchant for the daring and the unexpected comes strongly to the fore. There is also service music: Magnificats and Te Deums that could substitute for vocal performance and canzonas that were played during church services.

Undoubtedly a great deal of Buxtehude's keyboard and chamber music has been lost. The sonatas of 1696 cannot be his earliest attempts. His sonatas are somewhat retrospective, compared to the already-existing model of Arcangelo Corelli, and Buxtehude's keyboard suites follow the model of Johann Jakob Froberger. It is in the specifically North German forms that Buxtehude dominates and represents the climax of his era.

Further Reading

Buxtehude's importance is discussed in Manfred F. Bukofzer, *Music in the Baroque Era: From Monteverdi to Bach* (1947). Good background studies are Paul H. Lang, *Music in Western Civilization* (1941), and Donald J. Grout, *A History of Western Music* (1960).

Additional Sources

Snyder, Kerala J., *Dietrich Buxtehude, organist in Lübeck,* New York: Schirmer Books; London: Collier Macmillan, 1987. □

Richard Evelyn Byrd

Richard Evelyn Byrd (1888-1957), American aviator, explorer, and scientist, was the first man to fly over both poles and for his daring feats became one of America's genuine folk heroes.

Richard E. Byrd was born in Winchester, Va., on Oct. 25, 1888, into a distinguished Tidewater family. His early education included study at the Shenandoah Valley Military Academy and a trip around the world alone at the age of 13. He attended Virginia Military Institute, the University of Virginia, and the U.S. Naval Academy, graduating in 1912. At the academy Byrd established himself as a class leader and athlete, although leg injuries suffered in football threatened his military career.

After briefly retiring from active duty, Byrd returned to the service when the United States entered World War I. He requested assignment to the Navy's aviation division. In 1918 Byrd developed a plan to fly the Navy's trimotored NC-1 flying boat across the Atlantic. His wartime assignment, however, was as commander of U.S. Navy aviation forces in Canada, where a submarine patrol was maintained. Byrd worked on improving aerial navigation when neither land nor horizon was visible, and developed a "bubble" sextant and a drift indicator. After the war he took charge of the navigational preparations for a one-stop transatlantic flight of three Navy planes but was not himself permitted to make the May 1919 flight.

Exploration from the Air

Eight years later Byrd would make one of the early nonstop transatlantic flights; in the meantime he influenced flight development in other important ways. He successfully lobbied for legislation to establish a Bureau of Aeronautics in the Navy; and he commanded the Navy flying unit that accompanied Donald MacMillan's Arctic expedition of 1925, during which over 30,000 square miles of northern Greenland and Ellesmere Island were explored.

Convinced of the practicability of the airplane for polar exploration, in 1926 Byrd undertook a privately sponsored expedition to the North Pole. Flying from Kings Bay, Spitsbergen, Byrd and his copilot circled the North Pole on May 9, 1926. Byrd returned to the United States to a tumultuous reception and promotion to the rank of commander.

Byrd's new goal was to demonstrate the scientific and commercial value of multiengine planes on sustained flight over long distances. He entered the "transatlantic derby" of 1927, but the crash of his new plane during tests delayed his departure until after Charles Lindbergh's flight. His aviation experiences are detailed in his first book, *Skyward* (1928).

Antarctic Expeditions

Byrd's subsequent career centered on his Antarctic adventures. Buoyed by scientific and technological developments, he planned a large-scale exploration of Antarctica. Reaching the Bay of Whales in December 1928, Byrd estab-

lished his camp, Little America, on the Ross Ice Shelf. In constant radio communication with the outside world, he and his companions carried out their scientific studies and aerial surveys. On Nov. 28-29, 1929, Byrd and three companions successfully completed a hazardous flight to the South Pole and back, a distance of 1,560 miles, discovering several new mountain ranges and obtaining valuable geological, meteorological, and radiowave propagation data. When Byrd came home in 1930, he was showered with additional honors and awards, including promotion to the rank of rear admiral. His *Little America* (1930) is a full account of the expedition.

Byrd returned to Antarctica in 1933-1935. He spent 5 months in solitude at Advance Base, making careful meteorological and auroral observations. This expedition nearly cost him his life when he was stricken by carbon monoxide fumes. Rescued in August 1934, Byrd could not return to Little America II until 2 months later. He wrote about this expedition in *Discovery* (1935) and later in *Alone* (1938).

In 1939 the United States government sponsored its first Antarctic expedition in a century, with Adm. Byrd in charge. He made several flights over the continent, delineated hundreds of additional miles of coastline, and mapped mineral deposits. Further work in the Antarctic awaited the cessation of World War II, a conflict in which Byrd served with distinction.

In 1946-1947 Byrd led his fourth expedition to the Antarctic as part of the Navy's Operation High Jump. Thirteen ships and 4,000 men participated, photographing and mapping vast areas of the ice continent. Byrd again flew over the South Pole, dropping a packet containing flags of all the members of the United Nations. Byrd's final labors in Antarctica were made in Operation Deep Freeze (1955-1956) and in planning the United States Antarctic Program for the International Geophysical Year (1957-1958). He died in Boston on March 11, 1957, survived by his wife and four children. A scientist and inventor as well as a daring adventurer, Byrd had also lent his name and energy to many humanitarian and world peace organizations.

Further Reading

The best biography of Byrd is Edwin P. Hoyt, *The Last Explorer: The Adventures of Admiral Byrd* (1968), although it was compiled only from the public record and should be read in conjunction with other accounts. See particularly Fitzhugh Green, *Dick Byrd: Air Explorer* (1928); Charles J. V. Murphy, *Struggle: The Life and Exploits of Commander Richard E. Byrd* (1928); and the brief appreciation by Alfred Steinberg, *Admiral Richard E. Byrd* (1960). Walter B. Hayward, *The Last Continent of Adventure: A Narrative of Gallant Men and Bold Exploits in Antarctica* (1930), puts Byrd's early work in context. □

William Byrd

The English composer William Byrd (ca. 1543-1623) was one of the greatest polyphonists of his time. He also excelled in the composition of keyboard music, stage songs, and instrumental fantasias.

William Byrd was born in Lincolnshire, probably in 1543. Nothing is known of his boyhood except that he became a child of the Chapel Royal some time after 1550, moving then to London, where he was "bred up under Thomas Tallis." At the age of 20 Byrd received his first appointment, returning to his native shire as organist at Lincoln Cathedral. Within a few years he succeeded Robert Parsons as one of the gentlemen of the Chapel Royal. The records are unclear as to whether Byrd moved to Westminster at this time. In 1572, however, he was replaced at Lincoln Cathedral by Thomas Butler, whom he himself had chosen, and it is clear that at that time he moved to London, where he shared the post of organist with Tallis.

In 1568 Byrd married Juliana Birley; they had a son in 1569 and a daughter in 1572. It was during this period that he was charged with recusancy, for which he was troubled the rest of his life, and that he acquired the first of his leases, which were to embroil him in litigation from this time forward.

These were years of close professional association with Tallis, his former mentor and senior by some 40 years. Together they received in 1578 a license "to imprint any and so many as they will of set songe or songes in partes, either in English, Latine, Frenche, Italian or other tongues that may serve for musicke either in Church or chamber, or otherwise to be plaid or soong. . . . " This license, a virtual monopoly for music printing, passed to Byrd's sole ownership upon the death of Tallis in 1585. The proprietary fervor it inspired no doubt was a factor in the extraordinarily productive period which followed. During the next few years Byrd published no less than four major collections, all devoted entirely to his own works: *Psalmes, Sonets & Songs* (1588), *Songs of Sundrie Natures* (1589), *Cantiones sacrae I* (1589), and *Cantiones sacrae II* (1591).

The music in these, along with that available only in manuscript, such as the important keyboard collection "My Lady Neville's Book," reflects his esthetic position as a transitional figure between medieval and modern times. The very fact that these collections were composed and prepared for circulation in print furnishes one aspect of their modernity. And that the composer himself was launching these editions as a financial venture is another. Both these considerations relate to innovative features on the esthetic side, which in turn signalize several new developments in the musical culture of 17th-century England.

No hint of a new praxis appears in the title of the first collection, *Psalmes, Sonets & Songs of Sadness and Piety, Made into Musicke of Five Parts* (1588). However, Byrd did provide for a glimpse of contemporary procedures in the circulation of music with his expressed resolve to expose untrue copies of his works then abroad. All this, music printing was to change.

In the body of the collection, one of the upper parts of pieces in all three categories indicated in the title is marked "the first singing voice." Byrd probably composed all these as solo songs with viol accompaniment (we know that "Though Amaryllis dance in green" originated thus), then adapted the accompanying viol parts to the text in preparing these for publication. Presumably his motivation was to increase sales by appealing to a wider public, or at least to a greater number of performers. On the whole, though, the effect of this procedure was to bring Byrd's compositions into alignment with the Italian madrigal, by then new only in England, and they are rather stiff and unwieldy part-songs compared to the livelier polyphonic works of the Italians.

More evidence of Byrd's concern for marketability appears with the *Songs of Sundrie Natures, Some of Gravitie and Others of Myrth, Fit for All Companies and Voyces* (1589). And the title of the last set of secular part-songs, that of 1611, is even more explicit with its prescription for aleatory performance: *Psalmes, Songs & Sonnets: Some Solemne, Others Joyful, Framed to the Life of the Words: Fit for Voyces or Viols* In other words, both content and medium are arranged for the largest possible number of hearers or performers.

In the *Cantiones sacrae* Byrd clearly though tacitly went against the policy of the English Reformation, intended not only to remove the political hegemony of Rome from England but also to expunge Latin from the liturgy. But in the two books of *Gradualia* which marked his next flurry of editorial activity, he publicly avowed the recusancy for which he and members of his family had already been called to account numerous times.

The first book of *Gradualia* we know only from the second edition of 1610. The second book, published in 1607 and also appearing in a second edition in 1610, consists of 43 motets for four, five, and six voices. Again, these motets are generally shorter than those in the *Cantiones sacrae* collections and are obviously intended for use by those who sought formal musical expression of their Catholic faith. That he would have dared publish two such books, particularly just after the Gunpowder Plot in 1605, which raised such a wave of anti-Catholic sentiment, testifies to the strength of his position at court and to the excellence of his general reputation as the "father of English music." Musically, these books represent the work of the greatest English polyphonic master of the 16th century.

The same may be said of his more than 60 English anthems, some being his own adaptations of Latin motets; of his 50 stage songs; of the keyboard works in the "Fitzwilliam Virginal Book," in "My Lady Neville's Book," and in the printed collection *Parthenia;* and, not least, of his miscellaneous canons, rounds, and music for strings.

Further Reading

The standard biography of Byrd is Edmund H. Fellowes, *William Byrd* (1936; 2d ed. 1948), which gives a full list of sources and discusses the main forms and the style in which Byrd composed. It is, however, out of date, as is Frank Howes, *William Byrd* (1928). Good background material is available in Paul Henry Lang, *Music in Western Civilization* (1941); Gustave Reese, *Music in the Renaissance* (1954; rev. ed. 1959); Jack A. Westrup, *An Introduction to Musical History* (1955); and Donald J. Grout, *A History of Western Music* (1960).

Additional Sources

Howes, Frank Stewart, *William Byrd,* Westport, Conn.: Greenwood Press, 1978. □

William Byrd

Colonial planter and merchant William Byrd (1652-1704) founded one of the most remarkable and enduring political dynasties in America.

The first of several generations bearing the name, William Byrd emigrated from England to the New World as a young man, fortified by an extensive inheritance from an uncle which permitted him to purchase a large estate on the James River (near modern Richmond, Va.). Later, as he became increasingly prominent, he removed to the "Old Dominion's" western frontier. In 1676 he jeopardized his growing economic and political position by joining briefly in Bacon's Rebellion against the troops of royal governor William Berkeley. He had undoubtedly shared in the frustration with the government's inability to prevent depredations by native peoples that had led to the rebellion.

However, connections and wealth helped to smooth over Byrd's involvement with Bacon, and a few years later he sat in Virginia's House of Burgesses, in 1683 moving up to the more elite Council of State—testimony to his growing prominence. He eventually served as auditor general of the colony and president of its council, but it was not in politics that he made his greatest mark.

From his plantation on the James, and later from Westover, his frontier estate, Byrd traded with the Native Americans, parlaying his inheritance into one of the great fortunes of colonial Virginia and setting the keystone for a prolific and powerful political dynasty. Pioneering and exploring even as he traded with the Native Americans, Byrd was one of a small band of white men to move beyond the Blue Ridge in the 17th century. Indeed, he pushed across the Allegheny Divide into Kentucky at the head of a trading company a full century before Daniel Boone.

For Virginians like Byrd, moreover, the Native Americans offered a somewhat risky but enormously profitable wellspring of trade, at a time when such trade was limited to those licensed by the royal governor. By the 1680s Byrd was sending pack trains far into hostile country to exchange pots, pans, guns, and rum for furs and hides that were quickly and profitably sold at Virginia's flourishing eastern ports.

So extensive was his knowledge of the Native Americans that Byrd frequently represented the colony at treaty-making ceremonies. This activity, in turn, led him to a high rank in the Virginia militia. Increasing wealth, meanwhile, opened other economic doors; eventually he augmented his fortune in several ways that became traditional for future colonial Byrds: he was part owner of several merchantmen, a well-known slave dealer, a planter of tobacco, and a dealer in public securities. By the time he died on Dec. 4, 1704, he had firmly established both his family and fortune.

Further Reading

The standard source on Byrd is the biographical sketch in *The Writings of "Colonel William Byrd . . . ,"* edited by John Spencer Bassett (1901). See also Louis B. Wright, *The Cultural Life of the American Colonies, 1607-1763* (1957), and Wesley Frank Craven, *The Colonies in Transition, 1660-1713* (1967). □

William Byrd II

The Virginia diarist and government official William Byrd II (1674-1744) revealed much about 18th-century American life in his important, charming, and witty diaries.

William Byrd II was the son of William Byrd, whose inheritance had enabled him to purchase valuable Virginia lands at the age of 18, and of Mary Horsmanden Byrd, daughter of a Cavalier gentleman. Born on March 28, 1674, near what is now Richmond, Va., the younger Byrd was educated at Felsted Grammar School in Essex, served as an apprentice in business in Holland and London, and studied law at the Middle Temple. He was admitted to the bar in 1695 after 3 years of study. At the Middle Temple, Byrd's contemporaries included the dramatists William Congreve and William Wycherly. Byrd also came to know notable men of science, such as Sir Robert Southwell and Hans Sloane. In 1696 he was elected to membership in the Royal Society, and a paper published soon afterward demonstrated his scientific abilities.

In the same year Byrd returned to Virginia, where he was elected to the House of Burgesses, but the next year he was back in London, representing the governor of Virginia and later the Virginia Council as agent. This time he remained until 1704, when his father died, leaving him not only his lands, including the site of Richmond and the 1,400-acre Westover plantation, but also his office of receiver general. In 1706 Byrd married Lucy Parke. After the death of his wife's father he made the mistake of seeking to acquire his lands and as a result acquired immense debts.

In time Byrd became a member of the governor's council and commander in chief of the Charles City and Henrico County militias. His life, public and private, during these years is well documented in a secret diary dating from 1709. From it emerges a vivid portrait of Byrd as a healthy extrovert interested in everything from books (his library eventually numbered more than 3,600 items) to the welfare of his many tenants.

In 1715 Byrd returned to England on business. The next year he sent for his wife, who died of smallpox soon after her arrival. She left him two daughters, whom he brought to

England. Another secret diary, now published like the earlier, demonstrates that Byrd took advantage of the opportunities London offered for sexual adventures. He also served again as agent for Virginia. Despite strenuous efforts, he did not find the wealthy wife he was looking for, though he remained in England until 1719. Another visit in 1721 brought him a wife, Maria Taylor, who in time gave him four children but no fortune. He returned to America in 1726 and remained there until his death on Aug. 26, 1744.

Byrd's cultivation of writing over the years is demonstrated by his care in letter writing. His most famous contribution to literature is his *History of the Dividing Line Betwixt Virginia and North Carolina Run in the Year of Our Lord 1728,* first published in 1841. It is a witty, frank, and informative narrative. (Another version, *The Secret History of the Line,* is inferior.) Byrd's other writings include *A Journey to the Land of Eden* and *A Progress to the Mines,* both also published in 1841.

Further Reading

Written without knowledge of the diaries, Richmond C. Beatty, *William Byrd of Westover* (1932), is the only full-length biography. The best brief biography is by Louis B. Wright in Byrd's *The London Diary* (*1717-1721*) *and Other Writings,* edited by Wright and Marion Tinling (1958). A sketch of Byrd as man of letters appears in Wright's edition of Byrd's *Prose Works* (1966).

Additional Sources

Lockridge, Kenneth A., *The diary and life of William Byrd II of Virginia, 1674-1744,* Chapel Hill: Published for the Institute of Early American History and Culture, Williamsburg, Va., by the University of North Carolina Press, 1987.

Perceval, John, Earl, *The English travels of Sir John Percival and William Byrd II: the Percival diary of 1701,* Columbia: University of Missouri Press, 1989. □

Jane Byrne

Jane Byrne (born 1934) won the most astounding political upset in Chicago's history when she unseated incumbent Michael A. Bilandic in the 1979 Democratic primary and went on to become the first woman mayor of Chicago.

Born in Chicago on May 24, 1934, Jane Margaret (Burke) Byrne showed little interest in politics until the 1960 presidential election. Raised on the north side of Chicago by her father Edward Burke, who was vice president of Inland Steel, and her mother, Katherine Burke, Byrne attended parochial schools. Upon graduation from Saint Scholastic High School, Byrne enrolled in St. Mary-of-the-Woods in Terre Haute, Indiana. On completion of her freshman year she transferred to Barat College in Lake Forest, Illinois. She graduated in 1965 with a bachelor's degree in chemistry and biology. Jane married William P. Byrne, a marine aviator, soon afterward. A little more than one year after the birth of their only child on December 31, 1957, Edward crashed his plane near a naval air station in Chicago and sustained fatal injuries.

Byrne's involvement in politics stemmed partly from that crash. Upon hearing John F. Kennedy talk about the loss of life due to the Cold War, she joined his campaign for president and became secretary-treasurer for the presidential contender's Chicago headquarters. Her efforts impressed the Kennedy organization so much that they offered her a job in Washington, but Byrne decided to remain in Chicago and pursue graduate studies at the University of Illinois, Chicago Circle Campus. Having taught for a while, she planned to pursue a teaching career, but her continued interest in politics and her Kennedy association led to a meeting with Mayor Richard Daley, who urged her to work for his organization. Thus began a political relationship which deeply affected Byrne's future.

After satisfying Daley that she worked hard at the ward level, in 1964 the mayor appointed Byrne to a job in the Head Start program. A year later he promoted her to a job with the Chicago Committee on Urban Opportunity. During this period she studied Chicago politics and became a fiercely loyal Daley supporter. He rewarded her in 1968 by naming her the first woman member of his cabinet. As commissioner of sales, weights, and measures, Byrne attempted to uproot corruption and return her office to its original purpose, consumer protection.

Although never accepted by the party regulars, Byrne served as delegate to the 1972 Democratic National Con-

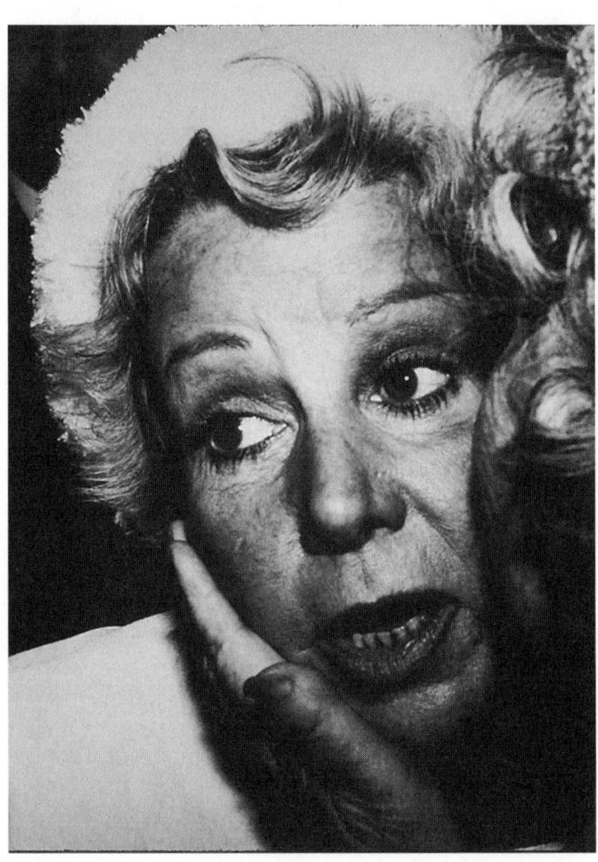

vention and chaired the resolutions committee for the Democratic National Committee the following year. In 1975 Daley named Byrne co-chairperson of the powerful Cook County Democratic Central Committee, much to the distress of many Democratic leaders.

When Daley died of a heart attack in December of 1976, Byrne's political future appeared clouded. Soon after Daley's passing, party regulars stripped Byrne of the Central Committee chair. And the riff between Byrne and the local Democratic Party "machine" widened after Byrne accused the new mayor, Michael A. Bilandic, of not looking out for the public interest and "greasing" a nearly 12 percent cabfare increase for the city. Shortly after hearing those charges, Bilandic fired Byrne from her job as commissioner of sales.

Byrne responded by announcing her decision to run for the Democratic nomination for mayor. Campaigning with funds mostly donated by her new husband, Jay McMullen, and lacking an efficient political organization, Byrne's chances of winning seemed nearly impossible. Even her major campaign issue, the taxicab fare increase, lost its potency when a federal grand jury found no wrongdoing. But snow, which started to fall on New Year's Eve, 1979, gave her an issue to win the mayoralty.

The heavy January and February snow brought Chicago to a near standstill, interrupting public transportation and garbage collection. The inability of the mayor to devise and implement an adequate snow removal plan angered the city's residents. Charging that under Bilandic Chicago was no longer "the city that works," the underdog rode the issue to victory. A break in the bad weather permitted a record turnout to the Democratic primary and secured Byrne the upset victory. In the general election the following April, heavily Democratic Chicago gave Byrne a landslide with 82 percent of the popular vote over Republican Wallace Johnson. Her victory, which included a sweep of all 50 wards, gave her the largest margin of votes in the history of Chicago's mayoral contests.

Byrne's triumph did not mark the end of the powerful Democratic organization, nor did it bring a new era of tranquillity to Chicago politics. Soon after her primary victory Byrne started mending ties with the organization, and after becoming mayor in April she dismissed many reformers who had worked diligently for her election. Furthermore, her acerbity and her politicizing of the mayor's office alienated many former supporters and a large portion of the press. Finally, the very magnitude of problems her administration faced in areas such as fire protection, education, and declining revenues made controversy almost inevitable. Always one for the spotlight, Byrne captured the imagination of many Chicagoans when she moved into the deteriorated Cabrini-Green public housing project in March of 1981. Her stay not only emphasized the horrible conditions many were forced to live with, but helped bring improved services to an area largely neglected by city workers.

Although actions like the Cabrini move increased the mayor's popularity, they were not enough for her to win the Democratic renomination in 1983. In a three-way race, Harold Washington, a Black Congressman, defeated Byrne and the machine's candidate Richard M. Daley, Jr. Unwilling to admit defeat, Byrne initiated a write-in campaign for the general election but called it off for lack of support. Washington won election as mayor, but his political struggles with a hostile city council encouraged Byrne to look forward to the 1987 election.

But in the 1987 Democratic primaries, Byrne lost to Washington again. She then gave the incumbent her support in his ultimately successful bid for reelection. In March 1988, she ran for clerk of the Cook County Circuit Court, but was again defeated in her party's primary, this time by Aurelia M. Pucinski. Once again on November 12, 1990, Byrne announced her candidacy in the 1991 Chicago mayoral elections, and once again she lost in the February 26, 1991 Democratic primary. Richard Daley, Jr., son of the former mayor, won the election. In 1992, Byrne published a mayoral memoir entitled *My Chicago,* which received favorable reviews from both *Publishers Weekly* and *Library Journal.*

Further Reading

Two biographies which focus on Byrne's pre-mayoral years are Kathleen W. FitzGerald, *Brass: Jane Byrne and the Pursuit of Power* (1981) and Bill and Lori Granger, *Fighting Jane: Mayor Jane and the Chicago Machine* (1980). Byrne told her own story in 1992's *My Chicago.* For more on Byrne's relationship with Daley, see Milton L. Rakove, *We Don't Want Nobody Sent: An Oral History of the Daley Years* (1979). Two books which explore Byrne's role in the 1983 election are Paul Kleppner, *Chicago Divided: The Making of a Black Mayor* (1984) and Melvin G. Holli and Paul M. Green, *The Making of the Mayor of Chicago 1983* (1984.) Other books which refer to Byrne's administration in a larger discussion of Chicago racial politics are *Fire On the Prairie: Chicago's Harold Washington and the Politics of Race* by Gary Rivlin (1992) and *Bitter Fruit: Black Politics and the Chicago Machine* by William J. Grimshaw (1992.) □

James Francis Byrnes

The American public official James Francis Byrnes (1879-1972) was a prominent political figure for some 40 years, serving under presidents Franklin Roosevelt and Harry S. Truman.

James F. Byrnes was born to immigrant Irish parents in Charleston, S.C., on May 2, 1879. His early years were difficult, for his father died a few weeks before his birth. His mother, left with two young children and almost penniless, took up dressmaking to support her family. To help, James left school when he was 14 to work as an office boy in a local law firm. Taught shorthand by his mother, he won a competition and obtained a job as a stenographer in the Second Circuit Court of South Carolina in 1900. In his free time he studied law and 3 years later was admitted to the South Carolina bar.

Byrnes opened his own law office in Aiken. He found few paying clients, however, and continued in his job as a court reporter. He also bought the *Aiken Journal and Review,* but his career in journalism was brief. In 1908 he was elected a circuit solicitor (an office equivalent to that of a prosecuting or district attorney) and sold his interest in the newspaper to his partner. Two years later he was elected to his first term in Congress. Before entering public life, Byrnes had married Maude Busch of Aiken in May 1906.

In 1911 Byrnes entered the House of Representatives, remaining until 1925, serving on the House Committee on Roads, the Banking and Currency Committee, and the Appropriations Committee. These experiences, together with his personal qualities, contributed to his political success. Byrnes was a genial and charming person, with a sense of humor, who quickly mastered the game of politics. "The art of legislating," he later observed," is the art of intelligent compromise."

Defeated for the Senate in 1924, Byrnes was elected in 1930. A realistic politician, a southerner, and a loyal Democrat, he supported Franklin Roosevelt in the election of 1932 and was tapped as a "brain truster" for budgetary matters. Byrnes strongly promoted New Deal legislation in the Senate during Roosevelt's first term, but after 1937 he adopted a more conservative position. He loyally defended the President's foreign policy, however, especially in the extension of trade agreements and defense appropriations. In 1940 Roosevelt considered Byrnes for the vice-presidential nomination but decided in favor of Henry Wallace. Following his third-term reelection, the President appointed Byrnes associate justice to the Supreme Court (June 1941).

But World War II was at hand, and Byrnes was on the Supreme Court for only 16 months before Roosevelt made him director of the Office of Economic Mobilization and, in the next year, head of the six-man War Mobilization Board. Byrnes now had considerable authority in the management of domestic affairs, while Roosevelt concentrated on the military conduct of the war. Byrnes's administrative performance was so outstanding that he became popularly known as "Assistant President." Roosevelt again considered Byrnes as a vice-presidential candidate in 1944 but chose Harry S. Truman. Byrnes, however, accompanied Roosevelt to the Yalta Conference in February 1945, and his detailed shorthand notes proved to be very helpful to President Truman. Shortly after Roosevelt's death in 1945, Truman appointed Byrnes secretary of state, a post he held until January 1947.

Byrnes's tenure coincided with the collapse of the wartime cooperation with the Soviet Union and the onset of the cold war. As secretary of state, he tried unsuccessfully to reconcile the conflicting interests between the United States and the Soviet Union. To satisfy the Soviet Union's demand for security against Germany, he proposed a four-power treaty of alliance to keep Germany demilitarized for 25 years; but the Kremlin rejected this offer. His effort to resolve the atomic energy issue between the two powers in 1945—he suggested the exchange of atomic information without absolute and effective agreement on inspection and control—met with opposition in Congress. Although unable to obtain solutions on either issue, Byrnes managed in 1946 to work out compromise peace treaties with the Soviet Union for Italy, Romania, Bulgaria, Hungary, and Finland. On Sept. 6, 1946, he delivered his famous Stuttgart speech, which called for the creation of an autonomous democratic German state. Increasingly, Byrnes adopted a tough posture toward the Soviet Union, but disagreements with President Truman led to his resignation on Jan. 10, 1947.

Following his departure from the Cabinet, Byrnes became associated with a Washington law firm, but in 1950 he ran for governor of South Carolina and was elected by an overwhelming majority. As governor, he fulfilled his campaign pledge to suppress the Ku Klux Klan in the state, but he resisted the efforts of the Federal government to desegregate public schools. Byrnes retired in 1955 and died on April 9, 1972, in Columbia, S.C.

Further Reading

There are no biographies of Byrnes. The most important sources on his life are his two memoirs, *Speaking Frankly* (1947) and *All in One Lifetime* (1958). The best account of Byrnes's tenure as secretary of state is the chapter by Richard D. Burns in Norman A. Graebner, ed., *An Uncertain Tradition: American Secretaries of State in the Twentieth Century* (1961). A brief, impressionistic vignette is in Raymond Moley, *27 Masters of Politics: In a Personal Perspective* (1949). □

George Gordon Noel Byron

The English poet George Gordon Noel Byron, 6th Baron Byron (1788-1824), was one of the most important figures of the romantic movement. Because of his works, active life, and physical beauty he came to be considered the personification of the romantic poet-hero.

George Gordon Noel Byron was born on Jan. 22, 1788, into a family of fast-decaying nobility. His lame foot, the absence of any fatherly authority in the household after Captain "Mad Jack" Byron's death in 1791, the contempt of his aristocratic relatives for the impoverished widow and her son, his Calvinistic up-bringing at the hands of a Scottish nurse, the fickleness and stupidity of his mother—all conspired to hurt the pride and sensitiveness of the boy. This roused in him a need for self-assertion which he soon sought to gratify in three main directions: love, poetry, and action.

On the death of his granduncle in 1798, Byron inherited the title and estate. After 4 years at Harrow (1801-1805), he went to Trinity College, Cambridge, where he became conscious for the first time of the discrepancy between the lofty aspirations of idealism and the petty realities of experience. "I took my gradations in the vices with great promptitude," he later reminisced, "but they were not to my taste." His obstinate quest for some genuine passion among the frail women of this world accounts for the crowded catalog of his amours.

Early Works

In 1807 Byron's juvenilia were collected under the title *Hours of Idleness;* although the little book exhibited only the milder forms of romantic *Weltschmerz,* it was harshly criticized by the *Edinburgh Review.* The irate author counterattacked in *English Bards and Scotch Reviewers* (1809), the first manifestation of a gift for satire and a sarcastic wit which single him out among the major English romantics, and which he may have owed to his aristocratic outlook and his classical education.

In 1809 a 2-year trip to the Mediterranean countries provided material for the first two cantos of *Childe Harold's Pilgrimage.* Their publication in 1812 earned Byron instant glory, as they combined the more popular features of the late-18th-century romanticism: colorful descriptions of exotic nature, disillusioned meditations on the vanity of earthly things, a lyrical exaltation of freedom, and above all, the new hero, handsome and lonely, somberly mysterious, yet strongly impassioned for all his weariness with life.

Social Life

While his fame was spreading, Byron was busy shocking London high society. After his affairs with Lady Caroline Lamb and Lady Oxford, his incestuous and adulterous love for his half sister Augusta not only made him a reprobate, but also crystallized the sense of guilt and doom to which he had always been prone. From then on, the theme of incest was to figure prominently in his writings, starting with the epic tales that he published between 1812 and 1816: *The Giaour, The Bride of Abydos, The Corsair, Lara, The Siege of Corinth,* and *Parisina.* Incestuous love, criminal although genuine and irresistible, was a suitable metaphor for the tragic condition of man, who is cursed by God, rebuked by society, and hated by himself because of sins for which he is not responsible. The tales, therefore, add a new dimension of depth to the Byronic hero: in his total alienation he now actively assumes the tragic fatality which turns natural instinct into unforgivable sin, and he deliberately takes his rebellious stance as an outcast against all accepted notions of the right order of things.

While thus seeking relief in imaginative exploration of his own tortured mind, Byron had been half hoping to find peace and reconciliation in a more settled life. But his marriage to Anna Isabella Milbanke (Jan. 1, 1815) soon proved a complete failure, and she left him after a year. London society could have ignored the peculiarities of Byron's private life, but a satire against the Prince Regent, "Stanzas to a Lady Weeping," which he had appended to *The Corsair,* aroused hysterical abuse from the Tories, in whose hands his separation from his wife became an efficient weapon. On April 25, 1816, Byron had to leave his native country, never to return.

His Travels

In Switzerland, Byron spent several months in the company of the poet Shelley, resuming an agitated and unenthusiastic affair with the latter's sister-in-law, Clare Clairmont. Under Shelley's influence he read Wordsworth and imbibed the high-flown but uncongenial spirituality which permeates the third canto of *Childe Harold.* But *The Prisoner of Chillon* and Byron's first drama, *Manfred,* took the Byronic hero to a new level of inwardness: his greatness now lies in the steadfast refusal to bow to the hostile powers that oppress him, whether he discovers new selfhood in his very dereliction or seeks in self-destruction the fulfillment of his assertiveness.

In October 1816 Byron left for Italy and settled in Venice, where he spent many days and nights in unprecedented debauchery. His compositions of 1817, however, show signs of a new outlook. The fourth canto of *Childe Harold* does not reject the cosmic pessimism of *Manfred,* but the mood of shrill revolt is superseded by a tone of resigned acceptance, and sizable sections of the poem are devoted to the theme of political freedom and national independence. Equally significant of Byron's renewed ability to face the world in laughter rather than in anger is the witty, good-humored satire of *Beppo,* which should be considered a preparation for *Don Juan,* begun in September 1818.

Spontaneous maturation had thus paved the way for the healing influence of Teresa Guiccioli, Byron's last love, whom he met in April 1819. The poet had at last begun to come to terms with his desperate conception of life, to the extent of being able to debunk all shams and to parody all posturing, including his own, in *Don Juan,* the unfinished masterpiece on which he was to work till the end of his life. But this new balance also found serious utterance in *Cain,* the best of the plays that he wrote in 1821. It is a closely argued dramatic restatement of Byron's lasting creed that as the universe is swayed by a loveless God, the only greatness to which man can aspire lies in his foredoomed struggle for reason and justice. *Marino Faliero* illustrates the same pattern in the field of action, exalting the selflessness of the man who sacrifices his life in the service of popular freedom.

It is characteristic of Byron's integrity that he increasingly sought to translate his ideas into action, repeatedly voicing the more radical Whig viewpoint in the House of Lords in 1812-1813, running real risks to help the Italian Carbonari in 1820-1821, and collaborating with Leigh Hunt in launching the *Liberal* in 1822. His early poetry had contributed to sensitizing the European mind to the plight of Greece under the Turkish yoke. In 1824 Byron joined the Greek liberation fighters at Missolonghi, where he died of malarial fever on April 19.

Further Reading

While Byron's tumultuous life has inspired many biographers, the standard work is Leslie A. Marchand, *Byron: A Biography* (3 vols., 1957). Byron's intriguing personality and his ambiguous ideological position are discussed in William J. Calvert, *Byron: Romantic Paradox* (1935); Edward Wayne Marjarum, *Byron as Skeptic and Believer* (1938); Ernest J. Lovell, *Byron, the Record of a Quest: Studies in a Poet's Concept and Treatment of Nature* (1949); and G. Wilson Knight, *Lord Byron: Christian Virtues* (1953).

General critical introductions are Herbert E. Read, *Byron* (1951); Paul West, *Byron and the Spoiler's Art* (1960); Paul West, ed., *Byron: A Collection of Critical Essays* (1963); Leslie A. Marchand, *Byron's Poetry: A Critical Introduction* (1965); and W. Paul Elledge, *Byron and the Dynamics of Metaphor* (1968).

No full-scale study of Byron's drama has appeared since Samuel C. Chew, *The Dramas of Lord Byron* (1915). However, much attention has been devoted to *Don Juan,* especially by Paul Graham Trueblood in *The Flowering of Byron's Genius: Studies in Byron's Don Juan* (1945) and by Elizabeth French Boyd in *Byron's Don Juan: A Critical Study* (1945).

For Byron's influence, William Ellery Leonard, *Byron and Byronism in America* (1905), and Samuel C. Chew, *Byron in England: His Fame and After-Fame* (1924), have not been superseded. For general background information see Ian R. J. Jack, *English Literature: 1815-1832* (1963). □

C

James Branch Cabell

The American essayist and writer of romantic fiction James Branch Cabell (1879-1958) played an important part in the battle against sexual taboos in American literature during the 1920s.

James Branch Cabell was born in Richmond, Va., into an aristocratic "Old Dominion" family. He graduated from William and Mary College in 1898, having taught French and Greek there. His first book, *The Eagle's Shadow* (1904), was a romance attacking contemporary materialism. However, he achieved greater success with *The Line of Love* (1905), *Gallantry* (1907), and *Chivalry* (1909), romantic tales of disillusionment set in the past. Both Mark Twain and Theodore Roosevelt praised the first of this series.

Cabell's most productive and popular period came in the 1920s with the continuation of his "Biography of the Life of Manuel." This saga chronicled the career of the pivotal character, Don Manuel, and the history of seven generations of his descendants. *The Soul of Melicent* (1913), revised as *Domnei* in 1920, was part of the saga, followed by *Jurgen* (1919), *Figures of Earth* (1921), *The High Place* (1923), *The Silver Stallion* (1926), *Something about Eve* (1927), *The White Robe* (1928), and *The Way of Ecben* (1929).

Cabell's best-known and most typical work was *Jurgen,* the story of a middle-aged pawnbroker wandering through a mythical realm known as Poictesme. When his youth is miraculously restored, Jurgen travels through other imaginary lands searching for "justice." In depicting these countries and the hero's adventures in them, Cabell satirized many contemporary beliefs and attitudes. As he recounted Jurgen's love affairs, he used Freudian symbols to make fun of sexual mores.

The guardians of American morality were outraged and acted to suppress the book. A hotly contested and widely publicized trial followed; sales of the book soared. Cabell became famous and his novel went through many editions. The publicity also increased the sales of his other books. Cabell fought hard to free literature from rigid values imposed by puritanical society, and for his forthrightness he was much admired. By 1932, however, Cabell's fame had waned, and his later books were not successful.

In his volumes of criticism, such as *Beyond Life* (1919), Cabell expounded the theory that fiction should allegorically interpret a dream life superior to sordid and meaningless actuality, thereby enlarging mankind's visions.

Further Reading

An 18-volume edition of *The Works of James Branch Cabell* (1927-1930) was published, but no collected edition has added books published after 1930. Isadore Rosenbaum Brussel, *A Bibliography of the Writings of James Branch Cabell* (1932) is also incomplete. A biographical and critical study which lists later books and perceptively surveys Cabell's career is Joe Lee Davis, *James Branch Cabell* (1962). Also illuminating are Arvin R. Wells, *Jesting Moses: A Study of Cabellian Comedy* (1962), and Desmond Tarrant, *James Branch Cabell: The Dream and the Reality* (1967).

Additional Sources

MacDonald, Edgar E., *James Branch Cabell and Richmond-in-Virginia,* Jackson: University Press of Mississippi, 1993. □

Étienne Cabet

Étienne Cabet (1788-1856) was a French radical whose utopian visions led him to found a community called Icaria in the United States.

Etienne Cabet was born on Jan. 1, 1788, in Dijon; his father was a cooper. After an excellent general education he studied medicine, then changed to law. He gained a reputation as a talented and eloquent lawyer in Dijon, but he was known also as an advocate of causes unpopular with the monarchy. By 1825, having lost his privileges in the courts of Dijon, Cabet had moved to Paris.

Cabet's involvement with republican opponents of the Bourbon monarchy grew bolder. He became a director of the Carbonari, a secret revolutionary society which had found its way from Naples into France. He headed an insurrectionary committee during the July Revolution of 1830, which resulted in the abdication of the last Bourbon king. It did not, however, result simply in republicanism. Instead, Louis Philippe ascended to "a throne surrounded by republican institutions," and in 1831 the new monarch, as part of his strategy to pacify the radicals, appointed Cabet to the post of procurer general of Corsica. But Cabet was too uncompromising to stay in favor long and was removed from office. He was then elected to the Chamber of Deputies. He also established a newspaper to give voice to the opinions of the radicals. Faced with intrigue and agitation, the administration adopted a course of repression. Cabet was given a choice between imprisonment and exile. He took asylum in London.

Away from the rapid pace of events in France, Cabet found time for reflection. He met the socialist Robert Dale Owen. Cabet gave up his faith in political reform and turned his imagination to new forms of social organization. In 1839 he published a fictional account of the travels of an English nobleman in a distant commonwealth named Icaria, after the heroic philosopher Icar who had led its successful revolution. The novel became a best seller. Returning to France, Cabet capitalized on its success with newspapers, magazines, and books publicizing the secrets of communal success in Icaria. He was neither a systematic nor a practical thinker. But by 1847 adherents of his doctrines reportedly numbered 400,000, and Cabet proposed a scheme for setting up his own Icaria in America. On Owen's advice Cabet acquired a million acres in Texas.

The first group of nearly 600 settlers found they had been swindled. The land was poor, isolated, and badly scattered in lots, rather than grouped in one large tract. Their discouragement abated, however, when they learned that the Mormons had abandoned the community of Nauvoo in Illinois. Cabet led the Icarians there in 1849. Still there were difficulties. French enthusiasts drifted away, and there was repeated criticism of the Paris office and Madame Cabet. Cabet returned to France to defend himself against charges of fraud. Then, in 1854, he became an American citizen. At the outset his experiment in forming a commune had seemed promising. Many of his followers were skilled French craftsmen, and the community had acquired a mill, library, printing press, distillery, and schools. But factionalism threatened their dreams.

Cabet was getting older and more dictatorial. He became critical of the morality of some Icarians, encouraged spying on other members, and would not listen to criticism of his economic doctrines. Opposition to his leadership grew. More democratic forms of government were demanded than Cabet, once so radical in his republicanism, would allow. In 1856, when Cabet refused to recognize the results of an election, he was himself expelled from Icaria. He took 180 disciples with him to St. Louis, where on Nov. 8, 1856, he was stricken with apoplexy and died. Icarian experiments on a smaller scale continued throughout the 19th century.

Further Reading

The most important books about Cabet are in French, the best being Jules Prudhommeaux, *Icarie et son fondateur, Étienne Cabet* (1907). A full-length study in English is Albert Shaw, *Icaria: A Chapter in the History of Communism* (1884). For background information and a good, brief chapter on Cabet's adventures see Mark Holloway, *Heavens on Earth: Utopian Communities in America, 1680-1880* (1951; 2d ed. 1966).

Additional Sources

Johnson, Christopher H., *Utopian communism in France: Cabet and the Icarians, 1839-1851,* Ithaca, N.Y.: Cornell University Press, 1974. □

Álvar Núñez Cabeza de Vaca

Álvar Núñez Cabeza de Vaca (ca. 1490-ca. 1557) was a Spanish explorer. Marooned on the Texas coast, he wandered for 8 years in a land no European had ever seen. His account is the earliest description of the American Southwest.

Álvar Núñez Cabeza de Vaca was born into a distinguished family in Jerez de la Frontera. His strange name, literally "head of a cow," was won by a maternal ancestor, Martin Alhaja, who showed King Sancho of Navarre a pass marked with a cow's skull. Use of this pass enabled Sancho to win the famous battle of Las Navas de Tolosa against the Moors in 1212.

Raised by his paternal grandfather, Pedro de Vera, one of the conquerors and governor of the Canary Islands, Cabeza de Vaca joined the Spanish army in 1511 and served in Italy, Spain, and Navarre. In 1527 he joined the Florida expedition of Pánfilo de Narváez as treasurer and chief constable. When the party landed in Florida in April 1528, Narváez unwisely split his land from his sea forces and led an expedition inland. Upon their return to the coast in August, they discovered the ships had left for Cuba. Desperately short of supplies and harassed by hostile Amerinds, the Spaniards built small boats and set sail along the Gulf coast, hoping to reach Mexico.

The voyage was a nightmare. There was little food or water, and the small flotilla was beset by storms. In November 1528, the tiny fleet was wrecked on Galveston Island. Many of the men were lost at sea, and most of the others died during the winter from cold and exposure. Captured and enslaved by the Karankawa tribe, Cabeza de Vaca managed to survive. In 1534, along with Alonso del Castillo, Andrés Dorantes, and the Moor Estevánico, he escaped and headed for Mexico. For 2 years the Spaniards lived by their wits, trading with wandering tribes and gaining a reputation as healers and medicine men. Their exact route is unknown, but modern scholars believe they wandered along the Texas coast to the Río Grande and turned first north and then west across present-day Texas and northern Mexico. Finally, in March 1536 the group encountered a small party of Spaniards near Culiacán in western Mexico.

After reporting to Viceroy Antonio de Mendoza in Mexico City, Cabeza de Vaca returned to Spain, where he sought a new post. In 1540 he became governor and captain general of Río de la Plata (Paraguay). During his 4 years in South America he made a 1,000-mile march into the interior, opening previously unexplored territory. Denounced by his subordinates, Cabeza de Vaca returned to Spain in 1544 as a prisoner, but later most of the charges against him were rescinded. He spent his remaining years writing and publishing the story of his remarkable exploits in the New World, *Los naufragios* (The Shipwrecked).

Further Reading

There are several translations of Cabeza de Vaca's Texas adventures, of which the best are Fanny Bandelier, *The Journey of Álvar Núñez Cabeza de Vaca* (1905; repr. 1964), and "The Narrative of Álvar Núñez Cabeza de Vaca" in Frederick W. Hodge, ed., *Spanish Explorers in the Southern United States* (1907). An excellent biography is Morris Bishop, *The Odyssey of Cabeza de Vaca* (1933). See also Cleve Hallenbeck, *Álvar Núñez Cabeza de Vaca* (1940), and John Upton Terrell, *Journey into Darkness* (1964). □

Antonio Cabezón

The Spanish organ composer Antonio Cabezón (1510-1566) was blind. But the conciseness, logic, drive, and consistency of his splendid "Obras de música" bespeak an interior vision of each piece in totality that sets him apart from all contemporary keyboard composers.

The supposition that Antonio Cabezón derived at least partially from Jewish ancestry, because he was born at Castrillo de Matajudios (near Burgos), remains unproved. Before the age of 16 he lost his sight. He studied organ at Palencia Cathedral, probably with Garcia de Baeza, and in 1526 was appointed organist to Isabel of

Portugal, who became Emperor Charles V's wife that year. About 1538 Cabezón married Luisa Núñez of Ávila, where they lived until 1560, after which the organist moved his household to Madrid.

In 1539 the Empress died, whereupon Cabezón alternated between service to her daughters and to Prince Philip. After 1548 he served the prince exclusively, traveling in his entourage to Italy, Germany, and the Netherlands during the next 3 years. He also accompanied Philip to England in 1554-1555. In both the Netherlands and England one of the royal keyboard players was Antonio's brother, Juan de Cabezón, and one of the choirboys was the blind organist's son Agustin. Cabezón's arrangement of the "hit song" *le file quant Dieu me donne de quoi* by Henry VIII's favorite lutanist, Philip van Wilder, was perhaps written during his English sojourn.

The *Libro de cifra nueva,* compiled in 1557 by Luys Venegas de Henestrosa, included 40 pieces by "Antonio," the blind virtuoso's fame already being so great that no other identification was needed. Cabezón's *Obras de música para tecla arpa y vihuela* was published in 1578 by his son Hernando. Among its varied contents are teaching pieces for beginners, hymn arrangements, 35 Kyries, 32 Psalm verses, 53 Magnificat verses, 32 *fabordones,* 12 *tientos,* 29 *glosas* of sections from Masses and motets by foreign masters, 10 variation sets (*diferencias*) on subjects ranging from Spanish folk tunes and French chansons to the Milanese galliard, and 18 *glosas* of French chansons. It also contains a *Pavana italiana* that in England became known throughout the rest of the 16th century as "The Spanish Pavan." The anthology provided "mere crumbs from my father's table," according to Hernando, who in his will dated Oct. 30, 1598, mentioned two other collections as ready for publication when royal bounty so allowed.

Cabezón's *Obras de música* began reaching the New World no later than 1586. In that year alone three copies were dispatched to Mexico City booksellers.

Further Reading

For information about Cabezón see Gustave Reese, *Music in the Renaissance* (1959), and John Ward, "Spanish Musicians in Sixteenth-century England," in Gustave Reese and Robert J. Snow, eds., *Essays in Musicology* (1968). □

George Washington Cable

The American novelist George Washington Cable (1844-1925) was an important regional writer whose best-received books were set in Louisiana. He was also an early Southern advocate of civil rights for African Americans.

George Washington Cable was born in New Orleans, the son of a Virginia-born father and a mother whose ancestors were New England Puritans. When his father died, 14-year-old George left high school and became the chief support of his mother and her sizable family. He served in the Confederate Army until the end of the Civil War. After working at several small jobs, Cable became a columnist and reporter on the *New Orleans Picayune.*

In 1869 Cable married Louise Stewart Bartlett, who would be his inspiration and assistant for 35 years. Stories sold to Northern magazines from 1873 to 1878 provided insufficient funds to support dependent relatives and a rapidly growing family (four daughters and a son by 1879), and he dropped writing for a time to work at three bookkeeping jobs. But payment he received for research for the U.S. Census and the success of *Old Creole Days* (1879), a collection of his stories, enabled him once more to devote full time to writing, the fruits of which were a novel, *The Grandissimes* (1880). Northern readers who particularly enjoyed regional literature delighted in Cable's uniquely graceful and delicate evocations of New Orleans and Louisiana plantation country.

By contrast, the Creoles, descendants of French or Spanish settlers of the Mississippi Delta country, disliked Cable's representations of them. He was fiercely criticized for having attacked various Southern practices and attitudes (including the treatment of African Americans) in his speeches, articles, and books such as *The Grandissimes, Madame Delphine* (1881), *Dr. Sevier* (1884), and *The Silent South* (1885). During Northern travels, notably a joint reading tour with Mark Twain in 1884-1885, Cable found the atmosphere friendlier, and in 1885 he moved his family

(eventually including eight children, seven surviving childhood) to Northampton, Mass., which was destined to be his home until his death.

Cable continued to champion african Americans rights in articles and lectures during years when the cause was not popular even in the North. Although *Bonaventure* (1888), a collection of stories, contained few social preachments, *The Negro Question* (1890) attacked racism. He founded the Home Culture Clubs, reading groups which dealt with Southern social problems.

Cable's best work appeared before 1890. *John March, Southerner* (1895) showed his weakness in portraying an area other than Louisiana, and *The Cavalier* (1901), though a financial success, was an inferior swashbuckling romance. *Gideon's Band* (1914) authentically pictures Mississippi River life but is theatrical. After many years of illness, Louise Cable died in 1904. In 1906 Cable married Eva C. Stevenson, who died in 1923; and in that year he married Hannah Cowing, who survived his death on Jan. 31, 1925.

Further Reading

Arlin Turner, *George W. Cable* (1956), is a splendid full-length biography. Cable's daughter, Lucy Leffingwell Cable Bicklé, stresses family life in *George Washington Cable: His Life and Letters* (1928). Charles Philip Butcher, *George W. Cable* (1962), and Edmund Wilson, *Patriotic George: Studies in the Literature of the American Civil War* (1962), provide excellent critical discussions. □

John Cabot

John Cabot (active 1471-1498), born Giovanni Caboto, was an Italian explorer in English service. He was once thought to have been the first to bear the English flag across the Atlantic, but recent evidence shows that another voyage preceded his.

John Cabot was probably born in Genoa. Venetian historical records show that between 1471 and 1473 he was admitted as an adult to citizenship in the republic. Naturalization in Venice presumed a residence of 15 years, but Cabot may have come with his family as a minor. By 1484 he was the father of Sebastian Cabot, who would achieve fame as an explorer, and another, older son.

A London acquaintance reported in 1497 that Cabot had once been as far east as Mecca and had attempted to learn the Oriental origin of spices. In view of his Italian birth and Christianity, it seems probable that Cabot visited Jidda, the port of Mecca, rather than the forbidden holy city itself.

Cabot was in Spain in the early 1490s and reached England by 1495, determined to make a voyage to Marco Polo's Cathay. He knew by then of Columbus's discoveries and believed the new land could not be China. English merchants from Bristol had been voyaging into the Atlantic since about 1480, and one expedition, either before or after 1492, had discovered the island of "Brasile," certainly Newfoundland. Cabot believed that this was the northeast corner of Asia, south of which would be found Japan and the Great Khan's empire. For his own voyage he received letters patent from Henry VII and financial backing in Bristol.

In 1497 Cabot sailed from Bristol in the little *Matthew* with 18 men. From the midpoint of Ireland he went as directly west as possible and made a North American landfall June 24. This was evidently Newfoundland again, perhaps Cape Race. Cabot then followed the coast in regions not precisely identified, but it is thought that he traversed part of Nova Scotia and possibly Maine. He returned to Bristol August 6. The amazing speed of the entire voyage has caused some scholars to doubt the accuracy of the computation, but it must be remembered that Cabot intended this only as a reconnaissance.

When the discoverer reached London, the city hailed him. King Henry, then on rather good terms with Spain, felt that the newly found lands lay far enough northward to be outside any legitimate Spanish sphere. The King granted Cabot a yearly pension of £20 and gladly gave his consent to a new voyage which would penetrate south of the regions already discovered.

In May 1498 Cabot sailed from Bristol again in command of five ships, and here knowledge of him virtually ends. Several of the vessels returned but the one in which Cabot traveled did not; those returning seemed not to know where or when Cabot's ship had been lost. Spanish evidence suggests that one English ship did reach the Carib-

bean, bearing out the fact that the intention had been to follow the American continent southward.

Further Reading

The most authoritative work on Cabot is James A. Williamson, *The Cabot Voyages and Bristol Discovery under Henry VII* (1962). This partly supersedes Williamson's earlier study, *The Voyages of the Cabots and the English Discovery of North America* (1929). An important contribution, in Italian, is Roberto Almagià, *Gli Italiani: Primi esploratori dell'America* (1937), which contains a long chapter on both John and Sebastian Cabot. Samuel Eliot Morison, *The European Discovery of America* (1971), discusses John Cabot. □

Richard Clarke Cabot

Richard Clarke Cabot (1868-1939), an American physician, pioneered clinical hematology, was an innovator in teaching methods, and introduced the concept of the medical social worker.

Richard Cabot was born in Brookline, Mass., on May 21, 1868. He studied at the Noble and Greenough School before going on to Harvard, from which he graduated with high honors in 1889. He graduated from Harvard Medical School in 1892 and interned there for the next 18 months. In 1894 he married Ella Lyman and settled in Boston.

Cabot's research during 1894 and 1895 indicated that the white blood cell count increases as a result of certain illnesses, like appendicitis; this was therefore a useful diagnostic aid. His first book was *A Guide to the Clinical Examination of the Blood for Diagnostic Purposes* (1896). He served aboard the U.S. Army hospital ship *Bay State* during the Spanish-American War. His interest in diagnosis continued, and in 1901 *Physical Diagnosis of Diseases of the Chest* was published. This book became a standard text.

In 1898 Cabot was appointed physician to outpatients at Massachusetts General Hospital, and in 1912 he became one of two chiefs of staff. It was here that he established medical social service as part of the total effective treatment of the patient when he organized, in 1905, a small group of social workers to attend to cases requiring observation at home. This was perhaps Cabot's greatest contribution to medicine. His ideas about social work are explored in *Social Service and the Art of Healing* (1909).

As an instructor at Harvard Medical School (1903), assistant professor (1908), and professor (1918), Cabot taught by presenting case histories to his students and asking for a diagnosis, an approach reflected in his *Exercises in Differential Diagnosis* (1902). These clinical exercises became the clinical pathologic conference, afterward used as a standard teaching method, when Cabot combined them with the results of postmortem examinations. In 1914 he published an important paper, "The Four Common Types of Heart Disease," in the *Journal of the American Medical Association,* in which he emphasized the etiologic diagnosis of heart disease.

From 1917 to 1919 Cabot served as chief of medicine at U.S. Base Hospital No. 6 in France. In addition to duties at the hospital, he established dispensaries for war refugees and lectured on social work at the Collège de France.

Cabot was appointed professor of social ethics at Harvard in 1919; he retired in 1934. He published essays in this field and held positions in organizations such as the National Conference of Social Work and the American Civil Liberties Union. He died in Boston on May 8, 1939.

Further Reading

There is no full-length study of Cabot. Frequent references to his work are in Frederic A. Washburn, *The Massachusetts General Hospital: Its Development, 1900-1935* (1939). Paul Buck, ed., *Social Sciences at Harvard, 1860-1920* (1965), describes Cabot's work at Harvard. For general background material see Henry E. Sigerist, *American Medicine* (1934), and Ida M. Cannon, *On the Social Frontier of Medicine: Pioneering in Medical Social Service* (1952). □

Sebastian Cabot

Sebastian Cabot (ca. 1482-1557), an Italian-born explorer in the service of England and Spain, made

significant discoveries in an age of geographical discovery.

Sebastian Cabot, the son of John and Mattea Cabot, was probably born in Venice, where he is documented as a small child in 1484. He accompanied his parents to Spain and England, but he would have been too young to sail with his father on the Atlantic voyages of 1497 and 1498. Although Sebastian had not yet commanded an expedition of his own by 1505, Henry VII of England awarded him an annual pension of £10, perhaps because of his growing proficiency in cartography and navigation.

Cabot almost certainly made a voyage for England in 1508-1509, in which he sailed far northward and discovered the entrance to Hudson Bay. He considered this to be the water passage leading around North America to the Orient. On his return to England, Henry VII had died, and Henry VIII showed no interest in pursuing the exploration further. In 1512, when in Spain with an English mission, Cabot transferred his allegiance to the Castilian service.

Cabot spent most of the next 36 years in Spain, though he several times considered returning to England and once offered to go to Venice. His restlessness was occasioned by his awareness that though Spain consulted him about voyages, it offered no encouragement for his favorite project of northern discovery.

In 1518, after the death of the Spanish navigator Juan Díaz de Solís, Cabot became pilot major for Spain. He sailed in command of his own expedition in 1526 with the intention of following the lead of Magellan and García Jofré de Loaisa to the Moluccas. While sailing off the coast of Brazil he encountered Spanish castaways, who reported the existence of a rich civilization. Cabot postponed his original project in favor of attempting to penetrate the interior of South America via the Río de la Plata and the Paraná, two rivers fed by the 1500-mile-long Paraguay River. Those reports, which caused him to abandon his search for a southern passage, concerned Inca Peru, as yet unpenetrated by Spaniards.

Cabot returned to Spain empty-handed in 1530. He was prosecuted and imprisoned for a short time. In departing from the original plan he had made bitter enemies. He managed to retain the confidence of the Spanish crown, however, and continued to hold the pilot's office.

Little is known of Cabot's career from 1533 to 1547. It is possible that he commanded unrecorded expeditions, but he was getting past the age for leading voyages of exploration and probably devoted his time to cartography. Soon after the death of Henry VIII in 1547, he accepted an offer to return to England. He did so without the consent of Charles V of Spain. Nothing bound him to Spain; his wife, Catalina Medrano, had died, and the Spaniards lacked interest in the northern discovery he still desired.

In 1553 about 200 English merchants under the patronage of John Dudley, Duke of Northumberland, formed what came to be called the Muscovy Company, with Cabot as governor for life. Their grant in the name of the boy king, Edward VI, empowered them to discover and possess lands to the northeast, north, and northwest.

Cabot, from his youth, had been mainly interested in a Northwest Passage, but his company decided to try the Northeast first. The first expedition which he planned was commanded by Sir Hugh Willoughby and Richard Chancellor. Willoughby discovered the Novaya Zemlya islands but died of winter hardship in Lapland. Chancellor reached the White Sea and from the port of Archangel traveled overland to Moscow, where he concluded a favorable trade agreement with the czar, Ivan the Terrible.

The Muscovy Company made another effort at finding a Northeast Passage. A single small ship, the *Serchthrift,* commanded by Stephen Borough, left England in 1556 for this purpose. Cabot performed his last-known act connected with navigation by going to wish the mariners a successful voyage. He died the next year.

Further Reading

All that is known of the place and time of Cabot's birth is furnished by James A. Williamson, *The Cabot Voyages and Bristol Discovery under Henry VII* (1962). His early career in English service is discussed by Williamson in *The Voyages of the Cabots and the English Discovery of North America* (1929). José Toribio Medina, *El Veneciano Sebastián Caboto al servicio de España* (1908), prints abundant documents concerning Cabot's Spanish career. Samuel Eliot Morison, *The European Discovery of America: The Northern Voyages* (1971), discusses Cabot's English service. □

Amílcar Lopes Cabral

Amílcar Lopes Cabral (1924-1973) was the father of modern African nationalism in Guinea-Bissau and the Cape Verde Islands and led Guinea-Bissau's independence movement, which was successful in 1975.

Amílcar Lopes Cabral was born on September 12, 1924, in Bafatá (Guinea-Bissau), on the western coast of Africa. His parents, Juvenal Cabral and Iva Pinhel Évora, were from Santiago, an island in the offshore Cape Verde archipelago. Cabral's parents trained him at home until he was seven, when they sent him to Cape Verde to attend primary and secondary school. An exceptional student, he completed his program in eight years, rather than the normal 11, and scored high enough on his final examinations to continue his studies in Lisbon. These formative years in Cape Verde significantly influenced Cabral's later commitment to the liberation of Guinea-Bissau and Cape Verde, which until 1973 and 1975, respectively, were Portuguese colonies.

Throughout their history the Cape Verde Islands suffered periodically from drought and the resulting famines. Cabral was still in Cape Verde during the drought of the 1940s. This disaster, complicated by the increased economic pressures World War II placed on all African colonies, made the islands a particularly difficult place to live. The catastrophic drought killed between 50,000 and 60,000 people, almost one third of the archipelago's population. This crisis, which was caused in part by Portugal's exploitative economic policies, affected Cabral and his contemporaries. One response Cabral's generation, like earlier ones, had to the crisis facing the islands was to write poetry, short stories, and other creative works about their situation. They discussed ways to improve their lives. Cabral's writings from this period show that even before his training in Portugal he had begun thinking about ways to free his people from the grips of this vicious colonial system.

Study in Portugal

After struggling for over a year to secure a scholarship, Cabral left for Lisbon in 1945. Because of the harsh economic realities in Cape Verde, he chose to study agricultural engineering at the Instituto Superior de Agronomia. While in Lisbon Cabral and other African students, including Vasco Cabral, Agostinho Neto, and Mário de Andrade, formed cultural associations in which they discussed their homelands. Cabral and his colleagues from Cape Verde, Guinea-Bissau, Angola, and Mozambique continued to write creative texts, reaffirming the beauty and vitality of their African cultures. These students, like some of their contemporaries from the French colonies in Paris, also questioned assimilation policies and talked about the need for political change.

When Cabral completed his training as an agronomist in 1951 he felt obliged to use his skills in Africa. He returned to Guinea-Bissau in 1952 with a contract from the Department of Agricultural and Forestry Services. Cabral's calculated decision to leave for Guinea-Bissau rather than to remain in Portugal or go to another colony reflected his desire to begin helping his people prepare for their struggle against colonial rule. In 1953 and 1954, Cabral conducted an agricultural survey or census of the colony. Cabral travelled throughout Guinea-Bissau talking with peasants about their economic activities, their problems as agriculturalists, and their histories and cultures. He analyzed the country's soils and crops and offered suggestions about how to improve the economic situation in the colony. Conducting this survey gave Cabral an opportunity to learn from the people themselves what colonial exploitation meant. The knowledge he gained from this intimate contact with peasants helped him later when the armed struggle against Portuguese colonialism began.

In 1955 Cabral returned to Lisbon and worked as an agricultural consultant in Portugal and her colonies until 1959. On a brief visit to Bissau in September 1956, Cabral, Aristides Pereira, Julio de Almeida, Elisée Turpin, Fernando Fortes, and Luiz Cabral (Amílcar Cabral's half-brother) founded the PAIGC (Partido Africano da Independência da Guiné e Cabo Verde). The PAIGC's goals were the liberation of both countries and the unification of these independent nations. The colonial authorities saw Cabral as a threat; consequently he returned to Lisbon. His compatriots stayed in Bissau and continued organizing the party underground.

In August 1959 a dock workers' strike at Pidjiguiti resulted in the massacre of 50 protesters. The authorities blamed the PAIGC of fomenting discontent among the workers, and the party's supporters had to rethink long range strategies for achieving their goals. In September 1959 Cabral and several PAIGC members met in Bissau and decided nonviolent protest in the city would not bring about change. They concluded that the only hope for achieving independence was through armed struggle. For their own protection they had to leave the country, but at the same time mobilize the people in the countryside—the majority of the population. The Republic of Guiné (Conakry), Guinea-Bissau's southern neighbor, gained its independence in 1958, and its leader Sékou Touré agreed to allow the PAIGC to use his country as a base.

The War for Liberation

From late 1959 until 1962 Cabral and the PAIGC built a military force to fight the national liberation war against Portuguese colonial rule. The PAIGC's guerrilla war began in late 1962 and lasted until 1973. The party sent cadres to Guiné to study in the schools it established. For more advanced programs, PAIGC militants went to supportive countries for military training and to study medicine, education, and engineering. The PAIGC infiltrated Guinea-Bissau slowly and mobilized the rural population.

Cabral's experience with the agricultural survey in the 1950s meant that he had contacts in the rural areas and that he understood how to appeal to the peasants. Cabral knew the party had to improve peasants' lives if it expected their support. As Cabral wrote, "keep always in mind that the people are not fighting for ideas, for things in anyone's head. They are fighting . . . for material benefits, to live better and in peace, to see their lives go forward, to guarantee the future of their children. . . . " Consequently, Cabral and his party developed programs designed to make life better in the areas the guerrillas liberated. By 1969 the PAIGC controlled two-thirds of the country. They established schools, medical clinics, and courts, as well as People's stores, in these areas. Cabral believed that political liberation in and of itself was not enough. Rather, he understood the need to create a new society with political, economic, and social structures that reflected the needs of the people. Operating the facilities established before the war ended prepared the party and its supporters for the independence period.

The PAIGC's army used their guerrilla warfare techniques to defeat the larger and better equipped Portuguese army. By 1972 the party's powerbase in the liberated zones was strong enough to hold elections in preparation for independence. The Portuguese were unable to admit defeat. In January 1973 the Portuguese secret police (PIDE) assassinated Cabral in the city of Conakry. PIDE believed by eliminating Cabral they could destroy the PAIGC and change the course of history. PIDE and its supporters in Lisbon failed to understand that even though Cabral was the guiding spirit of the party, he had anticipated that he might not live to see independence in Guinea-Bissau or Cape Verde. Therefore, throughout the struggle Cabral tried hard to build a party that could survive without him.

The party, dedicated to seeing Cabral's program for liberation through, declared Guinea-Bissau's independence in September 1973. Portugal refused to recognize their colony's declaration until after the 1974 coup d'état that ended almost 50 years of fascism in Portugal. Although Cape Verde ultimately gained its independence in 1975, the PAIGC's second goal of unification remained a long term and difficult program.

Cabral's vision and his ability to formulate a theory of liberation made him a unique statesman. His contribution to the national liberation war and the achievement of independence in Guinea-Bissau and Cape Verde was instrumental to their success. Furthermore, Cabral's writings continue to provide a framework for understanding colonialism and decolonization in the Third World generally.

Further Reading

Students interested in learning more about Amílcar Cabral should read his *Unity and Struggle* (1980), *Revolution in Guinea* (London, 1969), and *Return to the Sources* (1973). In addition, Basil Davidson's *No First Is Big Enough To Hide the Sky: The Liberation of Guinea and Cape Verde* (London, 1981) provides an excellent account of the war and Cabral's role in it. Two biographies on Cabral are also extremely useful: Mário de Andrade's *Amílcar Cabral—Essai de Biographie Politique* (Paris, 1980) and Patrick Chabal's *Amílcar Cabral—Revolutionary Leadership and People's War* (1983). □

Pedro Álvares Cabral

Pedro Álvares Cabral (c. 1467-1520) was a Portuguese navigator who discovered Brazil on a voyage to India.

Born on the family estate in Belmonte, Pedro Álvares Cabral grew up close to the Portuguese court. As a nobleman, he served in the council of King Manuel I and received the habit of the Order of Christ. Little is known of his activities before 1499, when Manuel appointed him the chief captain of a fleet being prepared to sail to India to follow the maritime route to the East charted by Vasco da Gama on his historical voyage of 1497-1499.

Amid colorful pageantry 13 ships with 1,200 men sailed from the Tagus River on March 8, 1500, en route to India. On April 22 the fleet unexpectedly sighted land in the west at 17° South latitude. Cabral explored the coast and claimed the new land for his sovereign. He christened it Ilha de Vera Cruz. Merchants, quickly attracted to its plentiful stands of brazilwood, the source of an excellent red dye, called it Terra do Brasil, and the name Brazil gained popular acceptance.

Cabral's discovery has raised a series of historical questions which have never been properly answered. Was he the first to reach Brazil or had the Spanish or French made prior visits? Had Portugal previously discovered Brazil and protected that discovery with secrecy? Did Cabral—who was far off the prescribed course to India—discover Brazil accidentally or intentionally? There is room for much speculation on each of these questions, but lack of documentary evidence to the contrary leads to the conclusion that Cabral was the first to discover Brazil and that he did so accidentally. The first cartographic notification of Cabral's discovery was the Cantino chart, finished no later than 1502.

After dispatching news of his discovery to King Manuel, Cabral proceeded to India, where he established a trading post at Cochin. He then returned to Lisbon laden with the coveted spices of the East. He helped to prepare the next fleet for India, which sailed under the command of Vasco da Gama. Cabral then apparently retired to his estate at Jardim, near Santarém, where he died about 1520.

Further Reading

The most complete information on Cabral and his voyage to the East is the translation, with an introduction and notes, by William Brooks Greenlee of *The Voyage of Pedro Álvares Cabral to Brazil and India: From Contemporary Documents and Narratives* (1938). See also Edgar Prestage, *The Portuguese Pioneers* (1933); Charles David Ley, ed., *Portuguese Voyages, 1498-1663* (1947); and Gilbert Renault, *Caravels of Christ* (1959). □

Juan Rodríguez Cabrillo

Juan Rodríguez Cabrillo (died 1543) was a Portuguese explorer in service to the Spanish. He is best known for his exploration of the coast of California in 1542-1543.

Juan Rodríguez Cabrillo (forefront)

Juan Rodríguez Cabrillo served under the command of Pánfilo de Narváez and aided him in the conquest of Cuba about 1518. When Narváez was sent to Mexico in 1520 to control the ambitious Hernán Cortés, Cabrillo went along. Once in Mexico, however, Cabrillo joined Cortés in his assault on the Aztec capital Tenochtitlán (Mexico City).

After the conquest of Mexico, Cabrillo remained in the Spanish service as an officer under Pedro de Alvarado. With Alvarado he journeyed through lower New Spain and into what is now Guatemala. When Alvarado was killed in 1541 during an rebellion by native peoples, Cabrillo was one of the most experienced military men in New Spain. He was authorized by Antonio de Mendoza, Viceroy of New Spain, to undertake an exploratory mission into the northern limits of New Spain along the Pacific coast. He was also instructed to discover and claim all new lands for Spain and, it was hoped, to meet with Francisco Vásquez de Coronado, who was crossing overland to the sea. Mendoza also instructed Cabrillo to try to find the opening of a trans-American strait like that described by Giovanni da Verrazano. Cabrillo hoped that he, like Cortés, would find a highly civilized, easily controlled native population.

Cabrillo left from the port of Acapulco in two primitive ships, the *San Salvador* and the *Capitana,* on June 27, 1542. Cabrillo's ships sailed north, reaching the coast of southern California. During his voyage he made the first known European contact with the natives of that area. His accounts contain the first European observations of such places as San Diego Bay, Santa Catalina Island, and Santa Barbara. There Cabrillo found the friendly Chumash tribe, who would subsequently serve as hosts for the Franciscan missionaries.

The expedition was not very successful in any of its larger objectives. He never met with Coronado, who was already returning to Mexico by the time Cabrillo reached California. He found friendly natives, but they were neither wealthy nor highly civilized. Further, he obviously never found the mythical strait that opened to the Atlantic Ocean.

Cabrillo's major contribution was the discovery and claiming of a rich new land for Spain. Until he traveled the coast of California, the Spaniards had no real idea of the enormity or the outlines of the lands they claimed to the north. The inaccuracies of his cartographical observations have not diminished the importance of his discoveries.

During an attack by hostile natives, Cabrillo fell and broke his leg; he died on Jan. 3, 1543, from complications. Before he died, Cabrillo named Bartolomé Ferrera (Ferrelo), his chief pilot, as his successor. Ferrera took the ships farther north to Oregon, through winter storms and hazardous conditions. The remnants of the Cabrillo mission returned to Mexico in April 1543.

Further Reading

A full-length study of Cabrillo is Henry R. Wagner, *Juan Rodríguez Cabrillo, Discoverer of the Coast of California* (1941). See also Wagner's *Spanish Voyages to the Northwest Coast of America in the Sixteenth Century* (1929) and Harold Lamb, *New Found World: How North America Was Discovered and Explored* (1955). □

St. Frances Xavier Cabrini

St. Frances Xavier Cabrini (1850-1917), Italian-born founder of the Roman Catholic Missionary Sisters of the Sacred Heart, became famous as the "the saint of the immigrants" during nearly 3 decades of service in the United States.

Maria Francesca Cabrini was born on July 15, 1850, at Sant'Angelo Lodigiano. The young girl was drawn toward a life of religious service at an early age, influenced by her older sister, a schoolteacher; her uncle, a priest who captured her imagination with tales of missionary work; and the Daughters of the Sacred Heart, who prepared her for a normal school diploma in 1870. Francesca, who had already vowed herself to virginity at the age of 12, tried to enter the Daughters of the Sacred Heart in 1872 but was denied on grounds of health. She had contracted smallpox while caring for the sick during an epidemic, and though recovered she did not seem physically strong. After brief employment as a teacher in Virdardo, she was persuaded to do charitable work in an orphanage at Codogno, where in 1877 she made her vows. In the same year she was appointed prioress of her new foundation, the Institute of Missionary Sisters of the Sacred Heart, which consisted at the outset of seven orphaned girls whom she had trained. As head of a religious order, she was entitled to be called "Mother."

Mother Cabrini had much to do in Italy, but she soon craved fulfillment of a lifelong wish to do missionary work in China. Pope Leo XIII and Bishop Scalabrini of Piacenza instead urged her to carry her talents to Italian immigrants in the slums of the United States, and dutifully but reluctantly she sailed in 1889 with six sisters. From modest beginnings in the New York City area Mother Cabrini and her followers gradually built a national and international network of some 70 institutions. In 1909 she became an American citizen. Her journeys in behalf of her mission, including 30 crossings of the Atlantic, occupied much of her time and energy, though she remained physically frail throughout her life. When World War I broke out in Europe, she dedicated her hospitals and nuns in Italy to the war effort there. On Dec. 22, 1917, after a brief illness, she died of malaria in her own Columbus Hospital in Chicago.

Cardinal George Mundelein of Chicago and others launched the process of her canonization in 1928. She was pronounced venerable in 1933, beatified in 1938, and canonized in 1946. Her remains, originally at West Park, N.Y., are now enshrined in the chapel of the Blessed Mother Cabrini High School in New York City. St. Frances Xavier Cabrini, though declared to have effected the two miracles necessary for canonization, is best remembered for her energetic labors among immigrants and the poor in the United States and for the establishment and staffing of orphanages, schools, hospitals, convents, and other facilities throughout the world.

Further Reading

There are many biographies of St. Frances Xavier Cabrini, including Frances Parkinson Keyes's popular account, *Mother Cabrini: Missionary to the World* (1959). More scholarly are the work by a Benedictine of Stanbrook Abbey, *Frances Xavier Cabrini* (1944); Theodore Maynard, *Too Small a World: The Life of Francesca Cabrini* (1945); and Pietro Di Donato, *Immigrant Saint: The Life of Mother Cabrini* (1960). □

Giulio Caccini

Giulio Caccini (ca. 1545-1618), an Italian singer and an early opera composer, wrote "Le nuove musiche," the first important and, in the 17th century, most influential publication of the new style of monodic recitative in vocal music with figured bass accompaniment.

Giulio Caccini was born in Rome, the son of Michelangelo Caccini. The only musical instruction that Giulio is known to have received was from Cipione del Palle (or Palla), a noted voice teacher in Rome, and it was as a singer that Caccini first made a name for himself. He was employed at the Medicean court in Florence, principally as a singer, from 1564 to his death on Dec. 10, 1618. He married twice, both wives being voice pupils of his. The first, Lucia, bore him three children: Pompeo, Francesca (called "La Cecchina," also a composer), and Settimia. He had no children by his second wife, Margherita.

Probably about 1579 Caccini became a member of the Florentine Camerata, a literary and musical society founded by Count Giovanni de' Bardi, who implies, in a letter to Caccini (ca. 1580), that he was the first to encourage Caccini to write in the new style. The letter bears out Caccini's claim in the dedication to Bardi (dated Dec. 20, 1600) of his opera *Euridice* that he had been composing in this style for more than 15 years, that is, at least as early as 1585.

In 1589 Caccini took part, as performer and conductor, in the wedding festivities of Ferdinand de' Medici. Three years later, when he visited Rome with Bardi as the later's secretary, Caccini sang some of the songs performed earlier at the Florentine Camerata, several of which he published in *Le nuove musiche* (1602).

When Maria de Médici married Henry IV of France in Florence, as part of the celebrations the nobleman Jacopo Corsi staged, on Oct. 6, 1600, what is sometimes regarded as the first opera—*Euridice,* with a libretto by Ottavio Rinuccini and music mostly by Jacopo Peri, also employed as singer and composer at the Medicean court. Caccini, who was in charge of the performance, unscrupulously replaced some of Peri's arias with his own. Three days later Caccini presented *Il rapimento di Cefalo,* for which he wrote most of the music, but it received little acclaim, unlike Peri's *Euridice.* Clearly spurred by jealously, Caccini hurriedly composed his own setting of the *Euridice* libretto and published it, probably in January 1601, shortly before the publication of Peri's version on February 6. Caccini's version was not performed until Dec. 5, 1602; it was not revived.

The success of Peri's *Euridice,* and his patronization by Corsi, Bardi's influential successor, resulted in Caccini's gradual decline in esteem during his remaining years, despite the importance and popularity of *Le nuove musiche,* and the publication of two other collections by Caccini—*Fuggilotio musicale* (2d ed. 1613) and *Nuove musiche e nuova maniera de scriverle* (1614).

Further Reading

Information on Caccini is available in Manfred F. Bukofzer, *Music in the Baroque Era from Monteverdi to Bach* (1947); Donald J. Grout, *A Short History of Opera* (1947; 2d ed. 1965); and *The New Oxford History of Music,* vol. 4; Gerald E. H. Abraham, ed., *The Age of Humanism, 1540-1630* (1968). There is an interesting chapter on the Florentine Camerata in Zesta De Robeck, *Music of the Italian Renaissance* (1928; repr. 1969). □

Alvise da Cadamosto

Alvise da Cadamosto (ca. 1428-1483) was an Italian trader and traveler from Venice who discovered the Cape Verde Islands and described the Canary Islands and the Senegal-Gambia-Geba area.

Alvise da Cadamosto sailed aboard Venetian galleys to North Africa, Crete, Alexandria, and Flanders between 1445 and 1452. On returning to Venice in 1454 he found his father banished and his family in distress. Because of Cadamosto's knowledge of the spice trade, Prince Henry the Navigator offered him a Portuguese caravel for a trading venture down the western African coast, with the right to keep half the products with which he returned.

Cadamosto, in a caravel of some 70 modern tons, left for Lagos in March 1455. He called at the Madeira and Canary islands, then traveled along the African coast. In his reports he observed that the Senegal River divided the arid Saharan region from the fertile, forested areas to the south. Beyond the Senegal Cadamosto encountered two caravels, one under the command of the Genoan Usodimare, and the three vessels proceeded past Cape Verde to the mouth of the Gambia River. In the estuary of the Gambia, Cadamosto sketched the Southern Cross, and he referred to the height of the Pole Star as a fraction of a lance-length above the skyline; this notation suggests that navigators were not yet measuring latitude in degrees.

In 1456 Cadamosto and Usodimare, with license from Prince Henry, equipped two caravels which, with a third provided by Henry, set out for the Gambia. Beyond Cape Blanc the vessels encountered a gale, and Cadamosto, steering as close to the wind as possible, headed out to sea. Off Cape Verde an island came into view which he named Boa Vista. A shore party observed an island to the north (Sal) and two to the south (Maio and São Tiago), and Cadamosto visited the last-named. Other islands of the archipelago were observed to the west.

Cadamosto sailed 60 miles up the Gambia and traded with a friendly chief until fever forced the vessels from the river. He named and charted several capes and rivers as far as the Rio Grande (Geba), which may have already been reached by Diogo Gomes; but he was the first to describe the Bissagos Archipelago.

Cadamosto's narrative, which was first published in 1507, gave valuable information about the caravan routes of the interior, from Mali via Ouadane to Morocco, from Mali via Timbuktu to Gao eastward, and from Timbuktu via Taghaza to Morocco and Tunis, and also described the trade, especially in gold and salt. G. R. Crone (1937) commented that Cadamosto's "is the first original account to have survived of a voyage into the regions opened up by European enterprise at the dawn of modern overseas expansion, and reflects the spirit of openminded enquiry characteristic of the new age."

Further Reading

The Voyages of Cadamosto was edited by G. R. Crone in 1937. Background studies include John W. Blake, *European Beginnings in West Africa, 1454-1578* (1937); Boies Penrose, *Travel and Discovery in the Renaissance, 1420-1620* (1952); Charles E. Nowell, *The Great Discoveries and the First Colonial Empires* (1954); and J. H. Parry, *The Age of Reconnaissance* (1963). □

Gaius Julius Caesar

Gaius Julius Caesar (100-44 B.C.) was a Roman general and politician who overthrew the Roman Republic and established the rule of the emperors.

At the time of Julius Caesar's birth the political, social, economic, and moral problems created by the acquisition of a Mediterranean empire in the 3d and 2d centuries B.C. began to challenge the Roman Republic. The senatorial oligarchy that ruled Rome was proving inadequate to deal with these new challenges. It could not control the armies and the generals and was unwilling to listen to the pleas of the Italian allies for equal citizenship and of the provinces for justice. The system also had no real answers for the growth of an urban proletariat and the mass importation of slaves. Caesar saw these inadequacies of the Senate and used the problems and dilemmas of the period to create his own supreme political and military power.

Caesar was born on July 13, 100 B.C. His father had been only a moderate political success, attaining the praetorship but not the consulship. Caesar's mother came from plebeian stock. The family could claim a long, if not overly distinguished, history. It was a patrician family on his father's side and therefore one of the founders of Rome and was entitled to certain traditional privileges and offices. However, in comparison with many other leading Roman families it had produced few distinguished people.

Early Training

Caesar received the classic, rhetorically grounded education of a young Roman at Rome and in Rhodes. He was considered one of the most cultured and literate of Romans by such an expert as Cicero himself. Caesar followed the traditional Roman practice of conducting some prosecutions in order to gain political attention. He served as a young officer in Asia Minor and was quaestor (financial official) in Farther Spain (69 B.C.).

Caesar first rose to political prominence in the internal struggles that followed the revolt of Rome's allies—the "Social Wars"—after Rome refused to grant them full citizenship in 90. Caesar's family was related to the revolt's leader, Gaius Marius, and joined his faction. Caesar married Cornelia, the daughter of Cinna, one of the leading Marians, and was nominated for the priesthood of *flamen dialis.* However, Marius died, and his followers were defeated by

the Roman general Sulla. Caesar was spared in the proscriptions that followed the victory of Sulla, even though he refused to divorce Cornelia, to whom he remained married until her death in 69.

First Political and Military Successes

In the following years Caesar emerged as one of the leading political and social personalities of Rome. Cultivated, charming, and handsome, vain about his appearance, he made his love affairs the talk of Roman society. He recognized the urban proletariat as one of the major sources of political power and cultivated this group assiduously. He maintained Marian connections, and in 65 B.C., when he was aedile, he restored the triumphal monuments of Marius that had been dismantled under Sulla. Caesar was famous for his hospitality and was often heavily in debt. His aedileship was especially noted for its lavish displays and games.

Caesar's first really important electoral success was his election as pontifex maximus in 63 B.C. This was regarded as the chief religious office in Rome and had important political possibilities.

Caesar was elected praetor for 62 B.C. and served his propraetorship in Farther Spain. For over a century Spain had provided Roman governors the opportunity for a triumph. Caesar was quick to take advantage of the situation by waging a successful campaign against some native tribes in Lusitania. His political enemies accused him of provoking the war—he would not have been the first Roman governor in Spain who had done so—but he was nevertheless awarded the right of a triumph for his victory.

First Triumvirate

In the meantime a political crisis was developing in Rome. Pompey had returned from the East after having eliminated Mithridates and made major political settlements. He was having difficulty persuading the Senate to ratify these settlements and provide compensation for his veterans. Caesar at the same time was setting his sights on the consulship for the year 59 B.C. He returned from Spain in 60 B.C. and waived his right of triumph in order to campaign for election. He won, together with a representative of the senatorial oligarchy, Bibulus. The Senate immediately moved to block his hopes of future political power by voting as his postconsular area of responsibility the care of the woodlands of the Roman state, a command with no possibilities for military glory. Caesar, desiring more glamorous political and military opportunities, saw that he would need allies to circumvent his senatorial opponents.

Out of the specific problems of two of Rome's great men and the general ambition of the third grew the political alliance known as the First Triumvirate. Pompey brought wealth and military might, Crassus wealth and important political connections, and Caesar the key office of consul along with the brains and skill of a master political infighter. Caesar was to obtain the necessary settlements for Pompey and was in turn to receive a choice province. The alliance was further cemented in 58 B.C. by the marriage of Caesar's only daughter, Julia, to Pompey.

Caesar showed soon after his election that he intended to ignore Bibulus, his weak consular colleague, by using the political and religious machinery to advance Pompey's requests. Caesar's land bills indicated an intelligent effort to solve the problem of Rome's urban proletariat by returning people to the land. Pompey's veterans were settled on their own land allotments; and Caesar received as a reward the governorship of the provinces of Cisalpine Gaul, Illyricum, and Transalpine Gaul for a period of 5 years after his consulship.

Proconsul in Gaul

At the time Caesar took command, Roman control in Gaul was limited to the southern coast, the area known as Gallia Narbonensis. However, Rome had political relations with tribes beyond the actual border of the province. Caesar quickly took advantage of these connections and the shifting power position in Gaul to extend the sphere of Roman control. At the request of the Aedui, a tribe friendly to Rome, Caesar prevented the Helvetii from migrating across Gaul and then defeated Ariovistus, a German chieftain, who was building his own political power among the Sequani, a rival tribe to the Aedui. From there, Caesar extended Roman arms north with military victories over the Belgi (57 B.C.) and the Venetic tribes on the north coast of Gaul (56).

Meanwhile political strains had appeared in the alliance of Caesar, Pompey, and Crassus. Caesar's 5-year command was coming to a close, and political enemies were demanding his recall to make him explain his often high-handed actions in Gaul in provoking war with the native tribes. Crassus had been viewing with jealousy the power base that Caesar was building in Gaul and desired his own military command.

The three men met at the northern Italian city of Luca in April 56 B.C. and recemented their political ties. Caesar received a 5-year extension of his command. Pompey and Crassus were to have another consulship, after which Crassus would assume the important post of governor of Syria and Pompey would receive the governorship of Spain.

Revolt in Gaul

Caesar turned his energies to Gaul again. He decided to undertake an expedition against Britain, whose tribes maintained close contacts with Gaul. These expeditions in 55 B.C. and 54 B.C. were probably not a complete success for Caesar, but they aroused great enthusiasm at Rome. For the first time Roman arms had advanced over the sea to conquer strange, new peoples.

Caesar probably thought that his main task of conquest was complete. However, in 52 B.C. Gaul arose in widespread rebellion against Caesar under Vercingetorix, a nobleman of the tribe of the Arverni. Caesar's power base was threatened.

At the same time the political situation in Rome was equally chaotic. The tribune Clodius had been murdered, and his death was followed by great civic disorder. Pompey was called upon to assume the post of sole consul for 52 B.C. Caesar had crossed the Alps to watch more closely the changing conditions in Rome, and when the news of the Gallic revolt reached him, he recrossed the Alps, still partly blocked by winter, and rallied his divided army. He won a striking victory by capturing the Gallic town of Avaricum but was repulsed when he tried to storm the Arvernian stronghold of Gergovia. This defeat added Rome's old allies, the Aedui, to the forces of Vercingetorix. However, Vercingetorix made the mistake of taking refuge in the fortress of Alesia, where Caesar brought to bear the best of Roman siege techniques. A relieving army of Gauls was defeated, and Vercingetorix was forced to surrender. He was carried to Rome, where he graced Caesar's triumph in 46 B.C.

Dissolution of the Triumvirate

Caesar's long absence from Rome had partially weakened his political power. He naturally kept numerous contacts in Rome through agents and through extensive correspondence. Profits from his conquests were used for building projects to impress the people and for personal loans to leading figures such as Cicero in order to win their allegiance. Caesar's conquests were well publicized; his *Commentaries,* which described the campaigns in a controlled, matter-of-fact, third-person style, circulated among the reading public at Rome. Recent scholarship has emphasized the propaganda aspects of the *Commentaries,* even claiming that Caesar seriously distorted facts to justify his actions. Certainly, Caesar sought to place his conquests in the best possible light, stressing their basically defensive nature and the importance of defending friends and allies of

Rome against traditional Roman enemies. He had made extensive additions to the Roman Empire (about 640,000 square miles) at the expense of peoples who had long been enemies of Rome.

Pompey, on the other hand, had remained in Rome and strengthened his political position by appearing as a savior in a time of chaos. Other tensions in the alliance were Julia's death in 54 B.C., which removed an important bond between the two men; and the death of Crassus in 53 B.C., which left Pompey and Caesar in a confrontation of power.

Caesar's second term as governor ended in 50 B.C. His enemies were awaiting the day when he lost the immunity of an official position and could be prosecuted for various actions during his consulship and proconsulship. This was the traditional republican method of breaking a political opponent by securing his condemnation and exile. Caesar countered this by requesting to stand for the consulship for the year 49 B.C. in absentia, thus moving directly from proconsulship to consulship without being exposed to the vulnerability of a private citizen.

Civil War

In 52 B.C. the bill allowing Caesar to run for consul in absentia was passed, but its effect was vitiated by a decree of the Senate which would have forced Caesar to yield his provinces to a successor before he was elected consul. The majority of the senators wanted peace but were pushed along by a determined minority who wanted to destroy Caesar. Pompey was caught in a dilemma. He did not want civil war, but he also did not want to yield his prime position in the state. Finally Caesar's opponents in the Senate won. A decree was passed in January 49 B.C. demanding that Caesar yield his province and return to Rome as a private citizen to stand for the consulship.

The proconsul now had two choices. He could bow to the will of the Senate and be destroyed politically, or he could provoke civil war. Caesar chose the latter course and led his troops over the Rubicon, the small river that divided Cisalpine Gaul from the Roman heartland. At the beginning the greater power seemed to rest with Pompey and the Senate. Most men of prestige, such as Cato and Cicero, joined Pompey's cause. Pompey had connections with the provinces and princes of the Roman East, where he could draw enormous resources. Furthermore, he was defending the cause of the Senate and the established order at Rome.

However, Caesar had at his command a tough and experienced army, as well as an extensive following in Italy. Most of all, he was fighting for his own interests alone and did not have to face the divisions of interest, opinion, and leadership that plagued Pompey.

Pompey quickly decided to abandon Italy to Caesar and fell back to the East. Caesar secured his position in Italy and Gaul and then defeated Pompey at Pharsalus on Aug. 9, 48 B.C. Pompey fled to Egypt and was killed by the young pharaoh, Ptolemy. Although his rival was eliminated, much work remained to be done to make Caesar's position secure.

Caesar followed Pompey to Egypt and became involved in the dynastic struggle of the house of Ptolemy. Caesar supported Cleopatra, but caught in Alexandria without sufficient troops, he was nearly destroyed before reinforcements could arrive. The main result of this sojourn was the affair that developed between Caesar and Cleopatra, which ultimately resulted in a son, Caesarion.

Caesar still had numerous unconquered enemies in Africa and Spain. Turning first to Africa, on April 6, 46 B.C., at Thapsus he crushed a republican army led by Cato the Younger, his old and bitter enemy. Cato retreated to Utica, where he committed suicide rather than surrender to Caesar. Caesar moved into Spain and on March 17, 45 B.C., defeated the sons of Pompey at Munda.

Consolidation of the Empire

Meanwhile Caesar had to define his political position in Rome. He adopted a policy of special clemency toward his former enemies and rewarded political opponents with public office. For himself he adopted the old Roman position of dictator. However, what had been traditionally a 6-month emergency magistracy he turned into an office of increasing duration.

There has been much debate about what political role Caesar planned for himself. He certainly regarded the old oligarchic government as inadequate and desired to replace it with some form of rule by a single leader. Significantly, just before his death, Caesar was appointed dictator for life. About the same time, he began issuing coins with his own portrait on them, a practice unparalleled in Rome up to that time.

Caesar was planning major projects and reforms. Public works, such as a new, massive basilica in the old forum complex, were progressing. Even more grandiose schemes, like the draining of the Pontine marshes, were planned. New colonial foundations were under way, including settlements in Carthage and Corinth, both destroyed by the Romans in 146 B.C. Among his reforms was the reordering of the inadequate Roman calendar.

However, Caesar's restless temperament was not satisfied by administration and legislation at Rome. He was preparing equally extensive military campaigns. Trouble was brewing in Dacia across the Danube, and the Parthians had not been punished for the destruction of Crassus' army.

Death and Legacy

In Rome dissatisfaction was growing among the senatorial aristocrats over the increasingly permanent nature of the rule of Caesar. A conspiracy was formed aimed at eliminating Caesar and restoring the government to the Senate. The conspirators hoped that, with Caesar's death, government would be restored to its old republican form and all of the factors that had produced a Caesar would disappear. The conspiracy progressed with Caesar either ignorant of it or not recognizing the warning signs. On the Ides of March (March 15), 44 B.C., he was stabbed to death in the Senate house of Pompey by a group of men that included old friends and comrades-in-arms.

With Caesar's murder Rome plunged into 13 years of civil war. Caesar remained for some a symbol of tyranny, and for others the heritable founder of the Roman Empire whose ghost has haunted Europe ever since. For all, he is a figure of genius and audacity equaled by few in history.

Further Reading

Two ancient biographies of Caesar survive: one by the Greek moralist Plutarch in his *Lives* and the other by the Roman courtier and bureaucrat Suetonius in his *The Lives of the Twelve Caesars.* Caesar speaks for himself in *Commentaries on the Gallic War* and *Commentaries on the Civil Wars.* For a vivid account of the politics of the period, with Caesar playing a major role, nothing surpasses the letters of Cicero.

The best modern biography of Caesar is Matthias Gelzer, *Caesar: Politician and Statesman* (1921; trans. 1968). Michael Grant, *Julius Caesar* (1969), is a detailed survey of Caesar's career. Other biographies include John Buchan, *Julius Caesar* (1932), and Alfred L. Duggan, *Julius Caesar: A Great Life in Brief* (1955; new ed. 1966). For an understanding of how Caesar operated in the politics of his time see Lily Ross Taylor, *Party Politics in the Age of Caesar* (1949). Ronald Syme, *The Roman Revolution* (1939; rev. ed. 1952), places Caesar in the political developments of the 1st century B.C. F. E. Adcock discusses Caesar's literary achievements in *Caesar as Man of Letters* (1956). T. Rice Holmes, *Caesar's Conquest of Gaul* (1899; 2d ed. 1911), is still the fullest commentary in English on Caesar's Gallic War. For general historical background see T. Rice Holmes, *The Roman Republic and the Founder of the Empire* (3 vols., 1923), and A. H. McDonald, *Republican Rome* (1966). □

Shirley Caesar

After hearing the voice of God during a college exam, Shirley Caesar (born 1938) believed it was her duty to spread the Gospel. This "calling" has developed into 150 concerts per year, volunteer work for the poor, numerous Grammy awards, and over 30 record albums.

With 150 concerts a year, 25 hours a week helping the poor in her Outreach Ministries, several Grammies, and 30 record albums to her credit, Shirley Caesar may seem to be a whole army of gospel singers instead of just one diminutive (5'1, 3/4") cherubic-looking woman. The "Queen of Gospel" packs a lot of wallop in her small frame. Backed by a sixty-person choir, rocking like a tempest, she is a bundle of fireworks on the Fourth of July. The gospel style of song and sermonette, singing that involves both the spoken word and dramatic acting, was developed primarily by Shirley Caesar. She journeys all over the world, sometimes traveling all night to return to her pulpit in Durham, North Carolina, the town where she was born. "It is not easy," said Shirley in her 1995 video *He Will Come* (Word Records), "In fact, sometimes it is downright mind-boggling. But, somehow, even though I'm wearing all of these hats, the Lord helps me to just barrel through it." Shirley has barreled through fifty years of touring and preaching, starting at age ten, and she continues to bring the house down every time she performs.

The tenth of 12 children, Shirley Caesar was born October 13, 1938. Her father James was a tobacco worker who was well-known in the Carolinas as the lead singer in a gospel quartet, the Just Came Four. Shirley began singing with the group at age ten. When she was twelve, her father died, and she began touring with an evangelist named LeRoy Johnson, who also had a television show in Portsmouth, Virginia. In 1951, at thirteen, she recorded her first song "I'd Rather Have Jesus." While still in high school, she toured throughout the Carolinas.

This was a time when Jim Crow laws were still in effect in North Carolina. Shirley remembers restaurants putting up the CLOSED sign when she would arrive. "I went to school in the days when all the white kids got things better," she told *People,* "I remember once when a lady gave cookies to all the kids in the state. The white kids got the fresh ones; we got the stale ones." Despite these obstacles, her beloved mother Hannah taught her to respect herself and to persevere.

Her determination took her to North Carolina Central College where she studied business education. She has said that she got the call to God's work in the middle of a typing test. According to Kim Hubbard of *People,* she heard someone call out her name. Shirley turned to the young woman next to her and asked if she had spoken. When Shirley went home, she lay on the bed, and heard the same voice: "Behold, I have called you from your mother's womb and I have anointed your lips to preach the gospel." Shirley believed that this was a message that foretold special work for her in spreading the Gospel. Around the same time,

Shirley heard Chicago's female gospel group, the Caravans, and she saw an opportunity to answer the call. She sought an audition with the group, was immediately hired, and left school for a life of singing and ministry.

The Caravans had several members who became famous in the history of gospel music: Albertina Walker, Inez Andrews, and Sarah McKissick. Each woman had a different style and Shirley's contribution was an energetic and dramatic approach where she would act out the songs and walk among the congregation, engaging the members directly. On the song "I Won't Be Back," she would run through the hall searching for an exit, then leave for a brief period. Her forte was the sermon in the middle of songs that addressed the subject of the song and expounded on its theme. She exhorted the listeners to reach out to God and to take the example of Jesus. On the subject of motherhood, she was particularly effective. Her song "Don't Drive Your Mama Away" tells of a son who is shamed for putting his mother in the rest home.

Along the way, Shirley found a male counterpart in the singer James Cleveland and they made several records together. They became known as the "King and Queen of Gospel." Shirley formed her own group in 1966 called the Caesar Singers, but she would reunite with the Caravans and the Reverend Cleveland occasionally throughout the years. In 1971, she won her first Grammy, for the popular song "Put Your Hand in the Hand of the Man from Galilee." On the night of the awards, she had returned very late from an engagement in Homer, Louisiana. People began banging on her door, and when she eventually answered, her sister Ann, one of her backup singers, shouted "You won!" It was the first Grammy for a black female gospel singer since Mahalia Jackson. Shirley went on to win the award in 1980, 1984, 1985, 1992 and 1994—for an astonishing total of seven Grammys.

Among her numerous honors are eight Dove awards, the Gospel Music Association's highest tribute. She was inducted into the Gospel Hall of Fame in 1982. She was the first female gospel artist to perform at Harvard University. In recent years, Shirley Caesar moved into other media, making several videos: *Live in Memphis, I Remember Mama,* and *He Will Come.* Broadway found that the gospel singer could conquer a big city when Shirley packed them in for the musical *Mama I Want to Sing* (1994). Her second Broadway musical in 1995 was titled *Sing: Mama 2* and her third in 1996 was titled *Born to Sing! Mama 3.* Perhaps her proudest achievement was the creation of a ministry in Durham to provide emergency funds, food and shelter for the needy, the Shirley Caesar Outreach Ministries. When Shirley ran for public office and was elected to the Durham City Council in 1987, she concentrated her efforts on housing and care for the poor and elderly.

Recently, Caesar went into the studio to help recording artist Bishop T.D. Jakes with his upcoming album, "Woman, Thou Art Loosed." The album, recorded live at Jakes' national conference in New Orleans, was released in the summer of 1997.

Her biggest fan, the Rev. Harold I. Williams, whom Shirley has called "my pastor, my best friend, my husband," assessed his wife's character in the 1995 video *He Will Come:* "After twelve years, I'm going to say the same thing I said after the first year I was married to Shirley: exciting! You never know what is coming next. I mean it is *exciting.* It is from one thing to another. She's an exciting person. She's a joy to be around." Most who have seen her perform would agree.

Further Reading

American Gospel, March/April 1992.

Ebony, December 1988; March 1994; February 1996.

Epic Center News: "http://www.epiccenter.com/EpicCenter/docs/artistbio.qry?artistid=235," July 17, 1997.

Essence, October 1990.

Jet, Jan. 8, 1990; Aug. 26, 1991; March 9, 1992.

Journal of American Folklore, Summer 1991.

People, November 9, 1987.

Heilbut, Anthony, *The Gospel Sound* (1985).

Cusic, Don, *The Sound of Light: A History of Gospel Music,* (1993). □

John Cage

American avant-garde composer John Cage (1912-1992) experimented with the nature of sound and devised new systems of musical notation. His innovative ideas on composition and performance influenced musicians, painters, and choreographers.

John Cage questioned all musical preconceptions inherited from the 19th century, and he flourished in an atmosphere of controversy. The teacher-composer Arnold Schoenberg once called him "not a composer, but an inventor—of genius." He received awards and grants; a few important music critics wrote perceptively and enthusiastically about his works. However, to most of the public and even to many musicians his compositions—especially the late ones—remain baffling and outrageous, an anarchic world of noise that cannot even qualify as music.

To Cage, "everything we do is music." He believed that the function of art is to imitate nature's manner of operation, and to this end he tried to make music that resembles forms of organic growth—taking into account ugliness, chaos, and accidents, as well as beauty, order, and predictability. In addition, the manner of nature's operation appears to change according to scientific advances. One can find roots of Cage's experiments with "chance" and "indeterminacy" in the work of such French Dadaists as painters Marcel Duchamp and Max Ernst and the surrealist poet André Breton in the early part of the 20th century, when quantum theory and the theory of relativity in physics were giving rise to new ways of conceiving space, time, and causality.

Cage was born in Los Angeles, California, on September 5, 1912, the son of John Milton Cage, an inventor and electrical engineer. John studied piano as a boy. After two years at Pomona College, he spent a year and a half in

Europe, trying his hand at poetry, painting, and architecture, as well as music.

Cage dedicated himself to music shortly after returning to the United States in 1931. His first composition teacher was pianist Richard Bühlig, a noted interpreter of Schoenberg. In a musical world then divided between the serialism of Schoenberg and the neoclassicism of Igor Stravinsky, Cage found himself in the Schoenberg camp. In 1933 Cage went to New York City to study with a former pupil of Schoenberg, and also took Henry Cowell's classes. In 1934 he returned to Los Angeles and was accepted as a pupil by Schoenberg himself.

During the years with Schoenberg, Cage developed three new interests: percussive music, silence, and dance. He started experimenting with percussion ensembles, discovering or adapting instruments as he went along. Finding Schoenberg's use of tonality as a structural principle inappropriate for percussion music, Cage sought a workable method. He decided that silence was the opposite coexistent of sound and determined that of the four characteristics of sound—pitch, timbre, loudness, and duration—only duration was also characteristic of silence; so he abandoned harmonic structure and began to use a rhythmic structure based on the duration of segments of time. Much of this early music is quiet, delicate, full of silences. *Construction in Metal* (1937) is a good example.

Rising Avant-garde Composer

Cage's interest in modern dance was immediately reciprocated; dancers were eager to collaborate. Cage spent two years in Seattle as composer and accompanist for the dance classes of Bonnie Bird. During this time he found that inserting screws between the strings of a piano would create a kind of one-man percussion ensemble. This "prepared piano" became one of his most admired contributions to music, and he wrote a good deal of music for it.

After spending a year in San Francisco and a year teaching at the Chicago School of Design, Cage moved to New York City in 1942. A concert at the Museum of Modern Art in 1943 established him as a rising avant-garde composer.

In 1945 Cage developed an interest in Eastern philosophy that soon had a profound effect on his work; he studied Indian music and attended Daisetz T. Suzuki's lectures on Zen Buddhism. About this time Cage became musical director for the Merce Cunningham Dance Company; this was the beginning of a long-term association.

In 1949 Cage won an award from the National Academy of Arts and Letters for the invention of the prepared piano and a Guggenheim grant. His *Sonatas and Interludes,* performed at Carnegie Recital Hall, was very well received. Cage and Cunningham gave recitals in Europe, which brought Cage into contact with the new generation of French musicians, including Pierre Boulez and Pierre Schaeffer. This year marked a culmination and a turning point.

Chance and Indeterminacy

Until 1950 Cage had been writing what he considered to be expressive music. Now his interest in Zen led him to question this. "When we separate music from life," he wrote in *Silence,* "what we get is art (a compendium of masterpieces). With contemporary music, when it is actually contemporary, we have no time to make that separation (which protects us from living), and so contemporary music is not so much art as it is life and anyone making it no sooner finishes one of it than he begins making another just as people keep on washing dishes, brushing their teeth, getting sleepy, and so on." To make his work consonant with the workings of nature and to free it from the tyranny of the ego, he experimented with "chance" procedures. Chance played a limited role in *Sixteen Dances* (for Merce Cunningham), but to create *Music of Changes* (premiered in 1952) Cage adapted methods from the *I Ching,* the Chinese *Book of Changes,* which involved tossing coins onto a series of charts to determine pitch, duration, and so forth. These experiments found little favor with the musical establishment, although Cage became closely involved with a circle of musicians with similar interests.

Cage swept forward into radical departures from all traditions, including his own. His *Imaginary Landscape No. 4* (1952) involved 24 men turning the dials of 12 radios. At Black Mountain College in the summer of 1952 he created a proto-"happening" that involved simultaneous dance, poetry, live music, records, films, slides, and an art exhibit. He produced his ultimate exploration of silence, *4'33"* (1952), in which the pianist sits immobile before the instrument, marking the beginning and end of each of the three sections in any way he chooses.

By 1958 Cage wished his music to be even more indeterminate in performance, that is, to give the performer a hand in the creation. Thus he did away with the usual score, instead devising a kit of materials: plastic sheets marked with predetermined codes, which the player was to superimpose in order to arrive at his "part." His improvisations did not endear him to the musical establishment. In 1958, when a group of artists presented a Cage retrospective at Town Hall in New York City, the audience that had enthusiastically applauded the earlier works expressed loud dissatisfaction during the performance of *Concert for Piano and Orchestra* (1958). And in 1964, when Leonard Bernstein presented Cage's *Atlas Enclipticalis* with the New York Philharmonic, not only members of the audience but also some of the musicians hissed the composer. This saddened Cage but did not deter him.

In 1954 Cage moved to a small art colony in Stony Point, New York. Here he developed an interest in mushrooms. He taught about them at the New School for Social Research and founded the New York Mycological Society in 1962. He also delivered a series of lectures. These talks, full of charm and wit, were, like his music, compositions of words and silence; they were not "about" anything so much as aggregates of thought on whatever interested him: music, mushrooms, Erik Satie, Buckminster Fuller, Marshall McLuhan, life.

Electronic Music

As early as 1939 Cage had been interested in electronics. He believed that his *Imaginary Landscape No. 5* (1952) was the first piece of magnetic-tape music to be created in America. In the 1960s Cage decided that pure electronic music might be boring for a concert audience, since there was nothing to look at. He experimented with placing contact microphones on conventional instruments; once he even placed a mike against his own throat, turned the volume up, and swallowed thunderously. The microphones, with the feedback used as a musical element, produce unbeautiful and often deafening effects. But Cage's belief that man must come to terms with the loud and ugly noises of modern life accords with his belief that if art has a purpose it is to open the mind and senses of the perceiver to life.

Cage's music became louder and more dense. One of his works, *HPSCHD* (produced in collaboration with Lejaren Hiller, finished in 1968), was created with the aid of a computer. It involves a possibility of playing up to 51 audio tapes and up to seven harpsichord solos simultaneously. A computer printout is supplied with the recording, which gives the listener a program for manipulating the controls of his stereo phonograph. Thus the music can still remain indeterminate in performance. *Cheap Imitation* (1969), based on a piece by the French composer Erik Satie, replaces the original pitches with randomly selected notes.

Continuing Experimentation

Cage's compositions of the 1970s continued to blend electronic noise with elements of indeterminacy. He created the score for the piano work *Études Australes* (1970) using astronomical charts. His 1979 piece *Roaratorio* incorporated thousands of sounds from James Joyce's novel *Finnegans Wake*

The increasing sophistication of computers helped shape Cage's work in the 1980s, most notably in the stage work *Europeras 1 & 2* (1987). The piece, written, designed, staged, and directed by Cage, is essentially a collage of snippets from existing operas woven together by a computer program designed by Cage's assistant, Andrew Culver. The opening performance of *Europeras 1 & 2* was itself a casualty of chance, however, when a vagrant set fire to the Frankfurt Opera House a few days before its debut. In all, Cage would complete five *Europera* works between 1987 and 1991.

Cage was also a prolific author. Drawing on influences like Gertrude Stein and Dada poetry, he created works such as *M* (1973), *Empty Words* (1979), *Theme and Variations* (1992), and *X* (1983). Some of these Cage designed as performance pieces, which he read aloud to the accompaniment of his own music. In other cases, he relied on computer assistance to generate evocative, semi-coherent poetry.

Cage also created and collected visual art: photographs, prints, paintings, and etchings. His musical scores, which eschew conventional notation in favor of idiosyncratic graphic markings, were exhibited in galleries and museums. A collection of his watercolors was exhibited at the Phillips Collection in Washington, D.C. in 1990.

Later Life

As he grew older, Cage was the recipient of numerous honors and awards. Each milestone birthday past the age of 60 was celebrated with a series of concerts and tributes the world over. He was elected to the American Academy of Arts and Sciences in 1978, and was one of 50 artists inducted into the American Academy of Arts and Letters in 1989. In 1981, he received the New York Mayor's Honor Award of Arts and Sciences. The following year, the French government awarded Cage its highest cultural honor when it made him a Commander of the Order of Arts and Letters. Cage traveled to Japan in 1989 to accept the prestigious Kyoto Prize.

A longtime New York City resident, Cage was known as an affable if soft-spoken man who was obliging toward young musicians and critics. He would often attend concerts in downtown Manhattan. Cage's only marriage ended in divorce in 1945. For the last 22 years of his life, he lived with his former collaborator, the choreographer Merce Cunningham. Cage died of a stroke on August 12, 1992.

Further Reading

Many of Cage's articles, lectures, and anecdotes were published in two collections: *Silence* (1961) and *A Year from Monday* (1967). The most detailed biographical account is the essay on him in Calvin Tomkins, *The Bride and the Bachelors: The Heretical Courtship in Modern Art* (1965). A brief but excellent discussion of Cage's position in 20th-century music is in Eric Salzman, *Twentieth Century Music: An Introduction* (1967). *John Cage,* a bibliography of his works compiled by Robert Dunn (1962), contains a brief biography, excerpts from reviews, an interview, lists of available recordings, and details of many first performances. Cage's philosophy and music are discussed in Peter Yates, *Twentieth Century Music* (1967). More recent studies of Cage include Fleming and Duckworth's *John Cage at 75* (1989) and Paul Griffiths, *Cage* (1981). A series of Cage's later lectures are collected in *Cage: I-VI* (1990). Cage's obituary appeared in *New York Times* on August 13, 1992. □

Abraham Cahan

The Jewish author and journalist Abraham Cahan (1860-1951) was a prominent Socialist leader and union organizer among Jewish immigrants in the United States.

Abraham Cahan was born in Podberezhie, near Vilna, Lithuania. His father was a storekeeper and later rabbi at Vidz, Vitebsk. In 1866 the family moved to Vilna, where Cahan was educated for the rabbinate and also studied Russian literature. After graduating from the Teachers Institute at Vilna in 1881, he taught for a short time. But, because he belonged to a Jewish idealist group connected with an assassination plot against Czar Alexander II, in 1882 he fled from Russia to the United States.

In New York, Cahan became a journalist and soon founded two Jewish journals, *Die neue Zeit* (1886) and *Arbeiter-Zeitung* (1890). From 1894 to 1897 he was editor of the Yiddish journal *Zukunft;* in 1897 he became the first editor of the Socialist *Daily Forward.* The following year he joined the staff of the *Commercial Advertiser,* where he remained until 1902. Cahan then returned to the *Forward* as editor in chief, a post he held until his death. Under his guidance the *Forward*'s circulation rose from 6,000 to 200,000.

Cahan's career as an author was not limited to journalism. His short story "The Providential Catch" appeared in 1895; it was followed by the novel *Yekl* in 1896 and *The Imported Bridegroom and Other Stories* in 1898. He subsequently published *The White Terror and the Red* (1905); two volumes on the history of Jewish immigrants in America (1910-1912); the novel *The Rise of David Levinsky* (1917); and his autobiography, *Bleter fun mayn Leben* (5 vols., 1926-1931). He also contributed many articles to periodicals.

Cahan was a Socialist and an outstanding advocate of what was known as the moderate right wing. He acted as a representative at international socialist congresses in Brussels (1891) and Zurich (1893). He engaged actively in organizing Jewish workers into trade unions. He used Yiddish as a medium to inform the ordinary immigrant of the possibilities for him in America while preserving the richness of his cultural heritage as a Jew. Under his direction the *Forward* became highly influential in the formation of the Jewish Labor movement.

Cahan also played a significant role in the development of the larger Jewish world community. After a visit to Palestine in 1925, he returned enthusiastic for the restoration of Israel as a national home for Jews. It was largely due to his influence that the State of Israel received the support of the American Jewish Labor movement at a later date.

Cahan died on Aug. 31, 1951, and his funeral was attended by over 10,000 people.

Further Reading

There is no full-length biography of Cahan. His autobiography was translated as *The Education of Abraham Cahan* (5 vols., 1926-1931; trans., 1 vol., 1969). Much of Ronald Sanders's study, *The Downtown Jews: Portraits of an Immigrant Generation* (1969), deals with Cahan. □

Auguste René Caillié

The French explorer Auguste René Caillié (1799-1838) was the first modern European to reach the famous Sudanic cities of West Africa, Timbuktu, and Djenné and to return and tell about it.

René Caillié was born in Mauzé. He never knew his father, and his mother died in 1810. Caillié left school at an early age to become an apprentice shoemaker. Life in the French provinces did not prevent him from reading and hearing about voyages of adventure; he early conceived the idea of visiting Africa and becoming an explorer. He eventually formulated a plan for gaining entry to the remote city of Timbuktu, a passion which shaped the rest of his life.

At 16 and with only 60 francs, Caillié left home for Senegal. He arrived at Cape Verde in July 1816, visited Saint-Louis, shipped to Guadeloupe in the West Indies, and finally returned to Senegal to join an expedition exploring the headwaters of the Senegal River. Caillié's first experience with the African interior left him exhausted. He returned to France, worked for a wine house in Bordeaux, and sailed to the West Indies several times. After regaining his health, he set out again for Senegal in 1824.

Caillié was unable to obtain official French backing to travel to Timbuktu. He decided nonetheless to prepare himself and spent 8 months living among the Brakna Moors, learning Arabic, studying the Koran, and becoming used to nomadic life in the Sahara. Unsuccessful in gaining British backing in Sierra Leone, Caillié finally set out on his own on April 19, 1827, from Kakandé (which became French Guinea) with only 2,000 francs. His experiences on the African coast and his knowledge of the customs enabled him to travel relatively unmolested.

Caillié reached the Niger River on June 10, 1827; the city of Djenné on March 11, 1828; and Timbuktu on April 20. He pretended to be an Egyptian Moslem pilgrim, and a prosperous local merchant befriended and protected him during his 2-week stay. Caillié made copious notes on the inhabitants, trade, buildings, and customs. Fearing detection in an intolerant city, he rented a camel and crossed the Sahara with a caravan which reached Fez in Morocco on Aug. 12, 1828. The French consul arranged for his passage to France in September, where he was received with excitement and adulation.

The Geographical Society of Paris awarded him its 10,000-franc prize for the first traveler to visit and return from Timbuktu. Caillié wrote a three-volume account of his travels afterward, which made him a famous man; yet he was unsuccessful in gaining support for further exploration in Africa. He lived a relatively quiet life with his wife and children on his farm in Mauzé until his death on May 17, 1838.

Further Reading

Caillié's account of his travels was translated into English as *Travels through Central Africa to Timbuctoo* (2 vols., 1830; repr. 1968). A popular account of Caillié's travels is Galbraith Welch, *The Unveiling of Timbuctoo* (1939). □

St. Cajetan

St. Cajetan (1480-1547), who was born Gaetano da Thiene, was one of the earliest Italian Catholic reformers of the 16th century. He was a cofounder of the Clerks Regular, a religious order popularly known as the Theatines.

Cajetan was born into an aristocratic family of Vicenza in October 1480. He studied at Padua and in 1504 received his doctorate in canon and civil law. In 1505 he went to Rome, where Pope Julius II invited him to join the papal service as a secretary. On Sept. 30, 1516, he was ordained a priest. Cajetan was a kind, energetic, and practical man whose life was marked by strict poverty and intense activity. With other men, including the humanist Pietro Bembo, he organized the Roman Divino Amore, or the Oratory of Divine Love—not to be confused with St. Philip Neri's Congregation of the Oratory. Cajetan's Oratory provided a program for common prayer and discussion of spiritual topics.

In 1518, because of his mother's sickness, Cajetan returned to Vicenza. Intent on helping others, especially the sick, he founded a hospital for incurables there. In 1520 he did the same at Venice, where he also initiated the practice of exposing the Blessed Sacrament in a monstrance for adoration by the congregation. Back in Rome, he again became an active organizer. In 1523, with Giampietro Carafa (later Pope Paul IV), Bonifacio de' Colli, and Paolo Consiglieri, he formed a group of priests who combined religious life with apostolic activity. So adamant was Cajetan on the vital place that poverty held in his ideal that he refused to allow even begging. To distinguish these priests from earlier organizations of religious, they became technically known as Clerks Regular. On June 24, 1524, Pope Clement VII gave them his approval. They were generally called Theatines, probably because the Latin form for Carafa's see of Chieti was Theate. Carafa was elected the first superior, and in 1527 Cajetan became the second superior.

The Theatines made a deep impression and soon spread to other cities of Italy. After the sack of Rome in 1527, during which Cajetan suffered great personal indignity, the Theatines moved to Venice and Verona. In 1533 they opened their apostolate in Naples, where Cajetan was the first superior. And there, with the exception of a few years in Rome and Venice, Cajetan spent the rest of his life. Ever the practical organizer, he was one of the first movers for a modern type of credit union to help the poor of the city. With his energetic life Cajetan united profound prayerfulness, severe penance, and adherence to the strictest kind of poverty. Toward the close of his life a riot broke out against the Inquisition, and Cajetan tried in vain to calm the disturbance. With this disappointment he died at Naples on Aug. 7, 1547. He was canonized on April 12, 1671.

Further Reading

A good biography of St. Cajetan is Paul H. Hallett, *Catholic Reformer: A Life of St. Cajetan of Thiene* (1959). Written in a popular style, which is at times pietistic, it provides a full and detailed study. See also Herbert Thurston and Donald Attwater's edition of *Butler's Lives of the Saints,* vol. 3 (1956). □

Calamity Jane

Martha Jane Cannary, known as Calamity Jane (1852-1903), was a notorious American frontier woman in the days of the Wild West. As unconventional and wild as the territory she roamed, she has become a legend.

The most likely date of Jane Cannary's birth is May 1, 1852, probably at Princeton, Mo. When she was 12 or 13, the family headed west along the Overland Route, reaching Virginia City, Mont., 5 months later. En route Jane learned to be a teamster and to snap 30-foot bullwhackers. Her father died in 1866 and her mother died a year later. Late in 1867 Jane was in Salt Lake City.

Until the early 1870s nothing more is known of Jane. Then she appeared at Rawlins, Wyo., where she dressed and acted like a man and hired out as a mule skinner, bullwhacker, and railroad worker. "Calamity" became part of her name; she was proud of it.

In 1875 Calamity went with Gen. George Crook's expedition against the Sioux, probably as a bullwhacker. While swimming in the nude, her sex was discovered and she was sent back. Excitement and wild adventure lured Calamity, whether it meant joining "her boys" at the bar or fighting with Native Americans. She was adept at using a six-shooter.

In Deadwood, Dakota Territory, in 1876 Calamity found a home. It was an outlaw town, so her escapades and drinking bouts did not seem out of place. One day she accompanied Wild Bill Hickok into town; apparently they had met before. Whether they were ever married, or lovers, may never be known. Jane later did have a daughter, but that she was fathered by Hickok (as the daughter claimed in 1941) is questionable. On August 2 Jack McCall shot and killed Hickok. Calamity took no revenge, as she later claimed, and McCall was legally hanged.

Yet this flamboyant woman was kind, and many remembered only her virtues. During the 1878 Deadwood smallpox epidemic Calamity stayed in the log pesthouse and nursed the patients.

Calamity Jane left Deadwood in 1880 and drifted around the Dakotas and Montana. She next appeared in California and married E. M. Burke in 1885, and her daughter was born sometime before or after this. Alone again in the later 1880s and the 1890s, she wandered through Wyoming and Montana towns, drinking, brawling, and working, even in brothels. Her fame began to grow. In 1896 she joined the Palace Museum and toured Chicago, St. Louis, and Kansas City; she was fired for drunkenness. Calamity came back to Deadwood in 1899, searching for funds for her daughter's education. A successful benefit was held at the Old Opera House. In 1900 Calamity appeared briefly at the Pan-American Exposition in Buffalo, N.Y., as a Western attraction, but she was homesick for the West and soon went back. In poor health, in July 1903 she arrived at the Calloway Hotel in Terry, near Deadwood, where she died on August 1 or 2. She was buried next to Wild Bill Hickok.

Further Reading

The work with the best scholarly research on Calamity Jane is Nolie Mumey, *Calamity Jane, 1852-1903: A History of Her Life and Adventures in the West* (1950), but the book is difficult to find because it was published in a limited edition. More readily available and also good is John Leonard Jennewein, *Calamity Jane of the Western Trails* (1953), which separates fact from fiction whenever possible. A short, interesting, debunking account of Calamity Jane is in James D. Horan, *Desperate Women* (1952). □

Alexander Calder

American sculptor, painter, and illustrator Alexander Calder (1898-1976), through his construction of wire mobiles, pioneered kinetic sculpture.

Alexander Calder was born in Philadelphia, the son of a well-known sculptor and educator and his wife, a talented painter. Calder's grandfather, also a sculptor, executed the figure of William Penn that graces the dome of the city hall in Philadelphia. Though he was brought up in an artistic atmosphere, Calder's own inclinations were mechanical. He trained as a mechanical engineer at the Stevens Institute of Technology in New Jersey, studying such things as descriptive geometry, mechanical drawing, and applied kinetics—the branch of science that deals with the effects of force on free-moving bodies—in preparation for receiving his degree in 1919.

After working at a number of jobs that allowed him time for travel and reflection over the next few years, Calder decided to explore his growing interest in art. In 1923, two years after beginning his study of drawing in night school, he enrolled full-time at the Art Students League in New York City. There he attended classes given by George Luks, Guy Pène Du Bois, and John Sloan, all important American painters of that period. Calder also did freelance work as an illustrator for the *National Police Gazette* for about two years. In 1926 he had his first one-man exhibition of paintings at the Artist's Gallery in New York City. While concentrating on painting, Calder also worked on wood sculpture, and when he visited Paris in 1926 he continued to carve.

Circus Brought Lasting Fame

Calder's first significant recognition as an artist came when he exhibited his now- famous miniature circus with its animated wire performers at Paris's Salon des Humoristes in 1927. The idea for the toy figures can be traced back to sketches he made in 1925 while reporting on the circus for the *Police Gazette* . Made from wire, rubber, cork, buttons, bottle caps, wood, and other small "found" objects, Calder's circus includes lions, acrobats, trapeze artists, elephants, a ringmaster, and numerous other figures. Unlike many art works of the period, the unusual creation drew crowds from outside the artistic community as well as within, and the thirty-year-old artist found himself suddenly widely known.

Calder's first wire sculpture, *Josephine Baker* (1926), a witty linear representation of the famous American-born chanteuse, was exhibited to the Paris art community during the same period that his circus was drawing attention. He decided to return to New York City late in 1927, where he gave a one-man show that included *Josephine Baker,* as well as several of his other wire portraits. Those portraits would grow increasingly three dimensional as the artist refined his technique.

Influenced by Modernists

In November 1928 Calder was again in Paris, supporting himself with performances of his miniature circus, one of which was attended by Spanish surrealist Joan Miró. Calder had his first one-man shows in Paris at the Galérie Billiet and in Berlin in 1929. In Paris he met a number of important modernists, including Fernand Léger, Theo Van Doesburg, and Piet Mondrian, the latter whose work particularly impressed him. By 1930 Calder was making large-scale abstract wire sculptures using flat metal ovals painted black or bright colors, as well as small balls or other shapes suspended by long wires. Many of these work suggested the solar system in their design. From these beginnings he developed motor-driven sculptures, which featured objects hanging from large bases, although the artist had no fondness for the regular, predictable motion provided by motors. An exhibition of Calder's kinetic sculptures was seen by Marcel Duchamp, who referred to them as "mobiles"—a term which became associated with this work. He made a number of sculptures during the thirties which employed the same forms as the mobiles but were static, and known as "stabiles."

Meanwhile, in 1931 Calder was married to Louisa James, who he had met on a voyage to New York City; that same year he illustrated an edition of *Aesop's Fables* . Two years later Calder made his first draft-propelled mobiles. Rather than following a monotonous path of motion as did his motor-driven sculptures, these pieces create myriad patterns once they are set in action by a breeze or gentle push. Their shapes, largely ovoid and biomorphic, may have been inspired by the art of Miró. In 1933 Calder and his wife bought a farm in Roxbury, Connecticut, where he established his studio. In 1935 and again in 1936 he designed stage sets for the dancer Martha Graham.

Commissioned Works Prompted Travel

The Museum of Modern Art in New York City gave a comprehensive exhibition of Calder's work in 1943, during which the artist gave performances of his famous circus; the show's catalog was the first extensive study on the artist. The following year he made sculptures out of plaster to be cast in bronze. These pieces moved at a slow, measured pace. During this period he illustrated *Three Young Rats* (1944), *The Rime of the Ancient Mariner* with Robert Penn Warren's essay on Coleridge (1945), and *The Fables of LaFontaine* (1946). At this time Calder's international reputation was reinforced by exhibitions in New York, Amsterdam, Berne, Rio de Janeiro, São Paulo, Boston, and Richmond, Virginia. In 1952 he designed the acoustical ceiling for the Aula Magna at the university in Caracas and received the first prize for sculpture at the Venice Biennale. Commissions for his designs continued to pour in as he created everything from jewelry to costume and stage-set designs for dance and theatrical performances. In the 1970s, at the height of Calder's fame, Braniff Airlines commissioned him to paint some of their jet planes with his unique, boldly colorful designs.

Calder's works are featured in permanent installations around the world. In 1955 he travelled to India to execute 11 mobiles for public buildings in Ahmadabad. He designed many monumental pieces, including those for Lincoln Center in New York City, for the Massachusetts Institute of Technology in Cambridge, for the gardens of UNESCO in Paris, and for Expo '67 at Montreal. In 1964, when the artist was in his late seventies, he was honored with a comprehensive retrospective at the Guggenheim Museum in New York City; a smaller one was given at the Museum of Modern Art in 1970. At his death in 1976, Calder was eulogized by Minneapolis, Minnesota, curator Marvin Friedman as "one of the greatest form-givers America has ever produced."

Further Reading

Excellent for its plates and its interpretations of Calder's sculptures is H. H. Arnason, *Calder* (1966). Also recommended are Calder's own *Calder: An Autobiography with Pictures* (1966), and James Johnson Sweeney, *Alexander Calder* (1943; rev. ed. 1951). □

Rafael Caldera Rodríguez

Venezuelan Rafael Caldera Rodríguez (born 1916) founded the Christian Democratic Party of Venezuela and served as his country's president from 1969 to 1974.

Rafael Caldera Rodríguez, the son of Dr. Rafael and Rosa Sofia Caldera, was born in 1916 in San Felipe in the north-central state of Yaracuy, Venezuela. An exceptional student, Caldera earned a doctor of philosophy degree in political science, taught at a leading Venezuelan university, and wrote a scholarly study of the distinguished Latin American educator Andrés Bello. His scholarly interests also included the rights and responsibilities of labor. He served in Venezuela's Ministry of Labor between 1936 and 1938 and published a comprehensive review of Venezuela's labor laws. In 1941 he married his wife, Alicia.

Caldera's political career began in 1936 when he was elected to the Chamber of Deputies. A devout Catholic, he organized Catholic civic groups, and, in 1946, helped establish the Christian Democratic Party of Venezuela or COPEI. Christian Democrats espouse that there is a third or middle way between *laissez-faire* capitalism and Marxist socialism. They reject Marxist ideas of dialectical materialism and class struggle. But they also fear that capitalism without social safeguards produces a grossly inequitable society. Christian Democrats accordingly believe that they must work for social justice by promoting democracy, fair taxation systems, and social welfare programs.

In 1947 Rafael Caldera ran for president and finished second behind Rómulo Gallegos of the Democratic Action Party. But in 1948 military officers overthrew the Gallegos government and established ten years of military dictatorship in Venezuela. The officers, led by Col. Marcos Pérez Jiménez, banned most political activity in Venezuela, closely monitored Caldera's activities, and in 1957 jailed and then exiled the Christian Democratic leader.

Caldera returned to Venezuela in 1958 following the overthrow of the Pérez Jiménez regime. He again competed for the presidency in 1958 and in 1963. Though he lost these two elections, Caldera and his party helped consolidate democracy in Venezuela. As committed democrats, they respected Venezuelans' decisions and served as the "loyal opposition" to the ruling Democratic Action Party in the Venezuelan legislature. Caldera, for example, presided over the Chamber of Deputies between 1959 and 1961. Caldera's persistency was finally rewarded in December

1968 when he won the presidency by garnering 29 percent of the vote in a multicandidate election.

President Caldera's domestic accomplishments were relatively modest. During the campaign of 1968 he had pledged to revitalize the agricultural sector of the economy and to build 100,000 homes a year. But his party did not command a majority in the legislature and his country lacked the resources for implementing such ambitious reforms. Therefore, Caldera continued the gradual socio-economic reforms that the Democratic Action Party had initiated. Perhaps his major achievement was to strengthen political democracy in Venezuela by encouraging citizens and organizations to speak up and by holding weekly television talks and press conferences.

In international economic affairs, however, significant change occurred during the Caldera presidency. In 1960 Venezuela had established, with Middle Eastern nations, the Organization of Petroleum Exporting Countries (OPEC). OPEC's major premise was that oil-exporting nations, like Venezuela, deserved a high price for the sale of a vital, nonrenewable natural resource. Throughout the 1960s industrial nations ignored OPEC because oil was abundant. But in the early 1970s demand for oil began to exceed supply, and Arab nations embargoed shipments of oil to the United States in protest against U.S. support for Israel during the Arab-Israeli (Yom Kippur) War of 1973. The price of oil shot up from $2.00 a barrel in 1971 to $14.00 by 1974.

Oil production was Venezuela's major industry, and President Caldera took advantage of these momentous developments in the international oil trade. He raised taxes on oil production, nationalized the gas industry, and enacted stringent laws regulating the U.S. oil companies that operated in Venezuela. By the time he left office in 1974 the government had, because of this oil bonanza, the income to improve the lives of Venezuelans.

The Venezuelan constitution prohibits a president from succeeding himself for ten years. In 1983 Rafael Caldera made his fifth bid for the presidency. He was badly defeated by Jaime Lusinchi of Democratic Action. While Venezuelans admired Caldera, they apparently blamed Christian Democrats, who had ruled since 1978, for a host of social and economic problems that bedeviled the country. As a former president, Rafael Caldera was a member of the Venezuelan Senate for life.

After leaving the presidency of Venezuela, Caldera continued to pursue both scholarly and political pursuits with remarkable vigor. For three years (1979-82) he served as the president of the Counselors for the World's Interparliamentary Union, and in 1979 he served as the president of the World's Congress of Agrarian Reform and Rural Improvement in Rome. He presided over a United Nations committee to create the University for Peace from 1980-1981, and over another Bicameral Commission (1989-1992) concerned with reforming the constitution. All together he published twenty-two books in his life, plus innumerable essays, articles, and booklets. Over the years his elaborate work on Andrés Bello was translated to French, Italian, Portuguese, Russian, and English (1975). He also wrote a number of pieces on Simón Bolivar, including *Bolivar Siempre* in 1987 for the National Academy of History in Caracas. Throughout his lifetime Caldera was bestowed with honorary doctorates, degrees, and professorships from a dozen universities and academies in Venezuela and from over a score of foreign universities including Hebrew University of Jerusalem, University of Notre Dame in Indiana, and University of Perugia (Italy) He was decorated many times both in Venezuela and abroad. His numerous distinctions and achievements require many pages to list in detail.

Caldera and his wife had six children and nine grandchildren.

Further Reading

There is no complete biography of Caldera in English. For background and information, see Donald L. Herman, *Christian Democracy in Venezuela* (1980) and Judith Ewell, *Venezuela: A Century of Change* (1985). For developments in oil, see Franklin Tugwell, *The Politics of Oil in Venezuela* (1975).

Other information can be accessed through the Venezuelan embassy's Web site at http://venezuela.mit.edu:80/embassy/politica/caldera.html □

Alberto P. Calderón

Alberto Calderón's (born 1920) revolutionary influence turned the 1950s trend toward abstract mathematics back to the study of mathematics for practical applications in physics, geometry, calculus, and many other branches of this field. His award-winning research in the area of integral operators is an example of his impact on contemporary mathematical analysis.

Widely considered as one of the twentieth century's foremost mathematicians, Alberto Calderón's career spans more than 45 years, during which he has left behind many seminal works and ideas.

Calderón was born on September 14, 1920, in Mendoza, Argentina, a town at the foot of the Andes. His father was a descendant of notable nineteenth-century politicians and military officers and was a renowned medical doctor who helped found and organize the General Central Hospital of Mendoza.

After completing his secondary education in his hometown and in Zug, Switzerland, under Dr. Save Bercovici, who encouraged Calderón's interest in mathematics, he enrolled in the School of Engineering of the National University of Buenos Aires, from which he graduated in 1947. He soon became a student of Alberto González Domínguez and of the celebrated mathematician Antoni Zygmund, who was a visiting professor in Buenos Aires in 1948. He continued his mathematical studies at the University of Chicago with a Rockefeller Foundation fellowship, and received his Ph.D. there in 1950.

Calderón began his academic teaching career as an assistant to the Chair of electric circuit theory at the University of Buenos Aires in 1948, and after graduating in the United States, continued it as a visiting associate professor at Ohio State University from 1950 to 1953. Calderón was also a member of the Institute for Advanced Study in Princeton (1954-1955) and later served as an associate professor at the Massachusetts Institute of Technology (MIT) between 1955 and 1959. He then moved to the University of Chicago, where he served as professor of mathematics from 1959 to 1968, Louis Block professor of mathematics from 1968 to 1972, and chairman of the mathematics department from 1970 to 1972.

By that time, Calderón's prestige was well established in scientific circles, and his research in collaboration with his longtime mentor Zygmund had already been dubbed "the Chicago School of Analysis," also known today as "the Calderón-Zygmund School of Analysis." Their contribution, which profoundly affected modern mathematics, included reversing a predominant trend towards abstraction and turning back to basic questions of real and complex analysis. This work, completed in tandem with Zygmund, came to be known as "Calderón-Zygmund theory."

A landmark in Calderón's scientific career was his 1958 paper titled "Uniqueness of the Cauchy Problem for Partial Differential Equations," which the American Mathematical Society has called "a real watershed in the theory of singular integral operators, taking it beyond its traditional role in the study of elliptic equations." Two years later, he used the same method to build a complete theory of hyperbolic partial differential equations.

His theory of singular operators, which is used to estimate solutions to geometrical equations, contributed to link together several different branches of mathematics. It also had practical applications in many areas, including physics and aerodynamic engineering. This theory has dominated contemporary mathematics and has made important inroads in other scientific fields, including quantum physics. Although some authors have introduced and used the notion of pseudo-differential operator, which is a sum of compositions of powers of the Laplacian with singular integral operators with kernels which are infinitely differentiable off the diagonal, the original idea and basic applications remain credited to Calderón.

Calderón's extensive work has transformed contemporary mathematical analysis. In addition to his work with singular integral operators, he also did fundamental work in interpolation theory, and was responsible, together with R. Arens, for what is considered one of the best theorems in Banach Algebras. Calderón also put forth an approach to energy estimates that has been of fundamental importance in dozens of subsequent investigations, and has provided a general model for research in this area.

A Brief Return Home

In 1971-1972, Calderón briefly returned to his home country to serve as professor and direct mathematical doctoral dissertation studies at his alma mater, the National University of Buenos Aires. He continued to encourage mathematics students from Latin America and the United States to pursue their doctoral degrees, in many instances directly sponsoring them. Some of his pupils, in turn, have become reputed mathematicians, as, for example, Robert T. Seeley, whose extension of the Calderón- Zygmund results to singular operators on manifolds became the foundation of the now-famous Atiyah-Singer index theorem.

After his stay in Argentina, Calderón returned to MIT as a professor of mathematics, and in 1975 he became University Professor, a special position, at the University of Chicago until his retirement in 1985. Between 1989 and 1992, he was a professor emeritus, with a post retirement appointment at that same institution. In 1979 he was awarded the Bôcher prize for a paper on the Cauchy integral on Lipschitz curves. In 1989 he shared the Mathematics Prize of the Wolf Foundation of Israel with his American colleague John W. Milnor. He received innumerable other honors around the world. The American Mathematical Society honored Calderón again with the prestigious Steele Prize (fundamental research paper category) in 1989, and former U.S. president George Bush, in granting him the 1991 National Medal of Science, cited "his ground-breaking work on singular integral operators leading to their application to important problems in partial differential equations."

Author and Lecturer

As an author, Calderón has published more than 75 scientific papers on various topics, from real variables to partial differential equations and singular integrals. A number of those papers were written in collaboration with his teacher Antoni Zygmund. Calderón has lectured in major cities the world over.

A member of the American Mathematical Society for over 40 years, Dr. Calderón has served as member-at-large of its Council (1965-1967) and in several of its committees. He has also been associate editor of various important scientific publications, such as the *Duke Mathematical Journal,* the *Journal of Functional Analysis,* and others.

Dr. Calderón married in 1950. With Mabel Molinelli, his first wife who died in 1985, he had two children: María Josefina, who holds a doctorate in French literature from the University of Chicago, and Pablo Alberto, also a mathematician who studied in Buenos Aires and New York. In 1989 Calderón married again. His second wife, Dr. Alexandra Bellow, is also a distinguished mathematician and a professor of mathematics at Northwestern University in Evanston, near Chicago.

Further Reading

Atiyah, M. F. and Singer, I. M., "The Index of Elliptic Operators on Compact Manifolds," *Bulletin of the American Mathematical Society,* 69, 1963, pp. 442-53.

González Domínguez, Alberto, "Dr. Alberto P. Calderón—Premio Bocher 1979," *Ciencia e Investigación,* 34, November-December 1978, Buenos Aires, pp. 221-23.

Beals, R. W., Coifman, R. R., and Jones, P. W., "Alberto Calderón Receives National Medal of Science," *Notices of the American Mathematical Society,* 39, No. 4, April 1992.

Chicago Tribune, September 17, 1991. □

Pedro Calderón

The Spanish poet and playwright Pedro Calderón de la Barca y Henao (1600-1681) is second only to Lope de Vega in Spain's Golden Age, 1580-1680. He used the stage to interpret and champion Catholicism, to battle the Reformation, and to exalt the monarchy.

Born in Madrid on Jan. 17, 1600, Pedro Calderón was orphaned by the age of 15. He studied first with Jesuits, then at the universities of Alcalá and Salamanca; his studies included rhetoric, logic, theology, the Bible, law, philosophy, grammar, the classics, and history. He obtained his degree in canon law from the University of Salamanca in 1619.

From 1638 until 1642 Calderón and his brother José were in the King's service, assigned to help quell an insurrection in Catalonia. Afterward, Pedro returned to Madrid, where sometime during the 1640s his inamorata bore him a son. She died during this decade, as did two of his brothers. Saddened and sobered, Calderón in 1651 took orders for the priesthood. He behaved decorously the remainder of his life and died in Madrid on May 25, 1681.

Literary Career

Calderón began his writing career in Madrid in 1622 by participating in a poetry competition sponsored by that city to celebrate the canonization of its patron saint, St. Isidro. About the same time, he produced his first play, *Love, Honor and Power* (*Amor, honor y poder*). In Madrid, then a great world capital, the theater district and King Philip IV's palace theater needed a constant supply of plays on varied subjects. To satisfy the demand for variety, Calderón searched through time, history, literature, and fantasy. At his death he left a considerable number and variety of plays—120 *comedias,* 80 sacramental plays (*autos sacramentales*), and several short pieces, including vaudeville skits with music (*zarzuelas*), and even comic curtain raisers of a mere few minutes' duration. A general classification, with accompanying exemplary titles, would be Spanish history and legend: *The Mayor of Zalamea* (*El alcalde de Zalamea*); honor plays: *The Physician of His Own Honor* (*El médico de su honra*); cape-and-sword plays: *The Phantom Lady* (*La dama duende*); philosophical plays: *Life Is a Dream* (*La vida es sueño*); religious plays: *Devotion to the Cross* (*La devoción de la Cruz*); hagiographic plays: *The Constant Prince* (*El príncipe constante*); sacramental plays: *Belshazzar's Feast* (*La cena del Rey Baltasar*); fantastic and mythological plays: *The Daughter of the Air* (*La hija del aire*).

Major Works

Calderón's most celebrated play is *Life Is a Dream* (1635), with a central theme of free will versus predestination, a burning issue of the day. The protagonist, Prince Segismundo of Poland, is born under the dismal astrological prediction that he will become a tyrant on reaching the throne. His father, King Basilio, a practicing astrologer, has him placed in chains in a remote prison. When Segismundo reaches his majority, his father relents and has his son drugged and brought to the palace, where he awakens to find himself on the throne. Segismundo in several violent actions shows himself cruel and vindictive as the stars had predicted, so his father has him returned to prison. Plunged back into this harsh environment after having tasted power and luxury, a bewildered Segismundo can no longer distinguish between the dreamworld and reality. The people of the kingdom, learning for the first time of the existence of their prince, overthrow King Basilio. Segismundo, once again enthroned, chastised by experience, proves triumphant over his darker and hateful self. *Life Is a Dream* ends optimistically—Segismundo, though inclined by the stars to tyranny, through his own free will overcomes evil. The play contains Calderón's most impassioned poetry.

Calderón's best play based on Spanish history and legend is *The Mayor of Zalamea* (1644?), in which he proves through convincing flesh-and-blood characters that common people may have both honor and pride and insinuates that, when circumstances justify, civil authority should overrule military authority.

Calderón's *Prodigious Magician* (*El mágico prodigioso,* 1637) relates the story of Cipriano, a student who mortgages his soul to the devil for the possession of the girl Justina. As he embraces a conjured-up pseudo-Justina, she turns into a skeleton; the deception brings about his conversion, and both he and Justina become martyrs. *Devotion to the Cross* (1633) portrays the career of a youthful gangster who is ultimately saved from hell through his devotion to the Cross, the symbol of divine grace. Albert Camus, who considered Calderón "the greatest dramatic genius Spain ever produced," was so drawn to the play and its message of "the grace which transfigures the worst of criminals" that he translated it into French.

No cape-and-sword plays surpassed Calderón's. He wrote them purely for entertainment, as the titles reveal: *The Phantom Lady, Everybody's Secret* (*El secreto a voces*), *April and May Mornings* (*Mañanas de abril y mayo*).

Calderón gave to the Spanish language the phrase "honor calderoniano" (Calderonian honor), meaning a sense of honor which forces a husband to take the life of a wife maligned by scandalmongers, even when he knows her to be innocent. "El honor con sangre, señor, se lava" ("A stain on one's honor, sir, is washed in blood") is the rigid creed of Don Gutierre in *The Physician of His Own Honor* (1635), who orders his suspected wife bled to death by a surgeon. Other plays depicting this same sort of bloodletting are *Secret Vengeance for Secret Offense* (*A secreto agravio, secreta venganza*) and *The Portrayer of His Own Dishonor* (*El pintor de su deshonra*). For many years Calderón had been censured for writing these plays because they seemed to condone undue violence committed by husbands on wives; only in recent times have critics begun to suspect that his honor plays are a condemnation of the seemingly mindless honor code.

Calderón's sacramental plays (*autos sacramentales*) were lyrically written poetic dramas of one act performed on *carros* (movable platforms) in open squares in honor of the Eucharist. Everyone, from the most arrogant aristocrat to the humblest beggar, shared the feeling of awe produced by these allegorical representations of the mystery of transubstantiation, and the populace saw Holy Writ become flesh and blood. Calderón produced over 70 *autos,* and perhaps the finest was *The Great Stage, the World* (*El gran teatro del mundo,* 1633), a vastly high-reaching, Scripture-girded interpretation of the origin and end of man.

Calderón was the last famous dramatist of Spain's Golden Age of literature and art, and after his death Spanish drama languished for a century.

Further Reading

In English the indispensable book on Calderón is Everett W. Hesse, *Calderón de la Barca* (1967). See also Salvador de Madariaga, *Shelley and Calderón* (1920); A.A. Parker, *The Allegorical Drama of Calderón* (1943); and A.E. Sloman, *The Dramatic Craftsmanship of Calderón: His Use of Earlier Plays* (1958).

Additional Sources

Gerstinger, Heinz, *Pedro Calderón de la Barc,* New York, Ungar 1973.

Comedias: a facsimile edition: with textual and critical studies, Farnborough, Eng.: Gregg International, 1973. □

Rafael Calderón Fournier

Rafael Calderón Fournier (born 1949) was elected president of Costa Rica in 1990, succeeding the popular Oscar Arias Sánchez, who had spearheaded the Central American peace plan. Calderón, who served until 1994, was president at a time of widespread national concern over economic decline and drug trafficking.

Rafael Calderón Fournier, son of former Costa Rican president Rafael Calderón Guardia y Muñoz (1940-1944) was born in 1949 in Nicaragua, where his father had taken refuge following the 1948 civil war. The elder Calderón's supporters had tried to reinstall him in the presidency after an election in which the opposition charged him with fraud. The young Calderón went to school in Mexico. The family returned to Costa Rica and he was elected to the National Assembly in 1974. From 1978 to 1980 he served as foreign minister. In 1982 Calderón lost in a bid for the presidency as candidate of Unidad (Unity) Coalition. Four years later he ran against Arias, nominee of the National Liberation Party.

In the late 1980s Costa Ricans often divided sharply over the country's relationship to the United States. Arias had warned that his predecessor's policies had compromised traditional Costa Rican neutrality. Arias won the election and as president shifted Costa Rican politics toward a centrist position in Central American affairs, thus antagonizing the Ronald Reagan administration. Calderón voiced more conservative views. He became executive secretary of the Costa Rican Association for the Defense of Democracy and Liberty, a conservative organization whose members were critical of Arias' Central American peace plans. This group had ties to conservative Republican leaders in the United States and, it was charged, received much of its financing from the National Republican Institute for International Affairs.

Exploiting his close ties to Republican advisers (among them political consultant Roger Ailes, who had managed George Bush's 1988 presidential campaign), Calderón conducted a successful bid for the Costa Rican presidency in 1990, defeating the National Liberation Party candidate Carlos Manuel Castillo, 52 percent to 48 percent. Eighty percent of the electorate of 1.6 million voted. (Arias was constitutionally prohibited from succeeding himself.) Unlike the 1986 campaign, where the divisions between the candidates had been great, that of 1990 displayed surprising agreement. Both Castillo (formerly president of the central bank) and Calderón, the leader of the Christian Unity Party (PUSC), expressed similar convictions about the need to confront social problems, particularly those wrought by the growing numbers of impoverished crowding into the towns and cities of the central valley. The National Liberation Party had emerged victorious in five of the six preceding elections, however, a departure from the post-1948 trend where the two major opposition parties alternated in holding power. Despite the similarity of the political agendas of the two candidates, many voters, suspicious of the long years of National Liberation rule, apparently wanted a change.

Calderón soon discovered that his campaign pledges of income distribution, subsidies for home buyers, and more welfare benefits could not be reconciled with budget slashing. In the 1950s and 1960s Costa Rica's government distinguished itself from its poorer Central American neighbors in its social policies that benefited the emerging middle class. In the 1980s, however, that middle class began to suffer a decline in its standard of living, just as the numbers of marginal peoples intruded more noticeably on the nation's vaunted social service institutions. The combination of these pressures and the cost of a decade of war (including the liability of caring for large numbers of Nicaraguan refugees) left Costa Rica more impoverished at the end of the decade.

There was some hope that the common economic problems of the Central American countries could be mitigated when presidents of the Central American republics (excluding Belize and Panama) met in June 1990 and declared a willingness to coordinate a regional approach to economic planning. Briefly, the plan included proposals for a reduction in regional tariffs, removal of restrictions on the movement of goods and people, incentives for foreign investment and tourism, and improved human rights standards. Despite these hopeful signs, the Costa Rican economy did not improve markedly, and Calderón's popularity diminished when he imposed austerity measures demanded by the International Monetary Fund (IMF). In June

1991 members of the National Liberation Party walked out of the National Assembly in solidarity with public sector workers who had struck for a pay increase and a restoration of food price controls. In response, Calderón created a labor council to look at labor and social issues. In October 1991 came further unrest by health workers and university students over anticipated budget cuts. A few weeks later the finance minister resigned, stating that the IMF would not continue its support to a financially irresponsible course.

Calderón's political troubles continued in 1992 and 1993, as the opposition hammered away at the president's austerity program and called for a genuine democratic plan to settle the country's profound social problems. Many were angered by the apparent contradiction between the president's rhetoric about free markets and the preferential treatment given to coffee and banana producers. The Colombian Government charged 14 Costa Rican companies with laundering drug money from 1990 to 1992. In November 1992 the Costa Rican Government, responding to an appeal from Guatemala, Honduras, and El Salvador for a Central American federation, declared that political unification was "inconvenient."

The announcement was a reminder of Costa Rica's ambivalence about its identity as a Central American nation. Those political and economic achievements that have historically distinguished the country from its isthmian neighbors have diminished before the depressing social and economic realities of the 1990s. But the Ticos are a proud and determined people. As Calderón entered his last year in office in January 1994, the economic crisis he inherited in 1990 had not been resolved, but there were signs that the country had discovered a way to confront its economic future by promoting tourism. In retrospect the figures show that inflation, which was at 25% in 1991 dropped to 9% in 1993. The growth of the economy was less encouraging. The 2.1% growth in 1991 and 7.7% rate in 1992 were followed by a drop to 5.4% in 1993 and 4.3% in 1994. In the long run, of course, tourism will not restore the middle-class democracy the Ticos fear they may be losing, nor will it prepare the country for entry into the modern market among the industrialized nations of North America and Europe. But tourism may permit Costa Ricans to stave off the social calamity some observers believe awaits them.

Calderón was succeeded in office by President Jose Maria Figuerres Olsen of the National Liberation Party (PLN) on May 8, 1994. Calderón continued as the leader of the PUSC.

Further Reading

Although Rafael Calderón is a contemporary personality, material on him in English is scarce. General information on the happenings in Costa Rica can be accessed through http://cliffie.nose.mil:80/~NAWFB/wfb/c/costa-rica.html (July 18, 1997). □

Erskine Caldwell

The American writer Erskine Caldwell (1903-1987) was one of the best-selling authors of all time. His novels and stories are distinguished by their brutally realistic depiction of the rural South; his early work was outstanding for a sexual candor uncommon in its time.

Erskine Caldwell was born in backwoods Coweta Country, in the town of White Oak, Georgia, on Dec. 17, 1903. His father was a Presbyterian minister, and the family moved frequently throughout the South. Caldwell's schooling was fragmentary; he attended high school sporadically and took college courses at the University of Pennsylvania, at Erskine College, in South Carolina, and at the University of Virginia.

As a young man, he worked in Atlanta, Memphis, New Orleans, Philadelphia, and Baltimore as a mill laborer, farmhand, cotton picker, cook, stagehand in a burlesque house, and book reviewer. In 1925 he left the University of Virginia to become a reporter for the *Atlanta Journal,* and he married the first of his four wives, Helen Lannigan, with whom he had two sons and a daughter. Discovering that newspaper work left him no time for creative writing, Caldwell retreated to Maine for four years. His prolific career as an author was launched by *The Bastard,* (1929), *Poor Fool* (1930), and *American Earth* (1931).

But it was the 1932 publication of *Tobacco Road* that assured Caldwell's success. The novel depicts the life of Jeeter Lester, a Georgia sharecropper, and his family as they stumble through a series of sexual and financial misadventures, culminating in the destruction by fire of their home and themselves. The novelistic treatment is comic, the structure is episodic, and the rural southern types appear childish, grotesque, and, ultimately, pathetic.

In 1933 *Tobacco Road* was dramatized and ran for a record- breaking seven years on Broadway, despite an obscenity charge that was brought against it by the New York Society for the Suppression of Vice. The charge was dismissed, as was a similar charge against Caldwell's next novel, *God's Little Acre* (1933), the story of Ty Ty Walden, a Georgia dirt farmer, and his sons and daughters, and the barren, useless acre of land that he dedicates to God. As in *Tobacco Road,* Caldwell's theme is the folly and promiscuity of rural southerners. *God's Little Acre* is one of the all-time best sellers in the history of book publishing.

In the mid-1930s Caldwell spent some years as a Hollywood script writer but continued his amazing book production. After a play, *Journeyman* (1935), he wrote *Kneel to the Rising Sun and Other Stories* (1935), *The Sacrilege of Alan Kent* (1936), and *Southways* (1938).

In 1938 and 1939 Caldwell was a newspaper correspondent in Mexico, Spain, and Czechoslovakia, and in 1941 a newspaper and radio correspondent in the Soviet Union. His strong social conscience is evidenced in his nonfiction: *Some American People* (1935); *You Have Seen Their Faces* (1937), with photographer Margaret Bourke-White, who in 1939 became his second wife, and who also collaborated with him on *North of the Danube* (1939), *Say, Is This the U.S.A.?* (1941), and *Russia at War* (1942). His Russian experience is also reflected in *Moscow under Fire* (1941), *All Out on the Road to Smolensk* (1942), and *All Night Long* (1942), a novel of Russian guerrilla warfare.

Two of Caldwell's best-selling novels appeared in the early 1940s, *Trouble in July* (1940) and *Georgia Boy* (1943). In 1942 Caldwell married his third wife, June Johnson, with whom he had a son. His postwar works included *The Sure Hand of God* (1947), *Episode in Palmetto* (1950), and *A Lamp for Nightfall* (1952).

In 1957 Caldwell married his fourth wife, Virginia Moffett Fletcher, who illustrated his travel book *Around about America* (1964). *In Search of Bisco* (1965) was an account of Caldwell's unsuccessful quest to locate a childhood friend.

After World War II Caldwell lived for many years in Tucson, Arizona.; in the late 1950s he moved to Rheem Valley, California. He finally settled in Scottsdale, Arizona in 1977. While he remained popular abroad, Caldwell and his plain style fell out of fashion in the United States. While he continued to publish new work, he shunned interviews and public appearances. His later books included the comical *Miss Mama Aimee* (1968), *Annette* (1973), and *Afternoons in Mid-America* (1976), a collection of his impressions of ordinary people.

Caldwell's later books failed to generate the excitement of his earlier works, but he had earned his niche as a serious if sensational regionalist. In 1982, the New American Library marked the 50th anniversary of the publication of *Tobacco Road* by releasing it and *God's Little Acre* in new paperback editions. In 1984, Caldwell was elected to the American Academy of Arts and Letters. In 1985, the Georgia Endowment for the Humanities invited him back to his native state for a series of teas and lectures in his honor. After his visit, Caldwell took note of the many economic and social changes that had taken place in the once destitute rural south.

Shortly before his death, Caldwell completed his autobiography, *With All My Might* (1987). A heavy smoker for all of his adult life, Caldwell twice underwent surgery for the removal of portions of his lungs. Lung cancer finally overtook him on April 11, 1987 in Paradise Valley, Arizona.

Further Reading

The best discussions of Caldwell's work are in Joseph Warren Beach, *American Fiction: 1920-1940* (1941); Leo Gurko, *The Angry Decade* (1947); and Wilbur M. Frohock, *The Novel of Violence in America* (1950; rev. ed. 1958). Caldwell himself penned the autobiographical *Call It Experience: The Years of Learning How to Write* (1951) and *With All My Might* (1987). Biographies of the writer include J.E. Devlin, *Erskine Caldwell* (1984), Harvey L. Klevar, *Erskine Caldwell: A Biography* (1993), and D.B. Miller, *Erskine Caldwell* (1995). □

Sarah Caldwell

Sarah Caldwell (born 1928) is the founder of the Boston Opera Group, now known as the Opera Company of Boston. She is also a conductor and artistic director of national renown. She has won international accolades for her use of the dramatic elements of opera and for expanding the operatic repertoire. She has headed several international exchange programs and was named National Medal of Arts recipient in 1996.

Sarah Caldwell, founder of the Boston Opera Group (1958), now known as the Opera Company of Boston, was born in the small town of Maryville, Missouri in 1924. Soon afterwards her family moved to Kansas City. Caldwell, a child prodigy in both mathematics and music, began violin lessons at the age of four and was holding violin concerts before the age of ten. She attended orchestral performances of the Kansas City Philharmonic as well as stage performances by the Kansas City Repertory Theater. She graduated from Hendrix College, University of Arkansas, then moved to Boston to attend the New England Conservatory of Music, the Boston Symphony's unofficial educational affiliate.

Caldwell was soon studying under Boris Goldovsky, head of the New England Conservatory of Music's Dept. of Opera. She also studied under Richard Burgin, concert master of the Boston Symphony Orchestra. Caldwell's love of

music and the theater found its focus in the artistic direction of opera. Goldovsky became her mentor and guide and Caldwell was instructed in all elements of opera, from chorus direction and stagecraft to orchestral conducting and costuming. By the age of 20, Caldwell had staged Vaughan William's *Riders to the Sea.*

As a member of the Conservatory, Caldwell participated in the annual Tanglewood Music Festival. (Tanglewood, Massachusetts has been holding an annual music festival for over sixty years. Musicians from the Boston Symphony traditionally perform in Tanglewood for eight weeks each summer.) She trained the choruses for various concerts.

Serge Koussevitzky, permanent conductor of the Boston Symphony (1924-49) and founder of the Berkshire Music Center (1940), admired Caldwell's work at Tanglewood and recommended that she be placed on the Berkshire Music Center faculty. Caldwell's success at the Berkshire Music Center led to her being named Director of Boston University's Opera Workshop (1953-57). She also created the Dept. of Music Theatre.

As director of the Opera Workshop, Caldwell was able to promote her concept of opera as a dramatic art form as well as search for compositions unfamiliar to American audiences. As one of her first productions, Caldwell staged the American premiere of German composer Paul Hindemith's opera *Mathis der Maler.* Caldwell also invited Igor Stravinsky to conduct his only full-length opera *Rake's Progress.* (Stravinsky's modern opera, composed to a libretto by W. H. Auden and C. Kallman, combines musical elements ranging from Mozart to Italian opera.) Caldwell proved to audiences that Stravinsky's opera could be successfully produced even though an earlier production by the Metropolitan Opera had been given poor reviews.

In 1957, Caldwell, with the help of supporters, founded the Boston Opera Group (renamed the Opera Co. of Boston in 1965). The difficulties of staging full-scale opera productions were considerable but Caldwell's unconventional approach to opera gave her productions an excitement and drama not characteristic of more traditional productions. She insisted upon extensive rehearsals which enabled singers to develop their characters both musically and dramatically. Her commitment to an expanded repertoire led her to stage premieres of several works that were only later put in the repertoire of other opera houses. Through research, she was able to locate and produce previously unperformed editions of familiar pieces. Her goal was to involve the audience by bringing out the inherently dramatic elements of an opera without sacrificing its musical content.

Several of the world's most sought-after opera stars were willing to participate in Caldwell's dramatic production even though they earned less money and had longer rehearsal times. Beverly Sills performed in *Manon* (1962) and Joan Sutherland made her Boston stage debut in *I Puritani.* The Opera Co. of Boston also presented the first east coast performance of *Lulu* (1964), the first American performance of Rameau's *Hippolyte et Aricie* (1966), and staged the American premiere of Schoenberg's *Moses und Aron* (1966).

From 1968-70, the opera company was without a home and was forced to hold performances at a variety of locations including the Kresge Auditorium at the Massachusetts Institute of Technology. In 1971 funding was received from The Ford Foundation and from the National Endowment for the Arts. The Orpheum Theater became the new home for the Opera Co. of Boston; another series of dramatic performances began. Operas produced by the Opera Co. of Boston under Caldwell's artistic direction included Kurt Weill's *Rise and Fall of the City of Mahagonny* (1973), the original French version of Giuseppi Verdi's *Don Carlos* (1973), Sergei Prokofiev's *War and Peace* (1974), and Roger Huntington Sessions' *Montezuma* (1976).

In 1978, after 21 years of rented space, the Opera Co. of Boston moved into its first permanent home in the Savoy Theater, now named The Opera House. Productions included Michael Tippett's English opera *The Ice Break* (1979), Leos Janacek's Czech opera *The Makropulos Affair* (1986), and the first American performances of Zimmermann's *Die Soldaten* (1982), and Puccini's *Madame Butterfly.*

Caldwell's reputation was gaining her both national and international recognition. In addition to conducting orchestras in almost every major concert hall in the United States, from Carnegie Hall to the Dallas Civic Opera House, she was appointed Director of the Wolf Trap Summer Music Festival in Virginia (1980). The first of her cultural exchange programs began as she became involved with special projects in Manila and in Tel Aviv in the early 1980s.

International interest in Caldwell's work took her to China in 1982 for a meeting with the Central Opera Theatre of Peking. Following their meeting, Ming Cho Lee of the Peking opera company produced costumes and sets for an Opera Co. of Boston production of *Turandot.* Caldwell also produced Shchedrin's opera *Dead Souls* as part of a Soviet-American Making Music Together Festival (1988). Despite the daunting logistics of rehearsing and preparing a production with artists who did not speak each other's language, the Festival was a great success.

Reviews of Caldwell productions were as widely diverse as her productions were original. Thor Eckert, Jr., of *Opera News* reviewed the 1984 production of *Turandot* and criticized the "details here and there [that] spoke more of haste than concept." In reviewing *The Makropulos Affair* (1986), Andrew Porter wrote that "the Boston company (was) at full strength presenting an opera that matters, and in a way to bring to life what matters about it most."

Caldwell's achievements with the Opera Company of Boston were astonishing, especially when one considers, as P. G. Davis said in a review, that it was "put together . . . out of chewing gum, rubber bands and sheer gall." It was Caldwell's ability not to let obstacles distort her vision that won her so many admirers. As she once remarked, "The secret of living is to find people who will pay you money to do what YOU would pay to do if you had the money."

Caldwell was the first recipient of the Kennedy Center Award for excellence. She is also recipient of the Rogers and Hammerstein Award and the 1996 National Medal for Arts.

Further Reading

There is not as yet a full biography of Sarah Caldwell but her career is outlined in *The New Grove Encyclopedia of Music,* Stanley Sadie, editor (London: 1980) and in *The American Music Handbook,* Christoper Pavlakis, editor (London: 1974). Other sources of interest include *Uncommon Women* by Joan Krufrin (1981), *Opera News, New York Magazine,* and *The New Yorker.* Both magazines have reviewed Caldwell's more unusual productions. An article by Winthrop Sargent *The New Yorker* (Dec. 24, 1973) presents an overall look at Caldwell's life and her work and describes how she created remarkable productions with only a minimal of financial backing and a whole lot of imagination. □

John Caldwell Calhoun

The American statesman John Caldwell Calhoun (1782-1850) became the most effective protagonist of the antebellum South. It was his tragedy to become the spokesman for the dying institution of slavery.

John C. Calhoun was born on March 18, 1782, in the uplands of South Carolina, the son of Patrick and Martha Caldwell Calhoun. The family was Scotch-Irish and Calvinist and was relatively wealthy; his father owned twenty or more slaves, was a judge, and served in the state legislature. John graduated from Yale in 1804. He studied in the law school of Tapping Reeves in Litchfield, Conn., and in an office in Charleston, S.C., and was admitted to the bar in 1807. He quickly established a practice in Abbeville near his family home.

In 1811 Calhoun married a distant cousin, Floride Bouneau, by whom he had nine children. The marriage brought him a modest fortune. He enlarged his holdings and in 1825 established a plantation, called Fort Hill, in his native area.

Handsome in early life and with a commanding presence and piercing eyes all his life through, Calhoun had a striking personality. He had a gracious manner, and Daniel Webster and others not his partisans paid tribute to his character and integrity. In later years he struck observers as a "thinking machine," speaking very rapidly and always terribly in earnest. The picture is conveyed in Harriet Martineau's phrase that Calhoun was a "cast-iron man who looks as if he had never been born and could never be extinguished." He was concerned almost exclusively with ideas, politics, and business; he had little humor and no broad, cultural interests. One Senate colleague said there was no relaxation with the man, and another complained that to be with Calhoun was to be made to think all the time and to feel one's inferiority.

Political Career

Calhoun was elected to the South Carolina Legislature in 1808 and 2 years later won election to the U.S. House of Representatives. Henry Clay made him chairman of the Foreign Affairs Committee, and Calhoun and other "War Hawks" moved the country to the unsuccessful War of 1812 against Great Britain. Calhoun led the effort in the House to supply and strengthen the Army, and after the war he continued to work for a stronger military establishment. He advocated measures which he would later denounce as unconstitutional: Federal encouragement of manufactures by means of a protective tariff, and internal improvements to "bind the republic together with a perfect system of roads and canals." To objections that the Constitution did not authorize such Federal expenditures, Calhoun replied that "the instrument was not intended as a thesis for the logician to exercise his ingenuity on. It ought to be construed with plain, good sense. . . . "

Calhoun was secretary of war in James Monroe's Cabinet (1817-1825). He became less and less militaristic through his life. In 1812 he had said that "a war, just and necessary in its origin, wisely and vigorously carried on, and honorably terminated," would establish "the integrity and prosperity of our country for centuries." But in 1846 he refused to vote for the declaration of war against Mexico; he asserted that the grounds for war given by the President were false and said simply, "I regard peace as a positive good, and war as a positive evil."

In Monroe's Cabinet, Calhoun was a nationalist. In 1821 John Quincy Adams appraised Calhoun as "a man of fair and candid mind . . . of enlarged philosophic views, and of ardent patriotism. He is above all sectional and factional prejudices more than any other statesman of this Union. . . . " Calhoun was Adams's vice president (1825-1829) and was elected to the office again in 1828 under Andrew Jackson. He had expectations of becoming president following Jackson's tenure, but there was a rupture between them during Jackson's first term. The social contretemps over Peggy Eaton was involved, but more important was Jackson's discovery that Calhoun had criticized his invasion of Florida in 1818. Even without these irritants the clash would have come. Calhoun had anonymously written the "South Carolina Exposition" in response to the so-called Tariff of Abominations of 1828. He argued the right of a state to "nullify" a Federal enactment injurious to its interests if the state believed the law to be unconstitutional. By 1830 Calhoun was known as the author of the doctrine, and at a Jefferson's birthday dinner that year Jackson glared at Calhoun and proposed the toast, "Our Federal Union—it must be preserved!" Calhoun replied, "The Union—next to our liberty, the most dear!"

Jackson threatened military force to collect the duties in South Carolina, and in 1832 Calhoun in an unprecedented action resigned from the vice presidency and was elected by South Carolina to the Senate to defend its cause. Henry Clay brought forth a compromise, which Calhoun supported, to lower the tariff gradually over a decade; the crisis subsided for a time.

In the Senate in the 1830s, Calhoun attacked the abolitionists, demanding that their publications be excluded from the mails, that their petitions not be received by Congress, and finally that a stop be put to agitation against slavery in the North as had been done in the South. By 1837 he was defending slavery as "a positive good" and had become an advocate for the suppression of open discussion and a free press.

Calhoun's shift from a national to a sectional position had virtually destroyed his chances for the presidency, but he continued to aspire to that office. He declared his candidacy in 1843 but withdrew to accept appointment as secretary of state for the last year of John Tyler's term. In his efforts for the annexation of Texas, Calhoun wrote a famous letter to the British minister in Washington, arguing that annexation was necessary to protect slavery in the United States and asserting (against the position of the British government, which was urging the emancipation of slaves throughout the world) that freed African Americans tended to be deaf, blind, and insane in far higher proportions than those in slavery. The letter did not help his cause in Congress. The treaty of annexation which he negotiated with the Republic of Texas was rejected by the Senate, where it was impossible to muster the required two-thirds vote in its favor. Calhoun then supported the device, of doubtful constitutionality, of admitting Texas by a joint resolution of Congress.

Calhoun returned to the Senate in 1845, where he first opposed the war against Mexico and then the Wilmot Proviso, which would have prohibited slavery in all the territories acquired from Mexico by that war. He denounced the Compromise of 1850, which did not guarantee the right of Southerners to take their slaves into all territories of the Union. He did not live to see that compromise adopted, dying on March 31, 1850. His last words were, "The South! The poor South!"

Political Philosophy

The political theory Calhoun had developed from the time of the Nullification Crisis of 1828 he began to organize in a formal treatise in the middle 1840s. His two works, *Disquisition on Government* and *Discourse on the Constitution and Government of the United States,* were published posthumously. Calhoun argued that government by mere numbers must inevitably result in despotism by the majority, a proposition supported by the men who drew up the Constitution. He also insisted that the Constitution should be based upon the "truth" of the inequality of man and on the principle that people are not equally entitled to liberty.

Calhoun said the U.S. Constitution lacked the necessary restraints to prevent the majority from abusing the minority. He proposed to give the minorities (the minority he had in mind was the Southern slaveholders) a veto power over Federal legislation and action by means of what he called the "concurrent majority." In the *Discourse* he proposed the device of dual executives for the Union, each to be chosen by one of the great sections of the country, with the agreement of both necessary for Federal action.

The 20th-century experience of the dangers of centralized governmental power has brought a renewed interest in Calhoun's proposals for the protection of minority rights. But although Calhoun's critical analysis was perceptive, his proposed solutions have not been regarded as serious contributions to the problem. Indeed, as critics have pointed out, although he spoke in general terms and categories, he was really interested only in defending the rights of a specific propertied minority—the slaveholding South.

Further Reading

Calhoun's own *A Disquisition on Government* and *A Discourse on the Constitution and Government of the United States,* originally published in 1851, are now available together in several editions. *The Works of John C. Calhoun,* edited by Richard K. Crallé (6 vols., 1851-1856), has been the basic published collection of his writings. However, a more recent, definitive collection of Calhoun's writings is *The Papers of John C. Calhoun,* edited by Robert L. Meriwether (4 vols., 1959-1969).

A representative collection of essays by Calhoun scholars is John L. Thomas, ed., *John C. Calhoun: A Profile* (1968). It provides an excellent introduction to the literature on Calhoun. The comprehensive biography is Charles M. Wiltse, *John C. Calhoun* (3 vols., 1944-1951); however, it denigrates his rivals and justifies Calhoun's actions throughout his career. The best one-volume biography, with a better interpretive balance, is Margaret L. Coit, *John C. Calhoun: American Portrait* (1950). For a more critical account see Gerald M. Capers, *John C. Calhoun, Opportunist: A Reappraisal* (1960). Richard N. Current, *John C. Calhoun* (1963), provides a good analysis of Calhoun's political theory.

To examine the changing interpretations of Calhoun over the last century see the biographies by John S. Jenkins, *The Life of John Caldwell Calhoun* (1852); H. von Holst, *John C. Calhoun* (1882); Gaillard Hunt, *John C. Calhoun* (1908); William M. Meigs, *The Life of John Caldwell Calhoun* (2 vols., 1917); and Arthur Styron, *The Cast Iron Man: John C. Calhoun and American Democracy* (1935). □

Caligula

Caligula (12-41) was the third emperor of Rome. At best, he was one of the most autocratic of Rome's early emperors; at worst, one of the most deranged.

Caligula was born Gaius Julius Caesar Germanicus in Antium (modern Anzio) on Aug. 31, A.D. 12. His mother, Agrippina, was Emperor Augustus's granddaughter, and his father, Germanicus, was Emperor Tiberius's nephew, adopted son, and heir. Gaius was brought up among the soldiers his father commanded on the Rhine. His mother dressed him in the uniform of a Roman legionnaire, and for this reason the soldiers called him Caligula ("Little Boots"), the name by which he is commonly known.

In A.D. 19 Germanicus died. His death was mourned throughout the empire because he was, by all accounts, an honorable and courageous man. After his father's death Caligula lived in Rome, first with his mother, then with Livia (Augustus's wife), and then with his grandmother. Finally, in 32, he joined Tiberius in his retirement on Capri.

By 33 those people with prior claims to the imperial position, including Caligula's brother Drusus, had died, and Caligula was next in line to succeed Tiberius. Caligula held public office in 31 and 33 but, apart from that brief experience, had no other training for political life. His experience at Tiberius's court seems largely to have been in the art of dissembling—hiding what his biographer Suetonius calls Caligula's "natural cruelty and viciousness."

Tiberius died in 37, and Caligula was acclaimed emperor in March. During the first months of his reign he distributed the legacies left by Tiberius and Livia to the Roman people, and after the austerity which Tiberius had practiced the games and chariot races Caligula held were welcomed. He was respectful to the Senate, adopted his cousin Tiberius Gemellus as his son and heir, and recalled political exiles who had been banished during the reigns of his predecessors.

But by the spring of 38 the character of Caligula's rule changed drastically. An illness late in 37 seems to have seriously affected his mind. Suetonius claims that, after the illness, Caligula succumbed completely to the role of Oriental despot. In all things he became arbitrary and cruel. He murdered, among others, Tiberius Gemellus, humiliated the Senate, and spent money recklessly. He revived treason trials so that he could confiscate the property of the convicted. Caligula's extravagances included building a temple to himself in Rome and appointing his favorite horse as high priest.

Caligula spent the winter of 39/40 in Gaul and on the Rhine and planned to invade Germany or Britain. His plans aroused some patriotic fervor, but the project was abandoned.

After his return to Rome, Caligula lived in constant fear and real danger of assassination. He was murdered by a tribune of the Praetorian Guards on Jan. 24, 41. His fourth wife and his daughter, who was his only child, were murdered at the same time.

Further Reading

The principal ancient source is the biography of Caligula in Suetonius's *The Lives of the Twelve Caesars.* The best full-length modern treatment is J. P. V. D. Balsdon, *The Emperor Gaius* (*Caligula*) (1934), which contains an extremely useful bibliography. The ways in which the Augustan system was changed are discussed in Mason Hammond, *The Augustan Principate in Theory and Practice during the Julio-Claudian Period* (1933; enlarged ed. 1968).

Additional Sources

Balsdon, J. P. V. D. (John Percy Vyvian Dacre), 1901-, *The Emperor Gaius (Caligula),* Westport, Conn.: Greenwood Press, 1977.

Barrett, Anthony, *Caligula: the corruption of power,* New York: Simon & Schuster, 1991.

Ferrill, Arther., *Caligula: emperor of Rome,* London: Thames and Hudson, 1991.

Hurley, Donna W., *An historical and historiographical commentary on Suetonius' Life of C. Caligula,* Atlanta, Ga.: Scholars Press, 1993.
Josephus, Flavius, *Death of an emperor,* Exeter, U.K.: University of Exeter Press, 1991.
Nony, D. (Daniel), *Caligula,* Paris: Fayard, 1986. □

Edward Morley Callaghan

The Canadian novelist and short-story writer Edward Morley Callaghan (1903-1990) was one of the major figures of 20th-century Canadian fiction. His work was linked with the development in American writing symptomatic of the 1920s.

Morley Callaghan was born on February 22, 1903, in Toronto into an Irish Roman Catholic family. He graduated from the University of Toronto in 1925. During his college years Callaghan held a summer job as a reporter with the *Toronto Daily Star,* where he met Ernest Hemingway. The two exchanged stories, and Hemingway encouraged Callaghan in his writing. In 1925 Callaghan enrolled in law school at Osgoode Hall in Toronto and was admitted to the Ontario bar in 1928.

First Successes

Callaghan's career as a writer began in 1921, when he sold a descriptive piece to the *Toronto Star Weekly.* In 1926 he published his first short story in the Paris magazine *This Quarter,* had another accepted by *transition,* and started on his first novel, *Strange Fugitive.* At this time Callaghan visited New York, and his friendships from this and subsequent visits included William Carlos Williams, Allen Tate, Ford Madox Ford, Katherine Ann Porter, and Sinclair Lewis.

Callaghan also attracted the attention of Maxwell Perkins of Scribner's, and his stories began to appear regularly in American and European magazines. In 1928 Scribner's published *Strange Fugitive* and in 1929 a collection of short stories, *A Native Argosy.* Callaghan married Loretto Dee in 1929 and went to Paris for eight months. He completed a novel, *It's Never Over* (1929), and a novella, *No Man's Meat* (1931).

From the Depression to World War II

The 1930s were an active and prolific period for Callaghan. He published four novels: *A Broken Journey* (1932), *Such Is My Beloved* (1934), *They Shall Inherit the Earth* (1935), and *More Joy in Heaven* (1937). He produced a second collection of stories, *Now That April's Here and Other Stories* (1936), and wrote two plays in 1939, *Turn Again Home* and *Just Ask for George.*

Callaghan's work of this period was strongly affected by the experiences of the Depression. But partly owing to the influence of the French philosopher Jacques Maritain, whom Callaghan knew in Toronto in 1933, it began to show a strain of Christian humanism and a strong sense of personal virtue coupled with deinstitutionalized Christian values. Father Dowling, the idealistic and naive Catholic priest who is the hero of *Such Is My Beloved,* is a good example.

During World War II Callaghan was attached to the Royal Canadian Navy and served on assignment for the National Film Board of Canada. He also became a well-known radio figure.

Change in Outlook

In 1948 Callaghan returned to writing with a fictionalized account of life at the University of Toronto, *The Varsity Show,* and a juvenile novel, *Luke Baldwin's Vow.* But it was not until 1951 and the publication of the Governor General's Award—winning novel, *The Loved and the Lost,* that Callaghan truly restaked his claim in the field of Canadian fiction.

In 1959 *Morley Callaghan's Stories,* a book comprising his best short fiction, appeared. Two novels followed, *The Many Coloured Coat* (1960) and *A Passion in Rome* (1961). *That Summer in Paris* (1963), an autobiographical reminiscence, deals with Callaghan's eight-month stay in Paris in 1929. It tells something of the novelist's relationship with the Paris expatriates and the complicated friendships of the leading writers of that day, prominent among whom were Hemingway and James Joyce. Callaghan also reveals his own ideas about writing and the writer's craft. This stage in Callaghan's artistic development showed a more refined, if sharper and more tragic, sense of moral responsibility presented in prose of richer texture and occasional symbolic overtones.

In 1967 Callaghan was named in the first Order of Canada honors list. In 1970 he won the Molson Prize and the valuable and prestigious Royal Bank of Canada Award for his contribution to the artistic and intellectual life of Canada.

While Callaghan's short stories continued to garner praise, his later novels met with mixed reviews. Ambitious ideas were often marred by clumsy plotting, stilted dialogue, and clichéd characterizations. In *A Fine and Private Place* (1975), Callaghan adopted the persona of a bitter novelist, Eugene Shore, to attack critics who refused to take him seriously as a writer. His next novel *Close to the Sun Again* (1977) shed the caustic veneer for a return to the humanistic themes of his earlier work. The novel relates the last days of Ira Groome, a widowed chairman of a municipal commission who comes to lament the loss of passion and joy in his life. Sitting in his hospital bed after a serious car accident, Groome drifts away into his wartime memories, recalling a time when sacrifice and suffering made his existence worthwhile. After experiencing a moment of epiphany, he dies.

The unsuccessful works *A Time for Judas* (1983) and *Our Lady of the Snows* (1985) did little to enhance Callaghan's reputation, or his bankbook. But he did have one last good novel in him, the vigorous swan song *A Wild Old Man on the Road* (1988). Set in Paris and Toronto, the novel returns to familiar Callaghan terrain in more ways than one. The story of an idealistic young Canadian writer who befriends—and grows steadily disillusioned by—his hero, a left-leaning British journalist turned neo-conservative, the novel brims with compassion and moral inquiry, the very stuff that had made Callaghan such a vital artist for so many years.

A longtime Toronto resident, Callaghan remained doggedly independent until the end of his life. He broke a hip in 1989 at the age of 88, but still persisted in walking to his neighborhood grocery store to do his shopping. He died of natural causes in Toronto on August 25, 1990.

Further Reading

Brandon Conron, *Morley Callaghan* (1966), is useful both for biography and criticism. Victor Hoar, *Morley Callaghan* (1969), concentrates on technique and themes in Callaghan's work. Edmund Wilson, *O Canada!* (1965), provides interesting material on Callaghan. A more recent biography is Gary Boire's *Morley Callaghan: Literary Anarchist* (1994). □

Leonard James Callaghan

Leonard James Callaghan (born 1912) was a Labor member of the British Parliament for over three decades and was prime minister from 1976 to 1979.

Leonard James Callaghan was born in Portsmouth, England, on March 12, 1912. His father, James Callaghan, was a chief petty officer in the Royal Navy. Upon his death in 1921 the family was plunged into poverty when instead of a pension only a small gratuity was forthcoming. A local Labor member of Parliament was instrumental in securing a weekly allowance of 26 shillings for Mrs. Callaghan and 10 shillings for the boy. As Callaghan said many years later, "after that we were staunch Labor for life."

His formal education ended at age 16. A year later he successfully passed a government test and began work as an income tax clerk. At 24 he became a full time trade union official with the Inland Revenue Staff Federation and became a specialist in the handling of arbitration cases. By 1938 he had risen to the position of assistant secretary in the union and was actively being considered as a prospective Labor Party candidate for Parliament.

Callaghan joined the Royal Navy in 1939 and served for the duration of World War II as a lieutenant in naval intelligence in the Far East. He was elected Labor member of Parliament (M.P.) for Cardiff south in the general election of 1945 and represented Cardiff south east uninterruptedly after 1950. He held two minor posts in the 1945-1951 Labor government: parliamentary secretary to the minister of transport (1947-1950) and parliamentary secretary to the admiralty (1950-1951).

The 1950s saw Callaghan's emergence as a national figure and spokesperson for Labor. He appeared frequently

on radio and television and was active as a free-lance political journalist. He was also a lobbyist for the Police Federation, a national policemen's interest group. First elected to the executive of the parliamentary Labor Party in 1951, he won election to the party's national executive committee in 1957, was opposition spokesperson on colonial questions from 1956 to 1961, and was shadow chancellor of the exchequer, 1961-1964. He stood unsuccessfully for deputy leader in 1960 and for leader in 1963 following Hugh Gaitskell's death. During this period he gained a reputation as a bitter opponent of Aneurin Bevan and of supporters of unilateral disarmament in the Labor Party.

Labor won a narrow victory in the general election of 1964, and Callaghan accepted Harold Wilson's offer to become chancellor of the exchequer. From the outset he opposed devaluation as a measure to help correct the British economy's sluggish growth rate and chronic tendency toward balance of payment deficits. He imposed a severely deflationary budgetary package in the aftermath of the 1966 sterling crisis, warning that unless it were implemented he might join the devaluers.

As late as July 1967 he was still insisting that "devaluation is not the way out of Britain's difficulties." However, in November 1967 there was another massive run on the pound, and Callaghan informed Wilson that the drain on the reserves was intensifying. On November 18, 1967, a 14.3 percent devaluation of the pound—from $2.80 to $2.40—was announced.

With the government's economic policy in disarray and the opposition demanding his resignation, Callaghan agreed to step down as chancellor, but remained in the government as home secretary. He was responsible for the Immigration Act of 1968, a hastily contrived piece of legislation prompted by Conservative assertions that an influx of Kenyan Asians would soon inundate the country. Rushed through the Commons in a week, it placed entry controls on holders of United Kingdom passports who had "no substantial connection" with Britain by setting up a voucher system. He was also responsible for sending troops to Northern Ireland in August 1969. The Catholic community welcomed him as a protector, and he successfully pressured the Northern Ireland parliament to abolish the "B-Special" paramilitary auxiliaries to the police.

When Labor returned to office in 1974, Callaghan accepted the post of foreign secretary. The sudden and unexpected resignation of Harold Wilson in March 1976 necessitated an election among Labor MPs to choose a successor, and Callaghan was chosen on the third ballot, winning 176 votes to Michael Foot's 137.

Callaghan's minority premiership was marked by the exceptionally difficult nature of the issues confronting the government and by an unusual constitutional arrangement with the Liberals by which they exercised a pre-emptive veto on proposed government legislation. Unemployment stood at a post World War II high, and the pound was once again falling. The government negotiated a $3.9 billion loan from the International Monetary Fund, raised interest rates to record levels, and made deep cuts in public spending. By 1978 inflation had fallen to single-figure levels and the balance of payments showed a small surplus.

Less successful was the government's industrial relations policy. A massive series of strikes in the winter of 1979 caused widespread disruption of public services and was settled on terms that far exceeded the government's stated pay guidelines. Finally, legislation providing for Scottish and Welsh elected assemblies with limited powers went down to defeat in referendums. Welsh voters rejected the measure outright by a 4 to 1 majority, while in Scotland it failed to gain a required affirmative vote by at least 40 percent of the electorate. On March 28, 1979, the government, having lost the support of the Liberals and nationalist MPs, was defeated in a dramatic vote, 311 to 310. In the ensuing general election Callaghan led the Labor Party to its worst electoral defeat since 1931, as the Conservatives, led by Margaret Thatcher, attained a majority of 43 over all other parties. (This episode, dubbed "the winter of discontent," was the subject of a symposium at the Institute of Contemporary British History in the late 1980s.)

In September 1980 Callaghan resigned the party leadership. During the 1983 general election he vehemently attacked Labor's stand on defense and disarmament in a speech that received blanket coverage in the media, delighted the Conservatives, and infuriated Labor Party activists. He was one of only four MPs returned in 1983 who had been first elected in 1945. In 1983 he was elected Father of the House of Commons, a largely honorific title. In 1987 James Callaghan was honored as a life peer.

Further Reading

There is no scholarly biography of Callaghan. Christopher Hitchens and Peter Kellner, *Callaghan, the Road to Number Ten* (1976) is polemical and hostile in tone. David Coates, *Labour in Power? A Study of the Labour Government of 1974-1979* (1980), and Alan Sked and Chris Cook, *Post-War Britain: A Political History* (1984) are informative and reliable guides to his years as prime minister. Richard Crossman, *The Diaries of a Cabinet Minister* (1975) contains many useful references.

James Callaghan has also written an autobiography. Callaghan, James, *Time and Chance,* Collins, (1987) was a useful resource as was the A & E Biography website http://www.biography.com (July 28, 1997). □

Daniel Callahan

Daniel Callahan (born 1930) was a philosopher widely recognized for his innovative studies in biomedical ethics. The co-founder of the Hastings Center, an internationally-acclaimed research institute for biomedical ethics, Callahan was best known for proposing that a looming crisis in health care resources would require society to set priorities and limits on medical care.

Daniel Callahan was born in Washington, D.C., on July 19, 1930. As a youth he was afflicted with a variety of maladies that resulted in several hospital stays. These experiences disposed him to an interest in matters of medicine, although this interest was not fully realized until later in his life.

Callahan's athletic prowess as a swimmer in high school led him to choose Yale University, the nation's best college for competitive swimming in the early 1950s, for his undergraduate education. At Yale he found himself drawn immediately to interdisciplinary studies, and he graduated in 1952 with a double major in English and psychology. A three-year stint with the U.S. Army counter-intelligence corps during the Korean War allowed Callahan to begin a Masters degree program at Georgetown University in Washington, D.C., where he was stationed for two years. In 1955 Callahan married Sidney deShazo, who shared many of his intellectual interests in psychology, ethics, and human behavior. Sidney Callahan subsequently became a distinguished social psychologist, teacher, and syndicated columnist in moral psychology. The Callahans had six children, five boys and one girl.

Following his army career, Callahan pursued his burgeoning philosophical interests in a doctoral program at Harvard University. Callahan very much believed the philosophic model was embodied in the person of the Greek philosopher Socrates: That is, the philosopher should be a person who enters the public forum and the marketplace and poses important and difficult questions for fellow citizens. However, Callahan soon discovered that this model clashed with the then-reigning methods of analytical philosophy at Harvard, which also precluded serious examination of questions of normative and applied ethics—that is, of how we ought to live our lives.

While completing his doctorate at Harvard, Callahan assumed a position as executive editor of *Commonweal* magazine, a lay-edited Roman Catholic weekly journal of opinion. During the 1960s the vast majority of Callahan's writings examined the Catholic encounter with the non-Catholic world in keeping with the religious ecumenical movement of the period. Despite the gradual diminishment and eventual cessation of his personal religious convictions by the 1970s, Catholic themes of community, tradition, nature, and metaphysical meaning continued to permeate his later writings. Callahan's eight years at *Commonweal* (1961-1968) enabled him to realize that the quest for philosophical insight could be pursued outside academia, and he turned away from his vocational plans to serve as a philosophical professor.

What Callahan turned towards was the emerging societal interest in the moral problems of a rapidly changing medicine and its new technology. A grant in 1968 from the Ford Foundation and the Population Council gave him an opportunity to examine ethical issues of population control and family planning programs. The publication of his research in *Abortion: Law, Choice, and Morality* (1970) firmly established Callahan as a pioneer in the new field of biomedical ethics. Callahan argued that the law on abortion should permit choice by a pregnant woman (at the time abortion was illegal in most states except to save the life of the pregnant woman), but both individuals and the community had a responsibility to engage in conscientious deliberation and justification regarding the morality of that choice. Callahan disagreed with the position that all abortions have equal moral validity. Despite many changes in law and social attitudes since its publication, this argument has had a continuing influence in philosophical discussions of abortion, as evidenced by its use in biomedical ethics anthologies in the mid-1990s.

In the late 1960s Callahan foresaw the need for an organization that could engage in systematic intellectual study of the ethical issues raised by the new technological medicine and the broader impact of this medicine on culture. A Christmas party conversation with a psychiatrist-neighbor, Willard Gaylin, soon led to the birth of the Institute of Society, Ethics, and the Life Sciences, eventually to be re-named the Hastings Center because of its original location in Hastings-on-Hudson, New York. Callahan has been the director of the Hastings Center for over 25 years. The Center has grown from a one-room entity in the basement of his house (supported by a small gift from his mother) into the pre-eminent research center for biomedical ethics in the world. The legacy of the Hastings Center lies not only in the quality of its own research projects on such issues as AIDS, death and dying, genetic engineering, organ transplantation, and reproductive technology, but also in the numerous other medical ethics centers it has spawned in the United States, Europe, and Asia. The story of contemporary biomedical ethics cannot be accurately told without identifying the central role of Daniel Callahan and the Hastings Center.

Callahan combined for over a quarter-century a rare mix of capacities for organization, administration, and stimulating scholarship. His trilogy of award-winning books, *Setting Limits* (1987), *What Kind of Life* (1990), and *The Troubled Dream of Life* (1993), set an innovative agenda for biomedical ethics. That agenda requires us to first ask what the goals and purposes of medicine should be: The prolongation of life at all costs by technology? The defeat of illness and the slowing of aging in a war against death? Callahan instead proposed that medicine be devoted to *caring,* including the relief of pain and suffering, rather than curing all afflictions of the human condition. The primacy of caring requires that social priorities and limits be set on the use of health care resources and that the culture support in attitude and practice an idea of a "peaceful death." To accomplish this, Callahan asks society to draw upon the moral traditions of caring communities rather than the adversarial claims of individual rights. He applied these concepts to the subject of old-age in *A World Growing Old: The Coming Health-care Challenges* (1995) which is based on the results of a worldwide research project dealing with medical care for the elderly.

An accomplished speaker, Daniel Callahan lectured at over 700 universities in the United States, Canada, and Europe and before some 300 professional and academic associations. He held honorary doctoral degrees from the University of Colorado, Williams College, and the University of Medicine and Dentistry of New Jersey. Callahan was also an elected member of the Institute of Medicine, the National Academy of Sciences, and the American Association for the Advancement of Science, and he was a member of the Director's Advisory Committee, Centers for Disease Control. He contributed his thoughts in the forward to *Life Choices: A Hastings Center Introduction to Bioethics* (1995), a collection of essays, and to the Hasting Hastings Center's *Living with Mortality,* a sound recording. In his own view, however, his most significant accomplishment was to foresee the importance of biomedical ethics and to undertake the initiative to begin a movement that achieved international renown.

Further Reading

A prolific author, Daniel Callahan is the author or editor of 30 books and the author of over 250 articles, reviews, and public policy testimony. Recommended readings include: *The Troubled Dream of Life: Living with Mortality* (1993); *What Kind of Life: The Limits of Medical Progress* (1990); *Setting Limits: Medical Coals in an Aging Society* (1987); *Abortion: Understanding Differences* (1984); and *Abortion: Law, Choice, and Morality* (1970). Also recommended is *A Good Old Age? The Paradox of "Setting Limits"* (1990), edited by Paul Homer and Martha Holstein. See also Warren T. Reich, ed., *Encyclopedia of Bioethics,* 4 vols. (1978).

Other useful articles can be found in *The Lancet,* June 15, 1996 and *Change,* November-December 1996. □

Rafael Leonardo Callejas Romero

Rafael Leonardo Callejas Romero (born 1943) was president of Honduras from 1990-1994, continuing constitutional civilian rule of the country and promoting economic development along neoliberal lines.

Rafael Leonardo Callejas Romero, born November 14, 1943, in Tegucigalpa, was the son of a landowning family. His elementary education was at the American School in Tegucigalpa, and he graduated from the San Francisco Institute (high school) of that city. Callejas received his B.S. (1965) and M.S. (1966) in agricultural economics from Mississippi State University, which in 1989 awarded him an honorary doctorate. He also studied agricultural development at the Social Studies Institute in The Hague, Holland, in 1967. Callejas married Norma Gaborit. They had three children.

Upon returning to Honduras he served on the Higher Council for Economic Planning, 1967-1971. In 1968 he became head evaluator in the Office of Agricultural Planning, then deputy secretary of the department of Natural Resources, 1972-1975; secretary of that department, 1975-1980; and director of agricultural planning, 1983-1984. He was also president of the board of directors of the National Bank for Agricultural Development, president of the board of the Honduran Institute for Agricultural Trade, and a member of the boards of the National Utility Company, the National Port Authority, the National Water Works and Sewerage Service, the Honduran Corporation for Forestry Development, and the Honduran Banana Corporation.

In 1980 he became treasurer of the National Party. When the military agreed to free elections in 1981, Callejas became the National Party candidate, but lost to the Liberal Party's Roberto Suazo Córdova. Four years later Callejas headed the National Renovation Movement, a conservative faction of the National Party. It favored private sector development in collaboration with Ronald Reagan's Caribbean Basin Initiative. The election of 1985 was bitter. Internal divisions in both major parties resulted in an electoral plan that essentially combined the primary with the general election. In a field of nine candidates, Callejas won a strong plurality of 41 percent against only 27 percent for the leading Liberal, José Azcona Hoyo. But the combined Liberal total (772,661) exceeded the National total (686,494), allowing Azcona to claim the presidency. Although this outcome angered Callejas' National Party, it accepted the decision in return for a power-sharing arrangement by which the National Party held several cabinet posts and five of the nine Supreme Court seats. This bipartisan government was notably unsuccessful in reversing Honduras' serious economic problems, rising crime rate, and unpopular involvement in the Contra war in Nicaragua.

Finally, Callejas won the election of November 1989, winning an absolute majority of 51 percent over the Liberal Carlos Flores Facussé (who received 43 percent). His campaign promised economic reform, an end to corruption, and demilitarization. He enjoyed strong U.S. support in an electoral campaign that was remarkably free of the fraud and violence that had accompanied the 1985 election. Callejas' inauguration on January 27, 1993, marked the first constitutional transition to an opposition leader in Honduras since 1932. Callejas' party also won a congressional majority.

Callejas cultivated close ties with the industrial nations and was popular among those advocating conservative (neoliberal) economic policies. The 4th International Democratic Association, meeting in Tokyo September 21-23, 1989, had elected him as its vice president upon the nomination of British Prime Minister Margaret Thatcher. Credibility in the international community earned Honduras favorable treatment by the International Monetary Fund, the World Bank, and the U.S. and European governments.

Callejas' victory came amid problems arising from Honduras' involvement in the Contra war against the Nicaraguan Sandinistas. That struggle stimulated large-scale immigration of Nicaraguan refugees, and the influx of U.S. aid in support of the Nicaraguan Contras contributed to inflation, uneven economic development, and political turmoil in the country. The defeat of the Sandinistas in the February 1990 Nicaraguan election allowed Callejas to achieve prompt removal of Contra bases in Honduras.

Callejas enjoyed high popularity and some economic improvement during the initial phases of his economic reforms. He reduced government expenditures and increased exports, especially of non-traditional *maquiladora* (processing) production, which by 1992 accounted for 35 percent of Honduran exports. He encouraged investment with lower taxes and tariffs. One of Callejas' first actions as president was to devalue the lempira to close to the black market rate and to begin structural adjustments according to recommendations by the U.S. Agency for International Development (AID). He sought to decrease capital flight from the country and undertook to privatize the National Production Development Agency (INFOP), various natural resources, the National Agrarian Institute, public works and transportation enterprises, and possibly the entire educational system. Callejas favored expansion of the North American Free Trade Agreement to include all of Latin America. He reduced tariff rates from a maximum of 135 percent in 1989 to a maximum of 20 percent by 1992. Threatened with curtailment of favorable U.S. trade privileges, his government in 1993 enacted an intellectual property law aimed at curbing the widespread piracy of television cable and video services.

Callejas faced opposition to his economic policies from organized labor. Under his pro-business policies many workers suffered declining living standards. While exports grew, the lower tariffs let imports pour into the country, displacing some local industry. By late 1993, according to a World Bank report published in Tegucigalpa, Callejas' structural adjustment policies had caused 20 percent of the Honduran population to be poorer, even as the macroeconomic situation improved. Devaluation of the lempira had reached 300 percent, and interest rates of 30 percent discouraged investment. Callejas argued that major increases in export earnings would soon ease the problem, but bank credit had virtually ceased and serious shortages of staple foodstuffs were causing social unrest.

Although Callejas was the third elected civilian president to rule Honduras in succession since 1980, the armed forces remained a strong force in Honduran politics. Military expansion accompanying the Contra war contributed to this, but it also reflected the shallowness of Honduran democracy. The army remained autonomous under Callejas, a fact emphasized by its arbitrary replacement of his armed forces chief in December 1990. The cost of Honduras' large military establishment contributed to the country's serious debt, but Callejas was powerless to reduce its size. Right-wing political violence during Callejas' administration was associated with the military's secret police, the National Investigation Directorate (DNI). Finally, in 1993, in response to popular animosity toward the military, Callejas' administration formally ended its connection to the DNI.

The Honduran presidency is limited to a single four-year term. In November of 1993 Carlos Roberto Reina, an opposition candidate, was elected to replace Callejas. Reina assumed the presidency in January of 1994.

Further Reading

For a detailed overview of recent Honduran political history see James Dunkerley, *Power in the Isthmus, A Political History of Modern Central America* (London: 1988); Alison Acker, *Honduras: The Making of a Banana Republic* (1988); and Tom Barry and Ken Norsworthy, *Honduras: A Country Guide* (1990). More detail on Callejas' presidential administration may be found in Howard H. Lentner, *State Formation in Central America: The Struggle for Autonomy, Development, and Democracy* (1993). □

Plutarco Elías Calles

Plutarco Elías Calles (1877-1945) was a Mexican revolutionary leader and president whose constitutional and key economic reforms provided a solid base for Mexico's later governmental stability.

Plutarco Calles was born in Guaymas, Sonora, on Sept. 25, 1877, and orphaned 4 years later. Stocky and iron-jawed, he taught school briefly and was a bartender before entering the ranks of the revolution supporting Francisco Madero against Porfirio Diaz and aiding Venustiano Carranza against Victoriano Huerta and Francisco "Pancho" Villa.

As military commander, provisional governor, and then constitutional governor of Sonora from 1915 to 1919, Calles established a record for the implementation of revolutionary ideals in terms of anticlericalism, agrarian reform, and educational progress. In 1919 he became secretary of industry, labor, and commerce in the Carranza government, resigning to participate in Álvaro Obregón's presidential campaign.

A key mover of the rebellion of Agua Prieta which overthrew Carranza, Calles served as secretary of war in the De la Barra interim government and as secretary of the interior during the presidency of Obregón (1920-1924). Obregón successfully backed Calles as his successor against the political and military challenge of Adolfo de la Huerta, who attracted conservative and dissident revolutionary support.

Calles began a decade of dominance of Mexican political life—4 years as president and 6 years as the "power behind the throne." His policy was foreshadowed by his record in Sonora. Agrarian reform was pushed, with the goal of establishing ultimately a nation of individual landholders. Labor was favored, Luis Morones and his Regional Confederation of Mexican Labor dominating the scene. The educational experimentation of the Obregón period now became national policy. Calles moved to implement and enforce constitutional provisions regarding religious matters and foreign ownership of petroleum resources.

One result was conflict between the Church and the state in the form of an economic boycott, suspension of religious services, and the armed rebellion of the *Cristeros*. Through the mediation of U.S. Ambassador Dwight Morrow an arrangement with the Church was worked out and made effective in 1929. Important for Mexico's future development were the establishment by Calles of the Central Bank of Mexico and the National Bank of Agricultural Credit and the initiation of programs for the construction of roads, dams, and irrigation projects.

Calles effected a constitutional change which made possible Obregón's return to the presidency. However, after election and prior to inauguration Obregón was assassinated by a religious fanatic. Calles publicly proclaimed the end of the era of caudillos, or military strong men. While not again occupying the presidency, he did remain the *jefe máximo,* or most powerful chief, behind three successive executives between 1928 and 1934. These were years of transition, with rule by a wealthy clique, a slowing down of revolutionary reform, and cynicism, corruption, and depression. A major military challenge in 1929 was suppressed, the official party was established as a means of ensuring peaceful transfers of power, and the Federal Labor Code was promulgated. The need for a reaffirmation of revolutionary commitment resulted in the drafting of an official Six-Year Plan in 1934 and the election of Lázaro Cárdenas as president. When Calles criticized the new executive's handling of labor disturbances, Cárdenas forced him to leave the country. Calles was permitted to return to Mexico in 1941 and died there on Oct. 19, 1945.

Further Reading

There is a serious need for biographical studies of the Mexican leaders of the 1920s. A good chronicle of political events of that period is in John W. F. Dulles, *Yesterday in Mexico: 1919-1936* (1961). Howard F. Cline, *United States and Mexico* (1953; rev. ed. 1963), gives an excellent analysis of the policy and importance of the Sonoran "dynasty." Harry Bernstein, *Modern and Contemporary Latin America* (1952), discusses economic and social changes during the period. Ernest Gruening, *Mexico and Its Heritage* (1928), is rich in material on regional and local politics. Harold Nicolson, *Dwight Morrow* (1935), discusses the diplomatic negotiations between Morrow and Calles. General surveys containing relevant material include Henry Bamford Parkes, *A History of Mexico* (1938; 3d ed. rev. 1960), and Lesley Byrd Simpson, *Many Mexicos* (1941; 4th ed. rev. 1966). □

Callimachus

The Greek poet Callimachus (ca. 310-240 B.C.) is regarded as the most characteristic representative of Alexandrian poetry. Learning, polish, and contemporaneity characterize his work, which had enormous influence on the Roman elegiac poets.

Very little is known about the life of Callimachus. What is known comes primarily from the 10th-century encyclopedist Suidas, not all of which is reliable, and from other, limited references in ancient sources. Callimachus was born in Cyrene; he apparently claimed descent from Battus, the founder of Cyrene, and lived during the time of Ptolemy II Philadelphus (reigned 285-247 B.C.) and survived into the reign of Ptolemy III Euergetes (reigned 246-221 B.C.).

Prior to his introduction into the Ptolemaic court, Callimachus, who many scholars argue had been poor, taught school in the Alexandrian suburb of Eleusis. Among Callimachus's more famous pupils were Eratosthenes of Cyrene, Aristophanes of Byzantium, and Apollonius of Rhodes. Callimachus is most often mentioned in connection with Apollonius because of a literary quarrel that eventually led to a personal feud. Apollonius believed in the viability of the Homeric tradition (in modified form) for epic poetry, whereas Callimachus argued for a learned modernized poetry, attuned to Alexandrian times, that was short and highly polished. From this quarrel resulted the poem of invective *Ibis,* after which Ovid modeled his own poem of the same name, and there is no doubt that it is Apollonius who is being castigated and viewed as a traitor.

Callimachus was also the librarian of the great library at Alexandria and is often said to have succeeded Zenodotus. Callimachus is credited with having compiled the first scientific literary history, the *Pinakes* (Tablets), an annotated catalog in 120 volumes of all the books in the library, from Homeric manuscripts to the latest cook-books—a feat of no mean accomplishment.

Suidas reports that Callimachus wrote some 800 works and mentions a wealth of titles, including satyric dramas, tragedies, comedies, and lyrics. Only a few hymns and epigrams have survived.

Style and Influence

At one point early in his career Callimachus had apparently been criticized for not writing anything of great length. He countered this criticism by producing the *Hecale,* a sizable work cited frequently by Greek and Roman authors but now lost. It narrated, with unusual digressions, Theseus's encounter with the Marathonian bull. However, it is clear that Callimachus was not primarily interested in bulk but in perfection of poetic form, refinement and purity of style, innovative ways of expressing the familiar, and graceful descriptions. Certainly one of the most influential figures in later ancient times, Callimachus outdistanced all contemporary poets in prestige and popularity, was quoted frequently by grammarians, metricians, and lexicographers, as well as scholiasts, and was studied by the Byzantines.

Callimachus's poetry seems to have survived till the time of the Fourth Crusade (1205). Modern critics have rediscovered Callimachus and have found true poetic genius in his works, even though he may not actually have been the most popular or most important poet as far as his contemporaries were concerned.

His Works

Since only a small portion of Callimachus's writings has survived, it is difficult for the modern reader to appreciate what a prodigious author he was. The six extant hymns are not necessarily his best work or even the most representative, but they do give an idea of his interests and range, dealing with Zeus's birth, raising, and might; a festival in Apollo's honor in Cyrene; Artemis; Delos, including the story of Apollo's birth, mythology, and Ptolemy's Gallic encounter; the bath of Pallas and how Tiresias saw her bathing and was struck blind; and Demeter's search for her daughter Kore and the punishment of Erysichthon.

The elegiac *Aitia,* in four books, also survives in fragments and deals with legendary origins of various localities and rites; it was much cited in antiquity. *The Lock of Berenice* survives in a Latin rendition by Catullus.

In Callimachus's hands the epigram emerges as a literary genre. Even though some of his epigrams are tomb inscriptions, the epigram now becomes a literary vehicle for real emotions, including love.

Further Reading

There are two Loeb Library editions of Callimachus: *Callimachus and Lycophron,* translated by A. W. Mair (1921), and *Aetia, Iambic, Lyric Poems, Hecale, Minor Epic and Elegiac Poems,* translated with notes by C. A. Trypanis (1958). Accounts of Callimachus in English are extremely limited and sometimes contradictory. The standard work, in Latin, is undoubtedly R. Pfeiffer's two volume study, *Callimachus* (1949, 1953). Georg Luck, *The Latin Love Elegy* (1959), is indispensable for students of Latin elegiac poetry; Luck includes a discussion of Callimachus as the Romans saw him. ☐

Cab Calloway

Cab Calloway (1907–1994), blues and scat legend, entertained generations of people with his jazzy big band sounds. Even in his golden years, Calloway still traveled on the road and performed for his fans.

Cab Calloway was a famous singer and bandleader beginning in the lively era of the 1920s, and he remained active in music throughout his golden years. At an age when most people retire and rest on old laurels, Calloway kept a full schedule of touring with a band and singing his signature song, "Minnie the Moocher." Long ago dubbed the "Dean of American Jive," Calloway brought the joys of the jazzy big band sound to many generations, helping to preserve the very style he helped to create.

Calloway was born Cabell Calloway III, in Rochester, New York. When he was six his family moved to Baltimore, Maryland, where his father practiced law and sold real estate. Although young Cab enjoyed singing solos at the Bethlehem Methodist Episcopal Church, it was assumed that he would follow in his father's footsteps and study law. Cab had other ideas, however. His older sister had found work singing with a show in Chicago, and he appealed to her for advice. Her guidance was substantial—she sent him a train ticket, and when he arrived in Chicago, she set him up as a singer with a quartet. He was still in his teens.

Calloway has noted that his career began in 1925. By that time he had become a talented drummer and secured a position with the Sunset Cafe orchestra in Chicago. He did not hide behind a drum set for long. Within two years—or by his twentieth birthday—he had organized his own orchestra and was singing lead vocals again. The group, Cab Calloway and his Alabamians, became quite popular in Chicago and eventually took a booking at the Savoy Ballroom in New York City. That engagement did not go well, and Calloway dissolved the band. He was about to return to Chicago when he landed a part in a Broadway comedy, *Connie's Hot Chocolates.* The show was an all-black revue, and Calloway brought the house down with his rendition of "Ain't Misbehavin'."

Broadway manager Irving Mills encouraged Calloway to form another band, so the young musician gathered another orchestra and immediately found work in the well-attended Harlem speakeasies and nightclubs. In 1929 he was invited to fill in for Duke Ellington at the Cotton Club, and thereafter the two band leaders alternated engagements at the prestigious venue. It was during his years at the Cotton Club that Calloway developed his crisp, jazzy song-and-dance style, and it was there that he composed and debuted "Minnie the Moocher."

Calloway was one of the first performers to make deliberate use of scat singing—random use of nonsense syllables—in his act. As with so many others, he began scat singing when he forgot a song's lyrics. Audiences loved the sound, however, so he began to write tunes with scat choruses. "Minnie the Moocher," his best-known song, is one such composition. Its refrain—"hi de hi de hi de ho"—invites the audience to sing along in the old call-and-response style. Recordings of "Minnie the Moocher" have sold in the millions worldwide.

Calloway's fame soared in the 1930s and 1940s. He appeared in such films as *International House* and *Stormy Weather,* he helped to popularize the jitterbug with tunes like "Jumpin' Jive," "Reefer Man," "It Ain't Necessarily So," and "If This Isn't Love," and he even wrote a popular book, *Hepster's Dictionary,* which sold two million copies and ran into six editions. Although Calloway's is not always associated with the big band era, he actually fronted a fine ensemble during the period. His ability to pay top salaries attracted a group of brilliant musicians, including sax players Chu Berry, Ben Webster, and Hilton Jefferson; trumpeters Dizzy Gillespie and Jonah Jones; bassist Milt Hinton; and drummer Cozy Cole. In his book *The Big Bands,* George T. Simon noted: "the *esprit de corps* of the Calloway band was tremendous, and the great pride that the musicians possessed as individuals and as a group paid off handsomely in the music they created."

The years of World War II found Calloway entertaining troops in the United States and Canada. After the war he returned to club work and to the Broadway stage, most notably as Sportin' Life in the George Gershwin operetta *Porgy and Bess.* In the late 1960s he took another important Broadway role, that of Horace Vandergelder in the all-black version of *Hello, Dolly!* His work with Pearl Bailey in that show was the culmination of a long friendship—he had helped Bailey get a start in show business in 1945 by hiring her to help him with vocals. Even though he was 60 when he appeared in *Hello, Dolly!,* Calloway never missed a step in the strenuous show. In fact, he was just hitting his stride.

The energetic performer's career received an enormous boost when he was asked to star in the 1980 film *The Blues Brothers.* The movie, which also starred John Belushi and Dan Aykroyd, gave Calloway the opportunity to perform "Minnie the Moocher" for an audience young enough to be his grandchildren—and, clad in a snazzy white zoot suit with tails, he made the number the highlight of the film. Critics who otherwise panned *The Blues Brothers* singled Calloway out for praise, and his popularity soared.

Into his 80s, Calloway stayed on the road most of the time, sometimes performing with his daughter Chris. *Philadelphia Inquirer* correspondent John Rogers observed that Calloway strutted around the stage "like some nimble tightrope walker." Rogers added: "[His] moves have slowed a bit since the '30s, a time when Calloway could have danced Michael Jackson or Mick Jagger into the ground. The hair is white and thinner now, the midsection thicker, and that classically handsome face lined and puffy after eight decades of full-throttle living. But every bit of his voice is still there—and every bit of the style and grace that made the legend."

In June of 1994 Calloway suffered a stroke and died that November. He was survived by his wife, Nuffie, whom he married in 1953. When once asked if he has any heroes in the music business, Calloway scoffed at the very idea. It is easy to undersand why he might not idolize Webster or

Gillespie—he helped give them their start, along with other notables such as Pearl Bailey and Lena Horne. "I'll tell you who my heroes are," he said. "My heroes are the notes, man. The music itself. You understand what I'm saying? I love the music. The music is my hero."

Further Reading

Calloway, Cab, *Of Minnie the Moocher and Me,* Crowell, 1976.
Simon, George T., *The Big Bands,* Macmillan, 1967.
Simon, George T., *Best of the Music Makers,* Doubleday, 1979.
Los Angeles Times, November 20, 1994, p. A1.
New York Times, November 20, 1994, p. 59.
Philadelphia Inquirer, August 16, 1990.
Times (London), November 21, 1994, p. 21.
Washington Post, November 20, 1994, p. B5. □

Charles Calvert

The English proprietor of colonial Maryland, Charles Calvert, 3d Baron Baltimore (1637-1715), tried unsuccessfully to impose feudal authority on his colony in the late 17th century.

Charles Calvert was born on Aug. 27, 1637, the son of Cecilius Calvert, 2d Baron Baltimore, and Ann Arundell, daughter of a prominent Catholic aristocrat. Calvert's life is inseparable from the colony projected by his grandfather, George Calvert, and settled by his father. Maryland was unique among the American colonies for the tenacity the Calverts exhibited in upholding their proprietary claims. Inasmuch as these claims were largely based on an outmoded system of feudal privileges, deriving from a royal charter, bitter controversies arose between each proprietor and his subjects. These conflicts wracked Maryland from its inception, but they developed greatest intensity under Charles Calvert.

Calvert was appointed governor in 1661, succeeding as proprietor when his father died in 1675. He brought to the governorship an unyielding concept of authority. Although compassionate and dedicated to Maryland's welfare, Calvert judged the value of every public act against his desire to protect his proprietary interests. He was unable to embrace the opposition or to reach out beyond his relatives and Catholic friends for help in governing Maryland. There were complaints about his alleged antagonism to Protestants and the disproportion of Catholics appointed to provincial offices. In 1670 Calvert restricted the franchise and called to the assembly only half the delegates elected. He interfered with the rights of the lower house, vetoed legislative acts years after they had been passed, and appointed to the highest offices men of little ability.

There were major upheavals in 1659, 1676, and 1681, during which Calvert's proprietary authority was seriously challenged. While Calvert was in England, a revolution occurred in the colony in 1689, partly triggered by the Glorious Revolution in progress in England. When Calvert failed to promptly proclaim William and Mary as the new rulers of England, insurgents in the Maryland colony, fed by fear of the Catholics and of Indian marauders, took over the government. Instead of giving power back to the proprietor, the new English monarchs accepted only Lord Baltimore's claim over the land and sent a royal governor to oversee the colony. Calvert spent the rest of his life in England trying unsuccessfully to regain political control of Maryland. He died in 1715. The Calverts secured limited political authority in the province under the 5th Baron Baltimore, who had been raised as a Protestant, but the full proprietary power under the old charter was never restored.

Further Reading

A concise biography of Calvert is offered in Clayton C. Hall, *The Lords Baltimore and the Maryland Palatinate* (1902). A detailed account of Maryland under Calvert can be obtained in Newton D. Mereness, *Maryland as a Proprietary Province* (1901). Of special value is the discussion in Charles M. Andrews, *The Colonial Period of American History,* vol. 2 (1936). A commentary with sources is provided by Michael G. Kammen in Michael G. Hall and others, eds., *The Glorious Revolution in America: Documents on the Colonial Crisis of 1689* (1964). □

George Calvert

The English statesman George Calvert 1st Baron Baltimore (ca. 1580-1632), was the founder of the colony of Maryland in America.

George Calvert was born in Yorkshire about 1580, the son of Leonard and Alice Crossland Calvert. He matriculated at Oxford in 1594 at the age of 14, graduating in 1597. Later, he became secretary to Robert Cecil, a leading figure in the English government. With Cecil's support and encouragement from the King, Calvert advanced rapidly, attaining a seat in Parliament, membership on the Privy Council, and the position of secretary of state. Prominent public service, however, brought difficult responsibilities. He was obliged to defend in Parliament the unpopular Continental diplomacy of James I, especially the rapprochement with Catholic Spain. His active part in examining Irish grievances led to knighthood in 1617. Following his conversion to Catholicism, Calvert resigned as secretary of state. As a reward for his service, James I gave him the Irish title of Baron Baltimore.

Calvert's interest in America was of long standing. He had held stock in the Virginia Company and was a member of the Council for New England. In 1623 Calvert obtained a royal charter to found a private colony in Newfoundland. He received the powers of a "Bishop of Durham," a medieval authority, which meant that the proprietor could exercise feudal control over the land, award titles of nobility, and dominate the government of any colony he established. Known as Avalon, the new colony received Lord Baltimore's firm support. He visited it in 1627 and later returned with his second wife and children, leaving in England only

his eldest son Cecilius. Because of the bitter arctic cold and French attacks, the colony proved a failure. Without giving up his proprietary hopes, Baltimore looked southward, arriving in Jamestown, Va., in 1629. However, his religion and interest in a proprietary colony antagonized the Virginians, who forced Baltimore to return to England. There he prevailed on Charles I to grant him another colony north of the Potomac River, with proprietary features similar to Avalon. Shortly before the charter gained final approval in 1632, Calvert died at the age of 52. The grant was completed in the name of his heir, Cecilius, who proceeded with the colonization of Maryland.

Lord Baltimore's activities in America indicate the profound impact which the New World had made in England. Some of the most influential men in the mother country were directly involved in western expansion. Moreover, the proprietary grants which Baltimore sought reveal that an interest in establishing feudal estates in America provided important motivation for colonization.

Further Reading

A biographical account of Calvert by a noted authority is Clayton C. Hall, *The Lords Baltimore and the Maryland Palatinate* (1902). For the English background of Calvert's life consult Godfrey Davies, *The Early Stuarts, 1603-1660* (1937; 2d ed. 1959). An excellent and concise interpretation of the background to the Maryland proprietorship is in Charles M. Andrews, *Our Earliest Colonial Settlements* (1933). □

John Calvin

The French Protestant reformer John Calvin (1509-1564) is best known for his doctrine of predestination and his theocratic view of the state.

John Calvin was born at Noyon in Picardy on July 10, 1509. He was the second son of Gérard Cauvin, who was secretary to the bishop of Noyon and fiscal procurator for the province. The family name was spelled several ways, but John showed preference while still a young man for "Calvin."

An ecclesiastical career was chosen for John, and at the age of 12, through his father's influence, he received a small benefice, a chaplaincy in the Cathedral of Noyon. Two years later, in August 1523, he went to Paris in the company of the noble Hangest family. He entered the Collège de la Marche at the University of Paris, where he soon became highly skilled in Latin. Subsequently he attended the Collège de Montaigu, where the humanist Erasmus had studied before him and where the Catholic reformer Ignatius of Loyola would study after him. Calvin remained in the profoundly ecclesiastical environment of this college until 1528. Then at the behest of his father he moved to Orléans to study law. He devoted himself assiduously to this field, drawing from it the clarity, logic, and precision that would later be the distinguishing marks of his theology.

In 1531, armed with his bachelor of laws degree, Calvin returned to Paris and took up the study of classical literature. At this time Martin Luther's ideas concerning salvation by faith alone were circulating in the city, and Calvin was affected by the new Protestant notions and by pleas for Church reform. He became a friend of Nicholas Cop, who, upon becoming rector of the university in 1533, made an inaugural speech which immediately branded him as a heretic. Calvin suffered the penalties of guilt by association and would certainly have been arrested had he not been warned to flee. In January 1534 he hastily left Paris and went to Angoulême, where he began work on his theological masterpiece, the *Institutes of the Christian Religion.*

Several turbulent months later, after a secret journey and two brief periods of arrest, Calvin was forced to flee from France when King Francis I instituted a general persecution of heretics. In December 1534 he found his way to Basel, where Cop had gone before him.

Calvin's Theology

Sometime during his last 3 years in France, Calvin experienced what he called his sudden conversion and mentally parted company with Rome. He proceeded to develop his theological position and in 1536 to expound it in the most severe, logical, and terrifying book of all Protestantism, the *Institutes of the Christian Religion.* Calvin followed this first Latin edition with an enlarged version in 1539 and a French translation in 1540, a book that has been called a masterpiece of French prose. The reformer continued to revise and develop the *Institutes* until his death.

Its theme is the majesty of God. There is an unbridgeable chasm between man and his maker. Man is thoroughly corrupt, so base that it is unthinkable that he could lift a finger to participate in his own salvation. God is glorious and magnificent beyond man's highest capacity to comprehend; He is both omnipotent and omniscient, and He has, merely by His knowing, foreordained all things that ever will come to pass. Man is helpless in the face of God's will. He is predestined either to eternal glory or eternal damnation, and he can do nothing, even if he is the best of saints in his fellow's eyes, to alter the intention of God. To suggest that he could would be to imply that the Creator did not fore-know precisely and thus diminish His majesty. To Calvin there could be no greater sacrilege. This doctrine of predestination did not originate with Calvin, but no one ever expressed it more clearly and uncompromisingly. He did not flinch from the terrible consequences of God's omniscience.

To those few whom God has chosen to save, He has granted the precious gift of faith, which is undeserved. All are unworthy of salvation, and most are damned because God's justice demands it. But God is infinitely merciful as well as just, and it is this mercy, freely given, that opens the door to heaven for the elect.

Calvin knew that this doctrine was terrifying, that it seemed to make God hateful and arbitrary, but he submitted that human reason is too feeble to scrutinize or judge the will of God. The Creator's decision on who shall be damned is immutable. No purgatory exists to cleanse man of his sins and prepare him for heaven. Yet Calvin counsels prayer, even though it will not change God's will, because prayer too is decreed and men must worship even though they may be among the damned. The prayer should be simple, and all elaborate ceremony should be rejected. The Catholic Mass is sacrilegious, because the priest claims that in it he changes the bread and wine into the body and blood of Christ. Calvin held that Christ is present whenever believers gather prayer-fully, but in spirit only and not because of any act undertaken by priests, who have no special powers and are in no way different from other Christians. There are only two Sacraments: Baptism and the Lord's Supper. Like Luther, Calvin rejects all other "sacraments" as not based on Holy Scripture.

Calvin makes a distinction between the visible Church and the true Church. The former is composed of those who participate in the Sacraments and profess their faith in Christ; the latter, invisible and unknown to all save God, is the community of the elect—dead, living, and yet unborn. One must belong to the visible Church in order to be saved, but belonging to it is no guarantee of salvation. Church and state are both ordained by God. The task of the former is to teach and prescribe faith and morals, while the latter preserves order and enforces the laws set forth by the Church. There is no separation of Church and state. Both must work in harmony to preserve the word of God, and to this end the state is enjoined to use force if necessary to suppress false teachings, such as Catholicism, Anabaptism, or Lutheranism.

That these ideas, particularly with their cornerstone of predestination, soon conquered much of the Christian world is baffling at first examination. But Calvin's followers were encouraged by hope of election rather than enervated by fear of damnation. It seems to be an essential part of human nature to see oneself as just, and Calvin himself, while he firmly maintained that no one is certain of salvation, always acted with confidence and trust in his own election.

Geneva Reformer

While publication of the *Institutes* was in progress, Calvin made preparations to leave his homeland permanently. He returned briefly to France early in 1536 to settle personal business, then set out for Strasbourg. Because of the war between France and the Holy Roman Empire, he was forced to take a circuitous route which brought him to Geneva. He intended to continue on to Strasbourg but was persuaded to remain by Guillaume Farel, who had begun a Protestant movement in Geneva. Except for one brief interruption he spent the remaining years of his life in Geneva, spreading the word of God as he understood it and creating a theocratic state unique in the annals of Christendom.

In 1537 Calvin was elected to the preaching office by the city fathers, who had thrown off obedience to Rome along with their old political ruler, the Duke of Savoy. A council, now operating as the government, issued decrees in July 1537 against all manifestations of Catholicism as well as all forms of immorality. Rosaries and relics were banished along with adulterers. Gamblers were punished and so were people who wore improper, that is, luxurious, clothing. The austere hand of Calvin was behind these regulations.

The new rules were too severe for many citizens, and in February 1538 a combination of *Libertines* (freedom lovers) and suppressed Catholics captured a majority of the council. This body then banished Calvin and Farel; Calvin went to Strasbourg and Farel to Neuchâtel, where he remained for the rest of his life.

At Strasbourg, Calvin ministered to a small congregation of French Protestants and in 1540 married Idelette de Bure. She bore him one child, who died in infancy, and she herself died in 1549. While Calvin was establishing himself at Strasbourg, things were going badly for the new Protestantism in Geneva. Strong pressure was being exerted on the council from within and without the city to return to Catholicism. Fearing that they might be removed from office and disgusted with the trend toward flagrant immorality among the citizenry, the councilors revoked the ban on Calvin on May 1, 1541. A deputation was sent immediately to Strasbourg to persuade the reformer to return, and he did so reluctantly, on Sept. 13, 1541, after being promised total cooperation in restoring discipline.

Rule of God

The law of a Christian state, according to Calvin, is the Bible. The task of the clergy is to interpret and teach that law, while the task of the state is to enforce it. Under this principle, while the clergy, including Calvin, were not civil magistrates, they held enormous authority over the government and all aspects of civil as well as religious life.

Immediately on his return to Geneva, Calvin set about organizing the Reformed Church. On Jan. 2, 1542, the city council ratified the *Ordonnances ecclésiastiques,* the new regulations governing the Church, formulated by a committee led by Calvin. The *Ordonnances* divided the ministry into four categories: pastors, teachers, lay elders, and deacons. The pastors governed the Church and trained aspirants to the ministry. No one could preach henceforth in Geneva without permission of the pastors.

The conduct of all citizens was examined and regulated by a consistory of 5 pastors and 12 lay elders elected by the council. The consistory had the right to visit every family annually and search its home; to summon any citizen before it; to excommunicate, which meant virtually automatic banishment from the city by the council; to force attendance at weekly sermons; to prohibit gambling, drunkenness, dancing, profane songs, and immodest dress; and to forbid all forms of the theater. The colors of clothing, hair styles, and amounts of food permissible at the table were regulated. It was forbidden to name children after saints, and it was a criminal offense to speak ill of Calvin or the rest of the clergy. The press was severely censored, with writings judged to be immoral and books devoted to Catholicism or other false teaching forbidden. Punishment for first offenses was usually a fine and for repetition of minor crimes, banishment. Fornication was punishable by exile, and adultery, blasphemy, and idolatry by death. Education, which Calvin regarded as inseparable from religion, was very carefully regulated, and new schools were established. Charity was placed under municipal administration to eliminate begging. Thus the whole life of Geneva was placed under a rigid discipline and a single Church from which no deviation was permitted.

The consistory and the city council worked hand in hand in enforcing the laws, but the moving spirit of all was Calvin, who acted as a virtual dictator from 1541 until his death. Calvin did not look the part of a dictator. He was a small, thin, and fragile man with an unsmiling ruthless austerity in his face. He was pale under a black beard and a high forehead. A poet would perhaps see these physical details as signs of enormous, orderly intellect and of little human warmth or appetite—a being all mind and spirit with almost no body at all. There were some ugly moments in theocratic Geneva. During these years 58 people were executed and 76 banished in order to preserve morals and discipline. Like most men of his century, the reformer was convinced that believing wrongly about God was so heinous a crime that not even death could expiate it.

Last Years

The last years of Calvin's life were spent in elaborating Geneva's laws, writing controversial works against spiritual enemies, and laboring prodigiously on the theology of the *Institutes.* Geneva became a model of discipline, order and cleanliness, the admiration of all who visited there.

Men trained to the ministry by Calvin carried his doctrines to every corner of Europe. The reformer lived to see his followers growing in numbers in the Netherlands, Scotland, Germany, and even France, the homeland he had been forced to leave. The impetus he gave to austerity, frugality, and hard, uncomplaining work may have had some influence in forming a capitalist mentality devoted to the acquisition but not the enjoyment of wealth. In any case his teachings have been carried to the present day and live on in the churches which descended from him, modified from their early severity by time but still vigorous in some of the more puritan aspects of modern life.

On May 27, 1564, after a long illness Calvin died. He left an indelible mark on the Christian world.

Further Reading

Calvin's clarity of expression makes him readily intelligible to the layman. His *Institutes of the Christian Religion,* translated by Ford Lewis Battles and edited by John T. McNeill (2 vols., 1960), provides an excellent introduction to the man and his work. Of the many biographies in English, two of the best are Williston Walker, *John Calvin* (1906), and Georgia Harkness, *John Calvin: The Man and His Ethics* (1931). For a thorough treatment of Calvin's teachings see John T. McNeill, *The History and Character of Calvinism* (1954).

There are many studies of the Reformation. Among those written from the Protestant viewpoint are James Mackinnon, *Calvin and the Reformation* (1936), and Roland H. Bainton, *The Reformation of the Sixteenth Century* (1952). Those with Catholic emphasis are Philip Hughes, *A Popular History of the Reformation* (1957; rev. ed. 1960); Henry Daniel-Rops, *The Protestant Reformation* (trans. 1961), which contains a large section on Calvin; and Christopher Dawson, *The Dividing of Christendom* (1965). See also Harold J. Grimm, *The Reformation Era, 1500-1650* (1954; with rev. bibl. 1965), and Geoffrey R. Elton, *Reformation Europe, 1517-1559* (1964). William J. Durant, *The Reformation: A History of European Civilization from Wyclif to Calvin, 1300-1564* (1957), is a popular history of the period. □

Melvin Calvin

American chemist Melvin Calvin (born 1911) did research that yielded important discoveries over broad areas of physical and biological chemistry, from metal-organic chemistry to the chemical origin of life.

Melvin Calvin was born in St. Paul, Minnesota, on April 8, 1911, to Russian immigrant parents. The family moved to Detroit, Michigan when Calvin was a child. He attended Michigan College of Mining and Technology, and, after a break of several years during the Great Depression that found him working in a Detroit brass factory, he graduated in 1931. He received his Ph.D. in chemical engineering from the University of Minnesota in 1935. His doctoral thesis concerned the electron affinity of iodine and bromide. A Rockefeller fellowship allowed Calvin the opportunity to do postdoctoral study at the University of Manchester, England, after which he joined the chemistry department of the University of California, Berkeley, in 1937, working as an instructor in chemistry before becoming a professor in 1947. He married Genevieve Jemtegaard in 1942; they had three children.

Organic Chemical Systems

At Berkeley, Calvin became interested in the structure and behavior of organic molecules, an interest that had been inspired by research on the catalytic reactions of the organic molecules involved in photosynthesis that he had undertaken while in England. He pursued his own studies in addition to his teaching duties, but was interrupted from both upon the United States entry into World War II. During the war, although he continued to teach, Calvin gave up his research to work for the National Defense Research Council and, later, as part of the Manhattan project charged with developing the atomic bomb, where he developed a process for procuring pure oxygen from the atmosphere that has since had significant peace-time applications for medical patients with breathing problems.

Resuming his research at Berkeley after the end of the war, Calvin studied the physical and chemical properties of organic compounds, writing *The Theory of Organic Chemistry* (1940) and *The Chemistry of Metal Chelate Compounds* (1952). His clear understanding of the nature of organic molecules was to prove valuable in his subsequent work in biological chemistry. He formed the bio-organic chemistry group, which later expanded to the Laboratory of Chemical Biodynamics, in the Lawrence Radiation Laboratory of the University of California in 1945.

Maps Process of Photosynthesis

Working with his University of California associates, Calvin used the radioactive isotope carbon-14—which had become available to scientists in 1945—as a tracer for investigations of complex organic chemical systems. They described these tracer techniques in *Isotopic Carbon* (1949). In Calvin's research, chorella, a green algae, was suspended in water and then exposed to light. Then carbon dioxide consisting of carbon-14 was added. When the algae went through its life processes, producing carbohydrates from the carbon dioxide, water, and minerals, the presence of carbon-14 could be traced using a new research tool, paper chromatography. The series of compounds containing the radioactive carbon at different stages of photosynthesis were thus identified, and the biochemical mechanism of photosynthesis was mapped. These discoveries were described in *The Path of Carbon in Photosynthesis* (1957) and *The Photosynthesis of Carbon Compounds* (1962). Calvin's proposal that plants change light energy to chemical energy by transferring an electron in an organized array of pigment molecules and other substances was substantiated by research in his laboratory and elsewhere.

Calvin tested his theories of the chemical evolution of life with studies of organic substances found in ancient rocks and of the formation of organic molecules by irradiation of gas mixtures, thus simulating the atmosphere thought to exist on earth billions of years ago. These findings were described in *Chemical Evolution* (1969). He was author of over 400 publications and held a number of patents.

Consulted widely in industry, Calvin became a member of the Board of Directors of the Dow Chemical Company in 1964. He served on many scientific boards for the United States government, including the President's Science Advisory Committee for presidents Kennedy and Johnson. He was president of the American Society of Plant Physiologists in 1963-1964, president of the American Chemical Society in 1971, and a member of the National Academy of Sciences and the Royal Society of London. In 1961 he received the Nobel Prize in chemistry for his work on the path of carbon in photosynthesis. The Royal Society awarded him the Davy Medal in 1964 for his pioneering work in chemistry and biology, particularly the photosynthesis studies.

Despite his important contribution to chemistry and biology, Calvin continued to involve himself in research. In the 1970s, as the shortage of the world's oil fuel supply was brought into sharp perspective by the Arab Oil Embargo, he began to contemplate the possibility of alternative nature-based fuels. From a farm in Northern California, he began testing the practicality of his theory: that a plantation growing certain species of rubber trees that secrete a sap with characteristics similar to petroleum, could produce enough of this sap to constitute a viable alternative fuel source. After retiring from the University of California, Calvin continued to be honored from his scientific peers, receiving the American Chemical Society's Priestly Medal in 1978 and that organization's Oesper Prize in 1981.

Further Reading

There is no full-length biography of Calvin. Melvin Berger's, *Famous Men of Modern Biology* (1968), written in nontechnical language, contains a section on Calvin that emphasizes his work in photosynthesis. William Gilman, *Science: U.S.A.* (1965), devotes a section to Calvin and his work in chemical biosynthesis. A useful background source is John F. Hemahan, *Men and Molecules* (1966), which contains no biography of Calvin but discusses his work. Other information can be found in *McGraw-Hill Modern Men of Science* (1984), H.W. Wilson *Nobel Prize Winners* (1987), and David Swift*SETI Pioneers* (1990). □

Italo Calvino

One of modern Italy's most important men of letters, Italo Calvino (1923-1985), blended fantasy, fable, and comedy in an effort to illuminate modern life, and in the process redefined the literary forms.

Italo Calvino was born in Cuba in 1923. His father, Mario, a botanist, was 48 when Calvino was born; his mother, formerly Eva Mameli, also a botanist, was 37. Shortly after his birth, his family returned to their native Italy. They raised Calvino on their farm in San Remo, and Mario taught at the nearby University of Turin. The lush vegetation of the San Remo area and his extensive knowledge of local flora are reflected in many of Calvino's writings.

After preparatory school, Calvino enrolled in the Faculty of Science at the University of Turin. However, soon after his matriculation, Calvino received orders to join the Italian Army. He promptly fled to the hills and joined the resistance. During the two years that Germany occupied Italy (1943-1945) Calvino lived as a partisan in the woods of the Alpi Maritime region fighting both German and Italian fascists.

At the war's end in 1945, Calvino joined the Communist Party. He also returned to the university; however, this time he enrolled in the Faculty of Letters. He began writing for left-wing papers and journals. Calvino also began to record his war experiences in stories that eventually became his highly acclaimed first novel, *The Path to the Nest of Spiders* (1947). Here he revealed the war as seen through the eyes of an innocent young soldier, the first of many youthful and/or naive protagonists he used to reflect life's complexity and tragedy. Considered a member of the school of neo-Realism, Calvino was encouraged to write another novel in this tradition by his literary friends, particularly writers Natalia Ginzburg and Cesare Pavese. They also invited him to join the staff of their new publishing house, Enaudi. He accepted and remained affiliated with Enaudi all his life.

However, Calvino's next books were very different. In *The Cloven Viscount* (1952) Calvino depicts a soldier

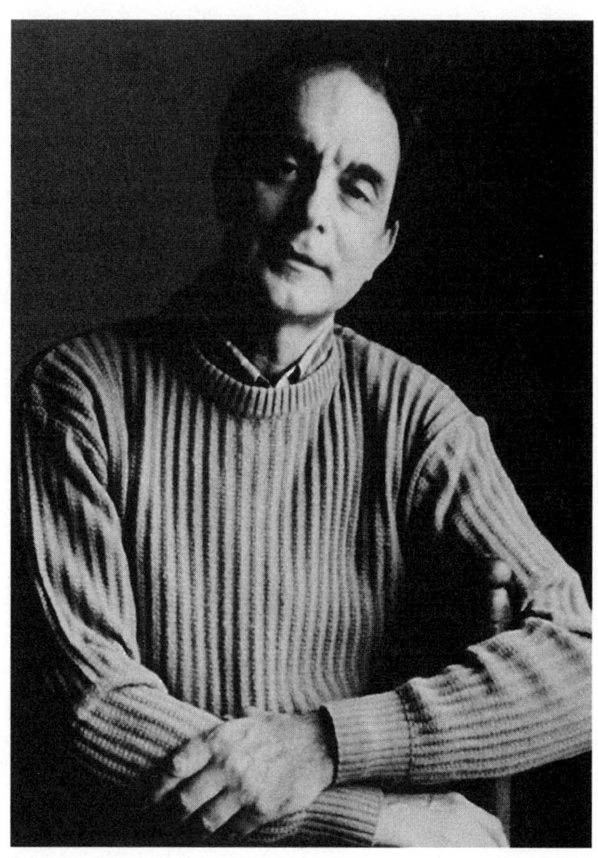

halved by a cannonball during a crusade. His two halves return to play opposing roles in his native village. *The Nonexistent Knight* (1959) details the adventures of a suit of armor occupied by the will of a knight who is otherwise incorporeal. And *The Baron in the Trees* (1957) recounts the saga of a boy who, rebelling against the authority of his father, spends the rest of his life living in the branches of a forest. All three works, set in remote times, rely on fantasy, fable, and comedy to illuminate modern life.

By the middle of the 1950s Calvino spent most of his time in Rome, the literary as well as political hub of Italian life. He resigned from the Communist Party, tired of writing tracts for Communist periodicals and disillusioned by the spread of dogmatic Stalinism and the savage crushing of the Hungarian revolt of 1956. As the years passed, Calvino became increasingly skeptical of politics.

Publication of *Italian Folktales* in 1956 did much to ensure Calvino's reputation as a major literary figure. Calvino compiled a complete and authoritative collection of 200 folk tales from all regions and dialects of Italy. Critics rank this anthology along with that of the Brothers Grimm in importance and appeal.

In 1959 Calvino visited America for six months, and in the early 1960s he moved to Paris. *The Watcher,* a collection of three short stories, was published in 1963. While living in Paris he met Chichita Singer, an Argentinian woman who had been working for years as a translator for UNESCO (the United Nations Educational, Scientific, and Cultural Organization). They were married in 1964.

In his writing Calvino continued to "search for new forms to suit realities ignored by most writers." In the comic strip he found the inspiration for both *t-zero* (1967) and *Cosmicomics* (1968). In these pieces, which resemble science fiction, a blob-like being named Qfwfq narrates the astronomical origins of the cosmos as well as the development of the species over millenia.

The 1970s saw the publication of *Invisible Cities* (1972), the story of Marco Polo's voyage from Venice to Cathay, including descriptions of many fictionalized cities; *The Castle of Crossed Destinies* (1973), which is organized around the imagery of medieval Tarot cards; and *If on a Winter's Night a Traveler* (1979). This last work consists of ten unfinished novels within a novel which is itself a wild romp through the worlds of academia, publishing, and criticism.

It was also during the 1970s in Paris that Calvino became a member of "the workshop for potential literature," a group of scholars and writers who met monthly to explore the possibilities of modern literature. During this period he and Chichita became the parents of a daughter whom they named Giovana.

Calvino returned to Rome in 1980. He and his family also enjoyed a country house at Pinetta Rocca Mare near the Riviera. In 1983 *Mr. Palomar* was completed. Calvino turned this novel into a dramatization of a mathematical formula categorizing the actions of the title character, named for the famous observatory, at a seaside resort. The book is at once a highly comic and abstract allegory.

During these years Calvino visited the United States again. In 1975 he became an honorary member of the American Academy and Institute of Arts and Letters; in 1980 *Italian Folktales* was included on the American Library Association's Notable Booklist; in 1984 he was awarded an honorary degree by Mount Holyoke College; and in 1985 he was to have delivered the Norton Lectures at Harvard. However, Calvino died at 61 on September 19, 1985, in Siena, Italy, following a cerebral hemorrhage.

Italo Calvino redefined the literary forms and in so doing breathed new life into the novel, the fable, and the folktale.

Further Reading

Most of his works are available in English. There are several books of criticism on Calvino's work. *Calvino: The Writer as Fablemaker* (1979) by Sara Maria Adler and *Contemporary European Novelists* (1968) edited by Siegfried Mandel are two in English. There are also numerous entries for Calvino in *Contemporary Literary Criticism.* However, a definitive biography has yet to be published, so periodicals, notably *The New York Times Magazine* and *Book Review,* as well as obituaries in major U.S. newspapers, remain the primary sources of data about Calvino's life. □

Michel Camdessus

Michel Camdessus (born 1933) was appointed Managing Director of the International Monetary Fund (IMF) in 1987. Prior to his position with the IMF, Camdessus pursued a financial career in France's political arena.

Michel Camdessus was born in Bayonne, France, on May 1, 1933 and has had a brilliant political career in international finance for more than 35 years. Camdessus followed the typical path for a brilliant young Frenchman by first studying at the University of Paris, then earning postgraduate degrees in economics at the Institute of Political Studies of Paris and the prestigious National School of Administration. He married Brigitte d'Arcy and they have six children.

Camdessus' first political appointment was as "Administrateur Civil" in the French civil service. He joined the Treasury in the Ministry of Finance and Economic Policies in 1960. From 1966-68, he served as financial attacheé to the French delegation at the European Economic Community (EEC) in Brussels and took an active role in Europe's first attempts to define a common value added tax (VAT). After completing his term with the EEC delegation, Camdessus returned to the Treasury, becoming Assistant Director in 1971, Deputy Director in 1974, and Director in 1982.

In the early 1970s, Camdessus' work focused on the internal aspects of the Treasury and he introduced several new solutions for channeling private savings into productive investments. His real interests, however, were in international finance. Beginning in 1978, Camdessus was deeply involved in the development of the European Monetary System (EMS). He became administrator of the Central Bank of West African States in 1978 and devoted much of his attention to these developing countries.

During the years 1978-84, Camdessus skill as Chairman of the Paris Club, the main forum for rescheduling debt between countries, gained him considerable respect from developing countries; he worked closely with both the World Bank and the International Monetary Fund (IMF) during these years. Camdessus was also instrumental in formulating economic and financial policies for industrial countries and he strongly endorsed efforts by the five major industrialized nations, known as the Group of Five, or G-5, to develop better monetary policy co-ordination. (The group of industrialized nations was later known as the Group of Seven, or G-7.) From December 1982 until December 1984 he served as Chairman of the Monetary Committee of the European Economic Community (EEC).

As the French socialist government moved from a previously loose monetary policy and protectionist tendencies to new policies during the early 1980s, Camdessus' influence helped shape his country's financial re-orientation.

At the Versailles summit in 1982, Camdessus negotiated an agreement with Beryl Sprinkel, then U.S. Secretary of the Treasury, that granted the IMF new responsibilities for surveillance of exchange rates between the major currencies. Then, in 1983, Camdessus was named Alternate Governor of the IMF for France, and in November 1984, he was appointed Governor of the Bank of France, a position that also entitled him to a seat on the EMS Governors' Committee. During this tenure he supported Tokyo's 1986 economic summit decision to use specific indicators to control the movements of exchange rates. He also supported the 1985 Plaza Hotel agreement.

By the time Camdessus assumed office as Managing Director of the IMF on January 16, 1987, he had considerable experience in managing both the monetary problems of industrial nations and the economic difficulties of the Third World. His first challenge was to seek long-term solutions to the global debt crisis. Camdessus had previously advocated "enlarged access" to IMF credits in addition to new Special Drawing Rights (SDR) allocations but member countries did not agree to the terms.

Under his leadership a number of new economic instruments were implemented, including an enhancement of the existing Structural Adjustment Facility (December, 1987), the creation of a Contingency and Compensatory Financing Facility (August, 1988), an improvement of the medium-term Extended Fund Facility (June, 1988), and the adoption of a new debt strategy (May, 1989). The new debt strategy included use of the IMF's own resources to help countries finance interest payments in debt reduction operations.

Camdessus also called for a doubling of member countries' total contributions, or quotas. However this latter plan was strongly resisted by the United States and other countries.

Camdessus' years as Managing Director of the IMF have not been without problems. In early 1997, the IMF's policy-setting Interim Committee reached a tentative agreement on the creation of new Special Drawing Rights (SDRs) that would benefit new member countries; no new SDRs had been allocated since the late 1970s. (Many countries, including the United States, fear that the creation of new SDRs would increase world liquidity and cause higher inflation.) Another of Camdessus' goals, also facing strong opposition, is to bring all member holdings up to 33% of their quotas. He has also called for a doubling of IMF quotas, the reserves of gold and currency that nations pledge to the organization and from which they can draw in the event of financial necessity. There have already been eleven unsuccessful reviews of quotas since the IMF was founded in 1945; Camdessus' goal is a difficult one. There are currently 181 member countries in the IMF with total SDR quotas equivalent to $200 billion U.S. dollars.

Over the past ten years, in an effort to revamp the IMF's public image and to keep the fund consistent with his own philosophical convictions, Camdessus, in his role as Governor of the IMF, has given increased attention to the impact of structural adjustments on the poor in developing countries. He has repeatedly urged private banks to adopt a more accommodating approach toward debtor countries, asking them to take part in debt relief schemes and provide new monies to aid the resumption of growth.

Camdessus' call for greater attention by the IMF to the social consequences of adjustment as well as for its increased commitment to long-term debt relief operations has drawn criticism from those who want the IMF to remain committed to only its original, narrowly-defined mandates, that of creating financial/monetary policies and providing for short-term adjustments.

Camdessus has frequently referred to the complex interrelationships of a global economy. His viewpoint of IMF's global role is reflected in comments made in 1995, as Mexico's devaluation of the peso began. "Financial globalization has heightened the challenges of fostering stable foreign exchange and financial markets, and of preventing and resolving financial crises. . . . Capitol flows don't move . . . capriciously. They move because financial markets feel somewhere something's wrong in the macroeconomic sectors in some countries."

In March, 1997, at a meeting with the Association of Southeast Asian Nations (ASEAN), Camdessus told the group that unless the ASEAN speeds the pace of its own financial liberalization, global economic stability and growth will be affected. Over the past ten years, Camdessus has repeatedly emphasized the shared responsibility of creditors and debtors in solving international debt crises, he has called upon industrialized nations to maintain orderly monetary policies, and he has insisted that debtor countries bear the primary responsibility for restoring their own economic health through sustained adjustment programs.

Further Reading

Michel Camdessus is listed in *The International Who's Who* and in the *European Biographical Dictionary*. Feature articles describing his approach to international economics appeared at the time of his election as IMF managing director in *The Banker* (January 1987) and *The Economist* (January 8, 1987). The policy changes he brought to the IMF are analyzed in *South* (No. 8, 1988). Most of his speeches and press conferences as IMF director can be found in the bimonthly *IMF Survey*. □

Simon Cameron

The American politician Simon Cameron (1799-1889) is best known for the efficient political machine he developed in Pennsylvania and for the way he used it to gain public office and financial rewards for himself and his friends.

Simon Cameron was born in Lancaster, Pa., on March 8, 1799. His family was poor and he had little formal education, so he apprenticed himself to a printing establishment in Harrisburg. Hardworking and ambitious, by the age of 21 he was editor of a local newspaper. Two years later he found employment with Gales and Saton, publishers of the congressional debates, in Washington, D.C. While there, Cameron spent his spare time in the houses of Congress, making friends and learning the ways of politics. In 1824 he was back in Harrisburg, where he became owner and editor of a local newspaper and launched a lifelong career of mixing business with politics.

Editor and Entrepreneur

Cameron took strong editorial positions on public issues, especially the protective tariff, and exercised considerable influence on state and even national politics. He was rewarded for his efforts with the lucrative position of state printer and, soon after, by appointment as adjutant general on the governor's staff.

Cameron saw enormous opportunity for wealth and political power in the internal improvement boom then sweeping the states. Without experience he became a contractor and made a fortune constructing a network of canals and railroads, which he ultimately brought together to form the Northern Central Railroad. To help finance this, he established his own bank.

Early Political Career

Cameron's interests in politics went hand in glove with his economic pursuits. He supported Democratic candidates in the Jackson-Van Buren period and evidently pulled strings that sent James Buchanan to the U.S. Senate. For yeoman service in support of Martin Van Buren, Cameron was appointed commissioner to settle Winnebago Indian claims in 1833. Though the scandal that followed led to his dismissal and temporarily damaged his political reputation, it did not change either his methods or his ambitions.

With the rise of the Native American party, better known as the Know-Nothing party, in Pennsylvania, Cameron shifted allegiance. In 1845, a coalition of Whigs, Americans, and protectionist Democrats elected him to the U.S. Senate. His career was undistinguished, and he was not reelected in 1849 or 1858. With the rise of the new Republican party he was able to weld a powerful Republican machine which sent him back to the Senate. Although his political shifts and intrigues brought opposition even from some Pennsylvania Republicans, Cameron's success and self-confidence allowed him to set himself up as a possible Republican candidate for the presidency in 1860. A Cameron-Lincoln club (with Abraham Lincoln as vice president) was formed but made little progress. Few who came to the Republican convention in Chicago thought of Cameron as a possible nominee, but all knew that the Pennsylvania vote was necessary for the success of any candidate. This gave Cameron enormous bargaining power.

Election of 1860

When the first ballot was taken, the votes for Cameron were almost wholly from the Pennsylvania delegates, and he was far behind William H. Seward and Lincoln. As the contest between those two developed into a struggle for the uncommitted states of Indiana, Pennsylvania, and New Jersey, Lincoln's campaign managers (against his firm instructions) began to bargain and make promises. To secure Indiana, they promised a place in Lincoln's Cabinet to Congressman Caleb B. Smith, and they promised the Pennsylvania delegation a place for Cameron at the President's "council table."

Lincoln was unhappy with these commitments but after his election found it necessary to keep them in mind. Pennsylvania and Cameron presented the most difficult problem. An important state could not be ignored; and Cameron was determined to see that the promise was kept, despite sharp opposition to him.

Lincoln attempted to avoid Cameron, but when Cameron appeared in Springfield, Ill., with the Pennsylvania men who had made the bargain, Lincoln yielded and gave him a letter saying that "by your permission I shall at the proper time nominate you to the United States Senate for confirmation as Secretary of the Treasury or as Secretary of War." Protests from all quarters convinced Lincoln of his mistake, and he wrote Cameron to recall this letter, saying it was impossible to take him into the Cabinet. His suggestion that Cameron write declining the appointment was never answered. Renewed pressure from the Pennsylvania Legislature consequently forced Lincoln to nominate Cameron for secretary of war; he could do less damage there than in the Treasury.

Lincoln's Secretary of War

As civil war became a reality, the War Department assumed new importance. The duty of organizing and equipping thousands of soldiers required the expenditure of millions of dollars and involved the exercise of enormous power. Cameron, as before, viewed his position primarily as a chance to reward friends, increase his own fortune, and create a powerful political machine. He rewarded more than 20 Pennsylvania politicians with jobs in the department. Then came contract scandals, the wasting of money on unneeded or inferior supplies, and even the awarding of commissions in the Army. Soon Congress was incensed, and the press began demanding Cameron's removal.

Cameron had at first followed Secretary of State Seward's lead on issues, but as his own situation grew desperate he turned toward Treasury Secretary Salmon P. Chase's position and became critical of Lincoln and devoted to fighting slavery. Although Lincoln made it clear that he opposed freeing slaves who escaped into the Union lines or who lived in conquered territory, Cameron openly defended generals who had done so. In his report to Congress in December 1861, Cameron included a passage recommending the creation of a slave army. Lincoln was not consulted, and the report was sent to the postmasters in the chief cities to be delivered to the press. This move behind the President's back was made to cloak departmental corruption and to give Cameron standing as a liberal. Although Cameron's report was recalled by telegraph as soon as Lincoln discovered the treachery, a few newspapers had already published it. The antislavery element responded and Chase approved, but it was apparent that Cameron could not remain in the Cabinet. On Jan. 11, 1862, Cameron received a letter: "My dear Sir: As you have more than once expressed a desire for a change in position, I can now gratify you consistently with my view of the public interest. I therefore propose nominating you to the Senate next Monday as minister to Russia. Very sincerely your friend, A. Lincoln."

Cameron's stay in Russia was short and uneventful. He soon returned to Pennsylvania and to the old political game. He ran unsuccessfully for the Senate in 1863 but regained his seat in 1867. He made certain that his son would succeed him as senator when he resigned in 1877. He then retired to his farm at Donegal Springs, Pa., where he died on June 26, 1889.

Further Reading

Erwin S. Bradley, *Simon Cameron, Lincoln's Secretary of War: A Political Biography* (1966), presents a sympathetic view of Cameron's political career. Lee F. Crippen, *Simon Cameron: Ante-Bellum Years* (1942), considers his career in relation to the times. Burton J. Hendrick, *Lincoln's War Cabinet* (1946), discusses Cameron's tenure as secretary of war. □

Luis Vaz de Camoëns

The Portuguese poet Luis Vaz de Camoëns (1524-1580), or Camões, is best known for "The Lusiads," which is among the best modern epics. He was a lyricist of rare perfection and is considered the greatest poet of the Portuguese language.

Luis de Camoëns was the son of Simão Vaz, from Coimbra, and Ana de Sá e Macedo. The date of his birth is fairly well established; however, such is not the case with his place of birth. Of the various cities which claim the honor, Lisbon has the best claim, with Coimbra a second possibility. He was a *cavalleiro fidalgo* (untitled nobleman) and was descended from a noble and wealthy family of Galician origin which had settled in Portugal in the late 14th century, as a result of the civil wars that raged in Castile. He was also related to the explorer Vasco da Gama, of whose heroic voyage to India he would sing in *The Lusiads.*

Camoëns spent his early years in Coimbra, where he studied at the university. He fondly remembered his life there in his poetry, and in later years he rightfully boasted of his studies. Chronological reasons make it doubtful that he studied with his uncle, the Augustinian friar Bento de Camoëns.

Early Career

About 1543, with his studies completed, Camoëns went to Lisbon, where he entered the court circles as the protégé of the great noble Don Francisco de Noronha, Count of Linhares. Camoëns became a friend of the count's son, Don Antonio, and according to tradition acted as his tutor. A thick web of legends obscures these years of Camoëns's life, but it is certain that he chose a military career (a most fitting vocation for an impoverished nobleman) and that he was in North Africa by 1547. It has been deduced from his poetry that he joined for a time the garrison of Ceuta, the most important Portuguese trading center and military post in North Africa, and that he lost his right eye in a skirmish with the Moors. The legendary explanation for this North African interlude has it that Camoëns was banished there from the court because of a love affair. The name that tradition has most frequently linked with Camoëns is that of Donha Caterina de Ataide, presumably the "Natercia" of his poems.

Voyage to India

Camoëns returned to Portugal, and it is from this period that the first document directly concerned with the poet survives—the *Carta de perdão a Luis de Camões,* issued by the King and dated Lisbon, March 7, 1553. According to this document, Camoëns, although very poor, was a gentleman in the royal household. The document further relates that in 1552 on the feast of Corpus Christi (June 16) Camoëns inflicted a sword wound on a royal servant and was arrested. The servant, however, eventually pardoned him, and the *Carta* represents royal ratification of the pardon.

The *Carta* also states that Camoëns was about to leave for India. In the last of four extant letters written from India, Camoëns wrote that he left his homeland without regret; once aboard ship he quoted the Roman general Scipio Africanus: "Ingrata patria, non possidebis ossa mea" (Ungrateful fatherland, you will not possess my bones). He described his life in Lisbon as "três mil [dias] de más linguas, peores tenções, danadas vontades, nascidas de pura inveja" (three thousand days of evil tongues, worse intentions, rampant ill-will, all born of sheer envy).

Camoëns sailed on the *São Bento,* and in September 1553, after a 6-month voyage, reached Goa, the commercial and military capital of Portuguese India. But he did not stay there long; in November he joined the viceroy Menezes in a punitive expedition against the Rei da Pimenta in Malabar. The viceroy led his forces to success, and Camoëns later wrote in his *Elegia VI,* "Com morte, com incêndios os punimos" (We punished them with death and fire). In February 1554 he set out on a new expedition, this time under the command of the viceroy's son, Don Fernando de Menezes. The armada sailed to the gates of the Red Sea and thence up the Arabian coast. Camoëns commemorated this journey in his *Canção VIII.* The expedition returned to Goa in November. When the new viceroy, Francisco Barreto, was invested in Goa in June 1555, Camoëns contributed to the festivities with his *Auto de Filodemo* and *Satyra do Torneio.*

Later Life

At this point facts concerning Camoëns's life again become scarce. Three years later, in 1558, however, he was in Macao, where he was in charge of the property in China of his dead or absent countrymen. There he started, or continued, to write *The Lusiads* (it is impossible to give an exact date for the poem's inception). Tradition has it that he wrote in a grotto that bears his name to this day. But he was soon accused of maladministration and was placed on board a ship for Goa.

On his return to Goa in 1561, Camoëns was jailed. After many vicissitudes he accompanied his friend Pedro Barreto to the latter's new post as governor of Mozambique. This was the beginning of Camoëns's long journey back to Portugal, which was started in 1567 and ended in 1570. His fortunes in Mozambique went from bad to worse, and in the course of the 2 years he spent there he was left almost destitute. The historian Diogo de Couto, who visited him there, relates that his friends had to give him food. With the help of Couto and others, however, Camoëns was able to embark on the *Sánta Clara* in November 1569, at long last homeward bound. He reached Portugal on April 7, 1570, after an absence of 17 years.

Camoëns brought back no fortune; all he had was the manuscript of his epic poem, which he was intent on publishing. Unfortunately, since Lisbon was still in the grips of the plague, the circumstances in Portugal were not propitious. But he forged ahead, and on Sept. 24, 1571, he obtained a royal license to print the poem. Published the following year, the poem met with immediate success. Sebastian, the young king of Portugal, tacitly recognized it as the national epic by awarding the poet an annual pension. By 1580 two different Spanish translations of the poem had been printed. The pension was renewed, and after the poet's death it was transferred to his mother. Camoëns died on June 10, 1580, on the eve of his country's annexation to Spain. He was buried in the church of St. Anna, but his tomb was destroyed by the famous earthquake of 1755.

Camoëns's Works

The works of Camoëns fall into the three categories of classical poetics: dramatic, lyric, and epic. His three extant dramatic works are his least important compositions. *Amfitrões* is a youthful work of little value; it does, however, show his thorough grounding in classical literature, since it is derived directly from *Amphitruo* by the Roman dramatist Plautus. *El rei Seleuco* (ca. 1545) is derived from the Greek author Plutarch; it has been traditionally believed that this play brought Camoëns the disfavor of King John III, who supposedly thought that the plot too closely paralleled his own life. *The Auto de Filodemo* (1555) is based upon a series of fantastic chivalresque adventures. Although Camoëns contributed to the development of Portuguese drama by giving restraint and depth to the *auto* (a short medieval play on a sacred or biblical subject) of Gil Vicente, he had little lasting influence.

As a lyric poet, however, Camoëns had a great number of imitators and disciples. He is one of the great European poets of love. He excels in his use of both the traditional Peninsular meters and of the recently imported Italian forms; he writes as well in Spanish as in Portuguese. Thematically and ideologically his place falls in the middle of that wide avenue of love poetry that extends from Petrarch through Neoplatonism well into the 17th century. Camoëns's inspiration was eclectic—he was influenced by the Latin poet Horace and the Italian poet Pietro Bembo, among others—but his sonnets have a texture and temperament completely his own.

Although the first edition of Camoëns's *Rimas* was not published until 1595 in Lisbon by Fernão Rodrigues Lobo Soropita, his poems had previously had wide circulation in various manuscript forms. Since Rodrigues Lobo was not working with an autograph copy, his edition contains alien material. Later collections of Camoëns's poetry, most notably the grossly inflated edition of the Viscount of Juromenha (1860-1869), contain a large number of inauthentic works. But the meticulous work of Wilhelm Stork and Carolina Michaëlis de Vasconcellos led to accurate attributions, and the text of the best modern editions (Rodrigues-Lopes Vieira, Cidade) is reliable.

Camoëns's masterpiece is, however, his epic poem *Os Lusiadas* (*The Lusiads or Sons of Lusus*). Cervantes called it "the treasure of Portugal." This work is in the manner of the Renaissance epic, as perfected by the Italian poets Matteo Boiardo and Ludovico Ariosto, and it is therefore written in ottava rima, with 1102 stanzas divided into 10 cantos. Since Lusus is the mythical and eponymous hero of Lusitania (the Latin name for Portugal), the poem's title indicates that Camoëns is concerned with Portuguese history and achievements. Unlike his Italian models, Camoëns did not choose a remote and legendary subject; but following the manner of the Spanish epics, from the anonymous *Cantar de Mio Cid* (ca. 1140) to Don Alonso de Ercilla's *La Araucana* (1569), he wrote of contemporary events or of those well documented by historical sources. Throughout *The Lusiads* Camoëns praises the courage and enterprise of the Portuguese explorers, and Vasco da Gama, the discoverer of the sea route to India, is the central figure of the epic. Camoëns sees Vasco da Gama and his Portuguese force as defenders of the Faith, martial evangelizers who triumph over man and nature. In a manner typical of the Renaissance epic, this heroic poem, which has a most Christian and historical subject matter, frequently uses elements taken from pagan mythology in order to enhance the epic stature of the Portuguese nation.

Further Reading

The standard modern study in English of Camoëns's life and works is the thoroughly researched, although sometimes outdated, book of Aubrey F. G. Bell, *Luis de Camões* (1923). More recent is Henry H. Hart, *Luis de Camoëns and the Epic of the Lusiads* (1962). Excellent approaches to the reading of *Os Lusiadas* from different perspectives are in C. M. Bowra, *From Virgil to Milton* (1945), and Gilbert Highet, *The Classical Tradition: Greek and Roman Influences on Western Literature* (1949). □

Tommaso Campanella

The Italian philosopher, political theorist, and poet Tommaso Campanella (1568-1639) was persecuted for his attempts to achieve utopian reforms.

Giovanni Domenico Campanella was born at Stilo in Calabria on Sept. 5, 1568; he assumed the name Tommaso when he entered the Dominican order about 1583. In Naples he made his first contact with the anti-Aristotelian doctrines of Bernardino Telesio. In 1592, after his first ecclesiastical trial, he was sentenced to return to his province and to abandon his Telesian sympathies. Campanella instead set out for the north, sojourning briefly in Rome, Florence, Bologna, and Padua. Between 1593 and 1595 he suffered several minor trials and periods of imprisonment on a number of charges.

After Campanella was released from prison in 1595, he passed the next few years in apparent quiet in a small monastery at Stilo. But this was actually a period of febrile secret activity. Campanella became the head of a conspiracy to overthrow the despotic Spanish rule of impoverished southern Italy and replace it with a theocratic republic, with himself as supreme priest and king. The plot was savagely repressed, and in 1602 he was sentenced to perpetual imprisonment. The subsequent 24 years of Campanella's life were spent in the bowels of various Neapolitan dungeons.

Despite discomforts and privations, this was a period of incredible literary productivity for Campanella, and many of his major works (the *Metaphysica,* the *Monarchia Messiae,* the *Atheismus triumphatus,* the *Apologia pro Galileo,* and others) date from this period. His best-known work, *Civitas solis* (*The City of the Sun*), was completed in 1623. This utopian work was based on Plato's *Republic,* and it presented Campanella's principal political ideal—universal theocratic monarchy, with its supreme head either the pope or the Spanish king. Regardless of who the ruler might be, the underlying principle remained constant: peace and well-being were impossible without unity.

In 1626, by order of the Spanish viceroy, Campanella was released from prison. When he reached Rome, he was imprisoned by the Pope but was soon freed. But the Curia's opposition to him because of his open defense of Galileo and his outspoken views, together with Spanish hostility, rendered his position in Rome precarious. Fearing further persecution, he fled from Rome in October 1634 and found refuge in France, where he was warmly welcomed in scholarly circles and at court. His central occupation now became the publication in 10 volumes of his writings, many of which had never appeared in print, while others had previously been brought out in unauthorized editions. This project was interrupted by Campanella's death on May 22, 1639.

Further Reading

The best comprehensive study of Campanella in English is Bernardine M. Bonansea, *Tommaso Campanella: Renaissance Pioneer of Modern Thought* (1969). It includes a good bibliography of the primary and secondary literature, with a listing of the writings by Campanella that are available in English translation. □

Alexander Campbell

Alexander Campbell (1788-1866) was an Irish-born American clergyman who, with his father, founded the Disciples of Christ, an indigenous American church movement.

Alexander Campbell, the first child of Thomas Campbell, a Presbyterian minister, was born Sept. 12, 1788, in County Antrim, Ireland. Educated in Ireland and at Glasgow University, Alexander brought his family to America in 1809, where they reunited with the elder Campbell, who had settled in western Pennsylvania. He joined in his father's rejection of Presbyterianism and in 1811 helped to organize a Christian Association Church at Brush Run.

In 1812 Campbell was ordained and within a few months assumed leadership of the religious movement that his father had started. The birth of his first child that year led him to question infant baptism, and intensive study convinced him that baptism by immersion was the only correct form. His father concurred, and after both were immersed they led the Brush Run congregation into affiliation with the Redstone Baptist Association in 1813.

Preaching for the sole authority of Scripture and against creeds and other additions of the institutional church, Campbell attracted both support and attack. His defense of immersion against Presbyterians in public debate in 1820 and 1823 popularized his views. His influence broadened after 1823, when he began to publish the *Christian Baptist.* Baptists began to dislike his anticreedal emphasis so Campbell changed his church's affiliation to a more favorable group, the Mahoning Association in Ohio. However, after 1827 all Baptist groups began to exclude the Campbellites.

By 1830 the Disciples of Christ (as they were now called) emerged as a distinct movement; all relations with Baptists were officially terminated. That year Campbell replaced his earlier paper with the *Millennial Harbinger,* which he edited until his death. Campbell's adherents were attracted by a similarity of purpose to the Christians in Kentucky associated with Barton W. Stone by 1832, and within a few years the two movements had largely merged.

Campbell was the key leader of the movement for a generation after this union. Having to guide the enlarged society led him to modify earlier ideas against church organization, and after 1849 he agreed to serve as president of the new American Christian Missionary Society. In 1840 he founded Bethany College and was its president for 20 years. Tirelessly, he published a translation of the New Testament and numerous theological works. His debates with Bishop Purcell on Roman Catholicism (1837) and the Rev. N. L. Rice on baptism (1843) gained him a national audience, and in 1850 he addressed both houses of Congress. The Civil War and failing health slowed his efforts, and he died March 4, 1866.

Further Reading

All accounts of Campbell rely on the basic biography by his friend Robert Richardson, *Memoirs of Alexander Campbell* (2 vols., 1868-1870). Winfred Ernest Garrison and Alfred T. DeGroot, *The Disciples of Christ* (1948; rev. ed. 1964), is the best history of the movement. □

Avril Phaedra Douglas Campbell

Avril Phaedra Douglas Campbell (born 1947), Canada's first woman prime minister and first prime minister born after World War II, held office for 132 days before her Conservative Party was crushingly defeated in the October 25, 1993, federal election.

The second daughter of George and Phyllis Campbell, Avril Phaedra Douglas Campbell was born on March 10, 1947, in Port Alberni, British Columbia, and raised in that province's largest city, Vancouver. Her father, a World War II veteran who was wounded during the Italian campaign, received a university degree after the war and became a lawyer. The parents divorced when their daughter was 12. In her own words, "My mother left a very difficult marriage . . . it had everything to do with the powerlessness of women in those days. The breakup . . . was very painful for me and being on my own as a teenager was very painful . . . . " It was during this period of emotional turmoil that Campbell began calling herself "Kim." She did not see her mother for a decade after the divorce.

The young Campbell was hard-driving, outgoing, and adventurous—among her interests were the piano, the guitar, and the musical theater—and she had an aptitude for academic pursuits. At the age of 16 she was elected the first "girl president" of Vancouver's Prince of Wales High

School student council, and she was the valedictorian of the graduating class of 1964. She earned a bachelor's degree in political science from the University of British Columbia (UBC), where she served as vice-president of the student government and developed a reputation for conservative, traditionalist views.

After beginning an M.A. in international relations at UBC, Campbell won a scholarship in 1970 to pursue doctoral studies in Soviet government at the London School of Economics. In 1972 she married her companion of five years, Nathan Divinsky, a mathematics professor almost twice her age; they divorced in 1983. She returned home in 1973 without her Ph.D., teaching political studies at Simon Fraser University, UBC, and Vancouver Community College, but not obtaining a permanent academic position. She would later express the opinion that this was because she was a woman and not because she had not completed a graduate degree. Campbell entered law school at UBC in 1980, began work at the influential Vancouver firm of Ladner Downs in 1983, and was called to the British Columbia bar in 1984.

Campbell launched her political career in 1980, winning a seat as a trustee on the Vancouver School Board. From 1982 to 1984 she chaired the board and presided over its $150 million annual budget, vigorously defending high profile cost-cutting measures. Her controversial commitment to restraint in the face of labor union opposition impressed the right-of-center Social Credit premier of British Columbia, Bill Bennett. Campbell ran unsuccessfully for a seat in the provincial legislature under the Bennett banner in 1983, and in September 1985 she left Ladner Downs to serve as executive director in the premier's office.

Against the advice of colleagues and although still a novice in politics, Campbell contested the leadership of the provincial Social Credit Party after Bennett resigned in May 1986. She finished last, obtaining a derisory 14 out of almost 1,300 votes cast by delegates at the convention, but impressed audiences with a powerful speech delivered on primetime television. Campbell was elected to the provincial assembly in October, but she had denounced the new leader in her convention address and she was never part of his inner circle. She married lawyer Howard Eddy during the summer of 1986; that marriage too did not last.

Campbell jumped to national politics in 1988, winning a Vancouver seat as a Conservative and attracting much favorable attention within the party and in the media. The prime minister, Brian Mulroney, took note and brought her into his cabinet as the junior minister for Indian affairs and northern development. On February 23, 1990, she became Canada's first woman minister of justice and attorney general. She championed tougher gun control regulations after the murder of women engineering students in Montreal, as well as legislation establishing stricter standards for the prosecution of rapists. Critics pointed to the compromises made along the way and to her support for the criminalization of abortion except when a woman's health was in danger. Campbell's growing list of admirers replied that she was adapting to the realities of politics, learning the flexibility and accessibility that she had always been accused of lacking.

In January 1993 Campbell was appointed Canada's first woman minister of national defense and minister of veterans affairs. Controversy quickly ensued. In the midst of a recession, and with millions of jobless Canadians, she determinedly defended the contract negotiated by her predecessor to buy $5.8 billion worth of sophisticated EH101 helicopters. Then, on March 16, a prisoner was tortured and beaten to death while in the custody of Canadian peacekeepers in Somalia. Campbell claimed that it was not until March 31 that she learned the death had been "characterized as a homicide." Her senior military commander contradicted her publicly.

Nevertheless, Campbell had transformed herself into the most striking politician in the country and the logical successor to retiring prime minister Mulroney. She had large quantities of charisma, humor, energy, intelligence—and, apparently, "winnability." One by one the stalwarts of the Conservative Party, including former prime minister Joe Clark, dropped by the wayside, leaving only one other serious candidate, 34-year-old environment minister Jean Charest, to oppose Campbell at the leadership convention. In the final analysis, Charest came within six percentage points of victory, but Campbell's superior organization and the early support of the party bosses was decisive. She was elected Conservative chief on June 13, 1993, and was named prime minister on June 25.

The new prime minister pared down the size of the cabinet, initiated a massive reorganization of government structure, attended the July G7 Summit in Tokyo, and criss-crossed the country to drum up support. Polls showed that she was well-regarded but that the weight of a decade of Conservative rule under the deeply unpopular Mulroney was enormous. The mandate of the Conservatives was almost up, and an election had to be called soon. When the campaign came in September-October 1993, the Conservatives lurched from disaster to disaster, and Campbell was herself not blameless. She had been chosen as a fresh face, but her inexperience showed, and she spoke frequently without sufficient thought or tact. The opposition leader, Jean Chrétien, meanwhile performed flawlessly, while regional parties in Quebec and the West further sapped Conservative strength.

The result was the greatest electoral defeat ever suffered by a major national party in Canadian political history. The Conservatives won only two of the available 295 seats, and Campbell's was not one of them. She left the premiership on November 4, 1993. Without a base in Parliament and hounded by a legion of detractors, she resigned as head of the party on December 13, 1993. Later, in the summer of 1996, Campbell was appointed by Prime Minister Jean Chretien to be the Canadian consul general in Los Angeles.

In 1995 Campbell, along with four other living Canadian Prime Ministers, was awarded her own coat of arms. Campbell's features the motto, "Seek Wisdom, Conquer Fear, Do Justice." It includes a white square with four Canadian Maple leaves in the center to signify that she served as prime minister. The international symbol for woman is also displayed on the shield, to show that she was the first woman to hold the office. She published her memoirs, *Time and Chance: The Political Memoirs of Canada's First Woman Prime Minister* in 1996, but the book proved to be less sensational than a 1994 book from her own senior advisor, David McLaughlin: *Poisoned Chance: The Last Campaign*.

Further Reading

The best study of Canada's 19th prime minister is Robert Fife, *Kim Campbell: The Making of a Politician* (Toronto, 1993). Murray Dobbin is more critical in *The Politics of Kim Campbell: From School Trustee to Prime Minister* (Toronto, 1993). E. Kaye Fulton and Mary Janigan, "The Real Kim Campbell," *Maclean's* (May 17, 1993) was helpful in preparing this biography.

Additional information is available in several issues of *Maclean's:* December 6, 1993; December 20, 1993; October 24, 1994; April 8, 1996; April 15, 1996; April 29, 1996; and August 19, 1996. □

Ben Nighthorse Campbell

As a result of his election on November 3, 1992, Ben Nighthorse Campbell (born 1933) of Colorado became the first Native American to serve in the U.S. Senate in more than 60 years. A member of the Northern Cheyenne Tribe, Campbell was also a renowned athlete and captained the U.S. judo team for the 1964 Olympics in Tokyo.

Ben Nighthorse Campbell was born in Auburn, California, on April 13, 1933, to Mary Vierra, a Portuguese immigrant, and Albert Campbell, a Northern Cheyenne Indian. He had a hard childhood, with a mother frequently hospitalized for tuberculosis and an alcoholic father. Indeed, by the time he turned ten years old Nighthorse had spent half of his life in St. Patrick's Catholic Orphanage in Sacramento, California. At home there was frequently no one to care for him or his younger sister, Alberta. As a result, the youngster spent much of his time in the streets getting into trouble.

While working as a fruit picker in the Sacramento Valley, Nighthorse befriended some Japanese youths who taught him judo. That sport, according to the senator, "kept me off the streets and out of jail." After graduating from high school, he served in the U.S. Air Force from 1951 to 1953. Stationed in Korea as an Airman 2nd class, he continued with his judo training. On completing his military service, Campbell entered San Jose State University and supported himself by picking fruit and driving a truck. He still was a member of the Teamsters and proudly displayed his union card while a senator. In 1957 he received a Bachelors degree in physical education and fine arts. Upon graduation, Nighthorse moved to Tokyo for four years to work on his judo and study at Meiji University.

Campbell's ability in judo not only won him All-American status in that sport and helped him become three-time U.S. judo champion but allowed him to win the gold medal in the Pan-American Games in 1963. The next year he captained the U.S. judo team at the Tokyo Olympics. Later, the Olympian coached the U.S. international judo team.

Although Campbell worked as a teacher, policeman, and prison counselor, as well as a farm laborer and a truck driver, his success came as a designer of Native American jewelry. He had been interested in this Indian art form since his childhood, but learned how to laminate different metals in Japan. Although traditionalists argued that this technique did not follow the style of Indian art, *Arizona Highways* recognized his creativity in a 1972 article that identified him as one of twenty Native Americans undertaking new forms of art. He won more than 200 design awards for his handcrafted rings, bracelets, and pendants. Some of his work has sold for as much as $20,000. In 1977 Campbell moved to a 120-acre ranch on the Southern Ute Indian Reservation near Ignacio, Colorado. With his wife, Linda Price Nighthorse (Campbell's third marriage), and their two children, Colin and Shana, Campbell trained champion quarter horses on the ranch until a severe injury, incurred while breaking a colt, put an end to that career.

Nighthorse's involvement in politics came about because of bad weather. Unable to fly his single-engine airplane to the West Coast to deliver some jewelry due to heavy storms, he visited a meeting of Colorado Democrats seeking a candidate for the state's 59th House District. At that meeting Democratic leaders persuaded him to run for that office. To nearly everyone's surprise, he defeated his better known opponent and served in the state legislature for four years. In 1986 voters of Colorado's 3rd Congressional District, a normally Republican district, elected Democratic Campbell to the U.S. House of Representatives. He defeated incumbent Mike Strang in a closely fought election to become only the eighth Native American ever elected to Congress. He won reelection to that post three times by large margins.

In Congress he earned a reputation for having a "straight-shooting approach," and his charm, sincerity, charisma, and political blend helped him gain support from a wide variety of factions within and outside Congress. Although a strong fiscal conservative (he supported a balanced-budget amendment), he was a liberal on social issues (strongly pro-choice). As a congressman he served on the House Committees on Agriculture and on Interior and Insular Affairs. He played an important role in securing legislation to settle Native American water rights, and in 1991 he won a fight to change the name of Custer Battlefield Monument in Montana to the Little Bighorn Battlefield National Monument, in honor of the Native Americans who died in battle. He also initiated and guided through Congress legislation to establish the National Museum of the American Indian within the Smithsonian Institution.

After six years in the House of Representatives, Campbell decided to run for the Senate seat vacated by Tim Wirth, a liberal Democrat who declined to run for a second term. He defeated Josie Heath and former Governor Dick Lamm in the Democratic primary. And on November 3, 1992, after a nasty campaign, he bested Republican state senator Terry Considine, a conservative, for the Senate. That victory made him the first Native American to serve in the U.S. Senate in more than 60 years. In that office he almost always supported the programs of the Clinton administration.

On March 3, 1995 Campbell made a decision which shocked much of the political world. He decided to change from his political affiliation from the Democratic to the Republican party. It has been stated that the balanced budget amendment persuaded Campbell to change his political views. Campbell will serve the remainder of his six year term as a Republican.

Further Reading

There are several good articles with excellent biographical data on Campbell. For instance, see "Big Ben," by Harland C. Clifford, in the *Boston Globe Magazine* (August 2, 1992). Also see a profile of him in the April 6, 1992, issue of *People* magazine. □

Joseph Campbell

A college teacher of literature, Joseph Campbell (1904-1987) was an editor and popularizer of comparative mythology. He created comprehensive theories of mythology that synthesized the discoveries of modern science, psychology, art history, and literature and used modern media, including television, to popularize his subject.

Joseph Campbell was born March 26, 1904, in New York City, the son of Charles William Campbell, a hosiery importer and wholesaler, and Josephine Lynch. He was raised Roman Catholic. He traced his lifelong fascination with mythology to his having seen Buffalo Bill's Wild West Show as a child and to trips with his brother and sister to the Museum of Natural History. At age nine he and his family moved to New Rochelle, New York, next to the public library, where he read exhaustively about Native American cultures and precociously educated himself.

He attended Dartmouth College in 1921-1922, then transferred to Columbia University and switched from science to the humanities. His Master's thesis (1927) compared the Arthurian legends with Native American myths. He read medieval French literature at the University of Paris in 1927-1928 and studied Sanskrit and Indo-European philosophy at the University of Munich in 1928-1929. While abroad he discovered modern art, literature, and psychology. He dropped his doctoral studies to work on integrating modern discoveries in archaeology, anthropology, art history, psychology, and literature into a comprehensive theory of the origins, functions, and meanings of world mythological themes.

For five years during the Great Depression of the 1930s Campbell lived a bohemian life between Woodstock, New York, and Carmel, California; sailed up the Alaskan coast; and read German philosophy. In 1934 he joined the faculty of literature at Sarah Lawrence College. By all accounts a charismatic teacher, he remained at Sarah Lawrence until he retired as professor emeritus in 1972. In 1938 he married Jean Erdman, a dancer in the Martha Graham dance troupe who later became a choreographer and founded a troupe of her own. They lived in Greenwich Village, New York City, and Honolulu, Hawaii.

Campbell's publishing and editing career started to flourish with *A Skeleton Key to Finnegan's Wake* (1944), a guide to the symbolic labyrinth of James Joyce's novel. Written in collaboration with Henry Morton Robinson (best-selling author of *The Cardinal*), it became a critical success.

After the death of his teacher and friend Heinrich Zimmer in 1943, Campbell edited Zimmer's collected works (1946-1955) and six volumes of the Jungian *Papers from the Eranos Yearbooks* (1954-1968) in the Bollingen Series, where his first solo work, *The Hero with a Thousand Faces* (1949), also appeared. *Hero* was a phenomenal popular success and won Campbell the National Arts and Literature grant (1949), but generated mixed reviews. It and successive projects revealed Campbell to be a complicated academic maverick, at once learned, romantic, and mystical, who wrote graceful, intelligible prose. An enormously gifted comparativist and popularizer, he bridged scholarly, scientific, and aesthetic disciplines with enthusiasm and with an intentional disregard for particular historical and local contexts of myths and rituals that rankled many specialist academics and scientists. With a broad brush he mixed the whole vast, esoteric, scholarly, and scientific apparatus of late 19th-and early 20th-century culture with modern literary and pictorial techniques of free association and taught an ambitious doctrine of underlying similarities and unities in world myth.

In his grand plan for the study and comprehension of all mythology, he oscillated idiosyncratically between being an energetic modernist and a scientific and political reactionary. He proposed an elaborate theory of the "monomyth" of the hero as the integrating structure of consciousness by which human beings organize personal psychic life and society in relation to the cosmos. He lamented the absence of viable mythologies and religions in the contemporary world and proposed in their place a planetary mythology, a gender-neutral ideal of individualist hero, and the practice of Buddhist compassion. He popularized the hypothesis of a pre-patriarchal goddess religion, but viewed it as an archetypal anachronism. He believed, however, in the therapeutic value of the wisdom of myth for modern individuals.

His works progressed as a set of variations on these and supporting hypotheses, among them a controversial theory of the geographical diffusion of major myth forms from a single fourth-millennium B.C.E. Mesopotamian source and a contention that significant differences between hunter and planter societies prefigured and determined contemporary forms of East and West. In *Hero,* Campbell introduced the hero "monomyth" in a poetic Jungian meditation that charmed and inspired readers (among them George Lucas, who made the *Star Wars* movies). *The Masks of God* (1959-1968), a four-volume synthesis of modern knowledge about human culture and mythology from 600,000 B.C.E. to the present, was a stylistic throwback to, and valuable updated rival of, such synthetic masterpieces as Oswald Spengler's *Decline of the West* and Sir James Frazer's *The Golden Bough. The Mythic Image* (1974), a Bollingen "coffee-table book," was a Jungian literary and pictorial exploration of the theories of *Masks.* Campbell's last major project, Volume I of the *Historical Atlas of World Mythology* (1983) and Volume II, completed by editors and published posthumously (1988), consists of five slim "oversize" books of text and pictures that repeat familiar Campbellian narratives and themes in a turn-of-the-century style. *The Flight of the Wild Gander* (1969) is an excellent selection of Campbell's major scholarly essays.

Between his retirement in 1972 and his death in 1987, Campbell lectured and published extensively and enjoyed growing popularity. His person, subjects, methods, and message fitted a post-1960 and increasingly media-oriented America. In 1988 a six-part public television interview series, *The Power of Myth,* and a subsequent rash of publishing spin-offs gave Campbell immense posthumous celebrity. Former friends and assorted academics raised caveats: Campbell was formally charged with being reactionary, anti-Semetic, anti-Black, inconsistently pro-and anti-West, and ingenuously partial to Eastern spirituality. He was attacked as a guru of a self-indulgent faith of self-realization and criticized for the slogan "Follow your bliss."

Ironically, Campbell's cross-pollination of academia and media both breathed life into esoteric and dated disciplines marred by exclusions and prejudices and helped pry them open for needed scrutiny. On balance, Campbell's final interdisciplinary breakthrough, his controversial television celebrity, was a major accomplishment. Through it, his alleged prejudices responsibly masked or not in evidence, he provided the model of a creative life enthusiastically and generously lived and gave millions of television viewers an experience of genuine intellectual adventure.

Further Reading

Robert Segal's *Joseph Campbell: An Introduction* (1990, Revised), a popular edition of an earlier scholarly text, presents and critiques Campbell's ideas in a piecemeal way, but compares them copiously with those of Jung, Freud, and others. The bibliography lacks the "Reviews" listing of the first edition. Campbell's own writings, especially his pre-retirement works, are the best guide to his thought. Magazine interviews in *Esquire* (September, 1977) and *Parabola* (Spring, 1976 and February, 1980) are recommended. The Brendan Gill article in the *New York Review of Books* (September, 1989) set off the posthumous controversies that surround Campbell's legacy. An academician's view of these controversies is in the *American Scholar* (Summer, 1990). Video tapes of the television series *The Power of Myth* are an indispensable record of Campbell's personality.

Additional Sources

Larsen, Stephen., *A fire in the mind: the life of Joseph Campbell,* New York: Anchor Books, 1993. □

Robert Campin

The Flemish painter Robert Campin (ca. 1375-1444), probably to be identified with the anonymous Master of Flémalle, was the first great innovator in early Netherlandish painting and one of the founders of the "new realism" in the north.

Robert Campin was probably born at Valenciennes in the north of France. He is first recorded in 1406, when he became a free master in Tournai. In 1410 he acquired citizenship in that city. In 1423 he was elected dean of the painters' guild and also chosen one of Tournai's three city councilors, a post he retained until 1428.

In 1432 Campin was charged with adultery; the sentence was banishment from Tournai for a year and a pilgrimage to the south of France. The personal intervention of the daughter of the Count of Holland, however, caused the sentence to be commuted to the payment of a small fine. This unusual action is generally interpreted as an indication of Campin's great artistic importance.

The Tournai records further state that Campin took two apprentices in 1427: Jacquelot Daret and Rogelet de le Pasture. The latter pupil is usually identified with the great Rogier van der Weyden. Perceiving a close stylistic proximity between the works of Rogier and the Master of Flémalle, some historians have grouped all the paintings under Rogier's name. Most authorities, however, are able to identify two distinct artistic personalities and to discern a clear master-pupil relationship between Campin and Rogier.

Among the earliest works attributable to Campin is a small *Nativity* (ca. 1420). In this panel, which shows one of the first uses of oil as a binding medium for pigments, he combines a mastery of weighty, material forms with the strong illusion of three-dimensional space. His robust and earthy sense of realism is revealed in both the figures and the landscape setting, through which he achieves an unprecedented degree of physical actuality and dramatic immediacy. Further advances in illusion and expression are also seen in the fragmentary *Betrothal of the Virgin* (ca. 1420).

Of Campin's surviving works, the so-called *Mérode Altarpiece* (ca. 1426) is generally considered his masterpiece. Investing each natural object in the painting with symbolic meaning, he has succeeded in presenting sacred and metaphysical events in terms of a thoroughly plausible earthly reality. A one-point perspective is employed for the first time in northern painting to organize the setting and provide compositional unity. Inconsistent lighting and active patterning of the surface at the expense of pictorial unity, however, produce minor disharmonies.

The *Virgin and Child before a Fire Screen* (usually dated ca. 1428) reveals more fully than any other work Campin's uncompromising spirit of materialism. In an attempt to eliminate all unreal conventions he has even employed a domestic fire screen to suggest a halo for the Virgin.

In the final phase of his career Campin appears to have fallen under Rogier's influence. *The Von Werl Altarpiece* (1438) shows the slender and idealized figure types of Rogier as well as the influence of his richer and warmer color scheme.

Among the few surviving portraits attributable to Campin, the panels of *A Gentleman and a Lady* are his finest. Strongly plastic and palpably real, these pictures represent major advances in characterization and individualization for the art of portraiture.

Further Reading

The most important book on the Master of Flémalle is Max J. Friedländer, *Early Netherlandish Painting,* vol. 2 (1924; trans. 1967). It contains a sensitive stylistic analysis of most of the artist's known works. Friedländer later revised his opinion and joined the ranks of those scholars who identify Rogier van der Weyden as the Master of Flémalle. Mojmir S. Frinta in *The Genius of Robert Campin* (1966) has attributed certain works traditionally associated with Rogier to Campin, but his arguments have not gained wide acceptance. Charles D. Cuttler, *Northern Painting: From Pucelle to Bruegel* (1968), contains a chapter on the Master of Flémalle, who is identified with Campin.

Additional Sources

Schabacker, Peter H., *Notes on the biography of Robert Campin,* Brussel: AWLSK, 1980. □

Albert Camus

The French novelist, essayist, and playwright Albert Camus (1913-1960) was obsessed with the philosophical problems of the meaning of life and of man's search for values in a world without God. His work is distinguished by lucidity, moderation, and tolerance.

Albert Camus may be grouped with two slightly older French writers, André Malraux and Jean Paul Sartre, in marking a break with the traditional bourgeois novel. Like them, he is less interested in psychological analysis than in philosophical problems in his books. Camus developed a conception of the "absurd," which provides the theme for much of his earlier work: the "absurd" is the gulf between, on the one hand, man's desire for a world of happiness, governed by reason, justice, and order, a world which he can understand rationally and, on the other hand, the actual world, which is chaotic and irrational and inflicts suffering and a meaningless death on humanity. The second stage in Camus's thought developed from the first—man should not simply accept the "absurd" universe, but should "revolt" against it. This revolt is not political but in the name of the traditional humane values.

Camus was born on Nov. 7, 1913, at Mondovi in Algeria, then part of France. His father, who was French, was killed at the front in 1914; his mother was of Spanish origin. His childhood was one of poverty, and his education at school and later at the University of Algiers was completed only with help from scholarships. He was a brilliant student of philosophy, and his major outside interests were sports and drama. While still a student, he founded a theater and both directed and acted in plays. Having contracted tuberculosis, which periodically forced him to spend time in a sanatorium, he was medically unable to become a teacher and worked at various jobs before becoming a journalist in 1938. His first published works were *L'Envers et l'endroit* (1937; The Wrong Side and the Right Side) and *Noces* (1938; Festivities), books of essays dealing with the meaning of life and its joys, as well as its underlying meaninglessness.

L'Étranger

At the outbreak of World War II in September 1939 Camus was unfit for military service; in the following year he moved to Paris and completed his first novel, *L'Étranger* (*The Stranger*), published in 1942. The theme of the novel is embodied in the "stranger" of its title, a young clerk called Meursault, who is narrator as well as hero. Meursault is a stranger to all conventional human reactions. The book begins with his lack of grief on his mother's death. He has no ambition, and he is prepared to marry a girl simply because he can see no reason why he should not. The crisis of the novel takes place on a beach when Meursault, involved in a quarrel not of his causing, shoots an Arab; the second part of the novel deals with his trial for murder and his condemnation to death, which he understands as little as why he killed the Arab. Meursault is absolutely honest in describing his feelings, and it is this honesty which makes him a "stranger" in the world and ensures the verdict of guilty. The total situation symbolizes the "absurd" nature of life, and this effect is increased by the deliberately flat and colorless style of the book.

Unable to find work in France during the German occupation, Camus returned to Algeria in 1941 and finished his next book, *Le Mythe de Sisyphe* (*The Myth of Sisyphus*), also published in 1942. This is a philosophical essay on the nature of the absurd, which is embodied in the mythical figure of Sisyphus, condemned eternally to roll a heavy rock up a mountain, only to have it roll down again. Sisyphus becomes a symbol of mankind and in his constant efforts achieves a certain tragic greatness.

In 1942 Camus, back in France, joined a Resistance group and engaged in underground journalism until the Liberation in 1944, when he became editor of the former Resistance newspaper *Combat* for 3 years. Also during this period his first two plays were staged: *Le Malentendu* (*Cross-Purpose*) in 1944 and *Caligula* in 1945. Here again the principal theme is the meaninglessness of life and the finality of death. Two more plays, *L'État de siège* (*The State of Siege*) and *Les Justes* (*The Just Assassins*), followed in 1948 and 1950, and Camus was to adapt seven other plays for the stage, the sphere of activity where he felt happiest.

In 1947 Camus brought out his second novel, *La Peste* (*The Plague*). Here, in describing a fictional attack of bubonic plague in the Algerian city of Oran, he again treats the theme of the absurd, represented by the meaningless and totally unmerited suffering and death caused by the plague. But now the theme of revolt is strongly developed. Man cannot accept this suffering passively; and the narrator, Dr. Rieux, explains his ideal of "honesty"—preserving his integrity by struggling as best he can, even if unsuccessfully, against the epidemic. On one level the novel can be taken as a fictional representation of the German occupation of France, but it has a wider appeal as being symbolical of the total fight against evil and suffering, the major moral problem of human experience.

Later Works

Camus's next important book was *L'Homme révolté* (1951; *The Rebel*). Another long essay, this work treats the theme of revolt in political, as well as philosophical, terms. Camus, who had briefly been a member of the Communist party in the 1930s, afterward maintained a position of political independence, from both the left and right-wing parties in France. In this book he develops the point that man should not tolerate the absurdity of the world but at the same time makes a careful distinction between revolt and revolution. Revolution, despite its initial ideals, he sees as inevitably ending in a tyranny as great or greater than the one it set out to destroy. Instead, Camus asks for revolt: a more individual protest, in tune with the humane values of tolerance and moderation. Above all he denounces the Marxist belief that "history" will inevitably produce a world revolution and that any action committed in its name will therefore be justified. For Camus, the end can never justify the means. *L'Homme révolté* was widely discussed in France and led to a bitter quarrel between Camus and Sartre, who at this time was maintaining the necessity of an alliance with the Communists.

In the early 1950s Camus turned back to his earlier passion for the theater and published no major book until 1956, when *La Chute* (*The Fall*) appeared. This novel consists of a monologue by a former lawyer named Clamence, who mainly sits in a sordid waterfront bar in Amsterdam and comments ironically on his life. Successful and worldly, he has undergone a moral crisis—the "fall" of the title—after failing to help a young woman who commits suicide by jumping off a bridge in Paris; afterward he gives up his career and moves to Amsterdam, where he lives as what he calls a "judge-penitent." The guilt he feels because of this "fall" makes him see and describe the whole of human life in terms of satirical pessimism.

In 1957 Camus received the great distinction of the Nobel Prize for literature for his works, which "with clear-sighted earnestness illuminate the problems of the human conscience of our time." In the same year he published a collection of short stories, *L'Exil et le royaume* (*Exile and the Kingdom*). Later he began to work on a fourth important novel and was also about to become director of a major Paris theater when, on Jan. 4, 1960, he was killed in a car crash near Paris, at the age of 46, a tragic loss to literature since he had yet to write the works of his full maturity as artist and thinker. Since his death important volumes of *Carnets* (*Notebooks*) have appeared.

Further Reading

There are a number of valuable studies of Camus's work: Robert de Luppé, *Albert Camus* (1957; trans. 1966); Thomas Hanna, *The Thought and Art of Albert Camus* (1958); Germaine Brée, *Camus* (1959; rev. ed. 1964); John Cruickshank, *Albert Camus and the Literature of Revolt* (1959); Philip Thody, *Albert Camus: 1913-1960* (1961); Adele King, *Albert Camus* (1964); and Emmett Parker, *Albert Camus: The Artist in the Arena* (1965). Donald R. Haggis, *Albert Camus: La Peste* (1962), is a perceptive short study. Germaine Brée edited a volume of extremely useful articles, *Camus: A Collection of Critical Essays* (1962). Recommended for general critical background are Henri Peyre, *French Novelists of Today* (1955; new ed. 1967), and John Cruickshank, ed., *The Novelist as Philosopher: Studies in French Fiction, 1935-1960* (1962). □

Canaletto

The Italian painter Giovanni Antonio Canal, called Canaletto (1697-1768), is known for his scenes of 18th-century Venice, executed with accuracy, precision, and luminosity.

Canaletto and Francesco Guardi between them created the image the world has held of Venice from the late 18th century to the present day. Guardi romanticized what he saw, but Canaletto did not. One of the many Englishmen who visited Venice in the 18th century said that Canaletto's excellence lay in painting things that fell immediately under his eye. What falls under the eye in Venice, then as now, is romantic enough. The buildings, built along canals instead of streets, seem to rise up out of the lagoon as if suspended between earth and water. From a distance, domes and towers appear to float. The colorful crowds that throng the main squares give Venice the air of being continuously in carnival. Canaletto painted his views not for Venetians but for foreign visitors, above all for the rich Englishmen taking the grand tour.

Canaletto was born in Venice on Oct. 18, 1697. He was trained by his father, Bernardo Canal, as a designer of stage sets. Most of the theatrical productions of the period called for sets representing palace interiors or palace gardens. Such scenes usually involved an intricate recession of pillars, pediments, porticoes, balustrades, and garden statues, and thus to execute them required a knowledge of the complexities of architectural perspective.

In 1719 Canaletto gave up designing stage sets and went to study in Rome. The following year he was back in Venice, where he was inscribed as a member of the painters' guild. From then on he was busy painting views of his native city. His most important patron was the English consul, Joseph Smith, who bought large numbers of Canalettos for resale to his countrymen.

Canaletto constructed his views of Venice with painstaking care. Usually he drew the scene on the spot and then made more detailed studies in his studio. These studies were then transferred to the canvas with the help of lines cut into the prepared surface as guidelines for columns, cornices, arches, and domes. We also know that Canaletto used the camera obscura, a darkened box or chamber in which the view is caught and reflected by lenses and mirrors onto a sheet of drawing paper so that the artist can render the perspective lines accurately simply by tracing the contours of the reflected image.

Pleased by his success with the English, Canaletto went to England in 1746. He stayed there off and on for a decade, but the results were disappointing. In Venice he had provided the English with scenes they considered exotic and picturesque, whereas in England he could provide them only with views of what they already knew.

Back in Venice, Canaletto continued to paint views for tourists. He also won acceptance from the Venetians themselves with a new form, the architectural caprice, in which famous landmarks were combined arbitrarily or (rarely in Canaletto's case) the architecture was invented altogether. With one of these as his reception piece he was finally admitted to the Venetian Academy in 1763. Five years later, on April 20, 1768, he died.

The *Stonemasons' Yard* gives a good idea of Canaletto's very early work. It is a Venice the tourist seldom sees, or tries not to remember: a view of disorder and poverty, of a vacant lot filled with stone and rubble, of gray buildings hung with damp laundry, of gray clouds closing off the sky. But it is also filled with gravity, dignity, and a sense of timelessness.

Far more typical are the sunlit scenes Canaletto painted so often of St. Mark's Square, the Ducal Palace, and the Grand Canal. In the best of these canvases the painted surfaces are beautifully modulated—the tan buildings touched with rose, and rose again in the blue of the sky. The open spaces come alive with festive clusters of bright little figures. These he brushed in broadly and made them sparkle with a scattering of white dots.

Under increasing pressure to turn out more and more paintings for the tourist trade, Canaletto took on assistants, who watered down his style. Many of his late canvases are overly rigid and dry.

Further Reading

The most complete study of Canaletto is W. G. Constable, *Canaletto, Giovanni Antonio Canal, 1697-1768* (2 vols., 1962), but it is difficult and dry. For a more sensitive interpretation see F. J. B. Watson, *Canaletto* (1949). K. T. Parker, *The Drawings of Antonio Canaletto . . . at Windsor Castle* (1948), is the best book in its area. A brief but highly readable account of Canaletto appears in Michael Levey, *Painting in XVIII Century Venice* (1959). □

St. Peter Canisius

The Dutch Jesuit St. Peter Canisius (1521-1597) was a leading figure of the Counter Reformation. A deeply prayerful man and indefatigable worker, he reanimated the Catholic Church in central Europe by preaching, writing, and founding Jesuit colleges.

Peter Canisius or Peter kanis, was born in the Dutch town of Nijmegen on May 8, 1521. He studied at the Latin school of St. Stephen there, and at 15 years of age he entered the University of Cologne. At the Carthusian monastery in Cologne he was influenced by the simple and ardent piety of the Devotio Moderna. In 1540 he became a master of arts and undertook the study of theology. In 1543 he heard about Pierre Favre, one of the first Jesuits, who was then at Mainz. He made the Spiritual Exercises of Ignatius of Loyola under Favre's direction and decided to become a Jesuit. He was ordained a priest in 1546.

Peter started a long career of apostolic labor in many countries of Europe. In 1546-1547 Peter participated in the Council of Trent; in 1548 he joined nine other Jesuits in opening a school at Messina; in 1549, with two other Jesuits, he joined the faculty of the University of Ingolstadt; and in 1552 he went to Vienna to assist the new Jesuit community there. To meet the challenge of Luther's popular catechism, Peter published his *Summary of Christian Doctrine* in 1555. Designed for boys in the upper classes and lucidly written in easy Latin, it rapidly ran into hundreds of editions. A German edition came out in 1556. The same year Peter published his *Tiny Catechism* for children, and 2 years later, his most popular work, *An Abridged Catechism,* planned for students in the middle grades. This he embellished through the years with engravings, verses, and prayers. In 1556 he became superior of the Upper German Province.

For the next 41 years, Peter's days were filled with the most diverse activity. He shared in the establishment of 18 Jesuit colleges, and in the Augsburg Cathedral alone he preached 225 long sermons in 18 months. He began the Catholic response to *The Centuries of Magdeburg* with two folio volumes of patristic learning, the forerunners of Baronius's *Annales ecclesiastici.* In 1557 he traveled about 2,000 miles through Italy, Austria, Bavaria, and the Rhineland. Prelates constantly sought his counsel.

Peter's correspondence, which fills eight large volumes, reveals a person of gentle patience, understanding, and ardent Zeal for the Catholic Church. He regarded heresy as "a plague more deadly than other plagues," but he insisted on a spirit of charity in meeting non-Catholics. At the age of 76 he died at Fribourg, Switzerland, on Dec. 21, 1597. Pope pius XI canonized him and declared him a Doctor of the Church in 1925.

Further Reading

A scholarly, sensitive, and delightfully written biography is James Brodrick, *Saint Peter Canisius* (1935). See also Edward McNall Burns, *The Counter Reformation* (1964), which has a brief biography of Canisius; and Martin P. Harney, *The Jesuits in History: The Society of Jesus through Four Centuries* (1941). □

George Canning

The English orator and statesman George Canning (1770-1827) opposed intervention by Continental powers in constitutionalist movements of other states. He successfully supported the insurgent Spanish-American colonies and the establishment of Greek autonomy.

George Canning was born in London on April 11, 1770, the son of a barrister who had been disowned by his well-to-do Londonderry family. When his father died a year later, his mother took to the provincial stage to support herself and her son. Fortunately his father's family relented and sent Canning to Eton and Oxford, where he won a reputation for his classical scholarship as well as for his wit, oratory, and Jacobin leanings..

Early Career

The excesses of the French Revolution modified Canning's political views, and when he entered Parliament in 1796, he was a supporter of Prime Minister Pitt. He was undersecretary for foreign affairs from 1796 to 1799; after serving in other offices he resigned with Pitt on the Catholic issue in 1801. His marriage to Joan Scott in 1800 relieved him from financial dependence on his political supporters.

In March 1807 Canning became foreign secretary in the Portland administration. Here he was chiefly responsible for the decision to seize the Danish fleet in 1807 to prevent it from coming under the control of Napoleon. He justified this action on the basis of secret articles of the Tilsit treaties but did not reveal his sources. He actively supported the Peninsular campaign but came into jurisdictional conflict with Lord Castlereagh, the minister of war. He privately urged the Prime Minister to transfer Castlereagh to another office, and finally, on Sept. 9, 1809, Canning resigned. At that point Castlereagh heard of the matter in such terms as to indicate that Canning had engaged in dishonorable intrigue against him. He demanded satisfaction and slightly wounded Canning in a duel on September 19. The illness and subsequent death of the Prime Minister removed the one person who could clear Canning, and he never quite lived down the mistrust that the episode both revealed and increased.

Canning's acid wit—Sir Walter Scott wrote that it could "penetrate the hide of a rhinoceros"—often gave offense. His great oratorical abilities were useful to a cabinet, but he was not always accepted with cordial confidence by Tory colleagues. He was offered the Foreign Office again in 1812 in the Liverpool ministry, but he demanded, unacceptably, the leadership of the Commons as well and lost his chance to the more tactful and unassuming Castlereagh. From 1816 to 1820 Canning was in the Cabinet as president of the Board of Control for India and served there with distinction, but he resigned in 1820 to support Queen Caroline in the divorce case. In 1822 he was appointed governor general of India and was about to embark when the suicide of Castlereagh in August 1822 opened the Foreign Office to him once more. Again he insisted on the leadership of the Commons, and this time he got it. From then until his death in 1827 he was the most influential member of the government.

Diplomatic Achievements

The immediate problem in foreign affairs was the Congress of the Great Powers (Russia, Austria, Prussia, Britain, and France) called for September to deal with the revolutions in Greece, Spain, and the Spanish colonies. The four Continental powers, after easy Austrian success in suppressing the constitutionalists in Naples, were now in full cry against popular movements. Castlereagh had planned to attend and make a major effort to dissuade them from any further interventions and, if necessary, to break openly with the alliance. Canning was in accord with this line, but he recognized that the Duke of Wellington would carry more weight on this mission. Wellington, however, was unable to deter the allies, who pledged their support to French intervention in Spain. The French success there in 1823 at once raised talk of another congress for French action against the rebellious Spanish-American colonies. In the British view, this would further disturb the balance of power and threaten British security as well as commerce.

Canning met this problem by giving a timely warning to the French that British sea power would be used to prevent any non-Spanish expedition across the Atlantic. He used his oratory to rouse Britain and to convince Europeans of his purpose. If it came to war, he declared, it would be a "war of opinions," a "civil war," in which Britain would find "under her banners all the discontented and restless spirits of the age."

In 1825 Canning extended British recognition to three Spanish-American republics, thus consolidating their independence and making the British money market more accessible to them. This situation inspired his most famous statement: "I resolved that if France had Spain, it should not be Spain 'with the Indies.' I called the New World into existence to redress the balance of the Old." Throughout, he avoided any special trade privileges from the new states, while his friend William Huskisson at the Board of Trade was doing much to liberalize British commercial policies.

Developments in the Greek revolt against Turkish rule soon led Canning to depart from the policy of nonintervention and to support the Greek national cause. The Turks had enlisted the army and navy of Mehemet Ali of Egypt and threatened to depopulate the Morea. This not only intensified British sympathy for the Greeks but also led to a threat of Russian intervention on their behalf, thus endangering the balance in the Near East. To meet this situation, in 1826 Canning enlisted Russian support for British mediation for Greek autonomy. Then, in July 1827, he formed an alliance with Russia and France to enforce Greek autonomy on the Turks. This new alignment, far too strong for Austria to resist, broke the fourpower front against national and constitutionalist movements and established Greek independence.

Canning himself did not live to guide this alliance to its fulfillment. After Lord Liverpool became paralyzed in February 1827, Canning succeeded him as prime minister but at the price of a serious split in the Tory party. Wellington, Peel, and others, mistrusting Canning in this office, refused to serve under him. Canning was able to recruit others, but the transition dragged out to 6 weeks of intense strain from which, bearing a heavy cold, he never recovered. His "hundred days" at the pinnacle ended in death on Aug. 8, 1827.

Further Reading

The best biography of Canning is H. W. V. Temperley, *Life of Canning* (1905). Josceline Bagot, ed., *George Canning and His Friends* (2 vols., 1909), contains interesting material. On Canning's foreign policy, H. W. V. Temperley, *The Foreign Policy of Canning, 1822-1827* (1925; 2d ed. 1966), is standard. Also well worth consulting is C. K. Webster, ed., *Britain and the Independence of Latin America, 1812-1830: Select Documents from the Foreign Office Archives* (2 vols., 1938).

Additional Sources

Dixon, Peter, *Canning, politician and statesman,* London: Weidenfeld and Nicolson, 1976; New York: Mason/Charter, 1976.

Hinde, Wendy, *George Canning,* New York, St. Martin's Press 1974, 1973. □

Annie Jump Cannon

The American astronomer Annie Jump Cannon (1863-1941) made her most outstanding contribution to modern astronomy in the field of stellar spectral classification.

Annie Jump Cannon was born in Dover, Delaware, on December 11, 1863, the daughter of Wilson Lee Cannon and Mary Elizabeth Jump Cannon. One of the first Delaware women to enroll in college, she attended Wellesley College (class of 1884). Back at Wellesley in 1894 after a decade at home, she did graduate studies in mathematics, physics, and astronomy. In 1895, Cannon registered as a special student in astronomy at Radcliffe College, staying there two years.

The newly elected director of the Harvard College Observatory, Edward C. Pickering, had put Williamina P. Fleming in charge of hiring a staff of women assistants. Between 1885 and 1900, Fleming selected 20 assistants—including Cannon, who joined the staff in 1896—to sort photographs of stellar spectra.

Cannon's early work dealt mostly with variable stars. Her greatest contributions remain in the field of stellar spectral classification. She discovered more than 300 variable stars on the photographic plates. A large number were detected from spectral characteristics. At Harvard the spectra of stars had been sorted into various groups, following the alphabetical order (A, B, C, and so on). Cannon created the definitive Harvard system of spectral classification. She rearranged groups, omitted some letters, added a few, and made new subdivisions. She proved that the vast majority of stars are representatives of only a few species. These few spectral types, with rare exceptions, can be arranged in a continuous series. Following five years of research (1896-1901), Cannon published in 1901 a description of 1,122 of the brighter stars.

Cannon's paramount contribution to astronomy was *The Henry Draper Catalogue,* named after the first man to photograph stellar spectra. In the Draper catalogue can be found spectral classifications of virtually all stars brighter than ninth or tenth magnitude, "a colossal enterprise embracing 225,300 stars" (Owen Gingerich).

She had described her classification in 1900 and, slightly modified, again in 1912. Most of the work of classifying the spectra was performed between 1911 and 1915. The first volume of the catalogue appeared in 1918, the

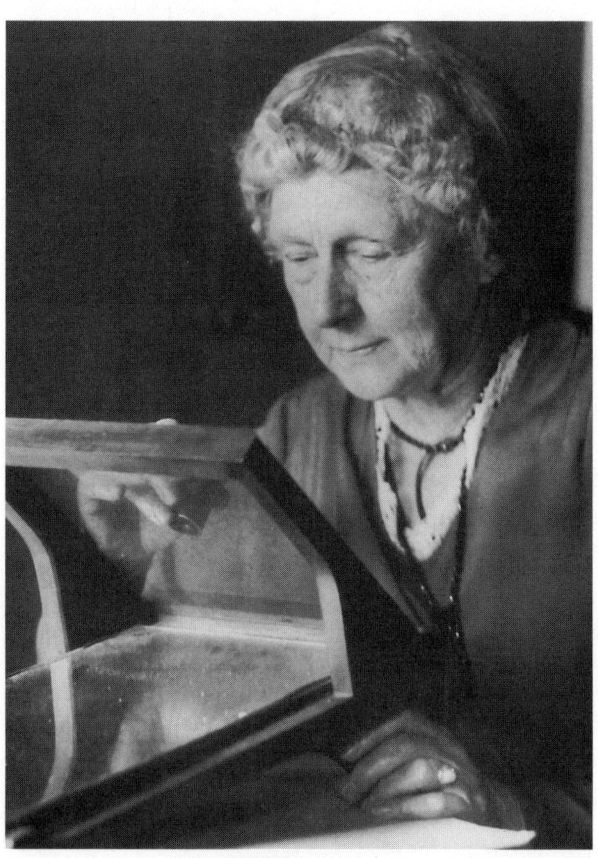

ninth and final volume in 1924. She published about 47,000 additional classifications in the *Henry Draper Extension* (1925-1936) and several thousand more in the *Yale Zone Catalogue* and *Cape Zone Catalogue.* Moreover, 86,000 were printed posthumously in 1949. In 1922 Cannon's system of classification was adopted by the International Astronomical Union as the official system for the classification of stellar spectra. That same year she spent half a year at Arequipa, Peru, photographing the spectra of the southern stars.

Throughout her career, in the absence of a hearing aid, Cannon suffered from complete deafness. In discussions about the election of a woman to the National Academy of Sciences, Raymond Pearl of Johns Hopkins declared he could not vote for Cannon on the grounds she was deaf. Incidentally, the first woman astronomer was not elected to the academy until 1978.

Cannon was curator of astronomical photographs in charge of the collection of Harvard plates starting in 1911. In 1914 she was elected an honorary member of the Royal Astronomical Society. At that time women could not become regular members.

Honors bestowed upon Cannon after 1920 resulted from initiatives taken by her director, Harlow Shapley (and also by Henry Norris Russel, professor of astronomy at Princeton University), due to the lack of recognition at Harvard itself. She received four American and two foreign honorary degrees: from the University of Delaware; Wellesley, her *Alma Mater;* Oglethorpe University; and Mount Holyoke College and from the University of Groningen (Holland) and Oxford University (the first woman ever to be granted such distinction).

In 1931 she was awarded the Draper Medal of the National Academy of Sciences. In 1932 she was the laureate of the Ellen Richards Prize. She turned it over to the American Astronomical Society for a triennal award for distinguished contributions to astronomy by a woman of any nationality. Margaret Rossiter wrote: "Perhaps because she had never won an award from the AAS or been elected its president (she was treasurer from 1912 to 1919), she wanted more recognition for younger women." In 1938 President James Bryant Conant of Harvard University made her the William Cranch Bond Astronomer, a nonfaculty appointment. In the summer of 1940 she retired officially but continued to work actively until a few weeks before her death, on April 13, 1941, in Cambridge, Massachusetts.

Her life and work inspired other women to follow in her footsteps, to dedicate their abilities to science, and, for many, to choose a career in the field of astronomy.

Further Reading

On Annie Jump Cannon as a woman scientist, see the classic work by Margaret W. Rossiter, *Women Scientists in America Struggles and Strategies to 1940* (1982). A biography of Cannon was written by Owen Gingerich: "Cannon, Annie Jump," in: *Dictionary of Scientific Biography* (1971). At the death of Cannon, two important obituaries were published, one by the first laureate of the Annie Jump Cannon Prize in 1934, Cecilia Payne Gaposchkin, in *Science* (May 9, 1941), and the other by R. L. Waterfield, in *Nature* (June 14, 1941). Apart from recalling the scientific career of Cannon, they paid homage to her personality. □

Joseph Gurney Cannon

Joseph Gurney Cannon (1836-1926) was the American politician whose arbitrary, often dictatorial, methods as Speaker of the House gave rise to the term "Cannonism."

Joseph Cannon was born in Guilford, N.C., on May 7, 1836, of old English and Huguenot stock. He grew up in Annapolis, Ind., studied 6 months at the Cincinnati Law School, and entered practice in Shelbyville, Ill., in 1858. He married Mary P. Reed in 1862.

A brilliant stump speaker in a racy, colloquial way, Cannon liked to pose as an untutored countryman. "I am," he said," one of the great army of mediocrity which constitutes the majority." More a standpatter than a reactionary, he was also a spoilsman, a protectionist, and an unqualified nationalist. "This country," he sometimes expostulated, is one "hell of a success."

After a long stint as an Illinois attorney general, Cannon was elected to Congress in 1872 and remained until 1923, except for the congresses of 1891-1893 and 1913-1915. He was known as "the hayseed member from Illinois," "foul-mouthed Joe," and, in later life, "Uncle Joe," He served 8 years as chairman of the Committee on Appropriations and 8 more as Speaker of the House, distinguishing himself in both posts for his high-handed geniality. In 1898, in a supreme moment of arrogance, he put through a $50,000,000 defense bill without consulting the other members of the Appropriations Committee.

Cannon had clashed with Theodore Roosevelt when the latter was civil service commissioner, and he was personally unsympathetic to much of the program of Roosevelt as president. Yet Cannon supported Roosevelt loyally until midway through the President's second administration. Cannon let some measures pass without opposing them, modified others, and worked to secure the enactment of still others. In 1906 he aided the passage of a number of reforms, including the Pure Food and Drug Bill. Conversely, his unwillingness to compromise on tariffs was largely responsible for the President's decision to abandon plans to reduce them. Holding that the government should spend "not one cent for scenery," Cannon fought Roosevelt's conservation program.

As Roosevelt became more progressive, Cannon parted with him completely. He fought bitterly and openly during Roosevelt's last 2 years in office, and in 1912 he was one of four Republicans to support consideration of an anti-third-term resolution aimed at Roosevelt. Cannon's relations with President William Howard Taft, whom he charged with being too nonpartisan, were bad from the beginning. Cannon's criticism of the tariff reciprocity treaty with Canada,

the President complained, was "the lowest politics I have ever seen in Congress."

Cannon's power derived from the strength of his personality and from his control of the House Committee on Rules, which had authority to appoint all other House committees. He became increasingly arbitrary as he aged, and in 1910 George W. Norris of Nebraska pushed through a resolution which stripped him of his seat on the Rules Committee and provided for election of the committee by the House. An effort to declare the speakership vacant failed, however, and Cannon continued in that position until 1911.

Defeated for reelection to Congress in 1912, Cannon was returned to office in 1914. Though the former bitterness gradually passed, he was never again a powerful factor in the House. He reluctantly voted for entrance into World War I in 1917 and scornfully attacked the League of Nations in 1919. He retired from Congress in 1923 and died on Nov. 12, 1926.

Further Reading

A political biography of Cannon is William R. Gwinn, *Uncle Joe Cannon, Archfoe of Insurgency: A History of the Rise and Fall of Cannonism* (1957). Blair Bolles, *Tyrant from Illinois: Uncle Joe Cannon's Experiment with Personal Power* (1951), concentrates on Cannon as Speaker of the House. Richard Lowitt, *George W. Norris: The Making of a Progressive, 1861-1912* (1963), offers the most authoritative account of the stripping of Cannon's power. L. White Busbey, *Uncle Joe Cannon: The Story of a Pioneer American . . .* (1927), is a discursive reminiscence by Cannon's private secretary.

Additional Sources

Bolles, Blair, *Tyrant from Illinois; Uncle Joe Cannon's experiment with personal power,* Westport, Conn., Greenwood Press 1974, 1951. □

Theodore Canot

Theodore Canot (1804-1860) was a French-Italian adventurer and slave trader. His memoirs, notable for their vividness and general accuracy, illustrate the conduct and character of every branch of the slave trade.

Theodore Canot, whose real name was Theophile Conneau, was born at Alessandria, Italy, the second son of an Italian mother and a French father who was a paymaster in Napoleon's army. Theodore went to sea in 1819 as cabin boy on an American ship which took him to Salem, where he learned navigation. After a series of West Indian adventures he joined the slave ship *Aerostatica* at Havana in 1826 and "plunged accidentally," as he put it, into the slave trade at age 22. Henceforward Canot—ambitious and intelligent, daring and unscrupulous, with "no religion, many vices, and few weaknesses"—became one of the more famous, though not the most successful, slavers of the 19th century.

Canot's story is filled with the lurid details and violent personalities of the new era of slave trading after the Napoleonic Wars, stimulated by Europe's revived demand for tropical produce, the expansion of slave systems in Brazil, Cuba, and the United States, and the enormous profits to be gained in the face of Britain's efforts to blockade the seas. The small operators of earlier centuries were now eclipsed by heavily capitalized "merchant princes" called mongos, established in huge depots or strongholds on the West African coast, able to embark a thousand and more slaves at a time.

Canot served these operations as clerk, agent, supercargo, and shipowner, seeking repeatedly to branch out on his own. Beginning on the Guinea coast as clerk for "Mongo John" Ormond at the Rio Pongo, he tried to succeed Ormond on the latter's suicide in 1828 but was burned out by hostile Africans. With a condemned schooner from Sierra Leone, Canot hijacked a cargo of slaves and took them to Cuba. After a series of successful voyages he was seized by the French and imprisoned at Brest. Pardoned by King Louis Philippe, he returned to Africa and joined Don Pedro Blanco, the Spanish nobleman and "prince of slavers," at the Gallinas River between Sierra Leone and Liberia.

After Don Pedro's retirement to Havana as a millionaire in 1839, Canot's fortunes declined. He tried legitimate enterprise for a time as a planter at Cape Mount in Liberia but failed and returned to slaving. Burned out of Cape Mount by the British, he was captured on a slaving voyage in 1847. Taken to New York for trial, he skipped bail and fled to Brazil, where the great coastal raid by Commodore Foote destroyed Canot's last ship in 1850.

Canot next appeared down but not out in the saloons of Baltimore in 1853, where he parlayed his acquaintance with the philanthropist James Hall of the African Colonization Society, for whom he had done favors when a planter at Cape Mount, into a second chance. Canot then recovered his fortunes with an unlikely marriage to socially prominent Eliza McKinley of Philadelphia and with the help of his brother, who had become personal physician to Napoleon III, pursued a career in the French colonial service as collector of Nouméa in New Caledonia, until he returned to Paris and died in 1860.

Canot's Memoirs

Through Hall, Canot had met Brantz Mayer, prominent journalist, who became his amanuensis and produced the book that made Canot famous: This memoir, as well as being a circumstantial account of the slave trade, is a document in the intellectual history of racism. Mayer saw in Canot's story a confirmation of his own facile assumptions concerning the slavery question, and he provided Canot's narrative of skulduggery with a moral for his times.

Slavery, said Mayer (1854), and the careers of men like Canot must be the fruit of Africa's own fatal flaws, whereby "one sixth of Africa subjects the remaining five sixths to servitude," long before the white man enters the picture. Mayer's was an Africa "unstirred by progress . . . full of the barbarism that blood and tradition have handed down from the beginning." For him, Canot's story demonstrated that slavery was not a white man's institution "except in so far as it is an inheritance from the system it describes"—an African-originated system which exhibited" an innate or acquired inferiority of the negro race in its own land."

Thus, in the creation of the 19th-century's image of Africa, the corrupt life of slaver Canot was turned against Africa and Africans. The victims became in effect the source of the transgression. The universal human and historical failure which the slave trade represented was attributed not to the shared responsibility of its white and black perpetrators alike but to the modern myth of race—the racial ghost of African inferiority.

Further Reading

Brantz Mayer's introduction to *Captain Canot, or Twenty Years of an African Slaver* (1854) summarizes Canot's ideas concerning Africa, Africans, and the slave trade in relation to the American slavery question. The 1854 edition is the complete account, while Malcolm Cowley, ed., *Adventures of an African Slaver* (1969), reprints the narrative with minor deletions up to Canot's decision to abandon slaving in 1840 (on which he reneged) and provides an epilogue summary of his subsequent career. Cowley's introduction is a useful assessment of Canot's place in the new slave trade. Daniel P. Mannix and Malcolm Cowley, *Black Cargoes: A History of the Atlantic Slave Trade, 1518-1865* (1962), includes a short account of Canot's career. □

Antonio Canova

The Italian sculptor Antonio Canova (1757-1822) was a leading exponent of the neoclassic style, which dominated the arts in the late 18th and early 19th centuries. Internationally famous, he was regarded as the most brilliant sculptor in Europe.

Antonio Canova was born in Possagno near Venice on Nov. 1, 1757. He displayed a talent for sculpture while still very young and by 1774 had established his own studio in Venice, where he produced portrait busts and other sculptures for the Venetian nobility. In 1779 Canova left Venice to travel and to study in southern Italy; during the following 2 years he worked in Rome and visited Herculaneum and Pompeii, ancient Roman cities which had been excavated in the middle of the 18th century. By 1781, the year he took up permanent residence in Rome, Canova was thoroughly committed artistically to the neoclassic style, which was sweeping all the arts.

During the first half of the 18th century the arts had been dominated by the rococo, a light, playful, and aristocratic style. By the 1760s, however, the rococo was under attack by intellectuals and critics as being trivial and frivolous, and at the same time several important books were published concerning ancient Greek and Roman art and architecture. Fashionable and artistic taste began to shift slowly from the rococo to the art of antiquity, and when Canova reached maturity as a sculptor, neoclassicism had achieved a virtually complete triumph in painting, sculpture, architecture, and the decorative arts. Canova's passion for ancient art and his study of it, combined with his particular talents and the taste of the period, led him to the heights of success as a champion of neoclassicism in sculpture.

Between 1783 and his death nearly 40 years later, Canova received important and extensive commissions from the popes, Napoleon, the Hapsburgs, and members of the English aristocracy. He traveled widely and worked in Rome, Paris, and Vienna. His statues became so popular that he utilized many assistants and various mechanical techniques in order to meet the demands made upon him. In 1805, by which time his reputation as the most eminent sculptor in Europe was firmly established, he was appointed by Pope Pius VII as inspector general of fine arts and antiquities for the Papal States. Five years later he became director of the Academy of St. Luke in Rome, the official art academy of the Papal States.

Canova's mature style derived specifically and directly from ancient Greek and Roman sculpture, and his subject matter was most often taken from classical mythology. *Perseus* (1801) reflects his classical taste for idealization, expressed in carefully controlled harmonies of proportion, clear line, smooth modeling, and sleek surfaces. Two famous and typical works which he created for the Bonaparte family are the monumental marble statues of Napoleon (1802-1810) and of Napoleon's sister, Pauline Borghese (1808). In the statue of Napoleon, which is nearly 12 feet

high, Canova presented the victorious Bonaparte as a nude Roman emperor, his facial features made to conform to the classical ideal. Princess Borghese, life-size and partly draped, is shown as Venus reclining on a couch. Both works are notable for dependence upon Hellenistic sources, idealized perfection of the forms, fluidity of line, graceful modeling, and exquisitely refined detail.

Canova died in Venice on Oct. 13, 1822. He created a classic ideal of human beauty which exerted a strong influence on academic sculpture during most of the 19th century. Late in the century, however, Canova's work was harshly criticized as cold, lifeless, uninspired, and a mere imitation of ancient art. This adverse critical judgment of Canova's sculpture prevailed well into the 20th century, but recent and more objective studies of the entire neoclassic movement have tended to restore to Canova's reputation some of the luster which it possessed during his lifetime.

Further Reading

The most important monograph on Canova is in Italian: Elena Bassi, *Canova* (1943). In English, an interesting and decidedly adverse evaluation of Canova's work may be found in Sir Kenneth Clark, *The Nude: A Study in Ideal Form* (1956). A different and more favorable view of Canova is expressed in Sir Osbert Sitwell, *Winters of Content* (1932). For examinations of Canova within the context of his era and for discussions of neoclassicism see Fritz Novotny, *Painting and Sculpture in Europe: 1780-1880* (1960); Robert Rosenblum, *Transformations in Late Eighteenth-Century Art* (1967); and Hugh Honour, *Neo-Classicism* (1968). □

Eddie Cantor

Eddie Cantor (1892-1964) was a singer and comedian in vaudeville and on stage and a radio and film star.

Eddie Cantor was born Isador Iskowitz on January 31, 1892, in the Lower East Side of New York City. His parents died before he reached the age of two, and he was raised by his maternal grandmother, Esther. Due to his poverty, Cantor was forced to drop out of school before he reached the sixth grade. He took on a variety of odd jobs—delivery boy, shooting gallery attendant, and, finally, performing in the streets for small change. At the age of 16 Cantor was in an amateur singing contest in which he won $5.00. He subsequently became a singing waiter in a saloon in Coney Island in which Jimmy Durante played the piano.

Cantor's first vaudeville appearance was in 1907 at the Old Clinton Music Hall in which he played with the juggling team Bedini and Arthur. He was picked up by Gus Edwards and played in his *Kid Kabaret* along with George Jessel and Lila Lee. In 1914 Cantor made his first London appearance at the Alhambra in *Not Likely.* He also pursued his vaudeville career in the act "Cantor and Lee" with Lila Lee from Edwards' company.

In 1916 Cantor made his first appearance in musical comedy with a minor role in *Canary Cottage* in Los Angeles. He also toured the same year playing the role of Sam in *US.* Cantor's big break came in 1917 when Florenz Ziegfeld, the famous theater impresario, hired him for his midnight revue, *The Frolics.* He rapidly moved to a featured role in *Ziegfeld's Follies* and success on the Broadway stage.

Cantor's association with Ziegfeld was a long and fruitful one for both of them. He starred in the *Follies* of 1917 through 1919. However, a rift occurred in their relations in 1919 when Cantor took an aggressive stand against management as one of the founders of Actor's Equity, a newly formed actors' union.

During his conflict with Ziegfeld Cantor worked for the rival producers the Shubert brothers. He was a great success in their productions of *Broadway Brevities* (1920), *She Don't Wanna* (1921), and *Make It Snappy* (1922). Finally Ziegfeld and Cantor resolved their conflict and Cantor returned to star in *Kid Boots* (1923), directed by Ziegfeld on Broadway. In this show Cantor played a clever caddie at a golf resort who sold golf lessons and, on the side, bootleg whiskey. This was his first full-length part on Broadway, and it proved to audiences and producers alike that his act could carry an entire show. In 1927 he was a smashing success in his return to *Ziegfeld's Follies,* and in the following year he starred in another Ziegfeld musical comedy, *Whoopee.* In *Whoopee* Cantor played the part of Henry Williams, a chronic hypochondriac travelling to a dude ranch. He sang "Makin' Whoopee," one of his all time favorite songs, and the success of this show led Eddie Cantor to film stardom.

Cantor had made his first film in 1911 in a test talking picture. In *Widow at the Races* he starred with his friend

George Jessel and was directed by none other than Thomas Edison. He started working seriously in film in 1926 (*Kid Boots*), but it was *Whoopee* (1930) which made him a film star. Among his best films were *Palmy Days* (1931), *Kid from Spain* (1932), *Roman Scandals* (1933), and *Kid Millions* (1934).

In 1931 Cantor had returned to the stage at the Palace (an old vaudeville house) and headed the bill with George Jessel. The show, which also starred the famous comedy team of Burns and Allen, was so popular that it was held over for six weeks. His next stage role was in *Banjo Eyes* (which became his nickname) in 1942.

Cantor frequently appeared on stage in blackface with a straw hat, wire-rimmed glasses, white gloves, black tie, and tight checked trousers. He had large popping eyes and used fast, mincing steps, jumping-jack antics, and hand clapping. He was known for his Jewish humor, for which he employed a Yiddish accent. In one sketch he announced, "I'd go to war for my mother country, Russia—darkest Russia—for all my relatives there, General Walkowitch, Hzkowitch, Eczema" When he was questioned about Eczema he answered, "Yes, that's another itch."

In addition to his stage and film career Cantor was host of the *Chase and Sanborne Hour* (1931), a popular radio show, and of the *Eddie Cantor Show* (1935-1939). He also made many recordings and wrote several books. He was co-author of *Silks and Satins* and author of such humorous books as *Earl Carroll's Sketch Book, Your Next President, Caught Short: A Saga of Wailing Wall Street, Between the Acts, Who's Hooey,* and *World's Book of Best Jokes*. With David Freedman he paid tribute to his mentor in *Ziegfeld, the Great Glorifier*. Cantor wrote two autobiographies, *My Life Is in Your Hands* (1928) and *Take My Life* (1930). He was also host of the television show *The Colgate Comedy Hour* . His life was recorded on film in 1953 in *The Eddie Cantor Story,* and in 1956 he was awarded a special Oscar for distinguished service to the motion picture industry.

Cantor was admired as a tireless, conscientious humanitarian. His outspoken criticism of what he called fascist government officials resulted in his being blacklisted for a year (1931). Nevertheless, always appreciated for his modesty, kindness, and generosity, he was granted, in 1951, an honorary Doctorate of Humane Letters by Temple University.

He was dedicated to many charities. Among his favorites were a summer camp for poor children, the March of Dimes (which he helped to create), and various Jewish causes. In 1962 the State of Israel gave him the Medallion of Valor for his extraordinary efforts on behalf of that nation.

He was a devoted family man who married his childhood sweetheart, Ida Tobias. They had five daughters. Cantor died October 10, 1964, at the age of 72.

Further Reading

Biographies of Eddie Cantor can be found in Daniel Blum's *Great Stars* (1952); Anthony Slide's *The Vaudevillians* (1981); and John Parker, editor, *Who's Who in the Theatre,* 9th edition, (1939).

The World of Flo Ziegfeld (1974) by Randolph Carter and *On with the Show* (1976) by R. C. Toll shed light on Cantor's career with Ziegfeld. *The Palace* (1969) by Marian Spitzer gives a description of his return to vaudeville in 1931.

Additional Sources

Koseluk, Gregory, *Eddie Cantor: a life in show business,* Jefferson, N.C.: McFarland, 1995. □

Georg Ferdinand Ludwig Philipp Cantor

The German mathematician Georg Ferdinand Ludwig Philipp Cantor (1845-1918) was noted for his theory of sets and his bold analysis of the "actual" infinite, which provoked a critical examination of the foundations of mathematics and eventually transformed nearly every branch.

Georg Cantor was born in St. Petersburg, Russia, on March 3, 1845. He was German only by tenure. His father was a Danish Jew who converted to Protestantism and made his fortune in merchandising; his mother was a Roman Catholic whose family was richly endowed with musicians and artists. The Cantor family moved to Frankfurt, Germany, when Georg was 11. When he entered the Wiesbaden gymnasium at the age of 15, his mathematical talent was already evident.

In 1862 Cantor entered the University of Zurich. After a year he transferred to Berlin, where he studied mathematics and received his doctorate in 1867. Two years later he joined the faculty of the University of Halle as a privatdozent, or unpaid lecturer, and in 1872 he was appointed assistant professor. He married Vally Guttman in 1874, and they had six children.

Up to this time Cantor's mathematical work was uniformly excellent but with no harbinger of the explosive things to come. Then, while pursuing a problem on trigonometric series originally raised by Georg Riemann, he was led to investigate the nature of infinite sets of numbers. Fascinated by what he saw and driven almost against his will, he dug deeper and came up with some outrageously paradoxical results. Among other things, he proved that the number of points within a square is no more "numerous" than the number of points on one of its sides. "I see it but I don't believe it," he wrote to a friend in 1877. Neither did many others, and some were quick to say so. Leopold Kronecker attacked Cantor personally and used his prestige to prejudice others against Cantor's ideas. What made these ideas so pernicious in Kronecker's eyes was Cantor's insistence on treating infinite sets as completed entities.

Cantor developed his theory of sets and transfinite numbers in a long series of papers from 1874 to 1897. In 1879 he was promoted to full professor, and after a time his work came to be appreciated by some mathematicians. But the general hostility caused him to suffer frequent nervous breakdowns and long periods of depression. In 1908 even the great Henri Poincaré remarked that later generations would regard Cantor's set theory "as a disease from which one has recovered." Poincaré was wrong. Today the power of set theory to illuminate and unify vast areas of mathematics is generally recognized.

Cantor died on Jan. 6, 1918, in a mental hospital at Halle.

Further Reading

The best biography of Cantor is in E. T. Bell, *Men of Mathematics* (1937). See also Ganesh Prasad, *Some Great Mathematicians of the Nineteenth Century: Their Lives and Their Works* (2 vols., 1933-1934). For an introduction to set theory and transfinite numbers see Richard Courant and Herbert Robbins, *What Is Mathematics* (1941). □

Canute I the Great

Canute I (ca. 995–1035) was a viking king who united the English and Danish people of England to become the first ruler since the fall of Rome to rule over all of England.

The life of Canute Sweynson (Cnut the Viking) King of England (1016-35), Denmark (1018-35), and Norway (1028-29), developed in a culture and setting shaped by over 100 years of interaction between the Danes and the English, for the Danish and Norwegian Vikings had used England and Ireland as a source of plunder and treasure. Violence dominated the relationship between the Anglo-Saxons and the Danes. The accession of Ethelred I to the English throne in 975 intensified the strife, as he proved to be neither a capable warrior nor an efficient administrator. The period of upheaval and civil war between 975 and 1015 was especially important for Canute and for England.

Inhabitants called the northeast section of England the Danelaw. This was the largest Viking settlement, a region occupied by Danes for over 100 years. By 975, the local English population had accepted the presence of these foreigners; indeed, English and Danish intermarriage was not uncommon. In this Viking settlement, the tribal leaders laid the groundwork for a Viking king to unite them.

Descended from the Shieldings, a long line of kings, Canute was also reputed by the Viking sagas to be descended from the Knytling dynasty, adding to his prestige. His grandfather was Harald Bluetooth, and his father Sweyn Haraldson, both kings of Denmark. When Canute was born (c. 995/998), his father was in the process of conquering more areas of England under Ethelred's rule. Canute's mother Gunhild was a Polish princess and sister to Duke (later King) Boleslav Chrobry. Gunhild became Sweyn's consort and mistress. Though they had no formal marriage

arrangement, Sweyn made their sons, Harald and Canute, his heirs.

Details of Canute's early life remain unclear because no written record exists. When the King married Sigrid the Haughty (the widow of King Eric of Sweden) in order to cement an alliance with Sweden, Gunhild had to leave Sweyn's court. Evidently, Gunhild took Canute—then no more than two or three years old—to the court of her brother. Though his childhood is shrouded in mystery, evidence points to a foster father, Thorkil the Tall, a distant cousin and brother to Earl Sigvaldi of Jomburg. Thorkil had also served as second-in-command to Sweyn on several raids during the years preceding Canute's birth.

Between 994 and 1007, Sweyn led a constant barrage of raids upon the beleaguered kingdom of England. Canute's brother Harald served as regent during the father's absence from Denmark. Sweyn resumed these attacks in 1009, and Canute appeared for the first time with his father in 1013. In that year, Canute held the fleet camp at Gainsborough in northeastern England while his father subdued all of northern and eastern England. Even London, which had lost no battles to the Vikings, submitted to Sweyn's authority, and in January 1014, Ethelred fled to Normandy and the court of his brother-in-law, Duke Richard.

On February 3, 1014, Sweyn's death, following a brief illness, set a number of events in motion. His elder son Harald received the crown of Denmark, while Sweyn's host ("army") at Gainsborough acknowledged Canute as his father's successor in England. Unfortunately, Canute needed the acceptance of both English and Danish nobles to claim the English throne. Though untested, the 20-year-old Canute must have displayed great promise or the Viking host would not have followed him.

Although they had given hostages to insure their submission to Sweyn and his son, the English nobles conspired with their exiled King. In April, Ethelred returned and gathered a large army to drive Canute from England. Realizing he could not hope for victory, Canute withdrew in May, taking revenge upon his unfortunate hostages. By his hasty retreat, Canute lost the Danelaw. He arrived in Denmark to find his brother in firm command with no interest in redividing the inheritance. Though both brothers agreed to assist each other in their endeavors to secure their kingdoms, Canute's claim remained more tenuous.

The following year, Canute (with assistance from another brother, Earl Eric, regent of Norway, and his foster father Thorkil) led an army which overran English territories of Wessex and Mercia. While this force was in England, Olaf Haraldson (the Stout), in the absence of Eric, began his quest to gain the throne of Norway. Because of his preoccupation with England, Canute could not spare Eric to return to defend Norway, and Eric would have to wait 15 more years for his chance to bring Norway under his sway.

Though Ethelred and his son, Saxon King Edmund Ironside, were no match for Canute, the Eadric of Mercia's change in allegiance gave Canute a significant edge. In the fall of 1015, Ethelred lost Wessex; in early 1016, Northumbria surrendered and was placed under the control of Earl Eric of Norway; by April, Canute was planning his attack on London. Before he could launch the assault, however, Ethelred died on April 23. Though in choosing a new king the English *witan* ("council of nobles") usually selected a successor in the line of Alfred of Wessex; they evidently had some powers of discretion. Before May's end, when over three-fourths of the kingdom had submitted to the Dane, many magnates and ecclesiastical leaders had met to designate Canute as their choice. At the same time, a similar body in London declared for Ethelred's son Edmund—an act which could only prolong the violence.

Using Mercia as a source of provisions, Canute besieged London over the course of the summer. In the fall, he led an attack on East Anglia, despite having to simultaneously besiege London. On October 18, 1016, Edmund's army found the Danes at Ashingdon and—against the advice of Eadric—attacked Canute's army. Edmund lost decisively. With England by then too exhausted to continue raising armies for him, Edmund's councillors suggested a division of England with peace. The "Compact of Olney" followed, dividing England into two sections: Edmund received Wessex while Canute held London, Mercia, and Northumbria. Edmund agreed in addition to levy a *Danegeld* ("tax") upon his lands to support Canute's army. Each ruler made the other his heir and exchanged oaths of friendship.

Edmund died on November 30, however, leaving Canute in undisputed control of England. For the first time in seven years, peace returned to the country, and at the

Christmas celebration in London all of England's nobles recognized Canute as England's king.

Not wishing to destroy the existing social order, Canute made England the center of a growing empire, governing the kingdom with the advice of English as well as Danish nobles. The new king would need strong English support for a stable rule, yet he brought with him from Scandinavia the custom of allowing considerable freedom to nobles. Indebted to his Danish and Norwegian nobles who had shown him strong support, he raised several Scandinavians to high court positions, while depending most heavily upon Earl Eric of Norway and his foster father Thorkil. To compensate for the loss of Norway in 1016, he made Eric the Earl of Northumbria. Thorkil became Earl of East Anglia and Canute's regent in Denmark in the King's absence. Canute also utilized the Mercian Eadric, despite Eadric's history of shifting allegiances; the Archbishop of York, Wulfstan II; and the newly made Earl Godwin of Devon. The use of such English councillors clearly indicated Canute's desire to rule the kingdom in the manner of his Anglo-Saxon predecessors.

Confirming the existing system, Canute's first act as king was to divide the kingdom into four great earldoms. While Eric, Eadric, and Thorkil held the above-mentioned positions, Canute held Wessex for himself, developing a division of power and land that would later provide a base for resistance by other such nobles against future kings. In addition to this system, Canute established a series of lesser earldoms along the Scottish, Welsh, and Cornish marches to protect those regions from raiders.

In July 1017, Canute married Emma, the widow of Ethelred. He had as well a consort in Denmark, Aelfgifu of Aelfhelm, with whom he had initiated a relationship in 1013 while holding charge of the fleet at Gainsborough. His marriage to Aelfgifu was after the Danish custom and not one sanctioned within the Christian church; together they had two sons, Harald Harefoot and Sweyn. When Canute then married Emma, a precondition was that the sons of their marriage would stand in line for the English throne before Canute's older sons or Emma's sons by Ethelred. The royal couple would eventually have two children, a boy, Harthacanute, and a girl, Gunhild, who later married Prince Henry of Germany.

During 1018, Canute sent most of his Scandinavian host back to Denmark. With the remaining 3,000 men, he established an elite bodyguard, which became the core of his army, and stationed these soldiers at strategic points around the kingdom. The defense of the peace against both English offenders and Danish raiders rested upon this force. In the summer his brother Harald died without heirs. Then in October, Archbishop Wulfstan drafted a law code for Canute; it reinforced the idea that Canute was ruling as an English successor to the line of Alfred of Wessex, thus making his rule more palatable to his English subjects.

Canute returned to Denmark in 1019 to establish a firm claim to the throne, but, regarding England as not yet stabilized, he did not remain long in his homeland. After making Thorkil his regent in Denmark in the spring of 1020, Canute journeyed back to London to contend with a plot led by the Earl of Devon whom he replaced with Godwin of Devon.

Among the problems Canute faced during his rule was the conflict between his Christian and pagan followers. In England, he ruled as a most Christian king, ordering his nobles to follow the advice of the bishops and abbots and having the holy relics of the martyred Archbishop Aelfheah transferred from London to Canterbury in June 1023. His outlawing of Thorkil, a determined pagan, in 1021, may also have been a concession to the Christian church in England; Thorkil was reconciled to Canute two years later but never returned to England. This period also found the King endowing many churches and rebuilding monasteries to secure the goodwill of the Church.

After Thorkil's fall from grace, Canute used his brother-in-law, Earl Ulf, and his Danish consort, Aelfgifu, to enforce the laws and collect the taxes in Denmark. He named Sweyn, his son by Aelfgifu, regent though the power resided with Earl Ulf and Aelfgifu. In 1023, Canute sent Harthacanute, his son by Emma, to the Danish court to learn Danish customs as would befit a future king of Denmark.

That same year, he began pressing his claims to Norway in opposition to King Olaf Haraldson the Stout. With Earl Eric of Norway dead, no one else could contest Canute's claim, and if Olaf meant to hold the kingdom, Canute said, then he would do so as a vassal to Canute—an idea which Olaf rejected. In preparation for the forthcoming war, Canute was able to forge an alliance with the Holy Roman Emperor Conrad the Salic. This alliance added some disputed territory to Canute's southern Danish border and gave Conrad support against dissident Slavs in the eastern part of his realm. This treaty also freed Canute from the worry of intervention by Conrad should an invasion of Norway be necessary.

By the autumn of 1025, Canute was in Denmark preparing a fleet and army for war. With large sums of money in hand, he also employed bribery as a means to change the loyalties of some Norwegian nobles. Six months later, Canute traveled to England, leaving Harthacanute as regent under the guidance of Earl Ulf. Unfortunately, Ulf's ambition outran his common sense; heavy-handed in ruling the Danes, he provoked some to rebel against the regent and declare their support for Olaf. Ulf even went so far as to declare Harthacanute king before an assembly of Danish nobles.

That summer Canute returned to Denmark with a large English force to suppress the rebellion and to press a war against Olaf. In the former act, Canute was successful, even forgiving Ulf; in the latter, however, Canute was defeated in battle September 1026 at the mouth of the Holy River. It was, however, a pyrrhic victory for Olaf. Badly outnumbered, he was forced to flee to Sweden for the winter.

During the war, Earl Ulf was assassinated in a church, and for this Canute had to repay the Church in Denmark and the widow, his sister. With this deed weighing on his mind, in 1027 Canute proclaimed that he would make a pilgrimage to Rome and ask forgiveness of the pope, John XIX, hoping that such a trip would repair the strain put on his relationship with the Roman Catholic Church by the murder of Earl Ulf. The trip would also offer Canute an opportunity to confer with the Holy Roman Emperor Conrad face to face.

Arriving in Rome near the end of March, Canute attended a Church synod at the Lateran Palace and requested a reduction in fees for the *palia* of English archbishops, to which the Pope consented under the condition of a more regular payment of Peter's pence. In addition, Canute managed to obtain lower charges for pilgrims at inns along the route from England through Burgundy, as well as a promise for better protection for English pilgrims traveling through that region.

His business concluded in Rome, Canute returned to Denmark quickly, perhaps fearing a renewal of hostilities with the spring thaw. Fortunately, Denmark was quiet enough to allow him to return to England in late 1027 to deal with Scottish raiders. With a large army, Canute forced King Malcolm of Scotland and Earl Macbeth to render homage.

By 1028, the English ruler was back in Denmark to pursue his conquest of Norway. He encountered little resistance when he finally invaded. Advancing through the kingdom, he summoned the assemblies of minor nobles, the franklins, who swore faith and gave hostages. At the *Erething* ("council meeting") in Throndheim, the franklins declared him the true king of Norway. At that meeting, many lords rendered homage to and received enlarged fiefs ("estates") from Canute.

In 1028, for the only time in his life, Canute called an imperial meeting at Nidaros, where the nobles from all three parts of his kingdom met. Creating a system of vassal earls and kings, he named his nephew, Haakon, earl of Norway and vice-regent while he made Harthacanute king of Denmark, with his foster brother Harald Thorkilson as chief advisor. As long as Canute reigned with an easy hand, his Norwegian nobles remained loyal. But when Aelfgifu, as regent for Harthacanute in Denmark and Norway, ruled with a heavy hand in Canute's name, the nobles of Norway began to turn away.

In 1029, Canute was again in England with his eastern portions of the kingdom once more secure. Unfortunately, his nephew Haakon perished during a storm in January 1030 and in his place Canute appointed Kalf Arnesson as vice-regent; his son Sweyn was named earl of Norway.

King Malcolm of Scotland renewed his homage during the year 1031, while many Welsh lords apparently submitted to Canute's overlordship as well. Yet the Empire had already grown too large for one man to rule easily. By 1033, problems were developing in Norway; Aelfgifu's rule had grown burdensome to Norwegian nobles, many of whom spoke of bringing Olaf Haraldson back. In the face of their growing rebellion, in 1035 Canute planned to travel again to Denmark in part to finalize the arrangements for a marriage between his daughter, Gunhild, and the son of Emperor Conrad, the future Henry III.

But the trip never took place. Following a period of illness, Canute died on November 12, 1035, at Shaftesbury while on an inspection tour of England; his remains were buried at Winchester. In the *Anglo-Saxon Chronicle*, the writer reported jaundice as the cause of death. During his 19-year reign, Canute had provided peace for England, as well as freedom from the savage raids which had marked his predecessor's reigns. His children did not long survive his death. Harthacanute reigned briefly as king of the entire realm but did not possess his father's strength or abilities. Harald also ruled briefly, but the great Anglo-Danish Empire depended upon a vigorous personality such as Canute. By 1040, the Empire was an idea of the past and in 1042, another Anglo-Saxon king, Edward the Confessor (son of Ethelred II), ascended the throne.

Further Reading

The main source of facts about Canute is *The Anglo-Saxon Chronicle*, edited and translated by G.N. Garmonsway (1953). For analyses of Canute's character, policies, and achievements see F.M. Stenton, *Anglo-Saxon England* (1943; 2d ed. 1947), and C.N.L. Brooke, *The Saxon and Norman Kings* (1963).

Additional Sources

Larson, Laurence Marcellus. *Canute the Great, c. 995-1035, and the Rise of Danish Imperialism During the Viking Age*. Putnam, 1912.

Loyn, H. R. *The Vikings in Britain*. St. Martin's Press, 1977.

Brooke, Christopher. *From Alfred to Henry III, 871-1272*. Norton, 1961.

Garmonsway, G. N. *Canute and His Empire*. University College Press, 1964. □

Robert Capa

One of the great war photographers, the photojournalist Robert Capa (1913-1954), born in Hungary, but a naturalized U.S. citizen, photographed the tumultuous 1930s and the wars that followed. After World War II he helped found Magnum Photos, an international photographic agency.

In a sense Robert Capa invented himself. The son of middle class Jewish parents, he was born Endre Friedmann in Budapest in what was then Austro-Hungary. He grew up under the dictatorship of Regent Nicholas Horthy but accepted the ideas of the artist Lajos Kassák, who spearheaded the avant garde movement in Hungary. Kassák's anti-authoritarian, anti-fascist, pro-labor, egalitarian, and pacifist beliefs influenced Capa the rest of his life. At age 18 Capa was arrested by the secret police for his political activities. He was released through the intervention of his father but was banished from Hungary.

Moving to Berlin in 1931, he worked as a darkroom assistant at Dephot (Deutscher Photodienst), the leading photo-journalist enterprise in Germany. This agency was distinguished by its use of the new small cameras and fast film that allowed photographers to capture fleeting gestures and to take pictures even in poor light. With these advances the photographer could focus on human events and move away from the carefully posed rows of diplomats that had characterized news photography until then. Capa soon mastered the new cameras and was occasionally sent out on small photographic assignments. In his first major break, he was sent to Copenhagen to photography Leon Trotsky. His photos of an impassioned Trotsky addressing the crowd captured Trotsky's charismatic oratorical style.

With Hitler's rise to power, Capa eventually moved to Paris. There he met Gerda Pohorylles, who called herself Gerda Taro, and fell in love with her. She wrote the text for his stories and acted as his agent. Taro found she could charge much more for a photo taken by a "rich American" photographer named Robert Capa than she could for the photographs of a poor Hungarian named Endre Friedmann. Thus the internationally known Robert Capa was born.

Capa and Taro were sent to Spain to cover the Spanish Civil War, where Capa took the picture that made him famous—a dying Loyalist soldier falling from the impact of a bullet. In July 1937 Taro was killed by a tank which sideswiped the car she had clambered onto in the retreat from Brunete. She was 26. Capa later dedicated his book *Death in the Making*, "to Gerda Taro, who spent one year at the Spanish front and who stayed on. R. C."

From 1941 to 1945 Capa photographed World War II in Europe as correspondent for *Collier's* and then *Life* magazine. On D-Day, 1944, he landed in the second wave on Omaha Beach. The soldiers, pinned down by unexpectedly heavy fire, sought shelter wherever they could. Capa, crouching with them, snapped pictures of the incoming troops. In London the lab assistant who was processing the films as quickly as possible turned up the heat in the print dryer and melted the emulsion on the negatives. The 11 that survived are slightly out of focus due to the melted emulsion, but the blurring adds to their effectiveness by conveying the confusion and danger.

After the war the photographer became what he always claimed he wanted to be—an unemployed war correspondent. He worked on a variety of projects, including a book about Russia with text by John Steinbeck. He returned to war photography briefly to cover the Israeli war of independence, 1948-1949.

In 1948 he had put into effect his long held dream of a cooperative photographic agency that would free photographers to concentrate on stories that interested them rather than spending their time scrounging assignments. The other founders of the Magnum Photo Agency were Henri Cartier-Bresson, David Seymour ("Chim"), William Vandivert, and George Rodger. Capa's legacy, beyond his wonderful photographs, included his commitment to nurturing young photographers, for his help extended beyond mere teaching to ensuring that they had enough to eat and the freedom to work as they pleased. Though he was often short of cash himself, he was extremely generous in his support of others.

While on an assignment in Japan Capa was asked to fill in for a photographer covering the French Indochina War. He was killed when he stepped on a land mine on May 25, 1954, at Thai-Binh.

For Capa, war always had a human face. His photographs, a deeply moving account of the boredom, terror, and insanity of war, are characterized by a direct appeal to the emotions, the response of average people to events beyond their control. Close up photos of a few people express the emotional impact of the whole. And his pictures were inevitably of people; beautiful compositions of inanimate objects did not interest him unless they somehow expressed the human element, as for instance his photo of an airplane propeller used as a German pilot's tombstone. He was impassioned, and therefore his photos always had a certain bias, but it was a humane bias. He hated war, never glorified it, and never saw himself as heroic. Despite his saying, "If your photos aren't good enough, you aren't close enough," he never took chances unless the photo demanded it.

Further Reading

Robert Capa's photographs appear in *Images of War* (1964), *The Concerned Photographer* (1968), and *Israel/ The Reality* (1969). The latter two were edited by his brother, Cornell Capa. Robert Capa published several books, including an autobiography, *Slightly Out of Focus* (1947), and a book of photographs for which he wrote the text, *Death in the Making* (1937). These texts should be taken with a grain of salt as a good story was more important to him than the truth. To understand the loyalty Capa inspired in his friends, read the essays in *Robert Capa* (1974) compiled by Cornell Capa. However, to help sort fact from fiction the best source is *Robert Capa* (1985) by Richard Whelan. Whelan, with Cornell Capa, edited *Robert Capa: Photographs* (1985), which includes many photographs before they were cropped by picture editors.

Additional Sources

Whelan, Richard, *Robert Capa: a biography,* Lincoln: University of Nebraska Press, 1994. □

Karel Čapek

The Czech author Karel Čapek (1890-1938) was a noted novelist, playwright, and essayist. He was perhaps the best-known Czech literary figure of the 1920s and 1930s.

Born in northeastern Bohemia on Jan. 9, 1890, Karel Čapek was the son of a physician. He studied philosophy at the Czech University of Prague, where he was influenced in his thinking by Henri Bergson and by modern American philosophy. In 1914 he earned a doctorate. He remained, except for numerous travels abroad, in Prague until the end of his life. In 1935 he married the well-known actress Olga Scheinpflugóva.

Literary Works

Čapek's first creative phase (1908-1921) was marked by close collaboration with his brother, Joseph, who later became a distinguished painter. This period in his writing career culminated in two collections of short stories. The central motif of *Wayside Crosses* (1917) is the mechanism of modern civilization—"Everything that we touch becomes a tool. Even man." The second collection, *Painful Stories* (1921; Eng. trans. *Money and Other Stories*), deals with middle-class life. It is no accident that the decisive role in almost all the stories is played by money. The characters in these books are, for the most part, helpless victims of forces that have overwhelmed them.

In his second phase (1921-1932) Čapek emerged as a dramatist, novelist, journalist, and writer of travel sketches. Some of his comedies as well as his novels from this period are utopian. Best known, especially to American theatergoers, is his visionary play *R. U. R.* (1920), a sharp criticism of capitalism which introduced the word "robot" into the English language. Another comedy of this period, portraying the postwar situation in the world, is the ballet or revue *From the Insect World* (1921), written in collaboration with his brother and translated into English as *The World We Live In.*

During this period Čapek also became prominent as an essayist. His deep humanity and his belief in ordinary man were expressed in an enjoyable book of humorous sketches, *Gardener's Year* (1922). Best known, however, and widely translated were his popular travel books on England, Italy, Spain, Holland, and Scandinavia.

In the collection entitled *Fairy Tales* (1931), a veritable treasure-house of pure storytelling, Čapek revealed his sincere understanding of childhood, his sense of humor, and the light touch characteristic of his fiction during the middle period.

His third and final creative phase (1932-1938) was marked by his highest achievement: a philosophical trilogy of distinguished novels which first appeared in serial form in newspapers between 1932 and 1934. The novels—*Hordubal, Meteor,* and *An Ordinary Life*—center on the problems of truth and reality. Čapek tells the same story from three different points of view, and in this respect he is sometimes compared to such masters of perspective in modern fiction as Henry James and Joseph Conrad.

Between 1934 and 1938 Čapek wrote a biography of Tomáš Masaryk, founder and first president of Czechoslovakia, told as far as possible in Masaryk's own words. The first two volumes of this popular work were translated into English as *President Masaryk Tells His Story* (1934) and *Masaryk's Thought and Life* (1938).

Čapek proved to be a bitter foe of dictatorship, attacking it forcefully in his last works written for the stage: *Power and Glory* (1937; Eng. trans. *The White Scourge*) and his last play, *The Mother,* written under the impact of the Spanish Civil War and the threat of Hitler against Čapek's own country. A few weeks after the occupation of Czechoslovakia, Čapek died in Prague on Dec. 25, 1938.

Further Reading

Two monographs on Čapek are available in English: William Edward Harkins, *Karel Čapek* (1962), a critical study; and

Alexander Matuška, *Karel Čapek: An Essay* (1964; trans. 1964), a biographical and critical survey.

Additional Sources

Zador, Andras, *Karel Čapek,* Budapest: Gondolat, 1984. □

Al Capone

Al "Scarface" Capone (1899-1947) was a notorious American gangster of the prohibition era. His career illustrated the power and influence of organized crime in the United States.

Al Capone, whose real name was Alphonso Caponi, was born to Italian immigrant parents on Jan. 17, 1899, in Brooklyn, New York. Like other young Americans from minority backgrounds, Capone was taught that the main purpose of life was to acquire wealth and that the United States was a land of opportunity. But he also discovered that his family background made it impossible to succeed in school and his ethnicity and working-class status resulted in discrimination, both in the business world and socially. Embittered by the gap between the American dream and his own reality, Capone began to engage in illegal activities as a means of achieving success in what he saw as an unjust society.

Capone was a natural leader. He possessed a shrewd business sense, gained the loyalty of those working for him by showing his appreciation for a job well done, and inspired confidence through his sound judgments, diplomacy, and "the diamond-hard nerves of a gambler." He left school at 14, married at 15, and spent the next ten years with the street gangs of his Brooklyn neighborhood. During a barroom brawl, he received a razor cut on his cheek, which gained him the nickname "Scarface."

Finds Success in Chicago

In 1919, the same year the U.S. government ratified the Eighteenth Amendment prohibiting the manufacture, sale, and transport of alcoholic beverages, Capone fled Brooklyn for Chicago to avoid a murder charge. In Chicago he joined the notorious Five Points Gang and quickly moved up its ranks to become the right-hand man of boss Johnny Torrio. After Torrio fled the country, Capone found himself in control of part of the bootleg operation in the city that had sprung up after prohibition. Chicago had voted 6 to 1 against passage of the prohibition amendment, and its citizenry—rich and poor, officials included—felt that liquor deprivation had been unfairly imposed. Capone took advantage of the popular willingness to break the law, and openly plied his trade. As he would tell reporter Damon Runyan, "I make money by supplying a public demand. If I break the law, my customers . . . some of the best people in Chicago, are as guilty as me."

Capone protected his business interests by waging war on rival gangs. During the legendary St. Valentine's Day

massacre in 1929, seven members of a rival gang led by George "Bugsy" Moran were gunned down in a Chicago garage. Other business strategies included bribing public officials, providing a ready market for the illegal home-brewed liquor produced by poor Italian ghetto residents, and becoming a supply source for the "respectable" customers of city speakeasies. Interacting in Chicago society in the manner of a well-to-do businessman rather than a shady racketeer, Capone gained a fabulously profitable bootleg monopoly, as well as the admiration of a large segment of the community, including members of the police and city government. Between 1927 and 1931 he was viewed by many as the de facto ruler of Chicago.

Seen as Common Thug outside Chicago

However, the rest of the country and certain elements in the Windy City regarded Capone as a menace. In the late 1920s President Herbert Hoover ordered his Secretary of the Treasury to find a way to jail Capone, who up until now had managed to evade being implicated in any illegal act. Perhaps more significantly than the efforts of the U.S. Treasury department, Capone's power had by now begun to wane due to both the coming of the Great Depression and the anticipated repeal of prohibition. Bootlegging was becoming less profitable.

After detailed investigations, U.S. Treasury agents were able to arrest Capone for failure to file an income tax return. Forced to defend himself while being tried for vagrancy in Chicago, Capone contradicted some previous testimony regarding his taxes, and he was successfully prosecuted for tax fraud by the federal government. In October 1931 Capone was sentenced to ten years' hard labor, which he served in a penitentiary in Atlanta, Georgia, and on Alcatraz. Because of syphilis Capone's mind and health deteriorated, and his power within the nation's organized crime syndicates ended. Released on parole in 1939, he led a reclusive life at his Florida estate, where he died in 1947.

Further Reading

John Kobler, *Capone* (1971), is the most thorough study of Capone's life. See also Fred D. Pasley, *Al Capone: The Biography of a Self-Made Man* (1930). For information on his life after imprisonment see James A. Johnston, *Alcatraz Island Prison, and the Men Who Live There* (1949). An excellent contemporary description of Capone's career and perhaps still the best analysis of the era is John Landesco, *Organized Crime in Chicago,* pt. 3 of the Illinois Crime Survey (1929). A reliable historical account is John H. Lyle, *The Dry and Lawless Years* (1960). Excellent for a sociological perspective is Kenneth Allsop, *The Bootleggers and Their Era* (1961). □

Truman Capote

Truman Capote (1924–1984) was one the most famous and controversial figures in contemporary American literature. The ornate style and dark psychological themes of his early fiction caused reviewers to categorize him as a Southern Gothic writer. However, other works display a humorous and sentimental tone. As Capote matured, he became a leading practitioner of "New Journalism," popularizing a genre that he called the nonfiction novel.

Because of his celebrity, virtually every aspect of Capote's life became public knowledge, including the details of his troubled childhood. Born in New Orleans, he seldom saw his father, Archulus Persons, and his memories of his mother, Lillie Mae Faulk, mainly involved emotional neglect. When he was four years old his parents divorced, and afterward Lillie Mae boarded her son with various relatives in the South while she began a new life in New York with her second husband, Cuban businessman Joseph Capote. The young Capote lived with elderly relatives in Monroeville, Alabama, and he later recalled the loneliness and boredom he experienced during this time. His unhappiness was assuaged somewhat by his friendships with his great-aunt Sook Faulk, who appears as Cousin Sook in his novellas *A Christmas Memory* and *The Thanksgiving Visitor* (1967), and Harper Lee, a childhood friend who served as the model for Idabel Thompkins in *Other Voices, Other Rooms.* Lee, in turn, paid tribute to Capote by depicting him as the character Dill Harris in her novel, *To Kill a Mockingbird* (1960). When Capote was nine years old, his mother, having failed to conceive a child with her second husband, brought her son to live with them in Manhattan, although she still sent him to the South in the summer.

Capote did poorly in school, causing his parents and teachers to suspect that he was of subnormal intelligence; a series of psychological tests, however, proved that he possessed an I.Q. well above the genius level. To combat his loneliness and sense of displacement, he developed a flamboyant personality that played a significant role in establishing his celebrity status as an adult.

Capote had begun secretly to write at an early age, and rather than attend college after completing high school, he pursued a literary apprenticeship that included various positions at *The New Yorker* and led to important social contacts in New York City. Renowned for his cunning wit and penchant for gossip, Capote later became a popular guest on television talk shows as well as the frequent focus of feature articles. He befriended many members of high society and was as well known for his eccentric, sometimes scandalous behavior as he was for his writings.

Capote's first short stories, published in national magazines when he was seventeen, eventually led to a contract to write his first book, *Other Voices, Other Rooms.* Set in the South, the novel centers on a young man's search for his father and his loss of innocence as he passes into manhood. The work displays many elements of the grotesque: the boy is introduced to the violence of murder and rape, he witnesses a homosexual encounter, and at the novel's end, his failure to initiate a heterosexual relationship with Idabel Thompkins, his tomboy companion, leads him to accept a homosexual arrangement with his elder cousin Randolph, a lecherous transvestite. Each of these sinister scenes is distorted beyond reality, resulting in a surreal, nightmarish quality. Despite occasional critical complaints that the novel lacks reference to the real world, *Other Voices, Other Rooms* achieved immediate notoriety. This success was partly due to its strange, lyrical evocation of life in a small Southern town as well as to the author's frank treatment of his thirteen-year-old protagonist's awakening homosexuality. The book's dust jacket featured a photograph of Capote, who was then twenty-three, reclining on a couch. Many critics and readers found the picture erotically suggestive and inferred that the novel was autobiographical.

Many of Capote's early stories, written when he was in his teens and early twenties, are collected in *A Tree of Night and Other Stories.* These pieces show the influence of such writers as Edgar Allan Poe, Nathaniel Hawthorne, William Faulkner, and Eudora Welty, all of whom are associated to some degree with a Gothic tradition in American literature. Like these authors, as well as the Southern Gothic writers Carson McCullers and Flannery O'Connor, with whom critics most often compare him, Capote filled his stories with grotesque incidents and characters who suffer from mental and physical abnormalities. Yet Capote did not always use the South as a setting, and the Gothic elements in some of the tales are offset by Capote's humorous tone in others. Critics often place his early fiction into two categories: light and sinister stories. In the former category are "My Side of the Matter," "Jug of Silver," and "Children on Their Birthdays." Written in an engaging conversational style, these narratives report the amusing activities of eccentric characters. More common among Capote's early fiction, however, are the sinister stories, such as "Miriam," "A Tree of Night," "The Headless Hawk," and "Shut a Final Door." These are heavily symbolic fables that portray characters in nightmarish situations, threatened by evil forces. Frequently in these tales evil is personified as a sinister man, such as the Wizard Man feared by the heroine in "A Tree of Night" or the dream-buyer in "Master Misery." In other instances evil appears as a weird personage who represents the darker, hidden side of the protagonist. The ghostly little girl who haunts an older woman in "Miriam" is the best-known example of this doubling device in Capote's fiction. In later years Capote commented that the Gothic eeriness of these stories reflected the anxiety and feelings of insecurity he experienced as a child.

In *The Grass Harp* (1951), Capote drew on his childhood to create a lyrical, often humorous novel focusing on Collin Fenwick, an eleven-year-old boy who is sent to live in a small Southern town with his father's elderly cousins, Verena and Dolly Talbo. At sixteen years of age, Collin allies himself with the sensitive Dolly and other outcasts from the area by means of an idyllic withdrawal into a tree fort. There, the group achieves solidarity and affirms the value of individuality by comically repelling the onslaughts of the ruthless Verena and other figures of authority. The novel, which achieved moderate success, is generally considered to offer a broader, less subjective view of society and the outer world than Capote's earlier fiction, and was adapted as a Broadway drama in 1952. A light and humorous tone is also evident in such works as the novella *Breakfast at Tiffany's* and the three stories published in the same volume, "House of Flowers," "A Diamond Guitar," and *A Christmas Memory. Breakfast at Tiffany's* features Capote's most famous character, Holly Golightly, a beautiful, waif-like young woman living on the fringes of New York society. Golightly, like the prostitute heroine in "House of Flowers," is a childlike person who desires love and a permanent home. This sentimental yearning for security is also evident in the nostalgic novella *A Christmas Memory,* which, like the later *The Thanksgiving Visitor,* dramatizes the loving companionship the young Capote found with his great-aunt Sook.

In some of his works of the 1950s, Capote abandoned the lush style of his early writings for a more austere approach, turning his attention away from traditional fiction. *Local Color* (1950) is a collection of pieces recounting his impressions and experiences while in Europe, and *The Muses Are Heard: An Account* (1956) contains essays written while traveling in Russia with a touring company of *Porgy and Bess.* From these projects Capote developed the idea of creating a work that would combine fact and fiction. The result was *In Cold Blood,* which, according to Capote, signaled "a serious new art form: the 'nonfiction novel,' as I thought of it." Upon publication, *In Cold Blood* elicited among the most extensive critical interest in publishing history. Although several commentators accused Capote of opportunism and of concealing his inability to produce imaginative fiction by working with ready-made material, most responded with overwhelmingly positive reviews. Originally serialized in *The New Yorker* and published in book form in 1965 following nearly six years of research and advance publicity, this book chronicles the murder of Kansas farmer Herbert W. Clutter and his family, who were bound, gagged, robbed, and shot by two ex-convicts in November, 1959. In addition to garnering Capote an Edgar Award from the Mystery Writers of America, *In Cold Blood* became a bestseller and generated several million dollars in royalties and profits related to serialization, paperback, and film rights. Written in an objective and highly innovative prose style that combines the factual accuracy of journalism with the emotive impact of fiction, *In Cold Blood* is particularly noted for Capote's subtle insights into the ambiguities of the American legal system and of capital punishment.

In the late 1960s, Capote began to suffer from writer's block, a frustrating condition that severely curtailed his creative output. Throughout this period he claimed to be working on *Answered Prayers,* a gossip-filled chronicle of the Jet Set that he promised would be his masterpiece. He reported that part of his trouble in completing the project was dissatisfaction with his technique and that he spent most of his time revising or discarding work in progress. During the mid-1970s he attempted to stimulate his creative energies and to belie critics' accusations that he had lost his talent by publishing several chapters of *Answered Prayers* in the magazine *Esquire.* Most critics found the chapters disappointing. More devastating to Capote, however, were the reactions of his society friends, most of whom felt betrayed by his revelations of the intimate details of their lives and refused to have any more contact with him. In addition, Capote's final collection of short prose pieces, *Music for Chameleons* (1983), was less than warmly received by critics. Afterward, Capote succumbed to alcoholism, drug addiction, and poor health, and he died in 1984, shortly before his sixtieth birthday. According to his friends and editors, the only portions of *Answered Prayers* he had managed to complete were those that had appeared in *Esquire* several years previously.

Critical assessment of Capote's career is highly divided, both in terms of individual works and his overall contribution to literature. In an early review Paul Levine described Capote as a "definitely minor figure in contemporary literature whose reputation has been built less on a facility of style than on an excellent advertising campaign." Ihab Hassan, however, claimed that "whatever the faults of Capote may be, it is certain that his work possesses more range and energy than his detractors allow." Although sometimes faulted for precocious, fanciful plots and for overwriting, Capote is widely praised for his storytelling abilities and the quality of his prose.

Further Reading

Dictionary of Literary Biography Yearbook: 1984, Gale, 1985.
Chicago Tribune, August 27, 1984.
Los Angeles Times, August 26, 1984.
Newsweek, September 3, 1984.
New York Times, August 27, 1984.
Publishers Weekly, September 7, 1984.
Time, September 3, 1984, September 7, 1988.
Times (London), August 27, 1984.
Washington Post, August 17, 1984.
Brinnin, John Malcolm, *Truman Capote: Deat Heart, Old Buddy,* Delacourte Press, 1986.
Clarke, Gerald, *Capote: A Biography,* Simon & Schuster, 1986.
Contemporary Literary Criticism, Gale, Volume 1, 1973, Volume 3, 1975, Volume 8, 1978, Volume 13, 1980, Volume 14, 1981, Volume 34, 1986, Volume 38, 1986, Volume 58, 1990.
Dictionary of Literary Biography, Volume 2, *American Novelists Since World War II,* Gale, 1978.
Dictionary of Literary Biography Yearbook: 1980, Gale, 1981.
Grobel, Lawrence, *Conversations with Capote,* New American Library, 1985.
Hallowell, John, *Between Fact and Fiction: New Journalism and the Nonfiction Novel,* University of North Carolina Press, 1977. □

Al Capp

Creator of "Li'l Abner," one of the most popular comic strips of all time, Al Capp (1909-1979) was also a satirist of remarkable talent.

Capp was born Alfred Gerald Caplin in New Haven, Connecticut, on September 28, 1909. Twelve years later he lost most of his right leg in a streetcar accident, an event which did not interrupt his progress as a student of drawing—self-taught in his early days. Capp married Catherine Wingate Cameron in 1929 while he was wending his way through a chain of art schools. After working for other cartoonists, Capp launched his own strip in 1934, succeeding on his first try. "Li'l Abner" was carried by only eight newspapers at the outset but soon became wildly popular. Before long it was giving Capp a yearly income of 150,000 solid gold depression-era dollars.

Set in the mythical hillbilly village of Dogpatch, with excursions to such places as Lower Slobbovia, "Li'l Abner" chronicled the adventures of a 19-year-old male of limited intelligence but much brawn who was relentlessly pursued by the beauteous Daisy Mae. Thanks to reader demand she caught up with him in 1952, when they were finally married. Other celebrated characters in the strip included Hairless Joe; Lonesome Polecat, distiller of the infamous "Kickapoo Joy Juice"; seductive Moonbeam McSwine; and the piteous Joe Btfsplk, whose life was lived beneath a cloud that perpetually rained down misfortune. Another creation, Evil-Eye Fleegle, possessed the dreaded triple whammy, a phrase that passed into the language. Perhaps his most unusual character was the shmoo, a ham-shaped but lovable herbivore that regularly fell dead at the feet of human beings, oven-ready and delectable. Sadie Hawkins Day (when women asked men for dates), an important event in the Dogpatch calendar, was observed not only in Capp's strip but at thousands of high schools and colleges.

Many Capp characters were loosely based on well-known personalities. Marryin' Sam bore some resemblance to New York City Mayor Fiorello LaGuardia. One Fault Jones reminded readers of President Herbert Hoover. By the 1950s, when Capp's strip reached its apex, even the names were similar. The columnist Drew Pearson was mocked as Drusilla Pearson. Secretary of State John Foster Dulles was immortalized as John Foster Dullnik. Capp's great popular-

ity in the 1950s owed much to his deft social and political satire. Liberals particularly relished his sendups of Eisenhower appointees and his cartoon war against McCarthyism. Everyone who read the "funnies" delighted in his parodies of other comics, the most famous being his strip within a strip, "Fearless Fosdick," inspired by Chester Gould's "Dick Tracy."

Capp's strip generated many by-products, as "Li'l Abner" became a motion picture in 1940 and a Broadway musical comedy hit in 1957. It was followed by a film of the musical comedy in 1959. There were also numerous published collections of his work. Together with the strip itself, which was carried by more than 900 newspapers at the height of his reputation, Capp's ventures earned him more than half a million dollars annually.

During the 1960s Capp became blatantly conservative. He also began to take himself more seriously—too seriously many thought—as a champion of traditional values. Senator Phogbound gave way to Joanie Phoanie—a character based on the liberal folk singer Joan Baez—while such organizations as Students for a Democratic Society were lampooned as S.W.I.N.E., Students Wildly Indignant about Nearly Everything. Although the number of papers carrying his strip declined as a result, Capp developed a second career as, oddly enough, a speaker at college campuses. Student organizations were willing to pay his very high fee (for the times) of $3,000 despite, or because of, the verbal abuse with which he showered them.

"The more I see of students," he once remarked, "the more I dislike them." He compared students to Nazi Brownshirts and attributed the spread of campus disorders to official leniency. When students "rip up one campus and all that happens is that their right to use the ice-cream bar machine is revoked for one hour, what do you expect?" Yet he appeared to enjoy these encounters, during which students would jeer while he delivered such observations as: "A concerned student is one who smashes the computer at a university, and an apathetic student is one who spends four years learning how to repair that computer." When asked if marijuana should be legalized, Capp said, "by all means. Also murder, rape and arson—then we could do away with all crime."

After four students at Kent State University were killed by a National Guard unit during a 1970 demonstration Capp expressed sympathy for the guardsman. At the same time, in an apparent effort to justify his view, he noted that the only students who were afraid to appear at their own college graduations were David and Julie Nixon Eisenhower.

In 1971 the fun came to an end when Capp pled guilty to the charge of attempted adultery when a woman student accused him of propositioning her. He subsequently gave up the talk-show and campus lecture circuits, becoming something of a recluse. Six years later he gave up "Li'l Abner" as well, explaining that for several years he had been losing his edge. "Oh hell, it's like a fighter retiring. I stayed on longer than I should have." He died on November 5, 1979, at the age of 70.

Whether he was a patriot or a betrayer of liberal principles, Al Capp deserves to be remembered not for his politics but, in the words of one news magazine, as "the Mark Twain of cartoonists."

Further Reading

Capp's memoirs, *My Well Balanced Life on a Wooden Leg,* was published in 1991, 12 years after his death. Obituaries appeared in *The New York Times* on November 6, 1979, and in *TIME* magazine's issue of November 19, 1979. *TIME* published an overview of his career at the time of his retirement in its issue of October 17, 1977.

Additional Sources

Caplin, Elliot, *Al Capp remembered,* Bowling Green, OH: Bowling Green State University Popular Press, 1994.

Capp, Al, *My well-balanced life on a wooden leg: memoirs,* Santa Barbara, Calif.: John Daniel, 1991. □

Frank Capra

Filmmaker Frank Capra (1897–1991) was 1930s Hollywood's top director, creating several immensely popular movies that captured the mood of the Depression-era United States and earning more Academy Award nominations than any of his contemporaries.

"Capracorn" is the term some use to describe Frank Capra's style of movie-making, but even if his films feel too sentimental to many critics and moviegoers, there is no denying the mastery he had of the film medium or that he developed a style uniquely his own. In the 1930s, he was the top director in Hollywood, turning out a series of films that touched the hopes and fears of the nation as it struggled through the Great Depression and, in the process, Capra garnered more Oscar nominations for himself and his pictures than any other filmmaker of the decade.

Stumbled Into Film Career

The youngest child in a large Sicilian family, Frank was six years old when his family joined the stream of European immigrants coming to the United States. Ending up in Los Angeles, he fought to go to college against his parents wishes; and he always looked back on his decision to attend the California Institute of Technology as one of the most important of his life. After serving stateside in the army, he had trouble finding well paying work, despite the being the only college-educated kid in a family that was otherwise fully employed. He was bumming around San Francisco when he answered an advertisement placed in the paper by an old Shakespearean actor looking for a director to shoot him in screen versions of his favorite poetry.

Capra turned out films based on poems such as Rudyard Kipling's "Fultah Fisher's Boarding House" and

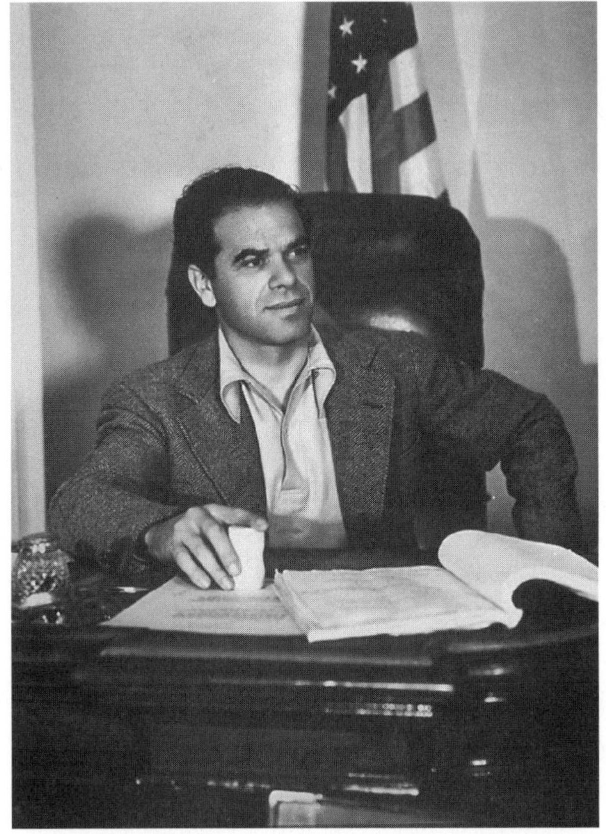

then sold them to the regular studios for a profit. After a series of these, Capra went to work for Harry Cohn who ran a small company called CBC that would grow into Columbia Pictures. For a while, Capra also worked in comedy, most notably with Harry Langdon, a silent clown usually placed fourth in the pantheon of great silent comedians after Buster Keaton, Charlie Chaplin, and Harold Lloyd. It was with Langdon that Capra made his first feature films, *Tramp, Tramp, Tramp, The Strong Man,* and *Long Pants.* All were successful, but Langdon wanted to direct his own movies, and he fired Capra. Langdon's career went into decline, and Capra went back to work for Harry Cohn at Columbia.

He turned out a series of action movies that did not really yet bear the Capra personal touches, but the films were well made and tended to do very well at the box office. It was in this period that Capra made his first "talkie," *The Younger Generation.* In 1930, Capra began working with a writer named Jo Swerling after Swerling attacked one of his scripts in front of Harry Cohn. Impressed with Swerling's criticisms, Capra asked Cohn to hire the New York writer. Swerling was an important influence on Capra, and their first film together, *Ladies of Leisure,* starred Barbara Stanwyck and showed Capra finding his distinctive voice.

Won Oscars

Although both Swerling and Stanwyck became regulars in the Capra stable, Capra's breakthrough project was written with another writer, Robert Riskin. *It Happened One Night* won the Best Picture Oscar and Oscars for Capra as director—one of three he would win, all in that decade—and for both of its leads, Clark Gable and Claudette Colbert. One of the most famous scenes takes place on a broken down bus in which the riders, to entertain themselves, begin singing together the old song, "The Daring Young Man on the Flying Trapeze." It is vintage Frank Capra material, offering a vision of a world in which social distinctions are broken down and a democratic camaraderie holds sway across class lines.

His next big film, *Mr. Deeds Goes to Town,* which won Capra another Oscar for Best Director, was also written by Robert Riskin. In it, Capra's belief in the goodness of the common man—as opposed to the greed of businessmen and the corruption of politicians—came even more to the fore. When Mr. Deeds becomes wealthy through an inheritance, he decides to give a significant part of his fortune to the poor. This leads his family to try to have him declared insane. At his trial, Mr. Deeds, played by Gary Cooper, refuses to speak in his own defense until his own faith in the goodness of humanity is restored. Of course as his faith is restored, so is the audience's; the film ends happily.

The next year he made *Lost Horizon,* a film that some critics say reveals some fascistic tendencies under his populism. In 1938, he turned a popular Kaufmann-Hart play, *You Can't Take It With You,* into a film very personal to himself. Picking up his third Oscar for Direction, he told the story of the love of a common, if eccentric, woman (Jean Arthur) saving the soul of a millionaire's son (Jimmy Stewart). It was Capra's first film with Stewart.

The next year they would make *Mr. Smith Goes to Washington.* It is the perfect expression of Capra's political belief that the innocent idealism of one man can beat the entrenched moneyed interests of cynical politicians and industrialists, even when the have a corrupt media on their side. The film culminates in the hero's 23-hour filibuster on the floor of the Senate where he refuses to be licked. The fact that no real political progress has been made by the film's happy conclusion seems to have occurred to Capra too. At one point, Mr. Smith admits that "the only causes worth fighting for are lost causes." Stewart was perfect in the title role.

World War II Intervened

With Jimmy Stewart, even more than with Gary Cooper, Capra found the actor capable of bearing the burden of Capra's exalted vision of the common man as hero in a bad situation. As Charles Affron has written in the *International Dictionary of Films and Filmmakers,* "In James Stewart, Capra finds his most disquieting voice, ranging in *Mr. Smith* from ingenuousness to hysterical desperation, and in *It's a Wonderful Life,* to an even higher pitch of hysteria when the hero loses his identity." A good case can be made that the change in America's self-image caused by the Second World War can be seen in the change in Jimmy Stewart's self-image in these two films. Mr. Smith in the end manages to maintain his idealism, but George Bailey of *It's a Wonderful Life,* goes through a much darker metamorphosis with a tacked-on happy ending. Capra's last film before the United States entered the war was *Meet John Doe,* starring Gary Cooper. As the editors of *World Film Directors* have written,

"*Meet John Doe,* made at the end of the isolationist period when war with the axis seemed imminent, has been taken as a deliberate reaffirmation of American values, but one that reveals a surprising uncertainty about their survival and perhaps even about their nature."

During the Second World War, Capra entered the armed services and made propaganda films for the Allies. Winston Churchill was a particular fan of Capra's propaganda films, considering them the finest made on the Allied side. After the War, Capra started his own film company, Liberty Films Inc., and made *It's a Wonderful Life,* the story of an extraordinary but profoundly discouraged man who around Christmas is allowed to see what the world would have been like if he had never been born. A sort of modern day *Christmas Carol,* the film would become one of the classics of the American screen; but on its release, it was not a success. His next film, the Spencer Tracy-Katherine Hepburn vehicle, *State of the Union* was a mean-spirited and confused political picture that did nothing to bolster Capra's sagging reputation.

He made only five more films, and none could be called an artistic success of the quality of his depression era films or of *It's a Wonderful Life.* He made his last film, *Pocketful of Miracles,* featuring a fine Bette Davis performance in 1961. It was another box office disappointment, and he would live another 30 years without going behind the camera again. In 1971, he published his autobiography, *The Name Above the Title,* which has remained one of the better selling movie industry reminiscences.

Although he does not have a critical reputation approaching John Ford's, Howard Hawk's or Orson Welles's , Frank Capra's best films are still popular with audiences; and if his vision of America is much simpler than John Ford's, perhaps just for that reason, it has remained especially popular with the young people who gravitate toward Capra's idealistic, non-materialistic heroes. In the end, it was probably the simplicity of his vision—wedded to a complex mastery of the film form itself—which has made him so enduringly popular. If the Second World War marked the point when his filmmaking went into decline—*It's a Wonderful Life,* not withstanding—it was probably because the naïveté of his world view could not live on long in the complex political realities of the Cold War.

Further Reading

Thomas, Nicholas, and Charles Affron, eds., *International Dictionary of Films and Filmmakers,* Vol. 2, No. 2, St. James Press, 1991, pp. 113-116. □

Jennifer Capriati

In March of 1990, Jennifer Capriati (born 1976) turned pro on the cutthroat women's professional tennis circuit.

"Even though I'm going to be playing older ladies, when I'm out there playing, I'm as old as they are," she told the *New York Times.* "I have no fear. I guess I was just born with that kind of mind." And that kind of talent.

Capriati, the youngest tennis player ever to turn pro, was met with overwhelming expectations from both the tennis world, the public, and the media upon her debut at the Virginia Slims tournament in Boca Raton, Florida. The pressure was not just for her potential in tennis, but for her potential as the best charismatic draw for the U.S. women's circuit since Chris Evert.

The question is whether or not Jennifer Capriati is capable of living through this. She seems more likely to stumble down the path of former tennis pros like Jimmy Arias, Andrea Jaeger, and Tracy Austin. There is a reason why that path is becoming somewhat of a cliché. Capriati's short life in this pressure cooker is one explanation.

Headlines trumpeted Capriati as the "Teen Queen of Tennis," "Eighth Grade Wonder," and "The Next Chris Evert." Her own coach, Tom Gullikson of the U.S. Tennis Association, said flatly to a *Los Angeles Times* reporter, "It's our viewpoint that [Capriati] is without question the most talented young pro in the world, man or woman." Interviewers scrounged for details of her life—she was five-foot-seven, 130 pounds, shoe size 8 1/2. Her favorite rap song: "Bust A Move." Favorite foods: hamburgers, chips, hot fudge sundaes. Favorite movie star: Johnny Depp. Favorite color: pink. Favorite pet: the family Shih Tzu, Bianca.

Meanwhile, Capriati just hoped she wouldn't look "dorky" on television, and she told the *Los Angeles Times* she'd like to be remembered this way: "I'd like, you know, when I retire, like, you know, when I go down the street, people would say, 'There's Jennifer Capriati, the greatest tennis player who ever lived.'" The concept of a young, pretty teenager who could sigh over Twizzlers licorice, white leather mini skirts, and the baby on the TV show, *The Simpsons,* while also blasting her way to the top of the tennis circuit, ignited thousands of new Capriati fans. One magazine writer wondered whether people wanted to see history in the making or really just had a weird fascination with seeing a player who might be a flash in the pan, used up, and burnt out by age 21. But those apprehensions were at first blotted out by the sheer talent and exuberance of Capriati's early play. In her first match she knocked off four seeded players and advanced to the finals before being beaten by Argentina's Gabriela Sabatini on March 11. With every later tournament, she showed her raw, powerful talent with booming ground strokes, a 94 m.p.h. overhead serve, and cool nerves that belied her young age.

In April, she reached the finals of the Family Circle Magazine Hilton Head Cup, finally losing to Martina Navratilova. Capriati was delighted, still, just to be there; she called Navratilova "a lege, you know, like, a legend." In June, seeded No. 17, she reached the quarterfinals of the French Open before she was beaten by No. 1 Monica Seles of Yugoslavia. In July she made it to the quarterfinals of Wimbledon, ranked No. 12, before losing to Germany's Steffi Graff. On July 16, she won her first professional title, at the Mount Cranmore International tournament in New Hampshire. In August, she was defeated in the early rounds at the U.S. Open, where she was ranked 16th. In September, as sixth seed, she made it to the quarterfinals of the Nichirei International Tennis Championship in Tokyo.

Though she didn't win any big matches, many believed Capriati had set the stage for her advancement to the pinnacle of women's tennis. It was a climb she was groomed for from infancy. Jennifer Capriati was born in 1976 on Long Island, New York, to Stefano and Denise Capriati. Her Bronx-born mother, who is a Pan Am flight attendant, met her father in Spain in 1972. Stefano Capriati, a native of Milan, Italy, was a resident of Spain, where he was a movie stuntman and a self-taught tennis pro. They married and settled in Spain. Stefano Capriati knew Jennifer would be a tennis player when she was still in the womb, says Denise Capriati, who played recreational tennis until the day she went into labor with Jennifer. "Stefano knew she would be a tennis player . . . just by the way I carried her," she told *Sports Illustrated.* They moved to New York so Jennifer could be born in the United States, then moved back to Spain. Another child, Steven, was born three years later.

When Jennifer was a baby, her father did cribside calisthenics, propping her backside with a pillow and helping her do situps. When she was four years old, the family moved to Fort Lauderdale, Florida, to further Jennifer's tennis. By then, she could hold her own with a ball machine. "Already she could rally a hundred times on the court," her father said. He took her to see Jimmy Evert, tennis star Chris Evert's father. Evert did not even want to meet her since she was only four, but when he saw her skill he agreed to take her as a student. He coached her from age four to age nine. Along the way, Jennifer became friends with Chris Evert. In 1987, the tennis star gave Jennifer a Christmas bracelet that reads, "Jennifer, Love Chris" that Jennifer wears in all her matches.

From age ten to 13, Jennifer was coached by Rick Macci in Haines City, Florida, then went to the Hopman Tennis Academy at Saddlebrook resort in Wesley Chapel, where she got a third coach, Tom Gullickson. But the driving force in her budding career was her father, whom she called her main coach and whom the other members of her entourage called "the main boss." Stefano Capriati considers himself a tennis father, in the best sense of the term, noting that there is a difference between pushing and aiding. "You try to direct her in the right way, and you see she has the potential," he told the *Los Angeles Times.* "I see she enjoys it. After 9-10 years old, you cannot direct them anymore. They must want it."

As a junior tennis player, Jennifer wanted it. She relished the competition. In 1988 at age 12, she won the U.S. 18-and-under championships on both hard and clay courts. In 1989 she won the 18-and-under French Open, made the quarterfinals at Wimbledon, and won the junior title at the U.S. Open. The rules said girls under 14 could not turn pro, but in 1989, her father, coaches, and tennis boosters thought she was ready. "People say she's only 13, but they miss the point. She's already put in 10 years," said tennis legend Billie Jean King, Jennifer's periodic doubles partner. "I'm telling you," said her former coach, Rick Macci, in *Sports Illustrated.* "She's scary."

However, the United States Tennis Federation was stubborn. It would not allow Jennifer to play until the month of her 14th birthday. Her father thought about challenging the rule in court, then changed his mind. Already, Jennifer Capriati was getting lucrative endorsement contracts. The Italian sportswear maker Diadora of Caerano Di San Marco gave her $3 million to endorse their line and Prince gave her $1 million to endorse their tennis rackets. Later in the year, she made a commercial for Oil of Olay face cream. "First, immortality, then the SATs," joked *Newsweek.* But it was no joke: before even turning pro, Capriati was the third highest endorsed tennis player behind Chris Evert and Martina Navratilova. John Evert, Chris Evert's brother, became Capriati's business manager.

Turns Pro

In between the relentless pace of tennis, Jennifer Capriati went through eighth grade at Palmer Academy in Wesley Chapel. When she couldn't go to school, she'd take her homework with her or have it sent to her on the road by fax machine. By March when she went pro, she still had to do homework in between matches. In September she started ninth grade at St. Andrew's School in Boca Raton, a 600-student private school. She was prepared to leave the Harry Hopman tennis facility of Saddlebrook and was offered a contract as touring pro at the Broken Sound Club in Boca

Raton. But later that month, her parents changed their minds.

Uncomfortable in a temporary home in Boca Raton, the Capriatis went back to Saddlebrook and Jennifer returned to the Palmer Academy, where she had attended eighth grade. The family intended to move to Broken Sound in January, then realized it would be better to remain at Saddlebrook. "There is life besides tennis," said Denise Capriati. "Jennifer was so happy to see her friends again. Jennifer's emotional happiness is the bottom line."

Also in September of 1990, ranked 12th in the world, Jennifer traveled to Tokyo for the Nichirei tennis championship. The remainder of the year she planned to do an exhibition match for former first lady Nancy Reagan, one for Chris Evert, and then hoped to make the Virginia Slims Championships in New York in November. The pace was grueling, but her spirits were high. "I feel like a kid, kidwise. But tenniswise, I feel I guess I have talent, I guess," she told the *Los Angeles Times*. "When I'm on the court, I just block out everything I'm thinking about and bring out my tennis stuff. When I'm off, I'm just a kid."

Her tennis stuff continued to wow observers. One coach praised her aggressive style, unpredictability, and power: "She was strong before, but her movement wasn't very good. Now she covers the court as well as any of the men I can think of," said Tommy Thompson, head tennis pro at Saddlebrook, to the *New York Times*. "She's going to be different than most women, who tend to play very defensively, because she's very confident at net. She has no fear when she's going in there to volley. Thompson said later in the *Washington Post,* "She's a kid off the court but a killer on it."

Whether the kid can continue life as a killer on the court without becoming overwhelmed is the question many had as her first six months on the circuit ended. While Capriati appeared to have a solid head on her shoulders, there were the inevitable comparisons with Andrea Jaeger and Tracy Austin, both of whom started tennis as young sensations but burned out from injuries and pressure. Jaeger won her first pro tournament at 14 but left the tour at 19 because of shoulder injuries. Austin, at 16, was the youngest player ever to win the U.S. Open, in 1979, but foot and back injuries sidelined her permanently at age 19. When asked about this by interviewers, Capriati sighs and replies wearily. "It's like, you know, it's not my fault," she says of Jaeger's and Austin's short-lived careers in the *Los Angeles Times*. "Why does everybody think it's going to happen to me? How do they know what my limit is?"

As time went on, she started to learn her limit. In 1991, Capriati peaked. She ranked in the Top 10 (No. 6) after reaching the finals of the U.S. Open and Wimbledon. In 1992, she won the gold medal in the Olympics at Barcelona, but no other tournaments. In September, after losing in the first round of the U.S. Open, Capriati returned to Florida from the tour to recover from bone chips and tendinitis in her elbow. In November, she moved out of her parents' home to an apartment. She later announced in January of 1993 that she was taking a leave from the tour to complete high school. In March, she dropped out of high school and moved to Boca Raton.

Enters Rehab

In May of 1994, Capriati was arrested in Coral Gables, Florida for possession of marijuana. According to *People* magazine, the arrest followed a weekend of serious partying with other teenagers. One of the teens, Thomas Wineland, was booked for possession of suspected crack cocaine and drug paraphernalia. He later claimed that he and Capriati smoked crack for a couple of hours, then smoked reefers, took painkillers, and drank. Two days after the arrest, Capriati started a drug rehabilitation program at Mount Sinai Medical Center in Miami Beach.

A flurry of criticism and "I told you so" articles followed from the media. Mike Lupica of *The Sporting News* wrote an article reflecting the thoughts of those who know Capriati. He had plenty of negative things to say about Stefano Capriati and the Capriati entourage. He wrote, "The short-term marketing was brilliant. The short-term thinking was stupid and greedy." *Tennis* magazine commented, " . . . the women's tour kept changing its rules to make sure Capriati played as often as possible. They were called by many 'The Capriati Rules.' Four years later, suddenly very concerned about little girls playing tennis for a living, the same group passed rules limiting play for teenagers. They also should have been called 'The Capriati Rules.'"

Capriati did come back and play one match in November 1994—losing to Anke Huber in Philadelphia. She then remained absent from tennis until February 1996. She won two matches in the Faber Grand Prix in Germany, finally losing in the quarterfinals. Anne Person Worcester, The Corel WTA Tour's chief executive officer, told *Tennis* magazine, "The hardest part about coming back for her is not the tennis, not the other players, not the fans; it's the media." Worcester believes that only Capriati's drug arrest, not her accomplishments will be highlighted in everything written about her. *Tennis* magazine suggested that Capriati will have to find the right support group to accompany her on the tour to keep the pressure at bay. Stefano Capriati, now divorced from Jennifer's mother, Denise, traveled with Jennifer to Germany, but insisted that he was not pushing her. He told *Tennis,* "She will decide what it is she wants. Whatever she will decide, I will give. Whatever she needs, I give."

Capriati lost in the first round of the French Open in May 1996. *The Sporting News* reported that five days later, she had another brush with the law. Capriati was at a nightclub in Miami with her boyfriend. Police said she got into an argument with him and tried to punch him. Her boyfriend ducked, and Capriati accidentally hit a waitress. Club security turned her over to the police. The state attorney will determine if charges will be filed.

In late June, Capriati decided not to play Wimbledon—one of the biggest tournaments of the year. She withdrew due to lack of preparation, according to her spokesperson. Also, Capriati will not be able to defend her Barcelona Olympic gold medal in Atlanta because her current ranking of 104 is too low. The women's coach, Billie Jean King, commented to *The Sporting News,* "I've told Jennifer all along, 'You've got no chance.'"

At 20 years old, Jennifer Capriati had won more tournaments and made more money in two years than most professional tennis players do in an entire career. Her success has also provided her with many options: she could take her money and pay for college and forget tennis; she could halfheartedly play a few tournaments a year, eventually leaving tennis; or she could come back and play tennis with everything she can muster because *she* wants it. Her true fans can only hope that she finds the courage and support she needs to live a normal life.

Further Reading

Detroit Free Press, June 6, 1990; June 8, 1990; June 30, 1990; July 3, 1990; July 16, 1990; August 31, 1990; September 4, 1990; September 14, 1990.

Fort Lauderdale News and Sun-Sentinel, September 16, 1990; September 25, 1990.

Los Angeles Times, May 27, 1990.

Newsweek, May 14, 1990.

New York Times, March 5, 1990; May 20, 1990.

People, May 30, 1994.

Sports Illustrated, February 26, 1990; March 19, 1990; April 16, 1990.

Tennis, January, 1996; May, 1996.

The Sporting News, February 7, 1994; June 5, 1996; June 19, 1996.

Time, March 26, 1990. □

Caracalla

Caracalla (188-217) was a Roman emperor whose reign was characterized by cruelty in his private life and irresponsibility in his public life.

Son of Emperor Septimius Severus and his Syrian empress, Julia Domna, Caracalla was originally named Bassianus. His father renamed him Marcus Aurelius Antoninus in 196 (Severus pretended to have been adopted into the prestigious Antonine family of emperors), but the boy was commonly called Caracalla from a Gallic cloak he affected.

Caracalla was named caesar (successor-designate) by his father in 196 during Severus's struggle with his rival, Albinus. Two years later Caracalla was promoted to the rank of augustus, or coemperor. His younger brother, Geta, received the same rank in 209. Both boys were with their father in Britain when he died in 211, leaving them corulers of the empire. Caracalla straightway returned to Rome, where the long-standing animosity between the brothers led Caracalla in 212 to assassinate Geta as he cowered in his mother's arms. Those that indicated disapproval were executed, but Caracalla secured the loyalty of the troops by a donative and raise in pay.

Caracalla fancied himself a military genius, the reincarnation of Alexander the Great. In 213 he led an expedition against the Germanic Alamanni, who threatened the northern frontiers. He defeated some and bought off others, while completing permanent fortifications in the area. In 214 he campaigned on the Danube. Meanwhile, he raised a phalanx of Macedonian troops so that he could proceed on an expedition to the East, in perfect emulation of his great hero, Alexander.

Caracalla reached Antioch in Syria in 215. But his ambition to create a Romano-Iranian empire was at first thwarted by the reluctance of the Parthian king to quarrel. Caracalla thereupon made a trip to Alexandria, where, in his resentment at the citizens' traditional liberty of speech, he assembled the city's youth and had them massacred by the army.

In 216 Caracalla decided to join Rome and Parthia by marriage, if he could not do so by arms, and asked for the hand of the Parthian king's daughter. A refusal was followed by an ineffectual invasion of Media. The Emperor wintered at Edessa and was preparing a more vigorous campaign for the following season when, in the spring of 217, he was assassinated near Carrhae at the instigation of his praetorian prefect and successor, Macrinus, who had information that Caracalla was planning his execution.

Caracalla is best known for the baths he built in Rome, which carry his name, and for an edict in 212/213 which granted full Roman citizenship to nearly all the free inhabitants of the empire, thus fulfilling centuries of legal progress. Some see in this a reflection of Caracalla's ideal of a world state, but ancient authorities found the motivation in in-

creased revenue: only Roman citizens paid an inheritance and manumission tax, and this tax was doubled at this time.

Further Reading

A discussion of Caracalla by S. N. Miller is in S. A. Cook and others, eds., *Cambridge Ancient History,* vol. 12 (1939). See also H. M. D. Parker, *A History of the Roman World from A.D. 138 to 337* (1935; rev. ed. 1958). □

Caravaggio

The Italian painter Caravaggio (1573-1610) depicted insolent boys and rough peasants in the guise of Roman gods and Christian saints. They are often portrayed as if emerging out of darkness, with part of their faces and bodies strongly illuminated.

Michelangelo Merisi is called Caravaggio after the tiny town in Lombardy where he was born on Sept. 8, 1573. His father, Fermo Merisi, who was a master builder for the local lord, died in 1584, and the young boy was apprenticed to Simone Peterzano, a mediocre painter in Milan. Caravaggio's contract with Peterzano ran until April 1588. He probably stayed on in Milan for another year, studying the paintings in his native Lombardy. By about 1590 he was in Rome.

During Caravaggio's first year in Rome he was desperately poor. For a brief period he worked for a certain Pandolfo Pucci, whom he called "Mr. Salad" since he said that was all Pucci ever gave him to eat. We know too that during his first years in Rome Caravaggio worked in the studio of Giuseppe Cavaliere d'Arpino as a painter of fruits and flowers.

Turbulent Life

From 1600 on it is easier to follow Caravaggio's career since his name appears with a certain regularity in the police records. That year he was arrested for a sword fight in which he wounded a captain of the guards at Castel Sant' Angelo. It seems, however, to have been a good-natured contest between two lovers of the sport, and there was a formal reconciliation in court. In 1603 Caravaggio was sued and jailed for libel for writing sarcastic and offensive verses about the painter and writer Giovanni Baglione. Prominent friends, who presumably recognized Caravaggio's great talent, secured his release. In January 1604 he was hailed into court for throwing an artichoke in the face of an insolent waiter, and in November he was jailed for stoning the police.

The police records for Rome of 1605 contain entries regarding a notary called Pasqualone, who reported that he had been wounded by Caravaggio in an argument over a girl named Lena "who stands in Piazza Navona." Following this incident Caravaggio fled to Genoa. But in 3 weeks he was back in Rome, where he and Pasqualone were formally reconciled.

During all these years Caravaggio was painting daring, revolutionary works unlike anything ever seen before. Such paintings naturally aroused a great deal of controversy. Some attacked them as being vulgar and indecent, but a few critics and connoisseurs praised them highly.

In May 1606 Caravaggio was playing tennis with one Ranuccio Tomassoni. There seems to have been an argument over the score, which turned into a brawl and then into a sword fight. Tomassoni was killed, and Caravaggio was badly wounded. Aided by friends, Caravaggio fled Rome. For a brief period he remained near the papal city, hiding in the Sabine Mountains. From there he set out for Naples, then under Spanish rule. By May 1607 his friends were already at work in Rome trying to obtain a pardon so that he could return.

Early in 1608 Caravaggio was on the small Mediterranean island of Malta, then ruled by the Knights of Malta, an aristocratic military order. Because of the portrait he painted of the head of the order, Alof de Wignacourt, Caravaggio was made a knight of Malta, a most unusual honor for a person of his modest background, and received a solid-gold chain and two Turkish slaves. A few months later he was again involved in a sword fight, this time with his superior officer, and was jailed. In some way that is still not explained, Caravaggio escaped from prison.

By Oct. 6, 1608, Caravaggio had reached Syracuse in Sicily. From this point on he was pursued by agents of the Knights of Malta, who sought to avenge what they considered an insult to their order. A hunted man, Caravaggio fled to Messina and then to Palermo. Somehow through it all he continued to paint. By fall 1609 he was back in Naples, where the Maltese agents trapped him and beat him so badly that he was disfigured almost beyond recognition. Reports reaching Rome said that he was dead, but he was still alive.

By summer 1610 a papal pardon appeared imminent. For this reason Caravaggio took a boat to Port'Ercole, a small Spanish outpost just north of Rome, where he was arrested in a case of mistaken identity. The Spaniards released him from jail after a few days, but the boat had sailed and with it, so he thought, the painting he carried with him and all his possessions.

Raging along the shore under the hot July sun, Caravaggio came down with a fever. As Roger Hinks (1953) wrote: "There was no one to care for him and in a few days it was all over. He died, as he had lived, alone. It was July 18, 1610. He had lived thirty-six years, nine months and twenty days, as Marzio Milesi records with the pious exactitude of a devoted friend. Three days later, by a tragic stroke of irony, his pardon arrived."

Revolutionary Paintings

The early works of Caravaggio show him in full revolt against both mannerism and classicism. He rejected the elongations and formal curvilinear shapes of the mannerists and ridiculed the concept of the classicists that the subject of a painting should be idealized and carry a moral message. What Caravaggio shows us in his *Bacchus with a Wine Glass* (ca. 1595) is no Roman god but a pudgy, half-naked boy draped in a bedsheet, who is identified as Bacchus by the vine leaves in his hair.

Sometimes the subject is a scene from everyday life. *The Fortune Teller* (ca. 1595) shows an elegant young dandy with a sword at his side having his palm read by a gypsy girl. He looks away with almost ostentatious boredom as she slips the ring off his finger. As in most of Caravaggio's paintings, the figures are hard, sculptural, and intensely three-dimensional. The realism is reinforced by the great clarity of detail, for instance, the hilt of the young man's sword and the seams of his glove.

Many of the paintings of this period have a momentary quality, as if Caravaggio had isolated a single instance in the midst of flux. In *Boy Bitten by a Lizard* (ca. 1593), for example, a wonderfully affected young man with a small girlish mouth and a rose behind one ear squeals with fright as a lizard comes out from behind a flower and bites him on the finger. In these works and others like them Caravaggio developed a new, totally secular iconography.

When Caravaggio did paint religious subjects, and he often did, he employed an immediacy and directness that has few equals. In the *Calling of St. Matthew* the saint, who was a tax collector in the ancient Roman Empire, is shown in contemporary Italian dress sitting at a table counting money. Around him at the table, as if in a gambling den, are a group of young swordsmen of the kind we associate with Caravaggio. In these years (ca. 1600-1606) Caravaggio's paintings are filled with deep shadows that absorb and conceal parts of the figures. At the same time the figures remain solid and powerfully three-dimensional where the light strikes them. This use of strong dramatic contrasts between light and shade is called tenebrism. In the *Calling* it is especially daring. Christ is far over to the right, almost totally lost in darkness, and all that emerges into the light is part of his face and one beckoning hand. They express his words to Matthew, "Arise, and follow me."

Here and elsewhere Caravaggio makes the scene look as if it is taking place before our very eyes. In his *Crucifixion of St. Peter,* for example, we catch sight of the saint at the moment when the executioners are just beginning to raise up the cross to which he has been nailed upside down. His bare feet are thrust toward us so we can see and almost feel the spikes that cut through them. The aged but powerful apostle lifts his head up from the cross in defiance.

Influence of Counter Reformation

Scenes such as these reflect the drive of the Catholic Counter Reformation to appeal directly to the masses through their emotions. It was chiefly the Jesuits who directed the Counter Reformation. Their founder, St. Ignatius of Loyola, laid great stress on the immediate perception of religious experience in physical terms. This he emphasized repeatedly in his famous, widely read *Spiritual Exercises.* In it, for example, Ignatius urges Catholics to imagine hell and in so doing to use all their senses: to see the flames, to hear the screams, to smell the smoke, to taste the tears, to feel the fires.

Other paintings by Caravaggio are quiet. In the *Madonna of Loreto* (1604) the Virgin, holding the Christ Child, miraculously appears before two peasants who have made a pilgrimage to her shrine. As the old man and woman, their gnarled hands clasped in prayer, kneel before the Virgin, their bare, dirty feet stick out toward the viewer. Again we see the influence of St. Ignatius but, even more, that of St. Philip Neri. While the Jesuits tended to align themselves with the powerful, Philip was especially concerned with the weak. He wished religion to be simple, joyful, easily understood, and expressed in the most common and natural terms. Above all he wanted it to be open to the humble and the poor. Pompousness and lavish display he ridiculed. Philip died in Rome in 1595. During Caravaggio's lifetime the saint's living presence seemed to hang over the city, and it can certainly be felt in Caravaggio's art.

Late Works

In Caravaggio's last works, painted when he was fleeing from one southern Italian town to another, his style changed. The modeling is softer; the paint is thinner and applied more rapidly; and the shadows are less profound. The expressive content is deeper. All this can be seen in the *Resurrection of Lazarus,* painted in 1609 at the very end of the artist's life. In it a small crowd huddles around the dim figure of Christ, which is almost phosphorescent where the light strikes it. The whole upper half of the picture is left dark and empty to serve as a sounding board that reverberates the shadowy moments between death and rebirth.

Though Caravaggio was never truly famous in his own lifetime, many who knew his work realized that they were seeing something amazingly new. His style spread rapidly throughout Europe. Without Caravaggio it is not possible to understand countless artists who followed.

Further Reading

The fullest work on Caravaggio is Walter F. Friedlaender, *Caravaggio Studies* (1955). It is especially valuable for an understanding of Caravaggio in his own era and above all for the influence of St. Philip Neri on his art. A much shorter book, Roger P. Hinks, *Michelangelo Merisi da Caravaggio* (1953), provides the most sensitive interpretation of the expressive content of his painting, especially the late works. The best color plates are in Roberto Longhi, *Il Caravaggio* (1952).

Additional Sources

The Age of Caravaggi, New York: Metropolitan Museum of Art: Electa/Rizzoli, 1985.

Bissell, R. Ward, *Orazio Gentileschi and the poetic tradition in Caravaggesque painting,* University Park: Pennsylvania State University Press, 1981.

Moir, Alfred, *Caravaggio,* New York: H.N. Abrams, 1989. □

Hattie Wyatt Caraway

Elected to the U.S. Senate in early 1931 to complete her late husband's term, Hattie Wyatt Caraway (1878-1950) won election to a full six-year term in 1932 (and again in 1938) to become the first woman elected to the U.S. Senate in her own right.

Hattie Wyatt Caraway was born on February 1, 1878, near Bakersville, Tennessee. When she was four years old, in 1882, her family moved to nearby Hustburg, Tennessee, where Hattie grew up working on the family farm and waiting on customers in her father's general store. A bright girl, she had already learned the alphabet before attending a nearby one-room school-house and entered Dickson (Tennessee) Normal College at the age of 14.

At Dickson she met Thaddeus Horatio Caraway, a fellow student several years older than she. She earned a B.A. degree in 1896. After graduation, Hattie, by now engaged to Thaddeus, set out to teach school. The couple married in 1902, after Thaddeus earned his law degree. They settled in Jonesboro, Arkansas, where Hattie gave birth to two sons, Paul Wyatt and Forrest, and managed the house while her husband established a legal and political career.

Thaddeus Caraway was elected to the United States Congress in 1912. While in Washington, D.C., Hattie gave birth to their third son, Robert Easley. She maintained their home in Washington, raising their children, seldom socializing outside the family, and leaving the business of politics to her husband. A Democrat, Thaddeus was elected to the Senate in 1920. A staunch supporter of his poor-white farm constituency, Thaddeus was reelected in 1926 but suffered a blood clot after kidney stone surgery and died unexpectedly in 1931, not completing his term.

Arkansas law required a special election to elect a senator to complete Caraway's term. In the interim Governor Harvey Parnell appointed Hattie to the post out of respect for her husband. Hattie Caraway entered the 72nd Congress in December 1931 with a commission from the governor to occupy her husband's Senate seat until the special election, called for January 1932.

The Arkansas Democratic Committee, unable to agree on a candidate for the special election, ended up nominating Hattie as a compromise. In Arkansas, part of the Democratic "Solid South," the Democratic nomination assured Hattie's election. Governor Parnell supported her with the understanding that she would step aside and make way for his candidacy in the election of 1932. In these strange circumstances Hattie Caraway became the first woman elected to the Senate. As an historic "first," this shy, quiet, at times awkward, 54-year-old housewife became the subject of enormous publicity. One journalist called her "one of the most visible women in America."

In sharp contrast to her voluble husband, Caraway would sit in the Senate chamber knitting or reading while she listened politely to the endless speeches. Despite her apparent diffidence, she was determined to continue her husband's work, to vote, as he would have, in unswerving support of the interests of the poor farm people now suffering through the deepening Great Depression.

As the deadline approached in Arkansas to announce candidacy for the regular senatorial election in 1932, seven men, including Governor Parnell, prepared to run for

"Fighting Thad" Caraway's Senate seat. They were dumbstruck when, at the very last moment, Hattie's application to run for the Senate arrived in Little Rock by special delivery. One opponent was quoted as saying that out of the estimated 300,000 votes, "she might receive 3,000" from feminists and personal friends.

Hattie found a powerful friend and champion in her neighbor in the Senate, the junior senator from Louisiana, Huey P. Long. Caraway supported Long's proposals for tax reform and redistribution of wealth to the farm poor. She launched her campaign with much fanfare but little success until Long arrived in Arkansas and in one week stumped with her across the state. Caraway visited 31 counties, giving 39 speeches and personally addressing more than 200,000 people. She won the Democratic primary, receiving 44.7 percent of the vote. In November 1932 Hattie Caraway became the first woman elected to a full six-year term in the United States Senate.

With a Democratic president in the White House, Senator Caraway worked devotedly if quietly in support of most of Franklin Roosevelt's New Deal programs. As a member of the Agriculture and Forestry Committee she was well positioned to help her people in Arkansas. "These are matters I know something about," she said. "You can tell by looking at me that I'm a farm woman."

In 1938 she edged out her opponent, whose slogan blatantly proclaimed, "Arkansas needs another man in the Senate," winning her second full term, this time without the aid of Huey Long, who had been assassinated in 1935. Caraway opposed Lend Lease for fear it would lead to war and defended local control against the president's policy to end the poll tax, which had disqualified many African-Americans in Arkansas from voting. But once World War II was declared she did much to help the grieving relatives of war victims and continued as one of Roosevelt's faithful backers.

Caraway lost the Democratic primary in her bid for a third term in 1944, but did not retire from politics. President Roosevelt named her to the Employees Compensation Commission and later to the Employees Compensation Appeals Board. Known forever as the first woman senator, if not for her forceful leadership, Senator Caraway's assessment of women in politics was characteristically simple and to the point. In 1943 she endorsed the Equal Rights Amendment (first introduced two decades earlier) by declaring, "There is no sound reason why women, if they have the time and ability, shouldn't sit with men on city councils, in state legislatures, and on Capitol Hill. Particularly if they have ability!" On December 22, 1950, Hattie Caraway suffered a stroke and died at the age of 72.

Further Reading

For additional information on Hattie Caraway see Hope Chamberlin, *A Minority of Members: Women in the U.S. Congress* (1973); Diane D. Kincaid, ed., *Silent Hattie Speaks, the Personal Journal of Senator Hattie Caraway* (1979); George Creel, "The Woman Who Holds Her Tongue," *Colliers* (September 18, 1937); and Hermann B. Deutsch, "Hattie and Huey," *Saturday Evening Post* (October 15, 1932).

Additional Sources

Caraway, Hattie Wyatt, *Silent Hattie speaks: the personal journal of Senator Hattie Caraway,* Westport, Conn.: Greenwood Press, 1979. □

Geronimo Cardano

The Italian mathematician, astronomer, and physician Geronimo Cardano (1501-1576) initiated the general theory of cubic and quartic equations. He emphasized the need for both negative and complex numbers.

Geronimo Cardano was born in Pavia on Sept. 24, 1501, the illegitimate son of a local jurist, Fazio Cardano. In spite of a boyhood filled with sickness and extreme poverty, he managed to attend the universities of Pavia and Padua, receiving his medical degree from the later in 1524. In 1532 he was appointed to the chair of mathematics in Milan but continued to practice medicine, albeit without much success. In 1536 he gained some notoriety by attacking the then-existing practices of medicine, but this aided rather than hindered him, for 3 years later he was admitted to the College of Physicians and later was appointed rector of the college. In 1543 he was professor of medicine at the University of Pavia.

Mathematical and Other Writings

In 1539 Cardano published two books on arithmetic, which were based on the lectures he had been giving at Milan, and they proved to be among the best mathematical texts of the time. Of more importance, however, was the *Ars magna* (*Artis magnae sive de regulis algebraicis*) of 1545, which was devoted solely to algebra and was the first important printed work on the subject. It was published in Nuremberg and contained the theories of algebraic equations as they were known at that time. Cardano wrote other mathematical works and a book on games of chance which discussed probability theory.

Cardano's most popular work was *De subtilitate rerum* (1550), an encyclopedia of physical inventions and experiments. It was followed by a companion piece *De varietate rerum* published in 1557. In both books Cardano shows himself to have been a man of many interests and possessed of a great curiosity. In his writings on magnetism he advanced the idea that magnets can grow old and lose their potency, and that a magnetized needle turns on its pivot spontaneously. He associated magnetism with the pull exerted by a star in the tail of the constellation Ursa Major (the Big Dipper). He distinguished between electrical and magnetic attraction, defining the former as the flow and return of a fatty substance to which dry things adhere.

The medical writings of Cardano covered a wide range of subjects and are again a mark of his intense interest in all aspects of science. He refused to rely on the authorities of the past, such as Galen and Hippocrates, and developed his own ideas in medical practice. He wrote about the instruction of deaf-mutes and blind persons, treatment of syphilis and typhus fever, causes of disease, and character determination from facial appearances. In his concern with life itself, he hinted at an evolutionary process and believed that there was infinite variability in animal species.

Later Years

Cardano may perhaps be regarded as typical, yet very special, among the men of the Renaissance. In spite of his accomplishments and devotion to science, he remained a strong believer in astrology and even cast the horoscope of Jesus Christ. He was also interested in philosophy and wrote two books on the subject. His character was anything but admirable, and he can be described as a liar, gambler, lecher, and possibly a heretic.

Following his professorship at Pavia, which he had to resign after his son's conviction for murder, Cardano was appointed professor of medicine at the University of Bologna (1562). However, here he again found difficulties and was jailed in 1570 on a charge of heresy. Upon his release he was deprived of his university chair and left for Rome. His fame had undoubtedly mitigated his punishment, and at Rome he was allowed to stay in the College of Physicians and was given a pension by Pope Gregory XIII. Cardano died in Rome on Sept. 21, 1576.

Further Reading

Recommended for information on Cardano are his autobiography, *The Book of My Life* (1643; trans. 1931), and Oystein Ore, *Cardano, the Gambling Scholar* (1953). For a general survey of the history of mathematics, E. T. Bell, *The Development of Mathematics* (1940; 2d ed. 1945), and Morris Kline, *Mathematics and the Physical World* (1959), are quite satisfactory.

Additional Sources

Fierz, Markus, *Girolamo Cardano, 1501-1576: physician, natural philosopher, mathematician, astrologer, and interpreter of dreams,* Boston: Birkhauser, 1983. □

Lázaro Cárdenas

Lázaro Cárdenas (1895-1970) was a Mexican revolutionary leader and president. During his administration he revitalized the people's faith in the revolution by implementing extensive land reforms, expropriating foreign-owned properties, and nationalizing the oil industry.

Lázaro Cárdenas was born of mixed white and Tarascan Indian ancestry in Jiquilpán de Juárez, Michoacán, on May 21, 1895. In order to support his family he worked in the local jail. When the Madero revolution broke out, he released his prisoners and together they went to join the *maderistas.*

After the Convention of Aguascalientes, Cárdenas fought briefly in the army of Pancho Villa but in 1915 joined the constitutionalists. In the revolt of Agua Prieta he took the side of Álvaro Obregón. During the 1923 rebellion he commanded loyal forces in Michoacán. The following year he was promoted to brigadier general and given command of military operations in the Huasteca, Michoacán, and the Isthmus. In 1928 he became governor of Michoacán, serving until 1932. He actively supported land reform. To his reputation for honest service in the military he added a comparable reputation in civil administration.

During the succeeding years Cárdenas served as president of the government party, minister of interior, and secretary of war and marine. In 1934 the Calles group, intending him to play the straw man for their continued control of the government, misjudged Cárdenas and selected him as the presidential candidate. Cárdenas, however, won and entered office with a radical mandate in the new Six Year Plan and proceeded to carry it out. He gave the people personal attention and patience. His 6-year term was marked by a reaffirmation of revolutionary faith and a revitalization of revolutionary processes.

When Calles challenged his leniency with labor, Cárdenas forced him to leave Mexico. Labor reached unprecedented power as it reorganized under Lombardo Toledano in the Mexican Confederation of Labor. Cárdenas expropriated 45 million acres of land and distributed them to the *ejidos,* including new collective types with large financial and technical support in the cotton region of La Laguna and the henequén area of Yucatán. The nationaliza-

tion of the railroads was completed, and in 1938, in an action described as Mexico's declaration of economic independence, foreign petroleum holdings were expropriated and nationalized.

A Department of Indian Affairs was established, and Mexico hosted the First Inter-American Indigenist Congress. After some initial friction a conciliatory policy was adopted toward the Church, and Bassol's strongly socialistic educational program was moderated with greater stress on nationalistic goals. In 1938, Cárdenas crushed the last significant regional revolt which was led by Saturnino Cedillo in San Luis Potosi. Mexico opened its doors to political exiles, including Leon Trotsky and a considerable number of Republican Spanish refugees.

In the presidential election of 1940 Cárdenas backed moderately conservative Manuel Ávila Camacho and served him as secretary of defense in 1943. For more than a quarter century Cárdenas remained a political force to be reckoned with. In 1960, at the time of the Bay of Pigs episode, he took a strongly pro-Castro position, consistent with his noninterventionist sentiments. However, Cárdenas consistently confounded those who have tried to associate his name with violence and the disruption of the political process. In October 1968 he strongly urged the students to end violence, and he remained an advocate of rapid reform, but by peaceful means. He died on Oct. 19, 1970, in Mexico City.

Further Reading

The definitive biography of Cárdenas remains to be written. A sympathetic view is William C. Townsend, *Lázaro Cárdenas, Mexican Democrat* (1952). An equally sympathetic account of the early years of his administration, written from a Marxist viewpoint, is Nathaniel and Sylvia Weyl, *The Reconquest of Mexico: The Years of Lázaro Cárdenas* (1939). Frank Tannenbaum, who was closely associated with Cárdenas, wrote one of the best analyses of his character and achievements in *Mexico: The Struggle for Peace and Bread* (1950). A specialized study of the labor movement is Joe C. Ashby, *Organized Labor and the Mexican Revolution under Lázaro Cárdenas* (1967).

Additional Sources

Townsend, William Cameron, *Lázaro Cárdenas, Mexican democrat,* Waxhaw, N.C.: International Friendship, 1979. □

Cuauhtémoc Cárdenas Solorzano

The son of the beloved reformist president, Cuauhtémoc Cárdenas Solorzano (born 1934) made two strong runs for the presidency of Mexico against the long entrenched Institutional Revolutionary Party (PRI). In 1997 he was elected Mayor of Mexico City during a landmark election marking the end of 70 years of one-party rule throughout that nation.

Cuauhtémoc Cárdenas Solorzano was born in Mexico City on May 1, 1934. The son of Mexico's legendary reformer President Lázaro Cárdenas, Cuauhtémoc (named for the first Aztec emperor) grew up in his father's shadow. Undoubtedly, Lázaro Cárdenas played a larger role than anyone else in shaping his son's political outlook. The younger Cárdenas' populism derived from his father's reformist policies. Lázaro Cárdenas holds an esteemed position in modern Mexican history because he, more than any other contemporary figure, fulfilled the redistributionist promises of the Mexican revolution. Rising to the presidency the same year that Cuauhtémoc was born, Lázaro Cárdenas expropriated the railroads, nationalized the petroleum industry, encouraged unionization, and impelled land reform. Known as one of Mexico's greatest reformers, Lázaro Cárdenas' political zeal lived on in his son.

Cuauhtémoc Cárdenas began his formal education in private schools and subsequently earned a civil engineering degree from the National Autonomous University of Mexico (UNAM). After graduating from UNAM, Cárdenas traveled extensively in Europe, studying in France, West Germany, and Italy. He returned home to begin his career and start a family. He spent most of his professional life working as an engineer and planner in the Secretariat of Water Resources. He eventually married Celeste, his Portuguese-born wife; the couple had three children—two sons and a daughter.

Predictably, the opportunity to enter politics lured Cárdenas away from engineering. In 1976 he won a Senate seat from his home state of Michoacán, and four years later he became the state's governor. Both times he ran as a candidate of the ruling Institutional Revolutionary Party (PRI). Like his father, Cárdenas captured the imagination of the people and inspired confidence through advocacy of social reforms. Like his father, he also developed an appreciation of the political rewards to be gained by advocating the cause of Mexico's poor. Most observers, however, found Cárdenas to be a mediocre chief executive of his home state.

In 1986 Cárdenas launched a democratic reform movement, known as the Democratic Current, within the PRI. The movement's chief aim was to include rank and file members in the party's presidential candidate selection process, long dominated by the incumbent president and party notables. PRI barons rebuffed Cárdenas' efforts. The cool reception to his views within the official party led Cárdenas and several dozen Democratic Current activists to break with the PRI in 1987 and enter a political coalition—the National Democratic Front (FDN).

Cárdenas used the FDN to wage what was to become the strongest challenge to the PRI nominee for president since the party's formation in 1929. In his bid for the nation's highest office, Cárdenas capitalized on popular dissatisfaction with the government, triple-digit inflation, and economic stagnation. In 1988 the Mexican economy was flat as a tortilla, corruption abounded, and half of the country's 82.7 million inhabitants lived as ragpickers in either fetid slums or postage stamp-sized plots of land. His calm demeanor, history-book name, and populist rhetoric—

incorporating the themes of honesty, nationalism, and redistribution—struck a powerful chord with the shantytown dwellers, peasants, and petty bureaucrats who had seen their purchasing power plummet amid soaring prices.

His campaign, which began in September 1987, was grass-roots in every sense. Denied full access to the officially-manipulated media, Cárdenas reached the people through mass rallies across Mexico. The FDN never evolved into a party but remained a coalition of left-leaning groups attracted to the son of Lázaro Cárdenas.

For all the enthusiasm sparked by his candidacy, Cárdenas delivered his speeches in a monotonous, undramatic fashion, largely devoid of imagination and imagery. This bland and earnest demeanor, at odds with the stereotype of a politician, proved a political advantage. He discovered that many voters identified with, and appreciated, his understated personality. Not even his public professions of atheism hurt him politically among rank-and-file believers in an overwhelmingly Catholic nation.

Officially, Cárdenas lost the 1988 election, gaining only 31.1 percent of the vote compared to 50.4 percent for Carlos Salinas de Gortari. Following the contest, *Los Angeles Times* pollsters found that a majority of responders believed that Cárdenas had actually won the contest. Emboldened by his strong showing, Cárdenas decided to seek the presidency again in 1994. (The constitution prohibited Salinas from seeking reelection.)

In contrast to running as the candidate of a front six years earlier, Cárdenas was the nominee in 1994 of the Democratic Revolutionary Party (PRD), a faction-ridden amalgamation of communists, socialists, nationalists, and ex-*Priistas*. Although Cárdenas' platform had changed little, Mexico had undergone a profound transformation since the last presidential contest. Above all, President Salinas had spearheaded sweeping reforms that privatized hundreds of state-owned firms, reduced federal subsidies, slashed inflation, revamped tax laws, tumbled trade barriers, and impelled Mexico's entry into the North American Free Trade Agreement, which also embraced the United States and Canada. A policy of modest *glasnost* accompanied Mexico's ambitious version of *perestroika*.

Salinas' innovations did not deter Cárdenas from again pursuing the position once held by his father. Unanimously nominated by the PRD on October 17, 1993, Cárdenas proclaimed that Mexico "will have to choose between the consolidation of a state party regime based on authoritarianism, corruption, and servility or a democratic system with respect of the votes, social equality, and an economic process that will benefit all." Despite social unrest in the southern state of Chiapas, few analysts believed that Cárdenas could defeat the PRI's candidate and his well-oiled political machine in the election scheduled for August 1994. They were right. After a tumultuous campaign which was marred by the assassination of PRI candidate Louis Donaldo Colosio, the machine of the incumbent Institutional Revolutionary Party emerged victorious once again as it had for decades.

Three years later Cárdenas ran successfully for Mayor of Mexico City, once again on the PRD ticket. Cárdenas' was not alone in his victory, as the election of July 6, 1997 resulted in the PRI's loss of control in the lower house of the national legislature (Chamber of Deputies). The historical election was hailed as the beginning of the end of the electoral abuses which had plagued Mexico for too long. After the election President Ernesto Zedillo stunned the nation by not only recognizing but congratulating Cárdenas' mayoral victory, thus sparking rumors that Cárdenas might still succeed in a third bid for the presidency.

Further Reading

There is little English-language material on Cárdenas. For election results see the *Los Angeles Times*. A good background book on Mexico is Michael Meyer and William Sherman's *The Course of Mexican History* (4th ed., 1990). □

Benjamin Nathan Cardozo

Benjamin Nathan Cardozo (1870-1938) was one of the greatest legal philosophers to serve on the Supreme Court of the United States.

Born in New York City on May 24, 1870, Benjamin Cardozo was of Jewish parentage. His ancestors had come to America in colonial times. On the maternal side, his great-great-uncle Rabbi Gershom Mendes Seixas was present at George Washington's presidential inauguration, and on the paternal side, his great-great-grandfather Aaron Nunez Cardozo emigrated from London in the 18th century.

Cardozo attended the public schools of New York City. At the age of 15 he entered Columbia College, where in 1889 he received his bachelor of arts degree. He delivered the commencement oration of *The Altruist in Politics*. Just 20 years old when he received his master of arts in political science, he went on to study at Columbia School of Law and graduated in 2 years with a bachelor of laws degree. Admitted to practice in 1892, he became an expert in the highly technical field of commercial law.

For 20 years Cardozo had a successful private practice, specializing in appellate law. He was constantly consulted by lawyers on intricate legal questions and was known as a "lawyer's lawyer," arguing complex points before the appellate courts.

Appellate Bench

Though not a politician in any way, Cardozo wanted to become a judge. In 1913, running as an independent Democrat, he was elected to a 14-year term on the New York Supreme Court. However, he was on the court for only a month when he was appointed to serve temporarily as associate judge of the highest court of the state, the Court of Appeals. His appointment came at the request of the court, which had been asked to nominate a candidate. The esteem in which he was held by his judicial colleagues is evident in

this most extraordinary move. On Jan. 15, 1917, New York's governor named him a regular member of the Court of Appeals. In November 1917 Cardozo was elected to a full term on the court, subsequently becoming chief judge. The New York Court of Appeals reached the height of its reputation during this period.

U.S. Supreme Court

In 1932 Associate Justice Oliver Wendell Holmes, Jr., retired from the U.S. Supreme Court. President Herbert Hoover invited Cardozo to serve because "the whole country demands the one man who could best carry on the great Holmes tradition of philosophic approval to modern American jurisprudence." The U.S. Senate confirmed the appointment unanimously. This was the same Senate that had rejected two previous Hoover nominees. Cardozo took his seat on Mar. 14, 1932.

A man with a mind as active as Cardozo's was bound to find an outlet in writing. In 1921 he published his first work, *The Nature of the Judicial Process,* and 3 years later *The Growth of the Law* appeared. *The Paradoxes of Legal Science* was published in 1928. Shortly after he moved to the U.S. Supreme Court his last work, *Law and Literature and Other Essays,* was published.

Cardozo's Opinions

Many of Cardozo's extraordinary qualities as a judge are revealed by his Supreme Court opinions. For example, his majority opinion in *Steward Machine Co. v. Davis* (1931) clearly indicated his belief that the Constitution must serve the changing needs of the people. In *United States v. Butler* (1936) Cardozo dissented, along with justices Louis Brandeis and Harlan Stone, declaring that the Agricultural Adjustment Act of 1933 was unconstitutional.

Justice Cardozo wrote for the majority in the 8-to-1 decision on the case *Palko v. Connecticut* (1937). Palko had been indicted and tried for murder in the first degree, but a jury found him guilty of second-degree murder, and he was given a life sentence. However, a Connecticut statute permitted the state to appeal rulings and decisions "upon all questions of law arising on the trial of criminal cases." The state appealed, and a new trial was ordered. Palko was again tried, found guilty, and sentenced to death and this second conviction was affirmed by the highest state court. Palko then brought the case to the Supreme Court on appeal, contending that he was being placed in double jeopardy in violation of the 5th Amendment.

The importance of this opinion was not in the fact that the Supreme Court found that Palko had suffered no loss of his rights under the Constitution, but in what Cardozo said about the 5th Amendment's self-incriminating clause. He wrote: "This (privilege against self-incrimination) too might be lost and justice still be done. Indeed, today as in the past there are students of our penal system who look upon the immunity as a mischief rather than a benefit, and who would limit its scope, or destroy it altogether. No doubt there would remain the need to give protection against torture, physical or mental. Justice, however, would not perish if the accused were subject to a duty to respond to ordinary inquiry."

Writing the majority decision in *Helvering v. Davis* (1937), Cardozo moved into the area of constitutional law. This case decided that the old-age pension phase of the social security program was constitutional. Cardozo made the issue clear when he declared, "Congress may spend money in aid of the 'general welfare.'"

Cardozo voted with the majority in a number of cases that set legal precedents. In *Nebbia v. New York* (1934) he agreed that a New York law establishing the price of milk was constitutional because: "Price control, like any form of regulation is unconstitutional only if arbitrary, discriminatory, or demonstrably irrelevant to the policy the legislation is free to adopt. . . . " In *West Coast Hotel Co. v. Parrish* (1937) the Court determined that a minimum-wage law enacted in the state of Washington was constitutional, overruling an earlier Supreme Court opinion. In finding for the plaintiff the Court opened the gates to social legislation passed by state legislatures.

Late in 1937 Justice Cardozo began to feel the pressures of his judicial responsibilities. He was tired. He had never married, and most of his family was dead. Judge Irving Lehman, who had been on the New York Court of Appeals with Cardozo, invited him to stay at his home. As the months wore on, Cardozo's health continued to fail, and early in 1938 he died.

An Evaluation

Cardozo's judicial career was one of the most illustrious in the annals of American law. Justice Felix Frankfurter, in his book *Of Law and Men,* stated, "Barring only Mr. Justice Holmes, who was a seminal thinker in the law as well as vastly learned, no judge in his time was more deeply versed in the history of the common law or more resourceful in applying the living principles by which it has unfolded than Mr. Justice Cardozo."

U.S. Attorney General Homer Cummings stated upon Cardozo's death: "His opinions spoke in tones of rare beauty. They might deal with things prosaic, but the language was that of a poet." Judge Learned Hand saw Cardozo as "a shy and sensitive man of great humility and compassion. It was a rare good fortune that brought to such eminence a man so reserved, so unassuming, so retiring, so gracious to high and low, and so serene."

Further Reading

Two works dealing directly with Cardozo and the law are Beryl H. Levy, *Cardozo and Frontiers of Legal Thinking* (1938; rev. ed. 1969), and George S. Hellman, *Benjamin N. Cardozo: American Judge* (1940). A well-documented work that praises Cardozo's decisions supporting Congress is Walter F. Murphy, *Congress and the Court: A Case Study in the American Political System* (1962). There is a chapter on Cardozo by A. L. Kaufman in Allison Dunham and Philip B. Kurland, eds., *Mr. Justice* (rev. ed. 1964). See also Joseph P. Pollard, *Mr. Justice Cardozo: A Liberal Mind in Action* (1935).

Additional Sources

Pollard, Joseph P. (Joseph Percival), *Mr. Justice Cardozo: a liberal mind in action,* Buffalo, N.Y.: W.S. Hein, 1995.

Posner, Richard A., *Cardozo: a study in reputation,* Chicago: University of Chicago Press, 1990. □

Giosuè Carducci

The Italian poet Giosuè Carducci (1835-1907) was awarded the 1906 Nobel Prize in literature. His gradual development from youthful revolutionary idealism to later acceptance of a conservative monarchy closely mirrors the course of 19th-century Italian history.

Born in the Tuscan village of Val di Castello, Giosuè Carducci spent his childhood traveling along the coastal plain, where his father was regional physician. Early studies in Florence, which afforded him a solid foundation in Latin and the Italian classics, prepared Carducci for the Teachers College of Pisa, from which he graduated in 1856. After several years of teaching and editing texts, Carducci was appointed to the prestigious chair in Italian literature at the University of Bologna, a post he held until 1904. During his years at Bologna, he participated fully in the intellectual life of his times as poet, critic, parliamentary deputy (1876), and senator (1890).

A powerfully built man whose prominent jaw accentuated an aggressive appearance, Carducci in his early writings proudly declared himself to be "a shield bearer of the classics," that is, a defender of traditional literary formation. In rejecting romanticism as a betrayal of the Italian artistic heritage and a servile imitation of foreign ideologies, Carducci's first poetry, *Juvenilia* (1850-1860) and *Levia gravia* (1861-1871), exalts nationalistic ideals of progress and freedom through satire directed against the political and clerical obstacles to the unification of Italy. Typical of this Risorgimento poetry is his Masonic, antipapal "Hymn to Satan" (1863), in which Satan personifies reason, progress, and rebellion against the oppressive force of religion. Only later, when national unity had been achieved, did Carducci evidence an appreciation for the religious traditions of his country.

The *Giambi ed epodi* (1867-1879) signals a new direction in Carducci's poetry. While still polemical and satirical, there emerges a freshness, a genuine tone which makes itself heard above "the bold verse which slaps the face" of the discredited past. The 32 poems of this collection champion the ideals of liberty against clerically imposed limitations, but they also reveal the initial traces of introspection and self-contemplation that characterize much of his mature writings. During this period Carducci began his first sympathetic studies of foreign romanticists (Hugo, Shelley, Heine, and others), whose works he had formerly rejected.

The 105 poems of Carducci's three-part *Rime nuove* (1861-1886; *New Rhymes*) develop more fully this intimate vein. These barely controlled expressions of his emotions are at times highly personal ("Ancient Lament," written on the death of his infant son) and are often delicately reminiscent of visions from his youth ("The Maremanno Idyl"). Several love poems, which suggest that Carducci frequently strayed beyond the boundaries of his marriage, afford the closest possible view of Carducci's inner self.

The *Odi barbare* (1873-1889; *Barbarous Odes*) constitutes his last major poetic achievement. "Barbarous" denotes the non-Italian meters employed in these verses, which are based on Greek and Latin models. This collection of 57 poems derives unity from its form, but its thematic content varies widely, from glorification of Rome's past ("The Springs of the River Clitumnus") to contemplative visions of the author's own experiences ("At the Station").

In addition to his poetry, Carducci made major contributions to literary criticism with several studies written largely during the first 10 years of his professorship in Bologna. His sound, if unsystematic, judgments are reflected in *The Development of a National Literature, The Varying Fortunes of Dante,* and *Essay on Petrarch.* Carducci died in 1907. A product of his times, he fulfilled his lofty conception of the civic mission of a poet—the expression and exaltation of the values of his people.

Further Reading

Relatively little scholarship in English has been dedicated to Carducci. Orlo Williams, *Giosuè Carducci* (1914), provides a general outline of his life and major writings. See also Ruth Shepard Phelps, *Italian Silhouettes* (1924), and S. Eugene

Scalia, *Carducci: His Critics and Translators in England and America, 1881-1932* (1937). □

Rod Carew

Rod Carew (born 1945) is widely recognized as one of the best hitters of his generation in professional baseball.

During his 19 seasons with the Major League's Minnesota Twins and California Angels, Carew lined, chopped, and bunted his way to 3,053 hits, winning seven batting titles and hitting .300 or better for 15 consecutive seasons. Thought by many sportswriters and fans alike to have elevated the skill of hitting a baseball to an art form, Carew was named to 18 straight All-Star teams and received American League Rookie of the Year honors in 1967 and the American League Most Valuable Player award ten years later.

In 1991, five years after his retirement, Carew became only the twenty-third player elected to the Baseball Hall of Fame in Cooperstown, New York, in his first year of eligibility. A national hero in both his native Panama—where he proudly retains his citizenship—and the United States, Carew has spent his retirement years running a batting school for young players in suburban Los Angeles.

Carew's early years were marred by illness and poverty. On October 1, 1945, Olga Carew went into labor and boarded a train in Gatun, Panama, hoping to reach a Gamboa clinic in time for doctors to attend to her child's delivery. The baby would not wait, however. Margaret Allen, a nurse, and Dr. Rodney Cline, a physician, both of whom happened to be on the train, delivered the woman's second son. While the excited mother asked the nurse to become the child's godmother, she honored the doctor by naming her son Rodney Cline Carew.

As a young boy, Carew was frequently ill and contracted rheumatic fever at the age of 12. The weakness that accompanied the disease brought only contempt and rejection from his father. Carew's uncle, Joseph French, who was a recreation official and Little League coach in Panama, attempted to fill the void. French cultivated the boy's interest in baseball and encouraged him to develop his athletic abilities despite the illness. As Carew grew stronger, he joined the other boys in pickup games played with a broom handle and rag balls wound in tape. His outstanding play in the local Little League even won him a Ted Williams bat, a prized possession that he often carried with him—even to bed, where he dreamed of traveling to the United States and becoming a big-league baseball player.

Sandlot Discovery Led to Tryout

When Carew was 15, his mother immigrated to New York City, where after finding a job and a place to live, she sent for her two sons. Once in New York, Rod enrolled at Manhattan's George Washington High School, but a part-time job at a grocery store to help support the family prevented him from trying out for school sports. The family's financial concerns, though, did not prevent Carew from participating in weekend sandlot games in Macombs Dam Park next to Yankee Stadium. It did not take long for him to show his skill at the plate; after a few weeks of play, a teammate's father—an unofficial scout for the Minnesota Twins—took notice of the talented kid from Panama and made a phone call to another scout. When the Twins came to town for a series with the Yankees, Carew came to Yankee Stadium for a tryout. Once inside the batting cage, the skinny 18-year-old demonstrated a hitting power that belied his six- foot, 170-pound frame. So many balls landed in the bleachers that Twins Manager Sam Mele—afraid the Yankees might offer him a higher signing bonus—halted the tryout. One month after the tryout, Carew signed with the Twins for a $5,000 bonus.

Moved Quickly to Major League

Unlike most players who need several years in the minor leagues to develop their skills, Carew spent only three years in the farm system before Twins owner Calvin Griffith brought him up to the big league club, inserting him into the starting lineup at second base for the start of the 1967 season. Although some within the organization—including Mele—did not believe the 21-year-old from the Class-A farm team was ready for the majors, Carew silenced the skeptics by hitting .292 his first season and winning the American League Rookie of the Year award. While quickly becoming one of the game's leading hitters, Carew also dazzled fans with his speed on the base paths with a record—breaking seven steals home. In one game that same season he stole second, third, and home in a single inning—a feat performed only once before in the previous four decades.

Despite his success on the field, Carew developed a reputation in his early years as "a loner who made friends slowly and suffered slights poorly," according to *Time*. Much of this changed, however, after he was introduced to Marilynn Levy at a local nightspot. At first the white Jewish woman was not interested in the black baseball player from Panama. As Marilynn told *Time,* "Sports? I didn't know from the Twins, and like a cocky little broad, I wasn't impressed." Despite the inauspicious beginning, the two began dating and married in October of 1970. While Carew was quickly accepted into the Levy family, he received a number of death threats and insults from Twins' followers. The two did not let racism prevent them from settling in Minneapolis, where they would have three daughters.

Although Carew won four batting titles between 1972 and 1975 and missed his fifth straight by .002 points, he did not receive the media attention granted to far lesser players. This was due in part to the fact that Carew prided himself in hitting singles rather than home runs. In 1975, Twins owner Griffith turned down Carew's request for a modest salary increase, claiming that the future Hall of Famer did not hit enough home runs to deserve the pay raise. The arbitrator sided with the Twins management and fixed Carew's salary at only $120,000—more than modest by league standards for a man of his ability. As if to prove his critics wrong, Carew hit 14 home runs the following season.

It was Carew's performance in 1977, however, that reserved him a position in the Hall of Fame and gained the respect of the national media. As Carew made his bid to become the first player in 36 years to hit .400, he appeared on the cover of *Time* as well as several sports publications and was featured in *Newsweek.* After one blazing hitting streak in late June that brought his average to .411, Carew told *Newsweek*'s Peter Bonventre that every pitch that came to the plate during that banner season "look[ed] like a basketball." When asked by Bonventre how to get Carew out, Gaylord Perry, a Hall of Fame pitcher for the Texas Rangers replied, "Greaseball, greaseball, greaseball. That's all I throw him, and he still hits them. He's the only player in baseball who consistently hits my grease. He sees the ball so well, I guess he can pick out the dry side." Although his average hovered above the mark well into the season, Carew finished at .388. But with 100 runs batted in and 100 runs scored to go with his lofty average, he was still the runaway winner of the American League's Most Valuable Player award.

Despite Carew's singular performance that season, he could not reach a contract agreement with management and was traded to the California Angels just two years later. After spending seven years in California, where he hit better than .300 five times, he was suddenly released after the 1985 season. Angered by the way Carew was treated, a Minneapolis media celebrity led an unsuccessful campaign to bring him back to Minnesota for a farewell season in 1986. No one was more disappointed than Marilynn Carew with the failed effort. "I'm still angry about it," she told the *St. Paul Pioneer Press-Dispatch.* "With the d.h. rule, Rod should still be playing. He would have done a lot for [Minnesota]." After the initial feelings of bitterness, however, her husband was ready for life on the other side of the basepaths. "Once I started coaching my daughters in softball and then started the hitting school," he said. "I found out I could get along without baseball."

Inducted into Baseball's Hall of Fame

The transition to civilian life was made easier in 1991 when Carew was elected to the Hall of Fame in his first year of eligibility, receiving more than 90 percent of the sportswriters' votes. "He was one of the best hitters I've ever seen." Twins owner Griffith told the *St. Paul Pioneer Press-Dispatch.* "He was just a natural up there. That's all there was to it. He had a stroke that God gave him and he took advantage of it." Former manager Mele, who initially opposed Carew's promotion to the majors, shared Griffith's sentiment. "I don't know who you could compare him with . . . ," he told the *Minneapolis Star and Tribune.* "You could put him in a tunnel with the lights out and you still know he's going to hit."

While many used the occasion of Carew's induction to remember his brilliance on the field, others recalled his regular travels to the Mayo Clinic to visit patients, his winning of the 1976 Roberto Clemente Award for distinguished community service, and his strong attachment to his Panamanian background. As former Twins Manager Gene Mauch stated in *Time,* "As impressed as I am with Rod Carew the hitter, Rod Carew the baseball player, I am more impressed with Rod Carew the man."

Carew faced perhaps his most difficult test off the field when his 18-year-old daughter, Michelle, died of leukemia on April 17, 1996. Since his daughter's diagnosis with the disease in September of 1995, Carew led a campaign to find an appropriate donor for a bone-marrow transplant. Unfortunately, because the donor pool is so limited in diversity, the operation was never performed. However, Carew succeeded in bringing media attention to the need for donors, and won even further admiration for his tireless efforts on behalf of his daughter.

Further Reading

Los Angeles Times, January 9, 1991.

Minneapolis Star and Tribune, January 9, 1991.

Newsweek, August 11, 1969, pp. 61-62; July 11, 1977, pp. 46-47.

People, December 4, 1995, p. 133.

Sports Illustrated, July 17, 1995, pp. 28-36.

St. Paul Pioneer Press- Dispatch (Minnesota), July 20, 1987; January 9, 1991; July 22, 1991.

Time, July 18, 1977, pp. 52- 62. □

George Leonard Carey

The Right Reverend George Leonard Carey (born 1935) was formally enthroned as the 103rd Archbishop of Canterbury in 1991. For the previous three years he had been Bishop of Bath and Wells, a region in southwest England.

Much of the world's religious community was surprised on July 25, 1990, when the announcement was made that Bishop George Carey would be the next Archbishop of Canterbury —head of the Church of England and symbolic leader of the worldwide Anglican Communion. When Carey was formally enthroned in 1991, he took responsibility for 70 million people scattered across 164 countries.

For many generations, the Archbishop's throne has been occupied by men born into England's upper classes and educated in the country's most elite schools. Those responsible for selecting Carey (a man with humble beginnings) to lead the church, may have been motivated by their recognition that the Church of England was a deeply troubled institution, badly in need of fresh perspectives.

Childhood and Training

George Leonard Carey was born on November 13, 1935. He came from a working-class family in the East End of London, whose inhabitants are known as Cockneys. His father was a hospital porter, and the family lived in public housing. Carey said that he could remember having to share shoes with his brother. He left school at 15 and became an office clerk with the London Electricity Board. At 18 he was called up for national service in the Royal Air Force, where he was a radio operator. At that time he had a conversion experience and decided to offer himself for the ordained ministry.

He worked at home to secure entry to King's College, University of London. There he secured a Bachelor of Divinity degree in 1962, and in that year he began to serve as curate (assistant) in the London evangelical parish of Islington. However, he also continued his academic studies. He was awarded a Master's degree in 1965 for a thesis on "Church, Ministry, Eucharist in the Apostolic Fathers" and, in 1971, a Doctorate for a thesis on "Church Order in the Shepherd of Hermas" (a second-century work).

This academic record led him to be appointed to the staff of three evangelical theological colleges: Oak Hill, London (1966-1970); St. John's Nottingham (1970-1975); and Trinity, Bristol (1982-1987), of which he was principal and where he had a profound effect in renewing the college. Meanwhile, from 1975 to 1982 he gained more parish experiences as vicar of St. Nicholas Durham. The city was a once-flourishing mining area in the north of England but was having a hard time when Carey came to the church. In 1988 he became Bishop of Bath and Wells.

His wife, Eileen, was a qualified nurse, and they had four children, two sons and two daughters. Carey was known to be a supporter of "green" issues, to be alert to the problems of inner-city parishes and urban renewal, and to be a lifelong supporter of the famous London Association Football (soccer) club, Arsenal.

History of the Anglican Church

In the modern world, all mainstream churches include a wide spectrum in understanding basic Christian beliefs, whether they acknowledge it or not. In the case of the Anglican Communion this has always been the case, because at the Reformation the Church of England took a conservative course in the conviction that the terms Protestant and Catholic were not antithetical but complementary. The term Protestant was understood as a protest in favor of a reformed Catholicism. However, in the Church of England there have always been those who emphasized one much more than the other, and this difference became sharper amid 19th-century controversies. Those on the Protestant side are usually referred to as Evangelicals and those on the Catholic side as Anglo-Catholics, but both also include a range of opinion within themselves. Together they represent, at the most, 40 percent of Anglicans; the remaining 60 percent or so are not and never have been of either party.

In recent years Evangelicals have gained ground while Anglo-Catholics have lost ground. This is largely because the new emphases in the Roman Catholic Church since the Second Vatican Council (1962-1965) have undermined most of what they stood for.

The Anglican Communion is made up of 29 self-governing provinces. They are linked together by three entities:

the Lambeth Conference of bishops every ten years; informal occasional meetings of the primates of the provinces; and the Anglican Consultative Council, which meets every two or three years and is made up of two or three representatives, clerical and lay, of each province. All three entities are advisory, which means that the personal influence of the Archbishop of Canterbury, while not decisive, counts for a lot.

The present process in England of appointing archbishops and diocesan bishops begins with the Crown Appointments Commission. This is made up of eleven members drawn from the General Synod (bishops, other clergy, and laity), who serve for the five-year life of the synod, together with four representatives, clerical and lay, of the vacant diocese. They meet (with advisors) in an atmosphere of retreat and send two names in order of preference to the prime minister, who is normally expected to choose the preferred name to submit to the Queen of England for nomination. The process is entirely confidential.

The vacancy at Canterbury aroused a good deal of interest in the national media. Most of the leadership in the Church of England had clearly been far from happy with the general lines of policy and the general tone of the Thatcher administration since it came to power in 1979.

Problems Within the Anglican Church

The population of the Anglican Communion is divided into 29 regional branches, and each branch has the authority to make its own rulings on the many controversies facing the modern church. Conflicting decisions on these issues, such as the ordination of women as priests, have already caused rifts between some of the member churches within the Anglican Communion. Other hotly debated issues within the Anglican Communion include the proper attitude toward homosexuality and the ordination of openly homosexual clergy, and the modernization of the liturgy.

Involved In Social Causes

Carey's appointment as Archbishop of Canterbury was significant for four reasons: First, at age 55, he could hope to have 15 years before retiring at 70, well past the next Lambeth Conference and long enough to exercise sustained influence. Second, his appointment marked a complete breakawayfrom the privileged backgrounds of the great majority of archbishops and bishops who have gone to public (U.S.A. "private") schools and then to the prestigious and wealthy ancient universities of Oxford and Cambridge. Third, Carey was an evangelical who was fairly conservative in his attitude to the Bible and to doctrine, but with a well-trained and open mind. In particular, he argued in speech and writing in favor of the ordination of women, against the evangelicals who said it was contrary to the Bible for women to have any authority over men. Several provinces of the Anglican Communion now ordain women, but so far in the Church of England the opposing minority has secured a blocking one-third vote. Carey's attitude may be of great importance when the issue is taken up again. Carey also had contacts with the charismatic Christian movement. Lastly, it seemed that Carey would be a "people's archbishop." He was a good communicator and had not lost touch with his roots. He said that the church was "light years away" from the kind of people among whom he grew up, and that instead of being a "Jesus movement" it had become identified with static church buildings.

While remaining a conservative theologian, Carey is involved with liberal social causes. As he told *Maclean's,* "Social and political issues are there, at the very heart of the Christian good news." His concern for suffering and his influence was made clear when, in 1994, he visited the Muslim country of Sudan, which suffered from civil-war and where Christians were persecuted. His desire to meet with only Christians there, not the government, was seen by the government as a snub. According to the *National Catholic Reporter,* "His visit has drawn attention to the persecution of Christians and the forgotten war in the southern Sudan."

Further Reading

Carey wrote eight books on such topics as Christology, ecumenism, relations with the Roman Catholic Church, and the existence of God. They are not of the long-lasting type and will not be easily obtainable. The best background reading is on Anglicanism as such. Here the Pelican *Anglicanism* by Stephen Neill is good (first published 1958). A series of 30 essays in *The Study of Anglicanism,* edited by Stephen Sykes and John Booty, an Anglo-American undertaking (S.P.C.K. and Fortress Press, 1988) covers almost every aspect. Nearly all the essays are good and some are outstanding. Further readings are also available in *Maclean's* (August 6, 1990); *Newsweek* (April 22, 1991); and *National Catholic Reporter* (January 14, 1994). ☐

Henry Charles Carey

Henry Charles Carey (1793-1879) was an American writer on economics who rejected the key ideas of the British classical economists. Instead of their free-trade policy, he advocated a policy of tariff protection.

Henry Charles Carey was born on Dec. 15, 1793, in Philadelphia, where his father was a leading bookseller and publisher. Largely self-taught, Henry left school at age 12 and while still a teen-ager joined his father's firm as a partner. After his early retirement from the publishing business in the 1830s, he devoted himself to his investments, to writing, and to public affairs.

A leader of the Pennsylvania protectionists, he supported their cause with a veritable flood of publications. Carey associated himself with the Republican party when it was established in the 1850s; the highly protectionist plank in the party platform of 1860 reflected his influence. His reputation spread, and Washington administrators, from President Lincoln on down, sought his advice on many occasions. It was frequently suggested that Carey make himself available for high public office, but he invariably refused. When he died in Philadelphia on Oct. 13, 1879, he was mourned as a national leader.

Reflecting the American Environment

Carey's fame rests on the books he published from 1835 to 1872. They reflected the influence of his father in their anti-British sentiment and espousal of protectionism. Their content ranged over the then barely divided fields of sociology and economics, with occasional glimpses of the order of the universe, which in Carey's opinion was ruled by the same laws that controlled social relationships.

Carey's ideas on economics were more optimistic than those of the classical economists. Compared with them, he laid greater stress on harmony than on potential conflict between economic groups. This reflected the American environment, where economic opportunities were plentiful and where class divisions were less rigidly drawn than in Europe. Like other American economists of the time, Carey rejected Thomas Malthus's view of the population relentlessly pressing against food resources. He had no use for David Ricardo's theory of rent, according to which the rental income of the more favorably situated landowners, who enjoyed low cost, would increase as less suitable land was taken into cultivation. On the basis of the American experience, Carey pointed out, the historical movement did not proceed from the most fertile lands to less fertile ones but in the reverse order. Carey directed his most pronounced criticism to the free-trade implications of Adam Smith's and Ricardo's doctrines, which in his opinion would perpetuate British economic power and stifle the economic development of the United States.

Carey saw his efforts rewarded by the tariff legislation of the United States. Abroad, and especially on the Continent, where the free-trade doctrine was less firmly established than in Britain, his works found many readers. His influence on academic economics was noticeable mainly at the University of Pennsylvania.

Further Reading

Carey's writings make 13 substantial books and about 6,000 pages of pamphlet and newspaper material; included are *Principles of Political Economy* (3 vols., 1837-1840) and *Principles of Social Science* (3 vols., 1858-1860). Arnold W. Green, *Henry Charles Carey* (1951), contains a list of his writings, a biography, and an appraisal of his contributions to social science. A. D. H. Kaplan, *Henry Charles Carey* (1931), discusses his economics. David Kaser, *Messrs. Carey & Lea of Philadelphia: A Study in the History of the Booktrade* (1957), treats Carey as a publisher.

Additional Sources

Kaplan, A. D. H. (Abraham David Hannath), *Henry Charles Carey, a study in American economic thought,* New York: AMS Press, 1982, 1931. □

Peter Carey

Australian writer Peter Carey (born 1943) won over twelve awards and received two major award nominations for his works of fiction (short stories, novels, and film adaptations) between 1981-1994. Carey was one of the first Australian writers to create a world of absurd realities by blending fantasy and dark humor; this style is now emulated by many other authors.

Australian writer Peter Carey, born in the small town of Bacchus Marsh, Victoria, in 1943, has won twelve awards in thirteen years (1981-94) for his short stories, novels, and film adaptations.

Carey found work in Melbourne as an advertising copywriter after graduating from Monasch University in 1961. Close contact with writers Barry Oakley and Morris Lurie provided the inspiration he needed to seriously start writing fiction. According to Oakley, who critiqued Carey's initial work, Carey's ability was obvious from the beginning but Carey himself had no idea of the magnitude of his own talent.

Carey lived in London for a brief time in the late 1960s, then returned to Australia in 1973. He married theater director Alison Summers in 1985.

Carey first made his mark on the Australian literary scene with a series of short stories that blended fantasy and dark humor, two characteristics which have since become trademarks of modern Australian fiction. Proclaimed an

Australian landmark at the time of its publication, the short stories assembled in *The Fat Man in History* (1974) move through macabre fantasy worlds that reduce reality to the level of absurdity.

Carey's second collection, *War Crimes,* solidified his reputation as a remarkable, new, fabulistic author. (Original stories from both works can also be found in an expanded collection of Carey's short stories, *Collected Stories,* 1994.)

Carey's first award-winning novel, *Bliss* (1981) is the story of advertising man Harry Joy's three drastically opposing experiences with death and resurrection. According to critics, Carey's storytelling created a world that hovered between fantasy and reality, a world that dismantled a reader's assumptions about time, reality, history, and character. One reviewer claimed, "Carey is arguing the necessity of constructing stories to live by, stories which emerge from and are given value by the community itself, rather than from the importation of American dreams." Carey's book *Bliss* has won the Miles Franklin Award (1981), the New South Wales Premier's Literary Award (1982), the National Book Council Award (1982), and the A.W.G.I.E. Award (1985).

Demonstrating some of the flexibility and inventiveness learned during his advertising days, Carey adapted quickly to the demands of other writing styles. He collaborated with film director Ray Lawrence to create a film adaptation of *Bliss.* The film achieved a moderate commercial success despite Carey's much-publicized conflict with the director and won three Australian Film Industry awards including best feature film (1985).

Carey later wrote a second screenplay, *Until the End of the World* (1992), for director Wim Wender.

The paradoxical nature of Carey's novels, the merging of lies with truth, fantasy with reality, is strongly reflected in his novel *Illywhacker* (1985) which sold 60,000 copies, 20 times the normal print run of an Australian novel. (The term "illywhacker" refers to a con-man or trickster.)

In *Illywhacker,* Carey draws upon the multiple strands of Australia's own culture and mythology. The story of 139-year-old illywhacker Herbert Badgery is the story of Australia itself. In an epigraph, Carey draws upon a line from Mark Twain, saying "[*Illywhacker*] does not read like history, but like the most beautiful lies." This popular novel was nominated for both the Booker Prize (1985) and the World Fantasy Award for Best Novel (1986) and was winner of the Ditmar Award for Best Australian Science Fiction (1986).

Carey's most critically-acclaimed novel *Oscar and Lucinda* (1988) also has a sense of historical allegory. As Carey develops the relationship between the story's two main characters, Rev. Oscar Hopkins and Lucinda Leplastrier, he creates an unsettling view of 19th-century Australia. Despite a bleak ending, Carey has called the novel a "celebration of the human spirit." *Oscar and Lucinda* won both the Booker Prize and the Miles Franklin Award in 1988.

Although Carey's stories have been compared to the works of Jorge Luis Borges and Donald Barthelme, the stories more strongly reflect that peculiar blend of "real *through* fantastic" noticeable in the writings of Gabriel Garcia Marquez. Similarities in style can also be found between Carey's books and the works of writers like James Joyce, Jack Kerouac, William Faulkner, Robbe-Grillet, Bob Dylan, and Graham Greene.

Throughout Carey's writings there is a sense of the absurd, of a paradox that reflects the contradictions in contemporary life. His writing is outstanding in its breadth of scope and its cultural significance as well as its offer of a new vision, a magical reality, a vision through which the author becomes the ultimate illywhacker.

Other works by Carey not mentioned above include {novels} *The Tax Inspector* (1991) and *The Unusual Life of Tristan Smith* (1994), winner of the Miles Franklin Award (1994) and Age Book of the Year Award (1994); {children's book} *The Big Bazoohley* (1995); {short stories and short story collections} "Room No. 5, Escribo," "Report on the Shadow Industry," and *Exotic Pleasures* (1990); {non-fiction} *A Letter to Our Son* (1994). Carey is currently working on the 1997 release of his sixth novel, *Mags,* a story based on the character Magwitch in Charles Dicken's *Great Expectations.* There are also indications that his novel *Oscar and Lucinda* will be produced as a film within the near future.

Further Reading

Beautiful Lies: a Film about Peter Carey (1985) is a biographical film about Carey. He has also been a popular subject for interviews in the Australian weekly press. A more substantial interview may be found in Candida Baker's *Yacker: Australian Writers Talk About Their Work* (Woollahra, N.S.W.: 1986). Van Ikin's interview, "Answers to Seventeen Questions," in *Science Fiction* (Sydney) (1977), explores aspects of speculative fiction in Carey's work.

John Maddock's interview with Carey (published in "Bizarre Realities: an Interview with Peter Carey" (*Southerly,* 1981) provides one of the most useful insights into the influences and literary antecedents which have influenced Carey. Other discussions of Carey's work include Graeme Turner's "American Dreaming: The Fictions of Peter Carey" in *Australian Literary Studies* (October 1986) and Teresa Dovey's "An infinite Onion Narrative Structure in Peter Carey's Fiction" in *Australian Literary Studies* (October 1983). A study of Carey's techniques and precedents may be found in C.K. Stead's "Careyland" in *Scripsi* (1989), while a view of Carey's 'metafiction' and post-modernism can be found in Wenche Ommundsen's "Narrative Navel-Grazing, Or How to Recognise a Metafiction When You See One" (*Southern Review,* 1989). □

William Carey

The English Baptist preacher William Carey (1761-1834), known as the father of modern Protestant missions, was a pioneer of new-style evangelism in India.

William Carey was born on Aug. 17, 1761, in a village in Northamptonshire, where he spent his childhood in poverty. He first was a shoemaker's apprentice. Although without formal education, Carey was an avid reader and a precocious linguist. He became a Baptist preacher and worked as a schoolmaster and was already on his way to becoming the leader who, in spite of the general reluctance of the Protestant churches of his day, devised new ways to obey the great commission "to go and evangelize the nations."

In one of the most surprising publications of missionary history, Carey expounded some practical guidelines "to use means for the conversions of the Heathens" (*Enquiry,* 1788). In a sermon to his colleagues (1791) he first used the words which would become the creed of modern missions: "Expect great things from God, attempt great things for God." In 1792 the first modern-style missionary society was founded: The Baptist Missionary Society. It was a model for the hundreds of societies to follow in the 19th century.

In 1793 Carey arrived in India, where he was confronted with the antimissionary attitude of the British colonial government. He settled in the Danish colony of Serampore, near Calcutta, where he inspired the teamwork of the "Serampore Trio" (Carey, William Ward, and Joshua Marshman). This "commune" attempted to translate the universality of the Christian faith into terms of practical involvement in all aspects of Indian life.

The basic principle of communal life was that every member should be, as far as possible, self-supporting. Carey paid for his missionary work (among other things) by acting as a director of an indigo factory and as a professor of languages in a secular institution. The objective of the community was to disseminate the gospel in all possible ways: by preaching, by teaching (in schools), and by literature (translating the Bible into more than 30 languages). Carey's translation service was noteworthy. He also made available some of the Indian classics and was instrumental in the renaissance of Hindu culture in the 19th century.

Carey believed that Indians could be authentically evangelized only by their own countrymen. He set out, therefore, to prepare converts for this task and broadened the scope of education in the mission schools. Serampore College was conceived not as a seminary but as a liberal arts college for Christians and non-Christians.

Carey died in Serampore on June 9, 1834, an internationally honored figure.

Further Reading

Carey's *An Enquiry into the Obligations of Christians* (1792) was republished in a new facsimile edition, edited by Ernest A. Payne (1961). The most complete biography is still S. Pearce Carey, *William Carey* (1923; 8th ed. 1934). A popular biography with an extensive bibliography is Walter B. Davis, *William Carey: Father of Modern Missions* (1963).

Additional Sources

Drewery, Mary, *William Carey: a biography,* Grand Rapids: Zondervan Pub. House, 1979, 1978.

Drewery, Mary, *William Carey: shoemaker and missionary,* London: Hodder and Stoughton, 1978.

George, Timothy., *Faithful witness: the life and mission of William Carey,* Birmingham, Ala.: New Hope, 1991.

Mangalwadi, Ruth., *William Carey: a tribute by a Indian woman,* New Delhi: Nivedit Good Books Distributors Pvt., 1993. □

Martha Carey Thomas

The American educator Martha Carey Thomas (1857-1935) was a proponent of woman's rights and president of Bryn Mawr.

Carey Thomas was born in Baltimore, Md., on Jan. 2, 1857, the oldest of 10 children of Dr. James Carey Thomas and Mary Whitall Thomas. Both parents were active members of the Society of Friends. Her intellectual development was strongly influenced by the militant feminism of her mother and her aunt Hannah Whitall Smith, a renowned preacher and reformer.

After attending private schools, Carey Thomas entered Cornell, then the only eastern university admitting women, as a junior, graduating in 1877 as a member of Phi Beta Kappa. Although admitted to graduate study at Johns Hopkins University by special vote of the trustees, she was dissatisfied with the policy that prevented her from attending seminars. In 1879 she went to Germany to continue her philological studies. She spent 3 years at Leipzig, which refused to grant degrees to women, as did Göttingen, where she also tried. Finally Zurich accepted her dissertation, and her brilliant defense won her a doctorate *summa cum laude* in 1882.

In 1884 Carey Thomas accepted the post of dean and professor of English literature at Bryn Mawr, then about to open as a college for women. She desired to build it into an institution that would encourage women to follow careers without having to face the difficulties with which she had struggled. Convinced that women deserved exactly the same education as men and needed even higher standards than men to succeed, she molded a curriculum that offered more advanced work than that given in many men's colleges and upheld the highest academic standards. She helped recruit an outstanding faculty which permitted offering graduate work modeled after that at Johns Hopkins. In 1894 she became president of Bryn Mawr, a post she held until her retirement in 1922. Her addresses to the student body were vividly remembered by many alumnae, inspiring them to strive for success in the professional careers that she had done so much to open to them.

Carey Thomas also helped open the Johns Hopkins Medical School to women by raising substantial sums on condition that no sexual discrimination be followed. She was active in the fight for woman's suffrage, helped organize the Summer School for Women Workers in Industry, and was the first woman trustee of Cornell. She played a major role in the League to Enforce Peace.

Carey Thomas never married. She died in Philadelphia on Dec. 2, 1935.

Further Reading

Barbara M. Cross, ed., *The Educated Woman in America* (1965), contains informative selections from Carey Thomas's addresses along with a perceptive introduction. An excellent biography, clearly presenting Carey Thomas's ideas and activities, is Edith Finch, *Carey Thomas of Bryn Mawr* (1947).

Additional Sources

Horowitz, Helen Lefkowitz., *The power and passion of M. Carey Thomas,* New York: Alfred A. Knopf, 1994. □

Tiburcio Carías Andino

Tiburcio Carías Andino (1876-1969) ruled Honduras as dictator (1932-1949) longer than any other president in his country's history. He was one of four Central American dictators of the 1930s and 1940s who comprised the socalled "Dictators' League" and, in collaboration with United States interests, brought stability and a degree of "modernization" to Honduras.

Tiburcio Carías Andino, was born in Tegucigalpa on March 15, 1876, the youngest son of Gen. Calixto Carías and Sara Andino de Carías. His father was active in the Liberal Party, which dominated Honduras through much of the late 19th and early 20th centuries, and Tiburcio worked for that party as early as the election of 1891 in political campaigning and military action related to the political struggles of the times. Along with his political and military careers, Carías excelled in the classroom. He obtained his law degree from the Central University of Honduras in 1898, but later became a professor of mathematics at the National Institute and conducted night school classes for poor children and workers.

Large for a Central American (Carías was 6′2″ tall), his physical stature complemented his talent for leadership. In 1903 he left the Liberal Party and joined in the founding of the Honduran National Party, essentially a successor to the 19th-century Conservative Party. Although he attained the rank of general for his role in the revolution of 1907, he was not primarily a military man, but rather an effective politician who made the military an important part of his machine. He was the most important leader of the National Party during the first half of the 20th century. He served in the Congress and as governor of several departments before becoming the National Party candidate for president in 1923. Although winning a plurality, he lacked the required majority. Political violence followed when the Congress failed to resolve the stalemate, and U.S. mediation ultimately established a compromise president. In 1928 Carías again ran, but lost to the Liberals by 12,000 votes. While his supporters called for revolt, Carías, even though he con-

trolled the military, respected the Liberal victory, a move that won him widespread respect.

Honduran politics of the era cannot be separated from the power of the North American banana companies, which intervened directly in Honduran affairs and were responsible for much of the political violence of the 1920s. The Liberal Party had the support of the fiercely competitive Samuel Zemurray and his Cuyamel Fruit Company, while the giant United Fruit Company backed Carías and the National Party. United's support was finally rewarded in November of 1932 when Carías won a convincing victory over Angel Zúñiga Huetes. Carías took office in 1933 after putting down a revolt aimed at keeping him from taking office. Zemurray, however, who had sold Cuyamel to United, soon emerged as the dominant figure at United.

Although the Honduran constitution prohibited reelection, the Congress amended it to enable Carías to extend his tenure first to 1943 and later to 1949. Carías was a strong, personalist *caudillo* who brought stability and order to a country noted for instability and frequent revolution. When he finally stepped down in January 1949 he turned over power to his protégé and minister of war, Juan Manuel Gálvez Durón, following the first presidential election (1948) in the country since 1932.

Five years later Carías, then 79, unsuccessfully sought to return to the presidency, suffering a major defeat at the polls. An ensuing coup reduced his still great political clout. He continued to live in Honduras until his death on December 23, 1969.

Carías's dictatorship has been compared to those of his contemporaries in other Central American states—Jorge Ubico of Guatemala, Maximiliano Hernández Martínez of El Salvador, and Anastasio Somoza of Nicaragua. Like them he had certain fascist characteristics and bought peace, order, and a measure of economic growth at the cost of civil liberties and the general welfare. There were many political prisoners and exiles; the press was shackled; and intellectuals and political activists found little opportunity for free expression. Angel Zúñiga kept up a steady propaganda campaign against Carías from exile in Mexico, and there was an occasional revolt attempted from within, but Carías's firm control of the military assured his continued rule. He cooperated closely with U.S. business and government interests, including support of the Allies in World War II. He also promoted notable expansion of road building and development of commercial aviation.

Unlike his "Dictators' League" counterparts in one important respect, Carías had abandoned the Liberal Party, which had become closely identified with economic policies that benefitted principally small oligarchies by the exploitation of native labor, often in collaboration with foreign capitalists. While Carías had close association with United Fruit and had himself come from a Liberal Party background, his National Party retained some of the 19th-century conservative philosophy which defended a curious alliance of the leading families of the elite with the masses. While all of the Central American dictatorships were repressive and often brutal, the Carías regime was somewhat more benign than the others, and he was the only one of them to step down gracefully from power. The overthrow of Hernández and Ubico by popular uprisings in 1944 probably were important in persuading Carías to leave the presidency in 1949, for he also began to face student and labor unrest after 1944. In reality, his National Party, which remains a force in Honduras today, represented a union of the 19th-century liberal and conservative elitist parties, allowing the Honduran Liberal Party of today to become more closely identified with middle-class interests. The heavy role of the military in modern Honduran politics is a major legacy of Carías's dictatorship.

Further Reading

There is little specifically on Carías in English, but James A. Morris, *Honduras, Caudillo Politics and Military Rulers* (1984) reviews his regime in some detail. See also William H. Stokes, *Honduras, An Area Study in Government* (1950); James D. Rudolf, editor, *Honduras, A Country Study* (1984); and Franklin Parker, *The Central American Republics* (1964). □

Giacomo Carissimi

Giacomo Carissimi (1605-1674) was an Italian composer of sacred and secular vocal music. His oratorios and chamber cantatas are of high importance musically and historically.

Giacomo Carissimi was born in Marino near Rome and baptized on April 18, 1605. In 1622 or 1623 he became a singer at the Cathedral of Tivoli, and from 1624 to 1627 he worked as organist there. He was chapelmaster at the church of S. Rufino in Assisi from 1628 to 1629. He was then appointed chapelmaster at the church of S. Apollinare in Rome and was simultaneously put in charge of musical instruction at the German College, an adjoining institution. Carissimi remained in this double position until his death on Jan. 12, 1674. He declined numerous invitations to other posts, and it seems that he never left Rome after 1630. His music was performed throughout Italy and abroad during his lifetime and well into the 18th century.

The extant works of Carissimi include 17 oratorios, about 150 chamber cantatas (that is, to Italian words), over 200 motets (to Latin words), at least 12 Masses, various liturgical works, some humorous Latin pieces, and a treatise on music. One or two pieces for instruments may be by Carissimi. But his music is virtually all for voices with instrumental accompaniment.

Of Carissimi's oratorios 15 are in Latin and 2 are in Italian. The majority are set to texts dealing with subjects from the Old Testament, and many include a part for a narrator, called the *testo.* His best-known oratorio is *Jephthe,* composed by 1649 at the latest, which is a masterpiece of expressive writing in both its solo and choral portions.

Most of Carissimi's chamber cantatas, in Italian, are for solo soprano voice and basso continuo; the remainder are for two or three voices and basso continuo. They are built of sections in recitative, arioso and aria style, which proceed in a manner at once varied and unified. The great majority are set to poems on amorous subjects, but some of the poems are religious in content and others are humorous. Carissimi's cantatas excel for their superb word setting and high musical quality.

In his Latin motets Carissimi used essentially the same forms and styles as in his Italian cantatas. His Masses reveal his firm mastery of contrapuntal writing in the then traditional church style.

Both directly, through his teaching at the German College, and indirectly, through the numerous copies made of his music, Carissimi was a leading influence on contemporary and later composers in Italy, France, Germany, and England.

Further Reading

Carissimi's music is discussed in Manfred F. Bukofzer, *Music in the Baroque Era: From Monteverdi to Bach* (1947), and Claude V. Palisca, *Baroque Music* (1968). An important general background study is Donald Jay Grout, *A History of Western Music* (1960).

Additional Sources

Dixon, Graham., *Carissimi,* Oxford; New York: Oxford University Press, 1986. □

Guy Carleton

The British statesman and general Guy Carleton, 1st Baron Dorchester (1724-1808), was one of the ablest British military leaders during the American Revolution. As governor of Quebec, he encouraged Canada's growth into a unified, self-governing nation.

Guy Carleton was born on Sept. 3, 1724, into a distinguished Irish family at Strabane in Tyrone County, Ireland. Entering the army as an ensign at 18, he was a lieutenant colonel 15 years later. In Canada he served under Gen. Jeffrey Amherst at the siege of Louisbourg, Nova Scotia, in 1758. A year later, in command of the regiment of grenadiers, he was with Gen. James Wolfe at the Battle of Quebec, where he was promoted to colonel and wounded. In 1761 he was wounded in the siege of Belle Isle, France; the following year he participated in the capture of Havana, Cuba, and was again wounded.

From 1766 to 1770 Carleton was lieutenant governor and acting governor of Quebec. He proved to be an able administrator who was successful in improving the relations between British and French Canadians. He was largely responsible for the passage of the Quebec Act of 1774, which established French and British law on equal footing in Canada. This infuriated the American colonists and helped provoke the American Revolution, but it also ensured the loyalty of French Canadians to Britain during the conflict.

Carleton became governor of Quebec in 1775. When Thomas Gage resigned as commander in chief of the British forces in North America, Carleton assumed command of the forces in Canada. American troops under Gen. Richard Montgomery advanced to threaten Montreal, and Carleton withdrew to Quebec with his small army. There he was besieged by an American force under Benedict Arnold, who was joined by Montgomery's troops. Carleton's leadership maintained the defenses of the city.

In spring 1776, reinforced by Gen. John Burgoyne's troops, Carleton counterattacked and drove the Americans out of Canada into New York. He defeated Arnold in October and then withdrew to Quebec. Disagreements with his superiors led to Carleton's removal from military command in 1777. The following year he resigned as governor and left Canada.

In February 1782, after the Revolution had effectively been ended, Carleton became commander in chief of the British forces in America. Using tact, firmness, and diplomacy, he successfully carried out the delicate tasks of suspending hostilities, withdrawing British forces from New York and Vermont, and protecting loyalists.

In 1786, as Baron Dorchester, he was appointed governor in chief of British North America, a post he held for 10 years. His major achievement was to redress the grievances of the American loyalists without antagonizing the French; he was also successful in promoting tolerance and cooperation between the English Protestant and French Catholic

populations. Under his leadership the Constitutional Act of 1791 was passed. This law instituted legislative councils, thereby giving Canada its first experience in self-government. Made a general in the British army in 1793, Carleton retired to England 3 years later. He died there on Nov. 10, 1808.

Further Reading

The standard biography of Carleton is A. G. Bradley, *Lord Dorchester* (1907; new ed. 1926). See also the appropriate volumes of Sir John William Fortescue, *History of the British Army* (13 vols., 1899-1930); relevant histories of the British in North America, such as James A. Williamson, *A Short History of British Expansion* (1922; 2 vols., 1945; vol. 1, 3d ed., and vol. 2, 5th ed., 1964); E. W. Sheppard, *Short History of the British Army* (1926; 4th ed. 1950); and V. T. Harlow, *The Founding of the Second British Empire, 1763-93* (2 vols., 1952-1964). □

George Carlin

Despite a lull in his career, George Carlin (born 1937) has secured his reputation as one of America's greatest comedians. He has performed regularly on television with the likes of Ed Sullivan, Tom Jones, Steve Allen, Jackie Gleason, and Carol Burnett, worked the major nightclub circuit, and starred in a Fox television sitcom, *The George Carlin Show.*

In the late-1960s, Carlin drifted into his thirties, dissatisfied and uninspired with comedy. Even Carlin's promotional literature admits: "[B]ecause of the influence television was having on his career, Carlin's material grew bland and safe. The rebellious, anti-establishment tone of some of his earlier routines had disappeared."

Anyone who has seen a Carlin performance knows his comedy turns on biting brilliance. As Richard Zoglin of *Time* noted about the funnyman's early days, "Carlin's unctuous radio deejays, TV newscasters and commercial pitchmen were not simple parodies: he used them to satirize a whole society that had its priorities out of whack." Fortunately, for Carlin and his fans, his early-thirtysomething career crisis was short-lived. By the age of 35, he had released a Grammy-winning album, *FM & AM,* appeared countless times on Johnny Carson's *Tonight Show,* hosted the first *Saturday Night Live,* and captured a corner of the cable market with his taped performances on HBO. Carlin has pushed his career at full-tilt ever since, and the payoff, as the comedian himself might say, has been "tangible recognition": a star on Hollywood's Walk of Fame, two Grammy awards, a popular book of his comedy, and movie roles. "He's at the top of his game now and the only comedian with his degree of fame who's doing standup exclusively 150 nights a year," the *New York Daily News* observed as Carlin approached 60. "He tapes an hour-long HBO special every two years and wishes he could do two hours every year. 'I've got a lot of things to say,' he insists."

Carlin realized the pleasures of humor as a kid growing up in New York City. "I remember being pretty young and

just saying something funny to my mother, and I remember I got a genuine laugh from her, you know how you can tell the difference?" he told the *New Jersey Herald* . "That's when I knew I could be funny." Armed with that homebred confidence, Carlin took his talent public, performing standup on his neighborhood streets, at high school, and in the Air Force. At the age of 19, while still in the Armed Services, he landed his first professional entertainment job working as a radio station disc jockey. Several years and radio stations later, Carlin joined up with newsman Jack Burns and developed a successful nightclub act that toured top stages around the country and earned a spot on *The Tonight Show* with Jack Paar. Two years later, Carlin struck out on his own.

For two years, Carlin honed his humor at a Greenwich Village cafe in New York City before breaking into television. Carlin's standup acts were a hit on shows hosted by the biggest names in the business: Merv Griffen, Mike Douglas, and Johnny Carson. Indeed, the performers Carlin joined on the stage reads like a "Who's Who of Post World War II Comics," including Steve Allen, Jackie Gleason, and Carol Burnett.

Eyes The Big Screen

Yet, despite his comic success on television, Carlin yearned for an acting career on the big screen, much like the comedians-turned-actors Bob Hope and Danny Kaye. Although he landed a role in the Doris Day film *With Six You Get Egg-Roll,* and a guest part on *That Girl,* Carlin was discouraged by his lack of success. Years later, he dabbled in the profession again—appearing in such flicks as *Car Wash, Bill and Ted's Excellent Adventure,* and *Prince of Tides,* with Barbra Streisand and Nick Nolte—but the experiences, coupled with a failed Fox network sitcom, only deepened his conviction that comedy was *his* calling. "I care a lot about my ideas," Carlin told the *Toldeo Blade* in 1995. "My mind is active, and I think hard and think a lot. I don't think a lot of stand-up people stay with it long enough to discover themselves. They see it as a stepping stone. Circumstances forced me to stay with it longer, and I discovered that I had something more to offer, and something else to do with myself. All of these guys that came out of *Saturday Night Live* and *Second City* on television—those two shows were always considered subversive, you know? They were the enemies of The Establishment. But the first thing they do when they come out here to Hollywood is start doing these crappy formula studio movies."

Though the material for Carlin's humor has changed during his long career, his fierce criticism of mainstream culture has not. He possesses a sensibility that has been described by writers as "caustic," "acerbic," "angry," and "irreverent." Carlin, during an interview with the *Denver Post,* admitted: "Anyone who's intelligent who isn't somewhat angry is probably missing the point somewhere along the way. The way I put it is this: This species is a failure that has organized itself incorrectly, and it's stuck and will never get out of it because the forces that keep it this way are much too powerful to change. So I gave up on this species, and I kind of try to look at it from a distance, but I can't completely give up because I'm a part of it. So there's this tension, and that creates a kind of anger that is easy to theatricalize." Such razor-sharp pessimism prompted at least one reporter from the *Bellingham Herald* to ask Carlin: "Is this all meant tongue-in-cheek?" To which the humorist replied, "No, it's not. I'm only being partly facetious. If you scratch any cynic, you'll find a disappointed idealist."

Challenges Audience

Carlin sharpened his comic focus in the early '70s. He emerged from his brief period of professional unrest with a new appetite for scathing commentary, for "testing the limits," as Zoglin of *Time* wrote, "challenging his audience, shouting from the depths of his social-activist soul." Carlin's most direct challenge appeared on the album *Class Clown* with a performance titled "The Seven Words You Can't Say on Television." After its release, community leaders tried to ban Carlin's concerts in their cities. "He was arrested several times for obscenity (all of which were dismissed), and fought the FCC [Federal Communications Commission] in a protracted legal battle," noted the *St. Petersburg Times.* Carlin's fight with the FCC ultimately was settled in a landmark Supreme Court ruling, which, according to *Time,* "upheld an FCC ban on 'offensive' material during hours when children are in the audience." Carlin, however, scored with his fans—*Class Clown* sold more than 100,000 copies. Moreover, Carlin continued to "keep a foot in the mainstream as well as the counterculture," as Zoglin of *Time* put it, by hosting the first edition of *Saturday Night Live* and subbing for Johnny Carson on the *Tonight Show.*

Thanks to cable television, Carlin also kept himself firmly entrenched in mass media. His first HBO show, a taped performance of *On Location: George Carlin at USC,* was so popular the cable company ran seven more Carlin shows, including a 1982 performance at Carnegie Hall and 1993 broadcast from the Paramount Theater at New York's Madison Square Garden called *Jammin' in New York.* Of that last performance, Zoglin of *Time* wrote, it "may not be his best, but it is almost certainly his angriest. Carlin's attack on America's war culture (complete with phallic interpretation of the gulf war) is too strident; his ridicule of golf ('an arrogant, elitist game that takes up entirely too much room in this country') too meanspirited. But he is, as usual, a whiz on the subject of language, this time our tendency to add unnecessary words to connote importance— 'shower activity' or 'emergency situation.' ('We *know* it's a situation. *Everything* is a situation.')"

Carlin is proud of his ability to offend—in fact, he considers it central to his success. "I don't care what happens to this planet, this race, the country," he told Jeff Rusnak of the Florida *Sun Sentinel.* "And being emotionally detached . . . gives the artist complete freedom to attack, to observe from a distance and not have this sort of echo in the background that 'this could be a lot better, folks.'" That "distance," he explained, has always existed in his life. "What really freed me was I began to realize that I don't identify with the human experience, with the national experience, and in fact, most of my life, didn't identify with the local group, no matter what it was, my school, the Air Force, my family, religion, commerce. Therefore I have no stake in the outcome."

Carlin's career has always been a high-wire act. He's a master of balancing his outrageous observations with enough humor to keep his fans laughing, and coming back for more. That his distinctive brand of comedy has weathered more than three decades, as well as his own personal struggles with "heavy drug use," according to *Time,* suggests Carlin delivers far more than a good joke. "I never understand why people ask whether I get tired of what I do. No, I don't get tired, I chose to do this," he once told the *New Jersey Herald.* "This is my art, to interpret the world."

Further Reading

Bellingham Herald, November 30, 1995, p. C1.
Denver Post, January 24, 1996.
New Jersey Herald, August, 11, 1995, p. 13.
New York Daily News, March 28, 1996, p.61.
New York Post, March 28, 1996, p. 12.
St. Petersburg Times, January 18, 1996.
Sun Sentinel, TK, 1996.
Time, May 18, 1992, p. 73.
Toledo Blade, September 22, 1995, p. 23. □

Chester F. Carlson

The American inventor Chester F. Carlson (1906-1968) invented the process of xerography which became the basis for the operation of the office copying machines first introduced by the Xerox Corporation in 1959.

Chester Floyd Carlson was born on February 8, 1906, in Seattle, Washington. Illness and poverty in his family forced him to become his parent's main financial support while he was in his teens. Despite these responsibilities and handicaps. Carlson worked his way through college, graduating with a Bachelor of Science degree in physics from California Institute of Technology in 1930.

After trying in vain to gain employment as a physicist in California he left for New York City, where the P. R. Mallory Company, an electrical manufacturing firm, offered him a position in its patent department. This job proved to be of crucial importance to Carlson's career as an inventor in two ways. First, he was introduced to patent law and procedures; second, the need to duplicate patent drawings and specifications made him aware of the inadequacies of the existing photostat process for copying documents.

Carlson stayed at Mallory until 1945, eventually becoming head of the patent department.

While working at Mallory, Carlson attended New York Law School at night, receiving his law degree in 1939. One year later he was admitted to the New York bar. At the same time he conducted research on a duplication process that would produce clean copies quickly without using the chemical solutions, film, and printing paper necessary for photographic reproduction.

Carlson began his search for an alternative process by reading the available literature on printing, photography, and various copying technologies. His study convinced him that in some yet unspecified manner it might be possible to duplicate documents by making use of photoconductivity. He decided that wet-process photography must be replaced by the dry techniques of what he called "electrophotography."

Using the little amount of money he possessed, Carlson bought chemicals and equipment and turned his New York apartment into a laboratory (1934). Unable to devote full time to this work, Carlson hired an unemployed German physicist and engineer named Otto Kornei to help him. Carlson and Kornei, limited to a research budget of $10.00 a month, were able in October 1938 to make the first electrophotographic copy. It read simply "10-22-38 Astoria."

This copy was produced by a primitive, but innovative, method that formed the foundation for Carlson's subsequent research and for the industry that grew out of it. First, a rabbit's fur or cotton cloth was rubbed vigorously over the surface of a metal plate coated with a layer of sulfur. The rubbing charged the plate with static electricity. The charged plate was then placed beneath a piece of glass upon which was inked the material to be copied. Metal plate and glass were next exposed to a bright light source for a few seconds. This exposure caused the sulfur coating to lose its charge in varying degrees depending upon how much light reached its surface. In effect, the intense illumination produced an invisible electrostatic image of the material being copied. This image could be made visible by dusting an electroscopic powder on the plate. The powder was attracted to the areas which had been less intensely illuminated. In order to make the fragile powder image permanent, Carlson carefully pressed a piece of wax-coated paper over the prepared plate. The powder adhered to, and fixed upon, the surface of the waxed paper.

Although there obviously remained much to be done in improving the new dry-copying technique—which came to be called "xerography"—Carlson applied for key patents on the process (1939, 1940). Carlson had neither the money, laboratory facilities, nor mechanical talent to transform his experiments into a working copy machine ready for public use. Therefore, in 1944 he reached an agreement with the Battelle Memorial Institute, a nonprofit industrial research laboratory, to develop his invention beyond its first stages. Three years later the Haloid Company of Rochester, New York, undertook the final conversion of xerography into a commercial product. Haloid, which became Haloid-Xerox and then Xerox, publicly demonstrated xerography in 1948 and offered the first Xerox copying machines for sale in 1959.

As xerography became a complex technical and business venture Carlson withdrew from active involvement with it, except for serving as a consultant to the Xerox Corporation. By 1945 his invention brought him sufficient financial security so that he could retire from Mallory. Royalties from his xerography patents made Carlson a multimillionaire, and in later life he engaged in many philanthropic endeavors.

Further Reading

For Carlson's life and work, and the commercial development of xerography, see John H. Dessauer, *My Years With Xerox: The Billions Nobody Wanted* (1971). The technical side of xerography is treated in John H. Dessauer and Harold E. Clark (editors), *Xerography and Related Processes* (London, 1965). □

Thomas Carlyle

The British essayist and historian Thomas Carlyle (1795-1881) was the leading social critic of early Victorian England. Disseminating German idealist thought in his country, with Calvinist zeal he preached against materialism and mechanism during the industrial revolution.

Thomas Carlyle was born at Ecclefechan in Dumfriesshire, Scotland, on Dec. 4, 1795. His father, a stonemason, was an intelligent man and a pious Calvinist. Carlyle was educated at Annan Grammar School and Edinburgh University, where he read voraciously and distinguished himself in mathematics. He abandoned his original intention to enter the ministry and turned instead first to schoolteaching and then to literary hackwork, dreaming all the while of greatness as a writer. A reading of Madame de Staël's *Germany* introduced him to German thought and literature, and in 1823-1824 he published a *Life of Schiller* in the *London Magazine* and in 1824 a translation of Goethe's *Wilhelm Meister's Apprenticeship* .

Meanwhile Carlyle had passed through a religious crisis similar to the one he was to describe in *Sartor Resartus* and had met Jane Baillie Welsh, a brilliant and charming girl, who recognized his genius and gave him encouragement and love. Through a tutorship in the Buller family Carlyle made his first trip to London, where he met Samuel Taylor Coleridge and other leading literary figures. He returned to Scotland, married Jane Welsh on Oct. 17, 1826, and settled first in Edinburgh and subsequently at Craigenputtock, an isolated farmhouse belonging to his wife's family. It was during this period that he wrote a series of essays for the *Edinburgh Review* and the *Foreign Review* which were later grouped as *Miscellaneous and Critical Essays.* Among these were essays on Burns, Goethe, and Richter and the important "Signs of the Times," his first essay on contemporary social problems.

"Sartor Resartus"

It was at Craigenputtock that Carlyle wrote *Sartor Resartus,* his most characteristic work. Originally rejected by London editors, it was first published in *Fraser's Magazine* in 1833-1834 and did not attain book form in England until 1838, after Ralph Waldo Emerson had introduced it in America and after the success of Carlyle's *The French Revolution.* The first appearance of *Sartor Resartus* was greeted with "universal disapprobation," in part because of its wild, grotesque, and rambling mixture of serious and comic styles. This picturesque and knotted prose was to become Carlyle's hallmark.

The theme of the book is that the material world is symbolic of the spiritual world of ultimate reality. Man's creeds, beliefs, and institutions, which are all in tatters because of the enormous advances of modern thought and science, have to be tailored anew as his reason perceives the essential mystery behind the natural world. Carlyle's concern is to allow for a change of forms while insisting on the permanence of spirit in opposition to the materialistic and utilitarian bias of 18th-century thought. Part of his thesis is exemplified in the career of an eccentric fictitious German professor, Teufelsdröckh, whose papers Carlyle pretends to be editing. He progresses from "The Everlasting No" of spiritual negation, through "The Centre of Indifference" of resignation, to "The Everlasting Yea," a positive state of mind in which he recognizes the value of suffering and duty over selfish pleasure.

Career in London

Carlyle came into his maturity with *Sartor* and longed to abandon short articles in favor of a substantial work. Accordingly, he turned to a study of the French Revolution, encouraged in the project by John Stuart Mill, who gave him his own notes and materials. As a help in his researches he moved to London, settling in Chelsea. The publication of

The French Revolution in 1837 established Carlyle as one of the leading writers of the day. The book demonstrates his belief in the Divine Spirit's working in man's affairs. Carlyle rejected the "dry-as-dust" method of factual history writing in favor of immersing himself in his subject and capturing its spirit and movement—hence the focus on the drama and scenic quality of events and on the mounting impact of detail. His ability to animate history is Carlyle's triumph, but his personal reading of the significance of a great event lays him open to charges of subjectivity and ignorance of the careful study of economic and political detail so admired by later schools of historical research.

Carlyle's great popularity led him to give several series of public lectures on German literature, the history of literature, modern European revolutions, and finally, and most significantly, on heroes and hero worship. These lectures were published in 1841 as *On Heroes, Hero-Worship, and the Heroic in Literature.* This work reflects his increasing hostility to modern egalitarian democracy and his stress upon the inequality of men's wisdom and the incorporation, as it were, of divine purpose. Carlyle's insistence upon the need for heroic leadership is the reason why he was attacked—often mistakenly—as an apostle of force or dictatorial rule.

Late Works

Carlyle's hero worship is responsible for the two largest projects of his later career. He first intended to rehabilitate Oliver Cromwell by means of a history of the Puritan Revolution but later narrowed his project to a collection of Cromwell's letters and speeches connected by narrative and commentary (1845). And from 1852 to 1865 he labored on a biography of Frederick the Great (1865) against the mounting uncongeniality and intractability of the subject. During these years Carlyle exerted a great influence on younger contemporaries such as Alfred Tennyson, Robert Browning, Charles Kingsley, John Ruskin, and James Froude. He published a number of criticisms of the economic and social conditions of industrial England, among them *Chartism* (1839), "Latter-Day" Pamphlets (1850), and *Shooting Niagara, and After?* (1867). His most significant social criticism, *Past and Present* (1843), contrasted the organic, hierarchical society of the medieval abbey of Bury St. Edmunds with the fragmented world of modern parliamentary democracy. It hoped for a recognition of moral leadership among the new "captains of industry."

In 1865 Carlyle was elected lord rector of Edinburgh University, but in his last years he was more than ever a lonely, isolated prophet of doom. He died on Feb. 5, 1881, and was buried in Ecclefechan Churchyard.

Further Reading

The standard biography of Carlyle is still James Anthony Froude, *Thomas Carlyle: A History of the First Forty Years of His Life, 1795-1835* (2 vols., 1882) and *Thomas Carlyle: A History of His Life in London, 1834-1881* (2 vols., 1884). For an account and assessment of the controversy occasioned by the biography see Waldo H. Dunn, *Froude and Carlyle* (1930). A short biography is Julian Symons, *Thomas Carlyle: The Life and Ideas of a Prophet* (1952). A good introduction to Carlyle's work is Emery Neff, *Carlyle* (1932). Also useful is Basil Willey, *Nineteenth Century Studies* (1949). Recommended for general historical background are George Macaulay Trevelyan, *British History in the Nineteenth Century and After, 1782-1919* (1922; new ed. 1937); David C. Somervell, *English Thought in the Nineteenth Century* (1929; 6th ed. 1950); G. M. Young, *Victorian England: Protrait of an Age* (1936; 2d ed. 1953); and Walter E. Houghton, *The Victorian Frame of Mind, 1830-1870* (1957).

Additional Sources

Campbell, Ian, *Thomas Carlyle,* New York: Scribner, 1975, 1974.

Clubbe, John, comp., *Two reminiscences of Thomas Carlyle,* Durham, N.C., Duke University Press, 1974.

Conway, Moncure Daniel, *Thomas Carlyle,* Folcroft, Pa.: Folcroft Library Editions, 1977.

Froude, James Anthony, *Froude's Life of Carlyle,* Columbus: Ohio State University Press, 1979.

Garnett, Richard, *Life of Thomas Carlyle,* New York: AMS Press, 1979.

Kaplan, Fred, *Thomas Carlyle: a biography,* Berkeley: University of California Press, 1993.

Lammond, D., *Carlyle,* Philadelphia: R. West, 1978.

Nicoll, Henry James., *Thomas Carlyle,* Philadelphia: R. West, 1977.

Sagar, S., *Round by Repentance Tower: a study of Carlyle,* Philadelphia: R. West, 1977. □

Stokely Carmichael

Stokely Carmichael (born 1941) was a "militant" civil rights activist and stood at the forefront of the "Black Power" movement. He soared to fame by popularizing the phrase "Black Power" and was one of the most powerful and influential leaders in the Student Non-Violent Coordinating Committee (SNCC).

Stokely Carmichael was born in Port of Spain, Trinidad, on June 29, 1941. His father, Adolphus, who died when he was in his late forties, moved with Stokely's mother, Mabel, to the United States when their son was only two-years-old. Although his father had been swept up by the cause of Trinidad's independence, he left his homeland to better his family's economic fortunes and moonlighted as a New York City cab driver, while Mabel found work as a maid. Young Carmichael was left in the care of two aunts and his grandmother and attended Tranquillity Boy's School. Carmichael joined his parents in New York City's Harlem when he was eleven-years-old and became the only black member of a street gang called the Morris Park Dukes. His status as a foreigner and his self-described "hip" demeanor assured him of popularity among many of his liberal, affluent white schoolmates. He said in an interview with *Life* that he dated white girls and attended parties on swank Park Avenue during this period. But Carmichael, a bright student, settled down after his family moved to the Bronx and he discovered the lure of intellectual life. After his parents moved to the Bronx, he

was admitted to the Bronx High School of Science, a school for gifted youths.

Carmichael was interested in politics even then, especially the work of African-American socialist Bayard Rustin, whom he heard speak many times. At one point, he volunteered to help Rustin organize African-American workers in a paint factory. But the friendliness, doctrinal and otherwise, of Rustin and other African-American intellectual leftists with the white liberal establishment would eventually alienate Carmichael.

Joined Civil Rights Movement

While he was in school the civil rights movement was gaining momentum. The Supreme Court had declared that school segregation was illegal, and African-Americans in Montgomery, Alabama, successfully desegregated the city's busses through a yearlong boycott. During Carmichael's senior year in high school, four African-American freshmen from North Carolina Agricultural Camp; Technical College in Greensboro, North Carolina, staged a sit-in at the white-only lunch counter in Woolworth's.

The action of these young students captured the imagination of African-Americans and some sympathetic white students throughout the United States. Some young people in New York City, including Carmichael, joined a boycott of the city's Woolworth stores which was sponsored by the youth division of the Congress on Racial Equality (CORE). CORE hoped that the boycott would pressure Woolworth's owners to desegregate all of its stores' facilities throughout the country. Carmichael traveled to Virginia and South Carolina to join anti-discrimination sit-ins and because of his growing sensitivity to the plight of African-Americans in the United States, especially in the segregated South, he refused offers to attend white colleges and decided to study at the historically black Howard University in Washington, D.C.

At Howard from 1960 to 1964, Carmichael majored in philosophy while becoming increasingly involved in the civil rights movement. He joined a local organization called the Non-Violent Action Group which was affiliated with an Atlanta-based civil rights organization, the Student Non-Violent Coordinating Committee (SNCC, called "Snick"). During his summers or whenever there was free time, Carmichael traveled South to join with the Congress of Racial Equality sponsored "freedom riders," composed of integrated groups riding interstate busses in an attempt to make the federal government enforce statutes which provided that interstate busses and bus terminals be desegregated. In bus depots there were separate toilet facilities for blacks and whites with signs that read something like "white ladies here, colored women in the rear."

Many southern whites were violently hostile to the efforts of these young people to force desegregation on them, and some of the freedom rider busses were bombed or burned. The riders were often beaten and jailed. A CORE leader remarked that for the seasoned freedom riders, jail was not a new experience, but that the determined exuberance of the young freedom riders was a shock to the jailers in Mississippi and other southern states. In the spring of 1961, when Carmichael was 20, he spent 49 days in a Jackson, Mississippi jail. One observer said that Carmichael was so rebellious during this period that the sheriff and prison guards were relieved when he was released.

After graduating in 1964 with a bachelor's degree in philosophy, Carmichael stayed in the South as much as possible, sitting-in, picketing, helping with voter registration drives, and working alongside of other leaders of SNCC. He was especially active in Lowndes County, Alabama, where he helped found the Lowndes County Freedom Party, a political party that chose a black panther as its symbol in order to comply with a state requirement that all political parties must have a visual symbol to assist voters. The black panther was indigenous to Alabama and seemed both a dignified symbol for empowered African-Americans and an effective response to the white rooster that symbolized the Alabama Democratic party. Southern response to the civil rights workers was often so violent that demonstrators were bruised, wounded, or even killed by policemen, by members of the Ku Klux Klan, or other individuals. There were six civil rights workers murdered that year, but this only made Carmichael, and others, more determined than ever to work for desegregation.

Turning From Non-Violence

The turning point in Carmichael's experience came as he watched from his locked hotel room while outside, African-American demonstrators were beaten and shocked with cattle prods by police. The horrified Carmichael began to scream and could not stop. As his activism deepened and he saw the violence doled out to violent and non-violent protesters alike, he began to distance himself from non-violent tactics and its proponents, including Martin Luther King, Jr.

In 1965, after Carmichael replaced the moderate John Lewis as the president of the SNCC, he joined Martin Luther King, Jr., Floyd McKissick of the National Association for the Advancement of Colored People (NAACP), and James Meredith, who had been the first African-American student to attend the University of Mississippi, on a "freedom march" in Mississippi which Meredith had first attempted alone. After he was shot during his solitary march, Meredith welcomed the help of other civil rights leaders. Carmichael and McKissick had trouble agreeing with King that the march would be non-violent and interracial. Carmichael had become increasingly hostile to the aid offered by white civil rights workers. During this march, Carmichael began to articulate his views about "Black Power" before the assembled television cameras. Americans reacted strongly to a slogan that seemed to indicate that African-Americans wanted to replace white supremacy with African-American supremacy. Carmichael later defined "Black Power" to mean the right of African-Americans to define and organize themselves as they saw fit and to protect themselves from racial violence. After the march, white members of the SNCC were not encouraged to stay and Carmichael and other SNCC leaders began to talk about "revolution."

Carmichael's articulation of "Black Power" evidenced by his 1967 book *Black Power* (co-written with Charles V. Hamilton), and his article "What We Want" advanced the idea that mere integration was not the answer to American racism, and that America formed only a piece in the puzzle. Carmichael and Hamilton linked the struggle for African-American empowerment definitively to economic self-determination domestically and the end of imperialism and colonialism worldwide. "What We Want" described the need for African-American communal control of African-American resources.

The term "Black Power," however disconcerting to moderate African-American leaders, absolutely terrified mainstream whites; many interpreted this term to mean not empowerment, but rather African-American domination and possibly even race war. Journalists demanded repeatedly that Carmichael define the phrase, and he soon began to believe that no matter what his explanation, they would interpret it as sinister. Pressed by *Life* magazine, Carmichael said "For the last time, 'Black Power' means black people coming together to form a political force and either electing representatives or forcing their representatives to speak their needs [rather than relying on established parties]. 'Black Power' doesn't mean anti-white, violence, separatism or any other racist things the press says it means. It's saying 'Look buddy, we're not laying a vote on you unless you lay so many schools, hospitals, playgrounds and good jobs on us.'" However, Carmichael sometimes gave the term a different spin when he spoke to African-American audiences. As James Haskins recorded in his book, *Profiles In Black Power* (1972), Carmichael explained to one crowd, "When you talk of 'Black Power,' you talk of building a movement that will smash everything Western civilization has created." Through statements like this, Carmichael and his movement continued to be seen by many in mainstream America as a movement not to build, but to destroy.

International Focus

As the revolutionary fervor of the 1960s deepened, the SNCC became a "Black Power" vehicle, more or less replacing the hymn-singing integration of earlier days. Yet Carmichael had gone as far as he could with the organization, deciding not to run for re-election as its leader in 1967, just before the organization fell apart. Carmichael's political emphasis had shifted as well; he began speaking out not only against the war in Vietnam, but against what he called U.S. imperialism worldwide. *Time* reported that Carmichael had traveled the world denouncing his adopted country, speaking to cheering crowds in Cuba, and declaring, "We do not want peace in Vietnam. We want the Vietnamese people to defeat the United States." *Time* called him a purveyor of "negritude and nihilism" and noted that many U.S. politicians wanted to jail him for sedition upon his return to the country he called "hell."

Upon his return in 1968, U.S. marshals confiscated his passport. Meanwhile, the radical Oakland, California-based Black Panther Party, a Black group which advocated African-American liberation by "any means necessary," had made him their honorary prime minister. He would resign from that post the following year, rejecting Panther coalitions with white activists. He based himself in Washington, D.C. and continued to speak around the country. In March of 1968, he announced his engagement to South African singer-activist Miriam Makeba. They were wed two months later and the Tanzanian ambassador to the United States hosted their reception. They were permitted to honeymoon abroad after they promised not to visit any "forbidden" countries; even so, many nations refused them entrance. In 1969, Carmichael left the United States for Conakry, Republic of Guinea, in West Africa. He moved there, in part, to assist in the restoration to power of the deposed Ghanaian ruler Kwame Nkrumah, who lived in Guinea and served as an exponent of the sort of anti-imperialist, pan-African empowerment Carmichael had espoused in the United States.

While in Guinea, Carmichael took the name Kwame Ture and, over the next decades, founded the All-African Revolutionary Party and continued to speak as an advocate of revolution to answer the problems of racism and injustice. In 1993, speaking at Michigan State University, he made it clear that he still considered capitalism the source of most of the problems he had been studying during his career as an activist. In a *Michigan Chronicle* interview he stated, "Those who labor do not enjoy the fruits of their labor, we know that to be slavery," but his 1992 afterward to a new edition of *Black Power* showed that he felt real progress had been made in certain respects in the U.S., "From 1965 to 1992, no one could deny that change has occurred."

In 1996 Carmichael was diagnosed with prostate cancer and was honored by his birth nation with a $1,000 a month grant, awarded to him by the government of Trinidad and Tobago. Benefits in Denver, New York, and Atlanta were also held to help pay his medical expenses.

Steeped in the civil rights struggle, Carmichael emerged as one of the firebrands of the African-American militant movement in the 1960s, and unlike many of his compatriots from that time, he has in the intervening years experienced neither burnout nor conversion; the years have only refined the flame of his convictions, even in the face of cancer.

He continues to advance revolution to answer the problems of racism and unfairness. "Since we shed blood continually and sporadically and in a disorganized manner for reforms," he stated in his afterward to *Black Power,* "let us permanently organize ourselves and make Revolution."

Further Reading

Carmichael discussed his views in *Black Power; the Politics of Liberation in America* (1967), co-authored with Charles V. Hamilton, and in *Stokely Speaks: Black Power to Pan-Africanism* (1971). Several authors have written about the history of SNCC. Two examples are Howard Zinn *SNCC, The New Abolitionists* (1964) and Cleveland Sellers with Robert Terrell *The River of No Return, the Autobiography of a Black Militant in the Life and Death of SNCC* (1973).

Further information on Carmichael and his views can be found in James Haskins *Profiles in Black Power* (1972), Jacqueline Johnson *Stokely Carmichael: The Story of Black Power* (1990), Milton Viorst *Fire in the Streets* (1979), and Robert Weisbrot *Freedom Bound: A History of America's Civil Rights Movement* (1990). For information on Carmichael's views in his own words, see the May 19, 1967 issue of *Life,* the February 24, 1993 issue of the *Michigan Chronicle,* the August 5, 1966 issue of the *New York Times,* and the December 15, 1967 issue of *Time.* Additional biographical material on Carmichael can be found in the April 14, 1996 issue of the *New York Times,* the February 8, 1992 issue of the *Chicago Defender,* and the March 30, 1997 issue of the *Denver Post.* □

Rudolf Carnap

The German-American philosopher Rudolf Carnap (1891-1970) was the most prominent representative of the school of logical positivism, sometimes called logical empiricism.

Rudolf Carnap was born on May 18, 1891, in Ronsdorf, Germany. From 1910 to 1914 he studied philosophy and science at the universities of Jena and Freiburg. At Jena, Gottlob Frege, the pioneering mathematical logician, directed his thinking. Carnap served as an officer in the Germany army during World War I, later resuming his studies at Jena, where he received his doctorate in 1921. As a student, Carnap came under the influence of Bertrand Russell and his writings on logic and epistemology.

In 1923 Carnap met Hans Reichenbach, with whom he later founded and edited *Erkenntnis* (1930-1940), the journal of the logical empiricists. Through Reichenbach he met Moritz Schlick, head of the Philosophical Circle at the University of Vienna. In 1926 Carnap became instructor of philosophy there and participated in the Circle. Ludwig Wittgenstein attended meetings of the Circle in 1927, becoming another influence on Carnap's thought.

Carnap won wide recognition among philosophers with the publication of the *Logische Aufbau der Welt* (Logical Structure of the World) in 1928. He offered a new methodology, which called for the reduction of all knowledge to private, subjective sense-data in order to construct a technical system to embrace all known-objects and to solve philosophical problems. In 1928 Carnap also published *Scheinprobleme in der Philosophie* (Fictitious Problems in Philosophy). Following Wittgenstein, he sought to show that metaphysical problems are pseudoproblems and that metaphysical sentences are "non-sense."

In 1931 Carnap became professor of natural philosophy at the German university in Prague. In 1933 he married Elizabeth Ina von Stöger.

Carnap's investigations into logic and mathematics came to fruition with the publication of *The Logical Syntax of Language* (1934). Utilizing the distinction between "metalanguage" and "object language" advanced by Polish logicians, Carnap sought to develop a metalanguage (which he called "logical syntax") to elucidate and formalize the basic terms, formation rules, and transformation rules of object languages—that is, systems of logic and mathematics. He proposed his famous "principle of tolerance," which permits anyone to construct any language he wishes.

Fleeing from Nazism, Carnap went to the United States in December 1935. A few months later he was appointed professor of philosophy at the University of Chicago. In 1941 he became a naturalized citizen. Except for leaves to research or to teach elsewhere, he remained at Chicago until 1952.

At the university Carnap joined Otto Neurath and Charles W. Morris to found and edit the *International Encyclopedia of Unified Science.* Carnap's contribution to the encyclopedia is entitled *Foundations of Logic and Mathematics* (1930). This work displays a radical shift in his thinking. Persuaded by Alfred Tarski, Carnap had become convinced that the logical analysis of language extends beyond logical syntax and includes semantics, which deals with the reference of language to objects and contains the concepts of meaning and truth. Thus Carnap initiated a series of studies in semantics: *Introduction to Semantics* (1942), *Formalization of Logic* (1943), and *Meaning and Necessity* (1947).

In 1950 Carnap's massive book, *The Logical Foundations of Probability,* climaxed his investigations into the logic of empirical knowledge. From 1952 to 1954 Carnap advanced his researches into the logic of science at the Institute for Advanced Study in Princeton. In 1954 he accepted the chair in philosophy at the University of California, Los Angeles, made vacant by the death of Reichenbach. Retiring from teaching in 1961, he continued as a research professor until his death on Sept. 14, 1970, in Santa Monica, Calif.

Further Reading

P. A. Schillp, ed., *The Philosophy of Rudolf Carnap* (1963), containing Carnap's intellectual autobiography, is basic. Carnap's views receive some attention in Julian Weinberg, *An Examination of Logical Positivism* (1936); Victor Kraft, *The Vienna Circle* (1950); and Joergen Joergensens, *The Development of Logical Positivism* (1951). See also Wolfgang Stegmuller, *Die Wahrheitsidee und die Idee der Semantik* (1957); B. H. Kazemeir and D. Vuijsje, eds., *Logic and Language* (1962); Alan Hausman and Fred Wilson, *Carnap and Goodman* (1967); and Arne Naess, *Four Modern Philosophers*. □

Carneades

Carneades (ca. 213-ca. 128 B.C.) was a Greek philosopher of the third school of academic skepticism. His combination of skepticism and empiricism can now be seen to have remarkable affinities with a good deal of post-Renaissance Western philosophy.

Carneades was born in Cyrene. Little is known of his personal life, except that in 156 B.C. he came to Rome, along with two other philosophers, to protest a recent fine imposed on Athens by Rome. Here he demonstrated with great effect the logic of skepticism by delivering two contradictory orations on justice. One of these praised justice, as a virtue grounded in nature; the other praised injustice, on grounds of expediency.

Carneades spent a large part of his long life as head of the so-called Third Academy, which like the second, started by Arcesilaus, was grounded in skepticism. In his attacks on "dogmatic" philosophies, particularly the stoicism of Chrysippus, Carneades went far beyond the skepticism of Arcesilaus. Accepting Arcesilaus's contention against the Stoics that "presentations" are just as likely to be untrue as true, he undermined the doctrine further by suggesting, in anticipation of George Berkeley, that at least one thing, color, has *no* absolute presentation at all but varies according to time and circumstance. He attacked the whole notion of a law of contradiction and may have been the first to suggest that the notion of "proof" in philosophy is chimerical.

In contrast with this, Carneades seems to have been more moderate than other Skeptics in his suggestion that some presentations are less misleading than others. He ridiculed the Stoics' belief in the gods, in providence, and in divine creation, and he undermined their belief in man's ability to predict the future by means of omens, dreams, oracles, and the like, by arguing that reference to chance alone is enough to account for any of their supposed successes. The determinism of stoicism he attempted to subvert by suggesting that man's free will is an independent cause, outside the scheme of physical cause-effect relationships.

Carneades suggested—in contrast with Chrysippus—that there is no such thing as a law grounded in nature, and he anticipated Thomas Hobbes in arguing that man is not just by nature. Skeptical of the whole notion of moral absolutes, he propounded a "social contract" theory of justice that has a remarkably modern ring, and his analysis of justice in terms of utility seems to antedate Jeremy Bentham and John Stuart Mill.

Further Reading

For the fragmentary remains of Carneades's doctrines the most convenient source is the third volume of C. J. de Vogel, ed., *Greek Philosophy* (3 vols., 1950-1959; 3d ed. 1963). See also Edwyn Bevan, *Stoics and Sceptics* (1913). □

Andrew Carnegie

The Scottish-born American industrialist and philanthropist Andrew Carnegie (1835-1919) was one of the first "captains of industry." Leader of the American steel industry from 1873 to 1901, he disposed of his great fortune by endowing educational, cultural, scientific, and technological institutions.

Andrew Carnegie typified those characteristics of business enterprise and innovation that changed the United States from an agricultural and commercial nation to the greatest industrial nation in the world in a single generation—between 1865 and 1901. The era has sometimes been called the "Age of the Robber Barons" on the assumption that because no public regulation or direction existed large fortunes were built by unprincipled men who corrupted officialdom, despoiled the country's natural resources, and exploited its farmers and laborers. Surely, there were some men who manipulated the corporate securities of the companies they controlled in the stockmarket for their own gain, but the only victims were their fellow speculators.

The entrepreneurs of the period not only built and modernized industry, but because they were technologically minded, they increased the productivity of labor in agriculture, mining, manufacturing, and railroading. As a result, the real wages of workers and the real wealth of farmers went up sharply.

In all this, Carnegie was a pacesetter. He was a stiff competitor; plowing back company earnings into new plants, equipment, and methods, he could lower prices and expand markets for steel products. In years of recession and depression he kept running his plants, undercutting competitors, and assuring employment for his workers.

These 19th-century entrepreneurs were successful in a dog-eat-dog world for several reasons. Government followed a hands-off policy: it did not regulate; it also did not tax. Government had not yet made commitments to social justice, protection of the poor, or more equitable distribution of the national product. At the same time, the customs,

attitudes, and sanctions of the period—and the law writers, courts, economists, Protestant clergy, and even the trade unionists affiliated with the American Federation of Labor—accepted the unequal distribution of wealth. In fact, success in the marketplace was equated with the virtues of hard work, thrift, sobriety, and even godliness.

It was in this kind of world that Carnegie, a man of boundless imagination and great organizational skills, built his companies and made steel efficiently and cheaply. He fought competitors and also efforts at market and price controls by the mergers and oligopolies that began to appear in the 1890s. Because he was successful, he had to be bought off: this was the origin of the U.S. Steel Corporation in 1901, the greatest merger of the era; and it was the end of Carnegie's career as a steel-master. But it was not his end as a citizen, for he closely followed national and international developments, particularly the search for world peace, and expressed himself forcefully in writings and before legislative committees on questions of the day; and he helped lay plans for the organizations he set up to use his very large endowments.

Youth and Early Manhood

Carnegie was born on Nov. 25, 1835, in Dunfermline, Scotland, the son of William Carnegie, a home linen weaver, and Margaret Morrison Carnegie, daughter of a tanner and shoemaker. It was a time of ferment in Scotland as machine looms displaced skilled cottage workers like Carnegie's father, and social and political inequalities radicalized such humble craftsmen. Because they lived in a caste-ridden society, agitations for reform were unsuccessful. When he came to contrast Britain with America in his *Triumphant Democracy* (1886), Carnegie said, "it is not to be wondered at that, nursed amid such surroundings, I developed into a violent young Republican whose motto was 'death to privilege.'"

In 1848 the family moved to the United States, settling in Allegheny City, across the river from Pittsburgh. The father obtained employment in a cotton factory, which he soon quit to return to his home handloom, peddling damask linens from door to door; Andrew, in the same mill, became a bobbin boy at $1.20 a week. The fierce desire to rise and to help take care of the family (he was soon its chief support for the father died in 1855) pushed Andrew to educate himself and to learn a craft. He became an indefatigable reader, a theatergoer who knew his Shakespeare so well he could recite whole scenes, and a lover of music with a cultivated taste.

At the age of 14 Carnegie became a messenger boy in the Pittsburgh telegraph office, and 2 years later a telegraph operator. So quickly did he improve himself that at 18 Thomas A. Scott, superintendent of the western division of the Pennsylvania Railroad, made Carnegie his secretary at $35 a month, soon raised to $50—a large enough salary to buy a house for his mother.

Carnegie stayed with the Pennsylvania Railroad until 1865, by which time he was a young man of real means. During the Civil War, when Scott was named assistant secretary of war in charge of transportation, Carnegie went to Washington to act as Scott's right-hand man and to organize the military telegraph system. But Carnegie soon was back in Pittsburgh, succeeding Scott as head of the Pennsylvania's western division. He was one of the backers of the Woodruff Sleeping Car Company, the original holder of the Pullman patents, and also bought into a successful petroleum company. He became a silent partner in a number of local small iron mills and factories; the most important was the Keystone Bridge Company, formed in 1863, of which he owned a one-fifth share.

Between 1865 and 1870 Carnegie became a self-designated capitalist. He traveled in and out of England, peddling the bonds of small United States railroads and publicly chartered bridge companies. He probably sold as much as $30 million in bonds and may have made in commissions from them, and from the iron products he also sold, $1 million.

During this time Carnegie watched the revolutionary changes taking place in the English iron industry as a result of the adoption of the Bessemer converter. Steel, he saw, was bound to replace iron for the manufacture of rails, structural shapes, pipe, wire, and the like.

In 1870 Carnegie decided that instead of being a "capitalist" with diversified interests he was going to be a steelman exclusively. Using his own capital, he erected his first blast furnace (to make pig iron) that year and the second in 1872. In 1873 he organized a Bessemer-steel rail company, a limited partnership. Depression had set in and would continue until 1879, but Carnegie persisted, using his own funds and getting local bank help. The first steel furnace at Braddock, Pa., began to roll rails in 1874. Carnegie continued building despite the depression—cutting prices, driving out competitors, shaking off faltering partners, plowing back earnings. In 1878 the company was capitalized at $1.25 million, of which Carnegie's share was 59 percent; from these policies he never deviated. He took in new partners from his own "young men" (by 1900, he had 40); he never went public, capital being obtained from undivided profits (and in periods of stress, from local banks); and he kept on growing, horizontally and vertically, making heavy steel alone. From 1880 onward, Carnegie dominated the steel industry.

Continued Growth

In the 1880s Carnegie's two most important acquisitions were his purchase of majority stock in the H. C. Frick Company with vast coal lands and over 1000 coking ovens in Connellsville, Pa., and the Homestead mills outside of Pittsburgh. Frick became his partner and, in 1889, chairman of the Carnegie Company. Carnegie had moved to New York City in 1867 to be close to the marketing centers for steel products; Frick stayed in Pittsburgh as the general manager. Frick and Carnegie made an extraordinary team. Carnegie, behind the scenes, planned the expansion moves, installation of cost and chemical controls, and modernization of plants. Frick was the working director who rationalized the mass-production programs necessary to keep prices down. It was Frick who saw that vertical integration was imperative and achieved the company's control (by purchase and lease) of iron ore mines in the Lake Superior area, linking Carnegie ore ships and railroads with the Pittsburgh complex of furnaces and mills.

Carnegie was wise enough to use his leisure for traveling, writing, and expanding his tastes. His first book, *Round the World* (1881), was a modest recital of widening horizons. His second, *An American Four-in-Hand in Britain* (1883), related a coaching trip through England and Scotland with his mother. The third, *Triumphant Democracy* (1886), surveyed the social and economic progress of the United States from 1830 to 1880, but woven in was a secondary theme: the contrast between American egalitarianism and the unequal, class societies of Britain and the other European countries. To Carnegie, easy access to education was the key to American democracy's political stability and industrial accomplishments. He said, "Of all its boasts, of all its triumphs, this is at once its proudest and its best."

In 1889 Carnegie published an important article, "Wealth" (republished in England as "The Gospel of Wealth"), in which he held that it was the duty of rich men to get rid of their fortunes, administering them personally for the welfare of the community. He did not gloss over the inequality of wealth, but he saw wealth as a stewardship to be employed productively, for modern industrialization and mass production had wide social benefits. As a result, he said: "The poor enjoy what the rich could not before afford. What were the luxuries have become the necessities of life."

Carnegie remained a bachelor until his mother died in 1886; a year later he married Louise Whitfield (their only child, Margaret, was born in 1897). The couple began to spend 6 months each year in Scotland, but Carnegie kept in close touch with developments and problems in the ramifying Carnegie Company, no minute detail of management escaping his attention.

Trials of the 1890s

The 1890s presented three serious challenges: two were surmounted, and one left a deep hurt and stained Carnegie's reputation. The bitter nationwide depression of 1893-1896 resulted in plant shutdowns, mass unemployment, and collapsing markets. But the Carnegie Company, by following Carnegie's famous injunction "Take orders and run full," pushed prices down, retained its workers, and made profits. Carnegie was hostile to pools, that is, collusive arrangements among steel companies to limit production and steady prices. He withdrew from them and undersold his competitors.

Carnegie's absence from the United States, together with his silence during the Homestead strike of 1892, was a tragic error. The Carnegie Company had acquired Homestead in 1883, invested $4 million in new plants and equipment, increased production 60 percent, and automated many of its operations, thus sharply stepping up productivity per man-hour but cutting down the number of skilled manual workers needed. These workers belonged to a craft union, the Amalgamated Association of Iron and Steel Workers, a member of the American Federation of Labor. From 1875 on the Carnegie Company had been negotiating wage and work agreements on a 3-year basis with this union. Thus, the Carnegie Company was not antiunion, and in two articles that Carnegie wrote in 1886 he declared that workers had a right to negotiate with management through their unions. He recognized the right to strike, as long as the action was peaceably conducted; management on its part was to shut down its plants and make no effort to use strikebreakers or protect them with private guards. Strikes, he said, should not degenerate into warfare but were to be regarded as trials of strength, with peaceful negotiation terminating the contest.

To show his good faith, Carnegie suggested a so-called sliding scale for wage determination in his own shops. There would be a guaranteed wage minimum, but rates would go up or down as market prices for steel products rose or fell. The union accepted such a contract for Homestead in 1889, but it was terminating on July, 1, 1892, and the union sought to renegotiate with the sliding scale. Frick had submitted a counterproposal calling for a lowering of the minimums from which wage rates were to be scaled, because modernization had resulted (in modern terminology) in more capital inputs and less labor inputs. Labor's contribution to the increased productivity had declined, as had the number of skilled manual workers. The two sides met head on; neither would yield, and on June 30, 1892, the Homestead mill shut down as a result of both a lockout and a strike.

Carnegie had departed for Scotland in the spring, having instructed Frick that in the event of a strike there was to be a complete shutdown and no strikebreakers. Apparently when Frick refused to meet with union spokesmen a second time, he meant to smash the union. Carnegie's silence, despite his previous statements, meant approval. In any event, Frick decided to open the company properties by force, and he hired the notorious strikebreaking Pinkerton Agency. It is beside the point whether Frick's intention was simply to protect the Carnegie properties (as he contended) or to recapture the plants and use strikebreakers (as the workers believed).

On July 6 two barges carrying 300 Pinkertons moved up the Monongahela River and were fired on from the hills and the shore. The Pinkertons also fired, but they were unable to land and surrendered, asking for safe conduct back to Pittsburgh. Five strikers were killed, three Pinkertons fatally wounded, and scores on both sides injured. The strikers had won the battle of Homestead; the company property was still virtually in their possession. Five days later the governor of Pennsylvania sent in 8,000 militia to restore order and open the plant.

Carnegie, from abroad, said nothing, except, in a letter dated July 17: "We must keep quiet and do all we can to support Frick and those at Seat of War. . . . We shall win, of course, but have to shut down for months." On July 27 the Homestead works reopened under military protection; new workers were hired, and old ones were permitted to return on an individual basis. The militia was withdrawn in September, and 2 months later the union called off the strike; thenceforth the Carnegie Company (and U.S. Steel which succeeded it) remained nonunion until the middle 1930s.

Carnegie never got over the consequences of Frick's actions. Years later he wrote: "I was the controlling owner. That was sufficient to make my name a by-word for years." But, as controlling owner, he had neither intervened nor repudiated Frick.

In the 1890s Carnegie, for the first time, began to meet with stiff competition from giant corporations which had been put together, recapitalized, and made public by the investment houses of J. P. Morgan and Company in New York and the Moore Brothers in Chicago. Because they were overcapitalized, these companies were interested in stability in an industry with excess capacity and fluctuating market conditions. They wanted controlled prices, prorations of the market, and tying agreements rather than Carnegie's ruthless competition with all comers.

The new combines made heavy steel and light steel; and because the second group was tied into the first by "communities of interest," they threatened to cut down their purchases from Carnegie unless he was willing to play their game.

Carnegie had thought of selling out and retiring in 1889: his annual income was $2 million, and he wanted to cultivate his hobbies and develop the philanthropic program that was taking shape in his mind. But the threats that now came from the West as well as the East were too much for his fighting spirit and his sense of outrage, and he took the war into the enemy camp. He would not join their pools and cartels; moreover, he would invade their territories by making tubes, wire and nails, and hoop and cotton ties and by expanding his sales activities into the West. He ordered a new tube plant built on Lake Erie at Conneaut, which at the same time would be a great transportation center with harbors for boats to run to Chicago and a railroad to connect with Pittsburgh.

Thus orignated the U.S. Steel Corporation in 1901, through the work of J.P. Morgan. The point was to buy Carnegie off at his own price—as he was the only disturbing factor that held back "orderly markets and stable prices." The Carnegie Company properties were purchased for almost $500 million (out of the total capitalization of the merger of $1.4 billion); Carnegie's personal share was $225 million, which he insisted upon having in the corporation's first-mortgage gold bonds. At last Carnegie was free to pursue his outside interests.

Development of Taste

Carnegie had started cultivating his interests in books, music, the fine arts, learning, and technical education early in life. He began to set up trust funds "for the improvement of mankind." The first were for "free public libraries"; some 3,000 were scattered over the English-speaking world. In 1895 the magnificent Carnegie Institute of Pittsburgh was opened, housing an art gallery (at his request, one of the first to buy contemporary paintings), a natural history museum (which also financed archeological expeditions), and a music hall. Originally under the institute (but separated in 1912) was a group of technical schools which blossomed into the Carnegie Institute of Technology, today the basis of the Carnegie Mellon University. The Carnegie Institution of Washington was set up to encourage pure research in the natural and physical sciences. He built Carnegie Hall in New York City. The Foundation for the Advancement of Teaching was created to provide pensions for university professors. Carnegie established the Endowment for International Peace to seek the abolition of war.

In all, Carnegie's benefactions totaled $350 million, $288 million going to the United States and $62 million to Britain and the British Empire. The continuation of his broad interests was put under the general charge of the Carnegie Corporation, with an endowment of $125 million. Carnegie died on Aug. 11, 1919, at his summer home near Lenox, Mass.

Further Reading

The *Autobiography of Andrew Carnegie* (1920) is fascinating. Burton J. Hendrick, *The Life of Andrew Carnegie* (2 vols., 1932), is an objective and sound account of Carnegie as man and steelmaster. Joseph F. Wall, *Andrew Carnegie* (1970), is the most recent life and very full; it is also critical of Carnegie as a businessman. Louis M. Hacker, *The World of Andrew Carnegie, 1865-1901* (1968), describes the times in which Carnegie flourished. The best discussion of the steel industry is Peter Temin, *Iron and Steel in Nineteenth-Century America: An Economic Inquiry* (1964). □

Hattie Carnegie

Hattie Carnegie (1889-1956) was a prominent fashion dress designer in the United States during the 1930s.

Hattie Carnegie, born Henrietta Kanengeiser in Vienna in 1889, was one of the premier dress designers of the 1930s. Not only did she make her mark through her elegant designs, she also trained a generation of fashion designers that shaped American style for decades. Carnegie started her career as a milliner. Her father, an artist and designer, introduced her to the world of fashion and design, and by age fifteen she had found work trimming hats. Five years later she opened a shop on East Tenth Street in New York called Carnegie—Ladies Hatter. The shop was successful, and within a few years she moved to the tony Upper West Side, where she took up dress design. However, she never learned to sew. A friend explained that "Hattie couldn't sew a fine seam, but she had a feeling about clothes and a personality to convey her ideas to the people who were to work them out." She changed the name of her business in 1914 to Hattie Carnegie, Inc., and by the 1920s was the toast of the fashion world from her new location in the Upper East Side.

"Simple, Beautiful Clothes"

Carnegie's belief in simplicity fit perfectly with the streamlining of 1930s design. She believed that "simple, beautiful clothes . . . enhance the charm of the woman who wears them. If you have a dress that is too often admired, be suspicious of it." The dress, she insisted, must fit and not overpower the woman who wears it. She was unabashedly devoted to Paris fashion and made regular buying trips throughout the 1920s and 1930s. Yet while she was a self-declared Francophile, she adapted French style to American tastes by offering a blend of style and comfort that suited many fashion-conscious Americans who still wanted their clothes to have a French flair.

Designing for the Middle Class

Carnegie's expensive original designer clothes were out of reach for many Americans, but this did not limit her influence on American design. Hers were among some of the most widely copied designs by popularly priced designers. As the decade wore on, Carnegie added a modestly priced, ready-to-wear line of clothing that proved to be the most lucrative of her enterprises. She made her modestly priced clothes more available to the average consumer by permitting some department stores to carry the new line, breaking from her usual practice of selling her clothes at her own shop. This practice secured her influence over both haute couture and popular wear.

Training a New Generation

Throughout the 1930s Carnegie's booming business attracted several young designers who trained under her. Norman Norell, Claire McCardell, Paula Trigére, Pauline De Rothschild, and Jean Louis, among others, spent years working under her tutelage. As her business grew, so did her interests. She added accessories, perfumes, chiffon handkerchiefs, silk hose, and cosmetics. By the 1940s Carnegie was well established as one of America's top designers.

Further Reading

L. H., "Profiles: Luxury, Inc.," *New Yorker,* 10 (31 March 1934): 23-27.

Caroline Rennolds Milbank, *New York Fashion: The Evolution of American Style* (New York: Abrams, 1989). □

Lazare Nicolas Marguerite Carnot

The French military engineer, soldier, and statesman Lazare Nicolas Marguerite Carnot (1753-1823) refashioned the French Revolutionary armies into an effective fighting force. For his invaluable services he was called the "Organizer of Victory."

Lazare Carnot was born on May 13, 1753, in Nolay, Burgundy, where his father was a lawyer, royal notary, and local judge. He was educated at Autun and at the École de Mézières. Upon graduation he joined the army as a military engineer. He first earned attention for his *Éloge de Vauban,* in praise of the Marquis de Vauban, Louis XIV's great military engineer and social critic, who became Carnot's ideal. His involvement in the controversies over the utility of frontier fortifications, on the side of innovator Marc René Montalembert, earned the displeasure of his superiors, and he was imprisoned for a short period. After marrying Marie Jacqueline Sophie Du Pont in 1791, he settled in Arras, where he became a member of the local academy and gained renown for his brusque revolutionary zeal. He condemned the flight of King Louis XVI as practical abdication and called for the establishment of a republic.

Carnot was elected to the Legislative Assembly as deputy from Pas-de-Calais and concerned himself with military affairs. His republican zeal caused him to condemn the accepted doctrine of passive obedience within the army. A soldier was a citizen, according to Carnot, and therefore should be accorded the same rights as a civilian, except in times of actual combat. In this way he registered his protest over the suppression of the revolt of the garrison at Nancy. He supported the declaration of war in 1792 as a means of stabilizing the Revolution. During most of his tenure in the Legislative Assembly and in the National Convention, Carnot was on missions to various military fronts, where he was actively involved in purging the army of disloyal or incompetent elements.

In 1793 Carnot became a member of the Committee of Public Safety, where he helped to direct the war effort by transforming the *levée en masse* (citizen army) into an effective military instrument. Working 17 hours a day, he managed 14 armies and was constantly involved with the creation and organization of the instruments of war. Later that year he was in Alsace and aided J. B. Jourdan in lifting the siege of Maubeuge. After that Carnot directed operations from Paris. Jourdan's victory at Fleurus in 1794 left France free from invasion for the next 20 years and was a tribute to Carnot's success as minister of war. His successes, however, intensified the rivalries and differences within the Committee of Public Safety, particularly between himself and Louis de Saint-Just.

Though Carnot served on the Thermidorian Committee, in the Five Hundred, and as a member of the Directory, his rigid personality and hatred of illegality led to his exile in 1797. With Napoleon's rise to power Carnot returned to France, where he served as minister of war for a short period in 1800. He retained his seat in the Tribunate (until its dissolution in 1807), where he displayed his courage by voting against the life consulate for Napoleon and the establishment of the empire. After his retirement he devoted himself to his mathematical interests and wrote his famous essay, *The Defense of Fortified Places* (1810).

Following the French defeats of 1813, Carnot offered his services to Napoleon and was appointed governor of Antwerp. After Napoleon's exile to Elba, Carnot successfully defended himself before Louis XVIII, but his opposition to the politics of the restored monarchy prompted him to again serve Napoleon during the Hundred Days as minister of the interior. After Napoleon's defeat at Waterloo, Carnot was exiled for life by Louis XVIII and died in Magdeburg in Prussian Saxony on Aug. 2, 1823. Finally, on June 10, 1899, the ashes of the "Organizer of Victory" were brought home to rest in the Pantheon.

Further Reading

The most authoritative account of Carnot is in French: Marcel Reinhard, *Le Grand Carnot* (2 vols., 1950-1952), a sensitive, critical analysis of Carnot's early years and his work in rebuilding the army. The biographies of Carnot in English are all inadequate. The best of these is Huntley Dupre, *Lazare Carnot, Republican Patriot* (1940), a sympathetic account emphasizing Carnot's intellectual and administrative capacities and his humanistic and republican sentiments. Background works which contain extensive discussions of Carnot are R. R. Palmer, *Twelve Who Ruled: The Committee of Public Safety during the Terror* (1941), and Georges Lefebvre, *The French Revolution* (2 vols., trans. 1961-1964).

Additional Sources

Amson, Daniel, *Carnot,* Paris: Perrin, 1992. □

Nicolas Léonard Sadi Carnot

The French physicist Nicolas Léonard Sadi Carnot (1796-1832), with his analysis of the working of an ideal heat engine, opened the road to the science of thermodynamics.

Sadi Carnot was born on June 1, 1796, in Paris. He was given the name Sadi because of the admiration of his father, Lazare Carnot, for Sadi (Muslihal-Din), a medieval Persian poet and moralist. Sadi entered the famed Polytechnique at the age of 16, and he graduated first the next year in the artillery section. In 1814 he went to Antwerp, where his father fought the British, made a successful stand against them, and became the only undefeated French general, as other Napoleonic armies fell to the Allies.

Following the peace treaty of 1814, father and son returned to Paris and from there Sadi went to Metz, where in the military school he wrote an able analysis of the use of theodolites. After Waterloo the elder Carnot was exiled, and Sadi was sent from one military fortress to another to do routine engineering work. In 1818 he made use of a new royal decree and successfully took the exams for admission to the corps of general staff officers. After that his life was spent largely in studies and in the cultivation of the arts, especially music.

Birth of Thermodynamics

The only interruption of Carnot's stay in Paris came in 1821, when he visited his father in exile in Magdeburg; his father died 2 years later. Carnot's interest turned more and more toward fundamental questions concerning industry, economics, and social organization. He kept visiting museums, factories, and offices, trying to find the key to the most efficient utilization of power.

These concerns led to the writing of Carnot's masterpiece, *Réflexions sur la puissance motrice du feu et sur les machines propres à développer cette puissance* (*Reflections on the Motive Power of Fire and on Machines Fitted to Develop That Power*), published in 1824. It stands as the beginning of the science of thermodynamics. This is not to say that Carnot wanted to write physics. His work had in view a wide audience and also contained many errors and half truths. Yet, as his analysis of the efficiency of heat engines aimed at fundamental elucidation of the problem, Carnot inevitably opened up new avenues in physics. He succeeded in making it clear that there was a theoretical limit to the efficiency of any heat engine: "The motive power of heat is independent of the agents employed to realize it; its quantity is fixed solely by the temperatures of the bodies between which is effected, finally, the transfer of the caloric."

The only favorable reaction to Carnot's work was a long review in the *Revue encyclopédique*. However, when E. Clapeyron returned in 1830 from Russia and began to work on his "Memoir on the Motive Power of Heat," he found that Carnot had anticipated him in several respects but that Carnot's ideas and experimental data needed considerable reworking. Clapeyron stated his indebtedness to Carnot at the beginning of his memoir, which contained the first diagrammatic representation of the so-called Carnot cycle. Still it was not until 1843, when Clapeyron's memoir appeared in German translation in the *Annalen der Physik und Chemie,* that the world of science began to take notice.

By then Carnot had been dead for 11 years. His last 8 years were spent in an intense search for an improved system of economics, of taxation, and of scientific education. In 1830, 2 years after his retirement from the army, he helped organize the Réunion Polytechnique Industrielle to promote collaboration among the alumni of the Polytechnique in support of the foregoing program. He was also an active member of the Association Polytechnique, devoted to the dissemination of useful knowledge among the wider segments of society.

Further Reading

The principal information on Carnot's life is the essay written in 1872 by his younger brother, Hippolyte. It was reprinted in 1878 in a new edition of Sadi Carnot's *Réflexions* (1824), together with some of his unpublished manuscripts. An English translation of Carnot's *Reflections on the Motive Power of Fire* (repr. 1960) contains a very informative introduction by the editor, E. Mendoza, on Carnot's life, on early thermodynamics, and on the significance of the Carnot cycle. □

Anthony Caro

The English sculptor Anthony Caro (born 1924) worked in steel and aluminum, often painted in primary colors. His welded and steel constructions explore the eccentricities of balance, weightlessness, and horizontal composition.

Anthony Caro was born in London on March 8, 1924. He took a degree in engineering at Cambridge and served in the navy during World War II. He studied at London's Regent Street Polytechnic School (1946-1947) and the Royal Academy Schools (1947-1952). He worked as a part-time assistant to the sculptor Henry Moore (1951-1953) and then began to teach at St. Martin's School of Art in London.

The period of training with Moore left its mark on Caro's work throughout the 1950s. Moore's impact was revealed not only in Caro's intense interest in the nature and inherent properties of the various materials with which he worked but also in his retention of the human form cast in bronze. It was not until 1959, the year of his first visit to America and his first-hand acquaintance with the new trends in art—principally the work of the painter Kenneth Noland and the sculptor David Smith—that Caro abandoned figurative sculpture.

Caro began working in steel and aluminum in 1960. First he used large metal shapes either cut with a torch or piled up off the ground as ready-made I beams. Then he moved away from these compact masses and began to stretch individual parts of a composition across the ground plane, often painting them in a single, unifying color. By 1962 he had enlarged his angular formal vocabulary by including in certain works thin ribbons of steel tubing, often gracefully bent and sometimes seemingly suspended in midair, which achieved a light and graceful mood. At the same time Caro continued to compose directly on the ground plane without any pedestal, and his compositions became increasingly complex and flamboyant. The culminating works of this period, *Bennington* and *Titan*, were executed in 1963.

Caro's work then took several directions. He began to simplify his compositions, often following a single directional line and using a variety of new shapes and materials, ranging from steel cylinders to metal mesh. But he simultaneously concerned himself with smaller, exquisitely refined pieces, adjusted to a more intimate space. These smaller works, executed in 1966 and 1968, are of polished and painted steel; they often have a boxlike support or pedestal not only to raise them to a more comfortable viewing height but to serve as a fulcrum for the compositions. Caro also continued to experiment with a vast repertoire of materials and to explore the full spectrum of scale relationships that made him one of the most formative influences on the younger generation of British sculptors.

Caro's career continued unabated well into the 1990s. In 1993 Caro returned to creating semi-figurative sculptures for the first time since the 1950s. These were clay figures made in combination with metal and wood; the subject of this series, which consisted of more than 40 pieces, was the Trojan War. At the same time, Caro continued to produce massive abstract steel sculptures, many of which are essentially architectural in nature. In 1996, his work *Goodwood Steps* was called Great Britain's largest work of sculpture. Located on the Sussex landscape, it was a series of massive forms marching across the countryside in a pattern that recalled the giant standing stones at Stone Henge.

Caro was awarded a knighthood in the Queen's Birthday Honors of 1987. He has also received honorary degrees from universities and art schools in Britain and around the world. In 1995, a large retrospective exhibition of his work was shown at the Metropolitan Museum of Art in Tokyo, the museum's inaugural show.

Further Reading

Although there is information on Caro in museum catalogs of his work, there is no monograph on him. Useful background sources include Michel Seuphor, *The Sculpture of This Century* (trans. 1960); Eduard Trier, *Form and Space: The Sculpture of the Twentieth Century* (trans. 1961; rev. ed. 1968); A. M. Hammacher, *Modern English Sculpture* (1967); and Jack Burnham, *Beyond Modern Sculpture* (1968).

Many articles and illustrations of Caro's life and work can be found on the Internet at www.sculpture.org.uk (July 23, 1997). □

Joseph ben Ephraim Caro

The Jewish codifier Joseph ben Ephraim Caro (1488-1575) is the most universally recognized authority on Jewish law and practice.

Joseph Caro was born in Spain or Portugal. His family was expelled from Spain in 1492 and then continued eastward with sojourns in Greece and Turkey before settling in Safed (now in Israel) about 1535. Caro received his early training from his father, Ephraim, an eminent Talmudist, and later added Cabala, or Jewish mysticism, to his basic interests. He aspired to become the highest authority in Judaism, and during the last 3 decades of his life he enjoyed a greater prestige than any rabbi since Maimonides. His opinions were accepted everywhere, and queries were addressed to him from both the Sephardi (Levantine and western European) communities and the Ashkenazi (eastern European) communities.

Although an eminent authority in the field of Jewish mysticism, Caro's abiding fame was engendered by his two major works. He wrote the *Bet Yosef* (The House of Joseph), an exhaustive commentary to the 14th-century code, *Arba Turim* (The Four Rows), of Jacob ben Asher. Caro's work also included all Talmudic and Gaonic sources in order to establish a legal regimen acceptable to all groups. The frequent migrations of Jews to all parts of the world and the diversity of *minhagim,* or local practices, emphasized the need for an all-embracing work.

The *Bet Yosef* was designed for scholars, but there were many who lacked the intellectual acumen to study it. For these people Caro compiled his other great work, the *Shulhan Aruk* (The Prepared Table). It has remained until the present time the official guide of rabbinical Judaism and is without a peer as the arbiter of all ritual and legal problems. The writings of Caro did not, however, replace the Talmud as the ultimate authority in Jewish law.

The *Shulhan Aruk* is divided into four parts, each bearing the titles provided by the *Arba Turim*. The *Orah Hayyim* (path of Life) covers the topics of prayer, synagogue ritual, Sabbath, and festivals. The *Yoreh Deah* (Teacher of Knowledge) deals with matters permitted and prohibited, and more especially with dietary regulations and the purity of women. The *Eben ha-Ezer* (Stone of Help) provides guidance for family relations, domestic affairs, marriage, and divorce. The *Hoshen ha-Mishpat* (Breastplate of Justice) is concerned with civil and procedural law.

A greatly simplified and popular condensation of the *Shulhan Aruk* known as the *Kitzur* (Abbreviated) *Shulhan Aruk* was compiled by the Hungarian scholar Solomon Ganzfried, and it has taken its place on the bookshelf of the Jewish home together with the Bible and the Prayer Book.

Further Reading

Caro's *Code of Hebrew Law* was translated into English with a commentary by Chaim N. Denburg (2 vols., 1954-1955). Studies in English of Caro and his work include Hirsch Loeb Gordon, *The Maggid of Caro: The Mystic Life of the Eminent Codifier Joseph Caro as Revealed in His Secret Diary* (1949), and Raphael Jehudah Zwi Werblowsky, *Joseph Karo: Lawyer and Mystic* (1962). □

Wallace Hume Carothers

The American chemist Wallace Hume Carothers (1896-1937) was an experimentalist in the organic and industrial branches. His researches into polymerization led to the invention of nylon, the first truly synthetic fiber.

Artificial fibers, in the sense of being man-made, had been known since the closing decades of the 19th century; the first patents for processes resulting in fibers of the type later known as rayon were taken out as early as 1885. Once it had been discovered by x-ray analysis that natural fibers were composed of molecules that were themselves long and narrow, the possibility of building up such long molecules from small units, so producing new fibers, had been envisaged. Wallace Carothers, who more than anyone enabled this possibility to be realized, died the year before the creation of nylon was announced by E. I. du Pont de Nemours and Company, whose research team he had led with such distinction.

Carothers was born on April 27, 1896, in Burlington, Iowa, to Ira Hume Carothers, teacher of commercial subjects, and Mary McMullin Carothers. In 1915 he entered Tarkio College, Mo., specializing in chemistry. After the outbreak of World War I he was asked to teach chemistry, no experienced instructor being available. After he obtained his bachelor of science degree in 1920, he enrolled in the chemistry department of the University of Illinois.

In 1921-1922 Carothers taught analytical and physical chemistry at the University of South Dakota. About this time he began to pursue independent research problems. He became interested in the recent valency theory of Irving Langmuir and investigated its relevance to organic chemistry. After receiving his doctorate in 1924 for research on the reduction of aldehydes with a platinum catalyst, he stayed on at Illinois for 2 years, teaching organic chemistry, and in 1926 moved to Harvard.

In 1928 the Du Pont Company, which had planned a new program of fundamental research, selected Carothers to lead the team in organic chemistry at its experimental station at Wilmington, Del. He was allocated a small group of trained research chemists to work on problems of his own choice. In the 9 years that followed, he made several major contributions to fundamental theory, as well as laying the foundations for the development of new materials.

Synthetic Rubbers

After the discovery in the 19th century that rubber on heating yields the liquid hydrocarbon isoprene, it gradually became apparent that its molecules were long chains of isoprene units; attempts to polymerize isoprene, however, merely produced sticky, rubbery substances of no commercial value. The exhaustive studies of acetylene compounds made by Carothers's team led to the crucial step about 1931, when they found a workable process for converting the hitherto little-known and unstable substance monovinyl acetylene to chloroprene (closely related to isoprene). This, on polymerization, yielded what is now known as neoprene, superior in many respects to the natural product.

Discovery of Nylon

Carothers's greatest accomplishment was his work in the related field of polycondensation, that is, the linkage of pairs of compounds, instead of identical units, with the elimination of some simple substance such as water. He prepared a number of polyester fibers, but these seemed to be unpromising, chiefly owing to their low melting points (later, however, this road led to Dacron and Terylene). The polyamide Carothers produced from adipic acid and hexamethylenediamine was eventually selected by Du Pont's textile experts for development and became known as Nylon-66 ("six-six"), since each of the constituent molecules contains six carbon atoms.

Carothers was elected to the National Academy of Sciences in 1936. He suffered from periodic fits of depression, which steadily grew worse; during one of these he ended his own life.

Further Reading

Roger Adams wrote a short biography of Carothers which was published in the National Academy of Sciences, *Biographical Memoirs,* vol. 20 (1939); this biography, slightly shortened and lacking the bibliography of Carothers's papers, is reprinted in Eduard Farber, ed., *Great Chemists* (1961). The development of synthetic rubbers and fibers, including the work of Carothers, is discussed in John Jewkes, David Sawers, and Richard Stillerman, *The Sources of Invention* (1958), and in James G. Raitt, *Modern Chemistry: Applied and Social Aspects* (1966); both books give useful references for further reading. For a history of chemistry which includes the work of Carothers see Aaron J. Ihde, *The Development of Modern Chemistry* (1964).

Additional Sources

Hermes, Matthew E., *Enough for one lifetime: Wallace Carothers, inventor of nylon,* Washington, D.C.: American Chemical Society, 1996. □

Jean Baptiste Carpeaux

The French sculptor and painter Jean Baptiste Carpeaux (1827-1875) stood apart from the neoclassic formulas of his time in the vehement expressiveness of his figures. The nude was a major motif of his large-scale allegorical works.

Jean Baptiste Carpeaux was born on May 11, 1827, in Valenciennes, the son of a mason. In 1842 he studied in Paris under the leading romantic sculptor, François Rude. The following year Carpeaux worked at the atelier of the sculptor Francisque Duret. Beginning in 1846 Carpeaux studied at the École des Beaux-Arts.

In 1854 Carpeaux won the Prix de Rome for his neoclassic statue *Hector Imploring the Gods for His Son, Astyanax.* At this time he also worked in a tempestuous romantic vein, as may be seen in *Ugolino and His Starving Sons* (1857-1861), which was executed and exhibited in Rome. The literary inspiration of this work was *Dante's Inferno,* where Carpeaux found the description of the suffering of Ugolino, who had to sit by in the Tower of Hunger as his sons starved to death. Its artistic inspiration was Michelangelo's *Last Judgment.* The group was well received in Italy but was criticized by the academicians in Paris, who held up its execution in marble until 1867, when it was financed by private funds to be shown at the Universal Exhibition at Paris.

Yet despite the conservative opposition Carpeaux was able to obtain important commissions. For the new wing of the Louvre, the Pavillon de Flore, he executed the pedimental figures (1863), comprising an *Allegory of Imperial France,* as well as a *Triumph of Flora,* a deeply cut relief in which light played dramatically over the surfaces of the ebulliently sensuous nudes.

Carpeaux's best-known work today is *The Dance,* a group in stone which the architect Charles Garnier commissioned in 1865 for the facade of his new Paris Opéra. Carpeaux worked on a series of models for 2 years. The work couples the intelligent control based on a neoclassic framework with a spirit of full-blown sensuousness. The rhythm of the figures, the effective openness of the composition, and the vigorous play of light and dark were ignored by many contemporary critics, who found only that the work was lewd. In his *Fountain of the World's Four Corners,* erected in Paris in 1874, four female nudes support a sphere above their heads. The vitality and animation of some of the figures show Carpeaux to be a precursor of Auguste Rodin and other pioneers of modern sculpture.

Carpeaux also produced a number of fine portrait busts, including those of the architect Vaudemer (1859); Charles Garnier (1869); Dr. Flaubert, the brother of the novelist Gustave Flaubert (1874); and the younger Alexandre Dumas (1874). Toward the end of his career he enjoyed the favor of Napoleon III and could take his pick of portrait commissions from the leaders of the Second Empire. Carpeaux died in Courbevoie on Oct. 12, 1875.

Further Reading

There is no biography of Carpeaux in English. Louise Clément-Carpeaux, *La Vérité sur l'oeuvre et la vie de Jean Baptiste Carpeaux* (2 vols., 1934-1935), in French, is the standard work. For background see D. Cady Eaton, *A Handbook of Modern French Sculpture* (1913), and *Fred Licht, Sculpture: 19th and 20th Centuries* (1967).

Additional Sources

Jouvenet, Nicole, *Jean-Baptiste Carpeaux: 1827-1875 . . . ,* Valenciennes (11, rue Saint-Jean, 59300): N. Jouvenet, 1974. □

Emily Carr

Emily Carr (1871-1945) was a Canadian painter and writer without equal as an interpreter of the native peoples and forests of British Columbia.

Emily Carr (she sometimes added the initial M in front of her name) was born in Victoria, British Columbia, on Dec. 13, 1871. About 1888 she persuaded her family guardian to let her study at the San Francisco School of Art. Returning to Victoria about 1895, she set up her studio in a barn on the family property and began to teach. In 1897 she made her first sketches of a native village, while on a visit to Ucluelet on Vancouver Island with a missionary friend. From her teaching in Victoria and Vancouver she saved enough money to study in England from 1899 to 1904, but her pictures of totem poles, painted on summer trips up the coast after her return to Victoria, are barely more than competent records of their subjects.

More influential on Carr's development was a period of study in France from 1910 to 1912, when she adopted the intense color of the Fauves. The new style of her French paintings shocked her former patrons in Victoria and Vancouver, and her painting classes dwindled. Finally, she was forced to open a rooming house, raise sheep dogs, and manufacture crude pottery to make ends meet.

The ethnologist Marius Barbeau first became interested in Carr's paintings of totem poles in 1921, and through him she lent 50 of them for an exhibition of West Coast Indian Art at the National Gallery of Canada in 1927. On her way to Ottawa for the opening she met the Group of Seven in Toronto, including Lawren Harris, whose bold simplifications of landscape forms were to inspire a new monumentality in her own paintings. From then on her work developed in mastery, and the timid records of native villages gave way to powerful interpretations of the forest itself, in which the totem poles united with their setting as expressions of the force of nature. In her later work, often painted on large sheets of brown paper, the rhythmic brush strokes give a pulsing vitality to forest, sky, and sea.

When failing health made expeditions into the forest impossible, Carr turned to writing, and her first book, *Klee Wyck,* won the Governor General's Award in 1941. In this and later books, such as *The Book of Small* (1942) and *The House of All Sorts* (1944), she tells with gusto and wry humor some of her adventures among her Indian friends, her animals, and the inhabitants of her rooming house. When she died in Victoria on March 2, 1945, she left a fine collection of her paintings to her native province, which is housed in the Vancouver Art Gallery.

Further Reading

The chief source of information on Carr's life is her own writings, particularly *Growing Pains: The Autobiography of Emily Carr* (1946), published after her death. The National Gallery of Canada, Ottawa, *Emily Carr: Her Paintings and Sketches* (1945), contains a biographical sketch, a study of her works, and plates. General works which discuss her include Richard S. Lambert, *The Adventure of Canadian Painting* (1947); Donald W. Buchanan, *The Growth of Canadian Painting* (1950); and J. Russell Harper, *Painting in Canada: A History* (1966).

Additional Sources

Blanchard, Paula, *The life of Emily Carr,* Seattle: University of Washington Press, 1987.

Gowers, Ruth, *Emily Carr,* Leamington Spa, UK; New York: Berg; New York: Distributed exclusively in the U.S. by St. Martin's Press, 1987.

Hembroff-Schleicher, Edythe, *Emily Carr: the untold story,* Saanichton, B.C.: Hancock House, 1978.

Neering, Rosemary, *Emily Carr,* Don Mills, Ont.: Fitzhenry & Whiteside, 1975.

Shadbolt, Doris, *The art of Emily Carr,* Seattle: University of Washington Press, 1979.

Tippett, Maria, *Emily Carr, a biography,* Toronto; New York: Oxford University Press, 1979. □

Carracci

The Italian painters and engravers Ludovico (1555-1619), Agostino (1557-1602), and Annibale (1560-1609) Carracci opposed the style of late mannerist painting and sought instead classically inspired realism. The style they created is called baroque classicism.

What the Carracci urged was a change from the artificial, antinaturalistic style then in vogue and a return to the realism, the richness, and in some cases the monumentality of the High Renaissance. This meant turning to examples of the work not only of Raphael, as is sometimes supposed, but of Titian, Correggio, and Michelangelo as well.

The movement began in Bologna. There is no doubt that Ludovico was the leader in the beginning. For a time he shared a studio with his cousins, the brothers Agostino and Annibale. Together they founded an art school or academy (the Accademia degli Incamminati) where their artistic principles were so convincing and their example so persuasive that they determined the course of Bolognese art throughout the following century.

Ludovico Carracci

Ludovico, who was baptized in Bologna on April 21, 1555, and remained there all his life, is most closely related to the northern Italian tradition. His *Madonna of the Scalzi* (ca. 1593), generally considered his masterpiece, takes both St. Jerome and the Christ Child from Correggio's *Madonna*

Annibale Carracci

of St. Jerome and the facial type of the Virgin from Veronese. In the interrelationship of the figures, however, we find a new intimacy that will come to be associated with the baroque. This intimacy is still more marked in the *Holy Family with St. Francis* (1591), where passages of deep color and white highlights in the Venetian manner are used in combination with unexpectedly deep shadows to create an effect that is still closer to pure baroque. Ludovico died in Bologna on Nov. 3, 1619.

Agostino Carracci

Agostino, who was baptized in Bologna on Aug. 16, 1557, is best known for his engravings. His most famous painting, the *Last Communion of St. Jerome* (ca. 1592), served as an inspiration for works by Domenichino and Peter Paul Rubens. Agostino was also a theoretician and a fine teacher, and he trained some of the better-known graduates of the Carracci school. He was working on the frescoes in the Palazzo del Giardino in Parma when he died on Feb. 23, 1602.

Annibale Carracci

Annibale, born in Bologna on Nov. 3, 1560, was the genius of the family, but he was slow to develop. His *Virgin with St. John and St. Catherine* (1593) repeats a whole series of High Renaissance formulas. The Madonna sits on a high throne with a saint on either side; together they form a symmetrical triangle. In the background a central niche and flanking columns provide tectonic stability. The gentle turning of the saints' bodies supplies just enough movement to loosen the composition a little. The pose of the Christ Child comes from Raphael, the relief on the pedestal from Correggio, and the facial types from Veronese. Paintings such as this, which are typical of Annibale's activity in Bologna, tell us much about his classicism but little about his originality.

In Rome, where he moved in 1595, Annibale's works took on a new inventiveness and monumentality. Under the impact of his intensive study of ancient sculpture and Raphael's frescoes his style became harder and tighter. At the same time he brought his figures close to the surface of the painting so as to give them immediacy and largeness of scale. In his *Domine, quo vadis?* (ca. 1600) Christ appears as a powerful, seminude athlete. With the cross borne lightly on his shoulder, he strides forward past an amazed St. Peter and on toward us as if he were about to break out of the canvas. Annibale's pictures are now filled with classical details, such as columns and temples, and his figures are rich in dignity. But there is also a preference for strong movement and a new sense of drama that belongs to the new age. Works such as this, which fuse two diverse stylistic currents, are apt examples of baroque classicism.

Annibale's masterpiece is in the Palazzo Farnese in Rome. He covered the ceiling of the great gallery with frescoes (1597-1604) that imitate framed easel paintings,

Agostino Carracci

Lodovico Caracci

bronze reliefs, marble statues, entablatures, balustrades, fruits, flowers, ox skulls, shells, masks—all crowding and overlapping one another in a kaleidoscopic display of lavishness that has few, if any, equals. Individual scenes, drawn from Greek and Roman mythology, are filled with the exuberant rhythms of Hellenistic sculpture. Many artists of the high baroque, among them Gian Lorenzo Bernini, Rubens, and Pietro da Cortona, turned for inspiration to this famous monument of 17th-century classicism.

Annibale's classicism is equally apparent in his landscapes. In his *Flight into Egypt* (ca. 1603) nothing is accidental. The eye is carried back into space along planes parallel to the surface. These are joined by connecting diagonals. A cluster of low stone buildings at the center of the picture intensifies the painting's underlying geometry. This is not ordinary nature but what is called *paysage composé,* or classical landscape, in which nature is shaped and modified by the hand and mind of man. Annibale's bold new concept of nature underlies the elaborations of Nicolas Poussin, which in turn provided a springboard for Camille Corot and Paul Cézanne.

In the last years of his life Annibale suffered a nervous collapse and, in the words of Bellori (1672), "was compelled to leave aside the brushes that melancholy had taken from his fingers." He must have suffered deeply, for his art was his whole life. "He was never avaricious or mean in regard to money," Bellori wrote. "Indeed, he appreciated it too little and kept it openly in his painting box so that anyone could dig their hand in it at will. He despised ostentation in people as well as in painting and sought the company of plain, ambitionless men. Thus he used to live shut up in his rooms with his pupils, spending hours at painting, which he was wont to call his lady." Annibale died in Rome on July 15, 1609.

Further Reading

Rudolf Wittkower, *Art and Architecture in Italy, 1600-1750* (1958; 2d ed. 1965), and Ellis K. Waterhouse, *Italian Baroque Painting* (1962), contain excellent studies of the Carracci and their work. See also Giovanni P. Bellori's fundamental work, *The Lives of Annibale and Agostino Carracci* (1672; trans. 1968). □

Venustiano Carranza

The Mexican revolutionary and president Venustiano Carranza (1859-1920) led the constitutionalist movement against the Huerta government and convoked the constituent assembly which drafted the Constitution of 1917.

Venustiano Carranza was born in Cuatro Ciénegas, Coahuila, on Dec. 29, 1859. He began his political career during the dictatorship of Porfirio Díaz, serving as municipal president, local deputy, and senator of his birthplace. During the political upheavals of 1908-1910 he became an early supporter of the presidential candidacy of Francisco Madero. The support of the Porfirian politico added prestige to the Madero rebellion of 1910. Carranza served in the revolutionary movement's cabinet and, subsequently, as governor of Coahuila. After Madero's assassination Carranza became the chief of the movement against the usurper Victoriano Huerta to restore constitutional government.

The revolutionary coalition of Carranza, Pancho Villa, and Emiliano Zapata began to dissolve even before Huerta fled into exile in 1914. Carranza sought to consolidate his control through a convention of the revolutionary generals, but the opposition of *villistas* and *zapatistas* forced removal of the gathering to Aguascalientes, where a rival regime emerged. Carranza had to evacuate the capital and withdraw to Veracruz.

Under the pressure of events both sides sought popular support. Carranza issued decrees in December 1914 and January 1915 detailing agrarian and other reforms. The tide turned in 1915 culminating in the victory of Carranza's forces under Álvaro Obregón at Celaya, and by autumn the United States had accorded de facto recognition to the Carranza regime.

The years 1913-1917 were characterized by uneasy relations with the United States. Initially, the problem was President Woodrow Wilson's opposition to the Huerta government and the resulting occupation of Veracruz by United

States troops. Subsequently, Villa's raid on Columbus, N. Mex., brought the Pershing Punitive Expedition. Carranza's Germanophile neutrality during World War I added to the difficulties. The grounds for differences shifted when the Constitution of 1917 was adopted, with its implied threat to American interests in Mexico.

Carranza had convened a constitutional convention in Querétaro in December 1916. A radical group of revolutionary soldiers revised his draft proposal to include articles strengthening the state and weakening the Church and restricting large landowners and foreign investors through national control of the subsoil, agrarian reform, and protection for labor. Carranza contributed significantly to the Mexican social revolution by his acceptance and promulgation of the Constitution, which provided the movement with its legal framework, even though the document differed so greatly from what he had proposed.

The bearded, stubborn Carranza, his thoughts and emotions masked behind dark lenses, did not aggressively enforce the new fundamental law after he was elected to the presidency. Land distribution was limited, and though the Mexican Regional Labor Confederation was established, the most serious strikes were dealt with by federal troops. Pacification of the countryside continued as guerrilla bands were brought under control and the economy began to revive.

In 1920 Carranza made a serious political error seeking to impose little-known civilian Ignacio Bonillas as his successor instead of the popular Obregón. Under the plan of Agua Prieta of April 1920 the Sonoran triumvirate of Obregón, Plutarco Calles, and Huerta rebelled. Carranza was forced to flee once again toward Veracruz. However, on May 21, 1920, he was assassinated in a peasant hut at Tlaxcalantongo, Puebla, betrayed by forces which had joined his escort.

Further Reading

There is no scholarly study of Carranza in either Spanish or English. However, studies of the revolution throw light on aspects of his career. Charles C. Cumberland describes the epic phase of the Mexican Revolution in *Mexico: The Struggle for Modernity* (1968). Frank Tannenbaum, *Peace by Revolution: An Interpretation of Mexico* (1933), contains a penetrating analysis of the 1917 Constitution. Two specialized studies by Robert E. Quirk are particularly significant: *The Mexican Revolution, 1914-1915: The Convention of Aguascalientes* (1960) and *An Affair of Honor: Woodrow Wilson and the Occupation of Veracruz* (1962). □

Alexis Carrel

The French-American surgeon and Nobel Prize winner Alexis Carrel (1873-1944) developed surgical techniques that marked the beginning of modern work in transplanting organs.

Alexis Carrel was born in Sainte-Foy-les-Lyon, France, on June 28, 1873. He graduated from the University of Lyons with a bachelor of letters degree in 1889, followed the next year by a bachelor of science degree; and, in 1900, by a medical degree. He taught anatomy and operative surgery at Lyons, beginning experimental research there. Carrel's particular interest in vascular surgery, however, met with little approval at Lyons. In 1904 he migrated to Canada and a year later to Chicago, where he was associated with the Hull Physiology Laboratory.

In 1906 Carrel joined the new Rockefeller Institute for Medical Research in New York. He became a fellow of the institute in 1909, a member in 1912, and member emeritus in 1939. Here he did research in vascular surgery, directing attention to organ transplantation and vascular suture. He recognized that the replacement or transplantation of organs was possible only if circulation without hemorrhage or thrombosis could be reestablished in the organ. For the successful techniques he developed in vascular anastomosis, Carrel was awarded the Nobel Prize in 1912.

In 1913 Carrel married Anna de la Motte. During World War I he served in the French Army Medical Corps and, with the chemist Henry Drysdale Dakin, developed sodium hypochlorite for the sterilization of deep wounds.

After the war he returned to the Rockefeller Institute. In 1935 Carrel and Charles A. Lindbergh, the aviator, announced methods by which the heart and other organs of an animal could be kept alive in glass chambers supplied by a circulation of artificial blood. In 1938 they published *The Culture of Organs.*

Carrel's most popular book, *Man the Unknown* (1935), deals with a range of scientific concepts and argues that man is in a position to control his destiny and reach perfection through eugenics, or selective reproduction. During World War II he was accused of Nazi sympathy because of these ideas.

Upon retirement in 1939 from the Rockefeller Institute, Carrel went to France. In 1940 he returned to the United States on a special mission to study man and the environment. At the time of his death in Paris on Nov. 5, 1944, he was director of the Vichy government's Carrel Foundation for the Study of Human Problems.

Further Reading

Carrel's *Reflections on Life* was translated from the French by Antonia White (1953). Two full-length studies of him are Robert Soupault, *Alexis Carrel, 1873-1944* (1952), and Joseph T. Durkin, *Hope for One Time: Alexis Carrel on Man and Society* (1965). A good introduction to Carrel is the chapter in Theodore L. Sourkes, *Nobel Prize Winners in Medicine and Physiology, 1901-1965* (1966).

Additional Sources

Malinin, Theodore I., *Surgery and life: the extraordinary career of Alexis Carrel,* New York: Harcourt Brace Jovanovich, 1979.

May, Angelo M., *The two lions of Lyons: the tale of two surgeons, Alexis Carrel and René Leriche,* Rockville, MD: Kabel Publishers, 1992. □

José Miguel Carrera

José Miguel Carrera (1785-1821), a Chilean revolutionary, was one of the leaders in the fight for his country's independence from Spain.

José Miguel Carrera was born in Santiago on Oct. 15, 1785, into a wealthy and socially eminent family. Sent to Spain to complete his education, he joined the army when the French invaded the Peninsula. Hearing of Chilean efforts to organize a national junta, he returned home and immediately sided with the small but vocal patriot group. Because of his military record, his family connections, and his charisma he emerged as its leader. He had little patience for the conservatism of the national congress, organized in 1811; and with the aid of his brothers, Luis and Juan José, who were officers in the army, and with the support of street mobs, he accomplished a coup on Sept. 4, 1811. Congress, intimidated by Carrera's forces, followed his bidding. Among the early reforms instituted was the abolition of slavery.

Carrera ruled Chile as dictator. In 1812 he released a constitution providing for a republican form of government although Chile remained nominally loyal to the Spanish king. The first national newspaper was started, the flag designed, and education encouraged. All reform efforts ceased when Spanish troops landed and quickly conquered almost half of the country by March 1813. Carrera was named commander in chief of the Chilean armies. Several defeats diminished his popularity, he was deprived of command, and Bernado O'Higgins was named to replace him. Carrera was captured by the Spanish.

By early 1814, both royalist and patriot forces were exhausted, and in May a truce was signed (Treaty of Lircay). Carrera was released, regained his popularity in Santiago, seized control of the government, and vowed to continue the war. Meanwhile, sizable royalist reinforcements arrived. On Sept. 30, 1814, a disastrous defeat was inflicted on the patriots at Rancagua, and Carrera was blamed for not committing reserves to aid the beleaguered O'Higgins. Spanish troops quickly took Santiago, and Carrera, along with other refugees, fled across the Andes to Mendoza, Argentina. Carrera claimed to head the Chilean exiles, but José de San Martín, governor of the province, discounted these pretensions and designated O'Higgins commander.

Carrera was ordered out of the province. He traveled to Buenos Aires to enlist support but was turned down. He then sailed to the United States to seek aid, managed to find assistance, and returned in February 1817. The head of the Buenos Aires government, Pueyrredón, refused to let him land. Carrera's two brothers, meanwhile, tried to organize a revolution to depose O'Higgins. They were captured, tried, and shot in April 1818. Carrera claimed that San Martín and O'Higgins had ordered the executions and he swore revenge. Deeply involved in plots to destroy his enemies, he was eventually captured by the governor of Mendoza and executed on Sept. 4, 1821.

Further Reading

There is no biography of Carrera in English. A valuable but brief portrayal is in Simon Collier, *Ideas and Politics of Chilean Independence* (1967). Supplementary material is available in Luis Galdames, *A History of Chile* (2 vols., 1906-1907; trans., 1 vol., 1941). □

José Rafael Carrera

José Rafael Carrera (1814-1865) was a conservative general-president of Guatemala. He was the first of the three long-term dictator-presidents who dominated the country during the 19th century.

Rafael Carrera was born in Guatemala City on Oct. 25, 1814, the son of parents of mixed Spanish, native, and African heritage. He was astute and intelligent but uneducated, and he found only menial employment until a backcountry revolt gave him national stature.

Rise to Power

Carrera attained prominence as leader of an insurrection against liberal governments in Guatemala and the Central American Federation, headed, respectively, by Mariano Gálvez and Francisco Morazán. The original grievance was a succession of unpopular reforms, especially anticlerical measures, which alienated the rural population and brought to their support elements of the clergy and of the old aristocracy. Excesses committed by the soldiery sent to subdue the initial outbreaks and the appearance of cholera increased the excitement, and soon the countryside was in a frenzy of fear and defiance. Certain disaffected liberals cooperated with the rebels to force Gálvez from office in February 1838. In March 1840 at Guatemala City, Carrera defeated Morazán in his last desperate effort to reassert federal control and drove him into exile.

Carrera followed separatist and even nationalistic policies. On April 17, 1839, Guatemala withdrew from the Central American Federation and on November 29 gave the chief executive the title of president. On March 21, 1847, Carrera declared Guatemala absolutely independent. Separatist movements within the state, however, he crushed mercilessly. When the western departments of the country had seceded and formed a sixth Central American state, of Los Altos, in 1840, Carrera had overwhelmed its armies and abused its leaders.

Although officially declared in 1847, independent status was not recognized by constitutional change until 1851. Then an *acta constitutiva* provided for an all-powerful president and an Assembly of Notables, whose principal function was to elect the president. Under that charter Carrera was elected in 1851. In 1854 he was given life tenure with the privilege of choosing his successor.

President for Life

Carrera first exerted his influence in Guatemala through nominal heads of state. In December 1844, however, an obedient council elected him president. Liberals briefly regained power in 1848 and forced him to resign, but they were unable to consolidate their position. Conservatives managed Carrera's return from exile in 1849 and the next year reinstalled him as president. From that time until his death he held the office. His rule, known as "the thirty-year regime," was an unrelieved absolutism.

From the president's chair, or near it, Carrera imposed internal order and enforced the tranquility of conformity. He ameliorated Guatemala's position with foreign creditors and improved roads and ports, particularly on the Pacific coast, but he tried without great success to diversify Guatemala's commercial monoculture. He also allowed public education to languish.

Carrera acted on the precept that Guatemalan society was composed of disparate racial and cultural elements, of which one had to be patronized, chastised, and driven by the other to perform its duty. He repudiated innovation to the sacrifice of progress, valued order over liberty, and forswore growth-producing dissent to attain a stultifying harmony.

Chief among Carrera's accomplishments was restoration of the Church to its ancient position of power and prestige. He permitted the return of monastic orders, reinstalled an archbishop, and in 1852 made Guatemala the first independent Latin American nation to sign a concordat with the Holy See. He also reestablished such corporate entities of special interest as the Consulado de Comercio and the Sociedad Económica.

The last years of Carrera's long incumbency witnessed a permanent decline of the market abroad for Guatemalan cochineal and initiation of a desperate search for a new agricultural staple. Coffee appeared to hold great promise, and the government took such means as its conservative philosophy suggested to encourage and extend cultivation of that crop.

Carrera was the Central American strong man during most of his tenure. He intervened repeatedly in neighboring countries to eliminate unfriendly liberal governments, and in turn he had to defend his own regime against their attacks, singly or in combination. He participated in the Central American coalition that drove William Walker from Nicaragua but took no leading role in it. In 1859 he reached with Great Britain an agreement on tenure and boundaries of Belize (British Honduras), the interpretation of which is still disputed. Carrera died on April 14, 1865.

Further Reading

There is no biography of Carrera in any language. The best treatment of Carrera in English is in Chester L. Jones, *Guatemala, Past and Present* (1940; repr. 1966). □

Wills Carrier

Willis Carrier (1876-1950) was the "father of air conditioning," developing both the theory and the applications of air conditioning systems.

Willis Haviland Carrier was born in Angola, New York, on November 26, 1876, a member of an old New England family. Young Willis was educated at Angola Academy and taught school for two years before entering Central High School in Buffalo, New York, to meet college entrance requirements. Carrier then won a state scholarship to attend Cornell University. He graduated from Cornell in 1901 with a degree in electrical engineering, whereupon he joined the Buffalo Forge Company in Buffalo as a research engineer. Carrier became chief engineer of the firm in 1906.

While associated with Buffalo Forge Carrier assisted materially in the development of blowers and of pipe-coil heaters manufactured for the company and formulated a technical method of testing and rating blowers and fan-system heaters. He also devised and published the first system of scientifically determined rating tables defining the capacities, speeds, and resistances of heaters at various steam pressures and air velocities. When the problem of providing clean air was encountered, Carrier invented a spray-type air washer, from which he later developed the spray-type humidifier or de-humidifier.

He next undertook an exhaustive study of a number of issues, including the first analysis of de-humidification by use of mechanical refrigeration. As a result of this, Carrier was able to make the first applications of his spray-type air washer. During studies of these applications, he realized the fundamental importance of humidification (that is, the control of air's moisture content) and developed dewpoint control, a method of regulating humidity by controlling the temperature of the spray-water in the conditioning machine. As a result of these investigations, Carrier presented two papers in 1911 to the American Society of Mechanical Engineers describing humidity control.

Carrier's work was not simply theoretical. Through the offices of Buffalo Forge he put his concepts into practice. Very early he designed for Sackett-Wilhelm Lithography and Publishing Company a system which maintained 55 percent humidity in the building throughout the year at a temperature of 70 degrees in winter and 80 degrees in the summer. By 1907 Carrier systems had been installed in several cotton mills and other plants. Therefore, later in that year Buffalo Forge decided to establish a wholly-owned subsidiary—the Carrier Air Conditioning Company—to engineer and market complete air conditioning systems. For the next six years Carrier was vice-president of the subsidiary and chief engineer and director of research for the parent firm. During this time Carrier equipment was installed in several industries: tobacco, rayon, rubber, paper, pharmaceuticals, and food processing.

Carrier, then, was the "father of air conditioning" in America in both a theoretical and a practical sense. Although the term "air conditioning" was first used by Stuart W. Cramer, a Charlotte, North Carolina, mill owner and operator, Carrier quickly adopted it, defining air conditioning as control of air humidity, temperature, purity, and circulation. In 1914 Buffalo Forge decided to limit itself to manufacturing and withdrew from the engineering business. Carrier then formed the Carrier Engineering Corporation. Shortly thereafter Carrier made an invention which would transform the industry. He developed a radical new refrigeration machine—the centrifugal compressor—which used safe, non-toxic refrigerants and could serve large installations cheaply. This opened the way for a system whose objective was human comfort.

During the 1920s Carrier began installing complete air conditioning systems. One of the earliest and most significant of these was in the massive J. L. Hudson department store in Detroit in 1924. This was followed in 1928-1929 by installations in the House and Senate chambers of the American Capitol. Of more local significance was the fact that by 1930 more than 300 movie theaters had installed air conditioning systems. The company, which Willis Carrier had started on a shoestring in 1915, prospered as a result of these and other installations and by 1929 was operating two plants in Newark, New Jersey, and a third in Allentown, Pennsylvania. In 1930 Carrier Engineering merged with two manufacturing firms—Brunswick-Kroeschell Company and the York Heating and Ventilating Corporation—to become the Carrier Corporation, with Willis Carrier as chairman of the board.

The depression of the 1930s, however, forced the company to fight for its survival. Bringing in business consultants, Carrier cut costs and systematized his operations, centralizing everything in a plant in Syracuse, New York. He also began to search out new markets. An obvious candidate was the tall skyscraper, but until the late 1930s no system could effectively provide this service. In 1939, however, Carrier invented a system in which conditioned air from a central station was piped through small steel conduits at high velocity to individual rooms. Although adoption was stalled by World War II, after the war there was a great boom in air conditioning, as it virtually became compulsory for any office building. Carrier Air Conditioning reaped a lion's share of this business, but a heart attack forced Carrier to retire in 1948. He died on October 7, 1950.

Carrier's achievements were manifold, and at his death he held more than 80 patents. Besides those things previously mentioned, he also played a significant role in the development of the centrifugal pump, determined and published basic data pertaining to the friction of air in ducts, developed practicable means to ensure uniform and effective air distribution and circulation within buildings, designed the diffuser outlet, and developed the ejector system of air circulation in which a relatively small volume of air is ejected through converging nozzles in such a manner that it induces the movement of air from three to five times its own volume, thereby providing an effective circulation within the given enclosure.

One of the most notable installations of Carrier equipment was made at the Robinson Deep in South Africa, the deepest mine in the world. By means of Carrier equipment, the owners were able to increase the mine's depth 1,500 feet to a total of 8,500, thereby increasing the available amount of gold. Carrier was awarded the John Scott medal by the city of Philadelphia in 1931 for his air conditioning inventions; the F. Paul Anderson medal of the American Society of Heating Engineers; and the American Society of Mechanical Engineer's Society medal in 1934.

Further Reading

M. Ingels, *W. H. Carrier: Father of Air Conditioning* (1927) provides a biography. Information on the air conditioning industry can be obtained from books published by Carrier Corporation. □

Baron Carrington

The British political figure Peter Carrington, sixth Baron Carrington (born 1919), became a major figure in Conservative politics during the second half of the 20th century. After occupying major ministerial portfolios, Carrington was named secretary-general of the North Atlantic Treaty Organization in 1984, and he served in that capacity until stepping down 1988.

Born into princely surroundings in Buckinghamshire, England, on June 6, 1919, Carrington was assured a high position in Britain by his pedigree. He was the only son of the fifth Lord Carrington and succeeded to his title in 1938. His ancestors were textile merchants, bankers, and elected members of Parliament. King George III created their baronage in 1796.

Carrington was educated at Eton and at the age of 19, with his peerage in hand, took officer's training at the Royal Military College in Sandhurst. He was commissioned in the Grenadier Guards and served throughout World War II. He took part in the campaign in France and the Low Countries, reaching the rank of major and being awarded the Military Cross (MC).

At the end of World War II Carrington chose to return to the family's country seat near Aylesbury, Buckinghamshire, to take a leadership role in reforming British farming practices and to occupy his seat in the House of Lords. His natural instinct for leadership not only led him into positions with the County Council, but also caused him to be made an opposition whip in the House of Lords during the two postwar Labour governments. When the Conservatives returned to power in 1951, Carrington became a parliamentary secretary at the Ministry of Agriculture and Fisheries. He was, at age 32, one of the youngest members of the government. British farm production was increasingly considered a key task for the government, which was faced with severe balance of payments problems. In 1951 he led the British delegation to the sixth conference of the Food and Agriculture Organization in Rome. He also served as chairman of

the Hill Farming Advisory Committee for England, Wales, and Northern Ireland and was a member of the working party on agricultural education set up by the ministry in 1952. He also served a relatively brief stint as parliamentary secretary to the minister of defense after October 1954; he was notable in that position for downgrading traditional shipbuilding in favor of modern electronic naval weaponry. But he made little apparent progress in that regard.

His first major diplomatic experience came in 1956 when he was appointed United Kingdom high commissioner in Australia. That country was not entirely strange to him: he had family interests there, and his father had been born in Australia. He was popular with the informal Australians and relinquished the post in 1959 only because he was made a privy councillor and first lord of the admiralty. As head of Britain's navy Carrington had the full support of Prime Minister Harold Macmillan to modernize and shake up the centuries-old traditions that governed most planning and procedures of Britain's navy. Carrington argued for a significant increase in resources, insisting that Britain's defense posture depended above all on its ability to compete with the best of the world's navies. That did not mean matching them submarine for submarine or ship for ship—but it did mean utilizing the best of new naval technologies to deter any possible aggressors against Britain. Carrington thus had less interest in maintaining aging capital ships and invested more resources in mobile, broadly applicable technologies. In addition to his naval duties, Carrington accepted the position of assistant deputy leader of the House of Lords in 1962.

In 1963 Carrington gave up his admiralty position to become leader of the House of Lords and minister without portfolio in the Cabinet (but with principal responsibilities in the area of foreign affairs). At the age of 44 he was recognized as having a bright political future, perhaps even as a future prime minister. His role as a statesman also grew: representing Britain at discussions of the Western European Union (and arguing for greater political integration across the continent) and leading foreign policy debates in the House of Lords (and arguing against arms sales to South Africa).

From 1964 until 1970 Carrington was a member of the Shadow Cabinet and leader of the opposition in the House of Lords. His reputation during this time was neither conservative nor liberal; indeed, his pragmatism sometimes disappointed doctrinaire members of the Conservative Party looking over his record for possible future leadership positions.

Nevertheless, when the Conservatives were put back into power in 1970, Carrington was made secretary of state for defence. He attempted to introduce economies into Britain's defense budgets and still maintain a global presence to meet the Soviet challenge. He worked especially closely with Australia, New Zealand, Singapore, and Malaysia to guarantee their security and to maintain the British presence in that region militarily. In 1972 he became chairman of the Conservative Party and then changed portfolios in the cabinet, to become secretary of state for energy. He lost both positions with the change of government in 1974 and spent 1974-1979 as leader of the opposition in the House of Lords.

Carrington was appointed secretary of state for foreign and commonwealth affairs following the return of the Conservatives to office in May 1979. He was chairman of the Lancaster House Conference at the end of 1979, which led to the negotiated transfer of white Rhodesia to Black-controlled Zimbabwe. From July to December 1981 he was president of the Council of Ministers of the European Community. He resigned as secretary of state in April 1982 and became chairman of the General Electric Company (of the United Kingdom) in 1983.

The foreign ministers of the North Atlantic Treaty Organization (NATO) Council elected Carrington secretary-general on June 25, 1984, succeeding Joseph M. A. H. Luns. He continued in that capacity until June 30, 1988.

Lord Carrington (his friends call him Peter) published *Reflect on Things Past: the Memoirs of Peter Lord Carrington* in 1988. The book went into a second printing in 1989. In his book Lord Carrington reserves the distinction of having served under every Conservative prime minister for a 31-year period, beginning in 1951. Lord Carrington continues to write and give interviews and provide commentary on public affairs.

Further Reading

Interesting profiles of Carrington's career and views can be found in *The New Yorker* (February 14, 1983) and in *The Economist* (November 21, 1981).

Carrington, Peter Alexander Rupert, *Reflect on Things Past: The Memoirs of Peter Lord Carrington,* Harper & Row, 1988. □

Anna Ella Carroll

Anna Ella Carroll (1815–1893) was a political writer and aid to Presidents Lincoln and Grant during the civil war and reconstruction. Her patriotism and diligence helped secure a victory for the north.

On August 29, 1815, Anna Ella Carroll was born in a lavish, twenty-two-room manor called Kingston Hall, which rested on a large Maryland plantation stocked with cotton, wheat, and tobacco. Anna was a bright, blue-eyed baby with dark red curls and a fair complexion. She had in girlhood a fierce temper and an independent spirit, balanced with an equally strong tendency to shower her family with love. Her sense of independence would remain with her, carrying her through the adventures that lay ahead.

For generations, the Carrolls had been an influential family in America. Thomas King Carroll and Juliana Stevenson Carroll, Anna's parents, were extremely wealthy and well-respected people of the South. As a teenager, Juliana had been an accomplished organist for the Episcopal church. Thomas Carroll was a powerful lawyer whose partners included Francis Scott Key, the composer of America's national anthem. Anna Carroll's paternal grandfather, Charles Carroll, signed the Declaration of Independence. Her maternal grandfather, Doctor Henry Stevenson, served as an officer and a surgeon in the British navy during the Revolutionary War. He operated on Tory soldiers and American prisoners of war alike, earning the respect of men on both sides.

Life at Kingston Hall

Anna Carroll was the first of eight children, only two of whom were boys. She soon became Anne to her family and friends, rarely using her real birthname, even in adulthood. Anne led a privileged life as a child, with a slave caretaker, Milly, to care for her every need from the time she was born. She also had a personal servant, a beautiful slave girl her own age named Leah, who tended her for many years. Anne and Leah became friends, yet they always observed the boundaries of their positions as mistress and servant.

From a very early age, Anne was the favorite of her well-educated father. In his eldest daughter, Thomas Carroll recognized the thirst for learning he had had as a boy. Proving that he did not subscribe to the popular notion that girls should not be educated, Thomas spent many hours reading Shakespeare's plays to his daughter. His readings continued as she grew older so that by the age of eleven she was reading with her father essays by the Scottish historian Alison. By the age of twelve, Anne had learned to assist her father in his work by finding legal passages from his law books for use in his debates with Southern legislators.

Father's secretary

In the spring of 1829, when Anne was thirteen, democrat Andrew Jackson was elected president, and Thomas ran for and was elected governor of Maryland by a Jackson-supporting legislature. His new position took him to Annapolis, Maryland, away from his family. Back at Kingston Hall, Anne took on new responsibilities as her father's secretary, screening visitors and answering letters on his behalf. She even started a book of newspaper clippings for him, selecting articles dealing with the ever-increasing tension between the Southern planters and the people in the North, whose views and life styles were very different. In the spring of 1831, Anne and her family traveled to Annapolis to visit Thomas. She was excited by this opportunity to observe firsthand the workings of the government.

Several years later, in 1837, after Thomas had returned home from his governorship, the nation fell into a terrible depression, and the Carrolls lost much of their fortune. The plantation and Kingston Hall were becoming too much to afford financially. Though they had at least 200 slaves to account for, they were not willing to sell them to slave traders who would separate the families that had been kept together. Luckily, a distant relative returning to the States from South America had enough money to buy the house and well over half the slaves. The remaining slaves went with the family to a smaller plantation, up the Choptank River, called Warwick Fort Manor.

Off to Baltimore

After her family was settled in their new environment, Carroll decided it was time to leave home and try to make her own way in the world. Now twenty-two, she announced to her parents that she and Leah would head for Baltimore, Maryland, the second-largest city in the United States at the time. She hoped they could not only support themselves but have enough money left over to send back home.

Leah, a skilled seamstress, found employment almost immediately working for wealthy families in Baltimore. As she worked in their homes, she would listen carefully to their gossip about new businesses and bring the word directly to Anne. Anne learned to act quickly on Leah's leads, tracking down new business owners and using her writing ability to compose letters for mailing lists, generate publicity, and create advertising. Her public relations work soon earned her enough to send home a few extra dollars to her brothers and sisters. She worked steadily for seven years in Baltimore, making a name for herself as a skilled publicity writer.

From railroads to politics

At the age of twenty-nine, Carroll began writing press releases for railroad companies in Baltimore. Her work for the railroads, as well as her family's strong political background, allowed her to easily slip into the world of politics that was so familiar to her. She became affiliated with the Whig party, meeting such people as the army chief of staff Winfield Scott. With Carroll, Scott discussed his war strategies in the invasion of Mexico, which resulted in the acquisition of California, New Mexico, and parts of Utah, Arizona, and Colorado.

Because of her acquaintance with Scott, Carroll began sitting in regularly at the visitors' gallery in the Senate, where she met many powerful men and future presidents, such as James Buchanan, whom she briefly dated. She also became close friends with Millard Fillmore in the early 1850s, shortly after he was sworn in as president following Zachary Taylor's death.

Frees slaves

In the midst of her budding political career, Carroll had many discussions with Northern abolitionists about slavery. To satisfy her personal belief that slavery was wrong, Carroll freed all twenty of her slaves, whom she had inherited from her father. This was a dangerous move in 1853, a year in which any freed slaves were considered fair game for recapture. So Carroll used her political influence to persuade abolitionists to accompany her former slaves to safety in Canada.

Confidante

In 1854 Fillmore began seeking Carroll out as a confidante and, because his first wife had died, as a possible second wife. But Carroll had a personal agenda to fulfill. She wanted to make an impact in the political world but not as the president's wife. Although she refused Fillmore's proposal, she continued to help him in his campaign for the presidency in 1856, which he lost to James Buchanan.

Also in 1856, Carroll met railroad mogul Cornelius Garrison. Her knowledge of railroads, which she had gained from writing press releases for various railroad companies, impressed Garrison so much that he hired her as an assistant planner for new railroad lines. Railroads, in fact, prompted Carroll to write her first major political essay, "The Star of the West," in which she discussed the importance of building railroad lines in order to keep the Union together and improve the economy.

"The Star of the West" was quite successful among Union supporters when it was published in 1856. Carroll's writing caught the interest of Republicans, many of them former Whigs, who shared her earnest desire for the Union to stay together. She met with Republican senators, wrote other pro-Union essays, and, in 1860, optimistically watched Abraham Lincoln sworn in as president of a nation divided by the argument over secession and slavery.

Politics over marriage

When she was forty-five, Carroll became romantically involved with Lemuel Evans, a member of the secret service assigned to protect President Lincoln. Evans offered Carroll her second marriage proposal, which she refused. She was concentrating on her political writing at the time. Carroll began working on a new document, *Reply to Breckenridge,* in which she spoke out against the anti-Lincoln Southerners, headed by such people as Senator Samuel Breckenridge, who wanted the nation divided. She even touched on strategies for keeping the nation united. In one part of the *Reply,* Carroll stated, "There can be no equivocal position in this crisis; and he who is not with the Government is against it, and an enemy to his country" (Wise, p. 110). Her powerful writing caught Lincoln's eye and, in the summer of 1861, he not only demanded government funding to publish 50,000 copies of the manuscript and distribute them throughout the states, but he also sent Carroll a telegram inviting her to the White House for a confidential interview.

A woman advises the president

Upon meeting Lincoln, Carroll was impressed by his loyalty to the Union, a sentiment which she fully shared. Although they had met in social situations before, this was the first time they were able to talk in depth about the state of the nation. Lincoln spoke frankly with Carroll about his need for her expert strategical mind and extensive political background. He had a war on his hands and he needed all the help Carroll could offer. Lincoln asked her to become an unofficial member of the Cabinet, acting as a top adviser to him, with access to the White House at any time of the day or night. She enthusiastically accepted the offer.

Carroll was immediately assigned to work directly with the Assistant Secretary of War Thomas Scott. Her first assignment was to travel by train to St. Louis, Missouri, to observe and report the general sentiment of the soldiers stationed along the Mississippi River. As a woman, she probably would not be suspected of being an informer to the president, for women in government were unheard of at the time. The trip proved to be a strenuous one for Carroll, with hours of traveling in hot, overcrowded railroad cars. The farther along the river she traveled, the more she discovered that hopes in the Union army were not high. Many of the soldiers confessed to her that the current plan of attack, to move down the Mississippi and take the Southern army head-on was simply too obvious. The Confederate army was ready and waiting at the mouth of the river. In the event that a Northern gunboat became disabled, it would float, with the southerly flowing current, right into the hands of the enemy. The soldiers feared that too many lives would be lost with this unimaginative battle plan.

By the time she arrived at her hotel in St. Louis, Carroll felt an impending sense of doom for the Union army. She knew that too much blood had been shed already and sought to hasten the end of the war. Under the light of an oil lamp, she studied the crude maps of the land for a better route, one that would take the South by surprise. After many hours, a brilliant alternative dawned on Carroll: the Tennessee River!

The Tennessee River Plan

Carroll worked all night on her discovery, devising a plan that would cut the Southern forces in half by intercepting the very railroad lines she had helped design years earlier. The South was now using these lines to transport supplies to their troops. If troops could not get food and ammunition from the Charleston and Memphis railroads, they would be forced to surrender immediately. The Union army could use the Tennessee River to surprise the Confederate army from an angle they were not expecting. Moreover, the Tennessee River flowed north, so any troubled gunboats would float with the current back to the safety of the Northern army bases.

Carroll had masterminded an amazing plan, but she still had some crucial questions to answer: Was the Tennessee deep enough to hold gunboats? What were the water current speeds? Where were the points of landing? She wasted no time in seeking out a river pilot loyal to the North. Charles Scott knew the Tennessee River well and he gave Carroll the information she needed to ensure that her plan would succeed. He even pointed out that the Tombigbee River, which flowed directly to Mobile, Alabama, was a short distance from the middle of the Tennessee. With this information, Carroll added to her outline the taking of Mobile via the Tombigbee. Wasting no more time, she drew up a comprehensive version of the Tennessee River Plan, and sent one copy to the secretary of war and one to the president in mid-November 1861.

"Relief, joy and hope"

According to Secretary of War Scott, when Lincoln received Carroll's proposed battle plan, he expressed "overwhelming relief, joy and hope" (Greenbie and Greenbie, p. 295). The president ordered the plan to go into effect as a military strategy in February 1862, keeping very silent about whose idea it was. Many gunboats under the command of Ulysses S. Grant were ordered up the Tennessee River and, within two weeks, two Confederate forts, 13,000 prisoners, and sixty-five guns were captured. The enormous success of the mission made people across the nation want to know who could have come up with such a successful scheme. There were rumors of a woman working in Washington, but Carroll's name was not leaked to the public. Meanwhile, Kentucky had been defeated, Tennessee was struggling, and, in accordance with Carroll's plans, Northern troops were heading for Vicksburg, Mississippi.

The war was far from over, however. As it raged on, Carroll continued to work side by side with Lincoln and Grant until the war's end in 1865. During the final months of war, Lincoln began planning the reconstruction of the country, with Carroll at his side offering advice.

On March 1, 1865, while Carroll and the president looked for ways to pick up the pieces of the shattered country, she received an anonymous letter from Fort Delaware. It read: "Madame: It is rumored in the Southern army that you furnished the plan or information that caused the United States Government to abandon the expedition designed to descend the Mississippi River, and transferred the armies up the Tennessee River in 1862. We wish to know if this is true. If it is, you are the veriest of traitors to your section, and we warn you that you stand upon a volcano. Confederates" (Greenbie and Greenbie, p. 415).

The warning worried Carroll, but everyone, it seemed, was receiving threats from bitter Confederates. She was never harmed in any way, unlike Lincoln. His plans for reconstruction were cut short with his assassination in April 1865. Exhausted from work and grief, Carroll was now fifty. Yet she by no means intended to quit the business of government simply because of the war's ending.

Carroll advises Grant

Grant, with whom Carroll had communicated by telegraph from Washington many times when he was in the battlefield, was being backed by an overwhelming number of people for the office of the presidency. Grant asked Carroll to do what she did best—advise him from his post as general of the Union army to his job as president of the United States.

The quest for recognition

Carroll needed Grant as much as he needed her. Feeling that the time had come for her to be officially recognized for her invaluable duties to the United States government, Carroll sought Grant's support. Also, she still had unpaid bills to printing companies, who printed copies of her speeches and pamphlets, equaling over $6,000. The Carroll family fortune had been used up, and Carroll had lived very modestly throughout her period of service to several presidents.

Carroll prepared a statement for Congress, "A Memorial," and published it on June 8, 1872. In it were quotes from some of the most influential men in government, who argued that she be given the recognition and monetary compensation she was rightly due. She quoted such statements as this one from Benjamin Wade, president of the Senate in 1869: "I know that some of the most successful expeditions of the war were suggested by you, among which I might instance the expedition up the Tennessee River. . . . I also know in what high estimation your services were held by President Lincoln . . . I [hope] that the Government may yet confer on you some token of acknowledgement for all these services and sacrifices" (Greenbie and Greenbie, pp. 436-37).

Secret remains a secret

Carroll also had the backing of Thomas Scott and Lemuel Evans, who was now chief justice of the supreme court of Texas. To their testimonies, she added her own: "I cannot . . . detract from our brave and heroic commanders to whom the country owes so much; and . . . I believe that . . . they would be gratified to see me or anyone properly rewarded" (Wise, pp. 189-90). This may have been true, but unfortunately there were too many men in the government who wanted this secret of a woman military adviser to remain just that. They would not recognize her role in any official sense.

Although Grant knew the truth about Carroll's responsibility in the war, other top advisers chose to bury the truth and promote Grant as the real war hero. Grant did not argue with this decision, causing Carroll to lose her faith in her former friend. Her "Memorial" and other claims for recognition disappeared from government files several times over, drawing the process out for years. In fact, Carroll did not receive any promise of payment from the government until James A. Garfield was elected in 1880 and Congress considered a bill demanding that Carroll receive back-pay as a major general in quarterly installments from November 1861 to the end of her life. However, this bill disappeared at the same time that Garfield was shot, and it was replaced with another in 1881, offering fifty dollars a month from the passage of this new bill until the end of Carroll's lifetime. This offer was financially incomparable to the salary of a major general, and an insult to such an important political figure. Nevertheless, Carroll had no choice but to accept it, for during her nine-year fight for recognition, she had grown ill and needed the money to take care of herself.

Final days

Carroll and her younger sister, Mary, lived together in Washington, D.C., on Carroll's meager government pension. Under Mary's devoted care, Carroll continued her writing well after she was bedridden. In a room piled high with books and letters, next to a vase of fresh flowers Mary brought almost daily, Carroll enjoyed the last years of her life by a window that gave her a view of the West. She accepted visitors until her last days, including her long-time love, Lemuel Evans.

On the morning of February 19, 1893, Anna Ella Carroll died, surrounded by family and friends. In accordance with her wishes, she was buried in the churchyard of the Old Trinity Church in Cambridge, Massachusetts, next to her father, mother, and other members of the Carroll family. She remains revered by those who recognize her selfless devotion and vital contributions to her country.

Further Reading

Greenbie, Sydney, and Marjorie Barstow Greenbie, *Anna Ella Carroll and Abraham Lincoln,* Tampa: University of Tampa Press, 1952.

Wise, Winifred E., *Lincoln's Secret Weapon,* New York: Chilton Company, 1961.

Young, Agatha, *The Women and the Crisis: Women of the North in the Civil War,* New York: McDowell, Obolensky, 1959. □

John Carroll

John Carroll (1735-1815) was the first bishop of the Roman Catholic Church in America. He designed the organization of the American Catholic Church, encouraged its educational activities, and emphasized its compatibility with democracy.

John Carroll was born in Upper Marlborough, Md., on Jan. 8, 1735, to Daniel Carroll, a wealthy merchant and landowner, and Eleanor Darnall Carroll. When he was 12 years old, John entered a Jesuit school in Maryland; in 1748 he went to Europe to continue his studies. He first attended St. Omers in France and then became a novice at the Jesuit college in Liège, Belgium, where he eventually taught. During this period he was ordained.

Carroll returned to America in 1774. Although he was a member of the colonial aristocracy, Carroll was active in behalf of the Revolutionary cause and the fledgling republic. In 1776 the Continental Congress asked him to join the Committee to Canada, consisting of his cousin Charles Carroll, Samuel Chase, and Benjamin Franklin, in its effort to persuade the Canadians to revolt against England. The mission failed and Carroll returned to Philadelphia with the ailing Franklin, who remained his lifelong friend. George Washington, Thomas Jefferson, and James Madison were among the many prominent men who welcomed his counsel. He worked to integrate his Church into the life of the country, urging that the liturgy be read in the vernacular and offering prayers for officials and the government.

Instrumental in obtaining religious tolerance for Catholics, Carroll worked to preserve the Church property which had belonged to the Jesuits before the order was disbanded. In 1784 he was appointed Supreme of Missions. Pius VI named him bishop of Baltimore in 1789, a post he accepted because he was convinced that an American bishop was needed.

Carroll's goal was to unify the disparate elements in the Church. In 1791 he called the first national synod for the purpose of coordinating the work of the clergy. Irish, German, French, and Spanish priests were jealous and distrustful of each other. The laity was even more seriously fragmented, for control of Church property was in the hands of lay trustees, who were not willing to use the property for the benefit of all Catholics. Carroll insisted that this practice be changed. By 1810 four additional sees had been created—Boston, New York, Philadelphia, and Bardstown, Ky. After Carroll consecrated the bishops, they worked out a pattern for uniformity of Catholic discipline. These regulations and those Carroll laid out at the synod of 1791 were the first canon law in the United States.

Carroll supported the establishment of parochial schools, academies, religious orders, and secular schools. Catholic colleges were established at Georgetown (1788) and Baltimore (1799). He was president of the board of trustees of St. John's College at Annapolis, Md. He died in Baltimore on Dec. 3, 1815.

Further Reading

Theodore Maynard, *The Story of American Catholicism* (1960), contains substantially sound information on Carroll, but there is little documentation. John Tracy Ellis, *Catholics in Colonial America* (1965), supplies additional detail and more documentation. Andrew M. Greeley, *The Catholic Experience: An Interpretation of the History of American Catholicism* (1967), contains numerous references to Carroll, but Greeley makes no attempt to be objective and there is no documentation. John Tracy Ellis, ed., *Documents of American Catholic History* (2 vols., 1956; 2d ed. 1962; rev. ed. 1967), is the best source for Carroll's statements.

Additional Sources

Shea, John Dawson Gilmary, *History of the Catholic Church within the limits of the United States,* New York: Arno Press, 1978, c1886-1892. □

Lewis Carroll

The English cleric Charles Lutwidge Dodgson (1832-1898), who wrote under the name Lewis Carroll, was the author of *Alice in Wonderland* and *Through the Looking Glass.* He was also a noted mathematician and photographer.

Born on Jan. 27, 1832, Lewis Carroll passed a happy childhood in the rectories of his father, the Reverend Charles Dodgson. For his nine sisters and two brothers he frequently made up games and wrote stories and poems, some of which foreshadow the delights of *Alice.* Although his school years at Rugby (1846-1849) were unhappy, he was recognized as a good scholar, and in 1850 he was admitted to Christ Church, Oxford. He graduated in 1854, and in 1855 he became mathematical lecturer at the college. This permanent appointment, which not only recognized his academic superiority but also made him financially secure, carried the stipulations that Carroll take orders in the Anglican Church and remain unmarried. He complied with these requirements and was ordained a deacon in 1861.

Photography and Early Publication

Among adults Carroll was reserved, but he was not a recluse. He attended the theater frequently and was absorbed by photography and writing. Beginning photography in 1856, he soon found that his favorite subjects were children and famous people; among the latter he photographed Alfred Lord Tennyson, D. G. Rossetti, and John Millais. Of Carroll's photographs of children Helmut Gernsheim wrote, "He achievers an excellence which in its way can find no peer." Though photography was a recreation, Carroll practiced it almost obsessively until 1880.

In the mid-1850s Carroll also began to write both humorous and mathematical works. In 1856 he created the pseudonym "Lewis Carroll" by translating his first and middle names into Latin, reversing their order, and translating them back into English. His mathematical writing, however, appeared under his real name.

Alice Books

In 1856 Carroll met Alice Liddell, the 4-year-old daughter of the dean of Christ Church. During the next few years Carroll frequently made up stories for Alice and her sisters. On July 4, 1862, while picnicking with the Liddell girls, Carroll recounted the adventures of a little girl who fell into a rabbit hole. Alice asked that he write the tale for her. He did so, calling it *Alice's Adventures under Ground.* After revisions, this work was published in 1865 as *Alice's Adventures in Wonderland* with illustrations by John Tenniel.

Encouraged by its success, Carroll wrote a sequel, *Through the Looking Glass and What Alice Found There* (1872). Based on the chess games Carroll played with the Liddell children, it included material he had written before he knew them. The first stanza of "Jabberwocky," for example, was written in 1855. More of Carroll's famous Wonderland characters, such as Humpty Dumpty, the White Knight, and Tweedledum and Tweedledee, appear in this work than in *Alice in Wonderland.*

Unlike most of the children's books of the day, *Alice* and its sequel do not contain obvious moralizing. Nor are they what critics have tried to make them—allegories of religion or politics. They are delightful adventure stories in which a normal, healthy, clearheaded little girl reacts to the "reality" of the adult world. Their appeal to adults as well as to children lies in Alice's intelligent response to absurdities of language and action.

Later Publications

Carroll published several other nonsense works, including *The Hunting of the Snark* (1876), *Sylvie and Bruno* (1889), and *Sylvie and Bruno Concluded* (1893). He also wrote a number of pamphlets satirizing university affairs, which appeared anonymously or under other pseudonyms, and several works on mathematics under his true name.

In 1881 Carroll gave up his lectureship to devote all his time to writing. However, from 1882 to 1892 he was curator of the common room (manager of the faculty club) at Christ Church. After a short illness, he died on Jan. 14, 1898.

Assessment of the Man

The Reverend C. L. Dodgson was a reserved, fussy, conservative bachelor who remained aloof from the economic, political, and religious storms that troubled Victorian England. Lewis Carroll, however, was a delightful, lovable companion to the children for whom he created his engrossing nonsense stories and poems. That both men were one has long puzzled biographers and psychologists.

One solution is that he was two personalities, "Lewis Carroll" and "the Reverend Mr. Dodgson," with the psychological difficulties that accompany a split personality. He did have peculiarities—he stammered from childhood, was extremely fussy about his possessions, and walked as much as 20 miles a day. But another solution seems more nearly correct: "Dodgson" and "Carroll" were facets of one personality. This personality, because of happiness in childhood and unhappiness in the formative years thereafter, could act in the adult world only within the limits of formality and could blossom only in a world that resembled the one he knew as a child.

Further Reading

Stuart Dodgson Collingwood, *The Life and Letters of Lewis Carroll* (1898), and *The Diaries of Lewis Carroll,* edited by Roger Lancelyn Green (2 vols., 1954), are dull but necessary. The sanest and most informative book on Carroll is James P. Wood, *The Snark Was a Boojum: A Life of Lewis Carroll* (1966), written for young people. Florence Becker Lennon, *The Life of Lewis Carroll* (1945; new ed. 1962), is contentious. Phyllis Greenacre, *Swift and Carroll: A Psychoanalytic Study of Two Lives* (1955), is too psychologically oriented. Alexander Taylor, *The White Knight* (1952), goes into too many explanations. Roger Lancelyn Green, *The Story of Lewis Carroll* (1950) and *Lewis Carroll* (1960), concentrates too heavily on Carroll's revisions and other bibliographical matters. Besides Wood, only Derek Hudson in *Lewis Carroll* (1954) maintains the steadiness and clarity of vision necessary when writing of Carroll. Helmut Gernsheim, *Lewis Carroll, Photographer* (1949), is an exciting demonstration of Carroll's ability with a camera. ☐

Sir Alexander Morris Carr-Saunders

The English demographer, sociologist, and academic administrator Sir Alexander Morris Carr-Saunders (1886-1966) pioneered in analyzing population problems and social structures. He contributed significantly to the development of higher education in Britain's colonies.

Youngest child of a wealthy underwriter in Milton Heath, Dorking, Alexander Carr-Saunders was educated at Magdalen College, Oxford, where in 1908 he took first-class honors in zoology. As Naples Biological Scholar, he was a laboratory instructor at Oxford for a year, but he became increasingly uncertain about his profession. Independently wealthy, he pursued mountaineering and a love of art and studied biometrics at the University of London.

In London before World War I Carr-Saunders was secretary of the Research Committee of the Eugenics Education Society; subwarden at Toynbee Hall, the university settlement house; an elected member of the Stepney Borough Council; and a member of the bar. During the war he was commissioned in the Royal Army Service corps and stationed in the Suez depot. He then returned to the zoology department at Oxford, became a farmer, and in 1921 participated in the marine biology expedition to Spitsbergen. In 1922 he received great critical acclaim for the publication of his *Population Problem: A Study in Human Evolution,* and the following year he was appointed the first Charles Booth professor of social science at Liverpool University. In 1937 he became director of the London School of Economics, remaining there until 1956.

As a member of the Asquith Commission on higher education in the colonies (1943-1955), Carr-Saunders worked to promote colonial universities of high caliber. He chaired the Colonial Social Science Research Council (1945-1951); the Commission on University Education in Malaya (1947); the Committee on Higher Education for Africans in Central Africa (1953); and from 1951 the Inter-University Council, which aided higher education in Malta, Hong Kong, and Malaya. He also served on the Royal Commission on Population (1944-1949) and was chairman of its Statistics Committee. He was knighted in 1946.

Carr-Saunders's earliest work applied the techniques and perceptions of natural science to social problems. *The Population Problem* developed the concept of an optimum number in relation to a country's social structure and discussed birth control as a problem in eugenics. In *Eugenics* (1926) Carr-Saunders argued that a more "satisfying state of society" depended on improving "the innate endowment of the race" as well as the physical and social enviornment. His *World Population: Past Growth and Present Trends* (1936) anticipated government control of population trends, and he urged the collection and analysis of demographic data as the basis for such policy.

Carr-Saunders's later work includes sociological analyses of the professions, discussions of the universities outside Britain, and a variety of studies of social problems. By the end of his life, in the Rathbone Memorial Lecture at Liverpool University, *Natural Science and Social Science* (1958), Carr-Saunders expressed his belief that social science, inherently imprecise in method and humanistic in purpose, could no longer be studied through the natural sciences, as he had done earlier.

Further Reading

There is no biography of Carr-Saunders and no study of his work. Background information is in Alfred N. Loundes, *The British Educational System* (1955). □

Christopher Carson

Christopher Carson (1809-1868), commonly called Kit Carson, was an American hunter, Indian agent, and soldier. He was one of the best-known and most competent guides available to explorers of the western United States.

Kit Carson's career in the West spanned the years from 1825 to 1868, a period of rapid national expansion, exploration, and settlement. His most important Western contributions came as a guide to the expeditions of John C. Frémont, as a messenger and soldier under Gen. Stephen W. Kearny in California, and as an Indian agent just prior to the Civil War. His name is inseparably connected with American expansion into the Far West.

The sixth child of Lindsay and Rebecca Robinson Carson, Kit was born on Dec. 24, 1809, in Madison Country, Ky. He spent his childhood in frontier Missouri and apparently received little formal education, because he was illiterate most of his life. In 1824 he became apprentice to a saddlemaker in one of the largest of the early Missouri river towns. After less than 2 years he deserted the saddlemaker and joined traders headed for Santa Fe, N. Mex.

Descriptions of Carson vary, but most agree that he was small, probably about 5 feet 8 inches, had blue-gray eyes, and light brown or sandy-colored hair. To the wife of explorer Frémont, Kit looked "very short and unmistakably bandy-legged, long-bodied and short-limbed." A quiet man with a soft voice, Carson was considered modest, brave, and truthful by contemporaries—characteristics which helped him acquire a reputation as a heroic frontiersman.

Career as a Trapper

Young Carson worked for several years as a teamster, cook, and interpreter in the Southwest. In 1829 he joined Ewing Young's party of trappers and for the next year and a half trapped along the streams of Arizona and southern California. This jaunt into the mountains served Carson as a sort of training exercise, and for most of the next decade he continued in this occupation. Trapping most of the major streams in the West prepared Carson for his later work as a guide.

While living in the mountains, Carson married an Arapaho woman, who bore him a daughter, Alice. When his wife died a few years later, he took the child to Missouri. In 1841 or 1842 he married a second Native American woman but soon left her and acquired a mistress in Taos, N. Mex. A year later he wed again.

Career as a Guide

In the summer of 1842 Carson met Lt. Frémont on a river steamboat. Apparently Frémont had hoped to hire the well-known Andrew S. Drips to guide him on an expedition, but when he could not find Drips he hired Carson. From June until September, Kit guided Frémont's party west through South Pass to the Wind River Mountains and then back to Missouri. When Frémont published his report of the expedition, Carson gained widespread fame.

The following year Carson rejoined Frémont traveling west on a second expedition. This time Carson shared the guide duties with Thomas Fitzpatrick, his former associate. The two mountain men led the Frémont party to Salt Lake, up the Oregon Trail to the Dallas River, south to Klamath Lake, then west across the Sierra Nevadas over Carson Pass to Sutter's Fort, Calif. From there the explorers moved south to the Mojave River and then northeast to Colorado, where Carson left them at Bent's Fort.

In 1845 Carson guided Frémont's third expedition across the Rockies to Salt Lake, across the Nevada desert to the Humboldt River, and to Sutter's Fort. This ended Carson's significant work as a guide, although on at least five other occasions he led army units or explorers through the Far West.

Career as a Soldier

Carson participated in skirmishes with Mexican forces in California in 1846. Returning to Washington, D.C., with messages from Frémont, Carson met Gen. Kearny, who was leading a small army to California. The general demanded that Carson guide his party west. This he did, participating in the battle and siege near San Pasqual. Later Carson was appointed a lieutenant in the Mounted Riflemen, but the Senate rejected this and he returned to Taos.

At the outbreak of the Civil War in 1861, Carson helped organize the First New Mexico Volunteer Infantry Regiment and became its colonel. He fought in the battle at Val Verde, participated in campaigns against the Mescalero Apaches and the Navahos, and led the campaign against the tribes of the southern plains. In 1865 he was breveted brigadier general of volunteers. For the next 2 years Carson held routine assignments in the West, and in 1867 he resigned from the army.

Career as an Indian Agent

Interspersed with this military activity, Carson also served the Office of Indian Affairs, first as agent and later as superintendent of Indian affairs for Colorado Territory. In 1854 he became the agent for the Jicarilla Apache, Moache Ute, and Pueblos. He worked to keep peace and to obtain just treatment for the Native Americans, but he also used his authority to punish those guilty of depredations and cooperated with military leaders to show the tribesmen that the U.S. Government meant business.

Carson often disagreed with his superior superintendent of Indian affairs, Territorial Governor David Meriwether, about polices. Carson suggested that the governor send the agents to live among the Native Americans, or at least within their area, so that tribesmen would not have to travel several hundred miles to talk with them. In fact, he went so far as to state that the Native Americans should not even enter the towns because every time one did he was hurt in some manner. However, Meriwether apparently liked to summon Native American leaders to councils, thus forcing the to travel long distances. Such continuing differences and Carson's Criticism of his superior caused Meriwether to arrest him in 1856. Meriwether suspended him and charged him with disobedience, insubordination, and cowardice. Carson soon apologized and was reinstated as agent, a position he held until 1861, when he resigned to enter the army. He was appointed superintendent of Indian affairs for Colorado Territory in 1868, but he never had a chance to assume the duties of that office for on May 23 he died at Fort Lyon, Colo.

Further Reading

Of the numerous "biographies" of Carson, those written before 1960 include half-truths and legendary materials. Somewhat more accurate are Bernice Blackwelder, *Great Westerner* (1962), and M. Morgan Esterngreen, *Kit Carson: A Portrait in Courage* (1962). A most useful addition is Harvey L. Carter, *Dear Old Kit: The Historical Christopher Carson* (1968). This includes a discussion of errors in earlier material and a newly edited and annotated version of Carson's memoirs.

Discussion of the Carson legends is found in Henry Nash Smith, *Virgin Land: The American West as Symbol and Myth* (1950), and in Kent L. Steckmesser, *The Western Hero in History and Legend* (1965). Carson's part in Western exploration is best discussed in Allan Nevins, *Frémont: Pathmarker of the West* (1939; new ed. 1955), and William H. Goetzmann, *Army Exploration in the American West, 1803-1863* (1959). For an understanding of the fur trade see Robert G. Cleland, *This Reckless Breed of Men: The Trappers and Fur Traders of the Southwest* (1950); Dale L. Morgan, *Jedediah Smith and the Opening of the West* (1953); and David S. Lavender, *Bent's Fort* (1954). □

Johnny Carson

Johnny Carson (born 1925), dubbed the King of Late Night Television, became a pioneer in show business as host of *The Tonight Show* for 30 years. His interviewing and comic techniques won over a huge audience and spawned numerous imitators.

There was no way of knowing the young magician performing before the local Rotary Club would one day become America's most recognized face. The Great Carsoni, or young Johnny Carson, had already begun to master the techniques that would become so useful when entertaining people like Bob Hope, Steve Martin, politicians, musicians, and other performers on *The Tonight Show*. Carson became a pioneer in the television industry when he got his chance to host the *Tonight Show* after Jack Paar left the show in 1962. After many memorable late night evenings with Carson, the King of Late Night Television stepped down from his throne May 22, 1992, after 30 highly successful years.

Johnny Carson came into the world October 23, 1925, in Corning, Iowa. At the age of eight, Carson's father, Kit, packed up the family: matriarch Ruth, older sister Catherine, Johnny, and his little brother Richard, and moved to Norfolk, Nebraska. It was there that Carson came of age and began nurturing his talent for entertaining. His first paid gig was at the Norfolk Rotary Club when he was 14 years old. With the Great Carsoni emblazoned on a black velvet cloth draped over his magician stand, Carson performed for his mother's bridge club and the Methodist Church socials.

Carson's ability to entertain came as no surprise to him or his family, according to a quote in *Carson, the Unauthorized Biography*, by Paul Cockery.

"I can't say I ever wanted to become an entertainer. I already was one, sort of—around the house, at school, doing my magic tricks, throwing my voice and doing Popeye impersonations. People thought I was funny; so I kind of took entertaining for granted . . . It was inevitable that I'd start giving little performances."

Carson was in his senior year of high school when Japan bombed Pearl Harbor on December 7, 1941. After graduating, he enlisted with United States Navy. For two years, he served in non-combative positions before being assigned to the *USS Pennsylvania,* which the Japanese torpedoed in Okinawa two days before his arrival. Carson also spent time on the island of Guam in the South Pacific, where he entertained the troops with his ventriloquist dummy named Eddie.

One favorite Johnny Carson anecdote came from his military period. On board the *USS Pennsylvania,* one of his duties was decoding and delivering messages. Once he had the opportunity to deliver a message to James Forrestal, the Secretary of the Navy. Forrestal, as the story goes, asked Carson if he wanted to make the Navy his career. Carson replied no and told him his dream was to become a magician and entertainer. Forrestal asked if Carson knew any card tricks and Carson was only too happy to oblige the Secretary of the Navy with some jokes and card tricks.

After the Navy, Carson returned to Norfolk and attended the University of Nebraska. He became a Phi Gamma Delta fraternity member and graduated in 1949 with a major in speech and a minor in radio. So enthralled with radio and comedy, Carson made a recording of all his favorite comedians like Bob Hope, Jack Allen, and Milton Belle, for his final thesis on "How to Write Comedy Jokes."

In the Beginning

Carson joined the forces of WOW Radio, Omaha, directly out of college, and on August 1, 1949, *The Johnny Carson Show* went on the air for in the morning for 45 minutes. Two months later, Carson married Jody Wolcott, his college sweetheart and the first of four wives. During his time at the radio station, Carson was becoming known for his cheerful banter while reading the news, but something bigger was about to begin in Omaha—television. Carson was about to embark on a new territory, a pioneer in television, just like everyone else at the time. But with his pleasant on-screen personality and satirical wit, he quickly became a recognizable figure in the small broadcast area of WOW-TV.

With the success of his television debut show *Squirrel's Nest,* Carson decided to take his talents on the road and see if he could make it in Hollywood, California. After months of rejection, Carson was offered a job at KNXT to read the station call letters, the time, and the weather. The job did not offer the notoriety or prestige he experienced in Omaha, but it was Hollywood and it was where he wanted to be. The *Carson's Cellar* was introduced a year later at 7:00 p.m. and many skits and characters seen by millions on the *Tonight Show* made their television debut.

Being a hard worker by midwestern nature, Carson diligently plugged away at his job, often putting in extra hours in and out of the studio. After *Carson's Cellar* went off the air, he became a game show host for *Earn Your Vacation,* and a comedy writer for Red Skelton. His tenacity payed off when he was asked to fill in for Skelton, who had become injured during rehearsals. He signed a contract for CBS shortly after, and a year later, Johnny Carson had his own half hour comedy show, aptly titled *The Johnny Carson Show.* Rumors were beginning to rumble about Carson becoming the next George Gobel, the very successful television comedian. But it did not last. The program was canceled four months later due to network lay offs and interference. CBS failed to renew his contract. Carson was left unemployed with a wife and three sons. His only option was to accept a job as game show host for *Do You Trust Your Wife?,* which eventually became *Who Do You Trust?,* on the ABC network and move to New York City.

New York was not as easy as Hollywood, but Carson kept plugging away. In 1957, Carson interviewed a man who would become synonymous with Johnny Carson and *The Tonight Show*—Ed McMahon. Carson substituted for Jack Paar on *The Tonight Show* for two weeks in 1958 and did a comedy routine for *The Perry Como Show.* Slowly, Carson was making a name for himself again, and when time came to restructure *The Tonight Show,* he wanted a chance to be involved.

The Tonight Show

The Tonight Show, which originated with Steve Allen on the radio in 1951 in Los Angeles, made the jump to television in 1954 in New York. Allen lasted two-and-a-half years and was replaced with Jack Paar. The show aired from 11:15 p.m. to 1:00 a.m. every night. Several millions of viewers watched every night—there was not a whole lot to choose from then. Johnny Carson took over October 1, 1962. The rest is television history.

Over thirty years, Carson had the perfect stage presence. An opening monologue and golf swing, his attention to comic details like timing, delivery, and gestures, plus his fair treatment of guests, made him a natural host of the most popular television show of the time. Carson believed that if the guest sparkled, so would the show. Over the years, many of the country's greatest entertainers, plus some local folks, came out from behind the stage curtain and sat between Carson and McMahon. The guest list was plentiful—Ethel Kennedy, Buddy Hackett, Ed Ames and his tomahawk, Pearl Bailey, Bob Hope, Dean Martin, and George Gobel all took time to talk with Carson about their newest projects. Carson and his show could make or break a struggling performer's career, and comedians like David Letterman , Jay Leno, George Carlin, and Joan Rivers all got their big break from appearing on *The Tonight Show.* Wild animals were special guests too, often creating hilarious disasters on Carson or his desk.

Carson's stage demure was quite different from his off-the-air personality. The pleasantries he bestowed to his guests were often not shared with anyone else. Carson preferred to remain aloof, almost shy, and small talk did not impress him. Carson preferred to save himself for his audience. He was divorced three times and often worked the proceedings and settlements into his monologues. Currently, he is married to Alex Mass, whom he met in 1984.

After hosting *The Tonight Show* 4,531 times for millions of people over 30 years, Carson was ready to retire from the show. On Friday, May 22, 1992, Johnny Carson did his famous golf swing for the last time. He resides in Malibu with his wife and manages to play a few games of tennis when he is not putting in time at his company, the Carson Production Group. He was reportedly entertaining thoughts of releasing *The Tonight Show* reruns for cable syndication.

Further Reading

Leamer, Laurence, *King of the Night: The Life of Johnny Carson,* 1989.

Corkery, Paul, *Carson: The Unauthorized Biography,* Randt & Co., 1987. □

Rachel Louise Carson

Rachel Louise Carson (1907-1964) was an American biologist and writer whose book *Silent Spring* aroused an apathetic public to the dangers of chemical pesticides.

Rachel Carson was born May 27, 1907, in Springdale, Pa. A solitary child, she spent long hours learning of field, pond, and forest from her mother. At college she studied creative writing and in 1932 obtained a master's degree in biology from the Johns Hopkins University. She did postgraduate studies at the Woods Hole Marine Biological Laboratory.

In 1936, Carson served as an aquatic biologist with the U.S. Bureau of Fisheries. After her first book, *Under the Sea Wind* (1941), she soon became editor in chief of the Fish and Wildlife Service, U.S. Department of the Interior. In 1951 *The Sea around Us* brought its author instant fame. At the top of the best-seller list for 39 weeks, it was translated into 30 languages. For it, the shy, soft-spoken Carson received the National Book Award, the Gold Medal of the New York Zoological Society, and the John Burroughs Medal.

The following year Carson left the government to undertake full-time writing and research. As a scientist and as an observant human being, she was increasingly disturbed by the overwhelming effects of technology upon the natural world. She wrote at the time: "I suppose my thinking began to be affected soon after atomic science was firmly established . . . It was pleasant to believe that much of Nature was forever beyond the tampering reach of man: I have now

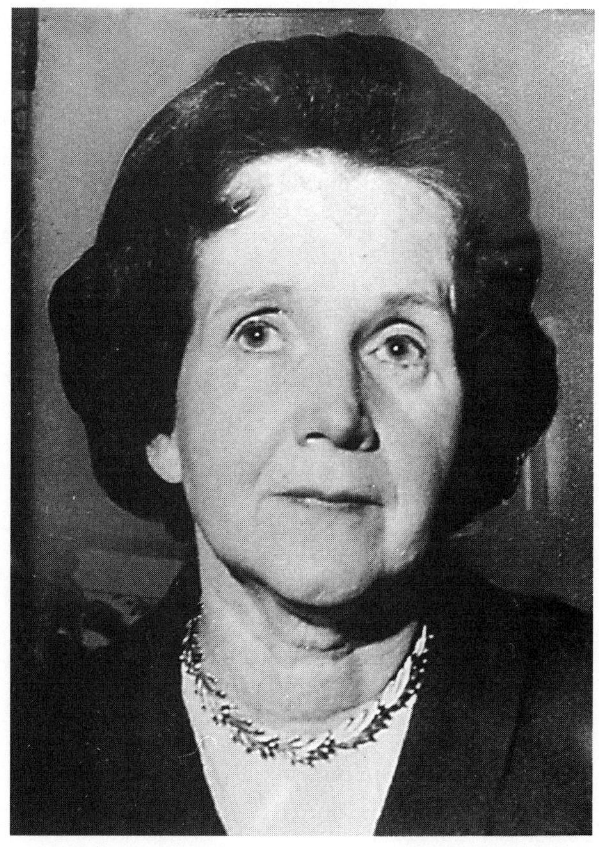

opened my eyes and my mind. I may not like what I see, but it does no good to ignore it."

When *Silent Spring* appeared in 1962, the lyric pen and analytical mind of Carson produced an impact equaled by few scientists; she aroused an entire nation. More than a billion dollars worth of chemical sprays was being sold and used in America each year. But when Carson traced the course of chlorinated hydrocarbons through energy cycles and food chains, she found that highly toxic materials, contaminating the environment and persisting for many years in waters and soils, also tended to accumulate in the human body. While target insect species were developing immunities to pesticides, because of these poisons birds were not reproducing. She proposed strict limitations on spraying programs and an accelerated research effort to develop natural, biological controls for harmful insects.

The pesticide industry reacted with a massive campaign to discredit Carson and her findings. Firmly and gently, she spent the next 2 years educating the public at large: "I think we are challenged as mankind has never been challenged before to prove our maturity and our mastery, not of nature, but of ourselves." She died on April, 14, 1964, at Silver Spring, Md.

Further Reading

The most authoritative book on Rachel Carson and the pesticide issue is Frank Graham, *Since Silent Spring* (1970). The references in the back of the book are recommended for up-to-date information on pesticides, their use, and control. □

Elliott Cook Carter Jr.

The American composer Elliott Cook Carter, Jr. (born 1908), developed an individual musical style, courageously ignoring many of the passing musical fashions to become one of the most respected composers of his time.

Elliott Carter was born in 1908 in New York, the son of a wealthy businessman. He was an English major at Harvard and, encouraged toward a musical career by his friend and mentor Charles Ives, he took his master's degree in music there, then spent 3 years in Paris studying with Nadia Boulanger. His first compositions, written upon his return to the United States, were a neoclassic ballet, *Pocahontas* (1939; rev. 1941), and *Holiday Overture* (1944).

Carter's Piano Sonata (1945-1946) is generally considered the first example of his mature style. It is highly dissonant and rhythmically complex, characteristics of all of his subsequent compositions. In his *Sonata for Cello and Piano* (1948) there is no attempt to "blend" the two instruments; each seems to go its own way. This manner of combining instruments is also used in his first String Quartet (1951-1952), in which the four instruments are treated like individual soloists, not sharing the same musical material. "I regard my scores as scenarios," the composer once said, "for performers to act out with their instruments, dramatizing the players as individuals and as participants in the ensemble." In this piece there are also examples of "metrical modulation," a method devised by Carter for precisely changing from one tempo and meter to another, giving a subtlety and flexibility to the time dimension of his music not achieved by other composers.

Variations for Orchestra (1955), a second String Quartet (1959), and a *Double Concerto for Harpsichord, Piano, and Two Chamber Orchestras* (1961) are later examples of his complex style. "I have tried to give musical expression to experiences anyone living today must have when confronted with so many remarkable examples of unexpected types of changes and relationships of character uncovered in every domain of science and art."

The Piano Concerto (1964-1965) continues the explorations of new tonal and temporal relationships. The composer described the piece as a "conflict between man and society. The piano is born, the orchestra teaches it what to say. The piano learns. Then it learns the orchestra is wrong. They fight and the piano wins—not triumphantly, but with a few, weak, sad notes—sort of Charlie Chaplin humorous." In his *Concerto for Orchestra* (1969) Carter achieves his complex texture by dividing the orchestra into four sections, each one different in composition and complete in itself.

Much of the composer's music since the 1970s took the form of solo and chamber works. His *A Mirror on Which to Dwell* (1978) is a song cycle based on the work of American

poet Elizabeth Bishop. His *String Quartet No. 5* was premiered by the Arditti Quartet in Antwerp, Belgium, in 1995. The same year also saw the premiere of a new song cycle, *Of Challenge and Of Love.* His later orchestral works include *Three Occasions* (1986-89) and his enormously successful *Violin Concerto* (1990). The latter piece has been performed frequently in more than a dozen countries. His *Partita* was commissioned by the Chicago Symphony Orchestra (1994) and around the same time his *Adagio Tenebroso* was commissioned by the BBC Symphony Orchestra for the 100th anniversary of the BBC Proms.

Carter has remained active well into his 80s. He has twice won the Pulitzer Prize and was the first composer to receive the United States National Medal of Arts. Carter was one of only four composers to win Germany's Ernst Von Siemens Music Prize, and in 1988 he was made a commander in the Orders of Arts and Letters by the French government. Among his other honors were Guggenheim fellowships, UNESCO citations, and several honorary doctorates. His compositions are performed and recorded as soon as they are completed. "I write for records," he said. "My last three pieces run about twenty-five minutes—the length of an LP side. They should be so rich that they can be played many times." It is this richness that makes a first hearing of Carter's music a confusing experience for many listeners, and the chief reason why it has not found popularity with a general audience.

Further Reading

Carter was the subject of *Elliott Carter, Collected Essays and Lectures, 1937-1995,* published by the University of Rochester Press. Edited by Jonathan W. Bernard, the book presents Carter's lectures and thoughts about music, literature, dance, film, philosophy, and his fellow composers such as Charles Ives and Igor Stravinsky. Joseph Machlis, *Introduction to Contemporary Music* (1961), contains a good chapter on Carter which discusses his String Quartet No. 2 in detail. David Ewen, *The World of Twentieth-Century Music* (1968), includes a critical essay on Carter and analyses of his works. See also Otto Deri, *Exploring Twentieth-Century Music* (1968), and Peter S. Hansen, *An Introduction to Twentieth Century Music* (3d ed. 1971).

Among the Internet web sites that contain biographical and critical data about Carter are www.ny.boosey.com and www.eyeneer.com. □

James Earl Carter

The first U.S. president to be elected from the deep South in 132 years, James Earl (Jimmy) Carter (born 1924) served one term (1977-1981). In 1980 he lost his bid for re-election to Republican candidate Ronald Reagan but went on to be a much admired worker for peace and human rights at home and abroad.

James Earl Carter was born in the small southern town of Plains, Georgia, on October 1, 1924. He was the first child of farmer and small businessman James Earl Carter and former nurse, Lillian Gordy Carter. When Carter was four, the family moved to a farm in Archery, a rural community a few miles west of Plains. At five, Jimmy was already demonstrating his independence and his talents for business: he began to sell peanuts on the streets of Plains. At the age of nine, Carter invested his earnings in five bales of cotton which he stored for several years, then sold at a profit large enough to enable him to purchase five old houses in Plains.

Following his graduation from high school in 1941, Carter enrolled in Georgia Southwestern College, but in 1942 he received word that a much desired appointment to the United States Naval Academy at Annapolis had been approved. Carter entered the academy in 1943, and showed a special talent for electronics and naval tactics, eventually going on to work on the nation's first nuclear powered submarines. During his time in the Navy he also met Rosalynn Smith who he married on July 7, 1947 and had four children with: John, James Earl III, Jeffrey, and a daughter born much later, Amy.

Civic Activist to Politician

Carter had ambitions to become an admiral, but in 1953, following his father's death from cancer, he returned to Plains to manage the family businesses. He took over both the farm and the peanut warehouses his father had established, enlarged the business and, in order to keep up

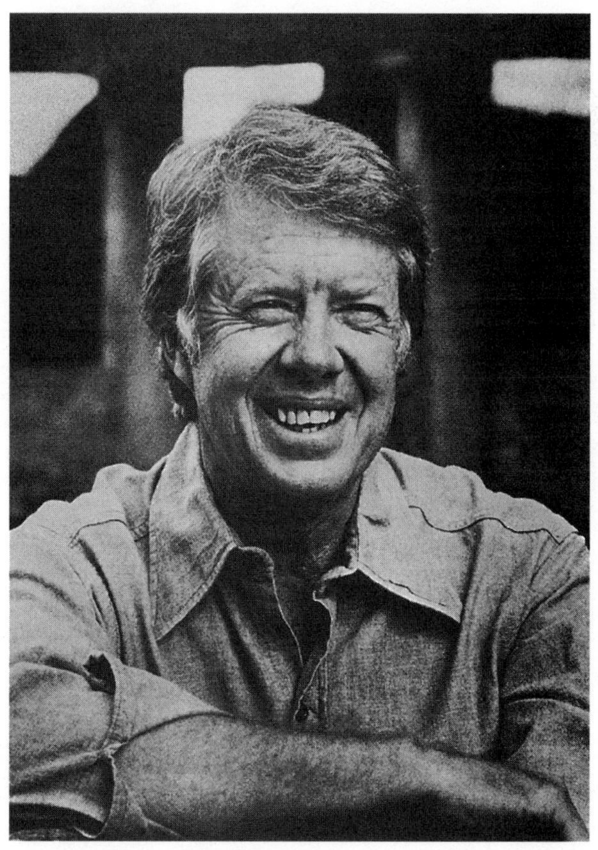

with modern farming techniques, studied at the Agricultural Experimental Station in Tifton, Georgia.

During these years in Plains, Carter began to play an active role in local civic affairs. From 1955 to 1962 he was active in a number of local functions and served on the boards of several civic organizations. In this civic life, Jimmy Carter distinguished himself by his liberal views on racial issues which could be traced back to his mother's disregard for many of the deep South's racist traditions.

As far as Carter's interest in politics goes, this may have come from his father, who had served for a year in the Georgia legislature. In 1962 Carter ran for a seat in the Georgia Senate and defeated his Republican opponent by about 1,000 votes. As a state senator, Carter promised to read every single bill that came up and when it looked as if he wouldn't be able to keep this promise due to the great volume of bills, he took a speed reading course to solve the problem. In government he earned a reputation as one of the most effective legislators and an outspoken moderate liberal. Carter was reelected to the state Senate in 1964.

In 1966, after first declaring himself as a candidate for the U.S. Congress, Carter decided to run for the office of governor of Georgia. He was beaten by Lester Maddox in the Democratic primary election though. Disappointed and spiritually bankrupt, Carter then became "born again" and pushed forward. Between 1966 and 1970 he traveled widely through the state, making close to 1,800 speeches, studying the problems of Georgia, and campaigning hard. In the 1970 gubernatorial election, Carter's hard work paid off and he won Georgia's top position.

Governor of Georgia

In his inaugural address Carter announced his intentions to aid all poor and needy Georgians, regardless of race. This speech won Carter his first national attention, for in it he called for an end to racial discrimination and the extension of a right to an education, to a job, and to "simple justice" for the poor. As governor, Carter worked for, and signed into law, a bill which stipulated that the poor and wealthy areas of Georgia would have equal state aid for education. Carter also worked to cut waste in the government, merging 300 state agencies into only 30. The number of African-American appointees on major state boards and agencies increased from three to 53 and the number of African-American state employees rose by 40 percent. During his term, laws were passed to protect historical sites, conserve the environment, and to encourage openness in government.

While governor, Carter became increasingly involved in national Democratic Party politics. In 1972 he headed the Democratic Governors Campaign Committee, and in 1974 was chair of the Democratic National Campaign Committee. That same year Carter officially declared his intention to run for president in the 1976 race. When Carter announced his intentions to seek the presidency, he was still little known outside the state of Georgia. As late as October 1975 a public opinion poll on possible Democratic candidates did not even list his name. Then, in January 1976, Carter's whirlwind rise to national prominence began and by March 1976 he was the top choice among Democrats for the presidential nomination.

The 1976 Election

Carter's success against ten other candidates began with a victory in the New Hampshire primary in February. He was successful in making himself a symbol of a leader without ties to the entrenched interest groups of the nation's capital. Carter convinced voters that without these ties he would be able to act independently and effectively. In his campaign he also vowed to restore moral leadership to the presidency which had been badly shaken in the wake of Richard Nixon and the Watergate scandal. Carter easily won 17 of 30 primary contests and was elected on the first ballot at the 1976 Democratic National Convention.

With his running mate, Minnesota liberal Democrat Walter Mondale, Carter made unemployment a central issue of his campaign, urging the creation of jobs through increased federal spending and the expansion of business. Carter also campaigned on promises of pardon for the draft evaders of the Vietnam War period, the reorganization of the federal government bureaucracy, and the development of a national energy policy.

When Carter defeated the incumbent, Gerald Ford, by 1,678,069 popular votes, winning 297 electoral college votes to Ford's 240, he became the first president from the Deep South since Zachary Taylor in 1844. Carter's victory was definitely regional and was definitely based on social and economic class as his winning margin came from African-Americans, those with low incomes, and others who thought that they were being hurt by the policies of the Ford administration. Four out of five African-Americans voted for Carter and he also did well among white southerners, receiving the highest number of votes for a Democratic candidate since Roosevelt, but lost over one-half of Catholic voters and 55 percent of the Italian vote. One of the challenges to Carter was to ease the regional and ethnic splits evident in the election and to create a unified support for his presidency.

His Record as President

The year 1977 began well for the new president with a series of quick victories for Carter-backed programs. These included congressional approval of his plans to eliminate or consolidate federal agencies which duplicated services and of legislation aimed at lowering federal income taxes. In August of 1977 Congress adopted Carter's proposal to establish the Department of Energy as a new executive department. At the same time, Carter used his executive powers to make good on campaign pledges, including the pardoning of Vietnam War draft evaders and ending production of the B-1 bomber, which he felt was wasteful.

The Carter Administration was not without its problems though. In 1977 economic conditions had improved somewhat and unemployment had fallen, but by 1978 inflation had, despite a variety of approaches to stabilize it, continued to rise, reaching 15 percent by mid-1980. Due largely to these economic problems, Carter's approval rating in a

July 1980 poll measured only 21 percent, the lowest recorded for any American president.

Carter's term was also marked by mixed success in foreign affairs. In 1977 Carter attracted worldwide attention and praise for his strong support of human rights wherein he limited or banned entirely any United States aid to nations believed to be human rights violators, but mixed reviews came for two 1977 treaties dealing with the Panama Canal. The first of these gave control of the canal to Panama on December 31, 1999 and the second gave the United States the right to defend the neutrality of the canal. Carter was influential in the Camp David Accords as well as in the creation of a peace treaty between Israel and Egypt in 1979 and in the negotiation of SALT (Strategic Arms Limitation Treaty) II with the Soviet Union, although these negotiations were ultimately delayed by the Soviet invasion of Afghanistan.

Carter's most dramatic moments in foreign policy affairs began in November 1979 when Iranian student militants seized the United States embassy in Teheran and took 52 U.S. citizens hostage. The hostages were to be held, their captors said, until the deposed Shah, who was in the United States for medical treatment, was handed over. Carter responded first by cutting diplomatic relations with Iran and stopping all imports from that country. When these measures failed he, in April 1980, ordered an attempt at armed rescue, which failed and led to the death of eight marines and the resignation of Secretary of State Cyrus R. Vance. In the end the crisis lasted for a total of 444 days with the hostages finally being released on January 20, 1981, the last day that Carter held office.

The hostage crisis overseas and economic difficulties at home left Carter vulnerable but still vying for the top spot in the 1980 presidential elections. Running again with Vice President Walter Mondale, Carter was defeated by former California governor and actor Ronald Reagan by a wide margin. He received only 35 million votes to Reagan's 44 million and lost the electoral college vote 489 to 44.

The Right Things to Accomplish Post Presidency

While seen as a somewhat lame-duck immediately following his departure as president in 1981, recent historical revisionism has cast him in a more favorable light, especially in lieu of his successor's later improprieties during the Iran-Contra scandal. Viewed as a basically honest man, not a small commodity in this age of popular mistrust of government, Carter has devoted his post presidential career to an array of peacekeeping and humanitarian efforts.

In 1981 Carter established the Carter Center which, with its sizable budget, has sponsored programs from promoting human rights in third world countries to maintaining databases of immunization for local Atlanta children. The Carter Center has also monitored elections in newly democratized countries, fought such diseases as polio and river blindness, and helped eradicate the harmful African Guinea worm in Pakistan. In addition to these humanitarian efforts, Carter and his wife, Rosalynn, have volunteered their summers building low-income housing through the Habitat For Humanity organization.

The international relations front has also been no stranger to Carter since his defeat to Ronald Reagan. In 1990 he persuaded Nicaraguan Sandinista leader Daniel Ortega to step down and let an elected president, Violeta Chamorro, step in, something that without the relative neutrality of Carter's position probably would not have been possible. Carter has also served as somewhat of a mediator between President Bill Clinton and various leaders of non-democratic nations. In the early 1990s Carter brought messages from Somali warlord Mohamed Farrah Aidid to President Clinton which helped avoid a military confrontation and in June 1994 Carter negotiated with North Korean dictator Kim Il Sung to freeze his country's nuclear program and allow inspection of their nuclear facilities. Interestingly enough, sometimes Carter's efforts haven't been completely appreciated. President Clinton was reportedly incensed at Carter going over his head in foreign matters and making statements that he wasn't authorized to make.

One further mixed victory from Carter came when in September 1994, he, with the help of former chairman of the Joint Chiefs of Staff Colin Powell and Georgia Senator Sam Nunn, negotiated an agreement with Haitian revolutionary leader Lt. Gen. Raoul Cédras. Haiti, since the ouster of their first democratically elected president, Jean-Bertrand Aristide, in 1991, had been a cesspool of violence and poverty since the revolution. Boatloads of Haitians seeking an escape from the myriad human rights abuses were arriving on U.S. shores daily and the situation was pointing towards a military invasion. President Clinton called on Carter to help, which he did with an agreement wherein military leaders relinquished power and handed it over to American forces until democracy could be restored. The downside of the agreement being Cédras and his cronies being given permission to stay in Haiti instead of being exiled which drew much criticism.

Whatever flak Carter has received for his methods of handling foreign affairs they fade from view when compared to the tireless work he has done for humanity since the end of his presidency. No other former president has worked so hard in the public arena while still maintaining personal pursuits which in Carter's case involve hunting, fishing, teaching adult Sunday school, and writing several books including one of his own poetry. As Carter's former speech writer, James Fallows, put it in 1990, "..what becomes . . . admirable is precisely the idealism of (Carter's) vision, the energy and intelligence and morality he has put into figuring out what is the right thing to accomplish."

Further Reading

There are several books that tell Jimmy Carter's story. Carter himself has written a number of books which include: *Keeping Faith: Memoirs of a President* (1982), *The Blood of Abraham: Insights into the Middle East* (1985), *An Outdoor Journal: Adventures and Reflections* (1988), *Turning Point: A Candidate, A State, and a Nation Come of Age* (1993), and his volume of poetry *Always a Reckoning* (1995). Edna Langford and Linda Cox have done a biography of Carter's wife, Rosalynn, entitled *Rosalynn, Friend and First Lady* (1980) and

Rosalynn tells her own story in *First Lady From Plains* (1985). Hamilton Jordan's book, *Crisis: The Last Year of the Carter Presidency* (1982) deals largely with the Iranian hostage crisis, while Jack Germond and Jules Witcover's *Blue Smoke and Mirrors: How Reagan Won and Why Carter Lost the Election of 1980* (1981) analyzes Carter's defeat in his bid for reelection. Carter's greatest diplomatic success—the 1978-1979 agreement between Israel and Egypt—is detailed in *Camp David* (1986) by William Quandt, a member of the Carter administration. Other accounts of Carter's life can be found in Peter G. Bourne's *Jimmy Carter: A Comprehensive Biography* (1997) and Rod Troester's *Jimmy Carter as Peacemaker: A Post Presidential Biography* (1996). For those inclined to go online, the Carter Center's Web site address is http://www.emory.edu/CARTER_CENTER. □

Sir George-Étienne Cartier

Sir George-Étienne Cartier (1814-1873) was a Canadian statesman who led French Canada into the federation of British North America in 1867.

George-Étienne Cartier was born in Saint-Antoine, Lower Canada, on Sept. 6, 1814. He studied at St-Sulpice College, Montreal, in preparation for a legal career. Called to the bar in 1835, he was immediately caught up in the political struggle of the French-Canadian *patriotes* against the English-dominated executive of Lower Canada. As an ardent supporter of the reform cause led by Louis-Joseph Papineau, Cartier fought in two of the sharpest encounters of the short-lived rebellion of 1837: the battles at Saint-Denis and Saint-Charles. The wholesale defeat of the rebels forced him to flee to the United States, where he settled for a time in Burlington, Vt. After an amnesty declared by the British government, Cartier returned to Montreal in 1838 and, as passions cooled after the rebellions, settled down to a legal career.

Corporation Lawyer

Cartier was remarkably successful as a lawyer, and he became the leading French-speaking corporation lawyer of Montreal, specializing in railway companies. In 1853 he reached the summit of his professional career, when he was asked to act as solicitor for the Grand Trunk Railway, the largest railway enterprise in British North America. At this time another side of Cartier's character was revealed when he wrote the lyrics for "O Canada," a song popular enough in his lifetime to become almost the Canadian national anthem.

Cartier and Macdonald

In 1848 Cartier had entered politics through his election as member for Vercheres County, which he represented until 1861, when he was chosen by a Montreal riding. A moderate Conservative, he reached ministerial rank in 1855 as provincial secretary for Canada East, in the united Province of Canada. A year later he was made attorney general of Canada East, and in 1857 he became the leader of the French-Canadian wing of the Conservative party. This brought him into close relations with John Alexander Macdonald, the Kingston lawyer who filled the same position in Canada West. The two found similar interest in the economic growth of Canada and agreed in applying the principles of a partnership of French and English-speaking Conservatives to the maintenance of a British North American identity. Each possessed a pragmatic approach to political questions, each was affable and urbane, and each was a master in the art of managing men. They developed a relationship of confidence that was to carry them through the critical times of Canadian federation and the launching of a new nation.

In 1857 Cartier teamed with Macdonald in the first of several ministries in which they functioned as joint leaders. The ministry was defeated in the Assembly on June 29, 1858, but came back to power on August 6 through a legal technicality, the "double shuffle." It then survived until 1862 but had increasing difficulties carrying out a legislative program against attacks from the "Grits" of Canada West, who objected to the French-Canadian influence in the government and wished to reconstruct the union on the basis of "representation by population" in the legislature instead of equality by territory.

The Confederation

Out of office for 2 years, Cartier resumed his old post of attorney general of Canada East in March 1864, again in alliance with Macdonald. In June he joined in a coalition ministry, in which George Brown and the Reformers of Canada West participated, to explore the possibilities of a federation of all the British American colonies. Cartier helped to work out the language and educational guarantees for the French-speaking minority in the projected new federal state. Then, tirelessly and skillfully, he used his considerable influence in Quebec to successfully persuade French-speaking Canadians to enter the wider union. The Confederation scheme was endorsed by the members of the legislature from Canada East in 1865. For his essential services to the cause of Confederation, Cartier was made a baronet by the British government in 1868.

The first federal cabinet was formed in July 1867, with Macdonald serving as prime minister. Cartier was minister of militia, his portfolio obscuring the fact that he was Macdonald's chief associate. In 1868 Cartier went to England to arrange the purchase of the Hudson's Bay Company lands in the West for the new Dominion. The acquisition of these lands was essential to the project of a transcontinental railway, which Macdonald envisaged as a necessary step in the creation of a new state across northern North America. Cartier, with his long interest in railways, was a strong supporter of the Pacific railway project.

"Pacific Scandal"

In the election of 1872 Cartier was imprudent in soliciting large campaign contributions for the Conservatives from Sir Hugh Allan, the leader of a syndicate interested in building the Pacific railway. Although no corrupt bargain was entered into, there is no doubt that Allan's expectations of receiving the railway charter were aroused through his dealings with Cartier. The Opposition raised the matter in Parliament in April 1873, an inquiry was instituted, and charges were voiced that eventually led to the resignation of Macdonald's government.

Cartier was a distant witness of these sorry events. He had gone to England in the spring of 1873 to consult physicians about his health, and he died suddenly in London on May 20, 1873.

Further Reading

The fullest biography of Cartier in English is John Boyd, *Sir George-Etienne Cartier, Bart.: His Life and Times* (1914). See also A.D. DeCelles, *Papineau; Cartier* (1904; reprinted as vol. 5 of "Makers of Canada" series, 1926). Background studies in Canadian history include Edgar McInnis, *Canada: A Political and Social History* (1947; rev. ed. 1959); Mason Wade, *The French Canadians, 1760-1945* (1955; rev. ed. 1968); and J. Bartlet Brebner, *Canada: A Modern History* (1960; rev. ed. 1970).

Additional Sources

Sweeny, Alastair, *George-Etienne Cartier: a biography,* Toronto: McClelland and Stewart, 1976.

Young, Brian J., *George-Etienne Cartier: Montreal bourgeois,* Kingston: McGill-Queen's University Press, 1981. □

Jacques Cartier

Jacques Cartier (1491-1557), French explorer and navigator, may truly be said to have discovered Canada. His voyages were the key to the cartography of the Gulf of St. Lawrence, and he named the land around it "Canada."

Born in Saint-Malo in Brittany, Jacques Cartier probably had already been on trading and exploring missions to Brazil and Newfoundland when Francis I of France first approached him about a French expedition to the New World in 1532. In April 1534 Cartier set out in two ships to discover, if he could, "certain islands and lands where it is said that a great quantity of gold and other precious things are to be found."

Cartier had a remarkably good run, reaching Newfoundland after a mere 20 days. It says much about Cartier's skill as navigator as well as about 16th-century navigation that his calculation of the latitude of Cape Bonavista, Newfoundland, was only about 11 miles off its true latitude. West of the Strait of Belle Isle, Cartier encountered a French ship from La Rochelle. It is clear from his account that French and Portuguese fishermen had frequented these coasts for some time past. It is altogether probable that western European fishermen had been fishing around Newfoundland well before even John Cabot's voyage of 1497.

Cartier disliked the inhospitable look of the land on the south coast of Labrador and turned southward along the west coast of Newfoundland, crossed the Gulf of St. Lawrence, sighted the fertile Prince Edward Island, and arrived in mid-July 1534 at Gaspé on the mainland. After exploring Anticosti Island in the St. Lawrence estuary but, because of bad weather, missing the St. Lawrence River, he returned to France, arriving in Saint-Malo in September 1534.

Almost at once he was recommissioned by Francis I for a more imposing expedition in 1535, this time with three ships, including the *Grande Hermine.* Leaving Saint-Malo in the middle of May, Cartier went straight for the estuary of the St. Lawrence where he had left off the year before. Using information gained from natives, he went up the great river, nothing how the water turned gradually from salt to fresh, and arrived at the site of the Iroquois village of Stadacona (modern Quebec City) early in September 1535. He continued up the river, anchored his ship, the *Emérillon,* at Lake St. Peter, and made the rest of his way to the native village of Hochelaga (modern Montreal) by longboat. There he arrived in October and found a thriving, fortified Iroquois village nestled at the foot of a hill which he called Mont Réal. From the top of this hill he could see the rapids, later to be called Lachine, that blocked further navigation westward.

Cartier spent the winter of 1535–1536 back at Stadacona, where his men had built a primitive fort. It was a cold winter even by Canadian standards. From mid-November until mid-April Cartier's ships were icebound. Worse still was scurvy, brought on by absence of fresh fruit and vegetables-basically the lack of vitamin C. Of Cartier's 110 men, only 10 were still well by February 1536, and 25 men eventually died. The the native peoples had a remedy for scurvy which Cartier learned about just in time: an infusion made from the bark of white cedar which produced massive quantities of vitamin C and by which the men were quickly restored.

Cartier returned to France in May 1536 and took 10 Indians (including 4 children) with him, promising to bring them back to Canada on his next voyage. However, all but one of them had died by the time the next expedition got under way in 1541. This time the expedition was under the leadership of Jean François de la Rocque de Roberval, and it was much larger than the earlier ones, with settlers included among about 1,500 men and with eight ships. Cartier left before Roberval, who was waiting for his guns, and arrived in August 1541 at Stadacona.

This time Cartier set up camp a few miles above Stadacona, wintered more comfortably than before, and, finding no sign of Roberval in the spring, set off for France in June 1542. At St. John's harbor, Newfoundland, Cartier met Roberval, who ordered him to return to Quebec. For a variety of reasons, some of them related doubtless to deteriorating relations with the native population, Cartier preferred not to return and slipped away for France under the cover of darkness. He settled down at a country estate not far from Saint-Malo. In 1520 he had married Catherine des Granches, but they had no children. Cartier died on Sept. 1, 1557, at Saint-Malo.

Further Reading

H. P. Biggar edited Cartier's record of his explorations, *The Voyages of Jacques Cartier* (1924). Biographical accounts of Cartier are in John Bartlet Brebner, *The Explorers of North America, 1492-1806* (1933); Lawrence J. Burpee, *The Discovery of Canada* (1944); and Alida Sims Malkus, *Blue-Water Boundary: Epic Highway of the Great Lakes and the Saint Lawrence* (1960). Cartier is discussed in Samuel Eliot Morison, *The European Discovery of America: The Northern Voyages* (1971), a readable and well-documented study. ☐

Peter Cartwright

The American preacher Peter Cartwright (1785-1872) was largely responsible for the rapid growth of Methodism in the Ohio River and Mississippi River valleys.

Born on Sept. 1, 1785, Peter Cartwright followed his pioneering father, Justinian, from their home in Virginia to Logan County, Ky., a brigand-infested locality near Tennessee. Justinian encouraged Peter's gambling habits, but his mother, who mourned the criminal debaucheries of two of her children, constantly urged repentance. At age 16 Peter converted to Methodism. After briefly studying at Brown's Academy, Cartwright began circuit riding in October 1803. In 1806 Bishop Francis Asbury ordained him deacon. At 23 "the Kentucky boy," as he was called, was ordained an elder. The low salary of an itinerant preacher encouraged bachelorhood, but Cartwright married 19-year-old Frances Gaines because, as he said, he thought it his duty.

As the Methodists spread throughout the South, their long-standing strictures against slave holding lost strength. Fearing the effects of slavery upon the moral character of his offspring, Cartwright moved his family to Illinois in 1824. He served two terms in the Illinois Legislature, where he successfully battled the introduction of slavery to the state. In 1846 Abraham Lincoln defeated Cartwright's only bid for Congress; Cartwright had centered his campaign upon Lincoln's alleged godlessness.

Cartwright's *Autobiography* (1856) chronicled his colorful career as "backwoods preacher." It provided glimpses of pioneer church life in the manner of tall-tale Western folklore. Often humorous, the *Autobiography* proudly recorded his "slaying" of countless sinners, besting rivals in conflicts both verbal and physical and riveting Methodist social taboos upon unruly frontiersmen. Yet Cartwright lived to lament the results his own success elicited. Prosperity and the consequent sophistication of rural life led his followers to demand settled clergy, fine buildings, seminaries, academies, and eastern luxuries, all of which, Cartwright believed, eroded the authority and simple faith of traveling revivalists and their flocks. Theologically, he denounced such "heresies" as predestinarianism, Second Coming millennialism, universalism, Catholicism, and, especially, Mormonism. He strongly approved expulsion of the Mormons from their settlement in western Illinois. While espousing a crude gospel of salvation, he deplored the

excess known as "the jerks," a phenomenon his vibrant sermons often aroused.

Cartwright was elected 12 times to the General Conference, where he argued against the Methodists' sectional split of 1844 and against attempts to curb the power of bishops over the circuit-riding system. Though opposed to ministers' owning slaves, he held abolitionists and proslavery apologists equally accountable for dividing church and nation. Cartwright represented the typical Western churchman's view of slavery as a moral evil but saw the black man as a member of "a degraded race." Cartwright died Sept. 25, 1872.

Further Reading

The Autobiography of Peter Cartwright, the Backwoods Preacher, edited by W. P. Strickland (1856), was republished as *Autobiography,* with an introduction, bibliography, and index by Charles L. Wallis (1956). General works which discuss Cartwright are Wade Crawford Barclay, *History of Methodist Missions,* vol. 2 (1950), and Emery Stevens Bucke, ed., *The History of American Methodism* (3 vols., 1964).

Additional Sources

Cartwright, Peter, *Autobiography of Peter Cartwright,* Nashville: Abingdon Press, 1986. ☐

Enrico Caruso

Enrico Caruso (1873-1921) was an Italian tenor who was an early recording artist and the foremost Metropolitan Opera attraction for a generation. For power, sweetness, and versatility his voice was without peer.

Born on Feb. 25, 1873, in Naples, Enrico Caruso was the eighteenth child of a poverty-ridden machinist. Early encouragement came from fellow workers who heard him sing Neapolitan ballads. Guglielmo Vergine, his first teacher, held small hopes for him as a professional, and Caruso's early efforts were not promising. He made his debut in *L'Amico Francesco* at the Teatro Nuovo, Naples, in 1894, and his apprenticeship was in small Italian theaters singing a variety of roles.

Selected for the tenor lead in the premiere of Umberto Giodano's *Fedora* in Milan in 1898, Caruso scored an electrifying success. Engagements at St. Petersburg, Moscow, Buenos Aires, and Bologna were climaxed by an invitation to sing at La Scala, the great opera house at Milan, directed by Giulio Gatti-Casazza and Arturo Toscanini. After triumphs with soprano Nellie Melba in *La Bohème* at Monte Carlo and *Rigoletto* in London in 1902, Caruso was engaged by the Metropolitan Opera Company. He made his New York debut in *Rigoletto* in 1903, and was connected with the "Met" for the rest of his life.

Idolized in every operatic center, the flamboyant Neapolitan was the subject of almost unprecedented publicity. In Berlin and Vienna "Caruso nights" were celebrated, and in Mexico City he received $15,000 for a single performance. At the peak of his career, his performance fees exceeded $500,000 annually. The earliest of his nearly 250 recordings dates from 1902, and his annual income from this source alone reached $115,000.

Caruso's liaison (never legalized) with Ada Giachetti, by whom he had two sons, was painfully ended by court proceedings in 1912. In 1918 he married Dorothy Park Benjamin, daughter of a wealthy New York industrialist. Stricken with a throat hemorrhage during a performance at the Brooklyn Academy of Music, Caruso sang only once more—a performance of *La Juive* at the Met in 1920. He died in Naples on Aug. 2, 1921.

Supremely gifted for opera by temperament and physique, Caruso was also single-minded, hard-working, and self-critical. An awkward actor in the beginning, he developed into a superlative artist. Certain roles, such as Canio in *Pagliacci* and Radames in *Aida,* became so indelibly his that all other tenors suffer by comparison. He had a remarkable range, but when the lighter quality of his early years darkened, his voice was less suitable for some of the lyric roles. In power and expressiveness, however, his abilities suffered no impairment despite a temporary loss of voice during the 1908-1909 season.

Among Caruso's many honors were commendatore in the Order of the Crown of Italy, the French Legion of Honor, and the Order of the Crown Eagle of Prussia. He was totally free from professional jealousies. A natural comedian, he was also a gifted caricaturist. His warmhearted generosity made him genuinely loved by his associates and the public at large to a degree almost unique in the lyric theater.

Further Reading

Enrico Caruso, His Life and Death (1945) is a beautifully written tribute by his wife, Dorothy Park Caruso. Pierre V. R. Key and Bruno Zirato, *Enrico Caruso, a Biography* (1922), lacks objectivity. T. R. Ybarra, *Caruso: The Man of Naples and the Voice of Gold* (1953), is packed with vivid reminiscences. More specialized works are Enrico Caruso, *Caricatures* (1906; new ed. 1914), and Aida Favia-Artay, *Caruso on Records* (1965). Other valuable sources are Frances Alda, *Men, Women, and Tenors* (1937); Giulio Gatti-Casazza, *Memories of the Opera* (1941); and Henry Pleasants, *The Great Singers: From the Dawn of Opera to Our Own Time* (1966).

Additional Sources

Barthelemy, Richard, *Memories of Caruso,* Plainsboro, N.J.: La Scala Autographs, 1979.

Caruso, Dorothy, *Enrico Caruso, his life and death,* Westport, Conn.: Greenwood Press, 1987.

Caruso, Enrico, *Enrico Caruso: my father and my family,* Portland, Or.: Amadeus Press, 1990.

Greenfeld, Howard, *Caruso,* New York, N.Y.: Da Capo Press, 1984, 1983.

Greenfeld, Howard, *Caruso: an illustrated life,* North Pomfret, Vt.: Trafalgar Square Pub., 1991.

Mouchon, Jean-Pierre, *Enrico Caruso: his life and voice,* Gap, France: Editions Ophrys, 1974.

Scott, Michael, *The great Caruso,* Boston: Northeastern University Press, 1989, 1988. ☐

George Washington Carver

George Washington Carver (1864-1943) started his life as a slave and ended it as a respected and world-renowned agricultural chemist.

Born in Kansas Territory near Diamond Grove, Mo., during the bloody struggle between free-soilers and slaveholders, George Washington Carver became the kidnap victim of night riders. With his mother and brother, James, he was held for ransom; but before they could be rescued the mother died. Merely a babe in arms, Carver was ransomed for a $300 racehorse by Moses Carver, a German farmer. Thus he was orphaned and left in the custody of a white guardian from early childhood.

Carver had responsibility for his own education. His first school was in Neosho, Iowa, some 9 miles from his home. Neosho had once been a Confederate capital; by now it had become the site of the Lincoln School for African American children. With James he walked there every day. His first teacher was an African American, Stephen S. Frost. He and his brother went faithfully to school for several years. Finally James tired of formal schooling and quit to become a house painter, but not George. He continued until he was 17. Then he went on to complete his high school work in Minneapolis, Kans.

Carver really wished to become an artist. His sketch of the rose *Yucca gloriosa* won him a first prize at the World's Columbian Exposition (1893).

Carver applied to study at the Iowa State College of Agricultural and Mechanical Arts but was turned down when it was learned that he was of African heritage. He then applied to Simpson College at Indianola, Iowa, where he was the second African American to be admitted. Tuition was $12 a year, but even this small amount was hard to come by. Carver raised the money by working as a cook at a hotel in Winterset, Iowa.

After 3 years' attendance at Simpson College, he once again applied for admission to Iowa State. He was admitted and was placed in charge of the greenhouse of the horticultural department while doing graduate work. He earned his master's degree in agriculture in 1896.

In April 1896 Carver received a unique offer from the African American educator Booker T. Washington to teach at Tuskegee Institute in Alabama. Said Dr. Washington: "I cannot offer you money, position or fame. The first two you have. The last from the position you now occupy you will no doubt achieve. These things I now ask you to give up. I offer you in their place: work—hard, hard work, the task of bringing a people from degradation, poverty, and waste to full manhood. Your department exists only on paper and your laboratory will have to be in your head."

Carver accepted the challenge. He arrived at the tiny railroad station at Chehaw, Ala., on Oct. 8, 1896. In a report to Dr. Washington he wrote: "8:00 to 9:00 A.M., Agricultural Chemistry; 9:20 to 10:00 A.M., the Foundation of Colors (for painters); 10:00 to 11:00 A.M., a class of farmers.

Additional hours in the afternoon. In addition I must oversee and rather imperfectly supervise seven industrial classes, scattered here and there over the grounds. I must test all seeds, examine all fertilizers, based upon an examination of soils in different plots."

Through the years Carver was gaining national and international stature. Chinese and Japanese farmers raised many unique problems for him. Questions were referred to him from Russia, India, Europe, South America. He later had to turn down a request to journey to the Soviet Union. In 1916 he was elected a member of the Royal Society for the Encouragement of Arts in England; he went to Washington to the War Department to demonstrate his findings on the sweet potato in 1918. He was awarded the Spingarn Medal of the NAACP in 1923.

An early close friend of Carver was Henry A. Wallace; the pair knew each other for 47 years. Wallace said that Carver often took him on botanical expeditions, and it was he who first introduced Wallace to the mysteries of plant fertilizers. Carver was a shy and modest bachelor. An attack of whooping cough as a child had permanently caused him to have a high-pitched tenor voice. He considered it a high duty to attend classes and was seldom absent. In 1908 he returned to the West to visit his 96-year-old guardian, Moses Carver, and to visit the grave of his brother, James, in Missouri.

A careful and modest scientist, Carver was not without a sense of humor. When one of his students, hoping to play a trick on him, showed him a bug with wings of a fly and body of a mosquito, Carver was quick to label it "a humbug."

Carver utilized the materials at hand. He was interested in crop rotation and soil conservation. From the clay soil of Alabama he extracted a full range of dyestuffs, including a brilliant blue. He created 60 products from the pecan. From the common sweet potato he extracted a cereal coffee, a shoe polish, paste, oils—about 100 products. From the peanut he developed over 145 products. Carver suggested peanuts, pecans, and sweet potatoes replace cotton as money crops. He published all of his findings in a series of nearly 50 bulletins.

The testimony of Carver before the congressional House Ways and Means Committee in 1921 led to the passage of the Fordney-McCumber Tariff Bill of 1922. Scheduled to speak a scant 10 minutes, he was granted several time extensions because of the intense interest in his presentation. (He appeared in a greenish-blue suit many seasons old, having refused to invest in a new suit: "They want to hear what I have to say; they will not be interested in how I look.")

In 1935 Carver was chosen to collaborate with the Bureau of Plant Industry of the U.S. Department of Agriculture. He received the Theodore Roosevelt Medal in 1939 for distinguished achievement in science. During his lifetime Carver had made many friends. Henry Ford was his frequent host. Carver was a treasured friend of Thomas A. Edison. It was Edison who offered to make him independent with his own laboratories and an annual stipend of $50,000. Other intimates of his were Luther Burbank, Harvey Firestone, and John Burroughs. He was also a friend of three presidents: Theodore Roosevelt, Calvin Coolidge, and Franklin Delano Roosevelt.

Dr. Carver had earned the salary of $125 a month from the beginning until the end of his service at Tuskegee. He might have had much more. In 1940 he gave his lifesavings, $33,000, to establish the George Washington Carver Foundation at Tuskegee Institute to perpetuate research in agriculture and chemistry. He later bequeathed his entire estate to the foundation, making a total of about $60,000. He died on Jan. 5, 1943.

At the dedication of a building in his honor at Simpson College, Dr. Ralph Bunche, Nobel Prize winner, pronounced Dr. Carver to be "the least imposing celebrity the world has ever known." Dr. Carver's birthplace was made a national monument on July 14, 1953.

Further Reading

Of the many studies of Carver the best is Rackham Holt, *George Washington Carver: An American Biography* (1943). Also useful is Shirley Graham and George D. Lipscomb, *Dr. George Washington Carver, Scientist* (1944). ☐

Jonathan Carver

The American explorer and writer Jonathan Carver (1710-1780) was one of the most famous travelers and travel writers of the 18th century.

Jonathan Carver was born on April 13, 1710, in Weymouth, Mass. The family moved to Canterbury, Conn., when Jonathan was a child. He entered military service in the French and Indian War as a sergeant and was wounded in 1757 in the horrible siege of Ft. William Henry, which became synonymous on the frontier with "atrocity." Two years later Carver was promoted to lieutenant and was raised to captain of a Massachusetts regiment the following year. Gen. Thomas Gage, particularly, thought highly of Carver's military ability.

When the French and Indian War ended, Carver began the travels which made him famous in America and Europe. He started from Boston and made his way to the British frontier post of Mackinac, where the commandant, Robert Rogers (of Rogers' Rangers fame), encouraged him and supplied trade goods to be used as presents for the Native Americans through whose country he would be traveling. Carver ascended the Mississippi River to the mouth of the Minnesota, which he then followed. He eventually reached Lake Superior and spent several months on its northern and eastern margins, exploring its bays and the rivers which entered the lake. He returned to Mackinac in 1767.

During the following year Carver took the journal of his wilderness travels to Boston in hopes of having it published. Disappointed, he sailed for London to announce his discoveries to the world. In England he petitioned the King for reimbursement of the money he had spent in his explorations. The result was an examination by the Board of Trade, which granted him permission to publish his journal. Although it was quite popular, the sales were insufficient to support him, and he had to take other work, such as clerking in a lottery office.

Carver remained in England the rest of his life, remarrying there though he had never bothered to divorce the wife he had left in America. He spent most of his time writing or trying to get more of his writings published.

His *Travels through the Interior Parts of North America* (1778) ran through numerous editions and was translated into foreign languages, becoming one of the most popular early travel accounts of America. But because Carver padded his journals with a section of information on Native American customs garnered from other authors, whom he did not identify, he was charged with plagiarism, and his reputation as both writer and explorer suffered. During 1778-1779 he lent his name to a work titled *The New Universal Geography* and wrote a technical work, *Treatise on the Culture of the Tobacco Plant,* but these books did not enjoy the sales of his *Travels.*

Carver died destitute on Jan. 31, 1780, and his English wife buried him in a paupers' field. His reputation has been hounded by charges of fictionalizing and plagiarism. Even today, historians are laboring to restore his once high standing.

Further Reading

The most useful work for the study of Carver is his *Travels through the Interior Parts of North America* (1778; repr. 1956). There is no adequate biography of him. William Francis Raney, *Wisconsin: A Story of Progress* (1940), includes a discussion of Carver. See also Larry Gara, *A Short History of Wisconsin* (1962).

Additional Sources

Carver, Jonathan, *The journals of Jonathan Carver and related documents, 1766-1770,* St. Paul: Minnesota Historical Society Press, 1976. □

Pablo Casals

In protest of dictatorships throughout the world, including the totalitarian Francisco Franco regime in Spain, cellist Pablo Casals (1876–1973) refused in 1946 to ever perform on stage again. He eventually returned to playing for audiences but would not perform in countries that supported the Franco government.

From the age of ten, Pablo Casals began each day with a walk, taking inspiration from nature. These outings were always followed by playing two Johann Sebastian Bach preludes and fugues on the piano when he returned home. It was, Casals expressed in *Joys and Sorrows: Reflections by Pablo Casals as Told to Albert E. Kahn,* "a rediscovery of the world of which I have the joy of being a part. It fills me with an awareness of the wonder of life, with a feeling of the incredible marvel of being a human being." A deeply reflective man, Casals imbued his life with his own spiritual triumvirate: the wonder of nature, the music of Bach, and God. This in turn informed his art. Technically masterful, revolutionary even, his cello playing was elevated by his belief, as he defined it for Kahn, that "music [was] an affirmation of the beauty man was capable of producing."

Casals always felt it his obligation to share with others this access to beauty that transcended languages and borders. When political and egotistical pursuits caused conflicts between his fellow men, however, Casals fought for peace by silencing that beauty. At the height of his artistic prowess he remained in exile, his cello quiet. Nobel Prize-winning writer Thomas Mann, quoted by Bernard Taper in *Cellist in Exile: A Portrait of Pablo Casals,* believed Casals's art was "allied to a rigid refusal to compromise with wrong, with anything that is morally squalid or offensive to justice."

Casals was born on December 29, 1876, in the seaside town of Vendrell, located in the Catalonian region of Spain. As a child he was surrounded by music. According to H. L. Kirk, author of *Pablo Casals: A Biography,* "The atmosphere

of music cradled Casals's earliest fantasies; much later he spoke of being bathed in it all the time." Casals's father, the local church organist and choirmaster, would play the piano while the infant Casals, barely old enough to walk, would rest his head against the instrument and sing along to the music he felt. By the age of four, Casals was playing the piano. The following year he joined the church choir. A year later he was composing songs with his father, and by the age of nine he had learned how to play the violin and organ.

When he was 11, Casals decided to study the cello after having seen the instrument in a chamber music recital. Though his father wanted him to apprentice to a carpenter, his mother insisted he follow his inclination toward music, enrolling him in the Municipal School of Music in Barcelona, Spain. The young Casals disagreed with the technical constraints advocated by his instructors, preferring to bow and finger the cello in his own manner. His progress was extraordinary, however, and soon Casals's revolutionary techniques had exposed "a range of phrasing, intonation, and expressiveness that had not previously been thought possible, and [made] the cello an instrument of high purpose," Taper noted in *Cellist in Exile.*

Among those impressed by the ability of the young virtuoso was the Spanish composer and pianist Isaac Albéniz. Upon hearing Casals play in a cafe trio, Albéniz gave him a letter of introduction to Count Guillermo de Morphy, secretary to the Queen Regent of Spain, Maria Cristine. In 1894 Casals traveled to Madrid and gave informal concerts for the queen and her court. Over the next few years, his reputation spread as he played with various orchestras in Paris and Madrid. With his formal debut as a concert soloist in Paris in 1899—where he appeared with the prestigious orchestra of French conductor Charles Lamoureux—Casals's career was assured.

What audiences heard in Casals's playing was a suffused reverence for everything around him. "I have the idea of God constantly," he declared in *McCall's.* "I find Him in music. What is that world, what is music but God?" Those feelings were heightened for Casals in nature and in the music of Bach, as he indicated when he continued, explaining his morning ritual: "I go immediately to the sea, and everywhere I see God, in the smallest and largest things. I see Him in colors and designs and forms. . . . [And] I see God in Bach. Every morning of my life I see nature first, then I see Bach."

Casals's devotion to the music of Bach was no more fully realized than in the Six Suites for solo cello. Sometime in 1890 while browsing through a Barcelona bookstore with his father, Casals found a volume of the suites. The discovery was enlightening. Previously the suites were considered merely musical exercises, but, even at that young age, Casals saw in them something deeper, richer. "How could anyone think of them as being cold, when a whole radiance of space and poetry pours forth from them," he marveled in *Joys and Sorrows.* "They are the very essence of Bach, and Bach is the very essence of music." Casals studied and practiced the suites every day for a dozen years before he exposed them to the public, and he continued to play at least one suite every day for the rest of his life.

His performance of the suites both shocked and astounded listeners. During the nineteenth-century revival of Bach's music, only the cantatas and the religious works were played in public. It was believed that the solo music for strings had no warmth, no artistic value. With these "exercises," however, "Casals displayed the [German] master as a fully human creator whose art had poetry and passion, accessible to all people," author Kirk stated in *Pablo Casals: A Biography.* "[Bach], who knows everything and feels everything, cannot write one note, however unimportant it may appear, which is anything but transcendent," Casals stressed to José Maria Corredor in *Conversations with Casals.* "He has reached the heart of every noble thought, and he has done it in the most perfect way."

Casals's interpretation of the suites, his true testament, came into disfavor after the 1940s when a more historically correct reading of lightness and spontaneity was advanced, in marked contrast to his dramatic renderings. "Almost every movement of the suites, in Casals's hands," William H. Youngren maintained in the *Atlantic,* "vividly projects the image of a powerful Romantic sensibility engaged in an unceasing, heroic struggle with itself and with the universe." However, in a *Strad* review of a recent remastering of Casals's performances for compact disc, Tully Potter justified his passionate, ennobling vision: "He builds up great waves of sound and tension, achieving an enormous physical and emotional release towards the end of each one—a Romantic approach, perhaps, but valid here because the player's heart, soul, and sinew are so completely behind every note. . . . [It is] a spiritual exaltation rare in any performance and still more so on record."

As he approached Bach and music, so did Casals approach life and other people. "The pursuit of music and the love for my neighbors have been inseparable with me, and if the first has brought me the purest and most exalted joys, the second has brought me peace of mind, even in the saddest moments," Casals affirmed to *Conversations With Casals'* s author Corredor. "I am everyday more convinced that the mainspring of any human enterprise must be moral strength and generosity." In 1891, while still in school, Casals came to understand the suffering and inequality of man as he walked among the poor on the streets of Barcelona. He vowed to use his gift from God—his music—for the welfare of his fellow people.

Throughout his career, Casals championed the oppressed and neglected by writing letters and organizing concerts. He refused to perform in countries practicing political tyranny and repression: the Soviet Union in 1917, Germany in 1933, and Italy in 1935. In 1920, for the benefit of the Catalonian people, Casals organized and led the Orquesta Pau Casals, using the Catalonian version of his name. He supported the Republican cause during the Spanish Civil War in the 1930s, and when Nationalist General Francisco Franco rose to power in 1939, Casals announced he would never return to Spain while Franco was in power. He settled in Prades, France, giving sporadic concerts until 1946 when he renounced the stage altogether. In order to take a stand against dictatorships, Casals vowed never to perform again. As author Kirk put it in *Pablo Casals: A Biography,* "His withdrawal into silence was the strongest action he felt he could make."

However, in 1950, urged on by friends, Casals resumed conducting and playing, taking part in the Prades Festival organized to celebrate the bicentennial of Bach's death. Though he picked up his cello again, he did not forget his cause—at the end of the festival and every concert he gave after that, Casals played his arrangement of the Catalonian folk ballad "Song of the Birds" as a protest to the continued oppression he saw in Spain.

Casals never returned to Spain. In 1956 he settled in Puerto Rico, his mother's homeland, where he inaugurated the world-famous Casals Festival that spurred artistic and cultural activities on the island, including the founding of a symphony orchestra and a conservatory of music. During the rest of his life, Casals balanced his stand on the issues with his creative impulses. In 1958 he joined his friend, Nobel Prize-winning French philosopher and musicologist Albert Schweitzer, in calling for peace and nuclear disarmament. Casals also spoke and played before the United Nations General Assembly. He appeared before the General Assembly again in 1971, at the age of 95, when he conducted the first performance of his "Hymn of the United Nations."

Though Casals had resumed performing, he refused to play in any country that officially recognized the totalitarian Franco government—as did the United States. Until he died in 1973, Casals did not waver from this position, but for one important exception—in 1961 he performed at the White House at the request of U.S. President John F. Kennedy, a man Casals greatly admired. In *Cellist in Exile,* Taper quoted Kennedy's introduction of Casals on that day, "The work of all artists—musicians, painters, designers, and architects—stands as a symbol of human freedom, and no one has enriched that freedom more signally than Pablo Casals."

Throughout his life, Casals exalted in the divine presence he found in music and in nature. He also sought to inspire and promote harmony among people, both with his cello and his silence. At his funeral, a recording of "The Song of the Birds" was played. "At that moment," Kirk recounted in *Pablo Casals: A Biography.* "the noble voice of Pablo Casals's cello commanded pause in the ceremony of the day, a last salutation, eloquent, profound, overwhelming."

Further Reading

Blum, David, *Casals and the Art of Interpretation,* Holmes & Meier, 1977.

Casals, Pablo, *Song of the Birds: Sayings, Stories, and Impressions of Pablo Casals,* Robsons Books, 1985.

Casals, Pablo, and Albert E. Kahn, *Joys and Sorrows: Reflections by Pablo Casals as Told to Albert E. Kahn,* Simon & Schuster, 1970.

Corredor, José Maria, *Conversations With Casals,* Hutchinson, 1956.

Kirk, H. L., *Pablo Casals: A Biography,* Holt, Rinehart, & Winston, 1974.

Littlehales, Lillian, *Pablo Casals,* Greenwood, 1970.

Quintana, Arturo O., *Pablo Casals in Puerto Rico,* Gordon Press, 1979.

Taper, Bernard, *Cellist in Exile: A Portrait of Pablo Casals,* McGraw-Hill, 1962.

American Record Guide, July/August 1991; November/December 1991; January/February 1992; March/April 1992.

Américas, July/August 1985.

Atlantic, November 1981.

McCall's, May 1966.

Musical America, July 1991.

New Yorker, April 19, 1969.

Strad, February 1989; September 1990. ☐

Giacomo Jacopo Girolamo Casanova de Seinglat

The Italian adventurer Giacomo Jacopo Girolamo Casanova de Seingalt (1725-1798) is best known for his memoirs, which are a most revealing record of 18th-century European society.

The first child of an actor and actress, Casanova was born in Venice. He set out to play the comedy of life with a short role as an ecclesiastic but was expelled from the seminary in 1743. He found refuge in Rome with Cardinal Acquaviva, the first of his many powerful protectors. By 1745 he had returned to Venice, where he practiced magic. Forced to flee prosecution for engaging in the black arts, Casanova drifted from city to city. In Lyons in 1750 he joined the Free Masons, an allegiance that gave him support in the noble, free thinking circles of cosmopolitan Europe. Gambling, profiteering, and amorous activities marked his first stay in Paris (1750-1753). His luck held until 1755, when he was imprisoned in Venice for "black magic, licentiousness, and atheism." His spectacular escape is chronicled in the only portion of his memoirs to appear during his lifetime (1788).

The years 1756-1763 brought Casanova his most brilliant successes in a society dedicated to games of love and chance. Voltaire, whom he met briefly, judged him to be a "mixture of science and imposture," a suspect combination which nevertheless brought Casanova in contact with Frederick II and Catherine the Great.

Casanova himself divided his life into "three acts of a comedy." The second, which he thought of as lasting from 1763 to 1783, was less droll than the first. Protectors were less willing, and as the adventurer's brilliance faded, his charlatanism became more evident. From 1774 to 1782 Casanova added to his repertoire the role of "secret agent" for the Republic of Venice, but he was less a spy than an informer.

Again obliged to leave Venice, Casanova began the third act of his comedy penniless and on the road. But in 1785 he gained the protection of the Count of Waldstein, in whose château at Dux (Bohemia) he stayed until his death in 1798. There he wrote his celebrated *History of My Life,*

ending with the events of 1774, after which he had "only sad things to tell." Written in sometimes imperfect French, this work moves rapidly and frankly through vast amounts of personal and social detail. Besides tales of the 122 women whose favors he claims to have enjoyed, Casanova offers a chronicle of social extravagance and decline and a vision of Europe as complex and colorful as the bawdy, elegant, naively rational, desperately pretentious, and comic figure of "Seingalt" himself.

Casanova's writings also include miscellaneous gallant verse, several treatises on mathematics, a three-volume refutation of Amelot de la Houssaye's history of Venetian government (1769), a translation of the *Iliad* (1775), and a five-volume novel of fantastic adventure to the center of the earth, *Icosameron* (1788).

Further Reading

Long limited to bowdlerized editions derived from a first German translation of the manuscript (acquired by Brockhaus in 1821), Casanova's *History of My Life* may now be read in a faithful translation by Willard R. Trask (4 vols., 1966-1967). The dean of Casanova scholars, James Rives Childes, wrote the definitive *Casanova: A Biography* (1961). The richly illustrated book by John Masters, *Casanova* (1969), provides valuable evocations of his life and times.

Additional Sources

Buck, Mitchell S. (Mitchell Starrett), b. 1887., *The life of Casanova from 1774 to 1798: a supplement to the Memoirs,* Brooklyn: Haskell House, 1977.

Casanova, Giacomo, *The life and memoirs of Casanova,* New York, N.Y.: Da Capo Press, 1984.

Childs, J. Rives (James Rives), *Casanova, a new perspective,* New York: Paragon House Publishers, 1988.

Ricci, Seymour de, *Jacques Casanova de Seingalt: an address to the Philobiblon Club of Philadelphia, 24 May 1923,* Norwood, Pa.: Norwood Editions, 1976.

Roustang, Francois., *The quadrille of gender: Casanova's "Memoirs,"* Stanford, Calif.: Stanford University Press, 1988. □

William J. Casey

William J. Casey (1913–1987) former CIA director, Casey is most known for his involvement in the Iran-contra affair.

William J. Casey was director of the Central Intelligence Agency (CIA) from 1981 to 1987. Basically a throwback to an earlier era of the Cold War, Casey attempted to revitalize the CIA from the torpor it had been in since the early 1970s. He played a murky role in the Iran-contra affair, President Ronald Reagan's greatest foreign policy debacle.

William Joseph Casey had a colorful background that easily made him the most interesting person in the Reagan cabinet. He was born on 13 March 1913 in Elmhurst, New York, in a middle-class Irish-Catholic family. He received degrees at Fordham University in 1934 and Saint John's University Law School in 1937. Rather than practice law, Casey went to work for a company that published digests of federal regulatory and tax matters. He proved to have a natural talent for sifting through reams of information to distill what was important. In 1950 Casey left the company to found a competing business, which eventually made him rich. His specialty was writing, virtually overnight, how-to guides on accounting and tax questions. Casey is credited with coining the term "tax shelter."

Commissioned a lieutenant in the navy in 1943, Casey ended up in the Office of Strategic Services (OSS), the CIA's forerunner. He successfully ran a network of agents who parachuted into Germany to radio back information about bombing targets.

After the war Casey elected not to remain in intelligence work, despite considering it the most exciting thing he had ever done. He returned to New York and for most of the next twenty years devoted himself to making money. He was a venture capitalist, investing in a variety of start-up businesses. Again he was successful, but he also earned a reputation for his fast and loose methods. He was frequently sued, something he regarded merely as an occupational hazard.

By the mid-1960s Casey was ready to enter politics. He tried his hand at elective politics, losing a 1966 race for Congress. An early and heavy contributor to Richard M. Nixon's successful 1968 campaign for president, he was finally rewarded in 1971 when Nixon nominated him to

become chairman of the Securities and Exchange Commission (SEC). It was an unlikely appointment, and many regarded Casey as the fox sent to guard the henhouse. But Casey quickly surprised his critics, as he aggressively enforced the securities laws. His role in cajoling a reluctant Justice Department into accepting SEC documents as part of a ploy to keep them out of the hands of congressional investigators almost brought a Watergate special prosecutor down on him. Casey, however, had cleverly managed to follow the letter of the law while evading its spirit.

Bored with the SEC, Casey served briefly as under secretary of state for economic affairs. It was a do-nothing job, as Secretary of State Henry Kissinger was both uninterested in economics and distrustful of Casey because of his independent ties to Nixon. In 1974 Casey moved on to head the Export-Import Bank for twenty months.

Casey resurfaced in politics in 1980 when he was brought on to take over Ronald Reagan's presidential campaign after the Iowa caucuses in which rival George Bush won an upset victory. Reagan's campaign was in trouble. Casey's job was to keep the campaign afloat. Never really interested in political strategy, Casey maintained overall responsibility while giving considerable leeway to subordinates. He is credited with luring James A. Baker, later secretary of state under Bush, from the defeated Bush campaign. Casey ran a private intelligence operation that monitored whether the incumbent Jimmy Carter administration was planning a last-ditch effort to free American hostages held in Tehran by the Iranian government.

Casey was rewarded for his work with the CIA directorship, a post he had coveted since the 1960s. Casey was a romantic. His approach to intelligence gathering hearkened back to his OSS days when issues were clearly black and white and everyone knew what the stakes were.

Casey took over a CIA that had been bludgeoned since the end of Nixon's first term. The mid-1970s revelations of CIA misdeeds, going back to the 1950s, had demoralized the agency. Covert operations had been discredited. Many intelligence officers were let go. Casey's predecessor, Stansfield Turner, had placed greater emphasis on passive intelligence gathering and analysis. The agency became, as one historian put it, more bureaucratic and less enthusiastic. By 1980 conservatives worried that the agency was both operationally ineffective and too sanguine about Soviet intentions. Reagan's transition team had written a scathing report about the CIA, mentioning twelve areas where it felt the agency had clearly failed to do its job.

Covert Aid

Casey took over determined to reverse the drift and end the agency's malaise. He had no doubts about the agency's purpose. Reagan, moreover, as prepared to let the CIA involve itself in more aggressively conceived operations. The CIA soon funneled vast amounts of aid to the anti-Soviet guerrillas in Afghanistan, making it the largest covert operation undertaken since the Vietnam War. Indicative of the new public mood, Congress tripled Casey's original request for funds for the Afghan rebels. Congress was less forthcoming about CIA involvement in Central America, fearing that Casey's taste for covert operations was a little too much. In 1982 it passed the first of the so-called Boland amendments forbidding the CIA from supplying the contras, the rebels fighting the Marxist Sandinista government in Nicaragua, with lethal aid. Casey's attempts to weasel around the prohibition compelled Congress to pass an even tougher version the next year.

Iran-Contra Affair

This atmosphere helped create the Iran-contra scandal, revealed in November 1986. It was a murky fiasco. While it is still not clear just what happened, it is known that in July 1985 Reagan ordered an operation to see whether the United States could sell arms to Iran in return for the release of American hostages held in Lebanon by Iranian-controlled Shiite-Muslim extremists. There was also the hope of building bridges to Iran's moderates. The plan violated U.S. policy barring arms sales to Iran's Khomeini regime. Secretary of State George P. Schultz and Secretary of Defense Caspar W. Weinberger got wind of it and dismissed it as absurd. But Reagan and his national security adviser, Robert McFarlane, were intrigued, and the plan went forward. Operationally, the scheme was confined to the National Security Council, with McFarlane's assistant, Lieutenant Colonel Oliver North, assuming responsibility. Because Congress had overseen its covert operations, the CIA at first was not officially involved. Casey later testified that the CIA had only a support role and that he did not know all the details.

As the plan evolved, the United States, using Israeli go-betweens, would sell weapons to Iran, through other middlemen, in an effort to mend ties with Iran "moderates" presumably in position to take over after the Ayatollah Ruholla Khomeini's death. They would attempt to secure the release of the American hostages. The actual weapons would come from Israeli stocks, which would be replenished by the United States. Some of the profits from the sales would then be diverted to the contras, thus circumventing the Boland amendment. The various middlemen would supposedly help maintain the fiction that the United States had not traded arms for hostages or violated its own arms embargo against Iran.

Between August 1985 and October 1986 there were seven arms shipments, some made with Israeli aircraft, others with CIA planes. On 6 December 1985 the CIA was formally apprised of the operation by John M. Poindexter, the new national security adviser. The swaps were not bringing about release of sufficient numbers of hostages, and Reagan ordered them halted. In January 1986, however, Israeli officials met with North and urged their resumption on the grounds that the Iranian moderates needed the weapons to demonstrate their credibility in defending Iran in its war against Iraq. Reagan ordered the swaps to resume, this time with official CIA support. Schultz and Weinberger were to be kept in the dark. Casey was not to tell Congress anything. Two more shipments arrived in Tehran in May 1986, but no hostages were released. McFarlane and North then made a secret trip to Tehran that month, but made no progress. Relations between the various parties were deteriorating, but the shipment continued until October. The results were poor — seven shipments for three hostages.

On 4 November 1986 a Beirut magazine first reported the arms-for-hostages deals, their information coming from the Iranians. The result was the most embarrassing setback for the Reagan presidency. Poindexter resigned, North was fired. Together with McFarlane, they later stood trial and were convicted of violating various laws in connection with the sales. North's conviction was later overturned on appeal, the court ruling that the prosecution used material presented during a congressional hearing into the affair, material for which North had been granted immunity from prosecution.

After several investigations, details still remain unclear. Casey is believed to have had a role independent of the CIA's, but no one knows exactly what that was. His testimony to Congress on 11 December 1986 about the whole affair was flatly labeled incredible. The next day he collapsed and needed emergency surgery to remove a cancerous brain tumor. One writer claims to have interpreted Casey's bedside comments to indicate that he did indeed have a much larger role than he had testified. Casey resigned from the CIA on 29 January 1987 and died on 6 May 1987. He was survived by his wife, Sophia, and a daughter. □

Johnny Cash

"The Man in Black"—as Johnny Cash (born 1932) has long been known—has been one of the most influential figures in country music since the 1950s. In the 1990s he broke through to a younger, more alternative audience, performing songs by Soundgarden, Beck, and others.

He has also reached a substantial audience of rock fans, thanks to his outlaw persona, deep, authoritative voice, and dark songs like "Folsom Prison Blues." After enjoying a string of hits in the 1950s and even greater success in the late 1960s, when he was briefly the best-selling recording artist in the world, he saw his edgy, close-to-the-bone style go out of fashion. Even as his 1980s work was neglected, however, he appeared before adoring throngs worldwide. In 1994, well past his sixtieth birthday, he came roaring back with a sparsely recorded album that ranked among his best work and earned him a Grammy Award. "Can you name anyone in this day and age who is as cool as Johnny Cash?" asked *Rolling Stone* rhetorically. "No, you can't."

J. R. Cash was born into an impoverished Arkansas family in 1932 and grew up working in the cotton fields. His Baptist upbringing meant that the music he heard was almost entirely religious, and the hymns sung by country greats like the Carter Family and Ernest Tubb reached him on the radio and made an indelible impression. "From the time I was a little boy," he recollected to Steve Pond in a 1992 *Rolling Stone* interview, "I never had any doubt that I was gonna be singing on the radio." His brother Roy formed a band when he was young, increasing John's determination to do the same one day.

Cash had no idea, though, what path would lead him to his destiny. He held a few odd jobs after graduating from Dyess High School in 1950, but eventually opted for a four-year stay in the Air Force. Stationed in Germany, he endured what he would later describe as a lonely, miserable period. Fortunately, he learned to play the guitar and began turning the poetry he'd been writing into song lyrics. After seeing a powerful film about Folsom Prison, he sat down to write what would become one of his signature songs—"Folsom Prison Blues." His empathy for prisoners and other marginalized people would consistently inform his work. With his powerful position in a generally conservative musical world, he also championed Native American rights and other social ills.

Cash left the military in 1954 and married Vivian Liberto, whom he met before joining the air force; they had corresponded throughout his tour of duty. The two lived in Memphis, Tennessee, and he earned a meager living selling appliances. "I was the worst salesman in the world," Cash confided to Pond. Nonetheless, he summoned the passion to sell himself as a singer, playing with a gospel group and canvassing radio stations for chances to perform on the air.

Plays with Presley

Eventually Cash was granted an audience with trailblazing producer Sam Phillips, at whose Sun Studios the likes of Elvis Presley, Jerry Lee Lewis, Carl Perkins, and others made recordings that would help change the course of popular music. Phillips was a hard sell, but Cash won the opportunity to record his first single; "Cry, Cry, Cry" became a number 14 hit in 1955, and Cash's group played some local gigs with Presley. Pond describes Cash's early records as "stark, unsettling and totally original. The instrumentation was spare, almost rudimentary" featuring bass and lead guitar supplied by his Tennessee Two and Cash's rhythm guitar, which had "a piece of paper stuck underneath the top frets to give it a scratchy sound."

In 1956 Cash left his sales job and recorded the hits "Folsom Prison Blues"—containing the legendary and much-quoted lyric "I shot a man in Reno just to watch him die"—and "I Walk the Line." The next year saw the release of the one album released by Sun before his departure from the label, *Johnny Cash With His Hot & Blue Guitar.* He and the Tennessee Two left the label after a string of hits and signed with CBS/Columbia Records in 1958. Singles he recorded on Sun at Phillips's insistence just before his contract lapsed continued to chart for years afterward, much to Cash's chagrin. Yet he charted on CBS as well with a bevy of singles and such albums as *Blood, Sweat and Tears* and *Ring of Fire.*

In the midst of his success, however, Cash grew apart from Vivian and their children. He grew dependent on drink and drugs and became increasingly dissolute. Such misery no doubt contributed force to such work as 1963's "Ring of Fire," which was co-written by June Carter, who also performed on the track. Cash and Carter—of the famed Carter family—became increasingly close, both professionally and personally. His marriage collapsed in 1966 and he nearly died of an overdose. Cash has long attributed his subsequent rehabilitation to two factors: Carter and God. He and Carter wed in 1968 and later had a son, John.

Cash Sells

In any event, Cash expanded his repertoire as the 1960s unfolded, incorporating folk music and protest themes. He recorded songs by folk-rock avatar Bob Dylan and up-and-comers like Kris Kristofferson, but by the end of the decade, driven perhaps by his generally out-of-control life, his hits came largely from novelty songs like Shel Silverstein's "A Boy Named Sue." Even so, by 1969 Cash was the best-selling recording artist alive, outselling even rock legends The Beatles. That year saw him win two Grammy Awards for *Johnny Cash at Folsom Prison,* a live album for a worshipful audience of prisoners that led, perhaps inevitably, to *Johnny Cash at San Quentin.* From 1969 to 1971 he hosted a smash variety program for television, *The Johnny Cash Show.*

The 1970s saw more career triumphs, notably a Grammy-winning duet with Carter on Tim Hardin's "If I Were a Carpenter," a command performance for President Richard Nixon, acting roles in film and on television, a best-selling autobiography, and several more hit albums, including *Man in Black,* the title of which would become his permanent show business moniker. While this label has been associated with his "outlaw" image, he and his bandmates originally wore black because they had nothing else that matched; besides, as Cash informed *Entertainment Weekly,* "black is better for church."

In 1980 Cash was inducted into the Country Music Association Hall of Fame. He had become a music hero worldwide, appearing in eastern Europe before the fall of the Soviet empire and praising those who agitated for democracy. Yet during the 1980s, Cash became less and less of a priority for his record label; country music had come to be dominated by younger, pop-inclined artists who favored slick production. He continued to struggle with drugs, eventually checking into the Betty Ford clinic. There, he has said, he experienced a religious epiphany.

Cash wrote a novel, *Man in White,* about the life of the apostle Paul, and continued indulging his eclectic musical tastes, recording songs by mavericks like Elvis Costello. Alongside Kristofferson, Willie Nelson, and Waylon Jennings, he participated in a collaborative album, *The Highwayman;* he also joined Jerry Lee Lewis, Carl Perkins, and country-rock giant Roy Orbison for a reunion recording called *Class of '55 (Memphis Rock & Roll Homecoming),* which enjoyed solid sales. A daughter by his first marriage, Rosanne, became a country star in her own right; Johnny Cash, himself, even as his albums sold poorly, was firmly established as a living legend of country music and a profound influence on rock and roll. In 1992 he was inducted into the Rock and Roll Hall of Fame, and 1993 saw him contribute a vocal performance to *Zooropa,* by rock superstars U2.

Yet Cash tired of record-business priorities. "I kept hearing about demographics [market studies of consumers] until it was coming out my ears," the singer told Christopher John Farley of *Newsweek.* The first label representative who seemed to understand him after this bitter experience was, ironically enough, best known for his work with hardcore rap, metal, and alternative acts. Rick Rubin had founded his own label, first called Def American and later changed to American Recordings, to support acts he believed in. Though not intimately acquainted with Cash's work, he admired the singer's artistic persona. "I don't see him as a country act," Rubin told Farley. "I would say he embodies rock 'n' roll. He's an outlaw figure, and that is the essence of what rock 'n' roll is."

Rubin's appeal to Cash lay in his idea for a record. After seeing one of the country legend's performances, the producer "said he'd love to hear just me and my guitar," Cash told *Los Angeles Times* writer Robert Hilburn. These were the words the veteran artist had waited decades to hear; he had suggested such a minimal approach many times to country producers, only to have it vetoed immediately on commercial grounds. Rubin simply set up a tape machine in his Hollywood living room and allowed Cash to do what he does best.

Rubin "was a lot like Sam [Phillips], actually," Cash ventured to Hilburn. "We talked a lot about the approach we were going to take, and he said, 'You know, we are not going to think about time or money. I want you to come out as much as you can." Without such constraints—which had clipped Cash's wings in his Nashville years—he was free to experiment with a wide range of material. Recording over 70 songs, mostly at Rubin's house but also at his own cabin in Tennessee and at the trendy Los Angeles nightspot The Viper Room, Cash had a valedictory experience. He later told *Time'* s Farley that the work was his "dream album."

The material was culled to 13 tracks, including traditional songs, some Cash originals, and compositions by such diverse modern songwriters as Kristofferson, Leonard Cohen, Tom Waits, Nick Lowe, Glenn Danzig, and Loudon Wainright III. The leadoff track, "Delia's Gone," grimly describes the murder of a faithless woman; Rubin seemed to invite comparisons between Cash and the controversial metal and rap acts on his label. Titled *American Recordings,* the album was released in 1994; Johnny Cash was 62 years old. The liner notes contained testimonials from both Rubin and Cash. "I think we made a brutally honest record," the producer declared. "Working with Rick," Cash averred, "all the experimenting, kinda spread me out and expanded my range of material. This is the best I can do as an artist, as a solo artist, this is it."

Critics seemed to agree. Karen Schoemer of *Mirabella* praised it as "a daring, deceptively simple album" that "operates on a mythic scale, which suits someone who's always been larger than life. What is breathtaking is Cash's ability to analyze his aging self, and the failures, weaknesses, strengths and wisdoms that time bestows." *Village Voice* critic Doug Simmons praised it as "fiercely intimate," while *Rolling Stone*'s Anthony DeCurtis called it "unquestionably one of his best albums," one which "will earn him a time of well-deserved distinction in which his work will reach an eager new audience."

While *American Recordings* didn't take the charts by storm, it restored Johnny Cash's sense of mission. It also earned him a 1995 Grammy Award for best contemporary folk album. He played a sold-out engagement in Los Angeles just before his nomination, before an audience studded with such music stars as Tom Petty, Sheryl Crow, and Dwight Yoakam. And in September of 1996 he played a set at the CMJ Music Marathon in Manhattan, previewing songs from his album *Unchained* as well as performing cover versions from younger artists such as Beck and Soundgarden.

About the prospect of an "eager new audience" Cash himself—who seriously considered playing at the alternative-rock festival known as Lollapalooza before declining the offer—was philosophical. "I no longer have a grandiose attitude about my music being a powerful force for change," he told *Entertainment Weekly.* Even so, he allowed, "I think [today's youth] sees the hypocrisy in government, the rotten core of social ills and poverty and prejudice, and I'm not afraid to say that's where the trouble is. A lot of people my age are." One thing remained constant, as he told *Rolling Stone:* "I feel like if I can just go onstage with my guitar and sing my songs, I can't do no wrong no matter where I am."

Further Reading

Rees, Dafydd, and Luke Crampton, *Rock Movers & Shakers,* Billboard, 1991.

Entertainment Weekly, February 18, 1994, pp. 57-67.

Hits, May 2, 1994.

Los Angeles Times, April 25, 1994, pp. F1, F5.

Mirabella, July 1994.

People, May 16, 1994.

Rolling Stone, December 10, 1992, pp. 118-25, 201; May 5, 1994, p. 14; May 19, 1994, pp. 97-98; June 30, 1994, p. 35.

Time, May 9, 1994, pp. 72-74.

Village Voice, May 18, 1994. □

Lewis Cass

As governor of Michigan Territory, Lewis Cass (1782-1866) contributed importantly to the development of the Old Northwest. Twice a presidential nominee, he served as secretary of war, minister to France, and secretary of state.

Lewis Cass was born on Oct. 2, 1782, in New Hampshire, the eldest child of a Revolutionary War veteran, Maj. Jonathan Cass, and Mary Gilman Cass. He studied at Phillips Exeter Academy. In 1800 the family moved to the Ohio frontier, where he studied law and was admitted to the bar in 1803. In 1806 he married Elizabeth Spencer and was elected to the legislature in Ohio. In 1807 he became U.S. marshal for Ohio.

In the War of 1812 Cass advanced from colonel of militia to brigadier general and fought with distinction at the Battle of the Thames. In 1813 he was appointed governor of Michigan Territory. He made a fortune by buying land in Detroit and later selling it in city lots. He promoted universal education and the establishment of libraries, built roads, and speeded the work of surveying tracts for settlers; as Indian commissioner, he conducted expeditions to the northwestern area of the territory, studied Native American languages, and supported scholarly work on Native American culture. He had sympathy for the Native Americans, but he persuaded them to cede their lands; as President Andrew Jackson's secretary of war (1831-1836), he vigorously supported the forced removal of the Cherokee from their agricultural lands.

Appointed minister to France in 1836, Cass used his influence against British efforts to stop the international slave trade. In 1842 he resigned and sought the Democratic nomination for president but lost to James K. Polk. Elected to the Senate in 1845, Cass urged war against Britain, if necessary, to obtain all of Oregon. He defended Polk's aggression against Mexico and advocated the acquisition of Cuba.

With Southern support Cass was the Democratic nominee for president in 1848, but in a rather close election he lost to the Whig general Zachary Taylor. Cass was again in the Senate (1849-1856) and again, at the age of 70, a candidate for president in 1852; but the Democrats nominated a nonentity, Franklin Pierce.

Cass supported the Compromise of 1850, including the Fugitive Slave Law, which denied a jury trial to any African American claimed by a slave owner. He supported the "popular sovereignty" doctrine of Stephen Douglas. In 1856 the Republican legislature in Michigan removed him from the Senate.

President James Buchanan made the aged Cass his secretary of state, and in this position Cass remained an expansionist and continued to oppose British policies. But the sectional conflict now dominated the American scene. Cass lost Southern friends by referring, in Michigan, to slavery as "a great social and political evil"; and he finally broke with Buchanan and his Southern advisers and resigned his office in 1860. He supported the Union during the Civil War. He died on June 16, 1866.

Had Cass retired from public life at the age of 60, his place in American history would be higher than it is as a consequence of his support of, and affiliation with, some of the weakest and most disastrous administrations in American history.

Further Reading

The standard biography of Cass is Frank B. Woodford, *Lewis Cass: The Last Jeffersonian* (1950). The subtitle is misleading, the style journalistic, and the interpretation nationalistic, but Woodford provides the basic information. Andrew C. McLaughlin, *Lewis Cass* (1891), in the "American Statesmen" series, is still useful. The interpretation is generally logical and persuasive, although McLaughlin is sometimes harshly censorious of Cass and others.

Additional Sources

Burns, Virginia, *Lewis Cass, frontier soldier,* Bath, Mich.: Enterprise Press, 1980.

Klunder, Willard Carl, *Lewis Cass and the politics of moderation,* Kent, Ohio: Kent State University Press, 1996.

McLaughlin, Andrew Cunningham, *Lewis Cass,* New York: Chelsea House, 1980. □

Mary Cassatt

Mary Cassatt (1845-1926), an American painter, is considered a member of the French impressionist group. Best known for her series of paintings of a mother and child, she also portrayed fashionable society.

Mary Cassatt was born in Pittsburgh, Pa., on May 23, 1845. As a child, she lived for a time in France. She studied at the Pennsylvania Academy of Fine Arts in Philadelphia. In 1866 she began her travels in Italy, Spain, and Holland, finally settling in Paris. There she exhibited at the Salon and met Edgar Degas, who was her real teacher, as she was his only pupil.

Despite her success at the Salon, Cassatt's sympathies lay with the impressionists, and in 1877 at Degas's suggestion she joined the group and exhibited with them in 1879. Her work sold well, particularly in Philadelphia, and she in turn bought paintings by the French impressionists. She also helped American friends, such as the Havemeyers, form their collections of impressionist paintings. Cassatt remained strongly American in her sentiments, as many expatriates do, and she wrote the American painter J. Alden Weir that "at some future time I shall see New York the artists' ground."

Cassatt's brother, Alexander, brought his family to Paris in 1880, the first of many trips. Although she never married, she was enchanted by her nieces and nephews and excelled in painting children, who dominate her subject matter. Her early work, done with the impressionists, is probably her best, but she remains known as the painter and poet of the nursery.

The paintings of Mary Cassatt, filled with light and joy, give a false impression of this strong-minded and somewhat difficult woman. She was at her best in her relations with other artists, for only in this environment did she consider herself among her intellectual equals. In later life she suffered from ill health and failing eyesight and was totally blind at her death. She died in her château at Mesnil-Beaufresne on June 14, 1926.

Painting Style

Midway in her career Cassatt ceased to be an impressionist painter. Her early works have the delicacy, the atmospheric effects, the play of light and shadow associated with the style, but she never used broken color and her use of complementary colors was slight. Paintings like *La Lo* are indeed impressionist pictures and have the characteristic instantaneous effect of being caught out of the corner of the eye. But her paintings of mothers and children are fully realized and three-dimensional; the drawing is classical and complete; and the color, far from being light and separated into its component parts, is flat and sometimes rather acid, like the Japanese prints which influenced her so much. These careful figure studies, completely rendered, in no way reflect the infinite variety of nature or the passing world, as the paintings of the impressionists did; they exist entirely in the hothouse atmosphere of the nursery, with no sound except the little cries.

Further Reading

The only thorough treatment of Mary Cassatt's life is Frederick A. Sweet's excellent *Miss Mary Cassatt, Impressionist from Pennsylvania* (1966). Sweet had access to family letters and papers that provide the basis for a new understanding of her character. Other biographies include Forbes Watson, *Mary Cassatt* (1932), and Julia M. H. Carson, *Mary Cassatt* (1966). For general background see John Rewald, *The History of Impressionism* (1946; rev. ed. 1961). □

Flavius Magnus Aurelius Cassiodorus

The Roman statesman and author Flavius Magnus Aurelius Cassiodorus Senator (ca. 480-ca. 575) exerted great influence on the preservation of works of classical literature in Christian monasteries from the 6th century through the Middle Ages. He is also an important source of information on the period of Ostrogothic rule in Italy.

Cassiodorus was born on his family's estate at Scyllacium in southeastern Italy. He received the education in philosophy and rhetoric appropriate to the son of a noble family, and by 511 he held the office of quaestor (royal secretary) at the court of the Ostrogothic king Theodoric the Great in Ravenna. In 523 he was elevated to the post of master of the offices, which made him in effect the head of the civil service. From 533 to 537 he held the powerful position of praetorian perfect.

Cassiodorus documented his career as public servant in his *Variae* (*Miscellaneous Letters*), which contained correspondence and official documents written by himself in the names of the Ostrogothic rulers under whom he served. Upon the successful invasion of Italy by the Byzantine emperor Justinian, Cassiodorus realized that he must abandon his long-cherished goal of an Italy in which Romans would live in peace and trust under Gothic rulers, and he retired from public life about 540. Thereafter he devoted himself largely to religious and literary matters.

In the early 550s Cassiodorus founded a monastery at his ancestral home and named it Vivarium after some fishponds which he had constructed nearby. His purpose was to educate his monks in both sacred and classical pagan learning and to transmit this learning to posterity. Cassiodorus and his monks copied biblical and classical manuscripts, edited and assembled a text of the complete Latin Bible, wrote commentaries and marginal annotations for particular books of the Bible, and made Latin versions of works of Greek church authors.

Cassiodorus's most important single work is the *Institutiones.* This encyclopedic collection of sacred and profane learning is divided into two parts. The first is concerned with the interpretation of the Bible and with the lives and works of eminent Church Fathers; the second is a manual for the study of the seven traditional liberal arts.

Cassiodorus died about 575, when he was approximately 95. His practice of preserving and copying manuscripts was followed by a great number of medieval monasteries, and his *Institutiones* was for many medieval readers one of the few means of access to the classic liberal arts.

Further Reading

Leslie Webber Jones, *An Introduction to Divine and Human Readings* (1946), is a translation, with notes, of the *Institutiones* and includes a lengthy biographical introduction and a bibliography. See also Arnaldo Momigliano, "Cassiodorus and Italian Culture of His Time," in *Proceedings of the British Academy,* vol. 41 (1955).

Additional Sources

O'Donnell, James Joseph, *Cassiodorus,* Berkeley: University of California Press, 1979. □

Ernst Cassirer

The German philosopher and intellectual historian Ernst Cassirer (1874-1945) was the most distinguished member of the Neo-Kantian school of philosophy.

Ernst Cassirer was born in Breslau, Silesia, on July 28, 1874, the son of a wealthy and cultured Jewish tradesman. He was educated at the universities of Berlin, Leipzig, and Heidelberg. His varied interests finally focused on philosophy after hearing Georg Simmel's lectures on Kant. This led him to Marburg, where Hermann Cohen, the leading Neo-Kantian of the period, lectured. Cassirer set himself to master both Kant's voluminous writings and Cohen's interpretations; though he went well beyond both, they formed the essential foundation for his subsequent work.

In spite of early and brilliant publications Cassier was blocked by anti-Semitic prejudice from a professorship in Germany. By the time he was 30, he had finished the first two volumes of a monumental work tracing the history of epistemology. This won him wide recognition and finally acceptance at the University of Berlin, but only as a lecturer.

In 1910 Cassirer published his first systematic work, *Substance and Function,* a profound essay on the nature of concepts and generalization. Still he was passed over for professorial appointments. In 1914 Harvard University invited him, but the outbreak of World War I prevented his acceptance. When the war ended, however, the new University of Hamburg offered him a professorship. He taught there from 1919 to 1930 and served as rector from 1930 to 1933. At Hamburg the superb Warburg Library enabled him to begin his *magnum opus, The Philosophy of Symbolic Forms* (1923-1929). Warburg had gathered a unique treasure of books on primitive cultures and studies of imagery, magic, folklore, and mythology. With these source materials Cassirer began to fashion a systematic comparison of the fundamentally different kinds of "symbolic forms" through which men interpret their experience. Although a continuation of Kant's analysis of human powers of synthesis, Cassirer's work took into account types of thinking which Kant had ignored as irrational. Cassirer thus subjected mythical thinking to detailed analysis and undertook to revise the Kantian accounts of scientific, moral, and esthetic thinking. The principles and methods used to structure these different areas of experience, Cassirer argued, must be seen as flexible and developing.

With the electoral triumph of the Nazi party in 1933, Cassirer immediately resigned his position in disgust and went to Oxford University. After 3 months of intensive study he learned to speak English. He lectured at Oxford until 1935, when the University of Göteborg in Sweden offered him a personal chair. Becoming a Swedish citizen, he once again learned a new language and later wrote a book on Swedish philosophy.

In the summer of 1941 Cassirer came to the United States as a guest professor at Yale University. In these years of exile he wrote continuously—books on physics, on political philosophy, on the history of ideas, and finally *An Essay on Man* (1944), a systematic study written in English. At the time of his death Cassirer was a visitor at Columbia University and was preoccupied with plans for further applications of his central discovery: the functions played by symbolic forms. He left a rich legacy which has not yet been fully assimilated and exploited.

Further Reading

An inquiry into Cassirer's work should begin with Paul Schilpp, ed., *The Philosophy of Ernst Cassirer* (1949). It contains biographical essays, descriptive and critical essays on his philosophy, and an exhaustive bibliography of his works. Carl H. Hamburg, *Symbol and Reality* (1956), is a study of Cassirer's central conception.

Additional Sources

Itzkoff, Seymour W., *Ernst Cassirer: philosopher of culture,* Boston: Twayne Publishers, 1977.

Lipton, David R., *Ernst Cassirer: the dilemma of a liberal intellectual in Germany, 1914-1933,* Toronto; Buffalo: University of Toronto Press, 1978. □

Humberto Castelo Branco

Humberto Castelo Branco (1900-1967) was a Brazilian career soldier and president who became his country's first military dictator in 70 years.

Humberto Castelo Branco was born in Ceará on Sept. 20, 1900. He graduated from the Brazilian military academy and entered the army in January 1921. He did not participate in any of the military insurrections of the 1920s, and by 1943 he had risen to lieutenant colonel. He went overseas as chief of operations of the Brazilian Expeditionary Force which fought with the Allied armies in the Italian campaign of World War II. During the postwar years Castelo Branco rose to general of the army by 1962 and to chief of the general staff of the army in the last months of the Goulart administration.

Gen. Castelo Branco's support of those conspiring against the government of João Goulart, made known secretly to other high military commanders in late March 1964, was one of the decisive factors in bringing about its fall. With the overthrow of Goulart on April 1, the three military ministers, who constituted a revolutionary junta, decided that they would, for the first time in 70 years, alter the normal constitutional succession to the presidency.

Support for a military candidate for the presidency did not come only from the armed forces but also from powerful state governors. Their choice was ratified by the military leaders, and Castelo Branco, promoted to marshal, was formally elected president by Congress and was inaugurated on April 15, 1964.

Political and Economic Changes

The Castelo Branco regime was a modified military dictatorship. The President seemed to want to prepare for the return to a fully democratic regime. He insisted on municipal elections being held as scheduled in March 1965 and on holding state elections scheduled in October. However, his modification of the constitution deprived a sizable number of citizens of their civil rights, including former president Juscelino Kubitschek and Goiás governor Mauro Borges. The President also used the authority provided by a new electoral law to ban a number of potential candidates in the 1965 gubernatorial elections.

The Castelo Branco government sought to come to grips with a number of the country's economic and social problems. Economist Roberto Campos was given virtually dictatorial powers as minister of economy. He developed a program for social changes and economic stabilization and development. The part of the program which was most effectively applied was that dealing with the inflation. Price rises were brought down from a rate of over 80 percent in 1964 to 25 percent in 1966, but at the cost of a considerable fall in the level of living of the workers and the bankruptcy of a sizable number of firms.

The Castelo Branco government's ardor for social and political reforms was not as great as its support of economic stabilization. It did not press for passage of a law allowing illiterates to vote in municipal elections, which would have reduced the power of rural landlords; and the agrarian reform law passed under government pressure was exceedingly mild and did not, in fact, bring about agrarian reform.

When the October 1965 state elections went against the regime, the "hard-line" military men forced President Castelo Branco to modify the constitution once again. The changes dissolved all existing political parties; provided for election of the president by Congress instead of by the people; reinstated the right of the president to remove key government officials and to cancel citizens' civil rights; and provided for packing the Supreme Court. A new constitution was enacted in March 1967, shortly before Castelo Branco left office, incorporating most of the dictatorial measures which had been adopted since the military coup.

President Castelo Branco turned his office over to Marshal Arthur da Costa e Silva on March 15, 1967, but although officially retired, he remained an important element in national politics until his accidental death in an airplane crash on July 18, 1967.

Further Reading

Since Castelo Branco only recently became known outside his country, there is no adequate work in English on his life or influence. José Mario Bello, *A History of Modern Brazil, 1889-1964* (1966), contains a brief outline of his life and his role in the Brazilian revolution of 1964. For the economic, social, and political background of recent years see Irving L. Horowitz, *Revolution in Brazil* (1964).

Additional Sources

Dulles, John W. F., *Castello Branco: the making of a Brazilian president,* College Station: Texas A&M University Press, 1978.

Dulles, John W. F., *President Castello Branco, Brazilian reformer,* College Station: Texas A&M University Press, 1980. ☐

Baldassare Castiglione

The Italian author, courtier, and diplomat Baldassare Castiglione (1478-1529) is known primarily for his "Book of the Courtier." This work, which portrays the ideal courtier, was a chief vehicle in spreading Italian humanism into England and France.

Baldassare Castiglione was born on Dec. 6, 1478, in Casatico in the province of Mantua of an illustrious Lombard family. After receiving a classical education in Mantua and in Milan, he served at the court of the Milanese duke Lodovico Sforza from 1496 to 1499. Castiglione then entered the service of Francesco Gonzaga, Duke of Mantua. In 1503 he fought with Gonzaga's forces against the Spanish in Naples. On his way north he visited Rome and Urbino; both cities fascinated him. His request to transfer to the court of Guidobaldo da Montefeltro at Urbino was grudgingly granted in 1504 by Gonzaga.

At Urbino, Guidobaldo's wife, Elizabetta, presided over the noble company depicted in the *Libro del cortegiano* (*Book of the Courtier*). Castiglione's service there gave him an entree into the court of Pope Julius II, where he became a friend of the artist Raphael. He was sent as ambassador to Henry VII of England and in 1513 was made Count of Nuvolara by Guidobaldo's successor, Francesco Maria della Rovere. Castiglione married in 1516 but became a cleric in 1521 after the death of his wife. In 1524 he was sent by Pope Clement VII as ambassador to Charles V in Spain—an unfortunate mission in that Castiglione reported wrongly the Emperor's intentions in the period leading up to the sack of Rome in 1527. Castiglione died in Toledo, Spain, on Feb. 7, 1529.

"Book of the Courtier"

Published in 1528, though it was begun in 1507 and written mainly from 1513 to 1516, Castiglione's *Book of the Courtier* was a huge and immediate success. His idealized picture of society at the court of Urbino quickly became a book of etiquette for both the bourgeoisie and the aristocracy even beyond the confines of Italy. Translated into Spanish (1534), French (1537), English (1561), and German (1566), *The Courtier* saw some 40 editions in the 16th century alone and a hundred more by 1900. Through it, the broad values of Italian humanism—the ideal of the fully developed, well-rounded man, itself the rebirth of a classical ideal—were helped to spread throughout western Europe. Yet it must be admitted that in *The Courtier* the high qualities of *humanitas*—culture and virtue—are exalted not for themselves but as tools of self-advancement.

Dignified, melancholy, and idealistic (qualities that Raphael captured in his famous portrait), Castiglione tended not only to soften society's rough edges but also to avoid thorny practical and moral issues. For instance, he says of the Italians' recent poor reputation in arms, "It is better to pass in silence that which cannot be recalled without pain." As to the question of what a courtier should do when ordered by his prince to commit an immoral act such as murder, he states, "There would be too much to say; it must all be left to your discretion." Nevertheless, there is much that is positive in *The Courtier;* there is a lofty concept of human personality and dignity and of man's creative possibilities.

Castiglione's classical learning is deftly blended into the polite conversation of the courtiers and their ladies. His arguments in favor of literature are derived from those of Cicero in *Pro Archia,* and his description of the ideal courtier is strongly influenced by Cicero's *Deoratore.* The courtier should be noble, witty, pleasant, agile, a horseman and a warrior (his principal profession), and devoted to his prince. He should know Greek, Latin, French, and Spanish, and he should be skilled—though not ostentatiously so—in literature, music, painting, and dancing. The courtier's behavior should be characterized by grace and nonchalance (*sprezzatura*), and he should carefully avoid any affectation. As in Machiavelli and Guicciardini, there is a certain moral relativism: seeming is frequently more important than being.

Only a modest poet in both Italian and Latin, Castiglione wrote a fine sonnet on the ruins of Rome, *Superbicolli e voi sacre ruine,* which reappears in the *Antiquités de Rome* of Joachim du Bellay and in Edmund Spenser's *Ruines of Rome.* His poetry was published in 1760 and his letters in 1769 and 1771.

Further Reading

The most famous translation of *The Book of the Courtier* is by Sir Thomas Hoby (1561; many later editions); the most recent and readable, by Charles S. Singleton (1959). Castiglione's contribution to the Renaissance is described in Ralph Roeder, *The Man of the Renaissance: Four Lawgivers, Savonarola, Machiavelli, Castiglione, Aretino* (1933). See also Julia Cartwright, *Baldassare Castiglione, the Perfect Courtier: His Life and Letters, 1478-1529* (2 vols., 1908), and Ernest Hatch Wilkins, *A History of Italian Literature* (1954). □

Ramón Castilla

Ramón Castilla (1797-1867) was a Peruvian military and political leader. After a distinguished military career he became president of Peru and provided his country with its first period of order, progress, and reform.

Ramón Castilla was born on Aug. 31, 1797, of mixed European-native parentage in Tarapacá (now Chile). When the wars of independence began, he joined the royalist forces in Chile and served from 1812 to 1817, when he was captured by the Argentine-Chilean patriot forces. Sent to a camp near Buenos Aires, he escaped and made his way to Peru. His royalist service continued until 1820, when, shortly after José de San Martin's liberating expedition arrived from Chile, Castilla changed sides. He served with distinction under the command of San Martín and Simón Bolívar until the war ended in 1824.

For the next 20 years Castilla moved in and out of the army, occasionally holding civilian administrative positions but more frequently commanding units supporting one or another of the military chieftains dominating Peru. In 1845 he was elected president of Peru. He served from 1845 to 1851 and in 1854 resumed the office, remaining chief executive until 1862. With his presidency the pacification of Peru began.

As president, Castilla acted with great energy, but, at the same time, his programs were characterized by moderation and prudence, usually striking a balance between liberalism and conservatism. He attracted men of all political persuasions, showing a preference for talent rather than party affiliation.

During Castilla's presidency Peru adopted its first budget and reformed its fiscal procedures. His government initiated public works projects and expanded the educational system. He emancipated the African slaves and ended the collection of the centuries-old native tribute. His government improved the armed forces and, in fact, became so thoroughly identified with military preparedness that Castilla came to be considered the creator of the national military forces.

The major shortcomings of his administrations resulted from the adoption of what proved to be poor financial policies. Although the fiscal machinery had been reorganized, his government had assumed new financial burdens without creating new and more adequate tax bases. In abolishing the tribute of the native peoples (which had formerly produced at least 10 percent of the national revenues), compensating the owners of the emancipated slaves, consolidating the internal debt, and subsidizing education, the government had greatly increased its expenditures. In its need for funds it became ever more dependent upon the revenues produced from the extraction and sale of guano, and the government borrowed heavily against future guano receipts, setting a pattern to be followed by succeeding administrations.

Castilla retired from office in 1862 but kept an active interest in national affairs. In 1864 he was exiled after he had quarreled with the new president, Juan Antonio Pezet, because he considered that the recently negotiated Vivanco-Pareja Treaty with Spain was an affront to the national honor. In 1867 Castilla headed a revolt against Pezet's successor, Mariano Ignacio Prado, but died, apparently from overexertion, on May 25 before the campaign had reached its conclusion.

Further Reading

While there is an extensive literature in Spanish, there is no biography of Castilla in English. His life and career are discussed in Fredrick B. Pike, *Modern History of Peru* (1967), and in other general histories of Peru. For a favorable contemporary view of Castilla by a well-informed Britisher see Sir Clements Markham, *Travels in Peru and India* (1862). □

Vernon and Irene Castle

Ballroom dancers Vernon (1887-1918) and Irene (1893-1969) Castle led the craze for ragtime and Broadway routines adapted as social dances in the years before World War I.

Vernon Castle was born Vernon William Blythe in Norwich, England, on May 2, 1887. Although he graduated from Birmingham University with a degree in engineering, he also worked as a conjurer in clubs and at private parties. He came to New York with his sister

Coralie and her husband Laurence Grossmith, who were actors. Adopting the surname Castle, he appeared in a series of shows produced by Broadway comedian Lew Fields: *About Town* (1907), *The Girl Behind the Counter* (1907), *Old Dutch* (1909), *The Midnight Sons* (1909), *The Summer Widowers* (1910), and *The Hen-Pecks* (1911). Castle's specialty was slapstick comedy. He was often cast as "second banana" to Fields and served as dancing partner to Lotta Faust and Topsy Siegrist.

Irene Castle was born Irene Foote on April 17, 1893, in New Rochelle, New York. She was the second daughter of Dr. Hubert Townsend Foote and Annie Elroy (Thomas) Foote, whose father was press agent for the Barnum and Bailey Circus. She attended several boarding schools but did not graduate from high school. As a child she studied dancing with Rosetta O'Neill, who taught a generation of children ballroom dancing. When she was a teenager, Irene appeared in amateur theatricals, often singing "The Yama-Yama Man,"—the song made popular by Bessie McCoy in the Broadway show *The Three Twins* (1908). After attaining stardom, Irene credited certain aspects of her style to McCoy, "the high shoulder, the way I held my hands, and anything that looked well about my dancing."

The couple met in 1910 at the Rowing Club in New Rochelle, which was by then a popular place for show-people to live. He arranged an audition for her with Lew Fields, who engaged her as a dancer replacement for *The Summer Widowers,* her first professional appearance. Despite her father's doubts about welcoming an actor into the family, the couple was married in New Rochelle on May 28, 1911. They went to England for their honeymoon to meet his family, but returned to New York in time for the August opening of *The Hen-Pecks* with both Castles in the cast.

The Castles returned to Europe because he was engaged to appear in the barbershop sketch from *The Hen-Pecks* in a French revue (*Enfin . . . Une Revue,* Olympia Theatre, Paris, March 1912). The revue included a dance for the Castles set to the music of the young songwriter Irving Berlin's "Alexander's Ragtime Band." While in Paris the Castles tried out a ballroom dance routine at the Café de Paris and made an instant impression. Later, she attributed their popularity to being "young, clean, married and well-mannered," but their appeal was based also on her appearance—a slim, boyish figure dressed in simple but tasteful dancing frocks (as she called them). She was the image of "the girl next door." The Castles projected their delight in dancing with each other and made the new dances look easy.

The Castles sailed back to New York after six months in Paris. They were booked by Louis Martin for his fashionable Café de l'Opera, and New York went dance crazy over the Castles.

In the period after 1910 when the Castles were busy devising their many dances, Black music and Black dance—the Texas tommy, foxtrot, grizzly bear, and others—had started to filter into the mainstream of American life. Ragtime became the inspiration for the composers of Tin Pan Alley. The Castles were the first white entertainers to hire Black musicians. James Reese Europe's orchestra provided music at the various clubs opened by the Castles and for the nation-wide "Whirlwind Tour" (1914), on which the Castles and their entourage played 24 cities in 32 days.

The Castles were cast in Charles Dillingham's 1912 Broadway production of *The Lady of the Slipper,* but left the show. Next came *The Sunshine Girl* (Knickerbocker, February 1913) and the opening of Castle House, their dancing school across from the Ritz Hotel and Sans Souci, a supper club. Later they opened Castles in the Air on the roof of the 44th Street Theatre. He taught dancing to fashionable ladies during the day and performed with his wife in their current Broadway show. Afterwards they would finish up in the wee hours of the morning at one of their after-hours clubs where they also performed.

In 1914 the Castles made a silent feature film, *The Whirl of Life,* loosely based on their own rise to fame. They also made a series of short films of their own dances.

She became a fashion leader. When she bobbed her hair, millions of women followed. Irene's light, floating "Castle frocks," headache band, and Dutch bonnet were extensively photographed, described in the journals, and copied. She endorsed fashion designs and sewing patterns through the *Ladies Home Journal* and Butterick Patterns.

The Castles opened on Broadway in Irving Berlin's *Watch Your Step* (December 8, 1914, New Amsterdam Theatre). He played the role of Joseph Lilyburn, a dance teacher. She played herself in a number with the boys chorus, "Show Us How To Do The Foxtrot," but the hit of the show was Berlin's "Syncopated Walk," which gave America a foretaste of the jazz decade ahead.

After the start of World War I Castle, who was a British citizen, grew restless as the dark news poured in from Europe. He left *Watch Your Step* in 1915. The Castles gave two farewell performances at the Hippodrome in New York with an orchestra led by John Philip Sousa. Vernon sailed for England, where he joined the Royal Air Force.

While he was away, she continued playing in *Watch Your Step* until 1916, then made *Patria,* a 15-part silent film. (She appeared in 16 more films before 1923.) In 1917 she was one of the stars in the Broadway flop *Miss 1917,* produced by Dillingham and Flo Ziegfeld.

He became an aerial photographer and was awarded the Croix de guerre for bravery. He was killed in a plane crash at Fort Benbrook, Texas, on February 15, 1918, on a training mission with a student pilot.

She appeared in vaudeville with William Reardon (1921-1922) in an act which Fred Astaire helped create. Her public career ended by 1923 when she married her third husband, Frederick McLaughlin, and moved to Chicago. (An earlier marriage after Castle's death to Robert E. Treman ended in divorce). The McLaughlins had two children. Castle married her fourth husband, George Enzinger, after McLaughlin's death.

In 1939 Castle acted as adviser to the Fred Astaire-Ginger Rogers film *The Story of Vernon and Irene Castle.* She also performed in several summer stock plays. Her chief interest in later life was in the field of animal rescue work.

Irene Castle died in Eureka Springs, Arkansas, on January 29, 1969. She is buried next to her first husband at Woodlawn Cemetery, New York.

Further Reading

Vernon and Irene Castle published *Modern Dancing* (1914), which described the dances they created. After Vernon's death, Irene published *My Husband* (1919), based on Vernon's letters from the front; later she wrote *Castles In The Air* (as told to Bob and Wanda Duncan, 1958). Both *My Husband* and *Castles In The Air* have been reprinted by Da Capo Press, New York. A chapter describing the 1939 Astaire-Rogers film *The Story of Vernon and Irene Castle* can be found in John Mueller's *Astaire Dancing: The Musical Films* (1985).

Additional Sources

Castle, Irene, *My husband,* New York: Da Capo Press, 1979, 1919.

Castle, Irene, *Castles in the air,* New York, N.Y.: Da Capo Press, 1980. □

Viscount Castlereagh

The British statesman Robert Stewart Viscount Castlereagh and 2d Marquess of Londonderry (1769-1822), as foreign secretary did much to consolidate a firm final international alliance against Napoleon and to establish the framework for a remarkably durable European peace settlement.

Robert Stewart was born in Ulster on June 18, 1769, son of Robert Stewart and Lady Sarah Seymour. His father, a substantial landowner and member of the Irish Parliament, was raised to the Irish peerage in 1789. As the eldest son, Robert held the courtesy title of Viscount Castlereagh from 1796 until he succeeded as Marquess of Londonderry in 1821. His schooling in Ireland was followed by a year at Cambridge and by a good deal of contact with the influential English families of his mother and stepmother, the Hertfords and the Camdens. In 1794 he married Lady Emily Hobart, daughter of the Earl of Buckinghamshire. Entering the Irish Parliament in 1790, he at first advocated radical reform of that body. But increasing fear of French influence and finally the Wolfe Tone rebellion convinced him, and the British government, that the only way to cure political corruption in Ireland and Catholic grievances on representation and tithes was parliamentary union with Britain. Castlereagh became chief secretary for Ireland in 1798, and to him fell the distasteful task of "persuading" a majority in the Irish Parliament to accept the Act of Union (1800). He resigned with William Pitt in 1801, when George III opposed legislation to permit Catholic representation.

For the next 11 years Castlereagh was in and out of office. He served as president of the Board of Control for India (1802-1805) and briefly as secretary for war under Pitt.

In 1807 he returned to the War Office. In September 1809, believing that the foreign secretary, George Canning, had been secretly intriguing against him, Castlereagh insisted on a duel in which Canning was slightly wounded. Both had resigned from the Cabinet a few days earlier, and both remained out of office for several years.

In March 1812 Castlereagh began his long tenure as secretary of state for foreign affairs, and in June he also became government leader in the House of Commons. He carried this double burden until his death, but it was in foreign affairs that he found his greatest success.

Peace Settlement

Napoleon's disastrous losses in Russia in 1812 broke his spell, and Britain could again weld an alliance with Russia, Prussia, and Austria against his restless domination. By the end of 1813 the Allies had reached the Rhine and the Duke of Wellington had crossed the Pyrenees, but differences in aims and tactics were bubbling to the surface.

The great problem now was to unite the Allies for an agreed settlement that would ensure a durable peace. Castlereagh proposed that France be allowed the boundaries of 1792 but be contained by independent buffer states and by balanced Great Powers. If these objectives were reached, Britain would return the colonies captured during the Napoleonic Wars. When Napoleon spurned these terms, Castlereagh succeeded in 1814 in pledging the Allies at Chaumont to a continuing Quadruple Alliance. Napoleon could not rally the weary French against invasion, and the First Treaty of Paris (May 30, 1814), made with the restored Bourbon government, embodied Castlereagh's moderate terms without occupation or indemnity except private claims. France was also pledged a voice at the Congress of Vienna except on matters affecting the balance of power.

Castlereagh played an important part at the Congress of Vienna (1814-1815), which negotiated a peace settlement emphasizing security and respect for law and treaties. To Castlereagh these objectives could best be ensured by a "just equilibrium" of the Great Powers, which would leave neither serious grievances nor prospect of easy gains to tempt resort to war, and in which the independence of the small states would be preserved. Ethnic factors got little attention from the peacemakers except for France, where Castlereagh and Wellington threw all their influence on the side of a settlement that would not arouse lasting national feeling. Even after Napoleon's Hundred Days in 1815, punitive measures of the Second Treaty of Paris were kept short-term and symbolic. A new treaty of Quadruple Alliance publicly pledged immediate action if France crossed its frontiers in aggression or again accepted a Bonaparte and provided for periodic consultation by the four at top level (congresses).

Britain adhered to the Quadruple Alliance, and at the first Congress (Aix-la-Chapelle), in 1818, Castlereagh and Wellington were able to secure agreement to bring France into the congress system, to end the occupation, and to reduce the French debt for private claims by 80 percent while reaffirming the alliance against French aggression. This timely Congress put the capstone on the strategy of containing France within a settlement tolerable to the French nation.

Later Career

The next 4 years put Castlereagh under enormous strain. Severe economic depression and widespread agitation roused European governments to almost panic fear of revolution. In Britain the archconservatives in the Cabinet insisted on the repressive "Six Acts," for which Castlereagh bore the major responsibility in the Commons. The bill of divorce for Queen Caroline, on which George IV insisted, was also highly unpopular. And Castlereagh was attacked for consorting with the autocrats of the Alliance, who now repressed their own people and intervened in other states to suppress constitutionalist movements. Moreover, he was damaged by his icy reserve (attributed to shyness, for with friends and colleagues he had tact and charm), his disdain for criticism, and his stilted language. Actually, he was bending every diplomatic effort to dissuade the Austrian foreign minister, Metternich, from turning the congress system into an organization for suppressing constitutionalist movements.

In 1820-1821 Castlereagh withheld British representation from the Congress of Troppau-Laibach, making known to the governments of Europe that Britain denied any right of intervention. When another congress was called for September 1822 to deal with the Greek revolution and Spain and the Spanish colonies, he decided to try personally to dissuade the powers or, if need be, to break with them more openly. But it remained for his successor, George Canning, to carry out this policy, which he did with popular acclaim. Following a grueling term in the House of Commons, Castlereagh suffered a nervous breakdown, and on Aug. 12, 1822, he committed suicide.

Further Reading

C. K. Webster has influenced all subsequent biographies with the two most thorough studies of Castlereagh's major work: *The Foreign Policy of Castlereagh, 1812-1815* (1931) and *The Foreign Policy of Castlereagh, 1815-1822* (1925; 2d ed. 1934). Also valuable are Sir J. A. R. Marriott, *Castlereagh* (1936); Ione Leigh, *Castlereagh* (1951), particularly for the earlier years; C. J. Bartlett, *Castlereagh* (1967), a readable and balanced analysis of Castlereagh's career; and Bradford Perkin's important study, *Castlereagh and Adams: Britain and the United States, 1812-1823* (1964).

Additional Sources

Derry, John W. (John Wesley), *Castlereagh,* London: A. Lane, 1976.

Hinde, Wendy, *Castlereagh,* London: Collins, 1981. □

Antônio de Castro Alves

Antônio de Castro Alves (1847-1871) was the last of the prominent romantic poets of Brazil. He is best known for his poetic campaign in behalf of freedom for African slaves.

Antônio de Castro Alves was born in Curralinho (now Castro Alves) in the coastal province of Bahia on March 14, 1847, the son of a doctor. After receiving the best secondary education available, Antônio entered law school. He had begun to compose poetry even earlier and wrote some of his most impressive poems while a student. A hunting accident led to the amputation of a foot, and he dropped out of school. After 9 months of wandering through the backwoods of Brazil, he settled to write in the city of Salvador. He died of tuberculosis there at the age of 24 on July 6, 1871. Only one book of his poems, *Espumas flutuantes* (1870), was published before his death, but others were issued posthumously.

Some of the poetry of Castro Alves suffers from the worst qualities of 19th-century sentimentalism. Its exaggerated rhetorical quality reflects the Brazilian penchant for oratory and declamation. But, if some of his worst poems are omitted and some of the others are edited, his work emerges as highly lyrical yet restrained by a disciplined from (for example, *O gondoleiro do amôr*). His images are often powerful and deeply moving, as in *Crepúsculo sertanejo*. And even the declamatory tendency of his poetry indicates the degree to which it was rooted in the social and historical context.

Like most romantics Castro Alves saw the drama of man's destiny as an eternal conflict between good and evil. Man is caught by the maladjustments of history, and it was in this way that Castro Alves approached the problem of human slavery. Sinister forces larger than the individual had produced this institution, but Promethean struggle could perhaps destroy it or at least redeem the individual crushed between the grinding forces that produced it.

When Castro Alves was in law school, the issue of slavery was foremost in the public eye. Although the problem was not resolved for many years, law dealing with that institution were being hotly debated. And it was into this discussion that Castro Alves threw himself. Perhaps his most frequently recited poem is *O navio negreiro,* an account of the African slave trade in epic proportions. In many of his other poems, for instance, in the collection *Vozes d' Africa* (1880; *Voices of Africa*), he pictured the African not only as a hero but also as a lover, a truly human figure. To be sure, Castro Alves did not escape his times: he endowed his Africans with "white" qualities, even altering their physiognomy. But by this very means he was able to persuade some whites that, indeed, Africans were like them in love, in sorrow, in anger, and in tenderness; therefore, why not in law?

Further Reading

There is no book on Castro Alves in English, although some attention is given to him by Samuel Putnam in *Marvelous Journey: A Survey of Four Centuries of Brazilian Writing* (1948). The major study in Portuguese is Eugênio Gomes, ed., *Castro Alves: Obra completa* (1960).

Additional Sources

Oliveira, Valdemar de, *Castro Alves,* Recife: Universidade Federal de Pernambuco, Editora Universitaria, 1979. □

Fidel Castro Ruz

Fidel Castro Ruz (born 1926) was Cuban prime minister and first secretary of the Communist party of Cuba. A lawyer by training, Castro led the Cuban Revolution and transformed the island into the first Communist state in the Western Hemisphere.

Fidel Castro was born on Aug. 13, 1926, on his family's prosperous sugar plantation near Birán, Oriente Province. His father was an immigrant from Galicia, Spain. Castro studied in Jesuit schools in Oriente and in Havana, where one of his high school teachers, Father Armando Llorente, recalled him as "motivated, proud, different from the others.... Fidel had a desire to distinguish himself primarily in sports; he liked to win regardless of efforts; he was little interested in parties or socializing and seemed alienated from Cuban society."

Became Campus Activist

In 1945 Castro entered law school at the University of Havana, where student activism, violence, and gang fights were common occurrences. Protected by its autonomy, the university was a sanctuary for political agitators. Castro soon joined the activists and associated with one of the gangs, the Unión Insurreccional Revolucionaria. Although police suspected him of the murder of a rival student leader and other violent actions, nothing was proved. Castro acquired a reputation for personal ambition, forcefulness, and persuasive oratory. Yet he never became a prominent student leader. On several occasions he was defeated in student elections.

In 1947 Castro temporarily left the university in order to join in an expedition led by writer Juan Bosch to overthrow the government of Dominican dictator Rafael Trujillo, but the coup was called off during the ocean voyage to Dominica. The 23-year-old Castro jumped into the shark-infested waters and swam to shore carrying a gun over his head.

The following year he participated in one of the most controversial episodes of his life, the *Bogotazo*—a series of riots in Bogotá, Colombia, following the assassination of Liberal party leader Jorge E. Gaitán. Castro, who was attending a student meeting in Bogotá supported by Argentine dictator Juan Perón that was timed to coincide with—and disrupt—the Ninth Inter-American Conference, was caught up in the violence that rocked Colombia after the assassination. Picking up a rifle from a nearby police station, he joined the mobs and roamed the streets, distributing anti-United States propaganda and inciting the populace to revolt. Enrique Ovares, one of his student companions, denies that Castro was a Communist but claims that it was "a hysteric, ambitious, and uncontrollable Fidel who acted in those events." Pursued by Colombian authorities, the Cuban students sought asylum in the Cuban embassy and were later flown back to Havana, where Castro resumed his law studies at the University of Havana.

While still a student, Castro married Mirta Díaz-Balart, a philosophy student whose wealthy family had political ties to powerful Cuban military leader Fulgencio Batista. The couple would have one son, Fidelito, in 1949, but because Castro had no income with which to support his family, the marriage eventually ended.

At the university Castro was exposed to different ideologies. The authoritarian ideas of fascism and communism were widely discussed, but above all, the nationalistic program of Cuba's Ortodoxo party—economic independence, political liberty, social justice, and an end to corruption—captured the imagination of many students. The party's charismatic leader, Eduardo Chibás, became their idol, and Castro developed into his devoted follower, joining the Ortodoxo party in 1947. While he would graduate three years later and and begin to practice law in Havana, his interest in the law soon gave way to his passion for politics.

Assumed Leadership of Revolution

Early in 1952, in preparation for upcoming elections scheduled for June, Castro began campaigning for a seat in congress as a replacement for Ortodoxo party leader Chibás, who had publicly killed himself the previous summer. However, elections were never held. On March 10 General Batista and a group of army conspirators overthrew the regime of Cuban president Carlos Prío Socarrás. For Castro, violence seemed the only way to oppose the military coup. He organized a group of followers and on July 26, 1953, attacked the Moncada military barracks in Oriente Province. Castro was captured, tried, and sentenced to 15 years in prison. During his trial he delivered a lengthy defense in what would become his most famous speech, *La historia me absolverá,* attacking Batista's regime and outlining his own political and economic ideas, most of them within the mainstream of Cuba's political tradition.

After being released by an amnesty in 1955, Castro was exiled to Mexico City, where he began organizing an expedition against Batista dubbed the 26th of July Movement. On Dec. 2, 1956, Castro, his brother Raul, and 80 other men landed in Oriente Province. After encounters with the army, in which all but 12 of his men were killed or captured, Castro fled to the Sierra Maestra, forming in these mountains a nucleus for a guerrilla operation.

At the same time, urban opposition to the militaristic Batista regime increased. An attack on the Presidential Palace on March 13, 1957, led by students and followers of deposed President Prío, nearly succeeded in killing Cuba's new dictator. By 1958 a movement of national revulsion against Batista had developed. Castro emerged as the undisputed leader of the anti-Batista opposition, and his guerrillas increased their control over rural areas. On April 9, 1958, Castro called a national strike, which was called off after Batista ordered strikers to be shot on sight, causing massive shootings. Finally, defections in the army precipitated the fall of the regime on December 31.

Revolution Changed Course

On Jan. 1, 1959, Castro and his July 26th movement assumed power, proclaimed a provisional government, and began public trials and executions of "criminals" of the Batista regime. On February 15 Castro replaced José Miró Cardona as prime minister and appointed his own brother commander of the armed forces. A powerful speaker and a charismatic leader, Castro began exerting an almost mystical hold over the Cuban masses. As previous revolutionaries had done, he lectured the Cubans on morality and public virtue. He also emphasized his commitment to democracy and social reform and promised to hold free elections. Denying that he was a Communist, Castro described his revolution as humanistic and promised his followers a nationalistic government that would respect private property and uphold Cuba's international obligations.

Attempting to consolidate his support inside Cuba, Castro introduced several reforms. He confiscated wealth "illegally" acquired by Batista's followers, substantially reduced residential rents, and passed an agrarian reform law that confiscated inherited property. Although the avowed purpose of this law was to develop a class of independent farmers, in reality the areas seized developed into state farms, with farmers becoming government employees. By the end of 1959 a radicalization of the revolution had begun to take place. Purges or defections of military leaders became common, and their replacement by more radical and oftentimes Communist militants was the norm. Newspapers critical of these new leaders were quickly silenced.

This internal trend toward a Communist agenda was reflected in foreign policy too. Castro accused the United States of harboring aggressive designs against the revolution. In February 1960 a Cuban-Soviet trade agreement was signed, and soon after Cuba established diplomatic relations with the Soviet Union and most Communist countries. Several months later, when the three largest American oil refineries in Cuba refused to refine Soviet petroleum, Castro confiscated them. The United States retaliated by cutting the import quota on Cuba's sugar. Castro in turn nationalized other American properties, as well as many Cuban businesses. On Jan. 3, 1961, U.S. President Dwight Eisenhower broke relations with Cuba.

Declaration of a Socialist State

In April 1961 anti-Castro exiles, supported by the United States under the leadership of its newly elected president, John F. Kennedy, attempted an invasion of Cuba at the Bay of Pigs. The failure of that invasion consolidated Castro's power, and the Cuban leader declared his regime to be socialist. Economic centralization increased. Private schools fell under government control and educational facilities increased. There was a nationwide literacy campaign. Sanitation and health improved with the establishment of rural hospitals and clinics. Confiscation of private property brought virtually all industrial and business enterprises under state control. Religious institutions were suppressed and clergymen expelled from the island.

In December 1961 Castro openly declared himself to be a Marxist Leninist. He merged all groups that had fought against Batista into the Integrated Revolutionary Organizations, changed it later into the United Party of the Socialist Revolution, and transformed it into the Communist Party of Cuba—the island's only ruling party—in 1965.

In foreign affairs Castro moved closer to the Soviet Union, although the Cuban Missile Crisis of October 1962 severely strained Cuban-Soviet relations. Castro had allowed the U.S.S.R. to install within Cuba's borders medium-range nuclear missiles aimed at the United States, ostensibly for the defense of Cuba. When President Kennedy protested and negotiated the missiles' removal directly with Soviet leader Nikita Khrushchev, Castro felt humiliated. Shortly thereafter, pro-Soviet Cuban Communists were eliminated from positions of power. By 1964 the Organization of American States had ended all diplomatic relations with Cuba, effectively isolating that country in South America and increasing its dependence on the U.S.S.R.

Until the end of 1964 Castro had attempted to maintain a position of neutrality in the Sino-Soviet dispute. But following the 1964 Havana Conference of pro-Soviet Latin American Communist parties, the Soviet Union pressured Castro into supporting its policies. Cuba's relations with China deteriorated, and early in 1966 Castro denounced the Peking regime. By supporting the Soviet invasion of Czechoslovakia in 1968, he demonstrated his dependence on the Soviet Union as well as his determination to move closer to the Soviet camp.

Spread of the Revolution

Another source of conflict in Cuban-Soviet relations was Castro's determination to export his revolution. After the 1964 Havana Conference the Soviet Union was temporarily able to slow down Castro's support for armed struggle in Latin America. But by 1966 Castro founded in Havana the Asia-Africa-Latin America People's Solidarity Organization to promote revolution on three continents. In July 1967 he formed the Latin American Solidarity Organization, specifically designed to foster violence in Latin America. Castro's efforts, however, were mostly unsuccessful, as evidenced by the failure of Che Guevara's guerrilla campaign in Bolivia in 1967. Nevertheless, Castro's efforts in this regard continued through the 1970s.

Repression Culminated in Boat Lift

Despite the improvements that he brought to Cuba—the country boasted a 94 percent literacy rate and an infant mortality rate of only 11 in 1,000 births in 1994—Castro was constantly condemned for human rights abuses. Political prisoners crowded Cuban jails, while homosexuals, intellectuals, political dissidents, and others were constant victims of government-sponsored violence. In 1989, perceiving him a threat, Castro authorized the execution of former friend General Arnaldo Ochoa Sanchez on trumped-up drug smuggling charges.

One of Castro's goals was to remove opposition to his rule, which he accomplished not only with executions and imprisonments, but through forced emigrations. The largest of these, the Mariel Boat Lift, occurred in response to a riot outside the Peruvian Embassy in Havana. In mid-April of 1980, Castro opened the port of Mariel to outsiders, particularly exiled Cubans living in Miami, FL., who sailed into port to claim their relatives. Taking advantage of the situation, Castro loaded boats with prison inmates, long-term psychiatric patients, and other social undesirables. During the government-directed exodus, over 120,000 Cubans left their homeland for sanctuary in the United States, causing a small crisis upon reaching Miami.

With the collapse of the Soviet Union in the early 1990s, Castro's revolution began to lose momentum. Without support from its Soviet allies, who had subsidized much of Cuba's economy via cheap petroleum and a large, ready market for the country's all- important sugar industry, unemployment and inflation both grew. In addition to adopting a quasi-free market economy, encouraging international investment in Cuba, and developing a tourist industry designed to draw foreign currency into his country, Castro began pressing the United States to lift the trade embargo it had imposed upon Cuba since the revolution. The U.S. government remained firm, however, refusing to negotiate with Cuba on trade matters until Castro ended his dictatorial regime. In 1994, the U.S. Congress even tightened the embargo. "This country can only be ruled by the revolution," Castro responded, according to *U.S. News & World Report;* he reaffirmed his determination to retain control by threatening further emigrations of Cubans to Miami. Still, U.S.-Cuban relations had begun to show signs of warming by the latter part of the 1990s: Castro visited the United States in 1996, and invited Cuban exiles then living in the United States to return to their homeland and start businesses. Resolute in his determination to preserve some form of socialism in his country, Castro prepared to groom a new generation of Cuban leaders while also effectively restoring stability to the Cuban economy and regaining support among its people.

Further Reading

There is extensive literature on Castro. Herbert L. Matthews's sympathetic *Fidel Castro* (1969) contains valuable insights into Castro's personality. Jules Dubois, *Fidel Castro: Rebel—Liberator or Dictator?* (1959), has much information on Castro's early life and on his struggle against Batista. For the historical conditions of the events see Wyatt MacGaffey and Clifford R. Barnett, *Twentieth Century Cuba: The Background of the Castro Revolution* (1965); and Earle Rice, *The Cuban Revolution* (1995).

Other recommended titles on Castro include Marta Harnecker, *Fidel Castro's Political Strategy: From Moncada to Victory* (1987); Sebastian Balfour, *Castro* (1990; 2nd edition, 1995); Georgie Anne Geyer's *Guerilla Prince: The Untold Story of Fidel Castro* (1991); Robert E. Quirk's *Fidel Castro* (1993); Warren Brown, *Fidel Castro: Cuban Revolutionary* (1994); and Esther Selsdon, *The Life and Times of Fidel Castro* (1997). Recommended for background on the revolution are Robert Taber, *M-26: Biography of a Revolution* (1961); Theodore Draper, *Castroism: Theory and Practice* (1965) and *Castro's Revolution: Myths and Realities* (1962); Bruce D. Jackson, *Castro, the Kremlin, and Communism in Latin America* (1968); Jaimie Suchlicki, *University Students and Revolution in Cuba, 1920–1968* (1969); and Hugh Thomas, *Cuba: The Pursuit of Freedom* (1971). See also Lee Lockwood, *Castro's Cuba, Cuba's Fidel: An American Journalist's Inside Look at Today's Cuba in Text and Picture* (1967; revised edition, 1990). □

Willa Sibert Cather

The American author Willa Sibert Cather (1873-1947) is distinguished for her strong and sensitive evocations of prairie life in the twilight years of the midwestern frontier. Her poetic sensibility was in sharp contrast to the naturalistic and Freudian-influenced literary movements of her time.

Willa Cather was born in Winchester, Va., but at the age of 9 moved to Nebraska, where her father had bought a farm. Her immediate response to the stark grandeur of the prairie and her involvement in the life of the Bohemian and Scandinavian immigrants provided her with both the material and an unadorned manner of expression for her novels. Although she was educated largely by her mother, her knowledge of English literature and Latin was sufficient for her to do excellent work at the University of Nebraska. Leaving the prairie for the first time in 1900, she moved to Pittsburgh and found employment as editor, drama critic, and high school teacher.

In 1903 Cather published a collection of poems, *April Twilights,* and in 1905 a collection of short stories, *The Troll Garden,* neither of which indicated her considerable talent. Her first novel, *Alexander's Bridge* (1912), the story of an engineer's love for two women, lacked emotional involvement.

In her poignant story of the prairie, *O Pioneers!* (1913), Cather at last discovered her subject matter. This tale of Alexandra Bergson, daughter of Swedish settlers, whose devotion to the land and to her tragically fated younger brother precludes her own chance for happiness, is a major novel and an important source for Cather's subsequent work. In *Song of the Lark* (1915) she presents the story of a young woman's attempt at artistic accomplishment in the constricting environment of small-town life. *My Antonia* (1918), generally considered her finest novel, is based on a successful city lawyer's reflections on his prairie boyhood and his love for Antonia Shimerda, a warm, vibrant Bohemian girl.

Cather's next novel, *One of Ours* (1922), about a man who goes to war in order to escape his midwestern farm environment, won the Pulitzer Prize. *A Lost Lady* (1923) depicts the conflict of a cultivated and sensitive young woman with the crass materialism of the post-pioneer period, and *The Professor's House* (1925) is a study of the problems of youth and middle age. These three novels differ from Cather's earlier studies of prairie life in that the midwestern atmosphere is used as a force in opposition to the artistic aspiration and intellectual development of the gifted inhabitants.

With the passing of the frontier and its ugly transformation into "Gopher Prairie," Cather permanently left the Midwest, both literally and as a thematic vehicle for her novels. She lived intermittently in New York and Europe until the

late 1920s. Then she discovered the Southwest desert, which came to serve as an emotional substitute for the prairie. *Death Comes for the Archbishop* (1927), which describes the dedicated missionaries in Mexico during the 1850s, and *Shadows on the Rock* (1931), a vivid re-creation of French-Catholic life in 17th-century Quebec, represent Cather's interest in Roman Catholicism and her attempt to find a historical metaphor for the qualities of heroism and endurance that she had observed in actuality.

Willa Cather's devotion to the land and her respect for those rooted to it imbue her work with a mystical quality. Man and nature are viewed as dual protagonists in a somber cosmic drama. Despite her love for the prairie, she did not permit sentimentally and nostalgia to cloud the clarity of her vision. She presented the intellectual stagnation, moral callousness, and small-minded bigotry that existed side by side with the heroism of frontier life. "Miss Cather's novels portray the results of the pioneer's defeat, both in the thwarted pettiness to which he is condemned by material failure," observed Lionel Trilling, "and in the callous insensitivity of his material success."

In her last years Cather devoted herself to literary criticism. *Not under Forty* (1936) contains an eloquent expression of her philosophy of writing.

Further Reading

The authorized biography of Willa Cather is Edward K. Brown and Leon Edel, *Willa Cather: A Critical Biography* (1953). The best book-length critical study is David Daiches, *Willa Cather: A Critical Introduction* (1951). More recent studies are John H. Randall, *The Landscape and the Looking Glass: Willa Cather's Search for Value* (1960), and Edward A. and Lillian D. Bloom, *Willa Cather's Gift of Sympathy* (1962). James Schroeter edited an excellent collection of essays, *Willa Cather and Her Critics* (1967). For briefer analyses of her work see the relevant sections in Rebecca West, *The Strange Necessity* (1928); Alfred Kazin, *On Native Grounds* (1942); Edward Wagenknecht, *Cavalcade of the American Novel* (1952); and Maxwell Geismar, *The Last of the Provincials* (1947). □

St. Catherine of Siena

The Italian mystic St. Catherine of Siena (1347-1380) was a woman of intense prayer and close union with God. She was also active in political affairs and influenced the return of the papacy from Avignon to Rome.

The twenty-third child of the Benincasa family, Catherine was born in Siena. She was a cheerful, bright, and intensely religious child, who later said she had vowed her virginity to Christ at the age of 7 when she had her first vision of Him. At 13 she joined the Dominican Sisters of Penitence in Siena. By the time she was 20, Catherine had become so widely known for her personal holiness and asceticism that she attracted a group of spiritual disciples—priests and laymen, men and women.

The many letters she dictated during the next 10 years show that her interest broadened from the religious to the political affairs of the time. The city-state of Florence was at war with the Pope and was torn by opposing factions. In 1376 Catherine was persuaded to act as a mediator and bring peace to Florence. She visited Pope Gregory XI at Avignon, which had been the seat of the papacy for over half a century. Catherine believed that peace would not come to Italy until the Pope returned to Rome. Pope Gregory himself wanted to move the papacy back to Rome but he had been unable to summon sufficient courage in the face of considerable opposition from his advisers. Catherine's deep spirituality and insistent words provided just the right kind of gentle, forceful persuasion.

In 1377 the Pope returned to Rome. But he died a year later and his successor, Urban VI, was harsh, unyielding, and antagonistic. Catherine kept in touch with him, once writing, "For the love of Jesus crucified, Holy Father, soften a little the sudden movements of your temper." The Pope did not follow her advice and lost the allegiance of the cardinals. Declaring that he had not been validly elected, they returned to Avignon to elect another pope. This was the beginning of the Great Schism. Catherine was crushed, and she attempted to win the allegiance of some political leaders to Urban. Her strength failed, however, and she died in Rome on April 29, 1380, surrounded by her spiritual "children." She was canonized in 1461.

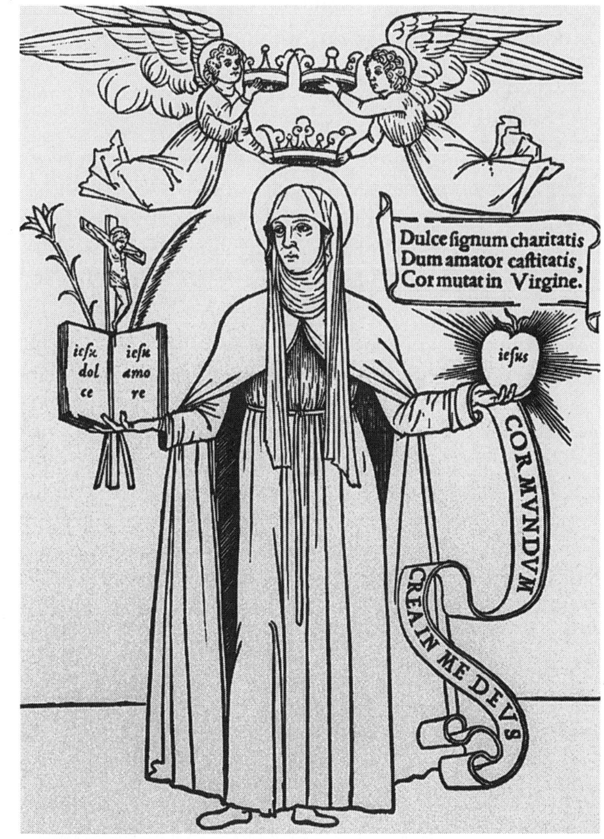

Catherine wrote of her religious experiences in a series of "dialogues" with God. This work, which became an Italian classic, is still read with respect.

Further Reading

Of the many biographies of Catherine available in English, two of the best are Sigrid Undset, *Catherine of Siena* (trans. 1954), which stresses her spiritual importance, and Michael de la Bedoyère, *The Greatest Catherine: The Life of Catherine Benincasa, Saint of Siena* (1947), which shows the woman as she appears in her letters.

Additional Sources

Baldwin, Anne B., *Catherine of Siena: a biography,* Huntington, Ind.: Our Sunday Visitor Pub. Division, 1987.

Meade, Catherine M., *My nature is fire: Saint Catherine of Siena,* New York, N.Y.: Alba House, 1991.

Noffke, Suzanne, *Catherine of Siena: vision through a distant eye,* Collegeville, Minn.: Liturgical Press, 1996.

Raymond, of Capua, *The life of . . . Sainct Catharine of Siena,* Ilkley Eng.: Scolar Press, 1978. □

Catherine the Great

The Russian empress Catherine II (1729-1796), known as Catherine the Great, reigned from 1762 to 1796. She expanded the Russian Empire, improved administration, and vigorously pursued the policy of Westernization. Her reputation as an "enlightened despot," however, is not wholly supported by her deeds.

Born in the German city of Stettin on April 21, 1729, Catherine was the daughter of Prince Christian August of Anhalt-Zerbst and Princess Johanna Elizabeth of Holstein-Gottorp. Her education emphasized the subjects considered proper for one of her station: religion (Lutheranism), history, French, German, and music.

When Catherine was 15, she went to Russia at the invitation of Empress Elizabeth to meet—and perhaps marry—the heir to the throne, the Grand Duke Peter, an immature and disagreeable youth of 16. As the Empress had hoped, the two proved amenable to a marriage plan; but Catherine later wrote that she was more attracted to the "Crown of Russia," which Peter would eventually wear, than to "his person." When Catherine had met the important condition imposed upon her as a prospective royal consort, that she be converted to the Russian Orthodox faith, she and the young Grand Duke were married in 1745.

The marriage turned out to be an unhappy one in which there was little evidence of love or even affection. Peter was soon unfaithful to Catherine, and after a time she became unfaithful to him. Whether Peter was the father of Paul and Anna, the two children recorded as their offspring, remains a moot question.

Although amorous interests were important in Catherine's personal life, they did not overshadow her intellectual and political interests. A sharp-witted and cultivated young woman, she read widely, particularly in French, at that time the first language of educated Europeans. She liked novels, plays, and verse but was particularly interested in the writings of the major figures of the French Enlightenment, such as Diderot, Voltaire, and Montesquieu.

Catherine was ambitious as well as intelligent. She always looked ahead to the time when Peter would succeed to the throne and she, as his empress, would be able to exercise great political influence. In anticipation of her future status she sought the reputation of being a true Russian. She worked diligently at mastering the Russian language and took care to demonstrate devotion to the Russian Orthodox faith and the Russian state. Thus she gave prominence to a significant difference between her attitude and that of her husband, who displayed open contempt for the country he was to rule. She assured herself of further advantage by the studied use of her charm and vivacity in cultivating the goodwill of important personages.

Ascent to Power

When Empress Elizabeth died on Dec. 25, 1761, Peter was proclaimed Emperor Peter III, and Catherine became empress. Friends warned that she might not enjoy her status for long since Peter was planning to divorce her, and she was advised to flee. She decided to ignore the warning, and the wisdom of her decision was soon demonstrated. Within a few months after coming to the throne, Peter had aroused so much hostility among government, military, and church leaders that a group of them began plotting a coup to remove him, place his 7-year-old son, Paul, on the throne, and name Catherine as regent until the boy should come of age. But they had underestimated Catherine's ambition—she aimed at a more exalted role for herself. On June 28, 1762, with the aid of her lover Gregory Orlov, she rallied the troops of St. Petersburg to her support and declared herself Catherine II, the sovereign ruler of Russia (she later named Paul as her heir). She had Peter arrested and required him to sign an act of abdication. When he sought permission to leave the country, she refused it, intending to hold him prisoner for life. But his remaining days proved few; shortly after his arrest he was killed in a brawl with his captors.

Early Reign (1762-1764)

Catherine had ambitious plans regarding both domestic and foreign affairs, but during the first years of her reign her attention was directed toward securing her position. She knew that a number of influential persons considered her a usurper and her son, Paul, the rightful ruler; she also realized that without the goodwill of the nobility and the military she could be overthrown by a coup as readily as she had been elevated by one. Her reaction to this situation was to take every opportunity for conciliating the nobility and the military and at the same time striking sharply at those who sought to replace her with Paul.

As for general policy, Catherine understood that Russia needed an extended period of peace during which to concentrate on domestic affairs and that peace required a cautious foreign policy. The able Count Nikita Panin, whom she placed in charge of foreign affairs, was well chosen to carry out such a policy.

Attempts at Reform (1764-1768)

By 1764 Catherine felt sufficiently secure to begin work on reform. In her thinking about the problems of reform, she belonged to the group of 18th-century rulers known as "enlightened despots." Influenced by the ideas of the Enlightenment, these monarchs believed that a wise and benevolent ruler, acting according to the dictates of reason, could ensure the well-being of his or her subjects.

It was in the spirit of the Enlightenment that Catherine undertook her first major reform, that of Russia's legal system, which was based on the antiquated, inequitable, and inefficient Code of Laws, dating from 1649. For more than 2 years, inspired by the writings of Montesquieu and the Italian jurist Beccaria, she worked on the composition of the "Instruction," a document to guide those to whom she would entrust the work of reforming the legal system. This work was widely distributed in Europe and caused a sensation because it called for a legal system far in advance of the times. It proposed a system providing equal protection under law for all persons and emphasized prevention of criminal acts rather than harsh punishment for them.

In June 1767 the Empress created the Legislative Commission to revise the old laws in accordance with the "Instruction." For the time and place, the Commission was a remarkable body, consisting of delegates from almost all levels of society except the lowest, the serfs. Like many others, Catherine had great hopes about what the Commission might accomplish, but unfortunately, the delegates devoted most of their time to the exposition of their own grievances, rather than to their assigned task. Consequently, though their meetings continued for more than a year, they made no progress, and Catherine suspended the meetings at the end of 1768. The fact that she never reconvened the Commission has been interpreted by some historians as an indication that she had lost faith in the delegates; others feel, however, that she was more interested in having the reputation of being an "enlightened" ruler than in actually being one.

War and Revolt (1768-1774)

Foreign affairs now began to demand Catherine's major attention. She had sent troops to help the Polish king Stanislas (a former lover) in suppressing a nationalist revolt aimed at reducing Russia's influence in Poland. In 1768 the Polish rebels appealed to Turkey for aid, and the Turkish sultan, grateful for an opportunity to weaken a traditional enemy, declared war on Russia. But his act was based on serious miscalculation, and his forces were soundly beaten by the Russians. This turn of events led Austria to threaten intervention on Turkey's behalf unless Catherine agreed not to take full advantage of her victory. Faced by this dangerous alternative, she agreed to show restraint in return for a portion of Polish territory. Thus in 1772 Austria and Russia annexed Polish territory in the First Partition of Poland. Two years later, after lengthy negotiations, Catherine concluded peace with Turkey, restricting herself to relatively modest but nonetheless important gains. Russia received as a territorial concession its first foothold on the Black Sea coast, and Russian merchant ships were allowed the right of sailing on the Black Sea and through the Dardanelles.

Even before the conclusion of peace with the Turks, Catherine had to concern herself with a revolt led by the Cossack Yemelyan Pugachev. It proved to be the most ominous internal threat she ever had to face. The rebel leader claimed that reports of Peter III's death were false and that he himself was the deposed emperor. He convinced many serfs, Cossacks, and members of other dissatisfied groups that when Catherine II was deposed and "Peter III" was returned to the throne their oppression would be ended. Soon tens of thousands were following him, and the uprising, which started in the south and spread up the Volga River, was within threatening range of Moscow. Pugachev's defeat required several major expeditions by the imperial forces, and a feeling of security returned to the government only after his capture late in 1774. The revolt was a major landmark in Catherine's reign. Deeply alarmed by it, she concluded, along with most of the aristocracy, that the best safeguard against rebellion would be the strengthening of the local administrative authority of the nobility rather than measures to ameliorate the condition of the lower classes.

Domestic Affairs (1775-1787)

Much of Catherine's fame rests on what she accomplished during the dozen years following the Pugachev uprising, when she directed her time and talent to domestic affairs, particularly those concerned with the administrative operations of government. Her reorganization in 1775 of provincial administration—in such a way as to favor the nobility—stood the test of time; but her reorganization of municipal government 10 years later was less successful.

Catherine attached high importance to expanding the country's educational facilities. She gave serious consideration to various plans and in 1786 adopted one providing for a large-scale educational system. Unfortunately she was unable to carry out the entire plan; but she did add to the number of the country's elementary and secondary schools, and some of the remaining parts of her plan were carried out during succeeding reigns.

Another of Catherine's chief domestic concerns was the enhancement of Russia's economic strength. To this end she encouraged trade by ending various restrictions on commerce, and she promoted the development of underpopulated areas by attracting both Russians and foreigners to them as settlers.

The arts and sciences received much attention during Catherine's reign not only because she believed them to be important in themselves, but also because she saw them as a means by which Russia could attain a reputation as a center of civilization. Under her direction St. Petersburg was beautified and made one of the world's most dazzling capitals. With her encouragement, theater, music, and painting flourished; stimulated by her patronage, the Academy of Sciences reached new heights. Indeed, during her reign St. Petersburg became one of the major cultural centers of Europe.

Foreign Affairs (1787-1795)

Catherine gradually came to believe that it would be possible to strip Turkey of both Constantinople and its European possessions if only Austria would join Russia in the undertaking. And, having gained Austria's lukewarm support, she began the deliberate pursuit of a policy so intolerably aggressive toward Turkey that in 1787 the Sultan finally declared war on Russia. As in past encounters, the Russian forces proved superior to the Turks, but they required 4 years to achieve victory. By the Treaty of Jassy (1792) Catherine won from Turkey a large area on the Black Sea coast and gained Turkish agreement to Russia's annexation of the Crimean Peninsula. But she was not able to carry out her original plan of annexing Constantinople and Turkey's European territory, since Austria had withdrawn its support of this action and other powers vigorously opposed it.

While the Russo-Turkish War was in progress, Polish nationalists again tried to strengthen the Polish state and end Russian influence within it. As before, their efforts were futile, leading only to unqualified disaster for their unfortunate country—the Second Partition of Poland (1793), in which Russia and Prussia annexed Polish territory; and the Third Partition (1795), in which Russia, Austria, and Prussia divided what remained of an independent Poland.

Problem of Succession

As she grew older, Catherine became greatly troubled because her heir, Paul, who had long been given to violent and unpredictable extremes of emotion, was becoming so unsettled and erratic that she doubted his fitness to rule. She considered disclaiming him as heir and naming his oldest son, Alexander, as her successor. But before she was able to alter her original arrangement, she died of a stroke on Nov. 6, 1796.

Further Reading

The Memoirs of Catherine the Great, edited by Dominique Maroger (trans. 1955), covers her life until 1762. *Documents of Catherine the Great,* edited by W. F. Reddaway (1931), includes the texts of the "Instruction" and her correspondence with Voltaire. Ian Grey, *Catherine the Great: Autocrat and Empress of All Russia* (1962), is a thorough and sound biography. Gladys S. Thomson, *Catherine the Great and the Expansion of Russia* (1947), provides a useful, brief survey of Catherine's reign. Kazimierz Waliszewski, *The Romance of an Empress: Catherine II of Russia* (1894), is still a fascinating and important work. □

Catiline

Catiline (ca. 108-62 B.C.), or Lucius Sergius Catilina, was a Roman politician and revolutionary. Cicero blocked his attempt to overthrow the government in 63 B.C.

Although Catiline traced his patrician lineage to Sergestus, a companion of Aeneas, no member of the family had held the consulship in Rome for several generations. His early life and career are shrouded in obscurity and misrepresentation. He may have served as military tribune in the Social War in 89 B.C. When Sulla returned to Rome in 83, Catiline joined him.

Catiline held the praetorship in 68 B.C. For the next 2 years he served as governor of Africa. When he returned to Rome in 66, he attempted to run for the consulship, but his candidacy was refused because he was under indictment for extortion in his province. Acquitted of extortion in 65 and of the charge of murder during the proscriptions in 64, Catiline ran for the consulship of 63 with financial support from M. Licinius Crassus. But senatorial leaders rallied behind Cicero, and Catiline lost. He campaigned again in 63, making a broad appeal on a platform of cancellation of debts. Again he failed because of the opposition of Cicero and heavy bribery by his senatorial competitors.

Disappointed and disgruntled, Catiline turned to revolution. With a small group of senatorial backbenchers and equestrians, he made plans to recruit an army in Etruria, march on Rome, and take control of the state after murdering Cicero and other leading senators.

Cicero learned of the plot from one of the conspirators and obtained concrete evidence of it from Crassus. On Oct. 21, 63 B.C., Cicero exposed Catiline's plans in the Senate, which declared a state of emergency and voted Cicero full power to deal with the conspiracy; his defensive measures in Rome and elsewhere in Italy foiled Catiline's plans on October 27. On November 7 Cicero denounced Catiline in the Senate in the first of his four Catilinarian orations. Catiline promptly left Rome to join his troops in Etruria. Early in December, Cicero arrested four of the conspirators left in Rome, and they were put to death on his orders. This action broke the back of the conspiracy. In January 62 B.C., two senatorial armies trapped Catiline at Pistoria in northern Etruria as he tried to flee to Gaul, and he died fighting at the head of his troops.

Though ambitious for power, Catiline saw himself as the champion of the poor and oppressed against an entrenched and unresponsive oligarchy. His economic program attracted small landholders in many parts of Italy, especially Etruria, who had been ruined in the Sullan confiscations.

Further Reading

Ancient sources on Catiline include Cicero, Plutarch, and Sallust. E.G. Hardy, *The Catiline Conspiracy in Its Context* (1924), and Arthur Kaplan, *Catiline: The Man and His Role in the Roman Revolution* (1968), offer good analyses of the problems connected with the conspiracy. Lester Hutchinson, *The Conspiracy of Catiline* (1966), is a well-written but uncritical account of Catiline's life.

Additional Sources

Beesly, Edward Spencer, *Catiline, Clodius, and Tiberius,* Tustin, Calif.: American Reprint Service, 1985.

Zullino, Pietro, *Catilina,* Milano: Rizzoli, 1985. □

George Catlin

The American painter George Catlin (1796-1872) made the most extensive and important record of life among Native Americans in North America through his drawings, paintings, and writings.

George Catlin was born on July 26, 1796, in Wilkes-Barre, Pa. His father, a retired lawyer, sent George to Connecticut to study law in 1817. Two years later he began practicing law in Wilkes-Barre. But he was more interested in painting, natural history, and Native Americans and by 1821 had taught himself portrait painting. In 1823 he painted miniatures in Philadelphia, and on seeing a delegation of Native Americans from the Far West, he determined to become their historian. He went to Albany, N.Y., to paint a portrait of Governor DeWitt Clinton, who later assisted Catlin in many ways. A frequent guest at the governor's mansion, Catlin met there Clara Bartlett Gregory, whom he married in 1828.

The famous Seneca orator, Red Jacket, was the first Native American to pose for Catlin. During the next 4 years he divided his time between commissioned portraits and studies of Native Americans. Finally he gave up his lucrative career as a portraitist and in 1830 went to St. Louis to study and depict Native Americans before they were changed by civilization. After 7 years of hard work under very difficult circumstances, he fulfilled his ambition. For the first 2 years he painted portraits of tribal delegates who came to St. Louis to talk with Gen. William Clark, governor of the vast Indian Territory (a close friend of the affable artist). In 1832 he traveled 2,000 miles up the Missouri River by steamboat, later making a trip to Texas and also to the upper Mississippi River. During these trips he worked at a frantic pace, so that he had about 500 portraits and sketches, a superb collection of Naive American artifacts, and notes and impressions of 38 different tribes to be used later in his lectures and books.

Catlin had early exhibitions of his work in Pittsburgh, Cincinnati, and Buffalo. In 1836 he moved this material home to Albany, where he finished paintings and made additional ones from field sketches. He planned to hold an exhibition and lecture in New York and other big eastern cities and then take his unique collection to Washington, where he hoped it would become the nucleus of a great national museum financed by the U.S. government.

In New York City, "Catlin's Indian Gallery" in 1837 was a tremendous success. This was the first "Wild West" show—one of the most durable popular interests America was to experience. Catlin's message of the noble Native American corrupted by the white man disturbed many people. Although he used all his brilliance and charm on influential friends in Washington, Congress did not purchase his collection, which he exhibited in the capital in 1838. To his disappointment his Indian Gallery had little success in Baltimore, Philadelphia, Boston, or in its second showing in New York.

In 1839 he took his gallery to London, where he again met with financial success. His wife and two daughters joined him. In 1841 he published his first book on Native Americns in North American. In 1845, when London tired of the show, he went to Paris, where his wife died. Except for a painting trip to South America from 1852 to 1857, financed by Baron Wilhelm von Humboldt, Catlin lived in Europe until his return to New York in 1870. He died on Dec. 23, 1872.

Further Reading

Catlin's most important work, *Letters and Notes on the Manners, Customs, and Condition of the North American Indians,* which first appeared in London in 1841, has had numerous reprints and subsequent editions. Loyd Haberly, *Pursuit of the Horizon* (1948), is an interesting biography, and Harold McCracken, *George Catlin and the Old Frontier* (1959), is scholarly and well illustrated. Thomas Donaldson, *The George Catlin Indian Gallery in the U.S. National Museum* (1885), is the basic reference book on Catlin's work. □

Cato the Younger

Marcus Porcius Cato Uticensis (95-46 B.C.), known as Cato the Younger, was a Roman political figure whose opposition to Pompey and Caesar helped hasten the collapse of the Roman Republic.

Orphaned when a child and raised in the house of his uncle M. Livius Drusus, the reformer, Cato early cultivated habits of austerity and made a great show of political and moral probity. After serving as military tribune in Macedonia (67-66 B.C.), he toured Asia to prepare himself for public life. As quaestor, or minister of finance, Cato was notable for his punishment of corrupt treasury clerks and the strict rectitude of his accounts. But he was not free of favoritism. As tribune elect in 63, he prosecuted for electoral bribery one of the men who defeated Catiline for the consulship, exempting the other because he was a relative.

Cato's fiery speech on December 5 led the Senate to vote for the execution of the Catilinarian conspirators who had been caught in Rome after an unsuccessful attempt at seizing control of the state. As tribune in 62, Cato blocked attempts by Metellus Nepos and Julius Caesar to recall Pompey to deal with Catiline and his army in Etruria.

When Pompey returned from the East, Cato led the senatorial opposition against him. He also outraged Crassus and the equestrians by refusing to allow reconsideration of the tax contract for Asia. The result was the formation of the First Triumvirate by Pompey, Crassus, and Caesar to attain their political ends. During Caesar's consulship in 59 Cato bitterly opposed the triumvirate's bills for the redistribution of land and the grant of an extraordinary command to Caesar. So violent were Cato's tactics that Caesar at one point had him imprisoned only to think better of it later. In the following year the triumvirs rid themselves of Cato by offering him a special command in Cyprus. Though Cato was aware he was being removed from the center of power, his exaggerated sense of duty made it impossible for him to refuse.

When he returned to Rome in 56 B.C., he attempted to block the election of Pompey and Crassus to their second consulship. They therefore prevented Cato's election to the praetorship, for which he had to wait until 54. To check the rioting and anarchy which developed in 53 and 52, Cato supported the proposal of the senatorial leaders to make Pompey sole consul. Thereafter he continued to back Pompey but only as a counterforce to the growing power of Caesar. Because Cato refused to cultivate the great politicians, he failed to win the consulship for 51.

In the civil war between Pompey and Caesar, Cato chose Pompey and was given command in Sicily, which he evacuated after the arrival of the Caesarian forces in order to avoid bloodshed. He garrisoned Dyrrachium for Pompey during the Battle of Pharsalus and after Pompey's defeat joined the Pompeian refugees in Africa. There he refused military command because he had not held the consulship but took charge of the city of Utica (whence he derived his surname) and organized its defenses. When Caesar crushed the Pompeians in the Battle of Thapsus in 46 and approached the city, Cato committed suicide.

After his death Cato became a symbol of republicanism in the continuing struggle against Caesar, Antony, and Octavian. But during his lifetime his conservatism and obstructionism served only to strengthen the forces he opposed.

Further Reading

The chief ancient sources for Cato are the speeches and letters of Cicero and the biography in Plutarch's *Lives*. There is no full-length study of Cato in English. For details see S. A. Cook, F. E. Adcock, and M. P. Charlesworth, eds., *Cambridge Ancient History,* vol. 9 (1932), and H.H. Scullard, *From the Gracchi to Nero: A History of Rome from 133 B.C. to A.D. 68* (1959; 2d ed. 1963). □

Marcus Porcius Cato the Elder

Marcus Porcius Cato (234-149 B.C.), known as Cato the Elder and Cato the Censor, was a Roman soldier, statesman, orator, and author. His stern morality in office as well as in his private life became proverbial.

Cato called "the Elder" to distinguish him from his equally famous greatgrandson, Cato the Younger, was born in Tusculum in the Sabine mountains. After growing up in the sturdy discipline of farm life, Cato, from the age of 17, participated in the Second Punic War, distinguished himself in various battles, and served as military tribune in Sicily. After gaining considerable fame for his oratorical ability in court, he was the first of his family to run for public office. Elected quaestor in 204 B.C., he was assigned to the proconsul Publius Cornelius Scipio (Africanus Major) during the war in Africa. On his return he met the poet Quintus Ennius in Sardinia and brought him to Rome.

In 199 Cato became plebeian aedile, and in the following year praetor in Sardinia, where he proceeded sternly against moneylenders. He won the consulship in 195 together with his patrician friend and supporter Lucius Valerius Flaccus. Before his departure for the province of Spain he opposed the repeal of the Appian Law against feminine luxury. As proconsul, in the following year he successfully quelled the rebellion of the Spanish tribes, settled Roman administration, and concerned himself with the Roman profit from the Spanish iron and silver mines. Returning to Rome later in 194, he celebrated a triumph.

In the war against the Syrian king Antiochus III, Cato served once more as military tribune under Manlius Acilius Glabrio, consul of 191 B.C. During his travels in Greece, Cato acquired his anti-Hellenic attitude. After brilliant operations at Thermopylae he was sent to Rome to report the victory, and soon afterward he began a series of accusations directed against the progressive and pro-Hellenic wing of the Senate, which centered on Scipio Africanus. His indefatigable attacks upon what he considered the demoralizing effects of foreign influences and his attempt to steer back to the "good old Roman ways" led to his becoming censor in 184.

Having reached the culmination of his career at the age of 50, Cato gave full scope to his doctrines of social regeneration. As censor, he introduced taxes on luxuries and revised rigorously the enrollment of the Senate and the equestrian order. On the other hand, he spent lavishly on public works such as the sewerage system and built the first Roman market hall, the Basilica Porcia, next to the Senate house. Through the sternness of his censorship he made so many enemies that he had to defend himself in court to the end of his life in at least 44 trials. He pursued a vigorous anti-Carthaginian policy after he returned from an embassy to Carthage, where he witnessed to his great dismay the economic recovery of Rome's former enemy. He died in 149 B.C. at the age of 85, 3 years before the final destruction of Carthage.

As an author, though following in his *Origines* (Foundation Stories) the Hellenistic foundation stories of Italian cities, Cato was the first Roman historian to write in Latin, thereby inspiring national historiography in Rome. He did not hesitate to include his own speeches (of which Cicero knew more than 150), and fragments of 80 are still preserved. Not a detractor of his own praises, he refused to include the names of other generals in his work. His didactic prose work *De agricultura* (*On Farming*) provides a mine of information on the changing conditions from small landholdings to capitalistic farming in Campania. It is also an invaluable source book for ancient customs, social conditions, superstitions, prayer formulas, and archaic Latin prose.

Cato was undoubtedly one of the most colorful characters of the Roman Republic, and his name became synonymous with the strict old Roman morality for generations to come.

Further Reading

The major ancient sources for the life of Cato the Elder are Livy's Books 31-45, "Cato Major" in Plutarch's *Lives,* "Cato" in *The Lives of Cornelius Nepos,* and Cicero's "On Old Age." The definitive modern biography is in German, D. Kienast, *Cato der Zensor* (1954). For general historical background see H.H. Scullard, *Roman Politics, 220-150 B.C.* (1951). □

Carrie Chapman Catt

The American reformer Carrie Chapman Catt (1859-1947) designed the strategy for the final victory of the woman's-suffrage movement in 1920 and founded the League of Women Voters.

Carrie Lane was born in Ripon, Wis., on Jan. 9, 1859. She was raised in Iowa and graduated from the state college. Her first husband died soon after their marriage, and 4 years later, in 1890, she married George Catt, a prosperous engineer. In 1895 she became chairman of the Organization Committee of the National American Woman Suffrage Association (NAWSA), and in 1900 she succeeded Susan B. Anthony as president of NAWSA. Her husband's ill health forced Catt to resign in 1904, but after his death the next year she returned to active service as president of the International Woman Suffrage Alliance. Later she assumed command of the New York woman's-suffrage movement, then struggling to win a statewide referendum authorizing the vote for women. Although the New York campaign was not completed until 1917, Catt's brilliant management of it made her the obvious choice to become president of NAWSA in 1915, when discontent with Dr. Anna Howard Shaw's faltering leadership forced her to step down.

Catt reorganized NAWSA, installed her own people in key positions, and in 1916 worked out a 6-year plan to secure a constitutional amendment that would enfranchise women. America's entry into World War I forced the issue. No doubt women would have gained the ballot some day, but they got it in 1920 mainly because of Catt. Under her direction the amendment was lobbied torturously through Congress and then, in the face of substantial opposition, through the state legislatures. The issue was in doubt until Tennessee, at the last minute, became the thirty-sixth state to ratify the 19th Amendment on Aug. 26, 1920.

Catt was notable for her intelligence, strength of character, and self-discipline. An effective speaker, a superb organizer, a diplomat and a politician, she converted NAWSA from a loose coalition of societies into a tightly knit political machine. She had pacifist inclinations and helped launch the Woman's Peace party, but she broke with it when American entry into World War I was imminent. By the same token, although she served on the Woman's Committee of the Council of National Defense during that war, she did only enough work to establish her credentials as a patriotic American. In both cases her first loyalty and best energies went to the suffrage movement.

In 1919 Catt founded the League of Women Voters as a vehicle for nonpartisan suffragists and as an instrument to advance those reforms for which women had sought the ballot. Later she fulfilled her early pacifist ambitions by establishing a Committee on the Cause and Cure of War, which was the largest of the women's peace groups during the 1920s. A lifelong internationalist, she supported both the League of Nations and the United Nations. Unlike many feminists, Catt was not discouraged by the modest gains women made after receiving the vote. She never thought that enfranchising women would revolutionize the human condition, and as long as her strength held out she continued to work for social justice and social welfare in a variety of fields. She died on March 9, 1947.

Further Reading

The only biography of Catt is Mary G. Peck, *Carrie Chapman Catt* (1944). The fact that the author was a friend and colleague of Catt for 40 years gives the book a special authority, but a full study of this important woman based on the extensive documentary material now available is needed. Carrie C. Catt and Nettie R. Shuler, *Woman Suffrage and Politics* (1923), is informative since it draws on some of Mrs. Catt's own experiences. Volumes 4 (1903), 5 (1922), and 6 (1922) of the *History of Woman Suffrage,* edited by Ida H. Harper, contain much useful material. □

James McKeen Cattell

The American psychologist and editor James McKeen Cattell (1860-1944) was a pioneer in American psychology who influenced the profession to use objective methods of study and to apply psychology to practical aspects of life.

James McKeen Cattell was born on May 20, 1860, in Easton, Pennsylvania. His father was president of Lafayette College in Easton, and his family supported Cattell's education and his early desire to travel and work abroad.

During the eight years following acquisition of a B.A. degree from Lafayette College in 1880 Cattell studied in Europe at Leipzig and at Göttingen under the famed European psychologist Wilhelm Wundt. Moving to England, Cattell worked with Sir Francis Galton, who strongly influenced him. Cattell also admired the American psychologist and philosopher William James. Returning to the United States Cattell worked at Johns Hopkins University.

From 1888 to 1891 Cattell held the first professorship in psychology at the University of Pennsylvania at Philadelphia. He made his greatest personal contributions to the field of psychology during 1891-1917 when he was professor at Columbia University. He died in Lancaster, Pennsylvania, on January 20, 1944.

Cattell had a strong and lasting impact on psychology in at least three ways. First, he began his career at a time when psychology and other behavioral sciences were allied with philosophy. Cattell championed the notion that psychology and other behavioral, biological, and social sciences could carry on rigorous, objective, scientific research. His impetus hastened a turning point in methodological practices in these disciplines. Some say Cattell probably did more than anyone else of his time to foster the development of the behavioral and biological sciences in the United States.

In his own work, Cattell demonstrated the rigor of a scientific approach as he researched reading and perception, psychophysics, individual differences, and individuals' reaction times to various stimuli. Examples of findings from his research still cited today are that eyes jump during reading, that words in print are only perceived when the eyes are at a standstill, that many words can be learned and remembered more easily and accurately than most letters, and that words and phrases can be read in a small fraction of a second.

Second, Cattell advocated that scientific findings could and should be utilized in practical ways. His conclusions from his study of reading, for example, along with others on reaction time revolutionized some educational practices such as methods of teaching reading and spelling. In 1921 Cattell founded, and for many years served as president of, the Psychological Corporation, the first of many groups applying psychological techniques to practice. Psychological Corporation became and remained a leader in the development of tests for use in education and industry.

Third, Cattell made a mark in history through his service to professional organizations and journals. He was one of the founders of the American Psychological Association and of several other scientific societies. He launched and published several scientific journals, including *Psychological Review, Science, Scientific Monthly, School and Society,* and *The American Naturalist.* He also prepared and published the first and subsequent editions of *American Men of Science* and *Leaders in Education.*

Further Reading

Complete reports of Cattell's life and work are in *James McKeen Cattell; 1860-1944: Man of Science.* Volume one, *Psychological Research,* contains Cattell's own reports of his research and volume two, *Addresses and Formal Papers,* consists of Cattell's own presentations.

An Education in Psychology: James McKeen Cattell's Journals and Letters from Germany and England, edited by Michael M. Sokal (1981), gives an interesting personal accounting of the beginnings of Cattell's career. The book also contains brief sections on Cattell at Columbia, Cattell as psychologist, Cattell as editor, and the Cattell family. □

Gaius Valerius Catullus

Gaius Valerius Catullus (ca. 84-ca. 54 B.C.) was a Roman lyric poet. He is best known for the intense poems which reflect various stages in his love affair with "Lesbia."

Catullus belonged to a circle of *neoteroi,* or "new poets," who used as their models the learned Greek poet-scholars at Alexandria in the Hellenistic period and wrote elegant, allusive, and highly finished poems on love, mythology, and other topics. They cherished the epithet *docti,* "learned." Catullus's friends were the poets C. Licinius Macer Calvus, Furius Bibaculus, and C. Helvius Cinna; the orator Q. Hortensius, Cicero's rival in the law courts; and the biographer Cornelius Nepos, to whom Catullus dedicated his book of poems.

Catullus was born in Verona. St. Jerome gives the year 87 B.C. and says that he died at age 30. Since events of 55 B.C. are referred to in several of Catullus's poems, however, and no poem can be said with certainty to be later than 54, scholars accept the dates 84-54. Catullus's family was prominent and well-to-do. They owned a villa at Sirmio, and his father entertained Caesar when the later was governor of Gaul.

When Catullus went to Rome in 61, he met and fell in love with Clodia, the "Lesbia" of the poems, who was a member of the old aristocratic Claudian family and the wife of Metellus Celer. For this upper-class sophisticate 10 years older than Catullus, the young poet from Verona was but another liaison in her constant search for diversion.

After a brief affair Clodia replaced Catullus with Caelius Rufus, who traveled in the same fast set as Catullus and was a protégée of Cicero. When Caelius threw her over (a new experience for her), Clodia brought charges against him in order to ruin him politically and socially. Cicero defended him in a masterpiece of character assassination (*Pro Caelio*) in which he repeated the rumors that Clodia had murdered her husband and slept with her brother and implied, among other things, that she was an insatiable prostitute. Before accepting as true Cicero's portrait of Clodia, one must remember that at one time the orator had thought of divorcing his wife in order to marry her. Whatever this woman was like, Catullus's experience with her was the source of some of the finest Latin lyric poems.

In 57 Catullus went to Bithynia on the staff of Memmius, who was to be governor of that Eastern province. While there Catullus traveled to the Troad to perform rites at the tomb of his brother, who had died in the East, recording this act of devotion in a moving poem. After a year in Bithynia he returned to Italy and probably lived in Rome the rest of his life. Despite complaints of poverty in his poems, he seems to have owned a villa near Tibur (modern Tivoli).

The collected 116 extant poems—18 to 20 are spurious—while arranged neither by chronology nor by subject, can be divided into three categories: The first, poems 1 through 60, is a group of short poems in various meters, with the hendecasyllabic and "limping" iambic predominating, among which are love poems, erotic poems, lampoons, and poems on a variety of other topics. The poems 61 to 64, the second group, are longer poems, including two wedding hymns (61 and 62); the Attis poem (63), about a youth who emasculates himself in order to become a priest of Cybele, then regrets his act; and the "Marriage of Peleus and Thetis" (64), an epyllion, or little epic, of some 400 hexameters. The poems of the third category, 65 to 116, are all written in elegiac meter. A few of these poems are elegies (65-68,76), the rest short poems of epigram type, as in 1-60, on a variety of topics.

Poems about Lesbia

Catullus's most memorable poems are the ones about "Lesbia." It is highly tempting to arrange them in an order that chronicles the poet's affair with Clodia: intense joy at the beginning, a break, reconciliation, then Catullus's awareness of his mistress's congenital faithlessness. Next comes bitterness and despair. The poet nearly loses his sanity but manages, by a great effort of will, to gain control of himself and is then slowly healed of his passion. To read these poems as autobiographical documents is a mistake, however. Catullus did not record this experience factually but, rather, used it as a source for poetry. Art and life were not the same for him. Rather, life was the matrix out of which a highly wrought art was formed.

Perhaps best known is 5, *Vivamus, mea Lesbia, atque amemus* ("Let us live, my Lesbia, and let us love"). The English poets Marlowe, Campion, Jonson, and Crashaw, to name a few, wrote imitations of it. Nearly as well known are 7, *Quaeris quot mihi basiationes* ("You ask me how many kisses"); 8, *Miser Catulle, desinas ineptire* ("Poor Catullus, stop acting foolishly"); 85, *Odi et amo* . . . ("I hate and I love"); the poems on Lesbia's sparrow (2 and 3); and the two in Sapphic meters, one an adaptation of a poem by Sappho (11), and the other, one of his most affecting, an address to a friend to carry a message to Lesbia (51). These poems are appealing by their direct, apparently unreflective, outpouring of emotion. But they have been carefully composed with an art that conceals art. One critic speaks of their "controlled lyricism," which produces a fine tension between intellect and the emotions.

View of Love

Catullus's vision of love in his poems is far different from the casual, frequent, and merely sensual liasions represented in the elegant dilettantish poems of the "new poets." In his poems Catullus imagines a kind of relationship with a woman which may be called total involvement, intellectual as well as physical. This concept of love, taken for granted today, combines friendship with sensual pleasure. Catullus's affair with Clodia was itself probably not unique, but it did provide the poet with a starting point from which to develop his concept of an ideal love.

Catullus could be witty and charming, as in poem 13, an "invitation" to one Fabullus to dine with him—but he must bring his own dinner, for the poet's wallet is full of cobwebs. Nonetheless the host will provide a scented ointment, on smelling which Fabullus will pray to the gods to become all nose. Catullus could be witty and obscene, as in poem 39, on a certain Egnatius, who continually grins, whether appropriately or inappropriately, in order to show off his brilliant white teeth. The secret of his beautiful smile, however, is the urine with which he cleans them. Many of the poems are forthrightly obscene to a degree that may shock even modern readers (32, 33, 37, 80, 97). There are two lampoons of Caesar (29 and 57), which the great man conceded had hurt him. When Catullus apologized for them, however, Caesar promptly invited him to dinner.

Other Themes

The long poems exhibit another side of Catullus's talent. Poem 61, a wedding hymn written in honor of the marriage of a friend, has a grace and sensitivity which make it one of his most delightful poems. The same holds true of 62, another wedding hymn but without reference to a particular marriage. Poem 64, on the marriage of Peleus and Thetis, is highly finished and subtle and was written for, and best understood by, a learned elite. In addition there are 76, the poet's plea to the gods to allow him to gain an ultimate perspective on the love that has consumed him like a disease, and 101, commemorating a visit to his brother's tomb and ending with the simple but expressive *atque in perpetuum, frater, ave atque vale* ("But now for all time, my brother, good luck and farewell").

A critic called Catullus's little book of poems "maddeningly scrappy." The poems are indeed uneven in quality, and many are difficult to understand. Nevertheless he wrote a new kind of poetry which influenced poets for two generations after his death. His direct personal lyricism gives a quality to many of them which makes them similar to modern lyric poems.

Further Reading

A biography that considers the political and cultural milieu of Catullus's works is Tenney Frank, *Catullus and Horace: Two Poets in Their Environment* (1928). Two of the best studies of Catullus in English are E. A. Havelock, *The Lyric Genius of Catullus* (1939), and Arthur Leslie Wheeler, *Catullus and the Traditions of Ancient Poetry* (1934). Kenneth Quinn, *The Catullan Revolution* (1959), assesses the poet's importance in the development of Roman poetry. A later work is David O. Ross, Jr., *Style and Tradition in Catullus* (1969).

Additional Sources

Stoessl, Franz, *C. Valerius Catullus: Mensch, Leben, Dichtung,* Meisenheim am Glan: Hain, 1977. ☐

Augustin Louis Cauchy

The French mathematician Augustin Louis Cauchy (1789-1857) provided the foundation for the modern period of rigor in analysis. He launched the theory of functions of a complex variable and was its authoritative pioneer developer.

Augustin Louis Cauchy was born in Paris on Aug. 21, 1789, 38 days after the fall of the Bastille. His father, Louis François, was a parliamentary lawyer, lieutenant of police, and ardent royalist. Sensing the political wind, he moved the family to his country cottage at Arcueil, where they lived for nearly 11 years. Here young Cauchy received a strict religious education from his mother and an elementary classical education from his father, who wrote his own textbooks in verse.

By 1800 the political situation had stabilized and the family moved back to Paris. At the age of 16 Cauchy entered the École Polytechnique, at that time the best school in the world for a budding mathematician. Originally designed to produce military engineers for the Revolutionary armies of France, the school developed as a revolutionary (in method) educational institution. Teaching was linked with research as the nation's finest mathematicians created pure mathematics in discussion with their students and showed them how mathematical theory and practice nourished one another at the very edge of invention.

As Lagrange and Laplace had predicted, Cauchy was a brilliant academic success. In the realm of personal relationships he was not so successful. The generally anticlerical polytechnicians simply could not believe that a brilliant student as aggressively pious and evangelically Catholic as Cauchy could exist. His imperturbability on the matter progressively amused, bewildered, irritated, and infuriated them. It was a pattern of responses that was to become typical in his social relationships. Many years later, after Cauchy had become the most influential mathematician in the world, the naive young genius Abel would conclude that Cauchy was insane. How else could a man of science be so bigoted in religious matters?

From Engineer to Mathematician

From the Polytechnique, Cauchy passed to the École des Ponts et Chaussées, where he studied engineering for 3 years. Upon graduation in 1810, he was sent to Cherbourg as a military engineer. But he could not stay away from pure mathematics. In his spare time he began to review all mathematics, "clearing up obscurities" and inventing new methods for the "simplification of proofs and the discovery of new propositions." He displayed the power and originality of these methods in a series of papers that impressed even the sophisticated mathematical community of Paris. Among these researches were two on polyhedrons, one on symmetric functions, and one on determinants. In the last paper Cauchy reorganized all that was then known about the subject and gave the word "determinant" its modern meaning. All this spare-time work had two results: it broke Cauchy's health, and he abandoned engineering to devote his life to mathematics.

If the mathematical community had been impressed by Cauchy the hobbyist mathematician, it was dazzled by Cauchy the full-time professional. In 1815 he proved a Fermat conjecture on polygonal (figurate) numbers that had defeated some of the world's best mathematicians. In the following year he demonstrated his versatility by winning the grand prize of the Académie des Sciences with a mathematical treatment of wave propagation on the surface of a fluid. Meanwhile, he had obtained his first teaching position, at the Polytechnique. He was appointed professor there in 1816, and before long he was also lecturing at the Collége de France and the Sorbonne.

At the age of 27 Cauchy was elected to the Académie des Sciences-an unusual honor for so young a man. In his case, there were some who insisted that there was nothing honorable about it. The chair which Cauchy filled had belonged to Gaspard Monge, the father of descriptive geometry, first director of the École Polytechnique, and loyal follower of Napoleon I. The restored Bourbon regime demanded that Monge be expelled from the academy. The academicians complied and elected Cauchy in his place. Cauchy, as rigidly ultraroyalist in politics as he was ultra-Catholic in religion, could never see anything improper about the procedure.

In 1818, securely established as the outstanding mathematician of France, Cauchy married Aloise de Bure. They had two daughters.

Prolific Decade

Cauchy worked as if he expected his worth to be measured by the sheer weight of his publications. His ideas, touching upon nearly every branch of mathematics, pure and applied, seemed to materialize as fast as he could write them down. There were occasions when he would produce two full-length papers in one week.

One of Cauchy's major interests in these years was the attempt to repair the logical foundations of analysis in such a way that this branch of mathematics would have "all the rigor required in geometry." This was a problem of long standing. In his devastating criticism of the Newton-Leibniz calculus, Bishop Berkeley had suggested that the faulty reasoning of the calculus led to correct results because of compensating errors. Maclaurin and Lagrange accepted the criticism and both made heroic efforts to construct a logical justification for the methods of the differential calculus. Neither succeeded.

Cauchy did not quite succeed either. But he took a great step in the right direction when he made the concept of limit the basis for the whole development. His definition of continuity and the derivative in terms of limit was quite modern. But to say that Cauchy" gave the first genuinely mathematical definition of limit, and it has never required modification" is quite wrong.

Cauchy defines "limit" as follows: "When the values successively assigned to the same variable indefinitely approach a fixed value, so as to end by differing from it as little as desired, this fixed value is called the limit of all the others."

As a rough description of the limit idea, Cauchy's "definition" may have merit. But it is verbal, intuitive, crammed with undefined terms, and therefore absolutely nonmathematical in the modern sense. Strangely enough, Cauchy did give a precise mathematical definition of convergent series, and he went on to establish criteria for convergence. It is said that Laplace, after hearing Cauchy's first lectures on series, rushed home in a panic, barred his door, and laboriously tested all the series in his masterpiece, the *Mécanique céleste,* using Cauchy's criteria. This story, perhaps apocryphal, nevertheless indicates how Cauchy's methods began to set new standards of rigor in analysis.

Between 1825 and 1831 Cauchy published a series of papers which created a new branch of analysis, the theory of functions of a complex variable. It is the principal mathematical tool used in vast domains of physics.

A Matter of Principle

The Revolution of 1830 sent Charles X into exile. The new king, Louis Philippe, demanded oaths of allegiance from the professors of France. Cauchy refused. He had already sworn his oath to Charles. Stripped of all his positions, he exiled himself to Switzerland, leaving his family in Paris.

In 1831 Cauchy was appointed professor of mathematical physics at Turin. Two years later Charles summoned him to Prague to tutor Henri, his 13-year-old grandson. Cauchy, ever the faithful legitimist, agreed to supervise the education of the future pretender. His family joined him in Prague in 1834. Playing Aristotle to Henri's Alexander consumed most of Cauchy's waking hours and sharply curtailed his mathematical output. It never ceased entirely, however. Among the important papers of this period were a long memoir on the dispersion of light, and the first existence proofs for the solution to a system of differential equations.

In 1838 Cauchy and family returned to Paris. Charles had baroneted him, but the title was no help in getting a position, since Baron Cauchy still refused to take the oath. At last, after the Revolution of 1848, the oath was abolished, and Cauchy resumed his old professorship at the Polytechnique. Louis Napoleon reinstituted the oath in 1852, but Cauchy was specifically exempted.

Meanwhile Cauchy's rate of publication reached and even surpassed previous limits. Of special merit in the more than 500 papers that appeared after 1838 were treatises on the mechanics of continuous media, the first rigorous proof of Taylor's theorem, a remarkably modern representation of complex numbers in terms of polynomial congruences, and a collection of papers on the theory of substitutions.

Cauchy's Influence on Mathematics

If the worth of a mathematician were to be measured by the number of times his name appeared in modern college textbooks, Cauchy might be ranked as the greatest of them all. His long-standing influence and fame are due in part to the fact that he swamped the competition with the published word. He was the first mathematician to realize that the greatest material engine of mathematical progress was the printing press. He knew that the entire mathematical community, from professor to arithmetic teacher, took its cue from published papers and textbooks. He literally imprinted his ideas upon a generation.

This practice of rapid publication, together with Cauchy's rather flowery style, had its dangers. Abel, for one, had difficulty in understanding some of Cauchy's papers. "His works are excellent, but he writes in a very confusing manner." But Cauchy's style of writing was the least of the offenses he committed against Abel in particular and mathematics in general. The 15-year delay in the publication of Abel's masterpiece—from 1826 to 1841—was largely due to Cauchy's cavalier treatment of it. Abel died in 1829, the same year in which Cauchy contributed to the suppression of young Galois's epochmaking discoveries. Galois died in 1832. It was this contemptuous attitude toward younger mathematicians, together with his religious and political bigotry, that made Cauchy unpopular with many of his colleagues. After all, it was difficult to overlook the fact that Galois had been a radical republican.

Cauchy died on May 23, 1857, after a short illness. His last words were, "Men die but their works endure."

Further Reading

There is no full-length biography of Cauchy, but E.T. Bell, *Men of Mathematics* (1937), contains a biography and a discussion of his place in the history of mathematics. An older source, David Eugene Smith, *History of Mathematics* (2 vols., 1925), gives a brief but adequate account of Cauchy's life. Herbert Westren Turnbull, *The Great Mathematicians* (1961), although it contains no biography of Cauchy, discusses him in relation to the life and work of Joseph Louis Lagrange. See also Jane Muir, *Of Men and Numbers* (1961), written in a lively and popular style and containing numerous references to Cauchy.

Additional Sources

Belhoste, Bruno, *Augustin-Louis Cauchy: a biography,* New York: Springer-Verlag, 1991. □

Constantine P. Cavafy

Constantine P. Cavafy (1863-1933) was the first modernist Greek poet. He revolutionized Greek poetry, but his work shows clear affinities with Hellenistic poetry of the Alexandrian era.

Constantine P. Cavafy was born in Alexandria, Egypt. His father, a prosperous export merchant from Constantinople, died in 1870, and two years later the family moved to England. They returned to Alexandria in 1879 and, except for three years in Constantinople and brief visits to Athens and other cities, Cavafy spent the rest of his life there. Between 1892 and 1922 he supported himself in clerical and minor administrative posts in the Egyptian Ministry of Irrigation. He died in 1933 of cancer in Alexandria.

As a poet, Cavafy was an exceptionally meticulous, slow worker, completing to his satisfaction only 24 poems before he was 48 (when he believed that he had reached his poetic maturity) and only 154 before his death. Aside from occasional magazine publication, the poems were privately printed, and a collected edition was not available until 1935. A complete English translation did not appear until 1951.

In order to understand Cavafy, one must have some knowledge of Alexandria, for the spirit of that city and its history contributed much to Cavafy's poetry. Alexandria was founded by Alexander the Great in 331 B.C. and served as the capital of the Ptolemaic empire. It was the center of the Hellenistic world. It was particularly famous for the Mouseion (in effect a research university) and associated library, which may have had as many as 700,000 rolls (including Aristotle's library), the largest in the world. Euclid, Aristarchus of Samothrace, and Callimachus were among the great scholars who worked there.

In Alexandria differences of opinion were not only tolerated but encouraged. Gnosticism, Neoplatonism, Judaism, and Christianity all had followers here—traditionally St. Mark founded Christianity in Alexandria—and the population was an eclectic mixture, as it was again in Cavafy's day, of Greeks, Egyptians, Jews, and others. An indication of the curious blend of cultures and ideas in Alexandria was the local worship of Serapis (mentioned by Cavafy in his poems), a god whose characteristics showed traces of both Greek and Egyptian influences. The complex, always changing culture of Alexandria gave its citizens little sense of stability or permanence, and for that they turned to art, to the well crafted artifice of a poem.

For Cavafy, as for the ancient Alexandrians, permanence was principally the property of art, not civilization or nature. In this, he was undoubtedly influenced by Mallarmé and other symbolist poets, but the Alexandrian view surely had its influence as well. Cavafy's poems are often self-consciously antiquarian, dealing with obscure corners of history, and this trait he also shares with famous Alexandrian predecessors. Furthermore, like his predecessors, he created his own highly artificial poetic language, a mixture of demotic and purist Greek, deliberately employing archaisms and colloquialisms. Also like the poetry of the ancient Alexandrians, Cavafy's is less the result of sudden inspiration than the result of the most scrupulous craftsmanship. It is the poetry of a very learned, very intelligent man.

Most modernist poets did their greatest work in lyric poetry, but Cavafy turned to the elegiac epigram, which had been perfected by Callimachus and his contemporaries. The elegiac epigram was originally intended for inscriptions on funerary monuments, but the Alexandrians developed it into an objective, cool, and often ironic poetic form. Robert Browning achieved similar poetic effects in his dramatic monologues, and these certainly had their effect on Cavafy, but the primary influence seems, as always, to have been Alexandrian. One persistent theme in ancient elegiac epigrams, particularly in the highly regarded work of Strato, is homosexuality, and this is also a principal theme for Cavafy. Most of his best poems, in fact, which do not deal with episodes, real or imagined, from the Hellenistic world deal with homosexuality.

Cavafy is rarely concerned in his poetry with great figures and incidents which have altered history. He is instead concerned either with people and incidents of no historical importance or at best with people who lived on the edge of great events but who contributed little to them. One of Cavafy's central achievements lies in his ability to invest such individuals and events with emotional consequence and passion. Similar achievements can be found in the works of other Alexandrians.

Cavafy began, like his Alexandrian predecessors, as a relatively traditional or conventional poet, his work rhymed and metrically regular, but he later experimented with new verse patterns and free verse. Because of this experimentation and his highly personal and idiosyncratic use of Greek, he was able to transform thoroughly and revitalize Greek poetry. Modernist Greek poetry begins with Cavafy. But while acknowledging this fact, it must always be remembered that his poetry is essentially conservative in important respects: it represents in many ways a reawakening of certain aspects of the Alexandrian and Hellenistic culture Cavafy profoundly admired.

Cavafy's own epitaph might well be the concluding lines of his own "Epitaph for Antiochos." To be Greek, says Cavafy in this poem, is to have the best there is except for what belongs only to the gods.

Further Reading

Cavafy's poetic voice, as W. H. Auden pointed out, is one of the few that survive translation, and there have been three major translations of the poems, the first by John Mavrogordato (published 1951), the second by Rae Dalven (with a superb introduction by Auden, 1961), and the third—and by most accounts the best—by Edmund Keeley and Philip Sherrard (1975). Robert Lindell's *Cavafy: A Critical Biography* (1976) is a good source for factual information on Cavafy's life as well as commentary on the poetry. Among other studies which should be consulted are Edmund Keeley's *Cavafy's Alexandria: Study of a Myth in Progress* (1976) and Jane Lagoudis Pinchin's *Alexandria Still: Forster, Durrell, and Cavafy* (1976).

Additional Sources

Kolaitis, Memas., *Cavafy as I knew him: with 12 annotated translations of his poems and a translation of the Golden verses of Pythagoras,* Santa Barbara, Calif. (1201 Alta Vista Rd., Santa Barbara 93103): Kolaitis Dictionaries, 1980.

Liddell, Robert, *Cavafy: a biography,* New York: Schocken Books, 1976, 1974.

Liddell, Robert, *Cavafy: a critical biography,* London: Duckworth, 1974. □

Guido Cavalcanti

The Italian poet Guido Cavalcanti (ca. 1255-1300) was one of the originators of the dolce stil nuovo, or sweet new style, in Italian poetry of the late 13th century. He was a contemporary of Dante, who called him his "first friend."

Guido Cavalcanti was born in Florence not later than 1259, the son of a wealthy Guelf. In 1267 the boy Guido was married to Bice, the daughter of the Ghibelline leader Farinata degli Uberti, possibly in a peacemaking attempt between the Guelfs and the Ghibellines. Guido was one of the Guelf guarantors of a peace concluded between the two factions in 1280. In 1284 he was a member of the General Council of the commune.

Contemporary chroniclers portray Cavalcanti as a disdainful, solitary, studious man, courtly and daring, and a good philosopher. His fiery temperament is evident in his animosity toward Corso Donati, the leader of the Black Guelfs of Florence. While Cavalcanti was on a pilgrimage to Santiago de Compostela-a trip which took him to Toulouse, where he met a young woman, Mandetta, to whom he wrote two poems, and to Nîmes but not beyond-it is said that Corso attempted to have him assassinated. Cavalcanti tried in vain to avenge himself by spurring his horse against Corso in a Florentine street and throwing a dart. A general fight ensued, involving also the Cerchi, leaders of the White Guelfs, whom Cavalcanti supported. On June 24, 1300, the priors of Florence (Dante among them) exiled some of the leaders of both factions, and Cavalcantri went to Sarzana with other followers of the Cerchi. His ballad of farewell, *Perch'i' no spero di tornar giammai,* a masterpiece of grace and tenderness, could have been written during this exile. He returned to Florence 2 months later, mortally ill. His death was recorded on Aug. 29, 1300, in the church of S. Reparata.

Poetic Works

The poems which can be attributed positively to Cavalcanti are 36 sonnets, 11 ballads, 2 canzoni, 2 isolated stanzas, and 1 motet. Almost all his poetry is concerned with love. In his famous canzone *Donna me prega . . .*, he develops his theory of love within an elaborate poetic structure and in complex philosophical terms. Original in Cavalcanti is his concept of love as a cruel, overpowering force with a violent potentiality for destruction. Love is a dark passion of the senses which arises from the contemplation of an image of ideal beauty abstracted by the possible intellect at the sight of a beautiful woman. From such love, death often result-a true state of death, in which the mind is destroyed and the poet moves about like an automation. The themes of fright and death predominate in Cavalcanti.

Cavalcanti incorporated into his poetic language a term from scholastic philosophy, "spirit" (*spirito* or *spiritello*), to indicate the various movements of the heart and the human faculties. The spirits become poetic personages by which Cavalcanti dramatically represents the psychology of the lover. The technique of personified spirits was adopted by Dante and other poets of the *dolce stil nuovo.*

Further Reading

There is no full-length biography of Cavalcanti. Ernest Hatch Wilkins, *A History of Italian Literature* (1954), deals with his life and work, and Domenico Vittorini, *The Age of Dante* (1957), contains numerous references to his influence on Italian poetry and his relationship to Dante. For both political and literary background of the period see John Addington Symonds, *Renaissance in Italy* (2 vols., 1935). □

Pietro Francesco Cavalli

The Italian composer Pietro Francesco Cavalli (1602-1676), the most outstanding figure in Venetian opera of his day, ushered in the style known as bel canto.

In *bel canto,* melody is typified by smooth-flowing, sensuous lines, sequential patterns, a slowish tempo, and predominantly triple meter; harmony is unobtrusive, with occasional flashes of chromaticism; and an overall unity prevails, underlined by the character of the bass, which tends to that of the melody, with the former often imitating the latter or arranged in the form of an ostinato. The importance of melody results in few ensembles, choruses, or purely instrumental numbers; even the recitatives are lyrical and arioso-like compared with the rapid patter of *secco* recitative favored in later baroque opera. Following in Claudio Monteverdi's footsteps, Pietro Francesco Cavalli fused music and drama, with musical and dramatic climaxes coinciding, whereas in most later baroque operas the emotional peaks were largely determined by the composer, not the librettist.

Cavalli was born in Crema on Feb. 14, 1602, the son of Gian Battista Caletti-Bruni, director of the cathedral choir. In his early teens he enjoyed the patronage of a Venetian nobleman, Federigo Cavalli, who took him to Venice in 1616. Later, in recognition of his patron's kindness and in accordance with a common practice of the time, he adopted the nobleman's name. In 1617 Cavalli joined the choir of St. Mark's Cathedral, Venice, under Monteverdi, whose pupil he became. Cavalli remained at St. Mark's for the rest of his life, becoming second organist in 1640, first organist in 1665, and *maestro di cappella* in 1668. He died in Venice on Jan. 14, 1676.

No music by Cavalli is known before his first opera, *Le nozze di Teti e di Peleo* (1639), produced when he was 37 years old. During the next 30 years he wrote 42 operas, of which 28 have survived, the last being *Coriolano* (1669). All but four of these were first performed in Venice, although many of them were revived elsewhere, notably *L'Egisto* (1643), *Giasone* (1649), *Il Ciro* (1654), and *L'Erismena* (1655).

Cavalli's reputation was not confined to Italy, for as early as 1646 *L'Egisto* was performed in Paris, and in 1660 he was invited there for the wedding of Louis XIV, where he produced his *Serse* (first performed in Venice in 1654), with Jean Baptiste Lully providing the ballet music that was an indispensable part of any opera in France. Two years later Cavalli visited Paris again to supervise the performance of his opera *Ercole amante,* originally written for Louis XIV's wedding but not staged for that event; again Lully wrote the ballet music.

During his last 8 years Cavalli wrote no operas, only a Vespers for eight voices (1675), though it is likely that a Requiem, also for eight voices, and sung at his funeral, was composed about this time.

Further Reading

Information about Cavalli is available in Manfred F. Bukofzer, *Music in the Baroque Era, from Monteverdi to Bach* (1947); Donald J. Grout, *A Short History of Opera* (1947; 2d ed. 1965); and Simon T. Worsthorne, *Venetian Opera in the Seventeenth Century* (1954). □

Henry Cavendish

The English physicist and chemist Henry Cavendish (1731-1810) determined the value of the universal constant of gravitation, made noteworthy electrical studies, and is credited with the discovery of hydrogen and the composition of water.

Henry Cavendish was born on Oct. 10, 1731, the elder son of Lord Charles Cavendish and Lady Anne Grey. He entered Peterhouse, Cambridge, in 1749 and left after 2 years without taking a degree. He never married and was so reserved that there is little record of his having any social life except occasional meetings with scientific friends. His death (Feb. 24, 1810) he faced with the same equanimity with which he faced the unavoidable breaking of apparatus in the course of increasing knowledge. He was buried in All Saints Church, Derby.

Cavendish's work and reputation have to be considered in two parts: the one relating to his published work, the other to the large amount he did not publish. During his lifetime he made notable discoveries in chemistry mainly between 1766 and 1788 and in electricity between 1771 and 1788. In 1798 he published a single notable paper on the density of the earth, but interest in this subject was evidently of long standing.

Contributions to Chemistry

At the time Cavendish began his chemical work, chemists were just beginning to recognize that the "airs" which were evolved in many chemical reactions were distinct entities and not just modifications of ordinary air. Cavendish reported his own work in *Three Papers Containing Experiments on Factitious Air* in 1766. These papers added greatly to knowledge of the formation of "inflammable air" (hydrogen) by the action of dilute acids on metals. Cavendish also distinguished the formation of oxides of nitrogen from nitric acid. Their true chemical character was not yet known, but Cavendish's description of his observations had almost the same logical pattern as if he were thinking in modern terms, the principal difference being that he used the terminology of the phlogiston theory (that is, a burning substance liberates into its surroundings a principle of inflammability).

Cavendish's other great merit is his experimental care and precision. He measured the density of hydrogen, and although his figure is half what it should be, it is astonishing that he even found the right order of magnitude, considering how difficult it was to manage so intractable a substance. Not that his apparatus was crude; where the techniques of his day allowed, his apparatus (like the splendid balance surviving at the Royal Institution) was capable of refined results.

Cavendish investigated the products of fermentation, showing that the gas from the fermentation of sugar is indistinguishable from the "fixed air" characterized as a constituent of chalk and magnesia by Black (both are, in modern language, carbon dioxide).

Another example of Cavendish's technical expertise was *Experiments on Rathbone-Place Water* (1767), in which he set the highest possible standard of thoroughness and accuracy. It is a classic of analytical chemistry. In it Cavendish also examined the phenomenon of the retention of "calcareous earth" (chalk, calcium carbonate) in solution, and in doing so he discovered the reversible reaction between calcium carbonate and carbon dioxide to form calcium bicarbonate, the cause of temporary hardness of water. He also found out how to soften such water by adding lime (calcium hydroxide).

In his study of the methods of gas analysis Cavendish made one remarkable observation. He was sparking air with excess oxygen (to form oxides of nitrogen) over alkali until no more absorption took place and noted that a tiny amount of gas could not be further reduced, "so that if there is any part of the phlogisticated air of our atmosphere which differs from the rest, and cannot be reduced to nitrous acid, we may safely conclude, that it is not more than 1/120 part of the whole." As is now known, he had observed the noble gases of the atmosphere.

One of Cavendish's researches on the currently engrossing problem of combustion made an outstanding contribution to fundamental theory. Without seeking particularly to do so, in 1784 Cavendish determined the composition of water, showing that it was a compound of oxygen and hydrogen ("dephlogisticated air" and "inflammable air"). Joseph Priestley had reported an experiment of Warltire in which the explosion of the two gases had left a dew on the sides of a previously dry vessel. Cavendish studied this, prepared water in measurable quantity, and got an approximately correct figure for its volume composition.

Electrical Researches

Cavendish published only a fraction of the experimental evidence he had available to support his theories, but his contemporaries were convinced of the correctness of his conclusions. He was not the first to profound an inverse-square law of electrostatic attraction, but Cavendish's exposition, based in part on mathematical reasoning, was the most effective. He founded the study of the properties of dielectrics and also distinguished clearly between quantity of electricity and what is now called potential.

Cavendish had the ability to make an apparently limited study yield far-reaching results. An example is his study of the origin of the ability of some fish to give an electric shock. He made up imitation fish of leather and wood, soaked in salt water, with pewter attachments representing the organs of the fish which produced the effect. By using Leyden jars to charge the imitation organs, he was able to show that the results were entirely consistent with the fish's being able to produce electricity. This investigation was among the earliest in which the conductivity of aqueous solutions was studied.

Cavendish began to study heat with his father, then returned to the subject in 1773-1776 with a study of the Royal Society's meteorological instruments, in the course of which he worked out the most important corrections to be employed in accurate thermometry. In 1783 he published a study of the means of determining the freezing point of mercury. In it he added a good deal to the general theory of fusion and freezing and the latent heat changes accompanying them.

Cavendish's most elaborate (and celebrated) investigation was that on the density of the earth. He took part in a program to measure the length of a seconds pendulum in the vicinity of a large mountain (Schiehallion). Variations from the period on the plain would show the attraction exerted by the mountain, from which the density of its substance could be calculated. Cavendish also approached the subject in a more fundamental way by determining the force of attraction of a very large, heavy lead ball for a very small, light ball. The ratio between this force and the weight of the light ball would furnish the mass of the earth. His results were unquestioned and unsurpassed for nearly a century.

Unpublished Works

Had Cavendish published all his work, his great influence would undoubtedly have been greater, but in fact he left in manuscript form a vast amount which often anticipated that of his successors. It came to light only bit by bit until the thorough study undertaken by Maxwell (published in 1878) and by Thorpe (published in 1921). In these notes is to be found such material as the detail of his experiments to examine the law of electrostatic force, the conductivity of metals, and many chemical questions such as a theory of chemical equivalents. He had a theory of partial pressures before Dalton.

However, the history of science is full of instances of unpublished works which might have influenced others but in fact did not. Whatever he did not reveal, Cavendish gave his colleagues enough to help them on the road to modern conceptions. Nothing he did has been rejected, and for this reason he is still, in a unique way, part of modern life.

Further Reading

The Scientific Papers of the Hon. Henry Cavendish: Edited from the Published Papers and the Cavendish Manuscripts was published in two volumes: vol. 1, *The Electrical Researches,* edited by J. Clerk Maxwell (1879), and vol. 2, *The Chemical and Dynamical Researches,* edited by Sir Edward Thorpe and others (1921). A straightforward account of Cavendish's life and work is A. J. Berry, *Henry Cavendish* (1960), which includes a useful select bibliography. George Wilson, *The Life of the Honble. Henry Cavendish* (1851), is available in many libraries. James R. Partington, *A History of Chemistry,* vol. 3 (1962), contains a very full account of Cavendish's chemical work and some discussion of his electrical work. □

Conte di Cavour

The Italian statesman Camillo Benso, Conte di Cavour (1810-1861), devoted himself to the liberation of northern Italy from Austrian domination. A brilliant and steadfast diplomat, he played a leading role in the unification of Italy.

Camillo Benso di Cavour was born on Aug. 1, 1810, at Turin. As a younger son in a noble family, he was trained to be an officer in the army. But moved by a restless dissatisfaction with Italian social and political conditions, he resigned his commission in 1831, when he was only 21 years old. He applied himself to the agricultural improvement of his family estate. Then, widening his sphere of activity, he founded the Piedmontese Agricultural Society and became one of the chief promoters of railroads and steamships in Italy. The liberal Cavour grew ever more distrustful of the reactionary politics in force throughout Europe, particularly their manifestation in the repressive rule of Austria over a large area of Italy.

The Journalist

Cavour believed that liberalism and love of country could be combined to cause a revolt against Austrian dominion in the north and then to establish an Italian constitutional monarchy. To spread his views, in 1847 at Turin he established the newspaper *Il Risorgimento* (the resurgence—the name given to the Italian movement for unification and freedom).

In January 1848 revolution did break out, but in Sicily, against the ancient and decadent Bourbon regime, rather than in the north. Cavour, however, saw this as an opportunity to press in public speeches and in *Il Risorgimento* for a constitution for the Piedmont. Charles Albert, King of the Piedmont, yielded to this pressure and on February 8 granted a charter of liberties to his kingdom. Within 6 weeks of this memorable day Cavour's principal hope was realized when the Milanese rose against the Austrians. He then threw all his journalistic power into persuading the King to enter the war. Cavour, more than anyone else, was responsible for Piedmont's March 25 declaration of war on Austria.

Elections were held during the hostilities, and Cavour became a member of Parliament, beginning a career of public service that would end only with his death. On March 23, 1849, almost exactly a year after the war had begun, the Piedmontese were decisively defeated. King Charles Albert abdicated in favor of his son Victor Emmanuel II, who had no recourse but to make a loser's peace with Austria. Although the effort to throw off the foreign yoke had failed, Cavour did not slacken his efforts to achieve Italian independence.

Diplomatic Activity

By 1851 Cavour was serving as minister of agriculture, industry, commerce, and finance. On November 4 he became prime minister. He brooded over the Austrian repression of Lombardy in retribution for the abortive revolt of that possession. He waited for a situation in which he could successfully oppose Austria, and his opportunity came with the Crimean War (1853-1856). This conflict allowed the Piedmontese statesman to use diplomacy on a broad international scale and thus force the Great Powers to take cognizance of Italy's plight. He decided to enter the war against Russia, and on Jan. 10, 1855, over serious objections within the Piedmontese government, a treaty with France and England was signed. A contingent of Piedmontese soldiers was sent to the Crimea, and the distinguished combat record of these troops enabled Cavour to assume a prominent position at the Congress of Paris after the war. Through his diplomatic skill at this meeting he succeeded in making the Italian question a chief topic of discussion and in making Austria appear in an unfavorable light.

Anticipating war with Austria, Cavour began strengthening the Piedmontese army and negotiating an alliance with the French emperor, Napoleon III. He agreed to cede Nice and Savoy to France in return for French help in ousting Austria from northern Italy. By 1859 the plans had been completed, and volunteers under the guidance of Cavour and Giuseppe Garibaldi were ready to spring into action throughout Italy. But Napoleon III then threw Cavour into despair by accepting a Russian proposal to convene a congress to settle the Italian question.

The Austrians, however, made the mistake of rejecting this plan and on April 23, 1859, sent an ultimatum to Piedmont. This had the effect of sealing the alliance between that state and France, and Cavour delightedly led the Piedmontese into war. When the French unexpectedly signed an armistice with Austria on July 8, Victor Emmanuel II, over the objections of Cavour, ended Piedmontese hostilities after only a partial victory. Lombardy was to be ceded to the Piedmont and Venetia to remain Austrian.

Unwilling to see such a good beginning go to waste, Cavour secretly encouraged revolutions against the petty tyrants of central Italy. He also remained in communication with Garibaldi. In May 1860, acting in the name of King Victor Emmanuel, whom Cavour had persuaded to cooperate, Garibaldi and his force of "Red Shirts" sailed to Sicily and in a few days demolished the tottering structure of the Bourbon government. When Garibaldi crossed to the mainland and took Naples, Cavour feared that the Red Shirts might complicate matters by attacking the Papal States. To avoid this action, he sent troops to annex the papal holdings. Cavour believed in a free Church but not in one whose territories cut Italy in half.

Cavour lived to see Victor Emmanuel II proclaimed king of a united Italy in 1861. But the statesman's strength was waning, and on June 6, 1861, he died. There were many problems in Italy still unsolved, but Cavour's brilliance had transformed his country from a collection of feudal principalities into a modern state.

Further Reading

The formative years of Cavour are analyzed in Arthur James Whyte, *The Early Life and Letters of Cavour, 1810-1848* (1925). Denis Mack Smith, *Cavour and Garibaldi, 1860: A Study in Political Conflict* (1954), is useful. A penetrating analysis of the major achievements of Cavour combined with primary source materials is Arthur James Whyte, *The Political Life and Letters of Cavour, 1848-1861* (1930). William de la Rive, *Reminiscences of the Life and Character of Count Cavour* (trans. 1862), is still valuable. For a more general picture of the unification see Sir J. A. R. Marriott, *The Makers of Modern Italy: Napoleon-Mussolini* (1889; rev. ed. 1937). A solid recent study of the unification is Edgar Holt, *The Making of Italy, 1815-1870* (1971). ☐

Duque de Caxias

Luiz Alves de Lima e Silva Duque de Caxias (1803-1880), was the most famous soldier in Brazilian history. He led the Brazilian army in the pacification campaigns during the regency and served as allied commander in the Paraguayan War.

Luiz Alves de Lima e Silva was born on Aug. 25, 1803, into a respected military family. He compiled a brilliant record in the military school in Rio de Janeiro, took part in the independence campaigns, fought in Uruguay in 1825 against Juan Antonio Lavalleja, and by the age of 25 had risen to the rank of major. In April 1831, following the abdication of Pedro I, Lima e Silva was called upon to organize and command the national guard to maintain order in Rio and its environs.

During the hectic regency period Lima e Silva methodically extinguished insurrections in rebelling provinces and in 1841 was named Baron of Caxias for his distinguished service. Rio Grande do Sul was still racked by the War of the Farropos, begun in 1835. Appointed president of the province and commander of imperial forces in 1842, Caxias combined lightning cavalry raids with superior infantry and artillery to force the insurgents to a peace settlement 3 years later. In 1852 Caxias led the Brazilian army at the victorious battle of Monte Caseros against Argentina's Juan Manuel de Rosas.

Caxias's military genius and sense of political moderation were highly regarded by the Conservative party. He was often called into government service—a traditional ploy of the monarchy to placate powerful military figures. In 1855 he was named minister of war, and in 1862 he became president of the council, a position he held on three separate occasions.

In 1866 Caxias was recalled to active duty to command the Brazilian army in the Paraguayan War against Francisco Solano López. Caxias replaced Argentina's Bartolomé Mitre as commander in chief of the allied armies in 1868. By the end of 1868 he dealt López's army a crushing defeat at Itá-Ibatay and proclaimed the war's end. He neglected to cut off López's escape, however, and the enemy retreated to the Chaco and continued to fight. On Jan. 12, 1869, he returned to Rio to face a Senate investigation for his conduct of the war. Absolved of all charges, Caxias was decorated, and on March 26 Pedro II raised him to the rank of duke, the only holder of that title in the history of the empire.

After the Paraguayan War perhaps only the influence of Caxias subordinated the increasingly arrogant military to civilian control. His death in Rio on May 7, 1880, unleashed the militarism which Brazil had been able to escape for over half a century. Caxias is remembered in Brazilian history as the "Pacifier" and "Patron of the Army," and his birthday is celebrated as the *Dia do soldado* (Army Day).

Further Reading

There is no study of Caxias in English. General works which discuss him include João Pandia Calogeras, *A History of Brazil* (1930; trans. 1939), and Alva Custis Wilgus, ed., *Argentina, Brazil and Chile since Independence* (1935). ☐

William Caxton

The first English printer, William Caxton (1422-1491), printed a total of about 100 different works. He also translated some 24 books, all but one of which he printed.

William Caxton said that he was born in the Weald of Kent, but his exact birthplace is unknown. In 1438 he became an apprentice to a prominent London mercer, Robert Large. Shortly after Large's death in 1441, Caxton moved to Bruges, where he worked as a merchant for 30 years. His success won him an important place in the Merchant Adventurers Company. He became governor of the English Nation, a company of English merchants, at Bruges. In 1469 he entered the service of Margaret, Duchess of Burgundy, the sister of King Edward IV of England. Margaret asked him to complete an English translation of Raoul le Fevre's history of Troy. Caxton finished his translation during 1471-1472 at Cologne, where he also learned the trade of printing.

When Caxton returned to Bruges, he and Colard Mansion set up a printing press. There the first book printed in English was made. It was Caxton's translation of Le Fevre, called *The Recuyell of the Historyes of Troye.* During his 2 years with Mansion, Caxton also printed his translation of the work of Jacobus de Cessolis, *The Game and Playe of the Chesse,* a moral treatise on government that he dedicated to the Duke of Clarence.

In 1476 Caxton returned to London, where he set up a printer's shop. Wynkyn de Worde became his foreman and, on Caxton's death in 1491, his successor. Among Caxton's early books was an edition of Chaucer's *Canterbury Tales.* He also printed Chaucer's translation of Boethius in 1479. Dissatisfied with his text of the *Tales,* he issued a second edition about 1484, when he also printed *Troilus and Criseyde.* About the same time he printed the *Confessio amantis* by John Gower. Malory's *Morte d'Arthur* was issued from his press in 1485. King Henry VII asked Caxton to translate the *Faits d'armes et de chevalrie* of Christine de Pisan, which he printed in 1489. Many of Caxton's books were religious. One of the most important of these was *The Golden Legend,* an enormous collection of legends of the saints.

As a translator, Caxton had to work with an unsettled medium, the English of his time. Recognizing that "English that is spoken in one shire varyeth from another," he sought, not always successfully, to employ "the common terms that do be daily used." Caxton and his successors among the printers did much to stabilize literary English, and especially to regularize its spelling.

Further Reading

The standard account of Caxton and his work, now somewhat outdated, is William Blades, *The Biography and Typography of William Caxton* (1877; 2d ed. 1882). There is a simplified biography by H.R. Plomer, *William Caxton* (1925). George Parker Winship, *William Caxton and His Work* (1937), provides a brief introduction. A lively essay together with a facsimile reprint of Caxton's preface to his *Eneydos* may be found in C. F. Bühler, *William Caxton and His Critics* (1960).

Additional Sources

Blake, N. F. (Norman Francis), *Caxton: England's first publisher,* New York: Barnes & Noble Books, 1976, 1975.

Childs, Edmund Lunness, *William Caxton: a portrait in a background,* New York: St. Martin's Press, 1979 1976.

Deacon, Richard, *A biography of William Caxton: the first English editor, printer, merchant, and translator,* London: Muller, 1976.

Knight, Charles, *William Caxton and Charles Knight; with an introd. by Kenneth Da,* London: Wynkyn de Worde Society, 1976.

Painter, George Duncan, *William Caxton: a biography,* New York: Putnam, 1977, 1976.

Painter, George Duncan, *William Caxton: a quincentenary biography of England's first printer,* London: Chatto & Windus, 1976.

Pearman, Naomi, *The Lincoln Caxton,* Lincoln: Lincoln Cathedral Library, 1976. □

Nicolae Ceausescu

Nicolae Ceausescu (1918-1989) was a Romanian leader whose attempts to fuse nationalism and communism resulted in such a brutal dictatorship that the Romanians overthrew his regime.

Nicolae Ceausescu was born of a peasant family on Jan. 26, 1918, in Scornicesti in the Olt country. At the age of 11 he began working in the factories of Bucharest. He participated in the social movements at the beginning of 1930s and joined the revolutionary working-class movement in 1932. The following year Ceausescu became a member of the Union of Communist Youth (UCY) and of the Romanian Communist party (RCP). He was successively secretary of Prahova and Oltenia regional committees of UCY and was a representative of the democratic youth in the Antifascist National Committee (1934).

Met Influential Communists in Prison

Between 1936 and 1938 Ceausescu was imprisoned several times for his revolutionary, patriotic, and antifascist activities. It was there that he met and became close with Gheorghe Gheorghiu-Dej, who led the Romanian Communists and took Ceausescu under his wing. Ceasescu took part in organizing the huge antiwar demonstration in Bucharest on May 1, 1939, in defense of Romania's independence against the Nazi danger. He then was elected member and secretary of the Central Committee of the UCY (1939-1940). Sentenced in absentia (1939), he was later arrested and imprisoned (1940-1944). During World War II he took an active part in the struggle to overthrow his country's fascist regime, to force Romanian withdrawal from the anti-Soviet war, and to free Romania from Hitler's domination.

After Romanian liberation from fascism, Gheorghiu-Dej helped Ceausescu again become secretary of the UCY Central Committee (1944-1945). Ceausescu then worked as secretary of the regional party committees of Dobrogea and later of Oltenia; in 1948 he was appointed general secretary. After serving as deputy minister of agriculture (1949-1950), Ceausescu joined the army staff and became deputy minister of the armed forces, holding the function of head of the Army High Political Department (1950-1954). Around this time, he married Elena Petrescu.

Used Power to Weaken Rivals

When Gheorgiu-Dej died suddenly in 1965, Ceausescu became first secretary of the RCP. Although many in the party felt Ceausescu was weak enough to be controlled, he used his new power to weaken his rivals. Subsequently, on Dec. 9, 1967, the Grand National Assembly elected him president of the State Council of the Socialist Republic of Romania, thus making him head of state.

Ceasescu's first years of authority were good for the country and people believed he was a bright ruler. When he boycotted the Soviet Union's 1968 invasion of Czechoslovakia, he won international support. However, these times belied his true nature. Armed with complete power, he began to impose his version of the ideal Communist society on the Romanians: rapid industrialization in the manner of Stalin, pursuit of Puritanism concerning individual and family life, and systemization, which included destroying churches and housing the population in concrete high-rise buildings. These actions were especially harsh in Bucharest, whose history was bulldozed to make way for Ceausescu's ideal city. In keeping with his luxurious lifestyle, Ceausescu began constructing the largest building in the world, "The People's Palace." All the while, life was crumbling for the average Romanian, many of whom had to survive without heat or electricity. In December, 1989, the Romanian people revolted, and killed both Ceausescu and his wife.

Further Reading

Galloway, George, and Bob Wylie, *Downfall: The Ceausescus and the Romanian Revolution,* Futura Publications, 1991 □

Viscount Cecil of Chelwood

The English statesman Edgar Algernon Robert Cecil, Viscount Cecil of Chelwood (1864-1958), received the Nobel Peace Prize in 1937, in large part because of his untiring efforts to establish the League of Nations and ensure its continuing success.

Robert Cecil was born in London on Sept. 14, 1864, the third son of Lord Salisbury, Disraeli's successor as leader of the Conservative party. Cecil was educated at Eton and University College, Oxford. While preparing for the bar, he served as private secretary to his father. Cecil was admitted to the Inner Temple in 1887, and until 1906, when he was elected to Parliament, he carried on a successful parliamentary law practice.

Cecil's victory in 1906 was not shared by most of his Unionist party colleagues, for they were deeply divided over protective tariffs. Cecil himself supported free trade. He also supported the state church, a concept to which he was always devoted. Defeated twice in 1910 in two different constituencies, he regained his seat in the Commons in a by-election in 1911.

In 1915 Cecil was appointed undersecretary in the Foreign Office, where he worked under the foreign secretary Sir Edward Grey and his successor Arthur Balfour. From 1916 Cecil also held Cabinet rank as minister of blockade, and in 1918 he became assistant foreign secretary, acting in Balfour's place for extended periods when the foreign secretary was ill. Cecil's smooth handling of British blockade was an outstanding contribution to the war effort. His maintenance of satisfactory relations with the United States was particularly important.

After the war Cecil turned his attention to the League of Nations. He led the British delegation to the League, and he and Gen. Smuts of South Africa were primarily responsible for drafting the League Covenant. For the next 20 years Cecil devoted much of his energy to the League and was widely recognized for his contribution to peace-keeping efforts. Although holding a position in the Cabinet in 1923 and from 1924 to 1927, he spent most of his time on League affairs.

In 1937 Cecil was awarded the Nobel Peace Prize in recognition of his dedication to the international amity and cooperation; but his hopes for the League were not fulfilled. He had been a delegate to the League's first assembly in 1920, and he was present at its dissolution in 1946. Having been raised to the peerage in 1923 as Viscount Cecil of Chelwood, he was a member of the House of Lords until his death on Nov. 24, 1958.

Further Reading

The best account of Cecil's life is his autobiography *All the Way* (1949). His earlier autobiography, *A Great Experiment* (1941), emphasizes his experience with the League of Nations. Cecil and his most important work can be examined in F. P. Walters, *A History of the League of Nations* (2 vols., 1952), and in A. J. P. Taylor, *English History, 1914-1945* (1965). □

Camilo José Cela y Trulock

The Spanish author Camilo José Cela y Trulock (born 1916) was a prose stylist of extraordinary ability. He is generally considered the major Spanish literary figure of the post-Civil War generation.

Camilo José Cela was born in Iria Flavia, Galicia, where his father's ancestors—some renowned, some of peasant stock—had lived for generations. His mother was of English ancestry. When he was 9, his family moved to Madrid, where Cela later attended a number of secondary schools run by religious orders, finally graduating with an undistinguished record. At the University of Madrid he studied, in turn, medicine, liberal arts, and law but abandoned all three fields without earning a degree.

In 1942 Cela's short novel *The Family of Pascual Duarte* exploded upon the literary scene in Spain. After the upheaval of the Civil War the Spanish novel had almost ceased to exist. Baroja, Azorin, and Pérez de Ayala had little new to say, and Unamuno and Valle Inclán had both died in 1936. *The Family of Pascual Duarte*, somewhat like Albert Camus's *The Stranger*, which appeared in the same year, presents an alienated character whom fate seems to drive to unbridled violence. The violent actions of the protagonist, which cannot be fully explained sociologically or psychologically, are generally symbolic of the hopeless chaos of post-Civil War Spain.

This novel introduced the Spanish literary manner known as *tremendismo*, a neobaroque and neopicaresque style, which concentrates on the violent and grotesque. *Tremendismo* is marked by extravagant and strident diction pointed toward the ugly, by sallies of grimly ironic humor, and by the presentation of irrational and alienated characters.

After *Rest Home* (1943), which is based on Cela's experience in a tuberculosis sanitarium, and *Las nuevas andanzas y desventuras de Lazarillo de Tormes* (1944; The New Fortunes and Misfortunes of Lazarillo de Tormes), Cela changed directions and published *The Hive* (1950), which many regard as his greatest novel. In the beehive of metropolitan Madrid more than 200 characters, all of them fearful and lonely, pursue the necessities of food and sex. The novel emphasizes the grim impersonality of human relations and the pettiness of man's existence.

Since Cela preferred not to develop sustained characters in his novels, he turned to another type of literature, the travel book. His first, *Viaje a la Alcarria* (1948; Journey in

the Alcarria), became a minor classic, and he published several others. In these books the author as wayfarer trods the roads of ancient Spanish regions such as the Alcarria, attempting to discover the heart of the Spanish land and people.

Cela also wrote short fiction with marked success. His *Apuntes carpetovetónicos* (1955) contains penetrating snapshots of provincial life. Of this type, his *El gallego y su cuadrilla* is a minor masterpiece. Cela's talents also lent themselves to novelettes, among which his best are probably *Timoteo el incomprendido* and *Café de artistas*, included in the volume *El molino de viento* (1956; The Windmill).

After 1956 Cela lived with his wife in Palma de Mallorca, where he edited the literary journal *Papeles de son Armadans* and continued to write a variety of literary works, none of them, however, novels. Cela's outstanding achievement was the cultivation of a style and manner which expressed not only his original and complex personality but also the preoccupations of modern man. After the Spanish dictator Franco died, Cela served as a delegate to the new constitutional convention. He also became somewhat known for a high lifestyle, driving at different times a Rolls Royce, a Bentley, and a Jaguar. In an interview around the time of his 80th birthday, he derided the notion of inspiration as a necessary ingredient for writers. "Picasso once said, I don't know if inspiration exists, but when it comes, it usually finds me working.' What a person has to do is sit himself down before a stack of blank papers, which is in itself terrifying. There is nothing as frightening as a stack of blank pieces of paper and the thought that I have to fill them from top to bottom, placing letters one after the other."

Further Reading

There are two studies of Cela's work in English: Robert Kirsner, *The Novels and Travels of Camilo José Cela* (1964), and David W. Foster, *Forms of the Novel in the Work of Camilo José Cela* (1967).

Among the Internet sites devoted to Cela's work is the Spanish language site maintained by La Fundación Camilo José Cela, found at www.celafund.es. The 80th birthday interview quoted above can be found at www.voyagerco.com. □

Louis Ferdinand Céline

The controversial French novelist Louis Ferdinand Destouches (1894-1961), who used the pen name Louis Ferdinand Céline, produced works marked by a black pessimism about humanity, violent diatribes, and an increasingly hysterical desperation.

Louis Ferdinand Céline was born on May 27, 1894, just outside Paris, where he spent his childhood in humble circumstances. He left school in 1905 but continued to study by himself for the *baccalauréat* (university entrance) examination while working as apprentice and office boy. In 1912 he enlisted for military service and was badly wounded and decorated during World War I. Discharged because of his injuries, Céline undertook medical studies and qualified as a doctor in 1924. Extensive travels in Europe, Africa, and North America followed until he set up his practice in a poor district of Paris in 1928.

Célinés first novel, *Voyage au bout de la nuit* (*Journey to the End of Night*), was published in 1932, when he was 38. It brought him immediate fame. Written in ungrammatical, colloquial language, including slang and obscenities, it has had a great stylistic influence on later writers, both in France and in North America. It describes the adventures, at once implausible yet convincingly portrayed, of the semiautobiographical hero, Bardamu, in the war, in the African jungle, and in America, and finally as an unsuccessful doctor in France. Above all, the novel communicates Céline's disgust and anger at what he considered the stupidity and hypocrisy of society.

It is this aspect of Céline's work which came increasingly into evidence in a second novel, *Mort à crédit* (1936; *Death on the Installment Plan*), dealing with the experiences of Céline's childhood and adolescence. A growing disillusionment and bitterness at the world around him led him to write works-shrill and hysterical pamphlets more than novels-containing incoherent political diatribes and a good deal of anti-Semitic propaganda. The paranoiac side of his personality was to dominate increasingly in the years which followed.

During the German occupation of France in World War II, Céline compromised himself politically by siding

with collaborators. After the liberation of France in 1944 he escaped with great difficulty through Germany to Denmark, but there he was imprisoned for over a year on charges of collaboration with the Nazis. In 1951 he was allowed to return to France; he spent the last 10 years of his life in a Paris suburb, still practicing medicine, impoverished and deeply embittered. During this time he wrote several other books based on his experiences during and after World War II. He now viewed life as a frightening nightmare, a world of hallucination and insanity, where hideous ugliness and death were the only true realities. Céline died on July 1, 1961.

Further Reading

There are four full studies of Céline in English: Milton Hindus, *The Crippled Giant* (1950); David Hayman, *Louis-Ferdinand Céline* (1965); and Erika Ostravsky, *Céline and His Vision* (1967) and *Voyeur Voyant: A Portrait of Louis-Ferdinand Céline* (1972).

Additional Sources

McCarthy, Patrick, *Céline,* New York: Penguin Books, 1977, 1975.

Vitoux, Frederic, *Céline: a biography,* New York, N.Y.: Paragon House, 1992. □

Benvenuto Cellini

The Italian goldsmith and sculptor Benvenuto Cellini (1500-1571) is considered the greatest goldsmith of the Italian Renaissance. He was also the author of the celebrated "Autobiography."

Given the immense pride that Benvenuto Cellini took in his talents, it is ironic that very few certain examples of his art as a sculptor exist today and that he is best known for his *Autobiography.* It is an extraordinary record of absorbing interest on many levels: a spirited and candid revelation of a complex character; a narrative of historical importance for its account of the working life of a 16th-century artist in his relations with his family, friends, enemies, and patrons; and a document of great interest for a description of the techniques of sculpture which has still not been fully investigated. Cellini stopped working on his *Autobiography* in 1558, and it was not published until 1728. It enchanted the poet Johann Wolfgang von Goethe, who wrote the first of countless translations; served as the basis for an opera by Hector Berlioz, *Benvenuto Cellini* (1837); and even stimulated the production of films for the 20th century centered on this colorful life that seems to fulfill every demand of the romantic conception of the artist.

However colorful the Cellini myth has become and however significant the response to this legend as an indication of the concept of the artist as romantic hero, the actual facts of Cellini's life remain at least as interesting as the stories. The son of an architect and musician, Benvenuto Cellini was born in Florence on Nov. 3, 1500. Trained as a goldsmith and early proficient in that craft, at 16 he had to leave Florence because of a street fight and spent some months in Siena. In 1519 he moved to Rome, the center of his activity for the next two decades, although his Roman years were frequently interrupted by journeys to Pisa, Bologna, Venice, Naples, and Florence, the city to which he always remained loyal.

In Rome, Cellini served popes Clement VII and Paul III, working chiefly on portrait medallions, coins, and jewels. By his own account Cellini was a notable fighter, and in the sack of Rome (1527) he fought against the imperial troops. An increasingly tense relationship with Paul III and a series of violent incidents led to Cellini's imprisonment in the Castel Sant'Angelo, from which he made a dramatic escape.

Works for the French King

Cellini spent the years 1540-1545 in France, serving Francis I as sculptor, decorator, and designer of architectural projects for the royal château of Fontainebleau. In 1543 he completed the famous and elaborate *Salt Cellar* from a model prepared earlier for Cardinal Ippolito d'Este. Cellini made models for a series of 12 silver statues of gods and goddesses and executed two bronze busts and silver vases (all now lost). He cast the bronze lunette of the *Nymph of Fontainebleau* (1545).

The gold *Salt Cellar* demonstrates extremely well the technical virtuosity in which Cellini delighted; the architectural relief of the *Nymph* reveals that even when he was working on a large scale as a sculptor his art was still essentially that of a goldsmith. These two examples of the few extant works by Cellini display the hallmarks of his style: intricately wrought surfaces alternating with highly polished smooth areas bounded by carefully chiseled contours. The precise and elegant effect achieved by such contrasts was enhanced by the use of graceful, elongated figures. Works of art such as these as well as Cellini's actual presence in France, along with other artists working under the enthusiastic patronage of Francis I, played an important part in forming the style of French art in the late 16th century and helped to create an international courtly style favored throughout Europe in this period.

Return to Italy

Cellini returned to Florence in 1545. For Duke Cosimo de' Medici he executed a bronze portrait of the duke, some marble statues of classical themes, and his most ambitious creation, the bronze *Perseus* in the Loggia dei Lanzi. The rigid, tense pose and biting characterization of the portrait of Cosimo were tempered in the more austere portrait of Bindo Altoviti (ca. 1550). Cellini's love of classical allusions, elaborate decorative effects, and formal elegance makes the *Perseus* appear more constrained and more stylish than the artist's tempestuous account of its casting would suggest.

These later Florentine years of the sculptor's life saw reenacted the earlier pattern of gradually increased difficulties with his patron, Duke Cosimo, and bitter conflicts with other artists, especially Baccio Bandinelli and Bartolommeo Ammanati. At the same time Cellini's admiration for Michelangelo, his constant concern for his family, and the carving of a large ivory *Crucifix* (1562) as the realization of a vision he had years before in prison reveal other facets of his many-sided character.

Cellini's *Autobiography* broke off in 1558, the year in which he took preliminary religious vows, but these were never carried further. In 1565 he began work on his treatises on the goldsmith's art and on sculpture; they were published in 1568. He died in Florence on Feb. 13, 1571.

Cellini lived during a period of religious, political, social, and military strife and tension. This stormy atmosphere is nowhere more vividly described than in Cellini's *Autobiography* and nowhere more apparent than in the evidence of his own life with its sharp contrasts of egoism and religious faith, worldly ambition and filial devotion, and spirited pride in his own talents and genuine humility in his admiration for the greater genius he saw in the work of Michelangelo and the ancients.

Further Reading

C.R. Ashbee translated *The Treatise of Benvenuto Cellini on Goldsmithing and Sculpture* (1888; repr. 1967). *The Life of Benvenuto Cellini Written by Himself,* edited by John Pope-Hennessy (1949), is the most useful recent edition of the basic translation by J. A. Symonds. The major work, in French, upon which less important studies have been based, is Eugène Plon, *Benvenuto Cellini* (1883). A brief but important critical summary is in volume 2 of John Pope-Hennessy, *Italian High Renaissance and Baroque Sculpture* (1963).

Additional Sources

Cellini, Benvenuto, *The autobiography of Benvenuto Cellini,* New York: Modern Library, 1985.

Cellini, New York: Abbeville Press, 1985. □

Anders Celsius

Anders Celcius (1701–1744) was an astronomer who invented the celcius temperature scale the most widely used in the world today.

Celsius is a familiar name to much of the world since it represents the most widely accepted scale of temperature. It is ironic that its inventor, Anders Celsius, the inventor of the Celsius scale, was primarily an astronomer and did not conceive of his temperature scale until shortly before his death.

The son of an astronomy professor and grandson of a mathematician, Celsius chose a life within academia. He studied at the University of Uppsala where his father taught, and in 1730 he, too, was given a professorship there. His earliest research concerned the aurora borealis (northern lights), and he was the first to suggest a connection between these lights and changes in the earth's magnetic field.

Celsius traveled for several years, including an expedition into Lapland with French astronomer Pierre-Louis Maupertuis (1698-1759) to measure a degree of longitude. Upon his return he was appointed steward to Uppsala's new observatory. He began a series of observations using colored glass plates to record the magnitude of certain stars. This constituted the first attempt to measure the intensity of starlight with a tool other than the human eye.

The work for which Celsius is best known is his creation of a hundred-point scale for temperature, although he was not the first to have done so since several hundred-point scales existed at that time. Celsius' unique and lasting contribution was the modification of assigning the freezing and boiling points of water as the constant temperatures at either end of the scale. When the Celsius scale debuted in 1747 it was the reverse of today's scale, with zero degrees being the boiling point of water and one hundred degrees being the freezing point. A year later the two constants were exchanged, creating the temperature scale we use today. Celsius originally called his scale centigrade (from the Latin for "hundred steps"), and for years it was simply referred to as the Swedish thermometer . In 1948 most of the world adopted the hundred-point scale, calling it the Celsius scale. □

Aulus Cornelius Celsus

Aulus Cornelius Celsus (ca. 25 B.C.-A.D. 45) was the Roman author of the first systematic treatise on medicine. It is the most important historical source for present-day knowledge of Alexandrian and Roman medicine.

Of Celsus the man little is known. It is surmised that he was born at Narbonne in the south of France. He was active during the time of the emperor Tiberius (reigned A.D. 14-37) and, judging by his style, may have been writing as late as the early years of Claudius (reigned A.D. 41-54). There is great dispute as to whether he was even a physician.

W. G. Spencer, the most recent translator of his works, supports an older, minority view that the details of medical procedure, the experienced judgment shown in the selection of treatment, and the not infrequent use of the first person reveal an author with an intimate acquaintance of clinical medicine who must have been himself a practitioner. The majority opinion holds that Celsus was a compiler who, like Cato the Elder and M. Terentius Varro, wrote his work on medicine as part of a general encyclopedia. His near contemporaries Columella and Quintillian record that Celsus wrote works on philosophy, rhetoric, military strategy, jurisprudence, and agriculture as well as medicine—a group of works apparently intended, says Alexander of Padua, to constitute a whole entitled *The Arts.* Although mentioned by Pliny the Elder, Celsus is not placed among the physicians. Indeed, neither any physician of antiquity, whether writing in Latin or Greek, nor his near contemporaries Galen and Caelius Aurelianus, nor the later compilers Aetius, Oribasius, and Paul of Aegina mention him. The weight of evidence is with the majority view.

There is even uncertainty about Celsus' name. Traditionally he is called Aurelius, but Aurelius is a clan name, not a prenomen; hence Aulus, a common first name among the Cornelii, has been suggested and has manuscript support.

The fame of Celsus rests entirely upon his *De medicina,* in eight books. Because of its clarity and elegant Latinity, its author has been called the "Cicero of medicine"—not a good sobriquet since Celsus, like Livy and Suetonius, followed the older and more direct, rather than the periodic, style. *De medicina* was among the first medical books to be printed (Florence, 1478), and more than 50 editions have appeared; it was required reading in most medical schools to the present century. It is the principal historical authority for the doctrinal medical teachings of Roman antiquity. The surgical section, which even Joseph Lister studied in the 19th century, is perhaps the best part of the treatise.

Further Reading

Two excellent English translations of Celsus' *De medicina* are by Alexander Lee (2 vols., 1831-1836) and by W. G. Spencer (3 vols., 1935-1938). The former edition contains a translation of J. Rhodius's *Life,* which expresses the 17th-century view of Celsus. There are no full-length works on Celsus in English. Good discussions of him are in Sir T. Clifford Allbutt, *Greek Medicine in Rome* (1921), and in Benjamin Lee Gordon, *Medicine throughout Antiquity* (1949). See also Arturo Castiglioni, *A History of Medicine* (1927; 2d ed. 1947), which contains a chapter on Celsus; George Sarton, *Introduction to the History of Science* (2 vols., 1927); and Cecilia C. Mettler, *History of Medicine* (1947). □

Marco Vinicio Cerezo Arevalo

In 1986, Marco Vinicio Cerezo Arevalo (born 1942) was elected as the first civilian president of Guatemala following 15 years of military rule. Cerezo Arevalo's term of office lasted through 1990. The significance of these two facts, that he was a civilian president who remained in office for five years, is best understood by examing the violence and political turmoil that was part of daily life in Guatemala for over forty years.

In 1986, Marco Vinicio Cerezo Arevalo was elected as Guatemala's first civilian president in fifteen years (1986-1990). The importance of his election and subsequent five year tenure is best understood by viewing the forty years preceding his election. Guatemala had experienced constant and violent political turmoil, swinging radically to the left and just as radically to the right, from the 1940s onward.

Born in Libertad, Guatemala, in 1942, Cerezo earned an undergraduate degree at the Salesian College of Don Bosco, and then went on to earn advanced degrees in law and public administration from the University of San Carlos. Cerezo joined the Christian Democratic Party in 1964, while still a college student, and was elected to his first office in the organization in 1970. This was the start of Cerezo's political career. He is married and the father of four children.

The first signs of serious political struggle surfaced in 1944, during Cerezo's youth, when a group of students, professionals, and dissident military officers overthrew dictator Gen. Jorge Ubico. Juan Jose Arevalo was elected as civilian president in 1945.

Political unrest continued during the next few years. In 1948, after registering protests with the United Nations, the Pan-American Union, and other American countries over British ownership of British Honduras (now Belize), the Guatemalan republic closed its border to British Honduras.

During this period of civil unrest a coalition of left-wing parties saw their candidate, Col. Jacobo Arbenz, win a decisive presidential victory (1950). Despite strong opposition, Arbenz' administration moved steadily leftward (pro-Communist) in its domestic policies. In 1952, a government order forbade anti-Communist demonstrations and the communist Guatemalan Labor Party was given legal status. By the end of 1953, more than a half million acres of land had been seized from private and government ownership and distributed to landless workers.

At the Tenth Inter-American Conference in March, 1954, the United States secured approval of an anti-Communist resolution condemning the Guatemalan government. Pro-Communists controlled important peasant organizations, labor unions, and government positions. In April, the Roman Catholic archbishop of Guatemala wrote a pastoral letter to the predominantly Catholic population, appealing for an uprising against Communism. In retaliation for these anti-Communist pronouncements, Arbenz' government began a round-up of all opposition leaders. Within days, all civil rights were suspended.

A few weeks later, a group of political and military exiles led by Col. Carlos Castillo Armas and headquartered in British Honduras (Belize) invaded Guatemala. The army refused to defend the government because of political disagreements between Arbenz and key social and military leaders. The coup was successful. By the end of June, Arbenz had resigned as president, the legislature had been dissolved, important Communist leaders had been arrested, and over 600 political prisoners were freed. In November, Castillo Armas was formally installed for a five year term as president and the government party won all 66 national assembly seats in the December elections. Anti-Communist forces were once again in control of Guatemala's government.

But in July of 1957, Castillo Armas was assassinated. Although the Guatemalan Congress named Vice-President Louis A. Gonzalez Lopez as provisional president, the validity of his re-election was challenged. A three-member military junta seized control of the government and the former Minister of Public Works, Gen. Miguel Ydigoras Fuentes, who was a bitter foe of Arbenz, was named president (1958).

Political revolts wracked the Guatemalan government during the next few years. Diplomatic relations between Guatemala and Cuba were severed (1960) when each country accused the other of trying to overthrow the government. The United States became involved once the military unrest became a perceived threat to U.S. lands. (For more information about U.S. involvement and the role of the U.S. secret intelligence forces, refer to the Bay of Pigs invasion.) Several Guatemalan junior military officers, in hiding after a failed revolt, became the nucleus for a Guatemalan guerrilla movement that established close ties with Cuba.

Demonstrations preceding the 1963 elections opened the door for another military coup and Defense Minister Col. Enrique Peralta Azurdia seized power. Peralta declared a state of emergency, cancelled the elections, and began a harsh crackdown on leftist insurgents. His unconstitutional seizure of power fomented a great deal of unrest, particularly with students (of which Cerezo was one). By the end of 1965 a constituent assembly had drafted a new constitution. When Julio Cesar Mendez Montenegro of the moderate Revolutionary Party won the 1966 presidential election, Guatemala was again ruled by a civilian president.

During Montenegro's reign, right-wing counter-terrorist groups, sanctioned by the army, killed hundreds of left-wing guerrillas. In retaliation, guerrilla forces attacked Guatemala City. Following a very violent campaign, rightist candidate Gen. Carlos Arana Osorio won the 1970 election. He immediately declared a state of siege and enforced intense anti-terrorist measures. Political murders conducted by both groups continued throughout Montenegro's term and that of his successor, Gen. Kjell Laugerus Garcia (1974-78). Two devastating natural disasters, a hurricane and an earthquake, struck Guatemala between 1974 and 1976, adding to the misery of Guatemala's people.

Civil savagery and death squads marked the presidential term of Gen. Fernando Romeo Lucas Garcia (1978-82). Left-wing guerrilla groups concentrated on violent sabotage attacks, destroying government installations. Right-wing vigilante groups tortured and murdered anyone suspected of taking part in leftist activities. Students, professionals, and peasants were targeted by both extremist parties.

Only two weeks after the March 1982 election, the National Palace was surrounded by army troops. Military coup leaders accused Defense Minister Gen. Angel Anibal Guevara of winning the election through fraud. A three-man junta led by Gen. Efrain Rios Montt was installed. Shortly afterwards, two junta members resigned. Montt took over complete control as president-dictator. He cancelled both the election and the 1965 constitution, dissolved Congress, and suspended all political parties.

When guerrilla forces spurned an offer of amnesty, Montt fought them with a combination of military action and economic reforms, or, in his own words, "rifles and beans." New atrocities were committed daily by both government troops and rebellious guerrilla forces. With Guatemala's economy suffering a severe decline and military infighting steadily increasing, Montt imposed a state of siege, severely restricted civil liberties, and established his own series of special courts.

A military coup led by Defense Minister Gen. Oscar Humberto Mejia Victores (August, 1983) removed Montt from office. Cerezo of the Christian Democrat Party won the following 1985 run-off election with 68% of the presidential ballots. Cerezo's inauguration, held on January 14, 1986, marked a return to civilian government after 15 years of violent military rule.

As the new president, Cerezo faced enormous social, economic, and political problems. The nation's financial equilibrium had long rested on a combination of agricultural exports and tourism but the international demand for coffee, cotton, and sugar had not increased during the five year period preceding Cerezo's election and long-term political violence had discouraged tourism. As a result of these negative economic factors, Guatemala, on the eve of Cerezo's inauguration, suffered a badly depressed economy with an inflation rate of almost 60%, unemployment/ underemployment running close to 50%, and a foreign debt of some $2.3 billion.

These economic problems, however, paled in comparison with the generations-long social disequilibrium which had produced a badly fragmented and polarized society. As a reformer, the president would be under pressure from the far left, which advocated radical revolutionary change, and a far right military-backed conservative private sector that viewed even moderate reform as a dangerous opening to their revolutionary opponents.

Although Cerezo believed that armed confrontation should be resolved through political negotiation he found it difficult to curtail the domestic violence that had plagued Guatemala for so many years. Since 1954, more than 100,000 civilians had been killed by either left-wing or right-wing terrorists. As many as 250,000 Guatemalans had gone into exile, with some 40,000 clustered in refugee camps across the border in neighboring Mexico.

Two attempted coups launched by dissident military forces (May 1988 and May 1989) showed the fragility of Cerezo's position. Negotiations held in Madrid between the rebel leadership and representatives of Guatemala's major political parties resulted in a tentative agreement in which the rebels promised to enter the political process if the government imposed certain restrictions on the military. But the agreement could not be implemented. Even though the position of Human Rights Ombudsman was created in 1987, Cerezo's administration was heavily criticized for its reluctance in investigating and/or prosecuting human rights violations.

Cerezo's efforts at peacemaking in the Central American region met with more success than did his internal peacemaking efforts. Cerezo was able to assume the role of a disinterested broker for contending factions elsewhere on the isthmus partly because of Guatemala's strategic geographic position. His peacemaking efforts were demonstrated at various isthmian conferences (Esquipulas, Tela, San José) as well as at the Organization of American States and the United Nations.

During the last two years of his presidency, Cerezo was faced with a failing economy, protest marches, strikes, and serious allegations of financial corruption and mismanagement of support funds from other countries, especially from the United States. Other problems such as a high infant mortality rate, deficient social services, illiteracy, and a renewed increase in violence contributed to the general discontent.

Cerezo's legacy was one of an uninterrupted five-year term and the smooth transition of one elected civilian government to another, as well as significant contributions to the cause of Central American peace. After leaving office, Cerezo, like other former Guatemalan presidents, became a member of the Central American parliament.

Further Reading

A biography of Cerezo Arevalo appears in the 1989 edition of *The International Year Book and Statesmen's Who's Who.* For background information on Guatemala see Tom Barry, *Guatemala, a Country Guide* (Albuquerque: Inter-Hemispheric Education Research Center, 1989). Other sources (in Spanish) are: Secretaría de Relaciones Públicas de la Presidencia, *Guatemala en la Democracia* (Guatemala, 1989); *Prensa Libre* (Guatemala, 1985-1990); *El Gráfico* (Guatemala, 1985-1990); *El Siglo Veintiuno* (Guatemala, 1990); *La Crónica* (Guatemala, 1990). □

Miguel de Cervantes Saavedra

The Spanish author Miguel de Cervantes Saavedra (1547-1616) is the greatest novelist of the Spanish language. His masterpiece, "Don Quixote," is one of the most important and influential books in the history of the novel.

Miguel de Cervantes was born in the university city of Alcalá de Henares in the old kingdom of Toledo. His baptismal record is preserved (he was christened on Oct. 9, 1547), but his birth date is unknown. It is generally surmised, however, because of the Christian name he was given, that he was born on Michaelmas (September 29). He was the second son and the fourth of seven children of the apothecary-surgeon Rodrigo de Cervantes and his wife, Leonor de Cortinas. On his father's side he was of Andalusian extraction, and Castilian on his mother's side. Rodrigo de Cervantes was not very successful in his profession, and he traveled quite frequently. In 1552 he was imprisoned in Valladolid for debts (a familiar lot, later on, for his most famous offspring), and in 1564 he was in Seville. It is possible, however, that the family had moved to Madrid in 1561, when Philip II made it the capital of his empire.

Nothing is known of Miguel's life until 1569. In that year the humanist Juan López de Hoyos brought out a commemorative volume to mark the death of Queen Isabel de Valois in 1568. Cervantes contributed three indifferent poems to this work, and López de Hoyos wrote of him as "nuestro caro y amado discípulo" (our dear and beloved pupil). López de Hoyos was a reader and admirer of the humanist Erasmus, and a connection has been drawn between this fact and some critical attitudes about religion later shown by his beloved pupil. This is all that is known about Cervantes' education. It is reasonable, however, to conjecture that he studied in Seville with the Jesuits, since some statements in *El coloquio de los perros* (one of the *Novelas ejemplares,* 1613) would bear this out.

Cervantes was in Rome by Dec. 22, 1569, (the date of a certificate made out by his father attesting to his son's legitimate birth and Christianity). In the dedication of his *Galatea* (1585), Cervantes states that he had been chamberlain to Cardinal Giulio Acquaviva. It has therefore been surmised that he traveled to Italy in 1569 in the cardinal's retinue, when Acquaviva returned to Italy from Spain, where he had been papal legate.

Military Career

In 1570 Cervantes joined the company of Diego de Urbina in the Spanish forces at Naples. As a soldier, he participated in the great naval victory of Lepanto (Oct. 7, 1571), in which the armada commanded by John of Austria destroyed the Turkish fleet. Cervantes was aboard the *Marquesa* in the thick of the battle, and in spite of being ill he obtained permission to fight in the most dangerous spot. He was wounded three times, twice in the chest and once in the left hand; the last wound maimed his hand for life. With justifiable pride Cervantes often mentioned this momentous victory in his works.

The triumphant fleet returned to Messina, and there Cervantes convalesced. He saw action again in 1572, this time in the company of Don Lope de Figueroa (famous in Spanish literature as one of the protagonists of Calderón's *El alcalde de Zalamea.* With his younger brother Rodrigo he participated in a naval battle off Navarino (October 1572). In early 1573 he was on garrison duty in Naples, but later that year, again under the command of John of Austria, he took part in the capture of Tunis (October 8-10). Tunis was shortly after recaptured by the Turks, and Cervantes participated in the unsuccessful expedition of relief in autumn 1574. That November he was on garrison duty in Palermo. By this time he felt ready for a promotion to captain, and in order to negotiate in the Madrid court he got letters of recommendation from John of Austria and the Duke of Sessa, one of his generals, and obtained leave to sail back to Spain. With his brother Rodrigo he sailed from Naples on the Sol in September 1575.

Five Years of Captivity

On September 26 the *Sol* was assailed by three Turkish galleys, in a place that has traditionally been identified as off the coast near Marseilles but which was more likely off the Costa Brava in Catalonia. The ship was captured with its crew and passengers, who were taken as captives to Algiers. Cervantes lived in slavery for 5 years; he was closely watched since his letters of recommendation suggested that he was a high-ranking person. In captivity he demonstrated an unbreakable will and exemplary courage, and he led an abortive escape attempt in 1576. In 1577 some priests of the Order of Mercy arrived in Algiers with 300 escudos sent by his family for his ransom, but this sum proved insufficient. Cervantes suggested that the money be used to rescue his brother, as was done on Aug. 24, 1577.

A month later Cervantes once more led a group in an attempt to escape but again met with no success. He remained undaunted by punishments and threats, and the captives looked to him for inspiration. While in captivity Cervantes reached near-legendary stature, as is attested by the narrative of his exploits written by Fray Diego de Haedo, Archbishop of Palermo. By 1579-1580 his family had raised a new sum of money for his ransom, and they entrusted it to two Trinitarian monks. The sum fell short of the 500 escudos demanded by his master, the viceroy of Algiers, Hassan Pasha, but Christian merchants in that city supplied the difference. On Sept. 19, 1580, Cervantes was rescued on board the ship that was to take him to Constantinople, his master's new destination. On October 10, before leaving Algiers, Cervantes wrote his *Información,* which described his conduct while in captivity. He sailed for Spain at the end of that month, and on December 18 in Madrid, he signed a statement about his release. He had proved himself to be a true Christian soldier, equally heroic in battle and in captivity.

Early Works

In 1581 Cervantes was in Portugal, which had been annexed to Spain the year before. On May 21, 1581, in Tomar, he was advanced 50 ducats to accomplish a royal mission to Oran. This he did, but the royal service, whatever its nature, was not very rewarding. In an autograph letter, addressed to the royal secretary and dated Madrid, Feb. 17, 1582, Cervantes tells of his misfortunes in trying to obtain a post in the Peninsula and states that he is ready to apply for some post in the Indies. He also reports some progress in the composition of the *Galatea.* This pastoral novel was to be his first published book, but it did not appear until 1585. The novel is somewhat experimental in tone; Cervantes' attachment to it is attested by the fact that on his deathbed he still promised its continuation. Furthermore, the importance of the pastoral theme in his works is undeniable.

About this same time, Cervantes turned to writing for the theater, an activity that guaranteed a certain income if the plays were successful. In the *Adjunta* to his *Viaje del Parnaso* (1614) and in the prologue to his *Ocho comedias y ocho entremeses* (1615), he tells of his dramatic successes and his eventual downfall, caused by Lope de Vega's increasing popularity. Of these early plays only two have survived, in a manuscript discovered in 1784: *Los tratos de Argel* and *La Numancia.*

On Dec. 12, 1584, Cervantes married Doña Catalina de Palacios Salazar y Vozmediano, from the wine-making town of Esquivias, in the old kingdom of Toledo. She brought him a modest dowry, and being 18 years his junior, she survived the novelist (she died in 1626). The marriage had no issue. But it was probably a year or two before his wedding that Cervantes had an affair with Ana Franca de Rojas, with whom he had a daughter, Isabel de Saavedra, who figured prominently in his later years. His daughter died in 1652, the last of his line.

Royal Service

In 1587 Cervantes was in Seville. The preparation of the Armada for its disastrous expedition against England was going on in a grand scale, and Cervantes had come to help in the enterprise. But his new post as commissary to the navy brought him only grief, shame, and discomfort. He was excommunicated by the dean and chapter of the Cathedral of Seville for requisitioning their grain in Ecija. He traveled considerably in Andalusia, but his finances went from bad to worse. On May 21, 1590, he petitioned the King for one of four vacant posts in the Indies. The petition was denied with the note, "Let him look around here for a job." As once before, he turned for financial help to the theater, and on Sept. 5, 1592, he signed a contract in Seville with the producer Rodrigo Osorio. Cervantes agreed to write six plays at 50 ducats each, but payment would be withheld if Osorio did not find each of the plays to be "one of the best ever produced in Spain." Nothing is known of the outcome of this extraordinary contract. Shortly after, Cervantes was jailed in Castro del Río, again for overzealous requisitioning. He was by now in dire financial straits, a situation considerably complicated by his unhappy handling of official accounts and by dealings with fradulent bankers. Thus he landed back in jail in September 1597 in Seville. He was released in December. In 1598 he seems to have remained in Seville, but his government employment seems to have come to an end, although the officials in Madrid summoned him twice (1599 and 1601) to clear up his accounts. The summonses were not obeyed.

"Don Quixote"

The documentation for the years from 1600 to 1603 is scanty. It is very probable that Cervantes was jailed again in Seville in 1602, once more for financial reasons. But most of his time must have been taken up by the composition of *Don Quixote.* In 1603 he was in Valladolid, where the new king, Philip III, had moved the capital. There Cervantes started negotiations for the publication of his manuscript, and the license was granted on Sept. 26, 1604. In January 1605 *Don Quixote* was published in Madrid; it was an immediate success, receiving the dubious honor of having three pirated editions appear in Lisbon in that same year. In the words of the German philosopher F. W. J. von Schelling, *Don Quixote* is "the most universal, the most profound and the most picturesque portrait of life itself."

But Cervantes did not bask in his success for long; on June 27, 1605, a Navarrese gentleman, Don Gaspar de Ezpeleta, was killed outside Cervantes' house in Valladolid. The novelist and his family were taken to jail on suspicion of murder but were soon released. The extant criminal proceedings show that Cervantes' financial difficulties were far from over.

There follows another documentary hiatus, from 1605 to 1608, when Cervantes reappears in Madrid, once again the capital of the kingdom. At this time his illegitimate daughter, Isabel de Saavedra, entangled him in a series of lawsuits having to do with financial matters. Once more Cervantes sought escape from Spain, and in 1610 he tried to go to Naples in the retinue of its newly appointed viceroy, the Count of Lemos. He was turned down, but nevertheless he displayed a lifelong affection for the Count of Lemos, to whom he dedicated five books, including the second *Quixote.*

Later Works

About this time Cervantes entered a period of extraordinary literary creativity, all the more admirable because he was close to 65 years of age. His *Novelas ejemplares* were published in Madrid in 1613. They are 12 little masterpieces, with which Cervantes created the art of shortstory writing in Spain, as he readily admitted in the prologue. Even if Cervantes had not written *Don Quixote,* the *Novelas ejemplares* would suffice to give him a prominent place in the history of fiction.

The year 1614 saw the publication in Madrid of Cervantes' burlesque poem *Viaje del Parnaso,* a lively satire of the literary life of his time. But that year also saw the publication in Tarragona of a spurious continuation of *Don Quixote,* signed with the pseudonym Alonso Fernández de Avellaneda. The identity of this author remains the greatest riddle of Spanish literature. Cervantes' rhythm of composition was unaffected by the insults Avellaneda piled on him, and in 1615 he published in Madrid his *Ocho comedias y ocho entremeses,* concrete proof of his early and lasting devotion to the theater. Some of the plays are from his early period, but he polished them for publication. He added eight one-act humorous plays (*entremeses*). Later in 1615 Cervantes published in Madrid his own second part of *Don Quixote.* The only fitting praise of the authentic second part of *Don Quixote* is to say that it is even better than the first part.

Cervantes then put all his energy into finishing *Los trabajos de Persiles y Sigismunda,* a novel of adventures along the lines of the Byzantine novel. He had probably begun it at the turn of the century; he signed the dedication to the Count of Lemos (dated Apr. 19, 1616) on his deathbed. He died 4 days later in Madrid. It was left to his widow to publish his last work, and the book appeared in Madrid in 1617. Cervantes' unmarked grave is in the Trinitarian convent of the old Calle de Cantarranas, now called Calle de Lope de Vega.

Further Reading

Luis Astrana Marin wrote an exhaustive biography of Cervantes in Spanish. In English there is no really good, up-to-date biography. The standard work is James Fitzmaurice-Kelly's outdated *Miguel de Cervantes Saavedra: A Memoir* (1913). See also A. F. Calvert, *The Life of Cervantes* (1905), and Rudolph Schevill, *Cervantes* (1919). Two interpretative studies are William J. Entwis tle, *Cervantes* (1940), and Aubrey F. G. Bell, *Cervantes* (1947). For an appreciation of Cervantes' art, Edward C. Riley, *Cervantes' Theory of the Novel* (1962), is indispensable. For the literary background see Ernest Mérimée, *A History of Spanish Literature* (trans. 1930), and Richard E. Chandler and Kessel Schwartz, *A New History of Spanish Literature* (1961). □

Carlos Manuel de Céspedes

The Cuban lawyer and revolutionary Carlos Manuel de Céspedes (1819-1874) initiated Cuba's Ten Years War of Independence against Spain in 1868, and the following year he became the first president of a provisional rebel government.

On April 18, 1819, Carlos Manuel de Céspedes was born in Bayamo, Oriente Province, the son of a wealthy landowner. In 1834 the young Céspedes went to Havana to attend secondary school and later enrolled in the University of Havana. After a short trip to Bayamo to marry his cousin, Maria del Carmen Céspedes, he traveled to Spain. There he received a bachelor of law degree from the University of Barcelona and a doctorate of law from the University of Madrid.

In Spain, Céspedes had his first taste of revolution. The Iberian nation was undergoing a period of political turmoil, and Céspedes joined the conspiratorial activities of army general D. Juan Prim against the Espartero regime. The failure of an anti-Espartero uprising in 1843 forced Céspedes to leave the country.

Céspedes returned to Cuba in 1844. Handsome, cultured, and energetic, he opened a law practice and engaged in business in Bayamo. But law soon gave way to politics. Cuba was experiencing the beginning of a strong anti-Spanish movement. Narciso López's unsuccessful filibuster expeditions against Spanish power in Cuba and his subsequent execution in 1851 had an impact on Céspedes. Arrested because of his anti-Spanish statements and banished from Bayamo, Céspedes began to organize a war for independence in Oriente Province. But his independence ideas were not shared by many of his compatriots. Some still hoped for reforms from Spain; others wanted annexation to the United States. Even those few who advocated complete independence felt that a war for independence should be carefully organized, and they cautioned against ill-prepared attempts.

Unsuccessful Revolution

But Céspedes and his group were determined to strike a blow at Spanish control of Cuba. When they learned that their conspiratorial activities had been discovered by the Spanish authorities, they were forced to act. On Oct. 10, 1868, Céspedes issued the historic *Grito de Yara* from his plantation, La Demajagua, proclaiming the independence of Cuba. He soon freed his slaves and incorporated them into his disorganized and ill-armed force and made public a manifesto explaining the causes of the revolt. The manifesto stated that the revolt was caused by Spanish arbitrary government, excessive taxation, corruption, exclusion of Cubans from government employment, and deprivation of political and religious liberty, particularly the rights of assembly and petition. It called for complete independence from Spain, for the establishment of a republic with universal suffrage, and for the indemnified emancipation of slaves.

The manifesto was followed by the organization of a provisional government with Céspedes acting as commander in chief of the army and head of the government. His almost absolute power as well as his failure to decree the immediate abolition of slavery soon caused opposition within the revolutionary ranks. Facing mounting pressure, Céspedes relinquished some of his power and called for a constitutional convention to establish a more democratic provisional government.

A constitutional convention met at Guáimaro in April 1869 with delegates from several eastern towns. A constitution was adopted which provided for a republican type of government. The legislative power was vested in a House of Representatives. Unhappy with Céspedes and fearful of concentrating too much power on the office of the president, a faction led by Camagüey's rebel chieftain, Ignacio Agramonte, obtained for the House a large degree of authority as well as control over presidential decisions. This group was also able to legalize the abolition of slavery by introducing Article 24 of the Constitution, which declared "all inhabitants of the republic to be absolutely free." Céspedes was elected president of the new republic, and Manuel Quesada was appointed commander in chief.

The war in eastern Cuba soon intensified. Céspedes decreed the destruction of cane fields and approved the revolutionary practice of urging the slaves to revolt and join the *mambises,* as the Cuban rebels were then called. Numerous skirmishes occurred, but Cuban forces were unable to obtain a decisive victory against the Spanish army. Simultaneously, Céspedes was unable to obtain United States recognition of Cuban belligerency.

For the next few years the Cubans continued to harass the Spanish forces. The war left untouched the rich western provinces and failed to cripple Spanish power in Cuba. By 1873 the *mambises* were actually retreating. With most members of the House of Representatives either dead or in hiding, Céspedes had regained almost absolute power.

Dissension in the Revolutionary Camp

Yet, despite his control, Céspedes had become alienated from most revolutionary groups. The more conservative elements resented his abolitionist stand and the destruction of cane fields. The more liberal groups disliked his attempts at absolute control. The followers of Gen. Máximo Gómez became particularly unhappy when Céspedes began interfering in military matters and ordered the removal of the able Gómez from command.

Dissension within the revolutionary ranks and personal jealousies finally led to Céspedes's removal as president. The remaining members of the House of Representatives called a meeting in October 1873 and refused to invite Céspedes. It soon became clear that the main objective of the assembly was Céspedes's removal. This was accomplished with little opposition and the president of the House, Salvador Cisneros Betancourt, was appointed new president of the republic.

For the next several months Céspedes sought refuge from Spanish forces in San Lorenzo, a farm in Oriente Province, awaiting an opportunity to leave the island. But on Feb. 27, 1874, a Spanish force surrounded the farm, killing Céspedes after a brave but futile struggle.

Further Reading

Most of the literature on Céspedes is in Spanish. Valuable information on him in English is in Philip S. Foner, *A History of Cuba and Its Relations with the United States* (2 vols., 1962-1963). □

Pietro Cesti

The Italian composer Pietro Cesti (1623-1669), also called Marc' Antonio Cesti, was the most cosmopolitan representative of the Venetian opera school in the generation following Monteverd.

Pietro Cesti is supposed to have written more than 100 operas, but only 15 have survived, and of these the ones composed for Italian audiences were heavily influenced by Pietro Francesco Cavalli. Cesti also composed a great many cantatas to both sacred and secular texts, as well as some occasional pieces. His cosmopolitanism is demonstrated in the operas he wrote while residing in Innsbruck and Vienna, which differ from the typical Venetian opera in the number of choruses, the enlarged orchestra, and the inclusion of ballets, this last showing the influence of French taste, an influence that was very powerful in Germany and Austria at that time.

Cesti was born in Arezzo on Aug. 5, 1623. He was a chorister in the Cathedral and later at the Pieve di S. Maria in his native city. He became a Minorite friar in 1637 and remained in the order until 1662.

From 1640 to 1645 Cesti studied with A. M. Abbatini and Giacomo Carissimi in Rome and then became music director at the seminary and Cathedral in Volterra until 1648. The following year saw the production of his first opera, *Orontea,* in Venice, and 2 years later his *Cesare amante;* extremely successful, they established his fame. He was in Venice, Florence (at the Medicean court), and Lucca from 1648 to 1652, when he became *maestro di cappella* to Archduke Ferdinand of Austria at Innsbruck, a position he retained until 1665. The appointment did not, however, prevent Cesti from serving as a member of the papal choir in Rome from 1659 to 1662. Three operas composed for Innsbruck are extant, of which the first, *L'Argia* (1655), was performed in honor of the conversion of Queen Christina of Sweden to Catholicism. During this period he wrote *La Dori* (1661), also extant; first produced in Florence, it was his most successful opera and is generally regarded as his masterpiece.

In 1665 Cesti moved to Vienna and in the next year became vice kapellmeister at the imperial court, a position he held until a few months before his death, when he settled in Florence, dying there on Oct. 14, 1669. In Vienna he wrote at least five operas, the most famous being *Il pomo d'oro* (1667), which demonstrates, though in an admittedly extreme form, the kind of opera favored north of the Alps. Commissioned for the wedding of Emperor Leopold I of Austria, the work is divided into 67 scenes, requires 48 characters, and necessitates 24 stage settings, some of them very elaborate. In addition there are numerous ballets and choruses (one for eight parts), and an exceptionally large orchestra is required, including trumpets, trombones, cornetts, lutes, and a regal organ, as well as the normal strings and harpsichord.

Further Reading

Information on Cesti is available in Manfred F. Bukofzer, *Music in the Baroque Era, from Monteverdi to Bach* (1947); Donald J. Grout, *A Short History of Opera* (1947; 2d ed. 1965); and Simon T. Worsthorne, *Venetian Opera in the Seventeenth Century* (1954). □

Cetshwayo

Cetshwayo (ca. 1826-1884) was the last independent Zulu king, whose reign ended in war against the British and in the collapse of Zulu unity.

Cetshwayo was a nephew of the first two Zulu kings, Shaka and Dingane. When his father, Mpande, displaced Dingane in 1840, Cetshwayo was brought into the line of immediate royal succession. But his prospects remained uncertain, for although the eldest son of Mpande's first wife, he was closely matched in age by a half brother, Mbulazi, the eldest son of Mpande's more favored second wife.

Mpande evaded choosing between the youths, but factions formed, and in 1856 they resorted to arms. Cetshwayo's Usutu faction won an overwhelming victory that was as much a triumph over Mpande as it was over Mbulazi. Thereafter, Cetshwayo was an independent power in the land although Mpande lived on until 1872 without being deposed.

A man of intelligence and considerable force of character, Cetshwayo infused a new vigor into the administration of the Zulu state and its military organization. The besetting problems of his reign arose in connection with his white neighbors. Faced by a border dispute with the Transvaal, he cultivated good relations with the British colony of Natal. In 1878 he agreed to an inquiry into the dispute by a commission of Natal officials. Though the inquiry favored Cetshwayo's claims, the British high commissioner seems to have feared that an award against the Transvaal might antagonize white opinion and so jeopardize the cause of a southern African federation, which he had been appointed to promote. He therefore withheld a decision until he had furthered preparations for war and then accompanied the boundary award with an ultimatum that Cetshwayo could not possibly accept.

Hostilities began in January 1879. Cetshwayo had no hope of success against an enemy that was better armed and could campaign without regard for plowing and harvesting seasons. In August he was defeated and exiled and Zululand was divided into 13 petty kingdoms under appointed rulers.

In 1882, when it was clear that this settlement was unworkable, Cetshwayo went to London for discussions, and in 1883 he was restored to the central portion of Zululand. By then deep divisions had opened within Zulu society. In the north he faced a dangerous rival, his cousin Zibebu, and Cetshwayo's own Usutu supporters seem to have been unwilling to accept the truncated kingdom assigned him. Within months there was bitter fighting that ended when Cetshwayo fled to the British reserve in the south of the Zulu country.

There Cetshwayo died in February 1884. The officially assigned cause was heart disease, but it is possible that he was poisoned. He was a spent force by the end, and his death cleared the way for new leadership.

Further Reading

C. T. Binns, *The Last Zulu King: The Life and Death of Cetshwayo* (1963), is an interesting and sympathetic, but somewhat inadequately researched, biography. It should be supplemented by Donald R. Morris, *The Washing of the Spears* (1965). Also useful are Edgar Harry Brookes and Colin deB. Webb, *A History of Natal* (1965), and Colin deB. Webb's "Great Britain and the Zulu People" in *African Societies in Southern Africa,* edited by Leonard Thompson (1969). □

Paul Cézanne

The French painter Paul Cézanne (1839-1906) was one of the most important figures in the development of modern painting. In particular, the evolution of cubism and abstraction was largely due to his innovations.

During the second half of the 19th century French impressionism created a dramatic break with the art of the past. In conception and appearance the style was radically new and, although it initially inspired public ridicule, it soon affected nearly every ambitious artist in western Europe. The new vision emerged during the 1870s, chiefly in the art of Claude Monet, Auguste Renoir, and Camille Pissarro. For each of these artists impressionism was an illusionistic style which differed from the tradition of Renaissance illusionism in its greater emphasis upon vibrant, natural color and on an immediate confrontation with the phenomena of the visible world.

As the style developed during the 1880s, however, it increasingly became characterized by paintings which were flat rather than illusionistic. In other words, the impressionists' insistence upon a direct application of pigment to canvas resulted in surfaces which declared themselves first of all as surfaces—and, consequently, in paintings which declared themselves first of all as paintings rather than as windows which looked out upon the natural world.

The tendency toward flatness persisted into the last years of the 19th century, its pervasiveness giving the impression that illusionistic space—fought for, won, and defended since the very beginning of the Renaissance—had finally been sacrificed by the medium of painting. Paul Cézanne worked within and finally emerged from this trend. As a painter, he matured slowly, his greatest works coming during the last 25 years of his life. During this period he scored a remarkable and heroic achievement: he restored to painting the space and volume that had seemingly been lost

to it. But he did it in a totally unprecedented way: not by return to the illusionism of the past but by the creation of a spatial illusionism that did not violate flatness.

Cézanne was born on Jan. 19, 1839, in Aix-en-Provence. His father, Philippe Auguste, was the cofounder of a banking firm which prospered throughout the artist's life, affording him financial security that was unavailable to most of his contemporaries and eventually resulting in a large inheritance. In 1852 Cézanne entered the Collège Bourbon, where he met and became friends with Émile Zola. This friendship was decisive for both men: with youthful romanticism they envisioned successful careers in the Paris art world, Cézanne as a painter and Zola as a writer. Consequently, Cézanne began to study painting and drawing at the École des Beaux-Arts in Aix in 1856. His father opposed the pursuit of an artistic career, and in 1858 he persuaded Cézanne to enter law school at the University of Aix. Although Cézanne continued his law studies for several years, he was simultaneously enrolled in the School of Design in Aix, where he remained until 1861.

In 1861 Cézanne finally convinced his father to allow him to go to Paris. He planned to join Zola there and to enroll in the École des Beaux-Arts. But his application was rejected and, although he had gained inspiration from visits to the Louvre, particularly from the study of Diego Velázquez and Caravaggio, Cézanne experienced self-doubt and returned to Aix within the year. He entered his father's banking house but continued to study at the School of Design.

The remainder of the decade was a period of flux and uncertainty for Cézanne. His attempt to work in his father's business was abortive, and he returned to Paris in 1862 and stayed for a year and a half. During this period he met Monet and Pissarro and became acquainted with the revolutionary work of Gustave Courbet and Édouard Manet. Cézanne also admired the fiery romanticism of Eugène Delacroix's paintings. But he was never entirely comfortable with Parisian life and periodically returned to Aix, where he could work in relative isolation. He retreated there, for instance, during the Franco-Prussian War (1870-1871).

Works of the 1860s

Cézanne's paintings from the 1860s are peculiar, bearing little overt resemblance to the artist's mature and more important style. The subject matter is brooding and melancholy and includes fantasies, dreams, religious images, and a general preoccupation with the macabre. His technique in these early paintings is similarly romantic, often impassioned. In the *Man in a Blue Cap* (also called *Uncle Dominique,* 1865-1866) pigments have been applied with a palette knife and the surface is everywhere dense with impasto. The same qualities characterize the weird *Washing of a Corpse* (1867-1869), which seems to picture the events in a morgue and to be a pietà as well.

A fascinating aspect of Cézanne's style in the 1860s is its sense of energy. Although the works are groping and uncertain in comparison to the artist's later expressions, they nevertheless reveal a profound depth of feeling. Each painting seems ready to explode its limits and its surface. Moreover, each seems the conception of an artist who could be either madman or genius. That Cézanne would evolve into the latter, however, can in no way be known from these examples. Nor was it known by many, if any, of his contemporaries. Although Cézanne received encouragement from Pissarro and some of the other impressionists during the 1860s and enjoyed the occasional critical backing of his friend Zola, his pictures were consistently rejected by the annual Salons and frequently inspired more ridicule than did the early efforts of other experimenters in the same generation.

Cézanne and Impressionism

In 1872 Cézanne moved to Pontoise, where he spent 2 years working very closely with Pissarro. During this period Cézanne became convinced that one must paint directly from nature, with the result that romantic and religious subjects began to disappear from his canvases. In addition, the somber, murky range of his palette began to give way to fresher, more vibrant colors.

As a direct result of his stay in Pontoise, Cézanne decided to participate in the first exhibition of the Société Anonyme des Artistes Peintres, Sculpteurs et Graveurs in 1874. This historic exhibition, which was organized by radical artists who had been persistently rejected by the official Salons, inspired the term "impressionism"—originally a derogatory expression coined by a newspaper critic. It was the first of eight similar exhibits which took place between 1874 and 1886. After 1874, however, Cézanne exhibited in only one other impressionist show, the third, which was held in 1877 and to which he submitted 16 paintings.

After 1877 Cézanne gradually withdrew from his impressionist colleagues and worked in increasing isolation at his home in southern France. This withdrawal was linked with two factors: first, the more personal direction his work began to take, a direction not basically aligned with that of the other impressionists; second, the disappointing responses which his art continued to generate among the public at large. In fact, Cézanne did not exhibit publicly for almost 20 years after the third impressionist show.

Cézanne's paintings from the 1870s clearly show the influence of impressionism. In the *House of the Hanged Man* (1873-1874) and the *Portrait of Victor Choquet* (1875-1877) he painted directly from the subject and employed the short, loaded brushstrokes which are characteristic of the style as it was forged by Monet, Renoir, and Pissarro. But Cézanne's impressionism never has the delicate look or the sensuous feel that the style has in the hands of its originators. Rather, his impressionism is strained and discomforting, as if he were trying fiercely to coalesce color, brushstroke, surface, and volume into a more tautly unified entity. In the *Portrait of Victor Choquet,* for instance, the surface is achieved in the face of an obvious struggle: to give each brushstroke parity with the brushstrokes adjacent to it, thereby calling attention to the unity and flatness of the canvas ground; and, at the same time, to present a convincing impression of the sitter's volume and substantiality. Mature impressionism tended to forsake the latter value in favor of the former; Cézanne himself spent most of the 1880s developing a pictorial language which would reconcile both, but for which there was no precedent.

Mature Work

During the 1880s Cézanne saw less and less of his friends, and several personal events affected him deeply. In 1886 he married Hortense Fiquet, a model with whom he had been living for 17 years, and his father died the same year. Probably the most significant event of this year, however, was the publication of the novel *L'Oeuvre* by his friend Zola. The hero of the story is a painter (generally acknowledged to be a composite of Cézanne and Manet) whom Zola presented as an artistic failure. Cézanne took this presentation as a critical denunciation of his own career and, bitterly hurt, he never spoke to Zola again.

Cézanne's isolation in Aix began to lessen during the 1890s. In 1895, owing largely to the urging of Pissarro, Monet, and Renoir, the dealer Ambroise Vollard showed a large number of Cézanne's paintings, and public interest in his work slowly began to develop. In 1899, 1901, and 1902 the artist sent pictures to the annual Salon des Indépendants in Paris, and in 1904 he was given an entire room at the Salon d'Automne. While painting outdoors in the fall of 1906 Cézanne was overtaken by a storm and became ill. He died in Aix on Oct. 22, 1906. At the Salon d'Automne of 1907 his achievement was honored with a large retrospective exhibition.

Cézanne's paintings from the last 2 1/2 decades of his life established new paradigms for the development of modern art. Working slowly and patiently, he transformed the restless power of his earlier years into the structuring of a pictorial language that has affected almost every radical phase of 20th-century art. This new language is apparent in many works, including the *Bay of Marseilles from L'Estaque* (1883-1885), *Mont Sainte-Victoire* (1885-1887), the *Cardplayers* (1890-1892), the *White Sugar Bowl* (1890-1894), and the *Great Bathers* (1895-1905).

Each of these works confronts the viewer with its identity as a painting; that is, the images of landscape, still life, or human figure are spread in all directions across the surface so that the surface compels attention in and of itself. The consistency of short, hatched brushstrokes helps to ensure this surface unity. Likewise, individual colors are scattered throughout a given composition, and their repetition generates a color web across the canvas ground.

But color and brushstroke serve other ends as well. Cézanne's brush stroke, for instance, is used to model individual masses and spaces as if those masses and spaces were carved out of paint itself. It is these brush strokes which the cubists employed in their analysis of form. And color, while unifying and establishing surface, also tends to generate space and volume, because, as various colors are juxtaposed, some tend to recede into space while others appear to project toward the viewer. What this means is that Cézanne achieves flatness and spatiality at the same time. By calling primary attention to the painting's flatness, however, he denies the possibility that his space or volume can be read as if it were being seen through a window. In other words, his space and volume belong exclusively to the painting medium. Cézanne's insistence on the integrity and uniqueness of painting as a medium has additionally meant that the demands of visible reality must ultimately give way when they meet the demands of the pictorial surface. This was a crucial step in the development of abstract art in the 20th century.

Further Reading

There are many important books dealing with Cézanne. Two early studies are particularly crucial: Roger Fry, *Cézanne: A Study of His Development* (1927), and Lionello Venturi, *Cézanne: Son Art—Son Oeuvre,* in French (2 vols., 1936). All recent studies have had to deal directly with these two seminal works. Two excellent monographs are John Rewald, *Paul Cézanne: A Biography* (1936; trans. 1948), and Meyer Schapiro, *Paul Cézanne* (1952). A work which probes Cézanne's psychological motivations is Jack Lindsay, *Cézanne: His Life and Art* (1969). For Cézanne's drawings see Alfred Neumeyer, *Drawings* (1958). A comprehensive view of impressionism and Cézanne's relation to the movement is John Rewald, *The History of Impressionism* (1946; rev. ed. 1961). □

Chadli Benjedid

Chadli Benjedid (born 1929) was elected president of the Algerian Republic and was a compromise can-

didate in 1979. Representing a so-called middle of the road faction, Chadli steered Algerians on a moderate path in foreign and domestic matters until he was deposed by a junta in 1991.

On April 14, 1929, Chadli Benjedid was born in Boutelda in the Annaba area. The son of a small landowner, he attended school near his home. Chadli was deeply moved by the Setif massacre of May 1945 when French police fired into crowds of Muslim Algerians. He became caught up in the rise of revolutionary nationalism in eastern Algeria, and, after fighting broke out in November 1954, he joined the FLN (National Liberation Front) and the ALN (Army of National Liberation).

His career during the war of liberation was a steady one, marked by efficiency and dedication. His competency attracted the then chief of staff Col. Houari Boumediene, who appointed Chadli to command of the Northern Military Zone in 1961. After the war Chadli was promoted to the rank of major, and at the end of 1962 he took command of Algeria's Fifth Military District. In June 1964 Chadli Benjedid was transferred to the important Second Military District headquartered in the city of Oran. Five years later Chadli achieved the rank of colonel at the age of 40.

As an indication of the esteem in which Chadli was held, he was selected to head Algeria's first mission to the Peoples' Republic of China in 1963. Chadli was also selected at that time to head the Algerian army's military tribunal. In 1965 he supported Boumediene's coup which toppled Ahmed Ben Bella from power, and when Boumediene organized the Council of the Revolution Chadli, as commander of the Second District, sat on the council with the other four regional commanders.

During the Boumediene years (1965-1978) Chadli remained a mainstay of the army supporting Boumediene's policies. When it was officially announced that President Boumediene was seriously ill, rule over Algeria was transferred to the Defense Ministry on November 22, 1978. Two influential colonels—Chadli and Abd-Allah Belhouchet, who was commander of the First District with headquarters at Blida—assumed legal control of the Algerian Republic. On December 27, 1978, Boumediene died of a rare blood disease and, according to the constitution, the powers of the executive were passed to the president of the National Assembly (ANP), Rabah Bitat, the last remaining member of the Nine Historic Chiefs of the Algerian Revolution. Bitat held the reigns of power until the FLN could convene a congress in late January 1979. The FLN, as the single party of Algeria, had a number of ideological factions, but on the last day of the congress, January 31, moderates succeeded in nominating Chadli Benjedid as the single candidate to stand for election to replace Boumediene as president. On February 9, 1979, Chadli Benjedid was elected as Algeria's third chief of state, with over 94 percent of the vote, representing moderate and army interests.

Chadli inherited a nation which was highly respected in the Third World, with a vigorous economy and a history of political stability. On the other hand, Algeria had some problems which the new chief executive spent considerable time coming to grips with. While Chadli consolidated his power by weakening the politburo by reducing its membership from 17 to nine, by weakening the position of the prime minister, and by recreating the army general staff, he remained, on the whole, committed to being accommodating, pragmatic, moderate, and outward looking. Chadli, unafraid of dealing with pressing social issues, in 1981 appointed Zhor Ounissi, an Egyptian educated writer, to be Algeria's first woman cabinet minister. As minister of social affairs, Ounissi, with Chadli's support, continually called for the passage of a liberalized personal status law for Algerian women. Chadli gave his blessing to a personal status law, but in June 1984 the ANP passed a *Code de la Famille* which was conservative and Islamic in nature. Not even the president's support could alter the rising tide of Islamic revivalism, another area Chadli had to face.

In July 1979 Chadli ordered the release of former President Ahmed Ben Bella from his long term house arrest. Ben Bella, who ruled Algeria from 1962 to 1965, was forbidden to engage in politics or grant interviews to the press. The release of Ben Bella was seen as an example of Chadli's willingness to be a leader bent on healing old wounds. In the area of education Chadli continued Boumediene's policies of Arabization, and he maintained Algeria's ties with the remainder of the Arab world in their support of the Palestinian cause. In foreign affairs, Chadli continued a policy of non-alignment and reconciliation. The Algerian government assisted the United States in obtaining the 1981 release of U.S. embassy personnel held in Teheran, Iran. Hoping to see a better era in U.S.-Algerian relations, the Chadli government found itself disappointed in rather cool receptions in Washington over a number of issues. Algeria refused to take sides in the Iran-Iraq War and tried several times to act as a mediator between the two Muslim states.

When Chadli Benjedid had been in power only a short time the strong tone of his administration reflected his background. His consolidation of power had to take into consideration trends in Algeria. Chadli had to deal with the West, but at the same time take note of the devotion of his people to Islam. When oil revenues fell due to a surplus of oil, Algeria remained a vital force within the Organization of Petroleum Exporting Countries (OPEC). Algeria, however, under Chadli had to find ways to diversify its economy. Most important of all was Chadli Benjedid's desire to maintain Algeria's position as one of the most stable and influential nations in the Third World with a strong voice in Arab and in international councils.

Benjedid's good intentions in these areas of reform met with slow progress. He was seriously hampered by a lack of bona fide presidential power. As a result Algeria was wrought by heavy rioting in 1985. Renewed fervor among Islamic fundamentalists billowed widely throughout the populace. Benjedid's sluggish implementation of desperately needed democratic principles resulted in a new outbreak of violence in 1988. The FLN government responded with the passage of a new constitution early in 1989. Islamic activists were not appeased however, and the local and provincial elections in 1990 resulted in widespread victories for the Islamic Salvation Front (FIS). In December of 1991 the FIS secured 188 Assembly seats. The reigning FLN party meanwhile, able to secure only 15 seats in the first round of elections, was toppled before the second round ever took place. A junta took power and forced Benjedid to resign. Parliament was suspended, and a Higher Council of State was instituted in its stead. The FIS was banned, and turmoil ensued.

Further Reading

Most of the works on the Chadli period in Algerian history deal extensively with the Boumediene period and slightly with the Chadli transition. David and Marina Ottaway, *Algeria: The Politics of a Socialist Revolution* (1970) and William B. Quandt, *Revolution and Political Leadership: Algeria, 1954-1968* (1969) are informative. I. William Zartman, et al., *Political Elites in Arab North Africa* (1982) offers a good view of Algerian leadership in a comparative framework. Alf Andrew Heggoy's *Historical Dictionary of Algeria* (1981) is a must for those seeking a handy reference for names, terms, and events.

Information on the government of Algeria can be accessed through the Internet on the "Arabnet Home Directory" at http://www.arab.net/algeria/govt (July 1997). □

Sir Edwin Chadwick

The English utilitarian reformer Sir Edwin Chadwick (1800-1890) sponsored legislation in the areas of public health, factory reform, and poverty relief. He was one of the founders of the modern British administrative state.

Edwin Chadwick was born at Longsight, Lancashire, on Jan. 24, 1800. Largely self-educated, he entered an attorney's office and was called to the bar. He was also a journalist and was influenced by the writings of Jeremy Bentham, the founder of English utilitarianism. Bentham in turn admired Chadwick's articles (especially those on preventive police) and took him on as his assistant.

When Bentham died in 1832, Chadwick carried on his work through membership on several royal commissions. Chadwick and the political economist Nassau Senior drafted the Poor Law Commission's report which led to the adoption of the New Poor Law of 1834. This legislation, however, was bureaucratic and harsh. It was popular with the propertied classes because poor rates dropped, but it was unpopular with the working classes since relief was not easily available.

Chadwick was also in the forefront of the movement to improve conditions of public health. He worked closely with Southwood Smith in publishing a series of reports which pointed up unsanitary conditions. In his *Report on the Sanitary Condition of the Labouring Population of Great Britain* (1842) Chadwick compiled a grim record of slum housing, unclean water, and undrained streets, all of which he concluded formed the basis of crime, disease, and immo-

rality. The Public Health Act of 1848, passed by Parliament in the wake of a threat of a cholera epidemic, fell far short of Chadwick's proposals, but a board of health was created which Chadwick headed from 1848 to 1854. Factory reform also attracted the attention of Chadwick and the Benthamite reformers. The acts of 1833 and 1847 were to a great extent a result of their work.

Chadwick was the most famous British civil servant of his time and the chief proponent of government intervention in the solution of social problems. His obsession with organization, centralization, and efficiency led a critic to charge that Chadwick planned to abolish the counties and cut up the map of England into "Benthamite rectangles." Local objections to government interference led to Chadwick's dismissal from the board of health in 1854. Although he never again held a government post, he continued to testify before royal commissions and, like Bentham before him, continued to draw up reform plans and programs until his death in 1890. He was knighted in 1889. Chadwick was a tactless man, but his passion for administrative efficiency brought the national state to a position of social responsibility.

Further Reading

The major study dealing with Chadwick and the social reforms he was associated with is Samuel Edward Finer, *The Life and Times of Sir Edwin Chadwick* (1952). Richard Albert Lewis, *Edwin Chadwick and the Public Health Movement, 1832-1854* (1952), concentrates on one of these reforms.

Additional Sources

Brundage, Anthony, *England's "Prussian minister": Edwin Chadwick and the politics of government growth, 1832-1854*, University Park: Pennsylvania State University Press, 1988. □

Sir James Chadwick

The English physicist Sir James Chadwick (1891-1974) made his most outstanding contribution to modern physics by demonstrating the existence of the neutron.

James Chadwick was born in Manchester on Oct. 20, 1891, the eldest son of John Joseph and Anne Mary Knowles Chadwick. In 1908 he enrolled at Victoria University in Manchester. Although his intention was to study mathematics, Chadwick was admitted to the physics programs and was too shy to correct the error. He graduated from the Honours School of Physics in 1911. During the next 2 years his education was continued in Ernest Rutherford's laboratory at the same university. It was there that Rutherford outlined his planetary theory of the atom. Chadwick's acquaintances in the physics department included Hans Geiger and Niels Bohr.. After Chadwick received his master's degree in 1913, he was awarded the 1851 Exhibition Scholarship, which he used to finance his studies under Geiger in the foremost German research institute, the Physikalisch-Technische Reichsanstalt in Charlottenburg near Berlin. An early result of his work there was the establishment of the first energy spectrum of beta particles. Years later, subsequent developments along these lines prompted Wolfgang Pauli to postulate the existence of the neutrino.

Discovered the Neutron

After spending the years of World War I in a civilian internment camp in Ruhleben, Chadwick returned to England and used his fellowship at Gonville and Caius College to work with Rutherford at Cambridge University's Cavendish Laboratory. In 1920 he became the first to use a direct method in determining the electric charge on the nucleus. In 1922, he became assistant director of research under Rutherford. Together they spent much of their time experimenting with the transmutation of elements, attempting to break up the nucleus of one element so that different elements could be formed.

Throughout the years of work, Chadwick and Rutherford struggled with an inconsistency. They saw that almost every element had an atomic number that was less than its atomic mass. Rutherford suggested this might be due to the existence of a particle with the mass of a proton but with a neutral charge. However, their attempts to find such a particle were in vain. But in 1932 Chadwick found the answer in the work of the Joliot-Curies, who observed that beryllium had become radioactive after being exposed to alpha particles. Chadwick showed, by using a cloud chamber filled with nitrogen, that the radiation caused the nitrogen atoms

to recoil with such energy as could be imparted only by collisions with uncharged particles having approximately the mass of protons. Chadwick had proven the existence of the neutron and received the Nobel Prize in physics in 1935.

From 1935 until 1948 Chadwick held the Lyon Jones chair of physics at the University of Liverpool. From 1943-1946, he also served as head of the British mission to the Manhattan Project and was present at the first atomic test in the New Mexico desert. He was knighted in 1945 and in 1948 was elected master of Gonville and Caius College, a post from which he retired in 1959. Three years later he retired also from the United Kingdom Atomic Energy Authority, on which he had served as part-time member from 1957. Sir James Chadwick died in Cambridge, England, on July 24, 1974.

Further Reading

Pais, Abraham, *Inward Bound,* Oxford University Press, 1986.
Rhodes, Richard, *The Making of the Bomb* Simon & Schuster, 1986. □

Marc Chagall

Marc Chagall (1887-1985), Russian painter, was one of the great masters of the School of Paris and was also acclaimed as a forerunner of surrealism.

Marc Chagall was born Moishe Shagal on July 7, 1887, in Vitebsk to a poor Jewish family. The years of his childhood, the family circle, and his native village became the main themes of his art. These first impressions lingered in his mind like primeval images and were transformed into paintings with such titles as the *Candlestick with the Burning Lights,* the *Cow and Fish Playing the Violin,* the *Man Meditating on the Scriptures,* the *Fiddler on the Roof,* and *I and My Village.* According to André Breton, with Chagall "the metaphor made its triumphant return into modern painting." And it has been said that Pablo Picasso was a triumph of the mind but Chagall was the glory of the heart.

In 1907 he moved to St. Petersburg, where he attended the school of the imperial Society for the Protection of the Arts and studied briefly with Leon Bakst. These were years of hardship and poverty for Chagall. In Bakst's studio he had his first contact with the modern movement which was sweeping Paris, and it liberated his inner resources. His pictures of this early period are lyrical evocations of his childhood.

With some help from a patron, Chagall went to Paris in 1910. The avant-garde poets Blaise Cendrars, Max Jacob, and Guillaume Apollinaire and the painters Roger de La Fresnaye, Robert Delaunay, and Amedeo Modigliani became his friends. Chagall participated in the Salon des Indépendants and the Salon d'Automne in 1912, but it was his first one-man show in Herwarth Walden's Der Sturm Gallery in Berlin which established him internationally as a leading artist.

Travels Inspired New Works

Chagall spent World War I in Russia. During the Revolution he was made a commissar for art but resigned after a clash with the suprematist painters in 1919. In 1922 left Russia for good, going to Berlin and then back to Paris. The art dealer Ambroise Vollard commissioned him to illustrate Gogol's *Dead Souls* (96 etchings) in 1923 and La Fontaine's *Fables* (100 etchings) in 1927.

A journey to Palestine and Syria in 1931 gave Chagall firsthand knowledge of the land, which he depicted in his illustrations for the Bible (1931-1939 and 1952-1956). He was the greatest interpreter of the Bible since Rembrandt, and he used biblical themes in paintings, graphic works, and stained glass (2 windows for the Cathedral in Metz, 1960 and 1962; 12 windows for the medical center in Jerusalem, 1961). Chagall started a new series of large paintings, the "Biblical Message," in 1963.

Chagall traveled extensively in France and elsewhere from 1932 to 1941, when he settled in the United States, where he remained until 1947. He designed the sets and costumes for the ballets *Aleko* (1942) and *The Firebird* (1945). Bella, his beloved wife, inspiration, and model, whom he had married in 1915, died in 1944.

In 1948, the year after Chagall returned to France, he started his series of lithographs, *Arabian Nights.* He began working in ceramics in 1950 and made his first sculptures the following year. He married again in 1952 to Valentina "Vava" Brodsky. His famous "Paris" series, a sequence of fantastic scenes set against the background of views of the city, was created between 1953 and 1956.

Honored for His Work

Chagall continued to create great artworks throughout the later years of his life. In the 1960s and 1970s, his stained glass art appeared in such buildings as the United Nations. In 1973, a museum of his works alone was opened in Nice, France. In 1977, the Louvre exhibited 62 of his paintings, an extremely rare event for a living artist. Chagall died at the age of 97 in 1985.

Further Reading

Alexander, Sidney, *Marc Chagall: A Biography* G.P. Putnam's Sons, 1978.

Chagall, Marc, *My Life* Peter Owen, 1965.

Compton, Susann*Chagall* Harry N. Abrams, 1985. □

Ernst Boris Chain

Ernst Boris Chain (1906–1979) was instrumental in the creation of penicillin, the first antibiotic drug.

Ernst Boris Chain was instrumental in the creation of penicillin, the first antibiotic drug. Although the Scottish bacteriologist Alexander Fleming discovered the *penicillium notatum* mold in 1928, it was Chain who, together with Howard Florey, isolated the breakthrough substance that has saved countless victims of infections. For their work, Chain, Florey, and Fleming were awarded the Nobel Prize in physiology or medicine in 1945.

Chain was born in Berlin on June 19, 1906 to Michael Chain and Margarete Eisner Chain. His father was a Russian immigrant who became a chemical engineer and built a successful chemical plant. The death of Michael Chain in 1919, coupled with the collapse of the post-World War I German economy, depleted the family's income so much that Margarete Chain had to open up her home as a guesthouse.

One of Chain's primary interests during his youth was music, and for a while it seemed that he would embark on a career as a concert pianist. He gave a number of recitals and for a while served as music critic for a Berlin newspaper. A cousin, whose brother-in-law had been a failed conductor, gradually convinced Chain that a career in science would be more rewarding than one in music. Although he took lessons in conducting, Chain graduated from Friedrich-Wilhelm University in 1930 with a degree in chemistry and physiology.

Chain began work at the Charite Hospital in Berlin while also conducting research at the Kaiser Wilhelm Institute for Physical Chemistry and Electrochemistry. But the increasing pressures of life in Germany, including the growing strength of the Nazi party, convinced Chain that, as a Jew, he could not expect a notable professional future in Germany. Therefore, when Hitler came to power in January 1933, Chain decided to leave. Like many others, he mistakenly believed the Nazis would soon be ousted. His mother and sister chose not to leave, and both died in concentration camps.

Chain arrived in England in April 1933, and soon acquired a position at University College Hospital Medical School. He stayed there briefly and then went to Cambridge to work under the biochemist Frederick Gowland Hopkins . Chain spent much of his time at Cambridge conducting research on enzymes. In 1935, Howard Florey became head of the Sir William Dunn School of Pathology at Oxford. Florey, an Australian-born pathologist, wanted a top-notch biochemist to help him with his research, and asked Hopkins for advice. Without hesitation, Hopkins suggested Chain.

Florey was actively engaged in research on the bacteriolytic substance lysozyme, which had been identified by Fleming in his quest to eradicate infection. Chain came across Fleming's reports on the penicillin mold and was immediately intrigued. He and Florey both saw great potential in the further investigation of penicillin. With the help of a Rockefeller Foundation grant, the two scientists assembled a research team and set to work on isolating the active ingredient in *penicillium notatum.*

Fleming, who had been unable to identify the antibacterial agent in the mold, had used the mold broth itself in his experiments to kill infections. Assisted in their research by fellow scientist Norman Heatley, Chain and Florey began their work by growing large quantities of the mold in the Oxford laboratory. Once there were adequate supplies of the mold, Chain began the tedious process of isolating the "miracle" substance. Succeeding after several months in isolating small amounts of a powder which he obtained by freeze-drying the mold broth, Chain was ready for the first practical test. His experiments with laboratory mice were successful, and it was decided that more of the substance should be produced to try on humans. To do this, the scientists needed to ferment massive quantities of mold broth; it took 125 gallons of the broth to make enough penicillin powder for one tablet. By 1941 Chain and his colleagues had finally gathered enough penicillin to conduct experiments with patients. The first two of eight patients died from complications unrelated to their infections, but the remaining six, who had been on the verge of death, were completely cured.

One potential use for penicillin was the treatment of wounded soldiers, an increasingly significant issue during the Second World War. However, for penicillin to be widely effective, the researchers needed to devise a way to mass-produce the substance. Florey and Heatley went to the United States in 1941 to enlist the aid of the government and of pharmaceutical houses. New ways were found to yield more and stronger penicillin from mold broth, and by 1943 the drug went into regular medical use for Allied troops. After the war, penicillin was made available for civilian use. The ethics of whether to make penicillin research universally available posed a particularly difficult problem for the scientific community during the war years. While some believed that the research should not be shared with the enemy, others felt that no one should be denied the benefits of penicillin. This added layers of political intrigue to the scientific pursuits of Chain and his colleagues. Even after the war, Chain experienced firsthand the results of this dilemma. As chairman of the World Health Organization in the late 1940s, Chain had gone to Czechoslovakia to supervise the operation of penicillin plants established there by the United Nations. He remained there until his work was done, even though the Communist coup occurred shortly after his arrival. When Chain applied for a visa to visit the United States in 1951, his request was denied by the State Department. Though no reason was given, many believed his stay in Czechoslovakia, however apolitical, was a major factor.

After the war, Chain tried to convince his colleagues that penicillin and other antibiotic research should be expanded, and he pushed for more state-of-the-art facilities at Oxford. Little came of his efforts, however, and when the Italian State Institute of Public Health in Rome offered him the opportunity to organize a biochemical and microbiological department along with a pilot plant, Chain decided to leave Oxford.

Under Chain's direction, the facilities at the State Institute became known internationally as a center for advanced research. While in Rome, Chain worked to develop new strains of penicillin and to find more efficient ways to produce the drug. Work done by a number of scientists, with Chain's guidance, yielded isolation of the basic penicillin molecule in 1958, and hundreds of new penicillin strains were soon synthesized.

In 1963 Chain was persuaded to return to England. The University of London had just established the Wolfson Laboratories at the Imperial College of Science and Technology, and Chain was asked to direct them. Through his hard work the Wolfson Laboratories earned a reputation as a first-rate research center.

In 1948, Chain had married Anne Beloff, a fellow biochemist, and in the following years she assisted him with his research. She had received her Ph.D. from Oxford and had worked at Harvard in the 1940s. The couple had three children.

Chain retired from Imperial College in 1973 but continued to lecture. He cautioned against allowing the then-new field of molecular biology to downplay the importance of biochemistry to medical research. He still played the piano, for which he had always found time even during his busiest research years. Over the years, Chain also became increasingly active in Jewish affairs. He served on the Board of Governors of the Weizmann Institute in Israel, and was an outspoken supporter of the importance of providing Jewish education for young Jewish children in England and abroad—all three of his children received part of their education in Israel.

In addition to the Nobel Prize, Chain received the Berzelius Medal in 1946 and was made a commander of the Legion d'Honneur in 1947. In 1954 he was awarded the Paul Ehrlich Centenary Prize. Chain was knighted by Queen Elizabeth II in 1969. Increasing ill health did not slow Chain down initially, but he finally died of heart failure on August 12, 1979.

Further Reading

Clark, Ronald, *The Life of Ernst Chain,* St. Martin's, 1985.

Curtis, Robert H., *Great Lives: Medicine,* Scribner, 1993, pp. 77–90.

Chain, Benjamin, "Penicillin and Beyond," *Nature,* October 10, 1991, pp. 492–94. □

Thomas Chalmers

The Scottish church reformer and theologian Thomas Chalmers (1780-1847) was a central figure in the 1843 secession of the Free Church from the Presbyterian Establishment.

Thomas Chalmers was born in Fife on March 17, 1780. While attending the University of St. Andrews, he was drawn both to the study of mathematics and science and to a clerical vocation. After Presbyterian ordination in 1803, he was a successful preacher and instructor. In his late 20s he became aroused to evangelical fervor; for the first time he was struck by his own incorrigible depravity, the imminence of death, and the promise of salvation through faith in Christ. This position was characteristic of the intellectually simple, scripturally bound, evangelical awakening typical of many of his generation. Chalmers, however, attempted to broaden evangelicalism by reconciling its zeal with secular ethics, science, and philosophy and with concern for social and economic issues.

In this spirit Chalmers delivered his "Astronomical Lectures" and preached to large congregations of the educated and well-to-do from his pulpit in Glasgow, where he became minister in 1816. Four years later he took a new parish in the poorest section of the city. By reviving the methods of personal visitation and private, church-directed charity, he provided relief for the poor while drastically reducing expenditure.

In 1823 Chalmers became professor of moral philosophy at St. Andrews. From 1828 to 1843 he was professor of theology at the University of Edinburgh, and during this period he wrote many of his 34 volumes of published works. But more important was his leadership of the reformers in the crisis over patronage in the Scottish Church. The issue involved the right of lay proprietors to appoint clergymen over Scottish congregations. This practice had been imposed by British law in 1712 and reinforced through the next century by the domination of "moderate" clerics in the national church.

At the annual Presbyterian General Assembly in 1832, with Chalmers as moderator, a proposal to change the patronage system failed. Finally, in May 1843, Chalmers regretfully led the famous secession of 470 ministers, who then began the Free Church of Scotland. As the first moderator, Chalmers raised substantial sums to finance the building of hundreds of new churches for the schismatics. From 1843 to 1847 he also served as principal of the Free Church's New College. Chalmers died suddenly on May 31, 1847. It is said that half the population of Edinburgh attended his funeral. Parliament later reversed the offensive act of 1712, and ultimately the Free and Established Churches were reunited.

Further Reading

Two early sources on Chalmers and the Free Church are still important: Chalmers's son-in-law William Hanna wrote *Memoirs of the Life and Writings of Thomas Chalmers* (4 vols., 1849-1852), and Robert Buchanan wrote *The Ten Years Conflict: Being the History of the Disruption of the Church of Scotland* (2 vols., 1857). The most recent study is Hugh Watt, *Thomas Chalmers and the Disruption* (1943).

Additional Sources

Brown, Stewart J. (Stewart Jay), *Thomas Chalmers and the godly commonwealth in Scotland,* Oxford Oxfordshire; New York: Oxford University Press, 1982. □

Arthur Neville Chamberlain

The English statesman Arthur Neville Chamberlain (1869-1940) was prime minister of Great Britain in the years preceding World War II. He is associated with the policy of appeasement toward Nazi Germany that culminated in the Munich Agreement of 1938.

Neville Chamberlain was born on March 18, 1869, at Edgbaston, Birmingham, the son of Joseph Chamberlain, colonial secretary from 1895 to 1903, and Florence Kenrick Chamberlain. Neville's home and family were the most influential aspects of his education and upbringing. He went to Rugby and then attended Mason College (later a part of the University of Birmingham) for 2 years to study science and engineering, but he did not distinguish himself in his studies. He then worked briefly and more successfully as an apprentice with an accounting firm.

In 1890 his father sent Neville to the island of Andros in the Bahamas to manage his 20,000-acre sisal plantation. Although the venture failed, the 7 years of comparative social isolation contributed to young Chamberlain's natural reserve and also gave him confidence in his own decisions. After returning to Birmingham, he became a leader in the city's industrial and political life.

Political Career

In 1911 Chamberlain married Annie Cole. He was elected that year to the city council of Birmingham, and in 1915 he became lord mayor of Birmingham.

Chamberlain's record led Lloyd George, the Liberal prime minister, to appoint him as the first director general of National Service in December 1916. Chamberlain was in charge of voluntary recruitment of labor in war industry, but he found himself without authority or organization to execute his duties. He lost confidence in Lloyd George and soon resigned.

In 1918, at the age of 49, Chamberlain entered national politics and was elected to Parliament. As a Conservative, he supported the coalition but would not accept a post under Lloyd George. When a Conservative administration was formed in 1922 under Bonar Law, he accepted appointment as postmaster general; his administrative talents were at once evident, and within a year he advanced rapidly to paymaster general, then to minister of health, and finally to chancellor of the Exchequer. In 1924, in the administration of Stanley Baldwin, he chose to return to the Ministry of Health for he was convinced that the government would rise or fall on its record of social reform.

Social Reformer

Indeed, Chamberlain made his reputation as a "radical Conservative" and energetic legislator during these years. His guiding principle in social legislation was that national resources should be used to help those who help themselves. His achievements included the Rating and Valuation Act of 1925, which assisted both agriculture and industry; the Widow, Orphans and Old Age Pension Act of 1925, which extended the act of 1908; the Local Government Act of 1929, which transferred care of the poor from Poor Law Unions to county agencies; and the construction of 400,000 new houses.

In 1931 Chamberlain joined the National government under Ramsay MacDonald, first as minister of health, then as chancellor of the Exchequer. In 1932, when he secured approval for a general tariff of 10 percent, he was adopting proposals urged by his father in 1903. He was responsible for the significant Unemployment Act of 1934, which reformed the system of administering relief. It was with good reason that Winston Churchill called him "the pack horse" of the administration.

Prime Minister

If his career had ended in 1937, Chamberlain might well have been recorded as the Conservative who did most for social reform between the wars. Instead, he succeeded Baldwin as prime minister in May 1937 and had to turn his attention abruptly to foreign affairs. Not that he did so with hesitation; here, as always, he faced his task with confidence. He was determined to avert a war, for which neither England nor France was prepared, through a policy of pacification involving collaboration with Hitler's Germany and Mussolini's Italy. Since he believed the League of Nations had failed, he turned to direct negotiation, seeking by compromise and appeasement to dissipate tensions that might lead to war—an approach already accepted by most Englishmen. However, his efforts with Mussolini led only to the resignation of Anthony Eden, his foreign secretary. And as for Hitler, Chamberlain accepted the Nazi takeover of Austria in March 1938 but attempted through negotiation to avert a similar fate for Czechoslovakia.

Chamberlain and Hitler conferred at Berchtesgaden and Godesberg in September and then met at Munich with Mussolini and Edouard Daladier, the French premier. The Munich Agreement was hailed enthusiastically in Britain, and it gave the nation precious time to rearm. But when the Reich absorbed Czechoslovakia in March 1939, Chamberlain realized that his policy of appeasement had failed. He announced military support for Poland and sought to include Russia in a security system. But on Sept. 1, 1939, German forces moved into Poland, and on September 3 Chamberlain broadcast to the nation that Britain was at war.

As a wartime leader, Chamberlain had no talent. The Germans invaded Scandinavia in April 1940, and the fall of Norway, despite desperate British aid, brought a division in the Commons which Chamberlain survived, though some 100 Conservatives either voted against him or abstained. On May 10 he resigned and was succeeded by Winston Churchill. Chamberlain remained as lord president of the council until illness forced him to retire in October. He died a month later on Nov. 9, 1940. His ashes are interred in Westminster Abbey.

Further Reading

There are two useful biographies of Chamberlain, Keith Feiling, *The Life of Neville Chamberlain* (1946), and Iain Macleod, *Neville Chamberlain* (1961), although neither is objective. They should be supplemented by the relevant volumes of A. J. Toynbee, ed., *Survey of International Affairs* (1920), and by A. J. P. Taylor, *English History, 1914-1945* (1965). Additional background works are Edward Hallett Carr, *The Twenty Years' Crisis, 1919-1939: An Introduction to the Study of International Relations* (1939; 2d rev. ed. 1946); W. N. Medlicott, *British Foreign Policy since Versailles, 1919-1963* (1940; 2d ed. 1968); Alfred Leslie Rowse, *Appeasement: A Study in Political Decline, 1933-1939* (1961); and Martin Gilbert and Richard Gott, *The Appeasers* (1963; 2d ed. 1967).

Additional Sources

Dilks, David, *Neville Chamberlain,* Cambridge Cambridgeshire; New York: Cambridge University Press, 1984.

Hyde, H. Montgomery (Harford Montgomery), *Neville Chamberlain,* London: Weidenfeld & Nicolson, 1976. □

Houston Stewart Chamberlain

The English-born German writer Houston Stewart Chamberlain (1855-1927) formulated the most important theory of Teutonic superiority in pre-Hitlerian German thought.

Houston Stewart Chamberlain was born in Southsea, England, on Sept. 9, 1855. He was the son of an English captain, later admiral. Two of his uncles were generals, and a third was a field marshal. Educated in England and France, he suffered from poor health throughout his life. This prevented him from entering the British military service and led him to take cures in Germany, where he became an ardent admirer of the composer Richard Wagner. In 1882 Chamberlain met Wagner at the Bayreuth Festival, and he later became a close friend of Wagner's widow.

During the 1880s Chamberlain studied natural sciences in Geneva and Vienna. He wrote a dissertation on plant structure, which was accepted by the University of Vienna in 1889, but he never sought an academic position. In 1908 Wagner's daughter Eva became Chamberlain's second wife. Thereafter he lived at Bayreuth, the "home of his soul." He became a German citizen in 1916 and died on Jan. 9, 1927.

Literary Works

Chamberlain preferred to write in German, and his major works were composed in that language. His first published books were studies of Wagner: *The Wagnerian Drama* (1892) and the biography *Richard Wagner* (1896).

Chamberlain's most significant work is *The Foundations of the Nineteenth Century* (1899), which demonstrates his thesis that the history of a people or race is determined by its racial character and abilities. He conceives of race in terms of attitudes and abilities rather than physical characteristics. In general he views abilities and attributes of personality as inherited.

Unlike Joseph Arthur Gobineau, Chamberlain applies the term "Aryan" only to a language group and doubts the existence of an elite Aryan race. Instead he views the Teutons as the superior European race. For him the Teutons include most importantly the Germanic peoples, but also the Celts and certain Slavic groups. He holds that the Jews are fundamentally alien in spirit to the Teutons and believes that they should be allowed no role in German history.

Foundations, despite its scientific underpinnings, is essentially an eloquent, even poetic, vision of the German people. The modern reader may justly criticize this work as self-contradictory and sometimes nonsensical, but it had deep meaning for the Germans of Chamberlain's day. By 1942 *Foundations* had gone through 28 editions.

During World War I Chamberlain advocated the German cause, and his pro-German, anti-English writings were published in English as *The Ravings of a Renegade* (1916). Chamberlain met the young Hitler in 1923 and wrote several articles favorable to him.

Further Reading

Because of the highly controversial nature of Chamberlain's main thesis, most of the literature on him is biased. However, an introduction by George L. Mosse in a 1968 reprint of John Lee's 1910 translation of *Foundations of the Nineteenth Century* (2 vols., 1899) is useful. See also Jacques Barzun, *Race: A Study in Superstition* (1937; rev. ed. 1965).

Additional Sources

Field, Geoffrey G., *Evangelist of race: the Germanic vision of Houston Stewart Chamberlain,* New York: Columbia University Press, 1981. □

Joseph Chamberlain

The English politician Joseph Chamberlain (1836-1914) influenced the fate of the Liberal party and then of the Conservative party. He has been described as one of Britain's first "professional" politicians.

Born in London on July 8, 1836, of a middle-class family, Joseph Chamberlain moved to Birmingham when he was 18 to join his uncle's engineering firm. He was so successful in business that he was able to retire with a large and assured income at the age of 38 and devote the rest of his life to politics. His first political position (1873-1876) was as the reforming Liberal lord mayor of Birmingham, where he promoted a "civic gospel." The city acquired new municipally owned services along with new buildings and roads, and it became a mecca for urban reformers. Chamberlain worked through a Liberal caucus, a more sophisticated form of party organization than existed anywhere else in Britain. When Chamberlain was elected to Parliament in 1876, his stated object was to do for the nation what he had already done for his local community.

Liberal Party

Chamberlain's liberalism was different in tone and in content from that of his party leaders, particularly William Gladstone. Chamberlain was a radical in sympathy, with a Unitarian religious background, and he systematically set out to attract support not only from religious dissenters but also from workingmen. His proposals for social reform, entailing increased government intervention and expenditure, were attacked by old-fashioned radicals as well as by Conservatives and moderate Liberals.

When the Liberals were returned to power in 1880, Chamberlain became president of the Board of Trade and a member of the Cabinet. However, he was never at ease personally or politically with Gladstone, his prime minister. After pressing for his unauthorized radical program in the 1885 election, Chamberlain broke with Gladstone in 1886 over the issue of home rule for Ireland. Because of Chamberlain's vigorous opposition to Gladstone's Home Rule Bill, the Liberal party split and was unable to regain office, except for one brief interlude, for 20 years.

The nature of the Liberal split was important. There had always been an internal division between Whigs and radicals, and it had seemed on more than one occasion that the party would divide into a right and a left wing. Instead, as a result of the home rule crisis, many Whigs and radicals found themselves in league against Gladstone, who represented the middle. After 1886 there was little hope for accommodation between Gladstone and Chamberlain, and Chamberlain became the effective leader of a third force, the Liberal Unionists, of which the Whig S. C. C. Hartington (later the Duke of Devonshire) was titular leader. Chamberlain's position throughout the rest of his political life was greatly strengthened by the fact that Birmingham remained loyal to him. Indeed, many of the policies which he advocated had their origins in the politics of the city.

Colonial Secretary

In 1895 Chamberlain became colonial secretary in a predominantly Conservative government led by Lord Salisbury. In his new position Chamberlain pursued forceful policies promoting imperial development. Although he was interested in the development of the tropics and in the transformation of the empire into a partnership of self-governing equals, his colonial secretaryship is associated mainly with the Boer War (1899-1902). His critics called this conflict "Chamberlain's war"; this description was a drastic oversimplification, despite Chamberlain's belief that British "existence as a great Power" was at stake. After the Peace of Vereeniging ended the war, he visited South Africa and supported measures of conciliation between South Africans of British and Boer descent. Throughout this period he was keenly interested in wider questions of foreign policy and argued for closer relations with Germany and the United States.

In May 1903 Chamberlain once again disturbed the pattern of British domestic politics by announcing his support of tariffs favoring imperial products and his abandonment of belief in free trade. His motives were mixed, but the effect of his conversion was to split the Conservatives as well as the Liberal Unionists. In September 1903 he resigned from the Cabinet and began a campaign to educate the British public. The leading Conservative free traders resigned with him, but his influence was perpetuated by the appointment of his son Austen as chancellor of the Exchequer. Chamberlain himself never held office again, and his protectionist campaign failed. The Liberals were returned to power in 1906, the year Chamberlain became 70. Immediately after the birthday celebrations in Birmingham, Chamberlain had a stroke, which prostrated him for the rest of his life. He died on July 2, 1914, a few weeks before the outbreak of World War I. It was left to his son Neville to lead Britain away from free trade in 1932.

Despite Chamberlain's switches of party alignment, his political career was more consistent than it seemed on the surface. He preferred deeds to talk and candor to equivocation. He looked for issues with extraparliamentary appeal and never lost his belief in active government.

Further Reading

There are several collections of Chamberlain's speeches, including Charles W. Boyd, ed., *Mr. Chamberlain's Speeches* (2 vols., 1914). The standard biography, *The Life of Joseph*

Chamberlain (1932-1969), consists of six volumes, the first three by James L. Garvin and the final three by Julian Amery. Two recent studies are Peter Fraser, *Joseph Chamberlain: Radicalism and Empire, 1868-1914* (1966), and Michael Hurst, *Joseph Chamberlain and Liberal Reunion: The Round Table Conference of 1887* (1967). For material on the Chamberlain family see Sir Charles Petrie, *The Chamberlain Tradition* (1938).

Additional Sources

Jay, Richard, *Joseph Chamberlain, a political study,* Oxford: Clarendon Press; New York: Oxford University Press, 1981.

Judd, Denis, *Radical Joe: a life of Joseph Chamberlain,* London: Hamilton, 1977.

Marsh, Peter T., *Joseph Chamberlain: entrepreneur in politics,* New Haven: Yale University Press, 1994.

Powell, J. Enoch (John Enoch), *Joseph Chamberlain,* London: Thames and Hudson, 1977. □

Sir Joseph Austen Chamberlain

The English statesman Sir Joseph Austen Chamberlain (1863-1937) held a number of high offices, most notably that of foreign secretary. He received the Nobel Peace Prize in 1925.

Austen Chamberlain was born in Birmingham, England, on Oct. 16, 1863. His father, Joseph Chamberlain, was the famous reforming mayor of Birmingham and a powerful figure in the Liberal and then the Conservative party. His mother, Helen, died in childbirth. Neville Chamberlain, Conservative prime minister of Great Britain from 1937 to 1940, was his younger half brother. Austen was educated at Rugby and at Trinity College, Cambridge, and then studied in France and Germany.

Given his family background, it was inevitable that Chamberlain should enter politics. But as his contemporary Lord Birkenhead put it, "Austen always played the game and always lost it." In 1892 Chamberlain was elected to the House of Commons as a Liberal Unionist. When the Tories took office under Lord Salisbury in 1895, he rose rapidly from civil lord of the Admiralty (1895-1900), to a Cabinet seat as postmaster general (1900), to the chancellorship of the Exchequer (1903-1905). He later served as secretary of state of India (1915-1917), as a member of the coalition War Cabinet under David Lloyd George (1918), and again as chancellor of the Exchequer (1919-1921).

Chamberlain's most important work was done during the postwar years. In 1921 he succeeded Bonar Law as leader of the Conservative party. That year he also accompanied Prime Minister Lloyd George to a conference with the Sinn Fein and signed the Irish Treaty. But because of his stand on the "Irish question" and because many Tories wished to dissolve the coalition with Lloyd George, he was ousted from the leadership in 1922.

A Labour victory in 1924, however, did much to heal the split in the Conservative party. When the Tories returned to power later that year Chamberlain was named foreign secretary, a post which he held until 1929. In 1925 he negotiated the Locarno Pact, a series of mutual defense and arbitration treaties among the major European powers. He was convinced that only respect for, and consultation with, Germany would win lasting peace. He also helped Germany secure a seat on the council of the League of Nations.

This was the last time Chamberlain held an important office. In the National government of 1931 he accepted the minor post of first lord of the Admiralty. He spent his last years as a backbencher, respected for his views on foreign affairs. Chamberlain died on March 16, 1937.

Further Reading

Chamberlain's own writings are autobiographical: *Down the Years* (1935), *Politics from Inside* (1936), and *Seen in Passing* (1937). The standard biography is Sir Charles Petrie, *The Life and Letters of the Rt. Hon. Sir Austen Chamberlain* (2 vols., 1939-1940). □

Wilt Chamberlain

Wilt Chamberlain (born 1936) is considered one of the world's all-time greatest professional basketball players.

Wilt Chamberlain was born in Philadelphia and was one of nine children. His father lived in a racially-mixed middle class neighborhood, and Chamberlain had a relatively pleasant childhood. At Shoemaker Junior High School, Wilt began to play on the basketball team, and he also played on the playgrounds against older players who taught him a lot about the game. He later said, "I still think you could pick up a team from the street corners of Philly that would give most colleges a real hard time." Wilt attended Overbrook High School in Philadelphia beginning in 1952. At that time he was already 6'11" tall, and had developed what he termed a "deep love for basketball."

Recruited By More Than 200 Universities

Chamberlain's high school basketball career was astounding. In three seasons he scored more than 2200 points. More than two hundred universities recruited Chamberlain, but he wanted to get away from big cities and preferred to play in the midwest. After seriously considering Dayton, Michigan, Indiana, and Kansas Universities he chose Kansas because of the recruiting by Hall of Fame coach Phog Allen.

At the University of Kansas, Chamberlain continued his brilliant play on the basketball court, scoring fifty-two points in his first varsity game. During his first varsity season he led the Jayhawks to the finals of the National Collegiate Athletic Association tournament, but they lost to North Carolina in double overtime. During his college career he averaged over thirty points per game and was twice selected to All-American teams. Following his junior year, he decided to quit college and become a professional because, he said, "The game I was forced to play at [Kansas] wasn't basketball. It was hurting my chances of ever developing into a successful professional player."

Because he did not play his final season at Kansas, Chamberlain was not eligible to join an NBA team until one more year. So he joined the Harlem Globetrotters and spent the year traveling the world and entertaining adults and youngsters alike. He still claims that his year with the Globetrotters was his most enjoyable season of basketball.

Scoring Machine

In 1959, Chamberlain joined the Philadelphia Warriors of the NBA. The great centers of the day were Clyde Lovellette, Johnny Kerr, Johnny Green, and, of course, Bill Russell of the Boston Celtics. But Chamberlain made an immediate impact on the league. He could score almost at will, and opposing teams gave up trying to stop him and instead tried only to contain him. His scoring average during the 1959-60 season of 37.9 points per game was more than eight points per game higher than anyone else had ever scored in the history of the league. He was named both rookie of the year and most valuable player, the first person to receive both awards in the same season.

For the next six seasons, Chamberlain led the league in scoring. In 1961-62 he averaged 50.4 points and scored 100 in one game. In 1962-63 he averaged 44.8 points per game. Chamberlain was simply the greatest scoring machine in the history of basketball.

Despite his scoring achievements, Chamberlain and his teammates were not winning NBA championships. The late 1950s and 1960s were dominated by the Boston Celtics and their center Bill Russell. Russell had revolutionized basketball as much with his defense as Chamberlain had with his offense, and Russell always had a great group of supporting players, including Bob Cousy, Bill Sharman, John Havlicek, and Sam Jones. Chamberlain often had strong supporting players as well, but Russell always seemed to pull out the championship. Chamberlain always took a great deal of abuse from the media and fans because of his lack of success against Russell.

Wins Championship with the 76ers

Finally, in 1967, Chamberlain reversed his fortunes. The Warriors had moved to San Francisco, and Wilt had gone with them, but he was later traded to the new Philadelphia team, the 76ers. In 1967, the 76ers had a great supporting cast, including Chet Walker, Luke Johnson, Hal Greer, Wally Jones, and Billy Cunningham. They finished the regular season with the best record in the history of the league. In the championship series, the 76ers polished off the San Francisco Warriors to win the first world title for Chamberlain.

Several years later Chamberlain was traded again, this time to the Los Angeles Lakers. The Lakers had featured numerous great players through the years, including Elgin Baylor and Jerry West, but had not won a championship since moving to Los Angeles from Minneapolis in 1960 (they *lost* in the championship series seven times between 1962 and 1970). For the last two losses, in 1969 and 1970, Chamberlain was on the team. The 1969 loss was particularly devastating, since it was to Russell and the Celtics again. In the final game, Chamberlain was injured and played very little. Russell later criticized Chamberlain for not playing, thus infuriating Chamberlain and removing the last remnants of friendship between the two men.

In 1972, however, the Lakers seemed poised to finally win a championship. They finished the year with the best regular season record in history, breaking the record set by Chamberlain and the 76ers in 1967. In addition to Chamberlain, the team now featured Happy Hairston, Gail Goodrich, Jim McMillan, Jerry West, and a strong set of reserves In the playoffs, the Lakers first defeated the Milwaukee Bucks, with Chamberlain completely outplaying the Buck center, Kareem Abdul Jabbar. In the championship series, the Lakers played the powerful New York Knickerbockers, led by Willis Reed, Dave DeBusschere, Bill Bradley, and Walt Frazier. In the fourth game of the series, Chamberlain suffered a fractured wrist. Although the Lakers led the series three games to one the series still seemed in doubt because of Chamberlain's injury. Despite understandable pain, Chamberlain played the next game with football linemen's pads on both hands. He scored twenty four points, grabbed twenty-nine rebounds, and blocked ten shots. The Lakers won the game and the series, four games to one and brought the first world championship to Los Angeles. After the final game Wilt said, "For a long time, fans of mine had to put up with people saying Wilt couldn't win the big ones. Now maybe they'll have a chance to walk in peace, like I do."

Following the 1973 season, Chamberlain left the Lakers to become the coach of the San Diego Conquistadors of the old American Basketball Association (ABA). Chamberlain left the NBA as the all-time leader in points scored (more than 30,000) and rebounds (over 22,000), and with four Most Valuable Player awards and more than forty league records. The ABA was a different sort of challenge, however; the athletes were not generally as good as in the NBA, and Chamberlain had never been a coach before. The Conquistadors were a poor team, even by ABA standards, and Chamberlain left the coaching ranks shortly thereafter for a well-deserved retirement.

Controversial Book

In recent years, Chamberlain has been involved in a wide variety of activities. He has sponsored a lot of amateur athletic groups, including volleyball teams and track clubs. He has invested wisely through the years and remains a wealthy man. He has also kept in outstanding physical condition. When he walks into a room or onto a basketball court today, he is a legendary presence.

Chamberlain gained notoriety in 1991 with the release of his second and most talked about autobiography, *A View from Above.* The book contains observations on athletes of the 90's, gun control and his 14 years in the NBA, among other topics. But it's the claim that he has slept with 20,000 women that landed him in the celebrity spotlight and in the public hotseat. Reflecting upon this claim, Chamberlain regretted the way he discussed sex in the book and became an advocate of safe sex.

Further Reading

Chamberlain, Wilt, and David Shaw, *Wilt: Just Like Any Other 7-Foot Black Millionaire Who Lives Next Door,* MacMillan, 1973.

Libby, Bill, *Goliath: The Wilt Chamberlain Story,* Dodd, 1977.

Sullivan, George, *Wilt Chamberlain* Grosset, 1971.

Ebony, April, 1972, pp. 114-121.

Esquire, May, 1988, pp. 53-56.

Life, March 13, 1970, pp. 46-50.

Look, June 10, 1958, pp. 91-94; March 1, 1960, pp. 51-57.

Sports Illustrated, October 29, 1973, p. 44-48; August 18, 1986, pp. 62-76; December 9, 1991, pp. 22-26.

Time, May 22, 1972, pp. 47-50. □

Thomas Chrowder Chamberlin

Thomas Chrowder Chamberlin (1843-1928), the leading American geologist of his time, was known primarily as a glacialist and as an outstanding contributor to theoretical geology, particularly for his "planetesimal" theory of the origin of the planets.

Thomas Chamberlin was born on Sept. 25, 1843, in Mattoon, Ill., the son of a Methodist minister. In 1866 Chamberlin received a bachelor of arts degree from Beloit College and the next year married Alma Wilson. After a year of graduate study at the University of Wisconsin he became professor of natural sciences at the State Normal School, Whitewater, Wis. (1870-1873).

Chamberlin then went to Beloit College as professor of geology and began his career as a student of earth history. The glacial deposits around Beloit revealed dramatically that the climatic conditions in past ages differed sharply from current conditions. Chamberlin followed this obvious fact into a consideration of earth climates through the known range of geological time and finally into problems of cosmic physics.

While at Beloit, Chamberlin also served as an assistant on the Wisconsin State Survey (1873-1876) and as its chief (1877-1882). The results of the comprehensive survey, published in four volumes, attracted so much favorable attention that a Division of Glacial Geology was established in the U.S. Geological Survey, with Chamberlin as head (1882-1887). For the next 5 years he was president of the University of Chicago as head of the department of geology and director of the Waller Museum, becoming professor emeritus in 1919. In 1893 he founded the *Journal of Geology* and was editor in chief until 1922. He died on Nov. 15, 1928.

His "Planetesimal" Theory

In the late 1890s Chamberlin began the series of papers which led to his "planetesimal" hypothesis. This was stated in its final form in *The Origin of the Earth* (1916). He drew upon a wide range of investigations in mathematics and astronomy and brought practically the whole field of cosmic physics to bear upon the problem. His theory grew out of efforts to test the long-standing nebular hypothesis. Chamberlin proposed that a star crossing close to the path of the sun caused a partial disruption of the sun. Materials were expelled and formed into great and small masses. Swarms of the minute particles solidified into what Chamberlin called "planetesimals." These in turn were drawn into the larger masses, which, moving in elliptical orbits, formed the planets of the solar system.

Further Reading

The only full-length study of Chamberlin is George L. Collie and Hiram D. Densmore, *Thomas C. Chamberlin and Rollin D. Salisbury: A Beloit College Partnership* (1932). For Chamberlin's life and work see Carroll Lane Fenton and Mildred Adams Fenton, *Giants of Geology* (1952; 1945 ed. entitled *The Story of the Great Geologists*). A summary of Chamberlin's survey of Wisconsin in 1876 is included in George P. Merrill, *The First Hundred Years of American Geology* (1924). □

Whittaker Chambers

In 1948 TIME magazine editor Whittaker Chambers (1901-1961) testified that in the 1930s he helped organize a Communist spy ring in the U.S. government. His accusations against State Department official Alger Hiss stunned the nation.

Jay Vivian Chambers was born April 1, 1901, in Philadelphia. He took his mother's family name Whittaker when he entered Columbia University in 1920. Young Chambers loved literature and had a gift for foreign languages, but severe family crises, his increasingly radical political opinions, and his lonely and brooding personality caused him to drop out of Columbia and to drift without purpose. In 1925 Chambers joined the Communist Party and attended open party meetings in New York City. By 1929 he was an editor of the party's official newspaper *The Daily Worker,* and in 1931 he was named editor of the *New Masses,* the party's literary journal.

In 1932 Communist Party officials ordered Chambers to leave his position and to join the party's underground branch. For the next six years Chambers was a courier in the party's spy network. Chambers carried messages and stolen documents from American Communists and gave them to his Soviet superiors for them to transmit to Moscow. In April 1938 Chambers defected from the Communist underground and went into hiding with his wife and two children. A year later he found work as a writer for TIME magazine. Chambers was a senior editor at TIME in 1948 when he disclosed his secret past to a shocked American public. In August 1948 Chambers told congressmen at hearings of the House Committee on Un-American Activities (HUAC) that in the 1930s he had helped to organize a small group of Communist Party members to infiltrate the federal government in Washington, D.C.

Chambers's testimony centered on a young government lawyer named Alger Hiss. A Harvard Law School graduate and former secretary to Supreme Court Justice Oliver Wendell Holmes, Hiss was a junior State Department official in the 1930s. But by 1945 Hiss had become a principal adviser to the secretary of state, and he played an important role in the organization of the United Nations. In 1948 Hiss was president of the prestigious Carnegie Endowment for International Peace.

Chambers testified under oath that he knew Hiss as a fellow Communist between 1934 and 1938. He spoke in detail about Hiss's habits and household and claimed that he and his wife became close friends of the Hiss family. Appearing before HUAC Hiss denied that he had ever been a Communist. With reluctance he recalled knowing Chambers under a different name in 1934 and 1935. Hiss testified that he rented his Washington apartment to Chambers for several months in 1935 and that he gave Chambers his old car, but that their casual acquaintance soon ended. Faced with conflicting testimony, HUAC could not prove that Hiss was a Communist. But its investigation and rigorous questioning by freshman Congressman Richard Nixon demonstrated Chambers's intimate knowledge of Hiss's background and disclosed serious flaws in Hiss's account of his acquaintance with Chambers.

The case took a new turn four months later on December 3, 1948, when newspapers reported Chambers's disclosure of the "pumpkin papers." The day before Chambers had taken HUAC investigators to his Maryland farm and dramatically pulled several rolls of microfilm from a hollowed-out pumpkin lying in a field. Chambers said Hiss gave him the microfilm of confidential State and Navy Department documents in early 1938. They were included in the many packages of stolen documents that Chambers said he received regularly from Hiss and other members of the Washington spy ring from 1937 until his defection. For self-protection Chambers withheld some of these materials from his Soviet superiors when he quit the underground in April 1938. Besides the microfilm (hidden in the pumpkin for just one day), the materials included four pages of Hiss's handwritten notes and 64 pages of State Department cables retyped on what experts later identified as the Hiss family typewriter. The notes and cables covered military and diplomatic events in Asia and Europe 18 months before the start of World War II.

From 1938 to 1948 Chambers hid the documents at a relative's house. But he made several attempts to expose Communist infiltration of the federal government. Chambers named Hiss and others as Communists in a 1939 interview with Assistant Secretary of State Adolph Berle and in two interviews with the Federal Bureau of Investigation in 1942 and 1945. Government authorities, however, showed little interest in Chambers's stories. Americans became worried about Communism only after the U.S.-Soviet alliance collapsed at the end of World War II. With the onset of the Cold War Chambers's accusations against Hiss suddenly became politically important.

Chambers's revelations led to Hiss's conviction and imprisonment for perjury. The first trial of Alger Hiss produced a deadlocked jury. But on January 20, 1950, a second trial jury found Hiss guilty of lying to a grand jury when he denied giving Chambers State Department documents in February and March 1938. Defense attorneys at each trial contrasted Hiss's impeccable reputation with Chambers's admitted past treason. But they were hard pressed to explain how Chambers had possessed confidential State Department documents which the defense's own experts said were typed on the Hiss family's Woodstock model typewriter. Hiss defense efforts then and since have tried to proved that somehow the documents were typewriter forgeries.

The Hiss-Chambers conflict became a major symbol in the Cold War political debates of the 1950s. Hiss's defenders such as Secretary of State Dean Acheson had their judgment and patriotism called into question. Republican critics of the Roosevelt and Truman administrations such as Richard Nixon charged that Hiss's influence in the State Department was responsible for U.S. foreign policy failures. Many intellectuals used the case to confront their own illusions about radical politics and to question the trust they once placed in the Soviet Union.

Chambers took no pleasure in Hiss's conviction. For him the case represented the tragedy of modern history. Profoundly pessimistic about the ability of Americans to understand the dangers of Communism, he retired quietly to his farm. Chambers wrote a compelling autobiography, *Witness* (1952). He died July 9, 1961.

Further Reading

Besides *Witness* (1952) Chambers's reflections and letters have been posthumously published in *Cold Friday* (1964) and *Odyssey of a Friend* (1969) edited by William F. Buckley, Jr. The best of the many studies of the Hiss-Chambers case is Allen Weinstein's *Perjury* (1978), which offers the most thorough and well-reasoned account. Alger Hiss presents his defense in *In the Court of Public Opinion* (1957). Richard Nixon's recollections appear in *Six Crises* (1962). Earl Latham, *The Communist Controversy in Washington* (1966) is a useful overview.

Additional Sources

Chambers, Whittaker, *Witness,* Chicago: Regnery Gateway, 1984, 1952.

Worth, E. J., *Whittaker Chambers: the secret confession,* London: Mazzard, 1993. □

Violeta Barrios de Chamorro

Newspaper magnate, publicist, anti-Somoza leader, and titular head of the United National Opposition, Violeta Barrios de Chamorro (born 1930) was also the first woman president of Nicaragua (1990).

Violeta Barrios de Chamorro, known to friends and supporters as "Doña Violeta," was born in the rural southern Nicaraguan town of Rivas in 1930. One of seven children of a wealthy ranching family distinguished for its contributions to Nicaraguan politics, Violeta Barrios as a young girl lived an idyllic, protected life in the countryside where she early became an accomplished equestrian. In her childhood years Nicaragua was wracked by civil war, beset by United States military intervention, shocked by the murder of nationalist hero César Augusto Sandino, and crushed by the ascension of Anastacio Somoza to dictatorial power in 1936.

As a teenager, she was sent to the United States to broaden her education and learn English. She attended a Catholic girls' school in San Antonio, Texas, and a small college in Virginia before being called home in 1948 upon her father's unexpected death by heart attack.

Home less than a year, Violeta Barrios met the dynamic Pedro Joaquín Chamorro, young scion of another of Nicaragua's leading families and a journalist for *La Prensa,* the nation's leading opposition newspaper, which was owned by his father. That opposition had caused much of the Chamorro family to seek exile (1944-1948), but upon their return Pedro, now publisher of *La Prensa,* maintained its role as an anti-Somoza forum. In 1950 he and Violeta married.

Violeta Chamorro raised two girls and two boys in a tense political atmosphere. Her husband Pedro was jailed several times (once for two years), and several times threatened with death for his political views, which were thoroughly democratic. The Barrios and Chamorro clans joined many other Nicaraguans who cheered when dictator Somoza was assassinated in 1956, but democracy was not to be the outcome. Two of Somoza's sons maintained the family autocracy by force, and with *La Prensa* leading the way, a popular opposition movement grew apace—a revolution in the making. Pedro Chamorro, so vocal and visible a foe of the regime, was murdered by Somoza thugs in 1978, becoming one of the chief martyrs of the evolving Sandinista revolutionary movement.

Chamorro, undeterred by her husband's death, continued, with *her* newspaper, to help lead the opposition to Somoza, calling for a return to democracy. When Anastacio ("Tachito") Somoza, Jr., fled the country in 1979 in the face of a popular uprising, she was honored with membership in the powerful Sandinista Governing Junta. Dedicated as she was to the ideals and practice of democracy, Chamorro quit the Sandinista Junta within a year and began speaking out against its Marxist rhetoric and increasingly authoritarian rule.

Once again in opposition, she and *La Prensa* led the attack against the supposedly popular, but soon dictatorial and incompetent, regime, labeling Daniel Ortega and other Sandinista rulers as "*Los Muchachos*" ("The Boys"). Careful not to align herself openly with the anti-Sandinista guerrilla movement known as the "Contras" or with the United States, Violeta Chamorro achieved more with the pages of *La Prensa* than the rebels did with their bullets, and by 1988 she was the most prominent of the nation's opposition leaders. Around her figure rallied all those disturbed by the economic chaos (35,000 percent inflation in 1988!) and the Sandinistas' alignment with Cuba and the Soviet Union.

In 1989 she agreed to run for the presidency of Nicaragua when the Sandinistas, under pressure from world opinion, announced that they would permit free elections in 1990. Although hampered by lack of campaign financing and not-so-subtle Sandinista interference, Chamorro laboriously put together a loose coalition of 14 political parties and groupings under the banner of UNO (United National Opposition). This coalition, which embraced such disparate dissident factions as right-wing businessmen and ranchers and the nation's official Communist Party, was "united" by one single purpose—to remove the Sandinistas from power. There was no agreement on what policies to follow should they be successful.

The Chamorro family was itself far from united. While two children, Cristiana and Pedro Joaquín, helped their mother run *La Prensa* and worked for her election, Claudia and Carlos were avowed and active Sandinistas, Claudia serving in the government's foreign service and Pedro as editor of the regime's official newspaper, *La Barricada*.

With promised financial campaign aid from the United States trickling in, and with the Catholic Church's support, Chamorro and UNO became a force to be reckoned with by late 1989; all the more so as an unparalleled number of foreign observers arrived in Nicaragua to ensure an honest and open election on February 25, 1990. For the first time in its history, the United Nations sent a delegation to observe a member state's election.

Still, numerous polls showed as late as February 15 that the Sandinistas maintained a seemingly insurmountable lead (by as much as two-to-one) among voters, and Violeta Chamorro, with a kneecap broken in a fall, had difficulty campaigning full-time. "In the macho culture of my country," Chamorro writes in her autobiography *Dreams of the Heart: The Autobiography of President Violeta Barrios de Chamorro of Nicaragua,* "few people believed that I, a woman and an invalid, would have the strength, energy and will to last through a punishing campaign." And indeed, she barely did. Between trips abroad, many for treatment of her ailments, and then recovery in seclusion at home, Chamorro spent more time off the stump than on during the most crucial phase of the campaign. In the end, it didn't matter.

The results of the election were electrifying, and almost totally unexpected; the polls proven wrong. Indeed, the actual ratios were almost the opposite of those predicted, with Chamorro and UNO swept to victory with 55 percent of the votes cast, to only 41 percent for the incumbent Sandinistas and a smattering for several minor parties. A similar phenomenon took place in Assembly (Congress) elections, with UNO winning 51 (of 92) seats and the Sandinistas 39.

Inaugurated April 25, Violeta de Barrios Chamorro was immediately confronted by a host of truly critical problems. She had to disarm the Contra revolutionaries and reintegrate them peacefully into Nicaraguan life; gain control of the ideologically Sandinista military (Central America's largest, by far) and radically reduce its size; diminish a still four-digit inflation; combat the nation's staggering unemployment problem; seek rescheduling of the hemisphere's highest per capita foreign debt; negotiate a substantial foreign aid package from the United States; and heal Nicaragua's deep and bitter social and political divisions. Few new chief executives have faced such daunting tasks.

As a person, Chamorro possessed an arrogance that was perfectly common in someone of her high aristocractic—and Spanish—lineage. "Pedro and I are the descendants of men who were in the top echelons of Nicaragua's social structure," she writes proudly. "Ours was a ruling class of European-blood criollos (children of Spaniards born in America in which birth determined status.)" A Sacasa by birth and a Chamorro by marriage (the rough equivalent, in the United States, of being a descendant of Washington married to a descendant of Jefferson), she never doubted her family's vocation to rule nor the uniftness of others less blessed by high birth. Like the rest of her class, she could barely hide her contempt for the arriviste Somozas or, in a different way, for the far humbler Ortegas.

Social position meant a great deal to Chamorro. When she first allied herself with the Sandinistas in 1979, it was in part because the revolutionary leaders had cleverly attracted to their side a small but distinguished group of Nicaraguan elites, men Chamarro related to socially.

Relying on a savvy team of advisers which included a number of her own trusted relatives, she tried to keep UNO truly unified to achieve her goals. Most who knew her or had followed her career believed that the 60-year-old, silver-haired grandmother, with her articulate love of democracy and belief in moderation, would change the course of her nation's history for the better.

Opting not to run for re-election, Chamorro handed over the presidency to Arnoldo Aleman after the October 1996 democractic election. She left him a country that was in better shape than when she took over as president. In 1996, the economy grew an estimated five percent, the third year of growth after a decade of contraction. Despite significant foreign debt relief negotiated during the year, the country continued to have a precarious balance of payments position and remained heavily dependent on foreign assistance. Although investment increased, the slow and complicated resolution of confiscated property claims continued to hinder private investment. The unemployment rate was officially estimated at 17 percent, while total unemployment and underemployment may have reached 50 percent. The inflation rate was about 11 percent and estimated per capita annual income was $470.

Chamorro will take a place in her nation's history, but it remains to be seen whether her reign of democracy was an aberration in Nicaraguan history rather than a harbinger of things to come.

Further Reading

The election of Violeta Chamorro and the problems she faced were described by Johanna McGeary, "But Will it Work?" *TIME* (March 12, 1990). An assessment of her first year in office was made by Edward Cody, *The Washington Post* (April 7, 1991). A book that deals with both Violeta Chamorro and her martyred husband is Patricia T. Edmisten, *Nicaragua Divided: La Prensa and the Chamorro Legacy* (1990). The Sandinista decade that ended with the election of Chamorro is described by Stephen Kinzer, *Blood of Brothers: Life and War in Nicaragua* (1991). □

Samuel de Champlain

Samuel de Champlain (ca. 1570-1635) was a French geographer and explorer whose mission was to establish a joint French and Native American agricultural and fur-trading colony. In 21 voyages to New France he laid the foundations for modern Canada.

Samuel de Champlain was born at Brouage, a small Huguenot seaport town in Saintonge. He was probably born a Protestant, but sometime before 1603 he embraced the Roman Catholic faith. He had served against the Catholic League in the army of Henry IV until 1598. By 1601 he was indulging his love of travel and the sea and extending his expertise in navigation.

Early Travels

Champlain spent time during 1601-1603 on voyages as far as the West Indies, working out of Spain. In 1603 he went, probably as an observer, with François Gravé du Pont, whom Aymar de Chaste, holder of the trade monopoly for New France from King Henry IV, was sending on an expedition to the St. Lawrence.

Gravé du Pont's ships arrived at Tadoussac, at the mouth of the Saguenay River on the St. Lawrence, some 120 miles below Quebec, on May 26, 1603. Champlain and Gravé du Pont reached Montreal that summer; by questioning natives through an interpreter, Champlain made astonishingly accurate guesses about the network of the Great Lakes, including Niagara Falls. Both men were back in France by the end of September.

Champlain, however, had acquired some interest and curiosity about Acadia (the area of Newfoundland and around the St. Lawrence), where he hoped to find mines and perhaps a more effective route into the interior. De Chaste died and was succeeded in the monopoly by Pierre du Gua de Monts. De Monts was interested in finding a site with a warmer climate and invited Champlain to accompany a new expedition as geographer. Early in May 1604 the expedition made landfall at Port Mouton on what is now the southeast coast of Nova Scotia, some 100 miles southwest of Halifax. Champlain was asked to choose a temporary base for settlement, and he explored the south coast of Nova Scotia; the Bay of Fundy, including the Annapolis Basin;

and the St. John River. De Monts, however, chose an island in the estuary of the St. Croix, now called Dochet Island.

The winter of 1604/1605 was a bad one, the cold being exceptionally severe, and the island became surrounded by treacherous half-broken ice floes, making it more a prison than a place of safety. Scurvy was prevalent, but Champlain, as was to be usual with him, seems to have been hardy enough to have escaped it.

In the summer of 1605 De Monts and Champlain explored the American coast as far south as Cape Cod. Although one or two English explorers had preceded Champlain on this coast, he made such precise and excellent charts of it that he really deserves the title of the first cartographer of the New England coast. The winter of 1605/1606 was spent comparatively easily in the Annapolis Basin, in a fort protected from the savagely cold northwest winds by the long high ridge that lies between the basin and the Bay of Fundy. In 1606 new arrivals turned up, with whom Champlain again explored southward along the American coast, this time as far as Martha's Vineyard.

The winter of 1606/1607 was mild and easy, for the new arrivals, Jean de Biencourt de Poutrincourt, Marc Lescarbot, and others, had brought supplies and wine. In May 1607 the whole colony returned to France, stopping en route to explore the area of Canso at the eastern end of Nova Scotia.

In 1608 Champlain received his first official position. Up to now all his work had been as observer or geographer on an informal basis. Now he was made lieutenant to De Monts. This new expedition went once more to the St. Lawrence. Arriving in the St. Lawrence in June 1608, they began the construction of a fort at the site of what is now the Lower Town of Quebec City. In the summer of 1609 Champlain cemented the fateful alliance between the French and the Hurons by an expedition against the Iroquois, up the Richelieu River toward Lake Champlain. This alliance dated from about 1603; if the French wanted furs, they had to support the Native Americans who supplied the furs, or at least controlled access to them. Thus they were compelled to support the Hurons and Algonquins against their enemies.

Champlain was back in France over the winter 1609/1610, making a report to De Monts and the king. The story of Champlain's relations with a number of French backers is long and complicated. There were a variety of them and a good deal of quarreling between various groups seeking to get control of the fur trade. Champlain had less interest in money than in exploration and in the development of a colony. With immense patience and seemingly unwearying persistence, he traveled back and forth across the Atlantic for the next 2 decades. In all he made some 21 voyages across the Atlantic.

Travel to the Interior

In 1615 Champlain made his boldest and most spectacular venture into the interior of Canada. Bound, as he believed himself to be, by promises to the Hurons to help them against the Iroquois and driven by his own considerable curiosity, he began his epic voyage to the Huron country with two Frenchmen and Native American canoeists. He left Montreal in July 1615. Traveling up the Ottawa River and a tributary, he reached Lake Nipissing, continuing down the French River to the northeastern corner of Lake Huron. He was probably the first white man to see it. By August 1 he was in Huronia, a fertile, well-watered country, populated by Huron villages, between the foot of Georgian Bay and Lake Simcoe, some 40 miles southeast.

They met with the Huron raiding party at the main village of Cahiagué, on the north side of Lake Simcoe. On September 1 they canoed down the Trent River system to Lake Ontario, and then via the Oswego River to the Iroquois village at the eastern end of Lake Onondaga, not far from present-day Syracuse. Huron impatience and lack of discipline made a coherent assault on the Iroquois fort impossible. Champlain was wounded in the knee by an Iroquois arrow, and with support failing to come from the Susquehannas, the Huron allies, the raiders had to return home. Champlain, unable to walk, was at times carried like a baby on the back of a Huron.

Champlain was obliged to winter in the disagreeable habitat of a Huron village but continued his inveterate habit of travel and exploration, visiting other tribes that were neighbors of the Hurons. In addition, and perhaps more important, he provided a detailed and informed account of the Native American ways of living, one of the earliest and best available. He returned to France in 1616.

In 1619 enforced leisure owing to legal complications gave him opportunity to write accounts of his voyages, which he illustrated with sketches and maps. In 1620, as lieutenant to the viceroy of New France, the Duc de Montmorency, Champlain set out again for Canada, this time with his wife, some 30 years younger than he. In 1627 Cardinal Richelieu, Louis XIII's chief minister, established the Company of One Hundred Associates, chartered to run the fur trade and organize settlement. Champlain was a member and became, in fact, the commander of the colony under Cardinal Richelieu.

All would have gone well but for the outbreak of war between England and France in 1627. A London company formed to get at the St. Lawrence trade financed, and Charles I of England commissioned, an expedition under David Kirke and his brothers to displace the French from Canada. They took four critically important French supply ships off Gaspé and thus almost stopped the life of the colony. By the summer of 1629, with no relief in sight, Champlain was compelled to surrender to the English and leave.

Not until 1632, with the Treaty of Saint-Germain-en-Laye, did England agree to restore Quebec (and Port Royal in Acadia) to France. In 1633 Champlain returned to New France, again under the aegis of a revived Company of One Hundred Associates. He died at Quebec, the town he founded, on Christmas Day, 1635.

Champlain was physically a resilient, tough, capable man. He also had the moral essentials for his role, courage and indomitableness. He was good-natured and kind and a man of his word, which explains his considerable success with Native Americans. But he also could be ruthless.

When, in 1608, there was a plot against his life by the locksmith Duval, Champlain formed a council that tried Duval and his accomplices. Duval was executed on the spot and his head stuck on a pike at the fort at Quebec.

Champlain was a man of large ideas; his aim was to establish a joint French and Native American agricultural and furtrading colony. He contemplated the Christianizing of Native Americans and their intermarriage with the French. He is, of all the explorers, the real founder of Canada, and he himself would have been pleased to be thought so. It was certainly what he set out to do.

Further Reading

H. P. Biggar edited Champlain's writings: *The Works of Samuel de Champlain* (6 vols., 1922-1936). Two lively and well-written biographies are Samuel Eliot Morison, *Samuel de Champlain: Father of New France* (1972), and Morris Bishop, *Champlain: The Life of Fortitude* (1948). □

Jean François Champollion

The French Egyptologist Jean François Champollion (1790-1832) was the father of Egyptology and the decipherer of Egyptian hieroglyphs.

Born on Dec. 23, 1790, in Figeac, Lot Department, Jean François Champollion was educated at the lyceum in Grenoble (1801-1807). His interest in the civilization of ancient Egypt, and especially in the then-undeciphered hieroglyphic script of that land, was first aroused when as a boy he learned about the Rosetta Stone, a key monument having Greek and Egyptian versions of the same text. At the age of 16 he read a paper before the Grenoble Academy maintaining that Coptic was the ancient language of Egypt.

Champollion studied Oriental languages in Paris under the famous Orientalist Sylvestre de Sacy and during this period (1807-1809) produced the first parts of his *Egypt under the Pharaohs:* the *Religion and History of Egypt* and the *Geography of Egypt.* In 1809 he was appointed to a teaching post in history and politics at Grenoble and married Rose Blanc.

Despite his republican sympathies Champollion secured the patronage of King Louis XVIII and then of King Charles X and was thus able to concentrate on his studies of Egyptian language and archeology. In 1824 he went abroad, especially to Italy, to study Egyptian language and archeological finds. On his return 2 years later he was made conservator of the Egyptian collections at the Louvre Museum in Paris. Champollion and a team of assistants visited Egypt in 1828-1829 and made the first systematic survey of the accessible standing monuments. In 1831 the chair in Egyptian history and archeology was created for Champollion at the Collège de France. While preparing to publish the results of his Egyptian expedition, he suffered a stroke and died in Paris on March 4, 1832.

Champollion possessed a phenomenal flair for languages and a genius for deciphering texts. He took his first steps in this field in 1808, when he equated 15 demotic signs with those of the Coptic alphabet; by 1818 he had established a key to the hieroglyphic version of the Rosetta inscription. He was now ahead of all contemporary scholars in the field, and his famous *Lettre à M. Dacier* (1822) marked a turning point in the story of Egyptology. The centenary of the publication of the Dacier letter was celebrated by a volume of studies from 45 Egyptologists in 1922.

Champollion's brother, Jacques Joseph Champollion-Figeac, published a number of Champollion's works posthumously, including an Egyptian grammar (1836-1841), a hieroglyphic dictionary (1841-1844), and, the most famous, *Monuments de l'Egypte et de la Nubie . . .* (4 vols., 1835-1847).

Further Reading

Although there are works on Champollion in French and German, there is no full-length study in English. C. W. Ceram, ed., *The World of Archeology: The Pioneers Tell Their Own Story* (1966), reproduces an English translation of Champollion's letter to M. Dacier, in which he makes his first clear account of his decipherment. Ernest Doblhofer, *Voices in Stone: The Decipherment of Ancient Scripts and Writings* (1957; trans. 1961), provides biographical material, as does Warren R. Dawson, *Who Was Who in Egyptology,* revised edition by Eric Uphill (in press). □

Richard Chancellor

Richard Chancellor (died 1556) was the first Englishman to penetrate the White Sea and to establish relations with Russia.

Richard Chancellor, evidently a native of Bristol, acquired geographical and maritime proficiency from the explorer Sebastian Cabot and the geographer John Dee. Cabot had always been interested in making a voyage to Asia through the Arctic, and for this purpose King Edward VI chartered an association of English merchants in 1552-1553, with the Duke of Northumberland as principal patron. They hoped not only to discover a Northeast Passage but also to find a market for English woolen cloth.

Sir Hugh Willoughby was given three ships for the search, and Chancellor went as second in command. A Norwegian coastal storm separated them; Willoughby, with two ships, sailed east and discovered Novaya Zemlya but died with all his men on the Lapland coast. Chancellor, with the ship *Edward Bonaventure,* found the entrance to the White Sea and anchored at the port of Archangel. Englishmen had visited Russia earlier, but all recent contact had been through the German merchants of the Hanseatic League. Leaving the *Edward* at Archangel, Chancellor traveled overland to Moscow, where he was favorably received by Ivan the Terrible. The Czar seemed glad to help in breaking the Hanseatic trading monopoly.

When Chancellor returned to England in the summer of 1554, King Edward was dead, and his successor, Mary, had executed Northumberland for attempting to place Lady Jane Grey on the throne. No stigma attached to Chancellor, and the Muscovy Company, as the association now was called, sent him again to the White Sea in 1555. On this voyage he learned what had happened to Willoughby, recovered his papers, and found out about the discovery of Novaya Zemlya. Chancellor spent the summer of 1555 dealing with the Czar, organizing trade, and trying to learn how China might be reached by the northern route.

In 1556 Chancellor departed for England, taking with him the first Russian ambassador to his country. They left Archangel in autumn; the *Edward* reached the Scottish coast but was wrecked at Pitlago, where Chancellor lost his life. The Russian envoy survived to reach London. Chancellor had found a way to Russia, and though in time it was superseded by a better one it remained for years the only feasible route for the English.

Further Reading

There is no biography of Chancellor; little is known of his life other than his trips to Russia. A convenient summary of his and Willoughby's voyages is in James A. Williamson, *The Age of Drake* (1938; 4th ed. 1960). Joseph K. Hamel, *England and Russia: Comprising the Voyages of John Tradescant the Elder, Sir Hugh Willoughby, Richard Chancellor, Nelson, and Others to the White Sea* (trans. 1854; repr. 1968), provides extensive discussion of Chancellor's ancestry but few biographical details. The material on Chancellor in T. S. Willan, *The Early History of the Russia Company, 1553-1603* (1956), is based on Hamel's work. Eva G. R. Taylor, *Tudor Geography, 1485-1583* (1930), furnishes background for the English Northeast Passage search. □

Alfred Du Pont Chandler Jr.

Alfred Du Pont Chandler, Jr. (born 1918) was an American historian who specialized in both the biographies of American business leaders and in the organization and administration of large scale industrial enterprises.

Alfred Du Pont Chandler, Jr., was born in Guyencourt, Delaware, on September 15, 1918, the son of Alfred DuPont and Carol Remsay Chandler. He was educated at Harvard, receiving his B.A. in 1940 just in time to join the United States Navy. While serving in the navy, in 1944 he married Kay Martin. Mustered out in 1945, Chandler returned to Harvard to study history, earning his M.A. in 1947 and his Ph.D. in 1952.

His professional career began at the Massachusetts Institute of Technology in 1950 where he was a research associate. He then became a faculty member and remained at M.I.T. until 1963, with time off to be a research fellow at Harvard in 1953 and a Guggenheim Fellow in 1958.

Chandler served an apprenticeship as assistant editor of *The Letters of Theodore Roosevelt* under Elting M. Morison and John M. Blum from 1950 to 1953. This was later to stand him in good stead when an opportunity arose to edit the Eisenhower Papers. His first book was a biography, *Henry Varnum Poor, Business Editor, Analyst, and Reformer* (1956), which was indicative of his interest in the history of businessmen, businesses, and business organizations. This book also showed his belief in the middle-class nature of reform movements in the United States.

While at M.I.T. Chandler also served as an academic consultant to the Naval War College in 1954. His second book, *Strategy and Structure: Chapters in the History of the Industrial Enterprise,* was a study in organizational behavior which won a Newcomen Award for 1962. It also furthered his reputation as a business historian, and the following year he moved to Johns Hopkins University.

At Johns Hopkins Chandler continued his productivity even though he took on the added responsibilities of director of the Center for Study of Recent American History in 1964 and of department chairman in 1966. He also became chairman of the Historical Advisory Committee of the U.S. Atomic Energy Commission in 1969, a post he held until 1977.

While busy with these administrative tasks, Chandler still found time to write. In 1964 he published *Giant Enterprise: Ford, General Motors and the Automotive Industry,* and in 1965 he edited a book entitled *The Railroads.* His major intellectual energy, however, was devoted to the editing of *The Papers of Dwight David Eisenhower,* which appeared in five volumes in 1970. His assistant editor, Steven B. Ambrose, became a noted Eisenhower scholar.

In 1970 Chandler was the Thomas Henry Carroll Ford Foundation Visiting Fellow at Harvard. He remained at Harvard as the Strauss Professor of Business History in the Graduate School of Business, although he was also a visiting fellow at All Souls, Oxford, and a visiting professor at the European Institute of Washington. The same year he was a visiting fellow at Harvard he also was a member of the National Advertising Council's Committee on Educational and Professional Development.

During his tenure at Harvard, Chandler continued to write. In 1971, along with Stephen Salsbury, he published *Pierre S. du Pont and the Making of the Modern Corporation.* In 1977 he published what was his most famous book, *The Visible Hand: The Managerial Revolution in American Business.* The book was a culmination of Chandler's thinking on the operation of American business and earned the Pulitzer and Bancroft prizes in 1978. These were not the only honors Chandler garnered. He was a member of the American Philosophical Society and a Fellow of the American Academy of Arts and Sciences. In 1977-1978 he served as president of the Business History Conference. The most fitting accolade is that of John Higham, who exempted Chandler from "the deadly blight" which had prevented other senior historians from doing their culminating work in the 1960s and 1970s.

Since that time he wrote *The Essential Alfred Chandler: Essays Toward a Historical Theory of Big Business* (1988), and his *Scale and Scope: The Dynamics of Industrial Capitalism* was written with the assistance of Takashi Hikino (1990). *Scale and Scope* was hailed as an indispensable historical reference spanning three-quarters of the twentieth century. In the book Chandler compares the European business environment with that of the United States. He evaluated the significance of business structure to performance and success in the marketplace. Chandler was dubbed the "dean of American business history" by *Financial World* in 1991.

Alfred D. Chandler, Jr. retired from the Harvard Business School on June 30, 1989.

Further Reading

There is a scarcity of material on Chandler. John Higham's favorable comment is from the epilogue of his 1983 edition of *History,* but it is only a brief consideration. Equally brief are the references to Chandler in Georg G. Iggers and Harold T. Parker, *International Handbook of Historical Studies* (1979).

Additional Sources

Chandler, Alfred D. Jr., *The Essential Alfred Chandler: Essays Toward a Historical Theory of Big Business,* Harvard Business School Press, 1988.

Chandler, Alfred D. Jr., *Scale and Scope: The Dynamics of Industrial Capitalism,* Belknap Press, 1990.

Forbes, November 13, 1989.

The New Republic, December 10, 1990. □

Raymond Chandler Jr.

Raymond Chandler (1888-1959) was a leading exponent of the hard-boiled detective novel and, with Dashiell Hammett, a seminal figure in American crime fiction.

Raymond Chandler was born in Chicago on July 23, 1888, of parents of Irish Quaker descent. His parents were divorced when he was very young, and in 1895 his mother took him to England where they lived with relatives in South London. There he attended Dulwich School from 1900 to 1905, and the following year he went to business school in Paris. In 1907, in order to qualify for a civil service job, he was naturalized as a British citizen. A few years later he free-lanced as a journalist for the *Daily Express* and showed his first creative inclination with some poetry and satire for the *Westminster Gazette.*

As an American living abroad, Chandler had grown up with an ethnic ambivalence and a curiosity about his native land that finally, in 1912, prompted his return to the United States; his first jobs in the United States were in St. Louis and on the West Coast, as a bookkeeper. In World War I he served with the Canadian army and the Royal Air Force. After demobilization Chandler settled permanently in southern California, principally in Los Angeles, which was to be the setting of his stories and novels. He worked as a bookkeeper for a California oil syndicate and in 1924 became vice-president of the company; that same year he married Cissy Pascal, a woman 18 years his senior. In the economic crash of 1929 Chandler's business foundered, but he held on to his post until 1932, when drinking and womanizing got him fired.

Choosing a Writing Career

Ironically, the firing was almost immediately salutary. Caught in the widespread economic squeeze, Chandler reverted to his earlier interest in writing and, at the unlikely age of 44, joined the ranks of some 1,300 American pulp writers. Strongly influenced by Dashiell Hammett and encouraged by Joseph T. Shaw, editor of the best of the pulps, *Black Mask,* Chandler embarked on his new career fully armed with a philosophy of crime fiction: he had no high-flown ideas regarding its esthetic worth, but he did think it an important literary form which owed the public a greater degree of honesty and reality than it ordinarily provided.

He felt that too many mystery writers, including Agatha Christie, deliberately plotted their stories to throw the reader off, and that the British writers especially were guilty of making their detectives genteel snobs. Chandler's famous essay "The Simple Art of Murder" credits Hammett with giving "murder back to the kind of people who commit it for reasons, not just to provide a corpse." Chandler recognized, however, that there were pitfalls in the hard-boiled approach: "The realistic style is easy to abuse. It is easy to fake; brutality is not strength, flipness is not wit, edge-of-the-chair writing can be as boring as flat writing."

Chandler was a painstaking craftsman and therefore not at all prolific: he wrote only 20 stories in all, and his annual earnings during the 1930s averaged only about $1,500. His first story, "Blackmailers Don't Shoot," took him five months to write. Years later, after his novelistic successes, the best of his stories, originally printed in *Black Mask* and *Dime Detective,* were collected in *Red Wind* (1946) and *The Simple Art of Murder* (1950), but the chief importance of the stories is that he pirated them for his novels. Chandler's first novel, *The Big Sleep* (1939), begun when he was 50, is a re-working of two of his stories, "Killer in the Rain" (1935) and "The Curtain" (1936). The novel form gave Chandler a more literate audience than he'd had in the pulps, and it introduced his readers to Philip Marlowe, a wise-cracking, half-cynical, half-romantic, first-person narrator-detective. The novel sold pretty well, but earned Chandler only $2,000.

Chandler's second novel, *Farewell, My Lovely* (1940), a powerful study of obsession and duplicity, has Marlowe on a mission for an outsized ex-con named Moose Malloy. Even more than *The Big Sleep* it established Chandler as a master chronicler of Los Angeles—of its criminal world, its parasitical upper class, and its general pattern of social corruption.

The High Window (1942) had a pre-publication title of "The Brasher Doubloon" (the valuable coin that the plot revolves around). It is both wise-cracking and moralistic in delineating the ruthlessness and decadence of the rich, particularly their ability to pervert justice.

The Lady in the Lake (1943) was a best-seller and was probably Chandler's best novel. It is a superbly plotted story in which the police, never an object of Chandler's admiration, come off even worse than usual.

The first four novels, like the stories that had inspired them, showed off Chandler's greatest gift—his *style.* He was a more rococo writer than Hammett, and occasionally the figurative language is embarrassingly strained, but at his best he could get off some daring, delightfully apt similes: "I thought he was as crazy as a pair of waltzing mice, but I like him." "His long pale hands made gestures like sick butterflies over the top of his desk." "Pieces of plaster and wood flew like fists at an Irish wedding." "The sky was as black as Carrie Nation's bonnet."

Writing for Film and Radio

Movie adaptations of Chandler's novels began as early as 1941, and in 1943 Chandler started a long writing association with Hollywood, although he could never work up any respect for the film industry. He once described Academy Award night as "Hollywood's exquisite attempt to kiss itself in the back of the neck." His first screenplay was "The Blue Dahlia" (1945), which starred Alan Ladd as a returning World War II veteran surrounded by social sleaze who learns of his wife's infidelity and is implicated in her murder. In 1947 Chandler earned $4,000 a week for his work on the original screenplay "Playback" and royalties from several Philip Marlowe radio series; one, in 1947, starred Van Heflin; another enjoyed a substantial run from 1948 to 1951. This commercial success was achieved despite an uneasy relationship with radio and film companies, who disliked dealing with him because he demanded some measure of control over the scripts.

His fifth novel, *The Little Sister* (1949), was published by Houghton Mifflin after Chandler left his original publisher, Alfred A. Knopf, over their insistence on publishing a detective novel that he felt plagiarized both himself and Hammett. *The Little Sister* shows a falling off of Chandler's skills: it has too many wisecracks and too little tension.

In 1950 Chandler wrote a screen play of Patricia Highsmith's *Strangers on a Train* but director Alfred Hitchcock was displeased by it, and it was re-written by a second scenarist. Chandler's creative decline is further evident in his last two novels. The principal interest in *The Long Goodbye* (1953) is that it is Chandler's most autobiographical novel. Cast in his familiar murder mystery mold, it projects a bleak vision of southern California and a theme of lovelessness and failure close to Chandler's feelings about his own life. *Playback* (1958), based on his original screenplay, is the weakest of his novels.

Profile and Last Years

Chandler was a tweedy, boozing, remote intellectual. He was a lonely man, shy and irritable in company, sometimes sarcastic and rude. He had difficulty fitting in with his chosen California environment, but he also loathed New York, especially its cab drivers. In fact, he disliked most people and had few friends; he met Hammett only once and liked him and had great admiration for and a lengthy correspondence with Somerset Maugham.

The one abiding relationship Chandler had was with his wife, to whom he was, in his own fashion, strongly devoted. When she died in her 80s, in 1954, Chandler became depressed to the point of attempted suicide. His own health was poor: he suffered from a severe sinus condition and from a number of drink-related ailments.

He moved to London in 1955, but his depression only deepened and his drinking grew worse, so he returned to the United States in 1956. He died in La Jolla, California, on March 26, 1959, of pneumonia either caused or aggravated by heavy drinking and self-neglect. He died a disappointed, frustrated man despite his natural gifts as a writer and his considerable achievements.

Further Reading

The authorized biography is *The Life of Raymond Chandler* (1976) by Frank MacShane, who also edited *Selected Letters of Raymond Chandler* (1981). Also, the title essay in *The Simple Art of Murder* (1950) provides some valuable insights into Chandler's views on art and life.

Additional Sources

MacShane, Frank, *The life of Raymond Chandler,* Boston, Mass.: G.K. Hall, 1986, 197. □

Zachariah Chandler

A U.S. senator during the Civil War and Reconstruction, Zachariah Chandler (1813-1879) was a leading Republican and helped shape Reconstruction policy toward the South.

Zachariah Chandler was born on Dec. 10, 1813, on a farm in Bedford Township, N.H. After attending district schools, he joined the tide of westward migration from New England and settled in the frontier city of Detroit in 1833. He opened a general store, and by shrewd investments of his profits in banking, commercial enterprises, and land he became one of the richest men in the state.

Chandler entered politics as a Whig, served as mayor of Detroit in 1851-1852, but was defeated for the governorship. Increasingly hostile to the expansion of slavery, in 1854 he helped found the Michigan Republican party. Three years later the state legislature elected him to the U.S. Senate. In Washington he emerged as one of the foremost members of the Republican faction known as "Radicals" because of their demands for a vigorous antislavery policy. In 1860-1861 Chandler opposed compromise with Southern secessionists, even at the cost of war: he declared that "without a little bloodletting this Union will not, in my estimate, be worth a rush."

When war came, he helped organize and equip the first regiment of Michigan volunteers. In the Senate he obtained a position on the powerful Joint Committee on the Conduct of the War, which exerted pressure on the Lincoln administration for a more aggressive war policy and harassed cautious or conservative Union Army generals, especially George B. McClellan. Chandler was also chairman of the Senate Committee on Commerce; he promoted the passage of measures creating a national banking system, higher tariffs, and other legislation to finance the war and aid Northern industrial growth. He was critical of Lincoln's moderate conditions for restoration of the South to the Union and bitterly opposed to Andrew Johnson's Reconstruction policy. A roughhewn, grim-visaged, hard-drinking, plain-speaking man, Chandler denounced Johnson as a traitor and voted for the President's conviction on impeachment charges in 1868.

Chandler reached the height of his power in the Grant administration; he was influential in formulating policy and used Federal patronage to build a personal political machine in Michigan. But Democratic victory in the 1874 state elections cost Chandler his seat in the Senate. President Grant appointed him secretary of the interior in 1875, and he did much to clean up this notoriously corrupt department. As chairman of the Republican National Committee in 1876-1877, he played a key role in the victory of Rutherford B. Hayes in the disputed 1876 presidential election. Chandler was again elected to the Senate in February 1879 but served only a few months before his death on November 1.

Further Reading

There is no satisfactory biography of Chandler. The staff of the *Detroit Post and Tribune* compiled and published the laudatory *Zachariah Chandler: An Outline Sketch of His Life and Public Services* (1880) after his death. For hostile views of Chandler and other Radical Republicans see Claude Bowers, *The Tragic Era: The Revolution after Lincoln* (1929), and T. Harry Williams, *Lincoln and the Radicals* (1941). A sympathetic interpretation, reflecting the trend of recent scholarship, is in Hans Trefousse, *The Radical Republicans: Lincoln's Vanguard for Racial Justice* (1969). □

Chandragupta Maurya

Chandragupta Maurya (died ca. 298 B.C.) was the founder of the Maurya dynasty and the first historical emperor of India.

According to the Puranic tradition, Chandragupta, also known as Sandracottus, was the illegitimate son of the last Nanda king of Magadha by the maid servant Mura, hence the name Maurya. Jain and Buddhist sources declare him to be a scion of the Moriya clan of Pippalivana.

In his youth Chandragupta came under the influence of Chanakya, also known as Kautilya, a Taxilian Brahmin and the reputed author of *Arthasastra,* the celebrated work on Indian polity. Aided by Chanakya, Chandragupta conspired to usurp the Magadhan rule but failed in his first attempt. Exiled, he met Alexander in 326/325 B.C., studied the significance and success of the Greek invasion, and bided his time.

After Alexander's death in 323 B.C., Chandragupta put an end to the Greek rule in northwest India, returned to Magadha, killed the Nanda king, and proclaimed the Maurya dynasty in 322. The attempt of Seleucus Nicator, a Greek satrap, to recapture Punjab in 304 was foiled, and Chandragupta obtained present-day Afghanistan as part of the peace treaty. Seleucus also gave his daughter in marriage to Chandragupta and appointed Megasthenes as ambassador to the Maurya court. Scholars owe much information about Mauryan India to a detailed account written by Megasthenes.

The Magadhan state under Chandragupta was both opulent and totalitarian. The capital, Pataliputra, was a magnificent city, and the royal palace was, according to Megasthenes, filled with "wonders which neither Memnonian Susa in all its glory nor the magnificence of Ekbatana can hope to vie; indeed, only the well-known vanity of the Persians could imagine such a comparison." Having come to power through intrigue, the Emperor feared plots. He employed an army of secret agents, and no method was considered unscrupulous to destroy his enemies.

The people enjoyed a reputation for honesty; lying and stealing were generally unknown, and the Greek ambassador notes that litigation was seldom resorted to. Much of this was no doubt due to the harsh penal system. The death penalty was imposed for evasion of taxes, and maiming was inflicted for perjury.

The empire was divided into three provinces, each under a viceroy, usually a member of the royal family. Chandragupta had an army of 600,000, but it is likely the number also included camp followers. A palace guard of foreign Amazons kept watch over the Emperor, and Chandragupta seldom appeared in public.

Chandragupta's rule lasted 24 years. According to Jain tradition, in 298 he abdicated his throne, retired to the Jain retreat at Sravana Belgola in Mysore, and eventually fasted to death.

Further Reading

The original account by Megasthenes has perished, but copious extracts are preserved in such later works as J. W. McCrindle, *Ancient India as Described by Megasthenes and Arrian* (1877); and K. A. Nilakanta Sastri, ed., *Age of the Nandas and Mauryas* (1952). See also R. K. Mokerji, *The Gupta Empire* (1947). □

Subrahmanyan Chandrasekhar

Subrahmanyan Chandrasekhar (1910–1995) worked on the origins, structure, and dynamics of stars and earned a prominent place in the annals of science. The Nobel Prize-winning physicist's most celebrated work concerns the radiation of energy from stars, particularly the dying fragments known as white dwarf stars.

Subrahmanyan Chandrasekhar was an Indian-born American astrophysicist and applied mathematician whose work on the origins, structure, and dynamics of stars secured him a prominent place in the annals of science. His most celebrated work concerns the radiation of energy from stars, particularly white dwarf stars, which are the dying fragments of stars. Chandrasekhar demonstrated that the radius of a white dwarf star is related to its mass: the greater its mass, the smaller its radius. Chandrasekhar made numerous other contributions to astrophysics. His expansive research and published papers and books include topics such as the system of energy transfer within stars, stellar evolution, stellar structure, and theories of planetary and stellar atmospheres. For nearly twenty years, he served as the editor-in-chief of the *Astrophysical Journal,* the leading publication of its kind in the world. For his immense contribution to science, Chandrasekhar, who died in 1995, received numerous awards and distinctions, most notably the 1983 Nobel Prize for Physics for his research into the depths of aged stars.

Chandrasekhar, better known as Chandra, was born on October 19, 1910, in Lahore, India (now part of Pakistan), the first son of C. Subrahmanyan Ayyar and Sitalakshmi nee (Divan Bahadur) Balakrishnan. Chandra came from a large family: he had two older sisters, four younger sisters, and three younger brothers. As the firstborn son, Chandra inherited his paternal grandfather's name, Chandrasekhar. His uncle was the Nobel Prize-winning Indian physicist, Sir C. V. Raman.

Chandra received his early education at home, beginning when he was five. From his mother he learned Tamil, from his father, English and arithmetic. He set his sights upon becoming a scientist at an early age, and to this end, undertook at his own initiative some independent study of calculus and physics. The family moved north to Lucknow in Uttar Pradesh when Chandra was six. In 1918, the family moved again, this time south to Madras. Chandrasekhar was taught by private tutors until 1921, when he enrolled in the Hindu High School in Triplicane. With typical drive and motivation, he studied on his own and steamed ahead of the class, completing school by the age of fifteen.

After high school, Chandra attended Presidency College in Madras. For the first two years, he studied physics, chemistry, English, and Sanskrit. For his B.A. honors degree he wished to take pure mathematics but his father insisted that he take physics. Chandra resolved this conflict by registering as an honors physics student but attending mathematics lectures. Recognizing his brilliance, his lecturers went out of their way to accommodate Chandra. Chandra also took part in sporting activities and joined the debating team. A highlight of his college years was the publication of his paper, "The Compton Scattering and the New Statistics." These and other early successes while he was still an eighteen-year-old undergraduate only strengthened Chandra's resolve to pursue a career in scientific research, despite his father's wish that he join the Indian civil service. A meeting the following year with the German physicist Werner Heisenberg, whom Chandra, as the secretary of the student science association, had the honor of showing around Madras, and Chandra's attendance at the Indian Science Congress Association Meeting in early 1930, where his work was hailed, doubled his determination.

Upon graduating with a M.A. in 1930, Chandra set off for Trinity College, Cambridge, as a research student, courtesy of an Indian government scholarship created especially for him (with the stipulation that upon his return to India, he would serve for five years in the Madras government service). At Cambridge, Chandra turned to astrophysics, inspired by a theory of stellar evolution that had occurred to him as he made the long boat journey from India to Cambridge. It would preoccupy him for the next ten years. He also worked on other aspects of astrophysics and published many papers.

In the summer of 1931, he worked with physicist Max Born at the Institut für Theoretische Physik at Göttingen in Germany. There, he studied group theory and quantum mechanics (the mathematical theory that relates matter and radiation) and produced work on the theory of stellar atmospheres. During this period, Chandra was often tempted to leave astrophysics for pure mathematics, his first love, or at least for physics. He was worried, though, that with less than a year to go before his thesis exam, a change might cost him his degree. Other factors influenced his decision to stay with astrophysics, most importantly, the encouragement shown him by astrophysicist Edward Arthur Milne. In August 1932, Chandra left Cambridge to continue his studies in Denmark under physicist Niels Bohr. In Copenhagen, he was able to devote more of his energies to pure physics. A series of Chandra's lectures on astrophysics given at the University of Liège, in Belgium, in February 1933 received a warm reception. Before returning to Cambridge in May 1933 to sit his doctorate exams, he went back to Copenhagen to work on his thesis.

Chandrasekhar's uncertainty about his future was assuaged when he was awarded a fellowship at Trinity College, Cambridge. During a four-week trip to Russia in 1934, where he met physicists Lev Davidovich Landau, B. P. Geraismovic, and Viktor Ambartsumian, he returned to the work that had led him into astrophysics to begin with, white dwarfs. Upon returning to Cambridge, he took up research of white dwarfs again in earnest.

As a member of the Royal Astronomical Society since 1932, Chandra was entitled to present papers at its twice monthly meetings. It was at one of these that Chandra, in 1935, announced the results of the work that would later make his name. As stars evolve, he told the assembled audience, they emit energy generated by their conversion of hydrogen into helium and even heavier elements. As they reach the end of their life, stars have progressively less hydrogen left to convert and emit less energy in the form of radiation. They eventually reach a stage when they are no longer able to generate the pressure needed to sustain their size against their own gravitational pull and they begin to contract. As their density increases during the contraction process, stars build up sufficient internal energy to collapse their atomic structure into a degenerate state. They begin to collapse into themselves. Their electrons become so tightly packed that their normal activity is suppressed and they become white dwarfs, tiny objects of enormous density. The greater the mass of a white dwarf, the smaller its radius, according to Chandrasekhar. However, not all stars end their lives as stable white dwarfs. If the mass of evolving stars increases beyond a certain limit, eventually named the *Chandrasekhar limit* and calculated as 1.4 times the mass of the sun, evolving stars cannot become stable white dwarfs. A star with a mass above the limit has to either lose mass to become a white dwarf or take an alternative evolutionary path and become a supernova, which releases its excess energy in the form of an explosion. What mass remains after this spectacular event may become a white dwarf but more likely will form a neutron star. The neutron star has even greater density than a white dwarf and an average radius of about .15 km. It has since been independently proven that all white dwarf stars fall within Chandrasekhar's predicted limit, which has been revised to equal 1.2 solar masses.

Unfortunately, although his theory would later be vindicated, Chandra's ideas were unexpectedly undermined and ridiculed by no less a scientific figure than astronomer and physicist Sir Arthur Stanley Eddington, who dismissed as absurd Chandra's notion that stars can evolve into anything other than white dwarfs. Eddington's status and authority in the community of astronomers carried the day, and Chandra, as the junior, was not given the benefit of the doubt. Twenty years passed before his theory gained general acceptance among astrophysicists, although it was quickly recognized as valid by physicists as noteworthy as Wolfgang Pauli, Niels Bohr, Ralph H. Fowler, and Paul Dirac. Rather than continue sparring with Eddington at scientific meeting after meeting, Chandra collected his thoughts on the matter into his first book, *An Introduction to the Study of Stellar Structure,* and departed the fray to take up new research around stellar dynamics. An unfortunate result of the scientific quarrel, however, was to postpone the discovery of black holes and neutron stars by at least twenty years and Chandra's receipt of a Nobel Prize for his white dwarf work by fifty years. Surprisingly, despite their scientific differences, he retained a close personal relationship with Eddington.

Chandra spent from December 1935 until March 1936 at Harvard University as a visiting lecturer in cosmic physics. While in the United States, he was offered a research associate position at Yerkes Observatory at Williams Bay, Wisconsin, staring in January 1937. Before taking up this post, Chandra returned home to India to marry the woman who had waited for him patiently for six years. He had known Lalitha Doraiswamy, daughter of Captain and Mrs. Savitri Doraiswamy, since they had been students together at Madras University. After graduation, she had undertaken a master's degree. At the time of their marriage, she was a headmistress. Although their marriage of love was unusual, as both came from fairly progressive families and were both of the Brahman caste, neither of their families had any real objections. After a whirlwind courtship and wedding, the young bride and groom set out for the United States. They intended to stay no more than a few years, but, as luck would have it, it became their permanent home.

At the Yerkes Observatory, Chandra was charged with developing a graduate program in astronomy and astrophysics and with teaching some of the courses. His reputation as a teacher soon attracted top students to the observatory's graduate school. He also continued researching stellar evolution, stellar structure, and the transfer of energy within stars. In 1938, he was promoted to assistant professor of astrophysics. During this time Chandra revealed his conclusions regarding the life paths of stars.

During the World War II, Chandra was employed at the Aberdeen Proving Grounds in Maryland, working on ballistic tests, the theory of shock waves, the Mach effect, and transport problems related to neutron diffusion. In 1942, he was promoted to associate professor of astrophysics at the University of Chicago and in 1943, to professor. Around 1944, he switched his research from stellar dynamics to radiative transfer. Of all his research, the latter gave him, he recalled later, more fulfillment. That year, he also achieved a lifelong ambition when he was elected to the Royal Society of London. In 1946, he was elevated to Distinguished Service Professor. In 1952, he became Morton D. Hull Distinguished Service Professor of Astrophysics in the departments of astronomy and physics, as well as at the Institute for Nuclear Physics at the University of Chicago's Yerkes Observatory. Later the same year, he was appointed managing editor of the *Astrophysical Journal,* a position he held until 1971. He transformed the journal from a private publication of the University of Chicago to the national journal of the American Astronomical Society. The price he paid for his editorial impartiality, however, was isolation from the astrophysical community.

Chandra became a United States citizen in 1953. Despite receiving numerous offers from other universities, in the United States and overseas, Chandra never left the University of Chicago, although, owing to a disagreement with Bengt Strömgren, the head of Yerkes, he stopped teaching astrophysics and astronomy and began lecturing in mathematical physics at the University of Chicago campus. Chandra voluntarily retired from the University of Chicago in 1980, although he remained on as a post-retirement researcher. In 1983, he published a classic work on the mathematical theory of black holes. Afterwards, he studied colliding waves and the Newtonian two-center problem in the framework of the general theory of relativity. His semi-retirement also left him with more time to pursue his hobbies and interests: literature and music, particularly orchestral, chamber, and South Indian.

During his long career, Chandrasekhar received many awards. In 1947, Cambridge University awarded him its Adams Prize. In 1952, he received the Bruce Medal of the Astronomical Society of the Pacific, and the following year, the Gold Medal of the Royal Astronomical Society. In 1955, Chandrasekhar became a Member of the National Academy of Sciences. The Royal Society of London bestowed upon him its Royal Medal seven years later. In 1962, he was also presented with the Srinivasa Ramanujan Medal of the Indian National Science Academy. The National Medal of Science of the United States was conferred upon Chandra in 1966; and the Padma Vibhushan Medal of India in 1968. Chandra received the Henry Draper Medal of the National Academy of Sciences in 1971 and the Smoluchowski Medal of the Polish Physical Society in 1973. The American Physical Society gave him its Dannie Heineman Prize in 1974. The crowning glory of his carer came nine years later when the Royal Swedish Academy awarded Chandrasekhar the Nobel Prize for Physics. ETH of Zurich gave the Indian astrophysicist its Dr. Tomalla Prize in 1984, while the Royal Society of London presented him with its Copley Prize later that year. Chandra also received the R. D. Birla Memorial Award of the Indian Physics Association in 1984. In 1985, the Vainu Bappu Memorial Award of the Indian National Science Academy was conferred upon Chandrasekhar. In May 1993, Chandra received the state of Illinois's highest honor, Lincoln Academy Award, for his outstanding contributions to science.

While his contribution to astrophysics was immense, Chandra always preferred to remain outside the mainstream of research. He died on August 21, 1995, at the age of 82 in Chicago. The respected physicist once described himself to his biographer, Kameshar C. Wali, as "a lonely wanderer in the byways of science." Throughout his life, Chandra strove to acquire knowledge and understanding, according to an autobiographical essay published with his Nobel lecture, motivated "principally by a quest after perspectives."

Further Reading

The Biographical Dictionary of Scientists, Astronomers, Blond Educational Company (London), 1984, pp. 36.

Chambers Biographical Encyclopedia of Scientists, Facts-on-File, 1981.

Goldsmith, Donald, *The Astronomers,* St. Martin's Press, 1991.

Great American Scientists, Prentice-Hall, 1960.

Land, Kenneth R. and Owen Gingerich, editors, *A Sourcebook in Astronomy and Astrophysics,* Harvard University Press, 1979.

Modern Men of Science, McGraw-Hill, 1966, p. 97.

Wali, Kameshwar C., *Chandra: A Biography of S. Chandrasekhar,* Chicago University Press, 1991. □

Coco Chanel

Gabrielle "Coco" Chanel (1883–1971) was noted for her free-flowing, loose-fitting designs for women's clothing, first introduced in 1919, and again in 1954.

In 1919 French designer Gabrielle "Coco" Chanel released women from the tight corsets of the era and introduced them to comfortable jersey clothing. In 1954, after fifteen years of retirement and just six months before her seventy-first birthday, she made a comeback and freed women once again from highly structured, constricting designs—this time the clothing of the "New Look." Critics were lukewarm, but women, particularly American women, loved her casual, softly shaped clothes and snapped them up. These designs ushered in a new relaxation in fashion that continues today.

Early Years

Little is known of Chanel's early years except that she was orphaned as a young child. She started in fashion in 1910, making hats in Paris. Chanel opened her first dress shop in Paris in 1914 and closed it in 1939 at the onset of World War II. But in the period between the world wars she revolutionized women's fashion with her straight, simple, uncorseted, and, above all, comfortable "Chanel Look." She also popularized short hair for women in the 1920s and introduced shorter skirts. She created her famous Chanel No. 5 perfume in 1922.

Later Years

In 1954 Chanel said her competitive spirit was aroused because Parisian high fashion had been taken over by men. "There are too many men in this business," she told a magazine interviewer in May 1954, "and they don't know how to make clothes for women. All this fantastic pinching and puffing. How can a woman wear a dress that's cut so she can't lift up her arm to pick up a telephone?" She had a

knack for knowing what women wanted, and women responded enthusiastically. In the 1950s her famous Chanel suit—a collarless, braid-trimmed cardigan jacket and slim, graceful skirt—was an enormous hit. She also popularized pea jackets and bell-bottom trousers plus magnificent jewelry worn with sportswear.

In 1969 Coco Chanel's life was the basis for *Coco,* a Broadway musical starring Katharine Hepburn. Chanel died in 1971, working to the end on a new collection. □

Chang Chien

Chang Chien (1853-1926) was a Chinese industrialist and social reformer who was chiefly concerned with finding a means to strengthen the Chinese nation at a time when it was threatened by foreign imperialism. His pragmatic reforms offered an alternative to the political methods of others.

On July 1, 1853, Chang Chien was born in the province of Kiangsu in central China. His ancestors had long been illiterate farmers. His father, however, acquired some education, and he enabled his sons to study for the civil service examinations. Chang passed the first of these trilevel examinations at the relatively early age of 15. But then his fortune changed, for despite repeated attempts he did not succeed in the third and last examination until 1894, when he was 41 years old. In that examination, however, he was ranked the highest—a distinction that brought him fame throughout the nation and promised him opportunities to rise to the highest offices in the government.

In an action almost without precedent for one awarded such an honor in the examinations, Chang rejected a bureaucratic career. This was just at the time of China's humiliating war with Japan, and Chang knew that China could survive in a world of imperialistic nations only if it undertook domestic reforms. He therefore returned to his native district of Nantung near Shanghai and began the series of reforms which he hoped would become a model for the nation.

The most important of Chang's undertakings was the Dah Sun Cotton Mill, which began production in 1899. Cotton cloth manufacture, employing modern machine methods, had begun in China in 1890, but Chang's venture proved to be the most successful of all privately financed cotton mills. This was partly the result of Chang's skilled and paternalistic management of the factory and of the high quality of the cotton fiber grown in Nantung. Within the next 6 years Chang also established in the area around Nantung a flour mill, an oil mill, a shipping line, a distillery, and a silk filature.

Chang used the profits from these ventures to institute a host of social and educational reforms in Nantung. He established a system of schools, including two normal schools, an agricultural school, and a medical college. He also took the lead in founding such diverse institutions as a founding home, a paupers' workshop, a medical clinic, a home for the physically challenged, a school for the blind, a museum, a library, a weather station, and an opera house. Many of these projects were financed entirely by Chang.

A person of Chang's reputation and abilities inevitably became involved in politics. He was an adviser to high officials such as Liu K'un-i, and in that role he helped prevent the provinces of central China from participating in the disastrous Boxer uprising of 1900. After a visit to Japan in 1903, Chang became a fervent advocate of constitutionalism. When the Manchu government instituted a series of reforms leading to constitutional government in 1908, Chang became an active leader in the advisory provincial assembly established in Nanking.

Chang had not favored the activities of the revolutionaries prior to 1911. Like many constitutional reformers in China at this time, however, Chang easily acquiesced in the overthrow of the Ch'ing dynasty and the establishment of a presidential form of government. During the early years of the republic, he served in the new government as minister of industries and then minister of agriculture. He worked harmoniously with President Yüan Shih-k'ai, until Yüan attempted to establish himself as emperor in 1915.

Throughout his career Chang adhered to the traditional Confucian values but was in the forefront of the movement to import modernity to China. In contrast to most other modernizers, such as K'ang Yu-wei and Sun Yatsen, Chang tried to avoid the political arena, believing that the most meaningful reforms to strengthen the nation must be implanted at the local level. He died on Aug. 24, 1926.

Further Reading

The one work on Chang in English is by Samuel C. Chu, *Reformer in Modern China: Chang Chien, 1853-1926* (1965). See also Li Chien-nung, *The Political History of China, 1840-1928* (trans. 1956). □

Chang Chih-tung

Chang Chih-tung (1837-1909) was a Chinese official and reformer. A brilliant Confucian scholar, he was convinced of the peerless quality of China's traditional culture. However, to preserve it, he introduced Western-type industry, education, and military techniques.

During the 19th century China became progressively aware of the necessity of borrowing increments of Western civilization if the country was to remain independent of foreign domination. By the 1860s officials such as Tseng Kuo-fan favored only the manufacture of Western armaments. At the end of the century K'ang Yu-wei and others advocated even the adoption of Western political institutions. Chang Chih-tung stood between these two extremes, making significant economic and even educational innovations, but only as a means of preserving what he regarded as the essence of Chinese culture.

Chang Chih-tung was born on Sept. 2, 1837, in northern China near Peking. His family had served as government officials for generations, and he received a superb classical education in preparation to continue this family tradition. He began his official career in 1863 after passing the third, or metropolitan, civil service examinations with unusual distinction.

Early Conservative Career

In 1879 Chang became famous as a result of his vigorous defense of the empress dowager Tz'u-hsi for her choice of Kuang-hsü as the new emperor following the death of the T'ung-chih emperor. For his support Chang won Tz'u-hsi's undying gratitude, which partially accounted for his subsequent meteoric climb in the official hierarchy. In foreign affairs he became a leader of the "war party," which hated the foreigners and preferred to go to war rather than to encourage the imperialist powers by giving evidence of weakness. His belligerent memorials significantly affected the formation of China's foreign policy in the Ili crisis with Russia (1879-1880) and in the conflict with France over Vietnam (1884-1885).

Chang's Reforms

In 1882 Chang became governor of Shansi Province, and 2 years later he reached the pinnacle of the provincial bureaucracy when he was appointed governor general at Canton. He was transferred in 1889 to the governor generalship at Wuchang in central China, where he served for 18 years, except for two brief interludes (1894-1896 and 1902-1903) as acting governor general at Nanking.

Chang possessed great drive and imagination as a provincial administrator. In 1887 at Canton he founded a modern arsenal and military academy, for the war with France had convinced him—despite his xenophobic tendencies—of the need of borrowing from the West. Two years later he instituted at Canton the first modern mint in China.

Chang's most far-reaching attempts to modernize China occurred during his tenure in Wuchang. In 1890 he opened the iron foundry that subsequently evolved into the huge Han-Yeh-P'ing iron and steel works. He also established cotton mills, silk factories, and tanneries—industrial enterprises that have caused the area around Wuchang to be known as the "Chicago of China." Chang was one of China's leading proponents of railroad and telegraph construction, and the Peking-Hankow Railway was completed largely as a result of his extended efforts from 1889 to 1906. Chang was also China's leading educational innovator, and in Hupei he set up an experimental school system consisting of a teachers' college and a series of primary, technical, and high schools.

Rationale for Reform

In 1898 Chang wrote *Exhortation to Study,* which is one of the most significant pieces of reformist literature in China during the 19th century. Chang presented this treatise to the emperor Kuang-hsü during the midst of the Hundred Days Reform movement, and the Emperor was so pleased that he ordered it to be distributed throughout the empire.

Chang's basic reform philosophy was summed up in the famous phrase, "Chinese learning for the essential principles (*t'i*); Western learning for the practical applications (*yung*). " Chang meant that Western technology and learning (*yung*) should be adopted, but only to the extent that they helped preserve China's culture, morality, and sociopolitical system (*t'i*). In *Exhortation to Study,* therefore, Chang advocated the adoption of Western-style industries and modification of the traditional educational and examination system. But he vehemently opposed the adoption of Western democratic institutions or concepts of social egalitarianism.

Later Career

In 1900 Chang helped prevent another full-scale war with the foreign powers when he restrained the provinces of central China from participating in the Boxer uprising. Between 1901 and 1906 he played a key role in instituting a coherent, nationwide system of schools teaching both traditional Chinese and Western subjects. Perhaps regretting the spread of Westernization in China, he was instrumental in 1906 in having the sacrifices to Confucius raised to the unprecedented dignity of being on a level with sacrifices to heaven and earth.

In 1907 Chang left the post of governor general at Wuchang to fill the posts of grand secretary and director of the new Ministry of Education at Peking. He died on Oct. 4, 1909, 2 years before his beloved Ch'ing dynasty fell to the revolutionaries.

Further Reading

Chang's *Exhortation to Study* was translated by Samuel I. Woodbridge as *China's Only Hope* (1900). William Ayers, *Chang Chih-tung and Educational Reform in China* (1971), is an important study of Chang's career that also touches on aspects other than his educational reform. A short biographical sketch is in Arthur W. Hummel, ed., *Eminent Chinese of the Ch'ing Period,* vol. 1 (1943). For his role in the modernization of China see Albert Feuerwerker, *China's Early Industrialization* (1958), and John L. Rawlinson, *China's Struggle for Naval Development, 1839-1895* (1967). For his place in Chinese intellectual history see Joseph R. Levenson, *Confucian China and Its Modern Fate* (1958). See also Samuel C. Chu, *Reformer in Modern China: Chang Chien, 1853-1926* (1965); Yi C. Wang, *Chinese Intellectuals and the West, 1872-1949* (1966); and Mary Clabaugh Wright, ed., *China in Revolution: The First Phase, 1900-1913* (1968), and her own work, *The Last Stand of Chinese Conservatism: The T'ung-Chih Restoration, 1862-1874* (1957). □

Chang Chü-cheng

Chang Chü-cheng (1525-1582), grand secretary under the emperors Lung-ch'ing and Wan-li, was one of

the most outstanding Chinese ministers of the Ming dynasty.

A precocious child from an impoverished family in what is now Hupei, Chang Chü-cheng achieved the highest academic degree, the *chin-shih,* in 1547, at the age of 22. At this time China was crippled by official corruption and court extravagance and endangered by the threat of Mongol invasion. The country was overdue for reform, but the time was not yet ripe for Chang. He served for 7 years in the Hanlin Academy, interrupted his career for 6 years, and then became vice president of the National University in 1560 and tutor to the future emperor Lung-ch'ing in 1563. In 1567 he was appointed assistant minister of rites and concurrently secretary of the Grand Secretariat. His initial proposal for reforms in government, however, met with negative responses, as he was not yet in a position of influence.

The accession of the Wan-li emperor in July 1572, then a 10-year-old boy, was the starting point of Chang's career; as a senior official of the previous reign and as imperial tutor, he received the mandate of adviser on government affairs. After reaching a compromise with the eunuchs in power as well as with the imperial relatives, Chang became senior grand secretary, then the de facto chief executive under the Emperor. In the following decade, during which he became the most powerful minister in the nation, Chang executed a vigorous program aiming to revitalize the state and strengthen the national defense.

Chang reorganized the official establishment, introduced a merit system for promotions, and carried out periodic evaluation of officials. He then strengthened the treasury through an increased inflow of revenue. To achieve this, he ordered a nationwide land survey to eliminate tax evasion, curbed the accumulation of landed domains by the official class and members of the imperial family, and reorganized the tax structure.

Official efficiency was improved, corruption was kept in check, and the government enjoyed a regular surplus of revenue. Meanwhile, under Chang's leadership two great generals reorganized the frontier defenses and the military establishments, making China strong and secure as never before. As a pragmatic scholar of Legalistic bent, Chang pursued his policy with vigor and determination, heedless of attack and scandal, even at the risk of being denounced as ruthless and despotic.

Chang's high-handed manner, however, antagonized not only the Emperor but also many of his colleagues. Shortly after Chang's death in 1582, his enemies gained their revenge. The Emperor ordered the confiscation of his property and banished the immediate members of his family, and many of the reforms he had introduced were rescinded.

Further Reading

There is no full-length biography of Chang in a Western language. Chang's Confucian Legalism is the subject of a study by Robert Crawford in W. T. de Bary, ed., *Self and Society in Ming Thought* (1969). Aspects of Chang's administration are discussed in Charles O. Hucker, *The Censorial System of Ming China* (1966) and *Chinese Government in Ming Times* (1969). Recommended for general historical background is Edwin O. Reischauer and John K. Fairbank, *A History of East Asian Civilization,* vol. 1 (1960). □

Chang Chüeh

The Chinese religious and revolutionary leader Chang Chüeh (died 184) founded a Taoist religious movement which, as a political force known as the Yellow Turbans, shook the Later Han dynasty, 25-220, to its foundations and contributed to its final collapse.

The conditions of the time facilitated the rise of the religious rebel movements of Chang Chüeh and others. A large number of eunuchs at the court controlled the Emperor and many of the local officials. More and more officials held office not through merit but because they had bribed the powerful eunuchs. Government taxes were increasing at the same time that local officials were levying exorbitant exactions. Northeastern China, where Chang developed his following, suffered from other problems as well. During the 170s and early 180s the area was hit by a series of droughts, famines, and widespread epidemics. Furthermore, at the Han court, a three-way struggle for power involved the Confucian officials, the consort family members, and the eunuchs.

Chang Chüeh, whose name is sometimes romanized Chang Chiao, first appeared in history in the 170s, when he began to attract a religious following. Known as the T'ai P'ing Tao (the Way of Great Peace), the movement was based upon the healing of the sick. Illnesses were considered to be the results of wrongdoings; the afflicted repented of his sins and was thereby cured. Those not cured were held not sincere believers in the Way. By about 175 Chang Chüeh was sending disciples throughout three-fourths of the provinces of China. The sick and the homeless (who were fleeing from rapacious landlords and officials) flocked to his movement. Converts were organized into units under a carefully regimented hierarchy.

By 184 Chang Chüeh had announced the political objective of overthrowing the Han dynasty. The original plan was to coordinate uprisings in the provinces with a palace coup led by some of the eunuchs. When news of this plan leaked out, the rebellion was prematurely launched: within less than 10 days several hundred thousand converts rose in rebellion. They identified themselves in battle by wearing yellow turbans—hence the alternate name of the movement. Local government offices were attacked; villages and towns were sacked and burned. The government responded by creating large armies and placing them under the control of leading political figures. Within the year Chang Chüeh had died of illness, and most of the Yellow Turban leaders were slain in battle. Without its leaders the movement as a largescale force ceased to be a threat to the government. Local elements, however, continued sporadic uprisings.

The long-term consequences of Chang-Chüeh and his religiopolitical movement may be considered twofold. First, the generals who led the imperial armies developed local power bases that the central government was not able to control. Ultimately, these generals, dividing China among themselves, brought about the downfall of the Han dynasty in 220. Second, from Chang Chüeh's Taoist movement (and from another, contemporary one in western China) was to come the popular Taoist religion, which continued to attract a mass following throughout subsequent Chinese history.

Further Reading

There is no book-length study of Chang or the Yellow Turbans. However, for a very good discussion of both in the larger context of the history of Taoism see Holmes Welch, *Taoism: The Parting of the Way* (1957; rev. ed. 1966). □

Chang Hsüeh-ch'eng

Chang Hsüeh-ch'eng (1738-1801) was a Chinese scholar and historian. His ideas about historical methodology and the historical process were far more advanced than those of most of his contemporaries.

Chang Hsüeh-ch'eng was a native of China's coastal province of Chekiang. Both his father and his grandfather had been government officials, and they handed on to Chang an avid interest in history and literature, a belief in strict adherence to the principles of historical accuracy, and the conviction that one must write and teach on the basis of one's principles without regard for popular esteem. Although Chang achieved the highest civil service examination degree in 1778, he never held high office and, in fact, spent much of his life on the verge of poverty.

Philosophy of History

Chang's best-known publications are his local histories (*ti-fang chih*) and two major collections of his essays on historiography (*Wen-shih t'ung-i* and *Chiao-ch'ou t'ung-i*). Chang was a methodical historian, and he developed his own indexing system in order to assure proper attention to detail and accuracy. He became one of the most enlightened historical theorists during the Ch'ing dynasty. Unlike many Ch'ing historians, Chang spurned pedantic historical writing and urged historians to search for general interpretations through specific factual information.

It was Chang's argument that history was an evolutionary process of individuals and political and cultural institutions. He felt that historical development was underlain by a basic principle or "path" (*tao*), which was the human potential for living an ordered, civilized, and moral life. To Chang the good historian was a sage who could "apprehend the essential character of the past and present" and "understand the principles by which the world is ordered." Chang believed, furthermore, that the ideal society was one in which there was a total integration of the intellectual-literary world and the political-institutional world, in which scholars would be officials, and in which culture and state were synonymous. In this idea Chang was applying the thoughts of the great Ming philosopher Wang Yang-ming, who had advocated a "unity of thought and action." Relating his thoughts to the political conditions of his day, Chang firmly supported state control of scholarship and even endorsed the Emperor's literary inquisition of the late 18th century.

The last years of Chang's life marked a sad close to a life of brilliant thought. Few of his contemporaries accepted Chang's "radical" ideas, and he found himself in extreme poverty without the support of a patron. He died in 1801 with few friends and almost no disciples, and it was not until the late 19th century that Chinese scholars began to fully appreciate his genius.

Further Reading

A superb study of Chang is David S. Nivison, *The Life and Thought of Chang Hsüeh-ch'eng* (1966). Other works which provide substantial information about him are Arthur W. Hummel, ed., *Eminent Chinese of the Ch'ing Period, 1644-1912* (2 vols., 1943-1944); Liang Ch'i-ch'ao, *Intellectual Trends in the Ch'ing Period* (1959); and W. G. Beasley and E. G. Pulleyblank, eds., *Historians of China and Japan* (1961). □

Chang Po-go

Chang Po-go (died 846) was a Korean adventurer and merchant prince whose name was once synonymous with Korean maritime dominance in eastern Asia in the early 9th century.

Son of a fisherman from Wan Island off the southwestern coast of the Korean peninsula, Chang Po-go early migrated to T'ang China, where he rose to be a captain in Hsü-chou in the lower Huai River valley. Returning to Korea in 828, he alerted the throne over the danger of Chinese piracy in the Yellow Sea, whereupon the King appointed him commissioner of Ch'onghaejin, the military headquarters of Wan Island. Chang raised a private navy, which at times numbered 10,000 men, by which he controlled the ocean commerce between China, Korea, and Japan.

The ships engaged in this international trade were owned and manned by Chang, and Korean trading communities flourished along the southern coast of the Shantung Peninsula and the lower reaches of the Huai. Some of these colonies enjoyed extraterritorial privileges, such as the famous Mount Ch'ih community, which over looked the sea route between China and Korea. These communities often served as an intermediary between Chinese authorities and Japanese visitors, as in the case of the Japanese pilgrim

Ennin, who at one time addressed a letter to Chang for his assistance and shelter.

In 837 Chang was involved in a royal succession struggle. From the end of the 8th century on, the Silla court was beset by contention between the rising aristocracy and the authoritarian monarchy based on the bone rank (bloodline) system. Hence the throne, hitherto determined solely by bloodline, came to require political skill and military might. Often a contender, to bolster his claim, had to ally himself with local chiefs who were disillusioned nobles, depending for their power on private soldiers recruited from serfs and vagrants. In 839 the son of the former king's rival Kyunjong, with military assistance from Chang, succeeded in overthrowing his rival and ascending the throne as Sinmu.

History relates that the downfall of Chang was connected with his efforts to marry off his daughter to the King. The marriage alliance had probably been promised by Sinmu during his protracted sojourn on Wan Island, but because of his untimely death Chang sought to force Sinmu's successor-son to abide by the promise. Chang's attempt in 845 to force the throne to adopt his daughter as royal consort irritated the central aristocracy, who frowned upon such an alliance as unsavory and potentially dangerous. Chang's death by assassination is traditionally placed in 846, but it may have occurred a few years earlier. In 851 Ch'onghaejin was abolished as a military base, and thus ended the maritime kingdom of Chang Po-go, and with it the brief Silla maritime dominance in eastern Asia.

Further Reading

There is no full-length biography of Chang in English. He is discussed in Edwin O. Reischauer, *Ennin's Travels in T'ang China* (1955). □

Chang Tso-lin

The Chinese warlord Chang Tso-lin (1873-1928) unified Manchuria and brought it into the realm of national Chinese politics. Forced to contend with ambitious neighbors, he distrusted the Russians and leaned toward the Japanese.

Chang Tso-lin was born of peasant stock in the northeastern province of Fengtien. Lacking formal education, he joined the army and fought in the first Sino-Japanese War (1894-1895). By the time of the Russo-Japanese War (1904-1905), he had organized a large force of irregulars, which he led in support of Japan. The chaotic conditions that prevailed during the declining years of the Manchu dynasty and the early period of the republic enabled Chang to further enhance his military power in Manchuria through deft military and political maneuvers. When the death of China's president, Yüan Shih-k'ai, opened the way for undisguised warlordism (1916-1928), Chang became *tuchun,* or military governor, of Fengtien. With the cooperation of Tuan Ch'i-jui, leader of the Anfu Clique, Chang had, by mid-1919, extended his control to the rest of Manchuria. From then until his death Manchuria was his private domain.

Chang was less successful when he sought to extend his influence into adjacent areas. His efforts in Outer Mongolia collapsed in 1921, when a new government was established under Soviet auspices. The first Chihli-Fengtien war (April-May 1922) brought the collapse of Chang's first bid for hegemony of North China. In 1924 Gen. Feng Yü-hsiang's timely defection to his side enabled Chang to establish a short-lived triumvirate in Peking with Feng and Tuan Ch'i-jui.

However, within a year Chang's fortunes had changed. He had to withdraw a substantial portion of his forces from North China, and only Japanese intervention saved Manchuria from an attempted coup. The plot, which enjoyed at least the moral support of the Soviet Union, provoked Chang to move against the Russian-controlled Chinese Eastern Railway, but threat of military retaliation forced him to back down. Having reconsolidated his position in Peking, Chang struck once again against the Russians. In a raid on the Soviet embassy on April 6, 1927, he netted volumes of incriminating documents and seized for execution Li Ta-chao and other Chinese Communists.

After a lifetime of shrewd manipulation of friends and foes, Chang finally fell between the millstones of Chinese nationalism and Japanese expansionism. As Chiang kai-shek's Northern Expedition moved into North China in April 1928, the Japanese leaders attempted to halt the fighting

before it poured over into Manchuria by urging Chang to retire north of the Great Wall. Chang hesitated but finally left Peking on June 3. The following day his train was blown up by a bomb planted by Japanese conspirators. Chang's assassination was an ominous prelude to the Japanese invasion of Sept. 18, 1931, which terminated the reign of his son and heir, Chang Hsüehliang.

Further Reading

The literature on Chang is inadequate. An older work is Putnam Weale, *Chang Tso-Lin's Struggle against the Communist Menace* (1927). The papers that Chang seized in his raid on the Soviet embassy were translated and edited in C. Martin Wilbur and Julie Lien-ying How, *Documents on Communism, Nationalism, and Soviet Advisers in China, 1918-1927* (1956). Chang's maneuvers in the context of warlord politics are covered in Oliver Edmund Clubb, *Twentieth Century China* (1964).

Additional Sources

McCormack, Gavan, *Chang Tso-lin in northeast China, 1911-1928: China, Japan, and the Manchurian idea,* Stanford, Calif.: Stanford University Press, 1977. □

Edward Channing

The historian Edward Channing (1856-1931), a specialist in American colonial and Revolutionary history, is best known for his multivolume "History of the United States."

Edward Channing, born on June 15, 1856, in Dorchester, Mass., was the son of William Ellery Channing the younger, a poet. At the age of 4 Edward was sent to Boston to live with his grandfather, Walter Channing, the dean of Harvard Medical School.

Channing graduated from Harvard in 1878. After hearing lectures by the distinguished Harvard history professor Henry Adams, Channing decided to pursue a career as a historian. He received his doctorate of philosophy in history from Harvard in 1880 with a dissertation on the Louisiana Purchase.

Channing applied to President Eliot of Harvard to teach American history but was refused. After touring Europe for a year Channing returned to Harvard as an independent student. In 1883 he became an instructor at Harvard. He married Alice Thacher in 1886 and gradually climbed the academic ladder, becoming a full professor in 1897. It was not until 1896, however, that Channing could offer a course in his special field, colonial history.

Channing won the coveted Tappan Prize for *Town and County Government in the English Colonies* (1884), in which he argued that comparisons of American with European institutions rested upon erroneous analogies and meaningless similarities. That year Channing helped found the American Historical Association.

During the 1880s Channing became a close friend of Justin Winsor and wrote essays for Winsor's *Narrative and Critical History of America.* Channing wrote several textbooks in the 1890s: *English History for American Readers,* with Thomas Wentworth Higginson; a volume in the "Cambridge Historical Series," *The United States of America, 1765-1865;* and *Student's History of the United States.*

In 1899 Channing embarked upon the project that occupied him for the rest of his life—a multivolume history of the United States. He had conceived the idea during his undergraduate days, planning to cover the period from A.D. 1000 to the end of the Civil War in eight volumes. To accomplish this feat, he devoted himself almost exclusively to it and to his teaching. Channing was able to complete only six volumes of *The History of the United States* (1905-1925); the sixth volume, *The War for Southern Independence,* won the Pulitzer Prize.

Channing's history was based on original sources; its theme, as historian Samuel Eliot Morison wrote, was that "the single most important fact in our development has been the victory of the forces of union over particularism." Channing's nationalism led him to concentrate upon political and constitutional developments, although he did devote time to urban history as well as to religious and educational developments. Despite such methodological shortcomings as refusing to use contemporary newspapers as source material, Channing's was the most scholarly multivolume history of the United States that had been published to his day.

Channing retired from Harvard in 1929. He died in Cambridge on Jan. 6, 1931.

Further Reading

Samuel Eliot Morison, Channing's student, presented a warm, friendly view of his teacher in "Edward Channing: A Memoir," printed in Morison's *By Land and by Sea: Essays and Addresses* (1953). George W. Robinson compiled the *Bibliography of Edward Channing* (1932). Two other accounts that assess Channing as a historian are Ralph Ray Johrney's "Edward Channing" in William T. Hutchinson, ed., *The Marcus W. Jernegan Essays in American Historiography* (1937), and John Higham's comments in John Higham and others, *History: The Development of Historical Studies in the United States* (1965). □

William Ellery Channing

William Ellery Channing (1780-1842), an American minister, was a key Unitarian theologian for the mid-19th century.

William Ellery Channing came from what is known as "the best New England stock." That is, his ancestors arrived in New England early and soon distinguished themselves by their industry and decorum. He was born on April 8, 1780, in Newport, R.I., to William and Lucy Ellery Channing. He graduated from Harvard College in 1798. He spent some time as a tutor, and in 1802 he returned to Harvard to study for the ministry. Because he showed great promise, Harvard appointed him regent, a less lofty post than the title suggested. He acted as a proctor to the students, but the job left him time for books and helped him support himself. The next year he was ordained as minister of the Federal Street Church in Boston, where he remained until his death. He married his cousin Ruth Gibbs in 1814.

In a sense, leadership and eminence came to Channing not through aggressively seeking it but because he was born at the right time. Theology was in crisis during Channing's prime. Almost from the beginning there were two warring parties in New England. The Calvinists believed in a jealous God, the depravity of mankind, and the absence of free will. The anti-Calvinists believed in a merciful God, the potential redemption of all mankind, and the existence of free will. As the 19th century proceeded, the fight between the parties sharpened. Channing, after much deliberation, sided with the anti-Calvinists.

In Baltimore in 1819 Channing preached a sermon entitled "Unitarian Christianity." It was a masterly manifesto for the Unitarian cause and formulated the creed of Unitarianism; it consequently consolidated Channing's leadership. Other influential sermons followed. "The Moral Argument against Calvinism" was delivered and printed in 1820. "Unitarian Christianity Most Favorable to Piety" (1826) emphasized the relevance of the movement and its personal basis: "We regard Unitarianism as peculiarly the friend of inward, living, practical religion."

In 1820 Channing organized a conference of Unitarian ministers, which 5 years later fathered the American Unitarian Association. He helped found the Unitarian journal, *Christian Register,* and became one of its outstanding contributors.

For his increasing audience Channing prepared some essays which discussed the social and cultural questions of the time. He especially campaigned for a genuine American literature. In his essay "The Importance and Means of a National Literature" (1830) he called for cultural independence from England and for a new literature which would reflect the hopeful, expansive attitude that he himself took in theology. The tract was read the more respectfully because Channing himself had written on English literature in both English and American magazines and was friendly with some of the best British writters of his period.

Channing grew increasingly interested in politics, believing that political reform, like religious reform, had to start from within. He aimed his political efforts at humanitarian causes: the abolition of slavery, the crusade against drinking, and the improvement in the conditions of the poor. In the slavery dispute he appealed to the conscience of Southerners instead of attacking them. He believed a harmonious and happy nation could be achieved through appealing to man's innate goodness. Though his own congregation disagreed with his stand against slavery, his last public address, in August 1842, was on behalf of emancipation. He died the following October.

Further Reading

A satisfactory modern biography is Arthur W. Brown, *Always Young for Liberty: A Biography of William Ellery Channing* (1956). Other works include *Channing's Life . . . with Extracts from His Correspondence,* edited by W. H. Channing (3 vols., 1848); J. W. Chadwick, *William Ellery Channing, Minister of Religion* (1903); and Madeleine Hook Rice, *Federal Street Pastor: The Life of William Ellery Channing* (1961).

Additional Sources

Delbanco, Andrew, *William Ellery Channing: an essay on the liberal spirit in America,* Cambridge, Mass.: Harvard University Press, 1981.

Edgell, David P., *William Ellery Channing, an intellectual portrait,* Westport, Conn.: Greenwood Press, 1983, 1955.

Eliot, Charles William, *Four American leaders,* Philadelphia: R. West, 1977, c1906.

Mendelsohn, Jack, *Channing, the reluctant radical: a biography,* Westport, Conn.: Greenwood Press, 1980, 1971. □

Chao Meng-fu

The Chinese painter Chao Meng-fu (1254-1322) was a high official under the Yüan dynasty, 1279-1369, and helped to establish the tradition of amateur scholarly painting, wen-jen-hua.

Chao Meng-fu was born at Huchow in Chekiang Province. He was a descendant of the Sung dynasty imperial family and destined for a brilliant official career. But while he was still in a junior post, the Sung dynasty fell and he retired into private life. In 1286, however, he was persuaded to take office under the Mongol conquerors of China. He often regretted his decision, but in the course of his long career he helped to soften the attitude of the Mongols toward their Chinese subjects. He served under five emperors and held several important posts, including that of director of the Hanlin Academy of Letters and governor of Chekiang and Kiangsi provinces. He was greatly admired in his lifetime, and on his death he was canonized as Duke of Wei.

Chao Meng-fu was considered the leading calligrapher of his time. He was especially noted for his *hisiao-k'ai shu* (small formal script) and *Hsing-shu* (running script), in which he revived the fluid, harmonious style of the great 3d-century calligrapher Wang Hsi-chih.

Study and Development

As a youth, Chao Meng-fu studied under the obscure artist Ao Shan, but he was also influenced by his conservative friend Ch'ien Hsüan. In the course of his official journeys in North China after 1286, Chao Meng-fu saw and collected paintings by the great masters of the 10th and 11th centuries, such as Li Ch'eng, Tung Yüan, and Fan K'uan, who were largely unknown in the South. These pictures inspired him to break away from the conventions into which landscape painting had hardened at the end of the Southern Sung Dynasty. "The most important thing in painting," he wrote, "is the spirit of antiquity (*ku-i*). " By this he meant not simply copying ancient styles but reviving the spirit of the old masters and using their direct, unaffected approach to nature as a way of finding a new freedom of expression.

On his return from the North in 1295, Chao Meng-fu painted for a friend his most famous surviving had scroll, *Autumn Colors on the Ch'iao and Hua Mountains,* a landscape in which he interprets archaic conventions in a revolutionary way. Seven years later, in the hand scroll *Water Village,* he carried his new style still further: the composition is inspired by Tung Yüan and, more remotely, by the T'ang painter-poet Wang Wei; but the brushstroke is even more relaxed and spontaneous. Of his own paintings Chao Meng-fu wrote that "they may seem simply and carelessly done, but true connoisseurs will realize that they are very close to the old models."

Chao Meng-fu was noted as a painter of bamboo, and there is a beautiful hand scroll by him, *Bamboo, Rocks and Lonely Orchids.* He also painted animals, especially horses. The most original of his animal paintings is the *Sheep and Goat* executed in a dry and deceptively simple brushwork. Nearly all the surviving horse paintings that bear his name are forgeries, but there is, in the John M. Crawford, Jr., Collection in New York, a painting by him of a horse and groom in dry ink on paper. Several members of his family were noted painters in their day: on this same scroll are studies of horses and grooms by his son Chao Yung and grandson Chao Lin. His wife, Kuan Tao-sheng, was China's foremost woman painter of landscape and bamboo.

Chao Meng-fu expressed in his art and writing the ideals of the *wen-jen-hua:* a cool detachment and understatement, a lack of concern for realism and for obvious visual appeal, a close union of painting and calligraphy, a restrained self-expression, and a creative reinterpretation of the art of the past which could be fully understood only by the small circle of the scholarly elite. The revolution, both in painting and in attitudes to painting, which Chao Meng-fu epitomized was carried to fruition by the next generation of Yüan scholar painters, the "Four Masters"—Huang Kung-wang, Wu Chen, Ni Tsan, and Wang Meng.

Further Reading

There is no complete study of the work of Chao Meng-fu in any Western language, although a survey of his career and achievement is found in volume 4 of Osvald Sirén, *Chinese Painting: Leading Masters and Principles* (7 vols., 1956-1958). Two monographs by Li Chu-tsing deal in detail with certain aspects of Chao Meng-fu's work as a painter: *The Autumn Colors on the Ch'iao and Hua Mountains* (1965) and *The Freer Sheep and Goat and Chao Meng-fu's Horse Paintings* (1968). The most comprehensive account of Yüan art is Sherman E. Lee and Ho Wai-kam, *Chinese Art under the Mongols: The Yüan Dynasty, 1279-1368* (1968). □

(F.) Stuart Chapin

F.(rancis) Stuart Chapin (1888-1974) was one of the first American sociologists to try to apply the research procedures of the physical sciences and the techniques of statistics to studies of social behavior, particularly in the areas of social and cultural change and social status.

F. Stuart Chapin was born in Brooklyn, New York, in 1888. He was educated at Columbia University and received his Ph.D. in sociology in 1911 with additional training in statistics. He taught at Wellesley College in 1911-1912, at Simmons College in 1912, and from 1912-1914 was an instructor in sociology and statistics at Smith College. Promoted to assistant professor in 1914 and associate professor in the same year, he eventually became professor of sociology and statistics and director of Smith's School of Social Work in 1919.

Chapin joined the faculty of the University of Minnesota in 1922, where he served as director of that institution's School of Social Work from 1922 to 1949 and as professor and chairman of the Department of Sociology from 1922 until 1953. He retired as professor emeritus in 1953 to become president of Consumer Behavior, Inc. in New York, a post he occupied until 1963. He conducted a private practice as a social research consultant until 1972. He died in Asheville, North Carolina in 1974.

Chapin was a consultant to the League of Nations, to the United Nations Economic, Scientific and Cultural Committee (UNESCO) in France, and to the World Health Organization in Geneva. He served as a member of the Governor's Commission on Education Beyond High School (North Carolina). He was one of the founders of *Social Science Abstracts* (1928) and was its editor-in-chief from 1928 to 1932.

Chapin was recognized by his professional peers by election to membership in the Social Science Research Council (1922-1927) and by his elections as president of the American Sociological Association in 1935 and of the Social Research Association in 1936. His contributions to the cause of making sociology a more exact science was acknowledged by the American scientific community when he was elected vice president of the American Association for the Advancement of Science in 1943.

Chapin's concerns as a sociologist are suggested by advice he offered to younger sociologists as a former president of the American Sociological Association. He observed in the *American Sociological Review* in December 1953:

> You should seek to become known as a social scientist in the field of your specialty. Do not be misled by resistance to overspecialization. . . . Remember that research, scholarship and teaching are interacting behaviors, each one reinforces the other. Techniques are no more effective in the long run than the soundness of the basic logic that underlies them. Technique should not become an end in itself lest you remain a skilled artisan instead of a creative worker who invents and discovers. Techniques should not become a snobbish escape device in which you seek mere intellectual security. . . . Remember that social values are an important subject matter of study and value judgments contribute to decisions on what to study. But try to keep your value systems from undermining the objectivity of your research method. Do not mix your roles. . . .

Chapin's scholarly career centered on two major concerns: the use of the methods of physical and biological science—what is often referred to as "scientific method"—and the techniques of statistics to make social science in general and sociology in particular more rigorous, and, hence, more scientific; and the use of sociology to "prevent the recurrence of social ills." He studied phenomena as diverse as the personal adjustment of work relief clients, social effects of public housing, physical and social space as determinants of social status, social participation of Boy Scouts, and community leadership. He developed the Chapin Social Status Scale (1935) that attempts to measure objectively people's socioeconomic status through recording observations of the equipment, condition, and "cultural expression" of their living rooms (cleanliness or orderliness of room, kind of flooring, floor covering, furniture, and the like); and the Chapin Social Participation Scale (1937), that relates social status to participation in voluntary organizations (as social status rises, so does the number of voluntary organizations in which one is involved). He also contributed to greater understanding of social change and its relation to the development of social institutions.

Further Reading

Don Martindale, *The Nature and Types of Sociological Theory,* 2d ed. (1981) contains a penetrating analysis of Chapin's work. Chapin's concerns are mirrored in his own writings, which include the following books: *Field Work and Social Research* (1920); *Introduction to the Study of Social Evolution* (1923); *Cultural Change* (1928); *The Measurement of Social Status by the Use of the Social Status Scale* (1933); *Contemporary American Institutions* (1935, 1946); *Social Participation Scale* (1937); *Community Leadership and Opinion in Red Wing* (1945); and *Experimental Designs in Social Research* (1947). □

Charles Spencer Chaplin

The film actor, director, and writer Charles Spencer Chaplin (1889-1977) was one of the most original creators in the history of the cinema. His remarkable portrayal of "the tramp"—a sympathetic comic character in ill-fitting clothes and a trademark mustache—won admiration from international audiences.

Charlie Chaplin was born in a poor district of London on April 16, 1889. His mother, a talented singer, spent most of her life in and out of mental hospitals; his father was a fairly successful vaudevillian until he began drinking. After his parents separated, Charlie and his half brother, Sidney, spent most of their childhood in the Lambeth Workhouse. Barely able to read and write, Chaplin left school to tour with a group of clog dancers. Later he had the lead in a comedy act; by the age of 19 he had become one of the most popular music-hall performers in England.

Arrived in the United States

In 1910 Chaplin went to the United States to tour in *A Night in an English Music Hall* and was chosen by film maker Mack Sennett to appear in the silent Keystone comedy series. In these early movies (*Making a Living, Tillie's Punctured Romance*), Chaplin made the transition from a comedian of overdrawn theatrics to one of cinematic delicacy and choreographic precision. He created the role of the tramp, a masterful comic conception, notable, as George Bernard Shaw remarked, for its combination of "noble melancholy and impish humour."

Appearing in over 30 short films, Chaplin realized that the breakneck speed of Sennett's productions was hindering his personal talents. He left to work at the Essanay Studios. Outstanding during this period were *His New Job, The Tramp,* and *The Champion,* notable for their comic pathos and leisurely exploration of character. More realistic and satiric were his 1917 films for the Mutual Company: *One A.M., The Pilgrim, The Cure, Easy Street,* and *The Immigrant.* In 1918 Chaplin built his own studio and signed a $1,000,000 contract with National Films, producing such silent-screen classics as *A Dog's Life,* comparing the life of a

dog with that of a tramp, *Shoulder Arms,* a satire on World War I, and *The Kid* a touching vignette of slum life.

In 1923 Chaplin, D. W. Griffith, Douglas Fairbanks, and Mary Pickford formed United Artists to produce feature-length movies of high quality. *A Woman of Paris* (1923), a psychological drama, was followed by two of Chaplin's funniest films, *The Gold Rush* (1925) and *The Circus* (1928). Chaplin directed *City Lights* (1931), a beautifully lyrical, Depression tale about the tramp's friendship with a drunken millionaire and a blind flower girl, considered by many critics his finest work. His only concession to the new sound medium occurred in the hilarious scene in which the tramp hiccoughs with a tin whistle in his windpipe while trying to listen politely to a concert. The pathos of the closing scene, in which the flower girl, who has just regained her sight (thanks to the tramp) sees him for the first time, is described by James Agee (1958): "She has imagined and anticipated him as princely, to say the least; and it has never seriously occurred to him that he is inadequate. She recognizes who he must be by his shy, confident, shining joy as he comes silent toward her. And he recognizes himself for the first time, through the terrible changes in her face. The camera just exchanges a few quiet close-ups of the emotions which shift and intensify in each face. It is enough to shrivel the heart to see, and it is the greatest piece of acting and the highest moment in the movies."

Modern Times (1936), a savagely hilarious farce on the cruelty, hypocrisy, and greed of modern industrialism, contains some of the funniest sight gags and comic sequences in film history, the most famous being the tramp's battle with an eating machine gone berserk. Chaplin's burlesque of Hitler (as the character Hynkel) in *The Great Dictator* (1940), although a devastating satire, loses impact in retrospect. The last film using the tramp, it contains an epilogue in which Chaplin pleads for love and freedom.

It was with these more complex productions of the 1930s and 1940s that Chaplin achieved true greatness as film director and satirist. *Monsieur Verdoux,* brilliantly directed by Chaplin in 1947 (and subsequently condemned by the American Legion of Decency), is one of the subtlest and most compelling moral statements ever put on the screen. Long before European film makers taught audiences to appreciate the role of the writer-director, Chaplin revealed the astonishing breadth of his talents by functioning as such in his productions.

Political Views Stir Trouble

The love showered upon Chaplin in the early years of his career was more than equaled by the vilification directed toward him during the 1940s and early 1950s. The American public was outraged by the outspoken quality of his political views, the turbulence of his personal life, and the sarcastic, often bitter, element expressed in his art. An avowed socialist and atheist, Chaplin expressed a hatred for right-wing dictatorship which made him politically suspect during the early days of the cold war. This hostility was compounded when he released his version of the Bluebeard theme, *Monsieur Verdoux.* With its brilliantly sustained parallels between mass murder and capitalistic exploitation, the film is, as Agee said, "the greatest of talking comedies though so cold and savage that it had to find its audience in grimly experienced Europe."

During the next 5 years Chaplin devoted himself to *Limelight* (1952), a strongly autobiographical work with a gentle lyricism and sad dignity, in sharp contrast to the mordant pessimism of *Monsieur Verdoux.* "I was optimistic and still not convinced," he wrote, "that I had completely lost the affection of the American people, that they could be so politically conscious or so humorless as to boycott anyone that could amuse them." Further tarnishing Chaplin's image was a much-publicized paternity suit brought against him. Although Chaplin proved he was not the child's father, the reaction to the charges was overwhelmingly negative.

On vacation in Europe in 1952, Chaplin was notified by the U.S. attorney general that his reentry into the United States would be challenged. The charge was moral turpitude and political unreliability. Chaplin, who had never become a United States citizen, sold all his American possessions and settled in Geneva, Switzerland, with his fourth wife, Oona O'Neill, daughter of the American playwright Eugene O'Neill, and their children.

In 1957 Chaplin visited England to direct *The King in New York* a satire on American institutions, which was never shown in the United States. *My Autobiography,* published in 1964, is a long, detailed account that descends from a vivid, Dickensian mode to endless self apologies and name-dropping. Such an error, wrote John Mason Brown, "is only a proof of his modesty. He forgets that one of the biggest names he has to drop is Charlie Chaplin." Chaplin's

1967 film, *A Countess from Hong Kong,* was considered disastrous by most critics.

Return to the U.S.

By the 1970s times had changed, and Chaplin was again recognized for his rich contribution to film making. He returned to the United States in 1972, where he was honored by major tributes in New York City and Hollywood, including receiving an honorary Academy Award. In 1975, he became Sir Charles Chaplin after being knighted by Queen Elizabeth II. Two years later, on December 25, 1977, Chaplin died in his sleep in Switzerland.

In all his work Chaplin consistently displayed emotional expressiveness, physical grace, and intellectual vision characteristic of the finest actors. The classical austerity and deceptive simplicity of his directorial style (emulated by Ingmar Bergman and others) has not been surpassed. A film about Chaplin's life, titled *Chaplin* was released in 1992.

Chaplin's most conspicuous deficiencies as an artist were attributable more to personal limitations than to aesthetic insensitivity. His occasional sentimentality represented an attempt to conceal deep bitterness; his frequently irritating tendency to idealize the female sex betrayed, as critic Andrew Sarris noted, the mark of the confirmed misogynist. Chaplin was a lovable but unloving figure—a fascinating, elusive, and difficult human being.

Further Reading

Chaplin, Charlie, *My Autobiography,* Simon & Schuster, 1964

Kerr, Walter, *The Silent Clowns,* Alfred A. Knopf, 1975

Robinson, David *Chaplin: His Life and Art,* McGraw-Hill Book Co., 1985 ☐

George Chapman

The English poet, dramatist, and translator George Chapman (1559/1634) is best known for his rhyming verse translations of Homer's *Iliad* and *Odyssey*.

George Chapman was born in Hitchen, a country town near London. He may have attended Oxford, although he claimed to have been selftaught. He spent a few years in the household of a nobleman and in 1591-1592 was engaged in military service on the Continent.

Chapman became an important literary figure with the publication of his first work, *The Shadow of Night* (1594). This obscure philosophical poem has led some to speculate that Chapman at this time belonged to the "School of Night"—a group of avant-garde thinkers who supposedly challenged traditional beliefs. Although the existence of such a formal "school" is still in doubt, it is clear that Chapman was acquainted with some of the more exciting thinkers of his day.

Chapman's reputation as a man of letters was firmly established by *Ovid's Banquet of Sense* (1595) and his continuation of Christopher Marlowe's *Hero and Leander* (1598), both of them amatory, erotic poems in the vein of Shakespeare's *Venus and Adonis* (1593). He began writing for the stage about 1595 and in the following 10 years composed a number of comedies, including *A Humorous Day's Mirth* (1597), the earliest example of the "comedy of humours" closely identified with Ben Jonson. Chapman's best-known dramatic work, however, is the heroic tragedy *Bussy D'Ambois* (1604), which celebrates the lofty aspirations of Renaissance individualism. The title character, modeled on a Frenchman who died in 1579, claims to be superior to ordinary mortals. In *The Revenge of Bussy D'Ambois,* a sequel written some 6 years later, Chapman presents a different kind of heroic virtue in the person of Bussy's brother Cleremont, who is noted for his extraordinary stoic forbearance and self-control.

Despite his success as a poet and a dramatist, Chapman led a very insecure existence. In 1600 he was imprisoned for debt, and in 1605 he suffered the same punishment for his part in *Eastward Ho!,* a play written in collaboration with Jonson and John Marston. For a time he was patronized by Prince Henry; when Henry died unexpectedly in 1612, Chapman found himself again in precarious straits.

Chapman's literary energies after 1613 were devoted almost exclusively to his monumental translation of Homer, which he had begun many years earlier and which he considered his most significant literary achievement. The completed translation, published in 1624, has been immortalized by John Keats's sonnet "On First Looking into Chapman's Homer" (1816). Chapman died on May 12, 1634.

Further Reading

A full sketch of Chapman's life, with excerpts from his letters, is in Charlotte Spivack's *George Chapman* (1967). For an account of Chapman's ideas on the nature of poetry see Phyllis Brooks Bartlett's introduction to *The Poems of George Chapman* (1941).

Additional Sources

Hunt, R. A., *The Startup papers: on Shakespeare's friend,* Upton-upon-Severn: Images, 1993.

Ellis, Havelock, *Chapman,* Norwood, Pa.: Norwood Editions, 1976. □

Sydney Chapman

The English geophysicist Sydney Chapman (1888-1970) made fundamental contributions to gas theory, to analysis of geomagnetic variations and atmospheric tides, and to theories of magnetic storms, auroras, and ionospheric layers.

Sydney Chapman was born at Eccles near Manchester on Jan. 29, 1888. Winning university scholarships, he first took an engineering degree at Manchester (1907), then mathematics degrees at Manchester (1908) and Cambridge (1911).

Chapman began work on gas theory during his third year at Cambridge, and he continued this work when he returned to Cambridge in 1914, producing two trailblazing papers. He shared with David Enskog the credit for a new method of investigating transport phenomena in gases and the discovery of gaseous thermal diffusion. Gas theory provided the background for much of his later work.

Chapman's years at the Greenwich Observatory, where he became a chief assistant under Frank Dyson (astronomer royal) in 1911, largely determined his future bent. He began by supervising the reconstruction of the magnetic observatory. Finding that magneticians had been far readier to accumulate data than to interpret them, he set about to analyze geomagnetic variations. Since one type of systematic variation appeared to arise from a very small lunar tide in the ionosphere, he sought and found a lunar tide in the barometric records and with immense labor, extending over 30 years, determined its properties over the globe. He devised methods of data handling, now commonplace but then almost unknown.

In 1931 he published two classic papers on the formation of the ionosphere by radiation from the sun, describing the standard "Chapman layer." Other papers on the upper-atmosphere photochemistry followed.

Dyson at Greenwich drew Chapman's attention to the apparent connection between magnetic storms and solar flares, so setting in motion a further series of investigations, which continued for 50 years. The highlight of the results was the Chapman-Ferraro theory of magnetic storms (1930-1933), explaining the storms by the interaction of ionized solar streams with the geomagnetic field. The theory was correct but incomplete; only after the discovery of the Van Allen radiation belts could it be completed.

Chapman was professor of mathematics at Manchester (1919-1924), at the Imperial College (1924-1946), and at Oxford (1946-1953). Retiring from Oxford, he took posts at College, Alaska, at Boulder, Colo., and elsewhere. In 1957 he produced a paper on the sun's corona, foreshadowing the discovery of the solar wind, and began a series of papers on auroras. He presided over the special committee that organized the International Geophysical Year of 1957-1958, which owed an immense amount to his unflagging efforts and inspiration. He died on June 16, 1970.

Further Reading

Syun-Ichi Akasofu, Benson Fogle, and Bernhard Haurwitz, eds., *Sydney Chapman, Eighty: From His Friends* (1968), contains a large number of anecdotes about Chapman together with autobiographical notes covering the years up to about 1930. T. G. Cowling wrote a biographical note on Chapman for publication in *Biographical Memoirs of Fellows of the Royal Society* (1971).

Additional Sources

Alton, Jeannine, *Report on the papers of Professor Sydney Chapman, FRS (1888-1970): deposited in the Bodleian Library, Oxford: with memorandum on the location of other papers,* London: Reproduced for the Contemporary Scientific Archives Centre by the Royal Commission on Historical Manuscripts, 1974. □

Jean Martin Charcot

The French psychiatrist Jean Martin Charcot (1825-1893) specialized in the study of hysteria, using hypnosis as a basis for treatment.

Jean Martin Charcot was born in Paris on Nov. 29, 1825, the son of a carriage maker. He took his medical degree at the University of Paris in 1853 and was appointed professor of pathological anatomy there in 1860. In 1862 he was appointed senior physician at the Salpêtrière, a hospital for the treatment of the mentally ill. It became a center for psychiatric training and psychiatric care, for Charcot had a flair for theatrics in addition to his reputation for sound science, and his lectures and demonstrations attracted students from all over Europe.

Charcot's contributions fall largely into three categories. First, he studied the etiology and cure of hysterical disorders (psychoneuroses). These disorders involve what appear to be physiological disturbances such as convulsions, paralyses, blindness, deafness, anesthesias, and amnesias. However, there is no evidence of physiological abnormalities in psychoneuroses since the root of the problem is psychological. In Charcot's time hysteria was thought to be a disorder found only in women (the Greek word *hystera* means uterus), but his demonstrations were eventually influential in correcting this idea. Charcot, however, continued to think of hysteria as a female disorder. Freud was later to associate hysterical symptoms with sexual problems.

Charcot's second area of contribution was the correlation of various behavioral symptoms with physiological abnormalities of the nervous system. One of the major problems for early psychiatry was that of determining whether certain behavioral abnormalities had their origins in psychological or in physiological disturbances and, if physiological, where in the central nervous system the abnormality might be located. Charcot became noted for his ability to diagnose and locate the physiological disturbances of nervous system functioning.

Finally, Charcot made popular the use of hypnotism as a part of diagnosis and therapy. Hypnotism, known at the time as "mesmerism" (named for Franz Anton Mesmer), was regarded by the medical profession as charlatanism. Charcot found hypnotism useful in distinguishing true psychoneurotics from fakers and, like Mesmer, found that hysterical symptoms could be relieved through its use. In the hypnotic state the patient falls into an apparent sleep. While in this condition, the patient can sometimes recall events in his life which are not recalled in the waking state, and he is susceptible to the suggestions of the therapist. In 1882 Charcot presented a summary of his findings to the French Academy of Sciences, where they were favorably received. Scientific psychiatry was thus well on its way to being accepted by the medical profession. Charcot died on Aug. 16, 1893.

Further Reading

A biography of Charcot is Georges Guillian, *I-M Charcot, 1825-1893: His Life-His Work* (trans. 1959). For general background material see Fielding H. Garrison, *An Introduction to the History of Medicine* (1913; 4th ed. 1929).

Additional Sources

Goetz, Christopher G., *Charcot,* New York: Oxford University Press, 1995. □

Jean Baptiste Siméon Chardin

The French painter Jean Baptiste Siméon Chardin (1699-1779) is considered by modern critics one of the most important artists of the 18th century as well as one of the most distinguished painters in the history of French art.

Jean Baptiste Chardin was born in Paris on Nov. 2, 1699, the son of a cabinetmaker. He studied painting with Jacques Cazes, Nöel Nicholas Coypel, and Jean Baptiste Van Loo. In 1728 Chardin was admitted to the Royal Academy as "a painter of animals and fruit," not a high rank in the academy but one which satisfied the unpretentious artist. The two paintings which won him admission into the academy were *The Rayfish* and *The Buffet,* paintings of fish, fruit, jugs, and other objects decoratively assembled in rather rich compositions enlivened by the presence of animals; both works are in the tradition of 17th-century Dutch and Flemish still-life painting.

After about 1730 Chardin began to paint the genre subjects for which he is best known: small, humble scenes of the everyday life of the Parisian lower middle class with which he was so familiar and to which he belonged. These paintings depict women working in kitchens, children playing quiet solitary games, mothers serving meals; they are simple scenes of ordinary domestic events presented without drama and without emotional flourishes, but Chardin invests them with dignity and humanity. They reveal an aspect of 18th-century French life never seen in the work of the fashionable artists who were patronized by the court and the aristocracy and who produced decorative, elegant, sensual, and light-hearted paintings in the dominant rococo style established by Antoine Watteau in the early years of the century.

By the late 1730s Chardin's value as an artist was recognized, and he began to enjoy success in spite of the fact that his work set him apart from the mainstream of French painting. Connoisseurs and collectors purchased his work, and engravings of his paintings became extremely popular. Good examples of his genre paintings are *The Grace* (ca. 1740), which King Louis XV purchased; *Child with Top* (1738); and *Back from the Market* (1739). Chardin is equally famous for the still-life paintings which he did throughout his career. The best of these are arrangements of a few simple objects such as copper kitchen utensils, a wineglass, a pottery bowl, a peach; examples are *Still Life with Pipe* and *Kitchen Still Life.*

Chardin's style is one of restraint, understatement, and a simplicity that approaches the severe. His colors are often subdued and cool, and many of his later still lifes have an almost austere formality. Chardin cannot, however, be wholly divorced from the rococo style or from the traditions of his century, although he was never a decorative rococo painter like François Boucher or Jean Honoré Fragonard. The 18th century was fond of the small and the intimate, and Chardin's works have these qualities. The subtle complexity of his compositions, his love of refined textures, and his perception of the trembling tonal values of light are also manifestations of contemporary artistic taste. Chardin's style is uniquely his own, but analysis of it reveals the extent to which he belonged to his period.

In 1757 Chardin was granted an apartment in the Louvre, which was not used by the kings of France as a residence at that time and which housed the Royal Academy of Painting and Sculpture. In 1768 King Louis XV gave him a pension. By that time public taste had turned from Chardin's modest scenes to an enthusiastic reception of the melodramatic, sentimental, and moralizing peasant genre of Jean Baptiste Greuze. Chardin continued to paint, however, although during the 1770s his eyesight weakened; he turned to the use of pastel and during the last few years of his life produced impressive work in this difficult medium. He died in Paris on Dec. 6, 1779.

Further Reading

The most comprehensive work on Chardin in English is Georges Wildenstein, *Chardin* (1969), a combination and translation of his two earlier works, in French, of the same title (1933 and 1963). Other works in English include Bernard Denvir, *Chardin* (1950), and Pierre Rosenberg, *Chardin* (1963; trans. 1963), which contains many excellent illustrations. An older but useful work is E. Herbert and A. Furst, *Chardin* (1911). Roger Fry, *French, Flemish, and British Art* (1951), contains an analysis of Chardin's work by an important modern critic who admired it without reservation. An excellent and sympathetic examination of Chardin in the context of 18th-century painting is presented in Michael Levey, *Rococo to Revolution: Major Trends in Eighteenth Century Painting* (1966). References to Chardin can be found in Arno Schönberger and Halldor Soehner's handsomely illustrated *The Rococo Age: Art and Civilization of the 18th Century* (1959; trans. 1960).

Additional Sources

Conisbee, Philip, *Chardin,* Lewisburg N.J.: Bucknell University Press, 1986.

Roland Michel, Marianne, *Chardin,* New York: Abrams, 1996.

Rosenberg, Pierre, *Chardin,* Geneva: Skira; New York: Rizzoli, 1991. □

Erwin Chargaff

The American biochemist Erwin Chargaff (born 1905) discovered that DNA is the primary constituent of the gene, thereby helping to create a new approach to the study of the biology of heredity.

Erwin Chargaff was born in Austria on August 11, 1905. He graduated from high school at the Maximiliangynasium in Vienna and proceeded to the University of Vienna. In 1928 he obtained a doctoral degree in chemistry after having written a thesis under the supervision of Fritz Feigl at Spath's Institute. He went to the United States in 1928 as a Milton Campbell research fellow at Yale University. He stayed until 1930, when he went to the University of Berlin as an assistant in the public health department. In 1933 he transferred to the Pasteur Institute in Paris, and in 1935 he returned to the United States to become an assistant professor of biochemistry at Columbia University. He became a full professor 17 years later and was chairman of the department from 1970 to 1974, when he became an emeritus professor of biochemistry.

Chargaff's most important contribution to biochemistry was his work with deoxyribonucleic acid, more commonly known as DNA. At the time he was working it was not known that genes were composed of DNA. Instead, it was generally accepted that the 20 amino acids which compose the protein in the cell were the carriers of genetic information. Scientists reasoned that because there were so many different kinds of amino acids in the cell, they could combine in enough different ways to form a sufficiently complex basis for the gene. It was only in 1944 when O. T. Avery and his co-workers showed that DNA was a key agent in biological transformations that Chargaff realized that DNA could in fact be a major constituent of the gene.

Two major facts were already known about DNA. The first was that it is contained in the nucleus of every living cell. The second was that, in addition to sugar (2-deoxyribose) and phosphate, DNA is composed of two bases: pyrimidines, of which there are two types (cytosine and thymine), and purines, of which there are also two types (adenine and guanine). In addition, two important experimental methods involving paper chromatography and ultraviolet light absorption had recently been developed.

To test the idea that DNA might be a primary constituent of the gene, Chargaff performed a series of experiments. He fractionated out nuclei from cells. He then isolated the DNA from the nuclei and broke it down into its constituent nucleic acids. Then, using paper chromatography, he separated the purines and the pyrimidines. This was done on the basis of the solubility of the substances being analyzed (a piece of chromatography paper is dipped into the solution and the different components of the solution travel different distances up the paper: the most soluble component travels the farthest up, to the driest section of the paper, and so on). He next exposed the separate components of the solution to ultraviolet light. Because each base absorbs light of a different, "characteristic" wavelength, he was able to determine how much of which bases are present in DNA.

What Chargaff discovered was that adenine and thymine exist in equal proportions in all organisms, as do cytosine and guanine, but that the proportions between the two pairs differ depending on the organism. These relationships are usually expressed as follows: purines (adenine + guanine) equal pyrimidines (cytosine + thymine); adenine equals thymine; and guanine equals cytosine. Chargaff drew the conclusion that it is in fact the DNA in the nucleus of the cell that carries genetic information rather than the protein. His argument was that, while there were only four different nucleic acids, as opposed to 20 proteins, the number of different proportions in which they could exist and the many different orders in which they could be present on the DNA strand provided a basis of complexity sufficient for the formation of genes. He also realized that there must be as many different types of DNA molecules as there are species.

Chargaff's conclusions revolutionized the biological sciences. One extremely important result of his discovery was that it helped James D. Watson and Francis Crick of the Cavendish Laboratory in Cambridge, England, in their determination of the structure of DNA. They reasoned that because adenine and thymine always exist in the same proportion, they must always bond together, and similarly for cytosine and guanine. This conclusion led them to propose a double helix structure for DNA, for which they won the Nobel Prize in 1952. Their model showed DNA as consisting of two strands of sugar and phosphate (alternating on each strand) with the pyrimidine and purine bases attached to each sugar component and bonding the two strands together.

Though his main interest lay in the living cell and he liked to think of himself as a naturalist philosopher, Chargaff did research in many areas of biochemistry. He did a lot of work with lipids, the molecules that form fats, and in particular studied the role of lipid-protein complexes in the metabolism. He also did work with thromboplastic protein, the enzyme (biological catalyst) that initiates blood coagulation.

Chargaff received honorary degrees from Columbia University and the University of Basel in 1976. A member of many scientific societies including the National Academy of Science, he was a visiting professor in numerous universities around the world. He also won many awards, including the Pasteur medal in 1949, the Charles Leopold Mayer Prize from the Academy of Science in Paris in 1963, and the Gregor Mendel medal in 1973.

In his later years Chargaff eschewed scientific research and turned to writing. He gained popularity in Europe for his prize-winning essays and "doomsday" lectures. He mourns most emphatically the loss of "excellent science" in modern society. In a 1985 interview for *Omni Magazine* Chargaff emphasized his dismay at the contemporary evolution of scientific research into a modern commercial commodity. He repeatedly denied any bitterness in being overlooked for the Nobel Prize, despite the fact that his discoveries laid the cornerstone for the work of Watson and Crick. He rejects further any comparison between their work and his own.

Further Reading

A concise description of the function of DNA in the cell can be found in Maya Pines's *Inside the Cell* (1975), published by the U.S. Department of Health, Education and Welfare. In *The Double Helix* (1969) James Watson gives a lively and exciting account of his discovery of the structure of DNA with Francis Crick. General information on DNA can be found in *A View of Life* (1981), co-written by Singer, Luria, and Gould. Also see *Omni,* November 1982; June 1985. □

Charlemagne

Charlemagne (742-814), or Charles the Great, was king of the Franks, 768-814, and emperor of the West, 800-814. He founded the Holy Roman Empire, stimulated European economic and political life, and fostered the cultural revival known as the Carolingian Renaissance.

In contrast to the general decline of western Europe from the 7th century on, the era of Charlemagne marks a significant revival and turning point. Through his use of available resources (such as the Church, Irish missionaries, and manorial and feudal institutions), his alliance with the papacy, and his numerous governmental and ecclesiastical reforms, Charlemagne was able to halt the political and cultural disintegration of the early Middle Ages and lay the foundation for strong central government north of the Alps. Partially as a result of Charlemagne's activity, northern Europe emerged in the high and late Middle Ages as the dominant economic, political, and cultural force in the West.

Early Life

Charlemagne, the son of Pepin the Short and Bertrada, was born in 742. In 741 Pepin had become mayor of the palace, and in 751 he deposed the last Merovingian king and was declared king of the Franks. Little is known about Charlemagne's childhood; in 754, however, he participated in the anointment of Pepin as king by Pope Stephen II. He was educated at the palace school primarily by Fulrad, the abbot of St. Denis.

When Pepin died in October 768, Charlemagne came into his inheritance. According to a general assembly of the Franks, Charlemagne and his brother, Carloman, were both proclaimed king and were to rule the kingdom jointly. In the division of the realm, however, Carloman received a larger and richer portion. Under these circumstances ill feelings between the two brothers were inevitable, and the tension was heightened when Carloman refused to aid Charlemagne in his campaign against an uprising in Aquitaine. Toward the conclusion of the Aquitanian campaign, from which Charlemagne emerged victorious, a fraternal war

seemed certain; but Carloman died unexpectedly in 771 and left Charlemagne the ruler of the entire kingdom.

Territorial Expansion

Charlemagne moved aggressively to remove those who threatened his suzerainty and to expand his power, especially in Italy. He immediately attacked and vanquished Desiderius, King of the Lombards; and in 774 Charlemagne was received by Pope Adrian I in Rome. The two renewed the alliance between the Frankish monarchy and the papacy, and shortly thereafter Charlemagne was crowned king of the Lombards at Pavia. The Frankish conquest of Italy—first of Lombardy in the north and later of the southern duchy of Benevento—had a twofold effect: all threats to the independence of the Holy See were removed, and a large portion of Italy was annexed by Charlemagne, thus bringing new wealth and peoples into his kingdom.

During his Italian campaigns Charlemagne also declared war against the Saxons, who had menaced the northeastern frontier of Francia for several generations. Begun in 772, this cruel and bitter war was finally concluded in 804 by the annexation of Saxony by Francia and the enforced Christianization of the Saxon tribes.

In the midst of the continual struggles to subdue the Saxons, Charlemagne carried on several major campaigns that resulted in territorial expansion. Perhaps the most renowned of these was his expedition into Spain. In 778, during the return from this successful campaign, Charlemagne's rear guard, led by Count Roland of the Breton March, was ambushed by traitorous Basques near Roncesvalles. The story of this episode was immortalized in the epic poem *The Song of Roland.* The historical importance of this campaign was the establishment of a military district called the Spanish March, a territorial buffer zone between Frankish Gaul and Moslem Spain.

On his eastern frontier Charlemagne defeated Tassilo, the Duke of Bavaria, and made the duchy of Bavaria part of his empire. He divided the western portion of the duchy into counties, each administered by a count loyal to the king; the eastern half formed a march, or border zone, called the Ost Mark (Austria), protected by a military duke, or margrave.

Further to the east, the major power and ultimate threat to the Frankish realm was the vast Slavic kingdom of the Avars, or Huns, an Asiatic tribe which had settled along the upper Danube. Between 791 and 795 Charlemagne crushed the power of the Avars and made their kingdom a tributary state. This victory opened the entire Danubian Plain to German colonization and the eastern expansion of Christianity—the beginning of the *Drang nach Osten,* or push to the East.

Holy Roman Empire

By 800 Charlemagne had succeeded in extending his overlordship from the Elbe River in the northeast to south of the Pyrenees in the southwest and from the North Sea to southern Italy. He ruled all of the Christianized western provinces, except the British Isles, that had once been part of the Roman Empire. As the sworn protector of the Church, Charlemagne was in fact the political master of Rome itself. Thus his authority, which extended over a vast realm and included numerous peoples, rivaled that of the Roman emperors of antiquity.

The papacy, at odds with Byzantium and its empress Irene over the question of iconoclasm (the problem of image worship and the use of images in the Church), looked to Charlemagne for protection and political leadership and regarded him as the true emperor of Latin Christendom and as the divinely appointed ruler of the earthly sphere. Thus the Pope crowned Charlemagne Holy Roman emperor on Christmas Day, 800.

Charlemagne endeavored to create unity and harmony within his vast realm and to promulgate laws and promote learning that would achieve his goals of empire. In his effort to assure his equality of rank with the Byzantine emperor, Charlemagne borrowed much from his eastern counterpart. The Byzantine influence is most clearly seen in the Palace Chapel of Aachen (Aix-la-Chapelle), which was a conscious imitation of the imperial residence at Constantinople. In style, the building is based upon the church of S. Vitale in Ravenna, the former western Byzantine capital. Thus Charlemagne, in contrast to his Merovingian predecessors, who traveled incessantly throughout their realm, attempted to create a fixed capital parallel to that of Byzantium, and he resided at Aachen during most of his later years.

Character and Appearance

The major contemporary record of Charlemagne's personal attributes and achievements is the *Vita Caroli Magni,* the first medieval biography, written by Einhard between 817 and 836. This biography is largely a firsthand account, since Einhard was a member of the palace school during Charlemagne's reign and was his close associate.

In the *Vita* is the actual physical description of the man who has since become one of the greatest legendary heroes of the Middle Ages. The most striking feature about Charlemagne was his immense size in comparison to the average man of his day. Einhard believed him to be seven times the length of a foot, but with the opening of his tomb in 1861 scholars discovered that his actual height was 6 feet 3 1/2 inches. He was well built and admirably proportioned, except for his rather short thick neck and a protruding paunch. He took frequent exercise on horseback and enjoyed excellent health for most of his life. Einhard says that "his eyes [were] very large and animated, nose a little long, hair fair, and face laughing and merry."

Toward his friends Charlemagne was jovial, and he particularly enjoyed the company of others. Yet toward his enemies he was a stern and often cruel warrior to be feared for his strength and ability. Although primarily a man of action, he had great admiration for learning and "was such a master of Latin that he could speak it as well as his native tongue." He studied Greek and the liberal arts and thus combined to some extent the personality of a warrior and a scholar.

Charlemagne's Administration

In many respects Charlemagne's government, which proved so successful and which began the ascendancy of northern Europe, differed little in its institutions from the Merovingian era. In keeping with Frankish tradition, the monarchy was considered a matter of family inheritance; the government itself was personal, and its administration was founded on feudal oaths of allegiance between lord and follower. There was no distinction between the king's personal servants and the public officials. Thus the public and private nature of political control were inseparable, as were the secular and the religious aspects of kingship. Much as the Merovingians had done in the past, Charlemagne presided over ecclesiastical synods, depended upon the clergy for advice and counsel, and interfered in matters of Church discipline and property.

What is most striking about Charlemagne's rule of so vast a realm was that he was able to maintain, largely through the strength of his own personality, a centralized state wherein royal authority was primary. Power and political authority descended from the Emperor's *imperium* to his vassals. In this system the count, a direct vassal of the Crown, was the primary link between central and local government. Each count was in charge of an administrative district or county, which he governed with the help of lesser officials. There was always the danger that a count might become too powerful in his own district, and Charlemagne therefore created a group of special envoys, *missi dominici,* who inquired into abuses in the kingdom. He also maintained a small group of elite warriors, the *vassi dominici,* who acted as his personal retinue and helped him enforce imperial authority.

During the course of his reign Charlemagne sent a number of written instructions to his officials. These enactments, known as the *Capitularii* had the force of law and were implemented directly by the royal agents. They are exceedingly valuable as sources in understanding the social and legal structure of Carolingian France.

In general, the reign of Charlemagne, because of his military and political ability, was a period of internal tranquility and prosperity. He succeeded, through diplomatic negotiations, in having his imperial title recognized by the Byzantine emperor and, through his program of cultural revival and Church reform, in upgrading the level of civilization in the West.

Carolingian Culture

Charlemagne's support of art and letters had several purposes beyond the general improvement of culture and literacy in the empire. One of the major purposes was to provide an educated clergy that could undertake many of the administrative tasks of government. A second purpose, for which an educated clergy was also a necessity, was to ensure the acceptance of orthodox doctrine as well as a uniform liturgy throughout the empire. Such uniformity not only strengthened the Church but facilitated the political task of integrating and centralizing the administration of the empire. The spread of a uniform script known as the Caroline minuscule, the attempts at achieving uniformity of doctrine through the suppression of heresy, and the publication of a uniform Mass book, book of lessons, and monastic rule were sponsored as a means of furthering unity and integration. A third purpose of this cultural revival was to enhance the prestige and authority of Charlemagne himself, who thus appeared as the defender and protector of the Church, of orthodoxy, and of education.

The intellectual traditions and educational institutions supported by Charlemagne greatly influenced the development of Western culture. Grammarians and rhetoricians from northern Italy and English scholars, such as Alcuin, enhanced his court. This mixture of Italian and Anglo-Irish culture provided a broad foundation for the later stages of the Carolingian revival. Charlemagne expanded the number of schools, both monastic and episcopal, and the quality of education was greatly improved through the influence of the scholars who taught at the palace school.

Last Years

In 806, at the age of 64, Charlemagne took measures to provide for the succession of his empire. He divided the realm among his three sons—Charles, Pepin, and Louis. But the death of Charles in April 810 was soon followed by that of Pepin. The remaining son, Louis, later called "the Pious," who was the least warlike and aggressive of the three, was left as the sole heir to the empire, and he was crowned by his father in 813.

The last years of Charlemagne's reign saw difficult times. Civil disobedience increased; pest and famine created hard times; there were troubles on the frontiers. In many respects an era of crisis and decline loomed in the future. In 811 Charlemagne made his final will and gave a sizable portion of his treasures (more than to his own heirs) to various churches of the realm. He died, while fasting, on Jan. 28, 814, and was buried at his palace at Aachen.

Further Reading

Among the studies that focus on Charlemagne's life are Jesse L. Weston, *The Romance Cycle of Charlemagne and His Peers* (1901). Harold Lamb, *Charlemagne: The Legend and the Man* (1954); and Richard Winston, *Charlemagne: From the Hammer to the Cross* (1954). Recommended among the general, recent works are Donald A. Bullough, *The Age of Charlemagne* (1965), especially distinguished for its illustrations, and E. M. Almedingen, *Charlemagne: A Study* (1968). The best introduction to Charlemagne and Carolingian institutions is Heinrich Fichtenau, *The Carolingian Empire: The Age of Charlemagne* (trans. 1964).

The documents for the Carolingian period are abundant, many of them in translation. For a general collection of sources see Stewart C. Easton and Helene Wieruszowski, *The Era of Charlemagne: Frankish State and Society* (1961). One of the best translations of Einhard is S. Epes Turner, *The Life of Charlemagne* (1960). Because of the importance of the coronation of Charlemagne, scholars have devoted special attention to the subject. Many of the evaluations have been collected in Richard E. Sullivan, ed., *The Coronation of Charlemagne: What Did It Signify?* (1959). For the artistic achievement during Charlemagne's reign see Roger Hinks, *Carolingian Art: A study of Early Medieval Painting and Sculpture in Western Europe* (1935), and Kenneth John Conant, *Carolingian and Romanesque Architecture, 800-1200* (1959; 2d ed. 1966). One of the most stimulating works on Carolingian culture is M. L. Laistner, *Thought and Letters in Western Europe, A.D. 500 to 900* (1931; new ed. 1957). □

Charles, Prince of Wales

Charles, Prince of Wales and heir apparent to the British throne, was probably the most photographed and written about person in the Western world in the late 1970s but has since been eclipsed in popularity by his ex-wife, Princess Diana.

Prince Charles Philip Arthur George, the eldest child of Princess Elizabeth and Prince Philip, was born on November 14, 1948, in Buckingham Palace. He had a younger sister, Princess Anne, born in 1950, and two younger brothers, Prince Andrew and Prince Edward, who were born in 1960 and 1964, respectively. After the death in February 1952 of his grandfather, King George VI, and his mother's succession as Queen Elizabeth II, Prince Charles became the Duke of Cornwall, a dukedom which includes considerable—and lucrative—property, and the heir apparent to the throne of the United Kingdom.

Like all parents, Queen Elizabeth and Prince Philip were very concerned about their children's education, and the academic training of the future monarch naturally entailed much thought and planning. Like previous royal heirs, Charles, who was an obedient, sensitive, shy, and somewhat awkward child, was first taught at home by a governess. His parents broke with tradition in 1956, however, when they decided to send him to a local day school, Hill House in Knightsbridge. During his time at Hill House Prince Charles was much pursued by members of the London press. Despite severe warnings from the royal press secretary, this situation was not much alleviated by the prince's enrollment in 1957 at Cheam in Hampshire, an upper-class preparatory school which his father had attended.

On July 26, 1958, during his stay at Cheam, the queen named Charles Prince of Wales and Earl of Chester. Nonetheless, while at Cheam Prince Charles was treated as much like the other boys as possible, sharing a dormitory room with nine others and doing chores. It was also while at Cheam that the prince refined his sense of humor, developed his taste for practical jokes, and discovered his interest in and talent for acting.

More Education and Military Training

In part to avoid the overly-enthusiastic attentions of the press, Gordonstoun, located in a remote area of northern Scotland, was the public (British equivalent of our private) school selected for Prince Charles. It also was Prince Philip's alma mater and was noted for its strict discipline, its spartan living conditions, and its dedication to the ideals of social responsibility and community service. The prince attended Gordonstoun from 1962 to January 1966, when he was sent to Australia to attend Timbertop, the outback branch of the prestigious Geelong Grammar School. Here, in an egalitarian social milieu very different from that to which he was accustomed, the isolated location and rigorous physical activity provided the prince with an increased sense of self-reliance. "Australia", he was later to say, "conquered my shyness." Prince Charles returned to Gordonstoun in September 1966 and during his last year rose to become head boy of the school. He enjoyed acting in plays and became interested in classical music.

After consultations which involved Church of England dignitaries, the prime minister, Prince Philip's much-admired "Uncle Dickie," Lord Mountbatten of Burma, Queen Elizabeth, Prince Philip and Prince Charles, it was decided that Prince Charles would complete his academic education by attending Trinity College, Cambridge, which his grandfather George VI had also attended. The prince entered Trinity in October 1967 and lived very much like other well-to-do students there. He enjoyed his time at Cambridge, continuing his musical and acting pursuits and attaining satisfactory if undistinguished academic credentials in anthropology, archaeology, and history. In the spring of 1969 Prince Charles was sent to University College of Wales at Aberystwyth in order to learn Welsh history, language, and literature in preparation for his investiture as Prince of Wales in a spectacular ceremony at Caernarvon Castle on July 1, 1969. Prince Charles returned to Cambridge in the fall of 1969 and received his degree in 1970, the first member of the royal family to do so.

Following family tradition, Prince Charles spent the next seven years in the military. He attended the Royal Air Force College at Cranwell, receiving his wings in 1971, and then went to the Royal Naval College at Dartmouth. During his time in the Royal Navy the prince served tours of sea duty, learned to fly helicopters and to skydive, and in 1975 got a command of his own, the HMS *Barrington*.

Prince, Husband, and Father

In 1977, his preliminary education and training complete, Prince Charles began his real career as Prince of Wales. Up to this time the prince had taken some part in public events. In 1964, for example, he, Princess Anne, and Prince Philip had attended the wedding of King Constantine of Greece, and in 1965 he attended Sir Winston Churchill's funeral. On November 14, 1966, he constitutionally came of age and was designated prince-regent in case of his mother's absence or incapacitation. In October 1967 for the first time he went with the queen to the formal opening of Parliament, and in the same year he represented her at the funeral of Australian Prime Minister Harold Holt.

From 1977 on, however, his public activities as Prince of Wales took a qualitative and quantitative leap. As Prince of Wales he espoused many charitable causes, especially those having to do with youth, such as the Queen's Silver Jubilee Fund. He also promoted environmental causes. As Prince of Wales he represented the monarchy at home and served as a good-will ambassador abroad. In the spring of 1978 he visited South America and in the same year served as the queen's representative at the funerals of respected Commonwealth statesmen Sir Robert Menzies and Jomo Kenyatta. The prince went to Yugoslavia in 1979, to the Far East in the same year, to India in 1980, and to Australia in the spring of 1981.

On February 24, 1981, the official announcement of his engagement to the Lady Diana Frances Spencer, daughter of Earl Spencer, brought to an end one of the greatest matrimonial sweepstakes of the century. The royal wedding, on July 29, 1981, was a magnificently orchestrated yet touching event which was viewed via television by millions worldwide. Marriage and the birth of his two sons (Prince William on June 21, 1982, and Prince Henry on September 15, 1984) did not curtail the prince's activities in any way. Indeed, his wife accompanied him on several trips—a tour of Wales shortly after their marriage, an excursion to Australia and New Zealand (with Prince William) in the spring of 1983, and a trip to Canada in the summer of 1983—and because of her youth, beauty, and style developed a loyal following of her own which served to enhance and later eclipse her husband's position.

Troubles at Buckingham Palace

While there had always been rumblings about the shaky status of Charles and Diana's marriage, the royal couple rode out the rest of the eighties making the standard monarchic ribbon cuttings and raising their two sons. Reports indeed did began to emerge in the mid-1980s of Charles' continued affair with old girlfriend, Camilla Parker Bowles but none were substantiated until a series of love tapes surfaced in the early 1990s. The age difference between Charles and Diana, a presumed intellectual gap, and the claim that Charles was pressured into marriage by his father, Prince Philip, were several theories thought to be the reason for the breakup of the marriage. One thing that is for certain is that Charles never gave up his love for Camilla though his entire marriage to Diana.

Prince Charles met the former Camilla Shand at a polo match in 1970 and right away Camilla and Charles were a hot item of the British tabloids. It was never to be though, and after refusing Charles' marriage proposal Camilla, for reasons of privacy and the lack of which being a royal comes with, married cavalry officer Andrew Parker Bowles in 1973. Charles, who didn't attend the wedding, nonetheless became their son Tom's godfather in 1974. In spite of their commitments, Charles and Camilla's affair was said to have been reignited within six years of Camilla's marriage and carried out thoughout Charles' subsequent marriage. While discretion was used thoughout the 1980s, by the early 1990s a series of "love tapes" surfaced that blew the lid right off the royal scandal.

Showing Charles and Camilla trying to arrange a suitable place for a rendezvous, Charles' desire to "live inside of your (Camilla's) trousers", be reincarnated as her tampon, and other various royal naughtiness the tapes became the talk of the early 1990s and eventually led to Charles and Diana's separation on December 9, 1992. With Diana retaining custody of their two sons, it was originally speculated that she would still be able to be crowned Queen one day. However when the royal divorce was announced in 1995 these plans were shuttled, though she was able to retain the title of Princess of Wales. In addition to keeping her title, Diana was awarded a settlement of $23 million, plus $600,000 a year to maintain her private office, where she continued to do charity work.

While the prince's broken marriage threatened to dominate the public's perception of him, he had an eclectic range of interests. Like other members of his family he loved country life and polo, fast cars, flying, and fishing. He was also a devotee of the theater, classical music, an avid reader of history and English literature, and notably an outspoken critic of architecture. And surely he must be the only Prince of Wales who ever wrote and published a fairy tale—*The Old Man of Lochnagar* (1980)—based on a story he told his younger brothers when they were children. In addition to this the Prince's Trust was established to be an umbrella group to benefit various charitable interests.

Prince Charles, had the intelligence and dedication to carve out for himself an important role in the British monarchy based on a profound interest in and understanding of his country. Aware, as he told British author Anthony Sampson, that "something as curious as the monarchy won't survive unless you take account of people's attitudes . . . ," he dedicated himself to serve his people in his own way to the best of his ability. Despite his diminished popularity post-divorce, he took seriously the motto of the Prince of Wales, "Ich Dien," I serve, and did so by endeavoring "to show concern for people, to display interest in them as individuals, and to encourage them in a whole host of ways." As *Maclean's* Joe Chidley writes while talking about the Prince's rather underwhelming 1996 solo visit to Canada, "..the low-key response to Charles' visit seemed in keeping with the man himself—introspective, and preferring substance over ceremony."

Meanwhile, for Charles the major problem was how to get the British people used to Camilla after the continued popularity of his ex-wife. One positive signal in July 1997 was Britain's conservative newspaper, The Daily Telegraph's blessing, "She is good for his peace of mind, and is, therefore, performing a public service. It would make the best of a bad job if the public were to come gradually to accept this." The message seemed to be that Charles is preparing the British people to accept Parker Bowles as their possible future Queen. For her part, Parker Bowles has emerged slowly as a society fund-raiser, a definite prerequisite for royal-dom.

However, Prince Charles faced his biggest challenge after the August 31, 1997, death of his ex-wife, Princess Diana, as he became a single parent to Princes William and Harry. British newspapers warned him that he "must cast off his stiff upper lip and reach out to his sons and the people of Britain, or he could lose both."

Further Reading

There are several popular biographies of Prince Charles which provide little useful information for those seriously interested in him. Of limited value is Gregary Wakeford's *The Heir Apparent* (1967), which is largely concerned with his early education. Of more utility is Tim Heald and Mayo Mohs's *HRH: The Man Who Will Be King* (1979). This book, though rather outdated, is entertaining and perceptive. A book by Prince Charles' former valet, Stephen Barry's *Royal Secrets* (1983), is a gossipy, anecdotal, and ultimately not unflattering portrait of life with the prince and his family. The most recent account of the Prince can be found in Jonathan Dimbleby's *The Prince of Wales* (1994). Information can also be found in biographies of his mother. Of these, *Majesty: Elizabeth II and the House of Windsor* by Robert Lacey (1977) is a serious and well-documented volume. Highly recommended is Elizabeth Longford's *The Queen: The Life of Elizabeth II* (1983), which is both gracefully written and insightful. *Charles & Diana* (1985) is saved from superficiality by the professional writing of Ralph Martin. □

Charles I

Charles I (1600-1649), king of England from 1625 to 1649, was to witness and take part in the English civil war, or Puritan Revolution, which ultimately cost him his life.

The second son of James VI of Scotland (later James I of England) and Anne of Denmark, Charles I was born in Dunfermline, Scotland, on Nov. 19, 1600. He did not become heir apparent to the English throne until the death of his elder brother, Henry, in 1612. Whether it was his early physical infirmities or the stress caused by the antipathy between his parents, the future king showed signs of personality disturbance in childhood. He did not speak as a young child and later always stuttered. He betrayed deep feelings of inadequacy both in his formal silences and in his overdependence on self-confident favorites. From very early life he lied. This was to be the King's ultimate weakness.

Charles received a good education with tutors. His first emergence into public affairs came with the loss of the crown of Bohemia by his brother-in-law, Frederick V, in 1618. That loss and the subsequent occupation of Frederick's inheritance in the Palatinate by Spanish troops deeply shocked Charles. He conceived that if he were to marry the Spanish Infanta, the King of Spain would restore the Palatinate to Frederick. Charles went to Spain in 1623 with the 1st Duke of Buckingham, who abetted the scheme. In Madrid it took Charles 5 months to comprehend that the Spanish would never agree to marriage with a heretic, much less to the restoration of the Palatinate.

Early Reign

When Charles perceived the truth, he and Buckingham went to the opposite extreme and stampeded an unwilling King James and an eager Parliament into war with Spain. At the same time a marriage treaty with Louis XIII of France was arranged for the hand of Louis's sister, Henrietta Maria. Charles became king on March 27, 1625. His marriage occurred by proxy in Paris on May 1. The union was accompanied by an alliance between England and France against Spain. From the first, however, there were misunderstandings. The English believed that the French were not active enough in helping to expel the Spanish from the Palatinate. The French did not believe that Charles had lived up to the religious promises of the marriage contract—to allow freedom to the English Catholics. It is not surprising under these

circumstances that Charles found the gawky adolescent princess less than compatible. Relations with the Queen's brother deteriorated until Charles declared war on France as well as Spain in 1627.

These wars necessitated the frequent summonses of Parliament during the first years of Charles's reign. Differences over supplies, religion, and economic policy were frequent and led to the Petition of Right in 1628, in which the Commons condemned the King's policy of arbitrary taxation and imprisonment. But the chief cause of the King's difficulties with Parliament was the resentment of the English aristocracy over the continued ascendancy of the Duke of Buckingham. His ill-managed expedition against Cadiz, Spain, in 1625 and his disastrous attack in 1627 on the French forces besieging La Rochelle completely discredited the King's government in the eyes of the aristocracy.

Buckingham's assassination in 1628, although it was a bitter personal blow to the King, opened up a period of constructive rule, known as the period of personal government. An aftermath of constitutional disputes rocked Parliament in 1629, but many of the peers and their allies in the Commons such as Thomas Wentworth and Dudley Digges had thrown in their lot with the King. The earls of Arundel and Pembroke, Clifford, and Weston divided up administrative patronage. The wars against France and Spain were terminated, and so long as no new foreign crisis arose, royal finances were sufficient to conduct government without calling Parliament and reviving constitutional and religious opposition. After Buckingham's death, too, Charles fell in love with Henrietta Maria, and they were ever after a devoted couple.

Charles spent his time hunting and acquiring perhaps the greatest art collection in Europe. The quintessence of the King's royal policy during these years was the enforcement of order and a decorous service in the English Church by William Laud, Archbishop of Canterbury. The attempt to extend this religious order to Scotland in 1637, however, brought down the edifice of personal government. Parliament again had to be summoned in 1640, and to the residue of constitutional resentment from the earlier parliaments was joined the fear that the Earl of Strafford, the King's deputy in Ireland, would be an even more powerful and dangerous minister than the Duke of Buckingham had been. Until Strafford's execution for treason in 1641, the King faced a united aristocracy; and he was forced to relinquish most of his ministers, abolish the Star Chamber (councilors and judges who sat as a court) and High Commission, agree to triennial parliaments, and promise that no customs would be raised in the future without specific parliamentary grant.

Civil War

Following Strafford's death, the King's untrustworthiness still barred a stable settlement with the leaders of Parliament. His attempt to get evidence against them in Scotland during the autumn of 1641 coincided with the Irish rebellion. The parliamentary leaders could not trust him with an army. Their fears were confirmed when he entered the House of Commons on Jan. 4, 1642, in order to arrest five of their leading members for treason. Parliament then began on their own authority to make military provision to suppress the Irish and to defend themselves. Charles could not allow the heart of his prerogative to be thus torn from him, and so on August 14 the King raised his standard at Nottingham and called upon all his loyal subjects to defend his right. The civil war had begun.

Charles attracted a majority of the peers and many of the gentry to his side, and he commanded the military populace of Wales and the North. Under the generalship of his nephew Prince Rupert, the royal cavalry in particular bore down the parliamentary forces during 1642 and 1643. But Charles again fell victim to incompetent courtiers, as a whole the King's cause was ill-managed. By contrast the few but important peers who remained to command Parliament proved masters at gaining popular support, money, control of the navy, and a sufficient military response. On July 2, 1644, they won a surprise victory over Rupert at Marston Moor; in the following year they professionalized their military force as the New Model Army and decisively defeated Charles and Rupert at Naseby. In 1646 Charles surrendered to the Scots allies of Parliament.

During the succeeding years the King's main effort was to restore his royal authority. The means he chose were contradictory deals with various political groups, now the political Presbyterians in Parliament, now Oliver Cromwell and the Independent army generals, and at all times the Scots. Just as his letter commissioning an Irish army to land in England and requesting French troops during the civil war had discredited him after their discovery on the field of Naseby, so these incompatible negotiations from 1646 to 1648 destroyed his moral position in the eyes of many Englishmen. His negotiations with the Scots led to their intervention in the second civil war, of 1648, and this sealed Charles's fate in the minds of the army generals. On Dec. 6-7, 1648, the generals purged Parliament of all who were negotiating for the King's restoration to power and prepared to bring the "Man of Blood" to trial.

The Trial

There was in England no legal method to try a king. But Henry Ireton and the other officers devised a High Court of Justice, consisting of members of the purged Commons and other public officials, to try Charles Stuart for high treason. The King refused to recognize their jurisdiction and would not plead. During the trial he gave his finest defense of his kingship: "I do stand more for the liberty of my people, than any here that come to be my pretended judges." "I am sworn to keep the peace, by that duty I owe to God and my country, and I will do it to the last breath of my body; and therefore ye shall do well to satisfy first God, and then the country, by what authority you [try me]." By such words, when the court condemned him to death, he created the myth that he died for liberty under the law. On Jan. 30, 1649, he was led onto a scaffold, where he prayed with Bishop Juxon, and was beheaded. Thereby he also became the sanctified champion of the Anglican Church, despite his many promises to Catholics, Presbyterians, and Independents during the days of his adversity. After a decade under

Puritan military dictatorship, the King executed that day became the foundation for restored monarchy, established church, free Parliament, and the conservative rule of law in England.

Further Reading

C. V. Wedgwood, *The King's Peace, 1637-1641* (1955), *The King's War, 1641-1647* (1958), and *A Coffin for King Charles: The Trial and Execution of Charles I* (1964), are probably the best studies of Charles I for the years 1637-1649 and also provide excellent background material on other politicians of those years. Esmé C. Wingfield-Stratford's three volumes, *Charles: King of England, 1600-1637* (1949), *King Charles and King pym, 1637-1643* (1949), and *King Charles the Martyr 1643-1649* (1950), are standard treatments, although conservative and very favorable to the King. Good background studies of the period are G. M. Trevelyan, *England under the Stuarts* (repr. 1957), and Roger Lockyer, *Tudor and Stuart Britain, 1471-1714* (1964).

Additional Sources

Bowle, John, *Charles I: a biography,* Boston: Little, Brown, 1975.

Carlton, Charles, *Charles I, the personal monarch,* London; New York: Routledge, 1995.

Daniels, Christopher W., *Charles I,* Cambridge England; New York: Cambridge University Press, 1988.

Gregg, Pauline, *King Charles I,* Berkeley: University of California Press, 1984.

Higham, Florence May Creir Evans, *Charles I: a study,* Norwood, Pa.: Norwood Editions, 1978.

Morrah, Patrick, *A royal family: Charles I and his family,* London: Constable, 1982.

Ollard, Richard Lawrence, *The image of the king: Charles I and Charles II,* New York: Atheneum, 1979.

Charles, King of England, 1600-1637, Westport, Conn.: Greenwood Press, 1975. □

Charles II

Charles II (1630-1685) was king of England, Scotland, and Ireland from 1660 to 1685. Restored to the throne after the Cromwellian experiment, he prevented a renewed outbreak of civil strife for a critical generation.

Charles II, the son of Charles I and Henrietta Maria, was born in London on May 29, 1630. For the first 8 years of his life, he was heir apparent in what seemed a quiet land. By 1638 he must have been aware that the calm was that deceptive moment before the storm. By the time he was 12, his father's kingdom had been torn apart by civil war, and by 1646 Charles was in exile. In 1649 he watched helplessly from the Continent while his father was tried and executed in England. This set of circumstances, and the demeaning 10 years of poverty and plotting that followed, seemed to be the paramount influence in his life. Unlike his brother James, the Duke of York and later King James II, he developed a suspicion not of men but of the ideologies that moved men. Ironically it was lack of ideological commitment, and his suspicion of such commitment, that made him suspect in his own times and that has condemned him in the eyes of many historians.

After 1649 Charles's principal interest was the reestablishment of the monarchy, and he used whatever means he thought necessary to achieve this end. In March 1650 he accepted the Scots' offer of support in his effort and accepted the Scots' covenant and Presbyterianism as a concomitant to such support. With the failure of Charles and the Scots at the battle of Worcester in 1651, the prince never again evidenced any interest in Presbyterianism other than repugnance.

His Accession

On his accession in 1660 Charles ended the trails and execution of regicides long before royalist appetites were appeased, and he refused to sponsor any attempts to appropriate, from former supporters of the Commonwealth, land sold by royalists during the interregnum. Moreover, he tried without success to arrive at a broader Anglican religious dispensation in 1660 and to contradict the St. Bartholomew's Day oath, which turned Nonconformist ministers out of ecclesiastical livings in 1662. These actions proceeded from the declaration he had made at Breda in April 1660, in which he attempted to persuade Gen. Monck and Parliament to return England to the monarchical form. His attempts, however, to implement this declaration came long after Monck's army had disbanded and after the Cavalier Parliament had been elected. Historians point out that this declaration was in keeping with Charles's disposition,

which was marked by a reluctance to act and a tendency to make enemies and to mask intention with the appearance of wit and love of pleasure.

Although Charles could and did act decisively in moments of crisis, he preferred to act through ministers who would serve as lightning rods to consume popular displeasure. When it served his purposes, he would undermine and deceive his own ministries. Thus, although the Earl of Clarendon served as Charles's first minister from 1660 to 1666, during the last 3 of those years he could only partially depend on royal support. In 1666, because of the disgrace of defeat in the Dutch war and the loss of Clarendon's abilities to control the lower house and produce revenues, his enemies pushed for his impeachment. Charles, who had never approved of Clarendon's religious policies or his high-handedness in government, joined in the destruction of the ministry.

The Cabal

Following the attempted impeachment and the exile of Clarendon, Charles turned to the formation of a government whose chief ministers were those who sponsored the old opposition. This group, known collectively by the initials of their names as the Cabal, was never used in a truly collective sense. To Charles, the Cabal's principal function was to lead the lower house of Parliament to a more generous posture in funding the government and to an acceptance of the royal policy on religion. The members of the Cabal were more likely to be consulted individually rather than collectively by the King, and certain members of this ministry were privy to, and sponsors of, certain aspects of the royal policy in which the others had no knowledge or interest. The ministry was not successful in leading Parliament and was already breaking up when Charles promulgated his Declaration of indulgence in 1672. On this issue—the use of the royal power to suspend religious statutes and to establish by administrative fiat Charles's goal of religious toleration—the ministry was shattered.

To Charles, the Cabal had been disappointing from its earliest days. It had not produced a subsidy-granting majority from the anti-Clarendonians in the lower house. Further, the attempts by two of its members, the 2d Duke of Buckingham and the 1st Earl of Shaftesbury, to build a power structure through anti-Catholicism and suspicion of the heir apparent frightened both other members of the ministry as well as the King.

Later Reign

The failure of the King's Indulgence and the subsequent anti-Catholic Test Act of 1673 forced Charles to look for new ministerial leadership. In Sir Thomas Osborne, soon to be Earl of Danby, Charles found a new figure to lead his government. Danby had been instrumental in bringing down Clarendon, but his policy and supporters closely followed Clarendon lines with the single exception of an anti-French rather than an anti-Dutch foreign policy. Danby, however, demonstrated a genius at finance that had never been a strength of Clarendon's government.

From its inception Danby's coalition was faced with an opposition led by Shaftesbury and Buckingham and their followers. The principal issue used by this opposition was the suspected Catholicism of the King and court and the known Catholicism of the Duke of York, the heir apparent. From 1674 Parliament spent progressively more time on debating whether Danby and his supporters or Shaftesbury and his were more virtuously anti-Catholic. In the meantime the King was, in the late 1670s, forming a northern alliance against French expansion.

In 1678 Titus Oates appeared with the tale of a Popish Plot to assassinate the King. Although Shaftesbury and the opposition were not connected with Oates, they soon turned national hysteria over the plot to their advantage. They launched a double-pronged attack to overturn Danby and to exclude York as the heir apparent. Supplied with evidence and funds from the French ambassador, Shaftesbury's party demanded Danby's impeachment. At this point Charles was forced to take over the management of the government. With enormous skill, he used the controversy over Danby to distract Parliament from Shaftesbury's primary aim—changing the succession to the throne.

During the 3 years of the plot hysteria, the King used every device to divert, split, and madden the opposition with the hopes that in time the nation would become suspicious of Shaftesbury's intentions. By 1681, Charles was able to dismiss Parliament.

From that time until his death, on Feb. 6, 1685, Charles personally directed the government. He was able to destroy the opposition, and on his death he left a possibility for absolutism which was greater than any seen in England since the time of Henry VIII.

Further Reading

Arthur Bryant, *King Charles II* (1935; rev. ed. 1955), is the best study of Charles, but it is idolatrous and should be balanced with the more Whiggish general work by David Ogg, *England in the Reign of Charles II* (2 vols., 1934; rev. ed. 1962), and the neutral, disappointing volume by G. N. Clarke, *The Later Stuarts, 1660-1714* (1934; 2d ed. 1955), vol. 10 in "The Oxford History of England" series. Lord Acton, *Historical Essays and Studies* (1907), contains a highly romantic and not very trustworthy chapter on Charles II. Godfrey Davies, *The Restoration of Charles II, 1658-1660* (1955), is a specialized study.

Additional Sources

Fraser, Antonia, *Charles II: his life and times,* London: Weidenfeld & Nicolson, 1993.

Fraser, Antonia, *Royal Charles: Charles II and the Restoration,* New York: Knopf: distributed by Random House, 1979.

Hutton, Ronald, *Charles the Second, King of England, Scotland, and Ireland,* Oxford England: Clarendon Press; New York: Oxford University Press, 1989.

Jones, J. R. (James Rees), *Charles II: royal politician,* London; Boston: Allen & Unwin, 1987.

Miller, John, *Charles II,* London: Weidenfeld and Nicholson, 1991.

Ollard, Richard Lawrence, *The image of the king: Charles I and Charles II,* New York: Atheneum, 1979.

Palmer, Tony, *Charles II: portrait of an age,* London: Cassell, 1979.

Wheatley, Dennis, *"Old Rowley": a very private life of Charles II,* London: Arrow Books, 1977. □

Charles II

Charles II (1661-1700), the last Hapsburg king of Spain, reigned from 1665 to 1700. Known as "the Bewitched," he was a foolish and weak monarch at a time when Spain direly needed strong leadership.

Charles II, the son of Philip IV of Spain and his second wife, Mariana of Austria, was born in Madrid on Nov. 6, 1661. On his father's death in 1665, Mariana became queen regent, and until her death in 1696 Charles was almost completely under her control. He was a rachitic, ugly, and feeble-minded weakling who by the age of 6 could barely stand and could not walk at all. His education was very poor; when he was 14, he could read only with great difficulty. Throughout his life he remained an ignorant and sickly man.

In 1675 the 14-year old Charles was officially crowned king of Spain. For his country these were agonizing years. The economy was stagnant, there was hunger in the land, and the power of the monarchy over the various Spanish provinces was extremely weak. In foreign affairs Spain was experiencing defeat after defeat; in 1697 French armies would easily occupy Catalonia, one of the most important Spanish provinces.

Charles reigned but did not rule. Effective power was wielded either by the incapable Mariana or by powerful noblemen such as the Count of Oropesa, who later served as first minister from 1685 to 1691. In 1680 Charles married the pretty French princess Marie Louise, but she died childless in 1689. He then married Maria Ana of Neuburg, who became the controlling influence in his life after his mother's death.

As the century drew to a close, all Europe was aware that Charles was sterile and dying. France, Austria, England, and the Netherlands had designs on the Spanish Empire. In Madrid the dying king presented a pathetic spectacle. Afflicted with convulsive fits, Charles was believed to have been bewitched, and exorcists and visionary nuns employed every means known to the Church to free him from the devil.

The unfortunate monarch felt increasing pressure from those who wanted him to will his empire to Archduke Charles of Austria and from those who argued that the empire could be kept together only if it were willed to Philip of Anjou, the grandson of Louis XIV of France. Charles decided for Philip and on Oct. 2, 1700, named him heir. On November 1 Charles died. When his heir entered Spain as Philip V, however, England, Austria, and the Netherlands would not recognize him as the legitimate Spanish king. In 1703 they declared war against Philip and France, and the long and bloody War of the Spanish Succession began.

Further Reading

The life of Charles II, as well as the history of his reign, has been generally ignored by historians. In English, the only account of Charles II is John Nada's gloomy biography, *Carlos: The King Who Would Not Die* (1963). For a brief but scholarly account of the situation in Spain during Charles's reign, J. H. Elliott, *Imperial Spain: 1469-1716* (1963), is highly recommended. □

Charles III

Known as an enlightened despot, Charles III (1716-1788) was king of Spain from 1759 to 1788. His reign was marked by economic progress and political stability and is usually considered one of the greatest in Spanish history.

The son of Philip V of Spain and his second wife, Elizabeth Farnese of Parma, Charles III was born in Madrid on Jan. 20, 1716. His education was excellent—at the age of 4 he wrote a letter in French to his parents—and during his youth he developed a great interest in the arts and a consuming passion for the hunt.

Since Philip V had had two sons, Louis and Ferdinand, by his first wife, Elizabeth felt that Charles and her other children stood no chance of inheriting the throne of Spain. Therefore she looked for thrones for them in Italy. Through her influence Charles was recognized as Duke of Parma in 1731 and as king of Naples and Sicily in 1736 after the War of the Polish Succession.

Charles proved a successful and popular king in Italy. He surrounded himself with able advisers and did much for his kingdom. He was also influenced by the ideas of enlightened despotism then current in the Italian peninsula. In 1738 Charles married Maria Amalia of Saxony. After bearing five daughters, in 1747 she gave birth to Philip, who was an idiot. But in the following year their second son and heir, Charles, was born. A third son, Ferdinand, was born in 1751.

When Philip V died in 1746, he was succeeded by his son Ferdinand VI (Louis had died earlier). Ferdinand had no children, and on his death in 1759 Charles, his half brother, became king of Spain. The new monarch renounced the throne of Naples in favor of his third son, Ferdinand. Not long after his accession Maria Amalia died, and Charles never married again.

When he arrived in Spain, Charles was a vigorous and healthy man of 43, eager to pursue a policy of active royal statesmanship. Assisted by able and dedicated ministers such as the Count of Arenda and the Count of Floridablanca, he introduced a series of reforms that strengthened the authority of the Crown. He asserted the monarchy's power over the Church by expelling the Jesuits from Spain in 1767.

Charles brought about a general economic expansion, implemented important changes in the educational system, and modernized Spain's military forces.

Charles signed the Family Compact in 1761 with France, which led to Spain's involvement in the Seven Years War. In the Treaty of Paris of 1763 Spain lost Florida but was ceded Louisiana. In 1779 Charles was drawn into war with England in the American Revolution; by the Treaty of Paris of 1783 Spain recovered Florida.

Charles's internal and colonial reforms greatly benefited Spain. He died on Dec. 14, 1788, and was succeeded by his son Charles IV.

Further Reading

In English, Joseph Addison, *Charles the Third of Spain: The Stanhope Essay* (1900), is not entirely satisfactory. Far more useful and scholarly is the Spanish work by Enrique de Tapia Ozcariz, *Carlos III y su época: Biografía del siglo XVIII* (1962). For a brief account of Charles and his reign see Charles Petrie, *The Spanish Royal House* (1958). □

Charles IV

Charles IV (1316-1378) reigned as king of Bohemia from 1346 and Holy Roman emperor from 1355. He strengthened monarchical authority and increased intellectual and cultural contact between Bohemia and the West.

On May 14, 1316, Charles IV was born in Bohemia, the son of John of Luxemburg, King of Bohemia. Charles was taken by his father to France at the age of 7 to be educated at the French court. John, who spent the last 20 years of his reign outside Bohemia, wanted his son to have a broader experience of the world of knighthood than Bohemia could offer. After his French education (under a tutor who would later, as Pope Clement VI, crown Charles emperor), Charles was called by his father to Italy, where John had temporarily become governor of Lombardy. After 2 years in Italy, Charles was sent by his father to Bohemia, where he was named margrave of Moravia and given the administration of Bohemia and Moravia on his father's behalf. In 1341 Charles was recognized as heir to the Bohemian throne.

In 1342 Charles's former tutor became Pope Clement VI and, in collaboration with King John, arranged for Charles to be elected king of the Romans (the first step toward being elected Holy Roman emperor) in 1346. In the same year John and Charles went to France to fight against the English armies in the first major campaign of the Hundred Years War. King John, blind and aged, was led into battle at Crécy, where he was killed. Charles, who survived the battle, now became king of Bohemia. After a diplomatic and political struggle with his rivals for the imperial crown

and with the Pope himself, Charles went suddenly to Italy in 1355 and was crowned emperor by the papal legate.

Holy Roman Emperor

In the mid-14th century the title of Holy Roman emperor was useful more for dynastic aggrandizement than as a sign of political power. The series of emperors from hitherto obscure families—Hapsburgs, Nassaus, Wittelsbachs, and Luxemburgs—who had held the title from 1273 had been elected precisely because they were unlikely to create a genuine imperial monarchy. The real power in the empire lay in the hands of the princes (the electors) who elected each emperor and in the hands of the other aristocrats and individual cities who vied with them for rights and privileges. The imperial title gave its holder only certain rights to appoint some kinds of officials, to issue some privileges, and to receive certain incomes from Italy and Germany. It also attracted dynastic jealousy and political opposition from those who feared too powerful or too ambitious an emperor. Charles faced the same problems as his predecessors: lack of an imperial administration or legal structure, lack of money, and lack of a strong social or territorial base upon which to establish a stronger imperial title.

Charles attempted first to set the empire in order. At the imperial diets of Nuremburg and Metz in 1355-1356 he issued a series of ordinances, collectively known as the Golden Bull, which stabilized the privileges of the electors, gave them virtual independence from imperial authority, and intended that they become the basis of a stronger empire. Hostility on the part of those envious of the electors, however, and of the Wittelsbach and Hapsburg rivals of Charles prevented the Emperor from contributing much toward a real reform of German government. In addition, Charles was occupied with other imperial duties. The papacy, situated at Avignon since the beginning of the century, claimed Charles's assistance for its return to Italy. The great poet Petrarch wrote Charles imploring him to remember the Roman destiny and to return to pacify Italy. In 1367-1369 Charles made an unsuccessful entry into Italy. From his return to Prague until his death he concentrated upon establishing his sons in positions of power. He had his eldest son, Wenceslaus (later Wenceslaus IV), elected king of the Romans and named him his heir in Bohemia and arranged for the marriage of his second son (later the emperor Sigismund) to the heiress of the king of Hungary. His remaining efforts concentrated upon the extension of Bohemian power.

Bohemian Cultural Revival

The establishment of the house of Luxemburg on the Bohemian throne in the person of Charles's father, John, in 1310 had begun the rise of Bohemian power and prestige in Christendom. John, although away from Bohemia for the last 20 years of his life, had strengthened the power and, more importantly, the prestige of the Crown by his chivalrous adventures and by his judicious acquisition of territories for his kingdom. Charles's talent, administrative experience, papal connections, and genuine love for Bohemia led him to continue his father's policy. In 1348 Charles established the great University of Prague and, in the following years, rebuilt much of Prague, his capital, adding the famous New Town to the city by a spectacular bridge across the Vltava, and built the famous castle of Karlstein, from which he governed both empire and kingdom.

Charles's patronage of learning and the arts resulted in the fertilization of native Bohemian culture with the work of artists and scholars brought from France and Germany. Prague even witnessed an early stage of humanism under the influence of Charles's efficient and learned chancery. The scholar-king himself inspired much of the activity in his realm. He could speak Latin, French, German, Czech, and Italian, maintained an interest in theology and law, and lived a simple, pious-almost superstitious-life.

In following the imperial style of his age, which meant attending as much to the fortunes of his house as to the problems of the empire, Charles also enriched the kingdom which his house ruled. If his imperial reign was less than effective, he at least avoided being pulled into the insoluble problems of Italy and the papacy and managed to stabilize for a time the political rivalries in Germany. He died at Prague on Nov. 29, 1378.

Further Reading

The standard biography of Charles IV in English is Bede Jarrett, *The Emperor Charles IV* (1935). Another fullength study is Gerald G. Walsh, *The Emperor Charles IV, 1316-1378: A Study in Holy Roman Imperialism* (1924). There is a short account in the *Cambridge Medieval History,* vol. 3 (1932). Background works which include excellent studies of Charles IV are Denys Hay, *Europe in the Fourteenth and Fifteenth Centuries* (1966), and R. R. Betts, *Essays in Czech History* (1969). □

Charles IV

Charles IV (1748-1819), who was king of Spain from 1788 to 1808, was a weak and good-natured monarch who preferred hunting to governing.

Born in Naples on Nov. 11, 1748, Charles IV was the second son of Charles, King of Naples and Sicily, and Maria Amalia of Saxony. His education was not a particularly good one; he was more interested in riding and hunting than in reading. In 1759 the childless Ferdinand VI of Spain died after naming as his heir his half brother Charles of Naples. The new king arrived in Spain a few months later. On his death in 1788 his son Charles ascended the throne of Spain as Charles IV.

When he became king, Charles was 40 years old and had had no experience in the art of government. Furthermore, the somewhat timid monarch was almost completely dominated by his wife, Maria Luisa of Parma, whom he had married in 1756. She in turn was infatuated with Manuel de Godoy, a young and handsome officer of the Royal Guards. Charles too became very fond of Godoy; he made him Duke of Alcudia and in 1792 named him head of the government.

While Godoy governed, Charles busied himself with his two favorite pastimes: hunting and collecting clocks. A sizable part of his clock collection is still to be seen at the royal palace in Aranjuez.

Godoy's alliance with France in 1796 and the subsequent war with Britain damaged Spain and made him, as well as the monarch who kept him in power, very unpopular. In March 1808 Godoy's enemies forced Charles to dismiss Godoy and abdicate in favor of his son Ferdinand VII.

By this time Napoleon had decided to replace the Spanish Bourbons, his allies, with a member of his own family, and in April 1808 he lured Ferdinand to Bayonne. Soon Charles, Maria Luisa, and Godoy also arrived there. Napoleon forced the Spanish royal house to abdicate, and a few months later his younger brother entered Spain as Joseph I.

Ferdinand returned to Spain as king in 1814. But his father and mother and Godoy never again played roles in Spanish history. After the events in Bayonne the royal couple and their favorite lived in France and then settled in Italy. On Jan. 2, 1819, Maria Luisa died in Rome. Charles died in Naples on January 29. Godoy was with him until the end.

Further Reading

There is no full biography of Charles IV in English. The short account of Charles IV and his reign in Charles Petrie, *The Spanish Royal House* (1958), is useful, and Raymon Carr, *Spain, 1808-1939* (1966), is highly recommended. □

Charles V

The Holy Roman emperor Charles V (1500-1558) inherited the thrones of the Netherlands, Spain, and the Hapsburg possessions but failed in his attempt to bring all of Europe under his imperial rule.

Born in Ghent on Feb. 24, 1500, Charles V was the oldest son of Philip the Fair of Hapsburg, Lord of the Netherlands, and Joanna the Mad of Aragon and Castile. When Philip died in 1506, Charles was in line for the rich inheritance of the Netherlands as well as Hapsburg Austria and possibly the office of emperor. Spain—the product of the rather recent union of Aragon and Castile under the Catholic Kings—fell to him because of a series of deaths in the Spanish family, which made his mother, Joanna, the legal successor to the Spanish throne.

Charles's maternal grandfather, Ferdinand of Aragon, who had long tried to block a Spanish-Hapsburg union, favored the succession of Charles's younger brother, Ferdinand, to the Spanish crown. But the grandfather died in 1516 before he was able to alter the succession. Charles, who in 1515 had already taken over the government of the Netherlands, became regent of Aragon and Castile for his mother, who was confined because of mental illness to the castle of Tordesillas. In 1517 Charles went to Spain, where he met his brother, Ferdinand, for the first time. The 17-year-old Charles acted with remarkable authority and self-confi-

dence and firmly rejected the suggestions of his family that he give his brother either Spain or the Netherlands.

Although the medieval idea of universal empire captured Charles's imagination only later, he was already determined to play a major role in the European scene. When his paternal grandfather, the emperor Maximilian I, died in 1518, the elective imperial crown as well as the Hapsburg patrimonial lands (Austria) came within Charles's reach, and he again acted strongly. To suggestions that Ferdinand be elected emperor, Charles replied that the duties of emperor would be too much for his brother. But Charles had a dangerous rival for the imperial crown in the French king, Francis I, who had offered huge bribes to the seven electors. Charles, however, was able to outbid him, and on June 28, 1519, he was elected king of the Romans, or emperor designate. (His actual coronation as emperor by the Pope took place in 1530 in Bologna.)

Basic Problems

With each of his crowns Charles inherited enormous problems. Each country had a peculiar internal structure which gave rise to constitutional opposition to the ruler, and furthermore most of the countries had a tradition in foreign policy related to their specific interests and situation in Europe. As an Austrian prince, Charles inherited the continuous struggle against the Turks in Hungary and the Balkans. As emperor, he was directly involved in the preservation of imperial power against the German semi-independent princes; moreover, he had to defend the remnants of imperial suzerainty that were being challenged by France in northern Italy. As king of Aragon, he had to protect the commercial Mediterranean interests of his subjects and their traditional involvement in southern Italy. The Castilians wanted him to carry the conquest of the Moslems into North Africa; and the huge Castilian possessions in South America also made demands upon him. Traditionally, the Burgundian-Netherlands princes had been the foes of France, but now the majority of the Netherlands leaders wanted a policy of peace with both France and England, which would be advantageous to trade. Charles had to find a way to integrate all these interests, essentially an impossible task. Moreover, the jealously guarded privileges of his various lands did not allow him to create a universal imperial policy.

Wars with France

Charles V derived unparalleled power from his vast empire, "upon which the sun never set," but at the same time he was the victim of its conflicts. He spent most of his reign combating enemies in one section of his empire, thus allowing his enemies in other parts to organize. Among the foreign powers that opposed him, the most stubborn and dangerous was France under Francis I and later Henry II. Since the late 15th century France had tried to get a foothold in either Naples or Milan (which had been conquered by Francis I in 1515); later it attacked Alsace as well.

A series of French-Hapsburg wars (a continuation of the wars of Maximilian I) started in 1521. In that year the French king, Francis I, attacked Lombardy, but this conflict ended with a resounding Hapsburg victory. Francis was captured near Pavia and was forced to conclude a very unfavorable peace (Madrid, 1525). In 1526, however, he was back in the field, now supported by the Pope and other Italian powers. But again Charles's forces prevailed. In 1527 his predominantly Protestant armies sacked Rome, and in 1529 they recaptured Milan. Charles's domination of Italy was guaranteed by the treaty ending the war (Peace of Cambrai, 1529).

In 1526 Charles married Isabel of Portugal, and their son, Philip (later Philip II of Spain), was born in 1527. Before his marriage Charles had sired two illegitimate children: Margaretha, later Duchess of Pavia, and John of Austria, the future victor of Lepanto.

Conflict in Germany

The victory in Italy seemed to be convincing proof of Charles's power. During the same period, however, the deterioration of his position in Germany had all but offset this success. The main elements in the German situation were the continuous advance of the Turks in Hungary (in 1529 they even appeared before Vienna), the organization of the anti-Hapsburg princes, and the involvement of the forces of the Reformation with Charles's political opponents. Although Charles took literally his oath to protect the Church, he was a religious moderate and not averse to compromise with the Protestants. After the Diet of Worms (1521), when he had taken the unprecedented step of hearing Luther himself, he had continued a policy of moderation.

But Charles's continuous absence from Germany (1521-1529) gave the anti-Hapsburg princes the opportunity to consolidate their opposition to the Emperor. Although the princes were not in general concerned with theological subtleties, they used religious issues as a means of breaking with the Emperor. In 1526 Charles ordered Ferdinand to assert his authority in religious matters. But Ferdinand was constantly harassed by the Turks, and he left the settlement of disputes on religion to the discretion of the princes "until a general council" was convened.

In 1529 Charles V tightened his orthodox position (second Diet of Speyer), but the only result was the defiant "Protest," which gave the name to the dissenters. At the Diet of Augsburg in 1530 both the Emperor and the Protestants were in a mood for compromise, but attempts at reconciliation failed. Because of his plan to move against the Turks, however, Charles could not proceed with force against the Protestants. He tried instead to persuade the Pope to call a general council and meanwhile hoped to enlist the support of the German princes against Islam in Hungary and northern Africa. During the 1530s the situation did not improve. Charles lost the support of Henry VIII of England, who divorced Charles's aunt Catherine in 1533 and was subsequently driven into separation from Rome. In Germany the Protestant princes, led by Philip of Hesse, allied with France to wage a new war (1536-1538) against the Emperor. Charles's stubborn imperialism also alienated his brother. Charles had arranged for Ferdinand's election as emperor-designate (1531) but tried afterward to change the succession to his own son Philip, thus causing much resentment on Ferdinand's part.

Final Failures

The decade after the inconclusive 1530s showed more dramatic reversals. In Germany nothing had been solved, and the need for help against the Sultan had forced the Emperor to continue negotiations with the Protestants (Worms, 1541). Charles still hoped for a general council, but the Pope did not intend to convoke one unless he could control it himself. In 1542 Charles found himself opposed by the unlikely combination of France, Turkey, the Pope, and the Dutch Duke of Guelders. The Peace of Crépy (1544) ended this inconclusive war. The treaty, however, contained a secret clause in which Francis I promised support for the forceful eradication of German Protestantism, and in 1545 the Pope offered his support in this undertaking. Charles V also secured the support of the Protestant Duke Maurice of Saxony (the house rival of the electoral dukes of Saxony) by bribing him with the promise of the office of elector.

In 1547 the army of the Protestant Schmalkaldian League was beaten by Charles and his allies at the battle of Mühlberg. At last Charles appeared to have attained success; his plan for a new universal imperial authority, based on a unified Catholic Germany, seemed near fulfillment. But as before, fear of a universal empire under the Hapsburgs made his allies desert him. Henry II, who became king of France in 1547, pursued an anti-Hapsburg policy, and Pope Paul III again defected from the Hapsburg coalition. The Pope moved the general council from Trent to Bologna in order to escape the Emperor's influence. In Germany it soon became apparent that the victory had no real results; Charles's proposals of constitutional reform and of the creation of a more centralized German league were opposed by all the German powers, Protestant and Catholic alike. In religious matters Charles again had to be satisfied with compromise (Interim of Augsburg, 1548).

Charles's efforts to guarantee the unity of his empire after his death also ended in failure. He tried in vain to persuade Ferdinand to give up his right of succession to the imperial crown, and Charles's relations with Ferdinand and his son Maximilian grew strained. In 1551, however, a compromise was reached that established Charles's son Philip, rather than Maximilian, as the legal successor of Ferdinand. But neither Ferdinand nor his son felt bound by this agreement, and the Austrian lands and the imperial crown were lost for Charles's descendants.

At the beginning of the 1550s a formidable coalition—France and the German Protestant princes, including Maurice of Saxony, who had rejoined the party of the princes—rose against the Emperor. In early 1552 Maurice of Saxony penetrated into Austria, forcing Charles to flee. Ferdinand remained inactive, obviously sympathetic to the princes' party, and in 1552 Charles V was forced to sign the Treaty of Passau. This agreement, which was finalized by the Treaty of Augsburg (1555), gave Lutheranism equal status with Catholicism and left religious matters in the hands of the German princes, who were ultimately the victors in their long struggle with the Emperor.

The negotiations of Passau and Augsburg had been left mostly to Ferdinand, while Charles withdrew to his native Netherlands. In 1553, however, he achieved one last diplomatic success: the marriage of his son Philip to Queen Mary of England. This marriage created the possibility of a future union of England and Spain under one monarch. But Mary died childless in 1558, and thus England's independent existence under the Tudor monarchy was assured.

Abdication of Charles V

From October 1555 to January 1556, in the midst of another war with the French, Charles V abdicated his many crowns. He bequeathed the bankrupt states of the Netherlands and Spain to Philip and Austria and the empire to Ferdinand. He then left the Netherlands for Spain, where he lived near the monastery of Yuste until his death on Sept. 21, 1558. He had witnessed the total failure of his dream of a Catholic Europe united under his imperial rule. Charles's ideal was an anachronism, however, since Europe had become too complicated to be so governed. But the extraordinary willpower and dedication with which Charles pursued his impossible goal establish him as a man of impressive character.

Further Reading

The most useful recent survey of the empire of Charles V is the book by H. G. Koenigsberger, *The Habsburgs and Europe, 1516-1660* (1971). Royall Tyler, *The Emperor Charles the Fifth* (1956), is a useful chronology of Charles's life and travels. Other biographical studies are Francisco López de Gómara, ed., *Annals of the Emperor Charles V* (trans. 1912); W. L. McElwee, *The Reign of Charles V, 1516-1558* (1936); and Karl Brandi's classic study, *The Emperor Charles V* (1937; trans. 1939). For a scholarly, well-written account of the situation in Spain during the reign of Charles V consult the relevant chapters in J. H. Elliott, *Imperial Spain, 1469-1716* (1963). Background information is also available in Leopold von Ranke, *History of the Reformation in Germany* (1905; trans. 1966); R. B. Merriman's masterful *The Rise of the Spanish Empire,* vol. 3 (1926); and Hajo Holborn, *A History of Modern Germany,* vol. 1 (1959). □

Charles V

The French king Charles V (1337-1380) ruled from 1364 to 1380. He skillfully governed France during a critical phase of the Hundred Years War.

Son of John II and Bonne of Luxemburg, Charles V was born at Vincennes on Jan. 21, 1337. He was the first heir apparent to the crown of France to bear the title Dauphin. Although nothing is known of his education, his later activities as a patron of the arts, theoretician of monarchy, and founder of the royal library at the Louvre indicate an early interest in learning. In 1350 Charles married his cousin Jeanne de Bourbon.

Charles was born, grew up, and reigned in the shadow of the great Anglo-French conflict called the Hundred Years War (1337-1453). When he was 16, Charles was made Duke of Normandy by his father and was thus entrusted with one of the most vulnerable areas of warfare. At the age of 19, on Sept. 19, 1356, Charles with his father and two younger brothers led the French army, which was cut to pieces by the English at Poitiers. During the battle John II was taken prisoner and held for ransom. Charles, lacking power and financial resources, had to assume the office of regent during his father's captivity, which lasted until 1360. During this period Charles weathered the threat of an English invasion and, faced with domestic discontent, put down a number of internal revolts, among them the Jacquerie, a peasant uprising. Only his astute political judgment and diplomatic skill saved the crown of France. With the Treaty of Brétigny in 1360 he arranged the terms of his father's ransom and established a temporary truce with the English.

When Charles became king on his father's death in 1364, his experience as regent had prepared him to take on his first great task—undoing the disastrous results of the political ineptitude of his father and grandfather. Although he was not a good general and was always in ill health, he devoted intense energy to ruling. He chose able advisers and was fortunate in securing a number of effective military commanders, including Bertrand du Guesclin, to counter the continuing threat from England. Charles resumed the war in 1369, and by his death in 1380 he had fought the English to a standstill.

Apart from his activities against the English, Charles's last years were spent in strengthening the defenses of France and organizing matters of law and finance. For the first time since the death of Philip V in 1314, France had an effective and intelligent ruler. But Charles's early death on Sept. 16, 1380, brought far less able men to the throne, kings who would preside over even greater defeats at the hands of the English and who would witness the further disintegration of French society.

Further Reading

There is no biography of Charles V in English; the standard works are in French. The period is well depicted in Jean Froissart's 14th-century *Chronicles* (many English translations), as well as in Édouard Perroy's standard study, *The Hundred Years War* (trans. 1951), and Kenneth Fowler's well-illustrated work, *The Age of Plantagenet and Valois: The Struggle for Supremacy, 1328-1498* (1967). □

Charles VI

The French king Charles VI (1368-1422), who ruled from 1380 to 1422, is also known as Charles the Mad. His reign was marked by political disorder and a series of defeats by the English that culminated in their overwhelming victory at Agincourt in 1415.

The son of Charles V, Charles VI was born in Paris on Dec. 3, 1368. On his father's untimely death in 1380, he ascended the troubled throne of France. Charles's minority was marked by the rivalry and struggles for power of his uncles, the dukes of Berry, Burgundy, and Bourbon.

In 1385 Charles married Isabelle of Bavaria, and in 1389 he finally assumed personal control of his kingdom. French court life in the 14th century was a joyous world of public revelry and grandiose diplomatic designs. It was brusquely shattered in August 1392, when Charles was stricken with the first of the spells of insanity which afflicted him—and France—for the rest of his life.

The King's madness did not immediately have a disastrous effect on French foreign policy. France and England were observing one of their many truces during the Hundred Years War, and the continuation of their armistice was aided by the marriage of Charles's daughter Isabelle to Richard II of England in 1396. England was then weakened by the struggles which accompanied Henry IV's deposition of Richard II in 1399.

The most important consequence of the King's incapacity was internal political strife. The governance of France again became the object of princely dispute, and two major groups sought control. The Burgundian faction was led by the dukes of Berry and Burgundy, while the Orleanist faction was headed by the King's brother Louis, Duke of Orléans. The King's uncle Philip the Bold, Duke of Burgundy, gradually asserted his ascendancy over Charles. After Philip's death in 1404, his son and successor, John the Fearless, became leader of the Burgundians and continued their feud with the Duke of Orléans. With the duke's murder in 1407, his son Charles inherited his title. The Orleanist

partisans then became known as Armagnacs because they were led by the duke's father-in-law Bernard VII, Duke of Armagnac. A series of murders and disputes between 1407 and 1410 caused both the Burgundian and Armagnac factions to seek the aid of the English.

When the English invaded France in 1415, the Burgundians allied with the invaders, and the Armagnacs became the nationalist party. The English king, Henry V, defeated the French at Agincourt and in 1420 forced the Treaty of Troyes upon Charles VI. By the terms of this treaty Henry was to marry Charles's daughter Catherine, act as regent for his mad father-in-law, and eventually succeed to the French throne.

When Charles VI died on Oct. 21, 1422, his legacy was discord and chaos. France was divided internally and faced with the prospect of being ruled by an English king. Although Charles VI's son was crowned Charles VII in 1429, strife continued until 1453, when the French expelled the English and ended the Hundred Years War.

Further Reading

The best account of the reign of Charles VI is in French. Although there is no biography in English, the period is well covered in Jean Froissart's 14th-century *Chronicles* (many English translations); Édouard Perroy, *The Hundred Years War* (trans. 1951); and Kenneth Fowler, *The Age of Plantagenet and Valois: The Struggle for Supremacy, 1328-1498* (1967).

Additional Sources

Famiglietti, R. C., *Royal intrigue: crisis at the court of Charles VI, 1392-1420,* New York: AMS Press, 1986. □

Charles VII

The French king Charles VII (1403-1461) ruled from 1422 to 1461. His reign witnessed the expulsion of the English from France and the reestablishment of a strong French monarchy after the disasters of the Hundred Years War, 1337-1453.

Charles VII was born on Feb. 22, 1403, the son of Charles VI. His father, who suffered from recurrent madness, implied that Charles was illegitimate since his mother, Isabelle of Bavaria, was known to be a woman of loose morals. Nevertheless Charles was regarded as heir to the throne until the English victory over the French at Agincourt. By the Treaty of Troyes (1420) his father was forced to disinherit him in favor of the English king, Henry V. After Charles VI's death in 1422, Charles VII was scornfully called the "king of Bourges," since that city was the capital of the small part of France that still recognized Valois royal legitimacy.

Rise to Power

At the beginning of his reign Charles was impoverished, threatened by English armies, and without a loyal nobility. He was also opposed by the powerful nobleman Philip the Good, Duke of Burgundy, and his followers. At first Charles was not equal to his task; he was not warlike and was sickly, physically weak, and personally unattractive. At Bourges he was ruled by powerful and ruthless favorites, particularly Georges de la Trémoïlle.

From 1422 to 1428 English armies moved toward Bourges through Maine and Anjou, often with the cooperation of the Duke of Burgundy. Popular resentment of English rule, however, remained strong in some places and lacked only a focus, which Charles was as yet unable to become. Such a focus, however, was provided in part by the heroic defense of Orléans during the English siege of 1428-1429. But more important was the appearance of Joan of Arc, who was thought by many to personify French resistance. She succeeded in raising the siege of Orléans in 1429, and Charles was crowned at Reims in the same year. Joan was captured by the English in 1430. Since Charles was unable and unwilling to mount a counteroffensive, in 1431 she was tried and executed as a heretic in the Norman city of Rouen.

Political Accomplishments

Not until 1433 did Charles actively assume personal control of the war with England. In 1434 the Church recognized his legitimacy, and in 1435 he was officially reconciled with Philip the Good. Also by 1435 Charles had freed himself from the control of favorites, and his personal finances had been improved by his financial adviser, Jacques

Coeur. Thus the period of his reign characterized by indifference, ingratitude, poverty, and fear came to an end. He began a period of vigorous personal rule characterized by intense legislative activity and close attention to the economy. He was especially concerned with sweeping governmental reforms. In 1444 Charles secured a 5-year truce with England and turned even greater attention to the rebuilding of France.

Charles's political skill was also reflected in his policies. Encouraged by the higher French clergy, who had become increasingly independent of the papacy, he issued the Pragmatic Sanction of Bourges in 1438, which sharply limited papal control of the French Church. The Church in France therefore enjoyed greater freedom than any other national body of clergy, and more important to Charles, the papacy's role in French politics was severely curtailed.

But Charles's reign was not free of internal troubles. In 1437, 1440, and 1442, he suppressed internal revolts. His son (later Louis XI) participated in a number of these uprisings and was forced to take refuge with Philip the Good from 1456 until Charles's death.

By 1449 Charles had created a standing army, and in 1449-1450 this force won back Normandy for the Crown. By the end of 1453 Charles had also recovered Gascony, the strongest English possession in France, and for all practical purposes the Hundred Years War had ended. With the return of Normandy, Charles was able to survey the records of Joan of Arc's trial, and in 1456 he had her officially rehabilitated through the annulment of her sentence by the Church.

The last years of Charles's reign were spent in consolidating and strengthening royal authority. At the end of his reign, France was more stable than it had been in more than a century. Charles died on July 22, 1461, leaving a restored kingdom to his rebellious but efficient son, Louis XI.

Further Reading

The standard biography of Charles VII is in French. Although there is no biography in English, useful works include Édouard Perroy, *The Hundred Years War* (trans. 1951), and Kenneth Fowler, *The Age of Plantagenet and Valois: The Struggle for Supremacy, 1328-1498* (1967).

Additional Sources

Vale, M. G. A. (Malcolm Graham Allan), *Charles VII,* Berkeley: University of California Press, 1974. □

Charles VIII

The French king Charles VIII (1470-1498) ruled from 1483 to 1498. Struggles for control during his minority and his attempt to conquer Naples were detrimental to France's political and economic life.

Charles VIII was born in Amboise on June 30, 1470. He was only 13 when he succeeded his talented and ambitious father, Louis XI, and his older sister Anne de Beaujeu served as regent during the early years of his reign. At this time the most important problem facing Charles was the virtual independence of the duchy of Brittany, the last of the powerful feudal principalities whose independent policies seriously threatened the political stability of 15th-century France. Francis II, Duke of Brittany, rebelled against Charles in 1484, but the King defeated him in 1488. During this period Charles was also involved in putting down uprisings led by his cousin Louis, Duke of Orléans, who later succeeded him. In 1491 Charles annexed Brittany by marrying Anne of Brittany, who had inherited the duchy from her father on his death in 1488. This marriage brought the last of the independent principalities under control of the Crown.

By this time Charles was free of the regency's influence, but he was at best ill-equipped to deal with the great difficulties of ruling. A contemporary described him as "very young, weakly, willful, rarely in the company of wise men . . . endowed with neither money nor sense." Unlike most rulers of the time Charles was barely literate, and his interests appear to have been absorbed by the reading of tales of adventure, history, and chivalry rather than by study of state documents.

By 1491 Charles was faced with a number of important problems. Political institutions needed reform and change; the status of the Church was vague and a definitive policy of church-state relations was called for; and strong measures

were required to strengthen the economy. Unfortunately Charles did not give continuing attention to the political and economic problems of France; instead he was absorbed by a chivalric and foolhardy dream of acquiring yet another kingdom, Naples, for himself. Reviving an old and remote Angevin claim to the throne of Naples, he mobilized the resources carefully husbanded by his father, traded away most of the diplomatic advantages which France had gained in the preceding half century, and in 1494 launched the largest invading army ever to have entered northern Italy.

In 1495 Charles briefly held Naples, but he was defeated at Fornovo and made a hasty retreat into France. The war which Charles began in 1494 was to turn Italy into a battlefield upon which France and Spain were to contend until the Peace of Cateau-Cambrésis in 1559. Charles's Italian campaign caused him to neglect French internal affairs almost completely, and many of the gains made during his father's reign were wiped out. But his expedition also had important international consequences; his initial success had shown more astute rulers that Italy was a rich prize which could be taken by force. Charles's French army had been defeated in part by a Spanish one, and this was the first indication that the hitherto independent activities of the Italian principalities were to be drastically curtailed by intervention of stronger powers.

In spite of his commitment of French resources to a fruitless expedition into Italy, Charles VIII did not notably weaken the power of the French monarchy. The achievements of Charles VII and Louis XI had made the king the ruler of France in practice as well as theory. This great royal authority was wielded in a number of institutions which continued to proliferate and grow during Charles's reign, despite his use of royal power in ill-considered enterprises. A lesson, which continues to have validity, can be drawn from this: it is difficult, even for a weak and foolish king, to impair a governmental apparatus whose basis was established by astute and perceptive rulers. In areas other than that of royal authority, Charles obliterated many of his father's achievements. Perhaps the most disastrous effect of his foreign policy was the formation of the anti-French alliance of Spain and the Holy Roman Empire, which lasted until the 18th century.

Charles VIII died childless, at the age of 27, on April 7, 1498. He was succeeded by the Duke of Orléans, who became Louis XII.

Further Reading

There is no adequate biography of Charles VIII in English. The standard work, in French, is Claude Joseph de Cherrier, *Histoire de Charles VIII* (2 vols., 2d ed. 1870). John S. C. Bridge in *A History of France from the Death of Louis XI* (5 vols., 1921-1936) devotes the first two volumes to the reign of Charles VIII. The problems arising from the invasion of Italy are well treated in *The New Cambridge Modern History* vol. 1: *The Renaissance, 1493-1520,* edited by G. R. Potter (1957).

□

Charles X

The French king Charles X (1757-1836) ruled from 1824 to 1830. The younger brother of Louis XVI and Louis XVIII, he was the last Bourbon king of France.

Charles Philippe, Count of Artois, was born at Versailles on Oct. 9, 1757. He was the fourth child of the Dauphin Louis, son of Louis XV, and Marie Josephe of Saxony. Artois devoted his youth to dissipation and extravagance. He was the leader of the reactionary clique at the court of Louis XVI. But in July 1789, with the outbreak of the French Revolution and the fall of the Bastille, he left France.

Granted asylum in England, Artois lived first in London and then at Holyrood palace in Edinburgh before establishing his residence at Hartwell. Although he undertook several diplomatic missions for the royalist cause, his contribution to the struggle against Revolutionary and Napoleonic France was insignificant. In February 1814 he returned to France; after Napoleon's abdication in April, Artois acted as his brother's envoy and signed the armistice of April 23, which restored the monarchy.

During the reign of Louis XVIII (1814-1824), Artois was the leader of the ultraroyalists, who considered the King too moderate. After the ultras gained control of the Chamber of Deputies in November 1820, Artois's political role steadily increased as he influenced legislation, foreign affairs, and the appointment of ministers. On Sept. 16, 1824, Louis XVIII died, and Artois became Charles X.

Charles's accession did not signal a radical turn toward reaction as some have asserted. The new monarch possessed many admirable qualities, among them a gracious and warm personality and a strong sense of duty. He was frugal in his tastes and generous toward others. He began his reign by abolishing censorship and by granting a broad amnesty to political prisoners. Charles, indeed, promised to rule according to the Charles, indeed, promised to rule according to the Charter, and many of the bills that he proposed became law. The law which granted an indemnity to *émigrés* for property confiscated during the Revolution provided a reasonable settlement to the vexing problem of nationalized lands and thereby promoted national reconciliation. The law against sacrilege was never enforced, and the primogeniture bill—defeated by the peers—would have affected only 80,000 families out of 6,000,000.

But despite his many virtues, Charles had two fatal weaknesses: impatience and a lack of judgment, especially in the choice of advisers. A staunch defender of royal prerogative, he could not accept the doctrine of parliamentary supremacy. "I would rather hew wood," he once exclaimed, "than be king after the English fashion." The blunders and divisions of the ultraroyalists themselves constituted another cause of the July Revolution (July 26-Aug. 2, 1830), which overthrew the Bourbon dynasty.

On August 16 Charles sailed to England, where he again lived at Holyrood. Six years later, on Nov. 6, 1836, he died at Göritz in Styria, where he had gone for the winter.

Further Reading

Vincent W. Beach, *Charles X of France: His Life and Times* (1971), is based on British and French archival materials, and gives the most scholarly and complete account in any language. Guillaume de Bertier de Sauvigny, *The Bourbon Restoration* (1963 ed.; trans. 1966), gives the best defense of Charles X. The topical account by Frederick B. Artz, *France under the Bourbon Restoration, 1814-1830* (1931), presents a good synthesis and has an excellent bibliography. ☐

Charles XII

Charles XII (1682-1718) was king of Sweden from 1697 to 1718. A famous warrior king, he led his country during the Northern War.

The son of Charles XI and Ulrica Leonora, daughter of Frederick III of Denmark, Charles XII was born on June 17, 1682. He was carefully nurtured by his parents because his four younger brothers died as infants. Charles XI, conscious of his own neglected education, selected the best available teachers for the boy's instruction; the future king was well grounded in theology, military science, the classics, languages, mathematics, and history. The father himself had a profound influence on the son. Young Charles rode and hunted with his father on expeditions that tested his endurance. He could ride before he was 4 and constantly engaged in mock battles with his peers and his teachers. Not only was he hardened to fatigue and exposure, but he was also made familiar with the details of administration.

The young prince was like his father in many ways. He had the same untiring energy, the same stubborn will. He was reserved and like his father distrusted all things French. He was also impatient with the niceties of diplomacy and preferred direct talk and action to courtly innuendoes. From his mother Charles received a personal gentleness which he combined with unflinching devotion to duty. His father's hopes that the boy would be eased into the duties of kingship were thwarted on April 5, 1697, by Charles XI's death. His father's plans that Charles should be subject to a regency during which he could gain experience also were not realized. Rumors of internal troubles between the six regents and the Estates caused the latter to request that although underage Charles assume full responsibility. Before the end of the year he was crowned, and the adolescent prematurely became the man.

Soon Charles's abilities would be put to the test. The early days of the reign saw him warding off many marriage offers, but his sister Hedvig Sophia married Duke Frederick of Holstein-Gottorp. He indulged in exciting escapades and committed his country by alliance to England and the Netherlands, supporting their stand on the Spanish succession for a guarantee of Sweden's possessions in the Baltic and the integrity of Holstein-Gottorp.

Northern War

Meanwhile Charles's enemies were forging alliances against him. By the close of the century a Livonian discontent, Joann Reinhold Patkul, had persuaded Frederick IV of Denmark, Augustus II of Poland-Saxony, and Peter the Great of Russia to make a joint attack on Sweden to despoil the young ruler of much of his inheritance. Charles XII turned from sham battles and mock heroics to real war. He had tried to avoid battle, but once his enemies began it, he resolved to punish them. To Charles the defense of his realm was a mixture of honor, duty, and patriotism.

Leaving his garrisons in Finland, the Baltic Provinces, and parts of Swedish Germany to care for themselves, Charles turned first against Denmark. While a combined Anglo-Dutch fleet kept the Danish navy bottled up in Copenhagen, on July 24, 1700, Charles landed his troops on Zeeland. The road to Copenhagen lay open, and shortly that city was besieged from the sea and land. Under pressure from his allies Charles signed a treaty at Travendal which was a return to the status quo.

Poland's turn was next. In September, Charles crossed over to Livonia, but Augustus had already withdrawn. Consequently Charles deceided to relieve Narva, which was under attack by the troops of the Czar. Peter enjoyed great numerical superiority but fled the area before the battle was engaged. It was well he did, because on Nov. 19, 1700, Charles crushed the Russian army, taking so many prisoners he was forced to disarm them and send them home. He should have taken advantage of this victory and brought Russia completely to terms, but he turned once more against Augustus. In 1701 Swedish troops crossed the Dvina in full view of the enemy, inflicted a severe defeat on Augustus's forces, and cleared Livonia of Polish soldiers. Soon Charles occupied Courland. In 1702 he invaded Poland proper and occupied Warsaw, winning a decisive victory at Kliszow. A victory at Thorn in 1703 made Augustus's position untenable, and in September of the next year Charles placed Stanislaus Leszczynski on the Polish throne. He cleared the marshes around Pripetz of Russian auxiliaries and marched through Poland and Silesia into Saxony, where in September 1707 at Altranstädt Augustus was forced to abandon both his Polish throne and his coalition with Russia.

His Defeat

The next to be chastened was Peter, who had been rebuilding his forces since Narva. He also had been whittling at Swedish possessions in Finland and the Baltic Provinces while committing enough troops to Poland to gain time. Charles's advance, at first crowned with success, ran into trouble because of long supply lines and Russia's policy. The King himself was wounded, and while incapacitated he was badly defeated at Poltava on June 28, 1709. Even worse, his cavalry surrendered on July 1 at Perevolotjna. The Swedish king went into Turkey, where through diplomacy he might have been successful except that Peter was able to buy off Russia's Turkish adversaries. Meanwhile the jackal kings of Poland and Denmark rejoined the ranks of Sweden's enemies. Not to be outdone at the carcass, the electors of Brandenburg and Prussia also became Sweden's enemies.

Charles XII and his country, however, were not dead. Despairing of Turkish help, Charles, after a dangerous ride through enemy territory from Adrianople, arrived on Nov. 10, 1714, at Stralsund, his last important garrison in Germany. When that fell a year later, Charles, after thrilling adventures crossing the Baltic in a small boat, came home to Sweden. There he strengthened his defenses and in two campaigns attacked Norway. During the second attack, on Dec. 11, 1718, he was shot while besieging the Dano-Norwegian fortress of Fredriksten. His skull was pierced, and he died immediately. The Northern War was ended during the reign of his successor, his sister Ulrica Leonora.

His Character

Myths about Charles XII are legion. Perhaps a few facts should be noted. He was not a barbarian but enjoyed social gatherings when he had time for them. He had a real interest and flair for design and urban planning. His dress, though plain, was expensive. He did not neglect civil administration. Rather he was good at it. Yet military survival had to be his main objective. The Spartan life he affected fast to encourage his troops. He was not a homosexual and was not killed by one of his own men. He could be charming but knew that in diplomacy charm without strength was relatively useless. His firmness—often called stubbornness—was Sweden's greatest as set, and his death contributed appreciably to Sweden's denouement.

Charless XII, however, must bear some responsibility for the loss of Sweden's status as a great power. Still he did not begin a single conflict, and any court of international law must consider his stand just, though unrealistic. The aspiration of fellow monarchs rather than the King's obduracy was Sweden's curse. He did not ruin his country internally or economically. His use of artillery, his tactical innovations, and his strategy when placed in their European context show that he ranks high as a military leader. His plans for peace which never could materialize indicate he would have been an above-average ruler. His death rather than his actions was a significant cause of Sweden's decline.

Further Reading

Ragnhild M. Hatton, *Charles XII of Sweden* (1968), is the best study in any language. A dated but helpful work is R. Nisbet Bain, *Charles XII and the Collapse of the Swedish Empire* (1895; repr. 1969). Charles's diplomacy is considered in John Joseph Murray, *George I, the Baltic and the Whig Split of 1717: A Study in Diplomacy and Propaganda* (1969). A lively discussion of Charles's invasion of Russia is in Leonard Cooper, *Many Roads to Moscow: Three Historic Invasions* (1968).

Additional Sources

Bain, R. Nisbet (Robert Nisbet), *Charles XI,* New York: AMS Press, 1980.

Hatton, Ragnhild Marie, *Charles XII,* London: Historical Association, 1974.

Voltaire, *Lion of the North, Charles XII of Sweden,* Rutherford N.J.: Fairleigh Dickinson University Press; London: Associated University Presses, 1981. □

Charles Albert, King of Sardinia

Charles Albert (1798-1849) was king of Sardinia (Piedmont) from 1831 to 1849. He played an important part in liberalizing the institutions of the Piedmont and in starting it on its path as the leader of Italian unification.

Born on Oct. 12, 1798, Charles Albert was the son of Prince Charles of Savoy-Carignano and Princess Albertine of Saxe-Courland, and the cousin of the Piedmontese king Charles Emmanuel IV. In October 1798 the French seized Piedmont, and the entire court took refuge in Sardinia, where Charles Albert spent the first 16 years of his life. In 1802 Charles Emmanuel abdicated in favor of his brother Victor Emmanuel I. On Napoleon's defeat in 1814, the family returned to Turin, the capital of Piedmont, where Charles Albert was given rigorous training to prepare him for the throne.

On Oct. 1, 1817, Charles Albert married the archduchess Maria Theresa of Tuscany. In early 1821 he refused a request by the liberals to participate in a revolt against the reactionary government. On March 10, 1821, however, Turin was taken by the revolutionaries. Their aims were to establish constitutional government in Piedmont and to drive Austrian rule from Italy.

Victor Emmanuel abdicated at once in favor of his brother Charles Felix and named Charles Albert regent. Charles Albert then granted a constitution, but it was revoked when he was forced into exile by Austrian troops, who quickly put down the revolutionary movement. He was allowed to return to Turin, however, after promising to uphold the principles of absolute monarchy.

On the death of Charles Felix in 1831, Charles Albert became king of Piedmont. He promptly manifested considerable administrative ability in reforming the financial system and the army. In 1846, when the apparently liberal Pope Pius IX assumed office, Charles Albert became convinced that a government of broader freedom was needed and issued a decree to that effect. On Feb. 8, 1848, he finally granted the eagerly awaited constitution.

When Milan revolted in March 1848 against its Austrian rulers, Charles Albert also declared war on Austria. But Austrian power was too great, and by 1849 Piedmont was soundly defeated. Forced to accept bitter terms from the victors, Charles Albert believed he could be of no further help to his country and abdicated in favor of his son Victor Emmanuel II. Charles Albert died in a monastery in Oporto, Portugal, on July 28, 1849. The day of Italian liberation was not yet at hand, but it had been brought nearer by his work.

Further Reading

There is almost nothing specific in English on Charles Albert. The most thorough general treatment is in Bolton King, *A History of Italian Unity* (2 vols., 1899; rev. ed. 1924). The most complete account of the Risorgimento in English is George Martin, *The Red Shirt and the Cross of Savoy: The Story of Italy's Risorgimento, 1748-1871* (1969). □

Prince Charles Edward Louis Philip Casimir Stuart

Prince Charles Edward Louis Philip Casimir Stuart (1720-1788), called the Young Pretender and Bonnie Prince Charlie, was the last member of the Stuart line to prosecute actively the Stuart claim to the English and Scottish thrones.

Charles Edward Stuart was born in Rome on Dec. 31, 1720, the eldest son of James Francis Edward Stuart, commonly styled the Old Pretender. His mother was Princess Clementina. As a result of disagreements between his parents, Charles received a desultory education at the hands of Jesuit priests, Protestants, and Jacobite soldiers. However, he developed a taste for music and the other fine arts and was an intelligent conversationalist.

Charles served with credit under the Duke of Liria at the siege of Gaeta (1734), and as he grew up—charming, magnanimous, and brave—he increasingly became the focus of the waning Jacobite cause. In July 1745, encouraged by promises of French aid and Scottish sympathy, he sailed for Scotland with two ships, landing in the Hebrides on August 2. The Scots advised him to return to France. "I am come home," he replied, "and I will not return to France, for I am persuaded that my faithful Highlanders will stand by me." Most of the Highland clans joined Charles, and on August 19 the royal standard was unfurled and Charles began his march south. At the battle of Prestonpans the Jacobites defeated an English force sent against them, and for the first time they posed a serious threat to the English government.

Charles and his army then crossed into England. On November 27 they reached Preston, having avoided the government army under Marshal George Wade. News of the capitulation of Derby horrified London, where all business was suspended. The Jacobites, however, were already contemplating retreat because expected English sympathizers had not joined them and the French had sent no reinforcements. On December 6 the Highland army began to retreat. It defeated Wade's force at Falkirk, but a second government army under the Duke of Cumberland completely routed the Highlanders at the battle of Culloden Moor on April 16, 1746.

Culloden marked the end of Charles's hopes. For 5 months he wandered, a fugitive, in western Scotland, before escaping to the Continent with the help of Flora Macdonald aboard a French ship. The king of France continued to extend moral support to the Jacobite cause until 1748, when, in accordance with the Treaty of Aixla-Chapelle, Charles was expelled from France. His movements during the next few years remain uncertain. He lived for some time in Paris with his mistress, Mrs. Wilkenshaw, and several times during the 1750s he visited London in unsuccessful attempts to revive his cause.

By this time Charles had become an inveterate drunkard and an increasingly pathetic figure. After his father's death in 1766, Charles lived in Rome as the self-styled Duke of Albany. In 1772 he married Princess Louise of Stolberg-Gedern. They separated in 1780, and Charles, neglected and alone, lived chiefly in Florence. He returned to Rome a few months before his death on Jan. 31, 1788. Bonnie Prince Charlie's romantic career has been celebrated in a large body of Scottish and English poetry.

Further Reading

Among the mass of popular literature spawned by Stuart's romantic career, there is no adequate biography. Perhaps the most reliable is James C. Hadden, *Prince Charles Edward* (1913). Basil Williams, *The Whig Supremacy, 1714-1760* (1959; rev. ed. 1962), provides an adequate background to the rebellion of 1745. □

Charles the Bold

The French nobleman Charles the Bold (1433-1477) was Duke of Burgundy from 1467 to 1477. During his life the Burgundian state reached the height of its political, economic, and cultural power.

The last of the four Valois dukes of Burgundy, Charles the Bold ruled a heterogeneous collection of territories running from the North Sea and the Netherlands around the eastern edge of the kingdom of France and terminating near the Mediterranean coast in Provence. The "Great Duchy of the West," as Burgundy was called, possessed the greatest strategic and diplomatic importance, wealth, and culture of any 15th-century principality. The independent policy of Charles's predecessors, Philip the Bold, John the Fearless, and Philip the Good, had made Burgundy the key power in resolving the Hundred Years War between England and France, as well as the most important influence on the political stability of the French kingdom. The life and career of Charles the Bold represented the greatest threat to the efforts of Louis XI to stabilize the kingdom of France by restoring royal authority over that of the great princes.

Charles was born at Dijon, the capital of Burgundy, on Nov. 11, 1433, the son of Philip the Good and Isabella of Portugal. Made Count of Charolais while still an infant, he was from birth the only heir of the dukedom and was carefully educated for his role as arbiter of the fortunes of Burgundy. He read widely in history, became an effective administrator and speaker, and grew into a ruthless and ambitious ruler. The personality traits which he appears to have developed early—a strong will, obstinacy, and little control of his emotions, particularly when faced with per-

sonal or political setbacks—coincide well with his nickname, "*le Téméraire*" ("the Bold," or as some would have it, "the Rash"). Charles's political character was further shaped by his reluctance to consider himself a subject of the king of France and by his desire to follow an independent and dangerous diplomatic course in his relations with England and France, in French internal politics, and in the affairs of the German territories which bordered his own on the east.

Struggle with the King

Kept from exerting power in Burgundy by his father's long reign and by a persistent animosity which developed between the two, Charles continually intervened in the struggles between the French king Louis XI and his nobles, particularly during the rebellion known as the League of the Public Weal (1465-1466). After the first of his many truces with Louis, Charles married Margaret of York, sister of the English king Edward IV, and thereby reopened the threat of an Anglo-Burgundian alliance, a diplomatic maneuver which had effectively threatened France earlier in the century and still constituted the greatest danger to French royal power.

Charles's growing ambition caused Louis to take the unprecedented and dangerous step of forcing a personal interview by staging a surprise confrontation with Charles at Péronne in October 1468. But Charles learned of the King's attempts to foment rebellion in Burgundian territories precisely at the moment when Louis was his "guest." On this occasion Charles extracted a number of concessions from Louis which greatly strengthened the power of the rebellious French nobles and secured Charles's position as the leader of the nobility, and the chief rival—and threat—to the king.

Charles's overwhelming success at Péronne appears to have increased his ambition and to have either revived or generated his idea of separating Burgundy from France by negotiating with the emperor Frederick III to make Burgundy an independent kingdom. By the Treaty of St. Omer in 1469 Charles acquired a number of strategic territories linking his northern and southern holdings, even further establishing Burgundy as a power separate in all but name from France. With his German, English, French, and Aragonese allies, Charles attempted in 1471 and again in 1472 to assemble large military coalitions against Louis XI. Although these failed to materialize, by 1474 Charles was at the height of his power, a formidable threat to France and the single key force in the diplomatic arrangements of the West.

Defeat for Charles

In 1474, on the eve of yet another Anglo-Burgundian coalition against France, Charles's single-mindedness and obstinacy drew him into a sequence of diplomatic and military errors. Instead of supporting the invasion force of Edward IV, Charles pursued a fruitless military campaign in Germany, thus abandoning his ally and making it easier for Louis to induce Edward to make a final peace. The ensuing Treaty of Picquigny (1475) marks the final resolution of the Hundred Years War.

Humiliated at being outmaneuvered by Louis and faced with revolts in Alsace, Charles launched punitive attacks against the duchy of Lorraine and the Swiss, who had provided aid to Louis. In 1476 the Swiss defeated Charles at Grandson and again at Morat. Committed to a policy of punishing the allies of his enemies, Charles finally became the victim of his own temperament. "The more involved Charles became," wrote his contemporary Philippe de Comines, "the more confused he grew." Driven to a fury by his setbacks at the hands of the Swiss, Charles forced a third battle at Nancy in 1477, in which the Burgundian army was once again defeated and Charles killed. Charles's death left his 20-year-old daughter, Mary of Burgundy, as the only heir to the Burgundian wealth and territories.

Further Reading

There is no adequate biography of Charles the Bold in English. The standard work, in French, is J. Bartier, *Charles le Téméraire* (1944). A subsequent work, also in French, is Marcel Brion, *Charles le Téméraire, grand duc d'Occident* (1947). The life of Charles is adequately treated in Joseph Calmette, *The Golden Age of Burgundy* (1956; trans. 1963). A detailed picture of the rich court life of Burgundy is in Otto Cartellieri, *The Court of Burgundy* (1926; trans. 1929). The importance of Burgundian culture is described in the brilliant work of J. Huizinga, *The Waning of the Middle Ages* (1924). However, the most vivid account of Charles and Louis XI remains the *Memoirs* of Charles's contemporary Philippe de Comines (available in many editions and translations).

Additional Sources

Vaughan, Richard, *Charles the Bold; the last Valois Duke of Burgundy,* New York, Barnes & Noble Books 1974, 1973. □

Ray Charles

The American jazz musician Ray Charles (born 1932) was widely admired as a singer, pianist, and composer. He combined elements of jazz, gospel and rhythm-and-blues to create a new kind of African-American music, known as soul.

Ray Charles Robinson was born in Albany, Georgia, on September 23, 1932. His father, Bailey Robinson, worked as a mechanic and handyman; his mother, Reather Robinson, worked in a sawmill. In order to avoid being confused with boxing champion Ray Robinson, he dropped his last name and was known as Ray Charles.

Suffered Blindness and Loss

The family moved from Albany, Georgia, to Greenville, Florida, when Charles was still a child. In Greenville, at the age of five, he began to go blind. At the age of seven, his right eye was removed, soon after which he became totally blind. At the Saint Augustine School for the Blind, in Florida, he learned to read Braille and began his musicianship as a pianist and clarinetist/saxophonist. His blindness required that he exercise his formidable memory for music aided by his gift of perfect pitch.

At 15 years of age, Charles lost his mother; two years later his father passed away. Suffering, somehow, always produces the greater artist. Charles, early orphaned and blind, suffered and grew in the capacity for emotion which infused his music.

Began Career With Country/Western Bands

Upon graduation from the Saint Augustine School, Charles traveled with country/western road bands—an experience he was to capitalize on later when he added country/western songs to his repertoire. Shortly afterwards, he began touring with rhythm-and-blues bands, working as a pianist, clarinetist, saxophonist, arranger, and composer.

As a singer, Charles was early influenced by blues singers Guitar Slim and Percy Mayfield. At the piano he was influenced by the jazz arrangements of Lloyd Glenn. Forever present in his style was the idiom of gospel music, sometimes subsumed by the other styles he sang; sometimes emerging in his pronunciation; sometimes predominating, as soul music. Charles' romantic ballad singing continued fundamentally in the suave Nat Cole school, but was embellished by deep-throated gospel growls and phenomenal falsetto which was frequently mistaken for a female soprano voice. The texture of his voice, his mixing of styles, his consummate musicianship, his versatile falsetto range, and his emotional appeal produced a unique vocal artistry which crossed even language barriers, but for an English-speaking audience his story-telling power added the dimension of meaning that provided a totally emotional experience not often equaled in any quarter of musical art.

Invented Soul

In 1954 an historic recording session with Atlantic records fused gospel with rhythm-and-blues and established Charles' "sweet new style" in American music. One number recorded at that session was destined to become his first great success. Secularizing the gospel hymn "My Jesus Is All the World to Me," Charles employed the 8- and 16-measure forms of gospel music, in conjunction with the 12-measure form of standard blues. Charles contended that his invention of soul music resulted from the heightening of the intensity of the emotion expressed by jazz through the charging of feeling in the unbridled way of gospel. When "It Don't Mean a Thing, If It Ain't Got That Swing" combines with "Swing Low, Sweet Chariot," the result is a beat hard to beat, and Charles never sang a note that was not perfectly on pitch or did not swing in his exceptional rhythmical contexts.

In 1959, on the ABC-Paramount label, Charles recorded his legendary "Georgia on my Mind." In 1961 he won the first of five consecutive polls conducted among international jazz critics by *Downbeat* magazine. Charles won several Grammy Awards from the National Academy of Recording Arts and Sciences. His virtuosity was internationally recognized. In 1976, he recorded songs from Gershwin's *Porgy and Bess* with Cleo Laine.

A Pepsi endorsement in the 1990s ensured that Charles would be known to a new generation of music lovers. He kept the albums coming, including *My World, The Best of Ray Charles: The Atlantic Years,* and *Love Affair,* and he even had a cameo in the 1996 movie *Spy Hard.*

Views on Elvis

In 1994, Charles appeared on the NBC news show "Now," admitting that "I'm probably going to lose at least a third of my fans," but telling interviewer Bob Costas that Elvis imitated what African-American artists were already doing. "To say that Elvis was . . . 'the king,' I don't think of Elvis like that because I know too many artists that were far greater than Elvis." While this statement caused a stir, it was known that rock-and-roll, especially in the early years, was heavily rooted in blues, and many rock artists performed and popularized music that originally belonged to African-American blues singers.

Although described by Nat Hentoff as living within "concentric circles of isolation," Charles was married to the former Della Altwine, herself a gospel singer, with whom he had three children. He was also known to enjoy good friendship with Stevie Wonder and other musicians. Yet there was a loneliness in his music, a kind of self- intimacy which was, perhaps, best reflected in his 1961 recordings with Betty Carter and his recordings from *Porgy and Bess.*

Of course, loneliness is inherent in the blues, but so much in the art depends upon the feelings of the interpreter that it is clear that there was a kind of loneliness inherent in Charles, himself; a loneliness that we are reminded that we share whenever we hear him sing. There is no more existential art than the art of music, which exists as creative experience only in the time of its performance. As Charles best put it himself, in a 1989 *Downbeat* interview with Jeff Levinson:

> And then you have another kind of person like myself, for whom music is like the bloodstream. It is their total existence. When their music dies, *they* die. That's me. That's the difference.
>
> How can you get tired of breathing? Music is my breathing. That's my apparatus. I've been doing it for 40 years. And I'm going to do it until God himself says, "Brother Ray, you've been a nice horse, but now I'm going to put you out to pasture."

Further Reading

There is no full-length biography of Ray Charles at this time. Information can be found in *Downbeat* (January 1989); *Ebony* (April 1963); *New York Post* (January 4, 1962); *New York Times* (October 8, 1961); *Newsweek* (November 13, 1961); *Saturday Evening Post* (August 24, 1963); *Show Business Illustrated* (March 1962); *TIME* (May 10, 1963); Leonard Feather, *Encyclopedia of Jazz* (1960); *American Heritage* (August-September, 1986); *Esquire* (May, 1986); *Rolling Stone* (February 13, 1986); and *Jet* (July 25, 1994). □

Charles de Menou Charnisay

Charles de Menou Charnisay, Seigneur d'Aulnay (ca. 1604-1650), was a governor of Acadia, a territory in the northeast of Canada. He was responsible for a solid and well-rooted establishment of French colonists in Nova Scotia.

Charles de Menou Charnisay was the son of a councilor of state of Louis XIII. He served in the French navy and, when his cousin Isaac de Razilly was appointed governor of Acadia in 1632, went there with him to a settlement at the mouth of the La Have River on the south shore of Nova Scotia, not far from the present town of Bridgewater.

On the death of Razilly in 1635, Charnisay acted as the effective governor of Acadia, though he did not have the title, which had been passed to Razilly's brother, with whom Charnisay worked cordially. Gradually the weight of settlement was shifted from La Have to the sunnier and more fertile lands at Port Royal on the Annapolis Basin on the northwest coast of Nova Scotia.

By this time a rivalry with Charles de La Tour, another administrator across the Bay of Fundy at the St. John River, had arisen. Both Charnisay and La Tour were under the aegis of the Company of New France, a trading company. Each had a right to half the revenue from the whole Acadian area, and each had the right of inspection of each other's territory.

In 1638 their quarrel was aggravated, rather than settled, by an arbitrary and clumsy move made through King Louis XIII, who granted Charnisay the title of lieutenant general in Acadia, with jurisdiction over La Tour's settlement at St. John. This led to a minor war between the two rivals and endless litigation. Further interventions of the court strengthened Charnisay's legal and financial position, but La Tour refused to give in. La Tour went to Boston in 1642 and chartered four ships, which he used to force Charnisay to give up a siege of starvation that he had laid against St. John.

In 1645 Charnisay again laid siege to St. John, apparently deliberately choosing a time when La Tour was absent in Boston. The fort was stormed and finally captured at Easter, 1645. The defenders, who had fought bitterly, were mostly hanged; Madame de La Tour, who had helped to defend her husband's fort, was taken prisoner and died shortly afterward.

By 1647 Charnisay became the governor of the whole of Acadia from the St. Lawrence as far south as he could get his writ to run. In the north he ran afoul of Nicholas Denys, whose trading empire had been established at what is now Bathurst on the northeast coast of New Brunswick. This too produced a lawsuit; but Charnisay's standing at court was very good, and he might have prevailed here too; but in May 1650 his canoe capsized in the Annapolis Basin, and he was rescued only to die of exhaustion. He was buried at Port Royal, leaving a widow, eight children, and a troubled estate. By a strange irony Charnisay's widow married Charles de La Tour in 1653.

Further Reading

The feud between Charnisay and La Tour has passed to the historians, who still tend to side with one or the other. John Bartlet Brebner, *New England's Outpost: Acadia before the Conquest of Canada* (1927), and Andrew Hill Clark, *Acadia: The Geography of Early Nova Scotia to 1760* (1968), are reasonably objective, while Bona Arsenault, *History of the Acadians* (trans. 1966), sides with Charnisay. □

Enguerrand Charonton

The French painter Enguerrand Charonton (ca. 1410-still active 1466), or Quarton, was one of the finest masters of the school of Provence. His "Coronation of the Virgin" is the most magnificent French altarpiece of the 15th century.

The origin and training of Enguerrand Charonton are unknown. He left Laon for the south of France in 1444 and worked in Aix, Arles, and Avignon until 1466. The contract for his *Virgin of Mercy* (1453), a long rectangular panel, is still preserved; it states that it was to be painted by Charonton and Pierre Villate of Limoges as a votive offering to a convent in Avignon.

The detailed contract for Charonton's *Coronation of the Virgin* (1454) has also survived. It specified that the zones of hell and purgatory, earth, sky, and paradise should be shown and that paradise was to be the locale of the crowning of the Virgin Mary by God the Father and the Son, identical in appearance, and by the dove of the Holy Ghost. This Trinitarian coronation expresses the Filioque doctrine (the Holy Ghost proceeds from the Father and the Son), which had become Church dogma in 1439.

On either side of the Virgin are ranks of adoring angels, saints, innocent children, and the blessed—in short, the entire Christian community. The apparition occupies more than three-quarters of the surface of the panel. Below, on earth, Jean de Montagnac, commissioner of the work, kneels before a crucified Christ. Against a Provençal landscape Jerusalem appears at the right and Rome at the left, both cities being abbreviated fantasies of Charonton. On the side of Rome, as the contract specified, are two revelations of God to man: the Mass of St. Gregory and Moses and the burning bush. The bottom stratum reveals many little figures in the zones of hell and purgatory. The composition is dogmatically and hieratically conceived, like a sculptured Gothic tympanum, and it is iconographically related to St. Augustine's *City of God.*

The picture is a blaze of bright color, especially red, blue, white, and gold. Noteworthy aspects of Charonton's style are the simplified, sculptural forms, linear patterning, stereometric construction of the distant landscape, balancing of hues, delicacy of shadowing, and an elegance that has always been a hallmark of French art. These characteristics are also evident in the great *Pietà* from Avignon (ca. 1460), with which Charonton has been credited.

Further Reading

The only book devoted exclusively to Charonton, a thorough study of his masterpiece, is in French: Charles Sterling, *Le "Couronnement de la Vierge" par Enguerrand Quarton* (1939). General works in English which discuss Charonton include R. H. Wilenski, *French Painting* (1931); Grete Ring, *A Century of French Painting, 1400-1500* (1949); and Michel Laclotte, ed., *French Art from 1350-1850* (1965). □

Marc Antoine Charpentier

The works of the French composer Marc Antoine Charpentier (1634-1704) are generally considered to be the epitome of the formal, learned style cultivated in French music in the late 17th century.

Marc Antoine Charpentier was born in Paris. He came from a family of painters and went to Italy to study painting when a very young man. During a stay in Rome he came under the spell of the famous Italian composer of oratorios Giacomo Carissimi, with whom Charpentier is reputed to have studied. He then changed his allegiance from painting to music and spent several years in Italy perfecting his musical skills.

On Charpentier's return to Paris he collaborated with the playwright Molière on comedy-ballets after the latter's break with Jean Baptiste Lully; Charpentier was responsible for the music for *La Mariage forcé* (1672) and *Le Malade imaginaire* (1673). Following Molière's death in 1673, Charpentier passed through a series of appointments as music teacher and conductor to several aristocratic families. In 1679 he became music master to the Dauphin, only to lose this rich post allegedly because of Lully's opposition. Between 1686 and 1688 Charpentier served in a similar position in the establishment of Mademoiselle de Guise. After 1684 he was also involved in the musical life of several Jesuit foundations in Paris. His *tragédies spirituelles,* written to be performed during Lent, brought him considerable fame. In 1698 Charpentier became director of music at Ste-Chapelle, Paris, and in this post he served until his death on Feb. 24, 1704.

While generally acclaimed for his sacred music, Charpentier's masterpiece is acknowledged to be his most successful opera, *Médée,* based on the drama by Pierre Corneille and mounted in Paris in 1693. Although *Médée* was lauded as the best dramatic work to be produced in France after Lully's death, Charpentier was not to enjoy a similar success with any of his other operas.

In general, Charpentier was acknowledged to be a learned but talented composer. He was considered by La

Cerf de Viéville (1709) to be the superior of any Italian musician, but his music was nonetheless described as very "dry and stilted." Charpentier's formal, learned style found its best expression in church music. He was particularly acclaimed for his solution to problems involved with musical realizations of Latin prosody. His talent was unsuitable for the exigencies of the music theater, despite his attempts to prove otherwise. Since it would seem he incurred the hostility of the all-powerful Lully, Charpentier did not secure a court appointment and hence passed his life in the service of the aristocracy and the Church.

Further Reading

Most of Charpentier's music remains in manuscript. His contributions to French music are discussed in Manfred F. Bukofzer, *Music in the Baroque Era: From Monteverdi to Bach* (1947). See also Donald J. Grout, *A History of Western Music* (1960). □

Pierre Charron

The French philosopher and theologian Pierre Charron (1541-1603) wrote an influential study of skepticism. He was also a renowned preacher and reformer.

Born in Paris in 1541, Pierre Charron studied law at Paris and Orléans before receiving a law degree from Bourges. After a brief period of law practice in Paris he entered the priesthood. He then went to Montpellier, where he studied law and theology and received a doctor's degree in canon and civil law in 1571. The same year he returned to Paris and began to preach. His eloquent sermons soon brought him fame and a variety of new positions. He served as preacher to Margaret of Valois, Queen of Navarre, as theological adviser in several dioceses in southwestern France, and as canon in Bordeaux. In his capacity as an adviser, Charron succeeded in carrying out Church reforms in accordance with the decrees of the Council of Trent. While in Bordeaux, he formed a close and lasting friendship with Michel Eyquem de Montaigne. In 1589 he tried to fulfill an earlier vow to enter a monastery but was rejected, probably because of his age.

In his first major work, *Les Trois Vérités* (1593; *The Three Truths*), Charron defended the Roman Catholic Church against its Protestant opponents. His three basic truths were: the existence of God and the necessity of religion; the existence of a "revealed religion," founded by Christ; and the maintenance of the pure truth by Catholicism, the oldest of the Christian religions.

In 1600 Charron published *Discours chrestiens,* a collection of 16 eloquent sermons. In that year he gave up his active duties and retired to Condom in southwestern France. In 1601 he published his most famous work, the controversial *De la sagesse* (*Of Wisdom*). In this work he developed the idea of skepticism by insisting that man, by use of his own capacities, can know nothing. What man considers true principles are really only "dreams and smoke." This attitude does not undermine religion, however, since it leaves man's intellect blank and thus ready to accept the revealed truths of Christianity. In addition, Charron also developed the view that the man of wisdom (the skeptic) is guided not only by the commands of God but also by the dictates of nature. This emphasis on natural morality was an important step in the philosophical study of ethics.

While visiting Paris, Charron suffered a stroke and died on Nov. 16, 1603.

Further Reading

The only full-length biography of Charron is in French. There is a monograph in English by Jean D. Charron, *The "Wisdom" of Pierre Charron* (1961). Also valuable is a chapter in Eugene F. Rice, Jr., *The Renaissance Idea of Wisdom* (1958).

Additional Sources

Charron, Jean Daniel., *The "wisdom" of Pierre Charron: an original and orthodox code of morality,* Westport, Conn.: Greenwood Press, 1979, 1960. □

Philander Chase

The American clergyman Philander Chase (1775-1852) was a pioneer Episcopal missionary in the early years of westward expansion and the first Episcopal bishop in both Ohio and Illinois.

Philander Chase was born on Dec. 14, 1775, at Cornish, N.H., the last of 15 children. He grew up in the Congregationalist faith of his parents, but while a student at Dartmouth College he converted to the Episcopal Church. Following graduation in 1795 he married and soon after began his theological studies under a rector at Albany, N.Y. He was ordained deacon in 1798 and priest a year later.

Chase's career began as a missionary in central New York (1799-1805) and continued when he was appointed a rector in New Orleans (1805-1811), and later in Hartford, Conn. (1811-1817). Enthusiasm for westward migration encouraged him to set out on his own in 1817 for Ohio, still largely unsettled. Preaching and organizing parishes as he traveled, Chase soon became conspicuous among the few Episcopalians in the region, and in 1818 when Ohio was organized as a diocese, he was elected its first bishop.

Since Chase's episcopal duties received no compensation, he settled at Worthington, where he served St. John's Parish, was principal of a local academy, ran a farm, and still managed to travel throughout the state. During 1821-1822 he was president of Cincinnati College, but this limited his episcopal functions. To build up the diocese required more clergy, and there was little missionary help from the East. Consequently, he determined to educate his own clergy by creating a seminary in Ohio. Untiringly he

solicited funds for this purpose, first in the East without success and then in England, where he received enough support to start the venture. His dream was realized in 1828, when Kenyon College opened at Gambier.

Chase attempted to function as college president as well as bishop, but his autocratic nature aroused antagonism. Alienated faculty, students, and clergy worked to limit his dual authority, and in 1831 he resigned both positions, retiring to a farm in Michigan.

In 1835 the Church's problem of what to do with a bishop without a see was resolved when Chase accepted election as first bishop of the new diocese of Illinois. With characteristic determination he relieved his earlier experiences: traveling, preaching, organizing, raising money, and starting another school (Jubilee College near Peoria, now closed). By seniority he became presiding bishop of the Protestant Episcopal Church in 1843, lending his support to "Low Church" interests. Though he was authoritarian and contentious, his zeal and diligence were respected. He died on Sept. 20, 1852, at Jubilee College after being thrown from his carriage.

Further Reading

Chase's ponderous autobiography, *Reminiscences of Bishop Chase* (2 vols., 1848), is less appealing than the affectionate biography written by his granddaughter, Laura Chase Smith, *The Life of Philander Chase* (1903). Brief biographical summaries are in Raymond W. Albright, *A History of the Protestant Episcopal Church* (1964), and James Thayer Addison, *The Episcopal Church in the United States, 1789-1931* (1951). □

Salmon Portland Chase

The American statesman Salmon Portland Chase (1808-1873) was an ardent advocate of African American rights. He was appointed secretary of the Treasury by President Lincoln, who later made him chief justice of the Supreme Court.

Salmon P. Chase was born at Cornish, N.H., on Jan. 13, 1808. He attended public school at Keene, N.H., and, for a time, a private school in Vermont. He established a reputation for good behavior, scholarly interest, and deep religious feelings. When he was 9 years old his father died, and soon he was placed under the stern direction of his uncle, Philander Chase, one of the great pioneer leaders in the American Episcopal Church.

Philander, "a harsh, autocratic, determined man of God," conducted a church school near Columbus, Ohio, where Salmon pursued classical and religious studies. When Philander, now Bishop Chase, became president of Cincinnati College, Salmon was his student. In less than a year, for some unexplained reason, Salmon left the college and entered Dartmouth College as a junior. He graduated in 1826 "without marked distinction." He had by this time decided to become a lawyer, not a clergyman, but he had not lost his religious devotion.

For a time Chase conducted a school for boys in Washington, D.C., and read law "under the nominal supervision" of William Wirt, one of the nation's best lawyers. He was admitted to the bar in December 1829.

Young Lawyer

As a practicing lawyer, Chase made his permanent home in Cincinnati. It was a wise choice. Located on the north bank of the Ohio River, with its busy western trade and with slave territory on the opposite bank, Cincinnati offered splendid opportunities to a young lawyer of ability and strong moral views. Chase's legal talents were quickly recognized, and soon he was being called the "attorney for runaway Negroes." His most famous case was the defense of John Vanzant, who had been arrested while carrying a number of Kentucky runaways to freedom under a load of hay. Chase and William H. Seward, as unpaid lawyers, carried Vanzant's case to the U.S. Supreme Court, where their eloquent appeals for minority rights on constitutional grounds attracted national attention. Chase's insistence that no claim to persons as property could be supported by any United States law won antislavery support among those who rejected William Lloyd Garrison's extreme militant views. It also served to advance Chase's political standing in Ohio and led to correspondence with such national antislavery figures as Charles Summer.

Meanwhile Chase's private life was filled with gloom. His first wife died a year after their marriage, his second after 5 years, and his third after 6 years. Of his six children, only two daughters grew to womanhood. The effects of death, always so near, deepened his religious fervor. Days spent in

Bible reading and prayer, and soul torture for possible neglect of duty in not impressing others with the need of salvation, left a deep mark on the man.

Political Rise

As a young man, Chase had voted as a Whig, but when the Liberty party emerged, his strong antislavery feelings drew him into its ranks. He was active in its development but was always ready to change parties if slavery could be ended more quickly by another agency. In fact, as the said, he sympathized strongly with the Democratic party in "almost everything excepting its submission to slaveholding leadership and dictation."

This was good politics in the state of Ohio, where widely differing peoples and interests kept party lines fluid. When the Liberty party gave way to the Free Soil party in 1848, Chase cautiously followed and a year later was elected to the U.S. Senate by a coalition of Democrats and Free Soilers.

In the Senate, Chase worked "to divorce our National and State governments from all support of Slavery" and through constitutional means to "deliver our country from its greatest curse." He labored to unite all the antislavery groups in a futile effort to capture the Democratic party and to make it the champion of freedom. Chase viewed the steps leading to the Mexican War as a proslavery drive but supported war measures as an obligation to the soldiers. He backed the Wilmot Proviso, opposed the Compromise of 1850, and was one of the group that issued the "Appeal of the Independent Democrats," with its false charge that Stephen Douglas's Nebraska Bill had opened that territory to slavery.

Chase was important in creating the new Republican party. In his own state he molded dissenting groups into an efficient machine and in 1855 was elected governor. He was reelected in 1857 and, because of his antislavery political record, was widely considered as a presidential candidate. Because of his shifting political course, however, he could seldom count on solid support from the politicians in his own party. Apparent at the first Republican National Convention at Philadelphia in 1856, this became more clear at the Republican National Convention in Chicago in 1860. There, although a "favorite son" candidate, he could not muster a solid vote from his Ohio delegation. Yet Chase and his state were so important to the party that a place in Lincoln's Cabinet was a foregone conclusion. The same held true for William H. Seward and the state of New York. The difficulty was that each of these men thought of himself as superior to the other and even to Lincoln. Both wanted to head the Cabinet as secretary of state, and the rivalry continued even after Lincoln had named Seward to the State Department and made Chase secretary of the Treasury.

Secretary of the Treasury

Chase's task of directing the nation's finances during the Civil War was a difficult one. Vast sums of money had to be borrowed, bonds marketed, and the national currency kept as stable as possible. Interest rates soared; specie payments had to be suspended; and soon a resort to paper money was reluctantly accepted. Yet with the aid of banker Jay Cooke, Chase somehow met the crisis and capped his accomplishments by creating the national banking system, which opened a market for bonds and stabilized currency.

As a member of a Cabinet in which Seward attempted to play the part of "prime minister," Chase led the opposition. To check Seward, he demanded regular Cabinet meetings, gave guarded approval to the provisioning of Ft. Sumter, and openly criticized Seward's handling of foreign affairs. He was equally critical of Lincoln, whom he viewed as incompetent and confused. His main complaints were against the retention of Gen. George McClellan and the refusal to use Negro troops. His constant disagreement with administration policies gained him a following among the Radical Republican element in Congress. In 1862 this led to a Cabinet crisis.

A group of senators, influenced by Chase's complaints, held a secret caucus and drew up a document to be presented to the President, demanding "a change in and a partial reconstruction of the Cabinet." It was, in fact, an effort to remove Seward and to advance Chase. On learning of the plan, Seward sent his resignation to the President, who put it aside. Then, by bringing the protesters and the rest of the Cabinet together for a frank discussion, Lincoln skillfully led Chase to repudiate some of his charges. This hurt Chase with both friend and foe. The next morning he offered his own resignation. Lincoln now held both Seward's and Chase's resignations and, having gained the upper hand, refused to accept either.

As the war dragged on, Chase was increasingly convinced of the impossibility of Lincoln's reelection. The Emancipation Proclamation had been satisfactory as far as it went, he felt, but it had not gone far enough. A new leader with a new approach was needed. Chase decided that it was his duty to seek the Republican nomination. A group of Radical leaders issued a pamphlet declaring Chase as the man who best fit the party's needs. The Chase boom, however, collapsed as Lincoln's hold on the public became clear. This made Chase's place as a Cabinet member embarrassing, and soon Chase submitted his resignation. Lincoln accepted it.

Supreme Court Justice

In the campaign of 1864 Chase made several speeches for Lincoln, and when Chief Justice Roger Brooke Taney died in October 1864, Lincoln appointed Chase to that important office. Chase presided over the Supreme Court during the troubled Reconstruction period. The important tasks were to restore the Southern judicial systems and to uphold the law against congressional invasion. Perhaps Chase best revealed his devotion to justice in his insistence on the judicial character of the impeachment proceedings against Lincoln's successor, President Andrew Johnson.

Meanwhile Chase retained his ambition to become president, and with the aid of his beautiful daughter Kate, he made strenuous but futile efforts to secure the Democratic nomination in 1868 and the Liberal Republican nomination in 1872. He died of a stroke in 1873.

Further Reading

David Donald, ed., *Inside Lincoln's Cabinet: The Civil War Diaries of Salmon P. Chase* (1954), includes notes, commentary, and an introduction which assesses Chase's life. Thomas Graham Belden and Marva Robins Belden, *So Fell the Angels* (1956), is a composite biography of Chase, his daughter, and her husband. Older but still useful biographies are Albert Bushnell Hart, *Salmon Portland Chase* (1899), and J. W. Schuckers, *The Life and Public Services of Salmon Portland Chase* (1899).

Additional Sources

Blue, Frederick J., *Salmon P. Chase: a life in politics,* Kent, Ohio: Kent State University Press, 1987.

Hart, Albert Bushnell, *Salmon P. Chase,* New York: Chelsea House, 1980.

Niven, John, *Salmon P. Chase: a biography,* New York: Oxford University Press, 1995. □

Samuel Chase

Samuel Chase (1741-1811), American politician and member of the early U.S. Supreme Court, was the most controversial of the founders of the American Republic.

Samuel Chase was born on April 17, 1741, in Somerset County, Md. He was educated, primarily in the classics, by his father, the Rev. Thomas Chase, until 1759, when he began the study of law; 2 years later he was admitted to practice. In 1762 he married Anne Baldwin. He was a member of the assembly (1764-1784) from Annapolis, where he resided until moving to Baltimore (1786).

A Force for Independence

An early and active opponent of the British crown, Chase led the tumultuous demonstrations of the Sons of Liberty against the Stamp Act. After the Boston Tea Party controversy in 1774, he was a member of the Maryland Committee of Correspondence and a delegate to the First Continental Congress. The following year he returned to Philadelphia for the Second Continental Congress and served in the Maryland Convention and Council of Safety. In the congresses he was among the most active and zealous and was instrumental in causing the Maryland Legislature to change its instructions to its congressional delegation so as to vote for independence. John Adams described Chase in Congress as "violent and boisterous" in debate and "tedious upon frivolous Points." So violent were his attacks on a fellow delegate who was unenthusiastic about independence that his victim retired from Congress. Chase's own patriotism was questioned when Alexander Hamilton (under the pen name "Publius") revealed that Chase had taken advantage of knowledge gained in Congress to try to corner the flour market. Temporarily retired from national

politics, Chase remained a dominant figure in Maryland politics.

In 1784 Chase was married again, this time to Hannah Kilty Giles. Through the years he had diversified his business interests to include involvement in confiscated coal and iron lands. In 1789, however, he declared insolvency. He was concerned in drafting the Mount Vernon Agreement of 1785, which settled differences on the Potomac between Maryland and Virginia, but it might be a mistake to see this as a step toward nationalism; and Chase's attitude toward the Constitution bears this out. He was not a delegate to Philadelphia, but under the name "Caution" he assailed the document as undemocratic and voted against ratification. His faction, however, was easily outvoted. Ironically, in view of his later actions, he proposed amendments protecting freedom of press and trial by jury. He was appointed to state judgeships in 1788 and 1791, and his holding of dual offices and his overbearing manner on the bench almost led to his ouster.

Member of the Supreme Court

In the Continental Congress, Chase had helped thwart opponents of Gen. Washington, and when Chase's name was suggested for Federal office in 1795, the President may have remembered this support. Washington first considered appointing Chase attorney general but in 1796 selected him for the Supreme Court, in place of the resigned John Blair. The fact that Chase had converted to Federalism lends credence to the assumption that his democratic opposition to the Constitution was another instance of his demagoguery.

In the first 5 years on the Supreme Court he delivered several precedent-making opinions. In *Hylton v. United States,* 1796, he defined direct taxation much more satisfactorily than would be done by the Court 99 years later. In *Ware v. Hylton,* also 1796, he effectively asserted the supremacy of treaties over state law, and 2 years later in *Calder v. Bull* he provided the textbook definition of expost facto laws. He summed up differing attitudes on judicial review in *Cooper v. Telfair.* An important circuit opinion was his ruling in *United States v. Worrall* that Federal courts lacked jurisdiction over common-law crimes.

Impeachment Proceedings

Chase, however, is best remembered for the contentious behavior that he carried to the bench. He advocated passage of the Sedition Act and then acted almost like a prosecutor, especially in the case of James T. Callender. At the second treason trial of John Fries, Chase's action was so high-handed as to lead to a boycott of his Court by Philadelphia lawyers. The "hanging judge," as the Republican press called him, campaigned vigorously for President Adams in 1800 and probably reached the peak of judicial impropriety on May 2, 1803, when he delivered a blistering tirade against democracy and the Jefferson administration, while making a jury charge. This action prompted the Jeffersonians to impeach him, and he was tried but not convicted in 1805, despite intense pressure from Jefferson, the Senate taking a narrow interpretation of the phrase "high crimes and misdemeanors" of Article III of the Constitution. chase's conviction might well have been followed by the impeachment of Justice John Marshall, but impeachment became a dead letter with Chase's trial, although the prospect may have served to curb the justices' political activities.

Chase was often absent his last 10 years on the bench due to gout, and his productivity was far less than that of his first 5 years. His stormy life ended on June 19, 1811.

Further Reading

There is no biography of Chase. Philip A. Crowl, *Maryland during and after the Revolution: A Political and Economic Study* (1943), provides useful background material, as does the biography of one of his closest friends, *Luther Martin of Maryland,* by Paul S. Clarkson and R. Samuel Jett (1970). The volumes in preparation on the history of the Supreme Court by Julius Goebel and Gerald A. Gunther will supersede existing works.

Additional Sources

Elsmere, Jane Shaffer, *Justice Samuel Chase,* Muncie, Ind.: Janevar Pub. Co., 1980.

Stormy patriot: the life of Samuel Chase, Baltimore: Maryland Historical Society, 1980. □

William Merritt Chase

William Merritt Chase (1849-1916) was one of the leading artists of America at the end of the 19th century as well as a distinguished teacher.

Born in Franklin, Ind., on Nov. 1, 1849, William Merritt Chase received his first art instruction in Indianapolis under B. F. Hays. He then attended the National Academy of Design in New York City, after which he studied in St. Louis, where his family had moved. Through friends impressed by his ability, he went abroad in 1872 and spent 5 years at the academy in Munich. American painters Frank Duveneck and John H. Twachtman were fellow students. Chase took a trip to Spain, where he copied the work of Velázquez, then spent several months in Venice with Duveneck.

In 1878 the Art Students League in New York City invited Chase to become a painting instructor. Knowledge of his European success had preceded him, and his class was an immediate success. He then founded his own school and continued for years as the most prominent art teacher in America.

Chase had his winter studio in New York City and held a summer school on Long Island. He was a prolific painter, active in the field of portraiture and landscape, as well as making a great success of fish still lifes. He soon gave up the muddy brown tonalities of the Munich school and adopted the silvery gray tones of Velázquez, gradually adopting lighter tones applied with much the same bravura as John Singer Sargent. Chase's portrait of Miss Dora Wheeler shows penetrating character analysis as well as facile handling of the exotic setting. *A Friendly Call,* showing Mrs.

Chase receiving a beautifully gowned visitor, is perhaps his most brilliantly conceived composition of figures in an interior.

Chase was very elegant in appearance and had a great deal of dash and style. His New York studio was a favorite gathering place for prominent artists and other notable people. On one occasion in 1890 Sargent was permitted to exhibit his portrait of the great Spanish dancer Carmencita, in the hope of making a sale to one of the notables who had gathered to view the painting and witness a private performance of her dancing. Chase asked Carmencita to pose for him, but she refused when he did not give her expensive presents such as those lavishly bestowed by Sargent. The portrait had to be finished from photographs. During visits to London, Chase became a close friend of James McNeill Whistler and painted a distinguished full-length portrait of the expatriate artist.

Over the years Chase probably had more students than any other painting teacher of his day. His influence was far-reaching, and he was responsible for establishing dashing, freely brushed canvases reminiscent of both Édouard Manet and Sargent as the accepted style of painting.

Further Reading

Katherine Metcalf Roof, *Life and Art of William Merritt Chase* (1917), is a useful, if uncritical, biography written by a student and friend of the artist. More recent exhibition catalogs that provide some biographical data in addition to representative illustrations of his work are Art Association of Indianapolis, *Chase Centennial Exhibition* (1949); *William Merritt Chase: A Retrospective Exhibition* (1957), a catalog of an exhibition held at the Parish Art Museum, Southampton, N.Y.; and University of California, Santa Barbara, The Art Gallery, *William Merritt Chase* (1964). Edgar P. Richardson in *Painting in America* (1956) briefly discusses Chase's importance as a teacher.

Additional Sources

Bryant, Keith L., *William Merritt Chase, a genteel bohemian,* Columbia: University of Missouri Press, 1991.

Pisano, Ronald G., *A leading spirit in American art: William Merritt Chase, 1849-1916,* Seattle: Henry Art Gallery, University of Washington, 1983.

Pisano, Ronald G., *William Merritt Chase,* New York: Watson-Guptill, 1979.

Roof, Katharine Metcalf, *The life and art of William Merritt Chase,* New York: Hacker Art Books, 1975. □

Vicomte de Chateaubriand

François René, Vicomte de Chateaubriand (1768-1848), one of the first French romantic writers, was a master stylist. Through the poetic prose of his voluminous work he was able to evoke exotic places and to transform and idealize his own life and times.

René de Chateaubriand was born in Brittany on Sept. 4, 1768, the son of an insignificant provincial nobleman. He grew up first on the Atlantic coast at Saint-Mâlo, later in the gloomy family château of Combourg. As one of 10 children, he was largely neglected and spent his days roaming the woods with his devoted sister Lucille, who first encouraged him to write poetry; by night he slept fitfully, isolated by a whim of his father in a haunted tower.

Chateaubriand attended the nearby College of Dol for 4 years. After acquiring a good classical background, he was sent to the Jesuit college at Rennes for more thorough preparation in mathematics. Following this he studied first for a naval career, later for the priesthood; Chateaubriand then joined the army, only to soon weary of military life.

Leaving the army, Chateaubriand went to Paris, where his brother introduced him at court and his first verses were published in 1789, the year of the fall of the Bastille. Though Chateaubriand was Catholic and royalist, he hated despotism and soon professed sympathy for the ideals of the French Revolution. But the revolutionary violence appalled him, and in 1791 he went to America in search of true liberty, of simplicity, and of the wilderness, where he expected to find American Indians living pure and simple lives. He dressed like a trapper and explored the Great Lakes and the regions around the Ohio and Mississippi rivers. The exotic color of his later works derives from diaries he kept at this time. Several American epics were the fruit of this journey.

Chateaubriand returned to France in January 1792, and in March he married Céleste Buisson de la Vigne, a sharp-tongued and witty young heiress. He joined the French

émigré army in the Rhineland, was wounded, and dragged himself half dead to France. In 1793, the year of the Terror, he escaped to London. At first he was miserably poor and almost starved to death; at this time, while a resident in the home of a British pastor, he was involved in a pathetic love affair with Charlotte Ives, the pastor's daughter.

Literary Career

Chateaubriand's first book, *Essai sur la Révolution* (Essay on the Revolution), was written in London and published in 1797. From the viewpoints of the Philosopher and the historian he examined ancient revolutions, compared them to the crisis in France, and attacked the conservative factions. The book shocked the monarchists in London, grieved and stunned his own family, but brought him new friends among French moderates.

One such friend, Louis de Fontanes, a neoclassic poet, was convinced that France was returning to Catholicism. His ideas struck a responding chord in Chateaubriand. Soon after, the death of his mother made Chateaubriand's religious conversion complete: "I wept and I believed." *Le Génie du Christianisme* (1802; *The Genius of Christianity*) struck like a flash of lightning when the French public was groping in the dark. This work, which established Chateaubriand as a major figure, defends Christianity not by appeal to reason but rather by appeal to the heart and the imagination. The cameo-like novels, *Atala* and *René,* intended merely as illustrations of the author's theses, are the works of Chateaubriand most widely read today.

Napoleon was pleased by this brilliant defense of Catholicism, and he named Chateaubriand secretary to the ambassador of Rome in 1803. When Napoleon had the Duke of Enghien assassinated, Chateaubriand had the courage to resign in protest from his new post in Valais.

Chateaubriand rejoined his wife after 12 years of virtual separation, but he discovered that her mocking gaiety had grown more biting as the years had passed. She was especially acerbic on the subject of his many mistresses, among them Madame de Beaumont, Madame de Custine, Madame de Noailles, and the celebrated Madame de Recamier, who had once refused the advances of Napoleon. These women used their influence to support Chateaubriand in politics and to spread his literary fame.

Chateaubriand and his wife retired to the secluded Valley of Wolves in the region of Sceaux outside Paris. Here he finished *Les Martyrs* (*The Martyr*), began his autobiography, *Mémoires d'outre-tombe* (*Memoirs*), and wrote in its entirety *L'Itinéraire de Paris à Jerusalem* (1812; The Journey from Paris to Jerusalem), the story of his pilgrimage to the Holy Land.

Political Career

Under Louis XVIII, Chateaubriand became minister of state without portfolio. This minor post displeased him, and he managed to be appointed minister to Berlin in 1821. He became ambassador to London in 1822, represented France at the Congress of Verona, and as minister of foreign affairs helped in 1823 to bring about the war with Spain. He was dismissed in 1824. He then engaged in bitter opposition to Louis XVIII but at the King's death and the advent of Charles X rallied back to the monarchy. He became ambassador to Rome in 1827 but resigned in 1829. In 1830 he refused to support the government of Louis Philippe (the "Bourgeois King").

Final Works

In 1831 Chateaubriand published his *Études historiques* (Historical Studies) and in the same year went back to his memoirs with greater seriousness. Chateaubriand's *Mémoires d'outre-tombe* manifest his desire to link his personal history with that of France. He constantly dramatizes his life, enlarging upon his role in events to the point of comparing himself to Napoleon. The book combines features of the confession ("to explain my inexplicable heart") and the historical essay. It is a masterpiece not only as an example of the genre but also as an expression of the 19th-century spiritual quest and its permanent malaise, the *mal du siècle.*

Chateaubriand's influence was immense; he dominated the literature of his time, to which he taught a fluid prose, intimately molded to the emotions. His *Génie du christianisme* imprinted a Christian character on the romantic movement; his exotic novels are both the source and the example of the *mal du siècle.*

Chateaubriand died in Paris on July 4, 1848, and was buried, according to his wish, opposite Saint-Mâlo, where he had played as a boy, on the isle of the Grand-Bé.

Further Reading

The best source of information on Chateaubriand is his own memoirs, *Mémoires d'outre-tombe;* the 1961 translation by Robert Baldick is handsome, exact, and highly readable. Two useful biographies are Joan Evans, *Chateaubriand: A Biography* (1939), and André Maurois, *Chateaubriand: Poet, Statesman, Lover* (trans. 1940). See also F. C. Green, *French Novelists from the Revolution to Proust* (1931), and Friedrich Sieburg, *Chateaubriand* (trans. 1961).

Additional Sources

Conner, Tom, *Chateaubriand's Memoires d'outre-tombe: a portrait of the artist as exile,* New York: P. Lang, 1995.

Painter, George Duncan, *Chateaubriand: A biography,* London: Chatto and Windus, 1977.

Painter, George Duncan, *The longed-for tempests: (1768-93),* New York: Knopf: distributed by Random House, 1978, 1977.

□

General Chatichai Choonhavan

As prime minister (1988-1990) General Chatichai Choonhavan (born 1922) tried to lead Thailand in its internal economic expansion and in its enhanced political and economic roles in Southeast Asia.

Born on April 5, 1922, to a military family (his father was Field Marshal Phin Choonhavan), Chatichai Choonhavan had a distinguished career both in the military and in public service. It was under the leadership of his government that Thailand began to play a more important role in the politics and economic life of mainland Southeast Asia.

Chatichai Choonhavan was educated at the Chulachomklao Royal Military Academy, graduating in 1940. His military education continued at the Royal Thai Army Cavalry Officer School in 1946 and at the Armored School of the United States Army in 1948. His active-duty career included action in the Thai-Indochina conflict of 1940, World War II, and the Korean War. He started as a sublieutenant in 1940 and a year later was promoted to lieutenant. He became a captain in 1943, a major in 1947, lieutenant colonel in 1951, colonel in 1954, brigadier general in 1956, and major general in 1973.

Military and Diplomatic Duties

In addition to his extensive military duties, which included serving as the commander of the 2d Cavalry Regiment in 1954 and as commandant of the Armored School in 1955, General Chatichai Choonhavan also held concurrently a variety of diplomatic and executive positions. He was minister plenipotentiary to Argentina in 1960, and thereafter ambassador concurrently to Austria, Turkey, and the Vatican, posts he held for eight years. In 1968 he was appointed ambassador concurrently to Switzerland, Yugoslavia, and the Vatican and permanent representative of Thailand at the United Nations office in Geneva.

By 1962 he became director general of the Political Department of the Ministry of Foreign Affairs, and in 1972 he became deputy minister of that ministry. In 1975 he became a member of Parliament from Nakhon Ratchasima Province and minister of foreign affairs; then the minister of industry.

Throughout most of the remainder of his career he retained his political role as a parliamentary member from Nakhon Ratchasima Province, and in 1986 became the leader of the Char Thai political party. He was appointed deputy prime minister in 1986, and prime minister in 1988.

Election as Prime Minister

The strengthening of the political process under the long tenure of Prime Minister Prem Tinsulanond from 1980 to 1988 gave a measure of stability to a nation that had witnessed a continuous intervention of the Thai military into leadership roles in the government since 1932. Beginning in 1980, elections and the military's involvement in the political process through parliamentary politics contributed to internal stability and an expanded Thai role internationally. Thailand had a history of military coups, and although there were two unsuccessful coup attempts by younger officers under the Prem regime, the emerging pattern was indicative of greater political stability through a strong military presence, but also with its governmental involvement through the political process.

Under the leadership of the prime minister, Thailand began to reassert a much more positive economic and political role in the region, while maintaining its strong support for ASEAN (Association of Southeast Asian Nations) and Thai membership. The enrichment of the country produced a growing and policially ambitious middle class opposed to the exploitation of the military government. In 1988 this began to have an impact, with the appointment for the first time in decades of an elected prime minister in Chatichai. Chatichai took some measures to curtail the practices of the military, but his government was widely seen as corrupt.

Thai Economics

Internally, the Thai economy was one of the healthiest in the region, with the gross national product expanding at an average rate of about 10.9 percent in 1989. Thailand was regarded as the newest of the "newly industrializing countries" (NICs) of the region, following Korea, Taiwan, Singapore, and Hong Kong. In 1989 international forces caused difficulties for Thailand. The income from tourism became threatened by the worldwide AIDS epidemic. In Bangkok, as many as 40 percent of the thousands of male prostitutes and 600,000 female prostitutes were infected with the HIV virus. In 1991, tourism was adversely affected by fear of travel generated by the Persian Gulf War.

Thailand had continuously been concerned over the expansion of Vietnamese influence over Indochina, specifically the Vietnamese invasion of Cambodia and its role in Laos, states bordering Thailand. Thailand was alarmed not only because of the military power of the Vietnamese, but also because a significant number of peoples of Lao and Cambodian ethnic descent live in Thailand and there had been historical Vietnamese and Thai rivalry on the mainland of Southeast Asia. The economic liberalization in Laos and the withdrawal of the bulk of Vietnamese military forces from Cambodia allowed a relaxation of tensions in the region, and in fact provided lucrative opportunities for Thai traders to play a dominant economic role in the region.

At the funeral of Emperor Hirohito in Tokyo on February 25, 1989, Prime Minister Chatichai presented President Bush with an *aide memoire* in which Thailand requested United States cooperation in an expanded diplomatic and economic Thai role in the Indochina states of Vietnam, Cambodia, and Laos and in Burma as well. All of these countries had recognized the need for major economic liberalization, a process in which Thailand believed it could play a most important role. The United States did not respond positively to the Thai interest, because the United States at that time did not recognize the Vietnamese or Cambodian regimes and had cut economic and anti-drug assistance to Burma (now called Myanmar) because of human rights violations by the Burmese military. After the Burmese coup of September 18, 1988, there were close Thai-Burmese military relations leading to major Thai economic investments in Burma.

A Coup

The careers of General Chatichai Choonhavan and other retired Thai military leaders seemed to indicate a shift to democratic processes in politics. However, sudden military pressure forced Chatichai Choonhavan to resign his post December 9, 1990. Chatichai was ousted in a coup d'etat that installed a mlitary junta, the 17th coup or attempted coup since 1932. A military junta took control of Thailand, calling itself the National Peacekeeping Council. Within days King Bhumibol Adulyadej recognized the new government. The former prime minister, his family, and some of his aides were charged with corruption and imprisoned.

A civilian diplomat, Anand Panyarachun, was appointed the prime minister pro tem by the junta that deposed Chatichai. But as new parties formed, the leading role was taken by a military party, Samakkhi Tham. In 1992, their choice for prime minister fell on General Suchinda Kraprayoon. Protests among university students and the middle class began immediately. Those opposed to a continuation of military rule rallied in Bangkok in the hundreds of thousands. In May the government declared a state of emregency and ordered troops to fire into the crowds of demonstrators. In the four days of turmoil, a number of people, somewhere between 40 (the government's figure) and 1,000, were killed by government troops. Violence was quelled when the king stepped in to call for an end to confrontation. Suchinda lost the support of the political coalition in charge of the government and resigned, replaced once again by Anand in the role of prime minister pro tem. In elections held in September, an anti-military pro-democracy coalition of parties, led by Chuan Leekpai of the Democratic Party, won a majority of seats despite violence and vote-buying that were manifest in many areas in Thailand.

Chatichai remained a vocal and active leader of the Char Thai political party, speaking out frequently on matters of Thai economic policy as it related to foreign relations and the development of Thailand. In September of 1996, just before elections, Chatichai publicly criticized Prime Minsiter Banharn Silpa-Archa for failing to fully pursue Mekong river sub-regional economic development projects, which, if properly managed, would enable Thailand to serve as a gateway to Indochina. The quadrangle project in the north and the seaboard development projects in the south had virtually come to a halt under the Banharn administration, Chatichai said. He added that the Banharn government has paid little attention to Indochina, and other countries have moved into what is supposed to be Thailand's backyard. He also said that Banharn lacks vision in foreign ecnomic policy-making. Just a week later, however, a new prime minister was selected: Chavalit Yongachaiyudh. Chatichai had also been in consideration for the position. The new prime minister selected Choonhavan as his special advisor for economic and foreign affairs.

Further Reading

Except for brief references in the daily press there is no biographical material in English for Chatichai Choonhavan. The Royal Thai Government has published a booklet, *The Thai Prime Minister and His Task* (Bangkok, no date). An analysis of Thai writing can be found in Herbert P. Phillips, *Modern Thai Literature: An Ethnographic Interpretation* (1987). □

Bankimchandra Chatterji

The Bengali novelist Bankimchandra Chatterji (1838-1894) was the first writer to use the Western form of the novel successfully in an Indian language.

Bankimchandra Chatterji was born on June 26, 1838, in the village of Kanthalpara near Calcutta. His father, Jadavchandra, an orthodox Kulin Brahmin, was a deputy collector of revenues. Bankimchandra received much of his early traditional Hindu education from a family priest. He was married at the age of 11 to a girl of 5 and in the same year, 1849, was enrolled in Hooghly College.

At Hooghly College, and later at Presidency College, Calcutta, Bankimchandra's education became almost entirely Western, with an emphasis on science, history, language, law, and philosophy. In 1858 he became one of the first two students to earn a baccalaureate from newly founded Calcutta University. Immediately after graduation he was appointed a deputy collector by the British colonial government and remained in that position without promotion for 33 years. He retired in 1891. But while he was a government official, he began to write novels in his spare time. He is said to have suffered from diabetes for some years, and he died 2 years after his retirement, on April 8, 1894.

Historical Novels

Bankimchandra wrote his first novel, *Rajmohan's Wife* (1864), in English. Thereafter he wrote 14 novels in Bengali from 1865 to 1884. He combined Sanskritized and colloquial Bengali in a manner that made it for the first time an adequate vehicle for expressing a wide range of subjects that hitherto had had to be stated in Sanskrit or English. His first Bengali novel, *Durgeshnandini* (1865), is said to have created a sensation in Calcutta. Bengalis had read English novelists, like Sir Walter Scott, but Bankimchandra's novels were the first that gave them a satisfying semblance of their own world in fictional form. His first three novels were pure romance decked out in historical costume. While the history in these and in later novels with historical themes was often inaccurate, the bravery of the heroes and the beauty, endurance, and self-sacrifice of the heroines served to inspire Bengalis with notions of a glorious past.

Social Issues

In his social novels Bankimchandra was bold for his time in creating characters who broke with traditional codes of behavior, but he was careful to see that in the end the conventional prevailed over the unconventional. In his two best social novels, *Vishavriksha* (1873) and *Krishnakanter Will* (1878), he explores the questions of extramarital love and remarriage of widows, but by means of suicide and murder he clears the way for convention to win out. He was guilty of helping the right as he saw it to overcome the wrong by undisguised authorial intervention in the affairs of his characters. However, Bankimchandra's works possessed vitality. In the numerous, short chapters, dramatic events happened frequently, humor appeared everywhere, and there was movement, action, and feeling. Many of the names of his fictional characters have passed into the idiom of the language.

Advocate of Hinduism

Bankimchandra became an adult at a time when the educated people of Bengal were beginning seriously to reexamine their ideals. The easy acceptance of everything Western and the derogation of everything Hindu had by this time given rise to a strong Hindu reaction. Bankimchandra became a spokesman for the orthodox point of view. He wrote a book on the Lord Krishna which showed a personal God with attributes more lofty than those of the Christian God. Bankimchandra defended the institution of caste, though he acknowledged some of its evils. In one of his last novels, *Anandamath,* he described a strongly disciplined order of *sanyasis* who revolted against the medieval Moslem rulers of Bengal. These *sanyasis* worshiped the mother-goddess Durga, who became to Bengali readers a powerful symbol of religion and patriotism. A long poem in this book, *Bande Mataram* (Hail to the Mother), became after Bankimchandra's death the anthem of Hindu nationalists in the early 20th century.

Bankimchandra's impact on nationalist thought and action was based on his teaching of a renewed faith in Hinduism, and occasionally this was used to exacerbate communal antagonism between Hindus and Moslems. Though he proposed no specific plan for gaining independence or for governing the country after independence, his ideas blossomed in other men's minds and were a force in the Indian nationalist movement.

Further Reading

Most of Bankimchandra's novels have been translated into English. Biographical and critical works on Bankimchandra in English are generally uninspiring. Jayanta-Kumara Dasa Gupta, *A Critical Study of the Life and Novels of Bankimcandra . . .* (1937), is readily available in university libraries. More enjoyable to read and more detailed biographically, although undocumented and marred by faulty English, is Mati-Lala Dasa, *Bankim Chandra, Prophet of the Indian Renaissance: His Life and Art* (1938).

Additional Sources

Bose, Sunil Kumar, *Bankim Chandra Chatterji,* New Delhi: Publications Division, Ministry of Information and Broadcasting, Govt. of India, 1974. □

Thomas Chatterton

The major works of the English poet Thomas Chatterton (1752-1770) are a group of poems that he claimed had been written by Thomas Rowley, a 15th-century priest.

Thomas Chatterton, born in Bristol on Nov. 20, 1752, was the posthumous son of a schoolmaster. In 1727 his father had acquired many 15th-century parchments, and in these documents Chatterton later pretended to find the poems and records of Thomas Rowley and his circle.

In 1760 Chatterton was enrolled in Colston's Hospital School, a charity school restricted to teaching reading, writing, arithmetic, and the principles of the Church of England. The narrowness of this education was somewhat relieved by the influence of the junior master, Thomas Phillips, who encouraged the older boys to read history and poetry and to write. According to Chatterton's sister, "he was more cheerful after he began to write poetry," when he was about 10 years old. His first published verses appeared in *Felix Farley's Journal* on Jan. 8, 1763.

On July 1, 1767, Chatterton was apprenticed to a scrivener. Although the boy did his work dutifully, much of the time there was nothing for him to do except write his own compositions and read chronicles, charters, Chaucer, and dictionaries, the sources of his antiquarian knowledge. While an apprentice, he discovered the store of 15th-century parchments in his mother's house. Exclaiming that he had found a great treasure, he carried them off for use in producing and authenticating his Rowley myth. Most of the

Rowley poems appear to have been written in 1768-1769, though they were not published until after the poet's death.

Anxious to try his luck in the literary world, in 1770 Chatterton set off for London. He wrote cheerful letters home about the people he had met and the welcome accorded his works, and it appears that he produced, in addition to poems, every kind of Grub Street writing. He also wrote the last-and one of the best-of the Rowley poems, "An Excelente Balade of Charitie." Unlike his hackwork, it was rejected. While Chatterton's acknowledged poems are often imitations of Pope's satires, the Rowley poems have such romantic qualities as a taste for the medieval, a rejection of social injustice, and a preference for loose or stanzaic forms rather than heroic couplets.

Chatterton's voluminous writings brought less fame than he claimed, and far less money than fame. On Aug. 24, 1770, alone in London, not having eaten for several days, Chatterton tore up his papers, drank arsenic, and died.

Further Reading

Joseph Cottle and Robert Southey, eds., *The Works of Thomas Chatterton* (3 vols., 1803), includes the earliest biography, the "Life of Chatterton" by George Gregory. *The Poetical Works of Thomas Chatterton* (2 vols., 1871) was edited by Walter W. Skeat; it includes an essay on the Rowley poems by Skeat and a memoir by Edward Bell. New biographical material is in John H. Ingram, *The True Chatterton* (1910), and Sir Ernest Clarke, *New Lights on Chatterton* (1916). A more recent full-length study is John C. Nevill, *Thomas Chatterton* (1948).

Additional Sources

Dix, John Ross, *The life of Thomas Chatterton including his unpublished poems and correspondence,* London: Routledge/Thoemmes Press, 1993.

Ellinger, Esther Parker., *Thomas Chatterton, the marvelous boy: to which is added The exhibition, a personal satire,* Norwood, Pa.: Norwood Editions, 1976. □

Geoffrey Chaucer

The English author and courtier Geoffrey Chaucer (ca. 1345-1400) was one of the greatest poets of the late Middle Ages and has often been called the father of English poetry. His best-known works are *The Canterbury Tales* and *Troilus and Criseyde.*

The exact date and place of Geoffrey Chaucer's birth are not known. The evidence suggests, however, that he was born about 1345, or a year or two earlier, in his father's London house. This was located on Thames Street adjacent to the west bank of the Walbrook. It is probable that young Geoffrey attended school at St. Paul's Cathedral. If he did so, his early training must have been strongly influenced by men whose intellectual tastes were shaped by their association with Richard de Bury, one of the most learned Englishmen of his time and the author of a treatise on the love of books called *Philobiblon.* But our first record of Chaucer reveals that in 1357 he was a page in the household of the Countess of Ulster, the wife of Prince Lionel. From this time forward we find Chaucer associated in one way or another with the royal family.

During 1359-1360 King Edward III campaigned in France, hoping to better the terms of what would become the Treaty of Bretigny (1360), and even to be crowned king of France at Reims. But the campaign was a failure, and during it Chaucer, who was in the retinue of Prince Lionel, who was in the retinue of Prince Lionel, was taken prisoner. The King ransomed him for the substantial sum of £ 16 on March 1, 1360. Later in the year Chaucer was again in France on a mission for Prince Lionel. We should not be astonished that in the late 14th century a young man of about 15 should be entrusted with considerable responsibility—boys did not then experience the uneasy period of adolescence that we know today.

Chaucer's Marriage

After 1360 we lose sight of Chaucer for several years. There is an old tradition to the effect that he studied at the Inner Temple, where apprentices at law were trained. This kind of education would have been especially appropriate for a young man destined for royal service. However, he may have been engaged with Prince Lionel in Ireland. He tells us in the "Retractions" at the close of *The Canterbury Tales* that he had made "many a song and many a lecherous lay." It is likely that such songs and lays were the

product of his youthful years, and that he acquired an early reputation for songs and jocular tales.

Recently discovered documents indicate that in 1366 Chaucer was traveling in Spain, and it is probable that soon after his return he married a lady of the queen's chamber, Philippa, the daughter of Sir Payne Roet. Philippa later entered the service of Constance of Castile, the second wife of John of Gaunt, Duke of Lancaster. Her sister, Katherine Swynford, had been in the service of John's first wife, Blanche. After the death of Blanche, Katherine became John of Gaunt's mistress, and many years later (1396) his third wife. Chaucer's ties with the Duke of Lancaster were thus very close. In 1368 Chaucer was again on the Continent, probably on a mission for the King. Chaucer was now a royal squire.

The Book of the Duchess

The year 1369 marks a turning point both in the fortunes of England and in the career of young Chaucer. Edward the Black Prince had won a singular victory at Nájera in 1367, but it was to be his last great chivalric achievement. He soon became subject to a debilitating and lingering illness. In 1369 the war with France was resumed, and the French were increasingly successful. On August 15 Queen Philippa died of the Black Death, which ravished England in that year. King Edward was becoming increasingly feeble both as an administrator and as a chivalric leader, and he soon fell under the domination of a mistress, Alice Perrers. The years between 1369 and 1400 witnessed a steady decline in English prestige abroad and in the integrity of English society at home.

On Sept. 12, 1369, Blanche, Duchess of Lancaster, also died of the plague. John of Gaunt, who was campaigning on the Continent, did not return until December. When he did so, however, he established two chantry priests in St. Paul's Cathedral to sing Masses for Blanche, ordered a tomb to be erected for her and for himself in the choir north of the altar, and established a memorial service to be held annually for her on September 12. It seems probable that he also asked Chaucer to compose a memorial poem to be recited in connection with one of these services.

Before the death of Queen Philippa, poetry in the English court had been customarily written in French. French was the natural language of both King Edward and his queen. Her secretary, Jean Froissart, was the most prominent poet associated with the court. Chaucer's memorial poem, however, was to be in English. It is possible that he had written his English devotional poem, "An A B C," which is a translation from a French source, for Blanche at some time before her death. We must not suppose that Chaucer dashed off his new poem, *The Book of the Duchess,* in a few days. It is a complexly structured allegory suited to the rather sophisticated court tastes of the time, and a fitting memorial to one of the highest-ranking ladies of the English royal household.

The King did not allow Chaucer to remain idle. He was sent abroad on diplomatic missions in 1370 and again in 1372-1373. The latter mission took him to Italy, where he visited Genoa and Florence. He may have deepened his acquaintance with the poetic traditions established by Dante and Petrarch.

John of Gaunt was able to attend a memorial service for Blanche for the first time in 1374. It may be that Chaucer's *Book of the Duchess* was read at this service. In any event, the duke granted Chaucer an annuity of £ 10, the normal income for a squire in an aristocratic household. The King granted Chaucer a daily pitcher of wine and appointed him controller of customs of wools, skins, and hides in the port of London. This position brought £ 10 annually and a bonus of 10 marks. The City of London granted Chaucer a residence above Aldgate; moreover, some wardships obtained in 1375 brought Chaucer a little over £ 175. He and Philippa were thus economically secure.

During the early years of his residence at Aldgate, where he remained until 1386, Chaucer went abroad several times on diplomatic missions for King Edward, who died in 1377, and for King Richard II. In 1380 Chaucer's name appears in some court records. He and three distinguished knights and two prominent merchants took one Cecily of Champaign before the chancellor, Archbishop Simon Sudbury, to swear that she had no charge of rape or other action to bring against Chaucer. This fact has given rise to a great deal of unwarranted speculation, but there is no evidence to show that Chaucer's relations with Philippa were not satisfactory. In the following year Chaucer probably witnessed the outrages of the Peasants' Revolt in London, during which Archbishop Sudbury was cruelly beheaded by a mob. In 1382 Chaucer was made controller of petty customs on wine and other goods with the right to employ a deputy. He obtained in 1385 a permanent deputy for the wool customs, which must have entailed many hours of onerous labor.

Troilus and Criseyde

The diplomatic business of the king and the regular affairs of the custom house must have kept Chaucer busy. Nevertheless, while he was living above Aldgate he completed his translation of Boethius's *Consolation of Philosophy,* a book whose phrases, figurative devices, and philosophical ideas echo throughout his poetry. It is almost impossible to understand Chaucer's original works without first obtaining a thorough understanding of this book. He probably composed some of his short poems during this period and almost certainly his "tragedy," as he calls it, *Troilus and Criseyde.* This long poem, set against the background of the Trojan War, is based on an earlier poem by the Italian Giovanni Boccaccio. But Chaucer uses the narrative for his own purposes. The story involves a young prince of Troy who, neglecting his obligations during the Greek siege of the city, falls in love with a widow named Criseyde, loses her, and dies in despair on the battlefield. The fate of the young prince serves as a warning to the chivalry of England.

Probably because of the influence of Thomas of Woodstock, Duke of Gloucester, Chaucer lost his controllerships at the custom house in 1386. He probably took up residence in Kent in that year. He served as a member of Parliament from Kent. It is probable that Philippa died in 1387. Certain evidence indicates that Chaucer was in straitened circumstances in 1388, but in 1389 he received his highest position, the clerkship of the royal works. Although the clerk of the works had an office in the palace grounds at Westminster, Chaucer must have traveled a great deal in overseeing the maintenance, repair, and construction of royal buildings.

Chaucer supervised the construction of lists for an important tournament at Smithfield, where matches were held in return for the jousts at St. Ingelvert. There Henry of Derby, John of Gaunt's son and the future Henry IV, distinguished himself before departing on a Crusade. The clerkship, which required a great deal of work organizing workmen, collecting and transporting materials, and consulting with masons and carpenters, was seldom held for a long term in the 14th century, and Chaucer resigned in 1391. For a time thereafter he served as deputy forester for the royal forest at North Petherton. The King granted him a pension of £ 20 in 1394, and in 1397 an annual butt of wine was added to this grant. These grants were renewed and increased by Henry IV in 1399.

The Canterbury Tales

Between 1387 and 1400 Chaucer must have devoted considerable attention to the composition of his most famous work, *The Canterbury Tales.* Some of the tales were probably modified versions of earlier works adapted for the new collection, while others were written especially for it. The original plan demanded two tales each for over 20 pilgrims making a journey from Southwark to the shrine of St. Thomas Becket at Canterbury and back. (The shrine was a favorite site for penitential observances on the part of English royalty.) The plan was later modified to require only one tale from each pilgrim on the road to Canterbury, but even this scheme was never completed. The tales survive in groups connected by prologues and epilogues, but the proper arrangement of these groups is not altogether clear. It is clear that in his final plan Chaucer intended the collection to begin with the "Knight's Tale," a short epic, and to close with a sermon on penance delivered by the Parson. The series is introduced in a "General Prologue" that describes the pilgrimage and the pilgrims taking part in it.

Pilgrimages were regarded as penitential acts reflecting the pilgrimage of the Christian spirit toward its Creator. The spiritual pilgrimage was said to be motivated by love and characterized by self-denial and contrition. Hence the Parson's closing sermon is appropriate. Chaucer gives his pilgrimage peculiarly national overtones by directing it toward the shrine of St. Thomas, a citizen of London and a national hero. Among the fictional pilgrims the Knight, whose campaigns reflect the glories of England before 1369; the Clerk, who is an ideal scholar; and the Parson, who clearly reflects the apostolic life, serve as reminders of the ideals associated with St. Thomas. Most of the other pilgrims exemplify in amusing ways the weaknesses of the groups they represent. Chaucer's chief weapon in criticizing these weaknesses is humor. The humor is sometimes very subtle, but it is also often broad and outspoken. We shall understand the pilgrims much better if we regard them as exemplifications rather than as realistic individuals or as personalities. Moreover, we should not be misled by the poet's laughter so that we miss the seriousness of his criticism. Chaucer's vigor and sanity have won him wide acclaim ever since his own time, when he was admired for his philosophy as well as for his poetic talent.

Chaucer must be ranked among the most learned and accomplished of English poets. Besides the translation and major works already mentioned, he wrote a number of shorter poems and translated at least part of the most successful late medieval French poem, the *Roman de la rose* by Guillaume de Lorris and Jean de Meun. Chaucer's interests also included the science of his time. He prepared a translation of a Latin treatise on the use of the astrolabe. He may also be the translator of a work concerning the use of an equatorium, an instrument for calculating the positions of the planets.

In December 1399 Chaucer leased a house for a long term in the garden of Westminster Abbey. He had known many of the prominent men of his day—knights, merchants, scholars, and members of the royal family. He undoubtedly looked forward to a quiet retirement in the London area he knew so well, but he died in October of the following year. He was survived by his son Thomas, who had served both John of Gaunt and King Richard and who was to enjoy a distinguished career in the 15th century.

Further Reading

The most convenient edition of Chaucer's works is by F. N. Robinson (1933; 2d ed. 1957). The earlier edition by Walter W. Skeat, in 6 volumes with a supplement (1894-1897), is still useful. Since so little is known about Chaucer's life, most studies focus on his work. Biographies tend to be speculative. See Marchette G. Chute, *Geoffrey Chaucer of England* (1946), and Edward Wagenknecht, *The Personality of Chaucer* (1968). Others combine a study of his thought with his literary development: John L. Lowes, *Geoffrey Chaucer and the Development of His Genius* (1934), and J. S. P. Tatlock, *The Mind and Art of Chaucer* (1966). Useful introductions and general views of Chaucer, his work, and his times are Paul G. Ruggiers, *The Art of the Canterbury Tales* (1965); D. S. Brewer, *Chaucer and Chaucerians: Critical Studies in Middle English Literature* (1966); and Beryl Rowland, ed., *Companion to Chaucer Studies* (1968).

Relevant documents concerning Chaucer's life are collected in Martin M. Crow and Clair C. Olson, eds., *Chaucer Life-Records* (1966). Other documents illustrating 14th-century life in general are collected in Edith Rickert, *Chaucer's World,* revised by Martin M. Crow and Clair C. Olson (1948). For Chaucer's London background see Durant W. Robertson, Jr., *Chaucer's London* (1968). Fairly full bibliographies of Chaucer are available to 1963: Eleanor P. Hammond, *Chaucer: A Bibliographical Manual* (1908); Dudley D. Griffith, *Bibliography of Chaucer, 1908-1953* (1955); and William R. Crawford, *Bibliography of Chaucer, 1954-1963* (1967). □

Charles Chauncy

The liberal religious views of the American clergyman Charles Chauncy (1705-1787) influenced 19th-century theology in New England.

Charles Chauncy was the great grandson of Charles Chauncy, second president of Harvard College. Young Charles was born and educated in Boston. He graduated from Harvard in 1721 and received his master's degree there in 1724. Ordained as minister to the First Church in Boston in 1727, he served in this prestigious position for 60 years. In 1727 he married the first of three wives, Elizabeth First; in 1738 he married Elizabeth Townsend; and in 1760 Mary Stoddard. He was a serious, diligent person and an energetic scholar of religion and the Bible.

Chauncy became the Great Awakening's most formidable critic. In 1741 he gave a lecture remarkably close in spirit to the thinking of New England clergyman Jonathan Edwards, but a year later Chauncy preached against the revivals. His *Seasonable Thoughts on the State of Religion* (1743) is a carefully built treatise against religious enthusiasm. Referring extensively to the Bible, he presented the Great Awakening as a time of runaway emotionalism, spiritual pride, delusion, and disorder. When George Whitefield, the great English evangelist, returned to New England in 1744, he was welcome neither at Harvard nor at Yale, and Chauncy, a member of the Harvard Board of Overseers, chose this moment to preach an excoriation of Whitefield and the Awakening.

Although Chauncy considered himself a Calvinist, he reinterpreted Calvinism at several major points, veering away from views held by his more orthodox contemporaries. He preached against an Anglican establishment in the colonies. Chauncy saw reason as the essence of "our character as men" and believed it would help guide a person to salvation. The contrast between faith and works as opposites, he felt, had been overemphasized.

Chuncy's belief in the essential reliability of common sense,even in the unredeemed, derived from his confidence in the benevolence of the Deity. He held that Christ's death was necessary for man's salvation, not to appease a vengeful God but because this cataclysmic event awakened sinners to God's authority. Chauncy felt that Christ died not to redeem a few chosen but to save all mankind, and that original sin was not an imputed condition but merely an inborn tendency. He moved gradually toward universalism and the concept of God as the single monarch of the universe rather than the three person God of Calvinism. These themese are basic to his influential *Compleat View of Episcopacy* (1771), as well as two other works, *The Benevolence of the Deity* (1784) and *The Mystery Hid fromm Ages . . . or the Salvation of All Men . . .* (1784), both published anonymously in London but apparently written before 1768. Chauncy's thinking significantly foreshadowed 19th-century developments in New England theology.

Further Reading

The best brief sketch of Chauncy is clifford K. Shipton, *Sibley's Harvard Graduates,* vol. 6 (1942). For a picture of Chauncy in the context of his times see Conrad Wright, *The Beginnings of Unitarianism in America* (1955).

Additional Sources

Griffin, Edward M., *Old Brick, Charles Chauncy of Boston, 1705-1787,* Minneapolis: University of Minnesota Press, 1980.

Lippy, Charles H., *Seasonable revolutionary: the mind of Charles Chauncy,* Chicago: Nelson-Hall, 1981. □

Carlos Chávez

Carlos Chávez (1899-1978) was a Mexican conductor and composer. By taking the lead in introducing national and folk elements to express the spirit of his country, he became the founder of modern Mexican music.

On June 13, 1899, Carlos Chávez was born in Mexico City, where he studied piano under Manuel M. Ponce and Pedro Luis Ogazón. But Chávez's ability as a composer was acquired primarily from direct observation and study of works by the great masters.

From a very early age Chávez felt the need to create a style and personality of his own. His first works, written in 1921, marked him as an innovator and alarmed the musicians who had been educated in the romantic European tradition. José Vasconcelos, minister of education, then commissioned Chávez to compose a ballet entitled *El fuego nuevo* (The New Fire), in which he introduced some instruments and elements which were considered to have existed in Mexico before the time of the Conquest.

In 1928 Chávez and the Mexico City Syndicate of Musicians founded the National Symphony Orchestra, which a few months later became the Mexican Symphony Orchestra. He devoted all his efforts to stimulating the musical life of the Mexican capital as well as, on a lesser scale, that of the rest of the country. In 1928 Chávez was appointed director of the National Conservatory of Music, and the following year he established the Conservatory Choir.

Becoming deeply interested in the problems of constructivist music depicting the machine age, Chávez composed his operatic ballet, *H. P.* (Horse Power), to symbolize the economic relationship between the industrial United States and the agricultural tropical lands. The ballet was first produced in Philadelphia in 1932.

Chávez was named chief of the Department of Fine Arts in Mexico City in 1933. The next year he left the conservatory to devote himself exclusively to the Mexican Symphony Orchestra. He was guest conductor of the Boston Symphony Orchestra in 1936 and of the New York Philharmonic Symphony Orchestra in 1937. In 1946 he became director of the National Institute of Fine Arts in Mexico City.

Chávez conducted the first performance (1953) of his Fourth Symphony with the Louisville Orchestra, which had commissioned it. During the academic year 1958-1959 he was Charles Eliot Norton lecturer at Harvard University; his lectures were published as *Musical Thought* (1960). In 1960 he helped implement the Composer's Workshop which is held at the National Conservatory. Before his death in 1978 he was awarded honorary memberships in the American Academy of Arts and Sciences and the American Institute of Arts and Letters.

Works by Chávez include six symphonies, a piano concerto, two violin concertos, a concerto for four horns, the *Ballet of the Four Suns,* the *Ballad of the Sun, Flames,* and the opera *Love Propitiated.* The *Toccata for Percussion* is perhaps his best-known work.

Further Reading

Chávez's *Catalogue of His Works* (1944) has a biographical introduction by Herbert Weinstock. Brief discussions of Chávez's life and work are in Paul Collaer, *A History of Modern Music* (trans. 1961), and David Ewen, *The World of Twentieth Century Music* (1968). □

Cesar Chavez

Cesar Chavez (1927-1993) was a Mexican-American labor leader who organized the first effective union

of farm workers in the history of California agriculture.

Cesar Chavez was born on March 31, 1927, near Yuma, Arizona. His grandfather had homesteaded some 112 acres there in 1904, but the family lost the ranch during the Depression in 1939, when they could not pay the taxes. The family then joined the migrant laborers streaming into California.

Early Organizing

Chavez quit school after the eighth grade to work full-time in the fields, but in 1944 he joined the U.S. Navy. He served for two years in the Pacific, but racism kept him in menial jobs, so upon discharge he rejoined his family and continued as a farm worker in California. In 1948 he married Helen Fabela of Delano, California.

In 1952 Chavez met Fred Ross, who was organizing Mexican-Americans in the barrios (quarters) of California into the Community Service Organization (CSO). They concentrated on voter registration, citizenship classes, and helping Mexican-American communities obtain needed facilities in the barrios as well as aiding individuals with such typical problems as welfare, contracts signed with unscrupulous salesmen, and police harassment.

Chavez's work in the voter registration drive in Sal Si Puedes, the notorious San Jose barrio, was so effective that Ross hired him as an organizer. Over the next 10 years Chavez rose to national director of CSO. In 1962, when the CSO rejected his proposal to start a farmworkers union, he quit the organization. At 35 years of age, with $1,200 in savings, he took his wife and eight children to Delano to begin the slow, methodical organizing process which grew into the National Farm Workers Association (NFWA). When, three years later, members of Agricultural Workers Organizing Committee of the AFL-CIO (American Federation of Labor and Congress of Industrial Organizations) struck the vineyards in Delano, they asked for support from Chavez's NFWA.

Thus began the great California table-grape strike, which lasted five years. In 1966, the two unions merged to form the United Farm Workers Organizing Committee (UFWOC) of the AFL-CIO, headed by Chavez. During the struggle to organize the vineyards Chavez initiated an international boycott of California table grapes that brought such pressure to bear on local grape growers that most eventually signed with his union. The boycott ended in September 1970. Soon after this victory, Chavez again employed the boycott strategy, this time against lettuce growers who used non-union labor. Chavez became the first man ever to organize a viable farm workers' union in California that obtained signed contracts from the agricultural industry.

Believed in Non-Violence

Chavez was an outspoken advocate of social change through nonviolent means. In 1968, to avert violence in the grape strike, he undertook a 25-day fast; the fast was broken at an outdoor Mass attended by some 8,000 persons, including Senator Robert F. Kennedy. Chavez also led a 200-mile march from Delano to Sacramento to dramatize the demands of the farm workers.

In July 1970 Chavez's union faced one of its most serious challenges when the Teamsters' union signed contracts that applied to farm workers with some 200 growers in California. Chavez met the challenge head on: within 3 weeks the largest agricultural strike ever to hit California had spread over 180 miles along the coastal valleys. About 7,000 farm workers struck to win recognition of Chavez's UFWOC as their bargaining agent, with the national boycott again used as the weapon.

From 1972 to 1974, membership in the union dwindled from nearly 60,000 to just 5,000. But Chavez's efforts were rewarded. From 1964 to 1980, wages of California migrant workers had increased 70 percent, health care benefits became a reality and a formal grievance procedure was established. Chavez continued to fight for the rights of workers up to the day of his death on April 22, 1993.

Further Reading

Collins, David R., *Farmworker's Friend: The Story of Cesar Chavez* Carolrhoda Books, 1996.

Ferris, Susan, et al, *The Fight in the Fields: Cesar Chavez and the Farmworkers Movement,* Harcourt Brace, 1997.

Gonzales, Doreen *Cesar Chavez: Leader for Migrant Farm Workers,* Enslow Publications, 1996. □

Dennis Chávez

The first Hispanic American to be elected to the United States Senate, Democrat Dennis Chávez (1888–1962) led a long and distinguished career in government service, first as a member of the U.S. House of Representatives and then as a senator from the state of New Mexico. Noted primarily for his long and unrelenting fight to create a federal Fair Employment Practices Commission, Chávez was also a staunch supporter of education and civil rights.

The third of eight children, Dionisio Chávez was born to David and Paz (Sanchez) Chávez on April 8, 1888. His family lived in in what was then the United States Mexican Territory. The area did not become the state of New Mexico until 1912. When he was seven, the family moved to Albuquerque. At school his name was changed to Dennis. Chávez quit school in the eighth grade and went to work. For the next five years he drove a grocery wagon to help support the family. He joined the Albuquerque Engineering Department in 1905, earning a substantial increase in income. Even after Chávez left school, he spent evenings at the local public library, reading about Thomas Jefferson and politics—his passions.

Chávez worked as an interpreter for senate candidate Andrieus A. Jones during the 1916 campaign. Jones rewarded him with a clerkship in the U.S. Senate in 1918-1919. While clerking, Chávez also entered Georgetown University through a special entrance examination to study law. He earned a Bachelor of Laws degree from Georgetown in 1920, and returned to Albuquerque, where he established a successful law practice.

Political Career Began with State Legislature

A Democrat in the tradition of his hero Thomas Jefferson, Chávez became active in local politics, winning election to the New Mexico House of Representatives. In 1930 he ran successfully for a seat in the U.S. House of Representatives, handily defeating the incumbent Republican, Albert Simms. He served as the thinly populated state's only representative. He was reelected once and then turned his sights toward the U.S. Senate. In 1934 he ran against the powerful Republican incumbent, Bronson Cutting. After a hard-fought, bitter campaign and a narrow defeat, Chávez challenged the validity of Cutting's victory, charging vote fraud. The issue reached to the Senate floor. The matter was still pending in May 1935, when Cutting was killed in an airplane crash. Chávez was appointed by New Mexico's Governor Tingley to serve in Cutting's place. Five senators expressed their disapproval by walking out of the Senate as Chávez was being sworn in. Chávez, however, was the people of New Mexico's clear choice when he was officially elected to the position in 1936, defeating a popular Republican candidate.

Served with Distinction

New Mexico voters showed their support for Chávez by reelecting him to the Senate five times. Although his often independent stands on various issues generated controversy, Chávez was a strong supporter of President Franklin Roosevelt's New Deal programs. His service on important Congressional committees allowed him to fight for causes he believed in. Chávez was a member of the Committees on Territories and Insular Affairs, the Education and Labor, Appropriations and Indian Affairs. In the last, he protested measures affecting Navajo grazing stock and also demanded an investigation of Indian Affairs Commissioner Collier.

In 1938 Chávez co-authored the Chávez- McAdoo bill, which established a federal radio station to counter Nazi and Fascist broadcasts into South America. In a curious move the following year, he advocated U.S. recognition of Spain's fascist leader, General Francisco Franco. He usually took a liberal stance on farm issues, voting for the draft deferment of farm laborers and against reductions in farm security appropriations. He was also active in measures regarding tariffs, employment programs, and unemployment benefits.

Chávez earned the nickname "Puerto Rico's Senator" in 1942 when he initiated an investigation into the causes of social and economic conditions in Puerto Rico. His support of a Senate bill to extend public works projects in that territory and the Virgin Islands was decisive in its passage.

Chávez attracted national attention during his long fight for enactment of a federal Fair Employment Practices Commission. The bill was designed to prevent employers or labor unions doing government work from discriminating on the basis of race, creed, color, ancestry, or national origin. The bill was eventually defeated in 1946—by only an eight-vote margin.

Dennis Chávez worked tirelessly to further the interests of the state of New Mexico. He is credited for garnering significant amounts of federal funding as well as key defense installations for the state. Chávez married Imelda Espinoza in 1911. They had three children: two daughters and a son. Chávez died of a heart attack on November 18, 1962, at the age of 74.

Further Reading

Hispanic-American Almanac, edited by Nicolás Kanellos, Detroit, Gale Research, 1993.

Mexican American Biographies, A Historical Dictionary: 1836-1987, edited by Matt S. Meier, Westport, Connecticut, Greenwood Press, 1988. □

Linda Chavez

Hispanic American civil rights activist Linda Chavez (born 1947) gained political attention for her conservative view that government policies such as affirmative action do a disservice to Hispanics and other minorities by perpetuating racial stereotypes. Originally a Democratic supporter, her ideas about civil rights and education reform were embraced by the Republican administration of president Ronald Reagan in the 1980s. After an unsuccessful bid for public office herself, Chavez became a prominent political commentator with writings such as her 1991 book, *Out of the Barrio: Toward a New Politics of Hispanic Assimilation.*

Driven by a desire to destroy negative stereotypes of Hispanic minorities in America as helpless, illiterate, and impoverished, activist Linda Chavez has fought to do away with government attitudes and programs that treat Hispanics as a homogenous unit. However, the conservative remedies she has supported, including the elimination of affirmative action and racial quota systems in various areas of society, have met with hostility from liberal politicians and civil rights activists in the Hispanic community. Originally a Democrat, Chavez switched her affiliation after finding more support for her ideas in the administration of Republican President Ronald Reagan, where she served as an advisor and White House staff member in the 1980s. Although her own attempt to win elected office was unsuccessful, as a political commentator and writer she has remained a prominent figure in the national debate on racial policy.

Chavez was born into a middle-class family in Albuquerque, New Mexico, on June 17, 1947. Her parents, both devout Catholics, came from different racial backgrounds; her mother was Anglo-American and her father was Hispanic. Racial prejudice was not a concern of her early years. The city of Albuquerque was predominately Hispanic, and so she did not encounter difficulties because of her race there. Her father was proud of his heritage as a descendant of seventeenth-century Spanish settlers and also took pride in his country, which he served as a soldier during World War II. But these were qualities that were considered part of private life, not subjects for the public sphere. Her father's quiet approach to his racial identity was influential in Chavez's own ideas later in her life.

Saw Reform Possibilities in Education

Chavez first came into contact with racial prejudice when her family moved to Denver, Colorado, when she was nine. The negative attitudes about minorities that she witnessed there inspired her to join in civil rights movements supporting the causes of Hispanics, African Americans, and women when she was a teenager. She also became to determined to excel in her schoolwork in order to overcome the low expectations of her as a Hispanic. After graduating from high school, she attended the University of Colorado, where she decided to pursue a career in teaching. Having tutored some Mexican American students through the college, she knew that teaching was a sometimes difficult job, but one that could play an important role in social reform. During her undergraduate studies, she was married to Christopher Gersten in 1967, but kept her maiden name. In 1970, she graduated from the University of Colorado with a bachelor's degree.

Chavez went on to the University of California at Los Angeles (UCLA), where she began a graduate program in English literature. She soon became frustrated, however, with the way she was treated by faculty and students because she was Hispanic. In one particularly negative experience, Chavez was given the task of teaching a course on Chicano literature, even though she initially resisted because of the lack of published material in the area. When the department insisted she go through with the course, she put together an appropriate reading list, but found many students in her class were unwilling to read the books or pay attention during her lectures. This disheartening situation reached a peak when some students she had failed in the course vandalized her home in an act of vengeance. Chavez left the university in 1972 and moved to Washington, D.C., with her husband.

Active in Education Issues

In the nation's capital, Chavez did not return to teaching but did remain active in educational issues. She worked with the National Education Association (NEA), the largest teachers' union in the country, and served as a consultant on education to the federal government's Department of Health, Education, and Welfare. In addition, she became an active member of the Democratic National Committee, participating in the promotion of a number of liberal causes. She eventually landed a position with the nation's second-largest teachers' union, the American Federation of Teachers (AFT), which was known as an influential force in education policy. Chavez became a well-known voice on the topic of education reform in her role as editor of the AFT's publication, *American Educator.* She began to attract notice among conservative politicians in Washington with her editorials calling for a renewed emphasis on traditional educational standards. Throughout the 1970s, Chavez also became increasingly dissatisfied with liberal views on the position of minorities in America. In her personal experience, she felt that liberals sought her out simply because of her symbolism as a Hispanic, not for her own ideas. Similarly, she felt that national programs that did not allow minorities to advance based on their own merits, but gave them financial assistance or employment preference solely because of their race, was demeaning. Hispanics should not be stereotyped as helpless minorities who could not get ahead without government aid, but should be encouraged to succeed through individual effort, she maintained.

With the election of Ronald Reagan to the presidency in 1980, Chavez found growing sympathy for her ideas among conservatives. She became a consultant for the Reagan administration in 1981, and in 1983 she was appointed by the president to serve as director of the U.S. Commission on Civil Rights. The commission was a nonpartisan body responsible for evaluating the government's success in implementing and upholding civil rights laws. Chavez criticized certain aspects of the country's civil rights laws, however, and strongly denounced the affirmative action programs that had been designed to ensure that minorities were represented in certain fields of employment. While she argued that her goal was to foster an unprejudiced environment that evaluated individuals solely by their ability, regardless of race, liberal activists accused her of supporting Republican efforts to dismantle the government's role in ensuring civil rights to minorities.

Views Supported by Republicans

Finding herself lacking support from most Hispanic activists and Democrats, Chavez officially joined the Republican Party after being hired onto Reagan's White House staff in 1985. As director of the Office of the White House Public Liaison, she was the most powerful woman on the staff. Her position gave her an increased level of influence with the president, and she also worked to lobby Congress and a variety of public groups to accept administration policies. She left this post after less than a year's time in order to run a campaign in Maryland for a U.S. Senate seat. Republican Party officials were enthusiastic about her run for senator, hoping that her image as a Hispanic, woman, and married mother of three children would win votes away from the single, white Democratic contender, Barbara Mikulski.

But Republican hopes that Maryland's primarily Democratic voters would abandon their party preference for a more conservative candidate were unrealized. The state's citizens were distrustful of Chavez's short residence in Maryland and her shift in political philosophy. Behind in the polls, the Republicans began a negative campaign, during which Chavez further alienated voters when she criticized Mikulski's unmarried status and her staff insinuated that the Democrat had ties to lesbian groups. After a major defeat on election day, Chavez decided to remove herself from the political arena.

Book Fuels Debate on Race

She returned to social and educational issues by becoming president of the organization U.S. English. The nonprofit group's aim was to gain the official recognition of English as the national language. After discovering the prejudices against Catholics and Hispanics of the founder of U.S. English, however, she resigned in 1988. Over the coming years, Chavez established herself as policy expert and political commentator. The Manhattan Institute for Policy Research, a conservative think-tank, made her a fellow, and she became a regular contributor of editorials on politics to periodicals. She also published a book on her ideas, *Out of the Barrio: Toward a New Politics of Hispanic Assimilation* in 1991, bringing her renewed attention from politicians and the press. The work reaffirmed her belief that affirmative action and other programs that focused on the lower socioeconomic levels of Hispanic society created an unrealistic and unflattering picture of Hispanics as a group. As had been the case throughout her career, Chavez's words were controversial with many, but nonetheless had the effect of bringing about serious discussions about the state of the nation's attitude toward minorities. She was the focus of a number of book reviews and also gained the national spotlight when she appeared on television programs such as *The McNeil/Lehrer News Hour.*

Despite the criticism she has received from many liberal and Hispanic American groups for her conservative views, Chavez has emerged as one of the most visible and influential figures fighting for civil rights and educational reforms. Her thought and example as a successful political personality has made her a role model for some in the Hispanic community, inspiring a growing number of politicians in the minority group to join the Republican Party in the 1990s. Chavez's insistence that racial equity cannot be accomplished by government policies based on stereotypes has given the American public and its leaders additional considerations in the debate on government's role in the welfare of minorities.

Further Reading

See also Arias, Maria, "Making People Mad," *Hispanic,* August 1992, pp. 11-16; Brimelow, Peter, "The Fracturing of America," *Forbes,* March 30, 1992, pp. 74-75; Chavez, Linda, *Out of the Barrio: Toward a New Politics of Hispanic Assimilation,* Basic Books, 1991; Grenier, Jeannin, "The Women Versus Woman Race," *Ms.,* November 1986, p. 27; and Telgen, Diane, and Jim Kamp, editors, *Notable Hispanic American Women,* Gale Research, 1993. □

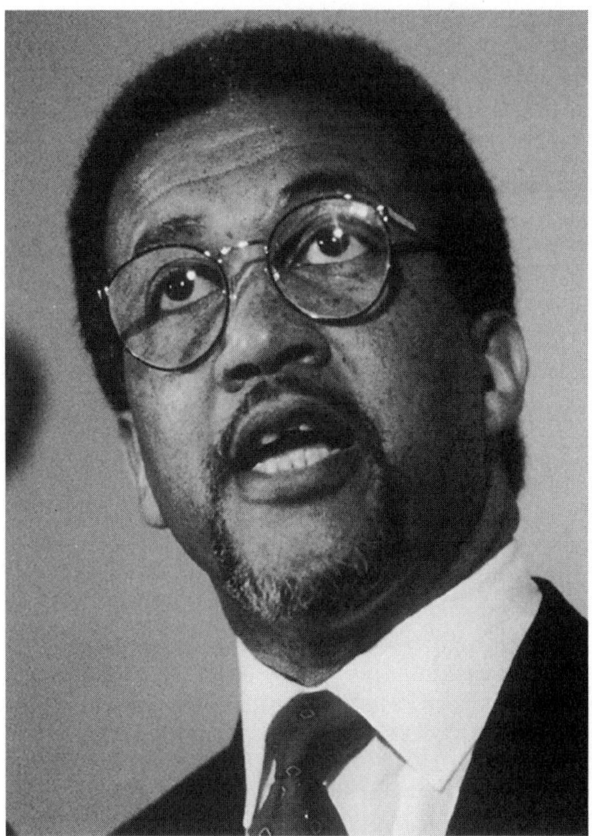

Benjamin Chavis

Lifelong political activist Benjamin Chavis (born 1948) overcame racial injustice and wrongful imprisonment to become a vocal leader in the civil rights movement.

The first political act of Benjamin Chavis came when he was a wide-eyed 13 year old. On his way home from school each day, Chavis would pass a whites-only library in Oxford, North Carolina. One day, tired of tattered hand-me-downs and desirous of a book with two intact covers on it, he boldly walked into the library. The librarians told him to leave, but he questioned that demand. "He asked why," a childhood friend told the *New York Times.* "A lot of us when we were told to go away . . . would just do so, but Ben would always challenge, always ask why." The librarians called his parents, but the incident, like the spunkiness of the boy at its center, could not be calmed, and tempers flared. In a short time, the library was opened to all races. A child's simple act of disobedience and intellectual curiosity had shattered the overt racism of an institution whose sole mission, young Chavis knew, should have been the enrichment of minds—those of blacks and whites.

Descended from Activists

The Reverend Benjamin Franklin Chavis, Jr., was born in 1948 in Oxford, North Carolina, into a long and distinguished line of preachers. His great-great-grandfather, John Chavis, is considered to be the first black graduate of Princeton University because he graduated from a New Jersey seminary that later became the university. John Chavis, according to Benjamin, was killed in 1938 for teaching black children to read and write.

In the mid-twentieth century, even as the walls of segregation began to tumble, many racist elements thrived in the United States, particularly in the South. But even though the nation's military services were integrated in the year of Benjamin Chavis's birth, and a judicial decision six years later struck down the practice of "separate but equal" education, closed-minded whites in some areas vehemently defended their racist institutions and laws. The worldviews of civil rights leaders like Chavis and Martin Luther King, Jr., were shaped against this backdrop of hatred and bigotry.

In 1968—the year of King's assassination, which some observers feel brought an end to the modern civil rights era—Chavis became a field officer for the United Church of Christ's Commission for Racial Justice. The Commission, organized in 1963 in response to the assassination of civil rights activist Medgar Evers and the infamous Birmingham, Alabama, church bombing, coordinated racial justice strategies for national and regional organizations and spearheaded community organization and criminal justice campaigns.

In February of 1971, Chavis was in Wilmington, North Carolina, to drum up support for a school desegregation lawsuit that had been brought by the NAACP. On a night of racial violence, one of many in a season of escalating tension, Mike's Grocery, a white-owned store in a black part of town, was firebombed. A year later, the Wilmington 10 (as the nine black men, including Chavis, and one white woman came to be known) were convicted of arson and conspiracy and sentenced to a combined total of 282 years in prison, with the lengthiest term, 34 years, slapped on Chavis.

World Focused on his Imprisonment

The case immediately garnered worldwide attention and became a celebrated focus of the civil rights movement in the United States. Defense attorneys cited 2,685 errors in the trial, but appeals were denied, and the convicted agitators went to prison in 1976. A year later, Amnesty International, the human rights watchdog agency, listed the ten as political prisoners. Ironically, the NAACP—the organization that Chavis had joined when he was only 12 years old and would one day head—was seen by some as offering one of the weakest responses to the obviously wrongful convictions.

While in prison, Chavis, who had been taught by King to see the positive in a negative experience, was frequently escorted in leg irons and handcuffs to Duke University, where he earned a master's degree from the divinity school under a study-release program. A disciplined student—he had taken his undergraduate degree in chemistry from the University of North Carolina at Charlotte in 1969—Chavis dodged the prison's strict, 10 P.M., lights-out rule by reading his school books in the bathroom, which was lighted all night.

The Wilmington 10 case took a dramatic turn when three principal prosecution witnesses from the trial admitted they had made up their stories after being pressured by local law enforcement authorities. North Carolina governor James Hunt reduced the sentences but left the convictions intact. Finally in 1980, after Chavis and the other activists had been paroled, a Justice Department investigation led to a federal appellate court's reversal of the convictions. "Our case was a victory for the whole movement," Chavis noted in *Newsweek.* "It showed people what is possible."

In 1983, two years after receiving his doctorate in divinity from Howard University, Chavis returned to the United Church of Christ's Commission for Racial Justice as deputy director. (The commission was one of several groups that had championed the release of the Wilmington 10.) By 1985, Chavis had been elected executive director of the commission and soon emerged as a national figure willing to exercise his preacher's oratory on a wide variety of racial and social justice issues in the United States. He organized gang summits to denounce the skyrocketing violence, high drop-out rate, and rampant drug involvement plaguing America's young people. He also participated in mainstream national politics, lobbying with other black leaders against U.S. aid to Angolan rebels fighting the Marxist regime of Jose Eduardo dos Santos, and serving as the clergy coordinator for the Reverend Jesse Jackson's 1984 presidential campaign.

Pioneered Concept of "Environmental Racism"

During his tenure at the Commission for Racial Justice, Chavis became most associated with the burgeoning environmental movement. In 1983 Chavis had joined in a protest against the depositing of tons of contaminated soil in rural Warren County, North Carolina, where the population was 75 percent black—the highest concentration of black citizens in the state—and mostly poor. Although the Warren County battle was lost, the protesters succeeded in shelving the state's plans to put another landfill and an incinerator in the area. Chavis, educated in school as a chemist and in the streets as an activist, saw the political issue clearly: industry's garbage was being foisted on the lower-class, politically unempowered members of society.

Coining the term "environmental racism," Chavis ordered a study that documented the extent of the crisis: three of the five largest toxic waste landfills in the country were in minority neighborhoods. Chavis spared few in his condemnation of this previously overlooked embodiment of racism. He chastised federal, state, and local governments; the mainstream environmental organizations, which were headed by whites and, in his view, cared more about the integrity of a wetland than the health of a black person; and big businesses that cavalierly promised jobs in impoverished communities in exchange for support of environmentally ruinous industries. "One of the responsibilities of the civil rights movement is to define the postmodern manifestations of racism," Chavis explained in *Ebony.* "We must not only point to overt forms of racism, but also to institutionalized racism."

Speaking at the 1987 First National People of Color Environmental Leadership Summit, which was attended by activists, professionals, and politicians, Chavis impressed upon conference participants the need to "rescue the environment from the clutches of persons and institutions gone mad with racism and greed," according to an account in *Audubon.* The summit cast much needed light on the environmental devastation plaguing minority communities—not only those of African Americans, but of Mexican American farmers, Native Americans, and the indigenous peoples of Alaska. Chavis thus became one of the most prominent spokespersons on environmental policy. After the election of President Bill Clinton in 1992, Chavis served as a senior advisor to the transition team studying the departments of Energy, the Interior, and Agriculture, as well as the Environmental Protection Agency.

Some observers noted that when Bill Clinton named of dozens of African Americans to top administration positions, he depleted the ranks of candidates qualified to fill the position of NAACP executive director, a post that Benjamin Hooks was vacating after 16 years in office. Still, the names under consideration were hardly minor league: Chavis; minister-activist Jesse Jackson; Jewell Jackson McCabe, founder and president of the Coalition of 100 Black Women; and Earl F. Shinhoster, a regional NAACP official. The appointment process began to look like a high-pressure political campaign. McCabe urged the predominantly male 64-member board to elect the first woman to the post, while

Chavis sent each board member a 14-minute videotape detailing his personal history, his commitment to the NAACP, and his vision of the organization's future. Most of the attention, however, focused on the controversial Jackson, who withdrew from the race two days before the election, apparently over a change in the NAACP's constitution that he felt would decrease the power of the executive director.

Upon his election in 1993, Chavis proclaimed: "Now is the time for healing. Now is the time for unity." However, it was soon discovered that Chavis had begun earmarking the organization's funds as hush money for a legal settlement on a sexual harassment case against him and for other controversial initiatives. In a bizarre twist of events, Chavis was fired by the NAACP's board of directors in 1994.

Further Reading

Audubon, January-February 1992, p. 30.
Black Enterprise, July 1993, p. 17.
Boston Globe, April 10, 1993, p. 3; April 18, 1993, p. 85.
Detroit Free Press, April 14, 1993.
Ebony, July 1993, pp. 76-80.
Economist, April 17, 1993, p. 27.
Emerge, June 1993, pp. 27-28; September 1993, pp. 38-42.
Jet, April 26, 1993.
Newsweek, August 1, 1983, p. 9; June 14, 1993, pp. 68-69; August 29, 1994, p. 27.
New York Times, April 10, 1993, p. 10; April 11, 1993, p. 20; May 2, 1993.
People, July 19, 1993, pp. 65-66.
Time, July 19, 1993, p. 33.
Wall Street Journal, April 12, 1993, p. B5.
Washington Post, April 10, 1993, p. A1; April 26, 1993. □

John Cheever

John Cheever (1912-1982) was an American writer known for his keen, often critical, view of the American middle class. Known primarily for his short stories, his attention to detail and careful writing found the extraordinary in the ordinary.

"I have been a storyteller since the beginning of my life, rearranging facts in order to make them more significant. I have improvised a background for myself—genteel, traditional—and it is generally accepted."—John Cheever, in his journal, 1961.

Only John Cheever the storyteller could have invented a character like John Cheever the author—as, indeed, he did. His life, like the lives of the people who populate the fictional world known as Cheever Country, was double-edged. Behind the pleasant facade of the country squire lurks a vision of deteriorating morality; the satisfied suburban gentleman falls away to reveal insecurity and ambiguity.

Cheever was born May 27, 1912, in Quincy, Massachusetts, to Frederick Lincoln Cheever and Mary Liley Cheever. His father owned a shoe factory until it was lost in the Great Depression of the 1930s. His mother, an Englishwoman who emigrated with her parents, supported her husband and their two sons with the profits from a gift shop she operated.

This is Cheever Country: a seemingly happy New England marriage that when poked reveals a relationship strained to the point of breaking. A man—a father—who prides himself on his ability to support his family is supported by his wife.

Cheever was sent to Thayer Academy, a prep school in Milton, Massachusetts. As a 17-year-old Harvard-bound senior he arranged his own expulsion for smoking and poor grades. The result was Cheever's first published work, "Expelled," a short story that appeared in *The New Republic* on October 1, 1930. The story is an embryonic version in style and approach of the Cheever to evolve over five decades; it revels in the details of ordinary lives with precise observation and disciplined language.

After leaving school Cheever toured Europe with his brother, Frederick, who was seven years his senior. He then settled in Boston, where he met Hazel Hawthorne and Henry Wadsworth Longfellow Dana, both of whom helped support the budding writer. In the mid-1930s Cheever moved to New York City, where he lived and worked in a bleak, $3-a-week boarding house on Hudson Street in Greenwich Village. During this period he helped support himself by writing synopses of books for potential M.G.M. movies. Malcolm Cowley, editor of *The New Republic,* also

arranged for Cheever to spend time at Yaddo, a writers' colony in Saratoga to which the author would often return. It was also during this time that Cheever began his long association with *The New Yorker.* In 1934 the first of 119 Cheever stories was published in this sophisticated magazine.

On March 22, 1941, Cheever married Mary Winternitz. He spent four years in the army during World War II and later spent two years writing television scripts for, among other programs, "Life with Father."

In 1943 Cheever's first book of short stories, *The Way Some People Live,* was published. War and the Depression serve as a backdrop for these stories which deal with Cheever's lifelong subject: simply, the way some people live. It was his next collection, however, that earned him the serious praise of critics. *The Enormous Radio, and Other Stories,* written in Cheever's Scarborough, New York, home, was published in 1953. The 14 stories plunge the reader deep into Cheever Country; the characters—nice people all—begin with a sense of well-being and order that is stripped away and never quite fully restored. The title story, for example, portrays an average young couple who aspire to move someday from their New York apartment to Westchester. Their sense of the ordinary is shattered, however, when they buy a radio that has the fantastic ability to broadcast bits of their neighbors' lives. The radio picks up the sounds of telephones, bedtime stories, quarrels, and tales of dishonesty. This peek behind closed doors serves to destroy the couple's own outward feelings of harmony, and the story ends with the young marrieds arguing as the radio fills the room with news reports.

In 1951 Cheever was made a Guggenheim Fellow. In 1955 his short story, "The Five-Forty-Eight," was awarded the Benjamin Franklin magazine award, and the following year he took his wife and three children to Italy. Upon their return the family settled in Ossining, New York, where Cheever meticulously embellished his image as a polished aristocrat. He was elected to the National Institute of Arts and Letters in 1957 and won the National Book Award for the first of his novels, *The Wapshot Chronicle.*

Cheever followed *The Wapshot Chronicle* with *The Housebreaker of Shady Hill* (1958), *Some People, Places and Things That Will Not Appear in My Next Novel* (1961), *The Wapshot Scandal* (1964), *The Brigadier and the Golf Widow* (1964), *Bullet Park* (1969), *The World of Apples* (1973), and *Falconer* (1977).

At the height of his success Cheever began a 20-year struggle with alcoholism, a problem he didn't fully admit to until his family placed him in a rehabilitation center in 1975. Earlier, in 1972, he had suffered a massive heart attack. After a long period of recovery he wrote the dark *Falconer,* which draws on his experience as a writing instructor in Sing Sing prison as well as on his recovery from alcoholism and drug addiction. This novel, with its rough language, violence, and prison setting, is a departure from Cheever Country and is the first of his works to deal directly with homosexuality. Cheever's journals reveal that, like the protagonist of *Falconer,* Cheever felt ambivalence about his sexual identity.

Like his characters, John Cheever did not fit the image he so scrupulously cultivated.

> "In the morning," his daughter, Susan, wrote, "my father would put on his one good suit and his gray felt hat and ride down in the elevator with the other men on their way to the office. From the lobby he would walk down to the basement, to the windowless storage room that came with our apartment. That was where he worked. There, he hung up the suit and hat and wrote all morning in his boxer shorts, typing away at his portable Underwood set up on the folding table. At lunchtime he would put the suit back on and ride up in the elevator."

John Cheever, who could find the extraordinary in the mundane, died on June 18, 1982, of cancer. His final work, *Oh What A Paradise It Seems,* was published posthumously.

Further Reading

Home Before Dark (1984) is a personalized biography by Cheever's daughter, Susan Cheever, that explores the many facets and ambiguities of the writer's private life. For more serious literary study, see *John Cheever* (1979) by Lynne Waldeland or *John Cheever* (1977) by Samuel Coale. Both books are strong on analysis and weak on biography. Cheever's first publisher, Malcolm Cowley, devotes some time to the author in *The Flower and the Leaf: A Contemporary Record of American Writing Since 1941* (1984). Cheever's own journals and letters, edited by one of his sons, are expected to be published.

Additional Sources

Cheever, Susan, *Home before dark,* New York: Bantam Books, 1991.

Donaldson, Scott, *John Cheever: a biography,* New York: Random House, 1988. □

Anton Pavlovich Chekhov

The Russian author Anton Pavlovich Chekhov (1860-1904) is among the major short-story writers and dramatists of modern times.

During the last half of the 19th century the old order in Russia was crumbling. Political institutions were out of line with actual developments, and the agrarian, aristocratic society was increasingly yielding to an urban bourgeoisie and a new capitalist class. Turgenev and Tolstoy, among other writers, had depicted the weakened social structure of the 1860s and 1870s; Dostoevsky had dramatically described the intellectual conflicts. Anton Chekhov, however, was the first to depict a world essentially without heroes and villains. A Chekhovian personage vacillates, often Hamlet-like, between what he should do and what he wants, meanwhile becoming ever more conscious of the wrongs he is helplessly suffering. Romantic illusion wars with disillusion. Time after time, the individual fails, almost fatalistically, but never without either discovering for himself or allowing the reader to discover the forces behind his contest with life. Dramatic understatement, a deeply poetic perception of loss and psychological impotence, exquisite and often gay humor, and extraordinary linguistic aptness characterize what has come to be called "the Chekhovian manner."

Chekhov was born in Taganrog in South Russia on the Azov Sea on Jan. 17/29, 1860, third of six children of a grocery store owner. Chekhov's grandfather was a serf who bought his family's freedom in 1841. While his father tried to improve his social status by attending to civic duties, the young Chekhov and his brothers and sisters worked in the family store and studied in the local school. In 1876 his father went bankrupt and fled to Moscow to start anew. Chekhov's mother soon joined his father in Moscow. Chekhov, then 16, was left behind to finish his schooling.

The blond, brown-eyed Chekhov was a self-reliant, amusing, energetic, and attractive young man. In August 1879 he joined his parents in Moscow, where his father was a laborer and his mother a part-time seamstress. Chekhov soon took his father's place as head of the household, a responsibility he shouldered all his life. He immediately entered the medical faculty of Moscow University. After graduating in 1884, he went to work in the hospital at Chikino, but by December of that year he had begun to cough up blood, the first symptom of the tuberculosis that was to kill him.

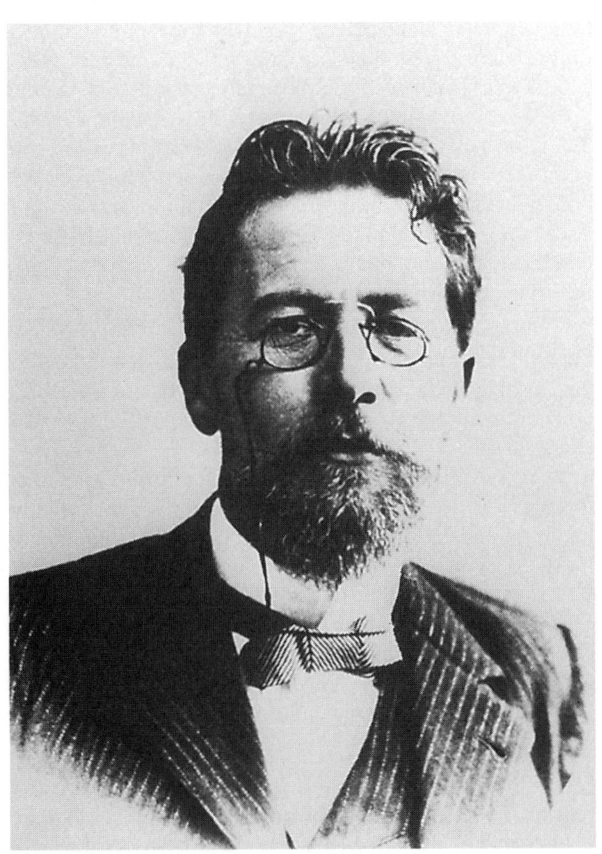

First Works

In the winter after arriving in Moscow, Chekhov decided to try to augment family income by writing for the humor magazines he himself liked to read. In March 1880 the *Dragonfly* published his first sketch. During that year it published nine more, most of them signed "Antosha Chekhonte." In the fall of 1881 he had stories accepted by the *Alarm Clock,* and he and his older brothers Aleksandr and Nikolai published in a new humor magazine, the Spectator. In the fall of 1882 he was introduced to Leikin, editor of *Fragments,* to which he was soon contributing regularly. His first book was *The Tales of Melpomene,* a collection of six of these sketches published with his own money (on credit) in mid-1884. Written for money under numerous pseudonyms, Chekhov's first sketches were the work of a gay, witty, enthusiastic reporter well aware of the dark side of life but unaware of his own literary promise.

Midsummer 1886 saw the appearance of Chekhov's first substantial book, *Motley Stories;* on the title page his real name stood beside his old pseudonym. The book did well, and Chekhov was recognized as a new literary talent. He practiced medicine less and wrote more. "On the Road" was a special success in the late fall of 1886. In February 1887 he was elected to the Literary Fund, an honor accorded only prominent authors. *In the Twilight,* a collection of short stories, appeared in August.

Chekhov's first completed play, *Ivanov,* was produced in Moscow in November 1887. He had given up writing for the light magazines in favor of serious fiction, art which would, as he stated in a letter, "depict life as it actually is. Its aim is truth, unconditional and honest. . . . A man of letters . . . has to . . . realize that dung heaps play a very significant role in a landscape and that evil passions are as inherent in life as good ones." Nostalgia, disharmony, and a sense of life's pervasive irony became elements of his writing in this transitional period.

Literary Success

"The Steppe" (1888), a lyrical paean to the Russian countryside revolving around the adventures that befall 9-year-old Egorushka on his way with his uncle to a distant town, began a new literary life for Chekhov. Not only was it accepted by the fashionable *Northern Messenger,* bringing Chekhov a considerable (for him) sum of money, but it also was highly praised by outstanding writers. At this time Chekhov wrote, "I regard medicine as my lawful wife and literature as my mistress, who is dearer to me than a wife." In October 1888 he won the Academy of Sciences' Pushkin Prize. "The Lights," "The Name-Day Party," and "An Attack of Nerves" all appeared in this year.

The one-act *The Bear* had a modest success, but the St. Petersburg production of a revised *Ivanov* in 1889 was a triumph. Another collection of stories, *Children,* was published in March. Chekhov calculated that he could now support his family by his writing. He spent the summer of 1888 in the Ukraine (where his consumptive brother Nikolai died) and at Yalta. The events of this period inspired the Tolstoyan "A Dreary Story" (1889), in which a dying old man muses on what he considers his pointless life.

In addition to some one-act plays (among them, "The Wedding"), Chekhov worked on *The Wood Demon,* but the St. Petersburg Theatrical Committee rejected the play, deeply wounding him. In March 1890 Chekhov's seventh book appeared, a collection of stories entitled *Gloomy People.*

Late in April 1890 Chekhov set out for the penal colony on the remote Siberian island of Sakhalin. After spending 3 months studying the island, Chekhov returned home and wrote *Sakhalin Island,* which was serialized in 1893-1894.

Chekhov, who had once asked his brother Aleksandr for literary advice, now willingly helped younger writers. In the summer of 1890 the young Ivan Bunin brought his manuscripts, and he and Chekhov soon became warm friends. In the spring of the following year Chekhov spent 6 weeks in Europe. By summer he was in the country again, working on the story "The Duel," which delves into the characters' isolation from each other and discusses political and moral themes in the life of the intelligentsia. Olga Ivanovna, an amateur artist and the central figure of "The Grasshopper" (1891), so desperately seeks for a great man that her sense of beauty and of moral worth is obscured. Chekhov was scornful of the philistine and of the frivolous side of art; he admired science and dedicated his life to helping people in need, like those who suffered cholera in the wake of the famine of 1891-1892.

Later Career

In February 1892 Chekhov bought the 675-acre "Melikhovo," 2 1/2 hours by train from Moscow. He, the grandson of a serf, had bought an estate, and he settled down on it with his family. To the local peasants he was a sympathetic doctor, but to his literary and theatrical friends he was the proprietor of a country retreat, and guests streamed out to visit him. By the end of 1893 he had paid off most of the mortgages on the estate and was supporting his family comfortably.

Chekhov began writing more slowly. "Ward No. 6" (1892), a powerful story of brutality and madness, added greatly to his reputation. "The Story of an Unknown Man" (1893), which tells of a love affair between a terrorist and another man's mistress, expressed new psychological care in portraiture. Unfortunately his health took a turn for the worse. To relieve his coughing, he went to Yalta in the spring of 1894 but quickly grew bored and hurried back to Melikhovo.

Stories by Chekhov regularly appeared in the leading St. Petersburg and Moscow magazines. Among his bestknown works of this period are "The Black Monk" (1894), "The Literature Teacher" (1894), "Three Years" (1895), "My Life" (1896), "The House with the Balcony" (1896), "The Peasants" (1897), "Ionych" (1898), "The Lady with the Dog" (1898), "The Gooseberry" (1898), "The Man in a Case" (1898), "The New Summer House" (1899), and "In the Ravine" (1900). The last years of his life, chiefly devoted to playwriting, saw revisions of his earlier stories for *Collected Works* (1899-1901) and creation of two new ones, "The Bishop" (1902) and "The Fiancée" (1903). Through most of them ran the haunting themes of human isolation, hopelessness, and want of understanding, which seem to reflect the Russian fin-de-siècle atmosphere with exceptional accuracy.

In Moscow, as in St. Petersburg, Chekhov was lionized. Long a bachelor and devoted to his sister Masha, who in turn idolized him, he had a number of vivacious, pretty, and talented women friends but none for whom he felt "love, sexual attraction, being of one flesh" in terms strong enough to propose marriage. But in 1898, when he was 38 and seriously ill, he met the actress Olga Knipper. By the time they married in May 1901, he not only was one of Russia's leading literary men, having been the first writer elected to honorary membership in the Academy of Sciences (January 1890), but was also engrossed in the theater, madly in love, and gravely tubercular.

Dramatic Works

The first draft of *The Sea Gull* (1896) drew heavily on a romance between Chekhov's former love Lidiya Mizinova and his writer-friend I. N. Potapenko. The play failed in its first presentation, but in 1898 in the new Moscow Art Theater it was such a spectacular success that the gull became, and remains, the theater's official emblem. Chekhov's other great plays followed quickly: *Uncle Vanya,* an extensive revision of *The Wood Demon,* in 1897; *Three Sisters* in 1900-1901; and *The Cherry Orchard* in 1903-1904. They all are about the passing of the old order. In each, a group of upper-class landowners, isolated in boredom and social impotence, struggles to preserve cultural values against the energetic social change insisted on by the middle-and lower-class teachers, writers, and businessmen to whom the new life belongs. Each character thinks chiefly only of himself, so that the conflict is expressed in the subtleties of small gestures, musically orchestrated, leading up to an overwhelming climax, usually a suicide, which is followed in a minor key by the general admission that nothing further can be done. The expressed hopelessness is counteracted by declarations of faith in an ideal. The audience perceives the difference between the esthetic harmony and the insurmountable pressures of moral choice and failure in everyday life.

Chekhov was at the height of his fame. He encouraged the writers Bunin and Andreyev, recommended writers for the Pushkin Prize, and was eagerly sought out for advice and comment. His wife acted in Moscow during the season while he stayed in Yalta. The letters between them indicate a deep and mutual passion. Chekhov's health worsened rapidly in 1904. Even in Yalta, where he lived in a villa he had built, little could be done. His doctors told him that he must go to a sanatorium. In June 1904 he set off for Badenweiler in the Black Forest. A friend who saw him in Moscow on the eve of departure for Europe quoted Chekhov as having said: "Tomorrow I leave. Good-bye. I'm going away to die." On July 2, 1904, he died in a hotel at Badenweiler; his body was returned to Moscow for burial.

Further Reading

Chekhov's plays and stories are available in many editions and translations. The best general work on Chekhov in English is

Ernest Joseph Simmons, *Chekhov: A Biography* (1962). An excellent study is Thomas Gustav Winner, *Chekhov and His Prose* (1966). See also Walter Horace Bruford, *Chekhov and His Russia: A Sociological Study* (1948); Ronald Hingley, *Chekhov: A Biographical and Critical Study* (1950); Maurice Jacques Valency, *The Breaking String: The Plays of Anton Chekhov* (1966); Daniel Gillès, *Chekhov: Observer without Illusion* (1967; trans. 1968); and Robert Louis Jackson, ed., *Chekhov: A Collection of Critical Essays* (1967). A good survey of Russian literature is D. S. Mirsky, *A History of Russian Literature* (1949). □

Frederic John Napier Thesiger Chelmsford

The English administrator Frederic John Napier Thesiger Chelmsford, 1st Viscount Chelmsford (1868-1933), was viceroy of India during a difficult period when British prestige there was at a dangerously low ebb. He initiated the course of Indian independence.

Frederic John Chelmsford was born in London on Aug. 12, 1868, the eldest of five sons. Educated at Winchester and at Magdalen College, Oxford, he won distinction in jurisprudence and a fellowship to All Souls in 1892. After a brief experience in local government, he became governor of Queensland, Australia (1905-1909), and governor of New South Wales (1909-1913).

In 1914 he went with the 4th Dorset Territorials to India. Though only a captain with no Indian experience, in 1916 he was offered the most important post of the empire, the viceroyalty of India, succeeding Lord Hardinge of Penshurst.

The government of India had undertaken a disastrous campaign in Mesopotamia, in which Chelmsford's oldest son had died; mismanagement was partially due to the overcentralized system of army administration instituted by Lord Kitchener, commander in chief from 1902 to 1909. "The disastrous effect" of Britain's defeat at "Mespot," as Chelmsford expressed it, led to the resignation of Austen Chamberlain, Secretary of State for India, in July 1917, and the appointment of E. S. Montagu in his stead.

Earlier in 1917 terrorism had broken out in Bengal, and Chelmsford had been forced to assume temporary powers of repression. On Aug. 20, 1917, the historic Montagu-Chelmsford Report announced Britain's ultimate goal in India as "the progressive realisation of responsible government." It drew the sting from a potentially explosive agitation and initiated the Government of India Act of 1919.

Because the Indian bureaucracy had always been slow to implement change and was largely unimaginative, Chelmsford and his council were especially criticized for institutional faults. But he guided his government through the unrest caused by Mohandas Gandhi's campaign of *satyagraha,* which was followed by serious disorders in the Punjab and by the Third Afghan War. Chelmsford used force and firm executive action in both crises, leaving the subsequent bitter Indian resentment to his successors.

After retiring in 1921, Chelmsford assumed a number of academic appointments which were interrupted only by his joining the first Labor government of Ramsay MacDonald in 1924. Chelmsford became first lord of the Admiralty, but the government fell within a year. He died of a heart attack on April 1, 1933.

Further Reading

There is no full-length biography of Chelmsford, but his career is fully discussed in Edwin S. Montagu *An Indian Diary,* edited by Venetia Montagu (1930). The official documents, *Indian Constitutional Reforms: The Montagu-Chelmsford Proposals* and *East India: Constitutional Reforms,* were published separately in 1918. □

Richard B. Cheney

Loyal service under four Republican presidents and a decade of leadership in Congress brought Richard B. Cheney (born 1941) to the inner circle in President George Bush's cabinet as secretary of defense. Assuming the post in March 1989, he faced Panamanian and Iraqi crises as well as an altered relationship with a disintegrating Soviet Union.

After weeks of contentious testimony, President George Bush suffered the first major defeat of his presidency when former Senator John Tower of Texas, his original choice for secretary of defense, was rejected by the full Senate. A day later, on March 10, 1989, the president nominated Representative Richard Bruce Cheney of Wyoming to the post. In a week the Senate confirmed him unanimously.

The 48-year-old legislator came to the office strictly through the political route, but both sides of the Senate aisle agreed that he brought to it an agreeable style, an amiable outlook on life, and a near flawless gift for dealing with people. A dedicated Republican, he left the 101st Congress as its newly-minted minority whip, a position second only to that of minority leader.

Born in Lincoln, Nebraska, on January 30, 1941, "Dick" Cheney was raised in Casper, Wyoming, by his parents, Richard H., a Department of Agriculture employee, and Marjorie L. Dickey. After a stellar secondary school career, he floundered at Yale, leaving in his sophomore year to return home, where he worked for the next two years before returning to college. Beginning again at the University of Wyoming in 1963, he quickly won his B.A. in political science in 1965 and one year later was granted the M.A. in the same discipline.

The Road to Washington Through Wyoming

While at Wyoming he undertook several internships, one with the state legislature and another in the governor's office. These whetted his appetite for government service and led him to apply for a coveted fellowship which brought him to the Washington office of one of the House's most highly respected members, William A. Steiger of Wisconsin.

The assignment drew him to the capital in 1968, a year of turmoil marking the end of eight years of Democratic control of both White House and Congress. While some careers were eclipsing, Cheney's was just beginning to rise. The Nixon administration, hungry for youthful blood, put him to work as special assistant to Donald Rumsfeld, director of the Office of Economic Opportunity. Cheney and Rumsfeld worked well together, the latter taking Cheney with him as deputy when he became White House counsel and as assistant director of operations when Rumsfeld became director of the Cost of Living Council. These positions, which Cheney held from May 1969 to March 1973, gave him an enviable education in government from the inside.

But Watergate Washington in 1973 was no place for a non-lawyer in his early thirties, particularly one with limited private employment experience. He took the vice presidency of an investment advisory group named Bradley, Woods and Company. Agnew's resignation in 1973 and Nixon's departure the following summer thus passed him harmlessly by and in fact opened new horizons.

Joining the Ford Administration

In August 1974 the call came to join Donald Rumsfeld on President Gerald Ford's transition staff. Cheney began life in the new administration at a considerably higher level than he had left the old. He was to serve as deputy assistant to the president, seconding yet again his close associate, Rumsfeld.

In the heady air of the White House, where absurdity is often called reality, Cheney remained himself: loyal, good-natured, pragmatically conservative, extremely civil, and extraordinarily hard-working. These traits brought him to the post of assistant to the president and chief of staff when Rumsfeld became Ford's choice to head the Department of Defense.

Cheney served the president from November 1975 until the end of his administration in January 1977. In the execution of his duties, he cultivated an old-fashioned "passion for anonymity" that would have done justice to many in the eras of Franklin Roosevelt and Eisenhower.

As chief of staff he was privy to the issues confronting Ford those days and had a direct role in advisement on political matters as well as responsibilities for scheduling the president and managing the White House staff. Once more, this was an education no graduate school could impart.

Return to Wyoming, Then a Return to Washington

Ford's defeat by Jimmy Carter sent Cheney back to Wyoming and private employment. But the lure of Washington was too great, and in 1978 he entered the Republican primary, winning it despite being stricken by a coronary attack in the midst of his campaign. Defeating his Democratic opponent in November, he entered the 96th Congress as his state's solitary member of the House of Representatives.

During the next decade of his life, from January 1979 until March 1989, Congressman Cheney consistently defined himself as a compassionate conservative. He made friends easily in both parties, assuming a leadership position early in his career. Re-election came easy to him, and he captured Wyoming's seat five times. Well-liked by his party, he was elected chairman of the Republican House Policy Committee in his second term, an unprecedented feat.

Cheney's political career as a congressman was benefitted greatly by the return of the Republicans to the White House in 1981. In domestic matters he joined right-of-center Republicans on issues such as abortion. In defense policy, he enthusiastically endorsed Carter, then Reagan, defense build up, including the Strategic Defense Initiative (SDI, or Star Wars). And in foreign policy he supported Reagan's stands on Nicaragua and Afghanistan. Nor did he neglect Wyoming, espousing popular positions on environmental issues while supporting reasonable use of the state's mineral and forestry resources. For example, Cheney once refused the requests of other congressmen who only wanted to "borrow" some of Wyoming's share of Colorado River water. They would give it back, they promised, and were even willing to put it in writing, after the water shortage eased. "No way," said Cheney. "Once they get it we'll never get it back. That's how things work."

His standing in Congress made him a natural choice for service on the House Select Committee to Investigate Covert Arms Deals with Iran. Elected as the ranking Republican, and therefore co-chair, he disagreed strongly with the majority report, defending the Reagan administration on the Iran-Contra episode without whitewashing it.

Secretary of Defense

His ten years of service in the House made him a widely respected national figure. The combination of executive-legislative experience gave him an uncommon perspective and compensated for some of the shortcomings which might have impeded his confirmation as defense secretary. Lack of personal military service and little experience in dealing with the Pentagon were built-in objections to his suitability. But these were not seriously entertained, partly because of the circumstances of the Tower rejection but most probably and principally because of the character and nature of Cheney himself. He was up to the job, even if his resume might not trumpet the fact.

He came to the position with a track record of enthusiasm for weapons systems but at a time of severe retrenchment made imperative by the deficit crisis at home and possible by the disintegration of the Soviet Union as a world-class antagonist. He early established control over the massive military-civilian bureaucracy, reprimanding one general and removing another for remarks he deemed beyond their authority. It was clear that civilian control of the military as a principle would not suffer under his tenure.

His capacity for crisis management was demonstrated in the invasion of Panama, a foreign policy-military operation that proceeded successfully to the seizure of Panama's free-wheeling chief of state, General Manual Noriega. But Secretary Cheney's most important test came in August 1990 with the Iraqi invasion and occupation of Kuwait. Responding to President Bush's call for American troop involvement in the defense of Saudi Arabia, Secretary Cheney undertook a massive movement of material and personnel to the Persian Gulf, where, in response to United Nations Security Council resolutions, they joined other nations from all quarters in pursuing the restoration of the Kuwait monarchy and the protection of America's interests. On January 16, 1991 these resources were employed in a violent air war against Iraq. This was followed by a ground attack launched February 23 that destroyed the bulk of Iraq's military forces in 100 hours. Cheney's key role, along with Chief of Staff Colin Powell, made both men popular heroes. With the formal surrender of Iraq, Cheney turned to the task of reducing the strength of the U.S. military, closing surplus military bases, and other cost-cutting devices. His solid reputation and stand-out professionalism helped him carry out these largely unpopular measures.

During his tenure, President Bush, Secretary of State James Baker, and Cheney shaped their party's national security policy. The Bush team reduced the military budget, shrank the size of U.S. military forces, and engaged in a flurry of negotiations that ultimately produced the START I and START II treaties, the Conventional Forces in Europe agreement, and the Chemical Weapons Convention. Bush and Baker led the way to a doubling of the number of U.N. peacekeeping operations across the globe. They all grappled with the issue of disarmament. Cheney's statement, reflecting the Bush administration's course, attested to no new or emerging policy on arms and security: "Arms for America's friends and arms control for its potential foes."

A Voice in Government

Cheney remained Secretary of Defense until 1994, through the political changing of the guard which resulted in the election of Democrat Bill Clinton as president. After leaving his official duties as Secretary of Defense, Cheney remained a voice in government affairs, and frequently commented on Clinton administration choices. In January 1994, Cheney said that the United States should avoid "getting consumed with the problems in Moscow" and instead concentrate on building strong relationships with all the republics of the former Soviet Union, especially Ukraine. In September 1994, he described the U.S. attempts to withdraw quickly from Haiti as "serious misjudgement" while pointing to the difficulties faced while attempting to leave Somalia. With tight budget times and downsizing at the Pentagon under way under the Clinton administration, Cheney was one of the eight civilian Secretaries of Defense invited to give "advice to the re-elected commander in chief" at a special event in Atlanta. In April 1997, he sent a letter to the Senate to protest the imminent ratification of the Chemical Weapons Convention.

Cheney was regarded as corporate America's choice for the 1996 Republican presidential nomination, although he removed his name from consideration almost two years before the election. His name was published as one of 15 possible vice presidential candidates as selected by Republican presidential candidate Bob Dole.

His wife, Lynne (Vincent) Cheney, whom he married in 1964, was a distinguished author and public figure and chairperson of the National Endowment for the Humanities. She has a doctorate in English, is a former editor of Washingtonian magazine and taught at several colleges and universities. They have two daughters, Elizabeth and Mary.

Further Reading

Some biographical data on Cheney's governmental career can be gleaned from accounts of his White House contemporaries and from those of journalists. Gerald Ford's account, *A Time To Heal* (1979), and John Osborne's *White House Watch: The Ford Years* (1977), fit those categories. For Cheney's part in the Iran-Contra investigation, see *Congressional Quarterly Almanac, 1987,* Vol. LXIII. His views on congressional responsibilities over national security, delivered at the end of his first year at the Department of Defense, can be found in "Legislative-Executive Relations in National Security," *Vital Speeches* (March 15, 1990). □

Cheng Ho

Cheng Ho (1371-ca. 1433) was a eunuch in the service of the Ming emperor Yung-lo and commander in chief of the Chinese expeditionary fleet to the South Seas in the early years of the 15th century.

Born into a family named Ma, presumably of Mongol-Arab origin, in central Yünnan Province, Cheng Ho was selected to be castrated by the general in charge of recruiting eunuchs for the court in 1381, when he was about 10. Assigned to the retinue of Chu Ti, who later became emperor, Cheng accompanied him on military campaigns, culminating in the usurpation of the throne by Chu Ti in 1402.

Because of a report that the former emperor Hui-ti had fled overseas, but probably with other good reasons, such as promoting Chinese influence or trade opportunities, Yung-lo sent out expeditions overseas under Cheng's command. In a period of 28 years, from 1405 to 1433, Cheng directed seven expeditions and visited no fewer than 37 countries, stretching from Champa in the east to the African coast in the west.

In preparation for these expeditions, some 1,180 ships of various types and measurements were constructed. The size of the fleet varied from voyage to voyage. The first expedition consisted of a 27,800-man crew and 62 large vessels and 255 smaller ones carrying cargoes of silk, embroideries, and other valuable products. Cheng took personal command of each voyage, but he often entrusted his lieutenants to undertake side trips away from the main itinerary. The countries visited ranged from the nearby states, such as Champa, Sumatra, and Java, to the faraway lands to the East, including Arabia and places on the east African coast, such as Mogadishu and Brawa.

The purpose of these trips was to assure foreigners of China's friendliness, extend imperial gifts and greetings to the chiefs of the foreign kingdoms, and report the conditions of these distant lands to the court. But at the same time, Cheng's fleet also managed to annihilate a powerful Chinese pirate, interfere in a Javanese war, and reinstate a legitimate ruler in Ceylon. Yielding loads of exotic native products, the expeditions were often followed by tribute-bearing envoys from across the sea.

Nonetheless, these voyages were criticized by Chinese officials as useless and wasteful of resources. After Yunglo's death in 1424, the expeditions were suspended, and Cheng was made a garrison commander of Nanking. The last voyage (1432-1433) took place under the auspices of Emperor Hsüan-te. Cheng is customarily said to have died in 1435/1436, at the age of 65, but one source holds that he died early in 1433.

Cheng's expeditions, undertaken almost a century before those of Christopher Columbus and Vasco de Gama, not only strengthened China's influence over its neighbors but also marked a unique achievement in the history of maritime enterprise. A navigational chart attributable to the expeditions has been preserved and translated into English.

Further Reading

There is no book-length biography of Cheng in any Western language. A translation of Cheng's biography in the Chinese official history of the Ming dynasty is included in W. P. Groeneveldt, *Notes on the Malay Archipelago and Malacca, Compiled from Chinese Sources* (1876), which was reprinted in 1960 as *Historical Notes on Indonesia and Malaya, Compiled from Chinese Sources.* Other scholarly evaluations of Cheng's expeditions include J. J. L. Duyvendak, *China's Discovery of Africa* (1949); Colin Jack-Hinton, ed., *Papers on Early South-east Asian History* (1964), which includes an article about Cheng by William Willets; and J. V. G. Mills, trans. and ed., *The Overall Survey of the Oceans' Shores* (1970). General historical background is in L. Carrington Goodrich, *A Short History of the Chinese People* (1943; 4th ed. 1969).

Additional Sources

Levathes, Louise, *When China ruled the seas: the treasure fleet of the Dragon Throne 1405-1433,* New York: Simon & Schuster, 1994. □

André Marie Chénier

The French poet André Marie Chénier (1762-1794) compressed into his brief life many kinds of experience and many poetic forms. He emerges in history as a rare poet-hero whose life is exemplary and tragic.

André Chénier was born in Constantinople. His father was French, and his mother claimed to be of Greek origin. André's early sense of affinity for Greece was vital in his development as a poet. He spent most of his childhood with an aunt and uncle in Carcassonne in Languedoc. When he was 11, he rejoined his mother in Paris and was exposed to the flamboyant society of her salon.

Chénier was an excellent scholar at the exclusive Collége Navarre. His earliest works are adaptations of Homer and Virgil and poems of adolescent love. He was always an affectionate and ardent man; he had many mistresses and a few great loves but never married.

In 1794 Chénier was arrested more or less by accident in Versailles and was sent to Saint-Lazare prison with no formal charges against him, though he was suspect through association with moderate groups. Eventually, he was accused of being an accomplice in a fictitious prison conspiracy and, more seriously, of subversive writings. He was guillotined on July 25, 1794.

His Works

Chénier's writings were not published until 25 years after his death, at which time he became the model for the romantic poets. Victor Hugo, Sainte-Beuve, Chateaubriand, Lamartine, and others nurtured the legend of the poet as hero which sprang up around Chénier's memory.

Chénier's *Bucoliques,* melancholy poems about love and sensual imaginings, were written in his late teens and early 20s. Later he wrote the erotic and witty *Elégies* as well as the *Odes* for his mistresses. His *Idylles,* which instinctively capture the beauty of Greek lyricism, include such famous poems as *L'Aveugle, Le Mendiant, La Liberté,* and the superb *Jeune Tarantine.*

Chénier's poetry is always vital and enthusiastic, since he believed that poetry must spring from genuine experience and lived emotions. The poet must be an inventor—yet Chénier's classical roots are always apparent. He borrowed not only from Homer and Virgil but from Racine, La Fontaine, Rousseau, and others.

During the Revolution, Chénier established himself as a great satirical poet. His poetry became a chronicle of the great events of the Revolution. Among the most outstanding poems are *Les Autels de la peur, Ode à Versailles, Ode à Charlotte Corday,* and *La Fête de l'Être Supreme.* In prison, where he wrote his *Iambes* and part of the *Odes,* Chénier withdrew into himself, yet did not fail to admire and to celebrate the courage of his fellow prisoners. The night before his execution Chénier wrote the last poem of *Iambes.* In this noble work, half elegy and half satire, he rises from a sense of his own separateness and melancholy to real self-forgetfulness, compassion, and courage.

Further Reading

Two major works on Chénier are Francis Scarfe's scholarly *André Chénier: His Life and Work, 1762-1794* (1965), which is devoted to close analysis of the poetry and to a study of poetic forms, rhetoric, and language; and Vernon Loggins, *André Chénier: His Life, Death and Glory* (1965), a more direct and simple, if adulatory, account of the poet's life, with less detailed discussion of the poetry. ☐

Ch'en Tu-hsiu

Ch'en Tu-hsiu (1879-1942) was a leader of China's cultural and political revolution. He helped found the Chinese Communist party and served as its first chairman from 1921 to 1927.

Son of a wealthy family in Huaining, Anhwei Province, Ch'en Tu-hsiu received a classical education. In 1896 he passed the lowest-level civil service examination but failed to obtain a higher degree. During the first decade of the 20th century he pursued a modern education in China, Japan, and France. He also helped to edit a series of magazines and served as a teacher and dean. After the Revolution of 1911 Ch'en headed the Anhwei Department of Education until forced by Yüan Shih-k'ai to flee to Japan in 1913. There he helped his friend Chang Shihchao to edit *Chia-yin tsa-chih* (Tiger Magazine). Upon the suppression of this publication, Ch'en went to the foreign concession in Shanghai. In 1915 he began to publish his most famous magazine, *Ch'ing-nien tsa-chih* (Youth Magazine).

Social Reformer

Though sympathetic to the revolution, Ch'en was concerned more with cultural and social changes than with political change. A Francophile, he championed equality, democracy, and science and denounced Confucianism. More a pamphleteer than a systematic philosopher, Ch'en was widely influential. In 1917 the chancellor of Peking University, Ts'ai Yüan-p'ei, invited him to become dean of the College of Letters at National Peking University (Peita). Surrounded by kindred souls of the literary renaissance, Ch'en made his magazine, now called the *Hsin Ch'ing-nien* (New Youth), the voice of the intellectual avant-grade.

In 1918, outraged at the misgovernment of Tuan Ch'ijui's Anhwei Clique, Ch'en and Li Ta-chao, professor and librarian at the University, formed the *Mei-chou p'inglun* (Weekly Critic) to serve as a platform of attack against the government's domestic and foreign policies. The paper helped prepare the ground for the May Fourth movement, a nationwide protest sparked by the Peking student demonstration of May 4, 1919. Targets of this assault were the Versailles powers, who had given Shantung Province to Japan, and the Peking officials, who had connived in this treachery.

Birth of the Chinese Communist Party

Swept along by the movement, Ch'en was jailed by the government for nearly 3 months. Upon release he resigned from Peita and returned to Shanghai. There he became a Marxist. In the summer of 1920, after discussions with Comintern agent Gregory Voitinsky, Ch'en organized a Communist nucleus and was instrumental in establishing similar groups elsewhere. In Shanghai he set about organizing students and workers, and in August the Socialist Youth League was formed to train future party members. A foreign-language school prepared students for study in Russia; one of its first graduates was Liu Shao-ch'i.

In December 1920 Ch'en accepted an offer from the progressive warlord Ch'en Chiung-ming to head Kwangtung's provincial education department. He took the opportunity to organize a Communist nucleus in Canton. In July 1921 the First Congress of the Chinese Communist party (CCP) unanimously elected Ch'en Tu-hsiu secretary of the Central Committee. Returning to Shanghai, Ch'en met with the Dutch Comintern representative, Maring. The Comintern agreed to provide funds, and Ch'en agreed to accept Commintern discipline. The implications of the agreement became clear a year later, when Ch'en reluctantly agreed to follow Comintern policy by joining an alliance with the Kuomintang.

Communist-Nationalist Coalition

Ch'en feared that the party of the proletariat would be swallowed up by this organ of the bourgeoisie. However, after attending the Comintern congress in Moscow in November-December 1922 and witnessing the weakness of the workers' movement in the Peking-Hankow railway strike of February 1923, he actively supported the new policy. In June 1923 he was elected secretary general of the party. Ch'en was nonetheless unenthusiastic about continued cooperation with the Kunomintang. Because the Kuomintang polarized after President Sun Yat-sen's death in March 1925, the alliance came under attack from within the Kuomintang as well.

After the anti-Communist purges by Chiang Kai-shek in March 1926 and April 1927, Ch'en pleaded for an end to the alliance but was overruled by the Comintern. With the split between Chiang's government in Nanking and the "left" Kuomintang regime in Wuhan, Ch'en followed Comintern orders and allied the CCP with the Wuhan faction. However, he came under growing opposition within the party, because of personal and regional jealousies and because he had become the scapegoat for the Comintern's miscalculations. Ch'en was branded a "Trotskyite," and, at a secured emergency conference on Aug., 7, 1927, he was replaced by Ch'ü Ch'iu-pai.

Expulsion and Imprisonment

For the next 15 years Ch'en lived in Shanghai, where he continued to write and to be active in party affairs. Ch'en followed an independent line which placed him at odds with the new leadership. He finally was expelled from the party for criticizing its support of the Soviet Union in the Chinese Eastern Railroad dispute of mid-1929.

Having been falsely branded a Trotskyite in 1927, Ch'en became a real Trotskyite in 1929. Though bitterly attacked as "liquidationists" by the Central Committee, in 1931 Ch'en and his followers finally brought several splinter groups together in a united Trotskyite organization, the Chinese Communist Party Left Opposition Faction. Though the new group suffered from factional rivalries and was completely ineffective, Ch'en was arrested by the Nationalists on Oct. 15, 1932, and charged with endangering the republic. Sentenced to 15 years' imprisonment, he turned a deaf ear to Nationalist supplications to cooperate with the Nanking government. While in prison he devoted himself to his old passion, linguistic studies.

After the outbreak of the Second Sino-Japanese War, Ch'en was released under a general amnesty. He announced his support of the united front against Japan and his refusal to identify with any political group. He fled from the advancing Japanese to Wuhan, Changsha, Chungking, and finally, because of poor health, to retirement in a small town 45 miles from the wartime capital.

In letters and essays written from 1940 to 1942 Ch'en reaffirmed his faith in individual freedom and democratic socialism, but he equated the repressive orthodoxy of Soviet communism with Confucianism, both being incompatible with these goals. Ch'en died on May 27, 1942.

Further Reading

A short treatment of Ch'en's life is in Y. C. Wang, *Chinese Intellectuals and the West, 1872-1949* (1966). Ch'en's role in the May Fourth movement and the founding of the Chinese Communist party is treated in Benjamin I. Schwartz, *Chinese Communism and the Rise of Mao* (1951), and in Chou Tse-tsung, *The May Fourth Movement: Intellectual Revolution in Modern China* (1960).

Additional Sources

Feigon, Lee, *Chen Duxiu, founder of the Chinese Communist Party,* Princeton, N.J.: Princeton University Press, 1983. □

Pavel Alekseevich Cherenkov

The principal contribution of the Russian physicist Pavel Alekseevich Cherenkov (1904-1990) was the explanation of a certain pale bluish radiation as a consequence of high-speed electrons passing through refractive mediums.

More is known about the Cherenkov effect than about Pavel Cherenkov himself. He was born on July 28, 1904, into a poor peasant family living in the village of Novaya Chigla, Voronezh Province. At the age of 20 he entered the State University of Voronezh, graduating 4 years later. In 1930 he was accepted as a postgraduate student at the P. N. Lebedev Institute of Physics of the Soviet Academy of Sciences. Cherenkov earned his doctorate in 1940.

As early as 1910, Marie Curie had noticed that radium salts dissolved in distilled water produced a bluish glow, but she did not pursue this observation further. During the late 1920s a French scientist, L. I. Mallet, examined the spectrum of the bluish-white radiation and discovered it was continuous instead of lines or bands usually associated with fluorescence; he failed to uncover the origin of the glow. Between 1934 and 1938 Cherenkov conducted a series of intensive investigations of the fluorescence of water bombarded by gamma rays. Before each experiment he would sit for 60 to 90 minutes in total darkness in order to increase his visual sensitivity to the feeble glow. He decided in 1934 that the bluish radiation was not a fluorescent phenomenon.

Sergei Vavilov's 1934 paper, which appeared at the same time as the Cherenkov study, suggested that the gamma-ray-induced glow was due to the slowing down of the electrons in the water (an example of the bremsstrahlung process). Vavilov then helped design a number of experiments for Cherenkov to carry out in the hope of determining the source of the luminescence. Under Vavilov's guidance Cherenkov arrived at the conclusion that the radiation was the result of light emitted by electrons liberated by the gamma rays as the electrons moved in a refractive medium at a speed faster than the propagation of light itself in that medium; the light was emitted not in random fashion but at a specific angle to the direction of the moving electron. The shock waves produced by bullets, missiles, or jet planes

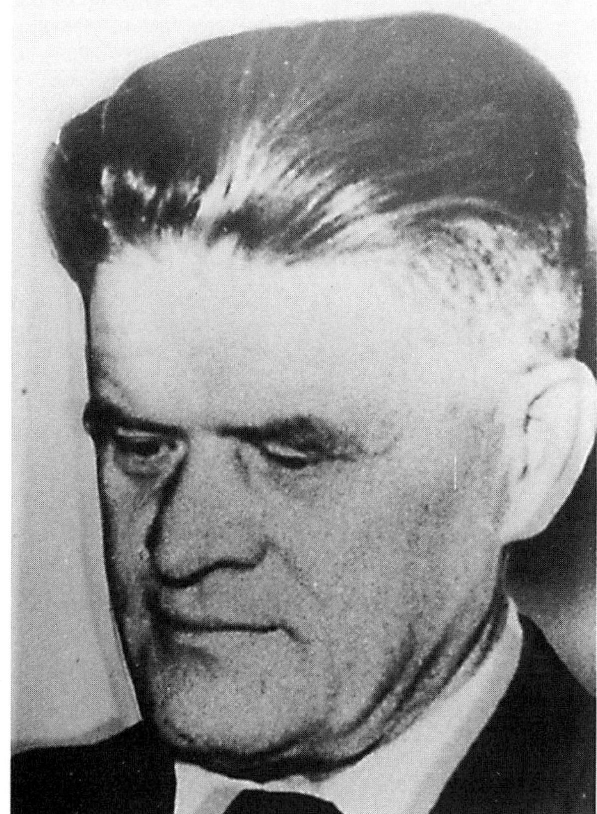

moving faster than the speed of sound are an acoustical analogy of the Cherenkov radiation.

The theory and the effect have been extended, refined, and modified; it has found increasing application in the physics of cosmic rays and high-energy particles. By employing photomultipliers, the Cherenkov effect has been successfully used in detectors for obtaining vital data on high-speed particles; a Cherenkov detector orbited the earth in *Sputnik III.* Cherenkov and Vavilov, together with Igor Evgenievich Tamm and Ilya Mikhailovich Frank, received the Stalin Prize in 1946 for their explanation, theory, and practical application of the Cherenkov radiation. In the former Soviet Union the "blue glow" is often referred to as the Vavilov-Cherenkov effect; Vavilov is usually given greater credit for its development than Cherenkov. In 1958 Cherenkov, Frank, and Tamm shared the Nobel Prize in physics. In 1964 Cherenkov was elected a corresponding member of the Soviet Academy of Sciences. He continued working in high energy physics and established a fine reputation for the training of research physicists. Cherenkov died in 1990.

Further Reading

Only brief and scattered accounts of Cherenkov exist. There is a biographical chapter on him in Nobel Foundation, *Nobel Lectures: Physics* , vol. 3 (1964). The most comprehensive work in English on the Cherenkov effect is J. V. Jelley, *Cherenkov Radiation and Its Applications* (1958). The Cherenkov radiation is discussed in J. G. Linhart, *Plasma Physics* (1960; 2d ed. 1961), and the Cherenkov detectors are presented in David M. Ritson, ed., *Techniques of High Energy Physics* (1961). □

Konstantin Ustinovich Chernenko

After many years as a loyal and effective member of the Communist Party, Konstantin Ustinovich Chernenko (1911-1985) ruled the Soviet Union as general secretary for 13 months between February 1984 and March 1985.

Born September 24, 1911, into a large and impoverished Siberian peasant family in the village of Bolshaya Tes, Novoselovo District, Krasnoiarsk Territory, Chernenko left home by his own account at age 12 to work as a farm hand. His formal grade and secondary school education may have ended at this time. Although his name is Ukrainian, his official biographers describe him as an ethnic Russian, and it has been suggested that his family at one point migrated from the Ukraine to South Siberia, where they came to consider themselves Russian.

As a teenager Chernenko became associated with the Communist Youth League (Komsomol), often an apprenticeship for future party officials. In 1929-1930, he was named to head the propaganda and agitation department of the Novoselovo District Komsomol committee.

The post was an important one. The year 1929 marked the beginning of forced draft collectivization in Soviet Russia, and a person in Chernenko's position would have played a role in the forceable creation of collective and state farms around Krasnoiarsk, as well as in the expulsion of those considered kulaks (wealthier peasants). In 1930 Chernenko began three years' service with the Red Army on the Chinese border. He became a full member of the party in 1931 and returned after his military service to Krasnoiarsk as a party propagandist, rising rapidly in the regional hierarchy and undoubtedly benefitting from Stalin's bloody purge of older party officials. Around the time of the German invasion in June 1941 he became secretary of the Krasnoiarsk Territory party committee responsible for political education.

Chernenko was apparently a successful local party boss. In 1943 he was selected to attend the Higher School for Party Organizers in Moscow, a stepping stone for promotion. Upon graduation in 1945 he was sent to Penza, where his work again apparently earned him a promotion to Moldavia, where he assumed the difficult task of heading the Moldavian Communist Party Central Committee's Propaganda and Agitation Division. The tasks of economic and ideological reconstruction in this largely Rumanian corner of Soviet Russia were formidable and put Chernenko to the test.

It was here that he developed his close association with Leonid Brezhnev, who headed the Moldavian party from

1950 to 1952 and whom Chernenko served as a loyal and competent aide. Soon after Brezhnev was brought to Moscow in 1956 as a party secretary, Chernenko was summoned as well, assuming a post in the Central Committee's Propaganda Section. In 1960 when Brezhnev became president of the Supreme Soviet, Soviet Russia's leading government position outside the party hierarchy, Chernenko became, in effect, his chief-of-staff. And as Brezhnev came to full power after the death of Khrushchev, Chernenko took on additional responsibilities in various party and state organs. He became a member of the Central Committee in 1971 and was elected a secretary of this all-important body in 1976. From 1978 onwards he also served as a full member of the ruling Politburo. Brezhnev apparently expected Chernenko to succeed him as general secretary and groomed him for this post. In 1979 Chernenko participated in the Vienna arms limitation talks and frequently met with foreign visitors and delegations.

It is still unclear how Iuri Andropov outmaneuvered Chernenko after Brezhnev's death in 1982, but this is not of great historical importance. Chernenko was known as a moderate and compromiser, a man unwilling or unable to initiate sharp changes in Soviet policy or to offend various groups of Kremlin leaders identified with competing policies or positions. He seemed to accept Andropov's success with good grace and political acumen, establishing a place for himself as party ideologist and chief theorist. With Andropov's illness, his position as successor was all but assured.

An aging and sick man when he was elected to succeed Iuri Andropov on February 13, 1984, his tenure in this all-powerful position was the briefest in Soviet history—and the least notable. No significant policy initiatives were begun under his direction, and no progress was made in improving chronic Soviet economic problems. No steps were taken to end the war in Afghanistan. When Chernenko died on March 10, 1985, from severe heart disease, Soviet citizens received the news with little apparent distress. Many probably felt conditions in the Soviet Union could begin to improve under new, more vigorous leadership.

Some in the West found it remarkable that a person with as little individual distinction as Chernenko could come, even for a brief period, to occupy one of the most powerful positions in the world. Unlike Andropov, Gorbachev, Romanov, and other of his Politburo colleagues, he never administered a major Soviet party organization or institution on his own. His personal life was also kept from public view. Many in both the former Soviet Union and the West saw his wife, Anna Dmitrievna, and his daughter, Elena Konstantinova, for the first time at his funeral. He was, however, a loyal and effective party aide, and his brief tenure as general secretary at age 72 rewarded his decades of devoted service as a career party politician.

Further Reading

An interesting study by Valerie Bunce, *Do New Leaders Make A Difference?* (1981) explores the general problems of executive succession and public policy under socialism in a comparative way and provides some clues to the listless nature of Chernenko's administration. George Breslauer, *Khrushchev and Brezhnev as Leaders* (1982) discusses Brezhnev's administration in detail. It is an excellent introduction to Chernenko's political milieu, as well as a good indicator of his own political style. See also Seweryn Bialer, *Stalin's Successors* (1980).

Additional Sources

Zemtsov, Ilya, *Chernenko: the last Bolshevik: the Soviet Union on the eve of Perestroika,* New Brunswick, N.J., U.S.A.: Transaction Publishers, 1989. □

Nikolai Gavrilovich Chernyshevsky

The Russian radical journalist Nikolai Gavrilovich Chernyshevsky (1828-1889) was a literary critic and social theorist. His best-known work, the novel *What Is To Be Done?*, became a classic of the Russian revolutionary movement.

The son of a priest, Nikolai Chernyshevsky was born on July 1, 1828, in Saratov. He started his literary career in 1855 with a master's thesis on esthetics which he submitted at the University of St. Petersburg. In this work Chernyshevsky attacked contemporary esthetic theory, which held that art was an independent transcendent realm. He argued that the arts in general, and literature in particular, could justify their existence only by accurately describing, explaining, and evaluating the actual in terms comprehensible to all—by being a "textbook of life." This utilitarian view made a strong impact and later assumed a quasi-official status under communism, serving to sanction government regimentation of the arts.

From 1855 to 1862 Chernyshevsky worked as a writer and editor for the radical journal *Contemporary.* His preoccupation with esthetic theory led to a series of literary studies. He then became increasingly engrossed in the domestic and foreign scene and wrote numerous essays on philosophy, politics, and economics.

For Chernyshevsky, ethics, like art, must be based on the philosophy of utilitarianism. He held that human behavior is motivated by self-interest. He believed that knowledge inevitably leads people to choose good rather than evil, and he attributed human wickedness to ignorance of the advantages of avoiding evil.

Chernyshevsky's economic theories were socialistic. He loathed the principle of laissez-faire, since he believed unrestricted competition sacrificed the weak to the strong and labor to capital. He held that free enterprise distributed goods unfairly and failed to stimulate production. Chernyshevsky's "toiler's theory" embodied his economic thought. By toiler he meant both the worker and the peasant; for him the *muzhik* (peasant) was the person of destiny for Russia.

The toiler's theory was based on Chernyshevsky's beliefs that the welfare of the individual was of paramount importance and that goods rightfully belonged only to those who had produced them. He advocated economic equality and elimination of unproductive social classes. Although he was ambiguous about the nature of the controls that would achieve these ends, Chernyshevsky did not call for a centrally planned, nationalized economy. Instead, he envisioned a loose aggregate of communities resembling phalansteries (voluntary associations, each engaging in both industry and agriculture on a cooperative basis). The voluntary associations were to be autonomous units, democratically administered and independent from central authority.

In 1862 Chernyshevsky published in *Contemporary* a series of open letters to an unnamed person who was clearly none other than Czar Alexander II. The Czar had emancipated the serfs in 1861, but Chernyshevsky pointed out that, although this reform had affected the appearance of the relation between master and serf, little real change had occurred. He hinted that revolution was perhaps the only way to completely abolish serfdom.

Because of his criticism of the government Chernyshevsky was watched carefully by the czarist secret police, and in 1862 his name headed the list of political suspects. That year he was arrested and imprisoned. While in prison he wrote the novel *What Is To Be Done?* (1863). In it he rejects such concepts as honor, conscience, duty, and self-sacrifice. *What Is To Be Done?* soon became the bible of the radical youth. It called for freedom in personal relations and for dedication to society, and it contained effective arguments for women's emancipation, for socialism, and indirectly for revolution. Lenin called it "one of those books the impact of which lasts a lifetime."

In 1864 Chernyshevsky was exiled to Siberia. Broken in health, he returned to civilization in 1883. He died in Saratov on Oct. 29, 1889.

Further Reading

Chernyshevsky's *Selected Philosophical Essays* (1953) contains a large collection of articles. His *What Is To Be Done? Tales about New People* (1961), with an introduction by E. H. Carr, is important as an intellectual document and as a prototype of later didactic radical novels. Recommended for general historical background are Tomas G. Masaryk, *The Spirit of Russia: Studies in History, Literature, and Philosophy* (2 vols., 1913; trans. 1919; 2d ed. 1955), and Franco Venturi, *Roots of Revolution: A History of the Populist and Socialist Movements in Nineteenth Century Russia* (1960).

Additional Sources

Paperno, Irina, *Chernyshevsky and the age of realism: a study in the semiotics of behavior,* Stanford, Calif.: Stanford University Press, 1988.

Pereira, N. G. O. (Norman G. O.), *The thought and teachings of N. G. Chernyshevsky,* The Hague: Mouton, 1975. □

Luigi Carlo Zanobi Salvatore Maria Cherubini

Luigi Carlo Zanobi Salvatore Maria Cherubini (1760-1842) was an Italian-born composer and teacher who lived in France. His dramatic compositions revitalized the French opéra comique. As a pedagogue, he had profound influence in shaping French music in the 19th century.

Luigi Cherubini was born in Florence on Sept. 12, 1760. He began his musical studies with his father, a musician of modest attainments. In 1778 Cherubini went to Bologna to study with the eminent opera composer Giuseppe Sarti. At a young age Cherubini had already begun to compose his own catalog, recording a "Mass" and an "Intermezzo" completed when he was 13. His first opera was produced when he was 20. After a brief attempt to establish himself in London, Cherubini settled in Paris in 1787 and remained there the rest of his life.

In 1789 Cherubini was named music director for the Théâtre Monsieur, founded to produce *opéra comique* (comic opera), and later, for the Théâtre Feydeau, an informal club for the aristocracy during the Revolution. In 1791 he electrified Paris with his first major "rescue opera," *Lodoïska.* This was followed by *Eliza* (1794), *Médée* (1797), and the immensely popular *Les Deux journées* (1800), known also under its German title, *Der Wasserträger* (The Water Carrier).

In the Napoleonic era Cherubini became more and more conservative in both his life and music. Described as moody and aloof, he made his most lasting friendship with J. A. D. Ingres, the great French painter of the neoclassic tradition. In 1808 Cherubini turned his attention to the composition of church music and became one of the few major composers active in the 19th century to write effectively in this genre. Long involved in pedagogical activities, he became director of the Conservatory in 1822, the institution he had been partially instrumental in founding in 1795. Elected to the Institut de France in 1815, he was named commander of the Légion d'Honneur in 1842 shortly before his death on March 15.

Cherubini is remembered more as a haughty, academic composer than as the creator of exciting revolutionary theater. He was a master contrapuntalist, was wary of innovation, and in an age which prized individual eccentricities, Cherubini became notorious as a reactionary traditionalist. In particular, he was the bane of the young Hector Berlioz. Beethoven, however, admired Cherubini above all his contemporaries, and *Médée* was not only a source of inspiration but a model as well for *Fidelio*. Cherubini's sense of decorum and propriety and his slavish respect for tradition have contributed to the beclouding in modern times of his genuine accomplishments.

Further Reading

The best study of Cherubini in English is Basil Deane, *Cherubini* (1965). His operas are discussed in Donald J. Grout, *A Short History of Opera* (1947; 2d ed. 1965). □

Mary Boykin Chesnut

Diarist Mary Boykin Chesnut (1823-1886) captured an intimate view of the political and personal struggles of the Confederate South during the Civil War. Her journal of the war years describes not only the difficulties of war, but also reveals her personal views on the similarities between the system of slavery and the position of women in the South.

The Civil War diaries of Mary Boykin Chesnut, a Southern woman from a well-to-do political family, provide an in-depth view of the attitudes and experiences of Southerners during the war between the states. After the war Chesnut recognized the literary and historic value of her observations and began to revise her diaries, but only one small excerpt was published during her lifetime. Following her death in 1886, heavily edited versions of her diary were released, and it was not until 1981 that a complete edition of her work appeared. Chesnut's writing is valued for its revealing personal anecdotes and candid opinions that reflect a strong support for women's rights and the abolition of slavery.

Chesnut was born Mary Boykin Miller on March 31, 1823, in Statesburg, South Carolina. She was the oldest child of Mary Boykin, the daughter of wealthy plantation owners, and Stephen Decatur Miller, a prominent politician who strongly supported states' rights. Her father was a South Carolina senator at the time of Chesnut's birth and had previously served as a member of the U.S. House of Representatives. During her early years, Chesnut and her family lived on the plantation of her maternal grandparents near Camden, South Carolina. When her father was elected governor of the state in 1828, the Millers moved to the capital city of Columbia, returning to Camden when Stephen Miller won a U.S. Senate seat in 1830. By the time her father resigned from the Senate in 1833 due to health problems, Chesnut had begun attending a local school in Camden.

When she was 12, Chesnut was sent to Charleston, South Carolina, to attend Madame Talvande's French School for Young Ladies. There she completed her education with academic courses in literature, science, and history as well as instruction in music, singing, and dancing. In 1836, she met James Chesnut, Jr., a Princeton University graduate who had come to the school to visit his niece. James took an interest in the lively and intelligent girl, and over the following years he began to court her despite objections from Chesnut's family. The two were married on April 23, 1840, and at the age of 17, Chesnut settled with her husband at his family's plantation, Mulberry, outside Camden.

Supported South's Stand on States' Rights

Chesnut had a flair for society life and a passion for literature. She found Mulberry to be a stifling environment where it was difficult to indulge in these interests. In 1848, she and James built a house in the town of Camden where she was able to escape the tedium of the plantation. Her husband had begun a promising career in state politics, and by 1854 they were able to move to a larger and more impressive home—called Kamchatka—in Camden. With James's election to the U.S. Senate in 1858, the couple left for Washington, D.C., where Chesnut enjoyed a thriving social scene. She also took an interest in the divisive political arguments over states' rights that had continued to gain intensity in the national government. Chesnut supported the position that her father had promoted during his career and that her husband now championed. Even though neither she nor James believed in the institution of slavery, they did uphold the right of states to make their own decisions on such matters. The election of Abraham Lincoln, who opposed slavery, to the presidency in 1860 angered Southerners, and with the secession of Southern states from the Union, the threat of a civil war loomed over the nation. When on November 10, 1860, her husband became the first Southern senator to resign from his post, Chesnut realized that a critical period of history was unfolding.

In February of 1861, Chesnut began a diary that recorded the explosive happenings around her as well as her own thoughts about the issues, events, and people that she encountered during the years of the Civil War, from 1861 until 1865. Her writings also captured Chesnut's spirited personality and her intolerance for the indecisive and foolish. Following her husband on his various duties in the South at this time, Chesnut provides a first-hand view of the political world of the Confederacy. In the first part of 1861, she went to Montgomery, Alabama, where James participated in the Confederate Provisional Congress. They then traveled to Charleston, South Carolina, where James was part of negotiations over the departure of Northern troops from nearby Fort Sumter. When Southern forces opened fire on the fort in the first battle of the war, Chesnut joined others in town in viewing the skirmish from a rooftop.

Recorded Experiences of Civil War

The novelty of war was soon replaced by a horror at the realities: destruction of property, political confusion, poverty and hunger, and the tremendous number of wounded and dead. Chesnut recorded the stories she heard about various battles as well as her personal experiences, such as tending sick and wounded soldiers and mourning the loss of friends and acquaintances. She had strong criticism for the fearful and conservative decisions of Southern leaders, including her husband. Chesnut was frustrated by James's lack of interest in the bloody conflicts in nearby Virginia and his reluctance to ask for the diplomatic posts in Europe that he wanted. In her diary she complained about her lack of power as a woman in the South, stating that she wished she could be a man so she could be more active in the war effort. She even admitted the hope that Confederate president Jefferson Davis would name her, instead of her timid husband, to a post in Paris.

James Chesnut was promoted to the rank of colonel and named an aide to Jefferson Davis in 1862. He and his wife moved to the Confederate capital of Richmond, Virginia, where they became close and loyal friends of Davis and his wife, Varina, whom Chesnut had known for many years. The pressures of his post in Richmond placed a great strain on James, however, and in 1864 he successfully arranged for a transfer to Columbia, South Carolina. There he attained the rank of brigadier general and organized reserve troops. By the beginning of 1865, Union troops under General Sherman had entered North Carolina and the defeat of the South appeared inevitable. Chesnut removed to Lincolnton, North Carolina, to wait out the war in safety.

With growing hopelessness she recorded the incoming news of the disintegration of the Confederate forces. In April of 1865, Confederate General Robert E. Lee surrendered at Appomattox Courthouse, ending the Civil War. Chesnut returned to her home state, settling in the town of Chester. Her house there served as a temporary place of refuge for Varina Davis and her four children as they attempted to escape arrest by Union forces in the war's aftermath.

Revised Diary for Publication

The Chesnuts returned to Camden, where the Mulberry plantation had suffered extensive damage at the hands of the Union Army. With few resources, they worked to piece together a new life, struggling to overcome the heavy debt into which both Mulberry and the family's Sandy Hill plantation had fallen. Both properties were inherited by James at the death of his father in 1866, and he and his wife returned to some level of comfort when they were able to build a new home, Sarsfield, in Camden in 1873. It was then that Chesnut began to evaluate the extensive diaries that she had compiled during the war. She hoped to use the material as the basis for novels, but after an unsatisfactory attempt at fiction, she decided to prepare her diaries for publication in their original first-person format. While working to edit the material and polish the prose over the next few years, she published one story from her diary in the *Charleston Weekly News and Courier* as "The Arrest of a Spy." This was the only item that Chesnut published during her life.

In the late 1870s and early 1880s, Chesnut's work was interrupted by a series of ailments of her lungs and heart. Her husband and mother also fell into poor health and died within a week of each other in January of 1885. This experience left her depressed and reduced in fortunes, due to a clause in James's father's will that required the plantations to be passed on to a male heir. Because Chesnut had never had children, she found herself in her final years with only the Sarsfield home and a small income of 100 dollars a year, which she supplemented by selling eggs and butter. Despite her hardships, she continued to rework various portions of the diary until her death of a heart attack in Camden on November 22, 1886.

Diary Published after Death

Editions of Chesnut's diary appeared in the early 1900s under the title, *A Diary from Dixie*. Early editors of the work, however, took great liberties in removing material they thought inappropriate or unnecessary. But even these incomplete versions became extremely popular for their wealth of information about the difficulties of Southern life during the Civil War. The diary also revealed a strong support for the end of slavery among Southern women, whom Chesnut felt were also enduring a kind of enslavement by the traditional male-dominated society of the South. The author reveals a strong revulsion for the moral lapses that such a system tolerated, giving the example of her father-in-law's liaison with one of his slave women. Readers also appreciated Chesnut's intellectual bent and her references to a wide range of literary works, as well as her often humorous jabs at what she perceived as the ridiculous side of society. A 1981 edition entitled *Mary Chesnut's Civil War* provided for the first time the complete version of the diary that Chesnut had intended for readers, revealing the full depths of her valuable personal history of the Civil War South.

Further Reading

For more information see Chesnut, Mary Boykin, *Mary Boykin's Civil War,* edited by C. Vann Woodward, Yale University Press, 1981; Chesnut, Mary Boykin, *The Private Mary Chesnut: The Unpublished Civil War Diaries,* edited by C. Vann Woodward and Elisabeth Muhlenfeld, Oxford University Press, 1984; and Muhlenfeld, Elisabeth, *Mary Boykin Chesnut: A Biography,* Louisiana State University Press, 1981.

□

Gilbert Keith Chesterton

The English author, journalist, and artist Gilbert Keith Chesterton (1874-1936) dedicated his extraordinary intellect and creative power to the reform of English government and society. In 1922 he converted to Roman Catholicism and became its champion.

On May 29, 1874, G. K. Chesterton was born in London. His father, gifted in many lines of amateur creativity, exerted no pressure on the boy to distinguish himself in either scholarship or athletics. Gilbert was a day boy at St. Paul's. The masters rated him as an under-achiever, but he earned some recognition as a writer and debater. From St. Paul's he went to the Slade School of Art, where he became a proficient draftsman and caricaturist; later he took courses in English literature at City College.

From art Chesterton drifted into journalism. He was vitally concerned with the injustices of Great Britain to its dependencies. He progressed from newspaper to public debate. He used logic, laughter, paradox, and his own winning personality to show that imperialism was destroying English patriotism. In 1900 he published his first literary works, two volumes of poetry.

In 1900 he met Hilaire Belloc, and in 1901 he married Frances Blogg. These events were two of the great influences in his life. From 1904 to 1936 Chesterton published nearly a dozen novels, the most important being *The Napoleon of Notting Hill* (1904) and *The Man Who Was Thursday* (1908). In 1911 Chesterton created the "Father Brown" detective stories. During his literary career he published 90 books and numerous articles. He poured out a wealth of lighthearted essays, historical sketches, and metaphysical and polemical works, together with such well-known poems as "The Ballad of the White Horse," "Lepanto," and the drinking songs from *The Flying Inn.* Among his major critical works are studies of Robert Browning (1903) and Charles Dickens (1906). Prodigiously talented, Chesterton also illustrated a number of Belloc's light works.

Chesterton spoke of himself as primarily a journalist. He contributed to and helped edit *Eye Witness* and *New Witness.* He edited *G. K.'s Weekly,* which advocated distributism, the social philosophy developed by Belloc. Chesterton's overriding concern with political and social injustice is reflected in *Heretics* (1905) and *Orthodoxy* (1909), perhaps his most important work.

Throughout his life Chesterton was one of the most colorful and loved personalities of literary England. To his intellectual gifts he added gaiety, wit, and warm humanity that endeared him even to his antagonists. Shortly after his marriage he had purchased a home in Beaconsfield, where he died on June 14, 1936.

Further Reading

A study of Chesterton requires these three basic books: his *Autobiography* (1936); Maisie Ward, *Gilbert Keith Chesterton* (1943), the official biography; and her *Return to Chesterton* (1952). Also valuable are Hugh Kenner, *Paradox in Chesterton,* with an introduction by Marshall McLuhan

(1947); Christopher Hollis, *G. K. Chesterton* (1950; rev. ed. 1964); and Garry Wills, *Chesterton: Man and Mask* (1961).

Additional Sources

Coren, Michael, *Gilbert, the man who was G.K. Chesterton,* New York: Paragon House, 1990.

Dale, Alzina Stone, *The art of G.K. Chesterton,* Chicago: Loyola University Press, 1985.

Dale, Alzina Stone, *The outline of sanity: a biography of G.K. Chesterton,* Grand Rapids, Mich.: Eerdmans, 1982.

Ffinch, Michael, *G.K. Chesterton,* San Francisco: Harper & Row, 1986.

The Riddle of joy: G.K. Chesterton and C.S. Lewis, Grand Rapids, Mich.: W.B. Eerdmans, 1989.

Titterton, W. R. (William Richard), *G. K. Chesterton: a portrait,* Folcroft, Pa. Folcroft Library Editions, 1974; Norwood, Pa.: Norwood Editions, 1978.

Wahlert Memorial Library, *Gilbert Keith Chesterton; an exhibition catalogue of English and American first editions on the occasion of the centenary of his birth, 1874-1974, along with appreciations and tributes to the man and his works by friends and critics,* Dubuque, La., 1974. □

Chiang Ching-kuo

Chiang Ching-kuo (1910-1988) became chairman of the ruling Nationalist Party (Kuomintang or KMT) in 1975 and president of the Republic of China in Taiwan in 1978. He was the elder son of Chiang Kai-shek, who led the KMT government until he died in 1975. Chiang Ching-kuo ruled until his death in 1988.

Chiang Ching-kuo was born in Fenghua, Chekiang Province. In early childhood he seldom saw his father and was brought up by his grandmother and mother in a Buddhist atmosphere. He was given a strict traditional Chinese education until he was 12 years of age when he left for Shanghai and Beijing to attend westernized schools. Chiang was a student activist and was involved in a number of anti-Japanese and anti-government protest movements.

In 1925 Chiang was one of 340 students elected to attend the Sun Yat-sen University of Moscow. At that time, his father was already a leading figure in the Kuomintang (KMT) which formed the first united front with the Chinese Communist Party (CCP) against the warlords and foreign imperialist powers. His Moscow education was mostly the studies of revolutionary theories, Marxism-Leninism, and military science. He joined the Soviet Communist Youth League and later became a probationary member of the Soviet Communist Party.

During the course of the power struggle between Stalin and Trotsky, Chiang might have professed sympathy with the latter. He antagonized Wang Ming, then the CCP representative in Moscow. More importantly, due to his father's strong anti-Communist policy Chiang was sent to a Siberian mining factory in 1931 where he met and married his Russian wife in 1935. His classmates in the Sun Yat-sen University included Deng Xiaoping (Teng Hsiao-ping), Liao Cheng-chih, Ulanfu, and Lin Chu-han, all of whom later became prominent CCP leaders. Chiang lost his probationary party membership in 1936.

Early Political Career

In 1937, after spending 12 years in the former Soviet Union, Chiang returned to China. Stalin decided to release him because the KMT under his father's leadership had just agreed to a second united front with the CCP in order to fight against the Japanese aggression. Upon return, Chiang spent one year in Fenghua with his mother (who was later killed by a Japanese bomb) under the guidance of Hsu Dao-lin, a brilliant scholarly official and aide to Chiang Kai-shek.

Chiang's political career began in 1938 when he was appointed to head the county government in Kanhsien, Kiangsi Province, and simultaneously assumed the post of administrative inspector to supervise nearby counties. He used iron-handed methods to put together a series of administrative, economic, and social reforms. He established a political institute to train administrative cadres. One of his pupil-proteges in Kiangsi—General Wang Sheng—later became a prominent leader in Taiwan. Chiang formally became a KMT member in 1938 and was baptized as a Christian in 1943. From 1941 to 1947 he devoted himself to the work of the youth league organization, which was conceived as an institutional arm of the KMT to recruit and train young cadres. Through these efforts he established himself as an important factor in the KMT power structure.

The KMT-CCP war broke out in 1948. In the face of mounting inflation and financial chaos, Chiang was sent by his father to stabilize the situation in Shanghai. The efforts failed; and as the political situation of the nation worsened, many ranking KMT leaders either locked into a power struggle against Chiang Kai-shek or defected to the Communist side. In 1949 the KMT forces lost to the CCP, and Chiang's Nationalist government was compelled to seek exile on the island of Taiwan, also known as Formosa.

Upon arrival in Taiwan President Chiang Kai-shek was determined to build the island into a military stronghold for the purpose of counter-attack against the CCP regime on the mainland. The experiences of KMT defeat in China had taught Chiang Kai-shek many lessons. In the subsequent years he rebuilt the KMT party, re-established a network of intelligence and security forces, reformed the economy, implemented a policy of party control over the military, and re-organized the youth league as an entrenched mass organization of the KMT. He weeded out the disloyal and the incompetent; political loyalty became the most crucial criterion for holding important public offices. Chiang Ching-kuo was entrusted by his father to be a pivotal figure in all of these institution-rebuilding efforts. In the process, the young Chiang was able to establish his own power base.

In 1954 Chiang became a member of the KMT Central Committee, vice-secretary-general of the National Security Council, and minister without portfolio in the cabinet headed by General Chen Cheng, Chiang Kai-shek's right-hand man. In 1964 he assumed the powerful post of minister of defense and subsequently became the vice-premier in 1969. In 1972 he was appointed premier.

As premier, Chiang implemented two major programs of lasting importance. He initiated the appointments of native Taiwanese as governor of the Taiwan provincial government, the vice-premier, and cabinet ministers. During 1972 and 1973 he also undertook the construction of ten major economic projects, including a freeway, harbors, a nuclear power station, and a large ship yard, thus laying a solid foundation for Taiwan's further economic growth.

Party Chairman and President

In 1975 President Chiang Kai-shek died. As the political strong-man in Taiwan, Chiang Ching-kuo succeeded his father as KMT party chairman, and, following the presidency of C. K. Yen (who had been Chiang Kai-shek's vice-president and became his immediate successor upon his death), was elected in his own right to be president of the Republic of China in 1978. During his presidential terms, he once again initiated the appointments of native Taiwanese as vice-presidents. The appointment of Cornell-educated Li Teng-hui as vice-president in 1984 received wide acclaim and was said to have won universal approval from Washington's political circle.

But political challenges remained. He had to find ways to fend off Communist China's aggressive "re-unification" campaign and to survive the nation's growing diplomatic isolation. Domestically, he faced growing Taiwanese demands for more democracy and better protections for civil rights. As more aging KMT leaders of mainland origins faded away, political succession, regime legitimacy, and continuing economic growth underscored what needed to be done in Chiang's remaining years. He succeeded admirably in the tasks that faced him. He retained the authoritarian regime that he inherited, but maintained a reputation for benevolence which took him far. Throughout his administration he was able to pacify persistent demands of the Democratic Progressive Party to lift the martial law (imposed since 1949) without sacrifice to his personal popularity. As for the economy, by 1986 Taiwan had achieved a trade surplus of $12 billion. When Chiang Ching-kuo died of a heart attack early in January of 1988 it was reported in *The Economist* that "the opposition has lost its most effective supporter." Before Chang's passing he designated Lee Teng-hui to be the next president.

President Chiang's Russian wife remained with him in Taipei. They had four children. The only daughter, Hsiaochiang, married and lived in California. His eldest son Hsiao-wen was seriously ill and inactive. Hsiao-wu and Hsiao-yung, two other sons, held important posts in the party-run communication and industrial enterprises. The president's only brother, Wego, was also active and held several important military posts.

Further Reading

There is no English-language publication on Chiang. The most reliable Chinese publication is Chiang Nan, *Chiang Ching-kuo chuan* (A Biography of Chiang Ching-kuo) (1985).

Additional Sources

Newsweek, January 25, 1988.
The Economist, January 16, 1988.
Time, June 1, 1987; July 27, 1987.
Forbes, August 11, 1986. □

Chiang Kai-shek

Chiang Kai-shek (1887-1975) was a Chinese nationalist leader. For 2 decades he was head of state on the Chinese mainland, and after 1950 he served as president of the Republic of China on Taiwan.

Chiang Kai-shek was born in Ch'i-k'ou, Chekiang, on Oct. 30, 1887. His father, a salt merchant, died in 1896, leaving his third wife with the burden of Chiang's upbringing. In 1905 Chiang went to Ningpo to study and decided on a military career. In 1906 he went to Tokyo but failed to qualify for military training. Returning to China, he studied at the Paoting Military Academy, continuing his military education in Tokyo at the Shikan Gakko Military Academy.

Protégé of Ch'en Ch'i-mei

In Tokyo, fellow Chekiangese Ch'en Ch'i-mei sponsored Chiang's entry into Sun Yat-sen's revolutionary party, the T'ung-meng hui. When the revolution broke out in

Wuhan on Oct. 10, 1911, Chiang returned to Shanghai to fight under Ch'en. A series of triumphs by Ch'en and other revolutionists in the lower Yangtze Valley set the stage for the installation in Nanking of Sun Yat-sen as provisional president of the Chinese Republic.

Ch'en Ch'i-mei and Chiang also fought in the 1913 abortive "second revolution," but by the end of the year both were back in Japan. In 1914 Chiang traveled to Shanghai and Harbin to undertake missions for Sun Yat-sen. In mid-1915 Ch'en and Chiang returned to Shanghai, but on May 18, 1916, Ch'en was assassinated.

Rootless Revolutionary

In the fall of 1917 Sun Yat-sen moved to Canton, where he tried to establish a military base via an alliance with a local warlord, Ch'en Chiung-ming. Chiang was assigned to Ch'en's staff, but as a Chekiangese, Chiang was not readily accepted among Ch'en's Cantonese followers.

Between 1918 and 1920 little is known of Chiang's career. He and other followers of Sun engaged in financial speculation, and it was also at this time that Chiang established cordial relations with the "Green Gang," a secret society that wielded great power in the Shanghai underworld.

Military Organizer

By early 1922 differences in policy between Sun and Ch'en had reached the breaking point and Sun and Chiang had to seek refuge on a gunboat. But before long, fortune turned once again in Sun's favor, and by February 1923 he was back in Canton. On April 20 Chiang assumed duties as Sun's chief of staff. Sun by now had turned for support to the revolutionary regime in Moscow, and Chiang headed a delegation to seek military assistance in the former U.S.S.R. Returning in December 1923, he soon was given an opportunity to put his newfound knowledge to use. When Sun's Kuomintang (KMT), reorganized along Leninist lines, held its first party congress in January 1924, Chiang was appointed to the Military Council.

On May 3 Chiang became commandant of the Whampoa Military Academy. There, with Soviet advisers and arms, Chiang organized a military elite, the Whampoa Clique, bound to Chiang by ties of personal loyalty. There too, by virtue of the KMT's united front with the fledgling Chinese Communist party (CCP), Chou En-lai and other future Communist luminaries gained experience as political commissars.

After Sun Yat-sen died on March 12, 1925, Chiang won out in the ensuing power struggle. With support from the chief Soviet adviser, Borodin, Chiang made the most of these circumstances and established himself on a par with Wang Ching-wei, the leader of the KMT's "left" wing. That Chiang's commitment to his radical allies was a matter of power rather than principle became apparent in the Chungshan gunboat incident of March 1926, when Chiang jailed alleged Soviet and Chinese Communist conspirators and forced Wang Ching-wei to retire. He also purged high party posts of leading Communists, including the acting head of the propaganda department, Mao Tse-tung.

Having consolidated his political position, Chiang prepared to carry out Sun Yat-sen's dream of national reunification. On July, 9, 1926, he became supreme commander of the Northern Expeditionary Forces. Chiang's troops struck northward through Hunan and Hupei, captured key Wuhan cities, and moved eastward through Kiangsi and Fukien toward the rich provinces of the lower Yangtze. Shanghai was occupied on March 22, 1927, Nanking on March 24. In less than a year Chiang had brought the wealthy and populous provinces of southern, central, and eastern China under Nationalist control.

However, success was complicated by new problems. A widening split had developed within the ranks of the expeditionary armies. On April 12, 1927, Chiang moved, swiftly and brutally, against Communists and Communist suspects in Shanghai, especially in the labor movement. This initiated a "party purification" movement that swiftly spread through other provinces controlled by Chiang or antipathetic to the Communists. On April 18 Chiang proclaimed a national government at Nanking in rivalry with the "left KMT" regime allied with Borodin and the CCP at Wuhan. Two months later Chiang precipitated the collapse of the Wuhan coalition with the cooperation of the powerful warlord Feng Yü-hsiang.

However, Chiang was unable to untangle the remaining political and military rivalries. He thereupon resigned his command and on Sept. 29, 1927, sailed for Japan to arrange his marriage to Soong Mei-ling. Chiang's bride was a member of a leading Christian family of Shanghai, and one of her sisters, Soong Ch'ing-ling, was the widow of Sun Yat-sen. As a condition of the marriage, Chiang agreed to study Christianity; he eventually became a devout Methodist.

Chiang's brief retirement proved politically useful, for his participation had become absolutely essential to the new regime. Having resumed command, Chiang launched the second stage of the Northern Expedition. Peking fell in June 1928, but since Chiang's power still rested in the lower Yangtze Valley, Nanking became the national capital while Peking ("Northern Capital") was renamed Peiping ("Northern Peace").

"Peacetime" Leader

The decade from 1928 to 1937 was peaceful only in comparison to what preceded it and what followed. Not a year passed without bloodletting among militarists, Nationalists, Communists, and Japanese invaders. For the Nationalist government these were, nonetheless, years of promise and accomplishment, and Chiang built up a formidable political and military machine. German advisers and arsenals helped build a modern army, which finally ousted the Communists from their principal base in Kiangsi and forced their decimated legions to flee to the distant northwestern periphery of China's heartland.

These were also years of promising developments in the urban sector of the country, especially in the lower Yangtze Valley and, until Sept. 18, 1931, Manchuria. With their emphasis on modern, urban development, the Nationalists secured the cooperation of many talented, foreign-educated intellectuals, and higher education flourished. At the same time Chiang initiated a "New Life Movement," seeking to infuse China's millions with enthusiasm for Confucian values revitalized with the spirit of puritanical Protestantism and military discipline. However, neither this nor the ideology of Sun Yat-sen provided an attractive alternative to Marxism. Moreover, two unresolved problems, the deterioration of rural China and the thrust of Japanese aggression, provided opportunities for the Communists.

Chiang, nonetheless, emerged from his first decade in power as the strong man of China. His good luck held when he needed it most. The Japanese, preoccupied with their conquests in Manchuria and adjacent areas of North China, slowed down the pace of aggression and appeared willing to come to an understanding. Chiang therefore concentrated on fighting the Communists and very often was able to capitalize upon the miscalculations of his rivals. Kidnapped at Sian on Dec. 12, 1936, by the Manchurian warlord Chang Hsüeh-liang, Chiang was forced to accede to Chang's demands that he join the Communists in a united front against Japan. But a fortnight later Chiang returned to Nanking a national hero.

Wartime Commander

During the first year of the Second Sino-Japanese War (1937-1945) Chiang's popularity soared. From August to December 1937 his German-trained armies fought a magnificent holding action around Shanghai and Nanking, allowing the government to withdraw briefly to Wuhan and, by the end of 1938, to Chungking. Proud and stubborn, Chiang symbolized China's dogged resistance against the Japanese juggernaut. His supremacy was confirmed in March 1938, when he assumed the title of *Tsung-tsai* (Party Leader)—successor to the *Tsung-li* (Party Director), Sun Yat-sen.

By 1941, however, the wartime élan was beginning to crumble. Inflation was sapping the country's economic and moral reserves, and the break with the CCP was almost complete. By the time the United States entered the war in December, war-weary Chinese were becoming disillusioned and cynical. The American alliance proved disappointing. Through the good offices of Roosevelt, Chiang was able to join the Great Powers in world diplomatic councils, but he received little respect from Churchill and Stalin. Chiang welcomed the efforts of Maj. Gen. Claire Chennault, whose Flying Tigers (the 14th Air Force) operated from Chinese bases, but Lt. Gen. Joseph Stilwell, the acerbic American chief of staff for the China-Burma-India theater, was a thorn in his side. When Chiang secured Stilwell's dismissal in October 1944, he could take but bleak satisfaction, for the last Japanese offensive of the war was cutting China in two and, in fact, validating Stilwell's criticisms. Even *China's Destiny,* Chiang's wartime political-historical treatise, was coldly received by Americans for its rejection of Western-style liberalism and democracy and its harsh condemnation of the unequal treaties.

Defeat in Victory

By V-J Day, unresolved prewar problems exacerbated by wartime conditions had weakened Chiang's government and allowed Mao Tse-tung to expand control over a population of some 100 million Chinese. The Marshall mission, sent by President Truman on Oct. 27, 1945, to mediate between the two sides, failed to prevent the outbreak of civil war. Overconfident at the outset, Chiang committed serious blunders on the battlefield.

Chiang was also under pressure from political rivals at home and American critics abroad, who urged him to democratize his government. On Jan. 1, 1947, a new constitution was promulgated. An elected National Assembly chose Chiang as president, though the Kwangsi general Li Tsung-jen won the vice presidency over candidates more to Chiang's liking. But the pomp and ceremony in Nanking occurred against a backdrop of disaster, because by 1948 the tide of battle had turned against the Nationalists. Mukden fell on Nov. 1, 1948, followed 2 months later by Peiping. On Jan. 21, 1949, Chiang retired from the presidency, leaving Li Tsung-jen with the thankless job of trying to salvage something from a situation beyond repair. Unable to build a bastion of resistance in southern or southwestern China, Chiang retired to Taiwan on Dec. 10, 1949.

Island Exile

Many of the goals that eluded Chiang on the vast mainland came within reach on the island of Taiwan (Formosa). There he gained unchallenged and virtually unlimited power. The National Assembly, under emergency law, reelected him to the presidency. His elder son, Chiang Ching-kuo, was groomed as his successor. Dissenters were jailed under martial law. The rugged central mountain range was free of rebel bands, and alliance with the United States protected the island from invasion. After 1954 the island enjoyed a spectacular economic boom, making its standard of living second only to Japan's among the nations of Asia.

Although, Taiwan, the largest of all islands which comprise the Republic of China, had many perquisites of independent nationhood, Chiang Kai-shek was not a man to surrender his youthful dreams. His diplomats tenaciously held on to the "China" seats in the United Nations, because Chiang saw Taiwan not as a nation but as a model province, where the teachings of Sun Yat-sen were being tested in preparation for the recapture of the mainland. But in 1972 representatives of Communist China replaced those of Nationalist China at the United Nations, the same year Taiwan's National Assembly elected Chiang Kai-Shek to a fifth six-year presidential term.

The year 1972 also proved to be pivotal for Chiang Kai-shek and Taiwan because United States President Richard Nixon visited the People's Republic of China. President Nixon also agreed that Taiwan was a part of China. These diplomatic setbacks, mixed with a long bout of pneumonia, had many questioning Chiang Kai-shek's ability to lead the country. His son, Chiang Ching-kuo, who was appointed premier in May, assumed most of Chiang Kai-shek's duties. For the last three years of his life, Chiang Kai-shek was the ceremonial leader of the Republic of China, but his son was the practical leader. Chiang Kai-shek suffered a fatal heart attack and died on April 5, 1975.

Further Reading

Chiang's two major books are available in English translation. *China's Destiny* (1943) was published in both authorized and unauthorized translations in 1947. The latter, edited with notes and commentary by Philip Jaffe, also includes Chiang's essay "Chinese Economic Theory." In *Soviet Russia in China: A Summing Up at Seventy* (1957; rev. abr. ed. 1965) Chiang interprets his country's experience with communism from 1924 to 1949 and discusses problems of anti-Communist strategy. Also useful are Mayling Soong Chiang, *Sian: A Coup d'Etat* (1937), in which Chiang and his wife present their account of the Sian incident, and *The Collected Wartime Messages of Generalissimo Chiang Kai-shek, 1937-1945* (2 vols., 1946).

Biographies of Chiang Kai-Shek include Brian Crozier *The Man Who Lost China: The First Full Biography of Chiang Kai-shek,* Scribner, 1976; and Owen Lattimore, *China Memoirs,* Columbia University Press, 1991. His second wife also wrote of his life, Chen Chieh-ju, *Chiang Kai-shek's Secret Past: The Memoir of His Second Wife, Chen Chieh-ju,* Westview Press, 1993.

Among the books that treat Chiang in his historical setting are Paul M. A. Linebarger, *The China of Chiang K'ai-shek: A Political Study* (1941), which is sympathetic to Chiang, and Theodore H. White and Annalee Jacoby, *Thunder Out of China* (1946), which is not. Ch'ien Tuan-sheng, *The Government and Politics of China* (1950), provides a good description of political institutions under Chiang's leadership. Tang Tsou, *America's Failure in China, 1941-1950* (1963), perceptively analyzes Chiang's relationship with his principal ally during the period of war and civil war. □

Roberto Chiari

Roberto Chiari (1905–1981) president of Panama (1960-1964), negotiated with two U.S. presidents in a futile effort to settle peacefully problems of the Canal Zone.

Roberto Chiari was born in 1905, a member of a well-known Panamanian family. His father, Rudolfo, was Panama's president from 1924 to 1928. But two years later the depression (which devasted the American economy) also wracked Panama, and Chiari had to go to work as a crew member aboard a ferry belonging to the Panama Canal Company. His job was that of a wiper in the engine room.

Such a job was quite a come-down for this proud young man who had gone to LaSalle School in Panama City and had served his father as an aide. The 1930s were tough times in Panama as well as elsewhere. But during World War II the Chiari family turned things around, and by the end of the decade its sugar plantations were prospering. In the late 1940s, a time of political turbulence in the country, his father served briefly as president but was tossed out after only five days in office. On October 1, 1960, he was inaugurated chief executive again.

In November 1959 serious disturbances over Panama's status in the Canal Zone had strained U.S.-Panamanian relations. The issue was symbolized by Panama's determination to fly its national flag over Zone territory to demonstrate that the ten-mile-wide strip was Panamanian soil. After the 1959 riots President Dwight D. Eisenhower announced that both the U.S. and Panamanian banners could fly in a small triangle at the Zone entrance, but Panamanians insisted that their flag should be raised in other places in the Zone.

Chiari began a program of limited social reform aimed at convincing Panama's rapidly expanding poorer classes that he cared about their situation. He gave his salary to the Red Cross. He improved public health services and pushed low-cost housing, though as a member of the elite he was slow to promote substantial reforms. In international affairs he was strongly anti-communist and pro-United States. However, he chided the United States for spending so much on neutral countries while neglecting its friends. When the "flag issue" came up again, he naturally sided with his country's citizens and further criticized the American government for its employment policies that, he argued, discriminated against Panamanians.

Pressed by the lower classes to move faster on social issues, Chiari began to press harder on the "flag issue." He went to Washington to discuss the matter with President John F. Kennedy. The two presidents created a joint commission to study the problem. The commission settled a few labor disputes in the Zone. Then it declared that Panama's flag would fly alongside the American flag at civilian buildings in the Zone. Americans in the Zone condemned this

decision. Angered, Chiari removed Panamanians from the commission.

As tensions mounted in late 1963 the Canal Zone governor ordered that neither flag fly over civilian institutions. This predictably angered the Americans, and on January 9 a group of students at Balboa (Canal Zone) High School defiantly raised the American flag. When Panamanian students heard about this, about 200 came into the Zone and tried to raise their flag alongside the American banner. The Americans stopped them and in retreat the Panamanians began trashing garbage cans. When news of the incident reached Panama City, 30,000 Panamanians rushed into the streets. The ensuing riot lasted for four days and spread to Colón and into interior cities. It took four American and 24 Panamanian lives and destroyed two million dollars in property before it ended.

Roberto's reaction surprised the Lyndon Johnson administration in Washington. Chiari suspended diplomatic relations on the grounds that American troops had committed aggression against Panama. He publicly challenged President Johnson to negotiate outstanding issues between Panama and the United States but privately assured the irritated American president that he would not demand revision of the hated canal treaty. Panamanians were afraid that the United States might construct another canal elsewhere.

Later in 1964 Chiari backed his cousin, Marco Robles, for president. Robles won a narrow victory over several-time candidate Arnulfo Arias and began serious negotiation for revision of the canal treaty (but it would take another 13 years to make an agreement). Roberto Chiari died in 1981.

Further Reading

For more on Roberto Francisco Chiari see John and Mavis Biesanz, *The People of Panama* (1955) and Walter LaFeber, *The Panama Canal* (1978). Chiari's obituary can be found in *The Annual Obituary,* St. James Press, 1981. □

Chia Ssu-tao

Chia Ssu-tao (1213-1275) was a Chinese statesman who served as chief minister in the closing years of the Sung dynasty and inaugurated a program of radical agrarian reform.

Chia Ssu-tao was born on Aug. 23, 1213, into a military family originally from T'ai-chou in Chekiang Province. Because of his father's distinguished service against the Chin, Ssu-tao was privileged to enter the bureaucracy, and he began his career as a granary superintendent in 1231. The influence of his elder sister, who became an imperial concubine in 1231, may have helped his career initially, but it was only after her death in 1247 that he received his most important posts. After a number of appointments involving financial and military affairs in the capital and in the provinces, Chia became an assistant state councilor in 1256 and right grand councilor in 1259. As right grand councilor, he dominated the government from 1259 until 1275, serving after 1267 concurrently as commander of all Sung forces.

Land Reform

The agrarian reform Chia initiated in 1263 went much further than earlier attempts. Limitations were enacted on the size of land holdings and one-third of the land held over the limit was purchased by the state, which affected payment in a combination of money, patents of office, and tax exemptions according to a formula which favored large landowners. The income from the resulting government estates went to pay for the expenses of the army, replacing the previous system of forced sale of grain to the state. At first applied only to land held by officials, the program was later extended to all land. In 1274 Chia undertook a further radical step when he made the landholdings of Buddhist and Taoist monasteries subject to taxation.

Chia's program earned him powerful enemies, and one critic charged that he intended "to subdue the mighty and impoverish the rich." His enemies also charged him with incompetence in foreign policy, accusing him of attempts to negotiate a secret peace treaty with the Mongols in 1259 to provide for the surrender of territories north of the Yangtze River and the payment of tribute. And they maintained that he misinformed the court about the military situation. These charges were, at best, exaggerated but contributed to the later image of Chia as a "bad last minister," responsible for the fall of the dynasty, a view propounded by Chinese historians and perpetuated, in embellished form, in literature and on the stage.

In his personal life Chia is portrayed by various sources as a sophisticated hedonist fully enjoying worldly pleasures, a connoisseur and collector of art and calligraphy, and an enthusiast for cricket fighting, on which he wrote a systematic treatise.

Chia's land program was rescinded 4 days after he lost office in disgrace after a disastrous defeat by the Mongols. He was banished but was murdered on the way to his place of banishment on Oct. 9, 1275.

Further Reading

The only study of Chia in English is Herbert Franke's excellent chapter "Chia Ssu-Tao (1213-1275): A 'Bad Last Minister'?" in Arthur F. Wright and Denis Twitchett, eds., *Confucian Personalities* (1962). See also Wolfram Eberhard, *A History of China* (1950; 3d ed. 1969). □

Judy Chicago

Judy Chicago (born 1939) was an American artist and activist best known for large-scale collaborative installation artworks—*The Dinner Party* and *The Birth Project*—both based on feminist themes and *The Holocaust Project*—based on the atrocities committed by the Nazi Party during World War II.

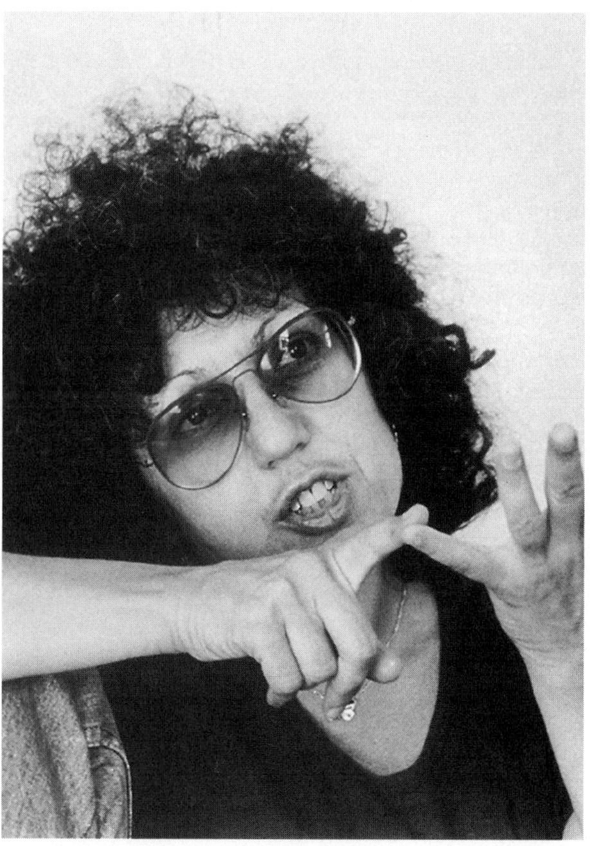

Judy Chicago was born Judith Cohen in Chicago, July 20, 1939. She assumed the surname of her hometown in 1969 to assert her independence from the patrilineal convention which gives a woman the surname of a father or husband. The daughter of political activists, her father was a union organizer, and her mother was a professional in a time when women working outside of the home were rare. Chicago studied at the Art Institute of California and later at the University of California at Los Angeles. Married three times, the artist lived and worked in Benicia, California.

Judy Chicago first gained recognition in the 1960s as Judith Gerowitz and did large, highly crafted sculptures of simple geometric forms that could be termed "minimalist." Eschewing the more traditional sculptural media of bronze and stone, Chicago worked in a variety of materials: painting on porcelain, airbrush painting on automobile hoods, and using fireworks to make drawings in the air. From the early 1970s her work focused on feminist themes, often using the motif of a flower or butterfly to symbolize a woman's sexuality and incorporating conversational language written directly on the artwork. Her work was always noted for its high level of technical finish. In addition to her artwork, Chicago taught college art classes, established the first feminist art programs and galleries, and very notably started *Womenspace,* an all-female art collective.

Controversy at the Dinner Party

Chicago is best known for three ambitious projects—*The Dinner Party,* completed in 1979, *The Birth Project,* completed in 1985, and *The Holocaust Project,* completed in 1993. The first two works summarized her stance as a feminist artist and her conviction that women have been left out of the telling of history. These projects were collaborations in which Chicago worked with teams of women artists and craftspeople in materials traditionally associated with women: quilting, needlework, china painting, and tapestry.

The *Dinner Party* took two years of work with a crew of 400 people. It was a three-sided table forming a triangle along which were 39 place settings with plate, goblet, and embroidered cloth. Each setting symbolized an illustrious woman from history or mythology ranging from a primordial goddess to the American painter Georgia O'Keefe. On the floor inside the triangular table were the names of 999 more women. Each place setting contained symbols of the woman, often derived from a flower-motif suggesting a vagina. The artwork opened at the San Francisco Museum of Art in 1979 and toured the United States, also being shown at the Brooklyn Museum. *The Dinner Party* met controversy and mixed critical response wherever it went, being variously described as visionary and Utopian or as obscene and overly didactic. Several museums withdrew offers to show the work in spite of record attendance rates, and Chicago drew criticism for perceived careerism and exploitation of her numerous volunteers.

Explorations into Birth and Death

Chicago's next major work was *The Birth Project.* Intended to celebrate the act of giving birth, which she observed is rarely treated in Western art while being common in the art of other cultures, it also drew controversy from male-based mainstream culture. Unlike *The Dinner Party,* this project was two-dimensional and consisted of approximately 100 needlework designs that summarized the birthing process as culled from interviews she conducted with women from around the country regarding their experiences giving birth. Chicago made this artwork, like *The Dinner Party,* a collaboration that challenged the idea of the artist as an isolated, individual creator. Begun in 1982, the needlework designs were executed by women from the United States, Canada, and New Zealand.

Chicago has also produced, with her third husband, Donald Woodman, a project confronting the horror of Nazi inflicted genocide during World War II. *The Holocaust Project* is described by Chicago as being her personal record of trying to understand this awful epoch of recent history. A multimedia piece consisting of painting, photography, needlework, silk-screen, tapestry, and stained glass, Chicago and Woodman spent over two years researching and visiting key sites of the Holocaust in Europe. 1993 saw the completion of this ambitious and rather uncomfortable project.

Late Nineties, Continued Shock

Into the nineties Chicago still incited controversy and outrage with her works. A 1990 attempt to find a permanent home for *The Dinner Party* at the University of the District of Columbia, was thwarted when she encountered much of the same opposition as before. A later exhibition in 1996 of *The Dinner Party* at the Armand Hammer Museum of Art at UCLA drew further criticism. As David Joselit wrote in *Art in America,* "ongoing theoretical and artistic disputes, not to mention the hostility of mainstream critics to an openly feminist project, conspired to engulf (the exhibition) in an often mean-spirited buzz of disapproval."

Despite the controversy surrounding them, these projects were immensely popular, but usually with audiences that do not regularly follow the arts. This populist appeal coincided with a general resurgence of feminist activity in the 1970s. Chicago's work was part of the movement within art circles to open up opportunities for women artists and to reinstate prominent artists such as Angelica Kauffman (1741-1807) and Artemesia Gentileschi (1590-1642) who had been written out of art history. In addition, museums organized retrospective exhibitions for contemporary artists Alice Neel and Louise Bourgeois.

Beyond the feminist aspects of Chicago's work, it also ran parallel with several aesthetic tendencies of the visual art of the 1960s. Artists in general were experimenting with all kinds of materials, challenging the conventional expectations of a work of art. Artists such as Claes Oldenburg and Robert Morris began to work with fabric and cloth. Sculpture could be soft, amorphous, and impermanent. Chicago's projects were collaborative and involved hundreds of people, like the wrapping projects of artist Christo, and went against the prevailing myth of the artist as an alienated loner. Judy Chicago's work called into question distinctions between high art (painting and sculpture) and crafts, between art made for its own sake and engaged activist art in the service of political ideas. It generated a great deal of critical discussion, and she had both ardent admirers and strident detractors.

Further Reading

Chicago wrote an autobiography, *Through the Flower, My Struggles as a Woman Artist* (1982), which chronicled her emergence as an artist and her involvement with the women's movement in the early 1970s. A sequel, *Beyond the Flower* was later written (1996). She had a retrospective exhibition in 1984 at the ACA galleries in New York accompanied by a catalog, *Judy Chicago, the Second Decade* (1984), which is the most complete record of her work up to that point. Chicago has also published books detailing her more recent works including *The Birth Project* (1985) and *The Holocaust Project: From Darkness into Light* (1993). Her joint exhibition with other female artists such as Yoko Ono and Mary Kelly is documented in *Sexual Politics: Judy Chicago's Dinner Party in Feminist Art History* (1996). Articles about *The Dinner Party* appeared in *Newsweek Magazine* (April 2, 1979), *Ms.* (June 1, 1979), and *Art in America* (April 1980). *Newsweek* also carried an article about *The Birth Project* (October 31, 1983), as did *Art in America* (November 1984). Later articles include pieces in *The New Statesman and Society* (March 25, 1994), *New York Times Book Review* (March 24, 1996), and *Art in America* (January 1997). A profile of Chicago is included in Eleanor Munro's *Originals: American Women Artists* (1979). For more information about women artists in history, see Anne Sutherland Harris' *Women Artists 1550-1950* (1976). □

Georgi Vasilyevich Chicherin

The Soviet statesman Georgi Vasilyevich Chicherin (1872-1936) guided Soviet foreign policy in the years following the foundation of the U.S.S.R.

Born in Tambov Oblast in 1872, Georgi Chicherin was a member of the Russian aristocracy—an unlikely background for a future Bolshevik. After graduating from the University of St. Petersburg, he trained for and later joined the foreign service. During the Revolution of 1905, however, he became involved in the socialist movement, and in 1907 he left Russia. He spent the next decade abroad, mainly in England, where he agitated against World War I. The Russian Revolution of 1917 converted him to bolshevism, and the British jailed him as a "hostile alien" but allowed him to return to Russia early in 1918.

As the only Bolshevik with formal diplomatic training and experience, Chicherin was assigned the post of people's commissar of foreign affairs, succeeding Leon Trotsky. He was strongly in favor of establishing friendly relations with other countries, most importantly Germany, in order to enhance the stability of the Soviet regime. After the failure of the Soviet march on Warsaw in 1920 and the initiation of Lenin's New Economic Policy in 1921, Chicherin was able to pursue his policy of strong ties with Germany and advantageous ties elsewhere.

Chicherin's crowning achievement was the Treaty of Rapallo (1922), in which the pariah nations of the Soviet Union and Germany ratified mutually advantageous diplomatic, economic, and military agreements. Chicherin secured diplomatic recognition of the Soviet Union from every major world power except the United States, and he was also successful in normalizing his country's relations with its Moslem neighbors, especially Turkey. He was not able, nor did he seek, to establish comprehensive ties, such as those with Germany, with other foreign powers; in fact, Soviet relations with many nations, notably England, remained very shaky. Chicherin's policies, however, did give the Soviet regime a needed degree of stability in international affairs and thus facilitated development of the New Economic Policy.

Chicherin avoided involvement in the intraparty dispute of the 1920s, but this conflict made his work at the Foreign Office difficult. Moreover, his failing health caused him to give greater power to his deputy Maxim Litvinov, and by the late 1920s Litvinov was in effect the director of Soviet foreign policy. Chicherin formally retired as commissar of foreign affairs in 1930 and spent the next years in semiseclusion. He died on July 7, 1936.

Further Reading

A highly sympathetic sketch of Chicherin is in Louis Fischer, *Men and Politics: Europe between the Two World Wars* (1966). Chicherin's tenure as commissar of foreign affairs receives considerable analysis in Fischer's *The Soviets in World Affairs . . . 1917-1929* (2 vols., 1930; 2d ed. 1951). Some of Chicherin's defenses of early Soviet foreign policy are in his own *Two Years of Foreign Policy* (1920; trans. 1920).

Additional Sources

O'Connor, Timothy Edward, *Diplomacy and revolution: G.V. Chicherin and Soviet foreign affairs, 1918-1930,* Ames: Iowa State University Press, 1988. □

Gaositwe Keagakwa Tibe Chiepe

Intellectual, educator, diplomat, politician, and cabinet minister of external affairs of Botswana, Gaositwe Keagakwa Tibe Chiepe (born 1926) was instrumental in the formulation of the Botswana educational system and represented Botswana as high commissioner and ambassador extraordinary and plenipotentiary to many European countries. Chiepe began serving as a cabinet minister of the ruling Botswana Democratic Party in 1974.

Gaositwe K. T. Chiepe was born in Serowe, daughter of T. and S. T. Chiepe (nee Sebina). She went to primary school in Serowe and then proceeded to Tigerkloof, South Africa, for secondary education, after which she went to the University of Fort Hare, where she obtained a Bachelor of Science degree and postgraduate Diploma in Education. She later went to the University of Bristol, England, for a Master's degree (1958). Her thesis for that degree was entitled "An Investigation of the Problems of Popular Education in the Bechuanaland Protectorate in the Light of Comparative Study of Similar Problems in the Early Stages of English Education and in the Development of Education in Yugoslavia and Uganda." She also held honorary doctorate degrees from the Universities of Bristol and DePaul. She was awarded national honors by both Great Britain and Botswana and was named Chief Councillor of the Royal Order of King Sobhuza II (Swaziland). She was a member of Parliament (M.P.) for Serowe South, Central District of Botswana.

G. K. T. Chiepe was the first woman education officer of Botswana. She served as assistant from 1948 to 1953; education officer from 1948 to 1953; education officer (with administration and inspectorate duties) from 1953 to 1962; senior education officer from 1962 to 1965; deputy director of education from 1965 to 1967; and director of education from 1968 to 1970. She was national deputy commander of Girl Guides in 1953, 1957, and 1963; chairman, Botswana Branch, Commonwealth Parliamentary Association (CPA), 1981; and chairman of the Africa Region of the CPA, 1981-1983.

Chiepe was the first woman to be appointed a cabinet minister. She was minister of external affairs, 1984-1995, after being previously cabinet minister of mineral resources and water affairs, 1977 to 1984, and minister of commerce and industry, 1974-1977. She had also been Botswana's high commissioner to the United Kingdom and Nigeria and ambassador extraordinary and plenipotentiary to France, Germany, Denmark, Norway, Sweden, and Belgium and to the European Economic Community (EEC). She actively participated in negotiations with EEC for Lome I, Lome II, and Lome IV and was chairman of the OAU (Organization of African Unity) council of ministers.

Chiepe traveled widely in southern Africa, Europe, the United Kingdom, the United States, Canada, China, the Caribbean, Asia, Australia, New Zealand, Japan, and the Pacific Islands. She was a fellow of the Royal Society of Arts (1973), honorary president of the Kalahari Conservation Society (1982), and patron, Forestry Association of Botswana (1984).

Further Reading

For additional information on G. K. T. Chiepe, see F. Morton, A. Murray, and J. Ramsay, *Who Is Who in Botswana* (1989); E. Kay, *Who Is Who in Southern Africa* (Gaborone, Botswana: 1987); *The International Who Is Who 1987-1988,* 51st edition (London); T. Tlou and A. Campbell, *History of Botswana* (Gaborone: 1984); and F. Morton and J. Ramsay, *The Birth of Botswana* (Botswana: 1987). □

Joseph Benedict Chifley

Joseph Benedict Chifley (1885-1951), prime minister of Australia, was one of the ablest and most successful leaders of the Australian Labour party.

Joseph Benedict Chifley was born of Irish-Australian parentage at Bathurst, New South Wales, on Sept. 22, 1885. He lived and worked on his grandfather's farm until he was 13 and then attended the Patrician Brothers' School at Bathurst for 2 years. In 1903 he joined the New South Wales Railways as a shop boy, rising to be the youngest first-class locomotive driver in the service.

Tall, rangy, and a convinced labor man, Chifley soon became an active spokesman for his union. During the 1917 railway and general strike he was discharged but reinstated on appeal. In 1920 he confounded the Australian Federated Union of Locomotive Enginemen. Well known as a union official, advocate, and expert witness before arbitration authorities, he won, in 1928, the federal seat of Macquarie in Parliament and was reelected in 1929 in a Labour landslide. Two years later Chifley became minister for defense and assistant to the federal treasurer in the Labour government of James Scullin.

Internecine party dissension and the political impact of the Great Depression led in December 1931 to Chifley's loss of his seat in the House of Representatives, and he did not return until 1940. During his absence from federal government Chifley was active in local government and prominent in the politics of divided Labour, which maintained a branch of the Federal party in opposition to the New South Wales State Labour group of Premier J. T. Lang. In 1936 Chifley was appointed member of the Royal Commission on Banking and Monetary Reform, and when World War II began, his recognized capacity, integrity, and experience made him a valuable director of labor regulation and supply in the Department of Munitions.

By 1941 Chifley was treasurer in the wartime government of John Curtin and a member of the War Cabinet. The following year he took over the additional portfolio of postwar reconstruction. He made such an effective mark that, after Curtin's death in 1945, he succeeded to the leadership of the party and the position of prime minister. He retained the Treasury post, having gained a reputation for financial judgment and high administrative ability.

After Labour's postwar victory in the general election of 1946, Chifley moved to expand the foundations of an Australian welfare state. Despite much positive legislation in this direction, his attempts to introduce a free medicine scheme, as in Britain and New Zealand, were frustrated by the opposition of the medical profession. At the same time his campaign to nationalize the banks came to legal and political grief. His government was defeated in December 1949, though Labour controlled the Senate until 1951. Chifley remained leader of the opposition until his death from a heart attack in Canberra on June 13, 1951.

Further Reading

A full-length study of Chifley is L. F. Crisp, *Ben Chifley.* General works which discuss Chifley are S. Encel, *Cabinet Government in Australia* (1962); Donald W. Rawson, *Labor in Vain? A Survey of the Australian Labor Party* (1966); Fred Alexander, *Australia since Federation: A Narrative and Critical Analysis* (1967); and Alan George Lewers Shaw and H. D. Nicolson, *Australia in the Twentieth Century: An Introduction to Modern Society* (1967). □

Chih-i

The Chinese Buddhist monk Chih-i (538-597) founded one of the most popular schools of Chinese Buddhism, the T'ien-t'ai.

Chih-i, also known as Chih-k'ai, was born Ch'en Wang-tao in South China in 538. He grew up in a chaotic period, during which North China was ruled by invaders from the northern steppes, while the Chinese held out in the south. Chih-i's father was an adviser to the Emperor of the Liang dynasty (502-557). When Chih-i's mother and father died about the time the dynasty was overthrown in 557, he became a Buddhist monk in his home province.

After several years in the South, Chih-i went north to study with Hui-ssu, a famous Buddhist monk. There he encountered a religious tradition which, unlike the scholarly approach of southern Buddhism, encouraged religious observances. He remained in the North until 568, at which time his teacher instructed him to return to the southern capital to gain imperial support for the religion.

Chih-i was not in the southern capital very long before his lectures began to attract notice, even coming to the attention of the court. He also gained increasing numbers of students. Perhaps because he received too much notice in the bustling capital, he decided to leave for the solitude of the T'ien-t'ai Mountains in southeast China, where he lived with a small group of close disciples.

Supported by wealthy and pious laymen, Chih-i remained in the T'ien-t'ai Mountains from 575 to 585. Because he produced his most important doctrines and works during that period, his school of Buddhism is known as the T'ien-t'ai sect. It was the first great synthesis in Buddhism of doctrine as well as scripture and method. One of the significant and central concepts of his school was a belief in the universal attainability of enlightenment. This belief opposed the view of other Buddhist schools that enlightenment was something very few believers could obtain even after a lifetime of religious devotion. The T'ien-t'ai sect gained a large following in China and Japan.

In 585 Chih-i was prevailed upon to return to the capital and was received with enthusiasm. Only 4 years after his return, the southern state was overrun by the Sui armies. In spite of this change, however, Chih-i was able to maintain a close relationship with the Sui. The Sui prince,

Yang Kuang, wanting to show his support for Buddhism, asked Chih-i to remain in Yang-chou, the Sui southern capital, but he soon returned to the seclusion of the T'ien-t'ai Mountains. Chih-i died while on another trip to the capital in 597.

Further Reading

The most complete discussion of the life and works of Chih-i can be found in Leon Hurvitz, *Chih-i (538-597): An Introduction to the Life and Ideas of a Chinese Buddhist Monk* (1963). A shorter piece which puts Chih-i in the context of his times may be found in Stanley Weinstein, "T'ang Imperial Patronage in the Formation of T'ang Buddhism," included in *Perspectives on the T'ang,* edited by Arthur F. Wright and Denis *Twitchett* (1972). □

Julia McWilliams Child

Chef, author, and television personality, Julia McWilliams Child (born 1912) probably did more for French-style food preparation than any other gourmet in history.

Julia Child was born to a well-to-do family in Pasadena, California, on August 15, 1912. Her parents, John and Julia McWilliams, raised Julia, her sister, and her brother in comfort; the family had servants, including a cook, and the children were sent to private schools. The children, all of whom were unusually tall, loved outdoor sports. In 1930 Julia went to Smith College in Massachusetts, where she majored in history. After graduation she took a job as a copywriter for a furniture company in New York City and enjoyed an active social life.

At the outbreak of World War II she joined the Office of Strategic Services, predecessor to the Central Intelligence Agency, seeking adventure in exotic locales. After a stint in Washington she was sent abroad as she had wished, but she worked as a file clerk, not as a spy, and her experience was distinctly unglamorous—she traveled on troop ships, slept on cots, and wore army fatigues. While in Ceylon (now Sri Lanka) in 1943 she met Paul Cushing Child, a member of a distinguished Boston family. Although his particular branch of the family was not rich, he had traveled widely, pursued several careers, and, at 41, was a sophisticated artist working as a cartographer and as the designer of Lord Mountbatten's headquarters. Although she was ten years younger and several inches taller, the two were immediately attracted to each other. He admired her unaffected manner, and she found his affectionate nature and cosmopolitan outlook irresistible. The romance bloomed when both were assigned to China, and it was while there that Child, a noted gourmet, introduced her to cooking.

Although they were in love, Julia and Paul were reluctant to commit to a permanent relationship during wartime. After the war she returned to California, where her conservative Republican father was unenthusiastic about her new beau, who was artistic and a Democrat. She was undeterred, however, and she began to study cooking at a school in Beverly Hills. On September 1, 1946, Julia and Paul were married, and the couple moved to Washington, D.C., where he had taken a position with the Foreign Service.

In 1948 her husband was posted to Paris. Child quickly came to appreciate the French way of life, especially French food. She decided she wanted to learn the intricacies of French cooking and, after studying French at the Berlitz School, enrolled at the famous Cordon Bleu. She made many friends who also were interested in French cuisine, and with two of these, Simone Beck and Louisette Bertholle, she formed a cooking school called L'Ecole des Trois Gourmandes (School of the Three Gourmets).

With Simone Beck, Child began working on a cookbook based on their cooking school experiences, and she continued her writing while she followed her husband on several postings throughout Europe. He retired in 1961, and the Childs settled in a large house with a well-equipped kitchen in Cambridge, Massachusetts.

The year 1961 was a landmark year for the Childs. In addition to her husband's retirement and a major move, Child's book, *Mastering the Art of French Cooking,* was published. The book, noted for the clarity and completeness of its instructions, its attention to detail and explanation, and its many useful photographs, was an immediate critical and popular success. Child was hailed as an expert and her views and advice were much sought after. She began writing articles on cooking for *House and Garden* and *House*

Beautiful and also had a regular cooking column in the *Boston Globe.*

In 1963, after an enjoyable appearance on a television panel show in Boston, Child expanded her efforts in television with a weekly 30-minute cooking program, "The French Chef." This proved even more successful than her book: with her admittedly eccentric style, good humor, knowledge, and teaching flair, she became a popular cult figure. Her work was recognized with a Peabody Award in 1965 and an Emmy Award in 1966.

The French Chef Cookbook, a cookbook based on the television series, was published in 1968. Additional television shows, notably "Julia Child and Company" (1978-1979), "Julia Child and More Company" (1980), and "Dinner at Julia's" (1983), were accompanied by well-received cookbooks, and in the 1970s and 1980s Child wrote regular columns for *McCalls* and *Parade* magazines and made frequent appearances on "Good Morning America" on ABC. In addition, she was a founder of the American Institute of Wine and Food, an association of restaurants dedicated to the advancement of knowledge about food and wine. In 1989 *The Way to Cook,* a lengthy cookbook dealing with both basic and advanced subjects, was published, and at age 77 Child happily undertook an extended tour to promote it. She recognized the need for advertisement and frankly enjoyed the attention: "You've got to go out and sell it," she declared. "No sense spending all that time—five years on this one—and hiding your light under a bushel. . . . Besides, I'm a ham."

Late in 1989 her husband suffered a stroke and had to be moved to a nursing home near Cambridge. She visited daily and called frequently, but found life without her constant companion lonely. Accordingly, she kept busy with a regular exercise routine, lecturing, writing, and working on television programs. She even provided a cartoon voice for a children's video. In 1992 her television show, "Cooking with the Master Chefs," was produced and in 1993 the accompanying cookbook was published. In August 1992, 170 guests paid $100 or more to attend her 80th birthday party (proceeds to the American Institute of Food and Wine). And her place as a gastronomic icon was assured when she became the first woman to be inducted into the Culinary Institute Hall of Fame in October 1993.

Child lost her lifelong friend and career partner when her husband died in 1994. Not long after that she was quoted as saying that she had nothing left to write. Nonetheless the years 1995 and 1996 each brought a new book and TV series combination from the indefatigable Child: *In Julia's Kitchen with Master Chefs* (1995), and *Baking with Julia* (1996). In 1997 she celebrated her 85th birthday, once again with a fund raiser for the American Institute of Food and Wine. This one-woman dynamo continues to host an annual luxury tour to Italy for food buffs

Although a staunch advocate of classic French cuisine, Child in the course of her career modified her approach to cookery to reflect contemporary needs and trends, such as developing a repertoire requiring less fat, red meat, and time. Above all, she supported a sensible approach to eating characterized by moderation and including all types of food. She rejected what she called "food fads," which she held responsible for widespread unhealthy attitudes toward eating in the United States. In her work she endeavored consistently and successfully to enhance the public's awareness and appreciation of, and need for, wholesome, skillfully prepared food.

Further Reading

The best single source of biographical information on Julia Child is contained in Mary Ellen Snodgrass' *Late Achievers: Famous People Who Succeeded Late in Life* (1992). Snodgrass' chapter on Julia Child is well-balanced and well-researched. A brief, breezily-written and appreciative sketch of Julia Child and her career is contained in Gregory Jaynes' "A Holiday Bird and a Free-Range Chat with Julia" (*LIFE,* December 1989). For a glimpse of the Childs at home, see Charles Grandee, "Grandee at Large: Julia Child—Still Cooking at 76," in *House and Garden* (June 1989). Julia's relationship with Paul Child is explored in Roberta Wallace Coffey's "Julia and Paul Child" (*McCalls,* October 1988), which also contains interesting information on Paul's background and career. In an interview, "Eat, Drink, and Be Sensible" (*Newsweek,* May 27, 1991), Julia Child explains her views on food and the goals of her career.

Additional Sources

Entertainment Weekly, December 10, 1993.
Town & Country Monthly , December 1994.
The Wine Spectator June 30, 1997.
Forbes, May 5, 1997. □

Lydia Maria Francis Child

The popularity and moral force of the American author Lydia Maria Francis Child (1802-1880) contributed to the impact radical abolitionists exerted on the antislavery debate that preceded the Civil War.

Lydia Maria Francis was born in Medford, Mass., of an old New England family, on Feb. 11, 1802, and revealed early her sensibilities and intelligence. Her novels of pioneer life, *Hobomok* (1824) and *The Rebels* (1825), opened a literary career for her. *Juvenile Miscellany,* an annual that she instituted in 1826, pioneered in its field, and her later publications appealed to girls and wives. In 1828 she married David Lee Child, a Harvard College graduate who had capped an idealistic, adventurous youth by becoming a lawyer. As a state legislator and editor of the *Massachusetts Journal,* he seemed on a successful path.

Both were converted to abolitionism by William Lloyd Garrison, but it was Lydia who most startled conventional circles with her *Appeal in Favor of That Class of Americans Called Africans* (1833). This tract made abolitionists of such noteworthy persons as the Reverend William Ellery Channing and Charles Sumner. It also, however, closed various social circles to her and caused her book sales to fall. Her *Juvenile Miscellany* suspended, she pressed on as author and abolitionist. She published several abolitionist compilations, as well as biographies of notable women and the groundbreaking *History of the Condition of Women in Various Ages and Nations* (1835). Her husband introduced beet sugar manufacture in the United States and penned important abolitionist pamphlets. However, he was impractically dedicated to agricultural experiments, and his wife was required to manage their often-constricted finances.

In 1840 Child assumed the editorship of the *National Anti-Slavery Standard,* representing Garrison in New York. While there she wrote *Letters from New York* (1843, 1845), which contained much of contemporary interest. Her husband joined her in the work in 1843. The next year, embittered by factional differences between abolitionists, she returned to private life, settling in Wayland, Mass. Among her later books was *Progress of Religious Ideas through Successive Ages* (1855), which once more broke ground in its religious liberalism.

When John Brown was wounded in the raid on Harpers Ferry, Va., in 1859, Child asked permission to nurse him; this resulted in an exchange of letters which were read nationwide. *Correspondence between Lydia Maria Child and Gov. Wise and Mrs. Mason of Virginia* (1860) exhibited her abolitionist prose at its strongest.

Child's later writings struck a summary note, as in *Looking toward Sunset* (1864). Many of her works were outmoded, but her own character evoked admiration. She survived her husband 6 years, dying on July 7, 1880. A memorial volume, *Letters* (1883), was introduced by John Greenleaf Whittier and included Wendell Phillips's funeral address.

Further Reading

Two biographies of Child are Helene G. Baer, *The Heart Is like Heaven: The Life of Lydia Maria Child* (1965), and Milton Meltzer, *Tongue of Flame: The Life of Lydia Maria Child* (1965). She is discussed in numerous works, including Thomas Wentworth Higginson, *Contemporaries* (1899), and Margaret Farrand Thorp, *Female Persuasion: Six Strong-minded Women* (1949). Her works are described in volume 2 of Jacob Blanck, *Bibliography of American Literature* (1957).

Additional Sources

Clifford, Deborah Pickman, *Crusader for freedom: a life of Lydia Maria Child,* Boston: Beacon Press, 1992.

Karcher, Carolyn L., *The first woman in the republic: a cultural biography of Lydia Maria Child,* Durham: Duke University Press, 1994. □

Vere Gordon Childe

The Australian prehistorian and archeologist Vere Gordon Childe (1892-1957) pioneered in the systematic study of European prehistory of the 3d and 2d millenniums B.C. and showed how technological advances marked the birth of human civilizations.

On April 14, 1892, V. Gordon Childe was born in Sydney, New South Wales. He studied at Oxford University under Sir Arthur Evans and John Linton Myers. His studies there concerning the relation of archeology and Indo-Aryan languages led to *The Dawn of European Civilization* (1925; 6th ed. 1957) and *The Aryans* (1926).

Childe became the first Abercromby professor of prehistoric archeology at the University of Edinburgh in 1927 and taught there until 1946. From 1928 to 1931 he supervised the excavation of the Skara Brae Stone Age village in the Orkney Islands, Scotland. In his evolution as a scholar Childe, like all 19th- and early-20th-century prehistorians, was strongly influenced by Charles Darwin's *Origin of Species* (1859) and by the positivism of Auguste Comte, Max Weber, and Sir Edward B. Tylor.

Childe's aim was to form a truly international approach to prehistoric studies in order to understand how civilizations arose. His method was based on an integrative principle. He related the known events of history to the data of natural history so as to form a total picture of how human civilization had developed. He studied the legal, political, economic, religious, and sociological structures of primitive and developing societies and linked the relevant studies with anthropology, geology, biology, zoology, and paleontology. His *Man Makes Himself* (1936) and *Social Evolution* (1951) are prime examples of his power of synthesis.

For Childe the invention of writing was a primary index of civilization. He maintained that the invention of writing by ancient peoples always coincided with a critical threshold in their economic and demographic structure. At that moment they had achieved a certain economic surplus, a definite preoccupation with such things as calendrical astronomy, geometry, and arithmetic, and some literary occupations mainly of a religious bent. In addition, their population involved a more complex sociopolitical organization than ever before. Childe used the term "civilization" to refer to this critical turning point rather than to any qualitative character of the civilization in terms of technological, artistic, and leisure indexes.

Childe was director of the Institute of Archaeology at the University of London from 1946 to 1956. He died on Oct. 19, 1957, on Mt. Victoria, New South Wales.

Further Reading

Stuart Piggott gives details of Childe's life in *Proceedings of the British Academy,* vol. 44 (1959). An assessment of his work is in Julian H. Steward, *Theory of Culture Change* (1955), and in Robert Redfield, *The Characterizations of Civilizations* (1956).

Additional Sources

Green, Sally, *Prehistorian: a biography of V. Gordon Childe,* Bradford-on-Avon: Moonraker, 1981.

Trigger, Bruce G., *Gordon Childe, revolutions in archaeology,* New York: Columbia University Press, 1980. □

Alice Childress

Alice Childress (1920–1994) is an author whose writing is characterized by its frank treatment of racial issues. Because her books and plays often deal with such subjects as miscegenation and teenage drug addiction, her work can be controversial.

Alice Childress's work is noted for its frank treatment of racial issues, its compassionate yet discerning characterizations, and its universal appeal. Because her books and plays often deal with such controversial subjects as miscegenation and teenage drug addiction, her work has been banned in certain locations. She recalls that some affiliate stations refused to carry the nationally televised broadcasts of *Wedding Band* and *Wine in the Wilderness,* and in the case of the latter play, the entire state of Alabama banned the telecast.

Childress notes in addition that as late as 1973 her young adult novel *A Hero Ain't Nothin' but a Sandwich* "was the first book banned in a Savannah, Georgia school library since *Catcher in the Rye,* which the same school banned in the fifties." Along with other contemporary and classical works, *A Hero Ain't Nothin' but a Sandwich* has been at the center of legal battles and court decisions over attempts to define obscenity and its alleged impact on readers. Among the most famous cases was *Board of Education, Island Trees Union Free School District v. Pico* (102 S. Ct. 2799) in which a Stephen Pico, then a high school student, and others sued the Board on the grounds that their First Amendment Rights had been denied. The case became the first ever of this type to be heard in the U.S Supreme Court. Justice Brennan found for the plaintiffs, having determined that a school board's rights were limited to supervising curriculum, but not the general content of a library. Despite special-interest groups' growing resistance to controversial subjects in books, Childress's writing continues to win praise and respect for being, as a *Variety* reviewer terms, "powerful and poetic."

A talented writer and performer in several media, Childress has commented about the variety of genres in which she writes: "Books, plays, tele-plays, motion picture scenarios, etc., I seem caught up in a fragmentation of writing skills. But an idea comes to me in a certain form and, if it stays with me, must be written out or put in outline form before I can move on to the next event. I sometimes wonder about writing in different forms; could it be that women are used to dealing with the bits and pieces of life and do not feel as [compelled to specialize]? The play form is the one most familiar to me and so influences all of my writing—I think in scenes."

In an autobiographical sketch for Donald R. Gallo's *Speaking for Ourselves,* Childress shares how theater has influenced her fiction writing: "When I'm writing, characters seem to come alive; they move my pen to action, pushing, pulling, shoving, and intruding. I visualize each scene as if it were part of a living play. . . . I am pleased when

readers say that my novels feel like plays, because it means they are very visual."

Alice Childress began her career in the theater, initially as an actress and later as a director and playwright. Although "theater histories make only passing mention of her, . . . she was in the forefront of important developments in that medium," writes *Dictionary of Literary Biography* contributor Trudier Harris. Rosemary Curb points out in another *Dictionary of Literary Biography* article that Childress's 1952 drama *Gold through the Trees* was "the first play by a black woman professionally produced on the American stage." Moreover, Curb adds, "As a result of successful performances of [her 1950s plays *Just a Little Simple* and *Gold through the Trees*], Childress initiated Harlem's first all-union Off-Broadway contracts recognizing the Actors Equity Association and the Harlem Stage Hand Local."

Partly because of her pioneering efforts, Childress is considered a crusader by many. But she is also known as "a writer who resists compromise," says Doris E. Abramson in *Negro Playwrights in the American Theatre: 1925-1959*. "She tries to write about [black] problems as honestly as she can." The problems Childress addresses most often are racism and its effects. Her *Trouble in Mind,* for example, is a play within a play that focuses on the anger and frustration experienced by a troupe of black actors as they try to perform stereotyped roles in a play that has been written, produced, and directed by whites. As Sally R. Sommer explains in the *Village Voice,* "The plot is about an emerging rebellion begun as the heroine, Wiletta, refuses to enact a namby-Mammy, either in the play or for her director." In the *New York Times,* Arthur Gelb states that Childress "has some witty and penetrating things to say about the dearth of roles for [black] actors in the contemporary theatre, the cutthroat competition for these parts and the fact that [black] actors often find themselves playing stereotyped roles in which they cannot bring themselves to believe." And of *Wedding Band,* a play about an interracial relationship that takes place in South Carolina during World War I, Clive Barnes writes in the *New York Times,* "Childress very carefully suggests the stirrings of black consciousness, as well as the strength of white bigotry."

Critics Sommer and the *New York Times*'s Richard Eder find that Childress's treatment of the themes and issues in *Trouble in Mind* and *Wedding Band* gives these plays a timeless quality. "Writing in 1955, . . . Alice Childress used the concentric circles of the play-within-the-play to examine the multiple roles blacks enact in order to survive," Sommer remarks. She finds that viewing *Trouble in Mind* years later enables one to see "its double cutting edge: It predicts not only the course of social history but the course of black playwriting." Eder states: "The question [in *Wedding Band*] is whether race is a category of humanity or a division of it. The question is old by now, and was in 1965, [when the play was written,] but it takes the freshness of new life in the marvelous characters that Miss Childress has created to ask it."

The strength and insight of Childress's characterizations have been widely acknowledged; critics contend that the characters who populate her plays and novels are believable and memorable. Eder praises the "rich and lively characterization" of *Wedding Band.* Similarly impressed, Harold Clurman writes in the *Nation* that "there is an honest pathos in the telling of this simple story, and some humorous and touching thumbnail sketches reveal knowledge and understanding of the people dealt with." In the novel *A Short Walk,* Childress chronicles the life of a fictitious black woman, Cora James, from her birth in 1900 to her death in the middle of the century, illustrating, as *Washington Post* critic Joseph McLellan describes it, "a transitional generation in black American society." McLellan notes that the story "wanders considerably" and that "the reader is left with no firm conclusion that can be put into a neat sentence or two." What is more important, he asserts, is that "the wandering has been through some interesting scenery, and instead of a conclusion the reader has come to know a human being complex, struggling valiantly and totally believable." And of Childress's novel about teenage heroin addiction, *A Hero Ain't Nothin' but a Sandwich,* the *Lion and the Unicorn*'s Miguel Ortiz states, "The portrait of whites is more realistic in this book, more compassionate, and at the same time, because it is believable, more scathing."

Some criticism has been leveled at what such reviewers as Abramson and Edith Oliver believe to be Childress's tendency to speechify, especially in her plays. "A reader of the script is very much aware of the author pulling strings, putting her own words into a number of mouths," Abramson says of *Trouble in Mind.* According to Oliver in the *New Yorker,* "The first act [of *Wedding Band*] is splendid, but after that we hit a few jarring notes, when the characters seem to be speaking as much for the benefit of us eavesdroppers out front . . . as for the benefit of one another."

For the most part, however, Childress's work, particularly her novels for young adults, has been acclaimed for its honesty, insight, and compassion. When one such novel, *Those Other People,* was published in 1989, it was acknowledged by very few of the traditional children's reviewing sources. The novel deals with a teenage boy's fears about admitting to his homosexuality. Childress has created characters who confront homophobia, racism, and social taboos honestly and with dignity. In her review for *School Library Journal,* Kathryn Havris notes that *Those Other People,* skillfully and realistically addresses young people's responses to these problems. This author, says Havris, "has presented the problems and reactions with a competence that deserves reading."

In *Crisis,* Loften Mitchell notes: "Childress writes with a sharp, satiric touch. Character seems to interest her more than plot. Her characterizations are piercing, her observations devastating." In his review of *A Hero Ain't Nothin' but a Sandwich,* Ortiz writes: "The book conveys very strongly the message that we are all human, even when we are acting in ways that we are somewhat ashamed of. The structure of the book grows out of the personalities of the characters, and the author makes us aware of how much the economic and social circumstances dictate a character's actions."

In discussing how she came to write books for teenagers, Childress remarks in *Speaking for Ourselves* that she wanted to "deal with characters who feel rejected and have to painfully learn how to deal with other people, because I believe all human beings can be magnificent once they realize their full importance." "My young years were very old in feeling," she comments elsewhere. "I was shut out of so much for so long. [I] soon began to embrace the low-profile as a way of life, which helped me to develop as a writer. Quiet living is restful when one's writing is labeled 'controversial.'

"Happily, I managed to save a bit of my youth for spending in these later years. Oh yes, there are other things to be saved [besides] money. If we hang on to that part within that was once childhood, I believe we enter into a new time dimension and every day becomes another lifetime in itself. This gift of understanding is often given to those wh constantly battle against the negatives of life with determination."

Childress died on August 14, 1994 in New York City. At the time of her death she had been at work on a novel about her African great-grandmother, who'd been a slave in her childhood, and her Scotch-Irish great-grandmother.

Further Reading

Abramson, Doris E., *Negro Playwrights in the American Theatre, 1925-1959,* Columbia University Press, 1969.
Betsko, Kathleen, and Rachel Koenig, *Interviews with Contemporary Women Playwrights,* Beech Tree Books, 1987.
Children's Literature Review, Volume 14, Gale, 1988.
Contemporary Literary Criticism, Gale, Volume 12, 1980, Volume 15, 1980.
Dictionary of Literary Biography, Gale, Volume 7: *Twentieth-Century American Dramatists,* 1981, Volume 38: *Afro-American Writers after 1955: Dramatists and Prose Writers,* 1985.
Donelson, Kenneth L., and Alleen Pace Nilson, *Literature for Today's Young Adults,* Scott, Foresman, 1980, third edition, HarperCollins, 1989.
Evans, Mari, editor, *Black Women Writers (1950-1980): A Critical Evaluation,* Doubleday-Anchor, 1984.
Gallo, Donald R., editor, *Speaking for Ourselves: Autobiographical Sketches by Notable Authors of Books for Young Adults,* National Council Teachers of English, 1990.
Hatch, James V., *Black Theater, U.S.A.: Forty-five Plays by Black Americans,* Free Press, 1974.
Mitchell, Loften, editor, *Voices of the Black Theatre,* James White, 1975.
Street, Douglas, editor, *Children's Novels and the Movies,* Ungar, 1983.
Crisis, April, 1965.
Freedomways, Volume 14, number 1, 1974.
Horn Book, May-June, 1989, p. 372.
Interracial Books for Children Bulletin, Volume 12, numbers 7-8, 1981.
Jet, September 5, 1995.
Lion and the Unicorn, fall, 1978.
Los Angeles Times, November 13, 1978; February 25, 1983.
Los Angeles Times Book Review, July 25, 1982.
Ms., December, 1979.
Nation, November 13, 1972.
Negro Digest, April, 1967; January, 1968.
Newsweek, August 31, 1987.
New Yorker, November 4, 1972; November 19, 1979.
New York Times, November 5, 1955; February 2, 1969; April 2, 1969; October 27, 1972; November 5, 1972; February 3, 1978; January 11, 1979; January 23, 1987; February 10, 1987; March 6, 1987; August 18, 1987; October 22, 1987.
New York Times Book Review, November 4, 1973; November 11, 1979; April 25, 1981.
School Library Journal, February, 1989, p. 99.
Show Business, April 12, 1969.
Variety, December 20, 1972.
Village Voice, January 15, 1979.
Washington Post, May 18, 1971; December 28, 1979.
Wilson Library Bulletin, September, 1989, pp. 14-15. □

Ch'in Kuei

Ch'in Kuei (1090-1155) was a leading Chinese government official during the early years of the Southern Sung dynasty (1127-1279) and was the foremost advocate of a peace policy toward the jürchen, the Tungusic people who had established the Chin dynasty in North China.

Ch'in Kuei was a native of Chiang-ning in Kiangsu Province. In 1115 he passed the highest civil service examination and obtained the *chin-shih* degree. After an assignment as an instructor in Shantung, he received the distinction "eloquent and virtuous scholar." His marriage to the granddaughter of a former chief minister, Wang Kuei (1019-1085), may have aided his career. During the closing years of the Northern Sung dynasty (960-1127), Ch'in held a number of government positions, and when the capital fell he was a censor. In 1127 he was taken north as a captive by the Chin because of his opposition to their establishment of the puppet state of Ch'u.

In 1130 Ch'in Kuei and his wife reappeared in the South after apparently being allowed to escape by Wangyen Ch'ang, also known as T'a-lan, a prominent, peace-minded member of the Chin royal house who had been given Ch'in as a slave. Welcomed by Emperor Kao-tsung, who was eager for information concerning the North, Ch'in soon won the Emperor's confidence, received the highest government positions in 1131, and championed peace. However, his opponents won a temporary victory when they forced him to resign in 1132. But Ch'in rapidly recovered his influence, received an important assignment in 1136, and was back in full power in 1138.

In 1141 Ch'in Kuei attained his goal in the form of a negotiated peace which established the Huai River as the boundary between the two states, called for an annual payment of silver and silk by the Sung, and included a Sung agreement to perform ceremonies of vassalage to the Chin. Before concluding the peace, the Sung government took the precaution of recalling three eminent generals and removing them from their commands. Among them was the famous Yüeh Fei, whose murder in prison has been blamed on Ch'in Kuei.

In 1150 an attempt to assassinate Ch'in Kuei failed, and he continued in power until his death of natural causes in 1155. Among his enemies were most of the prominent Confucians, who bitterly opposed his foreign policy and resented his practice of favoring his own followers. Held responsible for a peace which may have been realistic but was widely considered disgraceful and which did not prevent a new outbreak of fighting in 1161, Ch'in Kuei has been despised and condemned not only during the remainder of the Southern Sung dynasty but throughout subsequent Chinese history. Paralleling the growth of the reputation of Yüeh Fei until he became one of China's most glorified heroes, Ch'in Kuei came to be regarded as the villainous traitor par excellence.

Further Reading

There is no study of Ch'in Kuei in a Western language, but he is discussed in most histories of China. These include Wolfram Eberhard, *A History of China* (trans. 1950; 3d ed. 1969); Dun J. Li, *The Ageless Chinese: A History* (1965); and Harry Hamm, *China: Empire of 700 Million* (trans. 1966). □

May Edward Chinn

Mary Edward Chinn (1896–1890) is best remembered for the racial barriers she confronted as one of the first black women physicians in New York City.

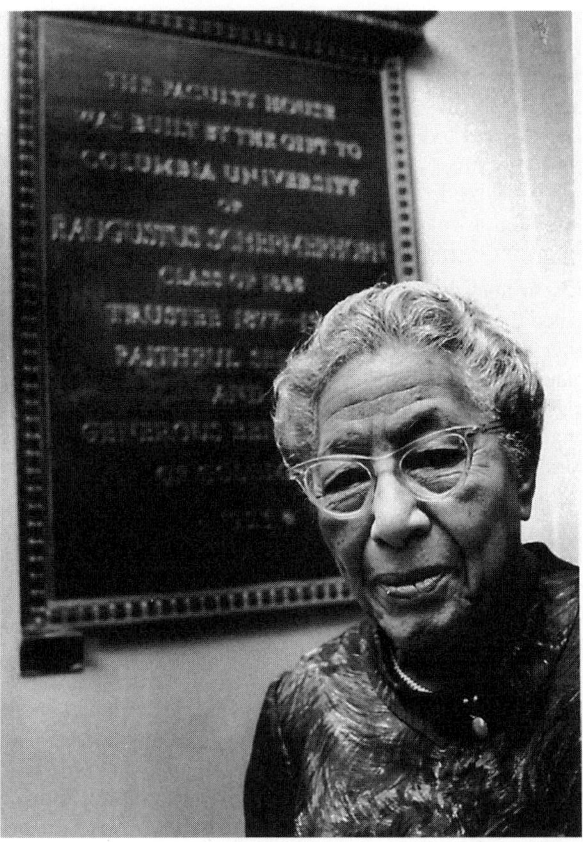

May Edward Chinn is best remembered for the racial barriers she confronted as one of the first black women physicians in New York City. Denied hospital privileges and research opportunities at New York City hospitals early in her career, she became a family doctor in Harlem, where she was the only practicing African American woman physician for several years. For her determination to provide medical care to the disadvantaged and for her work in cancer detection, she received honorary doctor of science degrees from New York University and Columbia University, and a distinguished alumnus award from Columbia Teachers College.

May Edward Chinn was born on April 15, 1896, in Great Barrington, Massachusetts. Her mother, Lulu Ann, was the daughter of a Chickahominy Native American and a slave. Her father, William Lafayette, was the son of a slave and a plantation owner. Chinn went to the Bordentown Manual and Training Industrial School, a boarding school in New Jersey, and spent one year of her childhood on the estate of Charles Tiffany, the jewelry magnate, where her mother was a live-in cook. The Tiffanys treated Chinn like family and took her to classical music concerts in New York City. She later learned to play the piano and became an accompanist to popular singer Paul Robeson in the early 1920s. Chinn played classical music and church music throughout her life and performed for African American soldiers during World War I. Although she never completed high school, she was admitted to Columbia Teachers College on the basis of her entrance examination. Originally intending to pursue a degree in music, Chinn quickly abandoned music for science because a music professor who believed that African Americans were unsuited for classical music ridiculed her, but another professor praised her for a paper she had written on sewage disposal. In 1921 she received a bachelor's degree in science from Columbia Teachers College, and in 1926 she became the first African American woman to graduate from Bellevue Hospital Medical College.

Upon graduation Chinn found that no hospital would allow her practicing privileges. The Rockefeller Institute had seriously considered her for a research fellowship until they discovered that she was African American. With her fair skin and last name, many assumed that she was white or Chinese. She later told Muriel Petioni, former president of the Society of Black Women Physicians, that African American workers often snubbed her because they assumed she was passing as white, and they did not want to jeopardize her position.

Though she was the first black woman intern at Harlem Hospital, racial and gender discrimination kept her from obtaining hospital privileges there. Chinn described her early practice in Harlem as akin to an old-fashioned family practice in the rural South a century earlier. She performed major medical procedures in patient's homes, while minor procedures were done in her office. She told George Davis of the *New York Times Magazine* "that conditions were so bad that it seemed that you were not making any headway." To get at the roots of poverty, she earned a master's degree in public health from Columbia University in 1933.

In the 1940s Chinn became very interested in cancer but was still prohibited from establishing formal affiliations with New York hospitals. Instead, she had her patients' biopsies read secretly for her at Memorial Hospital. In 1944 she was invited to join the staff of the Strang Clinic, a premier cancer detection facility affiliated with Memorial and New York Infirmary hospitals. She worked there for twenty-nine years and became a member of the Society of Surgical Oncology.

In her autobiographical paper written in 1977, Chinn noted that the committees established by Mayor LaGuardia after the Harlem riots of 1935 were pivotal in integrating blacks into medicine in New York City. As committee findings were reported in the newspapers, conditions began to change. Chinn saw this firsthand when she became the first African American woman granted admitting privileges at Harlem Hospital in 1940.

African American male doctors were another source of discrimination. In a *New York Times* interview with Charlayne Hunter-Gault in 1977, she described three types: "those who acted as if I wasn't there; another who took the attitude 'what does she think that she can do that I can't do?' and the group that called themselves support[ive] by sending me their night calls after midnight." Like other African American women physicians of her era, Chinn worked long hours but never got rich from her practice. By 1978 Chinn had given up her practice and begun examining African American students as a consultant to the Phelps-Stokes Fund. In late 1980 she died at age eighty-four at a Columbia University reception honoring a friend.

Further Reading

Brozan, Nadine, "For a Doctor at 84, A Day to Remember," in *New York Times,* May 17, 1980, p. 12.

Davis, George, "A Healing Hand in Harlem," in *New York Times Magazine,* Apr. 22, 1979, pp. 40+.

Ennis, Thomas W., "Obituary: Dr. May Edward Chinn, 84, Long a Harlem Physician," in *New York Times,* Sect. II, Dec. 3, 1980, p. 11.

Hunter-Gault, Charlayne, "Black Women M.D.'s: Spirit and Endurance," in *New York Times,* Nov. 16, 1977, pp. C1+.

Petioni, Muriel, *Interview with Laura Newman,* conducted on March 11, 1994. □

Ch'i Pai-shih

Ch'i Pai-shih (1863-1957) was one of the greatest Chinese painters of modern times. He led the revival of the traditional Chinese style of painting.

Ch'i Pai-shih, also called Ch'i Heng and Ch'i Wei-ch'ing, was born on a small farm near Hsiang-t'an, Hunan Province. His family was very poor, and the young boy was unable to obtain normal schooling. When Ch'i was 6 or 7, his grandfather, writing with fire tongs in the ashes of the stove, began teaching the boy characters. Aware of his desire to study, his mother carefully saved their meager resources and when he was 9 managed to send him to the village school run by her father. In less than a year, however, Ch'i was needed on the farm and had to leave school.

In order to continue his studies, Ch'i would hang a book from the horns of the water buffalo he tended and read in the fields. Ch'i also began painting at this time. By the age of 12 it was clear that the boy was too frail and weak for farm life, and he was apprenticed to a carpenter, progressing by age 15 from rough work to fine woodwork. In his late teens and early 20s Ch'i was widely known as a skillful professional craftsman. As was the custom among poor families, Ch'i had been married in 1874, at the age of 11, to a 12-year-old village girl. The first of their children was born about 7 years later.

Beginning as a Painter

While still an apprentice carpenter, Ch'i discovered a worn copy of *The Mustard Seed Garden Manual of Painting,* whose figural patterns were used in carving designs. His spare-time study of painting was rekindled by this discovery, his first true knowledge of the orthodox practice of painting. By the age of 27 he had achieved some success as a portrait painter and was able to support his family solely through his activities as an artist.

At the same time Ch'i met several of the leading scholars and artists of the region and with them started to study poetry, painting, and seal carving. Urged to study T'ang poetry, he did so only with the greatest difficulty because of his sparse early education. He persevered, however, and ultimately became a very accomplished poet.

Travel for Education

At the age of 40, leaving home for the first time, Ch'i embarked on a journey through China that took him to many of the hallowed scenic spots and sacred mountains of the country. During his travels he began to develop his interest in the variety of painting called *hsieh-i* ("expressing the idea"), a method different from the more orthodox mode of representation.

His journey kept Ch'i away for 7 years. When he returned home, he bought and renovated a large, old house, into which he now retired to study and to paint. Half of the old guide to a full education—"Travel 10,000 miles and read 10,000 books"—was fulfilled, and he was determined to read 10,000 books. He was now the father of three sons and two daughters, and shortly after his return the first of his grandchildren was born.

During his travels Ch'i had made countless sketches, and he began turning them into finished works. In his spare time he planted all manner of trees and shrubs around the house and kept fish, birds, shrimp, small animals, and insects. His affectionate study of these plants and creatures later resulted in some of the finest paintings of recent Chinese history.

Move to Peking

This was the period during which the Chinese Empire finally collapsed and the Republic of China was born. It was an age of great instability and disorder, and twice Ch'i was forced to flee to Peking for safety. From about the age of 60 he lived in Peking permanently, teaching at the Peking Institute of Art.

In 1919, Ch'i's wife presented him with a concubine named Precious Pearl. With Precious Pearl he had four more sons and several daughters, the last born when the painter was 78. In 1941, following the death of his wife, he married Precious Pearl.

The finest period of Ch'i's growth as a painter began with his move to Peking. He was now able to gain a much greater familiarity with the works of his noted predecessors, Tao-chi and Pa-ta shan-jen of the 17th century and Wu Ch'ang-shih and Chao Chih-ch'ien of the 19th. As he aged, his creativity, freshness, and artistic vigor seem only to have grown. Many of his finest works were done in his 80s and 90s.

During the Japanese occupation of Peking from 1937 to 1945, Ch'i withdrew from his teaching posts in protest and retired to his home. With the establishment of the People's Republic of China the old painter became a cultural hero. He was subsequently honored with every resource a grateful people could muster. In 1953 a state delegation called upon him to present congratulations on his ninetieth birthday. The frail, slender Ch'i, weak and sickly as a boy, died in 1957 at the grand age of 94. Only twice in his life had he gone as long as 10 days without painting, once at 63 when he lay ill and near death, the second time a year later when his mother died.

Further Reading

For Ch'i's paintings see Yakichiro Suma, *Ch'i Pai-shih* (1960). There is a good account of Ch'i Pai-shih's life and art in Michael Sullivan, *Chinese Art in the Twentieth Century* (1959). □